Lecture Notes in Networks and Systems

Volume 222

The series "Lecture Notes in Networks and Systems" publishes the latest developments in Networks and Systems—quickly, informally and with high quality. Original research reported in proceedings and post-proceedings represents the core of LNNS.

Volumes published in LNNS embrace all aspects and subfields of, as well as new challenges in, Networks and Systems.

The series contains proceedings and edited volumes in systems and networks, spanning the areas of Cyber-Physical Systems, Autonomous Systems, Sensor Networks, Control Systems, Energy Systems, Automotive Systems, Biological Systems, Vehicular Networking and Connected Vehicles, Aerospace Systems, Automation, Manufacturing, Smart Grids, Nonlinear Systems, Power Systems, Robotics, Social Systems, Economic Systems and other. Of particular value to both the contributors and the readership are the short publication timeframe and the world-wide distribution and exposure which enable both a wide and rapid dissemination of research output.

The series covers the theory, applications, and perspectives on the state of the art and future developments relevant to systems and networks, decision making, control, complex processes and related areas, as embedded in the fields of interdisciplinary and applied sciences, engineering, computer science, physics, economics, social, and life sciences, as well as the paradigms and methodologies behind them.

Indexed by SCOPUS, INSPEC, WTI Frankfurt eG, zbMATH, SCImago.

All books published in the series are submitted for consideration in Web of Science.

More information about this series at http://www.springer.com/series/15179

Nancy L. Black · W. Patrick Neumann ·
Ian Noy
Editors

Proceedings of the 21st Congress of the International Ergonomics Association (IEA 2021)

Volume IV: Healthcare and Healthy Work

 Springer

Editors
Nancy L. Black
Département de génie mécanique
Université de Moncton
Moncton, NB, Canada

W. Patrick Neumann
Department of Mechanical and Industrial
Engineering
Ryerson University
Toronto, ON, Canada

Ian Noy
Toronto, ON, Canada

ISSN 2367-3370   ISSN 2367-3389   (electronic)
Lecture Notes in Networks and Systems
ISBN 978-3-030-74610-0   ISBN 978-3-030-74611-7   (eBook)
https://doi.org/10.1007/978-3-030-74611-7

This Springer imprint is published by the registered company Springer Nature Switzerland AG
The registered company address is: Gewerbestrasse 11, 6330 Cham, Switzerland

Preface

The International Ergonomics Association (IEA) is the organization that unites Human Factors and Ergonomics (HF/E) associations around the world. The mission of the IEA is "to elaborate and advance ergonomics science and practice, and to expand its scope of application and contribution to society to improve the quality of life, working closely with its constituent societies and related international organizations" (IEA, 2021). The IEA hosts a world congress every three years creating the single most important opportunity to exchange knowledge and ideas in the discipline with practitioners and researchers from across the planet. Like other IEA congresses, IEA2021 included an exciting range of research and professional practice cases in the broadest range of Human Factors and Ergonomics (HF/E) applications imaginable. While the conference was not able to host an in-person meeting in Vancouver, Canada, as planned by the host Association of Canadian Ergonomists/*Association canadienne d'ergonomie*, it still featured over 875 presentations and special events with the latest research and most innovative thinkers. For this congress, authors could prepare a chapter for publication, and 60% chose to do so. The breadth and quality of the work available at IEA2021 are second to none—and the research of all authors who prepared their publication for this congress is made available through the five volumes of these proceedings.

The International Ergonomics Association defines Human Factors and Ergonomics (HF/E) synonymously as being:

> *the scientific discipline concerned with the understanding of interactions among humans and other elements of a system, and the profession that applies theory, principles, data and methods to design in order to optimize human well-being and overall system performance.*
>
> *Practitioners of ergonomics and ergonomists contribute to the design and evaluation of tasks, jobs, products, environments and systems in order to make them compatible with the needs, abilities and limitations of people.*
>
> *Ergonomics helps harmonize things that interact with people in terms of people's needs, abilities and limitations.* (https://iea.cc/definition-and-domains-of-ergonomics/)

The breadth of issues and disciplines suggested by this definition gives one pause for thought: what aspect in our lives is not in some way affected by the design and application of HF/E? For designers and managers around the world, a similar realization is growing: every decision made in the design and application of technology has implications for the humans that will interact with that system across its lifecycle. While this can be daunting, the researchers and professionals who participated in IEA2021 understand that, by working together across our disciplines and roles, we can achieve these lofty ambitions. This is especially relevant as we continue our collective journey into an increasingly "interconnected world"—the theme for the 21st IEA Congress. With the rise of a myriad of technologies as promulgated by Industry 4.0 proponents, we need now, more than ever, the skills and knowledge of HF/E researchers and practitioners to ensure that these tools are applied in a human-centric way towards resilient and sustainable systems that provide an enduring and sustainable road to prosperity—as advocated in the new Industry 5.0 Paradigm (Breque et al. 2021). Where the trend of Industry 4.0 aims primarily at encouraging technology purchasing and application, Industry 5.0 includes goals of resiliency and sustainability for both humans and our planet. These proceedings provide examples of research and development projects that illustrate how this brighter, human-centred future can be pursued through "*Ergonomie 4.0*", as stated in the French theme of the Congress.

While the theme of the Congress concerns human interactions within a rapidly evolving cyber-physical world, the devastating impact of the COVID-19 pandemic has given an added dimension to the Congress theme and its delivery model. As the pandemic began to engulf the world, the traditional in-person Congress became increasingly less viable and gave way to the creation of a hybrid model as a means to enhance international participation. In early 2021, it became clear that holding an in-person event would not be possible; hence, the Congress was converted to a fully virtual event. The uncertainty, mounting challenges and turbulent progression actually created new possibilities to engage the global HF/E community in ways that were never previously explored by the IEA. Indeed, one of the scientific tracks of the congress focuses explicitly on HF/E contributions to cope with COVID-19, and readers will find some submissions to other tracks similarly focus on what HF/E practitioners and researchers bring to the world during this pandemic period. This journey epitomizes broader transformative patterns now underway in society at large and accentuates the urgency for resilience, sustainability, and healthy workplaces. No doubt, the notion of globalization will be redefined in the wake of the pandemic and will have far-reaching implications for the connected world and for future society, and with new paradigms emerge a host of new human factors challenges. The breadth of topics and issues addressed in the proceedings suggests that the HF/E community is already mobilizing and rising to these emerging challenges in this, our connected world.

IEA2021 proceedings includes papers from 31 scientific tracks and includes participants from 74 countries across 5 continents. The proceedings of the 21st triennial congress of the IEA—IEA2021—exemplify the diversity of HF/E, and of the association, in terms of geography, disciplines represented, application domains, and aspects of human life cycle and capability being considered. Our diversity mirrors the diversity of humans generally and is a strength as we learn to weave our knowledge, methods, and ideas together to create a more resilient and stronger approach to design than is achievable individually. This is the strength of the IEA congresses, in the past, in the current pandemic-affected 21st occasion, and in the future. There is no other meeting like it.

A substantial number of works were submitted for publication across the Scientific Tracks at IEA2021. This gave us the happy opportunity to group contents by common threads. Each volume presents contents in sections with papers within the track's section presented in alphabetical order by the first author's last name. These proceedings are divided into five volumes as follows:

VOLUME 1: SYSTEMS AND MACROERGONOMICS (ISBN 978-3-030-74601-8)

Activity Theories for Work Analysis and Design (ATWAD)
Systems HF/E
Ergonomic Work Analysis and Training (EWAT)
HF/E Education and Professional Certification Development
Organisation Design and Management (ODAM)

VOLUME 2: INCLUSIVE AND SUSTAINABLE DESIGN (ISBN 978-3-030-74604-9)

Ageing and Work
Ergonomics for children and Educational Environments
Ergonomics in Design for All
Gender and Work
Human Factors and Sustainable Development
Slips Trips and Falls
Visual Ergonomics

VOLUME 3: SECTOR BASED ERGONOMICS (ISBN 978-3-030-74607-0)

Practitioner Case Studies
Aerospace Ergonomics
Agricultural Ergonomics
Building and Construction Ergonomics
Ergonomics in Manufacturing
HF/E in Supply Chain Design and Management
Transport Ergonomics and Human Factors

VOLUME 4: HEALTHCARE AND HEALTHY WORK (ISBN 978-3-030-74610-0)

Health and Safety
Healthcare Ergonomics

HF/E Contribution to Cope with Covid-19
Musculoskeletal Disorders

VOLUME 5: METHODS & APPROACHES (ISBN 978-3-030-74613-1)
Advanced Imaging
Affective Design
Anthropometry
Biomechanics
Human Factors in Robotics
Human Modelling and Simulation
Neuroergonomics
Working with Computer Systems Addenda (EWAT, HF/E Education and
Professional Certification Development, ODAM, Systems HF/E, Slips, Trips and
Falls)

These volumes are the result of many hours of work, for authors, Scientific
Track Managers and their reviewer teams, student volunteers, and editors. We are
grateful to Springer for making it available to you in book form and are confident
you will find these works informative and useful in your own efforts to create a
better, more human-centred future.

References

Breque, M., De Nul, L., Petridis, A., 2021. Industry 5.0: Towards More
    Sustainable, Resilient and Human-Centric Industry, in: Innovation, E.D.-G.f.R.a.
    (Ed.), Policy Brief. European Commission, Luxembourg, p. 48. https://ec.
    europa.eu/info/news/industry-50-towards-more-sustainable-resilient-and-
    human-centric-industry-2021-jan-07_en
International Ergonomics Association (2021) Definitions and Domains of
    Ergonomics. https://iea.cc/definition-and-domains-of-ergonomics/; accessed
    March, 2021

Nancy L. Black
W. Patrick Neumann
IEA2021 Scientific Co-chairs

Ian Noy
IEA2021 Conference Chair

IEA2021 Acknowledgements

The IEA Congress organizing committee acknowledges many individuals whose contributions to the event have been invaluable to its success.

First and foremost, we acknowledge with deep appreciation the tremendous work of Steve Marlin, CEO of Prestige Accommodations, International Inc. His firm, hired to assist with organizing and executing the Congress, delivered unparalleled service throughout the planning process. Tragically, Steve passed away in early 2021. He provided outstanding support and wise counsel, always with a smile. He is sorely missed. We remain indebted to the Prestige staff, whose expertise and outstanding professionalism guided us through the planning process. In particular, we are grateful to Laurie Ybarra, Sr. Meetings Manager, who oversaw the many diverse aspects of our ever-changing plans and Christine Reinhard, Director of Operations, who skilfully managed the budget, website and registration system. Laurie and Christine's friendly approach, and their unique combination of technical and interpersonal skills, made it a pleasure to work with them. Marie-Hélène Bisaillon, Executive Director of the Association of Canadian Ergonomists/ *Association canadienne d'ergonomie*, supported their work.

The Organizing Committee is also indebted to those contributors who were instrumental in developing and promoting IEA2021. Joanne Bangs, our freelance Communications Specialist, provided engaging news blogs and other promotional collateral to help get the word out about the Congress. Sadeem Qureshi (Ryerson University), Elizabeth Georgiou, Elaine Fung, and Michelle Lam (Simon Fraser University) helped to create widespread awareness of the Congress as well as the HF/E field and profession through creative use of digital and social media. We are also grateful to those who worked diligently to ensure that the Congress provided meaningful opportunities for students and early career researchers, including Daniel P. Armstrong and Christopher A.B. Moore (University of Waterloo), Owen McCulloch (Simon Fraser University), Dora Hsiao (Galvion, Inc.), Chelsea DeGuzman and Joelle Girgis (University of Toronto), and Larissa Fedorowich (Associate Ergonomist, self-employed). The ePoster presentation option, new to IEA triennial congresses in 2021, was defined with care by Anne-Kristina Arnold (Simon Fraser University). Colleen Dewis (Dalhousie University) was key to interpreting our technical submission software and adapting its capacities to our needs. Hemanshu Bhargav (Ryerson University), Rachel Faust (Université de Québec à Montréal), Myriam Bérubé (Université de Montréal), Charlotte Bate, Vanessa DeVries, Caleb Leary, and Marcelo Zaharur (Fanshawe College), Tobi Durowoju (EWI Works), Issa Kaba Diakite, Mariam Keita, Mouhamadou Pléa Ndour, Shelby Nowlan, Faouzi Mahamane Ouedraogo, Jenna Smith, and Israël Muaka Wembi (Université de Moncton), and the aforementioned Larissa Fedorowich assisted with technical submission database verification and clean-up. We are particularly grateful that so many came to us through the Association of Canadian Ergonomists/Association canadienne d'ergonomie, witnessing to the active and motivated ergonomics and human factors community in IEA2021's host country.

The organizers are especially grateful to our sponsors, whose generous contributions made the Congress possible and readily accessible to the global HF/E community. Their recognition of the Congress as a valuable opportunity to advance the field of HF/E, as well as their steadfast support throughout a very trying planning period, was critical to the success of the Congress. The IEA 2021 sponsors include:

Benefactor Level:
  Amazon.com, Inc.

Platinum Level:
  Anonymous

Diamond Level:
  Healthcare Insurance Reciprocal of Canada

Gold Level:
  Huawei Technologies Canada
  Institute for Work and Health (Ontario)
  WorkSafe BC

Silver Level:
  Fanshawe College
  Simon Fraser University
  Aptima, Inc.

Organization

IEA2021 Organizing Committee

IEA2021 Congress Chair

Ian Noy   HFE Consultant and Forensic Expert, Toronto,
                               Ontario

Technical Program Committee Co-chairs

Nancy L. Black   Department of Mechanical Engineering,
                               Faculté d'ingénierie, Université de Moncton,
                               Canada
W. Patrick Neumann   Human Factors Engineering Lab, Department
                               of Mechanical and Industrial Engineering,
                               Ryerson University, Canada

Media Outreach

Hayley Crosby   Options Incorporated, Canada

Developing Countries

Manobhiram (Manu) Nellutla   Actsafe Safety Association, Canada

ePosters Coordinator

Anne-Kristina Arnold   Ergonomics, Simon Fraser University, Canada

Exhibits Coordinator

Abigail Overduin   Workplace Health Services, The University
                               of British Columbia, Canada

Early Career Researcher Program Coordinator

Sadeem Qureshi   Human Factors Engineering Lab, Department
                                  of Mechanical and Industrial Engineering,
                                  Ryerson University, Canada

Media Relations

Heather Kahle   Human Factors Specialist/Ergonomist,
                                  WorkSafeBC, Canada
Jenny Colman   Human Factor Specialist, Risk Analysis Unit,
                                  WorkSafeBC, Canada

Events/Social

Gina Vahlas   Human Factors Specialist/Ergonomist,
                                  Risk Analysis Unit, WorkSafeBC, Canada
Era Poddar   Specialist Safety Advisor-Ergonomics,
                                  Manufacturing Safety Alliance of BC, Canada
Alison Heller-Ono   CEO, Worksite International, USA

French Language Coordinator

François Taillefer   Faculté des sciences, Université de Québec
                                  à Montréal, Canada

Communications Coordinator

Joanne Bangs   Free-lance consultant, USA

EasyChair Platform Technical Liaison

Colleen Dewis   Department of Industrial Engineering,
                                  Dalhousie University, Canada

Scientific Committee of IEA2021

Nancy L. Black (Co-chair)   Université de Moncton, Canada
W. Patrick Neumann   Ryerson University, Canada
  (Co-chair)
Wayne Albert   University of New Brunswick, Canada
Sara Albolino   Director Centre for Patient Safety Tuscany
                                  region, Italy
Thomas Alexander   Federal Institute for Occupational Safety
                                  and Health (BAUA), Germany
Anne-Kristina Arnold   Simon Fraser University, Canada

Rafael E. Gonzalez   Bolivarian University, Petróleos de Venezuela,
S.A. (PDVSA), Venezuela

Ewa Górska   University of Ecology and Management
in Warsaw, Poland

Maggie Graf   International Ergonomics Association -
Professional Standards and Education,
Certification Sub-committee, Switzerland

Alma Maria Jennifer Gutierrez   De La Salle University—Manila, Philippines

Jukka Häkkinen   University of Helsinki, Finland

Gregor Harih   University of Maribor, Slovenia

Veerle Hermans   Vrije Universiteit Brussel, Belgium

Dora Hsiao   Revision Military, Canada

Laerte Idal Sznelwar   Universidade de São Paulo, Brazil

Rauf Iqbal   National Institute of Industrial
Engineering (NITIE), India

Nicole Jochems   University of Luebeck, Germany

Marie Laberge   Université de Montréal, Centre de recherche
du CHU Ste-Justine, Canada

Fion C. H. Lee   UOW College Hong Kong, Hong Kong

Yue (Sophia) Li   KITE, Toronto Rehabilitation Institute—
University Health Network, Canada

Peter Lundqvist   SLU - Swedish University of Agricultural
Sciences, Sweden

Neil Mansfield   Nottingham Trent University, UK

Márcio Alves Marçal   Universidade Federal dos Vales do Jequitinhonha
e do Mucuri, Brazil

Blake McGowan   VelocityEHS, USA

Ranjana Mehta   Texas A&M University, USA

Marijke Melles   Delft University of Technology, Netherlands

Marino Menozzi   Swiss Federal Institute of Technology,
ETH Zurich, Switzerland

Francisco Octavio Lopez Millan   TECNM/Instituto Tecnológico de Hermosillo,
Mexico

Karen Lange Morales   Universidad Nacional de Colombia, Colombia

Ruud N. Pikaar   ErgoS Human Factors Engineering, Netherlands

Dimitris Nathanael   National Technical University of Athens, Greece

Yee Guan Ng   Universiti Putra Malaysia, Malaysia

Jodi Oakman   La Trobe University, Australia

Udoka Arinze Chris Okafor   University of Lagos, Nigeria

Paulo Antonio Barros Oliveira   Federal University of Rio Grande do Sul, Brazil

Vassilis Papakostopoulos   University of the Aegean, Greece

Maria Pascale   Uruguayan Association of Ergonomics
(AUDErgo), Uruguay

Gunther Paul	James Cook University, Australia
Chui Yoon Ping	Singapore University of Social Sciences, Singapore
Jim Potvin	McMaster University, Canada
Valérie Pueyo	Université Lumière Lyon 2, France
Sadeem Qureshi	Ryerson University, Canada
Sudhakar Rajulu	NASA - Johnson Space Center, USA
Gemma Read	University of the Sunshine Coast, Australia
David Rempel	University of California Berkeley; University of California San Francisco, USA
Raziel Riemer	Ben-Gurion University of the Negev, Israel
Michelle M. Robertson	Office Ergonomics Research Committee, Northeastern University, University of Connecticut, University of California, Berkeley, USA
Martin Antonio Rodriguez	Universidad Tecnológica Nacional Buenos Aires FRBA, Argentina
Gustavo Rosal	UNE (Spanish Association for Standardisation), Spain
Patricia H. Rosen	Federal Institute for Occupational Safety and Health (BAUA), Germany
Ken Sagawa	AIST, Japan
Paul M. Salmon	University of the Sunshine Coast, Australia
Marta Santos	Universidade do Porto, Portugal
Sofia Scataglini	University of Antwerp, Belgium
Lawrence J. H. Schulze	University of Houston, USA
Rosemary Ruiz Seva	De La Salle University, Philippines
Fabio Sgarbossa	Norwegian University of Science and Technology, Norway
Jonas Shultz	Health Quality Council of Alberta, University of Calgary, Canada
Anabela Simões	University Lusófona, Portugal
Sarbjit Singh	National Institute of Technology Jalandhar, India
John Smallwood	Nelson Mandela University, South Africa
Lukáš Šoltys	Czech Ergonomics Association, Czech Republic
Isabella Tiziana Steffan	STUDIO STEFFAN—Progettazione & Ricerca (Design & Research), Italy
Daryl Stephenson	Occupational Health Clinics for Ontario Workers, Canada
Gyula Szabó	Hungarian Ergonomics Society, Hungary
Shamsul Bahri Mohd Tamrin	Universiti Putra Malaysia, Malaysia
Andrew Thatcher	University of the Witwatersrand, South Africa
Giulio Toccafondi	Center for Clinical Risk Management and Patient Safety GRC, WHO Collaborating Center, Florence, Italy

Andrew Todd	Rhodes University, South Africa
Judy Village	University of British Columbia, Canada
Christian Voirol	University of Applied Sciences Western Switzerland, University of Montreal, Switzerland
Michael Wichtl	AUVA-Hauptstelle, Austrian Ergonomics Society, Austria
Amanda Widdowson	Chartered Institute of Ergonomics and Human Factors (CIEHF), Thales, UK
Sascha Wischniewski	Federal Institute for Occupational Safety & Health (BAuA), Germany

Contents

Part I: Health and Safety (Edited by Gyula Szabó)

Preliminary Findings on Handmade Rattan Baby Crib and Bassinet Designs Regarding Risk of Entrapment for Baby Safety

Ratriana Aminy and Lulu Purwaningrum[(✉)]

Faculty of Art and Design, Universitas Sebelas Maret, Ir. Sutami 36 A, Surakarta, Indonesia
ratrianaaminy@student.uns.ac.id,
lulu_purwaningrum@staff.uns.ac.id

Abstract. The demand for baby cribs and bassinets made from rattan is increasing, but consumer attention still tends to focus on the aesthetic design rather than on the safety of the product. Meanwhile, the designs of rattan bassinet and crib slats may pose potential risks of entrapment for baby's safety. This research was conducted to analyze the products' ergonomics by observing the babies' behavior when doing their activities in them. The crib and bassinet have variations in the gap sizes between the components on the crib sides. In terms of physical safety, the handmade rattan crib slats components, with 10 mm diameter rattan that is curved in form, have a risk of producing inconsistent rattan gaps that exceed 2 3/8 in. (60 mm). This results in the potential for injury to the limbs of infants aged 5–12 months. The baby's limbs can be trapped in the rattan slat decoration.

Keywords: Baby bed · Safety crib · Crib hazard · Rattan crib · Infant

Rattan crib and bassinet designs combine beauty, functionality, aesthetic natural materials, and skilled craftsmanship perfectly. The rattan decoration or crib slats are the visual point of a rattan crib [6, 7]. Even though the demand for baby cribs and bassinets made from rattan is increasing, consumer attention still tends to focus on the aesthetic design rather than on the safety of the product [1, 8].

The Consumer advocacy group in Australia (CHOICE) published a report on rattan bassinet products that have safety issues related to gaps that posed limb entrapment [3]. The condition that can lead to entrapment is also parallel to those of the American Academic of Pediatrics (AAP) report, stating that crib slats having gaps of more than 2 3/8 in. or 60 mm can get baby wedged between these slats. Anthropometric study for infants showed that 2 3/8 in. is the maximum suitable gap size for infant protection [4, 5]. In addition, the risk of injury such as limb entrapment is included as hazard in sleeping environments, which can cause Sudden Infant Death Syndrome (SIDS) [2]. Based on the findings of safety problems related to the rattan bassinet gap, when compared with the pattern of crib accidents that occur, there is a similarity in the type of risk condition related to the crib slat components. Therefore, it is necessary to identify the characteristics of unique rattan slat design in relation to the safety risk of its users, the babies.

There is no federal regulation for rattan crib slats mechanism. Although the full body rattan crib standard has referred to the Standard Consumer Safety Specification (CPSC),

N. L. Black et al. (Eds.): IEA 2021, LNNS 222, pp. 3–12, 2021.
https://doi.org/10.1007/978-3-030-74611-7_1

which states that there should be no more than 2 3/8 in. or 60 mm gaps between crib slats and other provisions such as no missing or cracked slats, there are still some types of risky condition for rattan crib slats [10, 11]. The slat component design, including rattan woven on the side of the crib, brings unique potential risks such as the inconsistent decor gaps due to the pliable material properties and handmade workmanship processes. This is an important concern in the issue of avoiding the risk of entrapment as previously described (AAP 2016). In addition, the provisions for rattan material have not been listed in the standard rules of the American Society for Testing and Materials (ASTM), which only mention wooden crib [25]. Therefore, a research to investigate the effects of rattan bassinets and cribs with several design variations related to the risk of entrapment and baby safety is essential. The findings of this research can be used to determine the risk of rattan cribs that have a unique variety of slat designs and to identify the safety standards for rattan crib slats.

1 Research Method

1.1 Variable

The National Electronic Injury Surveillance System (NEISS), operated by the CPSC, had reviewed the use of baby cribs and bassinets to classify the mechanism of injury [12]. The observation was limited to the potential risk of entrapment which led to the mechanism of injury so that the injured body region and type of injury categories did not occur under observation. In addition, it has been stated that safe baby crib products are those that do not cause the baby to fall when the baby climbs the side of the crib, do not cause the baby's limbs or head to get stuck between the slats and do not cause baby to fall into the gap of the mattress/bed base [13, 18]. Thus, the variables were adjusted in this research related to the potential risk of entrapment, including (1) the baby climbing the side of the crib (2) being hits or falling inside the crib and 3) being caught or wedged in the baby crib.

1.2 Participant

Indonesian babies who are healthy and with normal growth were chosen to represent the universal growth of all babies [14].

A total of 4 Indonesian babies were involved as participants to be observed in terms of the sleeping behavior and their interactions with the products. The infant participants were 0–12 months old, with mean ± SD of ages: 6.75 ± 3.4; weight 8.6 ± 2.8, and body length 60.5 ± 15.4. The selection of participant ages was based on the consideration that at that current age the babies were still using baby cribs during the time of the study. The conditions were observed when the babies were calm in their cribs, without any direction ahead and they were allowed to interact with their sleeping environment as well as their sleeping position.

1.3   Research Instrument

The research method was carried out in the field of ergonomics by observing the babies' behavior while doing their activities in a rattan bassinet and crib. The bassinet and crib have variations in the distance between the components of the slats. There are 4 types of designs that are in great demand by the market [8]. The designs studied consisted of 2 types of baby bassinet designs and 2 types of baby crib designs which were selected based on the variations of rattan decor and the users' age.

Type of Product	Rattan Decor or Slat Details
 Bassinet A	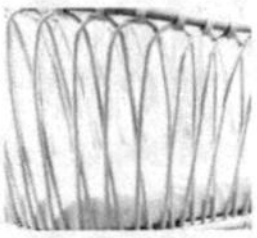
 Bassinet B	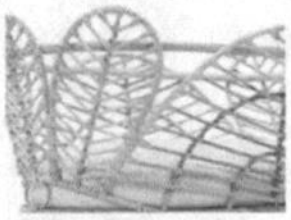
  Crib A	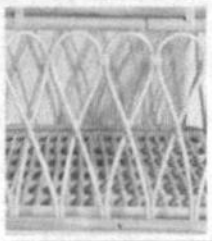
  Crib B	

Fig. 1. Bassinet and crib types (Left) and details of decor or slat of the bassinet and crib

In the details of the Slat components, there are differences in the size of the material used in the Bassinet and Crib (see Fig. 1). There are 4 types of products used, including: Type (1) Rattan Bassinet A & type (2) Bassinet B: the side of the bassinet, namely the slat decor using the 8–10 mm Rattan decor. The smaller sizes of rattan diameter are commonly used in some of the typical decor patterns for baby baskets aged 0–4 months.

And type (3) Crib A uses 10–12 mm rattan slats or decorations, while type (4) Crib B uses 20–22 mm rattan slats or decorations. These diameter sizes are used to adjust to the larger product proportion than those of the bassinets as well as the function of the crib which is used for babies aged 6 months and above so that bigger and stronger components are required. Natural rattan bark is used to tie joints between components. The products were made by hand of a highly skilled rattan maker.

The detail of the curved rattan decor with a 10 mm core type of rattan diameter (left) follows the standard reference for the Crib slat gap distance (see Fig. 2). It can be seen that the slat distance on the Crib side is inconsistent, namely a distance of 80 mm and 70 mm, or more than 60 mm. Rattan slats have a pliable nature with curved shapes and intersecting parts, resulting in inconsistent spacing (see Fig. 2).

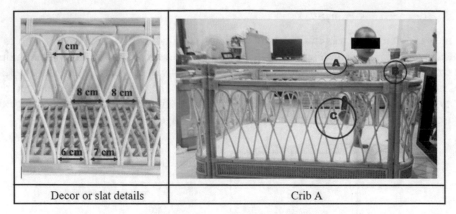

| Decor or slat details | Crib A |

Fig. 2. Spacing of rattan decor (left) and baby activities in crib A (right).

The physical body of the crib refers to the entire Crib section and the slat component parts that are the focus of the investigation. The red circle in section A is the outermost main frame, which is often held by babies. The red circle in section B is the corner of the connection of two parts, or it is called a corner post. The red circle in section C is a rattan decoration or Crib slat component that often gets pressure from babies' movements, such as from the legs while the babies are climbing/pushing the decorations on the Crib slat section.

1.4 Research Tools

Xiaomi Home Security Camera 360° 1080 P. Canon Camera 550 D.

1.5 Trial Tasks, Conditions, Procedures

The observations were done in 3 days. Each product was placed in each room of the participant's house for 3 days with environmental conditions that were familiar to the participants. The babies were then placed in the bassinet and crib, and all of their activities in the products were observed.

The baby's behavior was observed when they were awake to see their response when climbing and pushing with their feet on the Crib slat decoration (see Fig. 1). The red circle (section C) is a rattan decoration or Crib slat component.

The activities were recorded using photos and videos from the camera mounted on the front of the product. The recording device was placed at 150 cm above the floor, which made it possible to capture the entire product. With this placement, it was expected that the participants would not lose focus. The recording was done in the nursery room using a camera and portable CCTV.

For each task, all participants were given a simulation before the actual experiment. Brief instructions were given to the mothers of the babies to help direct and carry out the activities according to the protocol. Adult assistants accompanied them for safety precautions and would stop the activities when there was a dangerous situation and if the situation seemed impossible to continue. Participants' mothers were interviewed after the observation activity was complete to provide an evaluation regarding product use and problems that occur during product use. The video observation was considered successful if the children responded by getting closer to the crib slats within the specified duration. When there was a technical error, or delay in installing the camera, the video must be re-recorded at the next meeting.

2 Results

Potential Risk in Mechanism of Entrapment
Most of the potential risk found involved the Cribs (see Fig. 3). Climb up in the crib were the common risk potential of entrapment, accounting for 71.4% of entrapment among babies 5–12 months. The second most common risk potential in the mechanism of entrapment included a caught, wedged in crib with 28.5%.

Table 1. Potential risk in the entrapment mechanism of rattan bassinet and crib

Type	Age, Month	Hit, and fell in bassinet and crib	Climb up	Caught, wedged in crib
Bassinet	0–4 Month Male Female	– –	– –	– –
Crib	5–12 Month Male Female	– –	4x 6x	2x 2x
	TOTAL	–	10x	4x

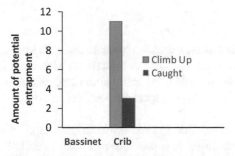

Fig. 3. Total potential risk activity in mechanism of entrapment

The results of the observations on the 2 physical designs of the small decor woven bassinet 8–10 mm did not show a potential risk of entrapment towards the safety of infants aged 0–4 months Table 1.

In the design of Crib A, with decorations made of rattan with a diameter of 10 mm which intersects each other (see Fig. 2), it was found that the gap between the components is more than 6 cm. When baby boys and girls (ages 5 months–12 months) tried to stand up, their hands and feet pressed the sides of the crib. During the 1 h observation, there were 10 times where the baby's feet attempted to play with the decor and attempted to climb by pressing the decor patterns that were intersected and joined by rattan ties Table 1.

Fig. 4. Picture of rattan ties on a crib slat decor

The pressure effect from the baby's movements on the rattan decor in Crib A (see Fig. 4) allows the rattan ties to loosen or even get loose. The loose ties may injure the baby's skin. Soft-tissue injury, including bruises and scrapes, is the most common injury, representing about one-third of all injuries reported [15].

In the Crib B design (see Fig. 1, where the slat crib decoration has 22 mm diameter rattan rods arranged in straight positions like a fence and resulting in a 60 mm gap, it was consistently recorded as safe and did not pose a potentially fatal risk. The placement of the mattress on the base of the bed was not obstructed by the rattan decor and the four corners of the bed base were suitable.

3 Discussion

Unlike other nursery products, the rattan bassinet and crib have a unique critical issue. Although many studies have examined non-fatal crib associated injury in infants, there is still little research on the potential risk of nonfatal crib associated injury. To our knowledge, this is the first study to report the potential risk of nonfatal rattan crib related injury among babies.

The investigation found that the red circle in section C is a decorative rattan or crib slat component that often gets pressure treatment from babies, such as when the babies climbed/pushed the decorations on the slat sections. This also carries the risk of loosening the rattan ties and the spacing of the plible rattan decor (see Fig. 4). The application of the curved decor intersecting over the crib (see Fig. 2) is not a suitable design for rattan with a diameter of 10 mm in the crib slat component. This allows the limb to be trapped by the rattan decoration in the slat component [16]. This is in line with the recommendation by the CPSC which states that there should be no more than

2 3/8 in. or 60 mm gap between crib slats and there should not be any missing or cracked slats to avoid limb entrapment. Furthermore, the CPSC advises parents to place babies to sleep in a sleeping environment that conforms to current standards; and be alert to the danger of choking and getting wedged in gaps between loose components, damaged blades, and other parts [17].

In the practice in the field, the production of rattan bassinet and crib still has shortcomings in terms of safety, namely the slat crib component that applies 10 mm diameter rattan material which is pliable with a curved decoration pattern intersected with rattan ties. These production processes have the risk of producing rattan décor with inconsistent gap spacing that is less or more than 6 cm (see Fig. 2). This creates a potential hazard when the baby's feet get caught between the decor gaps or allow the baby to climb over the side of the crib. This potential risk that leads to the mechanism of injury must be avoided, because it is related to the physical mechanics of the baby furniture design that can cause potential hazards where the child can climb and fall (13, 26). Children's development and coordination skills develop rapidly and motor skills improve in the first 2 years of their life. Children have the desire to explore their environment. Applying decorative webbing or rattan with a curved pattern over the crib allows the children to climb out. This potential risk is similar to the condition of placing netting over the crib because babies may become entrapped and strangled [20]. In addition n, the occurrence of children climbing out of the crib poses a risk of strangulation. The possibility of children's clothes getting stuck around the child's neck could happen. This has led to the incidence of clothing being caught around the neck and stuck on knobs and posts in the hardware sections projecting from cribs [16, 21, 29]. Recent studies have reported that almost all of the more than 2000 deaths in that study happened in such condition. Children were lying in bed and later found to be unresponsive, often lying face down on blankets or pillows or wedged between the mattress or base and the side of the bed. Although the cause of death was not always stated in the narrative or diagnosis of the NEISS cases, most were noted as anoxia or described in the narrative as sudden infant death syndrome or suffocation [4, 9, 22].

There were 10 activities in which the babies attempted to play with curved decorations that intersect with each other, and attempted to climb out within the 1 h observation time limit Table 1. This is an estimate of the potential risk of injury that has not been included in the variable mechanism of entrapment that was specified by the NEISS. Our findings illustrate the potential risk of limb entrapment contributing to the causes of infant jumping out or inside crib. Meanwhile, the choice of using a bumper or netting over the crib to prevent entrapment related to crib is also not recommended [20, 27, 28]. In some cases of other studies that involved the baby being stuck between the mattress and the mattress, the baby might also be caught between the netting and the side of the crib slats. The fact that baby's head is bigger and heavier than the small limbs and the neck muscles are in the developing stage allows the baby's head to get stuck and it is difficult to escape from the dangerous condition [4, 25]. The non-fatal issue in our study involving infants was the pressure on the slat crib caused by the infants' movements, such as when climbing/pushing the decoration on the slat section. This also has the risk of loosening the rattan ties and the pliable rattan decor slat spacing Fig. 4. The design of woven cribs or rattan decorations that intersect with gaps of more than 6 cm is strongly discouraged. Because this shape also triggers the interaction of the child to climb out of the crib. The loose gaps between slats pose a risk of injury, including suffocation and strangulation [2, 4]. Our findings support the recommendations of the American Academy of Pediatrics to reduce the risk of sudden infant death.

The safety of the rattan crib design is an important concern so that babies can sleep soundly, safely and avoid dangerous environments [6]. Of the two bassinet designs, a bassinet with small gaps between the slats, 2–3 cm, does not pose a risk to the safety of infants aged 0–4 months. Because babies of this age are still building muscle strength to move and do not cause much response to the motions in the bed environment [31–33]. For children aged 5 months and over, it is time to move from baby bassinet to baby crib, because babies can already change their own body position [29, 30]. Further research is needed in regards of the shape and distance between the components in a rattan baby crib to keep it safe even though it is processed using handmade crafts. ASTM recently revised its voluntary standards to reduce hazards associated with full-size cribs, bassinets and non-full-size cribs. Compared to the mandatory standards announced by the CPSC, voluntary standards can be applied more quickly and allow design changes to reach the marketplace faster [30]. Precautions through better product design must be achieved to effectively protect young infants in their sleeping environment.

4 Conclusion

Rattan baby crib with slat gaps that exceeds 60 mm and curved intersecting decor on the market that may threat baby's safety. Further research on the safety standards of handmade rattan baby bassinet and crib need to be established.

References

1. Mafra, S.C.T., et al.: ERGOBERÇO® (Ergonomics Crib) Evaluation of the Prototype for a Adaptation to Safety's Variables and Comfort. IOS Press, vol. 41, pp. 1–7. https://doi.org/10.3233/WOR-2012-0567-3085 (2012)
2. Moon, R.Y., et al.: SIDS and other sleep-related infant deaths: expansion of recommendations for a safe infant sleeping environment. Pediatrics 57(7), e1341–e1367 (2011)
3. Scheers, N.J., et al.: Reports of injury risks and reasons for choice of sleep environments for infants and toddlers. Matern. Child Health J. 23, 1613–1620 (2019)
4. American Academy of Pediatrics. SIDS and other sleep-related infant deaths: updated 2016 recommendations for a safe infant sleeping environment. Pediatrics 138(5), e20162938 (2016). https://pediatrics.aappublications.org/content/pediatrics/138/5/e20162938.full.pdf. Accessed 1 Aug 2020
5. Snyder, R.G., Spencer, M.L., Owings, C.L.: Selected Infant Anthropometry: Crib Slat Sub-Safety Study, February (unpublished report) (1973)
6. Burns, R.: Top Find Maison Object.1805_Roomy_Issue Two_Bermbach [article online], pp. 41–43. Bermbach Handcrafted, Paris (2017). https://presse.bermbach-handcrafted.com/1805_Rooomy_Issue%20Two_Bermbach.pdf. Accessed 10 Nov 2019
7. Crate and Barrel, Crate and Kids Exclusive: Rattan Bassinet. Crate and Barrel, US (2019). https://www.crateandbarrel.com/rattan-bassinet/s303882. Accessed 20 Aug 2020
8. WISANKA. Consumer Product Rattan Bassinet and Crib. PT Wirasindo Santakarya (WISANKA), Indonesia (2019)

9. Jodi, P., Rachel, Y.M.: Bassinet use and sudden unexpected death in infancy. J. Pediatr. **153**, 509–512 (2008)
10. Engel, P.: Two in three bassinets fail our key safety tests [article online]. Consumer advocacy group in Australia (CHOICE), Australia (2020). https://www.choice.com.au/babies-and-kids/baby-furniture/cots/articles/over-two-thirds-of-bassinets-fail-safety-tests. Accessed 15 Aug 2020
11. Smith, G.: Unsafe Nursery Design Trends [article online]. Consumer advocacy group in Australia (CHOICE), Australia (2020). https://www.choice.com.au/babies-and-kids/children-and-safety/avoiding-common-dangers/articles/unsafe-nursery-design-trends. Accessed 15 Aug 2020
12. US Consumer Product Safety Commission, NEISS: National Electronic Injury Surveillance System, A Tool for Researchers. Consumer Product Safety Commission. Washington, DC, US (2000)
13. Kravitz, H., Driessen, G., Gomberg, R., Korach, A.: Accidental falls from elevated surfaces in infant from birth to one year of age. Pediatrics **44**, 869–875 (1969)
14. Lansdown, G.: The Evolving Capacities of the Child. In: Boyden, J., Ling, B., Myers, W. (ed.) UNICEF, Florence (2005); originally amended from Boyden, J., Ling, B., Myers, W. What Works for Working Children, Radda Barnen/UNICEF, Florence p. 10–13 (1998)
15. Harris, T.S., et al.: Bruises in children: normal or child abuse? J. Pediatr. Health Care: Official Publ. Natl. Assoc. Pediatr. Nurse Assoc. Pract. **24**(4), 216–221 (2009)
16. Safety Research and Strategies, Inc. Crib tents: another hazard from the world of unregulated child products [article online]. Research Investigation Analysis Strategy Advocacy: Safety Research and Strategies, Inc., Washington, D.C. (2009). https://www.safetyresearch.net/blog/articles/crib-tents-another-hazard-world-unregulated-child-products. Accessed 10 Mar 2019
17. US Consumer Product Safety Commission. The safe nursery [article online]. CPSC publication no 202. CPSC, US (2009). https://www.cpsc.gov/cpscpub/pubs/202.pdf. Accessed 10 Mar 2019
18. Carroll, J.L., Siska, E.S.: SIDS: counseling parents to reduce the risk. Am. Family Physician **57**(7), 1566–1572 (1998)
19. Nelson, T.: Hazard analysis of injuries relating to Cribs. U. S. Consumer Product Safety Commision, pp. 61–62 (1975)
20. Scheers, N.J., Woodard, D.W., Thach, B.T.: Crib bumpers continue to cause infant deaths: a need for a new preventive approach. Pediatrics, pp. 93–97. https://doi.org/10.1016/j.jpeds.2015.10.050 (2015)
21. Ray, J.G., et al.: Birth weight curves tailored to maternal world region. Soc. Obstet. Gynaecol. Canada **34**(2), 159–171. https://doi.org/10.1016/S1701-2163(16)35159-3 (2012)
22. Consumer Product Safety Commission. CPSC Cautions Caregivers About Hidden Hazards for Babies on Adult Beds (2016) E-Print. https://cpsc.gov/s3fs-public/5091.pdf. Accessed 20 Aug 2020
23. Drago, D.A., Dannenberg, A.L.: Infant mechanical suffocation deaths in the United States. Pediatrics **103**(5) , 1980–1997 (1999). www.pediatrics.org/cgi/content/full/103/5/e59. Accessed 20 Aug 2020
24. Bureau Veritas Test Protocol. Full sizes baby crib. CPSD-TY-08102-USA-3 STAR. U.S. Consumer Product Safety Commission, pp. 7–8 (2020)
25. Pollack-Nelson, C., Drago, D.A.: Hazards associated with common nursery products. In: Liller, K., (ed.) Injury Prevention for Children and Adolescents. American Public Health Association, pp. 65–90. Washington, D.C. (2006)
26. Yeh, E.S., Rochette, L.M., McKenzie, L.B., Smith, G.A.: Injuries Associated With Cribs, Playpens, and Bassinets among Young Children in the US, pp. 1–10 (2011)

27. Safety Research and Strategies, Inc Crib tents: another hazard from the world of unregulated child products [article online] 2009. www.safetyresearch.net/2009/02/01/crib-tents-another-hazardfrom-the-world-of-unregulated-childproducts. Accessed 10 Aug 2020

28. Moore, L., Byard, R.W.: Pathological findings in hanging and wedging deaths in infants and young children. Am. J. Forensic Med. Pathol. **14**(4), 296–302 (1993)

29. Ridenour, M.V.: How do children climb out of cribs? Percept Mot Skills. **95**(2), 363–366 (2002)

30. Ridenour, M.V.: Catch-points as strangulation hazards in cribs. Percept Mot Skills **93**(3), 757–760 (2001)

31. WHO Motor development study: Windows of achievement for six gross motor development-milestones. Acta Paediatric Supplement **450**, 86–95 (2006)

32. Pollack-Nelson, C., Drago, D.A.: Hazards associated with common nursery products. In: Liller, K. (ed.) Injury Prevention for Children and Adolescents, pp. 65–90. American Public Health Association, Washington, DC (2006)

33. Scheers, N.J., Rutherford, G.W., Kemp, J.S.: Where should infants sleep? A comparison of risk for suffocation of infants sleeping in cribs, adult beds, and other sleeping locations. Pediatrics **112**, 883–839 (2003)

Implications of the Reform to the Colombian Health System in Employment Conditions, Working Conditions and Mental Health Status of the Health Workers: A Systematic Literature Review

Sara Baquero[✉] and Luz Pérez

Universidad Nacional de Colombia, Carrera 45 # 26-85, Bogotá, D.C., Colombia
{wlbaquero,laperezf}@unal.edu.co

Abstract. This study aims to describe the state of the art about the implications of the social security model in health, established with the Law 100 of 1993, in employment conditions, working conditions and mental health in Colombian health workers. A qualitative systematic literature review was carried out during the months of April and May of 2020. An electronic search of literature was made by consulting the REDALYC, SciELO, Google Scholar, DIALNET, ScienceDirect, Scopus and ELSEVIER databases. Considering the established inclusion and exclusion criteria, we used the PRISMA flow chart to select the studies. For the ordering of the data, we used a matrix for registration, extraction, and organization of information with the support of a spreadsheet (Excel software). 128 documents were identified and 45 were analysed. What we found indicates that the current state of employment and working conditions are harmful for the mental health of the Colombian health workers and those conditions are related to the proposals of Law 100 of 1993. Intrinsic motivation, social relationships, and leadership are noted as protective factors. The processes of outsourcing, deregulation of the labor market and job insecurity constitute the biggest problems and limitations for the mental well-being of the health personnel.

Keywords: Colombian health reform · Health workers · Mental health · Work conditions and employment conditions

1 Introduction

The current Colombian General System of Social Security in Health (henceforth SGSSS) was established with the Law 100 of 1993. This health system has remained intact, despite the regulatory adjustments after Law 100. The objective of this law was the adoption of the compulsory insurance figure, an objective that was reached thanks to the establishment of private agents and with the creation of two regimes: the contributory, for people who could afford health services, and the subsidized, aimed at the poor population [1–3, 6]. Among other things, the Reform of the Law 100 of 1993 facilitates

N. L. Black et al. (Eds.): IEA 2021, LNNS 222, pp. 13–20, 2021.
https://doi.org/10.1007/978-3-030-74611-7_2

the reduction of economic resources in the sector since this reform demands economic efficiency from health institutions. As a strategy, the health institutions have carried out restructuring processes that have led to fixed-term employment of health personnel, to its reduction and to the implementation of labor market flexibility. According to a survey conducted by the Colombian Medical College [8], 80% of physicians have some type of illegal hiring; 15% of rural physicians are not hired, although legally they should be. 54% of general practitioners and 56% of specialist physicians are hired under the figure of Service Provision employment modality. About salary, 40% of professionals in rural areas have received their salary late and 50% of them have had difficulties with the payments. For 67% of the specialist doctors, 59% of the general ones, 18% of the rural ones and 65% of the other health professionals, the main entity that owes them salary is the IPS. Frequently, health workers face lack of social security, compensatory days and overtime pay; exhausting working hours, low wages, outsourcing and shortages of work supplies. Also, they are pushed into the phenomenon of moonlighting. The described employment conditions negatively affect the health of workers because it exposes them to psychosocial risk factors, occupational diseases, low job satisfaction, decreased quality of life, anxiety, and burnout [9–15]. Usually, the analysis of workers mental health conditions focuses on the individual process, neglecting organizational context and structural factors that can harm their well-being. There is a need to describe the relationships between these processes that derived from the mentioned Law. With the purpose of contributing to this, we did a systematic literature review that aims to describe the advance of knowledge about the implications of the social security model in Health, established with Law 100 of 1993, in employment conditions, working conditions and mental health status in Colombian health workers.

2   Method

A qualitative systematic review of literature was carried out during April and May of 2020, following the adapted methodological proposal of Chicaíza et al. [16]. The search, results and findings were developed following the guiding question: What are the implications of the social security model in health, established with Law 100 of 1993, on employment conditions, working conditions and mental health in Colombian health workers? The answer to this question was addressed with the search for the following topics and keywords: employment conditions, working conditions and work-related mental health.

The inclusion criteria were studies that examined the health workers in Colombia, in the context of the Reform of Social Security in Health-Law 100 of 1993, in Spanish or English, in the period from 2010 to 2020, with access to the full text. We also considered papers that studied the nexus between employment conditions and working conditions, on the one hand, and mental problems—or disorders—in health workers, on the other hand. The type of studies included were primary studies and in gray literature, specialization, master's, or doctoral thesis. The exclusion criteria were studying whose participants were students, patients or health workers with comorbidity and a history of depression, anxiety, and suicide attempts. Similarly, studies that focused on hospital administration. Furthermore, opinion articles, graduate projects and letters to the editor were excluded.

An electronic search of the literature was carried out by consulting the REDALYC, Sci-ELO, Google Academic, DIALNET, ScienceDirect, Scopus and ELSEVIER databases. The keywords used were identified in the DeCS thesaurus. Considering the established criteria, we used the PRISMA flow diagram [62], according to the adapted methodology developed by Chicaíza et al. [16], for the selection of the studies. For the ordering of the data, we made a matrix of registration, extraction, and organization of information with the support of the Excel software. Note that the identified studies were evaluated with the inclusion criteria. The titles, abstracts, and introductory section of each document were then examined to determine their inclusion—or not—and subsequent analysis.

3 Results

We identified 128 documents. Among these, we dismissed 26 duplicate documents. A careful examination of each of the 102 eligible studies led to the final inclusion, for analysis, of 45 of them. Of the total of 45 documents included in the final analysis, 34 were primary studies, 4 corresponded to theoretical works, 6 were specialization, master's, or doctoral thesis, and 1 was a systematic literature review. Regarding the geographical distribution of the studies, in Bogotá D.C. 23 of the studies were carried out, while 22 were conducted throughout the national territory. The year of with the greatest number of publications was 2015 (20%), followed, in equal proportions, in 2010 (15%) and 2014 (15%). On the other hand, about the methodology used, 55% (25) of the studies used a cross-sectional quantitative approach; 29% (13) corresponded to a qualitative approach and 15% (7) used a mixed method design. With respect to the scope of research, 87% (39) of the studies were descriptive, 2% (1) explanatory, 9% (4) correlational and 2% (1) exploratory. The literature reviewed shows that the current employment conditions and working conditions of the Colombian health workers are derived from the Colombian Health Reform, Law 100 of 1993, since this is the regulatory framework to which the working conditions of health workers were adjusted.

The most important employment conditions identified as psychosocial risk factors are job insecurity, laboral contract types, the salaries, and the strenuous working hours of the health workers. Regarding working conditions, the following were identified as psychosocial risk factors for health workers: increased workload, high emotional demands, alterations in work rhythms, changes in life routines, variable work hours, little time available to dedicate to extra-work activities, physical and psychological aggressions, and cognitive psychological demands typical of a psychological burden, which outweigh emotional demands.

4 Discussion

Although the Law 100 of 1993 does not include aspects that are directly related to the labor market of the health sector, it is possible to ensure that, with its entry into force, the working conditions of these workers underwent important changes in terms of employment conditions and working conditions. The mentioned law does not indicate mechanisms that guides the operation of the health workers, nor does it offer them protection against outsourcing and job insecurity. Also, this law indicates that a salary regime must be established whose objective must be to achieve the gradual leveling of salaries for all the health workers. However, it does not offer a clear policy to achieve that and does not clarify the labor relations of these workers. At this point, it is necessary to emphasize that the employment conditionsand working conditions of the health workers are not only determined by the structure of the health system itself but also by different government entities, by labor legislation and by the economic resources available for the administration of the sanitary system [63].

About the employment conditions and their relationship with the mental health of these workers, some authors highlight that, with the entry into force of the Law 100 of 1993, processes of flexibilization and job insecurity have been carried out. Additionally, outsourcing, deregulation labor market and job insecurity processes constitute the greatest problems and limitations for the mental well-being of health workers [28, 29, 40–44, 58]. The employment conditions such as long working hours, the type of contracts; labor relations through work cooperatives and the social security shortcomings negatively impact the job satisfaction, working commitment, personal well-being, quality of life and, in addition, can cause emotional damage [30, 31, 33–35, 37, 38, 46–48, 50–54, 56, 60, 61]. As well, the evidence proves that if there is low extrinsic motivation, there will be negative effects at work [10, 26, 34, 38, 57]. Job insecurity and work overload are the most unfavorable factors risk for workers in the health sector, regardless of their functions. These factors are related to labor and health policies [37, 38, 46].

Relating to working conditions and their relationship with the workers' mental health, several authors affirmed that health workers have high work pressure due to the number of patients they must attend per day and the extension of the workday [28, 41–45]. Also, health workers deal with physical and psychological aggressions that harm their living and health conditions [30, 34, 35, 37–39, 46–48, 50–54, 60, 61].

Burnout syndrome is the most studied disorder when it concerns to the health of the workers. It has been established that in organizations in which workers face demanding—or hard—working conditions, such as those experienced by healthcare personnel, there are physical, social, and organizational demands that tend to produce discomfort and involve high cognitive effort, leading to the development of burnout [17–19, 23, 24, 27, 30, 32, 36, 39, 46, 50, 51, 54, 56, 57, 59].

To conclude, it is possible to affirm that the Law 100 of 1993, with its neoliberal perspective on health, radically changed employers, the nature of the medical work and the labor market of health workers. Under this change, mixed payments abound. The scope of this systematic literature review is descriptive and although it is an important input to the advance of knowledge about the implications of the Colombian health reform, further studies are needed. For this purpose, macro ergonomics and cognitive ergonomics could contribute to a systemic and holistic understanding of the situation, hence it is very important to develop new studies from organizational and cognitive ergonomics.

References

1. Hernández, M.: Reforma sanitaria, equidad y derecho a la salud en Colombia. Cad Saúde Pública **18**(4), 991–1001 (2002)
2. Gutiérrez, J., Restrepo, R.: El pluralismo estructurado de Londoño y Frenk frente a la articulación y modulación del Sistema General de Seguridad Social en Salud (SGSSS) en Colombia. Sociedad y Economía **23**, 183–204 (2012)
3. Cortés, A., Yepes, F., Agudelo, S., Gorbanev, I.: El sistema de salud colombiano: Grupos relacionados de diagnóstico, 21st edn. Editorial Pontificia Universidad Javeriana, Bogotá D.C (2018)
4. Ocampo, J.: Reflexiones sobre las ciencias económicas, 1st edn. Universidad Nacional de Colombia, Bogotá D.C (2010)
5. Estrada, J.: Construcción del modelo neoliberal en Colombia 1970–2004. Editorial Aurora, Bogotá D.C. (2004)
6. Urrea, F.: Trabajo y modelos productivos en América Latina, Argentina, Brasil, Colombia, México, y Venezuela luego de las crisis del modo de desarrollo neoliberal. In: Consejo-Latinoamericano de Ciencias Sociales - CLACSO: CLACSO, Buenos Aires, pp.137–203 (2010)
7. Barón, G.: Gasto Nacional en Salud de Colombia, 1993–2003. Composición y tendencias. Rev Salud Pública (Bogotá) **9**(2), 167–179 (2007)
8. Colegio Médico Colombiano: Encuesta de situación laboral para los profesionales de la salud. Epicrisis **12**, 1–10 (2019)
9. Ansoleaga, E., Castillo, A.: Riesgo psicosocial laboral y patología mental en trabajadores de hospital. Rev. Fac. Nac. Sad. Pub. **29**(4), 372–329 (2011)
10. Tejada, P., Gómez, V.: Factores psicosociales y laborales asociados al burnout de psiquiatras en Colombia. Rev. Colomb Psiquiatría **38**(3), 488–512 (2009)
11. Escriba-Agüir, V., Artacoz, L., Pérez-Hoyos, S.: Efecto del ambiente psicosocial y de la satisfacción laboral en el síndrome de burnout en médicos especialistas. Gac Sanit **22**(4), 300–308 (2008)
12. Aranda, C., Pando, M., Salazar, J., Torres, T., Aldrete, M., Pérez, M.: Factores psicosociales laborales y síndrome de Burnout en médicos del primer nivel de atención. Invest Sal. **6**(1), 28–34 (2004)
13. Cardona, A., Mejía, L., Nieto, E., Restrepo, R.: Temas críticos en la reforma de la Ley de seguridad social de Colombia en el capítulo de salud. Rev. Fac. Nac. Sad. Pub. **23**(1), 117–133 (2005)
14. Eslava, J., Barón, G., Gaitán-Duarte, H., Alfonso, H., Agudelo, C., Sánchez, C.: Evaluación del impacto en costo-equidad del Sistema de Salud en Colombia. Rev. Sal. Pub. **10**(1), 3–17 (2008)
15. Patiño, J.: La ley 100 de 1993. Reforma y crisis de la salud en Colombia. Rev. Gerenc. Polit. Sal. **9**, 173–179 (2009)
16. Chicaíza, L., Riaño, M., Rojas, S., Garzón, C.: Revisión sistemática de literatura en Administración. Documentos FCE-CID Escuela de Administración y Contaduría Pública **29**, 2–18 (2017)
17. Segura, O.: Agotamiento profesional: Concepciones e implicaciones en la salud pública. Biomédica **34**(4), 535–545 (2014)
18. Segura, O., Enciso, C., Gómez, M., Castañeda, O.: Agotamiento profesional en médicos intensivistas colombianos: Un estudio caso-control. Acta Colombiana de Medicina crítica y Cuidado Intensivo **16**(2), 1–10 (2016)
19. Segura, O.: Agotamiento profesional: Hacia una epidemiología social de la unidad de cuidado intensivo Burnout. Rev. Fac. Med. **64**(4), 721–725 (2016)

20. Robayo, E., Moncada, P., Murillo, L., Flórez, E., Barreto, M.: Análisis crítico de la deshumanización de la atención en salud en Colombia. Revista Opinión Pública **2**(2), 45–52 (2015)
21. Bruno, V., Bustamante, M., Jiménez, A., Maldonado, L., Segura, I., Tuesca, R.: Atención Primaria en Salud. Una mirada desde los profesionales de enfermería: Barreras, conocimientos y actividades. Salud Uninorte **31**(2), 295–308 (2015)
22. Solano, S.: Satisfacción laboral en profesionales de enfermería. Revista Cuidarte **1**(21), 53–62 (2015)
23. Eslava, J., Garzón, N., Tamayo, N., González, L., Rosero, E., Gómez, C.: Prevalence and factors associated with burnout syndrome in colombian anesthesiologists. Int. J. Prev. Med. **11**(5), 1–11 (2020)
24. Bonilla, D., Garzón, N., Carrasco, L., Florez, A., Martínez, L., Pardo, C.: Ausentismo laboral en el centro de atención médica inmediata Vista Hermosa I nivel, empresa social del Estado. Ciencia y Tecnología para la Salud Visual y Ocular **12**(1), 21–32 (2014)
25. Calderón, J.: Autonomía médica y ley estatutaria de salud. Acta médica colombiana **40**(1), 21–32 (2015)
26. Contreras, F., Espinosa, J., Hernández, F., Acosta, N.: Calidad de vida laboral y liderazgo en trabajadores asistenciales y administrativos en un centro oncológico de Bogotá (Colombia). Psicología desde el Caribe **30**(3), 560–590 (2014)
27. Sarsosa, K., Charria, V.H., Arenas, F.: Caracterización de los riesgos psicosociales intralaborales en jefes asistenciales de cinco clínicas nivel III de Santiago de Cali (Colombia). Rev. Gerenc. Polít. Salud **13**(27), 348–361 (2014)
28. Restrepo, F., López, A., Gutiérrez, L.: Condiciones laborales del personal de la salud en la región del Urabá- Colombia. Un análisis de la subjetividad laboral. Teuken Bidikay **6**(6), 145–161 (2014)
29. Cogollo, Z., Gómez, E.: Condiciones laborales en enfermeras de Cartagena, Colombia. Avances en enfermería **18**(1), 31–38 (2018)
30. Casto, N.R., Guío, M.M.S., (dir) García, J.E.L.: Condiciones Psicosociales Laborales del Personal de una Secretaría de Salud Territorial en Colombia [Thesis]: Universidad Distrital Francisco José de Caldas (2015)
31. Arango, G.: Conflictos éticos que se presentan a médicos de tres centros hospitalarios de Bogotá. Colombia. Revista Latinoamericana de Bioética **15**(1), 108–119 (2015)
32. Domínguez, L., Sanabria, A., Ramírez, A., Vargas, F., Pacheco, M., Jiménez, G.: Desgaste profesional en residentes colombianos de cirugía: Resultados de un estudio nacional. Rev. Colombiana de Cirugía **32**, 121–127 (2017)
33. Hackspiel, M., Paredes, O.: Dilemas bioéticos de médicos y enfermeras en la prevención de la atención primaria de salud en las ciudades de Bogotá y Valledupar. Colombia. Rev. Med. **2**, 101–114 (2012)
34. Garrido, J., Blanch, J., Uribe, A., Flórez, J., Pedrozo, M.: El capitalismo Organizacional como factor de riesgo Psicosocial: Efectos psicológicos colaterales de las nuevas condiciones de trabajo en hospitales y universidades de naturaleza pública. Resultados Santander, Colombia. Psicología desde el Caribe **28**, 166–196 (2011)
35. Hernández, J.Á., Cadavid, M.A.: Estrategias de afrontamiento del problema cognitivo bajo la nueva gestión pública en los profesionales del sector educativo y de salud de las instituciones públicas de Colombia, 2013 [Thesis]: Universidad de Manizales (2013). https://bit.ly/2TT X0bs
36. Sarsosa, K., Charria, V.H.: Estrés laboral en personal asistencial de cuatro instituciones de salud nivel III de Cali. Colombia. Univ. Salud **20**(1), 44–52 (2018)
37. Arenas, F., Jaramillo, V.: Factores de riesgo psicosocial y compromiso con el trabajo en una organización del sector salud de la ciudad de Cali. Colombia. Acta Colombiana de Psicología **16**(1), 43–56 (2018)

38. Castillo, I., Santana, M., Valeta, A., Alvis, L.R., Romero, E.: Factores de riesgo psicosociales del trabajo en médicos de una Empresa Social del Estado en Cartagena de Indias. Colombia. Rev. Fac. Nac. Salud Pública 29(4), 363–371 (2011)
39. Cañón, S., Galeano, G.: Factores laborales psicosociales y calidad de vida laboral de los trabajadores de la salud de ASSBASALUD E.S.E Manizales (Colombia). Archivos de Medicina 11(2), 114–126 (2011)
40. Molina, G., Oquendo, T., Rodríguez, S., Montoya, N., Vesga, C., Lagos, N., Almanza, R., Chavarro, M., Goenaga, E., Arboleda, G.: Gestión del talento humano en salud pública. Un análisis en cinco ciudades colombianas 2014. Rev. Gerenc. Polit. 15(30), 108–125 (2016)
41. Pinilla, M., Abadía, C.: Hospital San Juan de Dios: Actor y víctima de las políticas públicas en Colombia. Rev. Peru. Med. Exp. Salud. Publica. 34(2), 287–292 (2017)
42. Velandia, A.: La enfermería en Colombia 1990–2010. Ejercicio profesional y situación legal. Investigación en Enfermería: Imagen y Desarrollo 13(1), 287–292 (2011)
43. Ospina, J., Manrique, F., Martínez, A.: La formación de médicos generales según los requerimientos del sistema general de seguridad social en salud en Colombia. Revista Colombiana de Anestesiología 40(2), 124–126 (2012)
44. Florez, J., Atehortúa, S., Arenas, A.: Las condiciones laborales de los profesionales de la salud a partir de la Ley 100 de 1993: evolución y un estudio de caso para Medellín. Rev. Gerenc. Polit. Salud 8(16), 107–131 (2010)
45. Castro, M.V., Támez, A.R. (dir).: Limitaciones de la autonomía de los odontólogos en el sistema de salud colombiano actual 2011 [Thesis]: Pontificia Universidad Javeriana (2011). https://bit.ly/2Mg85iP
46. Luna-García, J., Urrego-Mendoza, Z., Gutiérrez-Robayo, M., Martínez-Durán, A.: Violencia en el trabajo del sector público de la salud: una visión desde las personas trabajadoras, Bogotá, Colombia. 2011–2012. Rev. Fac. Med. 63(3), 407–417 (2015)
47. Guerrero, J., Pulido, G.: Trabajo, salud y régimen contractual en personal de enfermería: un enfoque psicosocial. Bogotá, Colombia 2011–2012. Avances en enfermería 28(2), 111–122 (2018)
48. Bocanegra, J., González, L., Leguizamón, M., Eslava, J., Tamayo, N., Gómez, G.: Características sociodemográficas, académicas, laborales y satisfacción de los anestesiólogos en Colombia 2015, Bogotá, Colombia 2011–2012. Rev. Colomb. Anestesiol. 46(1), 11–18 (2018)
49. Atehortúa, S., Castaño, Y., Restrepo, R.: Situación de la enfermería en el desarrollo de la atención primaria en salud en Antioquia (Colombia): aproximación desde la perspectiva de los profesionales, Bogotá, Colombia 2011–2012. Revista Gerencia y Políticas de Salud 18(36), 1–35 (2019)
50. Ferrel, R., Sierra, E., Rodríguez, M.: Síndrome de desgaste profesional (burnout) en médicos especialistas de un hospital universitario, de la ciudad de Santa Marta, Colombia. Revista de la Facultad de Ciencias de la Salud 7(1), 29–40 (2017)
51. Abella, G.A., Furman, R. (dir): Síndrome de burnout en médicos residentes de psiquiatría en Bogotá (Colombia) [Thesis]: Universidad de Buenos Aires (2015). https://bit.ly/3gM4eI0
52. Cifuentes, J., Manrique, F.: Satisfacción laboral en enfermería en una institución de salud de cuarto nivel de atención, Bogotá, Colombia. Avances en enfermería 32(2), 29–40 (2014)
53. Uribe, A., Martínez, A.: Riesgos Psicosociales Intralaborales en instituciones de salud de nivel III de atención en Santander. Revista Interamericana de Psicología Ocupacional 32(2), 56–68 (2013)
54. Bustillo, M., Rojas, J., Sánchez, A., Sánchez, L., Montalvo, A., Rojas, M.: Riesgos Psicosocial en el personal de enfermería. Servicio de urgencias en Hospital Universitario de Cartagena. Duazary 12(1), 32–40 (2015)
55. Silva, D., Gutiérrez, A., Pando, M., Tuesca, R.: Relación entre factores psicosociales negativos y el síndrome de Burnout en el personal sanitario de Florencia (Caquetá, Colombia). Salud Uninorte 30(1), 52–62 (2014)

56. Ávila, J., Gómez, L., Montiel, M.: Características demográficas y laborales asociadas al Síndrome de Burnout en profesionales de la salud. Pensamiento psicológico **8**(15), 39–52 (2010)
57. Agudelo, C., Castaño, J., Arango, C., Durango, L., Muñoz, V., Ospina, A., Ramírez, J., Salazar, N., Serna, J., Taborda, J.: Prevalencia y factores psicosociales asociados al Síndrome de Burnout en médicos que laboran en instituciones de las ciudades de Manizales y la Virginia. Archivos de Medicina **11**(2), 91–100 (2010)
58. De la Cruz, G., Beltrán, E.: Flexibilización y precarización de los trabajadores de la salud en Santiago de Cali. Libre empresa1 **5**(2), 149–161 (2018)
59. Salgado, G.R., de Díaz M.A.L. (dir): Factores psicosociales de la organización del trabajo y su potencial influencia en la aparición de síndrome de burnout en profesionales de la salud responsables de actividades administrativas en Bogotá en el año 2014 [Thesis]: Universidad Nacional de Colombia (2015). https://bit.ly/2AtRKV2
60. Agudelo, J.R., Duque, G.A.C. (dir): Impacto de la reforma de la salud en colombia en la calidad de vida de los médicos en Caldas 2011 [Thesis]: Universidad Nacional de Colombia (2011). https://bit.ly/2Az7FkE
61. Abadía, C., Pinilla, M., Ariza, K., Ruíz, H.C.: Neoliberalismo en salud: La tortura de trabajadoras y trabajadores del Instituto Materno Infantil de Bogotá. Rev. Salud pública **14**(1), 18–31 (2012)
62. Moher, D., Liberati, A., Tetzlaff, J., Altman, D.G.: The PRISMA group (2019): preferred reporting items for systematic reviews and MetaAnalyses: the PRISMA statement. PLoS Med **6**(7) (2009)

Behavioral, Cognitive, and Psychophysiological Predictors of Failure-to-Identify Hunting Incidents

Karl E. Bridges(✉) ⓘ and P. M. Corballis ⓘ

University of Auckland, Auckland, New Zealand
kbri542@aucklanduni.ac.nz

Abstract. On average, a hunter is accidentally killed every nine months in New Zealand [1]. One of the most common causes of hunting fatalities in this country (up to 64%), are target identification failures - mistaking people for large game. Failure-to-identify incidents have no borders and occur primarily wherever a thriving recreational hunting industry exists. The USA and Canada experience similar incidence, with up to 75 fatalities per year [2]. Despite these statistics, no empirical research has been conducted on causation. Instead, researchers have focused on lag indications associated with incident rates and post investigative findings. Because of this, and in the wake of a pair of particularly troubling incidents in which a hunter shot and killed his own son [3] and in which a schoolteacher was killed while camping [4], we conducted a PhD study investigating the causes of failure-to-identify. This paper provides an overview of the findings and some of the resulting safety recommendations made to the hunting and firearms community.

Keywords: Hunting · Firearms · Functional resonance analysis · Neuroergonomics · Psychophysiology · Simulation

1 Introduction

Recommendations provided in the Arms Code [5] suggest refraining from discharging the firearm until the shooter is certain that their target has been fully identified; not shooting based on movement, color, sound, or shape alone. Despite being aware of the risk of failure-to-identify errors, many hunters believe they could not make such a mistake [6]. However, according to the Mountain Safety Council [7], a hunter is killed every seven months due to a failure-to-identify error. The danger is greatest during 'the roar' – a period from March to May (in New Zealand) when male deer will establish their rutting areas, and hunters have the greatest chance of shooting a stag [8–10]. During the roar male deer are less cautious around humans and are more likely to approach a hunter who is roaring to mimic another stag challenging their alpha status. The roar is a popular time of year for hunters, who hope to shoot a stag whose head is of high value and achieves a high score on the Douglas Score/Safari Club International/CIC System [11]. Unfortunately, this results in an increased concentration of hunters on public land during the roar, and the month of April alone accounts for 31% of yearly hunting fatalities [12].

© The Author(s), under exclusive license to Springer Nature Switzerland AG 2021
N. L. Black et al. (Eds.): IEA 2021, LNNS 222, pp. 21–26, 2021.
https://doi.org/10.1007/978-3-030-74611-7_3

It seems unlikely a hunter could genuinely believe they had correctly identified their target as a deer when in fact what they were seeing was a person [13]. Further, most of these types of incidents appear to occur at a surprisingly short distance. The New Zealand Mountain Safety Council [7] concluded that of the 58 daytime failure-to-identify incidents they analyzed, 37% occurred at a range of less than 25 m, 34% between 26 and 50 m, and the remainder at a distance exceeding 50 m.

Although anecdotes from the hunting community implicate old age, snap shooting (shooting too quickly), "buck fever" (over excitement) and personality in failure-to-identify incidents, there remains a clear information vacuum, with many challenges to understanding how these incidents can occur. We took our mandate to research this phenomenon from the lack of extant research into causation and the availability of technology to produce realistic and controlled simulations of hunting situations and the detect psychophysiological changes in both laboratory and field studies. Overall, our aim was to shed light on the psychological and physiological determinants of failure-to-identify incidents, and to replace anecdote with evidence in determining their causes.

2 Methods

The PhD consisted of four stages of research:

Stage 1 – Understanding the complexity of hunting using the Functional Resonance Analysis Method from a resilience engineering perspective [14]. The creation and calibration of the Hunting FRAM were supported by developing and facilitating a near-miss reporting system for hunters to report close calls of when they have misidentified their target [15]. The Hunting FRAM was also revisited at the end of the PhD to assess whether additional calibration was required taking into consideration all the experimental findings.

Stage 2 – Focusing on some of the preliminary steps associated with target acquisition to determine how hunters behave in field and simulation settings utilizing psychometric and physiological indices. We conducted a field-based pilot study in which hunters stalked and shot a deer. We then continued the study at a larger scale using an immersive simulation to understand how hunters behave and react to specific hunting-related stimuli [16].

Stage 3 – Focusing on whether targeting specific parts of a deer would cause hunters to react quicker and on identifying how they would react to seeing only a partial view of a deer under simulation. The study consisted of a computer-based test to determine how quickly hunters would identify their target based on partially obscured stimuli. The study continued in an immersive simulation to identify how they would react to moving images of deer.

Stage 4 – Focusing on the terminal stages of deciding whether to shoot or not, and to see if hunters' decision times could be affected by introducing specific and relevant cues including direct peer pressure, indirect (social comparison) pressure from social media and indirect pressure from context. This study was purely computer-based and involved hunters deciding to shoot by responding on a laptop keyboard.

Results Summary

A summary of the results includes the following observations:

- Hunting incidents and near misses appearing to be caused – at least in part – by hunters circumnavigating safety-critical steps, perhaps due to the belief of the hunter that deer are near, based on limited sensory data.
- Statistically significant sympathetic arousal upon sighting the first stag ($p < .01$), based on pupillometry.
- A further significant increase in arousal occurs around four seconds before shooting ($p < .01$).
- Time perception slows down for hunters, resulting in a perceived duration up to 27% longer than reality ($p < .01$).
- No significant evidence that personality, impulsivity, fatigue, food or water intake are associated with misidentification behavior across all experiments
- No significant evidence that age, sex or experience can cause failure-to-identify hunting incidents.
- Hunters recognize deer quicker based on sighting their forequarters compared to head and antlers ($p < .001$).
- 15% of hunters shot when a deer's head was obscured, but the rest of the body was visible.
- Hunters shoot significantly faster if subjected to direct peer pressure compared to social comparison based on social media exposure ($p < .001$).
- Hunters subjected to direct peer pressure have a 56% chance of shooting if presented with an animal other than the one they should be targeting. In contrast, social comparison increases the likelihood of shooting another animal by only 22% and the baseline at 29%.

3 Discussion

We took a pioneering approach to target identification in a hunting context. The thesis included a number of different and complementary qualitative and quantitative approaches. Psychophysiological data were obtained using modern technology in both field and simulator studies, which provided the opportunity to study hunters in environments that closely reflect real life. However, we also encountered some uncontrollable elements. Stages 2, 3 and 4 took place during a hunting show, and ambient noise was audible within the experimental testing area – possibly risking participant distraction or loss of immersion. Participant hunters were also under observation and accordingly may have performed differently given the context of the experiment. However, any such biases should have acted against our finding significant effects or observing unsafe activity taking place – so, if anything, our results are likely to underestimate effect sizes.

We found no evidence that a specific type of hunter is more at risk; there was no association between individual differences and failure-to-identify behavior. This suggests that any hunter could make an erroneous and fatal decision in the heat of the moment. The findings echo the anecdotes from hunting clubs suggesting that the most significant risk to hunters may be more associated with optimism bias and the attitude that target misidentifications will happen to others and not to oneself. This notion and the findings of this PhD are being discussed within the New Zealand hunting community to ascertain how it may benefit future hunter safety training.

Recommendations

This chapter provides an overview of research documented in the first author's PhD thesis (available on request), drawn together to provide an understanding of incident causation and prevention. While no definitive causal factors were discovered, utilizing theories associated with resilience engineering and psychophysiology, multiple contributing factors became evident.

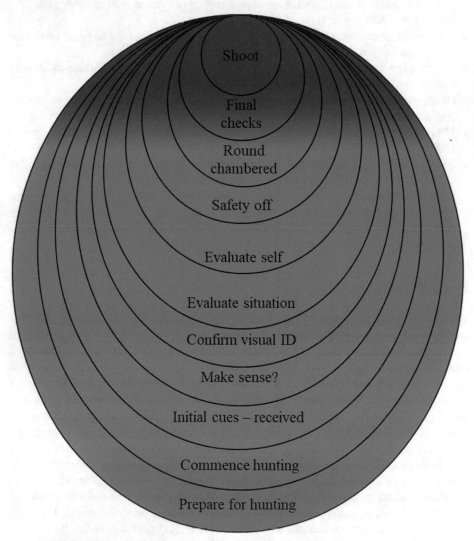

Fig. 1. Hunting layers of protection model – color coding reflects the hunting FRAM stages (green – sensing; amber – comprehending; red – committing)

Taking a risk-averse approach to the findings an adaptation of the Layers of Protection approach (LOPA) [17] was developed and presented in Fig. 1.

The Hunting LOPA was structured based on the following conclusions:

- Hunting is a bottom-up process built up from the smallest piece of sensory information – that being the initial 'desire' of the hunter to go hunting.
- The moment the hunter starts to receive initial cues of deer in the vicinity, their ability to make sense of those cues is the beginning of their journey towards identifying or misidentifying their target. Thus, the move from the green to amber stage of the process of hunting is appropriate.
- Layers of protection can be physical (safety on or off, semi-auto or bolt action rifle), cognitive (make sense? … of the information), or physiological (evaluate self). The model communicates the need to treat the situation uniquely regardless of their experience and the familiarity of the situation.
- As the hunter proceeds, each potential layer of protection peels back until no more layers remain except for the decision of whether to shoot. Each decision to remove a layer of protection is theirs, bringing them one step closer to shooting the correct target and thus the decision should be well thought out.
- A hunter can return to any layer, which may occur due to scenarios such as the deer being startled, the hunter deciding not to shoot a specific deer or becoming unsure of their situation, thus supporting the dynamic nature of hunting.
- If a hunter decides to take a top-down approach and shoot with little contemplation (often noticed in the near miss data of Appendix B), the layers of protection are thin to non-existent at the top of the model.
- The critical safety message is that peeling back each layer should be methodical and never expedited, supporting the need for hunters to take their time no matter what their perceptions are of the situation or of elapsed time. If hunters take their time this may help them to detect their target, or not as the case may be, with reduced bias and increased discriminability [18].

The model requires validation and testing but given it reflects the output and structure of the PhD research provides the basic message that the process of hunting should be meticulous, methodical, and thoughtful from the moment the decision has been made to go hunting to the moment the firearm is discharged. Even if deliberation on part of the hunter results in being too slow and thus losing the chance to shoot one's quarry.

It is hoped this research will continue by building on the need to obtain a detailed understanding of users of firearms in a hunting context. Until now the bulk of research has favoured military friendly fire incidents [19], and police shootings [20], which may provide insight into decision making, signal detection, situation awareness and target acquisition. However, drawing conclusions from other seemingly similar activities must be caveated by the understanding that the sense of self preservation which may exist in police and military operations is simply non-existent in hunters unless they are specifically hunting dangerous game.

References

1. Green, J.: To hunt and return – developing safe hunting practice, Wellington, New Zealand, New Zealand Police (2003)
2. International Hunter Education Association: Incident reports (2015). Retrieved September 2015 from https://www.iheausa.org/index.php/news-and-events/news/incident-reports
3. Southland Times. Stephen Phillip Long admits accidentally shooting son dead. Stuff, 22 May 2015. https://www.stuff.co.nz/national/crime/68763777/stephen-phillip-long-admits-accidentally-shooting-son-dead
4. Morton, J.: Rosemary Ives case: New findings. NZ Herald, 27 September 2012. https://www.nzherald.co.nz/nz/news/article.cfm?c_id=1&objectid=10836850
5. New Zealand Police: Arms Code. Wellington, NZ: New Zealand Police (2013)
6. Watson, M.: Hunter who killed friend was certain he was a deer, Stuff, 16 March 2013. https://www.stuff.co.nz/national/8433027/Hunter-who-killed-friend-was-certain-he-was-a-deer
7. Mountain Safety Council: A hunter's tale: A deep dive into hunting incidents in New Zealand, Wellington, New Zealand: Mountain Safety Council (2017)
8. Green, J., Boyes, M.: Deer hunting in New Zealand: lessons from the field. New Zealand J. Outdoor Educ. **2**(1), 34–49 (2006)
9. Points South: Good habits this roar, 17 March 2020. https://www.pointssouth.co.nz/blogs/news/good-habits-this-roar
10. Sunlive: Buck fever and the roar (2017). https://sunlive.co.nz/news/151399-buck-fever-and-roar.html
11. NZ Hunting Information: Trophy Scoring Systems (2016). https://www.nzhuntinginfo.com/trophy-scoring.html
12. Flahive, B.: Roar season is a risky time of year for deer – and also for hunters, Stuff (2018). https://www.stuff.co.nz/national/102908774/roar-season-is-a-risky-time-of-year-for-deer--and-also-for-hunters
13. Wilson, K., Bridges, K.E.: Mistaken-for-game hunting accidents—A human factors review (White Paper). Auckland, New Zealand (2015). Retrieved November 2016 from https://www.huntersafetylab.com/wp-content/uploads/2015/09/mistakenfor-game-hunting-accidents-a-human-factors-review1.pdf
14. Hollnagel, E.: FRAM: The Functional Resonance Analysis Method. Ashgate, Farnham, UK (2012)
15. Bridges, K.E., Corballis, P.M., Hollnagel, E.: "Failure-to-identify" hunting incidents: a resilience engineering approach. Hum. Factors **60**(2), 141–159 (2018). https://doi.org/10.1177/0018720817743851
16. Bridges, K.E., Corballis, P.M., Spray, M., Bagrie, J.: Testing failure-to-identify hunting incidents using an immersive simulation: Is it viable? Appl. Ergon. **93**, 103358 (2021)
17. Willey, R.: Layer of protection analysis. Procedia Eng. **84**(C), 12–22 (2014). https://doi.org/10.1016/j.proeng.2014.10.405
18. Green, D.M., Swets, J.A.: Signal Detection Theory and Psychophysics. Wiley, New York, NY (1966)
19. Munnik, A., Näswall, K., Woodward, G., Helton, W.S.: The quick and the dead: a paradigm for studying friendly fire. Appl. Ergon. **84**, 103032 (2020)
20. Mitchell, L., Flin, R.: Shooting decisions by police firearms officers. J. Cogn. Eng. Dec. Making **1**(4), 375–390 (2007)

Supporting the Development of Safety Culture at the Managerial Level

Willy Buchmann[✉] and Adelaide Nascimento

Research Center on Work and Development Le CNAM – Ergonomics Team,
41 Rue Gay Lussac, 75005 Paris, France
{Willy.buchmann,Adelaide.nascimento}@lecnam.net

Abstract. This paper reports an experience of formative intervention on a group of managers from a household waste collection organization in a French metropolis. In an organizational change management context, the objective is the integration of a safety culture adapted to the work activity. The intervention was based on the ergonomics of the activity in order to design a device allowing material and symbolic transformations in the way safety is managed. To do this, a three-stage process was implemented. Its originality lies in the integration of historical and cultural dimensions in the management of change. This historical-cultural approach offers a new perspective on the problems of work, through a configuration that gives depth to time (which is not only quantitative or chronological), to the articulation of events, and to the different temporalities. It allows us to understand the present and think about the future in the light of individual and collective experience of past successes and failures. We were able to identify that the group of managers was building new approaches to think about and to act on the relationships between change, work activity and safety.

Keywords: Safety culture · Formative intervention · Diachronical approach · Cultural historical activity theory · Managers

1   Problem Statement and Objectives

Referring to a recent publication by Nunem et al. (2018) who conducted a bibliometric analysis of safety culture research, it would appear that the concept continues to be of interest to at-risk organizations and scientists more than 30 years after its emergence in the aftermath of the Chernobyl accident (INSAG-4 1991). The concept of safety culture (SC) is classically defined in ergonomics as the set of practices developed and repeated by the main players concerned, to control the risks of their profession (Daniellou et al. 2010). From this perspective, the CS is situated in space (on the scale of practices in work situations) and in the immediate time. However, SC is also dynamic, in space (the practices of operational staff are largely influenced by the working conditions made available to them by management at different levels), and in time, insofar as the operating methods for carrying out the expected tasks can evolve and, as a result, the components for regulating the risks associated with the activity can change over time. In order to design a SC adapted to the activity and adaptive to future changes, it would therefore be useful to reconstruct a form of shared memory of the socio-technical system.

Considering SC as a historical-cultural process, we mobilized references to the past, present and future in a formative intervention. The analysis of the activity then took on social and historical dimensions where, more classically, it is situated in the here and now. As proposed by Gaudart (2016), this circular temporality of activity is a resource for understanding the origin of current practices and carries within it the seeds of possible wishes for the future. The temporal and spatial decompartmentalization proposed also implies thinking about the methodological device to be constructed.

In this context, how does security management change when approached from a temporal or diachronic perspective? This is what we wish to develop here, based on intervention research. The aim of this document is twofold: to present a formative intervention device that considers safety culture in its diachronic and historical-cultural dimensions, and to identify "markers" for the transformation of managers' representations towards a safety culture integrated into change management. We will try to answer these two questions:

1) What characteristics can a formative intervention have in order to develop a safety culture that is integrated into management, systemic, participative and coherent with production (or service) objectives?
2) What are the markers that indicate changes in meaning and significance towards the development of a safety culture?

2   Context and Field of Research Intervention

In France, the waste collection, treatment and disposal sector is among the occupational sectors reporting the most frequent and serious accidents at work. In 2008, faced with this observation, the french health insurance fund for workers published a five-page framework note (= the R-437) which recommends contractors and service providers to take into account a range of technical, organizational and social prevention measures. It does not, however, give precise keys to carrying out this mission.

The OPC is a public organization for the collection of household waste in a French metropolis (600,000 inhabitants), with around 280 workers (collection agents and management). The management of the OPC receives the R-437 prescription in a context of significant change, characterized by the transfer from a single historical site to 3 new sites spread around the metropolis. The request for assistance in ergonomics, made by the management of the OPC, concerns support for the implementation of a policy of continuous safety improvement, integrated with the technical, organizational and human changes made at different levels of the structure's hierarchy.

3   Methodolgy

The methodology presented below is part of a wider intervention (100 field days over 5 years): A working group (=WG) of 15 managers with a strategic influence on the safety policy within the establishment was set up, and followed a three-phase method:

– 1: Collective construction of a diagnosis on the conduct of past changes and on the current safety culture (2 meetings of 3 h each + 4 diachronic interviews)
– 2: Building on the phase 1 results, collective construction of a diagnosis on the strengths and weaknesses of the organization to lead change and provide security (1 meeting of 3 h)
– 3: Building on the phases 1 and 2 results, organizational simulations, to collectively identify the best change management scenarios (1 meeting of 3 h)

The 4 WG were recorded, then transcribed and analyzed according to the principle of a qualitative thematic analysis. The WG written productions were also analyzed.

4   Results

4.1   The Process and Tools Used

In order to identify the characteristics of an intervention aimed at developing a safety culture that is integrated into management, coherent and adaptive, integrated into a historical-cultural process, we looked at the process and the tools deployed in this intervention. Three major elements emerge from our data analysis:

The Temporalities of the Intervention
The intervention carried out is based on the construction of a collaboration over a long period of time (several months or even several years), but on a non-linear rhythm. The intervention was adapted to the rhythm of the needs of the applicants (sometimes it was necessary to be able to move quickly to solve urgent and important problems; or, on the contrary, the three-stage system, with a major strategic aim, was spread over 18 months, in order to give the stakeholders time to project themselves into another possible future).

The Tools of Intervention
Three main tools have been mobilized: the JDA (Nascimento and Falzon 2014), diachronic friezes for reconstructing the management of past changes (Buchmann 2013), and diachronic organizational simulations. The construction and use of these tools arises from the need for decision-makers (with distributed functions and variable seniority in the organization) to have intermediate objects at their disposal (Vinck 1999) in order to construct a more general representation of the situation, to question, debate and take decisions on different scales (operational, managerial, strategic).

Objects of the Intervention
The intervention articulated operational actions (actions on collection spaces, on equipment, on training, etc. to improve safety in waste collection) and actions aimed at the emergence of reflexive practices useful for building and evaluating change management strategies, in accordance with the expectations of the applicants (Deputy Director OPC, 1st meeting of the working group: we called on ergonomists to "help us move forward and help us watch ourselves move forward").

More specifically, the working group's discussions had the following objectives:

– To identify the temporalities and dyschronies of past changes at different levels of the organization;

– To reveal and discuss situations where safety and production trade-offs rather than regulations were made, in conditions where the protagonists did not necessarily have sufficient information or status to make informed decisions.
– To simulate and evaluate different possible future scenarios of change management (deployment methodology (working groups, field analyses, followed by data collection, etc.); prioritization of priorities; and temporality of changes).

4.2   Markers Indicating Changes in Significance and Importance for the Development of a Safety Culture

Four major developments have been identified in the way decision-makers view the change towards an integrated and adaptive safety culture, integrating historical and cultural dimensions:

(1)   From a prescriptive to a participative approach: For the OPC Director (Session 4 of the working group): "The gateway is real work. That's what makes people buy into changes in practice. It's not the injunction, it's not the big theories. We've gone from 20 years of injunctions to 10 months of practice exchanges between colleagues. And we can see that in 10 months we have achieved goals never achieved in 20 or 30 years of injunctions". We note here an evolution from a priority given to the implementation of safety rules and standards, to the priority given to the collective, clinical and adhoc construction of local and adaptive solutions.

(2)   From a reactive and immediate action towards a posture integrating different temporalities, leaving workers time to understand, learn and remobilize their experience in order to build new room for manoeuvre in the activity. For example, for the deputy director of the OPC it is necessary: "*to accept to be questioned (…) to accept not to work first on solutions, but on axes of progress (…) It forced us to take the time to think*" (session 4 of the working group).

(3)   From an individual approach to a collective problem-solving approach: working time and collective debates enabled participants to build a collective work team, with a common history and rules. Security no longer seems to be carried by a plurality of individuals, but by a collective. This is explained by a young prevention assistant participating in the WG: "*we have built up a relationship of trust, so that we can really go and ask questions. Saying to herself: good on this subject, what do you think about it? It was important for me*" (session 4 of the working group).

(4)   But tensions between participants and non-participants are emerging: given the evolution of their new vision of change management, some participants confide their fears of being out of step with the change management method prescribed by the higher hierarchical level. And this fear is verbalized by the deputy director: "*Now we see things differently, we have a different approach. But the problem is that I feel out of step with the parent company. We're starting to be more and more extraterrestrials*" (session 4 of the working group). This problem is not specifically related to our intervention, but arises in any participatory framework through representation, where one can ask oneself questions both about the different speeds of potential development and about the fact that the sample of participants may not account for all the collective dynamics.

5   Discussion Conclusion

In this last part we would like to highlight three contributions to the reflection:

(1) The intervention system presented is part of a broader framework of a singular clinical and systemic intervention including other methods of ergonomic analysis of work (Guérin et al. 2017; Falzon 2015) aimed at understanding and transforming work systems. More generally, however, we note that in any ergonomic intervention, and whatever the demand, studying historical and cultural dimensions broadens the understanding of the work situation: our approach aimed to integrate a diachronic perspective into the analysis of work. This approach proposes a new light on a problem, through a configuration that gives depth to time (which is not only quantitative or chronological), to the articulation of events, and to the different temporalities. It allows us to think about the present and the future in the light of individual and collective experience of past successes and failures (Degloulet, Buchmann and Gaudart, forthcoming). The methodological challenge then lies in the articulation between the ergonomic analysis of work in the here and now, the history of individuals in collectives and organizations, and possible future scenarios.

(2) We analyze the development of safety culture through the prism of the actors, i.e. when change is perceived as such by the people themselves. We believe that our approach thus contributes to the development of the "actors' agency" (Engeström et al. 2014) since, over the course of the intervention, we were able to identify that the actors were building new approaches to think about the relationships between change, work activity and safety, to debate them in the light of local histories and specificities, and to act on different scales (hierarchical, temporal, spatial). These new forms of practice are fundamental to progress towards an adaptive approach to safety at work.

(3) Finally, we can question the scope and generalization of our results with regard to the following elements: questioning the safety management to be supported in the short and long term leads us to question upstream the goals pursued by the managers themselves, in the more or less long term (Gaudart, Buchmann and Chassaing, forthcoming). This is because certain political, strategic, commercial and managerial choices, although a priori distant geographically or temporally from the work situations analyzed, can have a significant influence on activity and security. This means examining how the activity deployed in a situation is or is not supported by the organization's development project and its operational variations.

References

Buchmann, W.: Aspects de moyen et long termes dans la genèse et l'évolution des Troubles Musculo-Squelettiques au travail. Une recherche dans l'industrie aéronautique. Thèse de doctorat en ergonomie, CNAM, France (2013)

Daniellou, F., Simard, M., Boissieres, Y.: Human and organizational factors of safety: state of the art. Industrial safety manuals, Industrial Safety Culture found (ICSI). Issue 2010-02. Toulouse, France (ISSN 2100-3874) (2010)

Delgoulet, C., Buchmann, W., Gaudart, C.: Les parcours, une opportunité pour penser et agir sur le travail – Réflexions sur les échelles et le temps de l'intervention (to be published in 2021)

Engeström, Y., Sannino, A., Virkkunen, J.: On the methodological demands of formative interventions. Mind Culture Act. 21(2), 118–128 (2014). https://doi.org/10.1080/10749039.2014.891868

Falzon, P.: Constructive Ergonomics, p. 294. CRC Press, Boca Raton (2015)

Gaudart, C.: Activity, time and itineraries: for the integration of multiple times in the ergonomic analysis of work [1]. Le Travail Humain 79(3), 209–232 (2016). https://doi.org/10.3917/th.793.0209

Gaudart, C., Buchmann, W., Chassaing, K., et al.: Temps des marges de manœuvre, temps des changements. Pour une lecture diachronique du travail (to be published in 2021)

Guerin, et al.: Understanding and transforming work : The practice of ergonomics. Anact (ed.), p. 278 (2017)

INSAG, S.C.: Safety series no. 75-INSAG 4. IAEA International Nuclear Safety Advisory Group (1991)

Nascimento, A., Falzon, P.: Differential acceptability assessment and safety cultures in radiotherapy. Le Travail Humain 4(4), 325–349 (2014). https://doi.org/10.3917/th.774.0325

Nunem, K., Li, J., Ponnet, K.: Bibliometric analysis of safety cultureresearch. Safety Sci. 108(1), 248–258 (2018)

Vinck, D.: Les objets intermédiaires dans les réseaux de coopération scientifique. Contribution à la prise en compte des objets dans les dynamiques sociales, Revue Française de Sociologie. 11, 385–414 (1999)

Validation of a Visual Attention Test to Detect Driver Fatigue

Tanja Bärtsch$^{(\boxtimes)}$ and Marino Menozzi

Department of Health Sciences and Technology, ETH Zürich, Zürich, Switzerland
tanja.baertsch@hest.ethz.ch

Abstract. Fatigue is a high-risk factor for road accidents. It impairs driver's attention and performance and can thus compromise road safety. Unlike for alcohol, there are no objective measurements to detect fatigue during road a road traffic control, and thus it is difficult for the police to prove that a driver is too tired to drive. However, considering previous studies there are reasons to believe that a formerly developed visual attention test could be a possibility to detect sleepiness to a certain degree. This study investigates the effect of fatigue on the visual attention test. 21 participants drove 30 min on a driving simulator in order to get tired and performed the attention test before and after the drive. During the drive, subjective sleepiness, mental workload, and driving performance were recorded. Participants were divided into two groups with different test sequences to assess the effect of time elapsed between the drive and the second attention test. The results revealed that in young participants, the effect of fatigue induced by a 30-min drive in a driving simulator on visual attention is ambiguous. However, the results indicate that the effect of fatigue might be seen in the last third of the test. This study provides information on the sensitivity of the visual attention test and how the test might be adapted to detect fatigue.

Keywords: Fatigue · Visual attention · Road safety · Road traffic control

1 Introduction

Fatigue is severely affecting driving skills and belongs to the major causes of traffic accidents. Driving while fatigue limits the ability to drive, such as maintaining lane position [1], and impairs visual attention, a function, which is important in order to perceive what is happening in the environment. Therefore, drivers should refrain from driving in case of excessive fatigue. To increase road safety, road traffic polices conduct traffic controls to identify impaired drivers. In contrast to assessing driving under influence of drugs and alcohol, there is a lack of objective, rapid measurement techniques, which can be used considering the organizational and legal situation in police traffic controls, for measuring fatigue in drivers at traffic control stops. The fact that the Swiss Council for Accident Prevention (BFU) presumes that the dark figure of accidents caused by sleepiness is as high as 10–20%, underlies the severity of the lack of road safety caused by tired drivers [2].

© The Author(s), under exclusive license to Springer Nature Switzerland AG 2021
N. L. Black et al. (Eds.): IEA 2021, LNNS 222, pp. 33–38, 2021.
https://doi.org/10.1007/978-3-030-74611-7_5

In this study, the suitability of a formerly developed visual attention test [3] for detecting fatigue is investigated. The test is about detecting a signal, which appears either in the left, central, or right visual field. Based on previous studies, we have good reasons to believe that data recorded in people with fatigue, are affected in a particular manner. Faber et al. [4] showed that attention was affected by fatigue, in the form of a decreased ability to suppress irrelevant information, which resulted in decreased response accuracies. Moreover, a dominance of right hemisphere for visuospatial attention has been demonstrated [5, 6]. In addition, functional magnetic resonance imaging studies revealed that there is a substantial overlap between alertness network and visuospatial orienting network within the right brain hemisphere, leading to the strong believe that adverse factors, which impair the alertness, may also affect the visuospatial attention [7]. Fatigue therefore could affect the left visual field more pronounced as the right visual field.

We investigate how the attention performance changes after a 30-min drive, which aims to induce fatigue in participants. Considering the dominant theoretical framework postulating rightward shift in attention with declining alertness, we expect that the detectability of the signal and the reaction time to the signal is better in the right visual field compared to the left visual field when participants are tired.

2 Methodology

A total of 21 participants (13 m, 7 f) possessing valid driving license were recruited. Age range from 19 y to 43 y with a mean of 27.75 y (standard deviation [SD] 4.96 y).

Participants drove 30 min in our driving simulator on an oval shaped track. They were instructed to follow the car ahead at a constant distance. Before and after the 30-min drive, participants performed the visual attention test specified in Menozzi et al. (2012) (Fig. 1). The attention test is a computerized test, in which participants report whether a flashed 6-digit number appearing on a background movie showing a car drive includes the digit «3». Reaction time (RT) and response (hit, false alarm, miss, correct rejection) are recorder for each trial. At the end of the test, the detectability d' is computed based on given responses. Before, during and after the driving task, participants' sleepiness was recorded using the Karolinska Sleepiness Scale (KSS) (Akerstedt, et al. 2005), and their mental workload was recorded using the Instantaneous Self Assessment (ISA) questionnaire [8]. The KSS and ISA questionnaires were administered all 5 min during the 30 min driving task, therefore six times in total. After driving, the attention test was administered again. To investigate whether it matters if the test is performed right after the drive or a couple of minutes later, participants were randomly divided into two groups. Group I performed the second test immediately after the drive and Group II answered the presence questionnaire (PQ) [9] and the simulator sickness questionnaire (SSQ) [10] before taking the second test. In order to evaluate driving performance, the standard deviation of lateral position was recorded throughout the driving task.

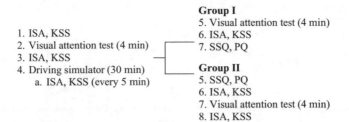

Fig. 1. Overview of the test procedure.

3 Results

The subjective sleepiness level recorded six times during the 30-min drive increased with time [Friedman test: $X^2(5) = 60.786$, $p < 0.01$, $n = 21$]. The ISA score did not change significantly over time [Friedman test: $X^2(5) = 7.846$, $p = 0.165$, $n = 21$]. One-way repeated ANOVA with the time-on-task separated into six 5-min periods revealed that the standard deviation of lateral position varied significantly with driving time [$F(5,90) = 3.696$, $p < 0.01$, $\eta2 = 0.170$]. Regarding the attention performance, a three-way ANOVA [location of presentation of the six-digit number (left/central/right), time (before/after the drive), Group of order in taking the second attention test (I/II)] showed a significant effect of the location on d' and RT (Table 1). Time and Group had no significant effect.

Table 1. Three-way ANOVA.

	Time	Location	Group
d'	p = 0.617	p < 0.01**	p = 0.744
RT	p = 0.355	p < 0.01**	p = 0.514

The post-hoc analysis (Bonferroni-corrected pairwise comparisons) revealed that d' and RT were better in the central visual field than in the periphery (Fig. 2). But there was no difference of the attention performance in the left and right visual field (d': p = 0.073, RT: p = 1.000). There was a tendency that the detectability in the right visual field (M = 2.481, SD = 0.121) was lower than in the left visual field (M = 2.772, SD = 0.113), p = 0.073.

Moreover, the first and last third of the attention test were analysed separately. Even if there were no significant findings, it is worth noting that regarding the left visual field in the last third, 68% of the participants showed a lower d' in the second attention test compared to the first attention test (Fig. 3). In average, d' decreased by 0.5 in the left visual field.

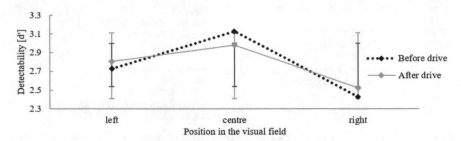

Fig. 2. Average and one standard deviation of d' for the task carried out in the left, central and right visual field before (dashed line) and after (solid line) the 30-min drive. For more clarity, the scale starts at d' = 2.3.

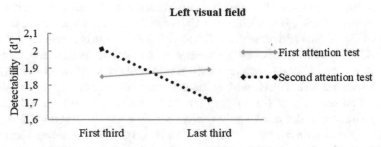

Fig. 3. Average of d' for the task performed in the left visual field in the first third and last third. The solid line indicates the change in d' from the first third to the last third of the attention test before the 30-min drive and the dashed line shows the change in d' in the attention test after the drive. For more clarity, the scale starts at d' = 1.6.

4   Discussion

The results indicate that a 30-min drive on a low-traffic road and in a monotonous environment on a driving simulator is a fatigue factor, manifested through increased KSS values and increased lateral movements of the car over time. The ISA values did not increase over time probably since the work demands during the performance of the task remain the same over time. Furthermore, the results revealed that it does not matter whether the attention test is performed immediately after a drive or a few minutes later. Regarding road traffic controls, this would mean that the police can apply the test directly after a driver has stopped or after the traffic control procedure.

As expected from many previous literature (e.g., [11]), the detectability and reaction time is better for central signals than for peripheral signals. However, the hypotheses that with increased fatigue, the detectability and reaction time generally deteriorate and are better in the right visual field than in the left could not be confirmed. There is even a tendency that the detectability is better in the left than in the right visual field, which indicates the so-called pseudo-neglect. This is a phenomenon that refers to the tendency to direct attention more to the left than to the right [12].

One reason for the lack of significant effect of fatigue on visual attention might be that the participants are between 19 and 43 years old, and that the effect of fatigue does not affect attention as much as it would in an older population. Menozzi et al. [3] showed that the performance in the central visual field did not depend on age, whereas the detectability in the periphery was shown to be an inverted U-shape function of age peaking in the fourth decade of lifespan. The visual attention performance might decrease in people older than 50 years compared to people between 20 and 50 since the psycho-motor and cognitive performance decreases [13]. In addition, it was shown that inhibitory performance is an inverted U-shape function of age [3]. Based on those facts and the assumption that fatigue reduces the ability to suppress irrelevant information [4], we hypothesize that the effect of fatigue on visual attention may have a more significant effect in people over 50 years of age than the effect in a younger population.

Another reason could be that the attention test is not sensitive enough to detect a small change in fatigue, which was on average 1.5 in the KSS scale. To improve the sensitivity, the difficulty level of the test could be increased by a shorter target presentation duration which would lower test performance scores [14].

However, the results indicate that the effect of fatigue might be seen in the last third time section of the attention test. An explanation could be that the background of the test is most complex in the last third. Thus, more attention is required and since the attention resource is limited due to fatigue, the capacity for maintaining the performance drop down. Another reason could be that the performance declines with time-on-task, which might be caused by depletion of cognitive resources, that can be exacerbated by fatigue. However, the time-on-task effect is unlikely, as the test duration is only 4 min [15].

In Conclusion, this study showed that abovementioned visual attention test is not sensitive enough to detect small changes in subjective sleepiness levels. However, by making the test more difficult, the sensitivity for detecting fatigue might be increased. In addition, further studies should be conducted to investigate the effectiveness of the last third of the visual attention test in detecting fatigue.

Acknowledgements. We would like to thank Jiahui An from Tübingen University (Graduate Training Centre of Neuroscience) for collecting the data.

References

1. Akerstedt, T., Peters, B., Anund, A., Kecklund, G.: Impaired alertness and performance driving home from the night shift: a driving simulator study. J. Sleep Res. **14**, 17–20 (2005)
2. Beratungsstelle für Unfallverhütung (BFU): Sinus 2019: Sicherheitsniveau und Unfallgeschehen im Strassenverkehr (2019)
3. Menozzi, M., Baumer-Bergande, E., Seiffert, B.: Working towards a test for screening visual skills in a complex visual environment. Ergonomics **55**, 1331–1339 (2012)
4. Faber, L.G., Maurits, N.M., Lorist, M.M.: Mental fatigue affects visual selective attention. PLoS One **7**(10), e48073 (2012)
5. Heilman, K.M., Valenstein, E., Watson, R.T.: Neglect and related disorders. Semin. Neurol. **20**, 463–470 (2000)
6. Heilman, K.M., Van Den Abell, T.: Right hemisphere dominance for attention: the mechanism underlying hemispheric asymmetries of inattention (neglect). Neurology **30**, 327–330 (1980)
7. Heber, I.A., Valvoda, J.T., Kuhlen, T., Fimm, B.: Low arousal modulates visuospatial attention in three-dimensional virtual space. J. Int. Neuropsychol. Soc. **14**, 309–317 (2008)

8. Hering, H., Coatleven, G.: ERGO (version 2) for instantaneous self assessment of workload in a real-time ATC simulation environment. EEC Note No 10/96 (1996)
9. Witmer, B.G., Jerome, C.J., Singer, M.J.: The factor structure of the presence questionnaire. Presence **14**(3), 298–312 (2005)
10. Kennedy, R.S., Lane, N.E., Berbaum, K.S., Lilienthal, M.G.: Simulator sickness questionnaire: an enhanced method for quantifying simulator sickness. Int. J. Aviation Psychol. **3**(3), 203–220 (1993)
11. Crundall, D., Underwood, G., Chapman, P.: Attending to the peripheral world while driving. Appl. Cogn. Psychol. **16**, 459–475 (2002)
12. Manly, T., Dobler, V.B., Dodds, C.M., George, M.A.: Rightward shift in spatial awareness with declining alertness. Neuropsychologia **43**, 1721–1728 (2005)
13. Davies, D.R., Taylor, A., Dorn, L.: Aging and human performance. In: Smith, A.P., Jones, E.M. (eds.) Handbook of human performance, vol. 3, pp. 25–61. Academic Press, London (1992)
14. Huang, Y.-Y., Menozzi, M., Favey, C.: A screening tool for occupations requiring a high level of attentional performance. Int. J. Ind. Ergon. **72**, 86–92 (2019)
15. Lim, J., Dinges, D.F.: Sleep deprivation and vigilant attention. Ann. New York Acad. Sci. **1129**, 305–22 (2008)

Integration of FRAM and Social Network Analysis to Analyse Distributed Situational Awareness in Socio-technical Systems

Moacyr Machado Cardoso Júnior[(✉)] [iD]

Technological Institute of Aeronautics, São José dos Campos, SP 12200-910, Brazil
moacyr@ita.br

Abstract. This paper proposes a method to integrate Functional Resonance Analysis Method - (FRAM) and social networks to analyse complex socio-technical systems and specially system´s Distributed Situational Awareness - (DSA). For this purpose an accident of a chemical process was revisited and social network analysis - (SNA) was used in order to measure Situational Awareness - (SA) of the system as well as DSA dynamics. The purpose of this paper is to show that SA is very important to maintain system's safety within a complex socio-technical system. More specifically, DSA which comprises all information provided by different actors in a system. FRAM's modelling is a powerful tool in order to understand what are the system's variabilities, to what extent that variability can produce resonance in the system, and from there measures should be adopted in order to enhance system's resilience. FRAM's model was established, and DSA was analysed using social network. It was possible to identify that the accident's root cause was linked to missing DSA. As future works, it is suggested that other industrial systems be analysed with the proposed method to verify contributions to system safety analysis of implementation of measures to better distribute SA within the entire system, as well as to analyse the multilayer network representation and its metrics to DSA.

Keywords: FRAM · Resilience · Situational awareness · Risk analysis · Social networks

1 Introduction

Situational awareness - (SA) which comprises perception, comprehension and projection of future status of a system is fundamental to process safety. All human, technological and organizational entities of a complex socio-technical system should have situation awareness - SA, or at least act as an element of distribution of SA to all other entities of the system. The Functional Resonance Analysis Method - (FRAM) provides a way to describe outcomes using the idea of resonance arising from the variability of everyday performance.

© The Author(s), under exclusive license to Springer Nature Switzerland AG 2021
N. L. Black et al. (Eds.): IEA 2021, LNNS 222, pp. 39–46, 2021.
https://doi.org/10.1007/978-3-030-74611-7_6

To do so FRAM modelling joins different functions, which are needed on a daily basis performance, linking functions aspects: Input, Output, Precondition, Resource, Time and Control to analyse possible variabilities that can influence system's performance. Based on FRAM's structure is possible to analyse Distributed Situational Awareness - (DSA) using social network analysis, and better understand how SA is distributed within a system and how it can be improved so that the resilience of the system is increased by making the distances between the situational awareness of different actors of the system closer and more available in order to improve process safety. This distance reduction will reduce mental workload as well, since functions of the system will share more SA from all the system's parts.

This paper proposes a method to model a complex socio-technical system, represented by a chemical process using FRAM to model interactions among Human, Technological and Organizational functions on a daily basis performance, free of accidents, and then transform this FRAM representation on a social network and analyse it using social network analysis - (SNA) tools in order to understand SA of the system as well as DSA dynamics.

This work has two main objectives: 1) To model FRAM functions of a past chemical accident in order to obtain all entities of the socio-technical system and their links, represented by FRAM's aspects; 2) To analyse DSA of the system based on that FRAM's model and using social network analysis - (SNA).

2   Theorethical Foundations

2.1   Situational Awareness

Several definitions of SA are provided in the literature (Chatzimichailidou et al. 2015), and one of most cited defines SA as a state of working knowledge of an individual; it is how much and how accurately he/she is aware of the current situation and concerns (1) the perception of the elements within a system, (2) the comprehension of their meaning, and (3) the projection of their future state (Endsley 1995). Another interesting definition (Jeannot and Kelly 2003) argue that SA is what someone needs to know in order not to be surprised. Salmon et al. 2008 and Stanton et al. 2010, state that SA is an emergent property of a collaborative system itself rather than an individual endeavour.

According to Chatzimichailidou and Dokas 2016 there are several SA measurement techniques, most of them based on individual SA models or team SA models.

In complex socio-technical systems, many parts of the system are controlled by human or automated agents, located in different hierarchical levels, and the primary goal is to assure system safety (Chatzimichailidou and Dokas 2016). The authors state that agents that control part of the socio-technical system should be capable of perceiving and comprehending threats and vulnerabilities, as well as projecting what they might entail, that is agents should make use of sensors, mental models and control algorithms to manage risk. If one agent of a socio-technical system becomes aware of a situation, it is common to disseminate this information, which contributes to the emergence of what is known as Distributed Situational Awareness - (DSA).

According to Salmon et al. 2008 DSA is an approach that sets the foundations for a systemic framework explaining the emergence of SA in collaborative systems. It also implies that no one system agent, namely humans and automated controllers that possess reasoning mechanisms and demonstrate a capability to influence other agents or situations, has a complete picture of the situation in which the system finds itself, but just a facet of the corresponding situation at any point in time.

2.2 Functional Resonance Analysis Method

The purpose of FRAM is to provide a method that recognizes successes as the flip side of failures, or better, a method that focus on the nature of everyday activities rather than on the nature of failures (Hollnagel 2012). FRAM allows systemic analysis of complex processes, based on the idea of resonance arising from the variability of everyday performance, and it has been used in aviation, railway and maritime accident analysis, environmental risk analysis, emergency response and in blood sampling activity, (Patriarca and Bergstrom 2017).

Functions in FRAM are classified in Human (H), Technological (T) and Organizational (O). Technological functions represented by "machinery" are considered very stable in variability, different from Human and Organizational functions that are considered to vary greatly in daily performance.

3 Proposed Method

In this section, a method for DSA measurement will be presented. The proposal for DSA measurement is based on social network analysis as proposed by Csardi and Nepusz 1695, and a plethora of measures are proposed in order to assess what DSA was in a complex socio-technical system, as in the T2's accident case that will be presented. In Table 1, several social network measures are presented and a correspondence to DSA are given. The starting point to the network construction is FRAM modelling of daily basis functioning of the system, including all Human, Technological and Organizational Functions that comprises the system.

From the FRAM model, an adjacency matrix is constructed, which allows the representation of the social network. Nodes represent FRAM's functions and the edges represent FRAM's aspects connections. The proposed metrics will be used to assess SA.

Table 1. Measure of DSA in network of a complex system.

Net measure	Meaning	DSA measure
Diameter	Longest geodesic distance (length of the shortest path between two nodes)	Provides the maximum distance between two system functions at the ends of the network. Gives the distance dimension of SA of two entities: Human and/or Artifacts
Degree	The number of adjacent edges (in, out or all)	Gives a notion of the importance of that Function for SA by the number of connections to/from other functions
Centrality	Measure how many steps are required to access every other vertex from a given vertex. (it is the inverse of the average length of the shortest paths to/from all other vertices in the graph)	Gives the idea of average length to any other vertex. (the greater, the more centrality, limited to 1). So the greater the score the greater SA is centralized in that Function
Betweenness	Measure defined by the number of geodesics (shortest paths) going through a vertex	Measures how SA is proximate to the vertex, and how a function is important to whole system
Hub Score Authority Score Kleinberg's Score	Hub tell us where to find Authorities; and Authorities contains reliable information on the topic of interest	Authorities represents central Functions in terms of DSA, and Hubs points to those functions
Distance	Gives the shortest path to/from the vertex of a graph	The number gives the separation of different SA in a system
Community	The idea of the edge betweenness based community structure detection is that it is likely that edges connecting separate modules have high edge betweenness as all the shortest paths from one module to another must traverse through them	The idea of important linkages and clusters for SA provision in a system

4   T2 Case Study Description

In order to apply the proposed method, an accident that has occurred at T2 Laboratories, Inc. on December 19, 2007 was analyzed. T2 was a chemical manufacturer in Jacksonville, Florida - EUA. A batch of methylcyclopentadienyl manganese tricarbonyl (MCMT) was in process when a powerful explosion occurred, resulting in four employees' deaths and complete destruction of T2 facility (CSB 2009).

CSB investigations found that a runaway exothermic reaction occurred during the first step of MCMT process, probably due a loss of sufficient cooling during the process, leading to an uncontrollable pressure and temperature rise inside the reactor. The pressure burst the reactor, its contents were ignited and consequently an explosion equivalent to 1,400 lb of TNT (CSB 2009).

5   Results of FRAM Modelling of T2

As presented in Sect. 2.2. FRAM modelling is primary intended to show how a complex socio-technical system performs on a daily basis. Considering the accident that occurred at T2 Lab, Inc. It is possible to enhance the FRAM analysis in order to incorporate all organizations that are part of the socio-technical system.

Figure 1, shows all the functions coupled, highlighting the three steps of MCMT process and final distillation (red).

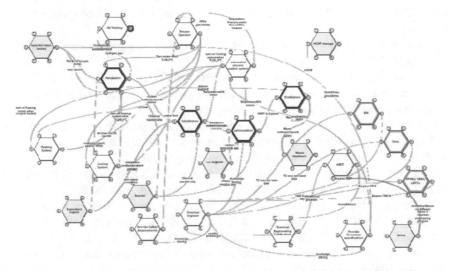

Fig. 1. FRAM modelling of T2 MCMT production, and instantiation of "metalation" Function.

In order to accomplish the first step of MCMT production, Metalation needs as Inputs: blocks of sodium metal, MCPD, diglyme (diglyme recycled from distillation). The Outputs: sodium methylcyclopentadiene, which is a Input for the next step, hydrogen gas, which is vented to atmosphere and Temperature & Pressure values that are informed to the automated process control system. As a Precondition the reactor has to be sealed by an operator, and Resources are circulation of hot oil to start reaction, water to cool the system and the Reactor. Finally this step is Tempo controlled by the information that sodium metal is molten at 98.9 °C, when a mixer should be initiated.

The concept of DSA of this instantiation - "Metalation" shows that different actors and artifacts in the system have distributed SA of the process that occurs on a daily basis. As stated by CSB (2009), up to the accident 174th batches of MCMT have been produced and although some variabilities do occurred along the process but the final result of producing MCMT was achieved.

Thinking about DSA of the system in Fig. 1, it is possible to use DSA measures from Table 1. The first one is diameter, which shows that there are 10 steps between the outers Functions, and they are represented in vector, D = {Aiche ABET cec ce apcs prop meta subs carb dist watr}. We can see that "Aiche" is in one corner of network and "Waste Treatment" - watr is in the other, so DSA from this Functions is far away the first one. Analyzing degree, or importance of Functions to DSA we have: in degree (DSA entering Functions) "metalation" with 8, "automated process control System", 6, "chemical engineer" and "Process Operator" with 4. On the other side the out degree (DSA exiting Function) "Chemical Engineer", 6, "Process Operator", 4, "Reactor", and "Operator hand-loaded" with 3. And finally considering all in-out DSA, "metalation" with 11, "Chemical Engineer", 10, "Process Operator", 8 and "automated process Control System", 7. From this measure we can establish that "metalation" step of process is one of the most important Function for providing DSA for the system, but "Chemical Engineer", "Process Operator" and "Automated Process Control System" are fundamental for DSA as well. In this case we have two Human and two Technological Functions interacting for better DSA.

The next topic, network centrality, which comprises that greater score, shows the centrality of DSA in a Function.

It is possible to see that apcs - "automated process control System" is the most centralized, as all status information and control passes through it, and it represents an important element for DSA.

Betweenness measures how DSA is proximate to the vertex, as SA has to pass through that Function. In this case "metalation-meta" and "process Operator - prop" have great importance to the system as both are "passing-through" SA.

One type of centrality is called hub-authority, which is hub nodes tell us where to find Authorities; and Authorities contains reliable information on the topic of interest.

"Metalation" is the most important Authority, with score 1, that is this node supplies the system with most of information to SA, the second one "Automated process control system" with 0.439. on the other side "Operator Hand-loaded" - ohol is the most important hub, that is indicates where are the Authorities, in a sequence there are other hubs "Process Operator", "Reactor".

"Metalation" has a reliable information about possible runaway reaction, and indeed it was the key function that needs to be managed in terms of information about reaction status to the "Process Operator" and to "Automated Control Process System" prevent a runaway reaction within the system design. It is noteworthy that "Process Operator" is both a Hub and a Authority, that is it represents reliable information, so partial SA of the system and points to "metalation", which is the most important part of SA of the system.

On the other side, it is possible to infer that the most important SA of the enhanced model to prevent runaway reaction is "Aiche", because it is a professional entity that gives training capability to engineers, as well as acts as an advisory to the "ABET" in order to engineering Courses program accreditation. Again if we look at the distance of SA of "Aiche" to "Process Operator" or "automated process control system" or "metalation", we have 5, 4, 5, respectively, that means that there are "5" steps from "Aiche" SA to "Process Operator" SA, 4 to "automated process control system" and 5 to "metalation". This SA distance should be diminished if one wants to enhance SA of the entire system. The average distance of entire network is 3.46.

Figure 2 - left shows the community structure of this system based on edge-betweenness, which represents a measure of the number of shortest paths through that function. "Aiche" is clearly the most important for system SA, but is the most outer Function of the entire system. Figure 2 - right shows the distances of different functions on a dendrogram, and it is possible to see that "Aiche", besides "chemical engineering certification" and "ABET" are the last Functions to be annexed to all others. And again it is clear that SA of those functions are totally apart of the system.

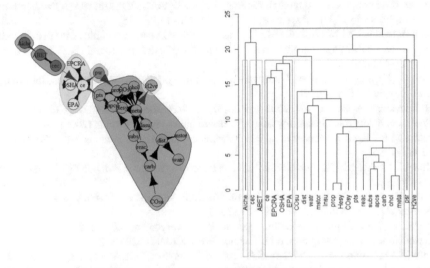

Fig. 2. Community structure based on edge-betweenness.

6 Final Conclusions

The purpose of this paper was to show that SA is very important to maintain system's safety within a complex socio-technical system. DSA which comprises all information provided by different actors in a system, and actors here means Human Operators, Technological Functions and Organizational and their interactions.

FRAM modelling is a powerful tool in order to understand what are the system's variabilities, to what extent that variability can produce resonance in the system, and from there measures can be adopted in order to enhance system's resilience. After FRAM model was established a social network analysis could be done in order to analyze all aspects of DSA in the system. As the root cause identified that T2 did not recognize the runway reaction hazard associated with the MCMT it was producing, but this knowledge was of domain of "Aiche", which had SA of a runaway reaction, but this SA was not distributed to the rest of system, culminating in a tragic accident. Other contributing factors: The cooling system employed by T2 was susceptible to single-point failures due to a lack of design redundancy and MCMT reactor relief system was incapable of relieving the pressure from a runaway reaction were causes derived from lack of SA from "Chemical Engineer".

As future works, it is suggested that other industrial systems be analysed with the proposed method to verify contributions to system safety analysis of implementation of measures to better distribute SA within the entire system.

References

Chatzimichailidou, M.M., Stanton, N.A., Dokas, I.M.: The concept of risk situation awareness provision: towards a new approach for assessing the DSA about the threats and vulnerabilities of complex socio-technical systems. Saf. Sci. **79**, 126–138 (2015)

Chatzimichailidou, M.M., Dokas, I.M.: Introducing RiskSOAP to communicate the distributed situation awareness of a system about safety issues: an application to a robotic system. Ergonomics **59**, 409–422 (2016)

Csardi, G., Nepusz, T.: The igraph software package for complex network research. InterJournal, Complex Syst. 1695 (2006)

CSB. Investigation Report No. 2008-3-I-FL, T2 Laboratories, Inc. Runaway Reaction., U.S. Chemical Safety and Hazard Investigation Board. jacksonville, Florida (2009)

Endsley, M.R.: Toward a theory of situation awareness in dynamic systems. Hum. Factors J. **37**, 32–64 (1995)

Hollnagel, E.: FRAM: The Functional Resonance Analysis Method. Ashgate Publishing Limited, Surrey (2012)

Jeannot, E., Kelly, C.: The Development of Situation Awareness Measures in ATM Systems. Technical report HRS/HSP-005-REP-01 (2003)

Patriarca, R., Bergstrom, L.: Modelling complexity in everyday operations: functional resonance in maritime mooring at quay. Cogn. Technol. Work **19**, 711–729 (2017)

Salmon, P.M., Stanton, N.A., Walker, G.H., Baber, C., Jenkins, D.P., McMaster, R., Young, M.S.: What really is going on? review of situation awareness models for individuals and teams. Theor. Issues Ergon. Sci. **9**, 297–323 (2008)

Stanton, N.A., Salmon, P.M., Walker, G.H., Jenkins, D.P.: Is situation awareness all in the mind? Theor. Issues Ergon. Sci. **11**, 29–40 (2010)

Risk Behaviours and Self-medication in Active Workers

Juan Alberto Castillo Martínez[1]([⊠]) [iD] and Andrés M. Pérez-Acosta[2] [iD]

[1] GiSCYT Research Group, Universidad del Rosario, Bogotá, Colombia
juan.castillom@urosario.edu.co

[2] Studies in Behavioural Sciences Research Group, Universidad del Rosario, Bogotá, Colombia

Abstract. The problem of self-medication at work has different nuances and raises serious questions about work practices. Self-medication behaviours are linked to cultural and social practices, however in workers it was related to pain management and to face the demands of their activity, self-medication can be seen as a resource in itself to maintain productivity at work. This study addressed self-medication behaviours and risk behaviours in three consecutive moments and in complementary perspectives, this in order to understand how they can be related. Specifically, when workers must place work at the center of their interests, leaving apart matters related to health, self-medication is also identified as a practice related to showing efficiency and productivity, especially in work environments where uncertainty about accessibility to work is critical. The study of self-medication in workers also highlights the problem of high consumption of pain medications, institutional data are just the tip of the iceberg, the high consumption of this type of medication indicates a problem that deserves to be studied in depth due to the profound implications for workers and their health, but also for security problems in organisations.

Keywords: Self medication · Risk behaviour · Addictions · Task analysis · Colombia

1 Introduction

Self-medication is defined as the use and consumption of medicines, whether industrialized or homemade, for the treatment of an illness or symptom, for the prevention of diseases or the promotion of health without a medical prescription [1]. In addition, due to the gradual decrease in the coverage of pharmaceutical benefits by the Social Security systems, the growth of soft medicines, and the increase of medicines in the media, self-medication is becoming increasingly strong in developed countries [2].

In Colombia, the National Institute of Health reported that about 1600 people were diagnosed with intoxication due to the inadequate intake of medicines during 2019. These results are supported by a study conducted with 625 students enrolled in the twelve semesters of the undergraduate program in medicine at a private university in Medellin-Colombia in order to explore their attitudes, knowledge and practices regarding the self-medication of herbal and psychopharmaceutical products. Of the people surveyed 67%

© The Author(s), under exclusive license to Springer Nature Switzerland AG 2021
N. L. Black et al. (Eds.): IEA 2021, LNNS 222, pp. 47–54, 2021.
https://doi.org/10.1007/978-3-030-74611-7_7

were women, the median for age was 20 years mostly single (97.3%), the analysis found that four out of ten students surveyed self-medicate to treat mental symptoms related to sleep, stress-anxiety and mood. In addition, it was found, that the most used medication was fluoxetine (5.1%), followed by zolpidem (3.7%), while of the phytotherapeutic drugs the most used was Soñax Forte (2.2%). Also, within the questionnaire it was asked if they will continue self-medicating and 78.6% answered affirmatively, which generates some questions and 90.1% stated that self-medicating is not a safe practice [3].

Self-medication practices include a diverse number of risks, among these are : "incorrect self-diagnosis, delays in seeking medical advice when necessary, rare but serious adverse medical reactions, dangerous drug interactions, incorrect administration, incorrect dosage, incorrect choice of treatment, masking of serious illness, and risk of dependence and abuse" [4]. In workers, the dangers associated with self-medication are numerous and varied, ranging from unforeseen reactions, intoxication and functional alterations from the physiological and cognitive point of view.

Self-medication affects workers of all social classes, it is a common practice in both the economically disadvantaged and the economically privileged population; there are multiple social, physical, cultural and psychological factors that explain the use of over-the-counter medications by people on their own initiative. For workers it goes from job fragility, work demands, consciously accepted work overload and permanent self-availability in the workplace, among other factors that drive permanent presence despite poor or precarious health conditions, for which self-medication is a means of maintaining presence and guaranteeing job retention or full availability of the worker.

1.1 Risk Behaviour

The risk behaviour, being defined as "an activity carried out by people with a frequency or intensity that increases the risk of disease or injury" [5]. Risk behaviours are behaviours for which people estimate a low probability of harm or consequence that, in most cases, do not result in injury, but occasionally do or, at least, have the potential to do so, for example, tobacco, alcohol or other health risk behaviours.

The use of non-prescription drugs can result in dangerous risk and events that could put not only the worker, but also those around him. This is especially concerning when there are mixtures of pharmaceutical drugs, traditional or natural medicines, and substance abuse habits before, during, or after work.

The study of risk behaviours implies understanding the notion of autonomy, which indicates the subject's capacity to act, either the physical and psychological capacity of the person (as opposed to the notions of dependence and handicap), or the recognition of his or her capacity to manage health or illness autonomously [6].

Autonomy also refers to the subject's capacity to decide to request or consent to care, and to participate in making decisions concerning his health. It could be said that self-medication is an expression of autonomy in which the individual estimates the risk he is taking, either by underestimating the consequences or overestimating the benefits of the treatment he is taking. Thus, when the uncertainty of the risk-benefit ratio is high, the question arises as to whether a worker whose life may be endangered in the short term by a specific health condition that could affect his competencies at work can act autonomously.

In risk behaviours it is equally important to take into consideration each individual's experience with past illnesses or health conditions, in those cases the way they have overcome those experiences will be taken into consideration, which will allow each person to autonomously copy or, on the contrary, reject certain treatments or curative practices, in other less experienced situations people will investigate medications in their environment with colleagues, friends, including neighbors [7]. Studies on the self-medication practices of Latino migrant workers show that "self-medication is not a purely pharmacological process, but a sociocultural one. When faced with a health problem, migrant workers rely on their own previous experience or the experience of family and friends, as well as on family traditions and cultural preferences" [8].

A simple notion of risk indicates that it refers to the undesirable consequences of a decision, event or activity, taking the risk then implies the consideration of the relationship between the possible consequences and the potential benefits, this simple relationship is key when studying the relationship between self-medication and work, especially for the balance that is made between the potential benefits of self-medication and the illusion of control of the effects of this practice in the execution of a work, that is, the worker tends to believe that by intensifying the behaviour, better benefits are obtained since the illusion of control is preserved.

2 Methodological Aspects

The study was carried out in three phases, for the first two of which an instrument consisting of three parts was used. Firstly, different sociodemographic and contextualization aspects of the respondent's state of health were investigated. Secondly, the respondent's position on self-medication and the different behaviours that comprise it is explored by means of 20 statements, using a five-point Likert-type scale, the reliability analysis of the self-medication risk questionnaire was 0.890 Cronbach's alpha and the KMO was 0.461 with a sigh of 0.000. Finally, the adaptation for Colombia of the Social Support scale [9] was used to determine the social support received by the subject, and also to make a relationship with the self-medication scale.

In the third phase, the analysis of a database collected with interviews conducted with workers in the process of recruitment in various Colombian companies was accomplished, the objective is to analyze among other three elements: the socio-demographic profile of the population, the behaviour regarding the consumption of medicines and other substances including alcohol, and the behaviour regarding risk. All persons gave their consent to obtain the data, and a polygraph was used in the process.

The first phase included a sample of 35 administrative workers in a public entity and workers in the industrial sector of flower growing. The second phase included 108 workers in the education sector and the third phase included 9000 workers in various areas.

During the application of the instruments in phases 1 and 2, a brief introductory talk about the questionnaire was given to the participants, providing them with general information about self-medication, and also mentioning that participation in this study was voluntary and anonymous. The application time was between 10 to 15 min. The data were recorded in an Excel database and subsequently analyzed using SPSS statistical software.

3 Findings

The three phases of the study sought to analyze and understand the presence of self-medication practices (SP) in people who are active in the workplace, In the first group, 21 women and 5 men were found to have no SP, while 5 women and 4 men showed evidence of such practices. The most common practices in the population participating in this study were that they knew a great variety of home remedies for any pain, discomfort or illness, and also that they knew the side effects that can be generated by any medication when taking it on their own initiative, and also the fact that they only go to the doctor when they feel sick.

In the second phase, of the group of 108 workers, 30.6% had a complete university education, 21.3% had a complete postgraduate degree, 20.4% had incomplete professional training, 10.2% had completed secondary school. In turn, 40.7% had their own home and 31.5% had a family home, 29.6% belonged to the middle stratum and 26.9% to the low stratum.

Of those surveyed, 40% had a permanent employment contract, 98.1% had health insurance, of which 34.3% had medical insurance while 23.1% had a government health subsidy. In addition, 65.7% said that their job offered them medical insurance, 31.5% said that because of their job they did not have time to go to the doctor; however, 90.7% considered that they would not lose their job to go to a doctor's appointment. On the other hand, it was found that gastrointestinal diseases were the main illnesses suffered in the last two years, with a prevalence of 33.3% and that 16.7% suffered from a chronic illness.

When asked about their perception of the health services they receive, it was found that 41.7% rarcly use health insurance, 61.1% stated that the medical center is partially close to them, 71.3% said they do not dislike going to the doctor, 85.2% believe that going to the doctor is not a waste of time, 41.6% stated that consultations are expensive, 26.9% said they would rather spend their time on other things than going to the doctor and 73.1% believed that doctors would prescribe medicines to improve their complaints.

Regarding the behaviour related to taking medications, it was found that 88.9% consider it essential to consult a doctor to decide which medications to take, 46.3% prefer to trust their instincts regarding their health and 42.6% prefer to ask the pharmacist. In turn, it was found that 50.9% of those surveyed consider that they can give suggestions as to which medicines to take.

19.5% of the respondents believe that the pharmacist can prescribe medications. In addition, it was found that 49.1% go to the pharmacy when they cannot stand pain, 51.8% stated that if they feel bad, they self-medicate, 13% buy medicines that they cannot obtain without a prescription from friends or relatives, 35.2% have all kinds of medicines at home, possibly because 69.4% state that it is very easy to obtain them, and 44.5% state that they do everything possible to obtain a medicine that they know will alleviate their pain.

On the other hand, the motivations or reasons for self-medication were found to be as follows: 37% state that they could not give up pain medication (whether prescribed or not), 72.2% state that taking medication docs not interfere with their life, 54.6% have tried to stop self-medicating, only 4.6% take medication for recreational purposes, 13% believe that medication helps them cope with their problems, 8.4% have been diagnosed with post-traumatic stress disorder and 13.9% with depression, 45.4% say that self-medication is common in their community, 21.3% take medication out of habit while 9.2% say they take it because it is a habit.

Finally, when analyzing the list of medications used for self-medication, it was found that the most commonly used medications were acetaminophen with a prevalence of 39% and ibuprofen with a prevalence of 15%. Among the reasons expressed for self-medication and consumption of medicines are the lack of time to go to the doctor (32.5%), the fact that 35.2% have all kinds of medicines at home and that 69.4% consider that it is very easy to obtain them.

The last phase focused on the analysis of the worker interviews, which were aimed at identifying risk behaviours that could affect in some way the work activities and performance of the workers. The group of participating workers was 9,997, of these 28% were women and 71.6% were men. 45% of the participants were between 15 and 25 years old, 34.7% between 25 and 35 years old and 15% between 36 and 45 years old. 70% had average income and 20% had low income (equivalent to minimum salary).

Regarding the consumption of drugs and self-medication, it was found that 35% (3579 workers) declared that they had self-medication, indicating that the decision to self-medication was taken by 13% looking for solutions on the Internet, 47% percent took it consulting a friend or a familiar person and 14% consulted the opinion of a pharmacist or druggist, the main drugs consumed were analgesics in 24% of cases and antibiotics in 3%. Regarding the age groups, 38.4% of the workers between 15 and 25 years old agreed to have self-medicated with the help of a friend or family; as well as 40% of workers between 26 and 35 years old, mostly consulting on the internet.

Concerning risk behaviours, 31% accept that they participated in hazard games at least during the last month, 8% in casinos. In addition, 97.8% agree to have consumed alcoholic beverages in the past, also indicating that 45% do so at least once a month and that 20% have worked with side effects of alcohol consumption, of which 3% I agree to have worked under the influence of alcohol. Regarding the consumption of hallucinogenic drugs, 18% accept having used them, however 36% (3643) accept having used marijuana.

Another important aspect that was studied regarding risk behaviours was the decision to make alcoholic drink mixes or hallucinogenic drug mixes. In this case, it was found that 62% of those who self-medicated made mixtures of different substances and 59% mixed alcoholic drinks.

The analysis of the variables associated with risk behaviours, shown in Fig. 1, the correlation between the significant variables allows to understand the link between some of the studied behaviours and self-medication behaviours. This should be analyzed in depth given the importance of these relationships in jobs where the control, surveillance and treatment of complex situations may be affected by such behaviours. In this sense, it is very important to understand the relationship between risky behaviours such as consuming mixtures of doras or alcohol, physical health estimation, and self-medication behaviours. Likewise, the decisions to take risks and their relationship with the consumption of drugs should be carefully observed in order to remain productive or available for work.

Chi-Square test summary	Sex	Self-Medication	Alcohol	Drugs	Marijuana	Casino	Alcohol Mixtures	Drugs Mixtures
Physical Health Self Qualification								
Mental Health Self Rating								
Have you ever self-medicated?								
Who made the drug decision?								
Have you ever played games of chance in your life?								
Select the last time you did it								
Select how often you do it								
Have you ever had alcoholic beverages in your life?								
Alcohol consumption (More than one) Mixtures								
Select the last time you did it								
Select how often you consume Alcohol								
Have you ever used an illegal drug								
Drug Use (More Than One) Mixtures								
Select the last time you did it								

No se rechaza la hipótesis de independencia a un nivel de significancia del 5%	
Se rechaza la hipótesis de independencia a un nivel de significancia del 5%, sin embargo, la prueba no es aconsejable	
Se rechaza la hipótesis de independencia a un nivel de significancia del 5%	
No Aplica	

Fig. 1. Summary of Chi-Square tests analysis of the correlation of the variables considered in the analysis

4 Discussion

One of the sources to understand how self-medication is expressed can be obtained from data related to the drugs dispensed, in Colombia according to the Ministry of Health, those that exceed the amount of one million units of disseminated doses are 26 drugs; among them the first 5, which were dispensed the most nationwide in 2018, appears in the Table 1.

These results obtained are similar to those obtained from various studies, one of them was carried out in 11 cities in Latin America, where it was found that the prevalence of self-medication is high, being a very common practice in more than half of the population evaluated. It was found that 26.87% indicate having received recommendations from a pharmacist.

In this sense, it is relevant to consider that workers who are overexposed or who reach levels of intensification or densification of their work (many hours or extension of work time invading private life, multiple tasks to attend, among others.), Externalize as the first symptom the phenomenon of "pain", this appears as an expression that their

Table 1. Number of doses dispensed, POS Populi, from the Ministry of Health Colombia

Tradename	Number of doses dispensed	Medication type
Acetaminophen	49.199.352,24	Analgesics
Fluoxetine	29.791.827,50	Antidepressant
Sertraline	21.702.493,00	Antidepressant
Rivastigmine	9.166.490,70	Antidementia
Escitalopram	6.978.067,00	Antidepressant

health conditions are compromised. However, it is necessary to analyze the origin of this "discomfort", which can come from various factors (motivation, stress, pressure from colleagues, cognitive or functional limitations, social, cultural, economic and/or family crossroads, etc.) or it can result from the combination of two or more of these. In fact, a worker may not present evident and obvious symptoms that his health is degraded, however he may be the victim of a poor health condition.

Workers for fear of losing their job and in the face of unsuccessful attempts at medical control, where repeated admissions to care services are evident, tend to develop different pain management. A study developed in 2011 by the CDCP (Centers for Disease Control and Prevention), found that around "12 million Americans admit to abusing the consumption of medicines", the use indiscriminate and overdoses of painkillers in the US exceed the admissions to medical emergencies for overdoses of cocaine and heroin combined. In this regard, in Colombia the third National Pain Survey (ACED, 2004) yielded some figures regarding the phenomenon of pain, there it was found that 47.7% of the population accepted having felt some type of pain in the immediately preceding month in the survey, of the declared pains, headache was found first. Followed by low back pain. 49%. Of the respondents who reported pain, they indicated that it was new (acute type), and 50% that it was already present (chronic type). Regarding pain interference, 52.4% indicated that their usual activity (work, academic, home, etc.) was affected or had to stop [10].

Losing the possibility of developing a job affects not only the individual's mood, it also affects his identity, affecting his intellectual and emotional stability, since losing his job can mean the loss of his home, family and friends. An individual with chronic pain demands modifications in her family circle, modifies the responsibilities of its members; In summary, chronic pain implies facing multiple scenarios and problems, these range from accepting the disability to making modifications to their ways of working and includes working on medication or on self-medication, with the implications of loss of skill and precision that this implies.

For workers, the challenges posed by an environment of uncertainty regarding the reality of their work leads them to make decisions regarding the balance between health and work, in fact the centrality of work overcomes concerns about health, the symptoms associated with Workers' activities are to a great extent treated through self-medication. This way out, as found in the study, allows them to ensure their physical presence at work and gives them certain certainty about the perception that they have of their productivity. Resorting to various forms of self-medication is nothing more than a way to ensure one's own productivity, however this behaviour is linked to other risk behaviours, as found in the final part of the study, these should be examined together when the responsibilities of the worker and the implications of their actions have important effects for all workers.

In short, the careful study of self-medication can help to understand risk behaviours, but also the reasons why workers report to work despite being reduced in their health conditions, be it due to an ongoing illness or discomfort, be it because of the delusions of consuming drugs on your own initiative. It is important to keep in mind the problem of productivity loss due to presenteeism, especially when it is mediated by self-medication. According to the work psychologist Sébastien Hof, "forced" presenteeism is the fact of no longer being able to work but of feeling obliged to stay at work. "We are trying to find efficiency, effectiveness," he explains. "In presenteeism there are also those who are sick, who should not be there and who come anyway," he adds. It is important to distinguish the involvement and motivation of the phenomenon of presenteeism.

References

1. Ruiz-Sternberg, A.M., Pérez-Acosta, A.M.: Automedicación y términos relacionados: Una reflexión conceptual. Revista Ciencias de la Salud **9**(1), 83–97 (2011)
2. Caamaño, F., Figueiras, A., Lema, E.L., Gestal-Otero, J.J.: La automedicación: concepto y perfil de sus «usuarios». Gaceta Sanitaria **14**(4), 294–299 (2000)
3. Mejía, M.C.B., Restrepo, M.L., Bernal, D.R.: Actitudes, conocimientos y prácticas frente a la automedicación con productos herbales y psicofármacos en estudiantes de medicina de Medellín-Colombia. Medicina UPB, **37**(1), 17–24 (2018)
4. Goldsworthy, R.C., Mayhorn, C.B.: Prescription medication sharing among adolescents: Prevalence, risks, and outcomes. J. Adolescent Health **45**(6), 634–637 (2009)
5. Steptoe, A.: Health behaviour and stress. In: Fink, G. (ed.) Encyclopedia of Stress, 2nd edn., pp. 263–266. Academic Press, San Diego (2007)
6. Sylvain Besle et Aline Sarradon-Eck, «Choisir le risque : l'autonomie du malade en situation d'échec thérapeutique», Anthropologie & Santé [En ligne], 19 | 2019, mis en ligne le 23 janvier 2019, consulté le 07 février 2021. https://journals.openedition.org/anthropologiesante/4817 https://doi.org/https://doi.org/10.4000/anthropologiesante.4817
7. Bacqué, M.-F.: L'automédication ou les mirages de l'autonomie. Psycho-Oncologie **6**(3), 183–184 (2012). https://doi.org/10.1007/s11839-012-0386-y
8. Horton, S., Stewart, A.: Reasons for self-medication and perceptions of risk among Mexican migrant farm workers. J. Immigrant and Minority Health No **14**, 664–672 (2012)
9. Sherbourne & Stewart (1991) Adapted and validated for Colombia by Londoño, N.H., Roger, H., Castilla, J.F., Posada, S., Ochoa, N., Jaramillo, M.A., Oliveros, M., Palacio, J., Aguirre, D.: International Journal of Psychological Research, **5**(1), 142–150 (2012)
10. Asociación Colombiana para Estudio del Dolor. Estudio Nacional de Dolor, Abril de 2004

Hierarchical Estimation of Occupational Accident Risks in a Brazilian Poultry Slaughterhouse

Sabrina Letícia Couto da Silva[1,2](✉) and Fernando Gonçalves Amaral[2]

[1] Federal Institute of Education, Science, and Technology of Rio Grande do Sul – Campus Porto Alegre, Porto Alegre, Brazil
sabrina.silva@poa.ifrs.edu.br
[2] Post Graduate Program of Production Engineering/UFRGS, Porto Alegre, Brazil

Abstract. Work accidents are events that must be controlled in a preventive manner through the planning, organization, and performance evaluation of two implemented control measures. A good performance in Health and Safety at Work is decisive for a company by promoting the reduction of risks of accidents and teaching to their employees, showing results and an internal and external image of the company. Despite being a subject investigated by researchers from different areas in interdisciplinary studies, there is still no emphasis, from an epidemiological point of view, on the different factors and levels (individual and environment) associated with the occurrences of accidents in work environments. The different factors and levels that may be associated with or related to accidents in the most diverse environments and workplaces. This work aims to present the estimates for occupational accidents among workers of a slaughterhouse, considering different factors and levels and using a hierarchical regression modeling. As a result, work accidents were associated with the variables gender; previous work experience in refrigerators; schooling; problems related to the circulatory system and respiratory system; taking breaks during the workday, and rotating activities. In the modeling, it was possible to identify some protective factors (gender, age, time in the company, previous experience in refrigerators, and taking breaks) and risk (schooling, problem related to the circulatory and respiratory system, and performance of rotation) for accidents at work in the company.

Keywords: Accidents · Risk · Hierarchical modeling · Poultry slaughterhouses

1 Introduction

The meat processing and slaughter industry stand out in terms of the Brazilian economy's importance and representation, given its production and exportation volume and its ample business management capacity. The Brazilian Animal Protein Association's annual report states that, in the year 2020, 13.2 thousand tons of Brazilian poultry meat was produced. Furthermore, this industry generates about 3 thousand businesses directly linked to refrigeration plants, being the State of Rio Grande do Sul or third-largest producer, responsible for 14.3% of poultry slaughter in the country [1].

© The Author(s), under exclusive license to Springer Nature Switzerland AG 2021
N. L. Black et al. (Eds.): IEA 2021, LNNS 222, pp. 55–62, 2021.
https://doi.org/10.1007/978-3-030-74611-7_8

Although the slaughterhouse sector has an essential economic relevance, there are still challenges regarding these companies' working conditions. However, improvements in working conditions have not kept pace with economic growth. Consequently, work activities are commonly associated with health and safety risks for workers [2]. They involve repetitive movements, unfavorable postures, high work rhythm, excessive use of force, and exposure to cold [3].

The study of the variables that influence occupational accidents' occurrence requires more in-depth analysis from an epidemiological perspective. The different factors and levels that may be associated with accidents in the most diverse environments and workplaces. Some researchers have used Multiple Linear Regression modeling for occupational safety and health studies [4, 5]. However, this analysis's problem is that the observations' independence may be compromised; the data collected in several areas are often from cases grouped in clusters [6].

Thus, they are likely to share similar characteristics. There is an underestimation of the regression coefficients' standard errors due to this dependence on the observations or measured attributes. An alternative that considers this similarity of characteristics is the analysis of Hierarchical or Multilevel Regression [7], a technique that simultaneously contemplates multiple aggregation levels, correcting problems by estimating standard errors and confidence intervals, and hypothesis tests that may be realized. This study aims to present the estimates for occupational accidents among workers of a slaughterhouse, considering different factors and levels.

2   Methodology

One hundred four cases of work accidents and respective controls, which occurred in 2018 and 2019 in a poultry slaughterhouse in southern Brazil, were analyzed.

Multilevel modeling was performed considering workers grouped by their sociodemographic, health, and work characteristics. In the construction of statistical models, it is usual and ideal to find the most parsimonious model for adjusting the data. Thus, the more variables are included in the model, the greater the error estimate and the more dependent the model is on the observed data [8].

This work's hierarchical model consisted of 3 levels and the variable work accident (yes or no). In level 1, we have included the variables age (years), time of service (months), gender, previous experience in slaughterhouses, and the worker's schooling. In level 2, there are characteristics related to the worker's health, such as a circulatory and respiratory system problem. At level 3, work activities were included, such as taking breaks and rotating activities.

Therefore, the variables were included in the modeling through the stepwise method, systematically adding significant variables and removing non-significant variables from the model. In addition to the stepwise method, the knowledge acquired after the interviews with the company's occupational, health, and safety specialists and managers was taken into account so that the results align with a more practical point of view.

With the modeling results, it was possible to test the association of the predictive factors for the outcome of the outcome by calculating the association's odds ratio - OR (adjusted), assuming 95% confidence intervals for the estimates. The Wald test was also calculated to verify the model's coefficients' statistical significance and the adjusted OR. Besides, the quality of the models' fit was analyzed using the Akaike Information Criterion - AIC [9] and Bayesian Information Criterion - BIC [10], and the lower the values for these criteria, the better the model will fit.

SPSS software version 18.0 for Windows and R Studio [11] was used to perform the statistical analysis.

3   Results and Conclusions

Table 1 shows the average (standard deviation) and n (%) statistics for the variables that make up the hierarchical logistic model. Also, the averages between injured and non-injured workers were compared (independent Student's t-test), and associations between qualitative variables and the outcome (Pearson's chi-square test) were tested.

Thus, it was possible to verify a statistically significant difference between the average age, with the injured young workers (p = 0.043), and between the average company times, with the injured workers having, on average, less time in the company (p = 0.038). According to the results of the Chi-square test, with a 5% significance level, the following factors were associated (all p-values < 0.010) with the work accident outcome:

i.   male workers;
ii.   to workers with no previous work experience in slaughterhouses;
iii.   workers with lower levels of education;
iv.   to workers with any problem related to the circulatory system;
v.   to workers with any problem related to the respiratory system;
vi.   to employees who do not take breaks;
vii.   to workers who rotate in their activities.

In Table 2, the estimates of the logistic regression equation's coefficients and the Odds Ratio (OR), adjusted for the gender and age variables, will be presented for each predictor in the hierarchical logistic regression models performed. The choice for this type of modeling is because the assumption of multivariate normality of the data is not necessary, of being a more generic and robust technique and its application suitable for a variety of situations [11].

Table 1. Statistics of the variables of the Logistic Regression model - by level.

Level	Variable	General (n = 208)	Work accident		p-value
			No (n = 104)	Yes (n = 104)	
1	Age (year)	32,3 (10,1)	33,6 (10,2)	31,0 (9,9)	0,043
	Time of service (month)	30,6 (9,2)	32,4 (8,7)	28,8 (10,3)	0,038
	Gender				
	Male	131 (63,0)	41 (39,4)	90 (86,5)	<0,010
	Female	77 (37,0)	63 (60,8)	14 (13,5)	
	Previous experience				
	No	116 (55,8)	16 (15,4)	100 (96,2)	<0,010
	Yes	92 (44,2)	88 (84,6)	4 (3,8)	
	Schooling				
	Illiterate	63 (30,3)	17 (16,3)	46 (44,2)	<0,010
	Elementary School	92 (44,2)	37 (35,6)	55 (52,9)	
	High School	44 (21,2)	41 (39,4)	3 (2,9)	
	University Education	9 (4,3)	9 (8,7)	–	
2	*Circulatory problem*				
	No	111 (53,4)	82 (78,8)	29 (27,9)	<0,010
	Yes	97 (46,6)	22 (21,2)	75 (72,1)	
	Respiratory problem				
	No	107 (51,4)	77 (74,0)	30 (28,8)	<0,010
	Yes	101 (48,6)	27 (26,0)	74 (71,2)	
3	*Break*				
	No	91 (43,8)	20 (19,2)	71 (68,3)	<0,010
	Yes	117 (56,3)	84 (80,8)	33 (31,7)	
	Rotation activities				
	No	95 (45,7)	72 (69,2)	23 (22,1)	<0,010
	Yes	113 (54,3)	32 (30,8)	81 (77,9)	

Table 2. Estimates of parameters and odds ratios for logistic model.

Variable	β	OR*	Low limit CI 95%	Upper limit CI 95%	p**
Gender					
Male	1	–	–	–	–
Female	−2,53	0,08	0,01	0,73	<0,050
Age (years)	−0,09	0,91	0,88	0,95	<0,050
Previous experience					
No	1	–	–	–	–
Yes	−2,55	0,08	0,02	0,40	<0,050
Time of service (months)	−1,02	0,36	0,19	0,69	<0,050
Schooling					
Illiterate	1	–	–	–	–
Elementary School	2,71	15,03	6,10	37,03	<0,050
High School	−3,22	0,04	0,01	0,22	<0,050
University Education	−4,05	0,02	0,01	0,04	<0,050
Circulatory problem					
No	1	–	–	–	–
Yes	1,89	6,62	5,55	7,90	<0,050
Respiratory problem					
No	1	–	–	–	–
Yes	2,09	8,08	3,99	16,37	<0,050
Break					
No	1	–	–	–	–
Yes	−2,37	0,09	0,01	0,98	< 0,050
Rotation activities					
No	1	–	–	–	–
Yes	2,72	15,18	12,73	18,11	<0,050

*Odds Ratio Adjusted; **Wald Test.

In model 3 (individual-level variables + health + environment), the results indicate that there is evidence that all predictors included in the model are associated with the outcome (occurrence of TA). As a result, we have to:

- The female worker is a protective factor for work accident (WA) (OR = 0.08, 95% CI: [0.02; 0.40]). That is, it is estimated that the chance of WA among workers in the female gender is 0.08 (or 92% lower) times the chance of WA among male workers;
- The unitary increase in the worker's age is a protective factor for WA (OR = 0.91, 95% CI: [0.88; 0.95]), that is, it is estimated that the chance of WA is reduced by 9% each year that the worker has increased his age;
- Having previous work experience in slaughterhouses is a protective factor for WA (OR = 0.08, 95% CI: [0.02; 0.40]). That is, it is estimated that the chance of WA among workers who already have previous experience is equal to 0.08 (or 92% less) times the chance of WA among workers who have no previous experience;
- The unitary increase in the employee's company time is a protective factor for WA (OR = 0.36, 95% CI: [0.19; 0.69]), that is, it is estimated that the chance of WA is reduced by 64% each month that the worker has added to his time with the company;
- The worker having elementary education level (OR = 15.03, 95% CI [6.10; 37.03]) was shown to be a risk factor for WA when comparing with illiterate workers, while the worker having high school (OR = 0.04, 95% CI: [0.01; 0.22]) and having a university education level (OR = 0.02, 95% CI: [0.01; 0.04]) were shown to be protection for WA, that is, it is estimated that when compared to illiterate workers, the chance of WA among high school workers is 96% lower and among workers with university education is 98% lower;
- The worker having problems with the circulatory system is a risk factor for WA (OR = 6.62, 95% CI: [5.55; 7.90]); that is, it is estimated that the chance of TA among workers with some circulatory system problem is 6.62 (562% higher) times the chance of WA among workers without circulatory system problem;
- The worker's respiratory system problems are a risk factor for WA (OR = 8.08, 95% CI: [3.99; 16.37]). It is estimated that the chance of WA among workers with a respiratory system problem is 8.08 (708% higher) than the chance of WA among workers without a respiratory system problem.
- The worker taking a break during the working day is a protective factor for WA (OR = 0.07, 95% CI: [0.01; 0.98]). That is, it is estimated that the chance of WA among workers who pause during the working day is 0.07 (93% lower) times the chance of WA among workers who do not take a break during the working day;
- During the workday, the worker rotating is a risk factor for WA (OR = 15.18, 95% CI: [12.73; 18.11]). That is, it is estimated that the chance of WA among workers who rotate during the workday is 15.18 (1418% higher) times the chance of WA among workers who do not rotate during the workday.

The results showed that the data's hierarchical adjustment proved fundamental for obtaining estimates free of possible confounding factors [12]. Thus, the improvement in adjustment depended on the variables available and a conceptual model for constructing the models (hierarchical structure) based on the company's emerging demand and information obtained in the interviews conducted previously.

Table 3 shows the statistics for comparing the models used (1, 2, and 3). For all indicators, model 3 (complete with three levels) showed the best fit for the data. The AIC and BIC criteria provide reasonable quality measures when comparing related or nested models, which is the model in question. Model 3 is composed of the predictors present in models 1 and 2 plus variables related to work activity (environment). The model with the lowest values of AIC and BIC should be chosen; thus, model 3 (complete) was the one that resulted in lower values for both AIC and BIC when compared to models 1 and 2.

The null deviation measure indicates how well the outcome (WA) is predicted by a model without predictor variables, relying only on the intercept. For this reason, the null deviation value is the same for the three adjusted models (288,349). The residual deviation measures the forecast quality for the outcome (WA) as the predictors are included in the modeling. Thus, adequate modeling will be one where the residual deviation is less than the null deviation when the insertion of predictor variables improves interest. According to Table 3, model 3 presented a residual deviation of 28.923 with nine predictor variables. Model 2 has a residual deviation of 42.452 with seven predictor variables, and model 1 resulted in a residual deviation of 81.351 with only five predictor variables.

According to the hierarchical levels, the residual deviation was reduced when including variables in the modeling; that is, the modeling proved to be better adjusted to the model's data with the three hierarchical levels (9 predictors).

Table 3. Adjustment statistics of logistic models.

Model	AIC	BIC	Null deviation	Residual deviation
1	97,351	124,051	288,349	81,351
2	62,452	95,827	288,349	42,452
3	50,923	87,636	288,349	28,923

Model 1: gender + age + previous experience + time of service + schooling.
Model 2: Model 1 + circulatory problem + respiratory problem.
Model 3: Model 2 + break + rotation activities.

The common and heterogeneous characteristics of WA's repercussions in different strata of workers were analyzed. This analysis of the different strata enabled the identification and definition of different groups according to the work process's characteristics. In this sense, it is mandatory to perform subsequent analyses of factors that define homogeneous groups' heterogeneity. It is a fundamental tool for epidemiological management in occupational health and safety.

In the studied company, it was possible to identify different strata of workers, through the different activities performed, forming different exposure groups that require diversified care.

The epidemiological action in Occupational Safety and Health (OSH) makes it possible, due to its results' clarity and incisiveness, to establish a dialogue with the management of a company, bringing indicators related to OSH built in an integrated way with safety issues. It was possible to demonstrate to the company which factors deserved more vigorous and urgent action, and the factors previously inexperienced in slaughterhouses and schooling could already be reviewed and controlled at the time of hiring employees.

Other factors listed as risk factors - carrying out activities and not taking breaks - signaled the company for necessary changes in the implemented work processes, the first of which proved to be something unexpected. Besides, it was interesting for the company to consider in its selection processes for new workers, in order to reduce the risk of work accidents, carry out the selection of female workers (performing more repetitive tasks and with greater precision of gestures and movements, with less use of force), with older ages, with a higher level of education and who have previous work experience in slaughterhouses.

The protection of workers against accidents and occupational diseases should be, mainly, a managerial responsibility together and in an equal degree of importance with other actions, such as the definition of production goals, the guarantee of product quality, and provision of services to customers. A strategic view on the part of management, with issues related to OSH linked to the organization's mission, can establish a context of growth, profitability, and production and generate value for workers concerning their OSH.

The OSH management system should be integrated with the culture and business processes of the company under study. However, although essential for the construction and monitoring of indicators and assessment of the risks inherent in the activities carried out, an epidemiological approach was very little or almost considered in the company object of the study.

Finally, the use of epidemiological foundations allowed the collection of OSH data to be better organized, but also so that it was possible to estimate the relationships between workers' health information and their linked work process.

References

1. Brazilian Animal Protein Association: Annual Report (2020)
2. Grant, K.A., Habes, D.J.: An electromyographic study of strength and upper extremity muscle activity in simulated meat cutting tasks. Appl. Ergon. **28**(2), 129–137 (1997)
3. Caso, M.A., Ravaioli, M., Veneri, L.: Exposure to biomechanical overload of the upper limbs: the assessment of occupational risk in poultry slaughterhouses. Prev. Today **3**(4), 9–21 (2007)
4. Araújo, C.C.: Identification of the level of importance of critical management factors for total quality in product quality results through multiple linear regression. Federal University of Ceará (2012)
5. Cavazotte, F.S.C., Duarte, C.J.P., Gobbo, A.M.: Authentic leader, safe work: the influence of leadership on safety performance. Brazilian Bus. Rev. **2**(10), 97–123 (2013)
6. Hair, J.F., Anderson, R.E., Tatham, R.L., Black, W.C.: Multivariate data analysis, 5th ed. Bookman (2005)
7. Harrel, F.E.: Regression Modeling Strategies: With Applications to Linear Models, Logistic Regression, and Survival Analysis. Springer, New York (2001)
8. McCullagh, P., Nelder, J.: Generalized Linear Models. Chapman and Hall, London (1989)
9. Akaike, H.: A new look at the statistical model identification. IEEE Trans. Automat. Contr. **19**(6), 716–723 (1974)
10. Schwarz, G.: Estimating the dimension of a model. Ann. Stat. **6**(2), 461–464 (1978)
11. Ripley, B.D.: The R Project in Statistical Computing. January, pp. 23–25 (2001)
12. Hosmer, D.W., Lemeshow, S.: Applied Logistic Regression. Wiley, New York (2000)

A Study of Attitudes and Behaviors in Industries Regarding Implementation of Low-Vibrating Machines and Measures to Reduce Vibration Injuries

Karin Fisk[1,2(✉)] (iD) and Åsa Ek[2] (iD)

[1] Occupational and Environmental Medicine, Department of Laboratory Medicine, Faculty of Medicine, Lund University, Lund, Sweden
karin.fisk@med.lu.se

[2] Ergonomics and Aerosol Technology, Department of Design Sciences, Faculty of Engineering LTH, Lund University, Lund, Sweden

Abstract. Vibration injuries are the most common approved occupational disease among men in Sweden. Vibration injuries often involves chronic nerve and vascular damage, reduced ability to work, and great personal suffering. In a project, new design solutions have reduced harmful vibrations for several hand-held machines. The machines were tested in demonstration environments in the construction, stone, and steel industry. Preliminary results on the environments' readiness for implementing the machines in their production will be reported in this paper. The objectives were to investigate the awareness about vibrations and the level of knowledge and acceptance of low-vibrating machines throughout the organizations. 28 interviews were conducted with persons on several organizational levels in a large steel works, a quarry, two construction companies, a construction machine rental company, and a dental engineering laboratory. Interview results showed that there was a great need for low-vibrating machines because it is the only way to significantly reduce the vibration exposure. The results however also showed a need for an increased awareness about the risks with vibrations and that the understanding and acceptance for new machines is important. Communication between employees and between employees and management needs to be strengthened. It is important to implement new low-vibrating machines in the organizations through well thought through change processes.

Keywords: Hand-arm vibrations · Risk awareness · Holistic approach · High frequency vibrations

1 Introduction

1.1 Background

Vibration injuries are the most common approved occupational disease among men in Sweden and about 400 000 persons are daily exposed to vibrations in their work [1].

© The Author(s), under exclusive license to Springer Nature Switzerland AG 2021
N. L. Black et al. (Eds.): IEA 2021, LNNS 222, pp. 63–69, 2021.
https://doi.org/10.1007/978-3-030-74611-7_9

Vibration injuries often involves chronic nerve and vascular damage, reduced ability to work, and great personal suffering [2]. Since afflicted often have to be redeployed, vibration injuries also account for large societal costs. Examples of occupational groups that are exposed to vibrations are in the automotive and construction industries as well as dental care.

The current European Union Vibration Directive, 2002/44/EC, regulates the obligations and rights of employers and employees regarding exposure to vibrations [3]. The responsibilities of the employer defined in the directive are among others to perform risk assessments of the vibration exposures and to inform and educate the workers about the risks of vibration exposure and the result of the vibration risk assessment. If there is a risk of injuries, workers must be offered regular health checks. For vibration exposure there is a limit value (5 m/s^2, 8h daily exposure) that must not be exceeded and an action value (2.5 m/s^2) which, if exceeded, means that measures must be taken. However, when assessing patients with vibration injuries it is often found that the proactive health and safety work has not been functioning at the workplace of the patient, and that the employer has not fulfilled its obligations according to the law [4].

In a project (supported by the Swedish innovation agency (Vinnova)) the aims were to through technical design solutions remove harmful vibrations in hand-held machines, to create an industry demand for low-vibrating machines, and to facilitate an attitudinal and behavioral change in industries that increases their readiness for implementing machines and measures to reduce vibration injuries. In the project, low-vibrating machine prototypes were introduced and used in antivibration demonstration environments, which are delineated industrial production environments at fully operational companies with associated productivity and quality assurance requirements. The demonstration environments were chosen to represent industries where vibration injuries are common and hand-held machines with high vibration levels are used, such as construction, quarries and steel industries.

For successful implementation of low-vibrating machines, it can be necessary to change leaders' and workers' attitudes and behaviours regarding vibrations in order to emphasize vibration exposure as a crucial physical work environment factor in a company. The aim is to achieve a holistic view in companies regarding vibration injuries, including direct technical machine solutions, increased understanding and acceptance throughout organizations of the need and use of low-vibrating machines, and to achieve an increased awareness of the risks of vibration exposures. An attitudinal and behavioural change is a way to yield increased exposure and injury awareness and to create a driving force in companies to reduce vibrations in machines and to implement measures against vibration injuries.

1.2 Objectives

The objectives of the study reported in this paper, were to yield increased knowledge on how low-vibrating machine prototypes were received in the demonstration environments. This included investigating a) the awareness about vibrations and vibration injuries on several levels in the organizations, b) the level of knowledge and acceptance of low-vibrating machines throughout the organizations, c) what obstacles or success factors there may be concerning future use of the low-vibrating machines in the organizations, and d) existing knowledge gaps about vibration risks, high-frequency vibrations, and the Swedish legislation on vibration exposure based upon the European Union Vibration Directive.

The aim of this paper is to report preliminary findings from interviews conducted in demonstration environments in six industries with high vibration exposure and with focus on a) and b) above.

2 Methodology

A methodology consisting of observations, interviews, and a short questionnaire was used in the study. It included field visits to six organizations: a large steel works, a quarry, two construction companies, a construction machine rental company, and a dental engineering laboratory.

At the dental engineering laboratory, a three-hour field visit through all departments at the company took place, led by a safety representative and the health and safety manager. During the tour there was opportunities to ask questions to dental technicians and other personnel. For the other companies, semi-structured and exploratory interviews were conducted with persons on several organizational levels in order to catch different views and perspectives from various functions in the organization. Interviews were conducted with professional workers (operators, machine users), health and safety representatives, health and safety managers, production managers, work supervisors, top management, as well as representatives of the machine purchasing organizations. The interviews included topics such as: vibration problem insight, risk awareness and work practice, knowledge of technical machine designs and supply of machines, change management work, attitudes to and willingness to use machines, knowledge and information about vibrations, and experiences of machine prototypes. A total of 28 interviews were conducted (Table 1). Interviews were analyzed using content analysis.

Table 1. Number of interviews conducted per company and the interviewees' professional role.

	Quarry	Steel works	Constr. comp.1	Rental comp.	Constr. comp.2	Dental lab.
Operator	2	3		1	2	
Safety representative		1	1	1		1
Supervisor	1	1			1	
Purchaser/renter	1			2		
Health and safety manager	1	1	1			1
Other management	2	3	1	1	1	
Total	7	9	3	5	4	2

A short questionnaire (12 items) with the aim of measuring the organizational readiness for change in the various demonstration environments were also included in the study. However, this paper will focus on reporting preliminary interview results.

3 Results

3.1 Overall Results

Generally, in all companies, knowledge about vibration risks, exposures, as well as obligations and rights regarding vibrations were low. The management in all companies requested more knowledge about machine solutions and supply, and more support from e.g. rental companies to enable considered choices when purchasing or renting machines.

3.2 The Quarry

At the quarry, granite products were mined and produced. The machine that would be replaced with a low-vibrating prototype was an air hammer used to split larger stones into material to be further processed.

Interview results showed shortcomings in the communication between stonemasons and managers about symptoms and problems in hands. The stonemasons talked about how they were all experiencing signs of vibration injury, but the managements' view was that there were no major problems with vibration injuries within the company. Instead, the management directed their attention and efforts to the quartz exposure, where the company performed regular measurements and health checks.

Stonemasonry is a profession with strong traditions and the stonemasons were clearly proud of their craftsmanship. The stone is a natural material and for a skilled stonemason it is important to "have a feel" for every stone. With changed work conditions, for example when introducing new machines, the stonemasons expressed worries of losing their feel when working with the stones.

3.3 The Steel Works

The demonstration environment at the steel works was the masonry hall where buckets for transporting molten steel were laid with refractory bricks on the inside. On the refractory bricks, an insulating mass was installed using a rammer. A rammer is a high-vibrating impact machine.

Results from the interviews showed that several other risks at the steel works overshadowed the risks of vibrations. There were many direct risks when handling steel melts with extreme heat, but also the long-term risk of dust exposure was perceived as a greater risk than vibrations.

From the interviews, it also emerged that knowledge and information about vibrations had not been communicated and dispersed throughout the company, but instead was possessed by a few key persons.

3.4   The Construction Companies and the Machine Rental Company

The construction work at the observed sites involved expansion of a sewerage system. During this work, vibration plates were used to compact the soil when backfilling.

In interviews, the site managers expressed expectations on the rental company to supply them with the, in terms of ergonomics and vibration levels, best machines. The site managers felt that they had neither enough time nor sufficient knowledge to look into which machines to choose. It also emerged that the skilled workers often chose the machines and brands that they were accustomed to use, and that there was a reluctance to use new machines such as low-vibrating machines. The rental company forwarded that in practice at the time of a machine rental, information about vibration levels or low-vibrating machines were never requested. The company had therefore stopped purchasing such machines.

3.5   The Dental Laboratory

At the dental laboratory, motor hand pieces with a speed up to 50 000 rpm were used.

Results showed that there was an awareness among dental technicians about high frequency vibrations and that it could cause injuries even though the measured levels are below the action value. On the other hand, the dental technicians were grinding using the hand pieces at least half of their workday, some as much as 70% of the day. During the field visit, communication deficiencies were revealed between employees and between employees and management regarding ergonomics issues and available aids at the workplace. Many technicians highlighted their ergonomics problems, and an in general neglected work environment.

4   Discussion

This paper reported preliminary findings on the awareness about vibrations and vibration injuries at visited demonstration environments in companies, and the level of knowledge and acceptance of low-vibrating machines throughout the organizations.

In all studied companies, knowledge deficiencies concerning vibration exposures and the current situations regarding injuries were discovered. The project described in the current paper has hopefully contributed to the spreading of information to the participating companies about vibration exposures and injuries. However, the knowledge and information need to be spread throughout the entire organisations so that it reaches middle management and not least the operators that are using the machines.

At the introduction of new low-vibrating machines the management has an important role. They must be clear and consistent in that the health of the employees is prioritized. It is important for management to support and encourage employees to raise concerns about health and safety, and to have an open communication between employers and employees is vital to safety [5]. It is also important that the management make sure that employees are involved when making changes to their work conditions. The interaction and cooperation of employees are important in relation to health and safety [6].

During interviews the question was raised about the machine manufacturers' influence on the supply and access to ergonomically safe machines. Some of the machines that was re-designed in the current project had very high vibration levels and could only be used for a few minutes per day before the vibration limit value was exceeded. In all companies there was therefore a great need for low-vibrating machines because it is the only way to significantly reduce the vibration exposures in their work environments. Today, many employers are unable to comply with the Swedish Work Environment Authority's regulation on vibration exposure because low-vibrating machine alternatives are often lacking. The current project meets the need to remove harmful vibrations in hand-held machines. However, low-vibrating machines must be developed, demanded, manufactured, purchased, and used.

5   Conclusions

In the industries that participated in this project, there was a great need for low-vibrating machines because it is the only way to significantly reduce the vibration exposure. The current project has shown that it is possible to technically reduce vibration levels in hand-held machines. However, in order to create a demand for low-vibrating machines, and generating an attitudinal and behavioural change in companies that emphasize measures to reduce vibration injuries the following can be concluded:

- **There is a need for an increased awareness about the risks with vibrations.** The knowledge and the awareness about injuries from vibrations needs to be strengthen in the participating companies. The risks with vibrations are often overshadowed by other, more prominent risks.
- **Understanding and acceptance for new machines is important.** Among the interviewees many knew that job rotation only was not enough to lower the vibration exposure sufficiently, but also better low-vibrating machines was needed. Although, sometimes can such a change affect the work and the craftmanship, so that understanding, acceptance and involvement from those using the machines will be necessary.
- **The communication needs to be strengthened**. Communication between employees and between employees and management needs to be functioning, so that employees receive information about risks and the management gets an overview over work conditions and health status. A good dialogue between employees and employers is needed for the introduction and use of new, low-vibrating machines to be as successful as possible.
- **Implement through well thought through change processes**. Change processes needs to be well designed, where information is given about upcoming measures and where the staff is involved and participating in the change work. This can increase the acceptance for new machines and the impact they have on the operative work. Such a change process may take time, but well implemented it can result in a changed workplace culture, where low-vibrating machines are used as a natural part of the work.

References

1. AFA Insurance: Severe occupational injuries and long-term sick leave. AFA Insurance, Stockholm (2020) (In Swedish)
2. Nilsson, T., Wahlström, J., Burström, L.: Hand-arm vibration and the risk of vascular and neurological diseases—A systematic review and meta-analysis. PLoS One **12**(7), e0180795 (2017)
3. Directive 2002/44/EC of the European Parliament and of the Council on the minimum health and safety requirements regarding the exposure of workers to the risks arising from physical agents (vibration). European Parliament and the Council of the European Union, Luxembourg (2002)
4. Gunnarsson, L-G., Mölleby, G., Porat, A-M.: Medical checks when using hand-held vibrating machines - a survey about the application of regulations in occupational health care units and companies. Swedish Work Environment Authority, Stockholm (2011) (In Swedish)
5. Cigularov, K.P., Chen, P.Y., Rosecrance, J.: The effects of error management climate and safety communication on safety: a multi-level study. Accid. Anal. Prev. **42**, 1498–1506 (2010)
6. Torner, M., Pousette, A.: Safety in construction–a comprehensive description of the characteristics of high safety standards in construction work, from the combined perspective of supervisors and experienced workers. J Safety Res. **40**(6), 399–409 (2009)

Future-Proof Commercial Vehicle Seat and Interiors Development

Susanne Frohriep[✉]

Global Ergonomics, Usability & Design, Grammer AG, Ursensollen, Germany
susanne.frohriep@grammer.com

Abstract. Future-proof commercial vehicle seats and interiors respect user groups with their scope of widely varying and constantly changing requirements, minimizing driver stress and strain by taking current and future use cases into account. This contribution presents user-centered development of commercial vehicle seats and interiors in logistics, agriculture and material handling. It shows how the manufacturer's development process ensures user involvement in the context of automation and digitalization of commercial vehicle work places. Associated user groups, usability methods and concepts are reported for a multifunctional truck cab interior, agriculture vehicle interiors facilitating a man-machine performance increase, and fork-lift truck seats with "haptic warning" for reducing driver stress.

Keywords: User-centered · Future-proof · Commercial vehicle seats · Usability · Use-case

1 Introduction: Commercial Vehicle Seats and Interiors in Focus

By taking current use cases into account and planning for future ones, commercial vehicle seats and interiors minimizes driver stress and strain. In order to be future-proof, they need to respect user groups with their scope of widely varying and constantly changing requirements. The entire cabin environment, consisting of the seat, controls and other components in the immediate bodyspace ("operator system") is relevant, and also the different personal and environmental conditions of its usage. Commercial vehicle seats and interiors for forklift trucks, construction machinery, agricultural vehicles, trucks, buses and trains are to be developed and optimized in a human-centric fashion. This paper presents Grammer AG's usability engineering and the results of user studies for specific vehicle types which were performed in the years 2018–2020.

2 Methods: Usability into Commercial Vehicle Seats and Interiors

Grammer AG uses a product development process based on ISO 9241–210 [1], which starts with user input studies and validates concepts and products during the process. Human beings with their abilities and needs always form the basis in this process,

© The Author(s), under exclusive license to Springer Nature Switzerland AG 2021
N. L. Black et al. (Eds.): IEA 2021, LNNS 222, pp. 70–77, 2021.
https://doi.org/10.1007/978-3-030-74611-7_10

which is described by the term "perceived quality" referring to the targeted positive user interaction for all relevant use cases. In the terms of comfort modeling, affinity and accommodation of users are achieved by the final product [2]. Capabilities united in the responsible team are design, usability and ergonomics, with the target of ensuring the users' ease, fit and comfort by their aligned approach. Defined test procedures, committee decisions and approvals are central parts of the development process [3] for validating new products. During product development, both laboratory and field tests are used. All aspects of interaction are considered in the final products, e.g. visual and haptic impression, adjustment ranges, thermal and vibration comfort, posture and usability. Respective suitable user collectives and rating criteria are determined by product maturity, project phase and focus of the respective evaluation. While lay subjects can be utilized for the validation of e.g. product dimensions and thermal properties, expert panels are needed to rate product interface aspects such as touch & feel and operation comfort, and professional users with work experience are needed to rate product features and general usability in their respective work context (efficiency, effectiveness and satisfaction). In designing for concrete applications and use cases, the parameters of usability [1] and the criteria of interaction according to Norman [4, 5] are used for evaluation. Usability data acquired during the process is analyzed and visualized following standardized procedures and reported during the phases of product development, forming the basis for product requirements and content.

This paper presents the results of studies from the years 2018 to 2020 for three different vehicle types in logistics, agriculture and material handling respectively. The studies were conducted in Germany and France. Methods used were partly-standardized interviews, focus group work, surveys, questionnaire-based seat comfort evaluations and ride & drives. Data analysis comprised numerical and frequency analysis of survey and questionnaire results, and contextualized qualitative analysis of verbatims yielding graphical visualization by pie, bar and spider charts as well as boxplots and word clouds. Visualized user ratings were reviewed by interdisciplinary teams including product development, customer managers, strategic planning, design and ergonomics, and then were processed and translated into product concepts for vehicle interiors. These concepts formed the basis for graphics and stories used in focus group reviews. Prototype seats with new integrated functions were built and then evaluated with professional drivers. In this way, user feedback was incorporated in various project phases through an iterative process.

Test persons taking part in the studies were professional drivers of commercial vehicles. They were recruited at their work places and on professional trade fairs. For the 2018 study on driving and living space in large on-road trucks, 208 truck drivers were consulted in total. 174 filled in a survey using 6 or 10-point ordinal scales to assess work satisfaction, stress and associated factors, as well as seat functionality, fit and adjustment. 30–90 min qualitative person-to-person interviews were performed with 34 drivers by company staff detailing use cases such as on-road meal consumption, communication, resting and personal hygiene. This was followed up in 2019 by interviewing 21 truck drivers at the company delivery gate concerning mobile office use cases. 7.4% of the entire trucker test subject sample were female. While this number seems low, women were overrepresented in the sample, as their number in occupational truck driving is currently much lower. Statista names a value of under 2% for Germany up to the year of 2018 [6]. The fact that there is a shortage of individuals wishing to become professional truck drivers justifies the over-proportional representation of women in the sample, as there is a growing need to recruit employees from this group in future.

For assessing usage and enabling performance increase of large tractors, farmers were surveyed. For determining the project focus, 10 farmers were recruited at a Southern German trade fair in 2018 and interviewed with a partly standardized questionnaire focusing on challenges in modern agriculture. This was followed up in 2019 with a study by a research partner institute. Two nationalities were included to address possible cultural differences. The first user group consisted of 25 participants from two European countries, Germany and France, over a total of four regions. 15 individuals were consulted in depth for four to six hours on their farm sites and in their tractors with partly standardized questionnaires and open ended questions, while ten were interviewed indoors in two focus groups in a later project phase. They named an average driving experience of more than 26 years and an annual driving time of more than 1350 h on tractors, and crop farming and grassland management was the main focus of their farm work. For a questionnaire based concept evaluation concerning relevance and affinity, commented 5-point ordinal scales were used in the focus groups. This project phase was concluded by a ride-and-drive assessment of a prototype seat with integrated functionality innovations by 14 internal comfort experts and 12 external professional drivers. These assessments used Likert and ordinal scales for rating seat features and associated (dis)comfort. Aspects of seat reaction like vibration insulation on rough terrain, seat position stability in emergency stops and seat height stability in hill terrain were rated and evaluated.

For a 2020 fork lift truck study, seven professional drivers were recruited in order to perform an evaluation of interface pressure and seat comfort of the newly implemented "haptic warning" system. The assessments were performed in static seats and ride and drives, employing partly standardized questionnaires with Likert scales and commenting. The developed system conveys two types of information via the haptic channel, an indication and an attention signal, by configured cushion vibration. Associated functions can be defined by forklift truck manufacturers, for example an indication signal to notify the correct position of the fork in the load and an attention signal for dangerous uneven load on the fork or as a snooze alarm. Signals are differentiated in activation time, cycle and alternation, and the system was implemented in three different seats to rate perception comparability and effectiveness for different seat sizes and versions. Goal of the analysis was to ascertain that the operator is in sufficient contact with the system in the occurring different seating positions to be able to safely perceive the signal. Positions that were tested were forward and rearward oriented sitting positions in which the seat occupant switch is activated, and thus the vehicle can be operated.

3   Results: Aspects of Future Seat and Interior Functionality

The purpose of the 2018 on-road truck study was the development of interior components specifically catering to cab use-cases in trucks to increase driver comfort during driving, breaks and rest activities. The agriculture project focused on the question of components or design variants that can further increase the performance of the man-machine system in the application of large tractors (>150 HP). The forklift-truck study was performed to verify the newly integrated feature of a "haptic warning" system using an alternative channel of perception to convey information to the driver.

3.1 A Multifunctional Truck Driver's Cab Interior

In the analysis of the 2018 driving and living space truck driver surveys, a generally high level of satisfaction with driving was found, however, a lesser well-being during breaks and rest periods. On a scale of 1–10, truckers gave a median rating of 8 points for comfort while driving, even though 28% of the surveyed group rated the driving task as "very strenuous". In comparison, comfort in the cab in non-driving activities was rated lower. With its median of 5, it indicated optimization potential of the truck interior. 2018 survey results identified associated stressors and positive aspects of truck driving: Unproductive waiting time was a major negative factor, technology a major positive one. 57% of the drivers report changing their seat settings while driving (from "rarely" to "every time"). The qualitative interviews showed over 50% drivers practice personal hygiene and over 88% consume meals in the truck cab, 64% even while driving. 50% of long-haul and 39% short-haul drivers read magazines or newspapers during their shifts. On the basis of these findings and the results from the qualitative interviews, use cases were specified, unfulfilled user needs identified and concepts for the further development of the interior were developed.

Fig. 1. Use-Case adapted interior for future large trucks: Mobile Office/Cooking & Eating

The 2019 truck driver survey researched aspects of the mobile office. It showed an average time of 25 min per day for office work in relation to freight handling, delivery and expenses. The vast majority of the sample (90%) completed this work in the driver's seat. The medium predominantly used for work is still paper (63% usage), while full transition to digital media was reported by 19%.

In the developed GRAMMER AG concept interior, the driver's seat becomes mobile for a more wide adaptation of driver position, it can be rotated up to 180° in order to be used not only for monitoring traffic, but also as workplace for office work or chair for consuming meals (see Fig. 1). Due to this range of orientations in the cab, its controls for seat settings are centralized in the left armrest by electric adjustment. Seat functions such as front-aft position, seat height, rotation, seatback and cushion angle are thus easily controllable from any position of the seat in the cab. Furthermore, the seat architecture is optimized for improved reclined position for the use cases of relaxation and recreation and for improved back support in a range of upright positions for the use cases of office work, reading and meal consumption. The seat is equipped with a state-of-the-art suspension to ensure road-induced vibration and shock management for maintaining driver wellbeing and health. Interior components cater to use cases of office work, personal hygiene, meal consumption, recreation and resting by integration of variable surfaces and components to facilitate these uses in the cab (see Fig. 1). Variable interior settings increase available personal space supporting activities associated with personal hygiene.

3.2   Man-Machine Performance Increase in Large Tractors

The international study conducted by GRAMMER AG in 2019 with a usability partner institution was performed to establish the context of changing conditions in modern agriculture. It focused on maximizing user performance and comfort during task execution and ensuring user health. Central topics identified by the users were interior design and equipment, the seat in its functions positioning, damping, comfort experience, and the multifunction armrest [7]. On the basis of the user interviews, concepts for these components of future operator systems for large tractor cabs were developed and visualized (see Fig. 2). Ratings by active farmer focus groups determined the elements with the highest affinity and relevance as concepts for centralizing the operation of the vehicle with its implementations and devices (smartphone, tablet) as well as multifunctional storage systems for various objects, also many features that are already implemented in personal cars, such as haptic warning, mobility and massage systems, and acoustic management. Non-explicit, underlying needs that were identified were a more refined interior design and maintaining driver health through preventive measures.

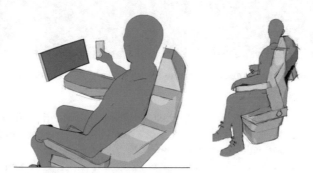

Fig. 2.   Feature integration and connectivity/evolved seat support for future tractors

Since vibration and shock isolation as well as driver health proved to be central user needs, a functional seat implementing suspension and adjustment innovations was developed and then rated by 12 expert users (farmers) in a follow-up ride & drive. The vibration insulation on rough terrain was rated with medians of 7 ("good") to 8 ("very good") on the 10-point comfort scale. Position and height stability received a rating of 8 ("very good") for both aspects.

3.3 A Haptic Warning System for Forklift Trucks

For industrial forklift trucks, where forward and reverse driving constantly alternates, literature states that collisions with people and obstacles constitute the most frequent number of accidents by far [9]. Drivers must continuously process high information densities on the acoustic and visual perception channels throughout their work days, and therefore, these channels are often overloaded [10, 11]. It was researched in the 2020 user study whether signals via haptics directly at the operator's body can be reliably detected independent of driver orientation on the seat (Fig.3).

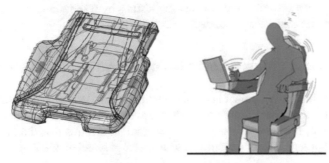

Fig. 3. Integrated haptic warning system position in seat cushions for forklift trucks/Symbolic image illustrating a possible application of a snooze alarm.

Drivers were able to detect and differentiate the two types of signals in the three different seats in different realistic sitting positions. In the given configuration, the intensity of the indication signal was overall rated as slightly too strong. The attention signal was classified as just right, and as a good alternative to an audio signal which might be overheard. Signal distinctiveness and effectiveness was thus confirmed by active forklift users in the prototype seat evaluations, and signal configuration changes were recommended to engineering based on the user feedback. The established configuration ensures that the signal is perceived when the seat occupant switch is activated and the vehicle is in operation.

4 Discussion

The user input gained in the usability projects serves as a basis for defining future products and equipment options, with the aim of optimizing user wellbeing and man-machine performance. Concepts become future-proof by incorporating users, understanding usage, detailing use-cases and forecasting future purposes of interior components and systems. Megatrends and environmental factors are taken into account, such as, in the described projects, future level 4 autonomous long-haul driving, digital smart farming and the continuous increase in signals and information processing.

In the context auf autonomous driving, the truck cab interior needs to become multifunctional in order to facilitate a range of uses, e.g. for personal nourishment, hygiene and mobile working. In the context of smart farming, the driver position needs to be more stable for information processing, and thus still increasing requirements for vibration management are being placed on the seat system. Information densities in modern and agile material handling require leveraging all possible sensory channels for information processing. Haptic channel information does not require directed attention from the drivers, only physical contact, so drivers do not have to be concerned about missing a signal [12]. Moreover, the information is "private", i.e. it can only be perceived by the driver and docs not additionally disturb the environment. Key contributions in the described studies were user-based concepts such as information management, connectivity and storage options, operation and signal implementation details, which form the basis for future projects, and verification testing by professional users for specific innovations in seat and interior concepts and products.

5   Conclusions: Future-Proof Seat and Interior Functionality

The goal of product development is to minimize driver stress and strain through product design. User needs are the basis for product evolution in order to continuously adapt them to changing use cases. Knowledge management ensures that the manufacturer's product development history advances and relevant parameters are continuously taken into account.

The results of the user studies have identified aspects that can further increase the performance of the human-machine system. Surveyed users expect that updated components and new designs can enable faster, safer, less fatiguing and accurate work. This is foreseen to have a positive impact on productivity, health and safety at work. These results are incorporated into company specifications as user requirements and are taken into account in product design. A further strength of user studies is that they can serve as company guard rails for choosing strategic projects and allocating resources strategically. The basis for product development is thus provided by the users, who in turn evaluate the developed solutions in order to offer products to the market that meet user needs.

Acknowledgements.   The Research presented here was made possible by Grammer AG. Not all details are presented due to company proprietary information.

References

1. ISO: ISO Standard 9241–210 Ergonomics of human-system interaction — Part 210: Human-centred design for interactive systems (2019)
2. Mansfield, N., et al.: Integrating and applying models of comfort. Appl. Ergon. **82**, 1–7 (2020)

3. Frohriep, S., Schneider, F.: People on tove: ccollaboration of ergonomics, usability and design in vehicle interior ddevelopment. In: Proceedings of the 2020 Aachen Colloquium Sustainable Mobility, pp. 1709–1721 (2020)
4. Norman, D.: The Design of Everyday Things. Basic Books, New York (1988)
5. Brodin, N.: Driver Seat Adjustment Control Design for Heavy Vehicles. Master Thesis. Lulea University (2004)
6. https://de.statista.com/statistik/daten/studie/202938/umfrage/hoehe-des-frauenanteils-bei-den-kraftfahrzeugfuehrern-in-deutschland/. Accessed 29 Jan 2021
7. Frohriep, S., Schneider, F.: Die Zukunft des Operatorsystems in großen Traktoren: Ergebnisse internationaler Nutzerstudien. Agroscope Sci. **94**, 171–178 (2020)
8. Volmer, D.: Development of a Mental-Stress-Reducing Excavator Cabin. Master tthesis. Delft University of Technology (2014)
9. Klinec, D., Zimmer, F.: Vorverarbeitung von 3D Daten in einer Kamera, zur effizeinten Automatisierung und Assistenz bei Flurförderzeugen. In: Proceedings FFZ VDI (2017)
10. Kuehner, M.L.: Haptische Unterscheidbarkeit mechanischer Parameter bei rotatorischen Bedienelementen. Dissertation, TU Munich (2014)
11. Dass Jr, D.E., Uyttendaele, A., Terken, J.: Haptic in-seat feedback for lane departure warning. In: Proceedings of the 5th International Conference on Automotive User Interfaces and Interactive Vehicular Applications. ACM, pp. 258–261 (2013)
12. Chang, W., Hwang, W., Ji, Y.G.: Haptic seat interfaces for driver information and warning systems. Int. J. Hum.-Comput. Interaction **27**(12), 1119–1132 (2011)

Design Thinking: A New Approach for OHS Professionals to Address Complex Problems

Sisse Grøn[(✉)] and Ole Broberg

DTU Management, Engineering Systems Design, Technical University of Denmark,
2800 Lyngby, Denmark
sgroen@dtu.dk

Abstract. Design thinking (DT) provides innovative tools that may be applied to manage complex musculoskeletal or psychosocial problems at work. In this project researchers trained OHS professionals to apply DT tools. The training included organizing and facilitating three design sprint workshops of 3–4 h duration. The sprint workshops created solutions to complex psychosocial or musculoskeletal problem in a company. The researchers kept track of the progress by observing the workshops and conducting semi-structured interviews. Data was coded and analyzed in accordance with the template analysis method.

This paper evaluates the outcome of the design sprint workshop processes.

Design thinking tools enabled the OHS professionals to solve complex problems in a different way than they normally would. Two main differences stood out. The first was the DT approach was more participatory and the second that it created a deeper understanding of the problem, before any solutions were created. The sprint workshop process resulted in planned and tested solutions that the companies could subsequently implement.

Keywords: Design thinking · Interventions · Problem solving · Participatory methods · Creativity

1 Introduction

Certain occupational health and safety problems are hard to manage with conventional methods. This is often true for musculoskeletal and psychosocial problems as these are characterized by being difficult to measure and having interdependent causes [1]. We propose that design thinking provides innovative tools that can be applied to manage complex musculoskeletal or psychosocial problems.

Design thinking is a term for the way designers work, when translated to fields outside design [2]. In a Scandinavian context it sits within the field of participatory design, which is characterised by the user being a partner in a co-creation process [3]. The participatory design tradition is a good foundation for the work of occupational health and safety committees as workplace democracy is a core prerequisite [4] for their role.

The design sprint is the key method in DT and often illustrated as a double diamond (see Fig. 1) [5], where the diamonds represents a non-linear and user-centred

N. L. Black et al. (Eds.): IEA 2021, LNNS 222, pp. 78–84, 2021.
https://doi.org/10.1007/978-3-030-74611-7_11

problem-solving process iterating through divergent and convergent phases of exploring a problem, defining the problem and then finding and testing solutions via prototypes.

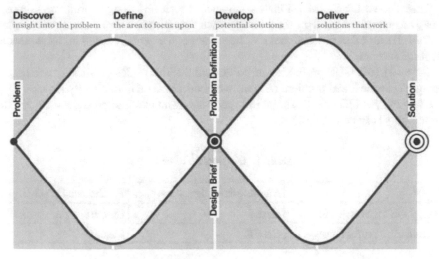

Fig. 1. The double diamond model from the British Design Council [5]

DT translated into fields such as health, where it was used to guide an innovation process by means of a series of compact workshops for a group of participants, based on rapid ethnography methods [6]. The project reported here has the similar aim to translate the DT approach to OHS management as a supplementary method.

The researchers trained OHS professionals to apply DT methods in four companies in a learning by doing process. Their task was to facilitate design sprints following the double diamond model, but centred on solving a complex work related musculoskeletal or psychosocial problem. This paper reports the preliminary evaluation of the outcome. The research question is:

- What characterizes the process of solving complex workplace problems with Design Thinking?

It is also relevant to pinpoint what is new and different about this approach, compared to how OSH professionals would normally do.

2 Methodology

The project design is a case study of four cases involving both internal and external OHS professionals and musculoskeletal and psychosocial work problems.

The researchers trained a small group of OHS professionals to apply DT tools and to organize and facilitate three design sprints. A design sprint within product and service companies takes a full week and follows the iterative double diamond process [7]. For this study the professionals compressed the process into 2–3 workshops of 3–4 h duration. The sprints aimed to solve a complex psychosocial or musculoskeletal problem, identified by the company.

Case I) Two OHS professionals conducted a series of design sprint workshops to manage a musculoskeletal problem in their own workplace - a pharmaceutical company.

Case II) An OHS professional did the same as an external consultant for a package distribution center.

Case III) Two OHS professionals conducted a series of design sprint workshops to manage a psychosocial problem in their own workplace - a municipality service.

Case IV) An OHS professional did the same as an external consultant for another municipality service (Table 1).

Table 1. Distribution of cases

	Musculoskeletal problem	Psychosocial problem
Internal OHS professionals	Case I	Case III
External OHS professionals	Case II	Case IV

The researchers collected various forms of qualitative data as summarized in Table 2 below. For each case, the researchers has compiled a detailed case report based on observation notes, creations from the workshops, photos and materials from the companies.

Table 2. Data collection

Respondents	Interviews	Observations
7 OHS professionals	Before and after full training program At time of evaluation	Case I: 8,5 h of sprint activities Case II: 15 h of sprint activities
9 OHS committee representatives from 4 case companies	Before and after sprint At time of evaluation	Case III: 4 h of sprint activities Case IV: 10,5 h of sprint activities

The data was coded in the software program Atlas.ti and analyzed following template analysis [5].

3   Case Settings

This section will zoom in on case I and IV as they represent the span of cases well. Case I was facilitated by internal professionals and focused on musculoskeletal health while case IV was focused on psychosocial health and facilitated by an external professional. Figures 2 and 3 outline the sprint process in each case.

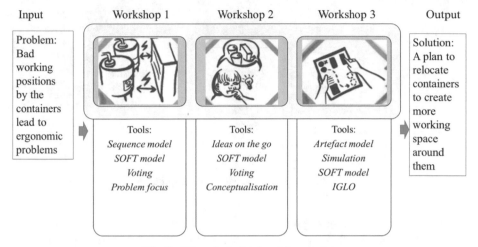

Input	Workshop 1	Workshop 2	Workshop 3	Output
Problem: Bad working positions by the containers lead to ergonomic problems	Tools: *Sequence model* *SOFT model* *Voting* *Problem focus*	Tools: *Ideas on the go* *SOFT model* *Voting* *Conceptualisation*	Tools: *Artefact model* *Simulation* *SOFT model* *IGLO*	Solution: A plan to relocate containers to create more working space around them

Fig. 2. Musculoskeletal problem sprint

In the first case two internal OHS professionals conducted a sprint to solve a long-standing musculoskeletal problem. The problem was vaguely defined as 'ergonomic issues in laboratory x'. The vagueness reflected that the OHS professionals only knew from annual risk assessments that there were a worrying number of complains and injuries connected to the work in one of their laboratories.

In an initial mapping of the area and problem, the work area surrounding two large containers was identified as the most problematic. The design sprint therefore focused on the work tasks connected to these containers.

The professionals planned and facilitated three workshops of 3–4 h duration. To participate they invited a group of directly affected employees with hands-on experience of the problem. They made sure to invite people representing the diversity of professions and experience within the workplace and the relevant manager. In the workshops, the ten participants applied DT methods in an iterative process following the double diamond model. By the end of the last workshop, they had developed and tested a solution to separate the containers. Subsequently the company followed the suggestion and moved the containers to a better position.

In case IV an external OSH professional was engaged to help a municipality health service address a problem of work pressure. This had been identified in their annual risk assessment and by the work authorities. The OHS committee obtained permission from their manager to engage an OHS professional and briefed him of the problem. Said professional planned and facilitated three workshops with the OSH committee members and their manager as participants; 5 in total. Thus the starting point was the vague knowledge that 'work pressure' had been selected as a problem in their risk assessment. In the course of the sprint, the participants realized that their collaboration interfaces were the best levers to improve their collaboration and thereby divide the work better,

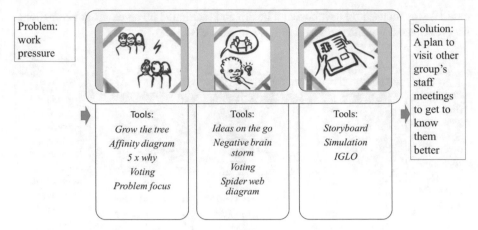

| Problem: work pressure | | Tools: Grow the tree / Affinity diagram / 5 x why / Voting / Problem focus | Tools: Ideas on the go / Negative brain storm / Voting / Spider web diagram | Tools: Storyboard / Simulation / IGLO | Solution: A plan to visit other group's staff meetings to get to know them better |

Fig. 3. Psychosocial problem sprint

which would lower the work pressure for those most affected. Also everyone would waste less time if the collaboration interfaces improved. So they drafted a plan to get to know the other teams and their tasks better. The municipality service has currently not carried out the plan, due to Covid 19 restrictions.

4   Results

One part of the data is self-reported from interviews with the professionals and OSH committee representatives, the other part is notes from the researchers' observations of the sprints. Both parts conveys information about the differences between a normal approach to solve a complex OHS problem and the design thinking approach.

4.1   Self-reported Differences

From the interviews the elements that stand out as different, in the design thinking approach were; the participatory element, the time spent, the engagement from the participants, the ownership to the solution and that the design thinking approach is more resource demanding.

The professionals described their normal procedure as 'by the book', meaning that they would normally follow the procedures that applies in their company. In the DT approach, they drew upon their own employees as experts in their specific problem.

A professional described the novelty in the design thinking approach this way:

'Normally we would have applied our company system in which we operate with only one cause, not interrelated causes, as we explored here. We also would likely have called upon an expert from outside instead of involving a group of our own employees. I would say the user participation is the difference.'

[Interview with professional in case I].

5 Observations

From the analysis of the observational data, the problem solving process stands out as the main difference.

In the sprints, the OHS problem was investigated as a design problem centred on defining the problem in the first diamond. The workshops illustrated very clearly the iterative nature, going back and forth in the double diamond. It was remarkable how the problem was framed and reframed by the participants during the process. In case IV, it started out as a matter of work pressure, then turned into a matter of imbalance between work requirements and personal resources, and then into how to ensure clear collaboration interfaces with other disciplines and collaboration partners.

Activities in the second diamond included developing many solution ideas. Creative tools like negative brainstorming facilitated this. Solution ideas were then tested by prototyping tools like storyboards, table-top simulation with LEGO and using simple mock-ups.

In both cases, the professionals and their participants managed to create tangible and simple solutions that were a good fit for their specific context.

In case I for example, the designed solution was to separate two containers to create better access for the ones working in their vicinity and avoid awkward positions.

6 Discussion

The main question is if the outcome of a design thinking sprint is worth the extra resources? The interviewed professionals stated that they spend more time on planning the sprints than they normally would for planning a process to manage a similar problem. But it was also a learning process for them and an unusual role to facilitate a sprint. Thus it is likely to get less time consuming with more practice. And even with the time it cost the interviewed company representatives stated that the created solutions were worth the extra resources.

The benefits included:

- The creative tools brought about new insights and ideas.
- The participating stakeholders took an active role. For example, the employees brought different context specific knowledge to the table and thus acted as experts of their own work situation. The participating managers were able to ensure that the created solutions were realistic.
- Fast feasibility evaluation of potential solutions by prototyping tools.
- Increased local ownership to solutions due to the participatory approach.

A limitation was that the participants in the sprints were not used to working creatively the way a designer would be; only few of the participants were able to draw a storyboard the way it was intended, for example.

7 Conclusion

We evaluated the design thinking approach as a method for OHS professionals to solve complex OHS problems in four real life cases. The professionals and their participants were able to find and test solutions that were feasible for their specific situations. However it is a new role for the professional as well as for the participants and requires training. The participants' engagement in creating the solution has the added benefit of ownership to the solution.

References

1. Jepsersen, A.H., Hasle, P., Nielsen, K.T.: The wicked character of psychosocial risks: implications for regulation. Nordic J. Working Life Stud. **6**(3), 23–42 (2016)
2. Dorst, K.: The core of 'design thinking' and its application. Des. Stud. **32**, 521–532 (2011)
3. Sanders, E.B.-N., Stappers, P.J.: Co-creation and the new landscapes of design. CoDesign **4**(1), 5–11 (2008).
4. Bødker, S., Kyng, M.: Participatory Design That Matters—Facing the Big Issues. *ACM Trans. Comput.-Hum. Interact.* 25 (1): 4:1–4:31 (2018).
5. Design Council: Eleven lessons: managing design in eleven global brands. A study of the design process, report (2007). https://www.designcouncil.org.uk. Accessed 21 Apr 2021
6. Guldbrandsen, M.: Design innovation: embedding design process in a charity organization: evolving the Double Diamond at Macmillan Cancer Support. In: Tsekleves, E., Cooper, R. (eds.) Design for Health (2017). Routledge
7. Knapp J, Zeratsky J, Kowitz B (2016) Sprint – how to solve big problems and test new ideas in just five days (2016). Simon Schuster
8. Brooks, J., McCluskey, S., Turley, E., King, N.: The utility of template analysis in qualitative psychology research. Qualitative Res. Psychol. **12**(2), 202–222 (2015)

Employees' Engagement in the Context of a Pandemic

Guimont Sophie[(✉)] and Therriault Pierre-Yves

Université du Québec à Trois-Rivières, Trois-Rivières, Québec, Canada
sophie.guimont@uqtr.ca

Abstract. The work organization is undergoing a major transformation amplified by the current pandemic and it is important to challenge these effects on employees' engagement towards their work environment. As a result of a scoping review, it is possible to consider that there is few elements present in the literature regarding the concepts of telework and employees' engagement. Therefore, it is suggested that the current context is studied in light of the new concept of enabling space to guide the ergonomic interventions.

Keywords: Engagement · Ergonomic · Enabling space · Teleworking · Work organization · Transformation

1 Introduction

Teleworking has been perceived as a way to reduce rush hour traffic congestion since the early 1970 [1]. This way of working remotely makes it possible to streamline the use of office spaces and tools. This allows the employee to perform his tasks in a place of his choice outside the organization's physical facilities. The challenge of communicating with others is then associated with the limits of the technological means available [2]. Subsequently, research shows several advantages to promote telework for certain tasks. Similarly, the studies indicate that telework foster work-life balance and a reduction in the stress level among employees [3, 4]. Gradually, the possibility of teleworking is considered by the human resources department of organizations as a recruiting or retaining factor for employees [5–7].

As of March 2020, organizations were disrupted by the COVID pandemic which added a range of occupational health and safety constraints. In this context, it is important to transform the way we work in order to respect health measures and to avoid physical contact as much as possible. Thus, the organizations that have the opportunity, opt for telework and a migration of work takes place. The private homes of employees not designed to do this become temporary workspaces. In connection with the tasks to be carried out, they set up a workstation based on the equipment needed to perform tasks in spaces shared with others, which they believe are best for carrying out their activity.

When does the idea of these improvised work environments continue? The understanding of this concept becomes more complex because the singular activity must

© The Author(s), under exclusive license to Springer Nature Switzerland AG 2021
N. L. Black et al. (Eds.): IEA 2021, LNNS 222, pp. 85–92, 2021.
https://doi.org/10.1007/978-3-030-74611-7_12

consider the personal sphere, the change in relations between colleagues the modification to the tasks performed as the layout of the workstation becomes a risk for health [8]. Are the benefits of telework still the same? Organizations need support in this necessary and major transformation in relation to the context, and ergonomics represents a useful field of knowledge.

The purpose of this communication is to identify how the choice of telework influences work engagement and how ergonomics can be useful in such a context. After presenting the methodology, the main results will be presented and discussed. Finally, the contribution of ergonomics will be put forward in relation to the working method that is telework.

2 Methodology

In order to conduct this scoping review, the five stages framework proposed by Arksey and O'Malley [9] has been selected. Their framework allows to rapidly define the underlying concepts of engagement and environment in relation with teleworking. This method is particularly useful when the issue is complex or that it is not subject to a comprehensive review, which is currently the case. The five stages are conducted iteratively, in a reflective process from the available literature.

2.1 Identification Research Question

The first phase of the scoping review is to articulate the research question. At this stage, there is a possibility that the search will generate a significant volume of studies and this could be resolved by narrowing the research question [9]. This review is to determine what factors are influencing the engagement of employees towards telework.

2.2 Identification of Relevant Studies

To complete the scoping review, two sources are consulted during the research studies. Keywords (see Table 1) related to the concepts of telework, work environment and engagement were used with the prefix "or" and "and". The research was further expanded to ensure that the term telework was present in the title. The following databases have been consulted: APA PsychInfo and Business source complete.

Table 1. Keywords used for research

Concepts	Telework	Environment	Engagement
Keywords	'telecommuting'	'management personnel'	'job satisfaction'
	'teleworking'	'human resource management'	'volition'
	'working from home'	'industrial and organisational psychology'	'employee motivation'
	'telework*'	'employee productivity'	'work commitment'
	'work-home'	'work environment'	'employee engagement'
	'virtual working'	'workplace'	'worker commitment'
		'working conditions'	'disengagement'
			'turnover'

2.3   Choice of Studies

A total of 144 items were identified in the databases, duplicates were removed leaving 135 references send in a bibliographic management software. The selected studies were written in English or French and covered at least one category of the work environment. The items related to the consequences, the advantages or disadvantages of teleworking, those written in another language as well as those which were not focusing on telework were excluded. The titles and abstracts of the items were read and 25 documents were kept, given the presence of a criterion sought against characteristic of the work environment. Finally, after the reading of these documents, 19 were retained. If the document had no summary, the table of contents or abstract has been consulted. The research and selection process of various steps are illustrated in Fig. 1.

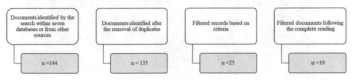

Fig. 1. Selection process

2.4   Map Data

As per the retained framework, each item included in the literature review has been analyzed using a grid of data extraction. The selected documents have been scanned and the data were extracted in a table according to.

1)   the authors, the year of publication and the place of origin of the study;
2)   the population concerned;
3)   the purpose;
4)   the methodology;
5)   the measurement of results; and
6)   key results.

The data have been processed through analysis of content [10]. The selected texts have been read in order to identify the segments related to environmental conditions which may influence the engagement. These segments have been decrypted and coded to identify the categories and subcategories as may be associated.

2.5   Assemble, Report and Synthesize the Results

Data were collected in a table outlining the characteristics of the studies and the characteristics of the work environment. The content analysis has highlighted the categories and subcategories to map and analyze results with respect to the objectives of this scoping review.

3 Conceptual Framework

The concept of enabling space, defined in recent years [11] may be partly related to a stage where the individual is allowed to act as he wishes regardless of the presence or absence of disability. As a result, the individual involved, undertakes and transforms community life in order to fully emancipated. This concept analysis identified antecedents (see Fig. 2) to take into consideration, such as legislation, policies, institutions and the work environment, to establish the presence of the enabling space concept.

Fig. 2. Enabling space characteristics

Attributes are also identified leading to the proposition of consequences in terms of enabling space, comprising of engagement, inclusion and wellbeing. The attributes defined in Table 2 are partnership, power to act, stimulating, security, tranquility as well as flexibility.

Table 2. Attributes definition

Attribute	*Partnership*	*Power to Act*	*Stimulating*	*Security*	*Tranquility*	*Flexibility*
Definition	Environment that fosters interaction and collaboration among the various players (work situation).	Environment that fosters the opportunity to choose and use freewill.	Environment that provides achievable and realistic challenges.	Environment that provides achievable and realistic challenges.	Environment that allows to live freely in a perceived comfort.	Environment that adapts to the existing conditions.

4 Results

4.1 Characteristics of Selected Texts

Data retrieved were gathered and organized based on the available information and characteristics of the texts and work environments. Among the characteristics of texts, the year and the country of publication were retained. For the characteristics of work environments, they have first been divided into categories based on home, work or social environments. These categories were distributed into subcategories, as a result

Table 3. Characteristics of texts and environments

Characteristics	Year of Publication			Country of Publication										
	Before 2000	2000-2010	After 2010	France	Canada	Finland	Belgium	USA	Germany	Sweden	UK	South Korea	New Zealand	Iran
N	2	6	11	1	1	1	1	8	2	1	1	1	1	1

Characteristics	Environment Category			Environment Sub-Category				
	Home	Work	Social	Isolation	Dedicated space	Communications	HR	Technical Support
N	2	15	3	3	1	2	13	2

of the content analysis. The texts have been allocated to one or more categories and subcategories as presented in Table 3.

The majority of documents presents elements in connection with the organization of work, including management. Effective communication promotes a better understanding of employees' reality, foster moral support as well as breaking down isolation. In addition, some results related to the social environment were considered mainly the work location (remote or office). Few elements were found in relation to the physical environment even if it is an important aspect to consider given that this is where the work activities are performed.

5 Discussion

This scoping review was to synthesize and disseminate the results of available research in connection with employees' engagement and telework. It appears that few elements are available and could possibly be explained by taking into consideration that the concepts of engagement to the workplace and telework are relatively recent.

5.1 Concept Enabling Space

The new concept of "enabling space" seems useful to better understand the major transformation required by the reorganization of work. This concept, defined as a stage where each of the actors, making or not, must be able to get involved in relation to the new reality of work, offers several avenues of reflection to address the transformation [11]. Indeed, the various attributes, which define the concept of enabling space make it possible to assess with precision the different characteristics of a work environment. This concept suggested the notion of engagement as a consequence to an enabling space. Each of the attributes is presented and illustrated with examples of application in order to understand the meaning. Since it is assumptions based on the fact that each environment as well as each position are different and variable, this new concept highlight how the engagement of teleworkers could be maintained or even promoted.

In the context of a pandemic, the various aspects of the environment can positively or negatively influence the engagement to work. Based on the attributes' definitions (Table 2), it is possible to demonstrate that the enabling space concept is applicable. Favorable work conditions can benefit of factors such as a mutual trusting environment, an better understanding of the employee's situation by its supervisor or the offering a flexible work arrangement either task-based or in permitting options to performing the position's deliverables [7]. Communication between colleagues is essential. The employee's autonomy and his entitlement to choose can also be considered beneficial for the engagement despite the pandemic context, Telework may introduce new professional challenges i.e. accepting a position in another geographical region since travels are reduced, which makes it more challenging [6, 7]. In contrast, the perceived isolation of the employee [12], modified and less stimulating responsibilities may hinder the engagement to work. The workstation, formerly adapted for the tasks and the employee, is now less adapted and increase the risk of developing musculoskeletal injuries due to the constraints of the work arrangement. The limited social contacts, the lack of informal meetings have a tendency to limit the opportunities for promotion and advancement which is hardly stimulating for employees [12].

5.2 The Role of the Ergonomist

For the organization, the ergonomist supports decision makers for better planning of operations, optimal choice of equipment and tools as well as to harmonizes social relationships in the work organization. In a pandemic, telework proved to be a vector of reorganization of enterprises and redefinition that the place of the work occupied in the life of every employee. In doing so, the traditional indicators of productivity and skills evaluation for employees have owed be re-evaluated. For example, the organization must be flexible with the tasks expected with regard to time limits, it must focus on sources of employee motivation and provide a fair challenge in the duties in order that the employee can maintain a sense of belonging, despite the absence of collective work.

For employees, the ergonomist provides the means to carry out their duties effectively, in a safe and comfortable manner. During pandemic, in order to conduct assigned work related tasks, employee shall install a dedicated work site in the space normally assigned for personal use [13]. In addition, the employee has to revise the time allocated between professional and personal obligations in order to reconcile them. This involve for employees, among other things, to obligation to be constantly available, and by extension, to put his physical and psychological health at risk in order to be able to complete the requested task. In this context, a true partnership is critical among policy-makers, employees and the ergonomist in a collaborative process that focuses on the overall health (physical and mental health of workers and health of the organization). As well, an organizational agility must be promoted to maintain the engagement of employees.

5.3 Limits

Despite all the precautions taken, when searching databases, it was found that the "Work-home" expression was a buzzword as it could be attributed to the work-life balance aspect without any consideration for teleworking. Other elements written in the literature were not considered such as personality traits and isolation in context of telework [14]. The possibility of including other concepts that may influence the engagement such as satisfaction or well-being could have bonified the results of the scoping review. That said, Kilic [15] submits that there is a close relationship between the work commitment and job satisfaction. However, in this study, the articles on the satisfaction of teleworkers have not been retained. Since the writings are scarce and inform us on only a few aspects of the concept, it seems important to broaden the research horizons in order to include factors that can be used to promulgate work commitment.

6   Conclusion

The role of the ergonomist is considerable at the organization level working on the one hand, to support decision makers and, on the other hand, to accompany employees. Beyond the pandemic, teleworking will remain, in whole or in part, so it is important to ask about how, the work organization and the employees, can foster commitment to work. In addition, a review of the management of workspaces will need to be carried out, as organizations can currently provide products or services while employees are outside the organization. As a result, requirement for large commercial spaces to lodge office spaces may not be necessary. Thus, the role of the ergonomist is important for the work organisation based on the acknowledgement of present and future transformation. The focus should be on the tasks performed in the physical environment of the organization, and outside of it. Considerations must be given to adequate equipment in order to reduce the constraints of this alternation between working environments. In addition, it appears that there is a need for further research, in relation to the concept of engagement which seems to offer an interesting avenue to better understand what promotes commitment to work [16]. Finally, teleworking is not a panacea since it can create risks for employees, whether it is physical ailments due to poor work arrangements, psychological ills since the personal and professional life boundaries are thinner. Conversely characteristics can be proposed in order to grant employees their emancipation, hence the importance of providing an enabling space and ensuring that the overall health is maintained.

References

1. Brown, J.E.: An empirical look at the relationship between personality type and the challenges of telecommuting. (71). ProQuest Information & Learning (2011). https://biblioproxy.uqtr. ca/login?url=https://search.ebscohost.com/login.aspx?direct=true&db=psyh&AN=2011-99030-449&site=ehost-live
2. Conner, M., Fletcher, W., Firth-Cozens, J., Collins, S.: Teleworking, stress and health. In: Schröder, H., Reschke, K., Johnston, M., Maes, S. (eds.) Health Psychology: Potential in Diversity, pp. 309–313. D-93018. S Roderer Verlag, Regensburg (1993)
3. Konradt, U., Hertel, G., Schmook, R.: Quality of management by objectives, task-related stressors, and non-task-related stressors as predictors of stress and job satisfaction among teleworkers. Eur. J. Work Organizational Psychol. 12(1), 61 (2003)
4. Vesala, H., Tuomivaara, S.: Slowing work down by teleworking periodically in rural settings? Personnel Rev. 44(4), 511–528 (2015)
5. Pearce, J.A.: Successful corporate telecommuting with technology considerations for late adopters. Organ. Dyn. 38(1), 16–25 (2009)
6. Radu, S.: How Soon Will You Be Working From Home? U.S. News—The Report, 28–30 (2018). https://biblioproxy.uqtr.ca/login?url=https://search.ebscohost.com/login.aspx?dir ect=true&db=bth&AN=128188396&site=ehost-live
7. Wolski, M.: Télétravail: Il reste encore du boulot. Stratégies, 44–45 (2019). https://bib lioproxy.uqtr.ca/login?url=https://search.ebscohost.com/login.aspx?direct=true&db=bth& AN=135971126&site=ehost-live

8. Palumbo, R.: Let me go to the office! an investigation into the side effects of working from home on work-life balance. Int. J. Public Sector Manag. **33**(6/7), 771–790 (2020)

9. Arksey, H., O'Malley, L.: Scoping studies: towards a methodological framework. Int. J. Soc. Res. Methodology: Theory Pract. **8**(1), 19–32 (2005)

10. Bardin, L.: L'analyse de contenu (1re éd. « Quadrige ». ed.). Presses universitaires de France, Paris (2007)

11. Therriault, P.-Y., Lefay, G., Guimont, S.: Le concept d'espace habilitant: une avenue théorique prometteuse en ergonomie. In: 2019 Annual Conference ACE Proceedings 10p. St. John's Newfoundland (2019)

12. Wilton, R.D., Páez, A., Scott, D.M.: Why do you care what other people think? a qualitative investigation of social influence and telecommuting. Transp. Rese. Part A: Policy Practice **45**(4), 269–282 (2011)

13. Hartig, T., Kylin, C., Johansson, G.: The telework tradeoff: Stress mitigation vs constrained restoration. Appl. Psychol. Int. Rev. **56**(2), 231–253 (2007)

14. Swigart, M.L.: Identifying successful telework factors through the study of the relationship between personality and workplace isolation. (73). ProQuest Information & Learning (2013). https://biblioproxy.uqtr.ca/login?url=https://search.ebscohost.com/login.aspx?direct=true&db=psyh&AN=2013-99090-495&site=ehost-live

15. Kilic, S.: Équilibre vie personnelle-vie professionnelle, Soutien social, Engagement et Satisfaction au travail: Une analyse des effets médiateurs. Revue de gestion des ressources humaines **107**(1), 23–33 (2018)

16. IRSST. https://www.irsst.qc.ca/media/documents/pubirsst/r-543.pdf. Accessed 01 Feb 2021

Comparison of Dose Models for the Assessment of Spinal Load and Implications for the Calculation of Cumulative Loading

Laura Johnen[✉], Alexander Mertens, Verena Nitsch, and Christopher Brandl

Institute of Industrial Engineering and Ergonomics of RWTH Aachen University,
52062 Aachen, Germany
`{l.johnen,a.mertens,v.nitsch,c.brandl}@iaw.rwth-aachen.de`

Abstract. In order to consider several work-related risk factors simultaneously when assessing work-related physical exposure, their relative influence on the resulting physical strain must be considered. An ergonomic assessment method in which multiple risk factors are relevant is by definition the concept of cumulative loading. As there is no standardized calculation method for cumulative loading, the objective of this contribution is to systematically compare different dose models proposed in the literature for the assessment of spinal cumulative loading. The dose models are compared regarding their ability to reflect physical strain resulting from two working tasks. Overall, results show that different work situations can be compared on the basis of cumulative loading estimates only if the same dose model was used for the assessment. Therefore, the results underline the need for a standardized and validated dose model for cumulative loading so that assessment results can be compared to assessment results from other work situations as well as to reference values.

Keywords: Cumulative loading · Lower back · Dose · Weighting factors

1 Introduction

In occupational settings, individuals are usually exposed to multiple work-related risk factors, so it seems reasonable to consider the relative importance of different risk factors when assessing work-related physical exposure [1]. An ergonomic assessment method in which multiple risk factors are relevant by definition is the concept of cumulative loading. As the calculation of cumulative loading follows the principle of integrating loading over time, both the intensity and the temporal aspect of the load are relevant for assessing the cumulative loading [2].

Still, there is no standardized calculation method for cumulative loading and the question remains as to how the interaction of both factors should be interpreted as the dose of cumulative loading acting on an individual [2–7]. The appropriateness of the dose model is crucial to obtain well-founded results when assessing a workplace and a prerequisite to make informed decisions within the ergonomic intervention process. Thus, the objective of this contribution is to compare systematically different dose models

© The Author(s), under exclusive license to Springer Nature Switzerland AG 2021
N. L. Black et al. (Eds.): IEA 2021, LNNS 222, pp. 93–100, 2021.
https://doi.org/10.1007/978-3-030-74611-7_13

proposed in the literature for the assessment of spinal cumulative loading regarding their ability to reflect the musculoskeletal, cardiovascular and psychophysical strain resulting from two dynamic lifting/lowering tasks. It was hypothesized that due to lack of standardization, assessment results may vary and lead to both overestimation and underestimation of the resulting strain.

2 Methodology

2.1 Data Collection and Data Processing

The analysis of this contribution is based on data obtained in a laboratory study which is described in detail in [8]. Briefly, participants performed a two-dimensional, symmetric lifting/lowering task in the sagittal plan with an external load (1 kg or 6 kg) in both hands. While performing both tasks, the participants' body posture was recorded at a rate of 30 Hz using Microsoft KinectTM V2. Based on the model by [9] for symmetrical activities, the compression force of the intervertebral disc at L5/S1was calculated and used as the load intensity. Prior to the study, the 12 participants' (8 female, 4 male) mean (SD) age (mean = 23.7 (2.7) years), height (mean = 172.0 (7.0) cm) and body weight (mean = 64.9 (10.2) kg) were recorded. The original aim of the study was to test systematically the suitability of the so-called non-weighted calculation method, which calculates cumulative loading as area under the loading curve without any additional weighting factors. Therefore, the lifting/lowering tasks were designed to have the same area under the loading curve. The area under the loading curve was calculated in real-time using rectangular integration by multiplying the load intensity by the duration of each frame and summing these products. Both tasks were stopped upon reaching a predefined value of 700 kNs.

This results in two experimental conditions examined here: Lifting/lowering task LI with low load intensity (external weight of 1 kg) and task HI with high load intensity (external weight of 6 kg). A higher external weight results in a higher level of spinal load intensity. Since the area under the loading curve was identical, this results in a shorter task duration and fewer movement repetitions for HI.

Muscle activity of the erector spinae longissimus (RES/LES) and heart rate (HR) were collected continuously via a Direct Transmission System (Desktop DTS Receiver, Noraxon, Scottsdale, AZ, USA) and the software MyoResearch 3.12 (Noraxon, Scottsdale, AZ, USA). Ag/AgCl self-adhesive and pregelled 8-shaped dual EMG-electrodes (diameter of adhesive areas: 1 cm; inter-electrode distance: 2 cm) and single ECG-electrodes (diameter: 4.3 cm) were used. Ratings of perceived exertion (RPE) were collected using the Borg RPE scale [10] after completing a task. Musculoskeletal exposure was analysed with regard to mean muscle activity normalized to the maximum voluntary contraction (%MVC). Cardiovascular exposure was analysed by calculating the percentage heart rate reserve ($HR_{task} - HR_{rest})/(HR_{max} - HR_{rest}$), with $HR_{task} =$ mean HR of a lifting/lowering task, $HR_{max} = 220 - $ age and $HR_{rest} = $ mean HR after a 10-min resting period in a sitting position.

2.2 Systematic Selection of Dose Models

Dose models were collected via a systematic literature search in accordance with PRISMA guidelines, using PubMed to access biomedical publications, and Web of Science and Scopus to access cross-disciplinary results published up to January 2021. The search terms used to identify methods that aim to accumulate physical exposure over time including weighting of risk factors were *cumulative* or *dose* and *weighting* or *weighted* and *compressi* * and *spine* or *spinal* or *low* * *back*. This paper focuses on compressive loading of the spine or the lower back, since this exposure is highly relevant for occupational stress assessment [11]. All citations identified were organized and the duplicates were deleted, resulting in 626 records. After screening the titles, 71 articles remained. After screening the abstracts, the full texts of 17 articles were retrieved. Moreover, reference lists of relevant articles were checked. Dose models were excluded that were not available in German or English, dealt with medical treatments, or required input data other than those available here. Articles containing only dose models from other authors or the authors' own previous publications without further development were also excluded to avoid duplication of dose models. The five different dose models, which were identified eventually, are shown in Table 1.

Table 1. Dose models that were identified via the literature search.

Ref.	Number of weighting factors $\neq$ 1 and type	Relative weighting of load intensity	Acquisition of time via		Author
			Parameter	Relative weighting	
A	1, Exponential	Squared	Load duration	None (exponent = 1)	[3–5]
B	1, Exponential	Cubic	Load duration	None (exponent = 1)	[4]
C	1, Exponential	Tetra-powered	Load duration	None (exponent = 1)	[4]
D	2, Exponential	Squared	Number of cycles	Exponent = 0.2	[6]
E	1, Multiplicative	Calculated via polynomial equation	Load duration	None (exponent = 1)	[7]

All dose models in Table 1 consider both the intensity and the temporal aspect of the load, although the latter is often not weighted relatively. For the dose models A, B and C, only the intensity of the load is weighted by an exponent (2, 3 or 4), while the duration of exposure is not weighted. The calculation of cumulative loading thus results in Eq. (1) with an exponent of 2 according to [3–5] or an exponent of 3 or 4 according to [4]. All three approaches are in particular based on in vitro experiments with human specimen by [12] which suggest a disproportionately higher overexertion risk of high forces. A clearly best-fit calculation method cannot be identified between A, B and C. While [13] concluded that a squared weighting would be more predictive of disc-related diseases, [14] found that a tetra-powered weighting of the load intensity also leads to a good overall prediction accuracy of disc-related diseases.

$$Cumulative\ loading = \sum \left(load\ intensity^{exp} * load\ duration\right),\ exp = \{2, 3, 4\} \quad (1)$$

In contrast, the two-factors exponential dose model D by [6] takes into account both load intensity and duration by means of a weighting factor. The calculation of cumulative loading is shown in Eq. (2). Since this model captures the time dimension via the number of cycles, its application is limited to cyclic activities. As the data this paper is based on refer to a cyclic activity, this model is included here.

$$Cumulative\ loading = \sum \left(load\ intensity^2 * number\ of\ cycles^{0.2} \right) \qquad (2)$$

The dose models presented so far have in common that the weighting factors are fixed for all levels. For the multiplicative dose model E by [7], different weighting factors are calculated individually depending on the load level to adjust for a different impact on injury development. The calculation is shown in Eq. (3). The use of this dose model in a study of [15] resulted in statistically similar cumulative loading estimates between different exposure conditions at the time of injury for porcine specimen. The weighting factor is calculated for each time frame using a fifth order polynomial equation that represents the weighting factor as a function of load magnitude. The load magnitude is determined as a percentage of the maximum compressive strength.

$$Cumulative\ loading = \sum (load\ intensity * weighting\ factor * load\ duration) \qquad (3)$$

2.3 Calculation of Cumulative Doses

The calculation of cumulative loading was performed for each task using all five dose models. For the single-factor exponential approaches (A, B and C), the cumulative loading was calculated according to Eq. (1) with exponents 2, 3 or 4, respectively. For the two-factors exponential dose model (D), the cumulative load estimate was calculated according to Eq. (2). A cycle was considered to be a complete lifting and lowering movement, and the maximum intensity of a cycle was used as load intensity. For the multiplicative dose model (E), the cumulative load estimate was calculated according to Eq. (3). To calculate the load magnitude as a percentage of the maximum compressive strength, which is needed to determine the weighting factor individually, the reference values for compressive strength from [11] were used.

2.4 Data Analysis

The dose models are compared regarding their ability to reflect the differences in musculoskeletal, cardiovascular and psychophysical strain resulting from the two lifting/lowering tasks. For this purpose, the percentage difference of the mean values for each indicator of strain is calculated using the formula in Eq. (4). The result indicates the percentage by which the mean value of the strain indicator of HI exceeds that of LI. In addition, the cumulative loading estimates were calculated for each participant and both tasks using the five dose models. For each dose model, the percent difference between HI and LI is calculated using the formula in Eq. (5). Again, the result indicates the percent by which the mean cumulative loading estimate of HI exceeds that of LI. For comparison purposes, the cumulative load estimates using the non-weighted method, which calculates cumulative loading as area under the loading curve, are also provided. As explained in Sect. 2.1, the two tasks were designed to have the same area under the loading curve, so the cumulative loading estimates are identical for the non-weighted calculation method.

It is assumed that a weighting factor reflects the resulting strain the better, the more the percentage difference of the calculated cumulative loading agrees with the percentage difference of the indicators of strain.

$$\left(\frac{Mean\ indicator\ of\ strain_{HI} - Mean\ indicator\ of\ strain_{LI}}{Mean\ indicator\ of\ strain_{LI}} \right) * 100 \qquad (4)$$

$$\left(\frac{Mean\ cumulative\ loading_{HI} - Mean\ cumulative\ loading_{LI}}{Mean\ cumulative\ loading_{LI}} \right) * 100 \qquad (5)$$

3   Results

Generally, cumulative dose estimates are higher for the task with higher load intensity HI due to the higher weighting of the load intensity relative to the temporal aspect, except for the non-weighted method. For each dose model, the percentage difference in the right column of Table 2a indicates by which the mean cumulative load estimate of HI exceeds that of LI. For the indicators of strain, the values are given analogously in Table 2b. The resulting musculoskeletal, cardiovascular and psychophysical strain is generally about 20% (mean muscular activity and HR reserve) to 25% (RPE) higher for the task HI with higher external weight.

Table 2a. Columns LI and HI show the cumulative loading estimates using to the indicated dose model. Column "Difference" indicates by what percentage the cumulative loading estimate of the condition with high external load (HI) exceeds the estimate of the condition with low external load (LI).

Dose model	Unit	Cumulative loading estimate		Difference (Increase HI over LI)
		LI	HI	
Non-weighted	[kNs]	700	700	±0%
A	[kN²s]	1.27E+6	1.45E+6	+14.5%
B	[kN³s]	2.66E+9	3.46E+9	+30.3%
C	[kN⁴s]	4.97E+12	7.39E+12	+48.7%
D	[kN²]	13.68	17.81	+30.2%
E	[kNs]	819.3	1132.3	+38.2%

Table 2b. Columns LI and HI show the mean value of the indicator of strain. Column "Difference" indicates by what percentage the mean value of the condition with high external load (HI) exceeds the mean value of the condition with low external load (LI).

Indicator of strain	Unit	Mean value of indicator of strain		Difference (Increase HI over LI)
		LI	HI	
Mean muscle activity, RES	[%MVC]	16.11	19.42	+20.5%
Mean muscle activity, LES	[%MVC]	18.93	22.46	+18.6%
HR Reserve	[%]	9.54	11.42	+19.7%
RPE	[-]	10.33	12.92	+25.1%

4 Discussion

The objective of this contribution was to compare systematically different dose models proposed in the literature for the assessment of spinal cumulative loading. Determining the correctness of an ergonomic assessment result is a well-known problem in ergonomics and generally hardly possible as already pointed out by [1]. A complicating factor for the five dose models examined is that the units differ in each case, as shown in Table 2a. The cumulative loading estimates are therefore physically different quantities, even though they all aim to represent the cumulative loading of the same two working conditions. Therefore, the dose models are not compared directly by their assessment results, but indirectly by how well the resulting strain was captured. From an ergonomic point of view, both systematic under- and overestimation of the resulting strain are problematic, as both human factors and economic efficiency should be considered when designing a workplace.

When comparing the cumulative loading estimates and their percentage difference in Table 2a, major differences between the five dose models are revealed, confirming the hypothesis, according to which the lack of standardization for calculating cumulative loading leads to differences in the calculation results. This is remarkable since all five dose models considered claim to represent the load acting on an individual over a certain period, taking into account the two risk factors intensity and temporal aspect of the load. As an implication for occupational practice, it can be concluded that different work situations can be compared on the basis of cumulative loading estimates only if the same dose model was used for the assessment.

The resulting strain values are generally about 20% to 25% higher for HI compared to LI. At the same time, all dose models using weighting factors result in higher cumulative loading estimates for HI compared to LI, so it can be stated that all dose models A-E represent the basic tendency of the resulting strain. Based on the assumption that a dose model reflects the resulting strain the better, the more the percentage difference of the calculated cumulative loading estimate (Table 2a) agrees with the percentage difference of the indicators of strain (Table 2b), the five dose models can be further evaluated. In this context, the results show that the resulting musculoskeletal, cardiovascular and psychophysical strain would be underestimated when using the single-factor squared dose model (A). Both the single-factor tetra-powered dose model (C) and the multiplicative dose model (E) lead to rather larger overestimation of nearly 20 to 30% points for the resulting musculoskeletal and cardiovascular strain and about 13 to 23% points for the resulting perceived strain. When using the single-factor cubic dose model (B) or the two-factors exponential dose model (D), the resulting strain would be better represented with only a slight overestimation of about 10 to 5% points.

With respect to dose models B and D, it is remarkable that they lead to almost identical results measured by the percentage differences of the cumulative loading estimates, although the dose models are based on completely different approaches. Since this analysis is based on only one, cyclic load profile, further research is needed to verify this observation with other load profiles before conclusions regarding the relative comparability of results of different dose models can be drawn.

Common to all dose models examined here is that development and validation of the model are based exclusively on results of in vitro studies on material failure of human or animal specimens. Therefore, it could be argued that a comparison of the dose models in terms of their ability to reflect the musculoskeletal, cardiovascular and psychophysical strain based on in vivo data is not meaningful. However, in view of the inherent problem of the possible overestimation of human capacity and the associated possible damage to the body, ergonomic assessment methods based on the principles of material failure of the human musculoskeletal system alone seem potentially disadvantageous [16]. In view of this argumentation, the evaluation of dose models for cumulative loading in terms of their ability to reflect short-term, reversible physical reactions such as musculoskeletal, cardiovascular and psychophysical strain seems appropriate.

5   Conclusion

Due to the lack of standardization for calculating cumulative loading, different work situations can be compared in occupational practice on the basis of cumulative loading estimates only if the same dose model was used for the assessment. Overall, the results underline the need for a standardized and validated dose model for cumulative loading so that assessment results can be compared to assessment results from other work situations as well as to reference values. Further research is therefore needed regarding a standardized dose model that captures the actual demands on an individual.

Acknowledgements. This article is part of the research of the Chair and Institute of Industrial Engineering and Ergonomics of RWTH Aachen University and the project 'workHEALTH', which is funded by the German Federal Ministry of Education and Research (BMBF, grant number 01EC1905B). The authors would like to thank for the support they have received.

References

1. Li, G., Buckle, P.: Current techniques for assessing physical exposure to work-related musculoskeletal risks, with emphasis on posture-based methods. Ergonomics **42**(5), 674–695 (1999)

2. Waters, T., Yeung, S., Genaidy, A., Callaghan, J., Barriera-Viruet, H., Abdallah, S., Kumar, S.: Cumulative spinal loading exposure methods for manual material handling tasks. Part 2. Theor. Issues Ergon. Sci. **7**(2), 131–148 (2006)
3. Jager, M., Jordan, C., Luttmann, A., Laurig, W.: Evaluation and assessment of lumbar load during total shifts for occupational manual materials handling jobs within the Dortmund Lumbar Load study. Int. J. Ind. Ergon. **25**(6), 553–571 (2000)
4. Jäger, M., Geiß, O., Bergmann, A., Bolm-Audorff, U., Ditchen, D., Ellegast, R., Elsner, G., Grifka, J., Haerting, J., Hofmann, F., Linhardt, O., Michaelis, M., Petereit-Haack, G., Seidler, A., Luttmann, A.: Biomechanical analyses on lumbar load within the German Spine study. Zbl fur Arbeitsmed **57**(9), 264–276 (2007)
5. Coenen, P., Kingma, I., Boot, C.R.L., Bongers, P.M., van Dieën, J.H.: Cumulative mechanical low-back load at work is a determinant of low-back pain. Occup. Environ. Med. **71**(5), 332–337 (2014)
6. Coenen, P., Kingma, I., Boot, C.R.L., Bongers, P.M., van Dieen, J.H.: The contribution of load magnitude and number of load cycles to cumulative low-back load estimations. Clin. Biomech. (Bristol Avon) **27**(10), 1083–1086 (2012)
7. Parkinson, R.J., Callaghan, J.P.: The role of load magnitude as a modifier of the cumulative load tolerance of porcine cervical spinal units. Progress towards a force weighting approach. Theor. Issues Ergon. Sci. **8**(3), 171–184 (2007)
8. Johnen, L., Mertens, A., Nitsch, V., Brandl, C.: Why the non-weighted integration method may not be suitable for calculating cumulative loading of the lower back: Empirical investigation of strain during lifting and lowering tasks (2020, Submitted)
9. Jäger, M., Luttmann, A.: Biomechanical analysis and assessment of lumbar stress during load lifting using a dynamic 19-segment human model. Ergonomics **32**(1), 93–112 (1989)
10. Borg, G.: Borg's Perceived Exertion and Pain Scales. Human Kinetics, Champaign (1998)
11. Jäger, M.: Extended compilation of autopsy-material measurements on lumbar ultimate compressive strength for deriving reference values in ergonomic work design. EXCLI J. **17**, 362–385 (2018)
12. Brinckmann, P., Biggemann, M., Hilweg, D.: Fatigue fracture of human lumbar vertebrae. Clin. Biomech. **2**, 94–96 (1988)
13. Jäger, M., Jordan, C., Voß, J., Bergmann, A., Bolm-Audorff, U., Ditchen, D., Ellegast, R., Haerting, J., Haufe, E., Kuß, O., Morfeld, P., Schäfer, K., Seidler, A., Luttmann, A.: Extended evaluation of the German Spine study. Zbl fur Arbeitsmed **64**(3), 151–168 (2014)
14. Seidler, A., Bergmann, A., Ditchen, D., Ellegast, R., Eisner, G., Grifka, J., Haerting, J., Hofmann, F., Jäger, M., Linhardt, O., Luttmann, A., Michaelis, M., Petereit-Haack, G., Bolm-Audorff, U.: Relationship between cumulative spinal load due to materials handling and lumbar disc herniation - results of the German Spine study. Zbl fur Arbeitsmed **57**(10), 290–303 (2007)
15. Zehr, J.D., Tennant, L.M., Callaghan, J.P.: Examining endplate fatigue failure during cyclic compression loading with variable and consistent peak magnitudes using a force weighting adjustment approach. Ergonomics **62**(10), 1339–1348 (2019)
16. Nussbaum, M.A.: Static and dynamic myoelectric measures of shoulder muscle fatigue during intermittent dynamic exertions of low to moderate intensity. Eur. J. Appl. Physiol. **85**(3–4), 299–309 (2001)

Fatigue Risk Assessment and Control

Heather Kahle[1]([⊠]), Chason Coelho[2], and Jennifer Colman[1]

[1] WorkSafeBC, Richmond, BC V7C 1C6, Canada
heather.kahle@worksafebc.com
[2] Exponent, Seattle, WA 98108, USA

Abstract. It is generally well accepted that fatigue can increase the likelihood of human errors and subsequent safety incidents. Managing fatigue-related risks has proven challenging, but such risks are indeed manageable. Oftentimes, the starting point to assess and control fatigue-related risk is the individual, with attempts to assess an individual's level of sleepiness and/or sleep hygiene. With this approach, countermeasures such as restricted hours of service or mandatory breaks of a certain frequency may be used. While some of these measures can be helpful, they may not be as effective or sustainable in reducing fatigue-related risks associated with performing work as more risk-based approaches.

This paper presents an alternative view on fatigue-related risk in a workplace setting, which may have implications for how it can be managed. One view holds that fatigue itself is a hazard, whereas as the other suggests it is a contributory factor. In the presence of workplace hazards, fatigue can escalate the potential for errors and safety incidents. This paper outlines a high-level fatigue risk assessment process that begins with identifying and prioritizing workplace tasks that are particularly vulnerable to fatigue-related performance impairment, such as safety critical work activities that involve vigilance, calculations, or recalling detailed information. The next steps are to assess (a) how fatigue may link with workplace hazards to escalate the potential for harm, (b) determine the possible consequences in those scenarios, and (c) then control both the workplace hazard(s) and factors that may decrease alertness with effective control measures.

Keywords: Fatigue-related risk · Safety · Error management · Systems

1 Fatigue Risk Management

Fatigue is common and the result of normal processes, and is therefore predictable in many cases. Human fatigue cannot be completely eradicated. Everyone, especially those who have to work when their drive to sleep is greatest, are subject to performance impairments when fatigued. These impairments can occur regardless of skill, knowledge, and training.

1.1 Workplace Aspects

Aspects of the workplace can influence personal alertness and fatigue levels. These aspects include, but are not necessarily limited to, the types of tasks being carried out, the

© The Author(s), under exclusive license to Springer Nature Switzerland AG 2021
N. L. Black et al. (Eds.): IEA 2021, LNNS 222, pp. 101–105, 2021.
https://doi.org/10.1007/978-3-030-74611-7_14

environment, and shift scheduling. Tasks that involve monotonous, repetitive activities, complex decision-making, or sustained mental or physical effort can decrease alertness levels. Environmental factors such as dim lighting, warm temperatures, and significant levels of vibration and noise can also promote decreases in alertness. Work schedules are relevant too. Shiftwork, and other irregular and extended hours of work can influence the quality and quantity of sleep an individual obtains, which in turn can impact fatigue levels.

1.2 Fatigue

Fatigue can be described as a change in physiological state that results from insufficient quality or quantity of sleep. Fatigue can negatively influence the ability to carry out even simple tasks. Fatigue is a human performance influencing factor. It is known to impair reaction time, alertness, decision-making, information processing, memory, recall, communication, and concentration. These mental and physical performance decrements can escalate the potential for adverse events and risk of harm [1].

Health and safety agencies, work organizations, and academic communities have developed various definitions and frameworks for fatigue. Identifying fatigue itself as a workplace hazard can lead to attempts to quantify and mitigate personal levels of fatigue. Attempts to quantify fatigue have resulted in the use of a wide array of tools to attempt to measure fatigue. However, the various tools available, ranging from sleep surveys to biomathematical models have limitations. As well, individuals can struggle to accurately assess their own fatigue levels. Efforts to mitigate fatigue often involve prescriptive hour-of-service (HoS) limitations and minimum rest break requirements.

2 Managing the Risk

To address risk emerging from work scheduling and other factors, a risk-based approach has been introduced in several safety-critical industries. This framework for managing fatigue is a 'fatigue risk management system' (FRMS). It is a management-system level administrative control including elements similar to a safety management system most often including the following elements: a policy statement outlining responsibilities, a fatigue-related risk assessment and control process, reporting, communication, investigation protocols, safe work procedures, as well as steps for continuous improvement. Collectively, these elements move the focus away from simply restricting HoS and toward proactively evaluating a series of defensive layers, including, but not necessarily limited to, sleep opportunity, sleep obtained, fatigue symptoms, and indicators of impaired performance [2]. Current limitations that can still be encountered within the FRMS framework are the challenges of developing practical, well-defined, accessible, and cost-effective methods for assessing fatigue-related risk and developing risk control measures.

Fatigue can also be viewed and treated as a personal or impairment issue that workers 'bring' to work. Viewing fatigue in this way can lead to mitigation efforts predominantly focused on 'fit for duty' issues, such as encouraging individuals to increase the amount and quality of sleep. While sufficient and good quality sleep are important, fatigue-related incidents are increasingly of interest to regulatory authorities. As such, non-work related fatigue factors and other personal prescriptive, alertness-boosting measures such as hydration, nutrition, fresh air, music, caffeine intake, fitness, and other personal efforts largely controlled by the individual fall within the health and wellness realm and lie outside of the scope of the safety regulator to influence or control. While some of these measures can be helpful to increase alertness, their use and overall effectiveness in the workplace to mitigate fatigue-related risk has limitations from the perspective of the regulator.

Alternatively to the characterization of fatigue as a direct hazard, fatigue can be viewed as a contributory factor (Fig. 1). Every workplace has hazards that can cause harm. If performing a task carries with it a certain risk, then performing the same task while fatigued likely increases the relative risk of making errors [3], which can lead to unwanted safety outcomes. If some tasks can be more vulnerable to fatigue and can therefore carry an increased risk of making errors if performed while fatigued, it begs the question as to what it is that makes the task more vulnerable. That is, what parts of the task are sensitive to fatigue and what potential outcomes could result? These questions can help safety practitioners understand how fatigue may interact with workplace hazards to increase the potential for harm. This perspective may be helpful because it creates learning opportunities to explore the workplace system, safety critical tasks and potential deficiencies. Then, the potential consequences that may result can be assessed to help inform, what and where lie the most effective areas to mitigate fatigue-related risk and prevention strategies that can fall within the purview of the safety regulator [4].

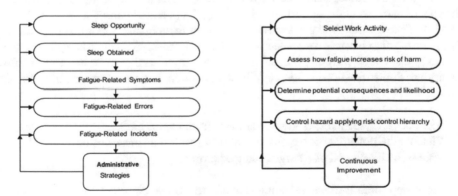

Fig. 1. Two fatigue risk management models.

Assessing fatigue-related risk using the alternate approach ultimately involves three core steps:

1. Select or identify work activities or tasks that are vulnerable or susceptible to fatigue;
2. For each task, assess whether and how fatigue increases the risk of harm from the hazard (identify consequences and determine likelihood); and
3. Control the hazard by implementing risk control measures

This process can be helpful in at least a few ways. It offers practical, accessible steps to mitigate fatigue-related risk. Second, it does not necessarily require highly specialized training in sleep and fatigue science or sophisticated technology, or development of a comprehensive safety management system and it can be applied across a wide range of industries. This straightforward method does not necessarily rely on operators or supervisors to observe indicators of impaired cognitive performance, which can be difficult to detect. It can be applied proactively offering a realistic and sensible starting place and options to help determine priorities. Paying attention to how human performance in work activities can be impaired by fatigue and then interact with other workplace hazards can help safety practitioners and regulators alike improve safety outcomes even when fatigue is not completely avoidable.

Evaluating the work activity helps identify ways to understand and alter tasks that may be especially sensitive to fatigue. Determining whether a task is even required, redesigning the task, changing aspects of the work environment that influence the task, such as lighting, noise or temperature, or changing when the task is performed, are all ways that can be helpful for practically and sustainably mitigating fatigue-related risk.

Some questions to help with the first core step of identifying tasks that involve characteristics sensitive to fatigue include, but are not necessarily limited to:

- Do the work activities rely on actions/activities known to be susceptible to fatigue?
- Do the workplace hazards increase the risk of harm when workers are fatigued?
- Is there elevated risk of errors and unwanted outcomes that could result due to fatigue?

The second core step identified above involves determining how fatigue may increase the risk of harm from the hazard and identifying the potential consequences and likelihood that fatigue-impaired performance could lead to an incident. For this step, identifying the existing hazards associated with the task is necessary. Any existing barriers or defenses that could prevent a fatigue-related error from leading to an incident are also identified. Some questions to help in this step, include, but are not necessarily limited to:

- How does fatigue increases the risk of harm from the hazard?
- What are the potential consequences that may result if an error occurs?
- What is the likelihood of a fatigue-induced error?

Core step three involves selecting risk control measures based on the findings of the previous two steps to help eliminate or mitigate the hazard at the source. Ideally, control measures reflect the risk control hierarchy to first eliminate the workplace hazard, followed by options to isolate or substitute, and then implement engineering solutions. Important in step three is determining whether or how aspects of the environment or work scheduling can be effectively changed to mitigate fatigue-related risk. Some questions to help in this step include, but are not necessarily limited to:

- Is the risk of committing a task-related error minimized if fatigue is present?
- How are workers and processes protected if fatigue is present?

- How will the current workplace system design or necessary changes accommodate or protect fatigued workers?

3 Summary

This paper presents two perspectives and ultimately two processes for managing fatigue-related risk. In one perspective, fatigue is viewed as a hazard. The starting point in the process is sleep opportunity. Underpinning this view is the idea that fatigue leads to errors. As such, attempts are made to identify at-risk individuals by trying to detect symptoms of fatigue. As well, efforts are made to measure fatigue levels with tools such as self-report surveys and symptom checklists. However, the tools to measure fatigue have limitations. In turn, efforts to control fatigue are introduced.

In the other perspective, fatigue is considered a 'contributory factor'. The starting point is the workplace activity. In this view, it is understood systems are not automatically safe. Hazards, poor design, and task characteristics can lead to errors which potentially can contribute to incidents and harm. In the presence of workplace hazards, human fatigue can escalate the potential for harm. If errors are made, it creates a learning opportunity. Understanding what makes tasks vulnerable to fatigue can be used to inform changes to existing defense measures or develop new measures to mitigate risk at the task level for effective and sustainable error prevention and overall improved system safety.

This panel discussion will help session participants develop an enhanced understanding of available options and explore examples of how the task-based approach can be adopted and successful in different workplace contexts.

References

1. Coelho, C., Lakhiani, S.D., Morrison, D.R.T. III: Staying alert: incorporating human fatigue in risk management. In: International Proceedings of the Human Factors and Ergonomics Society 2019 Annual Meeting, pp. 1819–1823 (2019)
2. Dawson, D., Chapman, J., Thomas, M.J.W.: Fatigue-proofing: a new approach to reducing fatigue-related risk using the principles of error management: 'sleep Medicine reviews (2004–2008). Chronobiol. Int. 27(5), 1013–1030 (2010)
3. Lombardi, D.A., Folkard, S., Willets, J.L., Smith, G.S.: Daily sleep, weekly working hours, and risk of work-related injury: U.S. National Health Interview Survey (2004–2008). Chronobiology International 27(5), 1013–1030 (2010)
4. International Association of Oil and Gas Producers. Assessing Risks from Operator Fatigue: A Guidance Document for the Oil and Gas Industry. Report No. 492 (2014). https://s3.eu-west-1.amazonaws.com/assets.stepchangeinsafety.net/Human-Factors-carousel/Assessing_risks_from_operator_fatigue_2014.pdf?mtime=20200422224120&focal=none

Psychological Assessment for Bus Captain Selection

Nga Man[1]([✉]), Siu Shing Man[1], Tingru Zhang[2], Wing Hong Chan[1],
and Alan Hoi Shou Chan[1]

[1] City University of Hong Kong, Kowloon, Hong Kong
ngaman2-c@my.cityu.edu.hk
[2] Shenzhen University, Shenzhen, China

Abstract. Bus drivers are parts of a safe transport environment. By selecting suitable humans for driving tasks, a work environment that boosts productivity and minimizes safety issues may be created. This paper reports the development and validation of the Bus Captain Aptitude Test (BCAT) for screening out bus captain applicants who have an inclination to drive aggressively in job selection process. The BCAT consists of 55 questionnaire items based on seven psychological factors which are considered as possible influencers of the disciplinary performance of drivers. A total of 387 bus captains are involved in completing the BCAT. The reliability assessment results show that the internal consistency reliability for all the seven factors in the BCAT is acceptable. Amongst the seven factors, the 'impulsivity' factor is significantly and negatively correlated with the disciplinary performance of the existing bus captains, implying a moderate level of the criterion-related validity of the BCAT. The results of reliability assessment and validity testing of the BCAT suggested that it is a psychologically sound instrument for effective bus captain selection.

Keywords: Aptitude test · Psychological factors · Occupational drivers

1 Introduction

Public buses, as one of the dominant modes of public transportation in Hong Kong, provide approximately 4 million daily passenger journeys. However, public bus had a high accident rate with a total of 2196 accidents which approximately 6 accidents happened per day in 2019 (Transport Department 2020). The occurrence of bus accidents not only results in injuries or deaths of bus passengers, captains and other road users, but also places a large financial burden on bus companies for the liability of loss of life and property caused. These adverse influences on the public and bus companies highlight the importance of reducing bus accidents.

One of the main causes of bus accidents is the aggressive driving behaviours of drivers (Özkan et al. 2010; Zhao et al. 2019). In Hong Kong, bus companies mainly assess bus captain applicants' driving skills and medical conditions in the present recruitment procedures. However, these procedures fail to consider their psychological characteristics

N. L. Black et al. (Eds.): IEA 2021, LNNS 222, pp. 106–111, 2021.
https://doi.org/10.1007/978-3-030-74611-7_15

which are believed to affect the driving behaviours in the actual complex bus driving environment. Cheng et al. (2016) found that licensed drivers with traffic offence records showed a higher degree of impulsivity and were more willing to make risky decisions compared with those who had no offence records in an event-related potential experiment, implying psychological characteristics of drivers may exert influence on their driving behaviours.

Inoue et al. (2009) suggested that a driving aptitude test can help the establishment of a safer transportation environment by taking psychological factors of drivers into consideration. Nevertheless, the number of aptitude tests established for occupational drivers is still limited. Amongst the few, Chan and Chen (2011) devised a driving aptitude test for assessing tram operators in the aspects of driving-related abilities and aptitudes to drive safely, and Tsang et al. (2012) attempted to validate the aforementioned test. However, these past studies lacked a detailed discussion on reliability and validity, which are important determinants of the quality of a test. Accordingly, a reliable and valid aptitude test for drivers is lacking.

Therefore, this paper aims to fill this research gap by providing a practical aptitude assessment called Bus Captain Aptitude Test (BCAT) for psychological testing of the bus captain candidates. The test is to screen out those who are inclined to drive aggressively or are easily provoked resulting in aggressive driving, with incorporating assessments on reliability and validity.

2 Methodology

2.1 Development of BCAT Items

A comprehensive literature review on risky, unsafe and aggressive driving of drivers was conducted to identify the psychological factors that were found to influence the driving behaviours of drivers (Iversen 2004; Moeller et al. 2001; Spinella 2005; Stephens and Sullman 2014; Swar et al. 2017; Ulleberg and Rundmo 2003; Wong and Law 2002; Zhang and Chan 2016). Seven psychological factors (Table 1), namely, driving anger expression, emotion appraisal, empathy, impulsivity, negative emotion, normlessness and risk-taking attitude were chosen, and they made up of a total of 55 questionnaire items for the BCAT. These fifty-five items for the BCAT were designed on the basis of previous studies with appropriate modifications to fit in the context of this research. All the items are measured in a seven-point Likert scale ranging from '1 = strongly disagree' to '7 = strongly agree'.

2.2 Data Collection: Pilot Study and Main Study

Subsequently, the BCAT questionnaires were randomly distributed to 41 bus captains from a bus company in Hong Kong in Nov 2019 for a pilot study. The pilot study was conducted to assess the feasibility of steps for distributing the BCAT and to ensure all the BCAT items could be understood easily. Specifically, each bus captain participant involved in the pilot study was asked by researchers for the views and comments concerning the BCAT items in terms of readability and understandability after he/she had

Table 1. Related psychological factors and definitions.

Psychological factor	Definition	Reference
Driving anger expression	How drivers express their anger while driving	(Stephens and Sullman 2014; Zhang and Chan 2016)
Emotion appraisal	Drivers' ability to understand their emotions and the emotions of people around them	(Wong and Law 2002)
Empathy	Drivers' tendency to vicariously experience others' emotional states	(Spinella 2005)
Impulsivity	Drivers' tendency to act without thinking	(Moeller et al. 2001)
Negative emotion	Drivers' unpleasant or unhappy emotion	(Swar et al. 2017)
Normlessness	Drivers' belief that socially unapproved behaviors are required to achieve certain goals	(Ulleberg and Rundmo 2003)
Risk-taking attitude	Drivers' tendency to evaluate risky driving behaviors with some degree of favor or disfavor	(Iversen 2004)

completed the BCAT. Some BCAT items may have been interpreted in unintended ways by the participants or not sufficiently comprehensive and thus were modified to improve their readability and understandability. Once the revised BCAT was ready for the main study, the BCAT was then randomly distributed to 387 bus captains in a period from January 2020 to June 2020. The sample size of the main study was determined by using the Cochran's formula (Cochran 2007) (Eq. 1). With a confidence level of 95%, ±5% precision and 50% population proportion, the minimum required sample size (n) would be 385.

$$n = \frac{t^2 p(1-p)}{d^2} \tag{1}$$

where:

n = sample size;
t = t value for selected alpha level;
p = population proportion or percentage picking a choice; and
d = acceptable margin of error.

2.3 Data Analysis

The data collected were adopted for assessing the reliability and validity of the BCAT. Reliability of a test is usually measured in terms of internal consistency reliability which describes the extent or degree to which the items in a scale measure the same construct or concept of interest with the use of Cronbach's alpha (Cronbach 1951; Tavakol and Dennick 2011). For validity assessment, the criterion-related validity of the BCAT was evaluated. Criterion-related validity can be used to provide evidence of a relationship between two measures (DeVon et al. 2007; Hinkin 1995). In general, there are three types of criterion-related validity, namely, predictive, concurrent and postdictive. In this regard, the disciplinary scores of the existing bus captains over the past five years provided by the mentioned bus company was chosen as the criterion for the validity assessment. The disciplinary score is a performance indicator of driving behaviours such as driving safety and customer service of bus captains during their working time. The higher the disciplinary score, the worse the disciplinary performance. Postdictive validity was used for this study as the disciplinary scores had been collected before the BCAT was done by bus captains. Significant correlation between the BCAT score and the disciplinary score was expected to be seen for verifying the acceptable validity of the BCAT (DeVellis 2016). The above analyses were performed with the use of SPSS statistical software package.

3   Results

The reliability assessment results (Table 2) showed that the internal consistency reliability for all the seven factors in the BCAT were acceptable (Cronbach's alpha values ranged from 0.704 to 0.884), indicating the items in each factor were unidimensional.

Table 2. Reliability test of psychological factors measured in the BCAT ($n = 387$).

Psychological factor	No. of items in the BCAT	Cronbach's alpha (acceptable: ≥ 0.7)
Driving anger expression	8	0.738
Emotion appraisal	6	0.812
Empathy	6	0.832
Impulsivity	8	0.734
Negative emotion	11	0.884
Normlessness	3	0.704
Risk-taking attitude	13	0.734

Amongst the seven psychological factors in BCAT, only the 'impulsivity' factor is significantly ($p < 0.05$) and negatively correlated (correlation coefficient (r) = -0.262) with the disciplinary score of the bus captains, implying a moderate level of criterion-related validity of the BCAT as shown in Table 3.

Table 3. Correlation between psychological factors and disciplinary score.

Psychological factor	Significance (2-sided)	Pearson correlation coefficient (r)
Driving anger expression	0.360	0.113
Emotion appraisal	0.777	−0.035
Empathy	0.621	0.061
Impulsivity	**0.031**	**−0.262**
Negative emotion	0.580	0.068
Normlessness	0.678	0.051
Risk-taking attitude	0.614	0.062

4   Discussion

The acceptable internal consistency reliability of the BCAT demonstrated its items could measure what it was assumed to measure. In addition, the significant and negative correlation between the impulsivity factor and disciplinary score of bus captains was found, suggesting bus captains who are unlikely to be impulsive tend to have lower disciplinary scores and drive safely. Accordingly, all the eight items related to impulsivity were comprised as the finalized version of the BCAT for screening out bus captain applicants who are likely to have high disciplinary scores at recruitment. The higher the total score of the BCAT achieved by bus captain applicants, the lower their degree of impulsivity.

This research can provide practical implications for the transportation industry. With the adoption of the reliable and valid BCAT at recruitment, effective bus captain selection may be made by choosing bus captain applicants who tend not to act impulsive easily. Specifically, the quality of bus captain candidates and the safety of the transportation environment could be better assured.

Despite promising contribution could be given in this study, its limitation should be admitted. The scope of investigation in the current research was confined to the transportation industry in Hong Kong only. In order to have higher applicability, further research is necessary to validate the BCAT across other countries.

5   Conclusion

This research successfully devised a reliable and valid psychological aptitude test named the Bus Captain Aptitude Test (BCAT) for the selection of bus captain applicants at recruitment in Hong Kong. The development of the BCAT consisted of three phases of activities, and they were item development, reliability assessment and validity assessment, respectively. The outcomes of this study are considered to be beneficial to personnel decisions in the transportation industry.

References

Chan, A.H., Chen, K.: Driving Aptitude Test (DAT): a new set of aptitude tests for occupational drivers. Paper presented at the International MultiConference of Engineers and Computer Scientists 2011, IMECS 2011 (2011)

Cheng, A.S., Ting, K.H., Liu, K.P., Ba, Y.: Impulsivity and risky decision making among taxi drivers in Hong Kong: an event-related potential study. Accid. Anal. Prev. **95**, 387–394 (2016)

Cochran, W.G.: Sampling Techniques. Wiley, Hoboken (2007)

Cronbach, L.J.: Coefficient alpha and the internal structure of tests. Psychometrika **16**(3), 297–334 (1951)

DeVellis, R.F.: Scale Development: Theory and Applications, vol. 26. Sage publications, Thousand Oaks (2016)

DeVon, H.A., Block, M.E., Moyle-Wright, P., Ernst, D.M., Hayden, S.J., Lazzara, D.J., Savoy, S.M., Kostas-Polston, E.: A psychometric toolbox for testing validity and reliability. J. Nurs. Scholarsh. **39**(2), 155–164 (2007)

Hinkin, T.R.: A review of scale development practices in the study of organizations. J. Manag. **21**(5), 967–988 (1995)

Inoue, T., Suzuki, H., Kioka, K., Akatsuka, H., Shigemori, M., Hida, W.: A new set of psychological aptitude tests for train operation staff. Q. Rep. RTRI **50**(1), 39–44 (2009)

Iversen, H.: Risk-taking attitudes and risky driving behaviour. Transp. Res. Part F Traffic Psychol. Behav. **7**(3), 135–150 (2004)

Moeller, F.G., Barratt, E.S., Dougherty, D.M., Schmitz, J.M., Swann, A.C.: Psychiatric aspects of impulsivity. Am. J. Psychiatry **158**(11), 1783–1793 (2001)

Özkan, T., Lajunen, T., Parker, D., Sümer, N., Summala, H.: Symmetric relationship between self and others in aggressive driving across gender and countries. Traffic Injury Prev. **11**(3), 228–239 (2010)

Spinella, M.: Self-rated executive function: development of the executive function index. Int. J. Neurosci. **115**(5), 649–667 (2005)

Stephens, A.N., Sullman, M.J.: Development of a short form of the driving anger expression inventory. Accid. Anal. Prev. **72**, 169–176 (2014)

Swar, B., Hameed, T., Reychav, I.: Information overload, psychological ill-being, and behavioral intention to continue online healthcare information search. Comput. Hum. Behav. **70**, 416–425 (2017)

Tavakol, M., Dennick, R.: Making sense of Cronbach's alpha. Int. J. Med. Educ. **2**, 53 (2011)

Transport Department: Vehicle Involvements in Accidents by Class (2020). https://www.td.gov. hk/filemanager/en/content_4970/table72.pdf

Tsang, S.N., Chen, K., Chan, A.H.: Driving aptitude test for personnel decisions: a case study. Iaeng Trans. Eng. Technol. **7**, 258–270 (2012)

Ulleberg, P., Rundmo, T.: Personality, attitudes and risk perception as predictors of risky driving behaviour among young drivers. Saf. Sci. **41**(5), 427–443 (2003)

Wong, C.-S., Law, K.S.: The effects of leader and follower emotional intelligence on performance and attitude: an exploratory study. Leadersh. Q. **13**(3), 243–274 (2002)

Zhang, T., Chan, A.H.: The association between driving anger and driving outcomes: a meta-analysis of evidence from the past twenty years. Accid. Anal. Prev. **90**, 50–62 (2016)

Zhao, X., Xu, W., Ma, J., Li, H., Chen, Y.: An analysis of the relationship between driver characteristics and driving safety using structural equation models. Transp. Res. Part F Traffic Psychol. Behav. **62**, 529–545 (2019)

The Safety Culture Assessment Process: Case Study on Offshore Platforms

Marina P. Mercado[1]([⊠]) [iD], Raoni Rocha[2] [iD],
and Francisco José de Castro Moura Duarte[1] [iD]

[1] Department of Production Engineering, Federal University of Rio de Janeiro, Rio de Janeiro,
RJ, Brazil
{marinapmercado,duarte}@pep.ufrj.br
[2] Department of Production Engineering, Federal University of Ouro Preto, Ouro Preto,
MG, Brazil
raoni@ufop.edu.br

Abstract. Safety culture has increasingly been discussed since the accident in Chernobyl, back in 1986. Studies made in this context have developed a number of definitions, approaches and diagnostic methods. However, there are few studies discussing transformations in safety practices, which can be brought about once diagnoses are applied. Thus, the purpose of this study is to analyze the methodological approach used in a safety culture assessment, which was applied to two offshore platforms and was based on an approach grounded in human and organizational factors related to industrial safety. This study was carried out and discussed based on document analysis, as well as on interviews made both with the researchers who developed and applied the diagnosis and with some key users who took part in the process. The main results show the challenges and advantages of the methodology used. The participatory approach used allowed for the development of action proposals intended to transform safety culture based on discussions on real work situations.

Keywords: Human and organizational factors · Industry · Oil and gas ·
Industrial safety · Quali-quantitative method · Diagnosis

1 Introduction

The safety culture is understood as a set of ways to do and think about the control the most severe risks related to their activities, being that such behavior is shared by stakeholders in a given organization [1]. The latest studies on safety culture have discussed the integration of human and organizational factors with industrial safety practice [2]. Diagnoses have been developed with the purpose of identifying factors which make efficient and safe human activity easier or more difficult. The human and organizational factors approach, which was the theoretical and practical basis for the diagnosis analyzed in this study, is strongly grounded in concepts presented in the Ergonomics of the Activity [3], such as prescribed and real work.

The studies on safety culture help understand the deeper causes leading up to major catastrophes and, in turn, human, environmental and financial losses [4]. Nonetheless, a

© The Author(s), under exclusive license to Springer Nature Switzerland AG 2021
N. L. Black et al. (Eds.): IEA 2021, LNNS 222, pp. 112–117, 2021.
https://doi.org/10.1007/978-3-030-74611-7_16

great deal of safety culture diagnoses applied in the oil and gas industry consist exclusively of questionnaires answered by workers of the organization being analyzed [5]. These methods, however, do not integrate the knowledge of real work situations in the development of transformations.

Human and organizational factors may be considered a new frontier in industrial safety [6]. The purpose is to effectively develop safer work practices based on detailed field analyses and thoroughly discuss the real work [7]. By analyzing a diagnosis made in oil platforms, the purpose of this study is to expand the understanding of this methodological approach and comprehend the transformation proposal developed.

2 Methodology

This study is a qualitative analysis of a case study related to the application of a safety culture diagnosis in two oil platforms. To that effect, semi-structured interviews were individually held with participants in the process, in addition to preliminary literature and document analyses. The study is descriptive, as it presents the characteristics related to project implementation and the perception of key users.

Thus, the research consists of the following sequence procedure: (i) document analysis of the safety culture assessment carried out; (ii) development of interviews; (iii) discussions with researches on the diagnostic method; (iv) analysis of interview questions; (v) visit to a unit owned by the same organization; (vi) interviews with participants; and (viii) critical analysis, as shown in Fig. 1.

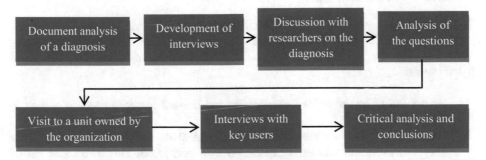

Fig. 1. Phases of the research method.

At the end of the diagnosis, researchers issued a report describing the application method and results. The data presented in this report were compared against data from the literature available. In the meantime, interviews with researchers allowed for a better understanding of details of the method and eliminated possible misunderstandings regarding document analysis interpretation.

Thus, document analysis and diagnostic method description helped the development of the interviews made with those taking part in the assessment process. The interview development and analysis processes are described below.

A guideline was developed for the exploratory interview, and was then used to make sure relevant questions were discussed, as well to maintain scope and direction.

Interviews were structured based on the type of function carried out by interviewees and directed according to the type of experience they had within the diagnosis. That being said, users were chosen for having acted in a given phase of the process, such as procurement, construction and/or diagnosis application. Each interviewee class was made up of two people, totaling eight interviews. Interviewees were selected based on the "key-informant" concept, as they had to be substantially familiar with the context and be able to help understand events and their causes [8].

Interviews with researchers lasted, on average, 30 min, and, those with other interviewees lasted, on average, one hour. Some interviews were made face-to-face, whereas others were held via video conference call or, in cases interviewees were deployed, over the phone. Due to the limitations of the research, it was not possible to interview representatives of the company's operation and maintenance crews. Thus, safety technicians participated both by applying and responding the diagnosis.

Our understanding is that the fact the current study does not contemplate all workers involved in the diagnosis does not interfere in the objectives established, which are related to providing new information that might contribute to improving the direction of future diagnosis. The representation of a given situation built by someone mainly depends on the nature of the information available, as well as on personal experience, action direction and interactions with the work collectivity [6].

3   Results

3.1   Diagnostic Method Used

The diagnosis analyzed used a quali-quantitative method and the conceptual approach provided by the ICSI (2017) [1]. The main results of this study show differences, challenges and advantages related to each one of the five phases of the process, which are listed below:

I.   Preparation: The use of local safety data and leadership engagement in questionnaire development.
II.   Quantitative analysis: The questionnaire was read together with participants and points requiring further clarification were addressed. This interaction led to improvements throughout the process.
III.   Exploring the answers: Researchers analyzed the answers given to the questionnaire.
IV.   Qualitative analysis: Answers were interpreted together with participants, according to the reality of the work in question.
V.   Feedback: Meetings with leaderships and reporting.

Ten meetings were held during the fourth phase, consisting of group discussions with overall participation of 67 people. Contributions made by these discussion groups will be presented in more details in the following topic (item 3.2). In addition to questionnaire data, concrete examples obtained from the ergonomic assessment of field activities contributed to discussions during this phase.

This diagnosis showed that spaces intended for discussions are essential to improve knowledge on actual field situations and, in turn, to transform local culture. Moreover, the constant development of initiative behaviors, as well as the teams' power to act, must always be addressed.

This method led to proposals of actions aimed at safety culture transformation, including: (i) Foster the integration between offshore and onshore teams, with the purpose of communicating and discussing project and transformation actions with the workforce; (ii) Transform existing safety meetings, addressing issues related to ongoing activities in the platform; (iii) Restructure the anomaly reporting system; (iv) Develop the power to act in all sectors; (v) Transform management tools; (vi) Restructure the standard development and alteration process, promoting collective discussions, for instance; (vii) Assert the right of refusal both for company and outsourced employees; (viii) Train the leadership in Industrial Safety Human and Organizational Factors.

Thus, the main actions proposed by the diagnosis address workers' learning process, identification of issues and solutions by field workers, and the right of refusal. To that effect, the organization must understand both organizational and system failures.

3.2 Contributions of Spaces Intended for Discussions on the Real Work

Spaces intended for discussions on the real work were identified, in a larger or smaller scale, throughout all phases of the diagnosis analyzed. For instance, leadership engagement was key in the preparation process, whereas the interaction between researchers and respondents in the quantitative phase led to improvements in the questionnaire. This session will focus mainly on the contributions made by the discussion groups.

The interviews with contracting parties and platform managers reinforced the fact that the culture is quite heterogeneous between company units, as mentioned by one of the interviewees:

"We are talking about a corporate area that deals with a company with facilities located all over the country. Thus, setting corporate standards, programs and procedures is extremely complex, as something may go very well in one location, may do ok in another location, and may be a total failure at a third location. So, the fact that corporate is making an effort to listen to us - and I believe this is the secret for success - allowing for a guideline, a program to fulfill its objective, but, at the same time, also allowing for some flexibility for this guideline or program to be absorbed by the culture. Because if it's not absorbed by the culture, it will eventually disappear."

Interviewees' perception is that face-to-face diagnosis have advantages when compared to a questionnaire sent by e-mail. The possibility of discussing, commenting, and understanding what was said provides information that is reflected in the answers, as well as feedback which is closer to the reality of the work.

Discussion groups were homogeneous and formed according to the hierarchy and function of each participant. This was done both to drive the discussion toward real work situations and to avoid any discomfort related to anyone's position. The issues that best represented each theme were chosen to foster group discussions.

The main issues raised were those whose answers showed more striking differences of opinion, when, for instance, "the boss believes one thing and subordinates believe something else." As safety culture is about shared values, whenever a major discrepancy in these values is identified, it means the points of view are extremely far apart and sharing might be compromised. However, other issues in which discrepancies were not identified were also discussed, as the purpose of group discussions was also to understand whether individual answers represented, in fact, what a single individual or the collectivity thought. These specificities, or exceptions, contributed to improving the understanding of work reality, as well as of the local safety culture.

Managers' perception was that the opportunity to have work teams taking part in the diagnosis made it possible to collect important information, because, according to one of the interviewees:

"We might create as many opportunities to listen to the workforce as we possibly can, but we aren't always able to streamline things as well as they did with the safety diagnosis, to capture major opportunities. Interaction with the workforce was extremely positive. The currently deployed leadership experienced the safety culture diagnosis and was able to enjoy its benefits, being able to rely on more openness, more interaction with the team, discussing the matters identified in the diagnosis."

Thus, the interviews held in this study showed that those who took part in the diagnosis have a good perception of the process. Such perception comes basically from the fact that a space was made available for field professionals to share their opinions, and also from the possibility of collecting information and opportunities more closely related to real work situations Thus, it consists of an in-depth work, for it is not always possible to collect opinions "that well", quoting one of the leaders interviewed.

4 Conclusion

The results show each diagnosis phase, from preparation to data treatment and presentation of results. This knowledge on the advantages and challenges related to the approach used contribute to a reflection on each and every step taken.

The work consisted of a participatory diagnosis, and the impact on social construction with a leadership turned up to be key since questionnaire development began. In addition, managers' involvement in the development of the diagnosis made it possible, for instance, to mobilize the participating teams, which were required to leave their work activities.

The questionnaire was built according to the unit's local reality and was adapted in a way for it to be better understood by workers. The interpretation of answers based on collective confrontation was crucial to allow for a representation which is closer to reality, as well as for new data related to real work situations to be collected, reflections which would not be likely to appear individually. The spaces intended for discussions with field teams made it possible for concrete everyday data to be extracted.

Throughout the process, the questions that made up the quantitative phase went through a critical analysis and the understanding of their applicability was improved. Following the spaces intended for discussions with homogeneous groups, meetings were held to provide feedback to the company, as well as to develop the report containing the results and later provide leadership training on the topic.

All of this process adopted a strategy to group up and adapt tools to discuss actual field work and activities. The several characteristics synthesized above were perceived by participants as advantages in terms of obtaining concrete data which is in line with the work reality. This data made it possible to improve existing work practices, which have been incorporated to the transformation proposals presented previously in item 3.1.

The main limitation of the current study was the lack of access to the platforms where the diagnosis was carried out, which happened due to bureaucratic and financial reasons. Despite that, interviews were made with participants who still work in such platforms and, as an alternative, a visit was made to another platform owned by the same company, with the purpose of gaining familiarity with the company's safety programs and everyday offshore safety activities. Thus, the reliability of the study was not affected, and it may be continued and serve as the grounds for future studies.

Even though there was no follow-up of the actions proposed proposed in the diagnosis, companies must prepare for that. Safety culture transformation and development is a long-term work that must be carried out in each and every production unit. The diagnosis process, with its quantitative and qualitative phases, allied with the knowledge stemming from detailed analysis of activities and discussion spaces fostered reflections on facilities' routine and safety conditions.

References

1. Besnard, D., Boissières, I., Daniellou, F., Villena, J.: ICSI - Institut pour une culture de sécurité industrielle. The essentials of Safety Culture. ICSI, Toulouse, França (ISNN 2554–9308) (2017). https://www.icsi-eu.org/docsi/fr/the-essentials-of-safety-culture-f534?id_cible=6. Accessed 31 Sept 2018
2. Duarte, F.: Safety culture in the ergonomics perspective: case study in offshore platforms. In: Arezes P. (eds.) Advances in Safety Management and Human Factors. AHFE 2017. Advances in Intelligent Systems and Computing, vol 604, Springer, Cham (2018)
3. Daniellou, F.: The French-speaking ergonomists' approach to work activity: cross influences of field intervention and conceptual models. Theoretical Issues Ergon. Sci. 6(5), 409–427 (2005)
4. Antonsen, S.: Safety Culture: Theory. Ashgate Publishing, Ltd, Method and Improvement (2009)
5. Mercado, M.P., Gallier, U., Alonso, C.M.C., Duarte, F.J.C.M.: Safety culture in oil and gas industry: a systematic review. Rio Oil and Gas 2018, ISSN 2525–7560, IBP1786_18, Brasil (2018)
6. Daniellou, F., Boissières, I., Simard, M.: Human and organizational factors of safety: state of the art. FonCSI., p.105, Les cahiers de la sécurité industrielle (2011)
7. Rocha, R., Mollo, V., Daniellou, F.: Contributions and conditions of structured debates on work on safety construction. Saf. Sci. 113, 192–199 (2019)
8. Patton, M.Q.: Qualitative Evaluation and Research Methods. 3ed. Sage Publications, Thousand Oaks (2002)

Occupational Exoskeletons: A New Challenge for Human Factors, Ergonomics and Safety Disciplines in the Workplace of the Future

Luigi Monica[1]([✉]) [iD], Francesco Draicchio[1], Jesús Ortiz[2], Giorgia Chini[1], Stefano Toxiri[2], and Sara Anastasi[1]

[1] Italian Workers' Compensation Authority (INAIL),
Via Roberto Ferruzzi, 38/40, 00143 Rome, Italy
l.monica@inail.it
[2] Advanced Robotics, Italian Institute of Technology (IIT),
Via S. Quirico, 19D, 16163 Genoa, Italy

Abstract. The growing interest in exoskeletons indicates that wearable robotic devices will represent one of the next changes in many occupational scenarios and new challenge for human factors, ergonomics and safety disciplines.

Despite the high interest in exoskeletons with an occupational application to prevent work-related musculoskeletal disorders (WRMSDs), large-scale implementation of this type of exoskeletons has still a long way to go, mainly because there is little knowledge of these wearable service robot devices and their real preventive effects on WRMSDs, and because of some technical and user acceptability issues.

The objective of the work is to represent the state of the art of occupational exoskeletons and to illustrate the new challenges for ergonomics and safety disciplines. So, The work provides same needs must be met and what requirements this typology of exoskeleton must possess, in order to maximize the user benefits and minimize potential negative impacts, using a human-centred design (HCD) and presents results of a joint INAIL/IIT project on collaborative exoskeletons.

Keywords: Exoskeletons · Human factors · Ergonomics

1 Introduction

1.1 Problem Statement

Robotic devices, such as exoskeletons, typically perform or support the performance of tasks to improve the quality of life of intended users. In particular, manual material handling (MMH) is a common physically demanding activity in many occupational contexts. MMH includes tasks such as dynamic lifting and prolonged stooped postures, can generate considerable compressive pressure on the lumbar spine and is one of the main risk factors for work-related musculoskeletal disorders (WRMSDs). WRMSDs not only increase the costs sustained by companies but, most importantly, have a severe impact

© The Author(s), under exclusive license to Springer Nature Switzerland AG 2021
N. L. Black et al. (Eds.): IEA 2021, LNNS 222, pp. 118–127, 2021.
https://doi.org/10.1007/978-3-030-74611-7_17

on workers' quality of life [1]. Safety and ergonomic guidelines for the workplace aim to reduce the workload on workers, often resulting in very strict limitations on MMH operations in terms of object weights and movement frequency [2]. With the use of technical devices, such as external manipulators, which unload all or part of the weight to be handled, the physical workload on workers can be reduced. Nevertheless, in some circumstances, such devices, and other technical and organisational measures to design workplaces, can be impractical or infeasible, and therefore it becomes necessary to consider the use of exoskeletons. As a matter of fact, there are many workplaces that are not tied to a specific location, where ergonomic design measures cannot be implemented because of the changing environmental requirements. In all these contexts, exoskeletons may offer a several of possibilities to improve working conditions and help prevent WRMSDs. Exoskeletons can be defined as personal assistance systems that affect the body in a mechanical way [3] and are normally classified as active or passive systems. Active exoskeletons (see Fig. 1) use actuators (mechanical drive components) to support human movements. Most active exoskeletons use electric motors. A computer program based on sensor information controls the action of the actuators during operation. In contrast, passive exoskeletons (see Fig. 2) use the restoring forces of springs, dampers, or other materials to support human movement. The movements of the user generate the energy stored in a passive exoskeleton. Furthermore, forces are redistributed to protect specific body regions. There are many possible applications of exoskeletons, which include physical therapy for clinical motor rehabilitation, assistance for people with motor impairments or those in the military, and even protective or enhancing gear for sports [4]. In general, an exoskeleton can be defined as a machinery in the field of the

Fig. 1. Examples of lumbar support Active exoskeletons: XoTrunk – INAIL/IIT project on collaborative exoskeletons

Fig. 2. Commercially available upper-limb passive exoskeleton: EksoVest by Ekso Bionics [6]

regulations of the Machinery Directive of the European Union (directive 2006/42/CE). Recently, there has been increasing interest in employing exoskeletons to reduce the physical load on workers carrying out demanding activities in several occupational sectors, because these devices may offer an alternative to existing solutions when the latter are not practicable. These exoskeletons are referred to as occupational exoskeletons. Despite the high interest in exoskeletons with an occupational application, large-scale implementation of this type of exoskeletons has still a long way to go [5], mainly because there is little knowledge of these wearable service robot devices and their real preventive effects on WRMSDs, and because of some technical and user acceptability issues. In fact, although the potential benefit of exoskeletons preventing WRMSDs could be significant, it is important to take into consideration several specific ergonomic issues, which need to be addressed to promote more widespread use of exoskeletons in the workplace.

2 Methodology

2.1 Occupational Exoskeletons: Difficulty of Acceptance by Workers

For workers wearing occupational exoskeletons (both active and passive), several risk scenarios can be defined relating to their prolonged use. In this regard, the French National Research and Safety Institute for the Prevention of Occupational Accidents and Diseases (INRS) has published an overview of the new risk factors encountered in the workplace while using exoskeletons [7]. New potential health risks could occur because of the redistribution of stress to other body regions. The use of exoskeletons also affects motor control, joint stability and altered kinematics. There are also some technical, safety and ergonomic issues that need to be considered and solved first to imagine large-scale implementation of occupational exoskeletons. One reason might be, for example, the level of discomfort associated with wearing the exoskeleton [8]. The elimination of discomfort at the physical user interface with the equipment could be the next challenge in the design of exoskeletons, bearing in mind that even a minimal level of discomfort might hinder acceptance by users. Another concern regarding passive devices is related to the potentially increased activity of leg or arm muscles. Active exoskeletons may have greater potential to reduce physical loads than passive exoskeletons, lightening the load on many joints throughout the body. However, with increasing numbers of joints and their actuators, and power supply, the weight of the exoskeleton will increase. The exoskeleton replicates the movements of the worker, i.e., the limbs of the human and the exoskeleton are aligned during motion. This requires the exoskeleton to detect how the human intends to move so that the actuators can respond appropriately. Distinguishing intended from unintended movements is often difficult and results in systems with many kinds of sensors and complex signal processing. Lazzaroni et al. [9] address the necessity for improved control strategies to enable smooth movements at a normal to fast pace, human–machine information exchange, real-time motion planning and safety control are the difficulties faced in building such a control strategy. Another concern is that international safety standards for occupational application of exoskeletons do not yet exist. This is a significant barrier to their adoption. To date, only the ISO/DIS 18646-4, which provides performance criteria and related test methods for medical lower-back support robots. In addition to the above technical challenges, and the safety and regulatory aspects of large-scale implementation of occupational exoskeletons, user acceptability is a crucial factor for the real implementation of these devices in the workplace. Recent publications looking at the barriers to acceptance and utilization of wearable technology noted that the device must not only be safe, comfortable, useful, and usable but, just as importantly, must be desirable to the end user [10]. For this reason, it is advisable to resort to a human-centred design approach to involve the users (companies and workers) directly in the exoskeleton design process.

2.2 Human-Centred Design and Occupational Exoskeletons

Human-centred design is an approach to interactive development that aims to make systems usable and useful by focusing on the users, their needs and their require-ments, and by applying human factors/ergonomics, and usability knowledge and techniques. This approach enhances effectiveness and efficiency, improves human well-being, user satisfaction, accessibility, and sustainability, and counteracts possible adverse effects of use on human health, safety and performance. The EN ISO 9241–210:2019 aims to make this information available to help to develop systems follow-ing an interactive process, where appropriate. This standard is specifically for managing hardware and software design and redesign processes, but the approach can also be useful for other complex systems such as the design of an occupational exoskeleton. In the literature, there are some applications of HCD to optimize the design of robotic exoskeletons, especially for rehabilitation purposes [11] or for general investigation [12]. Another useful standard for the scope of HCD is EN 614-2:2000 + A1:2008 (EN, 2008), which focuses on the interactions between the design of machinery and work tasks. This standard is a harmonized standard published in the Official Journal for the Machinery Directive (2006/42/EC).

3 Results

3.1 Design Characteristics of a Safe Occupational Exoskeleton

When adopting the HCD process, understanding and describing the user context is the first step to take. Therefore, for occupational exoskeletons it is of great importance to define the characteristics of the workplace and the MMH activities to be carried out by the worker. In this case it is useful to refer to the ISO/TR 12295:2014 technical report on the manual handling of loads and the evaluation of static working postures. Based on this procedure have to be define the tasks per-formed by the worker, such as:

- lifting and carrying weights,
- pushing and pulling weights,
- moving light weights at high frequency,
- static working postures.

Other aspects to consider at this stage relate to:

- the handling load (e.g. mass, size/dimension, grip/handles),
- environmental aspects (e.g. temperature, outdoor/indoor activity, restricted spaces, work space features),
- production conditions (e.g. times and working methods, price of the device),
- workers' characteristics (e.g. gender, age, qualifications, skill).

The second stage of the HCD process is specifying user requirements. In general, in the literature, the following main requirements have been identified:

- freedom of movement (e.g. body postures, dimensions of the device),
- comfort (e.g. postural and physiological comfortable angle),
- environmental conditions (e.g. interaction between operators, caloric/metabolic expenditure),
- wearability (e.g. material, shape of the device, adaptability),
- intuitiveness of use (e.g. cognitive resources required),
- biomechanical aspects (e.g. force/pressure in the different parts of the body, vibrations, noise, distribution of the weight on the operator's body),
- physiological aspects and effects (e.g. right balance between activity and in-activity).

Furthermore, other secondary aspects can encourage the acceptance of the system, such as the aesthetics of the occupational exoskeleton. In Table 1, the ergonomic standards useful for designing safe occupational exoskeletons are listed. After these activities, the HCD approach of EN ISO 9241–210:2019 gives other structured steps that the designer has to follow to target the design solutions to meet context and user requirements. One ideal choice for some of the abovementioned aspects is to develop anthropomorphic occupational exoskeletons to reflect the human anatomy, kinematics, and kinetics to enable natural and comfortable movements. Other ideas that can address the need for design solutions to meet the context and user requirements for an active exoskeleton could be:

- Power supplies with batteries and not cables to guarantee freedom of movement for the worker.
- Reduce the weight of the exoskeleton.
- Increase the adaptability, for example with gender-related assessment.

The last step of the HCD process is the evaluation of the gap between the design context and user requirements, reiterated as many times as necessary. Furthermore, as solutions evolve (e.g., lighter materials, smaller components, wearable computing, artificial intelligence), the designer, with the help of users, will continue to work on making a device acceptable and, more importantly, ensuring that it will be used.

Table 1. International standards for the design characteristics of safe occupational exoskeletons

Operator's variability	Physical dimension	EN 547-3:1996 + A1:2008 – Safety of machinery – Human body measurements — Part 3: Anthropometric data EN 614-1:2006 + A1:2009 – Safety of machinery – Ergonomic design principles – Part 1: Terminology and general principles EN 894-1:1997 + A1:2008 – Safety of machinery – Ergonomics requirements for the design of displays and control actuators – Part 1: General principles for human interactions with displays and control actuators EN 1005-1:2001 + A1:2008 – Safety of machinery – Human physical performance – Part 1: Terms and definitions EN 1005-4:2005 + A1:2008 – Safety of machinery – Human physical performance – Part 4: Evaluation of working postures and movements in relation to machinery access into machinery EN ISO 14738:2008 – Safety of machinery – Anthropometric requirements for the design of workstations at machinery EN ISO 15536-1:2008 – Ergonomics – Computer manikins and body templates – Part 1: General requirements EN ISO 7250-1:2017 – Basic human body measurements for technological design – Part 1: Body measurement definitions CEN ISO/TR 7250-2:2011 + A1:2013 – Basic human body measurements for technological design: Statistical summaries of body measurements from national populations
	Strength	EN 614-1:2006 + A1:2009 EN 1005-1:2001 + A1:2008 EN 1005-2:2003 + A1:2008 – Safety of machinery – Human physical performance – Part 2: Manual handling of machinery and component parts of machinery EN 1005-3:2002 + A1:2008 – Safety of machinery – Human physical performance – Part 3: Recommended force limits for machinery operation EN ISO 15536-1:2008
Space for movement	Posture	EN 614-1:2006 + A1:2009 EN 1005-1:2001 + A1:2008 EN 1005-2:2003 + A1:2008 EN 1005-3:2002 + A1:2008 EN 1005-4:2005 + A1:2008 – Safety of machinery – Human physical performance – Part 4: Evaluation of working postures and movements in relation to machinery access into machinery EN ISO 14738:2008 EN ISO 15536-1:2008

(*continued*)

Table 1. (*continued*)

Operator's variability	Physical dimension	EN 547-3:1996 + A1:2008 – Safety of machinery – Human body measurements — Part 3: Anthropometric data EN 614-1:2006 + A1:2009 – Safety of machinery – Ergonomic design principles – Part 1: Terminology and general principles EN 894-1:1997 + A1:2008 – Safety of machinery – Ergonomics requirements for the design of displays and control actuators – Part 1: General principles for human interactions with displays and control actuators EN 1005-1:2001 + A1:2008 – Safety of machinery – Human physical performance – Part 1: Terms and definitions EN 1005-4:2005 + A1:2008 – Safety of machinery – Human physical performance – Part 4: Evaluation of working postures and movements in relation to machinery access into machinery EN ISO 14738:2008 – Safety of machinery – Anthropometric requirements for the design of workstations at machinery EN ISO 15536-1:2008 – Ergonomics – Computer manikins and body templates – Part 1: General requirements EN ISO 7250-1:2017 – Basic human body measurements for technological design – Part 1: Body measurement definitions CEN ISO/TR 7250-2:2011 + A1:2013 – Basic human body measurements for technological design: Statistical summaries of body measurements from national populations
	Strength	EN 614-1:2006 + A1:2009 EN 1005-1:2001 + A1:2008 EN 1005-2:2003 + A1:2008 – Safety of machinery – Human physical performance – Part 2: Manual handling of machinery and component parts of machinery EN 1005-3:2002 + A1:2008 – Safety of machinery – Human physical performance – Part 3: Recommended force limits for machinery operation EN ISO 15536-1:2008
	Dynamics	EN 614-1:2006 + A1:2009 EN 1005-1:2001 + A1:2008 EN 1005-4:2005 + A1:2008 EN ISO 14738:2008 EN ISO 15536-1:2008
Work rate	Pace	EN 1005-3:2002 + A1:2008
	Speed	EN 894-1:1997 + A1:2008
Concentration	Mental operation	EN 614-1:2006 + A1:2009 EN ISO 10075-1:2017 – Ergonomic principles related to mental work-load – Part 1: General terms and definitions EN ISO 10075-2:2000 – Ergonomic principles related to mental workload – Part 2: Design principles EN ISO 10075-3:2004- Ergonomic principles related to mental workload – Part 3: Principles and requirements concerning methods for measuring and assessing mental workload

(*continued*)

Table 1. (*continued*)

Operator's variability	Physical dimension	EN 547-3:1996 + A1:2008 – Safety of machinery – Human body measurements — Part 3: Anthropometric data EN 614-1:2006 + A1:2009 – Safety of machinery – Ergonomic design principles – Part 1: Terminology and general principles EN 894-1:1997 + A1:2008 – Safety of machinery – Ergonomics requirements for the design of displays and control actuators – Part 1: General principles for human interactions with displays and control actuators EN 1005-1:2001 + A1:2008 – Safety of machinery – Human physical performance – Part 1: Terms and definitions EN 1005-4:2005 + A1:2008 – Safety of machinery – Human physical performance – Part 4: Evaluation of working postures and movements in relation to machinery access into machinery EN ISO 14738:2008 – Safety of machinery – Anthropometric requirements for the design of workstations at machinery EN ISO 15536-1:2008 – Ergonomics – Computer manikins and body templates – Part 1: General requirements EN ISO 7250-1:2017 – Basic human body measurements for technological design – Part 1: Body measurement definitions CEN ISO/TR 7250-2:2011 + A1:2013 – Basic human body measurements for technological design: Statistical summaries of body measurements from national populations
	Strength	EN 614-1:2006 + A1:2009 EN 1005-1:2001 + A1:2008 EN 1005-2:2003 + A1:2008 – Safety of machinery – Human physical performance – Part 2: Manual handling of machinery and component parts of machinery EN 1005-3:2002 + A1:2008 – Safety of machinery – Human physical performance – Part 3: Recommended force limits for machinery operation EN ISO 15536-1:2008
	Cognitive performance	EN 614-1:2006 + A1:2009 EN ISO 10075-1:2017 EN ISO 10075-2:2000 EN ISO 10075-3:2004
Human/machinery interface	Interaction	ISO 6385:2004 – Ergonomic principles in the design of work systems EN ISO 9241-910:2011 – Ergonomics of human–system interaction – Part 910: Framework for tactile and haptic interaction
	Visual	EN 614-1:2006 + A1:2009 EN ISO 14738:2008
	Auditory	EN 614-1:2006 + A1:2009
	Sensitivity	EN ISO 7730:2005 – Ergonomics of the thermal environment – Analytical determination and interpretation of thermal comfort using calculation of the PMV and PPD indices and local thermal comfort criteria ISO 7933: 2004 – Ergonomics of the thermal environment – Analytical determination and interpretation of heat stress using calculation of the predicted heat strain EN ISO 8996:2004 – Ergonomics of the thermal environment – Determination of metabolic rate

4 Discussion

As shown in this paper, exoskeletons can support workers in performing specific tasks in some working environments, and therefore can help prevent WRMSDs. Nevertheless, for several reasons the use of occupational exoskeletons in the workplace is still rather limited. On the one hand, there is little knowledge about these devices and their real preventive effects on WRMSDs. On the other, some "significant" technical challenges and user acceptability issues explain the current state of diffusion of these wearable service robot devices in the workplace. The HCD approach can be a tool to guarantee ever more widespread diffusion of these systems, responding more and more precisely to the real needs that users manifest.

5 Conclusions

The information in this paper can be identified as a potential foundation for future occupational exoskeleton human user research and provide critical insights that will ensure that occupational exoskeletons and their many potential benefits are here to stay instead of becoming merely the next ergonomic trend in the workplace of the future for the prevention of WRMSDs. Furthermore, the use of active and passive exoskeletons makes it necessary to develop new methodologies for biomechanical risk assessment. The redistribution of forces applied to the body and the changes in kinematics and motor systems that the use of exoskeletons entails do not allow the application of existing biomechanical risk assessment methodologies.

References

1. Peters, M., Wischniewski, S.: The Impact of using exoskeletons on OSH. Discussion paper, EU-OSHA – European Agency for Safety and Health at Work. Federal Institute for Occupational Safety and Health, Dortmund, Germany (2019)
2. Garg, A.: Revised NIOSH equation for manual lifting: A method for job evaluation. Am. Assoc. Occupational Health Nurses J. **43**(4), 211–216 (1995)
3. Liedtke, M., Glitsch, U.: Exoskelette – Verordnung für persönliche Schutzausrüstung. sicher ist sicher **3**, 110–113 (2018)
4. Roam Robotics Homepage. https://www.roamrobotics.com. Accessed 01 Feb 2021
5. Toxiri, S., Näf, M.B., Lazzaroni, M., Fernández, J., Sposito, M., Poliero, T., Monica, L., Anastasi, S., Caldwell, D.G., Ortiz, J.: Back-support exoskeletons for occupational use: an overview of technological advances and trends. IISE Trans. Occupational Ergon. Hum. Factors **7**(3–4), 237–249 (2019)
6. Ahsan Gull, M., Bai, S., Bak, T.: A review on design of upper limb exoskeletons. Robotics **9**(1), 16 (2020)
7. INRS. Acquisition et integration d'un exosquelette en entreprise: Guide pour les préventeurs. Institut National de Recherche et de Sécurité, Paris (2019). https://www.inrs.fr/media.html?refINRS=ED%206315

8. Poliero, T., Toxiri, S., Anastasi, S., Monica, L., Caldwell, D.G., Ortiz, J.: Assessment of an on-board classifier for activity recognition on an active back-support exoskeleton. In: IEEE International Conference on Rehabilitation Robotics, pp. 559–564 (2019)9. Lazzaroni, M., Toxiri, S., Caldwell, D.G., Anastasi, S., Monica, L., Momi, E.D., Ortiz, J. Acceleration-based assistive strategy to control a back-support exoskeleton for load handling: Preliminary evaluation. IEEE International Conference on Rehabilitation Robotics, pp. 625–630 (2019).
9. Lazzaroni, M., Toxiri, S., Caldwell, D.G., Anastasi, S., Monica, L., Momi, E.D., Ortiz, J.: Acceleration-based assistive strategy to control a back-support exoskeleton for load handling: Preliminary evaluation. In: IEEE International Conference on Rehabilitation Robotics, pp. 625–630 (2019)
10. Jacobs, J.V., Hettinger, L.J., Huang, Y.-H., Jeffries, S., Lesch, M.F., Simmons, L.A., Verma, S.K., Willetts, J.L.: Employee acceptance of wearable technology in the workplace. Appl. Ergon. **78**, 148–156 (2019)
11. Zhou, L., Li, Y., Bai, S.: A human-centered design optimization approach for robotic exoskeletons through biomechanical simulation. Robot. Autonomous Syst. **91**, 337–347 (2017)
12. Davis, K.G., Reid, C.R., Rempel, D.D., Treaster, D. Introduction to the human factors special issue on user-centered design for exoskeleton. Human Factors **62**(3), 333–336 (2020). Special issue: User-Centered Design for Exoskeleton & Exosuit Usage'

Acting in Safety from the Design to the Implementation of Helicopter Maintenance

Camille Murie[1,3(✉)], Willy Buchmann[1], Lucie Cuvelier[2], Flore Barcellini[1], Fabien Bernard[3], and Raphaël Paquin[3]

[1] CRTD, CNAM Paris, 41 rue Gay Lussac, 75005 Paris, France
{camille.murie,willy.buchmann,flore.barcellini}@lecnam.net
[2] 2C3U-Paragraphe, Université Paris 8, 2 rue de la Liberté, 93526 Saint-Denis, France
lucie.cuvelier@univ-paris8.fr
[3] Airbus Helicopters, Aéroport International Marseille Provence, 13700 Marignane, France
{fabien.bernard,raphael.paquin}@airbus.com

Abstract. In order to avoid helicopters accidents, maintainability engineers seek to identify, evaluate and solve what they called "the risks of maintenance errors" done by maintenance mechanics, and sometimes pilots performing simple pre-flight maintenance tasks. Here we will argue that beyond trying to avoid errors by following procedures, acting safely involves trade-offs between safety and performance within the engineers' and mechanics' activity. This papers show the relations between the mechanics' and engineers' work using the Critical Incident interview technique.

Keywords: Safety · Maintenance · Conception · Critical incident interview

1 Introduction

Saleh et al. (2019) presented maintenance as causal factors of accidents in 14% to 21% of helicopter accidents in the U.S. civil fleet between 2005 and 2015. In order to avoid these accidents, maintainability engineers in Airbus Helicopters' maintainability department seek to identify, evaluate and solve what they called "the risks of maintenance errors" done by maintenance mechanics. The maintainability team contributes to design helicopters and safe maintenance procedures within the complex process design of a helicopter involving many design actors (Bernard et al. 2019). In this context, the industrial thesis work presented here is based on an action research. Design science work emphasizes the distributed nature of design (Darses and Falzon 1996): in time, space, or in various organizations, and among various protagonists with their own goals and perspectives. As a result, design processes often take on a "conflictual" character. Designing then requires negotiations and the articulation of these different perspectives and goals. Negotiation is the process of elaborating rules through the construction of trade-offs that lead to agreements on the actions to be undertaken (Hollnagel 2009). The artefacts designed are thus the result of these different trade-offs in relation to the initial

© The Author(s), under exclusive license to Springer Nature Switzerland AG 2021
N. L. Black et al. (Eds.): IEA 2021, LNNS 222, pp. 128–135, 2021.
https://doi.org/10.1007/978-3-030-74611-7_18

design intent (Bucciarelli 1988). This design process continues in the use of the artefacts by users, who can develop new uses that can themselves be taken up by the designers (Bourmaud & Rétaux 2002). Reason's model (1990) highlights the primordial role of decision-makers and designers in the design of work situations presenting latent conditions of error that can lead to accidents. Workers are not passive but adapt the safety rules given to them by designers (Amalberti 2013; de Terssac and Mignard 2011). They adapt the rules in their work through processes of rule negotiation, which is done by establishing trade-offs between safety and performance. The notion of safety in action testifies to the fact that workers put these rules into action by deciding whether or not to integrate them into their action according to the context (de Terssac and Gaillard 2009). Here we will present the first part of the current thesis, which aims to provide answers to the following questions: In which situations maintainability engineers and maintenance operators build trade-offs between performance and safety? In what way is their work related?

2 Methods

Context - Most of the maintenance operations are carried out outside the manufacturer's premises, at the premises of customers who operate the aircraft or at approved maintenance workshops all around the world. We have therefore chosen a methodology for collecting information remotely from our workplace and for accessing the variability of the helicopter maintenance; the critical incident interview. The objective of the critical incident interview is to get closer to what the person has experienced by determining the critical requirements of a specific task (Bisseret Sebillotte Falzon 1999) through his or her subjectivity and experience. Butterfield et al. (2005) propose three operational criteria used in the choice of incidents: (1) the incident informs us about a past event; (2) it contains a detailed description of the experience as such; (3) it describes the results of the incident. The incident selected must have had a negative or positive impact on the activity. The concept of critical incident has been replaced by significant incident by some researchers in order to avoid resistance on the part of interviewees (Butterfield et al. 2005). During the interviews we did not use the term "incident" but "situation" because the term "already" has a meaning in the field of aeronautics. An incident is an event associated with an operation on the aircraft that affects or may affect the safety of the operation. We will therefore talk about significant events later on.

Development - In the literature, critical incident interviews usually take place during a single interview or questionnaire. We deviated from this method by proposing two interviews of one hour each to the interviewees. A first exploratory interview of the participants' activity enabled us to familiarize ourselves with the participants' profession and to create the bond of trust necessary for the second interview. The second interview, the critical incident interview, allowed us to collect significant events. We begin these interviews with the following instruction: "I will ask you to remember events you have experienced that have had an impact on your ability to secure the maintenance of the helicopter. You must have experienced them and they must have been significant in your work. They may be events that had a very positive impact, a very negative impact, or an event in which you almost failed to achieve your goal."

Material and Population - Depending on the availability of the participants and the logistical constraints, the interviews took place either in person, by telephone or using a videoconferencing software. Two types of population were targeted for these interviews: (1) Those who design maintenance safety rules through maintainability, engineers working in maintainability service, (2) those who carry out maintenance, mechanics and helicopter pilots. Eight people from the maintainability department were interviewed to have at least one person from each operational function on the team, three Maintainability Engineers, two Tooling Engineers, one Maintainability Expert, one Human Factor Specialist and one Maintenance Architect. We were also able to carry out these interviews with 5 mechanics and with a pilot as an end user of the helicopter. Four of the mechanics interviewed are mechanics employed by Airbus. One is currently an engineer in the maintainability department and 3 mechanics carry out maintenance operations at customers' sites. The fifth mechanic interviewed is external to the company.

Treatment - All significant events interviews have been transcribed. The analysis of these interviews seeks to answer the following question: On which critical requirements did the significant events have an impact? This categorization will then allow us to describe how maintainability engineers and maintenance operators construct safety trade-offs. We realized an inductive thematic coding as defined by the Braun and Clarke (2006) thematic analysis method. The categories and themes of critical requirements are constructed during the coding by including elements in the categories already identified and by creating new ones if these elements cannot be placed in an existing category.

3   Results

We have identified 43 significant events, 29 of which resulted from interviews with maintainability designers and 14 from interviews with maintenance operators. The Table 1 presents the functions, the participant's identification code and the number of significant events we identified in their interview.

Within the maintainability department there are 5 different functions including one of which is called Maintainability Engineer. From now on we will designate the group of people working in the maintainability department by "maintainability designers" to differentiate the Maintainability Engineers from the others. We will then present the themes and categorizations extracted of the critical requirements needed to secure the maintenance design and implementation and the events' code included in these categories in the Table 2. Each events is identify thanks to a code included the participant's identification code and the event's number preceded by the letter I (ex, M1I1 for the first event of the first mechanic). The Table 2 should be read as follow: The significant event GSE2I1 had a positive or negative impact on the understanding of the project's history. We will explain each categories briefly before discussing them.

Table 1. Number of significant events identified in the interview for each participants.

Function	Participant's code	Number of significant events
Extern mechanic	M1	1
Airbus mechanic	M2	3
Airbus mechanics working with clients	M3	3
	TR1	2
	TR2	2
Pilot	P1	3
Maintenance architect	A1	3
Human Factor Specialist	SFH1	4
Tools engineers	GSE1	1
	GSE2	2
Maintainability engineers	SM1	5
	SM2	8
	SM3	2
Maintainability expert	EM1	3

Table 2. Categorization of the critical requirements needed to secure the maintenance design and implementation

Select the intervention method and analyze the maintainability risk

Understand the project's history (GSE2I1, SM3I1) - The Maintainability designers wanted to understand the history of the project in order to be able to intervene into the design process and evaluate the resources that could be put at their disposal

Adapt the intervention to the project's constraints (EM1I1, SM2I8) - When the constraints of the project don't allow the Maintainability designers to do "the best [they] can do in maintainability", they proposed different forms of intervention

Taking advantage of resources to analyze the risk (GSE1I1, SM2I7) - With the right resources, they organized various forms of analysis according to the complexity of the maintenance task

Choosing the analysis' complexity according to the risk (SM2I6, EM1I3) - The maintainability designers found the maintainability task complex after its first analysis. They performed simulations of the task to identify risks that were invisible during the initial analysis and tested possible solutions

(*continued*)

Table 2. (*continued*)

Mobilize the collective around maintainability

Build the solution with the other designers (SFH1I4, SFH1I5, SM1I2, SM1I5) – This categorization shows how maintainability designers worked with other engineers to build solutions that work for everyone

Focus the discussion around maintainability to deal with conflicts (A1I1, A1I3, SM1I1, SFH1I1) - The maintainability designers identified points in conflict with the requests or objectives of other designers. Their solution was to highlight the maintenance constraints and the needs of maintainability

Ask help from authority figures (SFH1I2, A1I2) – Maintainability designers asked someone they think is an authority figure to support their message

---

Build an acceptable and accepted solution (Maintainability designers)

Include the solution in the design process (SM1I4, SM2I5, SFH1I3, EM1I2) – To be discuss a proposition of solution with the other designers, Maintainability designers tried to include it in an existing process of conception

Constrain the practice of maintenance (SM2I4) – The Maintainability engineer created a rule to be sur a maintenance operation will be done by the customers

Take into account the variability of helicopters (SM2I3, GSE2I2) – The Maintainability designers wanted to design for the most version of helicopters possible and not just the most current

Negotiate to promote design changes (SM1I3, SM2I1, SM2I2) – The Maintainability designers prioritized Design modifications because they are not based on the "will" of the operators who may deviate from the procedure

---

Compensate for a lack in design through maintenance

Add operations to the procedures (M3I1, M2I2, M2I3) - The mechanics added maintenance operations from the procedure in order to act safely

Remove operations from de procedures (M3I2) - The mechanic removed maintenance operations from the procedure in order to act safely

---

Manage an unforeseen situation

Assess the need for the aircraft's availability (M1I1, TR1I2) – The mechanics chose their action based on the customer's need for the helicopter

Repatriate a helicopter (P1I1, P1I2, P1I3) – The pilot helped to do maintenance tasks in order to repatriate damaged helicopters to their base the fastest possible

Manage the resources to be in time (TR2I1, TR2I2) – The mechanics had to organize their access to resources that helped them to be in time

---

Share experiences

Contact the maintenance organization (TR1I1) – The mechanic shared his conclusions after an incident to the customer's maintenance organization

Contact the helicopter manufacturer (M2I1, M3I3) – The mechanics communicated their experiences to the customer's support service

---

4 Discussion and Conclusion

The categorization of these significant events by critical requirements for safety highlight that the construction of safety is done in the very activity of maintenance operators and Maintainability designers. It is merged with it and is not a detached, separate and different action (Terssac and Gaillard 2009). Despite what their categorization may suggest, the critical requirements presented are interrelated. Trade-offs made in one category may affect trade-offs made in another.

4.1 Trade-offs in the Design Process

The choice of the analysis' form will impact the Maintainability designers' ability to identify risks more or less in detail and easily. They take into account the context in which their analysis and their work will be able to fit. This choice will condition their strategy to mobilize the designer collective. Maintainability designers can use several strategies to mobilize the designer collective, one of them is to focus the conversation around maintainability and convince them. They can organize collective workshops with other design actors in order to analyze the situation and build solutions with them. In one event, a maintainability engineer found his project complex and thought he needed to perform tests on a physical mock-up afterwards. He then organized working groups with the other design actors to co-construct the solutions. This allowed him to discover solutions that the maintainability engineer could not have found on his own. It also involved the other actors in the choice of solutions and facilitated the release of means for the tests because the participants were at the right hierarchical level. But highlighting the requirements and constraints of maintainability does not systematically lead to it being taken into account by the collective. That can be done according to the legitimacy that other designers give to risk analysis in the face of their own constraints. Oppositions may then persist and the engineer's solution proposals may be rejected. The collective mobilization around the constraints of maintainability conditions the process of building solutions.

Maintainability engineers build trade-offs between their goal of achieving an ideal solution from a maintainability point of view and the constraints and goals of other design actors with whom they may be in conflict. According to Benchekroun (2017), conflicts are not always an obstacle, they can be a resource of work if they are respected, listened to and worked on. For the maintainability designers an ideal solution is a solution that will be accepted by the other actors of the design, which gives the mechanic the possibility to carry out a maintenance procedure that is deemed to be risk-free. They can sometimes have the goal of constraining the mechanic's activity to avoid violations procedures. If the collective reject their solution, they will suggest alternative solutions that are either to add maintenance operations that can "lead to new human factors risks", to modify the work cards sent to the customer or to warn him of the identified risk. We can then put forward the role of conflictual cooperation in the development of conflicts in resources for activity (Benchekroun 2017). Fournier et al. (2001) define conflictual cooperation "as a mode of relationship based on critical collaboration ranging from the creation of alliances when possible to conflict when it becomes necessary to increase the power of influence". The notion of conflictual cooperation makes it possible to reflect on the collective work mechanisms of designers immersed in a system with contradictory injunctions.

4.2   Adapt Procedures to the Maintenance Situation

Maintenance operators show their ability to act safely through the mobilization of knowledge of prudence (Cru 2014) and by adapting the procedures to the situation. For example, during an inspection in a context where the availability of the aircraft was not urgent, the mechanic added dismantling operations to make sure he could do the task safely. He considered the elements on which he had to intervene were too difficult to access and that there was a risk of damaging the elements in the vicinity, which are very sensitive to shocks. The task he had to perform in 1h30 according to the procedure finally took him 1 day and a half. We can say here that the helicopter design, result of maintenance designers' work is at this event's root.

The trade-off between safety and performance is achieved by taking into account the time pressure and the resources available to the mechanic (Atak and Kingma 2011; Chang and Wang 2010). One of the significant events followed a planned maintenance operation. During an oil sampling that was supposed to take 10 min, the home-made hose used for the sampling fell into the main gearbox. The mechanic, with the help of his workshop manager, then spent 1 h finding a way to retrieve it in a context of high time pressure. Each time the operator re-evaluated the situation, he had to re-evaluate his decision not to request a replacement helicopter and to continue in the hope of being within the contractual time frame with the client. Here the mechanic finally manage to secure the helicopter but the event was initially caused by the lack of existence of a proper tool to realize the oil sample.

4.3   Build the Safety with Maintenance Operators' Feedback?

The parallel analysis of the significant events of maintenance operators and engineers shows us that maintainability engineers are looking for feedback on the work of mechanics by simulating the maintenance task or by interviewing in-house mechanics. At the same time, some maintenance operators their knowledge to the designers of these procedures in the hope of avoiding an incident in the future. When mechanics have to compensate for a lack of helicopter design and/or procedures and when they face an unforeseen situation they learn from the event, which impacts their future business to a greater or lesser extent.

Three significant events are centered on the sharing of this experience, either to the maintenance organization in their field or to the aircraft manufacturer. For example, during a visual inspection, a customer mechanic becomes aware of premature wear of an equipment. The element had not been correctly installed during the last maintenance operation. He remembered an older similar case in a different department than his own. The problem was due to the incomprehension from some mechanics of the procedure. The mechanic then contacted the manufacturer to trace the problem and propose modifications in the writing of the procedure and to put visual aids on a tooling concerned. One year later, the mechanic did not see any modifications and still does not understand what is preventing the manufacturer from carrying out what he considers to be simple actions. The mechanics' sharing of experience can, however, pay off. For a mechanic who is employed by the manufacturer and who maintains an aircraft that is in the process of being developed, his work of sharing his experience has led to the modification of the work card, which he believed to be false.

In fact, the conditions for the success of feedback both in its implementation and its effectiveness depend on the organizational and socio-cultural factors structuring it (Gaillard 2005). The main reasons for the difficulties of feedback "ie in the existence of different paradigms, cultural differences between disciplines and professions, but are also due to fear of sanctions, interference with the legal system and the media, as well as competition" (Gaillard 2005). Here too, we highlight the primordial role of a maintenance design result that takes into account feedback of maintenance operators for its durability.

References

Amalberti, R.: Navigating safety: Necessary compromises and trade-offs-theory and practice, vol. 13. springer, Heidelberg (2013)

Atak, A., Kingma. S.: Safety culture in an aircraft maintenance organisation: a view from the inside. Saf. Sci. **49**(2), 268–278 (2010)

Benchekroun, T.H.: Organiser la participation et l'agir collectif pour rendre le travail supportable. Sci. sociales et santé **35**(4), 97–104 (2017)

Bernard, F., Zare, M., Sagot, J. C., Paquin, R.: Using digital and physical simulation to focus on human factors and ergonomics in aviation maintainability. Human factors. **62**(1), 37–54 (2019)

Bisseret, A., Sebillotte, S., Falzon, P.: Techniques pratiques pour l'étude des activités expertes. Octarè (1999)

Bourmaud, G., Rétaux, X.: Rapports entre conception institutionnelle et conception dans l'usage. In: Proceedings of the 14th Conference on l'Interaction Homme-Machine, pp. 137–144 (2002)

Braun, V., Clarke, V.: Using thematic analysis in psychology. Qualitative Res. Psychol. **3**(2), 77–101 (2006)

Bucciarelli, L.: An ethnographic perspective on engineering design. Design Stud. **9**(3), 159–168 (1988)

Butterfield, L.D., Borgen, W.A., Amundson, N.E., Maglio, A.S.T.: Fifty years of the critical incident technique: 1954–2004 and beyond. Qualitative research **5**(4), 475–497 (2005)

Chang, Y., Wang, Y.: Significant human risk factors in aircraft maintenance technicians. Saf. Sci. **48**(1), 54–62 (2010)

Cru, D.: La prudence: des savoir-faire à la langue de métier. Clinique du travail, pp. 75–109 (2014)

De Terssac, G., Gaillard, I.: La sécurité en action. Toulouse: Octares (2009)

De Terssac, G., Mignard, J.: Les paradoxes de la sécurité. Le cas d'AZF. PUF (2011)

Falzon, P., Darses, F.: La conception collective: une approche de l'ergonomie cognitive. Coopération et conception, Octarès, 123–135 (1996).

Fournier, D., René, J.F., Duval, M., Garon, S., Fontaine, A., Chénard, J., Lefebvre, C.: La dynamique partenariale sur les pratiques des organismes communautaires dans le contexte de la réorganisation du réseau de la santé et des services sociaux. Nouvelles pratiques sociales **14**(1), 111–131 (2001)

Gaillard, I.: État des connaissances sur le retour d'expérience industriel et ses facteurs sociocul- turels de réussite ou d'échec. Cahier de l'ICSI (2) (2005)

Hollnagel, E.: The ETTO principle: efficiency-thoroughness trade-off: why things that go right sometimes go wrong. Ashgate Publishing, Ltd. (2009)

Reason, J.: Human Error. Cambridge University PRESS (1990)

Saleh, J.H., Tikayat Ray, A., Zhang, K.S., Churchwell, J.S.: Maintenance and inspection as risk factors in helicopter accidents: Analysis and recommendations. PloS one **14**(2) (2019)

Development of Non-contact Ubiquitous Monitoring System Embedded into Chair and Bed for Continuous Cardiac Monitoring

Priyadarshini Natarajan, Ananthakumar Balukkannu, and Venkatesh Balasubramanian[✉]

Indian Institute of Technology Madras, Chennai 600036, India
chanakya@iitm.ac.in

Abstract. Workplace stress and fatigue due to long working hours and prolonged cognitive workload has been reported to be a significant predictor of cardiovascular diseases. Continuous monitoring of cardiac activity could provide to be a way to identify the early onset of stress and fatigue. However, the discomfort brought by ECG measurement electrodes has been a challenge for long term ubiquitous monitoring at the workplace. In this study, we have developed tin-coated copper active electrodes embedded onto a mat that can be fastened to an office chair or bed allowing unobtrusive measurement of cardiac activity. The experimental results from filtering and R peak detection of cECG measurements show high accuracy, and the heart rate calculated had a very high correlation with the conventional ECG measurements for both chair ($r = 0.991$, $p < 0.01$) and bed ($r = 0.981$, $p < 0.01$) form factors. The decrease in the mean squared error of computed heart rates from cECG measurements on chair (MSE $= 0.43$ bpm) could be attributed to increased lumbar contact as compared to lying down on bed (MSE $= 1.13$ bpm). The developed cECG sensor and measurement system could be seamlessly integrated into everyday objects such as chair, bed and car seat for unobtrusive cardiac monitoring with no prior preparations. Further heart rate variability studies to identify the markers of changes in sympathetic nervous activity could provide an early indicator of stress and fatigue to promote an active and healthy lifestyle in the workplace.

Keywords: Workplace wellbeing · Capacitive ECG monitoring · Ubiquitous health monitoring · Sensor embedding · Chair/bed form factors · Signal appraisal

1 Introduction

Cardiovascular diseases (CVDs) have become the leading cause of mortality in India with a death rate of 272 per 100000 population higher than the global average [1]. Recently CVDs have been characterized with early onset of disease, rapid progression and high case fatality ratio. Work stressors characterized by long working hours and prolonged increased mental workload are associated with early-onset and elevated risk of CVDs [2, 3]. Fatigue and burnouts leading from long working hours have shown to decrease employee productivity and led to increased errors in the workplace. Though the manifestation of stress and fatigue is unique for each person, their characteristic markers could be observed from behavioural, electrophysiological or psychoneurological studies. Stress and acute fatigue have been characterized by an increase in sympathetic nervous activity and a decrease in the parasympathetic nervous activity [4–7]. The increase in sympathetic nervous activity raises the flight-or-fight response with the release of hormones which causes sweating, increased heart rate, muscular activation, increased respiration and blood pressure [8–10].

Electrocardiogram (ECG) is a widely used physiological measurement that provides instantaneous changes in sympathetic nervous activity through changing heart rate [8–10]. Conventionally, passive Ag/AgCl electrodes are widely used to obtain ECG signals. However, they require skin preparation and the application of gel to improve skin conductivity. Wires from the ECG system are connected to these electrodes reducing the mobility of a person and causes discomfort after some time. These requirements of conventional system limit its usage for long term unobtrusive and ubiquitous ECG monitoring [11].

The limitation of conventional passive ECG systems is overcome using capacitive based active electrodes, which provides a means of unobtrusive ECG measurement through cloths. Validation of capacitive electrocardiogram (cECG) sensors integrated into objects that people use regularly such as office chair, bed, bathtub and car seat has been published [6, 12, 13]. The unique advantage of this sensor system is that it allows unobtrusive ubiquitous cardiac monitoring without any interference to the user activities or behaviour providing seamless integration with the surrounding environment. Physical feasibility of the sensor system in comparison to the conventional ECG measurements have shown a high correlation between the extracted features.

In this paper, we have developed capacitive ECG electrodes and have embedded them on a mat which can be strapped to a chair or bed allowing long time unobtrusive ECG monitoring. An experiment was conducted to validate the quality of cECG sensor system and its signal conditioning unit against conventional ECG system in both sitting and lying down posture at a work or college environment.

2 Materials and Methods

2.1 Sensor and Signal Conditioning System

The developed capacitive electrodes are made of a tin-coated copper plate of dimensions 8 cm × 5 cm. The tin coating provides as an anti-corrosive layer against sweat and humidity required for long term monitoring [14, 15]. Behind the conductive electrode surface, signal conditioning unit containing impedance converter is designed with unity gain pre-amplification and a very high input impedance of 10GW. The active electrodes are embedded on a flexible cushioned mat which could be fastened to a chair or overlaid on a bed as required shown in Fig. 1. The common-mode signals are actively compensated using right leg driven flexible copper reference electrode [16, 17].

The signal conditioning unit consists of an instrumentation amplifier with a gain of 248, a fourth-order bandpass filter of 0.5–40 Hz with unity gain and a driven right leg circuit that provides negative feedback for noise reduction [6]. NodeMCU ESP-8266

Fig. 1. cECG sensors placed on the bed for continuous monitoring applications when the patient is lying down and placed on the seatback of a chair for quick screening.

with an operating voltage of 3.3 V was used to acquire data from the analogue signal conditioning unit. A bias voltage of 1 V is added to the filtered signal to shift the biphasic cECG signal to be monophasic for NodeMCU controller. The data from the controller is transferred to a laptop serially at a baud rate of 115200. The data is received using a Python program at a sampling rate of 80 samples/second and stored locally.

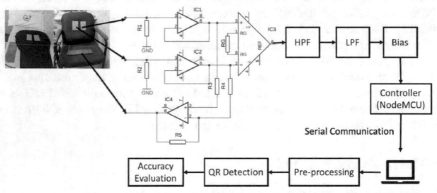

Fig. 2. Block Diagram representation of the locations of active cECG and driven right leg reference electrode embedded into a flexible mat. The blocks include a signal acquisition system, conditioning using, data acquisition system, serial communication and signal processing units.

Simultaneous ECG measurements were also recorded using the poly channel of Mitsar EEG Amplifier that allows ECG measurements. Gel-based Ag/AgCl electrodes were placed on the subject's right and left arm slightly below the wrist and the reference electrode was placed on the right ankle. Software provided with Mitsar was used for recording ECG signal at a default sampling rate of 2000 samples/second. A block diagram of the cECG sensor system, required signal conditioning unit and signal processing methods are given in Fig. 2.

2.2 Signal Processing and Validation

The capacitive ECG system is very prone to movement artefacts and any baseline wandering occurring due to limb or body movements were corrected through mean subtraction. Higher accuracy of QRS peak detection was achieved using Pan-Tomkins algorithm which applies bandpass filtering, differentiation, squaring and windowing operations to compute dynamic peak detection threshold [15]. The time interval between the detected R peaks was used to measure RR interval in seconds from which ECG and cECG heart rate were derived using their respective sampling rates. The validation was conducted in two steps, the first was to validate cECG R-peak detection accuracy through analysis of correlation with ECG signals measured through conventional Mitsar system. The second part was the comparison of mean squared errors between the detected R-peaks under different driving conditions.

2.3 Test Protocol

cECG measurements were carried out in two form factors. First using sensors embedded on a mat placed on the bed and next using sensors placed on the chair. The mat form factor of the sensor system enabled measurement flexibility from both bed and chair for unobtrusive long term monitoring. To validate the sensor system, six healthy volunteers of both gender (5 men and 1 woman), aged between 22 and 28 years were enrolled in the study. The subject was first asked to sit on a chair with cECG system for 30 min followed by lying down on a bed with cECG system for the next 30 min. Simultaneous measurements of both cECG and conventional ECG was conducted during the experiment. The accuracy of the measured cECG signal was then compared with the conventional ECG measurement from both form factors.

3 Results and Discussion

The data from capacitive electrodes were recorded on a laptop with simultaneous conventional Ag/AgCl-based electrodes. Both the active and passive electrodes were positioned in Lead I configuration of Einthoven/Goldberger triangle. Figure 3 shows the characteristic electrocardiogram waveform measured from one of the subjects when sitting on the chair. The active electrodes were positioned at the thoracic and lumbar level of the subject and the reference electrode was placed on the seat. cECG measurements from both the form factors show excellent goodness of fit and linearity when compared to conventional ECG measurements. The detected R peak using Pan-Tomkins algorithm marked on the measured cECG signal is shown in Fig. 3.

The experimental results from filtering and R peak detection of cECG measurements show high accuracy, and the heart rate calculated by the cECG system had a very high correlation with the heart rate computed using conventional ECG for both chair ($r = 0.991$, $p < 0.01$) and bed ($r = 0.981$, $p < 0.01$) form factors as shown in Fig. 4.

The mean square error (MSE) between the QRS peak detections of measured cECG signal and conventional ECG signal, has an error of 0.43 beats per minute when the measurements were conducted on the chair and 1.13 beats per minute when the measurements were conducted on the bed (Fig. 5). The results from Fig. 4 and Fig. 5 indicate

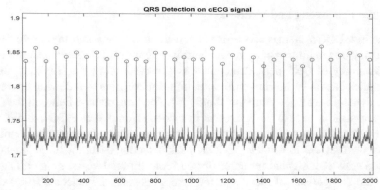

Fig. 3. Capacitive ECG measurements from active electrode system embedded on a flexible mat when the subject was sitting on a chair. Characteristic ECG waveform could be recorded with R peak detection using Pan-Tomkins algorithm.

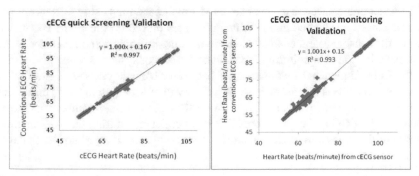

Fig. 4. A good correlation between cECG and conventional ECG were observed in both chair (99.7%) and bed (99.3%). The improved accuracy in QRS detection from the chair could be attributed to better lumbar contact with the electrodes

that a single lead configuration would be sufficient for a reliable measurement for long term continuous monitoring. Though both form factors show very high accuracy in R peak detection, a slight increase in the accuracy when the subject was sitting on a chair could be attributed to better lumbar contact. When lying down, the curvature of lumbar reduced the area of contact with cECG electrodes and thereby increasing the signal noise comparatively.

An advantage of using cECG system over conventional ECG assessment is that it involves non-contact electrodes which save the patient preparation time causing no skin irritation. Moreover, during continuous monitoring, the increased perspiration of the subject makes it difficult to stick the conventional ECG electrodes creating a loss of signal quality. Whereas Capacitive ECG works without any conductive electrical contact with the patient and increasing perspiration will only improve the signal quality [6]. Since measurements through clothing are possible in cECG system, it could be seamlessly integrated with the everyday objects to enable unobtrusive and ubiquitous cardiac monitoring in the workplace, during driving and at home.

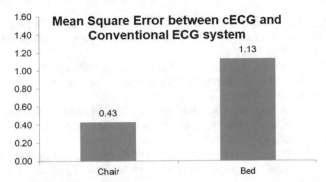

Fig. 5. Mean Squared Error between the computed heart rates of cECG and conventional ECG system. A higher error was recorded when the subject was lying on the bed with 1.13 beats per minute as compared to 0.43 beats per minute when sitting on the chair.

In this study, we have proposed an unobtrusive capacitive ECG system embedded into a chair and bed and validated it practicability in continuous monitoring at an office or a school environment. Further signal analysis to compute heart rate variability could provide information on the changes of sympathetic nervous activity for early detection of stress or fatigue in the workplace.

4   Conclusion

In this study, we have developed and evaluated the practicability of using a capacitive ECG sensor system on a chair and bed to unobtrusively and ubiquitously monitor cardiac activity. The obtained cECG signal quality and heart rate measurements were highly correlated with conventional ECG measurements. Further heart rate variability analysis could provide information on the changes of sympathetic nervous activity for early detection of stress or fatigue in the workplace. Application of this system would enable early warning of potential cardiac distress and promote employee well-being in the workplace. Future work will be aimed at long-term evaluations under real-life office workspace under realistic working conditions.

Acknowledgment. The authors would like to show gratitude to all the members of Rehabilitation Bioengineering Group (RBG) at the Indian Institute of Technology Madras, India, and other volunteers for their participation in this study.

References

1. Prabhakaran, D., Jeemon, P., Roy, A.: Cardiovascular disease in India: current epidemiology and future directions. Circulation **133**(16), 1605–20 (2016)
2. Kivimäki, M., Kawachi, I.: Work stress as a risk factor for cardiovascular disease. Current Cardiol. Rep. **17**(9), 630–638 (2015)
3. Huang, S., Li, J., Zhang, P., Zhang, W.: Detection of mental fatigue state with wearable ECG devices. Int. J. Med. Inf. **119**, 39–46 (2018)

4. Tanaka, M., Tajima, S., Mizuno, K., Ishii, A., Konishi, Y., Miike, T., Watanabe, Y.: Frontier studies on fatigue, autonomic nerve dysfunction, and sleep-rhythm disorder. J. Physiol. Sci. **65**(6), 483–498 (2015)
5. Tanaka, M., Mizuno, K., Yamaguti, K., Kuratsune, H., Fujii, A., Baba, H., Matsuda, K., Nishimae, A., Takesaka, T., Watanabe, Y.: Autonomic nervous alterations associated with daily level of fatigue. Behav. Brain Funct. **7**, 46 (2011)
6. Bhardwaj, R., Balasubramanian, V.: Viability of Cardiac Parameters Measured Unobtrusively Using Capacitive Coupled Electrocardiography (cECG) to Estimate Driver Performance. IEEE Sens. J. **19**(11), 4321–4330 (2019)
7. Tomoda, A., Mizuno, K., Murayama, N., Joudoi, T., Igasaki, T., Miyazaki, M., Miike, T.: Event-related potentials in Japanese childhood chronic fatigue syndrome. J. Pediatr. Neurol. **5**, 199–208 (2007)
8. Alberdi, A., Aztiria, A., Basarab, A.: Towards an automatic early stress recognition system for office environments based on multimodal measurements: a review. J. Biomed. Inf. **59**, 49–75 (2016)
9. Wijsman, J., Grundlehner, B., Liu, H., Penders, J. Hermens, H.: Wearable physiological sensors reflect mental stress state in office-like situations. In: Humaine Association Conference on Affective Computing and Intelligent Interaction, pp. 600–605, Geneva (2013).
10. Vrijkotte, T., Van Doornen, L., Geus, E.: Effects of work stress on ambulatory blood pressure, heart rate, and heart rate variability. Hypertension **35**(4), 880–886 (2000)
11. Searle, A., Kirkup, L.: A direct comparison of wet, dry and insulating bioelectric recording electrodes. Physiol. Meas. **21**(2), 271–83 (2000)
12. Lim, Y.K., Kim, K.K., Park, K.S.: The ECG measurement in the bathtub using the insulated electrodes. In: The 26th Annual International Conference of the IEEE Engineering in Medicine and Biology Society, pp. 2383–2385
13. Kim, K.K., Lim, Y.K., Park, K.S.: The electrically noncontacting ECG measurement on the toilet seat using the capacitively-coupled insulated electrodes. In: The 26th Annual International Conference of the IEEE Engineering in Medicine and Biology Society, pp. 2375–2378, IEEE EMBS, San Francisco, CA (2004)
14. Norlin, A., Pan, J., Leygraf, C.: Investigation of interfacial capacitance of Pt, Ti and TiN coated electrodes by electrochemical impedance spectroscopy. Biomol. Eng. **19**, 67–71 (2002)
15. Leonhardt, S., Aleksandrowicz, A.: Non-contact ECG monitoring for automotive application. In: 5th International Summer School and Symposium on Medical Devices and Biosensors, pp. 183–185, Hong Kong (2008)
16. Winter, B.B., Webster, J.G.: Driven-right-leg circuit design. IEEE Trans. Biomed. Eng. **30**(1), 6265 (1983)
17. Pan, J., Tompkins, W.J.: A real-time QRS detection algorithm. IEEE Trans. Biomed. Eng. **BME-32**(3), 230–236 (1985)

Exploring the Structure and Content of Pro Formas for Signal Passed at Danger Incidents in Australia and New Zealand

Anjum Naweed[1]([⊠]) [iD], Lorelle Bowditch[1] [iD], Janine Chapman[2] [iD], Jillian Dorrian[3] [iD], and Nora Balfe[4] [iD]

[1] Appleton Institute for Behavioural Science, Central Queensland University, Wayville, SA 5034, Australia
{anjum.naweed,lorelle.bowditch}@cqu.edu.au
[2] National Centre for Education and Training on Addiction (NCETA), Flinders University, Bedford Park, SA 5042, Australia
janine.chapman@flinders.edu.au
[3] Behaviour-Brain-Body (BBB), University of South Australia, Magill Campus, St. Bernards Rd, Magill, SA 5072, Australia
jill.dorrian@unisa.edu.au
[4] Centre for Innovative Human Systems, Trinity College Dublin, The University of Dublin, Dublin Dublin 2, Ireland
balfen@tcd.ie

Abstract. In rail transportation, managing and mitigating the risk of Signal Passed at Danger (SPAD) incidents is a perennial challenge, with causation reflective of a systems issue. However, very little research has evaluated the role of SPAD Pro Formas—the documents used to collect and analyse information during investigation. A total of 208 internal investigation reports were obtained for SPADs occurring over four years (2014–2018) from 10 organisations across Australia and New Zealand. Results revealed large variation across SPAD Pro Formas, and a notable paucity of multifactorial explanations for SPAD causation, creating key questions around organisational learning.

Keywords: SPAD prevention · Risk management · Tools · Systems thinking · Organisational behaviour · Investigation

1 Introduction

Rail is a complex system [1, 2] and SPAD management is a perennial challenge. SPADs can arise in response to conditions which, while complex and dynamic, are also opaque, meaning they rely on an in-depth investigation and application of systems thinking. A SPAD is a "near-miss" event which occurs when trains or light rail vehicles (e.g., trams) inadvertently exceed their movement authorities, typically by encroaching on signals showing stop/red/danger aspects [3]. SPADs are a weak link in an otherwise safe system and one of the few points in rail where a single failure can have catastrophic

© The Author(s), under exclusive license to Springer Nature Switzerland AG 2021
N. L. Black et al. (Eds.): IEA 2021, LNNS 222, pp. 143–153, 2021.
https://doi.org/10.1007/978-3-030-74611-7_20

consequences. Only a small proportion of SPADs have the potential to result in collision or derailment in most conventional rail networks, but by their very nature, even low-risk SPADs have far-reaching impacts (e.g., loss of service, timetable disruption, reduced driver wellbeing, lengthy incident investigation) [4]. Rail safety research has established a body of knowledge appealing to the underlying contributory human factors in the anatomy of a SPAD [e.g. 5–8]. However, one area that has been under-researched is the SPAD investigation process itself, specifically in terms of what Investigators do and do not look at when investigating these incidents.

Related research [9] highlights the existence of information gaps that may impact the investigation process, particularly from a systems thinking perspective [10]. This highlights a missing piece of the puzzle—what do specialist investigators look, or not look at when investigating SPADs? One of the best sources of information here is the organisational SPAD investigation *pro forma*—the document used to capture pertinent information and attribute causation by the Investigator.

1.1 SPAD Incident Investigation Pro Formas

An investigation pro forma is critical for understanding what happened in an incident. The efficacy of pro formas as tools for process and analysis has been established in other safety-critical contexts and now form part of systematic approaches to managing safety, including organisational structures, accountabilities, policies and procedure (i.e., safety management systems) [11, 12]. While the efficacy of pro formas for SPAD investigation has not been research foci in rail, long term documents used to support work activities, like pro formas, have been classified as incident factors in and of themselves when poorly defined, non-comprehensive, and badly presented [13, 14]. As an iterative tool, an investigation pro forma is not only critical for understanding what happened but extracting lessons that can be learned and shared with others.

This study examined rail organisational pro formas in Australasia (Australia and New Zealand) with the aim to understand what is/is not being looked at and is considered important/unimportant when investigating SPADs, and the extent to which systems thinking informs the overall investigative process.

2 Methodology

A qualitative cross-sectional multiple-case research design using conventional content analysis [15] was used to understand, categorise and analyse the structure and content of the pro formas, with reference to the RSSB Standard for Accident and Incident Investigation [16]. Multiple case studies are considered a highly informative research methodology but do not claim generalisability; rather, they offer in-depth and insightful comparisons between cases and contexts [17]. The pro forma was the focus of this study, but because of the possibility that organisations could have multiple types or versions of pro forma for investigating SPADs, the organisation itself was defined as the unit of analysis (i.e., the items and criteria pre-defined within the pro forma were viewed as a function of the foci and practices of its organisation).

Ten rail organisations took part in the study across Australia ($n = 8$) and New Zealand ($n = 2$). Each organisation was provided a one-page information sheet detailing the study. Safety professionals with responsibility for managing SPAD-risk at each organisation were requested to provide up to 25 completed SPAD pro formas. A total of 208 internal investigation reports were obtained for SPADs occurring over four years (2014–2018). Recruitment was facilitated by an Australasian SPAD Group focusing on continuous improvement and prevention [18].

Data analysis conformed to conventional content analysis [15] and was carried out inductively (i.e. without predefining categories prior to analysis) in multiple rounds of iterative coding. Use of the inductive approach in content analysis is determined by the purpose of the research, which was to look at areas of focus or emphasis, and differences across reports. This approach is recommended when knowledge about the phenomenon is insufficient or fragmented, and enables movement from the specific to the general, allowing for particular instances to be observed and combined in order to form a general statement [19]. Analysis followed a series of steps shown in Table 1.

Table 1. Overview of the data analysis process followed in the study.

Step	Primary activity	Description
One	Familiarisation	Every pro forma was read closely to familiarise with its layout, design and structure, and assembly of content. Key observations were noted
Two	Extraction & code creation	Each heading, sub-heading, tick-box and section prompt from every report was extracted onto a coding sheet ($n = 646$). Duplicate and almost-identical codes were removed ($n = 66$) to produce a consolidated list of codes
Three	Inductive grouping & refinement	Each code from the consolidated list of codes was analysed over multiple stages. Categories related to subcategories and the properties and dimensions of a category were specified to derive a single and final hierarchical categorization ($n = 492$). Major "nodes" and their subordinate categories were developed through refinement. This process was undertaken with NVivo (v.11) to determine the spread and variability across organisations and with concept mapping software (CMapTools v.6.01.01) to refine the categorization
Four	Mapping & representation	The final hierarchical description was checked against completed SPAD pro formas from each organisation to develop a broad representation of commonality (i.e., to comparatively identify what was, and was not, being featured across pro formas). This was carried out as an "item present/not present" scoring exercise

3 Results

Results revealed key differences in the style of pro forma used across organisations. While many pro formas were organised to include the sections reflected in the RSSB Standard, large variability featured in both structure and content across and within organisations. Long and short types of pro forma were used in both narrative and modulated styles, where narrative styles relied on the direction and expertise of the investigator and modulated styles were populated with information in a narrowly defined range (i.e., tick-boxes). As the period covering the SPAD reports spanned four years (2014–2018), it was common to see SPAD pro formas within the same organisation replaced by successive versions. However, pro forma differences within the same version/time period were also noted. Some of these arose from the use of database management systems (e.g., Microsoft Access), thus sections not populated during investigation did not necessarily carry over (i.e., were excluded) from a compiled PDF. However, in some cases, completely different forms were used within the same period in a manner reflective of poor document control.

A total of 13 pro forma nodes were identified. The spread of each section across organisations is given in Fig. 1, reflecting that many sections were represented, although 50% of pro formas (i.e., five organisations) did not feature a *Risk Assessment* or a *Damage/Cost Assessment* section, and 20% (i.e., two organisations) did not feature a *Vehicle Details* section, or a dedicated *Other Actors* section. A good level of commonality was thus apparent across the organisations and their pro formas, but the omission of *Other Actors* brings into question as to whether the full system was being represented during investigation in those organisations. An overview of each identified section is shown in Table 2, along with an indication of how many categories were coded within the hierarchical description.

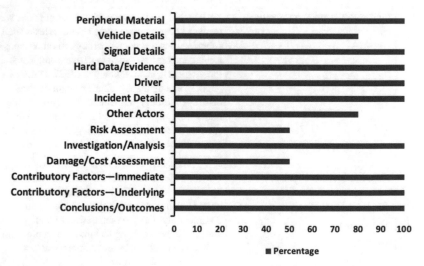

Fig. 1. Graph showing percentage of total coverage of overarching nodes in SPAD pro formas.

Categorisation under each node extended to four levels (i.e., a major category and up to three minor subcategory levels). *Contributory Human Factors—Underlying* was the most densely categorised node ($n = 177$), with nine major categories and many branches. The *Driver* node was also highly categorised ($n = 50$) but featured only two major categories (*Profile, Testimonial*). The third most coded node was *Contributory Human Factors—Immediate*, reflecting an assessment of all the things that were considered to immediately impact the SPAD as an outcome. Only two major categories were coded here: *Driver* and *Other Actors/Operational/Organisational Influences on the Driver*. Thus, the driver was the focus in the immediate contributory pathway, and while some

Table 2. Content overview of pro forma nodes and categories according to the hierarchical description, including number of codes in the major and subcategory levels.

Node number and title		Content overview	Number of subcategory levels and items coded		
			2	3	4
1	Peripheral material	Title and contents page, as well as providing context to the investigation. A brief summary of the evidence, and factual information that top and tails the report	2	14	–	–
2	Driver	Profile, factual information and testimony about the driver in control of the vehicle at the time of the incident	2	8	24	16
3	Signal details	Factual information about the SPAD signal, including the location, history and information about the surrounding track (road)	5	12	–	–
4	Vehicle details	Factual information about the vehicle involved in the incident, and the service information	3	17	–	–
5	Other actors	Profile, factual information and testimony of rail personnel or witnesses other than drivers involved in the incident	4	6	7	3
6	Hard data/evidence	Video, audio, photographic or logged data that supports the investigation	8	15	–	–

(*continued*)

Table 2. (*continued*)

Node number and title		Content overview	Number of subcategory levels and items coded		
			2	3	4
7	Damage/cost assessment	Factual statement of damage/cost associated with the incident	5	7	–	–
8	Incident details	Assimilation of the facts and summary of the events	12	27	2	–
9	Risk assessment	Summary of risk associated with incident and risk rating (score)	2	5	6	–
10	Contributory human factors—*immediate*	Assessment of the underlying factors that contributed to the incident	2	13	31	5
11	Contributory human factors—*underlying*	Assessment of the underlying factors that contributed to the incident	9	34	84	50
12	Investigation analysis	Assimilation of the facts and summary of the events	11	8	–	–
13	Conclusions & recommendations	Evaluation, corrective actions and recommendations related to the investigation	6	10	4	–

system elements and functions external to the driver were considered here, they were done so only in relevance to the driver. The *Incident Details* node was the fourth most coded ($n = 41$), and the rest featured minimal minor-level coding.

A high density of categories in the hierarchical description of the *Contributory Human Factors—Underlying* node was revealed, but this did not necessarily mean that this information was well-represented. Table 3 deconstructs the first-level minor category for each of the major categories and shows the individual and total representation of this node across organisations. Results here reveal that representation within the — *Underlying* node did not mean a particular category was expanded on within the pro forma. In these cases, a tick-box or open field textbox was used to denote whether or not the investigator felt the major category contributed to the SPAD, and if so, whether or not they had further information to add (i.e., open field textbox with or without an accompanying checkbox). One organisation (Org 4) did not feature any major categories within their pro forma, thus their pro forma relied entirely on investigator competency to apportion underlying contributory human factors in the course of their investigation.

The *Organisational/Operational* category of underlying contributory human factors featured in eight pro formas. With the exception of one organisation (Org 3), *Organisational/Operational* was subdivided into other areas. The most prevalent of these was *Failures* (six Orgs) and *Management* (five Orgs).

When present, the *Workload* subcategory featured within pro formas with denser categorisation of underlying factors (Orgs, 2, 3, 5 and 6). *Task* was the most represented subcategory in the four organisations, while *Mental* and *Physical* each featured in two.

Absent/Failed Defences was a major category across the pro formas of five organisations (Orgs 1, 3, 5, 6, and 9), decomposed beyond a header in three (Orgs 1, 5 and 9), but featured prevalently in only two (Orgs 5 and 9).

The *Workplace* category had the highest percentage of representation across organisations and reflected *Design*, *Condition*, and *Environment* features. Of these, *Environment* featured within pro formas of nine organisations and was the most represented category, while the *Design* aspects of the workplace were relatively minimal.

Outside Influences featured in the pro formas of just one organisation (Org 5), with a *Regulatory* subcategory. This was the only overt reference to regulatory influences as an underlying factor in SPADs.

Procedures featured in the pro formas of three organisations (Orgs 1, 2, and 5) with *Documentation* as the only common category. *Compliance and Misuse* (of procedures) each featured in only one pro forma.

While it featured prevalently in the nodes presented earlier, *Knowledge, Skills and Experience* was present in pro formas of only four organisations as an underlying factor (Orgs 2, 5, 7, and 10) and focused exclusively on the *Driver*.

As a category found in only three organisational pro formas (Orgs 2, 5, and 6), *Supervision* was minimally represented as an underlying factor and featured as more than a heading in only one organisation (Org 2).

The *Personal* category had the greatest number of subcategories across pro formas. It also dominated this node in five pro formas (Orgs 1, 2, 3, 7, and 10). The subcategory most represented here was *Lifestyle* (70%), followed by *Attention* (50%) and *Communication* (40%). However, in three organisations (Orgs 3, 4 and 8), the pro forma did not break the *Personal* category down beyond the title.

4   Discussion

The aim of this study was to understand what is/is not being looked at and is considered important/unimportant when investigating SPADs, and the extent to which systems thinking informs the overall investigative process.

The results provided comprehensive coverage of the similarities and differences in pro formas from 10 organisations and included broad information on the overall type and style and extent to which their flow and logic compared against established standards. More specific information included a complete hierarchical description, with a clear account of all the nodes and their densities across pro formas. The focus in this paper was placed on what information is being collected and documented around contributory human factors underlying the cause of the SPAD across the organisation.

It was apparent that organisations have different versions of pro formas, and in some instances, poor document control. The different styles and types of pro formas within

Table 3. Findings for the *Contributory Human Factors—Underlying* node showing frequency of representation across the pro formas of organisations.

Major category & global representation	Codes and representation at the first Minor category level	Specific organisation reference	Pro forma representation	
			Individual	Total
Organisational/Operational, 80% (8)	Goals	1, 5	20% (2)	70% (7)
	Management	1, 2, 5, 6, 9	50% (5)	
	Failures	1, 5, 6, 8, 9, 10	60% (6)	
	Organisational learning	5	10% (1)	
	Culture/normalisation	5, 9	20% (2)	
	Communication	9	10% (1)	
Workload, 40% (4)	Mental	2, 5	20% (2)	40% (4)
	Task	2, 3, 5, 6,	40% (4)	
	Physical	2, 5	20% (2)	
Absent or failed defences, 50% (5)	Control/recovery	5, 9	20% (2)	30% (3)
	Protection and containment	5	10% (1)	
	Escape and rescue procedure	5	10% (1)	
	Detection	5, 9	20% (2)	
	Awareness	1, 5, 9	30% (3)	
Workplace, 90% (9)	Design	2, 5, 9	30% (3)	90% (9)
	Condition	1, 2, 5, 9	40% (4)	
	Environment	1, 2, 3, 5, 6, 7, 8, 9, 10	90% (9)	
Outside influences, 10% (1)	Regulatory	5	10% (1)	10% (1)
Procedures, 30% (3)	Compliance	5	10% (1)	30% (3)
	Misuse	2	10% (2)	
	Documentation	1, 2	20% (2)	
Knowledge, skills and experience, 40% (4)	Driver	2, 5, 7, 10	40% (4)	40% (4)

(*continued*)

Table 3. (*continued*)

Major category & global representation	Codes and representation at the first Minor category level	Specific organisation reference	Pro forma representation	
			Individual	Total
Supervision, 30% (3)	Conflicting role	2	10% (1)	10% (1)
	Poor example	2	10% (1)	
	Inadequate knowledge, skills and experience	2	10% (1)	
Personal, 90% (9)	Goals	5	10% (1)	70% (7)
	Communication	2, 5, 7, 10	40% (4)	
	Behavioural beliefs	5	10% (1)	
	Confidence	5, 9	20% (2)	
	Personality/attitude	5	10% (1)	
	Attention	2, 5, 7, 9, 10	50% (5)	
	Lifestyle	1, 2, 5, 6, 7, 9, 10	70% (7)	
	Complacency/motivation	2, 5	20% (2)	

organisations co-existed in some cases (i.e., short version was not a summarised account of a SPAD investigated in a longer version).

A large emphasis was placed on capturing driver details during investigation and developing a driver profile. In the *Driver* node for example, *Other Actors/Operational/Organisational Influences* were featured, but only in the context of their influence upon the driver. In comparison to the *Driver* node, the *Other Actors* node did not appear in all pro formas, and where present, had less than half the same number of categories/items with shallower content. As the involvement of other systems functions have recognition in the anatomy of a SPAD, the level of information being captured about other personnel was limited and a secondary consideration. In all pro formas, the person operating the rail vehicle at the time of the SPAD was thus emphasised over persons controlling signals (i.e., Controllers) and others in the system, and this person was the focus of investigation leading to the assessment of underlying factors. In terms of systems thinking, the results for the —*Underlying* node revealed that the *Personal* category had the most space allocation, as well as the greatest number of subcategories across pro formas, showing that from a design perspective, the pro forma did not veer far from the individual level. As human error is well understood to be not a matter of personal control, but an emergent property from the overall system design [20], a lack of focus on other systems issues, particularly those placed at higher levels of the system (e.g., organisational factors), limits the amount of real learning and change that can be achieved. A persistent focus on the individual level has the effect of generating single factor causes that point to the person and promulgate a culture of blame [5, 21]. The design and structure of some pro formas did convey aspirations to get to the heart of underlying factors in SPADs, and some sought to establish multi-factorial explanations, even if it was not greatly represented. However, the presence of a particular category within a pro forma did not necessarily mean it was being considered a contributory factor and having a wide array of underlying factors was no guarantee of a shift toward consideration of deeper systems influences.

4.1 Future Research Directions

The study has mapped out a hierarchical description of a SPAD pro forma. Further work is needed to determine other meaningful insights to better parameterise these findings. Given the varied density of represented nodes across organisations, this should include a document analysis that provides some indication of how much space is allocated to different sections and categories, and more information on how much actual SPAD analysis is featured in the pro forma.

SPAD pro formas tended to distinguish between immediate and underlying human factors with the intention that the former was completed relatively quickly to suit business needs before more ostensibly detailed analysis was carried out. This study hints that triangulation with underlying contributory factors is reactive, relatively shallow, and multifactorial explanations for SPAD causation reflective of systems thinking currently do not feature greatly in the calculus of the investigation, but more work is required to investigate this. Further research could consider the actual outcomes in SPAD pro formas by considering the extent to which they shift towards systems influences by the end of the investigation.

Lastly, future research needs to undertake a more focused study on how investigators conduct SPAD investigations, and how investigators perceive systems thinking and conceptualise underlying contributory factors.

5 Conclusions

Currently, SPAD Pro formas in Australia and New Zealand have a paucity of multifactorial explanations for causation, creating key questions around organisational learning. At worst, lack of learning coming from SPADs may be hindering efforts to manage SPAD prevention, to the extent that a badly designed SPAD Pro forma may in itself be considered a contributing factor to SPADs.

References

1. Naweed, A., Dorrian, J., Rose, J.: Evaluation of Rail Technology: A Practical Human Factors Guide. CRC Press, Boca Raton (2017)
2. Read, G.J., Naweed, A., Salmon, P.M.: Complexity on the rails: A systems-based approach to understanding safety management in rail transport. Reliab. Eng. Syst. Saf. **188**, 352–365 (2019)
3. Naweed, A.: Psychological factors for driver distraction and inattention in the Australian and New Zealand rail industry. Accid. Anal. Prev. **60**, 193–204 (2013)

4. Naweed, A., Trigg, J., Cloete, S., Allan, P., Bentley, T.: Throwing good money after SPAD? exploring the cost of signal passed at danger (SPAD) incidents to Australasian rail organisations. Saf. Sci. **109**, 157–164 (2018)
5. Naweed, A., Rainbird, S., Dance, C.: Are you fit to continue? approaching rail systems thinking at the cusp of safety and the apex of performance. Saf. Sci. **76**, 101–110 (2015)
6. Stanton, N.A., Walker, G.H.: Exploring the psychological factors involved in the Ladbroke Grove rail accident. Accid. Anal. Prev. **43**(3), 1117–1127 (2011)
7. Balfe, N., Geoghegan, S., Smith, B.: SPAD dashboard: a tool for tracking and analysing factors influencing SPADs. In: Ergonomics and Human Factors 2017, Daventry, UK (2017)
8. Naweed, A., Rainbird, S.: Recovering time or chasing rainbows? exploring time perception, conceptualization of time recovery, and time pressure mitigation in train driving. IIE Trans. Occup. Ergonomics Hum. Fact. **3**(2), 91–104 (2015)
9. Ryan, B., Hutchings, J., Lowe, E.: An analysis of the content of questions and responses in incident investigations: self reports in the investigation of signals passed at danger (SPADs). Saf. Sci. **48**(3), 372–381 (2010)
10. Dekker, S., Cilliers, P., Hofmeyr, J.-H.: The complexity of failure: implications of complexity theory for safety investigations. Saf Sci. **49**, 939–945 (2011)
11. Shamsa, A., Jang, A.J., McGee, T.M.: Documentation of instrumental vaginal deliveries: the benefits of a pro forma. Health Inf Manag. **45**(3), 116–120 (2016)
12. Weichbrodt, J.: Safety rules as instruments for organizational control, coordination and knowledge: implications for rules management. Saf. Sci. **80**, 221–232 (2015)
13. Gibson, H., Mills, A., Basacik, D., Harrison, C.: Incident factor classification system and signals passed at danger. In: The Fifth International Rail Human Factors Conference. London, UK (2015)
14. Lowe, E.: A Guide to the 10 Incident Factors. London.Network Rail, UK (2013)
15. Hsieh, H.-F., Shannon, S.E.: Three approaches to qualitative content analysis. Qual. Health Res. **15**(9), 1277–1288 (2005)
16. RSSB. Rail Industry Standard for Accident and Incident Investigation [RIS-3119-TOM]. Ver 2.2 ed. RSSB, London (2019)
17. Yin, R.K.: Case Study Research: Design and Methods, 3rd edn. SAGE, California (2003)
18. RISSB: SPAD Working Group (2020). https://www.rissb.com.au/safety-tools/spad-working-group/, Accessed 2 Dec 2020
19. Elo, S., Kyngäs, H.: The qualitative content analysis process. J. Adv. Nurs. **62**(1), 107–15 (2008)
20. Ten, D.: Ten Questions About Human Error: A New View of Human Factors and System Safety. Lawrence Erlbaum Associates, New Jersey (2004)
21. Chikudate, N.: If human errors are assumed as crimes in a safety culture: a lifeworld analysis of a rail crash. Hum. Relat. **62**(9), 1267–1287 (2009)

Work System Design in Machine and System Safety with a Focus on Human-System Interaction

Peter Nickel[1,2](✉) [ID], Peter Bärenz[1,3], Hans-Jürgen Bischoff[1,4], Luigi Monica[1,5], Urs Kaufmann[1,6], Michael Wichtl[1,7], Era Poddar[1,8], and Siegfried Radandt[1,4]

[1] ISSA Section Machine and System Safety, WG Human Factors, Ergonomics and Safe Machines, Mannheim, Germany
peter.nickel@dguv.de
[2] Institute for Occupational Safety and Health of the German Social Accident Insurance (IFA), Sankt Augustin, Germany
[3] Research Centre for Applied System Safety and Industrial Medicine (FSA), Mannheim, Germany
[4] International Social Security Association, Section Machine and System Safety (ISSA MSS), Mannheim, Germany
[5] Italian Workers' Compensation Authority (INAIL), Rome, Italy
[6] Swiss Insurance Institution for Occupational Safety and Health (SUVA), Lucerne, Switzerland
[7] Austrian Workers' Compensation Board (AUVA), Vienna, Austria
[8] Manufacturing Safety Alliance of BC (MSA BC), Chilliwack, Canada

Abstract. Future work processes in digital transformation include dynamics in task design, digitised interfaces, and work system components interwoven in process chains and networks. This causes challenges for design according to human factors and ergonomics (HFE) and occupational safety and health (OSH) since it goes beyond anthropometry and biomechanics and calls for work system design and compatibility with human information processing. The Human Factors group of the International Prevention Section of the ISSA on Machine and System Safety is compiling HFE design requirements and solutions from international literature and standards at an internet platform to foster machinery and system safety. The platform structure for the Human Factors group is geared to the concept of work system design and already introduces work behavioural issues, work place issues, and work equipment issues. A given sample requirement for interaction interface design illustrates how good practice referring to HFE contributes to machinery and system safety. Compilation of HFE design requirements in the context of digital transformation is a cumbersome endeavour. While some HFE design requirements are available, others lack specifications for application at the shop floor level. Systematic research along work system design could result in differential design requirements regarding human-system interaction under conditions for work equipment, work place and work environment imposed by the work task.

Keywords: Work system design · Human information processing · Safety · Design requirements · Human factors · Ergonomics

1   Human Factors and Ergonomics in Work System Design

1.1   Findings and Knowledge Available

Work processes in digital transformation include dynamics in task design, digitised interfaces, and work system components interwoven in networks. This causes challenges for
design according to HFE and occupational safety and health (OSH) since it goes beyond
anthropometry and biomechanics and calls for compatibility with human information
processing. A systems approach seems promising in the given context and is available
in HFE as work system design, comprising humans who interact with work equipment
acting together to perform the system function in the workspace, in the work environment, under conditions imposed by work tasks [1]. For work system design in the context
of machine and system safety, HFE knowledge is available from different sources, i.e.
handbooks, textbooks, journal articles, guidelines and standards. With knowledge about
HFE design, in international standards some requirements are readily available (e.g.
arrangement of displays; [2, 3]), other call for specification (e.g. for robot control user
interfaces should be easy to understand; [4]), and some need extension for future work
systems (e.g. feedback design of controls; [5, 6]). In addition, for some design issues
(e.g. assisted obstacle detection around mobile machinery [7]) systematic findings and
knowledge are not yet satisfactory. Moreover, a work system design approach is frequently missing and it is not always clear, how to apply HFE findings for machinery
and equipment design suitable at the shop floor level or construction site, especially in
the context of occupational safety and health (OSH) and when combination of design
requirements is required. In summary, while some basis is available from HFE to improve
machine and system safety under digital transformation, it is not easy for the design of
machines and technical systems to take into account HFE knowledge, although in some
places also legally required (e.g. European Union [8, 9]).

1.2   Preparing Findings and Knowledge

Therefore, the International Prevention Section on Machine and System Safety (MSS) of
the International Social Security Association (ISSA) [10, 11] initiated a working group
to explore knowledge available for future human-system interaction in work systems
with regard to machine and system safety. The endeavour of the international working
group "Human factors, ergonomics and safe machines" (short: Human Factors; [12]) of
ISSA-MSS is to strengthen the ties between HFE and machine and system safety and vice
versa. Activities of the Human Factors Working Group aim at compiling and providing
some relevant and significant findings and knowledge available for early design stages
and modifications at the shop floor level.

2   Methodology

Findings and knowledge available is collected by reviews on design requirements and
recommendations available in the literature as well as national and international standards
related to HFE, research in OSH and OSH expertise on improving HFE and machinery

and system safety. Work system design serves as an approach to assign findings and knowledge available to dimensions and categories common in HFE and to establish a structure for systematic and demonstrative representation. An additional objective of the structure is to assess HFE solutions for machinery and system safety at the shop floor level, i.e. when scheduling adaptations or modifications of work system with machinery and technical installations.

With future work systems changing and the knowledge available increasing, the Human Factors Working Group preferred to establish dynamic web content rather than static documentation. Again, work system design provided orientation for an appropriate structure [12, 13]. The highest level of the structure represents the design approach referring to the work system as well as to system components. The lowest level intends to explain what, why, when, and how to apply HFE requirements and to illustrate good practice in machine and system safety by showcases and examples. A level in the middle provides relevant information from work system design towards solutions for early design stages.

The working group performed reviews of a broad range of HFE literature [e.g. 14–16], regulations [e.g. 8, 9] and standards [e.g. 17] including information available in varying subgroups related to OSH activities. Results were discussed in ISSA-MSS member institutions and in the working group before establishing content for dynamic presentation on the internet platform for open access. Contributions from individuals and parties interested in the objective of the working group are always welcome.

3 Results

3.1 Review of Findings and Knowledge

Reviews on design requirements and recommendations revealed several national and international standards relevant for OSH, especially machine and system safety, however, with the number falling when concentrating on HFE and future work systems [e.g. 18–20]. While some standards provide recommendations for machinery design at generic level (i.e. take into account "visibility of operations" [21] or "information presented on displays should be clear and concise" [22]), other standards inform about HFE requirements for safe and reliable application of controls referring to analogue knobs and dials only [2, 3]; not yet extended by digital representations. Research activities are ongoing in HFE, human-system interaction and design of future work activities. However, information about design fitting to and along human information processing often is not yet suitable for elaborated and clearly specified design requirements and recommendations in OSH or machine and system safety. In part, this may be due to increasing scatter and specificity of research studies and due to potential relevance of results still to be translated for practical application. Similar is true for findings and knowledge presented in ergonomics text books, journal articles and grey literature as information is often not yet very detailed for specific application in machine and system safety or because there are potentially moderating effects of a broad range of operational conditions not yet specified.

Nevertheless, HFE design requirements and recommendations including those along human information processing are available and several are identified as relevant in the given context. Therefore, an ongoing task for HFE scientists and practitioners is not to ignore them. Instead, more investigations, specifications and good practice would help adding to general requirements and extending ergonomic design principles and requirements for analogue interfaces (e.g. displays and controls) into those suitable for digital representation.

3.2 Selected Findings and Knowledge

Initial HFE findings and knowledge significant for machine and system safety is available at an internet platform of the Human Factors Working Group [12, 13]. The work system with its dimensions and categories common in HFE is presented at the platform in a hierarchical structure. Besides explanations about concept, criteria and strategies of work system design, the platform already informs about

- Work behavioural issues, with design for OSH, organisation and performance,
- Work place issues, with design that fits body dimensions, and
- Work equipment issues, with task, interaction and information interface design.

Presentations at three levels of granularity intent to provide explanations, to serve as illustrations and to give references; with the aim to show examples, good practice and sources for specific HFE requirements in the context of machine and system safety under digital transformation.

Work system design with an emphasis on design of work equipment refers to three different but interrelated interfaces; i.e. the task, the interaction and the information interface [18, 24]. The design of the task interface starts with an analysis of system goals, of information required, and so on, proceeds with function allocations to operators, to technical system components, and their interactions, before it ends with deducing task requirements for systems design according to HFE. The design of interaction interfaces explicitly refers to the design of the task interface and interfaces human operators for task interactions with technical systems. This process respects human performance capabilities and limitations and considers principles of human information processing. The design of information interfaces explicitly refers to the design of task and interaction interfaces. Information interfaces designed according to HFE requirements take into account information modalities (e.g. visual), objects (e.g. text) and passive or active (e.g. label, control, feedback) influences on human information processing.

HFE research identified a range of design requirements for interaction interface design (e.g. conformity with user expectations; [5, 6]), significant for an operator to perform his/her task. Operator interactions conform to user expectations if they correspond to predictable contextual needs of an operator and to commonly accepted conventions. Due to culture and stereotypes of the country of machinery use, interfaces shall be adapted to the prospective user population, i.e. for Europe and North America reading from left to right, right turn of dial increases volume, right turn of tap increases closure of water flow. A display indicating temperature measures of a distillation column conforms expectations of Europeans and North Americans, when temperature level increases to the right (see Fig. 1, left; [see 24]). At these places design of displays for temperature as presented in Fig. 1 (right) results in reading errors due to erroneous design and shall be avoided.

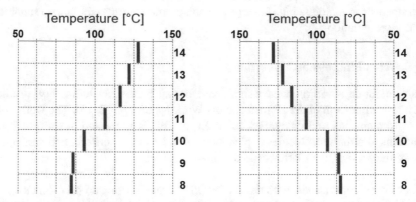

Fig. 1. Two displays with temperature measures of a distillation column (left, with temperature level increase to the right; right, with temperature level increase to the left).

4 Discussion and Conclusions

With the aim to inform machine and system safety, an internet platform has been launched that presents HFE design requirements and recommendations relevant in future work systems. National and international standards, textbooks and other publications provided content for presentation. The documentation at the platform is ongoing and it intends to cover issues structured by work system design from general level to detailed solutions for early design phases and application at the shop floor level.

Some requirements relevant for work system design in digital transformation have been identified, however, specification and translation for applications at the shop floor level is not yet available. This is because it is work in progress in terms of feeding the internet platform with content already available or in terms of HFE knowledge not yet available or not yet specified for practical applications, i.e. HFE design supporting human information processing. In addition, research in HFE is still required for requirement combination, especially when referring to multiple components in work system design, such as information presentation on displays in cabins of mobile machinery at construction sites. Cooperation with, participation in and contribution to activities of the ISSA International Prevention Section of the ISSA on Machine and System [10] is always welcome.

References

1. EN ISO 6385: Ergonomic principles in the design of work systems. CEN, Brussels (2016)
2. EN 894-3: Safety of machinery – Ergonomics requirements for the design of displays and control actuators – Part 3: Control actuators. CEN, Brussels (2008)

3. ISO 9355-3: Safety of machinery – Ergonomics requirements for the design of displays and control actuators – Part 3: Control actuators. ISO, Geneva (1999)
4. EN ISO 13482: Robots and robotic devices - Safety requirements for personal care robots. CEN, Brussels (2008)
5. EN 894-1: Safety of machinery – Ergonomics requirements for the design of displays and control actuators – Part 1: General principles for human interactions with displays and control actuators. CEN, Brussels (2008)
6. ISO 9355-1: Safety of machinery – Ergonomics requirements for the design of displays and control actuators – Part 1: General principles for human interactions with displays and control actuators. ISO, Geneva (1999)
7. EN ISO 16001: Earth-moving machinery - Object detection systems and visibility aids - Performance requirements and tests. CEN, Brussels (2018)
8. EU Machinery Directive 2006/42/EC of the European Parliament and the Council of 17 May 2006 on machinery, and amending Directive 95/16/EC (recast). Off. J. Eur. Union L 157, 24–86 (2006)
9. European Commission: Guide to application of the Machinery Directive 2006-42-EC (Edition 2.2, 10/2019). European Commission (EC), Brussels (2019)
10. International Social Security Association (ISSA), International Prevention Section of the ISSA on Machine and System Safety (MSS). https://www.safe-machines-at-work.org/
11. Nickel, P., Bischoff, H.-J.: Machine and system safety in digital transformation. In: Black, N., et al. (eds.) Proceedings of the 21st Triennial Congress of the International Ergonomics Association (IEA 2021), Lecture Notes on Networks and Systems (LNNS) 222, vol. 4, pp. x–y, Vancouver, Canada, 18–21 June 2021. Springer, Cham (2021). https://doi.org/10.1007/978-3-030-74611-7_22
12. ISSA-MSS Working Group Human Factors. Human Factors, Ergonomics and Safe Machines. https://www.safe-machines-at-work.org/human-factors/
13. Nickel, P., Bärenz, P., Radandt, S., Wichtl, M., Kaufmann, U., Monica, L., Bischoff, H.-J., Nellutla, M.: Human-system interaction design requirements to improve machinery and systems safety. Adv. Intell. Syst. Comput. (AISC) **969**, 3–13 (2020). https://doi.org/10.1007/978-3-030-20497-6_1
14. Kantowitz, B.H., Sorkin, R.D.: Human Factors: Understanding People-System Relationships. Wiley, New York (1983)
15. Stellman, J.: ILO Encyclopaedia of Occupational Safety & Health. International Labour Organization (ILO), Geneva (2015). https://www.iloencyclopaedia.org/
16. Lee, J.D., Wickens, C.D., Liu, Y., Ng Boyle, L.: Designing for People: An Introduction to Human Factors Engineering. CreateSpace, Charleston (2017)
17. EN ISO 10075-2: Ergonomic principles related to mental workload – Part 2: Design Principles. CEN, Brussels (2000)
18. EN 614-1: Safety of machinery - Ergonomic design principles - Part 1: Terminology and general principles. CEN, Brussels (2009)
19. EN 894-2: Safety of machinery – Ergonomics requirements for the design of displays and control actuators – Part 2: Displays. CEN, Brussels (2008)
20. ISO 9355-2: Safety of machinery – Ergonomics requirements for the design of displays and control actuators – Part 2: Displays. ISO, Geneva (1999)
21. EN ISO 10218-2: Robotics - Safety requirements for robot systems in an industrial environment - Part 2: Robot systems, robot applications and robot cells integration. CEN, Brussels (2021)
22. EN ISO 16090-1: Machine tools safety - Machining centres, Milling machines, Transfer machines - Part 1: Safety requirements. CEN, Brussels (2018)

23. EN 614-2: Safety of machinery – Ergonomic design principles – Part 2: Interactions between the design of machinery and work tasks. CEN, Brussels (2008)
24. European Commission: Guidance on the application of the essential health and safety requirements on ergonomics set out in section 1.1.6 of Annex I to the Machinery Directive 2006/42/EC, Ref. Ares(2015)1315566 - 25/03/2015 European Commission - Europa EU (2015)

Machine and System Safety in Digital Transformation

Peter Nickel[1,2(⊠)] ⓘ and Hans-Jürgen Bischoff[1,3]

[1] ISSA Section Machine and System Safety, WG Human Factors, Ergonomics and Safe Machines, Mannheim, Germany
peter.nickel@dguv.de
[2] Institute for Occupational Safety and Health of the German Social Accident Insurance (IFA), Sankt Augustin, Germany
[3] International Social Security Association, Section Machine and System Safety (ISSA MSS), Mannheim, Germany

Abstract. Human factors and ergonomics (HFE) is challenged by machine and system safety under digital transformation calling for sound solutions suitable for application at the shop floor level. HFE challenges will arise with future human-system interactions referring to dynamics in task design, digitised interaction interfaces, and work system entities interwoven in networks. Work system design, i.e. enclosing operator work task, workplace, equipment and environment, seems promising, especially with prevention through design early in construction of today and tomorrow machinery and technical installations. The Human Factors Group of the ISSA Section Machine and System Safety compiled some design requirements and recommendations available in the given context. The Scientific Symposium is likely to support collection of HFE knowledge available, discussion with HFE experts potentially interested and suggestions for research required to increase HFE contributions to machine and system safety in digital transformation. Contributions from, discussions and cooperation with those interested in HFE and objectives presented are always welcome.

Keywords: Health and safety · Work system design · Design principles · Human-system interaction · Human information processing · Prevention through design

1 HFE in Work System Design

Development and implementation of new technologies in production and services as well as evolution towards digitalised and dynamic industry 4.0 value-added networks call for human-centred design solutions according to human factors and ergonomics (HFE). In order to tackle HFE challenges related to developments in digitisation and to learn about solutions in design improving machine and system safety under digital transformation, a work system design approach is considered most promising [1, 2]. A system approach comprises humans acting together and interacting with work equipment to perform the system function in the workspace, in the work environment, under conditions imposed by

© The Author(s), under exclusive license to Springer Nature Switzerland AG 2021
N. L. Black et al. (Eds.): IEA 2021, LNNS 222, pp. 161–166, 2021.
https://doi.org/10.1007/978-3-030-74611-7_22

the work task [3, 4]. In addition, digitisation calls for HFE enclosing human information processing, dynamics call for ergonomic design of adaptations in allocations of functions to people and to technical systems, and networking calls for continuous communication between system components and mediation within and across organizational processes. Design strategies and principles with a HFE system perspective in digital transformation facilitate human well-being while addressing immobile and mobile as well as safe and secure task processing in human-system-interaction.

An IEA Scientific Symposium on "Machine and System Safety in Digital Transformation" in the given context may serve different purposes. First, it has the potential to inform about ergonomics findings and knowledge available for improving machine and system safety. By doing so, it intends to strengthen the ties between HFE and machine and system safety and vice versa. Next, it should encourage more HFE experts to engage in contributions towards machine and system safety. Moreover, it should allow learning from latest research and practice on how to improve machine and system safety and it should bring development of new technologies closer to requirements for machine and system safety. In addition, it should trigger research in HFE to engage in the design of human-system interaction focussing on human-information processing relevant in contexts of digital transformation at work. Finally, it should feed legal requirements calling for HFE in the design of machinery and technical installations [5–7]. As a result, it optimises operator physical and mental workload in human-system interaction, approaches a high-level occupational safety and health (OSH) and fosters overall system performance.

This provides a basis for taking on HFE challenges while at the same time contributing to machine and system safety in digital transformation. Solutions may demonstrate ergonomic design for new tasks, interfaces and technologies as well as integrate HFE design requirements early into prevention through design and construction of machinery and technical installations; i.e. ergonomic design of operator work task, workplace, equipment and environment is of relevance. In addition, HFE could become part of future systems in terms of tools and procedures adapting to digital transformation. HFE design and evaluation should foster safety and health in practice across the life cycle.

2   HFE in Prevention on Safety

The International Prevention Section on Machine and System Safety (MSS) of the International Social Security Association (ISSA) is committed to improving safety and health at work in the field of machine and system safety worldwide [8]. The section recognizes and integrates design requirements and recommendations when addressing assessment of systems regarding safety, security, health and well-being at work in the context of applications with machines, technical systems or plants in manufacturing. Section activities are divided in working groups. Work within the groups as well as information presented at the internet platform of the section [8] intends to promote an active and constructive discussion of design requirements, recommendations and solutions to improve OSH in today and future working world. Among different working groups on specific topics of the section, the Working Group "Human Factors, Ergonomics and Safe Machines" (short: Human Factors; [9, 10]) collects and promotes relevant findings and significant knowledge available from science and practice to machine and system safety. The Human Factors Group takes a HFE approach for work system design to present activities.

The role of the ISSA in the context is the world's leading international organization for social security institutions, government departments and agencies. The ISSA promotes excellence in social security administration through professional guidelines, expert knowledge, services and support to enable its members to develop dynamic social security systems and policy throughout the world. It provides an exclusive member community and promotes cooperation and exchange through on-site and on-line events, workshops and expert networks. The ISSA develops professional standards, undertakes research and analysis, identifies good practices, provides data on social security systems in 177 countries and offers practical services and support for social security administrations. Founded in 1927 under the auspices of the International Labour Organization, the ISSA today has over 320 member institutions from over 160 countries [11].

The Special Commission on Prevention links 14 sections to the ISSA, as it is one of 13 standing Commissions of the ISSA. The International Prevention Section on Machine and System Safety (MSS) of the ISSA is one among 14 international sections of the Special Commission on Prevention of the ISSA [12]. Each Section has its own work plan and contributes to the Special Commission's working program. The Special Commission coordinates joint activities across sections in the field of prevention of occupational risks. The Prevention Sections are key actors in prevention of traditional hazards and new and emerging risks within and across sectors in industry and services (e.g. construction, chemistry) as well as cross-sectional topics (i.e. information or research in OSH prevention). All sections support technical cooperation projects by providing expertise and specialized publications and participating in OSH conferences and training workshops. The Special Commission including its 14 sections follows ISSA's three-dimensional prevention approach that applies a concept of prevention in social security, consisting of risk management, health promotion and return to work measures [12].

3   HFE Contributions to Machine and System Safety

The Human Factors Group of the ISSA Section Machine and System Safety identifies and presents design requirements, recommendations and solutions for the design of human-system interaction according to HFE on an internet platform [9, 10, 13]. With the focus on work system design and the objective of improving machine and system safety, it refers to humans acting together and interacting with work equipment to perform the system function in the workspace, in the work environment, under conditions imposed by work tasks [3].

The HFE concept of work system design also provided orientation for an appropriate structure for presentation [3, 10]. A structure with three levels represents the design approach referring to the work system as well as to system components (see Fig. 1). The second level provides relevant information from work system design towards solutions for early design stages. A third level intends to explain what, why, when, and how to apply HFE requirements and to illustrate good practice in machine and system safety by showcases and examples.

The Human Factors group reviewed HFE literature [e.g. 2, 14, 15], regulations [e.g. 5, 6] and standards [e.g. 16] including information available in varying subgroups related to OSH activities [e.g. 17–19]. Before establishing content for dynamic presentation in the three-level structure, there are always discussions of results in the group and with member institutions of the ISSA-MSS.

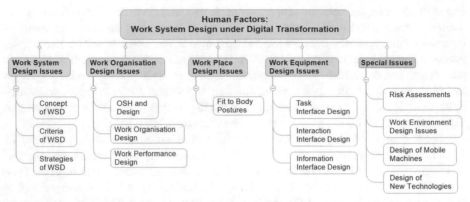

Fig. 1. Issues of the human factors group for work system design under digital transformation in a two-level structure (for three levels see [9]).

A broad range of papers indicated interest to join the IEA Scientific Symposium on "Machine and System Safety in Digital Transformation". Based on paper objectives and content, a draft layout for sessions has been suggested. The concept of work system design provides a structure to allocate papers and disclose potential contributions to the subject of the symposium. Consequently, new findings and knowledge integrates rather ideally into HFE and in addition, may inform machine and system safety. Although final decisions for programme details are pending, contributions are arranged as machine and system safety in automation, in transportation, and in manufacturing. Papers related to automation address the importance of human information processing and of prevention through design in the context of work system design and refer to HFE design in robotics ranging from exoskeletons to collaboration environments. Papers related to transportation refer to the design of traffic equipment and human-system interfaces in different vehicles (e.g. tram, bus, truck, and helicopter). Manufacturing is the context of papers covering cognition in assembly and interface design in manufacturing as well as focussing on risk assessment from analysis to redesign with some lessons learned.

4   HFE in Digital Transformation

HFE findings and knowledge are in the focus of the endeavour to support challenges and solutions in machine and system safety in digital transformation. Work system design seems to be a rather promising approach for not only structuring evidence available, discovering knowledge gaps and limitations, and addressing uncertainties, but also to improve operator well-being, safety and performance in today and tomorrow work environments [3, 10].

While the Human Factors group of the ISSA Section on Machine and System Safety uses this approach to inform about design strategies, principles, requirements and recommendations, for HFE design applications at the shop floor there is still lack of good practice. Especially in the given context on digital transformation, design specifications are rare and call for closer links to human information processing, dynamics in allocations of functions to people and to technical systems, and networking of more entities in human-system interaction. The Special Symposium and other contributions at the conference have the potential to facilitate the impact of HFE design for machine and system safety in digital transformation. Contributions from and discussions with those interested in HFE and objectives presented are always welcome.

References

1. Kadir, B.A., Broberg, O., Souza da Conceição, C.: Current research and future perspectives on human factors and ergonomics in Industry 4.0. Comput. Ind. Eng. **137**, 106004 (2019)
2. Lee, J.D., Wickens, C.D., Liu, Y., Ng Boyle, L.: Designing for People: An Introduction to Human Factors Engineering. CreateSpace, Charleston (2017)
3. EN ISO 6385: Ergonomic principles in the design of work systems. CEN, Brussels (2016)
4. EN ISO 10075–2: Ergonomic principles related to mental workload – Part 2: Design Principles. CEN, Brussels (2000)
5. EU Machinery Directive 2006/42/EC of the European Parliament and the Council of 17 May 2006 on machinery, and amending Directive 95/16/EC (recast). Off. J. Eur. Union L 157, 24–86 (2006)
6. European Commission: Guidance on the application of the essential health and safety requirements on ergonomics set out in section 1.1.6 of Annex I to the Machinery Directive 2006/42/EC, Ref. Ares(2015)1315566 - 25/03/2015 European Commission - Europa EU (2015)
7. European Commission: Guide to application of the Machinery Directive 2006-42-EC (Edition 2.2, 10/2019). European Commission (EC), Brussels (2019)
8. International Social Security Association (ISSA), International Prevention Section of the ISSA on Machine and System Safety (MSS). https://www.safe-machines-at-work.org/
9. ISSA-MSS Working Group Human Factors. Human Factors, Ergonomics and Safe Machines. https://www.safe-machines-at-work.org/human-factors/
10. Nickel, P., Bärenz, P., Radandt, S., Wichtl, M., Kaufmann, U., Monica, L., Bischoff, H.-J., Nellutla, M.: Human-system interaction design requirements to improve machinery and systems safety. Adv. Intell. Syst. Comput. (AISC) **969**, 3–13 (2020). https://doi.org/10.1007/978-3-030-20497-6_1
11. International Social Security Association (ISSA), Geneva, Switzerland. https://ww1.issa.int/
12. Special Commission on Prevention, Technical Commission of the ISSA, Geneva, Switzerland. https://ww1.issa.int/tc-prev
13. Nickel, P., Bärenz, P., Bischoff, H.-J., Monica, L., Kaufmann, U., Wichtl, M., Poddar, E., Radandt, S.: Work system design in machine and system safety with a focus on human-system interaction. In: Black, N., et al. (eds.) Proceedings of the 21st Triennial Congress of the International Ergonomics Association (IEA 2021), Lecture Notes on Networks and Systems (LNNS) 222, vol. 4, pp. x–y, Vancouver, Canada, 18–21 June 2021. Springer, Cham (2021). https://doi.org/10.1007/978-3-030-74611-7_21
14. Kantowitz, B.H., Sorkin, R.D.: Human Factors: Understanding People-System Relationships. Wiley, New York (1983)
15. Stellman, J.: ILO Encyclopaedia of Occupational Safety & Health. International Labour Organization (ILO), Geneva (2015). https://www.iloencyclopaedia.org/
16. EN 13861: Safety of machinery - Guidance for the application of ergonomics standards in the design of machinery. CEN, Brussels (2012)

17. Radandt, S.: Digital transformation of technical systems with explosion risk. ISSA Section Machine and System Safety, Mannheim (2021). https://www.safe-machines-at-work.org/exp losion-protection/
18. Stacey, N., Ellwood, P., Bradbrook, S., Reynolds, J., Ravetz, J., Williams, H., Lye, D.: Foresight on new and emerging occupational safety and health risks associated with digitalisation by 2025. European Risk Observatory (Summary). Publications Office of the European Union, Luxembourg (2018)
19. Flaspöler, E., Hauke, A., Pappachan, P., Reinert, D. et al.: The human-machine interface as an emerging risk (European Risk Observatory – A literature review). European Agency for Safety and Health at Work (EASHW), Bilbao (2009)

Occupational Health Assessment of Cement Handlers Exposed to Cement Dust in Enugu Metropolis Using the Micronuclei Assay

Anulika Onyemelukwe[1]([✉]), Samuel Ogenyi[2], Okechukwu Onwukwe[1],
Chinenye Okenwa[1], Echezona Nelson Dominic Ekechukwu[3,4,5], Harrison Asogwa[1],
and Peter Achukwu[1]

[1] Department of Medical Laboratory Science, Faculty of Health Science and Technology,
University of Nigeria Enugu Campus, Enugu, Nigeria
anulika.onyemelukwe@unn.edu.ng

[2] Department of Medical Laboratory Science, Faculty of Health Science and Technology,
Nnamdi Aziliwe University, Awka, Nigeria

[3] Department of Medical Rehabilitation, Faculty of Health Sciences and Technology, University
of Nigeria, Nsukka, Nigeria

[4] Environmental and Occupational Health Unit, Institute of Public Health, College of Medicine,
University of Nigeria, Nsukka, Nigeria

[5] LANCET Physiotherapy, Wellness and Research Centre, Enugu, Nigeria

Abstract. Cement handlers such as masons, cement loaders and cement sellers
are exposed to hazardous agents in cement dust daily over a long period of time.
This study evaluated the frequency of nuclear damage to the buccal cells of cement
handlers' exposed to cement dust in Enugu metropolis; by determining the frequencies of micronuclei (MN), binucleate cells (BNC) and Nuclear buds (NB)
in exfoliated buccal cells obtained from cement handlers and a control group.
A total of 238 apparently healthy male subjects, comprising 38 control subjects,
74 masons, 102 cement loaders, and 24 cement sellers were recruited for the
study. A structured questionnaire was used to obtain relevant demographic data
and exposure characteristics of participants. Buccal smears were obtained from
both cheeks for each participant using a sterile wooden spatula. The smears were
evaluated using micronuclei assay. Obtained data were statistically analyzed using
descriptive statistics, independent t-test and one-way ANOVA at $\alpha = 0.05$. All the
categories of cement handlers had a significantly increased micronuclei frequency
when compared to the control subjects. Factors such as age, years in occupation
and use of personal protective equipment did not significantly affect the frequency
of nuclear abnormalities among the cement handlers while the frequency of MN
and BNC was significantly increased by smoking and alcohol consumption habits.
Cement handlers may be exposed to toxic substances in cement dust that, when
compared to control subjects may have given rise to the observed increase in
micronuclei frequency.

Keywords: Cement handlers · Occupational health · Cement dust · Micronuclei
assay · Nuclear abnormalities · Binucleate cells

© The Author(s), under exclusive license to Springer Nature Switzerland AG 2021
N. L. Black et al. (Eds.): IEA 2021, LNNS 222, pp. 167–174, 2021.
https://doi.org/10.1007/978-3-030-74611-7_23

1   Introduction

One of the most commonly used substances on earth is cement. It is a powdery material used during construction to produce and keep blocks or bricks in place. It consists essentially of limestone, laterites, clay and gypsum [1, 2] Cement dust exposure is also common in the manufacture of cement and in the building industry [3]. Cement handlers such as masons, cement loaders and cement sellers are subjected to toxic agents in cement dust everyday for long period of time and exposure to this cement dust may pose unfavorable cellular effects to these cohorts [4]. The primary cement components are derived from heavy metals such as cobalt, lead, nickel, chromium and Silica which are harmful heavy metals [5–7]. Cement handlers are exposed to high levels of cement dust that are released into the environment of the workplace [8].

Invariably, dusty activities resulting in the exposure of these cement handlers to cement dust are the loading of cement bags onto delivery vehicles, the distribution of cements in stores and warehouses and the mixing of cement for building purposes by masons. One of the most efficient and minimally invasive methods to detect DNA damage is the Micronucleus (MN) assay, which have been used to examine the genotoxicity of a variety of toxic substances [9]. An elevated number of these micronuclei is an indication of chromosomal damage in buccal cells; and this finding can serve as an early warning for potential risk of developing long-term health problems [10]. The formation of binucleate cells is considered as a marker of cytotoxicity [11]. With oral cancer being the most common (90%) malignancy of the oral and maxillofacial region [12], the need for biological monitoring of nuclear changes in occupationally exposed workers can never be over emphasized. The quest for survival and contribution to socio economic development in the past few years, have added further complex issues relating to occupational health [13].

Cement handlers constitute a major workforce with a large population in Enugu metropolis, Nigeria. It is a basic key to the corporate social responsibility of researchers to ensure healthy and secure working conditions of cement handlers. This study therefore aimed to evaluate the frequency of nuclear damage to the buccal cells exposed to cement dust by cement handlers' and to address the need for regular effective health and safety training for these semi skilled and unskilled workers to reduce injury and occupational health hazards.

2   Materials and Methods

2.1   Ethical Consideration

Prior to recruitment and sample collection, the details of the procedures involved in the research was explained to the participants and volunteers who agreed to participate in the study signed an informed consent form.

2.2   Study Area and Design

Two hundred and thirty eight apparently healthy male subjects were recruited into the study as follows: - 38 control subjects, 74 masons, 102 cement loaders, and 24 cement sellers. A cross-sectional approach was adopted in the study.

2.3 Study Participants and Data Collection

The test group consisted of cement handlers who have actively been on the job for at least 1 year, while the control group was apparently healthy subjects who were not cement handlers. Individuals seen with oral lesion and those who reported any on-going ailment were excluded from the study. A structured questionnaire was administered before sample collection to obtain relevant demographic, exposure characteristics such as age, duration in occupation, lifestyle; drinking and smoking habits.

2.4 Buccal Smear Collection and Staining

Samples of buccal cells were collected by gently scrapping the inside of both cheeks with a sterile wooden spatula; each sample was suspended in a labeled universal container with 95% ethanol which served as a fixative. The samples were prepared in a laboratory by transferring into centrifuge bottles and centrifuging at 5000 rpm for 5 min, the supernatants were decanted, and the sediments were smeared on poly-L-lysine charged grease free slides. They were allowed to air dry and stained with hematoxylin and eosin staining technique.

2.5 Microscopy

Each slide was evaluated and scored independently by two individuals who had buccal cell cytology experience using the ×40 objective. At least 1000 intact buccal epithelial cells per slide were scored for micronuclei cells (MN), binucleate cells (BN), and cells with nuclear buds (NB) using guidelines described by Tolbert [14].

2.6 Statistical Analysis

Statistical analysis was performed using Statistical Package for the Social Sciences version 20.0. Data obtained from the assay were expressed as the mean $\pm$ standard deviations. Independent t-test (two-tailed) was used to compare nuclear abnormalities among test and control groups. The level of significance was set at $\alpha = 0.05$. Overall effects of age, number of years in occupation, alcohol consumption and smoking were determined using one-way analysis of variance, followed by post-hoc multiple comparisons.

3 Results

3.1 Frequency of Buccal Cell Nuclear Abnormalities

Table 1 compares the frequency of buccal cell nuclear abnormalities between cement handlers and control subjects. The cement handlers had a significantly higher MN than control subjects ($P < 0.001$). The cement handlers also had higher BNC and NB than the control subjects though it was not statistically significant.

Table 1. Comparison of the frequency of buccal cell nuclear abnormalities between cement handlers and control subjects.

Groups	Number	Nuclear abnormalities (mean ± SD)		
		MN	BNC	NB
Control	38	1.08 ± 0.85	0.00 ± 0.00	0.00 ± 0.00
Cement handlers	200	13.74 ± 10.22*	0.22 ± 1.19	0.08 ± 0.35
P-value		< 0.001	0.27	0.16

*P < 0.05 using the t-test statistics. MN: Micronuclei, BNC: Binucleate cells, NB: Nuclear buds.

3.2 Frequency of Buccal Cell Nuclear Abnormalities Among Various Categories of Cement Handlers

Table 2 compares the frequency of buccal cell nuclear abnormalities between the various categories of cement handlers and the control subjects. All categories of cement handlers had a significantly higher MN when compared with the control subjects (p < 0.001), with cement loaders having predominantly highest MN, while cement sellers had the least.

Table 2. The frequency of buccal cell nuclear abnormalities in various categories of cement handlers.

Groups	Number	Nuclear abnormalities (mean ± SD)		
		MN	BNC	NB
Control	38	1.08 ± 0.85	0.00 ± 0.00	0.00 ± 0.00
Masons	74	13.49 ± 9.70*	0.20 ± 0.81	0.11 ± 0.42
Cement loaders	102	14.57 ± 10.88*	0.27 ± 1.51	0.03 ± 0.17
Cement Sellers	24	11.00 ± 8.59*	0.00 ± 0.00	0.21 ± 0.59
F-ratio		20.40	0.83	2.99
P-value		< 0.001	0.48	0.32

*P < 0.05 using the t-test statistics. MN: Micronuclei, BNC: Binucleate cells, NB: Nuclear buds.

3.3 Effects of Exposure Characteristics and Lifestyle on Frequency of Nuclear Abnormalities Among Cement Handlers

The frequency of nuclear abnormalities among cement handlers was significantly affected by cigarette smoking and alcohol consumption, as shown in Table 3. Factors such as age, years in occupation and use of personal protective equipment did not signifi-cantly affect the frequency of nuclear abnormalities among the cement handler. However, cement handlers who had spent greater than 10 years in occupations that involves cement handling had increased frequency of MN though not statistically significant compared to their counterparts who had spent lesser years in cement handling occupations.

Table 3. Factors likely associated with increased frequency of nuclear abnormalities among cement handlers

Characteristics		Nuclear abnormalities (mean ± SD)		
Age	Number	MN	BNC	NB
21–30 years	118	13.90 ± 10.58	0.33 ± 1.51	0.60 ± 0.30
> 30 years	82	13.51 ± 9.74	0.05 ± 0.35	0.11 ± 0.42
T-value		0.27	1.96	0.94
P-value		0.79	0.05	0.35
Years in occupation				
< 5 years	26	13.85 ± 12.17	0.31 ± 0.93	0.12 ± 0.43
5–10 years	123	13.51 ± 9.43	0.24 ± 1.40	0.09 ± 0.36
> 10 years	51	14.24 ± 11.15	0.12 ± 0.59	0.04 ± 0.28
F-ratio		0.09	0.27	0.51
P-value		0.91	0.77	0.60
Use of PPE				
Yes	30	13.47 ± 13.43	0.20 ± 0.81	0.20 ± 0.61
No	151	13.28 ± 9.21	0.25 ± 1.32	0.05 ± 0.28
Sometimes	19	17.05 ± 12.03	0.00 ± 0.00	0.11 ± 0.32
F-ratio		1.11	0.36	2.26
P-value		0.33	0.70	0.01
Smoking status				
Yes	36	17.54 ± 11.25*	0.86 ± 2.60*	0.14 ± 0.50
No	164	12.96 ± 9.86	0.08 ± 0.46	0.07 ± 0.32
T-value		2.43	3.62	1.15
P-value		0.02	< 0.001	0.25
Alcohol consumption				
Yes		16.00 ± 7.39	0.78 ± 1.56*	0.22 ± 0.65
No		1349 ± 9.86	0.16 ± 1.13	0.07 ± 0.31
T-value		1.08	2.13	1.81
P-value		0.28	0.03	0.07

$^{*}P < 0.05$ using the t-test statistics. MN: Micronuclei, BNC: Binucleate cells, NB: Nuclear buds.

4 Discussion

Occupational and environmental exposure to toxic chemical agents presents a significant risk to human health and has become a global concern [15, 16]. Buccal epithelial cytogenetic damage due to environmental and occupational exposure, are monitored by micronucleus (MN) assay [4]. Mixing and loading of cement carry with it an inherent capacity to produce dust, which without effective control can lead to respiratory disease [17]. This study was performed to assess the occupational health of cement handlers exposed to cement dust using MN assay.

Higher frequencies of MN was observed in cement handlers when compared to the controls. This finding is similar to the report documented by a previous study which observed an increased level of MN in buccal epithelial cells of building construction workers when compared to the controls [18].

Comparing the various categories of cement handlers, it was observed that cement loaders had the highest frequency of MN, followed by masons while cement sellers had the least frequency of MN. This may be attributed to the fact that these cement handlers do not use their personal protective equipment (PPE). Moreover, cement loaders and masons are more inevitably in direct contact with these cement dust and inhalation during loading and mixing respectively is inevitable, unlike the cement sellers who retail the already finished cement products in sealed bags. This finding is similar to the findings of a previous study which documented a similar statistically higher frequency of micronuclei in cement factory workers involved in the various stages of cement production, such as; quarrying, crushing, milling and packing when compared with the control group [17].

A previous study also documented that older individuals are subjected to greater risks of developing oral pathological changes which may lead to cancer on prolonged exposure to toxic substances [19]. However, in the present study, there was no significant difference in the frequency of nuclear abnormalities between the older and younger cement handlers; this is similar to the finding documented by a previous study involving gas station attendants [20].

The increase in MN in participants who have worked longer in occupation requiring them to handle cement suggests that most direct and indirect genotoxic substances require chronic exposure to exert its damaging effect as opined by Beneditti [21].

The use of PPE such as boots, gloves, face masks and overalls, did not significantly affect the frequency of nuclear abnormalities, although the majority of workers sampled in this study did not strictly adhere to the use of PPE when working. Nevertheless, in preventing work related hazards due to occupational genotoxins, adequate use of PPE is very necessary.

According to some authors [9, 22], lifestyle factors such as alcohol consumption and smoking habits are considered as contributing factors for elevated levels of nuclear anomalies in individuals who are exposed to other environmental genotoxic substances. As observed in the present study, alcohol consumption and cigarette smoking were implicative factors to the significantly higher MN and BNC observed in cement handlers exposed to occupational genotoxins. Similarly, Khan and Sudha reported a higher degree of micronuclei and nuclear changes among cigarette smokers who were occupationally exposed to Polcyclic aromatic hydrocarbons (PAH) [23]. A previous study also showed a direct relationship between buccal mucosa nuclear anomalies and exposure to cigarette smoke and alcohol [24].

The relevance of these findings can not be overemphasized, it highlights the need of bio-monitoring of semi skilled and unskilled workers who are often not protected from toxic substances while at work and also the ergonomics need to develop strategies to ensure workers health and safety. Further immunocytochemical studies of the buccal epithelial cells of cement handlers to evaluate the expressions of p53 and ki-67 proteins for the detection of epithelial proliferation will elucidate these findings.

5 Conclusion

Cement handlers in Enugu Metropolis may be occupationally exposed to substances capable of inducing genotoxic changes which manifested as increased frequencies of buccal cell micronuclei and binucleated cells.

References

1. Amodu, A.E, Egwuogu, C.P.: Elemental characterization of Obajana Limestone deposit using energy dispersive x-ray fluorescence (XRF) technique. J. Appl. Sci. Environ., 65–68 (2014)
2. Krishna, L., Sampson, U., Annamala, P.T., et al.: Genomic instability in exfoliated buccal cells among cement warehouse workers. Int. J. Occup. Environ. Med. **11**, 33–40 (2020)
3. Sellappa, S., Shibily, P., Vellingiri, B.: DNA damage induction and repair inhibition among building construction workers in South India. Asian Pac. J. Cancer Prev. **11**, 875–880 (2010)
4. Arul, P., Smitha, S., Masilamani, S., Akshatha, C.: Micronucleus assay in exfoliated buccal epithelial cells using liquid based cytology preparations in building construction workers. Iran J. Pathol. **13**(1), 31–38 (2018)
5. Gbadebo, A.M., Bankole, O.D.: Analysis of potentially toxic heavy metals in airborne cement dust around Sagamu, South Western Nigeria. Appl. Sci. **7**, 35 (2007)
6. Baby, S., Singh, N., Shrivastava, P., Nath, S., Kumar, S., Singh, D., Vivek, K.: Impact of dust emission on plant vegetation of vicinity of cement plant. Environ. Eng. Manag. J. **7**(1), 31 (2008)
7. Gunbileje, J.O., Sadagoparamanujam, V.M., Anetor, J.I., Farombi, E.O., Akinosun, O.M., Okorodu, A.O.: Lead, mercury, Cdium Chromium Nickel Copper, Zinc Calcium, Iron, Manganese and Chromium (VI) level in Nigeria and United States of America cement dust. Chemosphere **90**(11), 2743–2749 (2013)
8. Sudha, S., Mythili, B.: Evaluation of genotoxicity through micronucleus assay among individuals exposed to cement dust. Biotechnol. Indian J. **3**(3), 184–187 (2009)
9. Holland, N., Bolognesi, C., Kirsch-Volders, M., Bonassi, S., Zeiger, E., Knasmueller, S., et al.: The micronucleus assay in human buccal cells as a tool for biomonitoring DNA damage: the HUMN project perspective on current status and knowledge gaps. Mutat. Res. **659**, 93–108 (2008)
10. Banerjee, S., Singh, N.N., Sreedhar, G., Mukherjee, S.: Analysis of the genotoxic effects of mobile phone radiation using buccal micronucleus assay: a comparative evaluation. J. Clin. Diagn. Res. **10**(3), ZC 82 (2016)
11. Collins, A.R., Oscoz, A.A., Brunborg, G., Gaivão, I., Giovanneli, L., Kruszewski, M., et al.: The comet assay: topic issues. Mutagenesis **23**, 143–151 (2008)

12. Johnson, N.W., Warnakulasuriya, S., Gupta, P.C., Dimba, E., Chindia, M., Otoh, E.C.: Global inequalities in incidence and outcomes for oral cancer: causes and solutions. Adv. Dent. Res. **23**, 237–246 (2011)
13. Joseph, M., Mehta, M.S., Thomas, M.D.: Effectiveness of structured teaching programme on knowledge of occupational hazards prevention and expressed practice of safety measures among frontline pharmaceutical industrial workers of Rajasthan. IOSR J. Nurs. Health Sci. **5**(3), 64–69 (2017)
14. Tolbert, P.E., Shy, C.M., Allen, J.W.: Micronuclei and other nuclear anomalies in buccal smears: methods development. Research **2/1**, 69–77 (1992)
15. Franco, S.S., Nardocci, A.C., Gunther, W.M.: PAH biomarkers for human health risk assessment: A review of the state-of-the-art. Cad. Saude Publica **24**, 569–580 (2008)
16. Akan, J.C., Abdulrahman, F.I.A., Ogugbuaja, V.O., Ayodele, J.T.: Heavy metals and anion levels in some samples of vegetable grown within the vicinity of Challawa industrial area, Kano, State Nigeria. Am. J. Appl. Sci. **6**, 534–542 (2009)
17. Ramakrishnan, V.: Increased frequency of micronuclei and sister chromatid exchange in cement factory workers. Asian J. Sci. Technol. **4**, 32–38 (2011)
18. Çelik, A., Çava, T., Ergene-Gözükara, S.: Cytogenetic biomonitoring in petrol station attendants: micronucleus test in exfoliated buccal cells. Mutagenesis **18**, 417–421 (2003)
19. Khan, M.R., Sellappa, S.: Elevated frequencies of micronuclei and other nuclear abnormalities in buccal epithelial cells of spray painters in South Indian. Int. J. Pharm. Life Sci. **4**, 2680–2684 (2013)
20. Benites, C.I., Amado, L.L., Vianna, R.A.P., Martino-Roth, M.G.: Micronucleus test on Gas station attendants. Genet. Molec. Res. **5**, 45–54 (2006)
21. Benedetti, D., Nunes, E., Sarmento, M., Porto, C., dos Santos, C.E.I., Dias, J.F., da Silva, J.: Genetic damage in soybean workers exposed to pesticides: evaluation with the comet and buccal micronucleus cytome assays. Mutat. Res./Genet. Toxicol. Environ. Mutagen. **752**, 28–33 (2013)
22. Diler, S.B., Ergene, S.: Nuclear anomalies in the buccal cells of calcite factory workers. Genet. Molec. Biol. **33**(2), 374–378 (2010)
23. Khan, M.R., Sudha, S.: Evaluation of genotoxicity in automobile mechanics occupationally exposed to polycyclic aromatic hydrocarbons using micronuclei and other nuclear abnormalities. Iran. J. Cancer Prev. **5**(2), 87 (2012)
24. Jyoti, S., Siddiquea, Y.H., Khan, S.: Effect on micronucleus frequency and DNA damage in buccal epiththelial cells of various factors among pan masala and gutkhaoral science. Int. J. Oral Sci. **12**, 9–14 (2015)

User Evaluation of a National E-library for Standardized Chemotherapy Regimens

Johanna Persson[1]([✉]) [iD], Ann-Sofie Fyhr[1,2], and Åsa Ek[1] [iD]

[1] Ergonomics and Aerosol Technology, Department of Design Sciences,
Lund University, Lund, Sweden
johanna.persson@design.lth.se
[2] Regional Cancer Centre South, Region Skåne, Lund, Sweden

Abstract. An e-library for standardized chemotherapy regimens has been developed and is, since 2015, available as a national resource for healthcare staff and patients in cancer treatment in Sweden. The library was developed in a user-centered design process and is now evaluated to understand how it is used and if it is used in the intended way. This paper presents the e-library in brief together with preliminary results from the ongoing user evaluation, including results from a web survey, web page statistics, and a heuristic evaluation to identify usability issues. The evaluation is a vital part in assuring that the library works as a patient safety barrier, matches the users' needs, and that it does not have design flaws that could introduce new risks in the already complex chemotherapy process. The results indicate that the library is being used in the intended way and the users do not have any problems interacting with it. With a broad national usage, the standardized chemotherapy regimens e-library can be a source for organizational and national learning, and a source for continuous improvement of cancer care in Sweden.

Keywords: Chemotherapy regimens · E-library · Patient safety · User evaluation · User-centered design

1 Introduction

The three most common cancer treatments are surgery, chemotherapy, and radiation. Chemotherapy include anti-cancer drugs as part of a chemotherapy regimen. A chemotherapy regimen defines the drugs to be used, the dosage, and the frequency and duration of drug administration for the treatment of a given cancer diagnosis. A regimen can include a single drug or a combination of drugs. For successful and safe treatment, it is necessary to know how to administer the drugs, what supportive drugs are needed, what precautions to take, and the checks needed. There is also a need for relevant pharmaceutical (e.g. how to prepare, stability) and medical (e.g. adverse reactions) information. Chemotherapy regimens are highly complex, and errors may cause serious harm among cancer patients, which is a particularly sensitive group due to impaired tolerance [1, 2].

Descriptions of chemotherapy regimens was earlier developed and compiled locally within health care organizations in Sweden. This was much due to Sweden being divided

© The Author(s), under exclusive license to Springer Nature Switzerland AG 2021
N. L. Black et al. (Eds.): IEA 2021, LNNS 222, pp. 175–181, 2021.
https://doi.org/10.1007/978-3-030-74611-7_24

into 21 county councils, representing different geographical regions, all having a far-reaching autonomy regarding the planning, financing, and operation of the region's health care. In total, there are 16 oncology clinics in Sweden managing chemotherapy regimens. Additionally, there are a number of smaller units at other health care clinics that also work with and manage regimens. The many autonomous clinics has resulted in the same chemotherapy treatments occurring under different names and with different dosages causing uncertainty and risks for mix-ups. To overcome these uncertainties and risks, a project was initiated with the aim to develop a national source for regimens (an e-library), with standardized nomenclature and content in chemotherapy regimens, also facilitating the exchange of information between hospitals, computerized prescription order entry (CPOE) systems, and patients.

A standardized national source for chemotherapy regimens can constitute a preventive safety barrier function in the chemotherapy process [3]. Leotsakos et al. [4] defines standardization as: 'the process of developing, agreeing upon and implementing uniform technical specifications, criteria, methods, processes, designs or practices that can increase compatibility, interoperability, safety, repeatability and, quality'. In the current case, the standardization is one way to ensuring that all involved health care units comply with the latest evidence on chemotherapy treatments, which may also allow for increased patient safety as well as health care cost reductions.

For the national e-library to serve as the intended safety barrier function, it needs to be designed and developed with accordance to user and usability criteria. The e-library was developed in a user-centered process and has been available since 2015 [5]. Representatives from different user groups were involved throughout the development process, including oncology nurses, physicians, hospital pharmacists, cancer patients, and software engineers. Since the information in the library is both complex and extensive it is central that the users can utilize the resource as intended. Otherwise, it might not be the source for improved performance and quality in cancer care that is envisioned. A user evaluation was therefore performed. The result from this will be used to draw conclusions about the initial use of the e-library, and will serve as input to continuous development and improvement. This paper presents the e-library in brief and preliminary results from the ongoing user evaluation. Especially, results from a web survey, web page statistics, and a heuristic evaluation to identify usability issues, are presented.

2   An e-library for Standardized Chemotherapy Regimens

The e-library can be found on www.regimbiblioteket.se. The library contains primarily three types of information: Chemotherapy regimens, Basic drug facts, and Supportive documents. Each document has a time stamp and is available in different formats to support different needs. There are PDF files for easy printing and reading but also XML files, which can be downloaded to the two CPOE systems used in Sweden. Users of the e-library are mainly physicians and nurses in the oncological clinics but pharmacist and representatives from pharmaceutical companies also use the resource.

The e-library contains more than 500 chemotherapy regimens (January 2021, with new ones added continuously). When creating the chemotherapy regimens the guiding principles are: it must be easy for users to grasp important information, and the information should be short, concise, and standardized. The information is therefore divided into three sections: 1) an overview of the regimen including precautions and recommendations for dose reduction, 2) adverse drug reactions, and 3) a schedule with administration details. Along with each regimen there is also a separate Patient information area addressed directly to the patient. An example of the overview section of one specific regimen is found in Fig. 1.

Fig. 1. The overview section of the Cisplatin-Docetaxel regimen for lung cancer.

3 Method

In order to ensure that the e-library is being used as intended and in a safe way, it is necessary to thoroughly evaluate it. A combination of methods was chosen in order to obtain a comprehensive view of the usage, including compilation of subjective views of the users, analysis of statistics from the website, and an expert evaluation of the usability of the webpage. The results will be used to understand where further development is needed or will have most impact. The six methods used are:

1. *Webpage statistics* collected from May 2020 showing number of users in total, unique users, when they visit the e-library and from where the visitors came.
2. A *web survey* for visitors to the e-library page conducted during January 2020. The survey consisted of questions about the role of the visitor, what information they were looking for and how pleased they were with the visit.
3. A *heuristic evaluation* of the user interface [6], performed in June 2020, to identify details in the user interface design that could be improved to increase usability.
4. *Spontaneous user feedback* collected in the form of e-mails sent to the development team/project leader during 2020, from user presenting their role and their questions or suggestions.
5. A *mapping of current regimens organisation*, i.e. identifying the existing variants of systems to manage regimens at each local clinic.
6. *Qualitative interviews* with users from user groups such as nurses, doctors, and pharmacists from various regions in Sweden. Questions about what parts of the e-library they use, how they use it, their experiences of the e-library compared to how they worked before, and their expectations for further development.

4   Results

The preliminary results presented in this paper contain data from parts 1–3, i.e. webpage statistics, the web survey, and the heuristic evaluation.

4.1   Webpage Statistics

During the last 8 months of 2020, the average number of visits to the website per month was just above 2500 and the number of unique visitors was 870. The majority of visitors came from Sweden with some users from other countries in northern Europe, especially Scandinavia. Visitors from Sweden's three largest cities (Stockholm, Gothenburg and Malmoe) accounted for more than 50% of all visits. Most visits took place on Mondays to Fridays but there were 5–10 visits per day on weekends.

4.2   Web Survey

From the survey with 292 answers it became clear that the visitors were mainly physicians but also nurses, and to some extent pharmacists. Almost 80% stated that they searched for regimens and 90% stated that they found what they were looking for. The majority of the users were satisfied with their visit. The less satisfied visitors lacked regimens or diagnostic areas that they were looking for.

4.3   Heuristic Evaluation

A heuristic evaluation according to the Nielsen & Molich [6] framework implies that a product or system is evaluated in a structured way following ten predefined usability heuristics. These are: 1) Visibility of system status, 2) Match between system and the real world, 3) User control and freedom, 4) Consistency and standards, 5) Error prevention, 6) Recognition rather than recall, 7) Flexibility and efficiency of use, 8) Aesthetic and minimalist design, 9) Recognize, diagnose, and recover from errors, 10) Help and documentation. A complete report of the evaluation is beyond the scope of this paper but three examples will be used to demonstrate the result of the heuristic evaluation.

Visibility of System Status. Visibility of system status implies that the system should keep users informed about where they are on the webpage, what is going on, and provide appropriate, timely feedback. The results from the evaluation showed that the information on the webpage is overall well structured, giving feedback on where in the system you are currently located. This feedback could, however, be clarified. The information to help the user orient on the webpage says "You are here: Home page", but as soon as you enter a subpage the name of the current position is not always consistent with the name that is used for this subpage in the menu bar. Such details may cause unnecessary confusion and should be avoided.

Consistency and Standards. This heuristic implies that the system should be consistent regarding terminology, layout, and actions and follow standardized ways of interacting. One example here is the arrows next to each regimen in the list of regimens (Fig. 2a). This type of arrow usually indicates a so called drop-down menu, where the content of the menu is displayed below (drops down) the top element (Fig. 2b). However, in this case the webpage does not work like that. Instead, a list of related regimens are displayed to the right (Fig. 2a) and is hence not used in a way that is consistent with the standardized usage.

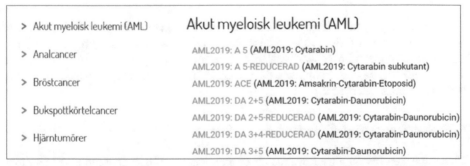

Fig. 2a. The arrows in the regimens menu (to the left) indicate that information will be expanded below the arrow when pressing it. Instead the list of elements are displayed to the right and the arrow changes colour to show that it has been clicked.

Fig. 2b. Example of the standardized use of an arrow in a drop down menu, with the elements of the menu expanding below the title element, and the arrow shifting angle to indicate that it has been expanded.

Help Users Recognize, Diagnose, and Recover from Errors. As the name of this heuristic indicates it is crucial to support the user when something is unclear or goes wrong. One example from the regimen e-library is the search function. If the user searches for a term that does not exist, the presented error message is clear and unambiguous. The problem is, however, that the user does not get any support in formulating the search string. Suggestions on possible strings could be displayed, based on the user writing one or two initial letters for example. And if no exact matches are found to the search string the user only receives an empty result, instead of receiving suggestions on resembling strings. This is especially important since the names of the regimens and the drugs are complex and similar to each other.

To summarize, the e-library follows many of the existing design principles and is usable in its current form. A list of improvement suggestions, based on issues such as the three examples above, was created as a result of this part of the evaluation. The suggestions will be used to improve the webpage interface in order to increase usability and cater for a safer usage.

5   Discussion and Conclusion

This paper reports on a user evaluation of a national e-library containing descriptions of complex chemotherapy regimens, built as a resource for users such as physicians and nurses in oncological clinics and units. The results from the preliminary parts of the user evaluation indicate that the e-library for standardized chemotherapy regimens is being used in the intended way and the users do not have any problems interacting with the resource. The heuristic evaluation showed that there were minor usability issues that should be taken care of to improve the overall usability of the webpage. The web survey showed that the users can find what they are looking for and their main feedback related to the content of the e-library. They wanted more regimens and more diagnostic areas to be covered, which is something that is continuously updated. The expressed needs from the users are useful in order to understand which areas and regimens that should be prioritized in the development. The number of visits indicate that the resource is used extensively and the geographical span shows that the e-library has emerged as the national resource it is intended to be. Users from almost all Swedish regions exist, although the two largest regions (Stockholm and Gothenburg) stand for the main usage. However, the introduction of the library has proceeded fairly quickly and it is believed it is only a matter of time before all regions has adopted the use of the e-library.

The comprehensive user evaluation that is being conducted is an important part of continuing the user-centred process that was started already during the development of the e-library. The combination of methods applied in the evaluation, including both usage statistics, expert methods for usability, and the users' subjective feedback provides a solid base for ensuring that the design and content of the e-library complies with the users' needs. The evaluation is also a vital part in assuring that the library as a patient safety barrier function is well designed and that general design flaws can be avoided, design flaws that otherwise could create new risks in the chemotherapy process.

The next step in the user evaluation includes analysing the spontaneous feedback that the users provide concurrently, and finalizing the interviews (including the mapping of current ways of how users organizes their work with regimens). This will contribute to a deeper understanding of users' judgements about the library content, and help to develop strategies for increasing the national usage of the library. With a broad national usage, the e-library can become a source for organizational and national learning, and a source for continuous improvement of cancer care in Sweden.

References

1. Müller, T.: Typical medication errors in oncology: analysis and prevention strategies. Onkologie 26(6), 539–544 (2003)
2. Weingart, S.N., Zhang, L., Sweeney, M., Hassett, M.: Chemotherapy medication errors. Lancet Oncol. 19(4), e191–e199 (2018)
3. Hollnagel, E.: Barriers and Accident Prevention. Taylor & Francis Ltd., London (2016)
4. Leotsakos, A., Zheng, H., Croteau, R., Loeb, J.M., Sherman, H., Hoffman, C., Morganstein, L., O'Leary, D., Bruneau, C., Lee, P., Duguid, M., Thomeczek, C., van der Schrieck-De Loos, E., Munier, B.: Standardization in patient safety: the WHO high 5s project. Int. J. Qual. Health Care 26(2), 109–116 (2014)
5. Fyhr, A., Borell, J., Jerkeman, M., Ek, Å.: National e-library for standardized chemotherapy regimens. Acta Oncologica 59(9), 1079–1083 (2020)
6. Nielsen, J., Molich, R.: Heuristic evaluation of user interfaces. In: SIGCHI Conference on Human Factors in Computing Systems, pp. 249–256. Association for Computing Machinery, Seattle (1990)

RAMP 2.0 – Further Development of the RAMP Tool

Linda M. Rose[1]([✉]) [iD] and Lina Kluy[1,2] [iD]

[1] KTH Royal Institute of Technology, Stockholm, Sweden
lrose@kth.se
[2] Karlsruhe Institute of Technology, Karlsruhe, Germany

Abstract. RAMP *(Risk Assessment and Management tool for manual handling – Proactively)*, a freely accessible MSD risk management tool for manual handling work, was launched 2017 to contribute to the reduction of musculoskeletal disorder (MSD) risks for manual handling work-tasks. The tool is currently developed further, using an iterative participative methodology, to: *i)* enhance the RAMP tool's application range, mainly to include hand-intensive work, *ii)* develop a system version of the tool, and *iii)* include key performance indicators (KPIs). A needs analysis resulted in 99 identified needs. Regarding *i)*, six needs were assessed as "very important to include" to enhance the application range. A literature study focusing on relevant risk factors and how exposure to them is associated with MSD risks was carried out and first drafts of a model for assessing risks in hand-intensive work are iteratively developed, using feedback from intended users. Regarding *ii)*, 50 needs and suggestions on what to consider when developing a databased system version of the RAMP tool were identified. Prototypes of parts of the system-version are iteratively developed, using intended users' feedback. Regarding *iii)*, the needs analysis resulted in 16 suggested KPIs, including KPIs based solely on RAMP results and KPIs which can be established combining RAMP results and company data. The project is ongoing. An enhanced RAMP tool, RAMP 2.0, with the abovementioned expansions could support MSD risk assessment and risk management in systematic MSD risks reduction work for a wide range of work tasks.

Keywords: Risk assessment · Risk management · MSDs · Tool · Participatory ergonomics

1 Introduction

1.1 Background

Work-related injuries are still a problem worldwide [1] and lead to negative consequences at many levels, including the societal level. With changing demographics, there is a need for prolonged working life to match peoples increased lifespan, which, in turn, leads to an increased need for sustainable jobs [2] and an urgency to deal with these types of injuries, to reduce their negative effects. As an example, within the EU, the societal costs

© The Author(s), under exclusive license to Springer Nature Switzerland AG 2021
N. L. Black et al. (Eds.): IEA 2021, LNNS 222, pp. 182–189, 2021.
https://doi.org/10.1007/978-3-030-74611-7_25

for such injuries are assessed to exceed 3 % of the GNP (Gross National Product) [3]. Musculoskeletal disorders (MSDs) constitute a large part of the work-related injuries [1] and in Sweden more than one third of the work-related diseases 2019 were attributed to factors known to increase the risks of developing MSDs, including monotonous or unusually strenuous movements or work postures [4].

Several tools have been developed to assess the risk of developing MSDs. Most of these tools can be applied for assessing the risks of developing MSDs in one or a few body parts, e.g. the upper extremities, as is the case with the RULA method [5], or assessing certain types of work, e.g. lifting, which can be done using the revised NIOSH equation [6]. Further, generally the tools only support parts of the systematic risk management process described in the ISO standard 31000 [7].

In a research and development project a more comprehensive risk assessment *and* risk management tool, RAMP (*Risk Assessment and Management tool for manual handling – Proactively*) [8] was developed to contribute to the reduction of MSD risks for manual handling work tasks. The RAMP tool was launched in 2017, is freely accessible globally via *ramp.proj.kth.se* and consists of four modules:

- *The checklist-based RAMP I for screening of MSD risks*
- *RAMP II which enables a more in depth analysis*
- *The Results module for presenting, visualising and communicating the results*
- *The Action module, supporting the development of risk reducing measures and systematic risk management*

In the RAMP tool, the assessment results are presented with a three colour coding system (for details see [8]). E.g. in RAMP II, "red" signals high risk for many employees and that risk reduction measures should be prioritized (red risk and priority level, RPL). In addition, yellow RPL signals elevated risk some and that risk reduction measures should be taken, while a green RPL signals that for most employees the risk is low, but that risk reduction measures may be needed for some employees.

The RAMP tool is part of the RAMP Package, which also includes the abovementioned website as well as online courses to train users in the tools use. Further, it was developed to be compatible with the with the ISO 31000 standard and is, to the best of our knowledge, the only tool in the area including risk assessments that supports the whole systematic risk management process [7, 8]. Since the launch in 2017, RAMP has been spread to over 100 countries. Feedback from RAMP users has highlighted wishes for further development of the tool. To meet these, the RAMP 2.0-project was started.

1.2 Objective

The objective of the RAMP 2.0 project is to develop RAMP further by: *i*) enhancing the RAMP tool's application range, mainly to assess MSD risks in hand-intensive work, *ii*) developing a system version (using a database) of RAMP, and *iii*) including key performance indicators (KPIs).

The objective can be visually illustrated as in Fig. 1, where the left-hand side illustrates the current RAMP (1.0) and the right-hand side illustrates the desired features in the RAMP 2.0 currently being developed.

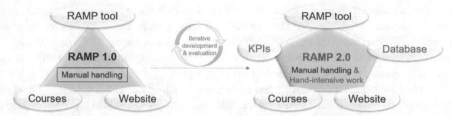

Fig. 1. The objectives of the RAMP 2.0 project: to develop the RAMP Package from the current RAMP 1.0 (left side) to the RAMP 2.0 (right side), by enhancing its application range to include hand-intensive work, develop a database-based system version of RAMP and include KPIs.

2   Methods

The project is carried out in collaboration between researchers and practitioners at organisations from five industrial sectors including manufacturing and dental care using an iterative methodology [9]. Practitioners with different roles, i.a. assembly line workers, OSH representatives, and company managers participate. Additionally, several expert groups with in total over 30 experts are linked to the project, including researchers and practitioners with expert knowledge in physical ergonomics and MSDs.

On a meta-level, a participatory methodological approach is used. First, a needs analysis was carried out among the participating organisations. They identified needs and weighed them using a three-graded scale on priority level, where: *1 = Very important to include; 2 = Would be good to include*; and *3 = Less important to include.*

Subsequently, a literature study focusing on hand-intensive work risk factors was carried out. This consisted of three parts: a scoping literature study in PubMed and Scopus focused on risk factors for developing MSD injuries in the upper extremities, literature recommended by researchers linked to the project and a review of the basis for some commonly used risk assessment tools.

Based on these, drafts of a hand-intensive work risk category model in the RAMP tool have been constructed and are currently under iterative development.

In the database development, an agile methodology is used, using e.g. user stories and user feedback, and usability workshops are an important part thereof.

In the KPI development, the identified needs have been structured into KPIs solely retrievable from RAMP results and KPIs which can be established by using combined results from RAMP and company in-house data.

3   Results

The main results so far are presented in the same order as the objectives above.

3.1   Enhancing the RAMP Tool's Application Range

The needs analysis resulted in 33 identified needs regarding enhancing the application range of the RAMP tool. Further processing of the needs, e.g. priority-weighing them

Table 1. Identified needs prioritized to include in RAMP 2.0 to assess hand-intensive work. with a weighing where "1" = "Very important to include" and "2" = "Would be good to include".

Need	Identified types of activities to include in the model	Weighing
S1	Gripping with & movements of fingers	1
S2	Hand activities affecting forearm supination & pronation	1
S3	Impact with hand or hand tool	2
S4	(High) Force exertion with tool	1
S5	Precision work	1
S6	Pushing/pulling with fingers/hand & arm	1
S7	Using tools with reaction parameters	1

	Type of parameter	Risk factors considered relevant to include
A	Grip	A1. Type of grip: from pinch to power 1
		A2. Contact area
B	Force amplitude	B1. Fingers
		B2. Hand
C	Time aspects (include some)	C1. Frequency
		C2. Duration
		C3. Duty-cycle
D	Postures	D1. Wrist Flexion/extension
		D2. Wrist Radial/ulnar deviation
		D3. Forearm rotation (Supination/pronation)
E	Exertion type (include some)	E1. Mainly exerting gripping force, e.g. with tongues, or
		E2. Exertion including reacting to kick-back, shock or impact, or
		E3. Hand or tool for impact exertion, e.g. hammers (w.vibration)
F	Combinations	F1, F2, etc., Research-based combinations for some of the above

Fig. 2. Suggested hand-intensive work model structure. Types of parameters (A–E) and combinations of them (F), each parameter with different possible risk factors considered for inclusion. Text within brackets ( ) provides information on design decisions to be made.

(see Methods), resulted in six needs assessed as "very important to include" and one assessed as "would be good to include" in the enhanced RAMP tool (Table 1).

In the literature study, relevant risk factors and how exposure to them is associated with MSD risks, e.g. repetitive forceful exertions, were identified. First drafts of a model for assessing risks in hand-intensive work have been constructed and are iteratively developed using feedback from intended users. Figure 2 illustrates the 1st suggested structure of a model (suggesting what type of parameters risk factors to include) to assess hand- intensive work including the identified needs in Table 1.

This suggested structure was iterated after feedback, thereafter the development work continued by grouping the results from the literature study according to the parameters and risk factors illustrated in Fig. 2. In the next step, several prototypes of a model based on the needs in Table 1, the suggested parameters and risk factors in Fig. 2 and the literature study results was developed. It is currently further developed iteratively in close collaboration with and through feedback from industrial participants as well as the different expert groups associated with the project. The development is still ongoing and the model for assessing risks in hand-intensive work will be presented once the model development is finished and the model shows satisfactory reliability and usability.

3.2   Developing a System Version of the RAMP Tool

The initial workshops with the organisations resulted in 50 suggestions on what to consider when developing a databased version of the RAMP tool, e.g. which user roles should be available. More than 65 user stories were developed. Based on these, first iterations of parts of the database, namely for one of the tool modules (RAMP I) and for the database authentication design were developed and presented for intended users. Table 2 presents a selection of the user feedback. This agile development is ongoing in collaboration with intended users, who mainly provide feedback at workshops.

Table 2. Examples of characteristics regarded to have high priority in the development of thesystem version of the RAMP tool by participants in the 1st usability workshop.

Characteristics	Example
Security	Only authorized users get access to and can change data
Authentication	Register and login to the system version of RAMP
Easy to make changes and save assessments as a different case	Make changes in an existing, saved assessment for a workstation after risk reduction measures have been taken and save the assessment under a new ID
Present results at different levels of detail & scope	Present results: in detail for production line managers and at a comprehensive, overview level to company management
Easy to export data from and into the database	Easy procedure for choosing results data to be included in presentations; easy transfer of data from the database to another software, e.g. Excel
Several ICT applications	Use RAMP on e.g. a laptop and a tablet
Integrated short user guide	Explanation of e.g. what "good grip" means in RAMP

3.3 Including KPIs

The needs analysis resulted in five suggested KPIs with data retrievable from RAMP assessments solely, e.g. the ratio between the number of "red" RPL assessments with RAMP II (see 1.1) at a department during a period of time and the number of all risk assessments ($\sum RA$) at the same department during that period of time. Figure 3 shows a visualization of this KPI, the $KPI_{R/\sum RA}$ (fictive data). Figure 4 displays the data used for calculating the $KPI_{R/\sum RA}$ in this example (the number of "green", "yellow" and "red" RPL assessments at the department and during the period of time (fictive data).

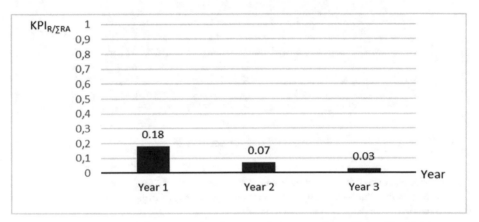

Fig. 3. Illustration of the $KPI_{R/\sum RA}$ displaying the ratio between the number of "red" risk assessments and the total number of risk assessments at a department, over a three year period (fictive data and results from using RAMP II).

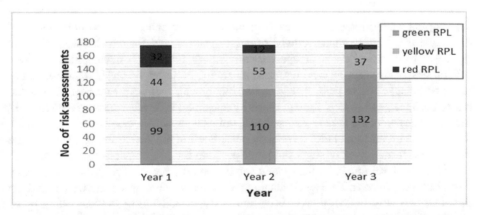

Fig. 4. Visualization of the the data used for calculating the $KPI_{R/\sum RA}$ in Fig 3 (fictive data).

In addition, 11 KPIs, which can be established combining RAMP results and company in-house data, e.g. combining elevated risk data and number of sick-leave days, have also been suggested. Figure 5 displays such a KPI ($KPI_{R/SL}$), defined as the ratio between the number of RAMP II risk assessments with a red RPL at a department and the number of sick-leave days at the same department for three subsequent years (fictive data).

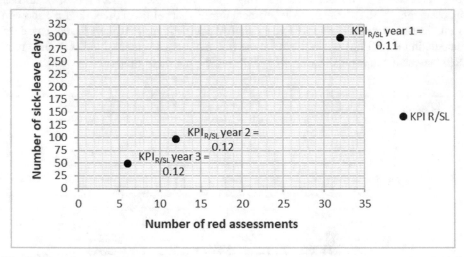

Fig. 5. Visualisation of the KPI showing the ratio of number of "red" assessments using RAMP II and the number of sick-leave days per year at a department, (KPI$_{R/SL}$) over a three year period (fictive data).

4 Discussion

Developing a hand-intensive risk assessment model is a delicate and complicated task, e.g. regarding how to model *combinations* of risk factors for which associations to increased MSD risks have been reported *individually*. Further, the development involves several design choices and can be seen as balancing between, on one hand, including as many relevant factors as possible and, on the other hand, keeping the number of included factors at a reasonable level for e.g. usability reasons. The needs analysis resulted in 99 identified needs for the RAMP 2.0, ranked at three levels. So far, mainly the needs ranked as "very important to include" have been considered in the development. However, the other needs form a bank of suggestions for possible future extensions of the tool.

Also, the development of the system version and the KPIs are not trivial, with many design choices to be made. Here, balancing, on the one hand, needs and wishes and, on the other hand, available resources is continuously needed during this four year project.

The iterative development continues and the RAMP 2.0 is planned to be launched in 2022. An enhanced RAMP tool, RAMP 2.0, with the abovementioned expansions could support MSD risk assessment and risk management in systematic MSD risks reduction work for a wide range of work tasks. This would enhance the current RAMP tools ability to contribute to achieving the UN Sustainable Development Goals (SDG) [2], e.g. SDG # 3: Good health and well-being and SDG # 8: Decent work and economic growth.

5 Conclusion

The development this far has resulted in a needs analysis and first drafts of the three parts: *i*) enhanced application range (a hand-intensive work model), *ii*) system version of the tool and *iii*) KPIs - both KPIs retrievable from RAMP results only and KPIs established by using results from RAMP and company in-house data.

References

1. International Labour Organization (ILO) Global trends on occupational accidents and diseases. World Day for Safety and Health at WorkPdf (2015). https://www.ilo.org/legacy/english/osh/en/story_content/external_files/fs_st_1-ILO_5_en.pdf, Accessed 26 Oct 2018
2. United Nations: Sustainable Development Goals. https://www.un.org/sustainabledevelopment/sustainable-development-goals/, Accessed 06 Feb 2021
3. Tan, B.K., Tan Wee, J., Remes, J., Takala, J.: cost estimates based on ILO global estimates on the burden of accidents and diseases at work and disability adjusted life years. In: Workplace Safety and Health Institute, Singapore (2017)
4. Arbetsmiljöverket, SCB: Arbetsmiljöstatistik Rapport 2020:01 Arbetsskador 2019. Occupational accidents and work-related diseases. Report 2020:01 (2020). (in Swedish)
5. McAtamney, L., Corlett, E.N.: RULA: a survey method for the investigation of work-related upper limb disorders. Appl. Ergonomics **24**(2), 91–99 (1993)
6. Waters, T.R., Putz-Anderson, V., Garg, A., Fine, L.J.: Revised NIOSH equation for the design and evaluation of manual lifting tasks. Ergonomics **36**(7), 749–776 (1993)
7. International Organization for Standardization (ISO): Risk Management - Principles and Guidelines. ISO 31000:2009 (2009)
8. Rose, L.M., Eklund, J., Nord Nilsson, L., Barman, L., Lind, C.M.: The RAMP package for MSD risk management in manual handling – a freely accessible tool, with website and training courses. Appl. Ergonomics **86**, 103101 (2020)
9. Martin, J.L., Norris, B.J., Murphy, E., Crowe, J.A.: Medical device development: the challenge for ergonomics. Appl. Ergonomics **39**(3), 271–283 (2008)

Development of Thumb Endurance Curves Applicable for Deadman Switches in Sandblasting Machines

Arijit K. Sengupta[✉], Ugur Oztas, and Anthony Krake

New Jersey Institute of Technology, Newark, NJ 07102, USA
sengupta@njit.edu

Abstract. Thumb operated deadman switches used in sandblasting machines are designed to prevent serious bodily injury from unintentional discharge of high velocity sand. The force required to hold down the switch is significant, causing fatigue and pain to set in very quickly in operator's thumb. The objective of this study was to determine the thumb force capacity and muscle fatigue curves for thumb flexion, applicable for design of these devices. Maximum thumb pressing force (MTPF) and endurance times (ET) for holding down at force levels of 10, 20, 40, and 60% of MTPF were measured from 10 male and 10 female participants in a laboratory experiment. The best fit curves of ET as a function of %MTPF were modeled with $R^2 > 95\%$. These models should be used in matching the worker strength capacity to the thumb force requirements in deadman switch design to improve safety standards in sandblasting.

Keywords: Thumb pressing · Muscle fatigue · Endurance time · Deadman switch · Sandblasting

1 Introduction

Sandblasting machines use a compressed air source connected to a container of sand, and a flexible hose with a hand-held nozzle to propel high velocity sand on a surface for cleaning or removing paint or rust etc. Apart from the health risks from dust inhalation, silicosis and high level of noise, accidental body contact with the sand discharge can develop serious injuries and death [1]. This type of accident can happen if the operator loses balance or trip on an uneven floor while sandblasting. To prevent such accidents, blast nozzles are equipped with a deadman switch that cuts of sand discharge in the event the nozzle is accidentally released from the operator's hand. Deadman switch shuts off the equipment when the worker is not holding it down. When it is properly used, a worker who drops a hose is protected because the flow of abrasive material is stopped by the switch not being held down. However, in some cases, workers bypasses the switch, and this can result in the equipment not shutting off, and the hose can spray everybody in the vicinity. Occupational Safety and Health Administration (OSHA) [2] mandates that "the blast cleaning nozzles shall be equipped with an operating valve which must be held

N. L. Black et al. (Eds.): IEA 2021, LNNS 222, pp. 190–195, 2021.
https://doi.org/10.1007/978-3-030-74611-7_26

open manually". An accident search in OSHA website with a keyword "sandblasting" [3] reveals a number of similar accidents in recent years with serious injuries and death.

A typical electrical deadman switch uses a thumb operated trigger (Fig. 1a) that needs to be actively pressed down (Fig. 1b) to maintain the sand discharge. The inch long trigger is stiff and guarded from two sides to prevent discharge if the nozzle is accidentally dropped from hand. This trigger creates a significant and static force on the user's thumb, and fatigue sets in very quickly. This muscle fatigue manifests as pain in the thumb muscles under static tension. To avoid pain, many operators modify these deadman switches by taping the trigger in an open position or placing a rock under the switch forcing it into an open position. Either of these two methods creates risk in the event of an accident.

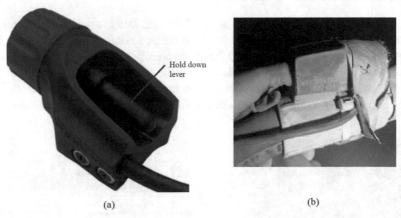

(a)   (b)

Fig. 1. (a) A Typical electrical deadman control switch; (b) assembled sandblasting hose with the deadman control switch.

Clearly the safety problem is related to thumb muscle fatigue. The only thumb fatigue model found in literature was developed by Choi et al. [4] for physiotherapist's work, and pipette-based laboratory work. The thumb positioning and the muscle group involved in their study were entirely different from operating a "deadman" switch in sandblasting. Many other muscle fatigue models, reviewed by El Ahrache et al. [5], were developed for different large muscle groups. Their review reported remarkable variances between ET values for different muscle groups. Thus none of the muscle fatigue data are applicable for deadman switch design. This lack of data in thumb muscle fatigue means that engineers designing these deadman switches do not have appropriate baseline of human capabilities to reference. Thus objective of this study was set to determine relationship between ET and the submaximal thumb pressing force (in terms of %MTPF) applicable to deadman switch design, with a goal to improve safety of sandblasting operation.

2   Methods

2.1   Participants

The experimental study was approved by the Institutional Review Board. Ten male and ten female subjects participated in this study with mean (standard deviation) of age 31 (11) years, height 67.3 (3.9) inches and weight 148.7 (33.3) lbs. Only healthy adults with no contraindicated health conditions or history of pre-existing thumb, hand or wrist injury, were eligible to participate in the study. The participants were paid $20 for their service.

2.2   Apparatus and Data Collection

A Datalog module (MVX8), a Pinch-meter (P200) and Datalite data acquisition system (Biometric Ltd.) were used to collect thumb force and holding time data. Participants pressed on the Pinch-meter (Fig. 2a) by the thumb area, between the interphalangeal joint and the middle of their nail plate, while keeping the wrist straight. The data acquisition software displayed real-time thumb force data on a moving timeline on the computer screen (Fig. 2b). The pinch-meter was calibrated prior to data collection.

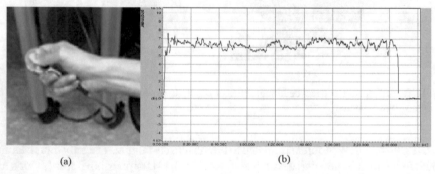

(a)   (b)

Fig. 2. (a) Pinch meter (P 200, Biometric Ltd.) is pressed by thumb, and (b) thumb force level display over time line for %MTPF trials.

2.3   Experimental Procedure

At the beginning of the experimental trial, the MTPF of a participant was measured over a duration of 4 to 6 s. The measurement was repeated three times with two minute rest pauses between trials. The maximum from these three trials was taken as the MTPF for the participant.

Following the MTPF measurement, endurance times (ET) were measured for targeted static exertions of 10, 20, 40, and 60% of MTPF, presented in a randomized order. Participants pressed the Pinch-meter to the targeted %MTPF force level and was instructed to hold the force level constant until they could no longer maintain the force level due to discomfort or pain from muscle fatigue. For time constraint, any trial that reached 20 min was terminated. Only three 10% MTPF trials reached 20 min. Five minutes or more rest pauses were given between trials to recover from muscle fatigue. During this time, participants filled in a feedback form noting down their level of pain, discomfort, numbness, and cramping in a scale of 0 (none) – 9 (highest). Each participant took about 1.5 h to complete the experiment.

2.4 Data Processing and Model Development

The participants tried to maintain the targeted %MTPF, however, there was some minor fluctuations of force over the ET, as seen in Fig. 2b. For fatigue modelling, the average thumb force over the ET was calculated, and %MTPF values were recalculated from the MTPF. The difference from the target %MTPF were nominal. For targeted %MTPF of 10, 20, 40, and 60% the corrected %MTPF's averaged at 10, 19, 37 and 54%, respectively, when calculated over all participants. The corrected %MTPF values were used in fatigue modeling.

Curve fitting function in Excel was used to obtain least square fit between ET and %MTPF values for all participants. The exponential function gave the best curve fit with coefficient of determination $R^2 > 0.95$.

3 Results

Figure 3 shows the least square fitted, exponential curves superimposed on the data points from male and female participants. As expected, the nonlinear curves show that when the %MTPF levels have decreased, the ET values have increased. In the range of 40 to 100% MTPF, the ET values were small, less than a minute. For lower than 40% MTPF, the endurance times have increased substantially.

The exponential functions for (i) combined male and female, (ii) male, and (iii) female populations are provided in Eqs. (1), (2) and (3), respectively. The coefficient of determinations R^2 were 0.95, 0.95 and 0.97, respectively.

$$Combined : ET = 18.177e^{-5.875*\%MTPF} \tag{1}$$

$$Male : ET = 13.823e^{-5.625*\%MTPF} \tag{2}$$

$$Female : ET = 24.381e^{-6.196*\%MTPF} \tag{3}$$

Participants noted different symptoms, ranging from shaking, numbness, tingling, burning, cramping, and pain at the end of ET measurement trials. The average discomfort levels (0–9 scale, 9 being most sever) at 10, 20, 40, and 60% MTPF levels were 6.4, 5.4, 5.5 and 5.4, respectively. At 10% MTPF, discomfort levels were generally higher. The discomfort levels indicated onset of localized muscle fatigue at the end of ET trials.

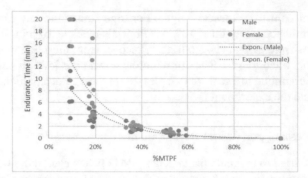

Fig. 3. Least square fitted exponential curves relating ET (min) to %MTPF values for both genders.

4 Discussion

The fatigue curves show that when %MTPF is less than 40%, the ET value increases noticeably – this trend was similar to the results from previous studies on muscle fatigue [5]. Female ETs were longer than males, especially at lower %MTPF levels (10 & 20%), which was also observed by other researchers [4, 5]. While the endurance time for female was 13.1 min at 10% MTPF, the male could perform 7.9 min for the same relative force level. The absolute thumb force was obviously higher for male compared to female. The average male MTPF (26.5 lbs) was 45% more than female MTPF (18.3 lbs). This study produced smaller ET values for 10% MTPF (7.9 min) and 20% MTPF (4.5 min) for male population, when compared to Choi et al. [3] results (12.4 and 6.1 min, respectively). This difference supports our hypothesis that different muscle groups of thumb will have different fatigue curves.

A typical deadman switch (Fig. 1a) requires approximately 3.4 lbs. of holding down force. At this force level, Eq. (2) predicts thumb fatigue would set in after 6.7 min for an average male, which is less than the usual continuous operating time of at least 15 min for sand blasting operations. With the present design, muscle fatigue and pain is unavoidable as the operating time exceeds ET. Equation (2) predicts that 3.2% MTPF can be maintained for an ET of 15 min. Similar calculation can be performed for any desired ET for combined male-female, male or female population using Eqs. (1), (2) and (3), respectively .

Sandblasting operators wear protective clothing, helmets, breathing apparatus, and they also experience high level of noise. All these factors, not been considered in present study, should adversely affect the worker's ET. Thus the ET values from this study should be further adjusted down when designing deadman controls.

This analysis shows that the design improvement of deadman switch is essential by substantially reducing the hold down force. Reducing hold down force may require an additional safety switch to prevent inadvertent actuation of the deadman switch. Two switch designs are used in many existing power tools to prevent inadvertent actuation. Another alternative could be using a lever that can be actuated by a power grip, instead of thumb alone to reduce muscle fatigue.

Acknowledgements. This publication was supported by the Grant Number, T42OH008422, funded by the Centers for Disease Control and Prevention. Its contents are solely the responsibility of the authors and do not necessarily represent the official views of the Centers for Disease Control and Prevention or the Department of Health and Human Services.

References

1. NIOSH publication # 75–122, Industrial Health and Safety Criteria for Abrasive Blast Cleaning Operations. https://www.cdc.gov/niosh/docs/75-122/pdfs/75-122.pdf, Accessed 2 June 2021
2. OSHA e-CFR 1910.244(b) Abrasive blast cleaning nozzles. https://www.osha.gov/laws-regs/interlinking/standards/1910.244(b), Accessed 2 June 2021
3. OSHA, Accident Search Results, Kewword; "Sandblasting". https://www.osha.gov/pls/imis/AccidentSearch.search?acc_keyword=%22Sandblasting%22&keyword_list=on, Accessed 2 June 2021
4. Choi, K., Lee, S., Lee, J., Kong, Y.: Development of thumb endurance curves associated with various exertion levels. Hum. Fact. Ergonomics Manuf. Serv. Ind. **27**(5), 249–255 (2017)
5. El Ahrache, K., Imbeau, D., Farbos, B.: Percentile values for determining maximum endurance times for static muscular work. Int. J. Ind. Ergonomics **36**(2), 99–108 (2006)

Hardiness Personality Disposition and Safety Citizenship Behaviour of Miners in the Ghana's Mining Industry

Joana Eva Dodoo[1] and Lilis Surienty[2(✉)]

[1] College of Distance Education, University of Cape Coast, Cape Coast, Ghana
[2] School of Management, Universiti Sains Malaysia, George Town, Penang, Malaysia
lilis@usm.my

Abstract. Contemporary safety literature points to safety citizenship behaviour (SCB) as a critical prevention behaviour against workplace incidents in today's high-risk industries. This paper seeks to investigate antecedents of two distinct dimensions of SCB (affiliation-oriented and change-oriented) among miners/employees. The objectives of the study are in threefold: (a) to explore the effect of resilient dispositional hardiness traits on psychological safety; (b) to examine the effect of psychological safety on SCB; and (c) to examine the mediating role of psychological safety on the relationship between hardy traits and SCB. Survey collected from a sample of 316 respondents drawn from six large-scale gold mining companies in Ghana found that, psychological safety has a positive and significant influence on the display of SCB among employees. Specifically, hardiness component of commitment, control and challenge were associated with psychological safety, significantly. The result showed that psychological safety mediated the relationship between commitment and control and SCB dimensions which are affiliation-oriented (safety stewardship) and change-oriented (employee safety voice). However, there is no supporting evidence for a mediation of psychological safety for the relationship between challenge hardiness trait and SCB. The findings have important implications for research and practice. In particular, it demonstrates the usefulness of psychological safety and SCB, and its role for developing current and future safety needs of organisations such as the mining companies. It sheds light on the differential effects of hardiness traits, and offers a more nuanced interplay between resilient disposition and SCB.

Keywords: Safety citizenship behaviour · Hardiness traits · Psychological safety · Safety stewardship · Employee safety voice · Mining

1 Introduction

High-risk industries such as the mining activities are in greater need of proactive employees who promote safety needs. One principle that could extend the safety practices to go beyond only safety compliance is the safety citizenship behaviour (SCB). SCB refers to voluntary and discretionary extra-role employee behaviours that are not contractually rewarded, yet promoted current and future workplace safety in organisations

N. L. Black et al. (Eds.): IEA 2021, LNNS 222, pp. 196–204, 2021.
https://doi.org/10.1007/978-3-030-74611-7_27

[1]. The relevance of SCB has been noted in its ability to inspire change-oriented and affiliation-oriented behaviours among employees in order to support risk management and decrease the occurrence of workplace incidents [2–4]. Yet, less scholarly attention has been devoted to exploring a wide-ranging antecedent of SCB in safety research.

Moreover, studies examining SCB have shown that employees perceive their relationship with their organisations as reciprocal. Reciprocal relationships are rooted in the social exchange theory (SET) [6]. For example, Reader, Mearns [7] confirmed that SCB was a product of social exchange relationship. Hofmann, Morgeson [1] and Didla, Mearns [3] found SCB as a consequence of SET. Their findings, pointed out that perceived quality of leader-member-exchange relationship, influenced by a positive safety climate inspired SCB among employees. Curcuruto and Griffin [2] and Laurent, Chmiel [8] demonstrated that demonstrated that SET underpinned SCB among steel workers.

Although past research has consistently addressed SCB as a consequent of SET, there is a call for adjustment to the traditional SET principles. Chernyak-Hai and Rabenu [9] indicated that to maintain the relevance of SET for the new era workplace relationship requires a consideration of the role of additional factors such as individual personal values. It was argued that personal values that relate to needs and goals of individuals have implication for citizenship behaviours. The current study is grounded on the SET and supported by hardiness trait theory. The study seeks to investigate the role of hardiness traits for generating SCB among employees. The objectives are in threefold: (a) to explore the effect of resilient dispositional hardiness traits on psychological safety; (b) to examine the effect of psychological safety on SCB; and (c) to examine the mediating role of psychological safety on the relationship between hardy traits and SCB.

1.1 Literature Review

The study applies the concept of affiliation-oriented and change-oriented SCB proposed by Curcuruto and Griffin [2]. Affiliation-oriented SCB concerns employee actions that seek to strengthen and preserve interpersonal relationship in the workplace. Research evidence suggests that affiliation-oriented SCB among employees influences safety compliance and overall safety management significantly [1]. Behaviours such as altruism and courtesy [10], helping co-workers with safety issues and safety stewardship [5] have been identified in the literature as variables that measure affiliation-oriented SCB. Ongoing SCB research measured all affiliation-oriented behaviours as safety stewardship [2, 4].

In relation to change-oriented SCB, the term employee safety voice is used to describe communications which are directed towards change and improvement to safety in the workplace [2, 11]. Change-oriented SCB involves speaking up [12], taking initiatives to improve safety, and whistle blowing [10]. Employee voice behaviours carries the potential to alter existing relationships, loss of image and career [13]. The recognition of the threats inherent in employee proactivity has prompted research to consider a supportive environment that provides cognitive and emotional security for employees. Morrison [14] identified disposition, job attitudes, psychological safety and leadership behaviours as antecedents of voice behaviours.

1.2 Hardiness Commitment, Control, and Challenge and Psychological Safety

Research considers hardiness disposition to comprise three sub traits namely, commitment, control and challenge [15]. Commitment refers to the extent of individual's engagement in different facets of life domain such as family, friends and work [16]. Control captures an intrinsic need to feel capable of managing events that surround an individual's life and environment. Thus, one's inability to control such events lead to stress [15]. Challenge refers to individual's interpretation of difficult situations, as either a challenge to overcome or a threat to their existence [16]. The three hardy traits are characteristic of core adult behaviours, and are critical for sustainable exchange relationship.

Employees in high-risk industries are exposed to varying degrees of stress and danger, and require sustained physical and psychological efforts to stay safe and alive [20]. Previous literature found association between dispositional traits and psychological safety [21]. Resilient traits constructs generally associated with psychological safety are proactive personality [22], emotional stability and locus of control [23]. Significant relationship was found for proactive personality, emotional stability, learning orientation and psychological safety [24]. Although a review of the literature does not suggest direct relationship between hardiness traits and psychological safety, yet it also suggests a theoretical linkage between dispositional traits and psychological safety. Thus, we envisaged that resilient hardiness traits will be associated with psychological safety. We propose the following hypotheses:

Hypothesis 1: Commitment has a positive and significant relationship with psychological safety.
Hypothesis 2: Control has a positive and significant relationship with psychological safety.
Hypothesis 3: Challenge has a positive and significant relationship with psychological safety.

1.3 Psychological Safety and Affiliation-Oriented and Change-Oriented SCB

Previous research considers psychological safety as a context factor that supports interpersonal risk-taking behaviours [13]. Psychological safety creates a context in which employees feel safe to interact with institutional structures in the workplace based on a belief that others will not punish them for it. Significant relationship was found for psychological safety and affiliation-oriented citizenship behaviours [24–26], and employee voice behaviour [27–29]. In line with above, we propose the following hypotheses:

Hypothesis 4: Psychological safety has a positive and significant relationship with affiliation-oriented safety citizenship behaviour.
Hypothesis 5: Psychological safety has a positively and significant relationship with change-oriented safety citizenship behaviour.

1.4 Psychological Safety as a Mediator for Hardiness Commitment, Control, Challenge, and Affiliation-Oriented and Change-Oriented SCB

Safety research captures dispositional traits as distal antecedents of SCB [30]. It has led to a consideration of psychological factors that facilitate workplace safety behaviour. Psychological safety strikes as a key mediator for the relationship between individual disposition and SCB. Psychological safety mediated the relationship between personality traits and OCB [24]. Previous research has shown that psychological safety mediates the relationship between disposition and affiliation-oriented and change-oriented citizenship behaviour [31]. Psychological safety mediated the link between core self-evaluation [32], proactive personality [33], locus of control [23] and employee voice behaviour. Thus, we propose that:

Hypothesis 6: Psychological safety will mediate the relationship between hardiness commitment, control, challenge and SCB.

2 Methodology

The study collected data from miners across six large-scale multinational gold mining companies in Ghana. Data collection was limited to only employees at the operational process of mining work. This was because, the daily work tasks of such employees make them subject to open risks and dangers associated with mining, thus are considered as the primary agents of SCB. Data was collected through self-reported rating. A multiple-item based survey instrument was distributed to employees. To ensure representativeness, participants were stratified into different departments such as exploration (geology), technical service (engineering), production, plant and metallurgy, heavy mining equipment, health, safety and environment and protection service. A sample of 382 were decided proportionately from each department. The first author spent 6 months in Ghana (from June to November, 2019) visiting the mines to distribute and collect completed questionnaires. Safety Officers or Site supervisors in each of the departments assisted with the distribution and collection of questionnaires. Three hundred and twenty-five (325) of the questionnaires were returned yielding a total of 70.6% rate of return. Three hundred and sixteen (316) were found usable and were analysed.

2.1 Measures

The proposed relationships among the key variables (see Fig. 1) were measured using a questionnaire based on validated scales. Hardiness traits sub-scales were assessed using the revised dispositional resilience scale (DRS-15) developed by Hystad, Eid [34]. The DRS-15 comprises 15 positive and negative closed ended statements which measure the three sub traits namely: commitment, control and challenge. Psychological safety (PS) was measured using the seven-item Likert scale developed by Edmondson (1999). SCB measures were adapted from Curcuruto and Griffin [2]. Five items were used to assess safety stewardship (ST) and employee safety voice (ESV) each. All measures had reported high reliability coefficient of between .62 to .92.

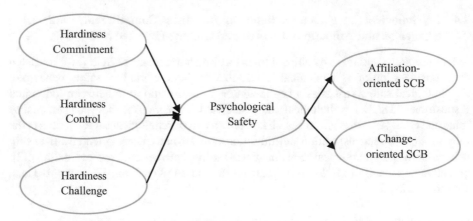

Fig. 1. Path diagram of hardiness traits, psychological safety, and affiliation and change oriented SCB

3 Data Analysis and Results

3.1 Assessment of Measurement Model

The study used the partial least squares structural equation model (PLS-SEM) approach via the SmartPLS 3.0 software [36] to examine each of the hypotheses. First, the reliability, convergent and discriminant validity analysis were performed to assess the quality of the measurement model. The factor loading, average variance extracted (AVE), and composite reliability (CR) exceeded the recommended threshold value of $>.7$ [35]. Discriminant validity was tested using the hetero-trait-mono-trait criteria (HTMT) ratio of correlation [37]. Results suggested that the required discriminant validity had been achieved since none of the values exceeded the conservative $HTMT._{85}$ threshold.

3.2 Assessment of Structural Model

The structural model was assessed by the following: assessment of collinearity, significance of structural model relationship, R^2 measures (coefficient of determination), effect size (f^2), and assessment of predictive relevance (Q^2) [35]. The results showed that all values ranged from 1.000 to 1.391, indicating that the collinearity for the structural model had not been violated [38]. A bootstrap analysis of 5000 subsamples was performed at statistical significance of $p < .05$ and path coefficients critical value of $t > 1.645$ (one-tailed) [38]. The results showed support for all the hypothesised relationships (see Table 1).

The results show that adjusted R^2 values of the combined effect of the independent variables (IV) on the dependent variables (DV) were: employee safety voice (.033), psychological safety (.233), and safety stewardship (.035). Applying Cohen [39] rule of thumb for interpreting R^2, the results suggest a close to substantial contribution (23.3%) of challenge, commitment and control for the variances in psychological safety. In addition, the results show weak variances (3.3% and 3.5%) in employee safety voice

Table 1. Significant relationships among study variables

Effect	Variable relationships	Beta	SE	t value	p value	f^2	Confidence interval (BC)	
							LL	UL
Direct effect	HCH > PS	.135	.055	2.469	.007**	.020	.037	.216
	HCM > PS	.224	.064	3.524	.000**	.051	.117	.326
	HCT > PS	.265	.058	4.608	.000**	.066	.165	.353
	PS > ESV	.191	.059	3.209	.001**	.038	.075	.266
	PS > SST	.195	.067	2.903	.002**	.039	.086	.280

$**p < .01$, $*p < .05$, LL 5.00% = lower limit; UL95.00% = upper limit, 5000 bootstrap samples one tailed test

Mediating effect	HCH –> PS –> ESV	.026	.015	1.694	.090		0.002	0.057
	HCM –> PS –> ESV	.043	.019	2.252	.024*		0.011	0.082
	HCT –> PS –> ESV	.051	.021	2.440	.015*		0.015	0.090
	HCH –> PS –> SST	.026	.015	1.692	.091		−0.005	0.056
	HCM –> PS –> SST	.044	.020	2.227	.026*		0.011	0.081
	HCT –> PS –> SST	.052	.023	2.235	.025*		−0.016	0.095

$*p < .05$, LL2.5% = lower limit; UL97.5% = upper limit, 5000 bootstrap samples two-tailed test

and safety stewardship (see Table 1). Regarding predictive relevance (Q^2), the Stone-Geisser's Q^2 analysis [38] results based on the blindfolding procedure ranged from .013 (employee safety voice), 0.112 (psychological safety) and .017 (safety stewardship). All values were > 0, signifying that the research model has good predictive relevance [35]. We tested mediation using Preacher & Hayes (2008) approach. Based on 5000 bootstrapping subsamples, two-tailed analysis assessed relationships at a significance of $p < .05$ and critical t value > 1.96. The results showed that psychological safety mediated the relationship between commitment and employee safety voice and safety stewardship (see Table 1 for details).

4 Discussion

This study found significant positive interactions among hardiness traits dimensions and psychological safety. We showed that employees in mining work context possessed a good amount of natural toughness, exercised more control over uncertainties contained in their work and were prone to psychological safety. Our findings were consistent with Mogelof and Edmondson [21] study that resilient dispositional trait reflects individuals who had thick skin and were naturally psychologically safer actors than others. Also, significant positive relationship was found between psychological safety and affiliation-oriented (safety stewardship). The finding demonstrates that an environment which gave psychological support mitigates the effects of unsolicited yet much needed voluntary moral obligation to look out for the safety of others and the display of altruistic and change-oriented behaviours to prevent workplace incidents from occurring. Our finding compared well with existing study by Leung, Deng [40] and Stoverink, Chiaburu [41] who found that citizenship behaviours of employees were associated with perceived sense of security experienced from the workplace.

We also demonstrated in this study that the theoretical distal relationship between dispositional traits and SCB [30] was mediated by psychological safety. Our results suggest that control trait energised employees to efficiently take spontaneous actions such as to protect co-workers from hazards and risky situations, promote cooperation, constructive criticism, speak-up, seek help, report errors through the influence of psychological safety. In addition, commitment disposition was related to affiliation-oriented and change-oriented SCB through the influence of psychological safety. The findings highlighted the value of a threat-free environment and interpersonal trust, and how it supports employees to broaden their roles beyond accountable job-roles in relation to safety. The study's findings were comparable to Frazier, Fainshmidt [24]'s meta-analysis study that found psychological safety mediated the effect of personality traits on organisational citizenship performances.

4.1 Limitations and Future Research

The study had limitations worthy of consideration. First, the study used cross-sectional design to collect data at one point of time, and all findings were correlational in nature. Therefore, any generalised cause and effect references to the study's findings must be done with caution. Future research might consider applying longitudinal methods to a cause-and-effect relationship. Second, all data for the study's variables were reported from a single-source, which limits SCB perspectives to only employees. Future research might consider an employee-supervisor dyad to explore a different perspective on the study's variables. Third, the study might have limitations with the use of only quantitative methods. Future research might consider a mixed-method approach to explore further nuances in the relationships among the variables.

5   Conclusion

The quest for zero-harm in high-risk industries is challenging. Our findings suggest that for a successful deployment of SCB, resilient hardiness disposition and psychological safety are critical antecedents. The overall results of this study provide support for the theoretical model that guided the investigation. We had shown that psychological safety deserved special attention for promoting organisational safety. We made a call to organisations, in particular high-risk industries to create environment that foster safety stewardship and safety voice behaviours.

References

1. Hofmann, D.A., Morgeson, F.P., Gerras, S.J.: Climate as a moderator of the relationship between leader-member exchange and content specific citizenship: safety climate as an exemplar. J. Appl. Psychol. **88**(1), 170 (2003)
2. Curcuruto, M., Griffin, M.A.: Prosocial and proactive "safety citizenship behaviour"(SCB): the mediating role of affective commitment and psychological ownership. Saf. Sci. **104**, 29–38 (2018)
3. Didla, S., Mearns, K., Flin, R.: Safety citizenship behaviour: a proactive approach to risk management. J. Risk Res. **12**(3–4), 475–483 (2009)
4. Curcuruto, M., Conchie, S.M., Griffin, M.A.: Safety citizenship behavior (SCB) in the workplace: a stable construct? analysis of psychometric invariance across four European countries. Accid. Anal. Prev. **129**, 190–201 (2019)
5. Griffin, M.A., Curcuruto, M.: Safety climate in organizations. Ann. Rev. Organ. Psychol. Organ. Behav. **3**, 191–212 (2016)
6. Blau, P.M.: Social exchange theory. Handb. Soc. Psychol. **3**(2007), 62 (1964)
7. Reader, T.W., et al.: Organizational support for the workforce and employee safety citizenship behaviors: a social exchange relationship. Hum. Relations **70**(3), 362–385 (2017)
8. Laurent, J., Chmiel, N., Hansez, I.: Jobs and safety: a social exchange perspective in explaining safety citizenship behaviors and safety violations. Saf. Sci. **110**, 291–299 (2018)
9. Chernyak-Hai, L., Rabenu, E.: The new era workplace relationships: is social exchange theory still relevant? Ind. Organ. Psychol. **11**(3), 456–481 (2018)
10. MacKenzie, S.B., Podsakoff, P.M., Podsakoff, N.P.: Challenge-oriented organizational citizenship behaviors and organizational effectiveness: do challenge-oriented behaviors really have an impact on the organization's bottom line? Pers. Psychol. **64**(3), 559–592 (2011)
11. Curcuruto, M., et al.: Voicing for safety in the workplace: a proactive goal-regulation perspective. Saf. Sci. **131**, 104902 (2020)
12. Tucker, S., Turner, N.: Sometimes it hurts when supervisors don't listen: the antecedents and consequences of safety voice among young workers. J. Occup. Health Psychol. **20**(1), 72 (2015)
13. Edmondson, A.C., Lei, Z.: Psychological safety: the history, renaissance, and future of an interpersonal construct. Annu. Rev. Organ. Psychol. Organ. Behav. **1**(1), 23–43 (2014)
14. Morrison, E.W.: Employee voice and silence. Annu. Rev. Organ. Psychol. Organ. Behav. **1**(1), 173–197 (2014)
15. Maddi, S.R., et al.: The personality construct of hardiness, V: relationships with the construction of existential meaning in life. J. Humanistic Psychol. **51**(3), 369–388 (2011)
16. Eschleman, K.J., Bowling, N.A., Alarcon, G.M.: A meta-analytic examination of hardiness. Int. J. Stress Manag. **17**(4), 277 (2010)
17. Sandvik, A.M., et al.: Psychopathy, anxiety, and resiliency–Psychological hardiness as a mediator of the psychopathy–anxiety relationship in a prison setting. Pers. Individ. Differ. **72**, 30–34 (2015)
18. Merino-Tejedor, E., et al.: Hardiness as a moderator variable between the Big-Five Model and work effort. Pers. Individ. Differ. **85**, 105–110 (2015)
19. Saksvik-Lehouillier, I., et al.: Hardiness, psychosocial factors and shift work tolerance among nurses–a 2-year follow-up study. J. Adv. Nurs. **72**(8), 1800–1812 (2016)
20. Nahrgang, J.D., Morgeson, F.P., Hofmann, D.A.: Safety at work: a meta-analytic investigation of the link between job demands, job resources, burnout, engagement, and safety outcomes. J. Appl. Psychol. **96**(1), 71 (2011)
21. Mogelof, J.P., Edmondson, A.C.: Explaining psychological safety in innovation teams: organizational culture, team dynamics, or personality? In: Creativity and Innovation in Organizational Teams, pp. 129–156. Psychology Press (2006)

22. Detert, J.R., Burris, E.R.: Leadership behavior and employee voice: is the door really open? Acad. Manag. J. **50**(4), 869–884 (2007)
23. Beus, J.M., Muñoz, G.J., Arthur, W., Jr.: Personality as a multilevel predictor of climate: an examination in the domain of workplace safety. Group Organ. Manag. **40**(5), 625–656 (2015)
24. Frazier, M.L., et al.: Psychological safety: a meta-analytic review and extension. Pers. Psychol. **70**(1), 113–165 (2017)
25. Frazier, M.L., Tupper, C.: Supervisor prosocial motivation, employee thriving, and helping behavior: a trickle-down model of psychological safety. Group Organ. Manag. **43**(4), 561–593 (2018)
26. Siemsen, E., et al.: The influence of psychological safety and confidence in knowledge on employee knowledge sharing. Manuf. Serv. Oper. Manag. **11**(3), 429–447 (2009)
27. Walumbwa, F.O., Schaubroeck, J.: Leader personality traits and employee voice behavior: mediating roles of ethical leadership and work group psychological safety. J. Appl. Psychol. **94**(5), 1275 (2009)
28. Frazier, M.L., Bowler, W.M.: Voice climate, supervisor undermining, and work outcomes: a group-level examination. J. Manag. **41**(3), 841–863 (2015)
29. Chamberlin, M., Newton, D.W., Lepine, J.A.: A meta-analysis of voice and its promotive and prohibitive forms: identification of key associations, distinctions, and future research directions. Pers. Psychol. **70**(1), 11–71 (2017)
30. Christian, M.S., et al.: Workplace safety: a meta-analysis of the roles of person and situation factors. American Psychological Association (2009)
31. Caniëls, M.C., Baaten, S.M.: How a learning-oriented organizational climate is linked to different proactive behaviors: the role of employee resilience. Soc. Indic. Res. **143**(2), 561–577 (2019)
32. Aryee, S., et al.: Core self-evaluations and employee voice behavior: test of a dual-motivational pathway. J. Manag. **43**(3), 946–966 (2017)
33. Xu, M., et al.: Supervisor-subordinate proactive personality congruence and psychological safety: a signaling theory approach to employee voice behavior. Leadersh. Q. **30**(4), 440–453 (2019)
34. Hystad, S.W., et al.: Psychometric properties of the revised Norwegian dispositional resilience (hardiness) scale. Scand. J. Psychol. **51**(3), 237–245 (2010)
35. Hair, J.F., Jr., et al.: Partial least squares structural equation modeling (PLS-SEM): an emerging tool in business research. Eur. Bus. Rev. **26**(2), 106–121 (2014)
36. Ringle, C., Wende, S., Becker, J.: Software SmartPLS 3.0. 2014. SmartPLS, Hamburg. www.smartpls.com, Accessed 30 June 2020
37. Henseler, J., Ringle, C.M., Sarstedt, M.: A new criterion for assessing discriminant validity in variance-based structural equation modeling. J. Acad. Mark. Sci. **43**(1), 115–135 (2015)
38. Sarstedt, M., Ringle, C.M., Hair, J.F.: Partial least squares structural equation modeling. Handb. Mark. Res. **26**, 1–40 (2017)
39. Cohen, J.: Statistical Power Analysis for the Behavioral Sciences, vol. 2. Lawrence Earlbaum Associates, Hilsdale (1988)
40. Leung, K., et al.: Beyond risk-taking: effects of psychological safety on cooperative goal interdependence and prosocial behavior. Group Organ. Manag. **40**(1), 88–115 (2015)
41. Stoverink, A.C., et al.: Supporting team citizenship: the influence of team social resources on team-level affiliation-oriented and challenge-oriented behaviour. Hum. Res. Manag. J. **28**(2), 201–215 (2018)

Rapid Assessment on Occupational Health and Safety Issues Faced by Young Workers in Indonesia Construction Sectors

Indri Hapsari Susilowati[1]([⊠]) [iD], L. Meily Kurniawidjaja[1], Mila Tejamaya[1],
Satrio Pratomo[2], Bonardo Prayogo Hasiholan[1], Amelia Anggarawati Putri[1],
and Akbar Nugroho Sitanggang[1]

[1] Universitas Indonesia, Depok 16424, Indonesia
indri@ui.ac.id
[2] LSPK3 – ICCOSH, Jakarta 12550, Indonesia

Abstract. The construction sector is a significant contributor to Indonesia's economy. However, this sector is a high-risk industry for Occupational Safety and Health (OSH), especially for young workers. This study aimed to analyze the OSH issues facing young workers in construction, including social & welfare issues, the knowledge and perceptions regarding OSH legal requirements, and the implementation. The sample size is 440 young workers aged 15–24 using Slovin's formula (95% CI). These data were collected from 4 large-scale public and private construction companies; power plants, transportation, residential, and office building projects using a questionnaire by interview, focus group discussion, and field visits to construction industry sites. The majority of respondents were male (86%), 21–24 years old (73,4%), and 1.8% were aged 15–17. 93% worked for >5 days per week. 71.6% worked overtime for <14 h per week. Another result showed that 83.6% had a single marital status (unmarried), and 54.5% are active smokers with about 11 cigarettes per day. The average smoking history is >5 years (35.8%). 9.8% consume alcoholic beverages, 74.3% sleep for <8 h per day, and 65.5% regularly exercise. The worker' perception found that 95.2% stated their company had provided OSH information properly. 83% said their company implements OSH's supporting factors (reward, information, rules, and engagement). Also, 74% revealed their company is good in compliance with OSH regulation, adherence in OSH implementation, and budgeting on OSH. There is a need for an occupational health program for young workers, mainly promoting health.

Keywords: Young · Worker · Health · Safety · Construction

1 Background

In Indonesia, young workers aged 15–24 years old amounts to 17,169,008 or 14.2% of the total number of workers [1]. According to the 2014 Indonesian Family Life Survey data, 60% of young workers are 21–24 years old, 31% are 18–20 years old, and 9% are

© The Author(s), under exclusive license to Springer Nature Switzerland AG 2021
N. L. Black et al. (Eds.): IEA 2021, LNNS 222, pp. 205–212, 2021.
https://doi.org/10.1007/978-3-030-74611-7_28

17 years old. The majority of young workers are single males [2]. Young workers face many challenges in the labor market in Indonesia. There are labor market differences for young people depending on their gender, residence type, and location. Around 56% of young workers work in the informal sectors, including daily workers in the agricultural or non-agricultural sectors who are not professional or technical jobs [3].

In Indonesia, a study found that young workers are a group of workers who are more vulnerable to get experience workplace injury to compare to workers in other age groups [4]. Workers at an age younger than 25 years old have a higher risk of injury at about 2,17 times than workers at age 55–65 years old.

Around 7,058,350 workers work in the construction sectors in Indonesia. This sector contributes to Indonesia's GDP, which is around 9.82%, or the 4th most significant contributor to Indonesia's economy, yet this sector is categorized as a high-risk industry from the aspect of OSH.

This study conducted a rapid assessment of Indonesia's occupational safety and health, particularly among young workers in the construction sector. This study aimed to analyze; (1) characteristics and background of young workers involved in hazardous workplaces and working conditions; (2) health and safety issues facing young workers in construction, including social and welfare issues, as well as recommendations on how to address them; (3) the roles and responsibilities of OSH stakeholders involved in the construction sector; and (4) knowledge and perceptions of young workers and employers in the construction sector regarding OSH legal requirements.

2 Methods and Material

2.1 Respondent Recruitment

According to the Statistics Center Agency, there are 7.06 million construction workers in Indonesia (2018). Using the 95% confidence interval (i.e., 0.05% error), the number of samples was 400 samples. This study adds 10% to the sample size as a buffer for lost respondents during follow-up; therefore, the final sample size is 440. The target sample in this study is young workers aged 15–24 years old.

This study collected data from 4 construction companies, from private companies and a public company in some areas of the project, including power plants, transportation, residential, and office building. All of the construction companies which agreed to participate in our study were large-scale construction companies, where the project was also large-scaled.

2.2 Instrument

A questionnaire was developed for this study, which was used to examine six variables under study. The composition of the final questionnaire consisted of 74 questions that include questions regarding:

1. Sociodemographic (22 questions).
2. The individual's perception of OSH (11 questions).

3. Supporting factors (10 questions).
4. Risk management:

   a. Compliance with the OSH regulation (5 questions)
   b. OSH implementation (8 questions)
   c. OSH versus production costs (18 questions)

Thirty young construction workers tested for the validity and reliability of the questionnaire. A statistical software (SPSS version 2.0) was used to calculate Pearson's correlation coefficients to measure validity. If the r calculation > r table, then the question is valid. Cronbach's alpha was calculated for the reliability test. If Cronbach's alpha coefficient is 0.70 or higher, the question is reliable.

The results for Pearson's correlation (r) were in the range of 0.407–0.911. Since the r table for 30 samples is 0.3061 (with 95% significance), questions with an r value less than 0.3061 were then removed. For the reliability test, it was found that the Cronbach's alpha coefficient was 0.844, higher than 0.70, which means that the questionnaire was reliable. For triangulation, a list of questions for the interview and focus group discussion, and observation checklists were developed.

3 Results

This study found that most young construction workers in Indonesia are men (86%), single, aged 21–24 years old (73%). The duration of work hours for young workers was mostly more than 8 h a day and more than five days a week, with the majority of overtime hours being less than 14 h per week. This study shows that most young workers are active smokers (54.4%) with an average of 11 cigarettes per day. Only 10% of the respondent consume a small amount of alcohol. Most workers sleep for less than 8 h per day, but most of them claimed they exercise regularly. Details can be found in Table 1.

Table 1. Characteristics of respondents

Characteristics		N	%
Sex	Male	378	85.9
	Female	62	14.1
Age	15–17	5	1.1
	18–20	112	25.5
	21–24	323	73.4
Marital status	Single	368	83.6
	Married	70	15.9
	Widow/Divorced	2	0.5
Employment status	Permanent	87	19.8
	Non-permanent	353	80.2

(*continued*)

Table 1. (*continued*)

Characteristics		N	%
Duration of work	0–2 Years	376	85.5
	3–4 Years	56	12.7
	5–7 Years	7	1.6
	>7 Years	1	0.2
Work hours per day	<8 h	22	5
	8 h	177	40.2
	>8 h	241	54.8
Workday per week	<5 Days	3	0.7
	5 Days	28	6.4
	>5 Days	409	93
Work shift	Yes	123	28
	No	317	72
Work shift rotation	Morning only	71	57.7
	Afternoon only	4	3.3
	Night only	48	39
Overtime	<14 h	315	71.6
	14 h	9	2
	>14 h	116	26.4
Smoking	No	163	37
	Ex-smoker	37	8.4
	Yes	240	54.5
Cigarettes per day (avg)	<11 Cigarettes	126	45.5
	≥11 Cigarettes	151	54.5
Duration of smoking	<Means (5 Years)	179	64.2
	≥Means (5 Years)	100	35.8
Alcohol consumption	Yes	43	9.8
	No	397	90.2
Alcohol consumption per day (avg) N = 43	1–2 glass standard	24	55.8
	3–4 glass standard	9	20.9
	5–6 glass standard	2	4.7
	7–10 glass standard	6	14
	11–12 glass standard	2	4.7
	>13 glass standard		
Frequency of alcohol consumption	Every day	0	0
	4–6 Days/Weeks	0	0
	2–3 Days/Weeks	5	11.6
	1 Days/Weeks	10	23.3
	2–3 Days/Months	7	16.3
	1 Days/Months	21	48.8

(*continued*)

Table 1. (*continued*)

Characteristics		N	%
Sleeping time per day (avg)	<8 h	327	74.3
	8 h	89	20.2
	>8 h	24	5.5
Exercise	Yes	288	65.5
	No	152	34.5
Freq. of exercise	3 Times/Weeks (@30 min)	34	11.8
	1–2 Times/ Weeks (@30 min)	254	88.2

The perception of OSH among young workers were asked by using questionnaires and focus group discussions. It was found that the individual perception of young workers towards OSH was good, meaning that young workers understood the importance of OSH prevention and agreed that OSH has been well-managed; OSH aspects are essential for their jobs; they understood their roles and responsibilities over OSH. Young workers also agreed that OSH's important factors include appropriate safety incentive systems, OSH information; OSH rules and policies; and moderate OSH engagement programs. Risk management activities conducted in their workplace were assessed to be effective in improving safety. Therefore, this study found a positive result regarding the perception of OSH from young workers. Details can be found in Table 2.

Table 2. Perception of young workers

Perception on OSH	Good	Moderate	Poor
1. Individual perception of OSH	419 (95.2%)	21 (4.8%)	0 (0%)
Provision of OSH at workplace	268 (60.9%)	171 (38.9%)	1 (0.2%)
Importance of OSH	201 (45.7%)	233 (53%)	6 (1.4%)
Roles and responsibilities in OSH	412 (93.6%)	27 (6.1%)	1 (0.2%)
2. Supporting factors	70 (15.9%)	365 (83%)	5 (1.1%)
OSH reward	29 (6.6%)	317 (72%)	94 (21.4%)
OSH information	33 (7.5%)	389 (88.4%)	18 (4.1%)
OSH rules and SOP	66 (15%)	322 (73.2%)	52 (11.8%)
Employee engagement program	96 (21.8%)	338 (76.8%)	6 (1.4%)
3. Risk management	329 (74.8%)	111 (25.2%)	0 (0%)
A. Compliance of OSH regulations	414 (94.1%)	20 (4.5%)	6 (1.4%)
Update OSH rule	407 (92.5%)	22 (5%)	11 (2.5%)
OSH policy, SOP	172 (39.1%)	259 (58.9%)	9 (2%)
Safety meeting and safety patrol	173 (39.3%)	262 (59.5%)	5 (1.1%)
Adherence of OSH implementation	180 (40.9%)	260 (59.1%)	0 (0%)
OSH rules & procedures' adherence	135 (30.7%)	291 (66.1%)	14 (3.2%)
Clarify OSH rules and programs	43 (9.8%)	388 (88.2%)	9 (2%)
C. OSH vs production cost	323 (73.4%)	117 (26.6%)	0
The necessity of OSH budget	257 (58.4%)	183 (41.6%)	0
Necessity of OSH TRAINING	356 (80.9%)	84 (19.1%)	0
Loss due to ignoring OSH	233 (53%)	207 (46%)	0

4 Discussion

Most of the young workers from this study were male because construction work uses muscle strength that requires energy [5]. A study showed that male muscle strength is stronger than women [6]. Therefore, female workers act as admin, inspectors, and drafter. Women who work in construction have long working hours and are prone to health problems that can affect women's fatigue [7].

Smoking and consuming alcohol are some lifestyles found among young workers in this research. Smoking indirectly causes fatigue and affecting sleep quality [8]. Moreover, the result found that young workers' time sleep was mostly less than 8 h, affecting their health and fitness during work [9, 10]. People intoxicated with alcohol will experience decreased alertness and coordination, like those who experience fatigue [11]. Another study found that alcohol consumption is indirectly related to work fatigue risk and associated with stress complaints, where stress can be a factor causing complaints of fatigue [12].

This survey indicates that the individual perception of young workers towards OSH was good, meaning that young workers understood the importance of OSH prevention and agreed that OSH has been well-managed. However, this result is in contrast with a study by Gyekye (2009), which showed that older workers seemingly have more positive attitudes towards safety than young workers [13]. A study about young workers in Italy also shows that young workers under 30 years have less access and lower awareness of OSH issues than older workers [14]. A previous study in Nordic (2017) found that young workers in the country are more at risk of getting occupational accidents than older colleagues, but young workers have a smaller chance of getting work-related illness [15].

In this survey, young workers believe that OSH aspects are essential for their jobs; they understood their roles and responsibilities over OSH. A study of 226 young workers in Australia showed similar results that these young workers can identify their concern about health and safety at the workplace, which indicates their understanding about OSH, but they lack the confidence to report their concerns and have limited information about it [16].

Young workers in this survey had a moderate perception of OSH's supporting factors, including appropriate safety incentive systems; OSH information; OSH rules and policies; and OSH engagement programs. OSH engagement program, which includes education and knowledge, is the key to reducing injury among young workers [17], thus making it one of the critical supporting factors.

In this study, it was said that young workers had a good perception of compliance with OSH regulations. This contrasts with a similar study in Italy [15], which stated that young workers are less aware of OSH's simple regulatory framework, including personal responsibility for safety and health and emergency procedures.

While the adherence of young workers to the implementation of OSH, including regulations, procedures, and programs, is still considered sufficient or not very good, this is in line with a study [13] which states that young workers tend to perform their work in unconventional methods which often appear more dangerous and risky.

Meanwhile, when young workers were asked regarding matters related to OSH's financial concerns, the majority considered OSH was necessary despite the budget that had to be spent, they even realized the more significant cost of loss caused by ignoring

OSH. Compared to a study in Pakistan [18], which aims to see OSH performance in companies from a stakeholder perspective, it is quite interesting because most adult respondents have no concern regarding budget allocation for OSH.

5 Conclusion

Continuous improvement on OSH implementation from surveyed companies combined well with a good perception of OSH from young workers needs to be supported by stakeholders, such as the government (via several ministries), professional associations, labor unions, academicians, etc. The insurance for work-related accidents and illness for young workers should be cover by the project site, while the social insurance has to cover by the construction companies. The policy of OHS approaches among young workers have issued by the Ministry of Manpower with asked the contribution from stakeholders, such as other ministries, Indonesian National Occupational Safety and Health Council, Labour Union, Organization/Association of Professional, Professional Certification Institution, the employees, and experts from University.

Acknowledgment. This study is supported by International Labour Organization (ILO) Jakarta.

References

1. BPS (2018) Penduduk 15 Tahun Ke Atas yang Bekerja menurut Lapangan Pekerjaan Utama 1986–2017. https://www.bps.go.id/statictable/2009/04/16/970/penduduk-15-tahun-ke-atas-yang-bekerja-menurut-lapangan-pekerjaan-utama-1986---2018.html
2. RAND Social and Economic Well-Being. IFLS Data and Documentation. In: RAND Soc. Econ. Well-Being (2014). https://www.rand.org/well-being/social-and-behavioral-pol icy/data/FLS/IFLS/download.html, Accessed 14 Jul 2019
3. Inter Agency Research Cooperation Project. Memahami pekerjaan yang dilakukan oleh anak dan pekerja muda di Indonesia (2012)
4. Ghani, T.L.: Determinan Kejadian Cedera pada Kelompok Pekerja Usia Produktif di Indonesia Determinants of Injury Among Productive Age Wokers in Indonesia. Bul. Penelit. Kesehat (2015)
5. Tarwaka. Ergonomi Industri, Dasar-dasar Pengetahuan dan Aplikasi di Tempat Kerja. Edisi Ke-2, 2nd ed (2014). https://doi.org/10.1007/978-1-4684-0104-2_6
6. Rodahl, K.: The Physiology of Work. Taylor & Francis, London (2003)
7. Saksena, H.T., Ophiyandri, T., Hidayat, B.: Identifikasi Tantangan dan Strategi Perempuan dalam Berkarir di Industri Konstruksi. Siklus J Tek Sipil. (2020). https://doi.org/10.31849/siklus.v6i1.3664
8. Theron, W.J., Van Heerden, G.M.J.: Fatigue knowledge-a new lever in safety management. J. South. African Inst. Min. Metall. **111**, 1–10 (2011)
9. Caldwell, J.A.: The impact of fatigue in air medical and other types of operations: a review of fatigue facts and potential countermeasures. Air Med. J. **20**, 25–32 (2001). https://doi.org/10.1067/mmj.2001.112420
10. Umyati, A., Yadi Y.H., Sandi, E.S.N.: Pengukuran Kelelahan Kerja Pengemudi Bis Dengan Aspek Fisiologis Kerja Dan Metode Industrial Fatique Research Committee (IFRC). Semin. Nas. IENACO (2015)

11. Kim, S., Cranor, B.D., Ryu, Y.S.: Fatigue: working under the influence. In: Proceedings of the XXIst Annual International Occupational Ergonomics and Safety Conference (2009)
12. Bültmann, U., Kant, I., Kasl, S.V., Schröer, K.A.P., Swaen, G.M.H., Van den Brandt, P.A.: Lifestyle factors as risk factors for fatigue and psychological distress in the working population: prospective results from the Maastricht cohort study. J. Occup. Environ. Med. **44**, 116–124 (2002). https://doi.org/10.1097/00043764-200202000-00006
13. Gyekye, S., Salminen, S.: Age and workers' perceptions of workplace safety: a comparative study. Int. J. Aging Hum. Dev. **68**, 171–184 (2009). https://doi.org/10.2190/AG.68.2.d
14. Hanvold, T.N., Kines, P., Nykänen, M., Thomée, S., Holte, K.A., Vuori, J., Wærsted, M., Veiersted, K.B.: Occupational safety and health among young workers in the Nordic countries: a systematic literature review. Saf Health Work. **10**, 180–187 (2019). https://doi.org/10.1016/j.shaw.2018.12.003
15. Dragano, N., Barbaranelli, C., Reuter, M., Wahrendorf, M., Wright, B., Ronchetti, M., Buresti, G., Di Tecco, C., Iavicoli, S.: Young workers' access to and awareness of occupational safety and health services: Age-differences and possible drivers in a large survey of employees in Italy. Int. J. Environ. Res Public Health **15**, 1511 (2018). https://doi.org/10.3390/ijerph150 71511
16. Clarkson, L., Blewett, V., Rainbird, S., Paterson, J.L., Etherton, H.: Young, vulnerable and uncertain: young workers' perceptions of work health and safety. Work **61**, 113–123 (2018). https://doi.org/10.3233/WOR-182788
17. Thamrin, Y.: Young workers health and safety : a summary of literature review. J Kesehat Masy Marit. **1** (2019). https://doi.org/10.30597/jkmm.v1i1.8702
18. Zahoor, H., Chan, A.P.C., Masood, R., Choudhry, R.M., Javed, A.A., Utama, W.P.: Occupational safety and health performance in the Pakistani construction industry: stakeholders' perspective. Int. J. Constr. Manag. **16**, 209–219 (2016). https://doi.org/10.1080/15623599. 2015.1138027

Analysis of Human Efficiency-Thoroughness Trade-Off Decisions in Approach Control

Tsubasa Takagi$^{(\boxtimes)}$ and Miwa Nakanishi

Keio University, Yokohama 223-8522, Kanagawa, Japan
tkg283@keio.jp

Abstract. New air traffic management systems are being researched throughout the world to enhance the safety and efficiency of the airspace. However, human air traffic controllers have been effectively balancing both safety and efficiency in their operations. In resilience engineering, this human trade-off characteristic is called the efficiency-thoroughness trade-off if efficiency is prioritized and thoroughness-efficiency trade-off if thoroughness or safety is prioritized. Moreover, understanding human decision-making is attracting attention in the field of air traffic control system design since it could be incorporated into autonomous systems to improve resilience and automation acceptance. In this study, we analyzed the mechanism of efficiency-thoroughness trade-off decisions in an approach control simulator experiment, so that the results could be applied to future air traffic management systems. The results showed that efficiency-thoroughness trade-off decisions were made when situational difficulty was under 3.5 times the difficulty of an easiest situation and when situational difficulty was over 3.5, a high ratio of thoroughness-efficiency trade-off decisions was observed.

Keywords: Efficiency-thoroughness trade-off · Decision-making · Resilience engineering · Approach control · Air traffic control · Safety

1 Introduction

Next generation air traffic management (ATM) systems are being developed throughout the world and they focus on making the airspace safer and more efficient [1]. Moreover, those projects try to optimize air traffic flow using advanced automation. However, human air traffic controllers have already been successful at achieving a high level of efficiency and safety. This is because they are able to prioritize efficiency and thoroughness at the correct timing.

In the field of resilience engineering, this trade-off between efficiency and thoroughness is called the efficiency-thoroughness trade-off (ETTO) if efficiency is prioritized over thoroughness, or the thoroughness-efficiency trade-off (TETO) if thoroughness is prioritized over efficiency [2]. By effectively balancing efficiency and thoroughness, air traffic controllers are capable of dealing with a wide range of situational difficulty.

N. L. Black et al. (Eds.): IEA 2021, LNNS 222, pp. 213–219, 2021.
https://doi.org/10.1007/978-3-030-74611-7_29

Furthermore, EUROCONTROL has stated that resilient human decision-making during air traffic control (ATC) needs to be understood and incorporated into the new ATM systems in order to enhance the system and add more flexibility [3]. Specifically, adding a human element into ATM systems could help maintain and enforce the strengths in human decisions. On the other hand, the automation element could focus more on supporting the weaknesses in human decisions. By adding the human element, not only will it make the airspace safer and more efficient, but it could also increase the acceptance of autonomous systems since their outputs are more likely to be closer to the preferred decisions of human air traffic controllers.

The purpose of this research is to analyze the human ETTO and TETO decisions under varying situational difficulty. We will be examining the ETTO and TETO decisions made during an experiment simulating an approach control environment. This research will mainly focus on why and how human ETTO and TETO decisions are made so that the results could be incorporated into future air traffic management systems with the aim of enhancing safety and efficiency using both human resilience elements and advanced automation.

2 Experiment Method

2.1 Experimental Setup and Task

We conducted an experiment simulating an approach control environment. Participants were seated in front of a 27-in. screen, a mouse, and a mousepad. They used the mouse to control the simulator displayed on the screen. The tasks were set up on a computer simulator depicting approach control operations at a single runway airport. The simulator screen is shown in Fig. 1. The air traffic radar had a weather radar function that could detect storms in the area, and a conflict detection function that could detect both future and present conflicting aircraft pairs.

The aircrafts entered from one of the four entry routes and the participants had to guide them to the exit waypoint. The participants could give speed change commands, heading change commands, and direct waypoint commands. In the simulator, participants had to avoid collisions at all cost, maintain at least a 5NM separation, keep all aircrafts within the airspace, and efficiently manage traffic so that the aircrafts passed through the airspace in order and as quickly as possible. If a separation violation or an airspace deviation occurred, the participant was asked to analyze the cause after the experiment and if a collision occurred, the participant had to start over the task from the beginning.

Before the experiment, all participants were given instructions and practice tasks so that they were able to operate within the rules of the experiment. The experiment had two 30-min tasks with various wind patterns, weather patterns, and emergencies. The scenarios created both easy situations as well as difficult situations. The details of the scenarios in the two tasks are organized in Fig. 2.

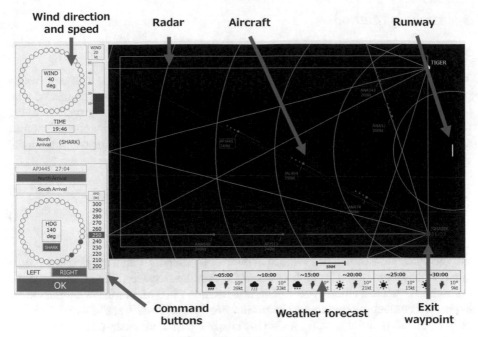

Fig. 1. Simulator screen

Fig. 2. Task scenarios

2.2 Measurements

The flight log data for all aircrafts were collected every second for all tasks and participants. In addition, each command given by the participants were recorded.

2.3 Participants

Ten healthy volunteers from ages 21 to 25 (female: 3, male: 7) were recruited for this experiment. They were not actual air traffic controllers, but one participant was a private glider pilot and had some experience managing glider traffic. Prior to their experiment, they were given information about the experiment including its risks, duration, and privacy. They also held the right to withdraw from their experiment at any time. All participants agreed to the experiment through a written informed consent. This experiment was approved by the local ethical committee.

3 Analysis Method

3.1 Quantification of Situational Difficulty

To generalize the difficulty of the situation so that the results could be analyzed from a practical point of view, situational difficulty of the airspace at time t was compared with the easiest in ATC. Specifically, the easiest situation is when only one aircraft is flying through the airspace. Upon defining situational difficulty, the total number of aircraft and the tendency towards conflicts were taken into consideration. Ultimately, situational difficulty was defined as Eq. (1).

$$x = \frac{\left(\dfrac{\sum_j m_{\beta j}}{\left(\sum_j s_{\beta j}\right)+1} + 1\right)^{n\beta}}{\left(\dfrac{\sum_i m_{\alpha i}}{\left(\sum_i s_{\alpha i}\right)+1} + 1\right)^{n\alpha}} \tag{1}$$

For the numerator, variable $n\beta$ is the total number of aircrafts within the airspace at time t, $m_{\beta j}$ is the nearest aircraft pair for aircraft j within the airspace at time t, and $s_{\beta j}$ is the separation of nearest aircraft pair for aircraft j at time t in NM. For the denominator, n_α is the total number of aircrafts within the airspace during the easiest situation, $m_{\alpha i}$ is the nearest aircraft pair for aircraft i within the airspace during the easiest situation, and $s_{\alpha i}$ is the separation of nearest aircraft pair for aircraft i during the easiest situation in NM. During the easiest situation, the total number of aircrafts is 1, the total number of nearest aircraft pair is 0, and the total separation of nearest aircraft pair is 0, so the denominator of Eq. (1) becomes 1 for all cases.

Using Eq. (1), situational difficulty was expressed as an exponential function of the number of aircraft and the tendency towards conflicts. The tendency towards conflicts was placed as the base and the number of aircraft was set as the exponent.

3.2 Classification of ETTO/TETO

For the determination of ETTO and TETO, we focused on the change in aircraft layout after each controller command. Particularly, we looked at the shortest separation between aircrafts associated with a command and compared the separation before the command and the separation after the command. The change in shortest separation was calculated using Eq. (2).

$$y = q - p \tag{2}$$

Variable p represents the separation between aircraft A and aircraft B at time t where aircraft A is the aircraft that received a controller command at time t and aircraft B is the nearest aircraft of aircraft A. On the other hand, q represents the separation between aircraft B and aircraft C at time $t + \Delta t$ where aircraft B is the aircraft from q and aircraft C is the nearest aircraft of aircraft B after Δt from the command to aircraft A in q. To allow the aircrafts enough time to change positions, 120 s was selected for Δt.

In theory, Eq. (2) should explain ETTO for commands directed towards the shortening of aircraft separation in the future and TETO for commands directed towards the lengthening of aircraft separation in the future. Therefore, we classified the command to be ETTO if the calculated value from Eq. (2) was negative and TETO if the final value was positive. Also, if there were multiple commands toward one aircraft within 15 s, the last command was selected, and the preceding commands were treated as command errors. Furthermore, the data was sorted based on if there was a separation violation in the airspace during the time when the command was given, and the two sets of data was analyzed separately.

4   Results and Discussion

4.1   Situational Difficulty and ETTO/TETO Excluding Separation Violation Cases

Using the analysis method in Sect. 3, we calculated the ratio of ETTO and TETO at various situational difficulty levels for cases where separation violation was absent. The results are shown in Fig. 3.

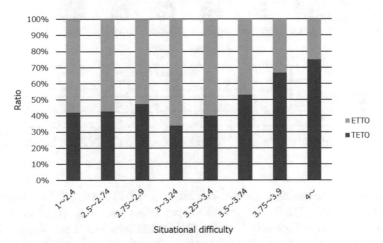

	Situational difficulty							
	1~2.4	2.5~2.74	2.75~2.9	3~3.24	3.25~3.4	3.5~3.74	3.75~3.9	4~
Number of TETO	641	86	45	17	10	9	2	3
Number of ETTO	878	115	50	33	15	8	1	1

Fig. 3. Relationship between situational difficulty and ratio of ETTO/TETO excluding separation violation cases

From the overall trend in Fig. 3, the ratio of ETTO decisions was above 50% for situational difficulty under 3.5 and the ratio of TETO decisions was above 50% for situational difficulty over 3.5. This suggests that when the airspace is not congested and easy to control, separation is shortened to create a layout that would increase efficiency. However, as the number of aircrafts and the likelihood of conflicts increase, the situation becomes difficult and separation is lengthened to create more margins in the layout.

4.2 Situational Difficulty and ETTO/TETO Including Separation Violation Cases

For cases where separation violation was present, we calculated the ratio of ETTO and TETO at various situational difficulty levels. The results are shown in Fig. 4.

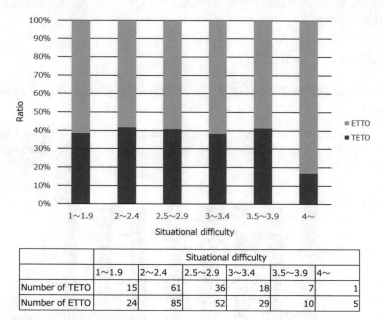

	Situational difficulty					
	1~1.9	2~2.4	2.5~2.9	3~3.4	3.5~3.9	4~
Number of TETO	15	61	36	18	7	1
Number of ETTO	24	85	52	29	10	5

Fig. 4. Relationship between situational difficulty and ratio of ETTO/TETO including separation violation cases

Compared to the results from Sect. 4.1, the ratio of ETTO and TETO did not change. In addition, the ratio of TETO never reached over 50%. Even though, the natural decision during a separation violation is to make TETO decisions and create more space, the results showed a contradicting trend. Therefore, it could be analyzed that the decisions in this case were mixed and contained improper or unrelated decisions. An improved classification of decision-making could allow further analysis for this category of data.

5 Conclusion

We analyzed the ETTO and TETO decisions in an approach control simulator experiment and discussed the reason and process behind the decisions. Specifically, we observed a high ratio of ETTO decisions when situational difficulty was under 3.5 but when situational difficulty became 3.5 times greater than the easiest situation, the trend switched and a high ratio of TETO decisions was present. In the future, refined results from this research could be applied to future air traffic management systems and make the airspace safer and more efficient by effectively combining human and machine.

References

1. CARATS: Long-term Vision for the Future Air Traffic Systems-Changes to Intelligent Air Traffic Systems (2010)
2. Hollnagel, E.: The ETTO Principle: Efficiency-Thoroughness Trade-Off: Why Things That Go Right Sometimes Go Wrong, 1st edn. Ashgate, Farnham (2009)
3. EUROCONTROL: White Paper Human Factors Integration in ATM System Design (2019)

Health and Safety Among Commercial Marine Fisheries in Québec: Navigating Through Haddon Matrix to Better Understand Accidents Causation

Mathieu Tremblay[1]([✉]) [iD], Martin Lavallière[2] [iD], Jérôme Pelletier[1] [iD],
Dave Bergeron[1] [iD], Valérie Dufresne Dubé[1,3] [iD], and Robert Fecteau[1,3] [iD]

[1] Université du Québec à Rimouski, Rimouski, QC, Canada
tremma11@uqar.ca
[2] Université du Québec à Chicoutimi, Saguenay, QC, Canada
[3] Transport Canada, CTC Rimouski, Rimouski, QC, Canada

Abstract. Despite its industry's importance and its impact on its community, commercial fishing did not receive much attention from the researchers. Little is understood about accident causations and safety issues among fishermen and their vessels. The paper' objective was to develop a conceptual framework based on accident analysis models and safety issues, adapted to commercial fishing activities. In this paper, Haddon matrix was used to conceptualize a *"man overboard"* accident which represents the primary cause of death among marine fisheries' workers in Canada. This reflective paper attempts to address the complex context of safety issues in the commercial fishing industry by providing a conceptual framework. This study highlights the need of a better understanding of accidental events and safety issues, hence also encouraging fellow researchers to investigate and explore further into health and safety domains.

Keywords: Accident analysis models · Work-related safety · Commercial fishery industry · Interventions

1 Introduction

Commercial fishing vessels are a complex work environment, as they are a means of transportation, as well as a work tool and a living environment [1]. Compared to safety gains obtained in several industries, commercial fisheries remain a high-risk profession with a deadly accident rate (around 9 fatalities per year between 2011 and 2017 in Canada) [2]. This fatality risk is 25 to 50 times higher than for onshore workers [3]. Even though multiple standards and recommendations exist, they are mostly oriented for the merchant shipping [4, 5]. Only a few recommendations were adapted for commercial fishing vessels. To study that problematic, a collaborative work was led by the *Comité permanent sur la sécurité des bateaux de pêche du Québec* (CPSBPQ) in partnership with Transport Canada (TC), Canadian Coast Guard (CCG), Fisheries and Oceans Canada

N. L. Black et al. (Eds.): IEA 2021, LNNS 222, pp. 220–224, 2021.
https://doi.org/10.1007/978-3-030-74611-7_30

(DFO), and the *Commission des normes, de l'équité, de la santé et de la sécurité du travail* (CNESST). They identified multiple issues in the commercial fishing industry in Québec. They found that each sector of the commercial fishing industry (e.g., lobsters, shrimps, scallops), as well as each geographical region (i.e. Îles-de-la-Madeleine, Gaspésie Sud, Basse-Côte-Nord), are unique in the way they handle their own safety culture. They concluded that an universal approach would fail at addressing sector- and region-specific issues, and thus tailored to local needs should be valorized [6]. The objective of this paper was to developed a conceptual framework based on accident analysis models and safety issues, adapted to commercial fishing activities, according to regional and sector specificities.

2 Conceptual Framework Challenges

To date, there is no such conceptual model existing in the literature. However, many approaches, such as occupational psychology, human factor-ergonomics or engineering, were used to conceptualized safety issues and accidents. One common way to conceive a model consist in using the quantification of the accidents. For instance, various explanatory models were drawn from transportation industry sectors (mainly aviation, surface transportation), then documented and categorized according to their data, in order to suggest explanatory models of accidents and trying to provide potential preventive measures for this sector. Nevertheless, with the commercial fishing industry, they are many challenges related to this method. First and foremost, each entity (e.g., TC, CCG, CNESST) records accidental events according to distinctive purposes using their own criteria, which makes the data-crossing complex or even impossible. Since there is no common identification key, database consolidation can only be achieved manually, thus limiting the ability to analyze accidental events [6]. This issue has long been acknowledged, as research on the fishing environment' accidents has always encountered this difficulty related to data' non-compatibility from various sources [7].

Undeniably, accessibility and knowledge of the data helps to understand how and why accidents occur. Though, the mechanisms explaining injuries and death or the intervention implementations to promote the fishery industry' adoption of safety behaviours were not clarified. A public health model caught our attention. In fact, Haddon matrix [8] has been used widely for decades to assist in developing strategies to prevent injuries and fatalities. Haddon matrix provides a conceptual framework for understanding the origins of safety problems and developing intervention strategies.

Furthermore, this model allows to include and apply the Hollnagel' model [1] to fishing vessels as well as to the sector and regional uniqueness that is highlighted by the CPSBPQ' report [6]. Thus, this model looks at intrinsic and extrinsic factors related to safety issues. More precisely, the individual and personal factors refer to the work at risk of injuries or deaths taking into account elements such as beliefs, fatigue, physical and psychosocial health, training, experience and resources. The main root agents for injuries and fatalities are often the vessel itself and the fishing equipment. Environmental factors encompass all the characteristics of the setting in which injury and death occurred, including physical aspects (e.g., environmental conditions, temperature), job demands (organization, physical, psychosocial), and social and legal environment, including safety culture practices.

Based on the CPSBPQ report [6] and TSB watchlist (2018) [2], an exhaustive list of these concurrent factors is presented in Table 1 anchored with the structure of work suggested by Haddon matrix' model. In Table 2, we showcase an example of the mechanism explaining a fatality caused by a fall overboard using Haddon' matrix. As we already mentioned, a man falling overboard stand for the main cause of fatalities between 2011–2017 [2] in the commercial fishing industry in Canada, as well as presenting the most expensive cost for the community, as averaging 3.2M$ per death [6]. This example demonstrates that the Haddon matrix is adaptable, by breaking multiple accident and

Table 1. Factors in the Haddon matrix based on the CPSBPQ report (2020) and TSB watchlist (2018)

Individual and personal	Vehicle and equipment	Environment	Socio-economic and organizational
- Age, - Health (physical, psychosocial, emotional), - Experience, - Fitness (physical, psychosocial, emotional) - Personal beliefs, attitudes, behaviours (safety culture) - Fatigue (physical, psychosocial, emotional) - Training, drills, knowledge - Drugs and alcohol usage	- Vessel maintenance and age - Fishing equipment maintenance and age - Maintenance, quality and quantity of safety equipment - Vessel design and construction - Vessel stability	- Coastal and midshore fishing areas - Climate - Temperature - Tide - Wave - Wind - Storm - Time of the day, luminosity -Regional specificity	- Emergency preparedness and access to healthcare - Job resources (crew support, training, safety drills, leadership) - Crew' belief (safety culture) - Vessel (living environment) - Laws, regulations - Economic context (quantity, quota, days off-shore) - Processing plant obligation (landing of the catch) - Natural resources viability and availability (halieutic resources) - Debt obligation - Organizational job demands (working shift, schedule) - Physical job demands (cumulative strain, strength, repeated motions, awkward postures) - Psychosocial job demands (stress)

safety issues into a single problem, hence easing its understanding and visualization. The presented case exposes all related factors before, during and after the unfortunate event of a man overboard, and therefore allows to target specific measures and interventions amongst all stakeholders.

Table 2. Example of Haddon matrix for the death of a crew member falling overboard.

	Individual and personal factors	Vehicle and equipment factors	Environment factors	Socio-economic and organizational factors
Pre-event	- Survival suit training - Health and fitness level - Safety behaviours - Age - Experience	- Safety equipment (quality, quantity, maintenance, age) - Guardrail - Hardness -Vessel design and construction - Vessel stability	- Height wave, wind, storm - Surface (wet) - Time of day (lighting conditions)	- Emergency drills and training - Muster list exercises - Emergency preparedness - Crew' belief - Leadership
During	- Ability to float/swim - Ability to stay warm - Ability to communicate	- Survival suit (availability, size, maintenance, training) - Wearing floatation device - Alarm - Life raft	- Visibility, audibility - Lighting conditions	- Rescue maneuvers and procedures - Safety equipment (availability) - Leadership
Post-event	- Age - Recovery capability - Health and fitness level	- DEA, first aids kit - Warming equipment - Communication device	- Coastal guard availability and proximity - Other vessels and proximity - Proximity to medical assistance	- Institutional regulations - Crew and community support

3 Discussion

Commercial fisheries industry would benefit from an in-depth study of the Haddon matrix model. In addition, the conceptualization of accidental events and safety concerns, this model offers several avenues of interventions suitable for education and awareness activities, and could lead to the reduction of fatalities and injuries in commercial fisheries. This model is not a panacea being limited by the information available (organizations, crews) that feed the model for understanding accident and safety issues mechanisms ("*what happened?*"). Despite the model' strength in addressing specific issues, the Haddon matrix might be limited by its capability to provide a broader perspective revealing systemic safety issues.

To address Haddon matrix' limitations and to develop interventions that are more tailored to sectors and regions specificities, the current work can help to guide an initial program theory development as part of research inspired by a realist approach. Realist approach helps to better understand the complexity associated with interventions by highlighting possible interactions between individuals and their social milieu [9]. Realist approach could enhance the present matrix by integrating the perspective of different stakeholders involved in the commercial fishing industry.

4 Conclusions

We need to better understand the fishing communities and the contextual reality of their profession in order to be able to support them and navigate with them along the continuum of the safety culture. Similar studies should be carried out in Canada' coastal provinces, which would enable comparisons of safety culture, health and safety indicators and assess if safety performances differ between provinces and sectors.

References

1. Hollnagel, E.: Understanding accidents-from root causes to performance variability. In: Proceedings of the IEEE 7th Conference on Human Factors and Power Plants, AZ, USA (2002). https://doi.org/10.1109/HFPP.2002.1042821.
2. Transportation Safety Board of Canada (TSB). Watchlist 2018. Factors associated with findings as to risk in TSB fishing vessel investigations, 2011–2017. Commercial fishing safety (2018). https://www.tsb.gc.ca/eng/surveillance-watchlist/marine/2018/marine.html
3. Jensen, O.C., Petursdottir, G., Holmen, I.M., Abrahamsen, A., Lincoln, J.: A review of fatal accident incidence rate trends in fishing. Int. Marit. Health **65**(2), 47–52 (2014). https://doi.org/10.5603/IMH.2014.0011
4. Transportation Safety Board of Canada (TSB). Statistical summary: Marine transportation occurrences in 2016 (2016). https://www.tsb.gc.ca/eng/stats/marine/2016/ssem-ssmo-2016.html
5. International Martime Organization (IMO). Guidelines on fatigue. 24 January 2019. MSC.1/Circ.1598.   www.imo.org/en/OurWork/HumanElement/Documents/MSC.1-Circ.1598.pdf
6. Pérusse, M., Cadieux, C., Lebeau, M., Fecteau, R., Francoeur, L.A., Dufresne Dubé, V., Drewitt, L.: Cap sur la prévention: Vers le développement d'une culture de sécurité dans l'industrie de la capture des pêches maritimes commerciales. Comité permanent sur la sécurité des bateaux de pêche du Québec (CPSBPQ) (2020). https://www.cpsbpq.org/informations.
7. Binkley, M., Bigney, K., Neis, B., Bornstein, S.: Lessons from offshore: challenges and opportunities in linking data to promote understanding of accidents and injuries among Newfoundland and Labrador fishers 1989–2001. Mar. Policy **32**(6), 905–912 (2018). https://doi.org/10.1016/j.marpol.2008.01.005
8. Haddon, W.: A logical framework for categorizing highway safety phenomena and activity. J. Trauma Injury Infect. Crit. Care **12**(3), 193–207 (1972). https://doi.org/10.1097/00005373-197203000-00002
9. Brand, S.L., et al.: Building programme theory to develop more adaptable and scalable complex interventions: realist formative process evaluation prior to full trial. Evaluation **25**(2), 149–170 (2019). https://doi.org/10.1177/1356389018802134

Part II: Healthcare Ergonomics (Edited by Marijke Melles)

Translating HFE into Action – Lessons from the Frontline

Sara Albolino[1], Peter Lachman[2]([⊠]), Christina Krause[3], and Allison Muniak[4]

[1] GRC, Florence, Italy
[2] RCPI, Dublin, Ireland
peterlachman@rcpi.ie
[3] BCC Council for Safety, Vancouver, Canada
[4] Vancouver Coastal Health, Vancouver, Canada

Abstract. Human Factors and Ergonomics (HFE) theory and methodology is well established in many industries. In healthcare it is still in its infancy and not well established, despite increasing evidence of the need to implement a HFE approach in day to day operations.

The COVID-19 pandemic demonstrated the need to implement HFE theories with clinical teams to ensure safety, be it for patients in clinical care or design of healthcare worker safety, or the procurement of supplies.

The examples of three different settings illustrate the key point of service design, development of situation awareness in clinical teams and the development of a culture of safety.

Keywords: Human factors · Clinical care · Safety · Situation awareness

1 The Human Factors Challenge

1.1 What at the Safety Challenge in Healthcare?

Human Factors and Ergonomics (HFE) has an important role to play in healthcare. Unfortunately, the principles and practice of HFE is not in widespread use by the administrators or the frontline clinicians. The aim of this workshop is to examine the potential for HFE to become an integral part of the healthcare design and delivery. We explore the reasons for the lack of HFE and use three examples to demonstrate how it can be come mainstream in healthcare.

1.2 Why Does This Challenge Exist Now?

At this time of the COVID-19 pandemic, the quality and safety of the care that clinicians provide, either in the hospital or in the community, is more important than ever. It requires an understanding of the sciences of improvement and patient safety. Safety and quality must be achieved within the increasing and competing demands for care, also with limited resources. This has been starkly demonstrated in the COVID-19 pandemic, with the reallocation of resources to the care of affected individuals, mainly the adult population. Care of people with long-term conditions or common acute ailments has been affected. In addition, the physical and psychological safety of the workforce has become a major issue.

The challenge is to care for people infected with COVID-19, protect staff and patients from infection, and to provide all the normal services for those with acute or long-term conditions. And with social distancing, the preservation of person centred care has become more challenging.

The current challenge has demonstrated the concept of healthcare being a complex adaptive system which undergoes continual change and must adopt new processes rapidly. Clinical teams do not have control over the whole care pathway, and it is difficult for clinical teams to provide care and continually improve care without taking a systems approach, either at a team or organisational level [1].

Improvement Patient Safety Science and HFE, provide a framework that allows clinical teams to make sense of the challenge that they now face. The methods provide an opportunity for continual learning from the current experience. Incorporating improvement methods with a human factors approach enables teams to maintain and improve care. This will have benefits for future service delivery and build resilience into the system, as post pandemic challenges will remain - they just may be different.

2   The value of Patient Safety Science

In the past twenty years the theories and methods of patient safety have developed and there are methods that can decrease harm. These include methodologies to manage clinical incidents, manage risk, improve the reliability of care, improve situation awareness of clinical teams with huddles, and to learn from what works well [1]. An example is the work on infection prevention, which is paramount now. Currently these methods have the potential to make a real difference in ensuring patients are safe. These require a system approach, which incorporates all the theories, and improvement methodology to achieve the outcomes.

2.1   Implementing Continual Improvement and Learning

The first step is to recognise that we need to plan for the quality of a service, have controls or measures of performance so that we know we are improving and delivering the desired outcomes. Then we need to actively improve the service delivery with the use of the methodologies of improvement, as part of our daily work [2]. The improvement theory has four lenses that clinical teams can use daily [3].

An understanding of how the work system works by breaking it down into its component elements. The Systems Engineering Initiative for Patient Safety (SEIPS) model incorporates improvement into human factors theory and looks at the environment, the culture of the team, the tools and technology required, the tasks to be undertaken and the people involved, staff and patients [4]. An example is for safe care of people with COVID-19, staff require Personal Protective Equipment (PPE), skills on using PPE, an environment that facilitates safe care, as well as the people who can deliver the care and complete the tasks.

Processes are designed to deliver outcomes and the study of variation in processes is a core element of improvement. Using run charts or time series measurement provides an opportunity to learn and improve over time. An example is measuring the variation in medication prescribing as medication harm is the most frequent harm for children, or how we will be able to maintain our services for children with long term conditions, studying the variation and how to minimise it.

Working with the people who provide the service is essential, and understanding their beliefs and attitudes is a core component. COVID-19 has highlighted the need to ensure wellbeing of staff both physical and mental. Resilience and caring for staff are essential if one wants to deliver a high quality and safe service [5].

A clear theory and method to improve care once variation has been identified is the final component. The lesson is, that if you apply the method i.e. studying the variation in the process, engaging the people involved and then collaboratively testing changes, change is possible. These simple lessons can be used now and in the future. As we respond to the new context of COVID-19, we must perform multiple small tests of change as the services are changed and have a measurement process to demonstrate improvement.

3 The Case Studies

Three examples demonstrate the value of using a combination of human factors, improvement, and patient safety science to make a real change.

3.1 Responding to COVID in Tuscany [6, 7]

COVID-19 in Italy to demonstrate how HFE made a real difference in the planning and response in Tuscany. The experience of the team in HFE knowledge and practice allowed them to work with clinical teams to facilitate a more effective response to the challenges of COVID-19. This real time development of a response can influence how HFE can become integral to healthcare in the future.

3.2 Case Study 2 Situation Awareness for Everyone [8–10]

S.A.F.E. (Situation Awareness for Everyone) programme demonstrate how HFE can become an integral part of day to day work introduction This programme aims to translate patient safety theory into practice and it relies on the SEIPS model as the foundation of building real time safety interventions. It has been applied in 50 paediatric units in England, 20 in Ireland and in Australia and Argentina. It is now being implemented in 14 adult clinical teams in Ireland. The COVID-19 pandemic placed exceptional demands on clinical staff and the need for situation awareness becomes even more important.The learning is that one can design for safety in a pragmatic way.

The aim is to allow clinical teams to develop situation awareness though the daily huddle. However the real innovation is the introduction of an adaptation of the Vincent model on measuring safety. Clinical teams incorporate the SEIPS model in a daily assessment of the workplace, an assessment of the resilience of the system by reporting what is working well, real time assessment of any harms that may have occurred in previous shift and constant review of the reliability of processes.

The main outcome has been an improvement of team safety culture as measured by Manchester Patient Safety Framework (MaPSaF) [11] as well as improved patient care and earlier response to deterioration.

3.3   Case Study 3 Responding to Infusion Harm in British Columbia

A high incidence of IV medication over-infusions was detected and investigated in British Columbia and ultimately led to a global recall of IV tubing sets. The team undertook a detail investigation journey demonstrating best practices for preservation of evidence, investigatory procedures and interdisciplinary collaborative approaches for "cracking the case" on medical device incidents. The main lessons were the need to look at the entire journey with necessary collaboration between patient safety, purchasing, human factors and medical device departments to ensure the issue was addressed in a timely manner.

4   The Challenge for Clinical Teams Now

As we move forward now during the pandemic and then after the pandemic, we need to ensure that the safety and quality of care is maintained. Although these scientific methods are not routinely included in medical education curricula or post graduate training, we can rapidly apply the methods. The challenge for those carrying out clinical care is to include these theories and methods into their daily work projects and programmes is to increase the rigour while not making it too difficult to implement. The desire to improve care and to spread results rapidly, without the required attention to theory and method, may result in the questioning of the validity of the outcomes by clinicians [12]. QI and HFE methodology should be applied with the rigour required to make a real difference in the care of patients. As way forward we recommend the following interventions as a start:

1. Continually use the SEIPS model to identify how the work-system is functioning [4].
2. Study variation in the process and develop programmes to improve the outcomes.
3. Use the huddle methodology to ensure that you have situation awareness, know what is working and be able to anticipate what needs to be improved [13].
4. Coproduce the solutions with staff and with patients and their families [14].

The dangers of delayed and missed diagnosis, clinical deterioration, medication harm, hospital acquired infections and safeguarding are still a threat to the safety of people. We need to use the Sciences of Improvement HFE and Patient Safety to help us deliver safe care now and in the future.

References

1. Cheung, R., Roland, D., Lachman, P.: Reclaiming the systems approach to paediatric safety. Arch. Dis. Childhood **104**, 1130–1133 (2019)
2. Bohmer, R.M.J.: The four habits of high-value health care organizations. New Engl. J. Med. **365**, 2045–2047 (2011)
3. Langley, G.J., Moen, R.D., Nolan, K.M., et al.: The Improvement Guide: A Practical Approach to Enhancing Organizational Performance. Jossey-Bass, San Francisco (2009)
4. Holden, R.J., Carayon, P., Gurses, A.P., Hoonakker, P., Schoofs Hundt, A., Ozok, A.A., Rivera-Rodriguez, A.J.J.: SEIPS 2.0: a human factors framework for studying and improving the work of healthcare professionals and patients. Ergonomics **56**(11), 1669–1686 (2013)
5. Wu, A.W., Connors, C., Everly, G.S., Jr.: COVID-19: peer support and crisis communication strategies to promote institutional resilience. Ann. Intern. Med. **172**(12), 822–823 (2020). https://doi.org/10.7326/M20-1236
6. Albolino, S., Dagliana, G., Tanzini, M., et al.: Human factors and ergonomics at time of crises: the Italian experience coping with COVID19. Int. J. Qual. Health Care (2020). https://doi.org/10.1093/intqhc/mzaa049, Accessed 13 May 2020
7. Albolino, S., Dagliana, G.: World patient safety day: the tuscany region at the forefront of quality of care. Int. J. Qual. Health Care **32**(3), 221–222 (2020). https://doi.org/10.1093/intqhc/mzaa010
8. Stapley, E., Sharples, E., Lachman, P., et al.: Factors to consider in the introduction of huddles on clinical wards: perceptions of staff on the safe programme. Int. J. Qual. Health Care **30**, 44–49 (2018)
9. Hayes, J., Lachman, P., Edbrooke Childs, J., et al.: Assessing risks to paediatric patients: conversation analysis of situation awareness in huddle meetings in England. BMJ Open **9**, e023437 (2019). https://doi.org/10.1136/bmjopen-2018-023437
10. Royal College of Paediatrics and Child Health. Situation Awareness for Everyone (S.A.F.E) toolkit. https://www.rcpch.ac.uk/resources/situation-awareness-everyone-safe-toolkit-introduction, Accessed 7 Feb 2021
11. Manchester Patient Safety Framework (MaPSaF). https://webarchive.nationalarchives.gov.uk/20171030124256/http://www.nrls.npsa.nhs.uk/resources/?EntryId45=59796, Accessed 7 Feb 2021
12. Dixon-Woods, M.: How to improve healthcare improvement—an essay by Mary Dixon-Woods. BMJ **367**, l5514 (2019)
13. Franklin, B.J., Gandhi, T.K., Bates, D.W., et al.: Impact of multidisciplinary team huddles on patient safety: a systematic review and proposed taxonomy. BMJ Qual. Saf. **29**(10), 1–2 (2020). https://doi.org/10.1136/bmjqs-2019-00991
14. Batalden, P.: Getting more health from healthcare: quality improvement must acknowledge patient coproduction—an essay by Paul Batalden. BMJ **362**, k3617 (2018)

Interface Design for Users with Spinal Cord Injuries and Disorders: An Interdisciplinary Research Program with the US Department of Veterans Affairs

Sam S. Anvari[✉], Gabriella M. Hancock, Nicole B. Mok, Aram Ayvazyan,
Carmen L. Machado, Rebecca M. E. Chompff, Kelsey M. McCoy, Matthew T. Nare,
Yuji Shiraiwa, Yoshiko Mizushima, Natalia Morales, and Loulya Alcharbaji

California State University Long Beach, 1250 Bellflower Boulevard, Long Beach,
CA 90840, USA
Sam.anvari@csulb.edu

Abstract. Assistive technologies such as environmental control units (ECUs)
enhance veterans' quality of life by enabling them to perform necessary tasks
independently. Previous research has identified usability problems regarding the
ECU's multimodal interface. This paper outlines an interdisciplinary team's program of research across academia, government agencies, and the private sector
to evaluate and re-design the ECU interface for improved usability/user experience. The ECU was evaluated in two phases based on established Interface Design
principles. First, heuristic analyses were performed to identify significant design
issues. Second, modifications were made as the result of these initial analyses, and
interactive digital prototypes of both the current and the enhanced ECU versions
were developed and implemented to facilitate remote usability testing during the
pandemic. The research program is currently in the A/B testing data collection
phase to evaluate both interfaces for usability and user experience outcomes across
defined tasks. This paper consequently provides an overview of each multidisciplinary partner's contribution to the program of research, complete with challenges, strategies, and recommendations for practitioners interested in launching
their own interdisciplinary projects.

Keywords: Interdisciplinary · User experience design · Interface design ·
Human factors · Department of Veterans Affairs · Environmental control unit

1 Introduction

This work details an on-going interdisciplinary design project between California State
University, Long Beach (CSULB), the Veterans Affairs' (VA) Long Beach Spinal Cord
Injuries and Disorders (SCI/D) Center, and an industry partner who manufactures the
device in question (Accessibility Services, Inc.). The VA has established 14 Cross-agency
Priority Goals to enhance the quality of care to citizens [1]. Improving the customer
experience is defined as one of these main goals [1; p. 11]. The VA promotes this goal

© The Author(s), under exclusive license to Springer Nature Switzerland AG 2021
N. L. Black et al. (Eds.): IEA 2021, LNNS 222, pp. 232–238, 2021.
https://doi.org/10.1007/978-3-030-74611-7_32

by utilizing tried and proven industry standards and applying them in order to enhance customer's experience in an appreciable and quantifiable way [1]. This collaborative design project focuses on enhancing the usability and user experience of autonoME Hospital Environmental Control Unit (ECU; Accessibility Services, Inc., Homosassa, FL). ECU is a device that helps individuals with functional disabilities (e.g. patients with spinal cord injuries) to undertake a set of tasks such as calling the nurse, adjusting the bed head or foot position, and controlling the TV, among others [2].

Veterans with spinal cord injuries and similar disorders have highly variable levels of motoric capacity. Therefore, assistive technologies, specifically environmental control units (ECUs), are used in veterans' care to facilitate the performance of necessary tasks, and thereby foster independence and enhance their quality-of-life. Given that veterans with SCI/D have a variable amount of control over their limbs, ECUs consequently include four modes of interaction to suit users' unique needs: touch-based, sip-and-puff (pneumatic tube), eye-tracking, and voice-control interfaces [3, 4]. The utility of these ECUs, however, is contingent on the efficiency and quality of users' interactions. Veterans with SCI/D typically find ECUs to be useful tools, yet previous research has identified numerous usability issues ranging from minor to catastrophic [3–5]. Thus, the challenge is to leverage input from an interdisciplinary research team (human factors/ergonomics, graphic design, and health care administration) and across agencies (academia, government, and industry) to effectively re-design these interfaces for improved usability/user experience. This project describes the challenges faced and lessons learned of an interdisciplinary line of research conducted by two CSULB departments in cooperation with a federal agency and the private sector. These include CSULB School of Art, CSULB Department of Psychology, VA Long Beach SCI/D Center, and Accessibility Services, Inc.

1.1 Our Interdisciplinary Design Research Team

This research is an interdisciplinary collaboration between the two faculty leads. The first is from the School of Art, an MFA in Graphic Design and BS in Biomedical Engineering, who specializes in interface design for mobile and digital platforms. The second faculty lead is from the Department of Psychology who holds a PhD in Applied Experimental and Human Factors Psychology. Combining these complementary backgrounds and fields of expertise, the nucleus for collaboration consequently focused on enhancing the usability and design of medical equipment. In 2019, initial contact was made with the Director of the VA Hospital at Long Beach with a research proposal to explore possibilities to evaluate and enhance the environmental control units (ECUs) used in the VA Hospital. As with most government facilities, all necessary operational and security protocols were observed. Receiving the appropriate credentials to gain access to the necessary areas required checking in with the VA Campus security department by every member of the research team during each visit. Additionally, as the VA is primarily a healthcare facility, all in-person collaboration has been put on hold during the pandemic for safety reasons and will only resume once the city's and VA's restrictive ordinances have been lifted. Keeping track of these protocols is essential for effective and safe collaboration. Having thus secured approval and support from the VA's administrative team at the local

Long Beach facility, undergraduate and graduate students from various disciplines were recruited to this project.

Ten students from various colleges at California State University, Long Beach (CSULB) are participating in this project. Two students from the BFA Graphic Design program are working on an alternative visual user interface design to help with the device's overall usability. Six students from the MS in Human Factors (MSHF) program are working on the research team to apply human factors methods for testing and evaluating design solutions in a remote manner. Two additional students have joined our research team from the CSULB Undergraduate Research Opportunity Program (UROP) with majors in the College of Natural Sciences and Mathematics (CNSM) at California State University, Long Beach. The students are research assistants with team doing work on communication, scheduling of user-testing sessions, and compiling a literature review. They also participate in the research as user testing facilitators. Our multi-disciplinary research team has brought together graduate and undergraduate students and faculty from a wide variety of backgrounds to take advantage of this opportunity for hands-on experience in team collaboration, applying design methods, and working with industry and government partners.

2 Methods

In the first phase of research, the original ECU interface was evaluated with a group of students and faculty using the testing methods based on commonly employed design principles from the classic human-computer interaction literature. Design adjustments were applied based on the issues identified in the first phase to enhance the ECU interface. In the second phase, the research team is using A/B user testing on common task sequences using the ECU interface to evaluate the performance of the enhanced design interface.

2.1 Phase 1

In the first phase of the project, seven trained evaluators from CSULB completed heuristic analyses of the ECU device's touch-based and eye-tracking modalities on the operational in-patient ECU system at the VA Long Beach SCI/D Center [3, 4]. The research team defined four typical tasks to simulate a patient's basic needs while interacting with the device's touch control interface:

1. Act out the steps required for the patient to make a phone call;
2. Compose an email to a medical professional, friend, or family member;
3. Turn on the television screen and navigate to a particular channel; and
4. Adjust the head and foot positions of the bed [3].

The touch-screen interface was evaluated based on Shneiderman's Eight Golden Rules for Interface Design [6] and Nielsen's 10 Heuristics for Interface Design [7]. The identified usability issues were categorized as either catastrophic, major, or minor by taking averages of the evaluators' severity ratings [3].

2.2 Main Issues with the Touch-Screen Mode

The research team categorized the results in three levels, namely catastrophic, major, and minor. This was done by averaging the evaluators' severity ratings. The evaluators found four catastrophic, eight major, and fifteen minor usability issues [3]. For catastrophic violations, the three most violated heuristics were "user control and freedom," "error prevention," and "offer informative feedback." The most important catastrophic usability issue was the lack of a dedicated "Go Back" button across screens which significantly hampered the efficacy of performance. The second catastrophic issue was the absence of help documentation when the user encounters an error message. The final catastrophic problems were the lack of informative system feedback given to the user when troubleshooting errors, and the inability to login and draft an email due to no internet connection/no offline mode [3].

2.3 Main Issues with the Eye-Tracking Mode

Based on the heuristic evaluations, in total thirty-eight issues were identified with the eye-tracking mode [4]. One of the catastrophic usability issues found when operating in the eye-tracking modality was the system's ineffective tracking of the pupil, and therefore the user's gaze is inconsistent due to excessive, unintended tracking [4]. Another major usability issue was identified when adjusting the bed positioning. There was no indication on the interface as to when the movements would begin or end. Another major problem was evident when inputting contacts for an email. The "at" symbol, though necessary and expected for this type of task, is not easily found, and the keyboard interface is confusing. It creates a poor user experience by requiring reliance on trial and error [4].

2.4 Phase 2 (On-Going)

Based on findings from heuristic evaluations on the touch screen mode in phase one, the design team applied modifications to the ECU interface in keeping with Nielsen's heuristics [7], Shneiderman's golden rules [6], and end-users' input from the first phase. To test the usability and user experience of two versions of the ECU interface, the design team built two interactive digital prototypes, replicating the currently implemented version at the Veterans Administration Hospital and a beta version designed by our research team (see Figs. 1 and 2). The team is currently conducting A/B testing to evaluate and compare two interfaces for task completion rates and times across four different tasks defined in the previous stage of the research. The researchers will administer validated questionnaires and assess various performance measures (speed, accuracy, stress, workload, frustration, and fatigue) to examine usability and user experience outcomes. Findings will facilitate the empirically driven re-design of the ECU interface to improve the user experience of the device.

Fig. 1. Left: actual ECU device – Right: Interactive digital replica made for A/B testing.

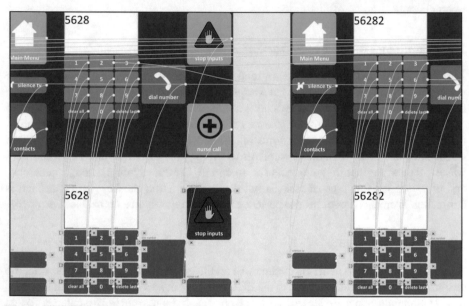

Fig. 2. ECU Digital Prototype Interface. Connection points indicating interactive prototype screen built based on user-testing scenarios for A/B Testing.

3   Discussion

This research project highlights the collaboration of an interdisciplinary team of faculty, students, industry, and government agencies that aim to enhance the usability and user experience of the autonoME ECU device. The research team shared its findings from the first phase of the research with the ECU manufacturer during the project's introductory phase. Frequent online meetings with the manufacturer were held to gain more technical insights in order to help build an interactive prototypes for online A/B testing, and also to plan for the next design phases. Additionally, the manufacturer sent one ECU device to the research team for in-person A/B testing. The team is currently in possession of the device, which will be installed in an on-campus facility once the stay-at-home orders are lifted and in-person research is safe to resume. The team will work closely with the manufacturer during the course of this research to implement and test new design solutions on the actual device as planned for the upcoming phases.

The research required expertise in various fields including interface design, graphic design, user experience, human factors, biomedical engineering, and usability. Therefore, the interdisciplinary nature of the faculty and student members of the academic team as well as those of the government and industry collaborators were all necessary to satisfactorily study, evaluate and propose solutions to meet all of the requirements for this unique ECU. This collaboration helped the team to gain insights into the functionality of the device and to set appropriate guidelines for improving the user experience of the interface design. Our efforts to incorporate students from the School of Art Graphic Design Program, Department of Psychology Master's in Human Factors Program, Department of Health and Human Services, and College of Natural Science and Mathematics have created a team that is successfully engaged in user-centered design research in an applied setting in collaboration with both the private sector and a federal agency.

Various academia and industry domains use shared methods for user experience and user interface design. This applied research project can bridge the gap between multiple practices and act as an incubator to train knowledgeable students. Students in the BFA Graphic Design program at the School of Art at Long Beach University learn visual design methods for communication design, digital interface design, and user-centered design research. Students in the Human Factors (MSHF) program learn applications of psychological principles to design human-machine systems, gaining skills in systems analysis, cognitive task analysis, rapid prototyping, and usability testing. This project has created an opportunity for students from diverse disciplines to experience the full process of design. Having an industry partner has strengthened the project by keeping it pragmatic and focused on realistic expectations for the outcome. Having a government partner allows for direct access to actual end-users of the design, and insight from other system stakeholders such as occupational therapy staff and at-home caregivers. Moreover, collaboration with the VA affords valuable observation of the utility of the system both in in-patient and out-patient operational contexts. The interdisciplinary nature of the project helps to put design ideas quickly into testing and allows the research team to receive quality usability feedback to identify areas for improvement. The collaboration has created a unique opportunity for academia, a government agency, and the private sector to shorten the feedback loop for design usability testing and ultimately benefit veterans and patients of the VA Hospital.

4 Conclusion

Implications from this work speak to the benefits and challenges of collaborative outreach efforts, community-based research, service-learning projects, and the generation and effective maintenance of multidisciplinary research programs involving academic, industry, and government agencies. Students and faculty researchers will also advance in their critical thinking skills, communication, creativity, pedagogy, and interdisciplinary techniques. However, the process is time-consuming and has its challenges. Still, it has the great advantage of training problem-solving students who have gained real, hands-on experience and are ready to emerge into the industry [8]. Interdisciplinary and inter-institutional research projects are also more comprehensive, meaningful, and applicable when conducted across ergonomic domains. Students gain real-world experience by engaging in hands-on research and design projects and the industry partners gain valuable research insights. Additionally, industry will benefit from these practitioners with broader knowledge bases and more extensive skillsets entering the field.

References

1. U.S. Department of Veterans Affairs FY 2020/FY 2018 Annual Performance Plan and Report [PDF file]. Retrieved from the website of the Middle Towship Government https://middletownship.com/wp-content/uploads/2019/07/VA-APPR.pdf. Accessed 10 Feb 2021
2. Bidassie, B., Vallette, M.A., James, T., Martinez, R., Etingen, B., Cozart, H., Weaver, F.M.: Evaluating the roll-out of environmental control units in veterans affairs spinal cord injury centers: workflow observations. Int. J. Healthc. **3**(2), 57–67 (2017)
3. Hancock, G.M., Anvari, S.S., Nare, M.T., Mok, N.B., Ayvazyan, A., McCoy, K.M., Bai, X., Mather, G.P., McBride, A.S., Morales, N.: Environmental control units for inpatient care at veterans affairs spinal cord injury centers: heuristic evaluation and design recommendations. In: Yamamoto, S., Mori, H. (eds.) Human Interface and the Management of Information: Proceedings of the 22nd International Conference of Human-Computer Interaction, pp. 23–38. Springer, Cham (2020a)
4. Hancock, G.M., Anvari, S.S., Nare, M.T., Mok, N.B., Ayvazyan, A., Bai, X., McCoy, K.M., Mather, G.P., Machado, C.L., Chompff, R. M.E., McBride, A.S., Morales, N.: A heuristic evaluation of usability for environmental control units' eye-tracking interfaces at veterans affairs spinal cord injuries and disorders centers. In: Proceedings of the 2020 International Symposium on Human Factors and Ergonomics in Health Care Virtual Conference: Springer (2020b)
5. Etingen, B., Martinez, R.N., Valette, M.A., Dendinger, R., Bidassie, B., Miskevics, S., Khan, H.T., Cozart, H.T., Locatelli, S.M., Weaver, F.M.: Patient perceptions of environmental control units: experiences of veterans with spinal cord injuries and disorders receiving inpatient VA healthcare. Disabil. Rehabil. Assistive Technol. **13**(4), 325–332 (2017)
6. Shneiderman, B.: Eight Golden Rules for Interface Design, Designing the User Interface, 3rd edn. Addison Welsey, Boston (1998)
7. Nielsen, J.: Ten Usability Heuristics for User Interface Design. Retrieved from the Nielsen Norman Group website. https://www.useit.com/papers/heuristic/heuristic_list.html.Accessed 10 Feb 2021
8. Jones, C.: Interdisciplinary approach - advantages, disadvantages, and the future benefits of interdisciplinary studies. Essai **7**(1), 76–81 (2009)

Resilience, Safety and Health: Reflections About Covid-19' Assistance

Vanessa Becker Bertoni[1] ⓘ, Natália Ransolin[1] ⓘ, Priscila Wachs[2] ⓘ,
and Angela Weber Righi[3(✉)] ⓘ

[1] Federal University of Rio Grande Do Sul, Rua Osvaldo Aranha, 99, 5 andar,
Porto Alegre, RS 90035-190, Brazil
natalia.ransolin@ufrgs.br
[2] Federal Institute of Education, Science and Technology of Rio Grande do Sul – Canoas
Campus, Rua Maria Zélia Carneiro de Figueiredo, 870, Canoas, RS 92412-240, Brazil
[3] Federal University of Santa Maria, Avenida Roraima, 1000, Santa Maria,
RS 97105-900, Brazil
angela.w.righi@ufsm.br

Abstract. There are growing concerns about how healthcare systems can adapt
in times of crisis. The overarching challenge lies in how resilience engineering
could be used to analyze and improve the performance of healthcare systems
concerning the Covid-19. This study aims to describe the relationship between
resilience potentials and health and safety aspects and its consequences on quality
and resilience in healthcare systems. This study has a quantitative methodological
approach using a survey with the Resilience Analysis Grid as an approach to
analyzing organizational resilience based on the idea that four potential (responding, monitoring, learning and anticipating) influence patient safety, occupational
health and safety and resilient system performance. As for this study results, anticipating and monitoring, overall resilience and occupational health and safety are
the variables that need more attention in healthcare systems. This study has a
dyad of contributions, as a practice, evaluate the resilience in a pandemic time,
and as theoretical, the identification of the importance of resilience four potential
connections in healthcare systems.

Keywords: Healthcare · Covid-19; resilience engineering · Human factors ·
Ergonomics

1 Introduction

Living in times of pandemic, as experienced since 2020 due to Covid-19, is a humanity
old challenge. However, the Covid-19 pandemic occurs in a scenario of unprecedented
interconnection between people, organizations and ecosystems [1]. Management skills
in all segments of public and private institutions are being challenged and the healthcare
systems were affected the most.

In the front line to deal with the disease, these institutions needed to quickly reorganize their practices, aiming at the services efficiency and, above all, the protection of

N. L. Black et al. (Eds.): IEA 2021, LNNS 222, pp. 239–245, 2021.
https://doi.org/10.1007/978-3-030-74611-7_33

its employees and patients. Elective surgeries needed to be canceled, areas for patients of different pathologies were transformed into exclusive beds for Covid-19 patients, employees were relocated from their previous sectors for exclusive care to these patients and the emergency hiring of many others needed to be done. In addition to the difficulties commonly experienced in the healthcare sector, such as emergency department overcrowding, scarcity of fundamental resources, high demand for personal protective equipment (PPE) and its real availability are a contributing factor to the installation of chaos in this system [2, 3].

Atypical situations such as the one currently experienced requests individual and organizational resilience, focused on the greater good: the population assistance. The term resilience presents different concepts in different areas of knowledge. In general, it is related to the materials, individuals, organizations, and systems ability to adapt. In safety management, resilience is perceived as "the system's ability to adjust their functioning before, during, or after changes and disturbances, so that the system can maintain the necessary operations, under expected and unexpected conditions" [4].

In this way, the discipline of Resilience Engineering (RE) aims to develop methods, techniques and tools to help complex socio-technical systems (CSTS), such as healthcare systems [5], to keep their operations safe and productive [6]. Resilience is a CSTC characteristic, enabling the CSTS to cope with its variability [5], and is even more necessary at a pandemic time like the one presented by Covid-19. Science-based approaches that consider human cognition and behavior in complex work systems are required to improve pandemic management [7].

Resilience is not something that the organization has, but something that it does [4]. Thus, for the organization to perform resiliently, four potentials (abilities) are essential: the ability to respond to system variability; the ability to monitor such variability, both in the system itself and in the external environment, identifying the need or not to activate the ability to respond; the ability to anticipate comprises knowing what to expect, anticipating possible threats and opportunities; and, finally, the ability to learn from past events. In this perspective, resilience cannot be measured from the count of results (e.g., number of accidents or incidents), but from its ability to respond, monitor, anticipate and learn from a situation [4, 8].

Still from the perspective of RE, analyzing the four potentials helps to understand the differences between the work-as-imagined (e.g., work policies and procedures) and the work-as-done (effectively performed by the workers). Thus, studying resilience in healthcare systems is essential to understand how healthcare systems are able to carry out their activities and to analyze or identify improvements opportunities in their processes [9–11].

Considering that more than 2 million people lost their lives as consequence of Covid-19 (as of 04 February 2021) [12] and that the world still struggles to control the disease, to understand how the frontline healthcare workers perceive the resilience potentials performance by their hospitals while assisting Covid-19 can be a significant indication of how the organization faces the challenges, manifested in health, safety and performance conditions.

Thus, the aim of this study is to identify the relationship between resilience potentials and occupational health and safety, patient safety and overall systems resilience in hospitals during the Covid-19 Pandemic, from the workers' point-of-view.

2 Method

This study is part of a main study, entitled "Organizational Resilience evaluation during COVID-19 pandemic: a study in the healthcare sector", approved by the Ethics Committee of the responsible institution (CAAE 32774620.0.0000.5346). The ethical precepts were respected in all phases of the study.

The study presented in this chapter is characterized as descriptive, with a quantitative approach, since it is concerned to describe a phenomenon in a specific context [13] (resilience during COVID-19 in the healthcare sector).

A survey was applied remotely to a snowball convenience sample. Invitations to participate in the study were sent through email and social media to potential participants, who could also invite other potential participants. The inclusion criteria for this study was: healthcare workers, working in Brazilian hospitals during the COVID-19 pandemic.

The questionnaire presented two categories of questions, the first one related to the participants and their hospital characterization (profession, hospital city, private or public hospital, hospital area) and the second one related to the resilience' four potential and based on the Resilience Analysis Grid (RAG), using 5-point likert scale [14]. RAG is focused on analyzing the resilience of an organization in everyday work based on how the organization responds, monitors, learns and anticipates in everyday activities [15]. The potential to respond is related to knowing what to do; the potential to monitor, knowing what to look for; the potential to learn, knowing what has happened; and the potential to anticipate, knowing what to expect [14]. No application of RAG in times of pandemic has been reported in the literature (yet).

The data collection occurred during the months of June, July and August of 2020. A total of 111 valid responses were obtained. 8% of the participants work in a private hospital, 62% in a public one and 30% in private/public one. 40% works in the Intensive Care Unit, 9% in the Emergency Department and 13% in the patient ward, 39% other hospital units. And 47% of the participants are nurses, 10% doctors, 14% physical/respiratory therapists, 5% others.

The data obtained were treated with simple descriptive statistics (mean) and multivariate statistics (Pearson's correlation). Pearson's analysis was used to study the relationship among the overall resilience of the system, the patient safety and the occupational health and safety. The measure of Pearson's correlation coefficient provides information on how closeness two variables are. All significance values are two-tailed [16].

3 Results and Discussion

3.1 The Four Potential

It is widely known in the field of resilience engineering that the four potentials are highly interconnected, being difficult and sometimes impossible to separate them [17].

Through the analysis of the questions' average of each potential individually, the radar graphic (Fig. 1) clearly shows that learning and responding are the ones highlighted by the institutions. In turn, monitoring and anticipating are the potentials that should require more efforts to increase, as they scored the lowest by the respondents. Next paragraphs will discuss the role played by each potential on the systems resilience when facing the COVID-19 pandemic.

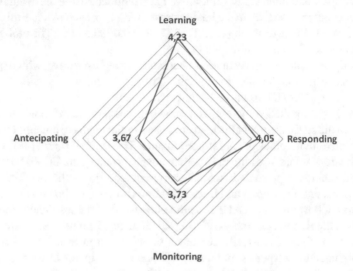

Fig. 1. Resilience four potentials radar chart diagram.

The learning potential is defined as the knowledge acquired from positive as well as negative aspects of a scenario [14, 18]. Learning was the highest scored potential by respondents (M = 4,23), which could be seen as a general aspect of this pandemic, as institutions, assistance, and even societal practices have been moving forward while taking into account the knowledge acquainted with desired and undesired outcomes.

Clinical workers agreed that lessons learned through negative (M = 4,35) and positive experiences (M = 4,43) in the past contribute to the promotion of patient safety as well as dealing with the pandemic as a whole, those questions being the top-ranked ones. On the other hand, the questions with the lowest scores were the ones regarding the contributions of learning from past situations for the occupational health and safety and health of workers who take care of infected patients (M = 4,08), and for the flexibility of the built environment in order to attend the increased demand (M = 4,00).

The potential to respond to problems is a healthcare workers' qualification and so could be expected to be well recognized in professional practice [14, 19]. Therefore, in this survey, it was highly scored when it comes to the creation and undertaking of safety measures for Covid-19 patients by the institutions (M = 4,41). Covid-19 is a highly contagious disease, so promptly acting to save the patient's life is related to the responding potential and consequently the patient's safety. However, this very same potential was not quite well ranked regarding its overall evaluation (M = 4,05) and efficiency when coping with infected patients' demands, such as the built environment conditions (M = 3,78). The potential to respond does not have the highest impact in the general resilience, although it significantly contributes (M = 4,05).

The potential to anticipate could involve foreseeing emerging problems or opportunities [14, 19]. The questions covered to analyze how workers evaluate this potential in their institutions scored the lowest among the four resilience potentials (M = 3,67). It seems that the anticipation of challenge scenarios is not a strategic practice incorporated in the healthcare systems. Within the anticipate potential, the top-ranked item was the one related to the contribution of reliable and updated information (M = 3,90), the same as for the previous potential to monitor. On the other hand, the lowest rated item was the institutions' capacity of anticipating situations that impact on Covid-19 patients' safety (M = 3,50).

Regarding the unforeseen, unknown and danger nature of this pandemic, the results indicate that the majority of healthcare organizations involved in this study are mainly concerned to quickly acquire the necessary clinical expertise and safety practices to adapt the evidence to their fields, where the need for responding the contextual demand is characterized by the increasing number of Covid-19 patients. Anderson [19] study aimed to develop a framework to guide future research into resilient processes, effects and interventions at all scales of healthcare activities. They have also found similar links with the results from the survey undertaken in this study, as they pointed out that anticipating task outcomes is an ability tightly connected to monitoring task performance.

3.2 Overall Resilience, Patient Safety, and Occupational Health and Safety

Finally, discussing how the general resilience score (Fig. 2), it can be stated that respondents strongly agreed that their institutions are resilient (M = 4,13). Regarding safety, participants do not totally agree they are safe (M = 3,33) as well as Covid-19 patients (M = 3,48), specifically speaking of chances of accidents, errors, and occupational diseases.

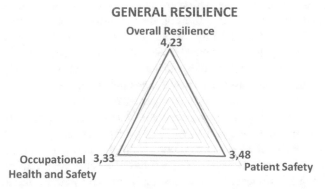

Fig. 2. Overall resilience, occupational health and safety, patient safety relations - radar chart diagram.

As for the four resilience potentials, they should be highly interconnected, reflecting directed in workers and patient safety [17]. As the resilience four potentials are promising and could provide means for thinking about how healthcare systems can be supported [20], they need to be present to compose the system's resilience, even with different intensities. The results obtained through Pearson's correlation presented the interaction between general resilience, patient safety, and occupational health and safety. The variables resilience (overall) and patient safety were highly correlated ($r = .680$, $p < .001$), while resilience (overall) and occupational health and safety were less correlated ($r = .600$, $p < .001$) compared to each other. Patient safety and occupational health and safety ($r = .764$, $p < .001$) were highly correlated. As safety can be treated as an emergent property resulting from the interactions among the aspects of a system, it acknowledged that safety means moving beyond human error and examining the deeper, system factors that affect clinical work in healthcare organizations [21, 22]. Also, it shows that when workers perceive their work environment as a safe place, they considered that patients are safe as well.

The four potentials are necessary and must be performed interconnected for supporting the system's resilience, as indicated by the result. Besides that, the resilience performance contributes to the patient safety and the occupational health and safety. Understanding the manifestation of resilience through the correlation of the four resilience potentials helps to understand the effectiveness of practices [22] used during the pandemic period, contributing to its dissemination. These results also suggest that organizations are not aware of emerging issues regarding their own systems, while they are taking into account external information regarding the Covid-19 pandemic, such as the recommendations of the World Health Organization.

4   Conclusions

Bringing up Resilience Engineering theory for safety in times of Covid-19, this paper suggests an approach to measuring resilience by means of RAG, a questionnaire-based tool based on the four cornerstones of resilience. The outcome-based on our data collected concludes that during the period of pandemic coping, institutions do not have enough time and resources to shed light on the monitoring and anticipating potentials, as they are dealing with Covid-19 by learning and responding to disruptions. The practice of following-up updated Evidenced Based Medicine (EBM) can be one hypothesis for these results, as workers from all organizational levels are constantly monitoring the Covid-19 unfolding, being aware of new procedures available. Anderson et al., 2020 have stated that "learning from previous experience of what works for a patient problem is linked to responding to future patients" (Anderson et al., 2020). To reinforce the potentials to monitor and anticipate is required a deeper understanding of the emerging phenomena, which can be seen as an outcome from the learning and responding potentials. Despite showing and discussing the results of the survey undertaken in this study, findings are unclear and deserve a detailed investigation by future research, including interviews and a mixed-method approach.

References

1. Saurin, T.A.: A complexity thinking account of the COVID-19 pandemic: Implications for systems-oriented safety management. Saf. Sci. **134**, 105087 (2021)

2. Randelli, P.S., Compagnoni, R.: Management of orthopaedic and traumatology patients during the Coronavirus disease (COVID-19) pandemic in northern Italy. Knee Surg. Sports Traumatol. Arthroscopy **28**, 1683–1689 (2020)
3. Zimmermann, M., Nkenke, E.: Approaches to the management of patients in oral and maxillofacial surgery during COVID-19 pandemic. J. Cranio-Maxillofacial Surg. **48**, 521–526 (2020)
4. Hollnagel, E., Paries, J., Woods, D., Wreathall, J.: Resilience Engineering in Practice: A Guidebook. Ashgate, Aldershot (2011)
5. Righi, A.W., Saurin, T.A.: Complex socio-technical systems: characterization and management guidelines. Appl. Ergon. **50**, 19–30 (2015)
6. Hollnagel, E., Woods, D., Leveson, N.: Resilience Engineering: Concepts and Precepts. Ashgate, Aldershot (2006)
7. Gurses, A.P., Tschudy, M.M., McGrath-Morrow, S., Husain, A., Solomon, B.S., Gerohristodoulos, K.A., Kim, J.M.: Overcoming COVID-19: what can human factors and ergonomics offer? J. Patient Saf. Risk Manage. **25**(2), 49–54 (2020)
8. Pecillo, M.: The concept of resilience in OSH management: a review of approaches. Int. J. Occup. Saf. Ergon. **22**, 291–300 (2016)
9. Ellis, L.A., Churruca, K., Clay-Williams, R., Pomare, C., Austin, E.E., Long, J.C., Braithwaite, J.: Patterns of resilience: a scoping review and bibliometric analysis of resilient health care. Saf. Sci. **118**, 241–257 (2019)
10. Braithwaite, J.: Changing how we think about healthcare improvement. BMJ **361**, 1–5 (2018)
11. Clay-Williams, R., Hounsgaard, J., Hollnagel, E.: Where the rubber meets the road: using FRAM to align work-as-imagined with work-as-done when implementing clinical guidelines. Implementation Sci. **10**(1), 1–8 (2015)
12. JHU (Johns Hopkins University). Coronavirus COVID-19 Global Cases by the Center for Systems Science and Engineering (CSSE) at Johns Hopkins University. https://coronavirus.jhu.edu/map.html. Accessed 04 Feb 2021
13. Gil, A.C.: Como elaborar projetos de pesquisa. Atlas, São Paulo (2020)
14. Hollnagel, E.: The Resilience Analysis Grid, In: Hollnagel, E., Paries, J., Woods, D., Wreathall, J. (eds.) Resilience Engineering in Practice: A Guidebook. Burlington, Ashgate (2011)
15. Patriarca, R., Di Gravio, G., Costantino, F., Falegnami, A.: Bilotta: an analytic framework to assess organizational resilience. Saf. Health Work **9**(3), 265–276 (2018)
16. Taylor, E.Z., Murthy, U.S.: Knowledge sharing among accounting academics in an electronic network of practice. Account. Horiz. **23**(2), 151–179 (2009)
17. Hollnagel, E.: Safety-II in Practice Developing the Resilience Potentials. Routledge, New York (2018)
18. Eppich, W., Cheng, A.: Promoting excellence and reflective learning in simulation (PEARLS): development and rationale for a blended approach to health care simulation debriefing. Simul. Healthc. J. Soc. Simul. Healthc. **10**(2), 106–115 (2015)
19. Anderson, J.E., Ross, A.J., Macrae, C., Wiig, S.: Defining adaptive capacity in healthcare: a new framework for researching resilient performance. Appl. Ergon. **87**, 103–111 (2020)
20. Wiig, S., Fahlbruch, B.: Exploring Resilience: A Scientific Journey from Practice to Theory. Springer, Heidelberg (2019)
21. Yang, Q., Tian, J., Zhao, T.: Safety is an emergent property: illustrating functional resonance in air traffic management with formal verification. Saf. Sci. **93**, 162–177 (2017)
22. Alders, M.D.L.: A reflective process for analyzing organisational resilience to improve the quality of care (Doctoral dissertation, King's College London). (2019)

Aligning and Forecasting Caregiver Needs Within Consumer Health Informatics Design: A Patient Ergonomics Perspective

Janetta C. Brown[✉]

Indiana University School of Medicine, 340 W 10th St. #6200, Indianapolis, IN 46202, USA
jancbrow@iu.edu

Abstract. Alzheimer's disease (AD) has subjected affected families to rigorous, unprecedented demands. Consumer health informatics (CHI) is suggested as a formidable intervention to aid in necessary health management for people with AD. Although CHI's have been developed to support chronic disease management, research is still needed to translate knowledge gained regarding patient work into CHI design in order to better represent the needs of AD caregivers. Patient ergonomics recognizes the efforts (i.e. work) that individuals put forth towards the treatment and maintenance of their health and thus was used to inform the design of targeted CHI. Participatory design and human factors methods were used to produce AD caregiver-generated data which were translated into recommended CHI application features for this population of health consumers.

Keywords: Patient ergonomics · Caregiving · Consumer health informatics · Alzheimer's disease · Chronic disease management

1 Introduction

1.1 Caring for Individuals with Alzheimer's Disease

Alzheimer's disease (AD) has subjected affected families to rigorous and unprecedented demands when contending with chronic disease management [1]. AD care includes assisting with daily living activities (e.g. bathing, dressing, and social support), taking extra measures to ensure safety at home, financial management, and care coordination with a care team (e.g. health care providers). These responsibilities can compound and evolve without warning as the disease progresses over time. The considerable responsibilities of AD caregivers warrant particular attention to their needs in order for these caregivers to be successful.

1.2 Patient Ergonomics

Patient ergonomics applies the human factors/ergonomics (HFE) discipline towards the study and improvement of non-professionals' performance and activities (i.e. work) for

© The Author(s), under exclusive license to Springer Nature Switzerland AG 2021
N. L. Black et al. (Eds.): IEA 2021, LNNS 222, pp. 246–250, 2021.
https://doi.org/10.1007/978-3-030-74611-7_34

treatment and health management [2]. Researchers have been compelled to further investigate the work performed by informal caregivers to achieve these health goals and are applicable to the AD caregiving context. Aging, chronic disease, and technology are established areas of patient ergonomics and influence modern approaches to healthcare provision for health consumers [2]. Consumer health informatics (CHI) (e.g. mobile health) are suggested as formidable interventions to aid in health management of individuals with AD [3]. Although CHI's have been developed to support chronic disease management, the problem remains that research is still needed to translate knowledge gained regarding patient work into CHI design in order to better represent the needs of the consumer.

This study sought to answer the following call to action [2] posed by patient ergonomics practitioners, but within the context of AD caregiving: 1) How do we systematically, efficiently, and effectively translate knowledge of caregivers' work activities into guidance for CHI application design? 2) How do we map specific caregiver work activities to 'feature sets' for CHI applications? 3) How can we best represent caregivers' illness-related experiences and perspectives as concrete design choices? Data gathered from this study were also translated into recommendations for specific CHI application features and design choices to reflect an AD caregiver user base.

2   Methods

Focus groups and questionnaires were the participatory design methods used to gather data regarding the work AD caregivers performed while caring for individuals at each stage of AD (i.e. Early, Middle, and Late stages) respectively.

Participants. Stratified sampling was conducted to recruit the caregivers representing the three stages of AD. The study criteria included informal AD caregivers who were a) 18 years of age or older and b) caring for individuals within each respective stage of AD. The stage of AD was self-identified by the caregiver and confirmed using the definitions of AD stages from the Alzheimer's Association [1]. Experience using smartphones or computer-based technology was not required.

Focus Groups. Three focus group sessions took place, one for each stage of AD. The caregivers were asked a series of open-ended questions in order to highlight their desired information and activities they conducted during care. The focus group sessions were audio recorded and transcribed manually. Open and closed card sorting analysis was conducted to derive themes from the discussion to use as recommended features for CHI design and content.

Questionnaire. A self-administered questionnaire was delivered electronically via Google Forms to AD caregivers, including the focus group participants, with the help of caregiver and medical programs in order to gather data from a larger sample size. Respondents rated the urgency of information they deemed critical at the stage of AD they were caring for to help prioritize content recommended for CHI design.

3 Results and Discussion

Tables 1, 2, 3, 4 and 5 display the results of the questionnaire respondents, focus group participants, caregiving activities, card sorting themes, and recommended CHI features. Text in italics represent information deemed critical at all three stages of AD.

Table 1. Questionnaire respondent demographics, n = 63

Stage of AD	Age	Gender	Race
Early: 20	$M = 59.62$ years	Male: 12	African American: 56
Middle: 25	$(SD = 12.79$ years)	Female: 50	Non-Hispanic White: 5
Late: 18		Preferred not to answer: 1	Asian: 2

Table 2. Focus group participant demographics, n = 17

Stage of AD	Age	Gender	Race	Length of care
Early: 6	$M = 53.7$ years	Male: 1	African American: 17	$M = 9.12$ years
Middle: 5	$(SD = 18.4$ years)	Female: 16		$SD = 8.6$ years
Late: 6	Range: 21–77 years			

Table 3. Recommended CHI application features for early-stage AD caregivers

Caregiving activity	Recommended CHI features	Themes
Caregiver self-care	*Caregiver self-care tool*	*Therapy, Anxiety/Stress solutions*
Family involvement	*Chatroom*	*Family care schedule, Care plan*
Safety	Safety tool	Technology, Wandering, Sensors

Table 4. Recommended CHI application features for middle-stage AD caregivers

Caregiving activity	Recommended CHI features	Themes
Legal planning	Legal information tool	Power of attorney, Wills, Elder law
Adult day centers	Respite care tool	Memory café, Lunch & Learn

Table 5. Recommended CHI application features for late-stage AD caregivers

Caregiving activity	Recommended CHI features	Themes
Safety approaches	Safety tool	Falls, Technology, Wandering
Financial planning	Informational support tool	Medicare, Medicaid, Veterans, Trusts
Doctor appointments	Health specialist tool	Care Team, Occupational therapy
Support groups	Chatroom, Social support tool	Support group programs, Conferences

The care activities discussed spanned and represented the evolving needs of caregivers as the disease progressed. The ages of the caregivers and years of caregiving experience also represented various generations (i.e. millennial and older) and relationship status (e.g. adult child vs. spouse) to the patient. These factors helped account for different care activities and should also be reflected in CHI design. The themes associated with the recommended CHI features from Tables 3, 4 and 5 reflect the keywords caregivers listed within the questionnaire that they would use when searching for these topics of information and depict the language caregivers are most familiar with. Topics such as Financial Planning, Support Groups, and Technology were only considered critical within advanced AD stages when proper preparation for these care activities was overdue. Early stage caregivers had less requests than those of other stages since the patient was still independent, but also discussed heightened levels of pressure associated with initially receiving the diagnosis and assuming the role of a caregiver with no prior experience. Similarly, a scoping review [4] of those transitioning into caregiver roles mirrored the paradox between caregivers needing, planning for, and securing reinforcement for care activities. Hence, anticipated topics of information being forecasted within CHI design could aid in proactive health management at all stages of AD.

Limitations of this study included only a 4% questionnaire response rate as 1600 total caregivers were contacted in North Carolina and Illinois. The geographic constraints also limited the inclusion of data from other regions, however, this study is scalable to include nationwide responses in the future. The cultural diversity of participants was low and largely African American, but gave insight into the plight of a largely marginalized population disproportionately affected by AD. This study did not focus on the education level, technical proficiency, or self-rated health of the caregivers and thus provides only a rationed depiction of caregiver characteristics.

4   Conclusion

By focusing on the work activities performed by AD caregivers, their associated informational needs were successfully translated into recommended features for CHI design using themes derived from focus group discussion. Supplemental data from the questionnaire helped to prioritize content critical for providing care in respective AD stages. These findings allow future CHI for AD management to optimize the performance and work of caregivers wanting to achieve proactive treatment and health outcomes.

References

1. Alzheimer's Association: 2020 Alzheimer's disease facts and figures. Alzheimer's & Dementia **16**(3), 391–460 (2020)
2. Valdez, R.S., Holden, R.J., Novak, L.L., Veinot, T.C.: Transforming consumer health informatics through a patient work framework: connecting patients to context. J. Am. Med. Inf. Assoc. **22**(1), 2–10 (2015)
3. Werner, N.E., et al.: Getting what they need when they need it: Identifying barriers to information needs of family caregivers to manage dementia-related behavioral symptoms. Appl. Clin. Inf. **8**, 191–205 (2017)
4. Lee, K., Puga, F., Pickering, C.E.Z., Masoud, S.S., White, C.L.: Transitioning into the caregiver role following a diagnosis of Alzheimer's disease or related dementia: a scoping review. Int. J. Nurs. Stud. **96**, 119–131 (2019)

Using a Systems Approach to Support the Redesign of an Inpatient Anticoagulant Medication Chart

Eva-Maria Carman[✉] [iD], Joannes Hermans, Selina Ladak, and Giulia Miles

Nottingham University Hospitals NHS Trust, Nottingham, UK
eva.burford@nuh.nhs.uk

Abstract. Human factors and a systems approach can offer unique insight into the redesign process of medical charts to enhance usability. This paper describes a mixed method approach utilising numerous HF tools and theories to support the redesign process for an inpatient anticoagulant medication chart. The system factors and error-producing conditions associated with the use of this chart were identified through a qualitative analysis, using the SEIPS 2.0 model, of 65 reported incidents associated with the use of this chart. To better understand the role of this document at a task level, the task 'first time prescription of anticoagulant medication' was analysed in more detail using Hierarchical Task Analysis and the Systematic Human Error Reduction Approach. The incident report data was then also mapped onto the HTA and SHERPA of the task. Based on studies that applied heuristic analyses and a human factors perspective to chart design and evaluation, key design characteristics were compiled that were used to evaluate the chart. The results from these three different analyses were used to compile recommendations for the next design iteration of this chart.

Keywords: Systems analysis · SEIPS 2.0 · Medication chart design · Task analysis

1 Introduction

Medication charts are essential tools in healthcare work, that are associated not only with medication prescription and medication administration but also often serve as a form of safety barrier. Due to this safety role, these documents have frequently been targeted as a potential area to enhance safety. However, studies on chart redesign seldom explore the system wherein the tool is used, how this may contribute to safety and the effect it may have on recommendations for the redesign process.

1.1 The Context

This piece of work originated as a result of an ongoing review and redesign of the inpatient oral anticoagulant chart used at a large hospital trust in the United Kingdom initiated in response to a serious incident. The Trent Simulation and Clinical Skills

© The Author(s), under exclusive license to Springer Nature Switzerland AG 2021
N. L. Black et al. (Eds.): IEA 2021, LNNS 222, pp. 251–258, 2021.
https://doi.org/10.1007/978-3-030-74611-7_35

Centre (TSCSC) was approached to offer some human factors insight as part of the review of the effectiveness of the redesigned chart and offer further potential redesign considerations. At the time the human factors team were invited into the project, an interim redesigned chart had already been rolled out and an initial redesign of the chart had already commenced. The human factors team were asked to provide an evaluation of this redesigned version (second iteration) and provide recommendations for future potential redesign cycles.

1.2   Study Aim and Objectives

This paper aims to describe the unique elements human factors and more specifically a system's approach can offer medical chart design, through the case study of the redesign and evaluation process of an inpatient anticoagulant medication chart. A unique aspect of this study was to bring a systems approach to the redesign process to compile a better understanding of the use of this chart and its potential effect on safety. The objectives included identifying contributing system factors associated with the use of this chart including associated reported incidents involving this chart, explore the potential risks of using this chart and evaluation of the design characteristics.

2   Method

A mixed methods approach was adopted to address the aims and objectives of this study. This included using numerous different data sources for different types of analyses. A summary of the approach, data sources, analyses, outputs and how these contributed to the development of the recommendations proposed has been depicted in Fig. 1. To identify contributing system factors and error-producing conditions, a qualitative analysis of 65 reported incidents associated with the use of the inpatient anticoagulant medication chart was conducted. This included all reported incidents that were related to the use of this chart for the date range of 04/05/2019 to 28/11/2019. At this time period, an interim redesigned chart was in use and the second iteration of the redesigned chart had not yet been rolled out. Although the design of the charts was different, the tasks associated with these charts are not and the interim chart already included the new task elements that the redesign chart required, namely the second prescriber requirement which was one of the key alterations made in response to the coroner's report on the serious incident that prompted this redesign. The Systems Engineering Initiative for Patient Safety (SEIPS) 2.0 model [1] was used to provide the system structure to guide the analysis.

To better understand the use of this chart, one task was explored in more depth, namely the task *'first time prescription of anticoagulant medication'*, using Hierarchical Task Analysis (HTA) [2] and the Systematic Human Error Reduction Approach (SHERPA) [3]. The task analysis was performed for the second iteration of the redesigned chart through a group interview with a lead pharmacist and consultant haematologist that were part of the chart design team. The task decomposition diagram was then verified by the same staff that participated in the task analysis in a follow-up meeting and the probable error states for this task were determined using the SHERPA method. The

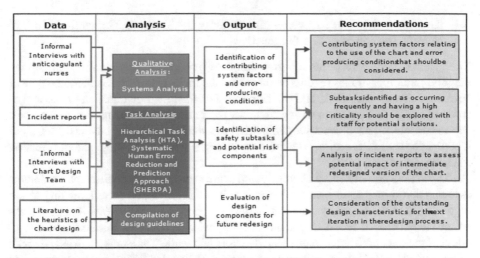

Fig. 1. The human factors analysis approach adopted including the data, analysis, output and how these contributed to the generation of recommendations.

incident report data was then also mapped onto the HTA decomposition diagram of the task.

Based on studies that applied heuristic analyses and a human factors perspective to chart design and evaluation [4, 5], key design characteristics were compiled that were used to evaluate the second iteration of the chart.

A key element of this piece of work was capturing the user's perspective. Unfortunately, due to the current pandemic it was not possible to capture work-as-done through the planned observation sessions and additional interviews with different staff groups that encounter this chart. Despite this, by using a variety of data sources the validity of the results was enhanced through data triangulation.

3   Results

Through the use of mixed methods and various data sources, a more comprehensive understanding of the chart within the system in which it is used could be generated. The systems analysis provided a broad perspective of the use of the chart not only by considering the work system but also along the whole patient-task pathway. The task analysis then focused specifically on one task within the patient-task pathway, namely the initial prescribing cycle. The results not only identified areas for consideration for the next iteration of the chart redesign process but also identified other potential areas of learning and improvement for the work system. Finally, the heuristic evaluation of the chart then provided specific design characteristics that could be applied at the next redesign phase.

3.1 The Inpatient Oral Anticoagulant Chart – the Types of Things that Go Wrong and the System's Perspective

The qualitative analysis of the reported incidents provided information not only on the negative outcomes of these events but also how the incidents were identified, the type of corrective actions staff took, and the learning staff identified that needed to occur. The types of things that could go wrong for tasks where the anticoagulant medication chart was used included documentation problems, prescription errors, dispensing errors, medication administration errors, procedure problems as well as discharge and information transfer-related problems.

The system components that contributed to error-producing conditions and problems associated at a task level identified from the incidents included factors relating to the organisation of work (e.g. staffing levels, timing of tasks), problems with tools and technology (e.g. delayed access to patient records), external environmental influences (e.g. effect of the weekend) and person-related factors (e.g. patient as a safety barrier, patient's behaviour, incorrect information from family, professional collaborative problems). It is essential to consider these other work system components in addition to the task-related aspects that went wrong as one cannot meaningfully separate these elements and as they may provide the context on why these task elements were not successful. The problem may not lie with the task but rather the context in which it was done.

The main learning opportunities identified by staff that filed the incident reports included education, training and improving communication. From a human factors perspective, this raises the question what organisational learning can be obtained from these incidents to enhance the work system to reduce error-producing conditions. Based on the systems analysis, an example of an additional area for consideration by the organisation included designing support for procedures and tasks that span temporal and shift boundaries (e.g. supporting staff completing tasks across shifts and over the weekend). To set up a robust and resilient system, the system needs to provide support for work as it occurs. Therefore, it is essential to understand when this task occurs and the conditions under which the task occurs.

Using the data, a simplistic task-patient pathway was created to identify where along a patient's journey the chart would be utilised and which tasks were involved with this patient type and related to this chart. The task stages included admitting the patient, generation of the initial documentation, the prescribing-testing cycle, dispensing and administering tasks and finally the chart would be used in the discharge process. At each of these stages different staff are involved, different tasks occur, and the chart is utilised in different ways.

3.2 The Task – 'First Time Prescription of Anticoagulant Medication'

The task analysis was done for one task that uses the inpatient anticoagulant medication chart, namely *'first time prescription of anticoagulant medication'* using the redesigned chart (second iteration) that was rolled out at the beginning of 2020. The task decomposition diagram is depicted in Fig. 2, and depicts the six necessary sub-goals needed to perform this task. The components of the sub-goals surrounded by a blue box in Fig. 2

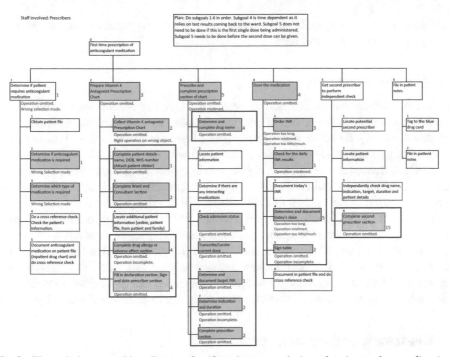

Fig. 2. The task decomposition diagram for *'first-time prescription of anticoagulant medication'* with the sub-goals associated with chart use (blue), safety elements (green) and the error types, and number of occurrences identified in the incident report data (red).

indicate subtasks that are associated directly with the chart. These are components of this task that are visible retrospectively as the chart requires input for these components.

Using the decomposition diagram and the data from the group interview held with a lead pharmacist and consultant haematologist as well as the incident reports, the error probability of the subtask was assessed using the SHERPA method. Of the 65 incident reports analysed, 42 reports contained problematic elements that could be connected with the sub-goals of the task decomposition diagram in Fig. 2. The incident reports revealed some additional potential error states for the sub-goals not initially identified in the SHERPA conducted with experts. Figure 2 also depicts the various sub-goals associated with safety and highlighted in the reported incidents. The sub-goals marked in green represent checking activities which are a form of safety barrier associated with this task, whereas the sub-goals marked in red are aspects that were identified as problematic in the incidents reported. Beneath and next to these sub-goals are the error types and number of occurrences identified in the incident report data. It is important to note that errors pertaining to sub-goals featured further upstream of the task (i.e. towards the left side of the diagram), may potentially result in the later sub-goals being omitted and possibly the error state not being pickup later in this task by safety-related sub-goals. The SHERPA method assisted in identifying which sub-goals have a high error probability and a high criticality level with regards to patient safety. By identifying these, this highlights the sub-goals that may need to be addressed to enhance patient safety. The next step would be to discuss these sub-goals, with frontline staff and expert groups to explore potential solutions to these safety problems.

3.3   Heuristic Evaluation

It has been shown that charts used in healthcare designed from a human factors perspective can result in fewer errors and may be adopted and used more quickly than familiar charts [6]. Based on studies that applied heuristic analyses and a human factors perspective to chart design and evaluation, specifically for the design of an observation chart [4] and insulin chart [5], some key design characteristics were compiled that would be relevant to any medical chart. The inpatient anticoagulant medication chart (second iteration) was evaluated against this compiled list of key design characteristics. The key design characteristics identified in this evaluation that may need to be considered in the next iteration of the redesigned chart included ensuring there is not a mixture of vertically oriented and horizontally oriented data points or text, that there is sufficient handwriting space, that the comprehensibility is assessed for basic functionality, that perceptually separate elements are adequately separated and that information does not need to be transcribed or compared over two pages, nor over different areas of one page.

4   Discussion and Recommendations

These results highlighted some of the breadth and depth human factors and a systems approach can offer to understanding the context in which medical charts are used. The wider context wherein these charts are used has important implications, not only for when things go wrong, but also for understanding the safety functions of these tools. By understanding these tools within the system in which they are used, key considerations can be identified that may assist in enhancing the design process of these tools. By first adopting a wider system's view, additional key system factors were identified that would influence the use of this chart and safety associated with this chart. The system's analysis highlighted that the type of things that go wrong span the whole patient-task pathway and not just the stages where documentation on the chart occurs. Furthermore, this identified elements of the patient-task pathway the redesigned chart may affect, and which other areas associated with safety that may need to be addressed using other means. Based on the results, recommendations for the next design iteration were compiled and have been summarised in Table 1.

The results highlighted that numerous other system components contribute to error-producing conditions and problems associated with this chart. By only addressing concerns at a task-level, the error-producing conditions may still be present. The task analysis provided an understanding of where within the task, safety activities are located and which sub-goals were associated with the incident reports. The systems analysis also provided additional information on why errors at these sub-goal levels may occur. The main areas of the chart that were not always completed (based on the incident report data and task analysis results) included the second signature and prescriber section as well as the target and duration section. The feature of a second signature was implemented in the interim design of the chart as a safety function. However, the problem associated

Table 1. The recommendations based on specific findings from the human factors and systems analysis for the inpatient anticoagulant medication chart.

Summary of findings	Recommendations
1. Numerous system components contribute to error-producing conditions and problems associated at a task level	• Reported incidents provide a potential untapped source of organisational learning as they provide information on system components that can contribute to error-producing conditions. By identifying aspects that may need to be addressed at a management or organisation level the context may be altered and thereby reduce error-producing conditions
2. The results from the task analysis and analysis of the incident reports highlighted areas of the chart that were not always fully completed	• It is recommended to explore these elements of the chart and the associated tasks in more detail using a systems approach to understand the changes and support staff may need to improve safety for the patient and ease of use for staff
3. The SHERPA identified which sub-goals have a high error probability and a high criticality level with regards to patient safety	• It is recommended that these sub-goals are discussed with frontline staff and expert groups to explore potential solutions to these safety problems • It is also recommended that alternative safety barriers be reviewed and identified for tasks associated with this chart

with a missing second signature, from a system's perspective, is more complex than at first glance as this is related to numerous organisation of work elements such as workload and staffing levels. This example highlights the need for a systems approach when adding elements in the redesign process, especially if they are to serve a safety function. Furthermore, by considering the interaction of the chart with the other work system components, the redesigned chart may be better implemented into the existing system and require less modification following implementation. The need for understanding the system in which the medical chart is to be used is further highlighted with the recent changes that have occurred in healthcare as a result of the COVID-19 pandemic. When redesigning medical charts there needs to be consideration of potential future use of this chart (i.e. the changes in procedure due to the COVID-19 pandemic) to ensure it can be used effectively and safely under new working conditions (e.g. effect of PPE while using the chart).

5 Conclusion

Based on the results, recommendations relating to specific findings were generated in addition to more general recommendations for the redesign of the inpatient anticoagulant medication chart. These included suggestions regarding general design of the chart based on the compiled literature on chart heuristics, identification of specific subtask components that need further exploration with staff to identify potential solutions and safety improvements based on the HTA and SHERPA, and consideration of additional system elements to enhance the safety and efficiency of this task and chart, based on the systems analysis conducted. Key strengths of this study included the utilisation of both a human factors perspective and systems approach. A systems approach is essential to improve safety, as tools such as medication charts need to be understood in the context within which they function [7]. Limitations of this study include those associated with qualitative research and limited involvement of the user's perspective. Although extensive user involvement had been planned, due to the outbreak of the Covid-19 pandemic, this was no longer possible.

References

1. Holden, R.J., et al.: SEIPS 2.0: a human factors framework for studying and improving the work of healthcare professionals and patients. Ergonomics **56**(11), 1669–1686 (2013)
2. Shepherd, A.: Hierarchical Task Analysis. Taylor & Francis, London (2001)
3. Embrey, D.: SHERPA: a systematic human error reduction and prediction approach. In: Contemporary Ergonomics 1984–2008 Selection Papier. an Overv. Ergonomics Society Annual Conference, pp. 113–119 (2009)
4. Preece, M., Hill, A., Horswill, M.S., Karamatic, R., Hewett, D., Watson, M.O.: Applying heuristic evaluation to observation chart design to improve the detection of patient deterioration. Appl. Ergon. **44**(4), 544–556 (2013)
5. Christofidis, M.J., Horswill, M.S., Hill, A., McKimmie, B.M., Visser, T., Watson, M. O.: Task Analysis and Heuristic Analysis of Insulin Charts: Final report prepared for the Australian Commission on Safety and Quality in Health Care: 2 February 2012," Sydney, (2012)
6. Christofidis, M.J., Hill, A., Horswill, M.S., Watson, M.O.: A human factors approach to observation chart design can trump health professionals' prior chart experience. Resuscitation **84**(5), 657–665 (2013)
7. Leveson, N.G., Samost, A., Dekker, S., Finkelstein, S., Raman, J.: A systems approach to analyzing and preventing hospital adverse events. J. Patient Saf. **1**, 162–167 (2016)

The Design of Work in Atypical Schedules: A Social Innovation Approach in Hospitals

Marlène Cheyrouze[1]([⊠]), Béatrice Barthe[2], and Jérôme Sartori[3]

[1] University of Toulouse Jean Jaurès, CLLE, UMR 5263 CNRS, 5 allée Antonio Machado, 31058 Toulouse Cedex 9, Toulouse, France
[2] University of Toulouse Jean Jaurès, PSDT, 5 allée Antonio Machado, 31058 Toulouse Cedex 9, Toulouse, France
beatrice.barthe@univ-tlse2.fr
[3] Pasteur Clinic, 45 Avenue de Lombez, BP 27617, 31076 Toulouse Cedex 3, Toulouse, France
jsartori@clinique-pasteur.com

Abstract. The transformation of schedules can be innovative if the actors concerned participate in it and if their professional logics are different. In activity ergonomics, it takes into account the content of the work and is discussed by all the actors to choose the best compromise. The objectives of this communication are to show that schedules and work content are interdependent, that the transformation of schedules is an opportunity to re-establish an inter professional discussion on current and future work, and that this discussion facilitates the appropriation of solutions. The methodology is deployed in a pneumology unit for three years. An inventory of the initial work situation is first constructed from observations and interviews. The design solutions are then projected in groups with work simulation. The three groups, which bring together the different professional logics of the service, are recorded and analyzed on Actograph®. The effects of the groups are studied during the testing of the new schedules, based on observations, interviews and internal data. The results first show that the increase in nurses' day-night overlap (schedules) is dependent on improved patient flow and coordination with physicians (work content). Inter professional discussions, equipped by the simulation, made it possible to project future working conditions, but above all to talk about current working conditions. They also enabled the actors to take ownership of the verbalized conditions for success: most of these conditions became a reality in the service during the test of the new schedules.

Keywords: Atypical schedules · Hospitals · Innovation · Temporalities

1 Introduction

This paper is the result of an action-research project on hospital work with atypical schedules. It is conducted in a private clinic that is seeking to design innovative schedules to reduce absenteeism among its healthcare staff.

1.1   Absenteeism of Healthcare Staff: The Impact of Working Conditions

Absenteeism is one of the most common causes of staff shortage in health facilities [1]. Several studies show that it is impacted by working conditions [2–4]. In France, the work of healthcare staff is subject to significant time pressure, frequently leading to overtime [5]. Part of this time pressure is linked to the acceleration of the flow of patients whose length of hospitalization is decreasing. Moreover, a recent study reveals that 70% of hospital staff and 60% of physicians feel that professional exchanges are insufficient [6]. Other studies show that exchanges on work conditions and organization are rare [7, 8] When faced with absenteeism among healthcare staff, reducing time pressure and increasing professional exchanges are as relevant as designing innovative schedules.

1.2   Schedule Design: Conditions for Innovation and Ergonomics

From a sociological point of view, innovation is a process of constructing meaning and appropriation of change, which produces the mobilization or disengagement of actors [9]. In Quebec, the organization of working time is recognized as a social innovation for its positive effects on living conditions [10]. However, social innovation is revealed both in the solutions chosen and in the way that they are constructed. Two conditions are necessary. First, the actors concerned must participate in order to take ownership of the solutions and give them meaning. Secondly, the actors' logics must be different, in order to create new forms of cooperation between them, and to enable them to build a common representation of problems and possible solutions [11–13]. From the point of view of the ergonomics of the activity, the design of schedules is inseparable from a reflection on the content of the work concerned [14, 15]. The proposed solutions must also be discussed with all the actors of the work situation to choose the best compromise [16]. The organization of working time is a delicate process because temporalities of schedules are interdependent with temporalities of work (rate, deadlines, flows, demands, etc.) and of workers (biological, social and family). The slightest change can disrupt their balance and produce deleterious effects. In addition, there are many temporalities in hospital work: there are those of the caregiver, the team, the patients, other professionals (managers, physicians, etc.) and other services [17]. Several professional logics must be coordinated and those of the physicians are dominant [18]. The design of new schedules can therefore be innovative if it is associated with an inter-professional discussion of work content.

1.3   Simulation as a Tool for Inter-professional Discussion

In activity ergonomics, work simulation has proven its worth in design projects. It invites participants to "play" their own work within the framework of design solutions, to help them project future working conditions [19]. The profiles of the participants are deliberately diversified in order to make them discover different points of view on the work situation [20]. Their debate gives rise to a new and shared representation of the work situation [21]. It gives meaning to the design solutions and facilitates their appropriation by the actors [22, 23]. The simulation method can therefore provide a tool for inter-professional discussion on the content of work and for the projection of new schedules.

2   Objectives

We want to show that the issues related to schedules and work content are interdependent, and that the proper design of schedules cannot be achieved without improving work content. We also want to show that the design of new schedules is an opportunity to rally the actors and their different professional logics in a discussion on the content of work. This inter-professional discussion, aided by simulation, not only allows the planning of future working conditions, but also underscores current working conditions. Finally, we wish to show that this inter-professional discussion can facilitate the appropriation of the proposed solutions.

3   Methodology

3.1   Field and Population

The action-research took place in a pulmonology unit. The nursing staff worked in 2 × 12 shifts. It was composed of six nurses, six nursing assistants and two hospital cleaners. The supervisory staff was composed of one day manager and two night managers. The medical staff was composed of eleven physicians divided into three teams. Each team employed several secretaries.

3.2   Year 1: Building an Inventory of the Initial Work Situation

Data Collection. The work of the caregivers, physicians, day manager and administrators was observed over 2 nights and 13 days. The duration of nurses' oral transmissions was recorded in an observation grid over 21 day-night overlaps. Patient discharge schedules were logged in a 6-day observation grid. Caregivers' and physicians' representation of the work situation was recorded in 17 interviews.

Data Processing. Data from observations and interviews were transcribed into a Word document and sorted by issue. The data from the observation grids were transferred and analyzed in an Excel table.

3.3   Year 2: Design and Project Design Solutions

Data Collection. The different professional logics of the service have been gathered in three groups, using different simulation models (Fig. 1). Five physicians, seven caregivers and one manager participated in Group A (13 participants). One physician, two caregivers, a manager and a secretary participated in group B (5 participants). Four physicians, two caregivers, two managers and three secretaries participated in Group C (11 participants). The groups were recorded with a Dictaphone.

Fig. 1. Photographs of the different simulation models (Groups A-B-C)

Data Processing. After several listening of the recordings, an analysis protocol was constructed using Actograph® software [24]. In each recording, the distribution of speaking time by profession was recorded continuously according to 5 possible items: caregiver (nurse, care assistant or hospital cleaner); manager (day or night); physician; secretary; others (researcher, hubbub, silence). The distribution of speaking time by purpose was continuously recorded according to 4 possible items: design solutions; current work situation; simulation model; others (informal discussion). Two other items were noted punctually when the participants were verbalizing: (a) the constraints of their work and (b) the conditions for the success of a design solution. The data relating to the distribution of speaking time were reported and analyzed in an Excel table. The data relative to the constraints and the conditions of success were transcribed in a Word document.

3.4 Year 3: Testing Schedules and Evaluating Group Effects

Data Collection. New schedules were tested for three months. During this period, the organization of 41 patient discharges was recorded in an observation grid. We retrieved the discharge schedule of all patients registered at the clinic. This allowed us to make a comparison between the test period and the same period of the previous year. Individual caregivers' views on the new work situation and on the effects of inter-professional groups were recorded in 12 interviews.

Data Processing. The data collected on the organization of the 41 patient discharges were reported in an Excel table and analyzed by task (e.g. dictate the prescription; order the ambulance). The discharge schedule of all patients registered during the test period (167) and during the same period of the previous year (177) were plotted in an Excel graph and compared by time slot. The data collected in the interviews were transcribed into a Word document and processed by theme (changes in work content, effects of inter-professional groups).

4 Results

4.1 The Inventory: Issues Identified in the Content of the Work

The inventory of the initial work situation (year 1) revealed a first problem in the schedules: the official duration of the day-night overlap between nurses (15 min) was inadequate for the actual duration of their oral transmissions. They lasted on average 45 min in the morning and 30 min in the evening. This added extra work time in the morning and in the evening. Extending the day-night overlap to 30 min was a necessary design solution, which the nurses unanimously validated. To achieve this, a day nurse's shift end had to be advanced by 15 min. This schedule change was difficult because of two issues identified in the work content. The first was related to the flow of patients: incoming patients - who arrived in the service from 2 p.m. onwards - were installed late in the beds. These beds were themselves released late by outgoing patients. Of the 11 patient discharges recorded in the observation grid, only one was recorded before 2:00 p.m. and seven were recorded between 2:00 p.m. and 3:00 p.m. This overlap of incoming and outgoing patients generated significant time pressure. The second problem was related to the coordination of physicians: the times at which they identified outgoing patients and formulated new prescriptions varied from day to day and from physician to physician. Without a joint improvement of these two issues, the new schedules risked worsening nurses' extra work time.

4.2 Simulation: A Framework for Discussing Future and Current Work

Distribution of Speaking Time by Profession and by Purpose. In the three inter-professional groups analyzed on Actograph® (Table 1), at least one-third of speaking time was held by physicians (Phy), regardless of their number. It was in group B that there was only one physician and that the caregivers (Car) expressed themselves the most. In all three groups, the participants spoke as much or more about the current work situation (Current) as they did about design solutions (Solut).

Table 1. Results of the analysis of the three inter-trade groups on issuers and objects of verbalization (without the "other" items)

Group	Participants				Speaking time (profession)				Speaking time (purpose)		
	Phy	Car	Man	Sec	Phy	Car	Man	Sec	Solut	Current	Mod
A	5	7	1	0	39%	13%	8%	0%	41%	47%	2%
B	1	2	1	1	34%	23%	6%	6%	24%	64%	2%
C	4	2	2	3	32%	13%	11%	3%	37%	46%	7%

Verbalization of Constraints. In the three groups, several constraints slowing down the anticipation of discharges and delaying the release of beds were verbalized. By the physicians: the late validation of the test results prevents confirmation of all discharges in the early morning; the digital incompatibility between the physician's dictaphones and the terminals in the infirmaries prevents the instantaneous transfer of dictated prescriptions to the secretaries. By the secretaries: the late transfer of dictated prescriptions to the secretaries prevents them from being written and transmitted to the nurses before the patient's departure time. By nurses: Late transfer of written prescriptions delays the patient's departure.

Verbalization of the Conditions for Success. In order to bring forward the installation of the incoming patients and the day nurse's shift (15 min earlier), several conditions for success were verbalised: (1) incoming patients must be summoned at 3 p.m. (not at 2 p.m.); (2) their beds must be available at 3 p.m.; (3) the nurse must inform the physician in advance of their arrival. In order to make outgoing patients leave earlier and to guarantee the availability of beds at the arrival of incoming patients, other conditions for success have been verbalized: (4) discharges must be identified the day before; (5) prescriptions must be dictated by physicians the day before; (6) physicians' dictaphones must be reconnected to the infirmary terminals; (7) prescriptions must be written earlier by secretaries; (8) the last biological tests should be prescribed on the day of discharge at 6 a.m.; (9) the ambulance should be ordered by the nurses the day before; (10) discharged patients should be prioritized by the doctors at the morning visit.

4.3 The Effects of New Schedules and Inter-professional Groups

Positive but Still Fragile Schedules. According to the testimony of the six nurses, the extension of the day-night overlap to 30 min allowed them to recognize the extra work time they invested in their oral transmissions. In the morning, the nurses were less overwhelmed with the first tasks of the day and the night nurses went home earlier. However, day nurses were not always able to leave 15 min earlier in the evening, due to the late arrival of some patients or late prescriptions from some doctors.

A Commitment of the Actors in the Transformation of the Content of the Work. Concerning the arrival schedule of incoming patients, the testimony of four daycare workers revealed that they were more often summoned at 3 p.m. (rather than 2 p.m.) (success condition 1). After their participation in Group A, the day nurses called the physicians to notify them of the arrival of incoming patients (success condition 3). In terms of discharge schedules, a comparison between the two years shows that discharged patients left earlier in the afternoon: discharges between 1p.m and 2 p.m. increased by 12% and discharges between 2 and 3 p.m. decreased by 7%. According to the testimony of eight caregivers, the outings were better anticipated at several levels. Firstly, doctors identified more outings the day before (success factor 4). Of the 41 outings identified in the observation grid, only 4 were identified for the same day. This allowed the nurses to order ambulances earlier (success condition 9). Secondly, the doctors dictated more prescriptions the day before (success condition 5), which allowed the secretaries to write them earlier (success condition 7). Thirdly, physicians prescribed more of the last biological tests at 6 a.m. (success condition 8), allowing them to check results earlier to confirm patient discharge.

Caregivers' Testimonials on Inter-Professional Groups. Group A made it possible to open "a dialogue with the doctors", and to "become aware of their difficulties", even if the physicians remained focused on their own difficulties. It was from group A that nurses encouraged the physicians to anticipate the discharge and that the physicians began to prescribe the last tests for the day of discharge at 6 am. Group B provided an opportunity to meet with the secretary, to identify solutions for moving the discharge forward, and to "really talk". Group C revealed the divergence of views held by the physicians on their work situation. Discussing the organization of work with the physicians was more interesting than changing schedules.

5 Discussion and Conclusion

Our results confirm that the temporal issues of a work situation - related to work schedules and work content - are interdependent. Indeed, the extension of the day-night overlap to 30 min could not have been tested without a joint improvement in patient flow and coordination with the physicians. Based on the difficulties encountered by the day nurses in completing their shift 15 min early, indicates the need for further inter-professional discussions on the content of the work [14, 15]. The importance of the speaking time held by the physicians confirms that their logic remains dominant and that their participation is indispensable to transform the content of the work [18]. Using work simulation as a tool, inter-professional discussions made it possible to identify the conditions that would allow the reusability of the new schedules. The example of discharge prescriptions - dictated by doctors, written by secretaries and then retrieved by nurses - shows the necessary coordination between all hospital work temporalities [17]. The participants used these groups to discuss current working conditions, giving visibility to each other's constraints. Based on the amount of speaking time devoted to the current work situation, opportunities to discuss current work with all professional logics are rare [7, 8]. By bringing together a diversity of professional logics, inter-professional discussions have created an uncommon cooperation between the actors from the care service. They have thus built up a shared representation of current and future work [21]. The inter-professional discussions also enabled the actors to give meaning to the conditions of success that they had verbalized and to appropriate them: most of verbalized conditions became a reality in the service during the test of the new schedules [9, 22, 23]. We confirm the interest of involving a diversity of actors from the care units, in the design of working hours, which inevitably links up with other work temporalities. Faced with the COVID-19 pandemic, which is calling into question all hospital organizations, our approach is a key topic of today's preoccupations, and can be fully considered as a social innovation [11–13].

References

1. Alreshidi, N.M., Alaseeri, R.M., Garcia, M.: Factors influencing absenteeism among nursing staff in the primary health care centers in hail: a preliminary study for enhancing staff commitment. Health Sci. J. **13**(4), 7 (2019)
2. Estryn-Béhar, M.: Santé et satisfaction des soignants au travail en France et en Europe. Presses de l'EHEPS, Rennes (2008)
3. Rajbhandary, S., Basu, K.: Working conditions of nurses and absenteeism: is there a relationship? an empirical analysis using national survey of the work and health of nurses. Health Policy **97**(2–3), 152–159 (2010)
4. Pollak, C., Ricroch, L.: Les disparités d'absentéisme à l'hôpital sont-elles associées à des différences de conditions de travail ? Revue française d'économie. **31**(4), 181–220 (2016)

5. Barlet, M., Marbot, C.: Portrait des professionnels de santé. DREES (2016)
6. Le carnet de santé des Français et des personnels hospitaliers. Un baromètre Odoxa pour la Mutuelle Nationale des Hospitaliers (MNH). Odoxa (2018). https://www.odoxa.fr/sondage/carnet-de-sante-francais-personnels-hospitaliers-2/
7. Acker, F.: Les infirmières en crise ? Mouvements **2**(2), 60–66 (2004)
8. Micheau, J., Molière, E.: Étude qualitative sur le thème de l'emploi du temps des infirmières et infirmiers du secteur hospitalier. DARES, Report No.: 132. (2014)
9. Alter, N.: L'innovation ordinaire. PUF, Paris (2000)
10. Klein, J.-L., Harrisson, D.: L'innovation sociale. Emergence et effets sur la transformation des sociétés. Québec: Presses de l'Université du Québec (2007)
11. Cloutier, J.: CRISES. Qu'est-ce que l'innovation sociale? CRISES, Montréal (2003)
12. Harrisson, D., Vézina, M.: L'innovation sociale : Une introduction. Ann. Public Coop. Econ. **77**(2), 129–138 (2006)
13. Lapointe, P.A., Bellemare, G., Briand, L., D'Amours, M., Grant, M., Laplante, N., et al.: Axe 1 - Travail et emploi. In: L'innovation sociale : émergence et effets sur la transformation des sociétés. Québec: Presses de l'Université du Québec, pp. 345-360 (2007)
14. Corlett, E.N., Quéinnec, Y., Paoli, P.: Adapting shiftwork arrangements. Dublin: European Foundation for the improvement of living and working conditions (1988)
15. Barthe, B., Gadbois, C., Prunier-Poulmaire, S., Quéinnec, Y. : Travailler en horaires atypiques. In: Ergonomie, PUF, Paris, pp. 129–144 (2004)
16. Quéinnec, Y., Teiger, C., de Terssac, G.: Repères pour négocier le travail posté. Octares Editions, Toulouse (2008)
17. Gonon, O., Barthe, B., Gindro, G.: Organisation du travail à l'hôpital : comprendre l'articulation des temporalités pour agir sur la transformation des situations de travail. In: Ergonomie et Organisation du Travail, Toulouse, pp. 183–190 (2009)
18. Raveyre, M., Ughetto, P.: Le travail, la part oubliée des restructurations hospitalières. Revue française des affaires sociales. **3**, 95–119 (2003)
19. Barcellini, F., Van Belleghem, L., Daniellou, F.: Les projets de conception comme opportunité de développement des activités. In: Ergonomie constructive. PUF, Paris, pp. 191–206 (2013)
20. Van Belleghem, L.: La simulation de l'activité en conception ergonomique : acquis et perspectives. Activités. **15**(1), 22 (2018)
21. Daniellou, F.: Des fonctions de la simulation des situations de travail en ergonomie. Activités. **4**(2), 77–83 (2007)
22. Van Belleghem, L., De Gasparo, S., Gaillard, I.: Le développement de la dimension psychosociale au travail. In: Ergonomie constructive. PUF, Paris, pp. 47–60 (2013)
23. Bobillier Chaumon, M-É., Rouat, S., Laneyrie, E., Cuvillier, B.: De l'activité DE simulation à l'activité EN simulation : simuler pour stimuler. Activités. **15**(1), 24 (2018)
24. Boccara, V., Delgoulet, C., Zara-Meylan, V., Gaillard, I., Barthe, B., Meylan, S.: The role and positioning place and role of observation in ergonomics approaches: a research and design project. In: Creativity in practice. Springer, Florence, pp. 1821–1828 (2019)

Remote Usability Testing of a Pediatric Trauma Dashboard

Sarah M. Coppola[1,2](✉) and Ayse P. Gurses[1]

[1] Johns Hopkins School of Medicine, Armstrong Institute for Patient Safety, Baltimore, USA
scoppola@jhu.edu
[2] University of Washington, Seattle, USA

Abstract. Health information technologies (HIT) can support care and coordination of pediatric trauma patients. This study adapted to a remote usability study protocol to test a HIT prototype that was designed using a participatory design process. The participants were mostly successful interacting with the prototype and were able to locate and understand necessary information. Several design and interaction issues were identified. The tests provided valuable feedback about the prototype's design that will inform the final prototype for testing in a team-centric in situ setting when it is safe to do so.

Keywords: Pediatric trauma · Health information technology · Usability testing · Participatory design

1 Introduction

Trauma is the leading cause of death for children in the US, and pediatric trauma care requires considerable communication and collaboration among multiple clinical teams [1–4]. A typical pediatric trauma patient travels through multiple clinical units and is cared for by a diverse multi-disciplinary team. Within the high stress, high stakes environment of the pediatric trauma bay (ED), the ability to communicate information in a timely and clear manner is of utmost importance to providing optimal care. This stream of communication containing patient information is not centered within the trauma bay but extends to the pediatric intensive care unit (ICU) providing ICU nurses advanced notice of the incoming patient. Health information technologies (HIT) can support coordination of care across different clinical teams and hospital locations. HIT, if designed for the end user, has the potential of easing the provider's burden to remember and transfer information within high stress environments. By supporting the users, HIT can move a system toward high patient safety by reducing communication error and providing accurate information efficiently.

Ideally, team-centric, computer-supported cooperative work tools should be tested in their use context and in a team environment. The Covid-19 pandemic has forced almost every aspect of life to be remote and has made testing HIT in situ unfeasible. While remote usability testing has become more common with improving technical capabilities, it is less common for a team-centric tool in a healthcare setting.

N. L. Black et al. (Eds.): IEA 2021, LNNS 222, pp. 267–273, 2021.
https://doi.org/10.1007/978-3-030-74611-7_37

We adapted our formative usability testing protocol from a team-centric in situ simulation to individual vignette usability tests over video conferencing. We used these to test specific design aspects and to elicit valuable feedback about a HIT prototype.

2 Methods

2.1 Setting and Sample

This formative usability study was part of a larger project aimed at understanding care and coordination of pediatric trauma patients [4–6]. We used a participatory design approach [7, 8] with key stakeholders to design a high fidelity prototype (Fig. 1) of the Trauma Dashboard HIT in InVision (New York, USA). It features a timeline of major events, vitals, and medications. The primary and secondary surveys are also displayed, and a mannequin displays height, weight, GCS, and the "problem list". Users can hover over icons on the screen to display more information. The dashboard will be displayed on a large screen in the trauma bay and will have desktop and mobile versions for distributed care team members. This study took place remotely with 11 healthcare workers who are involved in pediatric trauma care at an academic pediatric hospital in the Midatlantic USA. Three ED attendings, two ED fellows, three PICU attendings, one PICU fellow, one surgery attending, and one surgery nurse practitioner participated in the usability study. Nine healthcare workers participated in the questionnaire.

2.2 Study Procedure

We used a "Wizard of Oz" strategy [8, 9] and read a vignette [10] of a simulated pediatric trauma case with each participant over a video conferencing call. The research team shared their screen with the prototype and gave remote control to the participant who was able to control the screen. Because of the space limitations of the computer screen, participants had to scroll to see the entire dashboard. The researcher controlled the information that appeared on the screen as the case progressed. Participants were asked "What information do you need to know, and can you find that on the screen?" They were also asked for informal feedback after the simulation and answered an online questionnaire with a modified System Usability Scale (SUS) [11, 12]. Each video was recorded and audio transcribed. The study protocol was approved by the local institutional review board.

2.3 Analysis

A member of the research team categorized the transcripts into user needs, successes, and failures for each step in the vignette in a spreadsheet [13]. They also noted usability challenges mentioned by participants. Average values were calculated for the questionnaire results.

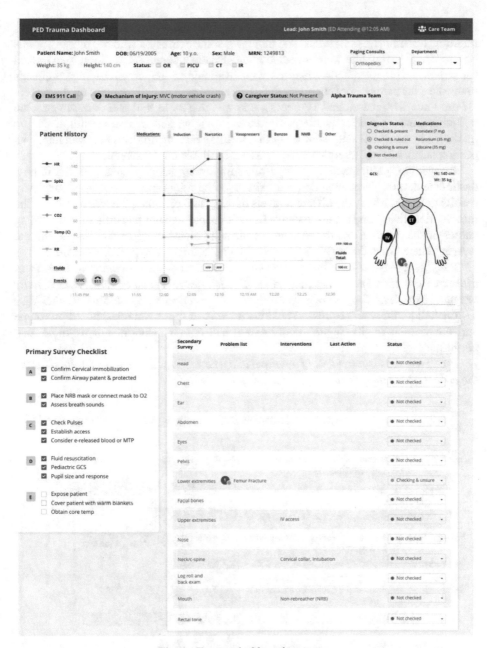

Fig. 1. Trauma dashboard prototype

3   Results

The usability study elucidated important design feedback. Five participants identified the Glasgow Coma Score (GCS) as a primary need, and all eleven participants mentioned having issues finding and deciphering it at some point during the study. Eight participants mentioned needing patient vitals, and there was some confusion whether missing points on the interface timeline were a device issue or patient signal. In addition, two looked for pulses and breath sounds which were not available on the screen. Eight participants mentioned the primary or secondary and were successful in finding them on the screen. Of the three who mentioned IV access, one was unable to find it on the screen. One participant mentioned medications, fluids, and imaging and was successful at finding medications and fluids and identifying that imaging information was not available. One participant mentioned allergies which was not available on the screen.

In addition, participants described other important design issues with the trauma dashboard design. These included confusion over the colors and symbols used to display medications and vitals, the different levels of diagnosis certainty, the temporality of the interventions listed, and resource status. In addition, participants had difficulty discerning values on the timeline due to the shared scale and pointed out potential issues with the "hover" interactions during an active trauma. For example, one participant said:

P2: *"I think it's a little hard for something like temperature when the scale is so different that-- like, I might not pick up the blood pressure and heart rate trends visually are most important. So, you're going to lose some discriminating ability with that"*.

Overall participants expressed positive reviews of the trauma dashboard prototype and the ways it might support coordination and communication. For example, one participant said:

P6: *"I like the visualization of a patient and where things are. So, the IV, the ET tube, the collar, where the injuries are, I think that is helpful."*

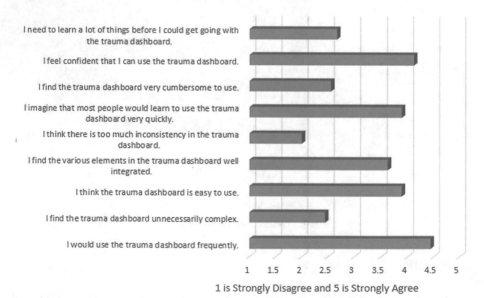

Fig. 2. Adapted SUS average scores

The survey responses (Fig. 2) to the adapted system usability scale were also positive. Participants agreed with the statements "I find the trauma dashboard easy to use" (66.7%), "I imagine that most people would learn to use the trauma dashboard very quickly (66.7%), and "I feel confident that I can use the trauma dashboard" (75%). Six participants (66.7%) rated that they were satisfied with the overall design.

4 Discussion

The Covid-19 pandemic has required shifting almost everything to be virtual. Social distancing posed significant challenges to our usability testing plan, and we were unable to test the dashboard in situ in a team environment as intended. However, remote testing over video conferencing did allow testing key design points, information architecture, and overall learnability of the system. In particular, remote testing identified missing information and issues related to color and icon choices.

Participants successfully navigated the prototype's interface and were able to understand and use the information displayed. In particular, the graphical displays of the timeline and the mannequin allowed participants to quickly learn information about the case. The redundant displays of information such as the medications and potential problems appears to have contributed to the successful location of these important pieces of information. Over time healthcare workers could likely learn the various elements of the dashboard and be successful in quickly identifying and utilizing the displayed information.

Other aspects of the prototype were less successful. The nature of pediatric trauma and the shared display make certain interactions such as hover over or clicking impractical. Participants were unclear what the categories to display diagnostic uncertainty (checked & present, checked & ruled out, checking & unsure, not checked) meant. The next design should have simpler language and fewer categories. The temporality of the interventions was also confusing, so the next design should have timestamps to be a more reliable narrator of the case's history.

Surprisingly, several design aspects that were identified as must haves from the user research such as patient demographics, family/caregiver status, and members of the care team were not mentioned or utilized. It is possible that the reduced complexity of the simulated case for the remote setting reduced the need for this information. These currently take up a lot of prominent space on the dashboard, so future testing is necessary to determine whether these can be reduced.

Our usability study was limited by the remote environment. The studies were done individually instead of in a team, and the vignette asked participants to imagine information that they would normally have visually in a trauma bay. We were further limited by the smaller screen which required participants to scroll up and down. One benefit of the scroll was that we were able observe that participants did not view the demographic information at the top. This will inform choices about what gets prime location on the next design. We were also limited in the number and diversity of available usability testers, so it is possible that these findings do not reflect all potential users. Future in-situ testing must include more team members from nursing and psychosocial staff.

5   Conclusions

We used a mixed methods participatory design process to design a pediatric trauma dashboard to facilitate communication and coordination of care for pediatric trauma patients. This study showed it is possible to do remote formative usability testing of a health information technology. Participants successfully found most of the clinical information they needed on the dashboard and generally reported satisfaction with the prototype.

Acknowledgments. This research was supported by the Agency for Healthcare Research and Quality R01 HS023837. We thank Amy Hushen and Jasmine McNeil in the Technology Innovation Center for their assistance with the design work. We especially appreciate our healthcare worker participants for participating in this study and for all they have done on the frontlines of fighting this pandemic over the last year.

References

1. Hose, B.-Z., Carayon, P., Hoonakker, P., Wooldridge, A., Brazelton, T., Dean, S., Eithun, B., Kelly, M., Kohler, J., Ross, J., Rusy, D., Gurses, A.: Challenges of disposition decision making for pediatric trauma patients in the emergency department. In: Bagnara, S., Tartaglia, R., Albolino, S., Alexander, T., Fujita, Y. (eds.) Proceedings of the 20th Congress of the International Ergonomics Association (IEA 2018): Volume I: Healthcare Ergonomics, pp. 339–345. Springer, Cham (2019)
2. Wooldridge, A.R., Carayon, P., Hoonakker, P., Hose, B.-Z., Ross, J., Kohler, J.E., et al.: Complexity of the pediatric trauma care process: implications for multi-level awareness. Cogn. Technol. Work **21**(3), 397–416 (2019)
3. Wooldridge, A.R., Carayon, P., Hoonakker, P., Hose, B.-Z., Eithun, B., Brazelton Iii, T., et al.: Work system barriers and facilitators in inpatient care transitions of pediatric trauma patients. Appl. Ergon. **85**, 103059 (2020)
4. Durojaiye, A.B., McGeorge, N.M., Puett, L.L., Stewart, D., Fackler, J.C., Hoonakker, P.L.T., et al.: Mapping the flow of pediatric trauma patients using process mining. Appl. Clin. Inf. **9**(03), 654–666 (2018)
5. Coppola, S., Webster, K., Gurses, A.: Team trust and performance in pediatric trauma. In: Proceedings of the International Symposium of Human Factors and Ergonomics in Healthcare, vol. 9 no. 1 pp. 93–97 (2020)
6. Durojaiye, A.B., McGeorge, N., Kristen, W., Oruc, C., Fackler, J.C., Gurses, A.P.: Characterizing the utilization of the problem list for pediatric trauma care. AMIA Annu. Symp. Proc. **2018**, 404–412 (2018)
7. Muller, M., Kuhn, S.: Participatory design. Commun. ACM. **36**(6), 24–28 (1993)
8. Hanington, B.M., Martin, B.: Universal methods of design: 100 ways to research complex problems, develop innovative ideas, and design effective solutions. In: Hanington, B.M., (ed.) Rockport Publishers, Beverly, MA (2012)
9. Kelley, J.: An iterative design methodology for user-friendly natural language office information applications. ACM Trans. Inf. Syst. **2**(1), 26–41 (1984)
10. Hughes, R., Huby, M.: The application of vignettes in social and nursing research. J. Adv. Nurs. **37**(4), 382–386 (2002)

11. Albert, B., Tullis, T.: Measuring the User Experience: Collecting, Analyzing, and Presenting Usability Metrics. 2nd ed. In: Albert B, (ed.) Morgan Kauffmann/Elsevier, Waltham, MA (2013)
12. Jordan, P.W., Thomas, B., McClelland, I.L., Weerdmeester, B.: Usability Evaluation in Industry. Taylor & Francis Group, Boca Raton (1996)
13. Chisnell, D., Rubin, J.: Handbook of Usability Testing: How to Plan, Design, and Conduct Effective Tests. 2nd ed. In: Chisnell, D. (ed.) Wiley Publication, Indianapolis, IN (2008)

IEA 2021 Patient Safety Design Competition

Chelsea DeGuzman[1], Joelle Girgis[1], Sadeem Qureshi[2], Michael Greig[2],
Amar Latchman[2], Audrey Benmergui[1], John Naismith[2], Maeesha Biswas[1],
Joseph Campos[2], Alyssa Iglar[1], Marcelo Degrazia[2], Karen Zhao[1], Jonas Shultz[3],
Peter Lachman[4], Sandi Kossey[5], Christine Quinn[6], Catherine Gaulton[7],
Philip DeSouza[7], Stefano Gelmi[7], Anthony Soung Yee[7], Trevor Hall[7],
and Mark Chignell[1]($\boxtimes$) (iD)

[1] University of Toronto, Toronto, ON M5S 3G8, Canada
`chignell@mie.utoronto.ca`
[2] Ryerson University, Toronto, ON M5B 2K3, Canada
[3] Health Quality Council of Alberta, Calgary, AB T2N 2A4, Canada
[4] International Society for Quality in Healthcare, Dublin, Ireland
[5] Canadian Patient Safety Institute, Gloucester, ON K1J 7S9, Canada
[6] Canadian Foundation for Healthcare Improvement, Ottawa, ON K1P 0E4, Canada
[7] Healthcare Insurance Reciprocal of Canada (HIROC), North York, ON M2N 6K8, Canada

Abstract. This paper reports on the Patient Safety Research and Application
Competition that was held in conjunction with the 2021 International Ergonomics
Association Conference. The objectives of this competition were to: (1) Formulate
research problem statements and innovative solutions to improve patient safety
through the application of human factors/ergonomics (HF/E) to the healthcare
system, (2) Showcase how the HF/E approach to this topic can lead to a useful,
usable, and satisfying user experience while simultaneously improving outcomes
relating to both functional and non-functional requirements, and (3) Provide an
effective way of engaging students and early career researchers in IEA activities
and initiatives. After reviewing the patient safety topics that motivated the design
competition, we then report on the work carried out by the two finalists in the
competition, and discuss lessons learned. We propose the continued use of design
competitions in the future to motivate and showcase ergonomic problem-solving
design by students and early career researchers and practitioners.

Keywords: Human factors · Ergonomics · Patient safety · Clinical
deterioration · Educating designers · Design competition

1 Introduction

1.1 Design Competitions

In recent decades considerable effort has been put into developing new methods for educating designers and creating innovative design technologies that can improve the way
we live and work while respecting the world around us. As a design-oriented discipline,
human factors and ergonomics needs to promote innovative design and to incorporate

best practices from other design-oriented disciplines. Design competitions of various types have come to be recognized as an important part of modern design pedagogy. Design of racing cars has been successful in motivating mechanical engineering students to learn about, and experience, design since 1981, when SAE International developed and managed the first Formula SAE student competition [1]. [2] discussed how to integrate this type of design competition within the design curriculum. Capstone design courses provide another kind of competition, having been part of the engineering curriculum for 40 years. Thus, design competitions of various kinds are a fixture of the engineering curriculum. They provide a way for students to put their knowledge into practice before they graduate [3] and typically have a competitive aspect, with prizes and recognitions for the best performing teams.

1.2 Design Competitions in Human Factors and Ergonomics

The Stanley Caplan User Centered Design Award is an annual award from the Product Design Technical Group of the Human Factors and Ergonomics Society (https://sites.goo gle.com/corehf.com/ucd-award/). This annual award emphasizes innovative and user-centered approaches to Human Factors and Industrial Design, but is not specifically student, or early-career, focused. Design competitions have sometimes been run at the ACM SIGCHI Conference (usually referred to as "CHI") often with a focus on students (e.g., [4]). The CHI design competition has also been explicitly linked to student design projects (e.g., [5]). [6] described the use of design competitions as a pedagogical tool. In view of the advantages of design competitions noted above, we decided to run a design competition for the IEA 2021 conference.

2 Design Competition Topic: Clinical Deterioration Examples

Although design competitions have been used in other venues, they have not been a feature of IEA conferences. We sought to address this deficit by creating a design competition that focused on an urgent problem of relevance to the IEA community. The objective of the competition was to encourage students and Early Career Researcher (ECR) teams to collaboratively use their knowledge/skills in human factors and ergonomics to design a solution to prevent clinical deterioration. Failure to prevent avoidable clinical deterioration leads to the loss of many lives and is a major threat to patient safety in healthcare systems. Safety leaders such as Healthcare Insurance Reciprocal of Canada (HIROC), the Canadian Patient Safety Institute (CPSI), the Canadian Foundation for Healthcare Improvement (CFHI), and the International Society for Quality in Health Care (ISQua) have all called for action on the patient safety issue of failure to recognize, or appreciate and act upon, patient status changes or deterioration. Clinical deterioration is a key contributor to mortality and is among the top patient safety concerns globally. The failure to recognize, monitor, interpret and respond to clinical deterioration is a systemic patient safety concern (e.g. failure to monitor/interpret/respond to abnormal fetal status; failure to appreciate and respond to a deteriorating condition). The design challenge asked:

1) How can good ergonomic design and innovative solutions contribute to reducing avoidable harm and subsequent mortality, through early recognition and intervention

for clinical deterioration, and increase quality of life for patients and their family caregivers?

2) How can we design innovative and ergonomically informed environments, tools, fixtures, devices, methods and applications that will improve early recognition and intervention for clinically deteriorating patients and improve patient safety?

There were two tracks for this design competition; Track One covered solutions relating to workplace design, industrial ergonomics, and occupational health, and Track Two covered HCI/UX (human-computer interaction/user experience) solutions. The competition was advertised through IEA, HIROC, and HFIG networks and social media channels. Professors were emailed with courseware examples and other resources to encourage implementation in their classes, as a class project.

2.1 Clinical Deterioration Examples

The following clinical deterioration example topics were provided (Table 1), although the design competition teams were free to choose other related topics. We prepared a one-hour training video with an associated slide deck to explain the concept of clinical deterioration. We also provided a short textual description of each of the topics (excerpts from two of these summaries, for falls and for mismanagement of neonatal resuscitation, are shown below), and we held online question and answer sections with experts, for those contestants who wanted it.

Patient Falls. Injuries caused by falls frequently result in significant disabilities with loss of independence and associated costs. Safety is fostered by both fall prevention and by reducing the severity of injury should a fall occur.

Table 1. List of suggested clinical deterioration topics.

Sample events
Failure to Monitor, Interpret or Respond to Atypical and Abnormal Fetal Health Surveillance (FHS) Patterns
Failure to appreciate status changes/deteriorating patients
Death by suicide while under care/Suicide attempts
Failure to identify/Manage neonatal hyperbilirubinemia
Failure to identify/Manage neonatal hypoglycemia
Delayed decision to delivery time for caesarean sections
Patient falls
Mismanagement of neonatal resuscitation
Failure to communicate/Respond to critical test results
Inadequate triage assessment/Reassessment
Failure to communicate fetal health status
Failure to identify/Manage postpartum hemorrhages and hemorrhagic shock

Mismanagement of Neonatal Resuscitation. Post-delivery neonatal resuscitation has become a significant liability exposure for hospitals, perinatal practitioners and the resuscitation teams, particularly in cases where the infant sustained neurological injury not arising from the management of pregnancy, labour or birth.

3   Design Competition Finalists

We selected two teams to be finalists and present their work at a special session of the IEA conference. As described below, one team proposed an ergonomic redesign within an oncology department, and the other team addressed mental health issues for women who have recently given birth.

3.1   Redesigning Procedures in an Oncology Department

The first team carried out an ergonomics study in the Oncology Department at Trillium Health Partners Hospital in Mississauga, Ontario. Their goal was to reduce the risk of clinical deterioration by improving the wellbeing of nurses and the operational performance of the department. The team conducted informal interviews with nurses, as well as collecting both quantitative and qualitative observation data about the current situation. Based on the results of this observation they decided to focus on the tasks of 1) transferring patients from beds to gurneys and vice versa; 2) retrieving items from the supply closet. The team focused on novel designs that could reduce physical load and mental strain while performing the tasks. Due to the ongoing COVID-19 crisis, it was not possible to evaluate the designs in the hospital setting. Thus the team proposed further work to demonstrate the extent to which the designs can improve nurse well-being and lead to better system performance. Two examples of the work performed are shown below.

1. A redesign of the patient transfer cloth would be implemented in order to ensure the posture used during patient transfers is an upright reach and pull rather than a bent-forward reach and pull. Implementing the change would result in a reduction in joint shear experienced by the 5th percentile female from 368N to 325N, representing an 11.7% reduction in joint shear as can be seen in Fig. 1 below.
2. To improve item retrieval, each supply room can be equipped with a Tablet for around $250 Cdn each at the time of writing. The tablets should have at least a 5-year lifetime and should be mounted on the wall with the charger in each supply room. An Excel file on the tablet would have multiple excel tabs that are coloured-coded, matching corresponding coloured sections of the storage cabinet, making it very easy to locate items.

3.2   A Postpartum Mental Health Tool

The second team focused on the issue of postpartum mental health. Approximately 85% of new mothers experience negative changes in their mood during the postpartum period,

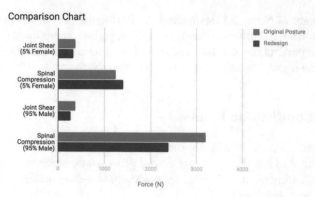

Fig. 1. Force comparison on human body for work postures

which may manifest as various mental health conditions including postpartum depression (PPD) and postpartum blues [7]. In researching literature, personal blogs, and available solutions, it was found that most existing technological solutions provide a range of resources for monitoring infant health but are lacking in features that promote maternal well-being for the postpartum period [8]. The team designed a mobile application, called *Nura*, to provide new mothers with tools and resources, encouraging them to focus on their own well-being, as well as their infant's.

To effectively promote maternal mental health during the postpartum experience, the *Nura* App aims to focus on the three user experience goals of (1) **Streamlining the flow of information**, which will lessen information overload for users (which can often lead to misinformation and additional stress for young mothers) [9]; (2) **Customizability**, which will allow the users to make specific changes, such as notification times for appointments, to fit their individual needs; (3) **System driven personalization** which will offer mothers a unique user experience based on data they provide while registering, throughout their use of the App.

In order to achieve these goals, the *Nura* team carried out a user-centered design process, starting with the objective to understand and empathize with the user. The team interviewed two potential users (mothers with young children) to gain additional perspective to aid in the formation of requirements and user personas. Based on the interviews and supplemental research of the e-health space, 6 technical and non-technical requirements were developed, as well as 2 personas to drive the design. After creating scenarios and use-cases, the team decided to re-frame the product from a "psychological" or "mental wellbeing" platform to a self-care application due to mothers feeling uncomfortable interacting with a "mental wellness" app. Next, the team created four low-fidelity prototypes, using a parallel design paradigm [10], leading to the example wireframes (one for each of the four prototypes) shown in Fig. 2.

The low-fidelity prototype alternatives were then narrowed down to create two unique and distinct medium-fidelity prototypes, which were evaluated with a comparative usability test to determine which design better met the team's usability, utility, and satisfaction goals. The usability tests were conducted remotely with two young mothers

Fig. 2. Four independent low-fidelity prototypes.

(the target audience) and two students (usability experts). The quantitative and qualitative data collection methods used were a System Usability Scale, Usability-Satisfaction Scale, Think-Aloud Protocol and a User Questionnaire.

After conducting comparative usability tests on the two designs, the team created a high-fidelity prototype which integrated desirable aspects of the earlier prototypes, while improving upon or eliminating features that were deemed unsatisfactory.

Fig. 3. Onboarding form before (left) and after (right) heuristic evaluation.

A heuristic evaluation was then done on the high-fidelity prototype, providing the designers with an opportunity to identify shortcomings within the design based on established usability principles. The prototype was evaluated based on Jakob Nielsen's set of 10 usability heuristics [11]. Various issues and strongpoints were identified and rated according to severity, and reflective changes were made in the prototype based on the discoveries from the heuristic analysis (an example of which can be seen in Fig. 3, where "Select all that apply" was added to cue appropriate input).

The next step in the development of the *Nura* app would be collaboration with subject-matter experts to determine how clinicians (primarily obstetricians) can best use the app to promote wellness of mothers postpartum.

4 Conclusions and Key Lessons

We faced a number of challenges in running the design competition, with the biggest challenge being the COVID-19 pandemic which was ongoing during the competition. Teams had difficulty carrying out the user research necessary for requirements analysis, and for user evaluation of design alternatives, although video conferencing was found to be a powerful tool to support the collaborative design work. Teams also had difficulty addressing the official topic of clinical deterioration, which was relatively unfamiliar to them, and typically picked topics of a more general nature that were likely easier for them to understand and get data on from secondary sources (which was not surprising given that their opportunities to collect data in hospitals were severely limited). Aside from the pandemic we also experienced problems in getting the design competition assigned as a project in university courses, which had been our preferred strategy for recruiting participants.

For many professors that we approached, the timing of the competition did not match the timing of their courses, particularly in different countries or in universities that had a quarter system vs. a semester system. Students and professors also had difficulties understanding, or perhaps warming to, the topic of clinical deterioration which was outside their general experience. Even when the design competition was assigned as a course project there were problems getting students to formally enter the design competition. For instance, in one course participation was voluntary, and as a result only one out of 7 project teams for that class submitted their work to the design competition. In spite of these challenges, we judge the design competition to be a success and we plan to keep running it in future years, and with a range of conferences, using iterative design to improve topic selection, communication with professors, and mentoring of teams. Our IEA 2021 design competition was a kind of "pop-up" competition which didn't have a history behind it and didn't have people planning to participate in advance of the competition launch. In future, having a regular design competition will encourage professors and students to plan ahead, and should lead to more adoptions of the design competition as a course project.

The sharing of good practice is essential for the principles of HFE to spread, and healthcare is just one of a number of important and highly relevant fields for design competitions to address. Having an annual competition, with accessible topics for university students, should increase uptake of the design competition within courses, not only increasing the size of the design competition but also enhancing its role as a pedagogical tool.

References

1. FSAE Michigan (2021). About Formula SAE Series. Downloaded from: https://www.sae.org/attend/student-events/formula-sae-michigan/about. 13 February 2021
2. Davies, H.C.: Integrating a multi-university design competition into a mechanical engineering design curriculum using modern design pedagogy. J. Eng. Des. **24**(5), 383–396 (2013)
3. Brackin, P., Knudson, D., Nassersharif, B., O'Bannon, D.: Pedagogical implications of project selection in capstone design courses. Int. J. Eng. Educ. **27**(6), 1164 (2011)
4. Churchill, E.F., Sykes, J., Zazelenchuk, T.: Recognizing student designers: ACM CHI's student design competition. Interactions **12**(5), 16–19 (2005)
5. Brumby, D.P.: (2012). Embedding the CHI Student Design Competition into Project- Based Learning. https://citeseerx.ist.psu.edu/viewdoc/summary?doi=10.1.1.665.1621 4 June 2020
6. Khare, R., Khare, A.: Design competition as a pedagogical tool to teach concepts of universal design in India. In: Proceedings of the Human Factors and Ergonomics Society Annual Meeting, vol. 57, no. 1, pp. 511–515. Sage CA: Los Angeles, CA, SAGE Publications (September 2013)
7. The MGH Center for Women's Mental Health. Postpartum Psychiatric Disorders (June 20 2019). https://womensmentalhealth.org/specialty-clinics/postpartum-psychiatric-disorders
8. Sadmin. Postpartum Apps You Will Love. Pregnant Pauses (8 June 2018). https://www.pregnantpauses.us/2018/06/08/top-apps-will-love-postpartum/Molina-Reci
9. Molina-Luque, R., Jiménez-García, A.M., Ventura-Puertos, P.E., Hernández-Reyes, A., Romero-Saldaña, M.: Proposal for the user-centered design approach for health apps based on successful experiences: integrative review. JMIR Mhealth Uhealth **8**(4):e14376 (2020). https://doi.org/10.2196/14376
10. Nielsen, J., Faber, J.M.: Parallel Design and Testing (01 February 1996). Retrieved 02 November 2020. https://www.nngroup.com/articles/parallel-design/
11. Nielsen, J.: (24 April 1994). 10 Usability Heuristics for User Interface Design. Nielsen Norman Group. Retrieved 22 November 2020. https://www.nngroup.com/articles/ten-usability-heuristics/

Energy Cost and Perception of Degree of Exertion of Use of Walking Aid Post Open-Reduction and Internal Fixation of Lower Limb Fracture in Young Adults

Victor Afamefuna Egwuonwu[1]([✉]), Nwanne Chiamaka[1], Chima Collins Ihegihu[2], and Richard Falade Busuyi[1]

[1] Department of Medical Rehabilitation, Nnamdi Azikiwe University, Nnewi Campus, Anambra, Nigeria
va.egwuonwu@unizik.edu.ng
[2] Department of Orthopeadics and Trauma Surgery, Nnamdi Azikiwe University, Nnewi Campus, Anambra, Nigeria

Abstract. Walking re-education is usually the first line of rehabilitation post open-reduction and internal fixation of lower extremity fractures. Assistive walking aid is prescribed for the patient while healing and recovery is ongoing. It is important that cost-effective rehabilitation interventions are adopted, which entail prescription of walking aid requiring minimal energy expenditure during rehabilitation phase of management, to guarantee fewer incidences of falls and re-fractures. The present study was a pretest-posttest research design that investigated the energy demand of assistive devices (Axillary Crutch (AC), Standard Walker (SW), and Wheeled Walker (WW) and degree of perceived exertion on fracture patients undergoing rehabilitation. Thirty patients undergoing rehabilitation for fractures of the lower limb were consecutively recruited from Nnamdi Azikiwe University Teaching Hospital, with mean age, height and weight of 23 years, 1.66 m and 64 kg respectively. Subjects were progressed into daily ambulation for nine (9) minutes with each assistive device and their Heart rates (HR), Blood Pressure (BP) were measured for six weeks eight-weeks after post-operative immobilization. Maximum oxygen uptake during training (VO2max) and energy expenditure were estimated from the subjects. Comparative analysis of data was done using descriptive statistics of mean and standard deviation, Kruskal Wallis Test was used to compare the demand of Assistive devices on energy expenditure, VO2max, HR and degree of perceived exertion, with alpha level of significance set at 0.05. There was a significant change in degree of perceived exertion, associated with the use of axillary clutch (AC), compared to that of standard walker (SW) and wheeled walkers (WW) during non-weight bearing. The use of AC during NWB ambulation revealed less energy expenditure, but it may not be appropriate for older population, since the degree of perceived exertion reported by participants was high.

Keywords: Energy-expenditure · Walking-re-education · Open-reduction · Internal-fixation · Assistive-devices

© The Author(s), under exclusive license to Springer Nature Switzerland AG 2021
N. L. Black et al. (Eds.): IEA 2021, LNNS 222, pp. 282–286, 2021.
https://doi.org/10.1007/978-3-030-74611-7_39

1 Background

Assistive devices (walking aid) provide advantages such as stability, augmentation of muscle action, and reduction of weight bearing load to patients post fracture surgeries (Faruqui and *Todd* 2010). In order to attain efficient and upright locomotion following an injury or surgery, patients with locomotor dysfunction may be mobilized with an assistive device (Dounis et al. 2000). The prescription of walking aid may be arbitrary or based upon the evaluation of patient's balance, coordination, mental status, strength, and age (El Hellou et al. 2012). The energy exertion of walking aids to these individuals has never been considered as a requirement to recommend the appropriate device for patient post open reduction surgeries. Walking re-education is usually the first line of rehabilitation post open-reduction and internal fixation of lower extremity fractures. Assistive walking aid is prescribed for the patient while healing and recovery is ongoing. It is important that cost-effective rehabilitation interventions are adopted, which entail prescription of walking aid requiring minimal energy expenditure during rehabilitation phase of management, to guarantee fewer incidences of falls and re-fractures. Assistive devices with efficient energy demand for locomotion poses reduced challenges to the cardiorespiratory system and fatigability which are important goals for health workers involved in orthopaedic management. Ergonomic research might provide a bird's eye view on ways of optimizing and enhancing cost-effective ambulatory aid prescription. Presently, in the low-to-middle income countries clinical settings, like Nigeria, assistive devices are mostly prescribed, with little knowledge of its energy demand and degree of perceived exertion on the patients, increasing the risk of fall during walking re-education.

2 Statement of Problem

Non weight-bearing ambulation with the aid of an assistive device is often prescribed in the clinical setting (Tappan 2002). Little is known about the energy expenditure, and perception of exertion of these devices when deployed by patients (Holder et al. 1993). Therefore, the present study compared the Energy expenditure measured by, oxygen consumption, heart rate (HR), blood pressure (BP) responses, and perception of effort [measured by ratings of perceived exertion (RPE)] of unassisted ambulation (UA), non-weight bearing ambulation using axillary crutches (AC), a standard walker (SW), and a wheeled walker (WW). Many patients may have compromised cardiovascular and/or respiratory systems, itis important to be aware of the energy expenditure and perception of effort (Baruch and Mossberg 1983).

3 Methods

The present study was a pretest-posttest research design that investigated the energy demand of assistive devices (Axillary Crutch (AC), Standard Walker (SW), and Wheeled Walker (WW) and degree of perceived exertion on fracture patients undergoing reha-bilitation. Thirty patients who had fractures of lower limb bones were consecutively recruited from Nnamdi Azikiwe University teaching hospital, Orthopaedics unit, with mean age, height and weight of 23 years, 1.66 m and 64 kg respectively. The choice of young adults was to ensure adequate exercise endurance, since patients are still recovering from long-term immobilization on in-patients bed rest associated with muscle wasting and reduced cardiorespiratory fitness. To prepare the patients for post-surgical rehabilitation, aerobic exercise was sustained to improve cardiorespiratory endurance. Exactly eight-weeks after post-operative immobilization, subjects were progressed into daily ambulation for nine (9) minutes with each assistive device and their Heart rate (HR), Blood Pressure (BP) were measured for six weeks using a hardwired Polar Electro PE 3000 h monitors and an OMRON BP monitors respectively. Additionally, their maximum oxygen uptake during training (VO2max) and energy expenditure were estimated from HR using the equation VO2max = 65.81 (0.1847XHR) for female participants and VO2max = 111.33 (0.42XHR) for male participants. Meanwhile, heart rate data collected were utilized to estimate the physiological workload for various categories of participants' ambulation modes.

4 Results

The mean VO2max of 49.33 kcal, 43.67 kcal, 41.53 kcal for AC, SW and WW respectively. Meanwhile the mean heart rates for AC, SW and WW respectively were 48.50 bpm, 44.67 bpm and 42.33 bpm See Table 1. There was a significant change in degree of perceived exertion, associated with the use of axillary clutch (AC), compared to that of standard walker (SW) and wheeled walkers (WW) during non-weight bearing (k = 20.03; p = 0.001). Meanwhile, there were significant changes in HR, and V02Max recorded during Auxiliary Crutch usage, compared to the use of Standard Walker and Wheeled Walkers during Non-Weight Bearing (NWB) ambulation (k = 14.06; p = 0.013 and k = 11.38; p = 0.085 respectively). Additionally, estimated energy cost of work estimated from heart rate reserve showed that the use of axillary clutch (AC), demanded

Table 1. Kruskal wallis test showing changes in heart rate, oxygen consumption, and rate of perceived exertion among the three modes of ambulation.

Variable	Ambulatory mode	Mean rank	K	p
Vo2max	Axillary crutch	49.30	11.38	0.085
	Standard walker	43.60		
	Wheeled walker	41.60		
% Heart rate reserve	Axillary crutch	58.33	14.06	0.013*
	Standard walker	44.67		
	Wheeled walker	42.50		
% Estimated energy cost	Axillary crutch	19.13	12.16	0.031*
	Standard walker	24.67		
	Wheeled walker	29.50		
Rate of perceived exertions	Axillary crutch	60.77	20.03	0.001*
	Standard walker	43.95		
	Wheeled walker	31.78		

α: P ≥ 0.05 *: Significant alpha value.

the lowest percentage estimated energy cost of locomotion compared to that of standard walker (SW) and wheeled walkers (WW) during non-weight bearing (k = 12.16; p = 0.031).

Table 2. Estimates of workload from working heart rate (HR) of ambulation mode (3).

Working HR	Ambulatory mode	Physiological workload
90–110	Axillary crutch	Moderate
110–130	Standard walker	Heavy
130–150	Wheeled walker	Very heavy

5 Discussion

The findings in the present study showed a significantly lower estimated gait energy cost of ambulation with crutches compared to standard and wheeled walkers. The consequential decrease in the energy expenditure during ambulation with axillary crutch, compared to walkers could be explained by the increase in step width and step angle thereby increasing the load exerted over the forearm, while using walkers, compared to the use of crutches. This agrees with findings of Jones et al. 2008 who compared the energy expenditure in patients with unilateral knee osteoarthritis while walking with canes of different lengths. The results of the present study observed a significantly higher Oxygen Cost, during Non-Weight Bearing Ambulation using axillary crutch compared to the use of standard walker and wheeled walkers. This result consistence with the report of Holder et al. (1993) on the effect of Assistive Devices on Cardiovascular stress and perception of degree of exertion among fractured patients placed on ambulatory aids who reported a significant change in the oxygen consumption in ml/kg.min^{-1} in AW, SW and WW. However, this is contrary to the study of Czerniecki and Morgenroth (2017) on cardiovascular responses that both compared oxygen consumption per minute during non-weight bearing ambulation with AC and SW and touchdown ambulation disabled and apparently healthy participants who showed no significant changes in oxygen consumption and Estimated Gait energy cost of ambulation with crutches and wheeled walkers. The findings from this study suggest that ambulating non-weight bearing using AC can be classified as having a moderate physiological workload demand compared to SW and WW that fell within heavy to very heavy physiological workload demands respectively.

6 Conclusion

The use of AC during NWB ambulation revealed less energy expenditure, but it may not be appropriate for older population, since the degree of perceived exertion reported by participants was high. Pre-operative aerobic training could be advocated for patients requiring ambulatory devises to induce substantial change in the cardiorespiratory and metabolic systems, consequently minimizing the effect of immobilization wasting and other complications of surgeries.

References

Abdalbary, S.A.: Partial weight bearing in hip fracture rehabilitation. Future Sci. OA. **4**(1). FSO254 (2017)

Adedoyin, R.A., Opayinka, A.J., Oladokun, Z.O.: Energy expenditure of stair climbing with elbow and axillary crutches. Physiotherapy **88**(1), 47–51 (2002)

Czerniecki, J.M., Morgenroth, D.C.: Metabolic energy expenditure of ambulation in lower extremity amputees: what have we learned and what are the next steps. Disabil. Rehabil. **39**(2), 143–151 (2017)

Baruch, I.M., Mossberg, K.A.:Heart rate response of elderly women to non-weight bearing ambulation with a walker. Phys. Ther. **63**(2), 1782–1787 (1983)

El Helou, A., Bastuji-Garin, S., Paillaud, E., Gracies, J.M., Skalli, W., Deco, P.: Determinants for the use of ambulation aids in a geriatric rehabilitation care unit: a retrospective study. J. Am. Med. Directors Assoc. **13**(3), 279–283 (2012)

Faruqui Safi, R., Todd, J.: Ambulatory assistive devices in orthopaedics: uses and modifications. Am. Acad. Orthop. Surgeon. **18**(1), 41–50 (2010)

Dounis, E., Rose, G.K., Wilson, R.S.E., Steventon, R.D.: A comparison of efficiency of three types of crutches using oxygen consumption. Rheumatol Rehabil (19), 252–255 (1980)

Holder, C.G., Haskvitz, E.M., Weltman, A.: The effects of assistive devices on the oxygen cost, cardiovascular stress, and perception of non-weight-bearing ambulation. J. Orthop. Sports Phys. Ther. **18**(4), 537–542 (1993)

Jones, A., Alves, A.C., de Oliveira, L.M., Saad, M., Natour, J.: Energy expenditure during cane-assisted gait in patients with knee osteoarthritis. Clin. (Sao Paulo). **63**(2), 197–200 (2008)

Tappan, R.S.: Rehabilitation for balance and ambulation in a patient with attention impairment due to intracranial hemorrhage. Phys. Ther. **82**(5), 473–484 (2002)

Detecting Abnormalities on Displays of Patient Information

Sydney Fleishman[1]([⊠]), Alexis Hess[2], Larry Sloan[2], Joseph J. Schlesinger[3] [iD], and Joshua Shive[2] [iD]

[1] Vanderbilt University, Nashville, TN 37235, USA
sydney.a.fleishman@vanderbilt.edu
[2] Tennessee State University, Nashville, TN 37209, USA
jshive@tnstate.edu
[3] Vanderbilt University Medical Center, Nashville, TN 37209, USA
joseph.j.schlesinger@vanderbilt.edu

Abstract. This project tested a new physiological information display that aims to improve a clinician's ability to detect vital sign abnormalities before those abnormalities trigger an alarm. The configural display integrates information about heart rate, blood pressure, and blood oxygen saturation into a visual representation of the patient's current state relative to alarm and "pre-alarm" thresholds. Eight participants were asked to monitor patient displays for six different types of emergency events under three display configurations (numerical, configural, and both) and two levels of cognitive load. The numerical display showed color-coded numerical values of each of the three patient parameters. Emergency events involved abnormal values of heart rate, blood pressure, and blood oxygen saturation that occurred approximately every thirty seconds during six ten-minute patient monitoring blocks. Cognitive load was manipulated using an N-back task with two levels ($N = 1$ and $N = 2$). Emergency event detection was faster when both the configural display and numerical display were present than when only the numerical display was present. Furthermore, a combined display showing both the numerical and configural information required the fewest number of alarms to facilitate correct detection of emergency events. In addition, reaction times to emergency events were slower in the high cognitive load condition than in the low cognitive load condition. These results suggest that the combination of numerical and configural displays has the potential to reduce the number of threshold alarms and reduce the time it takes clinicians to respond to emergency events.

Keywords: Configural display · Hospital alarms · Visual displays · Pre-alarm space · Cognitive load

1 Introduction

Intensive Care Units (ICU), operating rooms (OR), and emergency rooms (ER) in hospitals are busy, hectic environments. In the ICU, alarms have the important task of alerting clinicians of emergency events and keeping them informed of patients with deteriorating physiological status. Ultimately, their goal is to indicate a serious health risk (Imhoff and Kuhls 2006). Since alarms warn others of dangerous situations, they can be unnecessarily loud and overused out of caution (Schlesinger et al. 2018). However, this attempt to err on the side of safety results in alarm fatigue, in which there are too many disruptive, loud alarms that do not effectively communicate the important information they are supposed to, so clinicians begin to ignore them (Meredith and Edworthy 1995).

These problems with alarms, in addition to the cognitive strain of the ICU environment and patient data analysis, compromise patient care and safety (Faiola et al. 2015). A possible solution is using alarms that involve other senses in addition to hearing. In particular, vision remains a largely unexplored sense when it comes to multisensory alarms, that are more often multiple unisensory streams, in the ICU. The current visual information displays used by clinicians spread data out across multiple locations, and data is not organized in a way that one can understand efficiently (Anders et al. 2012). This hampers a clinician's ability to recognize ongoing patient physiologic trends, which makes it difficult to maintain a comprehensive view of a patient's state. Currently, quality care for patients is limited by these inadequate visual displays and auditory alarms that are loud and shrill, only mildly effective, largely uninformative, have poor positive predictive value, and cause numerous problems for both clinicians and patients (Cvach 2012; Meredith and Edworthy 1995; Schlesinger et al. 2018). These shortcomings call for implementing improved user-centered visual displays as part of multisensory alarms in healthcare settings.

2 Literature Review

2.1 Cognitive Load

Many clinicians in the ICU are put in high pressure situations and perform tasks with significant cognitive load. Much of this cognitive load is a result of insufficiently designed device interfaces, the complex ICU environment, and patients that require constant care and analysis (Faiola et al. 2015). These challenges force clinicians to use workarounds that reduce their analytical capacity and other mental capabilities (Faiola et al. 2015; Paas et al. 2003; Seaman and Erlen 2015). In situations where cognitive load is high, important details can be missed, and there is an association between cognitive load and medical error (Pickering et al. 2010; Wilbanks and McMullan 2018).

A study by Ahmed et al. (2011) showed that when clinicians tested a new user interface, specifically designed to reduce task load through fewer data points, they had reduced task completion time and fewer errors. However, most hospitals don't implement these designs, and the cognitive load of the ICU is further complicated by problems with hospital alarms and inadequate visual displays.

2.2 Problems with Auditory Alarms

Common negative consequences of alarms for physicians and patients are alarm fatigue and desensitization, damage from noise levels, and masking (Cvach 2012; Schlesinger et al. 2017; Hasanain et al. 2014).

Alarm Fatigue. Alarm fatigue occurs when a listener becomes desensitized from too many disruptive alarms. Alarm fatigue results in a lack of response to alarms and leads to missed or delayed action from clinicians (Cvach 2012).

Patient Harm. Moreover, current ICU alarms can be hazardous and intrusive, as they cause both discomfort and lasting psychological problems for patients including PTSD, delirium, and sleep disturbance (Lutter et al. 2002). Wade et al. (2014) also found that 88% of interviewed patients experienced some form of hallucination or delusion about the ICU after being discharged. This damage likely comes from their high frequency and shrillness, which is unpleasant for all those in the surrounding area (Schlesinger et al. 2017).

Signal to Noise Ratio. There is a prevalent belief that alarms must be louder than the surrounding background noise to do their job effectively. In reality, the acoustic features of a sound are a better determinant of whether the sound will be perceived (Schlesinger et al. 2018). Furthermore, alarms don't necessarily have to be loud to be effective. The idea that "louder is better" leads to increased and unnecessary noise that can cause stress, miscommunication, poor decision-making, and even negative health effects (van Kempen et al. 2002).

Poor Positive Predictive Value. Alarms are also largely uninformative and rarely predict patient distress. Lutter et al. (2002) demonstrated that 67.2% of alarms across 3 different ICU machines were false positives. Additionally, most of these general auditory alarms don't indicate to physicians what exactly the patient's problem is when the alarm goes off (Meredith and Edworthy 1995).

Masking. Alarm sounds in the ICU are often masked by other tonal sounds, which prevent the clinician from hearing the important alarm that requires their attention (Hasanain et al. 2014). The tones within the international medical alarm standard, IEC 60601-1-8, are especially susceptible to simultaneous masking (Bolton et al. 2018; International Electrotechnical Commission 2020). Studies by Toor et al. show that in operating rooms, low urgency sounds can mask high urgency sounds, potentially causing clinicians to miss these more important alarms (Toor et al. 2008).

2.3 Visual Displays

Certain visual components in alarm displays can benefit a clinician's perception of a patient's physiological status. Khairat et al. (2018) reviewed visualization dashboards in healthcare and found that flexible, human-centered designs that were logically organized, color-coded, and adapted for clinician rounds improved efficiency, accuracy, safety, and clinician satisfaction.

There are a variety of visual display types including numerical, configural, and integrated graphical information displays. Most hospitals use primarily numerical displays that present important vital signs (e.g., heart rate, blood pressure, blood oxygen saturation) using individual numbers that change with the patient's physiological variables (Drews and Doig 2014). These give a moment-by-moment picture of the patient's status.

Configural displays (see Fig. 1 for an example) add trendlines and visible data changes to these numeric physiological variables. According to Drews and Doig (2014), nurses who used configural displays showed a significant increase in data interpretation and accuracy as well as a significant decrease in mental demand. Since it is more common for patients to deteriorate in increments, the ability to see trendlines, a concept that has already been explored for sound, helps clinicians recognize deterioration faster than a simple numerical display (Deft Design Labs 2019). Ahmed et al. (2011) showed that use of an integrated graphical information display (IGID), a new form of display that logically organizes patient information along a timeline, was not only more usable than a traditional electronic chart, but more importantly, it helped nurses detect more patient abnormalities.

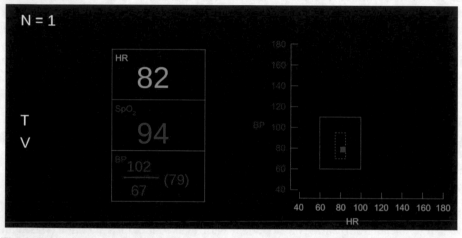

Fig. 1. Example display from the study. The N-back stimuli are shown at the left side of the display. The numerical display is shown at the center. The configural display is shown on the right-hand side of the display. The location of the small square on the configural display represents the current values of the patient's heart rate and blood pressure, while its color indicates the current blood oxygen saturation level. The dotted rectangle on the configural display indicates the pre-alarm thresholds for HR and BP. The solid rectangle on the configural display indicates the alarm thresholds for those parameters.

Furthermore, Wright et al. (2019) conducted a comprehensive review of patient information displays in healthcare and found that designing the displays around the users, who are mainly clinicians, can improve accuracy and efficiency outcomes. The best results were from improved information integration, organization, and trend display as well as the use of simpler shapes when incorporating geometric representations. These improvements ultimately led to conceptually-related information being grouped together, making the displays easier for clinicians to understand.

2.4 Multisensory Alarms

While conventional alarms are mostly auditory, multisensory alarms target additional senses, like vision and touch, to prevent overload of one sense. There are many indications of the potential benefits of introducing an improved multisensory alarm to ICU monitors (Burdick et al. 2019). Studies by Burdick et al. (2020) combined auditory and tactile stimuli to create a multisensory alarm that was tested in trials with tasks mimicked the attention needed in the ICU. The results showed a significant difference in correctly identifying parameters (heart rate, blood pressure, and blood oxygenation) and noticing a change in these parameters or multisensory alarms as compared to unisensory alarms. These results indicate the possibility that employing multiple senses in alarms can not only limit the auditory burden but also allow clinicians to better recognize patient problems that arise. In another study with a test of object identification, subjects were more accurate and faster at target identification when both visuals and sounds were present (Molholm et al. 2004). Furthermore, a study by Innes et al. (2019) tested auditory, visual, and multisensory stimuli and found that the human response to multisensory signals was significantly faster. The combination of auditory and visual stimuli gives stronger responses than each of the stimuli on their own, indicating the benefits of audiovisual integration.

2.5 The Current Study

This study introduced a visual component into auditory alarms through a new configural display with the goal of reducing aforementioned problems with current alarms (see right side of Fig. 1). Additionally, we hypothesized that a new configural display would show an improvement in abnormality detection compared to traditional vital sign displays under two cognitive load conditions because it has an easy to understand shape and color morphology. While current alarms force clinicians to react to the situation, this visual component gives clinicians a view of the pre-alarm space, or the changing physiological trends before an alarm sounds, allowing them to be proactive (Young et al. 2007). The display indicates that a patient's physiological status is deteriorating, so a clinician can tend to them before their physiological variables reach a dangerous level and an alarm sounds.

The configural display shows acceptable vital sign values, what vital sign is abnormal, and the acuity of the problem compared to traditional displays that leave acuity up to clinician interpretation and understanding of normal ranges. As a result, we predict that this new configural display will improve clinician perception of a patient's status and allow faster understanding of whether a patient's values are normal when clinicians are already occupied with other tasks and patients.

3 Method

3.1 Participants

Eight undergraduate students at Tennessee State University who reported normal or corrected to normal vision and normal color vision participated in the study. Participants were given course credit for their participation.

3.2   Materials

We developed two types of displays for use in the study: a numerical display that presented patient vital signs in a table, and a configural display that represented the same information using the position and color of a square on a two-dimensional graph.

Numerical Display. The center of Fig. 1 shows an example of the numerical display used in the study. The top row of the numerical display presented heart rate (HR) information, the middle row presented blood oxygen saturation (SpO_2), and the bottom row of the display presented systolic, diastolic, and MAP blood pressure ratio (BP). Heart rate, blood oxygen saturation, and blood pressure values were color-coded. The color codes for the patient values are displayed in Table 1. As Table 1 shows, heart rate and blood pressure values were printed in green and red, respectively. Normal SpO_2 values (between the range of 93 and 100) were indicated by shades of pink, whereas abnormally-low values that would trigger a threshold alarm (values lower than 93) were indicated by shades of blue.

In experimental conditions where participants were asked to monitor the numerical display, participants were also provided with the table of pre-alarm threshold values and alarm threshold values shown in Table 2. For each of the three monitored parameters, this table listed patient values that were abnormal but would not generate an auditory alarm (pre-alarm thresholds) during monitoring and alarm threshold values that would generate an auditory alarm during monitoring.

Configural Display. The configural display (see right side of Fig. 1) showed the same values as those shown on the numerical display, using a two dimensional figure based on the one developed by Drews and Doig (2014). A colored square represented the patient's current heart rate, blood pressure, and blood oxygen saturation. Heart rate was represented by the square's position relative to the x-axis, while blood pressure was represented by the square's position relative to the y-axis. The patient's current blood oxygen saturation was represented by the color of the rectangle, using the same color coding scheme used on the numerical display.

This study examines whether configural displays that present visual information about the patient's current value relative to pre-alarm thresholds can speed clinician responses to abnormal values, reducing the number of threshold alarms that are triggered in the ER or ICU. On the configural display, pre-alarm threshold values were indicated using a rectangle with a dashed-line border, while alarm threshold values were indicated using a larger rectangle with a solid-line border. The boundaries of these rectangles were the same as those represented in Table 2. The position of the patient marker (the colored rectangle) indicated the patient's current state relative to pre-alarm thresholds and alarm thresholds. If the patient marker was inside the boundaries of the pre-alarm threshold rectangle, as it is in Fig. 1, the patient's heart rate and blood pressure were within normal limits. If the patient marker moved outside the boundaries of the dashed rectangle, the patient's heart rate and/or blood pressure was in the pre-alarm space, indicating that one or both of those parameters was abnormal but had not yet triggered an alarm. Finally, if the marker moved outside of the solid-line rectangle, one of those parameters had become extreme enough to trigger an alarm.

Table 1. Colors used on numerical and configural displays

Value	RGB values
Heart rate (HR)	0, 255, 0
Blood pressure (BP)	255, 0, 0
Blood oxygen saturation (SpO$_2$) of 96–100	234, 63, 247
Blood oxygen saturation (SpO$_2$) of 93–95	196, 55, 238
Blood oxygen saturation (SpO$_2$) of 89–92	148, 58, 237
Blood oxygen saturation (SpO$_2$) of 85–88	93, 58, 237
Blood oxygen saturation (SpO$_2$) <85	28, 100, 232

Stimuli were displayed on a Dell Latitude E6530 laptop with a resolution of 1366 × 768 pixels. The experiment was programmed in the Psychophysics Toolbox for Octave (Brainard 1997; Pell 1997).

3.3 Design

The study used a 2 (cognitive load) × 3 (display configuration) × 6 (emergency event) experimental design to examine the speed and accuracy of emergency event detection. Cognitive load was manipulated with an N-back task with two levels: $N = 1$ (low) or $N = 2$ (high) load. The display configuration compared detection performance with the configural display, a numerical display, or both. Six emergency events were tested: 1) high or low blood pressure, 2) high or low heart rate, 3) low blood oxygen saturation, 4) high blood pressure/high heart rate, 5) high heart rate/low blood pressure, and 6) low blood pressure/low heart rate.

3.4 Procedure

Participants were seated in front of a laptop computer with the table of threshold values shown in Table 1 displayed below the screen. Participants completed six blocks of patient monitoring. During each block, participants were asked to divide their attention between two tasks: an N-back task designed to manipulate cognitive load during patient monitoring, and a patient monitoring task where participants were asked to respond as quickly as possible to simulated emergency events.

N-Back Task. During all blocks of the experiment, participants were asked to complete an N-back task (Jaeggi et al. 2010). Participants saw a pair of letters to the left of the patient monitoring displays (see left side of Fig. 1). Each pair of letters remained on the screen for two seconds, followed by a blank that lasted one second.

For each pair of letters, the participant was asked to report whether the letter on the bottom had appeared as the top letter of either the previous pair ($N = 1$) or the top letter of the pair that had appeared two pairs ago ($N = 2$). For example, in Fig. 1, the

Table 2. Alarm thresholds and pre-alarm thresholds

Value	Low alarm threshold	Low pre-alarm threshold	High pre-alarm threshold	High alarm threshold
Heart rate (HR)	60	75	85	100
Blood oxygen saturation (SpO2)	85	93	–	–
Blood pressure (BP)	60	70	95	110

participant would have to determine whether the "V" shown on the screen had appeared as the top letter of the previous pair (not shown). Participants were asked to press the "s" key on the keyboard if the bottom letter was the same as the one that had appeared in the top position on a previous screen and press the "d" key if the letter on the bottom was different than the one that had appeared in the top position on a previous screen. Participants were instructed to make a response for every pair of letters that appeared during an experimental block. Participants were encouraged to respond as quickly as possible and as accurately as possible. We recorded the reaction time to each test letter, as well as the accuracy of each response.

Normal Patient Monitoring. During the periods when no emergency event was occurring, patient parameter values varied slightly within normal ranges. Every second, heart rate, blood pressure, and blood oxygen saturation were each adjusted by a value of either $+1$ or -1. The direction of change for each parameter was chosen randomly. If changing one of the values in one direction would cause it to cross the pre-alarm space boundary, it was changed in the other direction. Thus, during normal patient monitoring, patient parameter values changed within the boundaries of the pre-alarm space.

Emergency Events During Patient Monitoring. Participants were instructed to monitor the patient displays for values that indicated an emergency event and press keys on the keyboard to identify the emergency event that had occurred as soon as they noticed it.

Emergency events occurred on average once every 30 s (plus or minus a randomly selected time between zero and six seconds). During an emergency event, the patient parameter values corresponding to the emergency event changed systematically in the direction of the emergency event. For example, during a high heart rate event, the simulated patient's heart rate increased by three beats per minute every second, while the other patient parameters remained constant.

Participants were instructed to identify an emergency event by pressing a pattern of keys on the number pad on a computer keyboard to indicate which values were abnormal. Five keys were labeled with buttons indicating high heart rate, low heart rate, low blood oxygen saturation, high blood pressure, and low blood pressure (Fig. 2).

Figure 2 shows an example emergency event as it would appear on the configural display, along with the correct keypad response associated with this event. The left side of the figure shows the configural display during an abnormal heart rate event where the patient's heart rate has increased past the boundaries of the pre-alarm space. The keypad

Example Configural Display

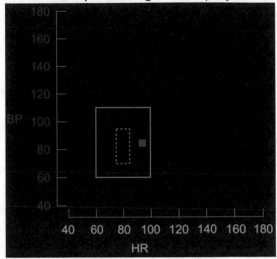

Fig. 2. Example emergency event and correct keypad response. The left side of the figure shows an example configural display screen showing an abnormal heart rate emergency event. The right side of the screen shows the correct keypad response, as indicated by the thick black square around the "high heart rate" key.

shown to the right of the configural display illustrates the correct response: pressing the high heart rate key. In the case of an emergency event where two of the patient values were abnormal, participants were instructed that they could press the keys in either order for their response to be counted as correct.

For the first few seconds of an emergency event (*i.e.*, while the patient's values were in the pre-alarm space), no auditory alarm was generated. However, once a patient's parameter passed the alarm threshold indicated in Table 1, an auditory alarm sounded. We used the crisis (red) alarm sound used on Philips (Eindhoven, The Netherlands) monitors played at approximate 60 dB. The alarm sounded for up to five seconds and was silenced when the participant used the keypad to record the details of the alarm or after the alarm had sounded for five seconds. At that time, the patient's values were reset to values within the pre-alarm space boundaries.

For each emergency event, we recorded the event that occurred, the participant's reaction time to the event, and the accuracy of the participant's key presses identifying the event.

Study Procedure. After obtaining participant consent, participants were trained on each of the experimental tasks used in the study. We first trained participants to complete the two conditions of the *N*-back task. Participants practiced each of the conditions for forty-five seconds. Next, we trained participants to recognize each of the six types of emergency events using the numerical display and configural display and enter the emergency event type using the keypad. Finally, participants practiced completing the *N*-back task and the emergency monitoring task at the same time for 45 s.

Participants then began the series of experimental blocks. The order of study conditions was chosen randomly for each participant. Each block lasted approximately ten minutes, and the total time for the study was approximately sixty minutes. Participants were encouraged to take breaks between experimental blocks. After completing all six blocks, participants were thanked for their participation.

4 Results

To examine whether display configuration and cognitive load produced differences in reaction time to emergency events, we calculated the average reaction time across all correctly-identified emergency events for each combination of display configuration and cognitive load.

Reaction Time to Emergency Events. The analysis of variance revealed a main effect of display configuration: emergency events were detected more quickly when the configural display and numerical display were present ($M = 3.33$ s, 95% C.I. [2.39, 4.27]) than when only the numerical display was present ($M = 6.03$ s, 95% C.I. [3.15, 8.90], $F(2,12) = 6.12, p = 0.01, \eta^2 = 0.50$). However, pairwise comparisons showed that there was not a significant difference between reaction times for correct detections with the configural display presented alone ($M = 3.44$ s, 95% C.I. [2.49, 4.40]) and the numerical display presented alone or between the configural display presented alone and the configural and numerical displays presented together.

Effects of Cognitive Load on Reaction Time to Emergency Events. The analysis of variance also revealed a main effect of cognitive load. Emergency event detection was faster under the lower level of cognitive load (N-back = 1: $M = 3.81$ s, 95% C.I. [2.62, 5.01]) than under the higher level of cognitive load (N-back = 2: $M = 4.71$ s, 95% C.I. [3.10, 6.33], $F(1,7) = 6.14, p = 0.04, \eta^2 = 0.47$). However, there was no interaction of cognitive load and display configuration. Figure 3 displays the results of this analysis.

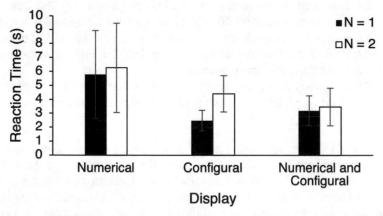

Fig. 3. Reaction times for each display configuration under different cognitive loads. The combination of numerical and configural display had the shortest average reaction times under both cognitive load conditions compared to the numerical display only.

Number of Triggered Threshold Alarms. Finally, we examined the number of triggered threshold alarms that occurred during a correct emergency event detection when each of the display configurations was used. For each of the display configurations, we identified the proportion of correctly-identified emergency events that triggered a threshold alarm. Next, we performed a one-way repeated-measures analysis of variance using the proportion of correctly-directed emergency events that triggered a threshold as the dependent variable and display configuration as the independent variable as the factor. The analysis revealed that only 17.1% of correctly-detected emergency events required a triggered threshold alarm when both the configural and numerical display were shown (95% C.I. [2.5%, 31.7%]), in comparison with 28% of emergency events when only the configural display was shown (95% C.I. [14.2%, 41.9%]) and 57.2% when only the numerical display was shown (95% C.I. [28.0%, 86.4%], F(2,7) = 7.52, p = 0.006, η^2 = 0.52). Figure 4 displays the results of this analysis.

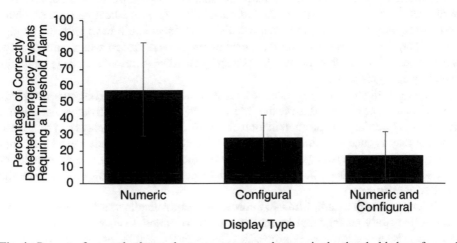

Fig. 4. Percent of correctly-detected emergency events that required a threshold alarm for each display configuration. Numeric displays presented alone required more triggered threshold alarms for correct emergency event detection than either configural displays by themselves or numeric and configural displays presented together.

5   Discussion

This study examined whether a display that combines information about patient vital signs into a visual representation can improve responses to emergency events that occur during patient care. We developed an existing configural display that represents information about heart rate and blood pressure to include information about blood oxygen saturation. Furthermore, we implemented pre-alarm space boundaries on the display to indicate values of these parameters that are abnormal but have not yet triggered a threshold alarm. We showed that the use of configural displays can speed correct responses to emergency events and reduce the number of threshold alarms that are triggered during the correct response to an emergency event in comparison with numerical displays that show the same information.

Reaction times to emergency events were fastest in conditions when the configural display and numerical display were present together and worst when only the numerical display was present. This indicates that the inclusion of a configural display helps clinicians detect emergency events more accurately and quickly than with only a numerical display. While this result may indicate a benefit of the configural display, it may also indicate a relative disadvantage for numerical displays in this study. This disadvantage may be due to the fact when only the numerical display was present, participants were asked to consult the threshold table to determine whether a value presented on the numerical display was in the pre-alarm space or try to determine which patient value had triggered the threshold alarm. We did not think it was reasonable to ask participants to memorize the ten pre-alarm and alarm threshold values. However, it is possible that participants who had already memorized these values (*e.g.,* medical personnel) would perform equally well with the numerical display as they would have with the configural display. In addition, the fact that reaction times were fastest when both displays were present indicates that the numerical display provides information that is useful for detecting emergency events.

Configural displays may reduce the time it takes to respond correctly to emergency events by allowing clinicians to see the "pre-alarm" space and respond before the alarm is triggered. As we showed, the combination of data from numerical displays and configural displays may reduce the number of alarms triggered during patient care. Configural displays of patient physiological data have the potential to aid in the development of multisensory alarms that speed the detection of patient abnormalities and reduce the number of alarms.

Future work will examine how to improve configural displays such as the one examined in this study so they can be incorporated into bimodal (visual + auditory) and trimodal (visual + auditory + vibrotactile) alarms and wearable devices. Improving the availability of multisensory information may improve clinicians' awareness of patients' physiological status, reduce alarm fatigue for clinicians, and improve patient outcomes and safety.

References

Ahmed, A., Chandra, S., Herasevich, V., Gajic, O., Pickering, B.W.: The effect of two different electronic health record user interfaces on intensive care provider task load, errors of cognition, and performance. Crit. Care Med. **39**(7), 1626–1634 (2011)

Anders, S., Albert, R., Miller, A., Weinger, M.B., Doig, A.K., Behrens, M., Agutter, J.: Evaluation of an integrated graphical display to promote acute change detection in ICU patients. Int. J. Med. Inform. **81**, 842–851 (2012)

Bolton, M.L., Edworthy, J., Boyd, A.D.: A formal analysis of masking between reserved alarm sounds of the IEC 60601-1-8 international medical alarm standard. In: Proceedings of the Human Factors and Ergonomics Society Annual Meeting, Vol. 62, No. 1, pp. 523-527. Sage CA: Los Angeles, CA: SAGE Publications (2018).

Brainard, D.H.: The psychophysics toolbox. Spat. Vis. **10**, 433–436 (1997)

Burdick, K., Courtney, M., Wallace, M.T., Baum Miller, S.H., Schlesinger, J.J.: Living and working in a multisensory world: from basic neuroscience to the hospital. Multimodal Technol. Inter. **3**(1), 2 (2019)

Burdick, K.J., Jorgensen, S.K., Combs, T.N., Holmberg, M.O., Kultgen, S.P., Schlesinger, J.J.: SAVIOR ICU: sonification and vibrotactile interface for the operating room and intensive care unit. J. Clin. Monit. Comput. **34**(4), 787–796 (2020)

CareTunes. Music as a nurses' monitoring tool - Critical Alarms Lab, 21 May 2019. Delft Design Labs. https://delftdesignlabs.org/projects/caretunes/

Cvach, M.: Monitor alarm fatigue: an integrative review. Biomed. Instrum. Technol. **46**(4), 268–277 (2012)

Drews, F.A., Doig, A.: Evaluation of a configural vital signs display for intensive care unit nurses. Hum. Factors **56**(3), 569–580 (2014)

Faiola, A., Srinivas, P., Duke, J.: Supporting clinical cognition: a human-centered approach to a novel ICU information visualization dashboard. In: AMIA Annual Symposium Proceedings, vol. 2015, p. 560. American Medical Informatics Association (2015)

Hasanain, B., Boyd, A.D., Bolton, M.L.: An approach to model checking the perceptual interactions of medical alarms. In: Proceedings of the Human Factors and Ergonomics Society Annual Meeting, vol. 58, No. 1, pp. 822–826. SAGE Publications, Los Angeles, CA, September 2014

IEC 60601–1–8:2006/AMD2:2020 Amendment 2 - Medical electrical equipment - Part 1–8: General requirements for basic safety and essential performance - Collateral Standard: General requirements, tests and guidance for alarm systems in medical electrical equipment and medical electrical systems. International Electrotechnical Commission Webstore (2020). https://webstore.iec.ch/publication/59648

IEC 60601-1-8:2006/AMD2:2020. International Electrotechnical Commission (2020). https://webstore.iec.ch/publication/59648#additionalinfo

Imhoff, M., Kuhls, S.D.: Alarm algorithms in critical care monitoring. Anesthesia Analgesia **102**(5), 1525–1537 (2006)

Innes, B.R., Otto, T.U.: A comparative analysis of response times shows that multisensory benefits and interactions are not equivalent. Sci. Rep. **9**(1), 1–10 (2019)

Jaeggi, S.M., Buschkuehl, M., Perrig, W.J., Meier, B.: The concurrent validity of the N-back task as a working memory measure. Memory **18**(4), 394–412 (2010)

Khairat, S.S., Dukkipati, A., Lauria, H.A., Bice, T., Travers, D., Carson, S.S.: The impact of visualization dashboards on quality of care and clinician satisfaction: integrative literature review. JMIR Hum. Factors **5**(2), e22 (2018)

Lutter, N.O., Urankar, S., Kroeber, S.: False alarm rates of three third-generation pulse oximeters in PACU, ICU and IABP patients. Anesthesia and analgesia **94**(1 Suppl), S69–75 (2002)

Meredith, C., Edworthy, J.: Are there too many alarms in the intensive care unit? An overview of the problems. J. Adv. Nursing **21**(1), 15–20 (1995)

Molholm, S., Ritter, W., Javitt, D.C., Foxe, J.J.: Multisensory visual–auditory object recognition in humans: a high-density electrical mapping study. Cereb. Cortex **14**(4), 452–465 (2004)

Paas, F., Tuovinen, J.E., Tabbers, H., Van Gerven, P.W.: Cognitive load measurement as a means to advance cognitive load theory. Educ. Psychol. **38**(1), 63–71 (2003)

Pelli, D.G.: The VideoToolbox software for visual psycho- physics: transforming numbers into movies. Spat. Vis. **10**, 437–442 (1997)

Pickering, B.W., Herasevich, V., Ahmed, A., Gajic, O.: Novel representation of clinical information in the ICU: developing user interfaces which reduce information overload. Appl. Clin. Inform. **1**(2), 116–131 (2010)

Schlesinger, J.J., Reynolds, E., Sweyer, B., Pradham, A.: Frequency-selective silencing device for digital filtering of audible medical alarm sounds to enhance ICU patient recovery. Georgia Institute of Technology (2017)

Schlesinger, J.J., Baum Miller, S.H., Nash, K., Bruce, M., Ashmead, D., Shotwell, M.S., Edworthy, J.R., Wallace, M.T., Weinger, M.: Acoustic features of auditory medical alarms–an experimental study of alarm volume. J. Acoust. Soc. Am. **143**, 3688–3697 (2018)

Seaman, J.B., Erlen, J.A.: Workarounds in the workplace—a second look. Orthopedic Nurs. **34**(4), 235 (2015)

Silent ICU // ICAS - Intensive Care Alarm System - Critical Alarms Lab Lab. Delft Design Labs (2019). https://delftdesignlabs.org/projects/icas/

Toor, O., Ryan, T., Richard, M.: Auditory masking potential of common operating room sounds: a psychoacoustic analysis. Anesthesiology **109**(A1207), A1207 (2008)

Van Kempen, E.E., Kruize, H., Boshuizen, H.C., Ameling, C.B., Staatsen, B.A., de Hollander, A.E.: The association between noise exposure and blood pressure and ischemic heart disease: a meta-analysis. Environ. Health Perspect. **110**(3), 307–317 (2002)

Wade, D.M., Hankins, M., Smyth, D.A., Rhone, E.E., Mythen, M.G., Howell, D.C., Weinman, J.A.: Detecting acute distress and risk of future psychological morbidity in critically ill patients: validation of the intensive care psychological assessment tool. Crit. Care **18**(5), 1–9 (2014)

Wilbanks, B.A., McMullan, S.P.: A review of measuring the cognitive workload of electronic health records. CIN: Comput. Inform. Nurs. **36**(12), 579–588 (2018)

Wright, M.C., Borbolla, D., Waller, R.G., Del Fiol, G., Reese, T., Nesbitt, P., Segall, N.: Critical care information display approaches and design frameworks: a systematic review and meta-analysis. J. Biomed. Inform. X **3**, 100041 (2019)

Young, J.S., Stokes, J.B., Denlinger, C.E., Dubose, J.E.: Proactive versus reactive: the effect of experience on performance in a critical care simulator. Am. J. Surg. **193**(1), 100–104 (2007)

The Effect of Mobile Phone Exposure in Two Memory Tasks

Joanna Fowler[✉]

School of Psychological Sciences, University of Bristol, Bristol, UK
psjenf@bristol.ac.uk

Abstract. The adoption of 5G technology networks provide users opportunities for faster broadband speed and reduced latency. Two memory experiments are considered in the context of future use of 5G technology for mobile phones. 120 participants are tested. A significant result of an effect is found in the change detection task. No effect is found in the Stroop task. Over the last 20 years many studies have shown inconsistent results of effect on cognitive performance. With the roll out of 5G, it is important to investigate this area further to gain a clear understanding of what these effects are. Caution is recommended for use of 5G mobile phones.

Keywords: 5G · Mobile phone · Memory · Electromagnetic · Hemisphere

1 Introduction

Many countries are adopting 5G technology networks which provide users opportunities for faster broadband speeds and reduced latency. The use of 5G promises far-reaching impact for future technological advancements such as artificial intelligence, telemedicine, autonomous cars, the internet of things and many other areas. However, scientific research continues to ask whether the use of mobile phones and other smart devices are safe to users who are exposed to radio-frequency electromagnetic radiation.

Recent experimental findings suggest that the effect of mobile phone radiation exposure show health concerns. Many human studies have found effects. Hematological analyses of human blood samples exposed to 1 h of mobile phone radiation in vitro showed significant changes [1]. A systematic review of studies investigating mobile phone emitted radiations on buccal mucosal cells and found markers of genotoxic effects [2]. Animal studies have shown effects. Mobile radiation caused considerable changes in the Bax/Bc/2 mRNA expression in laboratory mice hippocampus [3].

Studies on the effect of radio-frequency electromagnetic fields (RF EMF) on cognition, in particular, memory and attention have also shown effects. Some have found improved performance [4–6] and others impaired performance [7] whereas other studies have found no effect [8, 9]. Differential effects in the right and left hemisphere have been investigated [8, 10, 11].

This paper investigates if the presence of RF EMF exposure from a mobile phone effects cognitive performance in two visual memory tasks. It also tests for differential

© The Author(s), under exclusive license to Springer Nature Switzerland AG 2021
N. L. Black et al. (Eds.): IEA 2021, LNNS 222, pp. 301–308, 2021.
https://doi.org/10.1007/978-3-030-74611-7_41

effects in the right or left side by positioning the phone on alternate sides of the head. The first, a change detection task is a computer-based task that involves a conjunction of features of colour, shape and orientation [12]. It is thought to activate the parietal and right dorsolateral prefrontal cortex and category-selective regions of the extrastriata visual cortex, with involvement of dorsal-ventral interactions in visual awareness [13]. This is the first time the change detection task has been used to investigate the effect of RF EMF radiation from mobile phones. The second, the Stroop test, is a reading task that involves selective attention and speed of processing. It is used for the assessment of executive functions and demonstrates the interference of reaction time in a task. Areas in the brain thought to underlie the Stroop performance are the lateral and superior medial areas of the frontal lobes, [14].

2 Methodology

2.1 Participants

One hundred and twenty healthy, university students (100 female, 20 male) were tested. Ages ranged from 18 to 30 (M = 20.19, SD = 4.25) and all participants were mobile phone users with many years' experience (M = 8.41, SD = 3.40). Participants made on average 3 to 4 calls (M = 3.41, SD = 10.95) and sent over 40 texts a day (M = 44.02, SD = 63.93). Participants gave their informed consent prior to their inclusion in the study and confirmed that they had no known neurological condition or mental health issues.

2.2 Design

Possible lateralized effects of mobile phone exposure were investigated in a single blind, between subject design. Participants were randomly assigned to one of three conditions: active phone, inactive phone, and no phone by positioning the phone over the right or the left side of the head. Thus, there were 6 groups: active-right, active-left, inactive right, inactive left, control-right, control-left. Each group therefore had 20 participants and ages of participants were similar in all groups. All procedures had ethical approval from the University of Bristol Ethics Committee.

2.3 Materials

A recording, not heard by the participants, was played from a laptop to the phone to create an active phone condition. Three GSM 900 MHz Nokia 130 (RM-103) phones were used. The phones had a maximum specific absorption rate (SAR) of 1.28 kW/kg over 10 g when held against the head. Participants were aware that the phone was active or inactive, but they could not tell whether it was on or not. This was verified at the end of the experiment by asking participants if they thought the phone was active or not. A socket that is usually attached to the connection to make hands free operation of the phone possible had been cut. Participants wore a headband in all conditions to keep the phone in place, including the no phone condition. The antennae on the phones were on the outside of the phone, positioned 2 cm away from the top of the phone and over the area of the bottom of the posterior lobe, the side of the temporal lobe and the top of the occipital lobe.

2.4   Procedure

Participants sat 50 cm away from the computer monitor. The center of the monitor was positioned at eye level and the monitor screen was positioned vertical to the viewer. Participants carried out two visual short term memory tasks, a change detection task and a Stroop Test.

The Change Detection Task. Participants viewed a sample array of four shapes for 100 ms and a test array of four shapes on each trial, separated by a brief delay of 900 ms. They then identified whether the two arrays were identical (match accuracy) or differed in terms of a single feature (change accuracy). Participants identified any changes in the configuration of the object by pressing a key to indicate if there had been a change. The accuracy of this discrimination is assessed as a function of the number of items in the stimulus array to determine how many items are accurately retained in short-term memory. In this study, the task was selected to expand on the range of cognitive tasks that had investigated the effects of RF EMF exposure.

Analysis: Performance for the change detection task was recorded by measuring match accuracy and match reaction time and subsequently change accuracy and change reaction time. Reaction time was measured by the difference in milliseconds between the onset of the test display and the participant's response and was inbuilt into the programme. It was recorded using MatLabs 'GetSecs' function. Heterogeneity of variance was demonstrated: thus, data were analyzed using the Kruskal Wallis test (suitable for six independent groups, using error rank scores). A post hoc pairwise comparison using Dunn-Bonferroni correction was then used to adjust for multiple comparisons.

The Stroop Task. In the Stroop Task participants were required to read a few words in the same colour as the printed colour word (the congruent condition) and then read a list of words about colour in different colours to the printed word of the colour (the incongruent condition). Participants were timed with a stopwatch to see if there was a difference in the two conditions of congruency and incongruency.

Analysis: Performance was recorded by measuring the congruent and incongruent reaction times. Stroop effect RTs were calculated by subtracting the RTs in the incongruent task from the RTs in the congruent task. The data collected showed homogeneity of variance, so a one way independent, between subjects' ANOVA was carried out on the data.

3   Results

3.1   The Change Detection Task

Match Data. When the phone was positioned at the right ear, no effect of experimental condition for match accuracy was found, $X^2(2) = 1.254$, p $= .534$. Similarly, there was no effect for match reaction time, $X^2(2) = 0.096$, p $= .953$. The error rankings are depicted in Table 1. When the phone was positioned at the left ear, no effect of experimental condition was shown for match accuracy, $X^2(2) = 1.409$, p $= .494$ or match reaction time, $X^2(2) = 0.498$, p $= .780$.

Table 1. The effects of mobile phone exposure in a change detection task. Data shows results for match accuracy and match reaction times and change accuracy and change reaction times. Values depicted are error rankings based on a Kruskal Wallis Test performed on each ear.

Condition	Match accuracy	Match reaction time	Change accuracy	Change reaction time
Right control	29.70	31.30	35.78	27.95
InAct.	33.85	29.60	33.25	32.90
Activeleft	27.95	30.60	22.48*	29.05
Control	31.68	28.75	30.80	26.90
InAct	32.95	32.60	29.50	35.90
Active	26.85	30.15	31.20	28.70

InAct. Refers to the inactive condition. (n = 20) for all conditions.
*Significantly different from inactive and control phone conditions (p < 0.05).

Change Data. When the phone was positioned at the right ear, a significant effect of experimental condition for change accuracy was shown ($X^2(2) = 6.746$. p = .034). The error ranks are shown in Table 1. Upon finding the significant effect result of the Kruskal Wallis test, a post hoc pairwise comparison using Dunn-Bonferonni correction for multiple comparisons was carried out for all interactions. This showed that there was a significant difference between the active and the control condition Z = 2.45, p = .043, thus surviving multiple comparison analysis. There was no significant effect for reaction time $X^2(2) = 0.903$, p = .637 or for the left ear $X^2(2) = 2.98$, p = .23 (Table 2).

Table 2. The effects of mobile phone exposure in a change detection task. Data shows results for match accuracy and match reaction times and change accuracy and change reaction times. Values depicted are error rankings based on a Mann Whitney Test performed on each side of the head separately.

Condition	Match accuracy	Match reaction time	Change accuracy	Change reaction time
Right				
InAct.	22.43	20.45	24.18	21.70
Active	18.58	20.55	16.83*	19.30
Left	22.60	21.30	20.18	22.60
InAct.	18.40	19.70	20.83	18.40
Active				

nAct. Refers to the inactive condition. (n = 20) for all condition.
*Significantly different from inactive and control phone conditions (p < 0.05).

3.2 The Stroop Task

With the phone positioned at the right ear, an ANOVA comparing the three conditions, no phone (n = 20), inactive phone (n = 20) and active phone (n = 20) showed no effect of experimental condition for the reaction time value, F(2,57), p = 0.391, partial eta^2 = 0.032. With the phone positioned at the left ear, an ANOVA comparing the three conditions, no phone (n = 20), inactive phone (n = 20) and active phone (n = 20) also showed no effect of experimental condition for reaction time, F(2,57) = 0.560, p = 0.574, partial eta^2 = 0.19. These results are shown in Table 3.

Table 3. The mean and standard deviation for stroop reaction times in all phone conditions: control. inactive, active: exposure conditions for each side separately.

Side	Control	Inactive	Active	P
Right	M = 1.40 SD = 1.63	M = 1.74 SD = 2.58	M = 0.96 SD = 0.82	> .391
Left	M = 1.39 SD = 1.60	M = 1.74 SD = 2.51	M = 0.96 SD = 0.88	> .560

4 Discussion

The results in this study show a significant effect of RF EMF exposure from a mobile phone on cognitive performance in the change detection task but not in the Stroop task. Findings over the last 20 years on the effect of RF EMF exposure on cognitive performance have found variable effects. Evidence of the effects of RF EMFs on brain physiology from mobile phones have been observed in many visual tasks [4, 5] which is sometimes reflected in cognitive performance measures. Cognitive performance is a useful measure for discerning changes in human behavior, but RF EMF effects can be difficult to capture due to the sensitivity of RF EMF. The current evidence from previous studies is not conclusive; there are many inconsistencies. Furthermore, Zhang et al. [15] assessed the results of recent studies on neurocognitive functions [16, 17] and concluded that the effect of mobile phone RF EMF exposure on brain function and cognitive performance remain unanswered and essentially unaddressed. Curcio [18] has also commented on the heterogeneity of experimental evidence on the effect of exposure on neurocognitive function in attention tasks. The reasons for these inconsistencies are not fully understood and need further investigation. One problem that has pervaded empirical studies on the effects of RF EMFs is the lack of the ability to replicate data. If, however, the RF EMF effects are small, subtle and variable [19], results might be difficult if not impossible to replicate.

In the change detection task, a significant effect of RF EMF exposure was shown for experimental condition and hemisphere. Change accuracy performance improved in the active condition at the right ear by showing fewer errors in the task. A condition of change demands a higher cognitive load than no change. Previous findings with positive results suggest that significant effects of RF EMF on simple and choice reaction time depend on high cognitive load [19–22].

Eliyahu et al. [10] investigated possible differential effects of RF EMF on the right and left hemisphere and found that after 40 min exposure of the left side of the brain, responses were slowed down. Different tasks rely on different aspects of human information processing and region(s) of the brain to process task demands. It might be that RF EMF effects have different lateralized effect depending on the task. Further investigation of the lateralized effects of exposure is recommended for future studies with the addition of fMRI and/or PET scan analysis.

In the Stroop task, no significant effect of RF EMF exposure was found for experimental condition or hemisphere. Cinel et al. [8] and Thomas [23] also found no effect of exposure for the Stroop task. In contrast, however, Abramson et al. [24] found that the completion time for the incongruent condition of the Stroop task was longer for users showing high mobile phone exposure. This measurement was based on the number of voice calls made by participants. In addition, Deniz et al. [25] found a significant difference in effect in a high user phone exposure group in the Stroop test. It could be that the RF EMF effects of mobile phone exposure do not have immediate consequence, and that the effects of acute exposure have a delayed impact. This would mean that the effects might not be discernible in the current study, as measurements were only taken at the time of exposure. Regel et al. [22] recorded alpha activity in the n-back task and found that this increased 30 min after the end of RF EMF exposure. No effect was found immediately after or at 60 min after. Future studies could assess the impact of exposure at time intervals after the test, to see if delayed effects of exposure occur.

Further limitations in the current study include sample size (120), age and gender. There were six independent comparison groups with only 20 participants in each group and a 5:1 female to male ratio. This makes the possibility of a Type II error possible. Previous studies used a range of sample sizes from Vecchio et al. [5] with 11 participants and Preece et al. [21] with 18 participants through to Mortavazi et al. [4] with 120 and Russo et al. [11] with 168. To further develop this research, many experimental conditions can be improved through increasing sample, size, considering dosimetry measurements, control of the dose-response relationship, environmental conditions of use (temperature, noise, time of day), the differential effects between users brought about by the length of time the user has been using a mobile phone and which side of the head the user positions the phone for everyday use. In addition, temperature variations of the phone can be recorded with a double-blind experimental design.

5   Conclusion

In conclusion, the key contribution of this research is further knowledge about the effects of RF EMF on cognitive performance. The next steps are to experiment further to understand and clearly identify the reasons that contribute to an effect of RF EMF radiation from mobile phones as 5G becomes the dominant provider. This research is important because of the effect of the radiation emitted from 5G smart devices on the cognitive performance and health of mobile phone users. As 5G is rolled out, more users will be affected by possible radiation effects from using 5G phones.

The full implication of the effects of 5G on the health of users are unknown. Caution and health considerations are recommended for future use. This can include the use of headphones, short calls, and where possible, avoiding putting the phone next to the head and near the body.

References

1. Christopher, B., Mary, M., Khandaker, U., Bradley, D., Chew, D.A., Jojo, P.J.: Effects of mobile radiation on certain hematological parameter. Radiat. Phys. Chem. **166**, 108443–180447 (2020)
2. Revanath, M.P., Aparna, S., Madankumar, P.D.: Effects of mobile phone radiation on buccal mucosal cells: a systematic review. Electromagn. Biol. Med. **39**(4), 273–281 (2020)
3. Tohidi, F-Z, Sadr-Nabavi, A., Hagir, H., Fardid, R., Rafatpanah, H., Azimian, H., Bahreyni-Toossi, M.H.: Long-term exposure to electromagnetic radiation from mobile phones can cause considerable changes in the balance of Bax/Bcl2 mRNA expression in the hippocampus. Electromagn. Biol. Med. (2020)
4. Mortazavi, S.M.J., Rouintan, M.S., Taeb, S., Dehghan, N., Ghaffarpanah, A.A., Sadeghi, Z., Ghafouri, F.: Human short-term exposure to electromagnetic fields emitted by mobile phones decreases computer-assisted visual reaction time. Acta Neurologica Belgica **112**, 171–175 (2012). https://doi.org/10.1007/s13760-012-0044-y
5. Vecchio, F., Buffo, P., Sergio, S., Iacoviello, D., Rossini, P.M., Bablioni, C.: Mobile phone emission modulates event related desynchronization of alpha rhythms and cognitive-motor performance in healthy humans. Clin. Neurophysiol. **12**, 121–128 (2012)
6. Guxens, M., Vermeulen, R., van Eijsden, M., Beekhuizen. J., Vrijkotte, T.G.M., van Strien, R.T., Kromhout, H., Huss, A.: Outdoor and indoor sources of radiofrequency electromagnetic fields, personal cell phone and cordless mobile phone use, and cognitive functions in 5–6 years old children. Environ. Res. **150**, 364–374 (2016)
7. Keetley, V., Wood, A.W., Spong, J., Stough, C.K.K.: Neuropsychological sequelea of digital mobile phone exposure in humans. Neuropsycholgiae **44**, 1843–1848 (2006)
8. Cinel, C., Boldini, A., Fox, E., Russo, R.: Does the use of mobile phones affect human short-term memory or attention? Appl. Cogn. Psychol. **22**, 1113–1125 (2008)
9. Trunk, A., Stefanics, G., Zentai, N., Bacskay, I., Felinger, A., Thuroczy, G., Hernadi, I.: Lack of interaction between concurrent caffeine and mobile phone exposure on visual target detection: an ERP study. Pharmacol. Biochem. Behav. **124**, 412–420 (2014)
10. Eliyahu, I., Luria, R., Hareveny, R., Margaliot, M., Nachshon, M., Gad, S.: Effects of radiofrequency radiation emitted by cellular telephones on the cognitive functions of humans. Bioelectromagnetics **27**, 119–216 (2006)
11. Russo, R., Fox, E., Boldini, A., Defeyeter, M.A., Mirhikar-Syahkai, D., Mehta, A.: Does acute exposure to mobile phones affect human attention? Bioelectomagnetics **27**(3), 215–220 (2006). https://doi.org/10.1002/bem.20193
12. Luck, S.J., Vogel, E.K.: The capacity of visual working memory for features and conjunctions. Nature **390**, 279–281 (1997)
13. Beck, D.M., Rees, G., Frith, C.D., Lavie, N.: Neural correlates of change detection and change blindness. Nat. Neurosci. **4**, 645–650 (2001)
14. Alvarez, J.A., Emory, E.: Executive function and the frontal lobes: a meta-analytic review. Neuropsychol. Rev. **16**(1), 17–42 (2006)
15. Zhang, J., Sumich, A., Wang, G.: Acute effects of radio frequency electromagnetic fields emitted by mobile phone on brain function. Bioelectromagnetics **38**(5), 329–338 (2017)

16. Lv, B., Chen, Z., Wu, T., Shao, Q., Yan, D., Ma, L., Lu, K., Xie, Y.: The alteration of spontaneous low frequency oscillations caused by electromagnetic fields exposure. Clin. Neurophysiol. **125**, 277–286 (2014)

17. Goshn, R., Yahia-Cherif, L., Hugueville, L., Ducorps, A., Lemarechal, J.-D., Thuroczy, G., de Seze, R., Selmaoui, B.: Radio-frequency signal affects alpha band in resting electroencephalogram. J. Neurophysiol. **113**, 2753–2759 (2015)

18. Curcio, G.: Exposure to mobile phone-emitted electromagnetic fields and human attention: no evidence of a causal relationship. J. Microsc. Ultrastruct. **5**(4), 191–197 (2018)

19. Krause, C.M., Pesonen, M., Haraala, C., Hamalainen, H.: Effects of pulsed and continuous wave 902 MHz mobile phone exposure on brain oscillatory activity during cognitive processing. Bioelectromagnetics **28**, 296–308 (2007)

20. Koivisto, M., Krause, C., Revonsuo, A., Laine, M., Hamailainen, H.: (2000) The Effects of electromagnetic field emitted by GSM phones on working memory. Neuroreport **11**, 1641–1643 (2000)

21. Preece, A.W., Goodfellow, S., Wright, M.G., Butler, S.R., Dunn, E.J., Johnson, Y., Manktelow, T.C., Wesnes, K.: Effect of 902 MHz mobile phone transmission on cognitive function in children. Bioelectromagnetics **26**(Supplement 7), S138–S143 (2005)

22. Regel, S.J., Gottselig, M., Schuderer, J., Tinguely, G., Retey, J.V., Kuster, N., Landolt, H.-P., Achermann, P.: Pulsed radio frequency radiation affects cognitive pergformance and the waking electroencephalogram. Neuroreport **18**(8), 803–807 (2007)

23. Thomas, S., Benke, G., Dimitriadis, C., Inyang, I., Sim, M.R., Wolfe, R., Croft, R.J., Abramson, M.J.: Use of mobile phones and changes in cognitive function in adolescents. Occup. Environ. Med. **67**(12), 861–866 (2010)

24. Abramson, M.J., Benke, G.P., Dimitiadis, C., Inyang, I.O., Sim, M.R., Wolfe, R.S., Croft, R.J.: Mobile telephone use is associated with changes in cognitive functions in young adolescents. Bioelectromagnetics **30**, 678–686 (2009)

25. Deniz, O.G., Kaplan, S., Selkcuk, M.B., Terzi, M., Altun, G., Yurt, K.K., Aslan, K., Davis, D.: Effects of short and long-term electromagnetic fields exposure on the human hippocampus. J. Micros. Ultrastruct. **5**(4), 191–197 (2017)

Compensation Strategies Among Drop Foot Patients and the Effect of Ankle-Foot Orthosis on Gait Symmetry

Albert Qianyi Fu$^{(\boxtimes)}$ (ID), Albert J. Shih (ID), and Thomas J. Armstrong (ID)

University of Michigan, Ann Arbor, MI 48109, USA
qifu@umich.edu

Abstract. This work aims to investigate how different compensation strategies among drop foot patients affect the treatment performance of ankle-foot ortho-sis (AFO) regarding the symmetry of step length and swing time. Based on the literature review, two compensation strategies for the drop foot syndrome were identified during the swing phase: 1) excessive knee and hip flexion and 2) cir-cumduction of the leg. One drop foot patient of each compensation strategy was selected in this study to investigate the different effects of AFOs. Results showed that AFO could benefit patients who utilize excessive circumduction to compensate regarding the symmetry of step length and swing time.

Keywords: Drop foot · Ankle-foot orthosis (AFO) · Compensation strategy · Gait symmetry

1 Introduction

Drop foot affects about 80% of multiple sclerosis (MS) population experience gait prob-lems (Bulley et al. 2015; Pittock et al. 2004) and 20% of the stroke population during their rehabilitation (Benjamin et al. 2017; Wolf et al. 2008). Investigators (Don et al. 2007) demonstrated that drop foot patients used two compensatory strategies, increas-ing the hip abduction or knee flexion angle on the impaired side during the swing phase (SW), to avoid stubbing their toes. Passive-dynamic Ankle-foot orthosis (AFO) has been used to promote medial-lateral stability, correct gait abnormality, and improve gait quality of drop foot patients (Bregman et al. 2012; Novacheck et al. 2007). However, AFO's effect on gait was not detail investigated among different walking preferences and compensation strategies.

To evaluate pathological gait and the gait improvement made by AFOs, several quality metrics were developed. Gait symmetry index (SI), or Robinson Index (Robinson et al. 1987), was proposed to evaluate the quality of the patient's gait (Hendrickson et al. 2014; Patterson et al. 2010; Roerdink and Beek 2011):

$$SI = 2 \frac{X_R - X_L}{X_R + X_L} \times 100\% \tag{1}$$

© The Author(s), under exclusive license to Springer Nature Switzerland AG 2021
N. L. Black et al. (Eds.): IEA 2021, LNNS 222, pp. 309–313, 2021.
https://doi.org/10.1007/978-3-030-74611-7_42

where X_R is the gait parameter on the right side, and X_L is the gait parameter on the left side. Examples of X include the step length and swing time.

The goal of this work is to investigate the improvements in the symmetry of step length and swing time made by AFOs on patients with different compensation strategies.

2 Methods

Two drop foot patients (left ankle impaired due to spastic hemiparesis) with different gender and compensation strategies (Subject 1: male, excessive flexion; Subject 2: female, circumduction) were selected to measure their walking gait with and without AFOs. Each subject was prescribed with medium-(AFO1, 3.6 Nm/deg) and high-stiffness (AFO2, 4.5 Nm/deg) AFOs. The goal, experimental procedure, and possible risks were explained to the subjects before participation. Each subject signed the informed consent form approved by the Institutional Review Boards of the University of Michigan (HUM00090458).

A five-IMU system, LEGSysTM (BioSensics LLC, Newton, MA, USA), was used to measure thigh and shank movements at a 100 Hz sampling rate and calculate step length, knee flexion, and hip abduction.

Each subject was asked to perform level ground walking without AFO (NAFO), with AFO1, and with AFO2 on his/her impaired (left) ankle. For each trial, the subject was asked to walk for 6 eight-meter trips with comfortable self-selected speed. The symmetry of step length and swing time was calculated based on the left and right step lengths and swing time, respectively.

3 Results

The measured knee flexion and hip abduction of both subjects under three conditions are summarized in Table 1. It was found that Subject 1 tended to utilize excessive flexion to compensate for his impairment, while Subject 2 tended to utilize circumduction.

Table 1. The summary statistics of knee flexion and hip abduction of both subjects under three conditions.

Subject	1			2		
Condition	NAFO	AFO1	AFO2	NAFO	AFO1	AFO2
Knee flexion	66 ± 3	63 ± 3	61 ± 2	53 ± 7	60 ± 4	60 ± 5
Hip abduction	7 ± 3	5 ± 4	5 ± 4	15 ± 8	10 ± 2	12 ± 3

As shown in Fig. 1(a), Subject 1 (male, utilizing excessive flexion) had longer step lengths on his impaired side while Subject 2 (female, utilizing circumduction) had longer step lengths on her unimpaired side. The AFOs increased both subjects' impaired-side step lengths and decreased their unimpaired-side step lengths. As shown in Fig. 1(b), the symmetry of step length was improved by wearing AFOs for Subject 2 but worsen by wearing AFOs for Subject 1. On the other hand, the symmetry of swing time was improved by wearing AFOs for both subjects (Fig. 2).

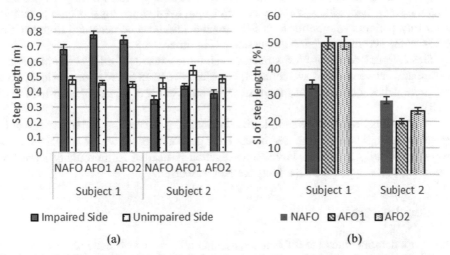

(a)   (b)

Fig. 1. (a) The observed step length of the impaired and unimpaired sides for both subjects, and (b) the calculated SI of step length for both subjects under three conditions.

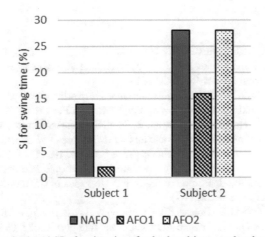

Fig. 2. The calculated SI of swing time for both subjects under three conditions.

4 Discussion

The results suggested that patients with different compensation strategies may receive different benefits. Patients who prefer to utilize excessive flexion may be benefited from wearing AFOs on the symmetry of swing time, but sacrifice some symmetry of step length. Because of more knee and hip flexion, the heel strike occurred later and further away from the stance leg, which led to longer step lengths of the impaired side. While the AFO shortening the unimpaired-side step length by constrain the impaired-side ankle and lengthening the impaired-side step length by releasing energy during the push-off. Thus the AFO makes the symmetry of step length even worse for this type of patient. Contrarily, patients who prefer to utilize circumduction can be benefited from wearing AFOs on the symmetry of step length and swing time.

The different compensation strategies can be the result of differences in walking preferences between males and females. Females have been found to have wider pelves and more pelvic obliquity ranges during walking (Smith et al. 2002; Stansfield et al. 2018).

This work is limited to its sample size. Variabilities in walking preference and compensation strategies may be caused by different gender, age, stature, body weight, background, and daily activities. Future investigation is needed to thoroughly learn how individual walking preference affects the AFO effect.

5 Conclusions

This work demonstrates the differences in AFO effects on two patients with different compensation strategies. The results showed that AFO could benefit patients who prefer to utilize circumduction to compensate based on the symmetry of step length.

References

Benjamin, E.J., Blaha, M.J., Chiuve, S.E., Cushman, M., Das, S.R., Deo, R., De Ferranti, S.D., et al.: Heart disease and stroke statistics' 2017 update: A report from the American heart association. Circulation **135**, e146–e603 (2017)

Bregman, D.J.J., Harlaar, J., Meskers, C.G.M., de Groot, V.: Spring-like ankle foot orthoses reduce the energy cost of walking by taking over ankle work. Gait Posture (2012)

Bulley, C., Mercer, T.H., Hooper, J.E., Cowan, P., Scott, S., Van Der Linden, M.L.: Experiences of functional electrical stimulation (FES) and ankle foot orthoses (AFOs) for foot-drop in people with multiple sclerosis. Disabil. Rehabil. Assistive Technol. **10**, 458–467 (2015)

Don, R., Serrao, M., Vinci, P., Ranavolo, A., Cacchio, A., Ioppolo, F., Paoloni, M., et al.: Foot drop and plantar flexion failure determine different gait strategies in Charcot-Marie-tooth patients. Clin. Biomech. **22**(8), 905–916(2007)

Hendrickson, J., Patterson, K.K., Inness, E.L., McIlroy, W.E., Mansfield, A.: Relationship between asymmetry of quiet standing balance control and walking post-stroke. Gait Posture (2014)

Novacheck, T.F., Beattie, C., Rozumalski, A., Gent, G., Kroll, G.: Quantifying the spring-like properties of ankle-foot orthoses (AFOs). J. Prosthet. Orthot. (2007)

Patterson, K.K., Gage, W.H., Brooks, D., Black, S.E., McIlroy, W.E.: Evaluation of gait symmetry after stroke: a comparison of current methods and recommendations for standardization. Gait Posture (2010)

Pittock, S.J., Mayr, W.T., McClelland, R.L., Jorgensen, N.W., Weigand, S.D., Noseworthy, J.H., Weinshenker, B.G., et al.: Change in MS-related disability in a population-based cohort: a 10-year follow-up study. Neurology **62**, 51–59 (2004)

Robinson, R.O., Herzog, W., Nigg, B.M.: Usc of force platform variables to quantify the effects of chiropractic manipulation on gait symmetry. J. Manipulative Physiol. Ther. **10**, 172–176 (1987)

Roerdink, M., Beek, P.J.: Understanding inconsistent step-length asymmetries across hemiplegic stroke patients: Impairments and compensatory gait. Neurorehabil. Neural Repair **25**, 253–258 (2011)

Smith, L.K., Lelas, J.L., Kerrigan, D.C.: Gender differences in pelvic motions and center of mass displacement during walking: stereotypes quantified. J. Women's Health **11**, 453–458 (2002)

Stansfield, B., Hawkins, K., Adams, S., Bhatt, H.: A mixed linear modelling characterisation of gender and speed related changes in spatiotemporal and kinematic characteristics of gait across a wide speed range in healthy adults. Med. Eng. Phys. **60**, 94–102 (2018)

Wolf, S.I., Alimusaj, M., Rettig, O., Döderlein, L.: Dynamic assist by carbon fiber spring AFOs for patients with myelomeningocele. Gait Posture (2008)

Mitigation of Risk of Patient Handling During Rehabilitation Tasks

Melanie Gee[(⊠)] and Remi Adejumo

Fraser Health Authority, Surrey, BC, Canada
melanie.gee@fraserhealth.ca

Abstract. There are a variety of risks associated with providing care in healthcare; some are associated with tasks and some are related to the environment. Rehabilitation staff are exposed to high risk patient handling tasks for longer durations when motivating patients through exercises to reach their mobility goals [1]. Meeting these rehabilitation goals while following Fraser Health (FH) safe patient handling policies can be challenging. Mechanical assistive devices can help mitigate risks while offering promising outcomes for patient rehabilitation.

We explored how to effectively mitigate the risk of musculoskeletal injury (MSI) due to excessive force and awkward posture of rehabilitation staff during patient rehabilitation activities.

The ergonomics team assessed and determined an X-Y ceiling mounted lift with motor locking mechanisms was the most appropriate mechanical assistive device for an in-patient rehabilitation setting based on the identified risk of injury to the rehabilitation team.

This equipment was installed and significantly reduced the exposure risk of MSI from excessive forces and awkward posture during rehabilitation activities. Concurrently, patients met their functional goals, resulting in faster recovery and discharge out of hospital.

Rehabilitation staff reported numerous positive patient outcomes that may not have been achievable without this equipment. Other benefits reported were related to faster patient recovery times improving patient flow.

Rehabilitation staff reported that the X-Y ceiling mounted lifts with motor locking mechanisms are useful tools for tasks like standing tolerance, endurance and gait training. With this equipment, patients and rehabilitation staff can safely achieve their goals while working within FH policies.

Keywords: Ceiling mounted lift · Ceiling lift · Safe patient handling · Rehabilitation · Early mobilization

1   Introduction

Rehabilitation services promote safe and successful early discharge from the hospital. A successful discharge is one in which the patient's functional and discharge goals are reached. To meet these goals, rehabilitation staff use safe patient handling equipment for activities designed to improve patient abilities with activities of daily living such

© The Author(s), under exclusive license to Springer Nature Switzerland AG 2021
N. L. Black et al. (Eds.): IEA 2021, LNNS 222, pp. 314–321, 2021.
https://doi.org/10.1007/978-3-030-74611-7_43

as transfers, gait, standing balance, weight bearing, and posture, as well as functional activities such as toileting, dressing and bathing [2]. These activities are longer in duration when compared to other patient handling tasks like transfers and bed repositioning which increases rehabilitation staff risk of injury [1]. Mechanical patient handling assistive devices, like ceiling lifts with motor locking mechanisms, substantially reduce the risk of excessive force and awkward postures by providing support and stabilizing the patient while the motor is locked in place on the gantry and the length of the sling strap is taut. As a result of the reduced physical demand when using mechanical patient handling assistive devices, rehabilitation staff report experiencing less fatigue and pain and the ability to accomplish more in therapy sessions [2].

2 Problem

Lifetime incidence of work related musculoskeletal disorders for rehabilitation staff is estimated to be 91% [3]. Rehabilitation staff are often at increased risk of developing injuries due to the range of patients they treat with varying degrees of functional impairment and medical acuity who benefit from early mobilization, such as those recovering from orthopedic or cardiac surgery or neurological events like strokes, all of whom tend to be more dependent for mobility. Other patients may have a Body Mass Index above 30 in addition to their medical condition, requiring even more assistance to mobilize.

Rehabilitation goals include safe early mobilization as it is well documented that hospitalization and the associated deconditioning due to inactivity is linked with functional decline [4]. Loss of muscle mass and strength is a consequence of immobilization, with the majority lost in muscles that maintain posture, aid in transfer and ambulation [5]. Performing rehabilitation activities frequently requires more than minimal assistance, putting significant force and postural stress on workers bodies [6].

This project explored how patient handling equipment can mitigate awkward postures, repetitive motions, and heavy lifting experienced by rehabilitation staff during the performance of rehabilitation activities in an acute care hospital facility.

3 Actions

Rehabilitation staff approached the ergonomics team to discuss the possibility of installing a ceiling mounted lift in the dedicated rehabilitation area on their medical unit. This request was seen as positive as it would increase the options for rehabilitation staff to provide safe, quality care, and, as has been reported in the literature, allow for the ability to mobilize patients earlier thus increasing patients' participation and activity [7].

A review of the area indicated rehabilitation staff mainly utilized the space for ambulating patients between parallel bars, assisted walking and standing training. Interviews were conducted with rehabilitation staff and they reported struggling with mobilizing very dependent patients recovering from neurological medical conditions such as a stroke, without sitting or standing balance. In line with current Fraser Health (FH) Clinical Practice Guidelines and WorkSafeBC Guideline for Minimizing the Risk of MSI when moving a physically–dependent person [8], these patients were assessed as being unsafe to mobilize without mechanical assistive devices, as they required more than minimal assistance.

The ceiling lift vendors were contacted to determine equipment options to best mitigate the specific risks related to anterior, posterior and lateral swaying of the ceiling lift motor that they experienced while performing rehabilitation activities with the ceiling lifts in traditional patient rooms. The equipment options were reviewed with rehabilitation staff and it was determined that an X-Y ceiling mounted gantry with a safe working load of at least 454 kg/1000lbs with motor locking mechanisms was recommended. This would provide more flexibility for use than a straight track as the motor moves along the boom and the boom moves along the rails. The motor can manually be utilized anywhere within the X-Y gantry. Portable mechanical equipment was not recommended as they fail to adequately protect workers from recommended exposure limits for push/pull forces [9] and require more space to maneuver. Further consultation with the equipment vendors was required to confirm that the environment (e.g. sufficient space, ceiling height, etc.) would support an installation and to provide cost information. Structural integrity of the space was also checked to ensure the equipment could be installed to accommodate all patient weights.

Department funding was requested and secured based on the requirements of the FH Safe Client Handling policy. The established FH Ergonomics Ceiling Lift Installation procedure was followed which involves coordinating all of the stakeholders: the equipment vendor, facilities maintenance & operations, infection control, rehabilitation staff, department manager and housekeeping to safely close the area for construction to install the equipment.

3.1 Patient Handling Equipment

A standard ceiling mounted lift system has a motor with a sling bar strap, carry bar and handset which controls the sling bar strap length. This motor moves along tracks that are mounted to the ceiling (e.g. Fig. 1a). For this particular installation of a ceiling lift system with locking mechanism, two stationary rails were mounted to the ceiling with a perpendicular boom that can move along the rails creating an X-Y gantry. The motor moves along the boom and the boom moves along the rails. The motor can manually be maneuvered anywhere within the X-Y gantry (e.g. Fig. 1b). The motor is composed of a sling bar strap with a 2-point carry bar attached.

Motor locking mechanisms are electronic locks installed on the rails and boom (e.g. Fig. 1c). They are controlled with a separate handset and provide you with the ability to lock the position of the boom and/or motor within the X-Y gantry. In this case, motor locking mechanisms provide the rehabilitation staff the ability to restrict the movement of the overhead equipment providing them more control over the patient's position during activities. For example:

- When the motor locks on the rails are engaged, the boom is stationary and the motor can traverse along the boom.
- When the motor lock on the boom is applied, the motor cannot move and the boom can traverse along the rails.
- When all three motor locks are on, the motor and boom position are locked in place.

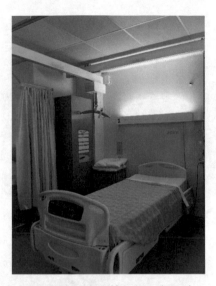

Fig. 1a. Standard ceiling lift system in patient room

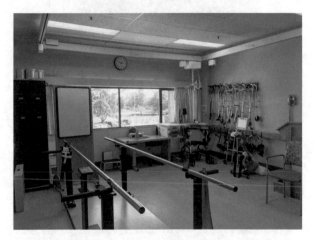

Fig. 1b. X-Y gantry ceiling lift over parallel bars

Slings are applied to patients and then attached to the carry bar on the ceiling lift motor. Specifically, for this case, walking slings are used to provide support to the patient's torso with straps that attach to the carry bar. With the handset, rehabilitation staff adjust the carry bar sling strap length so it is taut and the patient is safely supported in an upright position, with both feet making full contact with the floor (e.g. Fig. 2).

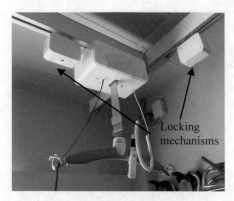

Fig. 1c. Ceiling lift motor with motor locking mechanisms

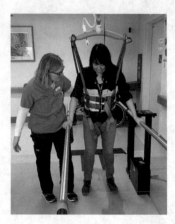

Fig. 2. Rehabilitation staff member with subject wearing a walking sling

4 Outcomes

Rehabilitation staff were surveyed post installation and reported the ability to use the equipment with neurological, orthopedic patients and those with increased body mass index for sit to stand practice, mobilization between parallel bars and with a platform walker. The motor locking mechanisms eliminated the swaying motion and patients could now perform these activities in a stable, upright position. Rehabilitation staff no longer had to spend time finding additional staff for manually supporting patients during these activities. Indications were that workload and risk of injury was decreased as they no longer had to manually support their patients, fatigue was eliminated as a limiting factor for treatment and patients were able to work to their potential, aligning with outcomes in the literature [7]. The ceiling lifts with motor locks allowed rehabilitation staff to use their hands for therapeutic touch, tactile cues, or other manual treatment techniques rather than struggling to hold the patient's body weight during treatments, another benefit of this technology [9]. Rehabilitation staff are also able to focus on patient facial expressions, watch for visual cues of fatigue and pain and remain in constant communication with their patient.

Patients experience the benefits of safe early mobilization and achieve their highest level or pre-disability function, primarily walking with an aid, which is a major determinant of whether an individual returns home following a stroke and has long lasting implications for the person's quality of life and ability to participate in activities of daily living [10]. An additional significant benefit was that patients had a private space that was clear of clutter for rehabilitation activities, as previously; they were utilizing ceiling lifts without motor locks, for therapy, in four bed rooms with limited space for a platform walker and other equipment, as well as minimal privacy.

Management, nursing staff and rehabilitation staff report that patients are able to meet their progressive functional goal in a timely manner and meet the admission requirements for specialized rehabilitation facilities and discharge out of the hospital sooner, improving patient flow.

5 Discussion

This installation provides an opportunity to evaluate staff and patient experiences, use information/data gathered to advocate for similar equipment in rehabilitation areas and shape the design of our future facilities.

Patients reported to rehabilitation staff that they no longer experienced fear nor felt unstable when using the standard ceiling lift to be raised up to an upright posture, as they no longer had to oppose the forces from the motor swaying within the gantry creating an unnatural motion. Having the ability to lock the ceiling lift motor in place on the gantry and adjusting the tension of the ceiling lift strap so the patient is secure, built trust and allowed the patient to fully engage in the rehabilitation training activities without worrying about falling or hurting rehabilitation staff. One physiotherapist explained that the design of the equipment centres the patient's weight naturally within their base of support while in a standing anti-gravity posture. Patients would arrive ready, motivated and smiled during treatment as they experienced progress in their abilities. To manage any patient anxieties, rehabilitation staff donned the sling to demonstrate to patients how the sling fits and how the equipment works. Family members were also welcome in the rehabilitation area to observe and provide support.

Providing this type of therapy takes substantial time for set up and execution of the therapy but rehabilitation staff reported that the benefits of patient and staff safety and achieving patient goals outweighed this cost. They also reported the sling was easy to apply and the equipment was easy to use. Negative feedback was only heard about the handset. Rehabilitation staff felt it could use some improvements on usability, as the symbols were not intuitive.

An unanticipated benefit for nursing was they could perform their nursing duties in spaces free of cluttered rehabilitation equipment like platform walkers in the four bed patient rooms.

Many of the successes of this project can be attributed to the teamwork and collaboration between the care staff, managers and the ergonomics team. Using a systems approach and allowing for stakeholder input at project outset, as well as feedback as the project progressed led to the desired outcome of optimization of the health and well-being of the rehabilitation staff by mitigating their risk of injury due to patient handling during rehabilitation activities.

The ergonomics team future plans include exploring other uses for ceiling lifts and motor locking mechanisms in rehabilitation. For example, this equipment can be used over plinths and beds for overhead exercises with bands, and other activities performed in a supine position. Rehabilitation staff plan to continue utilizing the equipment with any patient deemed appropriate, such as patients who have been diagnosed with Parkinson's disease, multiple sclerosis, acquired brain injury, etc. We will also disseminate our findings throughout FH rehabilitation teams. Developing good relationships with equipment vendors to keep well informed of new equipment developments, communicate clinical needs and engage with to improve future safe patient handling equipment design is a key consideration in the mitigation of risk of injury during patient handling.

5.1 Limitations

The ceiling lift with locking mechanism is a first for FH. It was installed on a 43 bed medical unit at a community hospital that provides primary, secondary and some specialty services such as emergency, surgical, inpatient and outpatient care. Due to the size and type of facility, the rehabilitation team is small therefore, we were limited in the number of rehabilitation staff who we were able to collect feedback from regarding use of the ceiling lift and locking mechanisms. This was intended to be a pilot project to evaluate the benefits of the equipment to support recommendations for replication throughout FH in similar areas. Further exploration is required to determine the impact this type of equipment has on work flow and patient rehabilitation outcomes.

6 Conclusion

This case study shows that ceiling lifts with motor locking mechanism is a promising practice for the rehabilitation environment. This system has the ability to positively affect multiple stakeholders; it can help achieve FH goals of timely discharge, rehabilitation team goals of safe early mobilization and patient goals of regaining a level of independence. For example, rehabilitation staff say "The current ceiling lift has enabled us as a team to make rehab and functional goals easier and refer patients to (high intensity) rehab earlier"; "This present model of ceiling lift with positioning lock allows patients to benefit from early mobilization and early rehab". Leadership support for funding and engagement for ongoing utilization of the system are essential. Additionally, understanding the specific challenges that need to be addressed from the clinical perspective as well as the specifications of ceiling lift installation to ensure that the installation meets the identified challenges are crucial for the success of this intervention.

References

1. Physiotherapy Association of British Columbia: Safe Patient Handling Physiotherapist Awareness Campaign (Alert 2 of 4) [Brochure]. Vancouver, BC: Author (n.d.).

2. Harwood, K.J., Darragh, A.R., Campo, M., Rockefeller, K., Scalzitti, D.: A systematic review of safe patient handling and mobility programs to prevent musculoskeletal injuries in occupational and physical therapists and assistants. Int. J. Safe Patient Handling Mobility (SPHM) **8**(1), 46–56 (2018)

3. Perlow, E., Tunney, N., Lucado, A.: Integrating safe patient handling into physical therapist education: reducing the incidence of physical therapist injury and improving patient outcomes. J. Phys. Ther. Educ. **30**(2), 32–37 (2016)

4. Wood, W., Tschannen, D., Trotsky, A., Grunawalt, J., Adams, D., Chang, R., Kendziora, S., Diccion-MacDonald, S.: A mobility program for an inpatient acute care medical unit. Am. J. Nurs. **114**(10), 34–40 (2014)

5. Ball Saunders, C.: Preventing secondary complications in trauma patients with implementation of a multidisciplinary mobilization team. J. Trauma Nurs. **22**(3), 170–175 (2015)

6. WorkSafeBC: MSI risk assessment and control for client handling. (2017). https://www.worksafebc.com/en/resources/health-safety/books-guides/msi-risk-assessment-control-client-handling?lang=en. Accessed 21 Sep 2020

7. Darragh, A.R., Campo, M.A., Frost, L., Miller, M., Pentico, M., Margulis, H.: Safe-patient-handling equipment in therapy practice: Implications for rehabilitation. Am. J. Occup. Ther. **67**(1), 45–53 (2013)

8. WorkSafeBC: Guidelines – Part 4 – Ergonomics (MSI) Requirements, Section G4.50–2 Minimizing the risk of MSI when moving a physically-dependent person. https://www.worksafebc.com/en/law-policy/occupational-health-safety/searchable-ohs-regulation/ohs-guidelines/guidelines-part-04?origin=s&returnurl=https%3A%2F%2Fwww.worksafebc.com%2Fen%2Fsearch%23q%3DMSI%2520ERGONOMICS%2520REQUIREMENTS%26sort%3Drelevancy%26f%3Alanguage-facet%3D%5BEnglish%5D#C9340ACF01684B669D80EC14E43ACB8C. Accessed 22 Jan 2021

9. Latvala, S.M., Masterman, R.: The evolution of the ceiling lift: A glimpse at how a single device has redefined caregiver safety and patient care. Int. J. Safe Patient Handling Mob. (SPHM) **10**(3), 91–97 (2020)

10. Ada, L., Dean, C.M., Vargas, J., Ennis, S.: Mechanically assisted walking with body weight support results in more independent walking than assisted over ground walking in non-ambulatory patients early after stroke: a systematic review. J. Physiotherapy (Australian Physiotherapy Association) **56**(3), 153–161 (2010)

Home Care Support for Older Adults in England: Perceptions of Quality and Safety Standards

Jan Healey(✉) 🆔, Sue Hignett 🆔, and Diane Gyi 🆔

Loughborough University, Loughborough, Leicestershire L11 3TU, UK
J.healey2@lboro.ac.uk

Abstract. Occupational Therapists (OTs), Social Work Managers and practitioners perceptions of the safety risks and quality standards in home care services (packages) that are funded by adult social care for older adults were explored in a descriptive, qualitative study using semi structured interviews and application of the CARE model (Concepts of Applying Resilience Engineering). Time pressures, skills and knowledge deficits and client dependency emerged as key themes impacting the delivery of safe, high quality care for older adults living at home. The next step is to investigate 'a day in the life of a Home care worker' and explore the views of independent care providers to develop an understanding of how the design of home care packages can be improved to promote safer and higher quality standards of care delivery.

Keywords: Home care safety and quality · Resilient home care · Healthcare ergonomics · Adult social care

1 Introduction

As the older population increases there will be more demand on home care to support over 65 + years population living with health conditions that affect their ability to complete basic activities of daily living (ADLs) independently [1].

Home care services (packages) that are commissioned by local authorities for older adults (clients) in England are predominantly provided by independent care agencies [2]. The home care service provider supports the client to remain living at home with the care package typically including assistance up to four times daily at key times of the day (breakfast/lunch/tea/bed) depending on the level of assessed need [3]. Home care workers (HCWs) support clients with ADLs such as personal care, moving around and nutrition [4].

In the UK the home care sector faces significant challenges as demand outstrips supply due in part to the mismatch between rising life expectancy and falling birth rates [5] and the constant pressures independent care providers experience due to the high workforce turnover amongst HCWs [4]. During 2018/19 the HCW turnover rate was 43.7% within the independent home care sector [6] and in 2018/19 the sector was estimated to have vacancy rates of 10% at any one time [6].

© The Author(s), under exclusive license to Springer Nature Switzerland AG 2021
N. L. Black et al. (Eds.): IEA 2021, LNNS 222, pp. 322–327, 2021.
https://doi.org/10.1007/978-3-030-74611-7_44

1.1 Home Care Support – the Role of HCWs

The services HCWs provide is based on a care plan by the commissioning Local Authority [7] specifying the activities the client needs assistance with, how these will be met, time of day and length of the care call [8]. The HCW, a non-professionally registered role [9], may use technology/equipment to assist with care and mobility needs, problem solve, recognize and respond to client variability including health deterioration, manage behaviors that challenge, the safe delivery of care or compromise the client's health, working alone or as part of a team (double handed care) [10]. Task shifting from registered health professionals (e.g. District Nurses) includes monitoring skin integrity, preparing food according to health professional guidance for example the client with swallowing difficulties, management of percutaneous endoscopic gastrostomy (PEG) feeds, urinary catheter care [11]. The HCW role also requires time management skills, communication skills with client, family, colleagues, health and social care professionals and documentation skills for maintaining care records [12].

2   Aims

The aim of this study was to capture the effect that challenges and the design of home care support services in England [13] imposes on standards of care for older adults by exploring the views and perspectives of adult social care practitioners.

Occupational Therapists (OTs) and Social Work Practitioners, the two professions who conduct assessment of needs for older adults [7], routinely collaborate with independent care providers throughout the care needs assessment process.

3   Methods

Semi structured interviews were conducted with OTs and Social Work Practitioners n = 10). The participants had 1–40 years working experience in adult social care (mean 22). They were recruited from County, Metropolitan and London Borough local authorities in England (Table 1).

Table 1. Participant characteristics

Participants	Number	Local authority type London county metropolitan		
OT Manager	4	3	1	
OT Practitioner	3	2		1
ASC Service Lead	1	1		
ASC Moving & Handling Manager	1			1
Social Care Assessor	1	1		

The CARE model (Concepts for Applying Resilience Engineering) [14] was selected to explore misalignments between work-as-imagined (WAI) and work-as-done (WAD). WAI is defined by the interplay between system demands and capacities and the misalignments between the two are the adaptations HCWs make to reconcile WAI mismatches (WAD) [15].

4   Results and Discussion

The interviews were transcribed and analyzed thematically using NVIVO 12 and the Quality improvement (QI) theory CARE. Figure 1a shows the demands and capacities (WAI) characteristic of prescribed or implied tasks [16] in home care commissioned by social care as perceived by adult social care practitioners and Table 2 presents results showing the adjustments HCWs make (WAD), according to social care practitioners, in response to WAI mismatches.

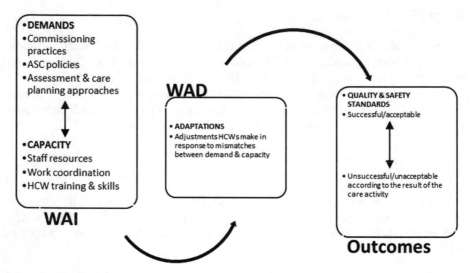

Fig. 1a. WAI misalignments in home care in England (Adapted from Anderson et al., 2020)

System demands were home care commissioning practices, adult social care policies, care support plans prescribed by local authorities and capacities related to home care providers organizational and operations processes [16] specifically staff resources, work coordination processes and HCW job design eg training, skills.

Three key themes emerged relating to adjustments HCWs make as a consequence of misalignments between demands and capacity (WAI) (Table 2);

- Time
- Skills and knowledge deficits
- Client dependency

Table 2. Summary of findings – Home Care for Older Adults

Themes WAI Misalignments	Themes HCW Adaptations
Demands	**Time adjustments**
Commissioning pricing strategy	Rushing care calls
Length of care calls inadequate	Cutting scheduled care times
Value for money	Using equipment instead of client participation
Capacity	Reducing/omitting client functional participation
Workforce turnover	**Skills & knowledge**
Back-to-back care calls	Management of complex clients
Care call cramming	Moving & handling safety
Zero hours contracts	Equipment operation/use
Inexperienced HCWs	**Client dependency**
Fragmented time	Training/skills & knowledge
Low pay	Workload demands
	Time deficits

Low pay, workload demands including high workload schedules, complexity of client and the physicality of the job were cited as influencing workforce turnover by all participants (Fig. 1b). The lack of professional status in the context of responsibility of the HCW role was also perceived by managers from both professions as a reason for workforce turnover rates.

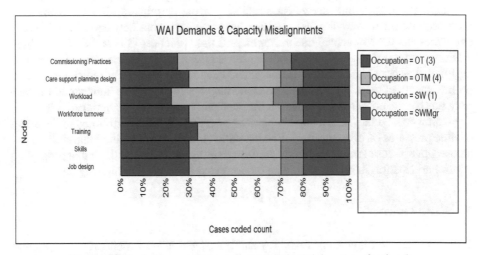

Fig.1b. WAI misalignments according to adult social care professionals

Time pressures were the most frequently cited problem by both professional groups (Fig. 1c). Care call cramming, back-to-back care calls and unpaid travel time were misalignments which participants attributed to commissioning practices. There was a general view that as payments were low and limited to client contact time many independent care providers were not able to pay for HCWs travel time. Inadequate time allocated to care calls was associated with the lack of understanding of client complexity by prescribers eg commissioners, social care practitioners, and a need to ensure value for money by the commissioning local authority. Clawing time back from care calls was considered a common deviation from prescribed tasks practiced by HCWs and was linked to quality and safety standards [16].

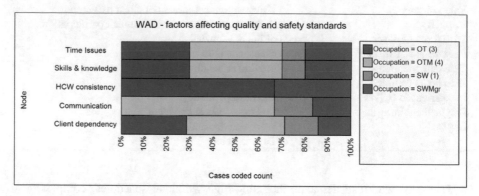

Fig.1c. WAD themes according to adult social care professionals

Skills and knowledge deficits were associated with deviations from the task prescribed due to time pressures and were linked with quality and safety standards by most participants. Quality and safety issues included errors culminating in unsafe practices using equipment for moving and handling clients, mismatches between scheduled care call times and time of arrival due to fragmented time practices [17] and HCWs rushing ADLs to recover time. Knowledge of health conditions, and effect on client's functional abilities, was considered to be lacking and OT managers especially felt this impacted on the quality of care. If prescribed tasks are not clearly defined or understood the task may not be carried out as implied resulting in quality and safety deviations.

Client dependency was a key factor cited by OTs which they attributed to the effect of time pressures on client participation in relation to maintaining functional skills. They also expressed concern about the standards of training for HCWs and felt that promoting client participation in ADLs should be incorporated in HCW training (Fig. 1c).

5   Conclusion

This study has identified some of the key challenges for HCWs in delivering high quality and safe home care support for older adults as perceived by adult social care practitioners and managers. The next step is to investigate 'a day in the life of HCWs' and explore the views of independent care providers to achieve an understanding of how human factors ergonomics can facilitate the design of home care packages to promote safer higher quality standards of care delivery.

References

1. Kingston, A., Comas-Herrera, A., Jagger, C.: Forecasting the care needs of the older population in England over the next 20 years: estimates from the population ageing and care simulation (PACSim) modelling study. Lancet Public Health **3**(9), 447–455 (2018)
2. Jasper, R., Hughes, J., Roberts, A., Chester, H., Davies, S., Challis, D.: Commissioning home care for older people: scoping the evidence. J. Long-Term Care **2019**, 176–1(2019)
3. National Institute for Clinical Excellence. https://www.nice.org.uk/guidance/qs123/resources/home-care-for-older-people-pdf-75545356896709 Accessed 16 Apr 2019
4. Vlachantoni, A., Shaw, R.J., Evandrou, M., Falkingham, J.: The determinants of receiving social care in later life in England. Ageing Soc. **35**(2), 321–345 (2015)
5. Office for National Statistics. https://www.ons.gov.uk/economy/governmentpublictaxes. Accessed 06 Jan 2019
6. Skills for Care. https://www.skillsforcare.org.uk/adult-social-care-workforce-data/Workforce-intelligence/documents/State-of-the-adult-social-care-sector/State-of-Report-2019.pdf. Accessed 20 Aug 2019
7. The Care Act 2014. https://www.gov.uk/government/publications/care-act-statutory-guidance/care-and-support-statutory-guidance#using-the-care-act-guidance. Accessed 12 Mar 2019
8. National Institute of Clinical Excellence. https://www.nice.org.uk/guidance/ng21/resources/home-care-delivering-personal-care-and-practical-support-to-older-people-living-in-their-own-homes-pdf-1837326858181. Accessed 06 Jan 2019
9. Kings Fund. https://www.kingsfund.org.uk/publications/new-models-home-care. Accessed 06 Feb 2019
10. Hignett, S.M., Otter, M.E., Keen, C.: Safety risks associated with physical interactions between patients and care givers during treatment and care deliver in home care settings: a systematic review. Int. J. Nurs. Stud. **59**, 1–14 (2016)
11. Denton, M., Brookman, C., Zeytinoglu, I., Plenderleith, J., Barken, R.: Task shifting in the provision of home and social care in Ontario, Canada: Implications for quality of care. Health Soc. Care Community **23**(5), 485–492 (2015)
12. Craftman, Å.G., Grundberg, Å., Westerbotn, M.: Experiences of home care assistants providing social care to older people: a context in transition. Int. J. Older People Nurs. **13**(4), 1–8 (2018)
13. Care Quality Commission. https://www.cqc.org.uk/sites/default/files/20191015b_stateofcare1819_fullreport.pdf. Accessed 25 Oct 2019
14. Anderson, J.E., Ross, A.J., Back, J., Duncan, M., Snell, P., Walsh, K., Jaye, P.: Implementing resilience engineering for healthcare quality improvement using the CARE model: a feasibility study protocol. Pilot Feasibility Stud. **2**(1), 1–9 (2016)
15. Anderson, J.E., Ross, A.J., Macrae, C., Wiig, S.: Defining adaptive capacity in healthcare: a new framework for researching resilient performance. Appl. Ergon. **87**, 103111 (2020)
16. Leplat, J.: Error analysis, instrument and object of task analysis. Ergonomics **32**(7), 813–822 (1989)
17. Rubery, J., Grimshaw, D., Hebson, G., Ugarte, S.M.: Its all about time: time contested terrain in the management and experience of domiciliary care work in england. Hum. Resour. Manage. **4**, 753–772 (2015).

Remote Design of a Pediatric Intensive Care Unit Dashboard in Time of Pandemics

Maxence Hébert-Lavoie[1]([✉]), Karine Ung[1], Lise Boudreault[1], Célia Mahmoudi[1],
Quynh Vu[1], Philippe Jouvet[2], and Philippe Doyon-Poulin[1]

[1] Polytechnique Montréal, Montréal, QC H3T 1J4, Canada
`maxence.hebert-lavoie@polymtl.ca`
[2] Sainte-Justine Hospital, Université de Montréal, Montréal, QC H3T 1C5, Canada

Abstract. To support the pediatric intensive care unit with the COVID-19 pandemic, we followed a user-centered design process to create a dashboard in a context where direct access to users was impossible. To this end, we applied contextual inquiry, user interview, requirement definition, iterative design with user validation and usability testing in a remote fashion. Being unable to be physically present at the hospital limited our understanding of the context of use, extended the duration of the study and limited the number of interviews and testing sessions. However, we were able to benefit from the experience of our team members, adopt an efficient decision-making method to select appropriate requirements and use remote moderated usability testing to conform our design process to an aggressive timeline.

Keywords: Remote usability evaluation · User-centered design · Medical dashboard · Covid-19 · Pediatric intensive care unit

1 Introduction

In Quebec, the COVID-19 pandemic exacerbated hospitals' condition. Healthcare personnel worked with an added pressure due to limited human resources, highlighting the need for efficient personnel management. At Sainte-Justine hospital (Montreal, Quebec) Pediatric Intensive Care Unit (PICU), the tools available to manage patient care were inadequate to deal with the pandemic. In 2017, the PICU developed a digital dashboard showing bed occupancy and medical staff on-duty on a large-screen television. However, the dashboard was unable to meet the needs brought by the pandemic: it did not manage the growth in the number of overflow beds, as the visualization was fixed to 32 rooms, and there was no information on zone separation between COVID-19 positive and negative patients. The dashboard also showed usability issues related to situational awareness, since it did not offer any trend information on staff load and nurse-patient ratios. A new digital dashboard was necessary to deal with the possible overflow of hospitalizations caused by the COVID-19 pandemic.

We partnered with Sainte-Justine hospital to develop a new visual dashboard that would meet the PICU medical staff's needs to face the COVID-19 pandemic. To this

N. L. Black et al. (Eds.): IEA 2021, LNNS 222, pp. 328–335, 2021.
https://doi.org/10.1007/978-3-030-74611-7_45

end, we followed the User-Centered Design (UCD) methodology prescribed in ISO 9241–210 (2019) [1]. All activities were conducted remotely, as the dashboard design happened during the shelter-home order and we were unable to go on-site for observations. Completely remote UCD activities with short deadlines in a medical setting posed a challenge that was not specifically documented in ISO 9241–210.

In this study, we present the UCD activities aimed at developing a dashboard in a completely remote context where access to users was limited. First, we provide a review on PICU and critical care management dashboard characteristics and describe the ISO 9241–210 process. Second, we present the main UCD design activities that were conducted. Third, we conclude with recommendations for the application of a UCD process in a completely remote context.

2 Literature Review

2.1 PICUs Characteristics

Efficiency of PICU relies on a quick and accurate communication of critical information between doctors, nurses and respiratory therapists [2]. PICU are characterized by a higher average nurse-to-patient ratio than in other ICUs, usually one nurse for one or two patients [3]. Since the risk of respiratory exhaustion is faster in children than in adults, having an efficient nurse bedside supervision is critical [4]. As bed occupancy increases and the number of available staff members becomes limited, the situational awareness decreases due to the demand in cognitive workload [5]. Efficient management of the PICU's resources is key to assure on-time healthcare services.

2.2 Critical Care Management Dashboard

A dashboard is a visual display of important information that has been consolidated on a single screen to be monitored at a glance [6]. Dashboards were first implemented in businesses as a competitive tool to monitor performance [7]. Since the 90s, they started to be increasingly present in healthcare establishments [8].

Hospital dashboards aim to meet the needs of strategic, tactical or operational resource management in hospitals [9]. However, a unified view of resource management and clinical management of patients is rare [10]. This leads to a situation where the hospital's resource management is not aligned with care management activities in the hospital's units. Therefore, in order to find a solution to the lack of technological integration of clinical and administrative resource management in the pediatric intensive care unit of a hospital, we developed a critical care management dashboard. To this end, we used the methodology prescribed in ISO 9241–210.

2.3 ISO 9241–210

ISO 9241–210 is an UCD approach that aims to improve the usability of interactive systems with defined requirements capture and user involvement throughout the design cycle [1]. Its use for the design of medical equipment showed to improve the device's overall usability and user performance [11, 12].

After considerate planning, the iterative approach consists of the following 4 main activities with their expected information outputs (in parenthesis):

1. Understand and specify the context of use (output: as-is scenario, personas)
2. Specify the user requirements (user needs, user requirements)
3. Produce design solutions to meet these requirements (scenarios of use, low- to high-fidelity prototypes)
4. Evaluate the design against requirements (usability test report, field report)

On-site observation and interview with end-users, such as contextual inquiry and usability evaluations, are preferred methods for capturing the context of use and the user requirements [13]. However, we were unable to go on-site as the design phase occurred during the stay-at-home order when the pandemic started. We therefore adapted the UCD activities to a remote setting.

3   Methodology

Since the intention was to offer the dashboard to the hospital in time to face the pandemic, an aggressive timeline was elected to complete all activities within 2 months. The size of the team, an efficient allocation of the resources and a good communication between its members permitted to address such a timeline.

The design team was composed of graduate students in User Experience (UX) programs and were responsible for defining the user requirements, designing the prototype and conducting usability evaluations. IT personnel from Sainte-Justine were responsible for implementing the prototype and integrating it with the hospital's digital record. The PICU staff that intervened in the design process were representative of the people

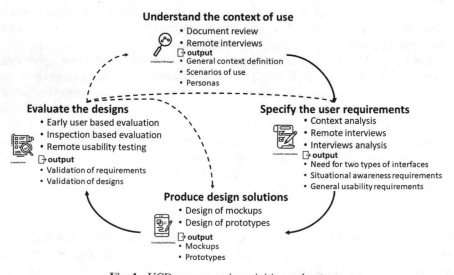

Fig. 1. UCD process main activities and outputs

working in the unit as it was composed of doctors, nurses, beneficiary attendants and administrative personnel.

Together, we worked on our main usability objective for the new dashboard: to improve the healthcare workers' situational awareness [14]. To this end, we followed the structure of the ISO 9241–210 closely, while adapting the activities to a remote context. Figure 1 illustrates the UCD process that was carried out during this study with its main activities and outputs.

3.1 Understand and Specify the Context of Use

To understand and specify the context of use in a pandemic context, the research team relied on two methods: document review and remote interviews.

The document review was based on a previous on-site evaluation of the existing digital dashboard done in 2019. It gave the design team an overview of the hospital's existing digital dashboard system and challenges that users were experiencing. The output of this work included: a definition of the context; list of the users and their role with the dashboard; review of usability problems with the existing dashboard and a proposition of design solutions to fix them. These information were the only data available captured directly on-site prior to the pandemic, all other information was captured remotely.

We conducted remote semi-structured interviews that lasted from 30 min to one hour. We followed an interview guide prepared to cover the research main goals: work organization, effects of COVID-19, existing tools in the unit and situational awareness requirements. We used a teleconference software (i.e., WebEx) to conduct and record the interviews that were then transcribed and categorized. 11 healthcare professionals took part in these interviews (6 from Sainte-Justine and 5 from other Quebec health-care institutions). At the end of the interviews, the team presented an iteration of the dashboard.

3.2 Specify the User Requirements

Usability and situational awareness requirements were first identified through an analysis of the context including the main tasks of the healthcare professionals related to the dashboard. They were then completed with more remote interviews which were also used to confirm that the requirements were aligned with the objectives identified at the start of the project. The users continued to specify their requirements throughout the design process as the interviews were carried out. About one month in the project, those were starting to be steady and seemed reliable.

3.3 Produce Design Solutions to Meet User Requirements

A user interface design tool (e.g. Adobe XD) was used to produce the design solutions shared on a common drive with the rest of the research team. In order to take into consideration the whole user experience while meeting user requirements, the production of design solutions started in the early phase of the project with the development of mockups. At first, they were based on the documentation review and refined following benchmark research, user interviews, and daily multidisciplinary team meetings.

Then, a more precise definition of the context of use and requirements allowed to produce concrete design solutions. These mockups were developed having in mind a scenario of a typical day in the PICU and multiple solutions were explored. At this point, the software developer and the IT personnel of the hospital started developing the back-end structure of the dashboard, while consulting with interface designers. This helped optimizing the workflow and making sure that the interface design was in concordance with the backend capabilities. Within a span of two months, mockups and prototypes were created, revised and validated with further interviews resulting in mature interfaces that were ready to be implemented.

3.4 Evaluate the Designs Against Requirements

The mockups and prototypes were subject to three types of evaluation: early user-based evaluation with mockups, remote inspection based evaluation with mockups and user-based evaluation with prototypes. Early user-based evaluation was done with the first mockups during the interview to help us understand the context and specify the requirements. Remote inspection based evaluation was done in two ways via screen sharing. The mockups were reviewed on a daily basis by the main team during meetings and also on a weekly basis by another Montreal hospital's design team that was also developing an interface to help with hospital resource management.

When a mature design was obtained, a moderated remote usability testing was used to identify persisting usability issues and to evaluate the design against situational awareness requirements. 6 individual tests were completed with 5 participants from Sainte-Justine hospital. The group was composed of pediatricians, intensive care doctors, a respiratory therapist and one head nurse. One participant was interviewed twice within a week to validate some of his ideas and modifications to the dashboard. Each session lasted one hour. The tests consisted of situational awareness tasks questionnaires that the users answered for both the old and the new dashboards followed by an open discussion on the efficiency of the proposed design. Using a teleconference software, the screen of the interviewer was shared to give the user access to the dashboard interface, questions were asked verbally and the session was recorded with the user's permission.

4 Results

The context specification allowed the team to define the dashboard as a tool mainly used to know where a specific room or a specific person is in the unit. It can be used by everybody in the PICU, either workers, patients or their relatives. During a shift, there are typically around 20 people who will be relying on the information provided by the dashboard. As such, the dashboard must display its content in a way that relevant information is quickly available for up to 16 different types of users (doctor, nurse, beneficiary attendant, parents, medical consultant, etc.). Based on the understanding of this context, the team elaborated scenarios of use and personas.

The understanding of the context along with the evaluation of mockups generated a document of over 80 pages. The report included requirements related to the context of use, general usability issues and the objective of improving the situational awareness of the PICU workers. The analysis of the requirements along with the evaluation of different mockups by the users and stakeholders enabled the team to produce the interface presented in Fig. 2.

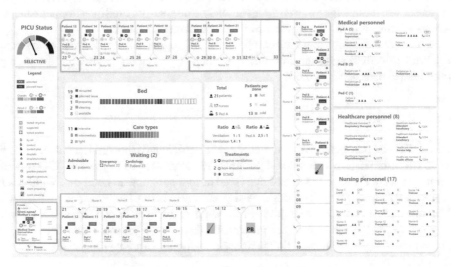

Fig. 2. Overview of the medical dashboard

5 Discussion

The results show that conducting the ISO 9241–210 process remotely is feasible. We successfully identified personas, defined scenarios and user requirements, as well as designed, tested and validated prototypes with the users. We were able to apply user-centered methods in time of pandemics for the design of a medical visual dashboard.

However, we experienced two main constraints. First, being unable to be physically present at the hospital limited our understanding of the context of use of the dashboard already in place and of the way the PICU operates. For instance, access to informal interactions between staff and observation methods such as contextual inquiry were not possible. Second, working remotely offers limited direct access to the users. We were unable to commute to their workplace and conduct interviews between their breaks. Instead, we had to plan the interviews in advance and make sure that they had the adequate equipment to complete an interview or remote testing. This extended the duration of the study and limited the number of interviews and testing sessions.

Nonetheless, three elements helped the team complete the design of the dashboard in these circumstances. First, a member of the team had worked on the previous iteration of the dashboard. Her work provided valuable information, such as identified users of the dashboard, which helped with the understanding of the context. Second, limitations related to user requirements specification were addressed by giving precedence to requirements that increased situational awareness offered by the dashboard. Some requirements were "nice to have" but would not have been possible to implement within the framework of the project. Third, the moderated usability tests proved useful given the circumstances. The fact that the questionnaires was oriented toward situational awareness encouraged the users to focus on accomplishing the tasks and acted as a visualization exercise. Even though the test was done remotely, this goal-oriented questionnaire helped the users focus on using the dashboard in its actual environment.

A next avenue for future research would be to investigate alternative methods to gather information faster in remote settings (e.g. video recording, diary logs, unmoderated user testings, etc.).

6 Conclusion

The COVID-19 pandemic raised the urgency for efficient dashboards in Quebec hospitals to better manage personnel and patients. We were able to follow an UCD process remotely during the lock-down and delivered design solutions to address such needs in a completely remote way. The dashboard is currently being implemented in the PICU of Sainte-Justine and will be subject to follow-up evaluations to confirm that it has met the goals defined at the start of the project. Furthermore, a journal paper detailing our approach to design a dashboard that increases situational awareness in a medical context will soon be published.

Acknowledgement. This research was carried out as part of the activities of the IVADO and TransMedTech Institutes, thanks, in part, to financial support from the Canada First Research Excellence Fund.

References

1. International Organisation for Standardisation. ISO 9241–210:2019 Ergonomics of human-system interaction—Part 210: Human-centred design for interactive systems (2019)
2. Flohr, L., Beaudry, S., Johnson, K.T., West, N., Burns, C.M., Ansermino, J.M., Görges, M.: Clinician-driven design of vitalpad–an intelligent monitoring and communication device to improve patient safety in the intensive care unit. IEEE J. Transl. Eng. Health Med. **6**, 1–14 (2018)
3. Ream, R.S., Mackey, K., Leet, T., Green, M.C., Andreone, T.L., Loftis, L.L., Lynch, R.E.: Association of nursing workload and unplanned extubations in a pediatric intensive care unit. Pediatr. Crit. Care Med. **8**(4), 366–371 (2007)
4. Randolph, A.G., Wypij, D., Venkataraman, S.T., Hanson, J.H., Gedeit, R.G., Meert, K.L., Arnold, J.H.: Effect of mechanical ventilator weaning protocols on respiratory outcomes in infants and children: a randomized controlled trial. Jama **288**(20), 2561–2568 (2002)
5. Koch, S.H., Weir, C., Haar, M., Staggers, N., Agutter, J., Görges, M., Westenskow, D.: Intensive care unit nurses' information needs and recommendations for integrated displays to improve nurses' situation awareness. J. Am. Med. Inf. Assoc. **19**(4), 583–590 (2012)
6. Few, S.: Information Dashboard Design: Displaying data for at-a-glance monitoring, 2nd edn. Analytics Press, Burlingame (2013)
7. Kaplan, R.S., Norton, D.P.: Putting the balanced scorecard to work. Econ. Impact Knowl. **27**(4), 315–324 (1998)

8. Pace, A., Buttigieg, S.C.: Can hospital dashboards provide visibility of information from bedside to board? a case study approach. J. Health Organ. Manage. **31**(2),142–161 (2017)
9. Buttigieg, S.C., Pace, A., Rathert, C.: Hospital performance dashboards: a literature review. J. Health Organ. Manage. **31**(3), 385–406 (2017)
10. Tan, K.W., Ng, Q.Y., Nguyen, F.N.H.L., Lam, S.S.W.: Data-driven decision-support for process improvement through predictions of bed occupancy rates. In: 2019 IEEE 15th International Conference on Automation Science and Engineering (CASE), pp. 133–139. IEEE August 2019
11. Martin, J.L., Clark, D.J., Morgan, S.P., Crowe, J.A., Murphy, E.: A user-centred approach to requirements elicitation in medical device development: a case study from an industry perspective. Appl. Ergon. **43**(1), 184–190 (2012)
12. Wanderer, J.P., Nelson, S.E., Ehrenfeld, J.M., Monahan, S., Park, S.: Clinical data visualization: the current state and future needs. J. Med. Syst. **40**(12), 275 (2016)
13. Goodman, E., Kuniavsky, M., Moed, A.: Observing The User Experience: A Practitioner's Guide To User Research (2nd ed.). Morgan Kaufmann, Amsterdam (2012)
14. Endsley, M.R., Jones, D.: Designing for Situation Awareness: An Approach to User-Centered Design (2nd ed.). CRC Press, Boca Raton (2011)

Patient Ergonomics in Hospital and Community Settings

Richard J. Holden[1](✉) and Rupa S. Valdez[2]

[1] Indiana University School of Medicine, Indianapolis, IN 46202, USA
rjholden@iu.edu
[2] University of Virginia, Charlottesville, VA 22908, USA

Abstract. Patient ergonomics is, simply put, the science (and design) of patient work. Patient work is the effortful, goal-driven, and consequential health-related activity performed by patients, families, and others independently or in concert with healthcare professionals. Patient work is hard work, occurs in context, unfolds as a journey, is a team effort, is distributed, goes beyond disease, can be invisible, and is not experienced invariably. Patient work, whether occurring in hospitals, homes, communities, or other settings, can benefit from the application of cognitive, physical, and organizational human factors theories and methods.

Keywords: Patients · Health · Human factors/ergonomics · Self-care · Design

1 Patient Ergonomics

Patient ergonomics is, simply put, *the science (and design) of patient work*. More formally, it is the application of human factors/ergonomics (HF/E) to study and design the effortful, goal-driven, and consequential health-related activities of patients, families, and other nonprofessionals, independently or in concert with healthcare professionals [1].

As healthcare embraces patient-centered care and patient engagement, HF/E research and practice have expanded to study and support the role of patients, their families, and members of their social network in health and healthcare [2, 3]. To the extent patients do work in the hospital, at home, or in other settings, HF/E experts are needed to provide theories, design technologies, and develop methods to study and support this work, the same way HF/E has proven useful for the work of professionals such as physicians and nurses [4, 5].

2 Patient work: The Target of Patient Ergonomics

Patient ergonomics aims to study and improve *patient work* [6]. This work is often unpaid, sometimes involuntary, and never bound by a formal contract—yet it adheres to Hendrick's definition of work as "any form of human effort or activity, including recreation and leisure pursuits" [7]. We have argued what defines patient work as work is that it is: (1) effortful; (2) goal-driven; and (3) consequential [8].

© The Author(s), under exclusive license to Springer Nature Switzerland AG 2021
N. L. Black et al. (Eds.): IEA 2021, LNNS 222, pp. 336–343, 2021.
https://doi.org/10.1007/978-3-030-74611-7_46

2.1 The Characteristics of Patient Work

We have observed the following characteristics of patient work to be generally true across contexts.

Patient Work Is Hard Work. It demands time, effort, and resources. The demands of patient work are multifaceted, spanning cognitive, physical, emotional, and other domains [9].

Patient Work Occurs in Context. Studies have posited work system models to describe the context in which patient work occurs (reviewed in [10]), including the people, environments, tasks, tools, and other system factors that interact to shape the performance of patient work [11–13].

Patient Work Unfolds as a Journey. Patient work is dynamic, temporal, and longitudinal in nature. It is characterized by adaptation and change, as over time people traverse and transition between various touchpoints and settings [5, 14].

Patient Work Is a Team Effort. Multiple social agents may be involved in patient work, contributing in various ways, from performing to assisting to observing, and more. These people include family, friends, members of a geographic or online community, healthcare professionals, and others [15–17].

Patient Work Is Distributed. Patient work can also be undertaken by or offloaded to non-human entities, including artifacts and environments. In the same way a cockpit remembers its speeds [18], *a pillbox remembers its meds* [19, 20].

Patient Work Goes Beyond Disease. The word patient—a derivation of the Latin "to suffer" that continues to perpetuate this meaning [21]—implies a sick individual needing care beyond usual daily activities. Health is more than disease and thus the work to achieve health is more than the work of managing disease [22]. Patient work minimally includes not only disease treatment but also disease prevention, slowing disease progression and complications, and work in the service of physical and mental wellness. Other types of patient work include managing one's illness identity, survivorship, advocacy, learning about health, and taking part in social activities with long-term health consequences (e.g., environmentalism or research).

Patient Work Can Be Invisible. Invisibility means the work that takes place is not seen, recognized, or valued by others [23] or indeed by the ones performing it, the latter being a case of *autoinvisibile* work [24]. Certain forms of patient work are generally less visible, for example, the work of arranging health and life priorities or recruiting energy to perform an undesirable health task, may be taken for granted or not at all recognized by outside observers.

Patient Work Is Not Experienced Invariably. Different groups and individuals may experience patient work differently, even if it appears similar on the surface. For example, managing a sexually transmitted disease, women's health, or mental illness can look very different in groups where these areas of health are stigmatized. Health disparities, including inequitable access to resources or exposures to risk factors, are also significant sources of difference in the experiences of patient work [25].

Patient Work Can Be Improved. Without belaboring the point, we contend patient work can be made better, easier, and more pleasant through intentional design [26].

3 Patient Ergonomics in Hospital and Community Settings

Patient work takes place in many settings. For example, Ye and Holden [27] identified 15 categories of locations: home, residential outdoors, friend/family house, clinic/hospital, pharmacy, grocery, restaurant, gym, neighborhood, community meeting place, community outdoors, in transit, work/volunteering, school, and travel.

Hospitals are an interesting location for patient work, because these spaces are often strongly associated with the work of professionals [28]. A layperson might even assume hospital patients are incapacitated, sedated, bedridden, or otherwise unable to perform work. This imagined reality of work at a hospital is represented in Fig. 1, a 19th century work of art in which hospital patients are generally passive or incapacitated while hospital staff actively plan and perform their care. The reality is that patients can and do contribute meaningfully in hospital settings and so can their families, friends, and other nonprofessionals. These parties play an important role in their therapy and recovery, in parallel and often in coordination with care provided by hospital care teams. For example, the standard of care is for patients with diabetes undergoing hospital procedures to continue to self-manage their diabetes during the hospitalization, when able [29]. As another example, older adult inpatients play a major role in their recovery and future health by engaging in physical mobility efforts [30].

Patient work also takes place in community settings, where over 99% of lifetime health-related activity occurs for the average person. In communities, everyday health or illness work intertwine with and resemble life and professional healthcare work (Fig. 2). As formal care in the 21st century is increasingly performed in people's homes as opposed to institutional settings such as hospitals, some have argued for the need to use HF/E methods to improve health and healthcare in this particular setting:

> The reorientation of the culture of health care to the home setting, as well as the range of individuals, tasks, technologies, and environments involved in home health care, heightens the importance of human factors. Care recipients and other caregivers, now expected to perform procedures previously executed only by trained professionals, bring a range of knowledge, capabilities, environments, and subsequent interactions to health care. Numerous issues arise in home settings that are not often considered in institutional-based practice[31].

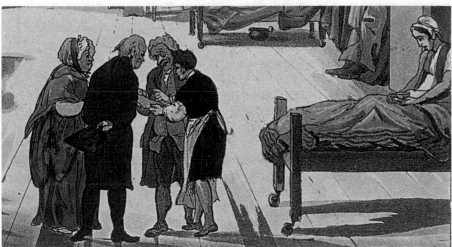

Fig. 1. An early 19th century painting (top) portrays in the background women patients in a hospital ward. The patients are as depicted passive or incapacitated, while hospital staff in the foreground plan and perform their care (detail in bottom panel). *The Middlesex Hospital: the interior of one of the female wards.* Colored aquatint by J. C. Stadler, 1808, after A. C. Pugin and T. Rowlandson. Credit: Wellcome Collection. Attribution 4.0 International (CC BY 4.0).

Fig. 2. A mid-19th century painting of children "playing doctor" in their home. The subjects imitate the activities of formal healthcare delivery, such as taking vitals and preparing medicine, in a clinician-centered manner remarkably similar to other Realist artwork of the same era [3]. *Children Playing at Doctors*. Oil on canvas by Frederick Daniel Hardy, 1863. © Victoria and Albert Museum, London, licensed for noncommercial reuse.

4   Patient Ergonomics Theories, Topic Areas, and Methods

Three branches of HF/E theory are applicable to patient work: physical; cognitive; and organizational [32]. Physical patient ergonomics addresses patient work activities "that require physical perception or function or interactions with physical tools or environments" [33]. Examples include studying a post-surgical walking aid, evaluating a lift assist technology for physical rehabilitation, or designing an intervention to improve inpatient mobility. Cognitive patient ergonomics refers to the study and design of patient work that involves perception, signal detection, decision making, problem solving, memory, and other cognitive functions, as well as interacting with technologies to perform cognitive tasks. This might include, for instance, usability evaluations of software applications for dementia caregivers [34]. Organizational patient ergonomics studies and designs patient work systems and processes that shape and comprise the patient journey [5]. An example is the study of the patient experience receiving care from multiple healthcare services. Often, these three patient ergonomics theories intersect, for instance in an interdisciplinary design study evaluating the user interface of environmental controls for inpatients with spinal cord injuries [35].

The topic areas of patient ergonomics that have been most frequently addressed in HF/E studies and design projects are consumer health information technology, patient-professional communication, self-care, and patient engagement in patient safety [1]. Other important areas have received lesser attention, for example, patient work in transitions of care, public health, and lifestyle behaviors such as diet and exercise.

Many methods from HF/E are applicable to studying and designing to improve patient work. These include traditional field methods such as interviews, focus groups, surveys, and field observation; design and usability methods including user-centered and participatory design; experimental and quantitative research studies; more novel methods such as those using sensors for data collection or studying internet communities; and participatory methods such as action research, community-based participatory research, and patient and public involvement studies. Although multiple methods apply, it is abundantly clear that methods developed and traditionally used in other areas of HF/E must be adapted [8] and strategically implemented [36] to accommodate the unique needs, characteristics, and settings of patient work.

5   The Future Value of Patient Ergonomics

Whatever the theory applied, topic addressed, or method used, patient ergonomics offers bidirectional value to HF/E and the domain of health. Patient ergonomics expands the scope of HF/E in health and healthcare beyond traditional interests in formal clinical work performed by healthcare professionals [37]. As the paradigms of health evolve, so can HF/E, by attending to patient work. Reciprocal value to health and healthcare comes from deliberate and scientific improvements by applying HF/E's human-centered and systems-oriented theories, methods, and approaches.

References

1. Holden, R.J., Cornet, V.P., Valdez, R.S.: Patient ergonomics: 10-year mapping review of patient-centered human factors. Appl. Ergon. **82**, 102972 (2020)
2. Holden, R.J., Valdez, R.S.: Town hall on patient-centered human factors and ergonomics. In: Proceedings of the Human Factors and Ergonomics Society Annual Meeting, vol. 62, no. 1, pp. 465-468 (2018)
3. Holden, R.J., Valdez, R.S.: 2019 Town hall on human factors and ergonomics for patient work. In: Proceedings of the Human Factors and Ergonomics Society Annual Meeting, vol. 63, no. 1, pp. 725-728 (2019)
4. Valdez, R.S., et al.: Transforming consumer health informatics through a patient work framework: connecting patients to context. J. Am. Med. Inf. Assoc. **22**(1), 2–10 (2015)
5. Carayon, P., et al.: SEIPS 3.0: Human-centered design of the patient journey for patient safety. Appl. Ergon. **84**, 103033 (2020)
6. Corbin, J., Strauss, A.: Managing chronic illness at home: three lines of work. Qual. Sociol. **8**, 224–247 (1985)
7. Hendrick, H.W.: An overview of macroergonomics. In: Hendrick, H.W., Kleiner, B.M. (eds.) Macroergonomics: Theory, methods and applications, pp. 1–23. Lawrence Erlbaum Associates, Mahwah, NJ (2002)

8. Holden, R.J., Valdez, R.S.: Patient ergonomics: The science (and engineering) of patient work. In: Holden, R.J., Valdez, R.S. (eds.) The Patient Factor: Theories and Methods for Patient Ergonomics, pp. 3–18. CRC Press, Boca Raton (2021)
9. Ponnala, S., et al.: Conceptualizing caregiving activities for persons with dementia (PwD) through a patient work lens. Appl. Ergon. **85**, 103070 (2020)
10. Werner, N.E., et al.: Human factors/ergonomics work system analysis of patient work: state of the science and future directions. Int. J. Qual. Health Care **33**, 60–71 (2021)
11. Holden, R.J., et al.: Self-care barriers reported by emergency department patients with acute heart failure: a sociotechnical systems-based approach. Ann. Emerg. Med. **66**, 1–12 (2015)
12. Holden, R.J., Schubert, C.C., Mickelson, R.S.: The patient work system: an analysis of self-care performance barriers among elderly heart failure patients and their informal caregivers. Appl. Ergon. **47**, 133–150 (2015)
13. Holden, R.J., et al.: Macroergonomic factors in the patient work system: examining the context of patients with chronic illness. Ergonomics **60**(1), 26–43 (2017)
14. Werner, N.E., et al.: Performance-shaping factors affecting older adults' hospital-to-home transition success: a systems approach. Gerontologist **59**(2), 303–314 (2018)
15. Mickelson, R.S., Holden, R.J.: Assessing the distributed nature of home-based heart failure medication management in older adults. In: Proceedings of the Human Factors and Ergonomics Society, vol. 57, no. 1, pp. 753-757 (2013)
16. Valdez, R.S., Brennan, P.F.: Exploring patients' health information communication practices with social network members as a foundation for consumer health IT design. Int. J. Med. Inf. **84**, 363–374 (2015)
17. Valdez, R.S., et al.: From loquacious to reticent: understanding patient health information communication to guide consumer health IT design. J. Am. Med. Inf. Assoc. **24**(4), 680–696 (2017)
18. Hutchins, E.: How a cockpit remembers its speeds. Cogn. Sci. **19**(3), 265–288 (1995)
19. Mickelson, R.S., Holden, R.J.: Mind the gulfs: An analysis of medication-related cognitive artifacts used by older adults with heart failure. In: Proceedings of the Human Factors and Ergonomics Society, vol. 59, no. 1, pp. 481-485 (2015)
20. Mickelson, R.S., Willis, M., Holden, R.J.: Medication-related cognitive artifacts used by older adults with heart failure. Health Policy Technol. **4**, 387–398 (2015)
21. Neuberger, J.: Do we need a new word for patients? lets do away with "patients." BMJ **318**(7200), 1756–1757 (1999)
22. Holden, R.J., Valdez, R.S.: Beyond disease: Technologies for health promotion. In: Proceedings of the International Symposium on Human Factors and Ergonomics in Health Care, vol. 8, no. 1, pp. 62-66 (2019)
23. Gorman, R.K., Wellbeloved-Stone, C.A., Valdez, R.S.: Uncovering the invisible patient work system through a case study of breast cancer self-management. Ergonomics **61**(12), 1575–1590 (2018)
24. Valdez, R.S., Holden, R.J.: Patient ergonomics: attending to the context of settings and populations. In: Valdez, R.S., Holden, R.J. (eds.) The Patient Factor: Applications of Patient Ergonomics, pp. 3–12. CRC Press, Boca Raton (2021)
25. Holden, R.J., Toscos, T., Daley, C.N.: Researcher reflections on human factors and health equity. In: Roscoe, R., Chiou, E.K., Wooldridge, A.R. (eds.) Advancing Diversity, Inclusion, and Social Justice Through Human Systems Engineering, pp. 51–62. CRC Press, Boca Raton (2020)
26. Faiola, A., Holden, R.J.: Consumer health informatics: empowering healthy-lifestyle-seekers through mHealth. Prog. Cardiovasc. Dis. **59**(5), 479–486 (2017)
27. Ye, N., Holden, R.J.: Exploring the context of chronic illness self-care using geospatial analyses. In: Proceedings of the International Symposium on Human Factors and Ergonomics in Health Care, vol. 4, no. 1, pp. 37-41 (2015)

28. Strauss, A., et al.: The work of hospitalized patients. Soc. Sci. Med. **16**, 977–986 (1982)
29. Clement, S., et al.: Management of diabetes and hyperglycemia in hospitals. Diabetes Care **27**(2), 553–591 (2004)
30. King, B.J., et al.: Getting patients walking: a pilot study of mobilizing older adult patients via a nurse-driven intervention. J. Am. Geriatr. Soc. **64**(10), 2088–2094 (2016)
31. National Research Council, Health Care Comes Home: The Human Factors. National Academies Press. Committee on the Role of Human Factors in Home Health Care, Board on Human-Systems Integration, Division of Behavioral and Social Sciences and Education: Washington, DC (2011)
32. Holden, R.J., Valdez, R.S. (eds.): The Patient Factor: Theories and Methods for Patient Ergonomics. CRC Press, Boca Raton (2021)
33. Steege, L.M., Cavuoto, L., King, B.J.: Physical patient ergonomics: understanding and supporting physical aspects of patient work. In: Holden, R.J., Valdez, R.S. (eds.) The Patient Factor: Theories and Methods for Patient Ergonomics, pp. 37–59. CRC Press, Boca Raton (2021)
34. Brown, J., Kim, H.N.: Usability of Alzheimer's mHealth applications. J. Best Practices Health Prof. Diversity **11**(1), 31–42 (2018)
35. Hancock, G.M., et al.: Environmental control units for inpatient care at veterans affairs spinal cord injury centers: heuristic evaluation and design recommendations. In: Yamamoto, S., Mori, H. (eds.) HCII 2020,12184, pp. 23–38. Springer, Cham (2020)
36. Valdez, R.S., Holden, R.J.: Health care human factors/ergonomics fieldwork in home and community settings. Ergon. Des. **24**, 44–49 (2016)
37. Holden, R.J., et al.: SEIPS 2.0: a human factors framework for studying and improving the work of healthcare professionals and patients. Ergonomics **56**(11), 1669–1686 (2013)

Human Computer Interaction (HCI) in General Radiography: A Case Study to Consider HCI Factors When Purchasing X-ray Equipment

Anita Jogia[1]([⊠]), Jean-Pierre Brunet[1], Dann Ramos[2], Julia Lintack[2], Luigi Di Raimo[2], Michael Sharpe[1], Karen Rowe[1], Narinder Paul[1], Derek Lall[1], Sherri Cheadle[1], Jill Smith[1], Ryan Macdonald[1], and Jerry Plastino[1]

[1] London Health Sciences Centre, London, ON, Canada
anita.jogia@lhsc.on.ca
[2] Fanshawe College, London, ON, Canada

Abstract. Human computer interaction (HCI) between medical radiation technologists (MRTs) and x-ray equipment influence the quality and safety of patient care with diagnostic procedures and should be considered during purchase of equipment. Practitioners from London Health Sciences Centre collaborated with a professor and students of the Fanshawe Advanced Ergonomic Program to complete a field study to identify HCI Factors in x-ray equipment that could be used as part of a hospital's centralized purchasing guide.

Keywords: X-ray · Human factors · Radiology · Healthcare · Ergonomics

1 Introduction

Hospitals generally use a centralized purchasing process for equipment, and a number of stakeholders are part of this process, specifically, when purchasing x-ray equipment. A previous paper examined inclusion of ergonomic factors such as force to operate x-ray machines into the purchasing process [1]. However, there is limited research on HCI between MRTs and x-ray equipment. These factors are important for health and safety but are rarely considered during the purchasing process. The challenge is to identify the HCI factors by observing how MRTs interact with the x-ray equipment, and to determine how this can impact staff and patient safety. This paper attempts to identify HCI factors in the use of x-ray equipment for inclusion in a centralized purchasing process.

2 Method

A field study methodology was used to gather relevant data. The hospital Ergonomist, x-ray department Coordinator and a Professor of HCI facilitated the project and mentored 2 students as they worked with MRTs to gather data. Additional stakeholders such as safety, planning and patient safety were consulted as required. Due to Covid-19, initial

N. L. Black et al. (Eds.): IEA 2021, LNNS 222, pp. 344–350, 2021.
https://doi.org/10.1007/978-3-030-74611-7_47

data was gathered remotely in June, 2020 with onsite review completed September, 2020. The study is limited to a single x-ray unit in the hospital's emergency department. The hospital's Adverse Event Management System (AEMS) was used to collected data with respect to incidents related to use of the x-ray equipment.

2.1 Remote Data Collection

Background Information. Students completed a literature review of x-ray equipment and medical imaging techniques using manufacturer user manuals and relevant online videos. They spent forty hours to complete an initial task analysis of the x-ray equipment and other prospective equipment by reviewing the same manufacturer user manuals and instructional videos. The students verified this analysis remotely by reviewing information provided to them by the hospital, this included: reviewing a Job Demands Description (JDD) of an MRT role, videos of a senior technologist doing a 'mock-x-ray', and photographs of key display features.

Video Analysis. Both students reviewed a total of seventeen videos of an experienced MRT performing a mock chest x-ray on a 'mock' patient (for confidentiality purposes). Three minutes and forty seconds of video displayed the physical manipulation of the x-ray machine, whereas two minutes and seven seconds of video displayed the MRT interacting with the x-ray console. The videos were used as a means of understanding how an MRT would typically interact with the x-ray system when taking an image of a patient.

The tasks shown in each video were broken down into specific actions and steps. Online discussion and written feedback from the experienced MRT helped to piece the steps determined in each video in sequential order for the whole imaging task. Reviewing the videos and breaking down the tasks took upwards of two hours to analyze and understand. The full task breakdown was compared against the JDD provided by the hospital. Using a flow diagram, the tasks were highlighted as either occurring in the x-ray room (typically tasks involving more physical manipulation of the machine/patient) or in the control room (typically operating the x-ray computer console). From here, the tasks involving operation of the computer console in the control room were focused on, as this is where the Human-Computer Interaction occurs when imaging patients. Then it was determined which decisions might be required at each step when interacting with the console.

A Repeat/Reject Analysis for Radiology report was provided to the students by the hospital. The report summarizes where an image may have had to be re-taken or the image wasn't used. The students analyzed this data against the components of the task breakdown involving HCI. Discussion with subject matter specialists helped to pinpoint specific actions at the console that might have resulted in waste images and which design principles might mitigate repeated/rejected x-ray images.

2.2 On Site Assessment

Observations. One student completed the on-site observation of MRTs using x-ray equipment with patients in the emergency department for a duration of one week. The student collected a total of six hours of data over the week. Data necessary to complete a heuristics evaluation was collected using direct observation of MRTs using the x-ray equipment, and formal discussions using Neilsen's 10 Heuristics Principles [2] with two experienced MRTs, five novice MRTs, and the department Coordinator. A limitation was the small sample size of MRTs, a total of seven with a large proportion of novice MRTs.

Analysis. There were some challenges in identifying the most appropriate tool to complete the HCI analysis. In consultation with a professor of HCI, heuristics evaluation and NASA TLX was recommended as the most appropriate method and tool given at the time. The NASA-TLX [3] was used to identify the sources of task workload when using the Emergency x-ray unit, and a Heuristic Evaluation based on Nielsen's principles [2] was used to evaluate overall usability of the emergency x-ray unit. The heuristics evaluation method as modeled by Zhang et al., 2003 [4] was adopted with additional modification to conduct this assessment. A NASA TLX pen and paper method was conducted after every x-ray assessment with a total of 3 MRTs participants, two of which are novice users. The type of x-ray assessment, its duration and when it occurs could not be controlled for the purposes of the NASA TLX survey study, as it varies according to real time patients' scheduled appointment, therefore, a 'mock' x-ray assessment was used. The MRT participants were told to complete any outstanding x-ray assessment then complete NASA TLX pen and paper method with an x-ray assessment of the spinal cord in mind. This type of assessment was used because the MRT participants noted that the most difficult x-ray assessments involve the spinal cord. A limitation was that the level of difficulty of the 'mock' spinal cord assessment varies with user experience. The emergency x-ray unit was compared against a newer model to assist in the identification of potential gaps in HCI between the two x-ray machines.

3   Results

From April 1, 2019 to August 31, 2020 a total of 118 incidents were reported in radiology via the hospital's Adverse Event Management System. See Fig. 1. Of note, 72% of incidents were related to patients/properties/visitors/affiliates. This category captures incidents impacting patients or others but not staff directly, as they generally report incidents related to physical injury in AEMS workplace/illness/injury category. They are also incidents are related to medical imaging procedures, treatment, preparation, transporting and reporting. The increase in reporting of these types of injuries in 2020 may be attributed to a combination of increased stress due to the large influx of patients during the COVID-19 outbreak and possible sources of workload that may be attributed to working with the computer console.

Investigation of the Repeat/Reject Analysis for Radiology report provided great insight as to where HCI issues might exist in emergency x-ray unit. The report noted images that were marked as waste or requiring a repeat as a result of both over- and under-exposure. According to the JDD provided, MRTs are "required to remember infrequently used information and/or sequences … on a regular basis." To control for human error due to chance, the task workload of the x-ray unit was estimated using NASA-TLX. The

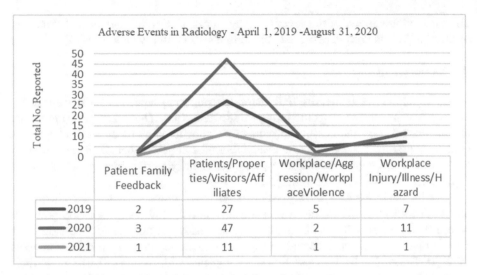

Fig. 1. Type of incidents in radiology reported through adverse event management system

sources of task workload as identified in the NASA-TLX assessment scores are, in order of magnitude: *mental demand, frustration,* and *performance.* See Fig. 2 below.

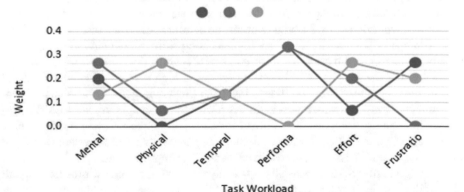

Fig. 2. NASA TLX task demand rating scores by weight (%). The MRTs place most of their concern with their performance, frustration and mental demand when working with the x-ray machine.

The most frequent heuristic violation that occurs in the console, a touch screen based in Windows 8 version, of the x-ray machine in the study involves problems concerning, *Consistency and Standards,* followed by problems concerning: *User Control and Freedom.* The greatest of severity rating involves problems concerning, *Error Recovery* followed by, *Help and Documentation,* then by, *Error Prevention* and finally by *Memory.*

To assist in the validity of the severity rating Norman's Seven Fundamental Principles of Design [5] was used in composite of Neilsen's 10 Usability Heuristics [6].

4 Discussion

This study attempted to identify HCI factors in using x-ray equipment with the intent to include them into an existing purchasing guide. Due to COVID-19, there were limitations in the methodology including: the number of students allowed on site to spend the necessary time to collect data, the availability of a large number of MRTs who may be experienced with the specific x-ray unit, and identifying the most applicable tool to capture HCI factors with x-ray imaging.

Due to time limitations, the heuristics analysis was completed with one evaluator and one MRT subject matter expert. It is estimated that only 35% of the usability problems would be identified with one evaluator [2]. Increasing the number of evaluators from 1 to 5 could increase the expected percentage of identified usability problems to about 75% [2]. The NASA-TLX assessment was completed with a sample size of three which includes both novice and expert MRT. Results may not represent a full perspective of the x-ray department due to the small sample sizes for either assessments.

Upon further consultation, the Professor of HCI has stated that aside from Nielsen's 10 Heuristics Principles [2] and Norman 7 Principles of Design [6] the following alternative HCI tools would be appropriate for this study: Tognazzini's 16 principles [7] and Shneiderman's 8 golden rules [8].

It was identified that a computer console with good feedback would provide the MRT with a complete and clear visual indication on how to recognize, diagnose, and recover from an error before it happens. Moreover, a computer console with a good conceptual model would provide the MRT with relevant and helpful audiovisual instructional aid on how to properly conduct a procedure. Implementing instructional aids would improve the understanding and mastery over the equipment specifically for the novice MRT.

Data from the hospital AEMs system showed a high number of incidents related to patients/properties/visitors/affiliates; incidents impacting patients or others but not staff directly, who generally report incidents related to physical injury via AEMS workplace/illness/injury category. It is difficult to trace back to see if these incidents may be a result of poor HCI with x-ray equipment. In general, the AEMs system would not directly capture HCI issues. This could be an area for improvement.

During this study, plans to install a new x-ray machine were underway at the hospital. One of the first items addressed in the project initiation phase was to identify the stakeholders and their involvement through the use of a stakeholder register. Categorization of stakeholders and their needs determined their involvement and input within the project.

The initial design and planning process consisted of extensive stakeholder engagement and collaboration meetings over a series of weeks. Preliminary meetings consisted of a functional planning focus capturing all requirements (both directly and indirectly) of the purpose-built state to support the departmental needs within the x-ray suite. Building from the collection requirement exercises, a high-level schematic design was developed and presented to the user group for further review and analysis.

Narrowing down into the granular details, the design was further exploited in the "design development" phase focusing on the finite details which addressed both patient and staff workflow in the space. Part of this process elaborated on how staff functioned through their daily tasks, focusing on precise placements of display monitors & aide tools to facilitate the precise and individualized x-ray scans. As well, lighting levels and their respective ranges were considered to ensure staff were equipped with optimal illumination to suit their needs. Once all of the requirements were identified and captured within the project scope, the drawings & specifications (contract documents) were finalized, then proceeding to the construction tender (procurement) phase of the project lifecycle.

Stakeholder engagement happens early on in the project lifecycle (initiation phase) ensuring their involvement and input is provided and captured. Typical tools and techniques used in the design process have historically been the use of AutoCad for drawing preparation and presentation. However, the use of Revit software is being introduced more frequently as it not only provides 2D drawing capabilities, but also 3D visuals and perspectives. This has proven to be an effective tool when proposing and conceptualizing specific design elements throughout the process. This has become effective in identifying potential safety concerns and risk mitigation tactics before it is realized in the built environment. Also, various architectural and interior design guidelines and standards are adopted to ensure an ergonomic focus for best practice design.

Every project is unique in nature and in order to ensure project success, stakeholder engagement early on must be carried out and in a tailored approach in order to ensure end user satisfaction.

Generally, a comprehensive review of equipment prior to purchase is lacking, and the focus can be on price, gift or grants for buying equipment. Appropriate stakeholders are required as subject matter experts (SME) to provide input and feedback as part of the process, but having vendors provide mock ups to simulate equipment in the room to be tested and evaluated to understand any ergonomic risks during the purchasing process would be beneficial.

Ergonomics is a key piece absent from evaluation on medical equipment and ends up being a big issue after the purchase and when in use. Providing defined ergo requirements and outcomes such as lower repetitive injures, measures of force and HCI factors during the purchasing process will allow a better product due to feedback and dialogue and allow a more informed design to be developed.

Taking the information discussed and finalized in the purchasing process during the mock up or "Learning lab" scenario will then get translated in the design through flow, furniture selection and implementation. It would allow the continuum of work that has occurred right from purchase to be translated to the design and ultimately to a better outcome-based solution that can be measured by various data points to understand if desired results were achieved. It is unclear at this time how HCI factors may or may not influence stakeholder engagement during the design of the x-ray suite but this may be a topic for future research.

5   Summary

New x-ray equipment had already been purchased for the emergency suite at the hospital using a standard purchasing guide that included physical ergonomic factors, and these factors are also considered by relevant stakeholders during the installation of the new unit. The question remains, could HCI factors be included in such a guide for future purchases, and could those factors be identified by applying the available HCI tools while observing MRTs working with the equipment, or by directly using the HCI tools during the purchasing process. One of the primary challenges was to identify the most appropriate method and tool to use in evaluating HCI between MRTs and the x-ray equipment.

Future work should consider evaluation of HCI with a large sample size of MRTs using different x-ray machines, and additional evaluators to complete the heuristic evaluation, and perhaps focus on specific HCI factors that can be readily identified/tested during the purchasing process that can translate to the final planning and design of an x-ray suite. Given the potential impact on system errors, patient and staff safety, it should be a topic of further research.

References

1. Brunet, J.P., Jogia, A., Brown, J., Stuyt, A., Perfetto, K., Leblanc, G., Plastino, J., Smith, J.: A multi-professional approach to investigating musculoskeletal injuries among medical radiation technologists: a case study for new equipment. In: 50th Annual Conference of the Association of Canadian Ergonomists, pp. 1–9. Association of Canadian Ergonomists, Nfld (2019)
2. Nielsen, J.: Heuristic Evaluation: How-To: Article by Jakob Nielsen (1994). https://www.nngroup.com/articles/how-to-conduct-a-heuristic-evaluation/. Accessed 05 Feb 2021.
3. NASA: NASA TLX: Task Load Index (2019). https://humansystems.arc.nasa.gov/groups/TLX/. Accessed 05 Feb 2021
4. Zhang, J., Johnson, T.R., Patel, V.L., Paige, D.L., Kubose, T.: Using usability heuristics to evaluate patient safety of medical devices. J. Biomed. Inf. **36**(1–2), 23–30 (2003)
5. Norman, D.A.: The Design of Everyday Things. (Revised and expanded ed.), Basic Books, New York (2013)
6. Nielsen, J.: 10 Usability Heuristics for User Interface Design (2020). https://www.nngroup.com/articles/ten-usability-heuristics/. Accessed 05 Feb 2021
7. Shneiderman, B., Plaisant, C., Cohen, M., Jacobs, S., Elmqvist, N.: Designing the user Interface: Strategies for Effective Human-Computer Interaction (Sixth ed.). Boston, Pearson (2018)
8. Tognazzini, B.: First Principles of Interaction Design (Revised & Expanded) (2014). https://asktog.com/atc/principles-of-interaction-design/. Accessed 05 Feb 2021

Evaluation of a Suspension System to Reduce Whole Body Vibration Exposures Which Can Be Used in Ambulances

Peter W. Johnson[1](✉), Greg Kiselis[2], Gary Ford[2], and Dean Bartolone[2]

[1] University of Washington, Seattle, WA, USA
petej@uw.edu
[2] LiquidSpring, Lafayette, IN, USA

Abstract. First responders and their patients can be exposed to high levels of whole-body vibration (WBV) during ambulance transport. Using vibration measurements over the front and rear axles of a shuttle bus, the purpose of this field-based study was to measure and compare the WBV exposures between a shuttle bus with a conventional, stock suspension and a shuttle bus with an alternative, vibration-mitigating suspension. This alternative suspension can be installed in ambulances. The WBV exposures measured from the rear of both shuttle buses were on average over 50% higher than those measured from the front of the vehicle. When comparing the floor-measured vibration levels, which were used as a surrogate measurement to compare the vehicle occupants' potential exposures, the WBV exposures were always lower in the shuttle bus with the alternative suspension. If these results can be translated to actual ambulances, relative to the ambulance cab, it appears that patients and first responders traveling in the patient compartment in the rear of an ambulance would likely have up to 50% higher vibration exposures. The alternative suspension demonstrated it would reduce the WBV exposures of all vehicle occupants compared to a vehicle with a conventional, stock suspension.

Keywords: Patient transport · First responders · Vehicle suspension design

1 Introduction

Previous work has shown that ambulance occupants (first responders and their patients) can be exposed to high levels of whole-body vibration during ambulance transport [1]. For the first responders, the prolonged exposure to movements and whole-body vibration (WBV) can contribute to some level of physical and cognitive fatigue—which may influence the quality of care they can provide. In addition, there is an inherent risk of motor-vehicle accidents when driving ambulances [2] and the first responders riding in the back of ambulances are vulnerable to injury while delivering critical patient care [3].

For the injured or ill patients, the exposure to movements and vehicle vibrations may further compromise their health, care and well-being during ambulance transport. The movements and vibration in the back of the ambulance may limit the emergency

© The Author(s), under exclusive license to Springer Nature Switzerland AG 2021
N. L. Black et al. (Eds.): IEA 2021, LNNS 222, pp. 351–354, 2021.
https://doi.org/10.1007/978-3-030-74611-7_48

personnel's ability to provide chest compressions [4] and to administer intravenous medicines and fluids [5]. The fore-aft accelerations and movements associated with rapid starts and stops and the side-to-side translational and roll movements can put ambulance patients under additional emotional and physiological stressors [6]. Solutions to reduce ambulance occupants' exposures to movements and high-levels of WBV are needed.

Using vibration measurements from the vehicle axles and floor, the purpose of this field-based study was to compare the WBV exposures between a shuttle bus with a conventional, stock suspension and the same bus with alternative, vibration-mitigating suspension. The alternative suspension system can be specified and installed in ambulances.

2 Methods

WBV exposures were measured from a shuttle bus built on a Ford 550 chassis with a conventional/stock suspension, and the same bus subsequently retrofitted with an alternative suspension system (LiquidSpring; Lafayette, IN). Each shuttle bus drove over the same 72 km standardized route which contained three different rough road segments, three different city street segments, and three different freeway segments.

Tri-axial, portable accelerometers with built-in memory (Axivity AX-3, Open Movement; Newcastle upon Tyne, UK) were used to measure the WBV exposures at 800 Hz from the front and rear of the shuttle bus on top of the axles and from the vehicle floor directly above the axles. The vibrations from the vehicle floor were used as surrogate measures for the vehicle occupants' potential exposures. A GPS logger collected vehicle speed and location to enable the analysis of the shuttle bus WBV data over identical road segments.

According to the ISO 2631-1 standard, the weighted average [A_w] and impulsive [VDV] WBV exposures at the axles and vehicle floor were compared between the two shuttle bus configurations with their respective suspension systems. The A_w and VDV exposure measures were normalized to 1-h of exposure [A(1) and VDV(1)] to reflect 1-h of travel on each road type. No inferential statistical analyses were performed due to the small number of measurements and data being from one vehicle.

3 Results

Table 1 below compares the two shuttle bus suspensions and shows the vibration exposures in the front and rear of the shuttle bus at the axle and floor levels based on 1-h of vehicle operation [A(1) and VDV(1)]. The floor-measured vibration levels provide a rough indication of the occupants' WBV exposures. The WBV exposures measured from the rear of both shuttle buses were on average over 50% higher than those measured from the front of the vehicle. When comparing the floor-measured vibration levels between the suspensions, the WBV exposures were almost always lower in the shuttle buses with the alternative suspension (14% lower on average). The GPS data indicated there were no differences in speeds between the two shuttle buses when traversing the various road types.

Table 1. Suspension comparisons based on the 1-h average weighted vibration [A(1)] and the 1-h weighted vibration dose value [VDV(1)]. Measurements from the axle and floor level from the front and rear of the shuttle buses. Con = conventional suspension; Alt = alternative suspension. RR = Rough Roads, CS = City Streets, FW = Freeway.

Road type		A(1) – m/s^2				VDV(1) – m/s$^{1.75}$			
		Front		Rear		Front		Rear	
	Loc	Con	Alt	Con	Alt	Con	Alt	Con	Alt
RR	Floor	0.76	0.55	1.13	0.82	11.3	7.8	17.7	13.0
	Axle	5.04	5.72	5.83	4.66	80.9	92.5	87.1	85.6
CS	Floor	0.38	0.35	0.58	0.50	5.5	5.1	8.5	7.3
	Axle	2.48	3.10	2.83	2.00	43.7	51.6	46.7	39.3
FW	Floor	0.36	0.34	0.55	0.55	4.8	4.5	7.7	7.3
	Axle	2.57	3.35	2.96	2.00	40.4	49.4	47.0	38.6

4 Discussion and Conclusions

This study identified that the shuttle bus with the alternative suspension typically lowered the floor measured vibrations in the front and rear of the bus by 28% on the rough roads, 10% on the city streets and 4% on the freeways. However, the floor-measured vibrations in the rear of both vehicles were on average 54% higher compared to the vibrations measured in the front.

With respect to the floor-measured vibration levels [A(1) and VDV(1)], if they were an accurate surrogate measurement for one-hour of first responder and patient exposures, the impulsive VDV exposures would have a greater influence on the time to reach the occupationally derived, daily vibration action limits [7]. On the rough roads, based on the impulsive VDV exposures, occupants in the rear of the vehicle would reach the occupationally derived, daily vibration action limit in 22 min with the conventional suspension and 43 min with the alternative suspension, almost a doubling of the time to reach the daily vibration action limit. In addition, all vehicle occupants would likely be better isolated from road vibration with the alternative suspension.

If these results are generalizable to ambulances, relative to the ambulance cab, it appears that the first responders and patients traveling in the patient compartment in the rear of an ambulance would likely have higher exposures to vibration. Reducing movements and vibrations in the back of the ambulance during transport would be beneficial, reducing the disruptions may better facilitate the administration of chest compressions and intravenous medications and fluids during transport [4, 5]. In addition, although not measured or characterized in this study, the alternative suspension also has the capability to reduce side-to-side vehicle sway and roll. This roll-reduction, if present, could increase vehicle stability, ambulance driver control and reduce the chances for vehicle crashes. It may be beneficial for future studies to measure and characterize the sway and roll properties of the conventional and alternative suspensions.

The ideal place to isolate vehicle vibration, when possible, is at the source of the vibration, as it protects everything above the vehicle suspension, including the vehicle occupants, vehicle electronics and any onboard equipment. In addition, isolating at the source reduces the chances of equipment, like stretchers in ambulances, from being excited at their resonant frequency, which results in unwanted amplification of the patient's vibration exposures [8]. Future studies could document and verify these benefits for first responders and the treatment of their patients. Finally, the systematic methods used in this study could be a model for future studies to evaluate vehicle suspension systems and vehicle occupant WBV exposures.

References

1. Sherwood, H.B., Donze, A., Giebe, J.: Mechanical vibration in ambulance transport. J. Obstet. Gynecol. Neonatal. Nurs. **23**(6), 457–463 (1994). https://doi.org/10.1166/jnn.2012.6247
2. Custalow, C.B., Gravitz, C.S.: Emergency medical vehicle collisions and potential for preventive intervention. Prehosp. Emerg. Care **8**(2), 175–184 (2004). https://doi.org/10.1016/s1090-3127(03)00279-x. PMID: 15060853
3. Slattery, D.E., Silver, A.: The hazards of providing care in emergency vehicles: an opportunity for reform. Prehosp. Emerg. Care **13**(3), 388–397 (2009). https://doi.org/10.1080/109031208 02706104
4. Lerner, E.B., Sayre, M.R., Brice, J.H., White, L.J., Santin, A.J., Billittier IV, A.J., Cloud, S.D.: Cardiac arrest patients rarely receive chest compressions before ambulance arrival despite the availability of pre-arrival CPR instructions. Resuscitation **77**(1), 51–56 (2008). https://doi.org/10.1016/j.resuscitation.2007.10.020
5. McEachin, C.C., McDermott, J.T., Swor, R.: Few emergency medical services patients with lower-extremity fractures receive prehospital analgesia. Prehosp. Emerg. Care **6**(4), 406–410 (2002). https://doi.org/10.1080/10903120290938030
6. Bouchut, J.C., Van Lancker, E., Chritin, V., Gueugniaud, P.Y.: Physical stressors during neonatal transport: helicopter compared with ground ambulance. Air Med. J. **30**(3), 134–139 (2011). https://doi.org/10.1016/j.amj.2010.11.001
7. European Union. Directive 2002/44/EC of the European Parliament and of the Council of 25 June 2002 on the minimum health and safety requirements regarding the exposure of workers to the risks arising from physical agents (vibration) (sixteenth individual Directive within the meaning of Article 16(1) of Directive 89/391/EEC). Official Journal of the European Communities L, vol. 177, pp. 13–19 (2002)
8. Ryan, D., Lokeh, A., Hirschman, D., Spector, J., Parker, R., Johnson, P.W.: The characterization and evaluation of an intervention to reduce neonate whole body vibration exposures during ambulance transport. In: Proceedings of the 20th Triennial Congress of the International Ergonomics Association, pp. 670–677. Florence, Italy (2018). https://doi.org/10.1007/978-3-319-96083-8_84

Comparing Update Assessment Results in EMRs Between Inside and Outside the Patient Room in an Intensive Care Unit

Alireza Kasaie[1(✉)], Jung Hyup Kim[1], Wenbin Guo[1], Roland Nazareth[1], Thomas Shotton[1], and Laurel Despins[2]

[1] Industrial and Manufacturing Systems Engineering Department, University of Missouri, Columbia, MO, USA
{skdx2,wgk95,rnbh6,tmsv22}@umsystem.edu, kijung@missouri.edu
[2] Sinclair School of Nursing, University of Missouri, Columbia, MO, USA
DespinsL@health.missouri.edu

Abstract. The primary objective of this study is to analyze the different patterns of electronic medical record (EMR) documentation corresponding to updating assessment results and how these patterns would be different inside and outside the patient room in a medical intensive care unit in terms of average process time. In this study, the real-time measurement system data was used to analyze ICU nurses' workflow related to the EMR documentation. After that, multiple hierarchical task analysis charts were developed to find different EMR documentation patterns for assessment results. The results revealed that the patterns of EMR documentation were significantly different in terms of average process time. The findings from this study might identify the areas of EMR where improvements can be made by preventing disruptions, incompleteness, and optimizing the EMR process efficiency in a medical ICU.

Keywords: Electronic medical record · Nursing workflow · Health information technology · Human-Computer interaction

1 Introduction

An intensive care unit (ICU) is one of the dynamic and problematic areas in a hospital. In ICUs, many nurses are exposed to a hectic environment where they need to provide timely and proper healthcare services to support urgent therapeutic interventions and monitoring intensive patients. According to a study done by Singer and Little [1], the mortality rate among patients who are not critically sick is more than 25%, while this ratio increases more than 40% in the case of patients who are experiencing a complication. Thus, reducing the probability of clinical risks is vital inside the ICU [2, 3].

Several strategies have been proposed to improve the quality of care and operational efficiency in ICUs [4]. One of these strategies is using healthcare information technology [5] to support clinical activities, improve efficiency, reduce errors, improve the quality of care, and reduce the cost of healthcare [6, 7]. An electronic medical record (EMR)

N. L. Black et al. (Eds.): IEA 2021, LNNS 222, pp. 355–362, 2021.
https://doi.org/10.1007/978-3-030-74611-7_49

system is a digital information equivalent of paper records, which typically contains general information such as treatment, assessment, orders, and patient medical history [8]. The EMRs enable nurses to access their patient's data over time, identify patients for preventive visits, monitor patients, improve healthcare quality, reduce medical errors, and predict drug interaction [9, 10]. The adverse consequences of HIT systems are including 1) more or new work for clinicians, 2) changes in clinicians' workflow, and 3) new types of errors regarding entering assessment and medical results [11].

EMR systems affect ICU nurses' workflow by increasing the documentation time, while decreasing communication time with patients [12]. ICU nurses have spent up to 60% of their time with computers [13], although getting to know the patient and family is essential for providing a good quality of care [14]. Having proper communication and spending more time with patients can help nurses improve their comprehension and retention of patient conditions [15]. However, EMR systems provide enormous digital information regarding their patient's treatment and conditions.

This study aims to identify the areas of EMR where improvements can be made by preventing disruptions, incompleteness, and helping nurses to have proper communication with patients and their relatives. Thus, having a good understanding of how ICU nurses perform EMR documentation related to updating assessment results will improve healthcare delivery processes. In this study, a time & motion study was conducted in a medical ICU at the University of Missouri Hospital. After that, by combining the data obtained from manual observation forms and real-time measurement system (RTMS), multiple hierarchical task analysis (HTA) charts were developed to understand ICU nurses' workflow. According to the previous studies [5, 16, 17], all nurses' activities related to the EMR documentation will be categorized into four main groups, including 1) update assessment results, 2) review documents, 3) check and update medication requests, 4) check lab specimen.

2   Methodology

In this study, the time & motion study was conducted at the University Hospital, University of Missouri-Columbia. Nine ICU nurses participated in this study, and one to three nurses were observed on each observation day from 7:00 a.m. to 7:30 p.m. for 15 days from 2/17/2020 to 3/11/2020. All participants were registered nurses with a range of 1 to 26 years of ICU work experience. All participating nurses were informed about conducting the time & motion study and all collected information related to the nurses and patients was kept confidential. To minimize the Hawthorne effect, observers maintained a considerable distance from the participants and did not initiate any conversation with them. Besides, to maintain patient privacy, observers were not allowed to enter a patient room. The studied ICU had eighteen single-patient rooms in two pods and a reception desk located in the middle of the unit. Each pod had a nurse station equipped with monitors, computers, telephones, tables, and a medicine cabinet.

All log information related to EMR documentation were recorded in the Real-Time Measurement System (RTMS) database. In this study, the RTMS log data was used to analyze nursing work patterns related to the EMR charting [5]. The University of Missouri IRB approved all procedures done in this study.

Three graduate students collected time and activity data with one undergraduate student and recorded the start and end time of each task done by ICU nurses by using an observation form (see Fig. 1).

Start Time:	End Time:	Date:					Nurse:							Observer:	
No	Activity	0	5	10	15	20	25	30	35	40	45	50	55	Total	Comments
	Verbal Reports	0	5	10	15	20	25	30	35	40	45	50	55	Total	
V1	Start of Shift Report (Big Report)														
V2	One-to-One Meeting (Nurse Handoff)														
	Primary Care (In-Room)	0	5	10	15	20	25	30	35	40	45	50	55	Total	
PC1	Initial Assessment(Vital)														
PC2	Focused Assessment														
PC3	Performing Procedure														
PC4	Patient Care (Turning/Bathing/Etc)														
PC5	Comforting/Teaching/Talking to Patients														
PC6	Preparing/Administering Medications														
PC7	Talking to Physician														
PC8	Talking to Family														
PC9	EMR Charting														
PC10	Teaching Residents/Students														
PC11	Using ASCOM Phone														
PC12	Transport Patient/Prepare for Transport														
PC13	Taking Notes About Patients (Brains)														
PC14	Taking Lab Specimens														
PC15	Stocking Room														
PC16	Cleaning Room														
PC17	Working on Monitors and Equipment														
PC18	Attending/Participating in Clinical Rounds														
PC19	Closed Curtain, Tasks Unknown														

Fig. 1. The manual observation form

All nursing activities are categorized into five main groups: verbal report, primary care, peer support, out-of-room activities, and non-nursing activities [18]. RTMS data shows the time and work patterns related to nurses' EMR documentation in an ICU.

3 Data Analysis

The collected data from the manual observation forms and RTMS system were combined to develop a hierarchical task analysis (HTA) chart to have a detailed view of the nurses' EMR documentation workflow inside and outside the patient room.

3.1 Hierarchical Task Analysis (HTA) Chart

By combining the data gained from the time & motion study and RTMS system, multiple HTA charts were created to show the process of updating assessment results in EMRs. HTA chart breaks down a nurses' task into sub-tasks. It provides a model for task execution to accomplish the goals of different tasks. For example, HTA might help us to have a better understanding of the ICU nurse work patterns related to updating the assessment results. Figure 2 shows the HTA chart for updating assessment results both inside and outside the patient room.

To construct the HTA chart, all nursing tasks related to updating the assessment results inside and outside the patient room were categorized into ten different processes. To update assessment results inside or outside the patient room, ICU nurses must complete all or a part of these tasks.

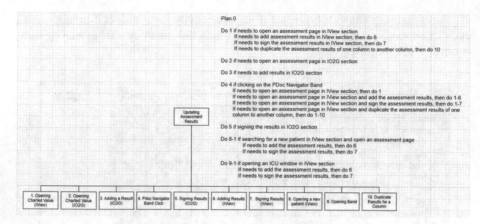

Fig. 2. The HTA chart for updating assessment results

In EMR systems, there are two different assessment pages, Interactive View (IView) and Intake and Output second Generation (IO2G), which are mostly used by bedside caregivers (i.e., a respiratory therapist, dialysis nurses, and registered nurses) to add or sign their assessment results. Interactive View (IView) window is a tab in EMR system that allows nurses to chart and organize patient assessment data in a meaningful manner. On the other hand, Intake and Output window is a tab in the EMR system used to document and share the information related to fluids taken and removed from a patient, like urine. Table 1 shows a brief description of each of the HTA chart tasks.

Table 1. The description of tasks in the HTA chart

Task ID	Task name	Description
1	Opening charted value (IView)	Opening the patient assessment page in IView section to add and sign the assessment results
2	Opening charted value (IO2G)	Opening the patient assessment page in Intake and Output section to add and sign the assessment results
3	Adding a result (IO2G)	Adding the assessment results, related to the amount of fluid taken by a patient and the amount of any fluids, like urine removed from the patient in IO2G section
4	PDoc navigator band click	A ribbon on the left side of each EMR window which is made up of several bands and sections and enables nurses to have access to other pages

(continued)

Table 1. (*continued*)

Task ID	Task name	Description
5	Signing results (IO2G)	Reviewing, confirming, and signing the results related to the Intake and Output assessment in IO2G section
6	Adding results (IView)	Adding results related to initial and focused assessments, like temperature, oxygen saturation, breath sounds, heart rate source, etc. in IView assessment window
7	Signing results (IView)	Reviewing, confirming, and signing the results related to the initial and focused assessments in the IView section
8	Opening new patient	Searching the name of the patient to have access to patient's documentation
9	Opening band	Opening a new section using the PDoc Navigator Band
10	Duplicate results for a column	Utilizing the EMR option for duplicating the previous assessments results of one column to another column or assessment page in IView section

4   Results

In this study, a one-way ANOVA was conducted to compare the patterns of EMRs for updating assessment results inside and outside the patient room in terms of average process time. Tables 2 and 3 show the results of ANOVA on the average process time of updating assessment results in EMRs. There are significant differences in average process time inside and outside the patient's room for sequences 4 ($P = 0.005$), 1–6 ($P = 0.002$), 4-1-7 ($P = 0.005$), and 8-1-7 ($P = 0.020$). In all these sequences, ICU nurses spent longer process time updating the assessment results in the EMR system outside the patient room.

Table 2. ANOVA results for the average process time of updating assessment results

Location	Avg process time (min)	StDev (min)	F	P
In-Room	5.581	7.134	12.49	**0.00**
Out-of-Room	7.509	7.751		

Table 3. ANOVA results for the average process time of HTA chart tasks

Sequence	Location	Average process time (min)	StDev (min)	F	P
4	In-Room	3.09	5.70	8.08	**0.005**
	Out-of-Room	4.47	5.91		
1–6	In-Room	2.07	2.96	9.75	**0.002**
	Out-of-Room	3.29	5.36		
4-1-6	In-Room	4.46	5.83	1.93	0.165
	Out-of-Room	5.27	6.56		
4-1-7	In-Room	4.71	4.71	8.08	**0.005**
	Out-of-Room	6.74	6.74		
4-1-10	In-Room	5.30	8.29	0.56	0.454
	Out-of-Room	6.00	6.13		
8-1-7	In-Room	4.55	6.25	5.01	**0.020**
	Out-of-Room	6.74	8.08		

5　Discussion

The primary objective of this study is to analyze the documentation patterns of EMRs for updating assessment results in a medical ICU and how these patterns can be different inside and outside the patient room in terms of average process time. Table 2 shows that ICU nurses prefer to spend more time on updating assessment results outside the patient room. Table 3 shows that ICU nurses spend more time on the PDoc Navigation band (task 4) when they use the EMR system outside the patient room. The navigation bar in this task is a ribbon located on the left side of the EMR window. It helps nurses and physicians to access other EMR windows, such as Intake and Output, IView, clinical notes, medication profile, etc. (see Fig. 3(a)). By clicking on these icons provided in this ribbon, ICU nurses will open other windows and navigate the system. This result indicates that ICU nurses might prefer to process more information while working outside the patient room. They accessed more pages, including patient's documentation, allergies, medication history, etc.

For Task 7, it is performed to check the accuracy of all inputted data [5]. After adding the results to the IView assessment page, ICU nurses must click on the checkmark button on the toolbar above the navigator band to confirm and sign the assessment results (see Fig. 3(b)). Table 3 shows a significant difference in average process time for sequences 4-1-7 and 8-1-7 compared to sequences 4-1-6 and 4-1-10. It means that nurses prefer to check and measure the vital signs and do the focused assessments and enter the assessment result when they work inside the room. On the other hand, they prefer to check the accuracy and consistency of the assessment results when they work outside the room because they spent a significantly longer time to check the accuracy of all inputted data.

 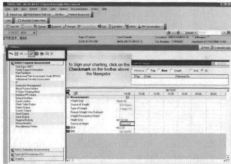

(a) PDoc Navigator Band ribbon   (b) signing the results in IView assessment window

Fig. 3. Screenshots of the EMR system

In a patient room, performing focused assessment and adding those results in the EMR system are the top priority tasks for ICU nurses. The key difference between sequence 1–6 and sequence 4-1-6 is whether to use the navigation bar or not. Table 3 also shows a significant difference in the process time for sequence 1–6 between inside and outside the patient room compared to sequence 4-1-6. Furthermore, the standard deviation of sequence 1–6 is increased from 2.96 to 5.36 when the location is changed from inside to outside the room. One possible explanation of this phenomenon could be the design issue related to the PDoc Navigation Band inside the patient room. According to the results, we found a large deviation of using the navigation bar for ICU nurses when adding results in the IView section inside the patient room.

Overall, the findings of the current study revealed that the location of EMR charting has a significant impact on the average process time while updating the assessment results in EMRs. We also identified one usability issue of PDoc Navigation Band ribbon in the EMR system related to adding results in the IView section.

6 Limitation and Future Research

Despite our findings, there are several limitations in this study. First, we only used data from day-shift nurses; so, it would be beneficial to include night-shift nurses and compare the current findings. Second, nurses' interruption was not considered in our data collection. Although ICU nurses experience multiple interruptions while working during a shift, we did not consider the source of disruption in our data collection. Third, we only collected data from nine ICU nurses. Hence, it would be recommended to have more participants in future studies.

References

1. Singer, M., Little, R.: ABC of intensive care: cutting edge. BMJ: Br. Med. J. **319**(7208), 501 (1999)
2. Chiozza, M.L., Ponzetti, C.: FMEA: a model for reducing medical errors. Clin. Chim. Acta **404**(1), 75–78 (2009)

3. Morelli, P., Vinci, A., Galetto, L., Magon, G., Maniaci, V., Banfi, G.: FMECA methodology applied to two pathways in an orthopaedic hospital in Milan. J. Prev. Med. Hyg. **48**(2), 54–59 (2007)

4. Hoot, N.R., Aronsky, D.: Systematic review of emergency department crowding: causes, effects, and solutions. Ann. Emerg. Med. **52**(2), 126–136 (2008)

5. Guo, W., Kim, J.H., Smith, B., Despins, L.: How nurse experience influences the patterns of electronic medical record documentation in an intensive care unit. In: Proceedings of the Human Factors and Ergonomics Society Annual Meeting, vol. 63, no. 1, pp. 708–712. SAGE Publications Sage CA, Los Angeles, CA (2019)

6. Likourezos, A., Chalfin, D.B., Murphy, D.G., Sommer, B., Darcy, K., Davidson, S.J.: Physician and nurse satisfaction with an electronic medical record system. J. Emerg. Med. **27**(4), 419–424 (2004)

7. Sittig, D.F., Kuperman, G.J., Fiskio, J.: Evaluating physician satisfaction regarding user interactions with an electronic medical record system. In: Proceedings of the AMIA Symposium. American Medical Informatics Association, p. 400 (1999)

8. USF Health. What is EMR. https://www.usfhealthonline.com/resources/key-concepts/what-are-electronic-medical-records-emr/. Accessed

9. National Coordinator for Health Information Technology: What are the differences between electronic medical records, electronic health records, and personal health records? https://www.healthit.gov/faq/what-are-differences-between-electronic-medical-records-electronic-health-records-and-personal. Accessed

10. Alpert, J.S.: The electronic medical record in 2016: advantages and disadvantages. Digit. Med. **2**(2), 48 (2016)

11. Campbell, E.M., Sittig, D.F., Ash, J.S., Guappone, K.P., Dykstra, R.H.: Types of unintended consequences related to computerized provider order entry. J. Am. Med. Inform. Assoc. **13**(5), 547–556 (2006)

12. Kossman, S.P.: Perceptions of impact of electronic health records on nurses' work. Stud. Health Technol. Inform. **122**, 337 (2006)

13. Cornell, P., Riordan, M., Herrin-Griffith, D.: Transforming nursing workflow, part 2: the impact of technology on nurse activities. JONA: J. Nurs. Adm. **40**(10), 432–439 (2010)

14. Luker, K.A., Austin, L., Caress, A., Hallett, C.E.: The importance of 'knowing the patient': community nurses' constructions of quality in providing palliative care. J. Adv. Nurs. **31**(4), 775–782 (2000)

15. Schillinger, D., et al.: Closing the loop: physician communication with diabetic patients who have low health literacy. Arch. Intern. Med. **163**(1), 83–90 (2003)

16. Smith, B., Sreeramakavacham, S., Kim, J.H., Despins, L.: Improving computerized charting in an intensive care unit. In: International Conference on Digital Human Modeling and Applications in Health, Safety, Ergonomics and Risk Management, pp. 537–546. Springer (2018)

17. Sreeramakavacham, S., Kim, J.H., Despins, L., Sommerfeldt, M., Bessette, N.: Effect of patient acuity of illness and nurse experience on EMR works in intensive care unit. In: International Conference on Digital Human Modeling and Applications in Health, Safety, Ergonomics and Risk Management, pp. 547–557. Springer (2018)

18. Song, X., Kim, J.H., Despins, L.: A time-motion study in an intensive care unit using the near field electromagnetic ranging system. In: IIE Annual Conference. Proceedings. Institute of Industrial and Systems Engineers (IISE), pp. 470–475 (2017)

Ergonomics and Job Retention of Workers with Chronic Disease

Joanie Maclure[1,2]([envelope]) and Pierre-Yves Therriault[2,3]

[1] Programme de Doctorat en Sciences Biomédicales, Université du Québec à Trois-Rivières (UQTR), Trois-Rivières, Québec, Canada
joanie.maclure@uqtr.ca
[2] Laboratoire de Recherche en Ergologie, UQTR, Trois-Rivières, Québec, Canada
[3] Département d'ergothérapie, UQTR, Trois-Rivières, Québec, Canada

Abstract. Work is a central activity among the working population. The presence of a chronic disease (CD) can influence working life by modifying people's capacities. Because CD is long lasting and rarely heals, job retention will be impacted. This research explore the process of job retention of people with CD. To meet this objective, grounded theory (GT) has been used. The study took place in an organization of the public health and social services in Quebec. The research participants are on one hand workers with CD and on the other, managers of the sectors in which workers with CD work. The data collection aim at understanding the phenomenon through individual interviews. The approximately 75-min interviews were digitally recorded and transcribed in their entirety into NVivo (version 12) for analysis. Constant comparative analysis of the data, collected through individual interviews, allows coding (open, axial, selective and theoretical). In the organization, managers and workers use ergonomic strategies for job retention. These ergonomic strategies can be societal, organizational or personal. The implementation of ergonomic strategies results in consequences on the job retention of people with CD.

Keywords: Ergonomics · Job retention · Chronic disease

1 Introduction

1.1 Increase of Chronic Disease in Population

In general population, there is a growth of CD [1]. CD is considered as a condition that lasts over time and that causes limitations in everyday life [12]. It can be related to specific diagnoses either link to physical or mental health. Along with the growth of CD in population, some cultural changes are operationalizing in the health and social services system in Quebec. These changes concern, among other things, the shift from paternal models which placed the person with CD in a passive role in CD management to models where active involvement is required of them. These changes require the management of CD in the different spheres of their life, including work.

1.2 Work, an Central Activity

Work is a central activity among the working population. During his work life, workers will experience few steps [2]. These steps can be influenced by the presence of CD. CD can influence the different stages of working life by modifying people's capacities. What are the impacts of changing capacities of workers with CD, among others, on occupational health and safety (OHS)?

1.3 Health and Safety at Work

OHS is define as follows: "aim to promote and maintain the highest possible degree of physical, mental and social well-being of workers in all trades, to prevent harmful effects on the health of workers due to their working conditions, protect workers against dangers that threaten their health, place and maintain workers in a working environment adapted to their physical and mental needs, adapt work to men"[1]. OHS covers all aspects of the physical, mental and social well-being of workers [3]. Habitually, more importance is given to safety concerns than to health concerns. However, being interested in health problems implies repercussions on safety problems since by definition a healthy environment is also a safe environment [3]. What actions can organizations and workers take to promote OHS? Since CD is long lasting and rarely heals, it is worth asking how people with CD manage to maintain their job and what are the impacts on their health?

2   Aims

The aim of this article is to explore the perceptions of workers with CD and managers about job retention in relation with of deploying ergonomic strategies. The article is part of a research project aimed at understanding the job retention of workers with CD from a perspective of preventing exclusion from the labor market.

3   Methods

3.1 Epistemological Framework

To meet this objective, grounded theory (GT) was selected. Inscribed in a constructivist paradigm, this research is based on the fact that reality is socially constructed. Participants and researchers construct categories by co-construction through their interactions. Thus, the representation of data is problematic, relativistic, situational and partial [4].

---

[1] Organisation internationale du travail (OIT). *Santé et vie au travail: un droit humain fondamental.* Organisation internationale du travail, Genève (2009) p. 5.

3.2 Methodological Framework

Context. The study took place in an organization of the public health and social services in Quebec. The participants in the research were workers with CD on one hand, and managers in which workers with CD work on the other part.

Sampling. The initial convenience sample is made of workers with CD and managers. The initial selection criteria for workers were: 1) aged between 35 and 65; 2) presence of one or more work difficulties related to a CD; and 3) have a regular full-time or regular part-time job. The initial selection criteria for managers was to be hired as a manager (regardless of the strategic positioning in the organization). Workers and managers in casual job were excluded from the search. Subsequently, the sampling became theoretical, the participants were selected by the researchers for their theoretical contribution. For example, following this sampling method, the 4th worker participant was selected according to a criterion related to age and the 4th, 5th, and 6th managers participants were selected according to their position in the organization. Finally, the 7th participants of the two categories were selected following a falsification strategy, the selection of an extreme case.

Data Collect. Sociodemographic data were collected by questionnaire while data aimed at understanding the phenomenon via individual interviews. The initial interview guide for workers included questions such as: How is your CD affecting your job? How do you think it is possible to keep your job despite the CD? While those for managers included questions such as: How do you see the job retention of people with CD? What does managing a worker with CD mean to you? The approximately 75-minutes interviews were digitally recorded and transcribed in their entirety into NVivo software (version 12) for analysis.

Analysis. A constant comparative analysis of the data (coding and analyzing) is begging with the first interview. There is four levels of coding in GT. As this article present a part of the research, only the three first level of coding are present. The first, open-ended, consist of assigning a word that simultaneously summarized and counted data transcribed from the interview. The second and the third, compare codes with each other in order to obtain categories and concepts. It is, ultimately, the relationship between categories and concepts that will allow the emergence of the theory.

Scientific Criterion. In this research, scientific criteria considered are credibility, consistency as well as applicability [5]. The credibility concerning the accuracy of the results was supported by continuous questions of analysists such as: Are the data sufficient? Are the data compared systematically? Are the links between categories and concepts logical? The strategy of falsification, the triangulation of the results with the scientific documentation as well as the fact that the concepts come directly from the interviews promote credibility [6]. In this research, to ensure consistency, the researchers constantly assessed whether the conceptualization corresponds to the workers perspective. To achieve this, they questioned themselves about the categories and emerging concepts, in order to know whether they cover the phenomenon studied. Likewise, other elements increase consistency, including knowledge of the environment by the principal investigator and the involvement of long-term researchers in the environment. Finally, concerning the criterion of applicability, the researchers tried to understand the retention in employment of people with a chronic disease by tending towards a theoretical saturation. During the coding process, the use of memos to define the different codes allowed, for example, the constant comparison of results.

4 Results

4.1 Ergonomic Strategies

In the organization, workers and managers use ergonomic strategies for job retention. These strategies can be societal, organizational or personal. Among the societal strategies is universal accessibility. Organizational strategies include work organization as well as workstation adaptations. As for individual strategies, they include self-management as well as attitudes of workers or managers. The ergonomic strategies are influenced by different organizational factors such as the availability of the workforce and by different personal factors such as the type of CD (Table 1).

Table 1. Societal, organizational and personal ergonomic strategies

Type	Ergonomic strategies	Definitions
Societal	Universal accessibility context	Adopt a culture conducive to inclusion for all with regard to the choice of physical environments
Organizational	Workstation adaptation	Adapt workstations for considering workers' capacities
	Work schedule modification	Ajust the work schedule for considering worker's individuals caracteristics
	Work organization flexibility	Ajust organizational demands in considering perspectives workers with CD
	Roles and responsibilities clarification	Clarifying roles and responsibilities of managers and workers
	Human resources augmentation	Add human resources in considering team workload
Personal (worker)	Energy conservation techniques utilization	Implement judicious techniques for use of energy conservation
	Articular protection techniques utilization	Implement judicious techniques for articular protection

4.2 Consequences of the Deployment of Ergonomic Strategies

The goal for workers with CD as well as managers is job retention. To pursue that goal they use wherewithal's as the deployment of ergonomic strategies. These can have consequences on the organization, the managers and the workers with CD. The consequences may be favourable (+), unfavourable (−) or both (±) but depend on the context (Fig. 1).

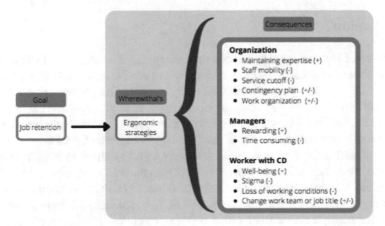

Fig. 1. Consequences of deployment of ergonomic strategies on the organization, the managers and the workers with CD.

Organization. The positive consequence of deploying ergonomic strategies on the organization is the maintenance of expertise. If the worker with CD manages to maintain his job, partly due to ergonomic strategies, the organization benefits from the worker's expertise. On the other hand, adverse consequences are also possible. These include the mobility of staff as well as service cuts. Indeed, it may be that through the implementation of ergonomic strategies such as the setting of the work schedule, this can have an impact on the composition of the work teams or the services rendered to the population. Finally, some consequences may be both favourable or unfavourable to the organization depending on the context. This is the case, among other things, for the implementation of contingency plans or for the revision of the organization of work.

Managers. For managers, the positive consequence of deploying ergonomic strategies for job retention is the recognition of the worker with CD for supporting him or her in the process. While the adverse consequence is the time managers must invest to deploy effective ergonomic strategies in a context where their agenda is already well-stocked. Management related to the implementation of ergonomic strategies can become a burden for managers.

Worker with CD. Worker with CD who wishes to remain employed will find that the implementation of ergonomic strategies gives him a sense of well-being since the strategies aim, among other things, to make the work more suited to his abilities. On the other hand, because ergonomic strategies may target workers with CD, they may experience stigma or in some cases even lose certain working conditions. Among the consequences that can sometimes be favourable and sometimes unfavourable is the change of work team or job title. Changing work teams or job titles can be an initiative of the worker to more closely match their job and abilities. In this context, the change is often favourable. It can, however, also be initiated by managers and, at that time, be unfavourable.

5 Discussion

The purpose of this text was to explore the perception of workers with CD as well as managers about the consequences of deploying ergonomic strategies for job retention. It is part of a research project aimed at understanding the phenomenon of keeping people with chronic illnesses in employment, with a view to preventing exclusion from the labour market. It appears that favourable, unfavourable or both context-dependent consequences affect the organization, managers and worker with a CD.

Workers with CD as well as managers want to allow them to remain employed. To achieve this, they will implement different ergonomic strategies. Although they want to avoid premature exclusion from the labour market, the implementation of these ergonomic strategies is not without consequences. Some of them will be positive and will increase, for example, the worker's well-being at work. While others will have a more detrimental effect such as an extra workload for the managers. Thus, although everyone is willing and the strategies deployed are ergonomic in nature, it seems impossible that the consequences on the organization, managers or worker with a CD are automatically favourable. It is thus possible to believe that the context in which these ergonomic strategies are deployed greatly influences their consequences.

The worker with CD is looking for a balance in order to be successful in remaining in employment. He experiences, to a certain extent, a new identity as a worker. He seeks a balance between his own well-being and that of the organization [7, 8]. The implementation of ergonomic strategies is, for him, a way of getting closer in the organization. Managers are looking for a balanced response between meeting productivity objectives, providing service to population and the well-being of workers with or without CD [9, 10]. They experience how CD influences the accomplishment of work within the team and ultimately the achievement of the organization's mission. The society is looking for a product or service to meet the needs of the populations. Society wants inclusion for everyone, regardless of the difference between individuals [11]. Is it a utopia to believe that inclusion of all is possible while maintaining the well-being of individuals and organizations?

It is hoped that people with CD could be fulfilled in meaningful work, but is this a paradox? All hope for it, but few succeed in updating it. Is this why ergonomic strategies can be both favorable or unfavorable for different persons and organizations involved in the process? Currently, ergonomic strategies are primarily focused on responding to the onset of CD. Can certain strategies be put in place even before the onset of CD? For example, elements related to organizational culture such as a specific direction, opportunities for advancement, etc. These constitute strategies favorable to the retention of all workers. Thus, ensuring the presence of these elements for everyone, with or without disease, would act before the apparition of a disease. Likewise, acting on the perceptions of managers or workers, through information sessions, can have a favorable impact on job retention even before a worker signifies that he is suffering from a CD.

6 Conclusion

The prevalence of CD is increasing in populations and CD creates an impact on lives of those who suffer from it. Among the possible impacts, limitations in carrying out a job are real. Several studies deal with socio-professional rehabilitation programs, self-management, work accommodation, etc. The establishment of anti-discrimination laws, policies, regulations aimed at inclusion are currently advocated by society. But what about the study of organizations? As the effectiveness of ergonomic strategies seem to depend on the context in which they are deployed, focusing on organizations open up a new understanding of this phenomenon.

References

1. World Health Organization (WHO). https://www.who.int/fr/. Accessed 30 Jan 2021
2. Riverain-Simard, D.: Étapes de vie au Travail. Éditions Saint-Martin, Montréal (1984)
3. Organisation Internationale du Travail (OIT): Santé et vie au Travail: un Droit Humain Fondamental. Organisation Internationale du Travail, Genève (2009)
4. Charmaz, K.: Constructing Grounded Theory: A Practical Guide Through Qualitative Analysis. Sage, London (2006)
5. Lincoln, Y., Guba, E.: Naturalistic Inquiry. Sage, Newbury Park (1985)
6. Drapeau, M.: Les critères de scientificité en recherche qualitative. Pratiques Psychol. **10**(1), 79–86 (2004)
7. Restall, G.J., Simms, A.M., Walker, J.R., et al.: Understanding work experiences of people with inflammatory bowel disease. Inflamm. Bowel Dis. **22**(7), 1688–1697 (2016)
8. Helgeson, V.S., Jakubiak, B., Van Vleet, M., Zajdel, M.: Communal coping and adjustment to chronic illness: theory update and evidence. Pers. Soc. Psychol. Rev. **22**(2), 170–195 (2018)
9. Amir, Z., Wynn, P., Chan, F., Strauser, D., Whitaker, S., Luker, K.: Return to work after cancer in the UK: attitudes and experiences of line managers. J. Occup. Rehabil. **20**(4), 435–442 (2010)
10. Varekamp, I., Haafkens, J.A., Detaille, S.I., Tak, P.P., van Dijk, F.J.: Preventing work disability among employees with rheumatoid arthritis: what medical professionals can learn from the patients' perspective. Arthritis Care Res. Official J. Am. Coll. Rheumatol. **53**(6), 965–972 (2005)
11. Chan, M., Zeollick, R.: Rapport Mondial sur le Handicap. Éditions de l'OMS, Genève (2011)
12. Beaglehole, R., Epping-Jordan, J., Durivage, S., Marlin, A., McCaffrey, K., Munro, A., Savitsky, C. et., Thompson, K.: Prévention des maladies chronique: un investissement vital. Genève : Éditions de l'OMS (2006)

Impact of Audio/Visual Guidance on Novices' Training with VR Orthopedic Surgical Simulators

Carolyn Mattes-O'Brien[1,2]([✉]) [iD], Marino Menozzi[3] [iD], Roger Gassert[1] [iD], and Markus Oelhafen[2]

[1] Rehabilitation Engineering Laboratory, ETH Zurich, Zurich, Switzerland
carolyn.obrien@hest.ethz.ch
[2] VirtaMed AG, Schlieren, Switzerland
[3] Human Factors Engineering, ETH Zurich, Zurich, Switzerland

Abstract. Minimally invasive surgery, specifically endoscopy, is a vital component in modern surgical healthcare. Due to the challenging nature of operating through a restricted endoscopic camera view, novice surgeons must master navigating surgical volumes effectively and efficiently. One of the specific focus areas for these inexperienced surgeons is maintaining the horizon of the camera in the surgical volume. Alongside traditional cadaver training, surgeons use mixed-reality surgical training simulators to improve their surgical skills. In this work, we propose a new method of training novice users in the proper method of maintaining camera horizon alignment in an arthroscopic knee procedure. We ran a study with 21 medical novices on a commercially available surgical simulator. We provided automated verbal cues, digital sine wave audio, or a commercially available visual horizon bar to see if an improvement in performance could be found over the control group that received no additional feedback for the camera horizon. We examined the Overall Workload of the participants, along with the misalignment time of the camera horizon and the procedure time. Results from the study showed that the verbal cues improved procedure time and Overall Workload, and the visual horizon bar improved the horizon misalignment time. Digital sine wave audio was not effective overall.

Keywords: Multimodal systems · Surgical training · Healthcare ergonomics · Workload · Simulator

1 Introduction

Obtaining proficiency in any field is challenging, but the cognitive abilities and fine-motor skills required in the operating room are a culmination of years of education and training. Minimally invasive surgery, often in the form of endoscopy, focuses on causing the smallest amount of damage to the patient, limiting trauma and recovery time. Endoscopy is difficult as it is only done through narrow view cameras inserted into the patient. Arthroscopy, or minimally invasive endoscopic surgery of the joints,

N. L. Black et al. (Eds.): IEA 2021, LNNS 222, pp. 370–379, 2021.
https://doi.org/10.1007/978-3-030-74611-7_51

is even more challenging than normal endoscopy as the surgeons must navigate very small surgical volumes. This space is often only several cubic centimeters. Gaining the appropriate skillset for these styles of surgery requires intensive effort.

During the training and education of novice endoscopic surgeons, special focus is often placed on holding the camera horizon parallel to the ground [1]. As one of the first skills learned in the operating room [2], maintaining this consistent camera horizon supports the identification of critical anatomical structures, since they resemble the structures shown in textbooks and literature in this position. The surgeon also benefits from a better orientation within the body.

Alongside traditional cadaver training, surgeons today practice arthroscopies on surgical simulators, e.g., for the knee or the shoulder. Several commercially available simulators exist for knee arthroscopy and have found commercial success around the world [3–5]. In the last few years, virtual reality has been applied to surgical training, with the intent of improving the efficiency and effectiveness of training, especially for novices [6].

Currently, the only implemented method of guiding novice users in holding the correct camera horizon angle is with a visual horizon bar, like those seen in flight simulators. Due to the sheer volume of information that is also being presented simultaneously during a training scenario, trainees may be put under a high cognitive load. As De Jong notes, "cognitive load theory asserts that learning is hampered when working memory capacity is exceeded in a learning task" [7]. As the intrinsic cognitive load of learning surgical procedures is high, by nature fewer resources are available for the trainees. To limit the cognitive overload, one focus can be on reducing the extraneous cognitive load. As Mousavi et al. note, "when students must split their attention between multiple sources of information, [it] results in a heavy cognitive load. Presentation-modality effects suggest that working memory has partially independent processors for handling visual and auditory material. Effective working memory may be increased by presenting material in a mixed rather than a unitary mode" [8].

When examining the horizon guidance, the information is only presented in visual form. The surgical simulators currently do not use the auditory pathway to convey training information. Performance and workload of novices may be improved if some information can be provided along a different modality. One obvious candidate for this alteration would be the horizon information that is currently communicated visually. One method of evaluating the workload of the participants is by using the simple but effective Overall Workload questionnaire created by Vidulich and Tsang [9].

In this work, we explore the application of two forms of audio guidance and one form of visual guidance in the field of knee arthroscopy. We address the following question: do verbal cues, digital sine wave audio cues, or a visual horizon bar help maintain the correct horizon, lower the procedure time, or reduce the Overall Workload compared to a control group training without the cues? We hypothesize that audio cues will have a greater impact on these metrics than the visual cues. Additionally, we hypothesize that both cue types will be an improvement when compared to the control group.

2 Methodology

2.1 Instrumentation

A commercially available mixed-reality arthroscopic knee simulator (ArthroS Knee, VirtaMed AG, Switzerland) was sourced and modified to support additional sound feedback. The system included training software, an arthroscopic camera and palpation hook, in addition to an anatomical knee model of a right, male, healthy knee, shown in Fig. 1. An additional training module was also provided, the Fundamentals of Arthroscopic Surgery Training (FAST) basic skills module.

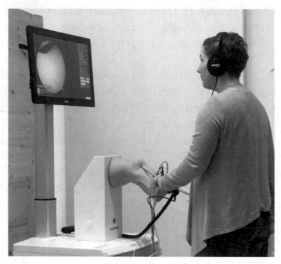

Fig. 1. The modified knee arthroscopy simulator is shown with a right, male knee model, arthroscope, palpation hook, and headphones.

Additionally, the participants were provided over-ear headphones (SRH440, Shure, USA) with an impedance of 44 Ω, foam isolation, and no active noise cancelation. The headphones were calibrated using the method prescribed by Pigeon, by playing a reference sound to the output of the headphones to a L_{max} of 68 dB(A) [10].

A digital sine wave was integrated into the training software, using the camera angle to create the appropriate pitch using the OpenAL library. A lower pitch indicated a better angle position, and a higher pitch indicated a larger deviation from the desired angle, from no audible sound at 0 Hz to 1 kHz, rendered continuously. The 1 kHz pitch as played at a deviation of 90° or more. The verbal cues were recorded with a Zoom H6 recorder (Zoom, Japan) and imported with version 2.3.3 of Audacity® recording and editing software (Audacity Team) in both German and English. The cues in both languages were "Caution", "Watch your horizon", or "Your camera is over 90° off". The cues were played based on the camera angle deviation from ideal. The "Caution" cue was triggered by 27 to 45° of deviation, a deviation of 45 to 85° triggered "Watch your horizon", and greater than 85° triggered the final message. The simulator already had the visual horizon bar integrated as part of the available software, which maintained a fixed horizon bar and indicated the level of deviation with green to red coloring, with green being acceptable deviation levels and red being unacceptable level of horizon misalignment, as seen in Fig. 2.

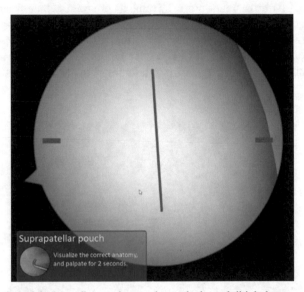

Fig. 2. A screenshot of the knee diagnostic tour shows the lateral tibial plateau, with the meniscus on the edge. The vertical bar shows that the horizon has an approximately 90° deviation. The horizon bar is implemented in the software additionally indicates deviation levels with color. This red color indicates higher levels of horizon misalignment.

2.2 Participants

Participants were informed about the procedure before the experiment, gave written consent, and were aware that the study was approved by the local ethics committee (ETH Zürich, EK-2020-N-07). A total of 21 participants (22.5 ± 6.6 years, 7 males, 14 females) were tested and their results analyzed. The participants were not medical personnel and had no previous knee arthroscopy experience.

None of the participants reported auditory, visual (including color deficiency), or motor impairments. A non-medical hearing evaluation was performed in which participants were given headphones and listened to stereo audio cues that were played from a laptop with a constant sound level setting. They indicated when they could detect a sound. Six sound cues were played: 250 Hz, 500 Hz, 1000 Hz, 2000 Hz, 4000 Hz, and 8000 Hz with increasing sound pressure levels of 0, 5, 10, 15, and 20 dB [10]. If a participant could not hear the sound at 20 dB(HL) at any of the tested frequency, there could be evidence of auditory impairment, based on the typical hearing range of humans being between-10 and 15 dB(HL) [11]. No participants were excluded for audio impairment.

2.3 Experimental Protocol

The sessions lasted approximately 90 min each. A between-subjects design was used, where each participant was assigned to one feedback group for the entire study. Each participant completed a standardized training and priming program using the FAST (Fundamentals of Arthroscopic Surgical Training) program, which focused on training instrument usage. The FAST Program was designed by the Arthroscopy Association of North America, the American Academy of Orthopaedic Surgeons, and the American Board of Orthopaedic Surgery [12]. The core functionalities of the camera and the hook were demonstrated (see Fig. 3). A minimum score of 50% was required by all participants.

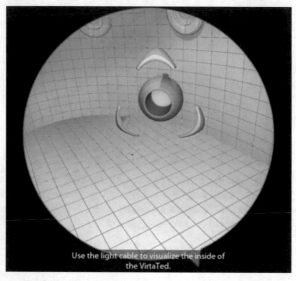

Fig. 3. The FAST basic skill training protocol was used to train user in basic tool manipulation and handling. The scenario shown here demonstrates periscoping, or manipulation of the angled optics. This image shows the target pyramid object that needs to be viewed, with the goal of seeing the inner circle of the pyramid object completely. This task is done by manipulating the camera and the 30° angled optics to change the viewing angle.

After the FAST training session, the three cues for maintaining the horizon were tested, along with one control group: digital sine wave audio cue, verbal cues, visual horizon bar, and no cues. The participants were assigned to only one form of cues for the entire experiment. The participants were instructed individually on how to perform a standardized diagnostic tour of the knee using the arthroscope and palpation hook included with the simulator. A proctor guided the first tour without any additional feedback cues. Following this training exercise, three independent tours were performed with the assigned feedback group, followed by a final tour without any feedback, as shown in Fig. 4. The training and priming lasted approximately 45 min. The five diagnostic tours were also approximately 45 min. After every diagnostic tour, participants reported their Overall Workload [9]. The simulator continuously recorded their horizon angle and procedure time at a sample rate of 30 Hz.

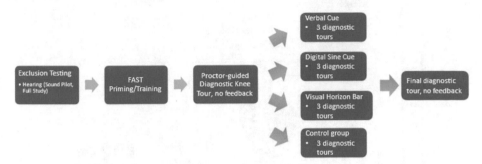

Fig. 4. The experimental protocol for the study. The participants followed one protocol path with one feedback cue group: verbal, digital sine, visual horizon bar, or control (no feedback).

2.4 Data Processing

Simulator data and OW questionnaires were exported and stored in a spreadsheet and analyzed in RStudio 1.1.463 (RStudio Team, Boston, MA, USA) and SPSS 25.0 (IBM Corp., Armonk, NY, USA). If discussed, the significance is at a level of 0.05. Data were analyzed using ANOVA. The ANOVA model considers the factors of feedback (4 levels: verbal, digital sine wave, visual horizon bar, or control). The means of the dependent variables were also tested using t-tests and the medians were tested with Mood's median test, to determine if the difference was significant, along with Tukey HSD post-hoc tests. Additionally, Wilcoxon and Kruskal-Wallis non-parametric tests were used.

3 Results

For the holding of the horizon angle in the correct position, we compared using the horizon bar (n = 6) to the control group (n = 5). The Wilcoxon test values, indicated by the pair bars above the box-whisker plots, revealed a significant effect ($p < 0.0084$; see Fig. 5). The horizon angle was misaligned less of the time at 26.5% ± 17.4 with the horizon bar, compared to the control group's misalignment of 41.4% ± 21.3. While not significant, the verbal cues (n = 5) showed a tendency to lower the misalignment to 29.4% ± 20.3, with $p < 0.091$. The digital sine wave (n = 5) was not significant ($p < 0.7$, 46.5% ± 27.4). Comparing the verbal cues to the horizon bar, the difference was not significant ($p < 0.66$).

The Overall Workload was significantly lowered ($p < 0.00036$) when using the verbal cues compared to the control group, as shown in Fig. 6. A mean score of 42.0 ± 19.6 with the verbal cues was found versus 70 ± 24.4 with the control group. The visual cue and digital sine wave were not significant ($p < 0.25$, 64.5 ± 14.7; $p < 0.71$, 72.4 ± 25.0). The difference between the verbal cues and the horizon bar was significant ($p < 8.9e{-}5$).

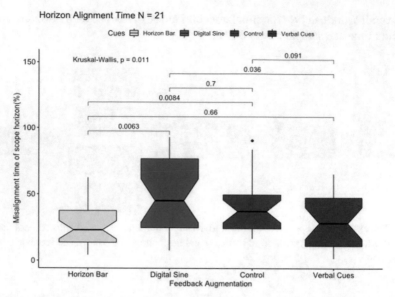

Fig. 5. The percent of time that the horizon was misaligned per feedback cue type. Outliers are shown with dots. The pair bars indicate the Wilcox test p-values.

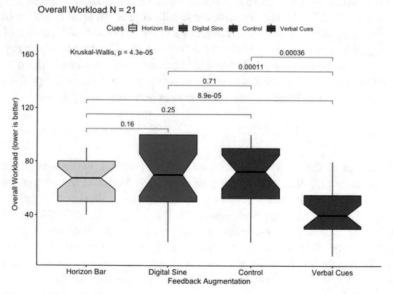

Fig. 6. The overall workload per feedback cue type. The pair bars indicate the Wilcox test p-values.

The procedure time was once again significantly lowered when using the verbal cues ($p < 0.015$, 393 ± 233) compared to the control group 553 ± 226 (see Fig. 7). The digital sine wave showed a tendency towards lowering the overall procedure time ($p < 0.075$, 434 ± 204). The horizon bar was not significant in lowering the procedure time ($p <$

0.11, 460 ± 212). The difference between the verbal cues and the horizon bar was not significant (p < 0.18).

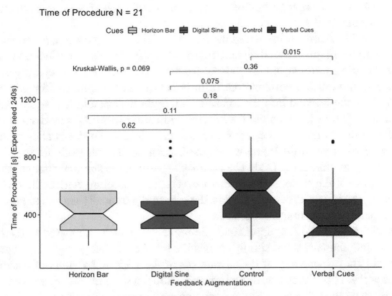

Fig. 7. The procedure time per feedback cue type, where an expert can complete the diagnostic tour in 240 s or less. Outliers are shown with dots. The pair bars indicate the Wilcox test p-values.

4 Discussion

Three forms of guidance were assessed in a mixed-reality reality knee surgery simulator. We examined their efficacy in holding the appropriate horizon angle during a diagnostic tour of the knee, along with examining the effect on procedure time and on Overall Workload. The participants were novices and received a brief proficiency training in the surgical instrument usage. Results show that the visual and auditory horizon feedback improved performance when compared to the control group. Additionally, verbal cues reduced procedure time and Overall Workload. These results follow the results of Mousavi et al., indicating that the auditory pathways can be used to lower overall cognitive load [8]. Visual cues helped reduce misalignment of the camera horizon most significantly.

Verbal cues shortened the procedure time and reduced the Overall Workload of the training scenario compared to the control group. However, the verbal cues only showed a tendency for improving the misalignment time of the camera. The verbal cues mimic the way feedback would be provided in actual surgery or training, with a human instructor regularly providing guidance or correction with verbal cues. This form of educational feedback is likely familiar to most trainees. The voice cues were given in a neutral tone, without intentional stress or negative tone in the recordings. These neutral-toned corrections lowered the Overall Workload score and procedure time (where lower is better for both metrics), indicating that the use of a different modality can provide helpful guidance without disrupting the training or distracting the trainee. Further research could delve into the tones, urgency, and other styles of verbal cues to see if this effectiveness can be expanded in the surgical simulators.

The visual horizon bar improved the holding of the correct camera alignment compared to the control group, but it did not improve the procedure time or Overall Workload compared to the control group. The visual feedback is a current commercially accepted method to communicate horizon control information. The inspiration for this horizon bar was likely the horizon information found on flight decks and flight simulators. One point of note is that in avionics, the horizon indication has two very distinct display methods: one from the perspective of the horizon where the plane is altered, and one from the perspective of the plane where the horizon is altered. Both are found in airplanes and flight simulators [13]. The approach found in the surgical simulator is from the perspective of the camera where the horizon is altered. Future work could investigate if switching the perspectives or allowing the user to dynamically chose the perspective has an impact on the training experience.

The digital sine did not significantly improve any metric compared to the control group. Despite the sine wave simply translating the visual horizon bar into an auditory form, it did not provide any of the advantages of the horizon bar and did not improve upon the horizon bar either. The digital sine wave did not support a better or more relaxed performance by the trainees. We do not recommend incorporating this form of feedback for holding the horizon angle or lowering the Overall Workload in future surgical training simulators without more design or research efforts to find an effective approach.

A limitation of the study was that the participants were not medical professionals. The participants were recruited from the local population, without requirement of previous medical training or knowledge. While it was the intent of the authors to include medical personnel, the concurrent COVID-19 pandemic unfortunately disrupted those efforts. Future work should explore the effects of these forms of feedback beyond non-medical novices.

Future works will apply verbal cues alongside the horizon bar in a multi-session study to examine the cues' impact on training over time. This effort, alongside other work in audio-tactile feedback, will be tested on commercially available systems to create a system that could provide a near-term impact on the market.

5   Conclusion

This work examines the application of verbal cues, sine wave audio, or a visual horizon bar on a commercially available surgical knee simulator to investigate the effectiveness of these forms of guidance compared to a control while performing an arthroscopic diagnostic tour of the knee. The presented study data partially support the hypothesis that these forms of feedback perform better than the control when examining holding the horizon, procedure time, and Overall Workload. Verbal cues were found to be overall more effective, especially with the Overall Workload and procedure time. The horizon bar was effective in maintaining the correct horizon angle. The digital sine wave was not effective in any of the metrics. The verbal feedback will be included in a follow-up study comparing it to the horizon bar and the control group to measure the impact on learning with novices.

References

1. Buzink, S.N., Botden, S.M., Heemskerk, J., Goossens, R.H., de Ridder, H., Jakimowicz, J.J.: Camera navigation and tissue manipulation; are these laparoscopic skills related? Surg. Endosc. **23**(4), 750–757 (2009)
2. Franzeck, F.M., Rosenthal, R., Muller, M.K., Nocito, A., Wittich, F., Maurus, C., et al.: Prospective randomized controlled trial of simulator-based versus traditional in-surgery laparoscopic camera navigation training. Surg. Endosc. **26**(1), 235–241 (2012)
3. VirtaMed. VirtaMed ArthroS™
4. 3D-Systems. ARTHRO Mentor (2019)
5. ToLTech ArthroSim Arthroscopy Simulator. https://www.toltech.net/medical-simulators/pro ducts/arthrosim-arthroscopy-simulator. Accessed 28 Dec 2020
6. Menozzi, M., Ropelato, S., Köfler, J., Huang, Y.-Y.: Development of ophthalmic microsurgery training in augmented reality. Klin. Monatsbl. Augenheilkd. **237**(04), 388–391 (2020)
7. De Jong, T.: Cognitive load theory, educational research, and instructional design: some food for thought. Instr. Sci. **38**(2), 105–134 (2010)
8. Mousavi, S.Y., Low, R., Sweller, J.: Reducing cognitive load by mixing auditory and visual presentation modes. J. Educ. Psychol. **87**(2), 319 (1995)
9. Vidulich, M.A., Tsang, P.S.: Absolute magnitude estimation and relative judgement approaches to subjective workload assessment. In: Proceedings of the Human Factors Society Annual Meeting, vol. 31, no. 9, pp. 1057–1061. SAGE Publications Sage CA, Los Angeles, CA (1987)
10. Pigeon, S.: Online Hearing Test and Audiogram Printout (2017). https://hearingtest.online/. Accessed 31 July 2020
11. Martin, F.N., Clark, J.G.: Introduction to audiology (1997)
12. Tauro, J., Pedowitz, R.: Arthroscopic skills training modalities. In: Motor Skills Training in Orthopedic Sports Medicine, pp. 53–64. Springer (2017)
13. Caro, P.W.: Aircraft simulators and pilot training. Hum. Factors **15**(6), 502–509 (1973)

The Lived Experience of Nurses Wearing Facemasks During COVID-19 Pandemic: An Ergonomic Study

Mohammed Mokdad[1]([✉]) [iD], Bouhafs Mebarki[2] [iD], Imed Eddine Mebarki[3] [iD], and Ibrahim Mokdad[4] [iD]

[1] College of Arts, University of Bahrain, Zallaq, Bahrain
mmokdad@uob.edu.bh
[2] Laboratory of Ergonomics, University of Oran 2, Oran, Algeria
mebarki.bouhafs@univ-oran2.dz
[3] The Public Hospital - Ain Turk, Oran, Algeria
[4] Mohammed Shaikhedine Establishment, Manama, Bahrain

Abstract. In times of pandemics, people are required to wear personal protective equipment especially facemasks to minimize exposure to hazards. The purpose of facemasks is to prevent the transmission of viruses through the respiratory system from one person to another. Besides their advantages, they have disadvantages too. They may cause facial complications and negatively affect communication. Wearing a facemask is considered a new experience around the world. Therefore, it is useful to know the experience of people who wear it, especially for long periods. This research aims to study the experience of nurses who wore facemasks for extended hours.

Researchers used the phenomenological method that explores the meaning that individuals give to the experiences they have had towards a particular phenomenon. The sample consisted of fifteen (15) adult nurses who were intentionally chosen from one hospital in the city of Oran (Algeria). Researchers used face-to-face semi-structured interviews with nurses. The following question: "What was your experience as a nurse wearing a facemask while working for more than eight hours a day?" was asked to each of them. Nurses were encouraged to speak freely while expressing their experience.

The analysis of the nurses' experience while wearing the facemask showed they were embodied in four major themes which are: 1- Health and safety concerns (headache and face wounds), 2- Physical ergonomic concerns (facemask design and anthropometric data), 3- Communication ergonomics concerns (communication disturbances) and 4- Aesthetic ergonomics (Appearance and Color). The research concluded with a discussion of all these four themes.

Keywords: The lived experience · Nurses · Facemasks · COVID-19 pandemic

© The Author(s), under exclusive license to Springer Nature Switzerland AG 2021
N. L. Black et al. (Eds.): IEA 2021, LNNS 222, pp. 380–388, 2021.
https://doi.org/10.1007/978-3-030-74611-7_52

1   Introduction

In times of pandemics, people need to wear personal protective equipment (PPE) to minimize exposure to hazards that cause serious health problems. With the COVID-19 pandemic, people, especially healthcare professionals, were required to wear PPE. Studies on COVID-19 pandemic outbreak have showed that medical work is not only stressful and tiring but is fearful too as healthcare professionals are facing death, going to a battle, without adequate PPE [1].

One of the PPE is the facemask. Interest in wearing facemasks is not recent. However, during the Covid-19 pandemic, great attention was paid to protecting the respiratory system and wearing facemasks. Most countries of the world mandated their citizens to wear facemasks, especially in public places.

No matter what type of facemask (surgical, cloth, or respirator), scientific studies indicate that facemasks limit the spread of diseases in the air to others, and prevent inhalation of harmful dust particles in the air. At the end, they do protect people from developing respiratory diseases [2].

However, how much time does an individual spend wearing the facemask? It should be noted that there are some individuals (health sector personnel, public institutions workers, closed areas workers) whose jobs compel them to wear the facemask for hours every day. In such cases, the facemasks will be harmful unless they are well ergonomically designed to suit those who use them.

According to Gefen [3], many medical devices including facemasks, may be associated with pain and leave some scars, which may be highly visible and cause distress "device-related pressure ulcers". Likewise, other researchers have warned of the possible negative effects of extended use of the facemask on the face [4].

Aside from the physical effects of the facemask, what are the psychological experiences of nurses (Males and females) who wear facemasks for prolonged period?

1.1   Research Aim

This research aims to study the psychological experiences of nurses who wear facemasks for extended hours (up to eight hours a day).

1.2   Theoretical Background

Broadly, there are three different types of facemasks usable for COVID-19 virus control: the cloth, the surgical and the N95 respirator facemasks (see Table 1).

Despite the fact that facemasks limit the spread of COVID-19 virus, they have other side effects such as making breathing more difficult and inhalation of carbon dioxide.

2   Methodology

2.1   Research Method

Researchers used the qualitative phenomenological approach. This methodology allows in-depth exploration of how phenomena occur in human consciousness.

Table 1. The three types of facemasks used during COVID-19.

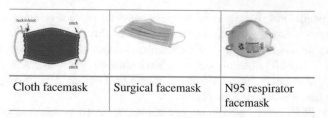

Cloth facemask	Surgical facemask	N95 respirator facemask

2.2 Sample

The sample includes a number of nurses (15 nurses: 09 females and 06 males) who were described as heroes during the COVID-19 epidemic era. They were chosen intentionally.

2.3 Data Collection Tool

Data were collected using semi-structured, in-depth, face-to-face interviews with each member of the sample. In addition, field observations of individuals were also recorded during the interview. The interview question was: "What was your experience as a nurse wearing a facemask while working for more than eight hours a day?"

For nurses who did not object to recording verbal answers automatically, we used a smart phone (Voice recorder). As for those who objected (two nurses), the answers were recorded manually.

2.4 Transcribing Interviews

Transcription is the conversion of oral text into written form. According to Gibbs, transcription is the first stage of data analysis in qualitative research [5]. Researchers tried as much as possible to transcribe all the interviews accurately, while preserving the verbal and non-verbal language of the interview. Two of the researchers (M.M & B.M) carried out the process of transcription. The whole process was done according to Oliver, et al. [6].

2.5 Data Analysis

Researchers carried out the data analysis based on the phenomenological analysis method proposed by Diekelmann, et al. [7], Table 2.

2.6 Ethical Consideration

To ensure that the current research is free from everything that could threaten the ethics of scientific research, the following measures have been taken:

- All members of the sample signed a statement of voluntary consent to participate in the research.

Table 2. Diekelmann et al. [7] stages of analysis.

Stage	Steps
Stage 1	All the interviews or texts are read for an overall understanding
Stage 2	Interpretive summaries of each interview are written
Stage 3	A team of researchers analyze selected transcribed interviews or texts
Stage 4	Any disagreements on interpretation are resolved by going back to the text
Stage 5	Common meanings are identified by comparing and contrasting the text
Stage 6	Relationships among themes emerge
Stage 7	A draft of the themes along with exemplars from texts are presented to the team. Responses or suggestions are incorporated into the final draft

- All respondents were informed of the main research objective and its sub-goals.
- It was confirmed to all members of the sample that the information they provide remains confidential and is used only for scientific research.

3   Results and Discussion

3.1   Sample Demographics Results

Fifteen nurses participated in this research. (09) of them are females, and (06) are males. The average age for females was (30.22) years, with a standard deviation (6.81), and a range of (23) years to (42) years. The average age for a male was (45) years with a standard deviation of (14.67) and a range of (26) years to (60) years. Table 3 provides more information about the sample members.

Table 3. Sample members' data.

Indicator	Type of work		Professional experience			Type of facemask worn		
	Part time	Permanent	More than 10 y	Between 5 and 10 y	Less than 5 y	N95	Cloth	Surgical
Males	0	06	02	01	03	00	00	03
Females	0	09	04	04	01	01	01	10
Total	**0**	**15**	**06**	**05**	**04**	**01**	**01**	**13**
	15		**15**			**15**		

It can be seen that all nurses are permanent employees, that (40%) possess a professional experience of less than five years, and that the vast majority of nurses wear the surgical facemask.

3.2   The Experience of Nurses

The phenomenological analysis of the nurses' experience while wearing the facemask showed that these experiences were embodied in four major themes. Moreover, each of these themes includes a number of sub-themes as seen in Table 4. Further, it also includes samples of the statements[1] that the respondents expressed while answering the interview questions.

Theme 1: Health and Safety Concerns. Sample members showed that at the end of the working day, wearing a facemask causes health problems especially for the face. Of these health problems, we refer to headache whose intensity ranges from light to severe. Sample members showed that this headache forces some of them to take some sedatives, such as aspirin and Tylenol (painkiller), to be able to continue working to the end of the day. In addition, it causes a feeling of suffocation.

The vast majority (N = 13) also showed that wearing the facemask causes them redness in the face accompanied by itching in the areas where the facemask comes into contact with skin, especially the area under the eye. Other nurses (N = 11) indicated that wearing the facemask for the entire length of time, in these days when there is an increase in the air temperature, causes them infections in the skin, especially in areas where the facemask rubs the face (the nose). Further, nurses expressed fear that the infections will remain in the face for a long time. (See Table 4 for some of the respondents' statements). Furthermore, a number of nurses (n = 09) have complained that the elastic cord of the facemask causes over time pain in the ear auricle.

These results are consistent with the results of many previous researchers, including, for example: Ong, et al. [8] who have unanimously approved that whoever wears the facemask for a period will have this kind of problems.

Theme 2: Physical Ergonomic Concerns. Sample members showed that the facemasks they wear (N95) did not seal tightly to their faces. They mentioned that the respirator rim does not conform to contours of their faces. They indicated that their sizes are large, because they are designed for other people, not for us. They do not fully protect us from the COVID-19 virus, which can reach parts of our respiratory system. For this reason, some nurses put pieces of cotton to fill these voids, so that the facemask fits tightly the face. In addition, nurses indicated that badly designed facemasks force them to keep readjusting them to the face. This constant touch to the facemask may contaminate it. Nurses, who wear glasses (vision correction, or eye protection), have complained of breathing vapor rising into the glasses, making the vision cloudy. It forces us to wipe them off from time to time. Nurses have also shown that the poor design is not only for facemasks, but also for all personal protective equipment such as gowns, helmets, gloves, face shields, goggles, etc. (See Table 4 for some of the respondents' statements). The fact that facemasks should be designed to who use them has been mentioned by other researchers [9].

Theme 3: Communication Ergonomics Concerns. Nurses (n = 15) indicated that wearing the facemask caused communication problems with some patients, especially

---

[1] These statements are translated from Arabic to English.

the deaf, the elderly and children. On the one hand, nurses have shown that wearing facemask prevented clients from reading the movement of the nurses' lips while dealing

Table 4. Samples of the statements that the respondents expressed.

Theme	Sub-themes	Samples of the respondents statements
Health and safety concerns	• Headache. • Face wounds. • Pain in the ear auricle	• "Imagine you wear the facemask almost all day long, and more than half of your face is covered. Don't you feel the headache?" • "Sometimes the headache I have is severe and requires medication to relieve it. I have Panadol in my bag" • "Wearing the facemask causes itching on my face" • "I am afraid that the traces of the facemask will remain on my face long and will not go away" • "Last month, when I entered the house, my children feared the effects of the facemask on my face"
Physical ergonomic concerns	• Facemask design. • Anthropometric data	• "Unfortunately, the mask I wear is bigger than my face, and it distorts it more than it protects it" • "I spend the day fighting with the facemask to secure it to my face" • "I hope facemasks are made in our country and do not need to be purchased from abroad"
Communication ergonomics concerns	• Communication disturbance	• "I'm confused if I wear the facemask, some patients don't understand what I say. If I took it out to clarify what was meant, the officials would blame me" • "Help me find another way to communicate with patients without having to take off the facemask"

(*continued*)

Table 4. (*continued*)

Theme	Sub-themes	Samples of the respondents statements
Aesthetic ergonomics	• Appearance • Color	• "I don't like the look of the facemask" • "I feel that my face shape has become ugly with the facemask" • "We do not have a chance to choose the color of the mask we prefer" • "I like the color, it is enjoyable" • "Everyone prefers to wear a facemask that is aesthetically pleasant"

with them. On the other, they also showed that they experienced many problems related to understanding the messages their clients wanted to convey because they also wear facemasks. Consequently, the communication problem associated with the facemask is paired with which both nurses and patients suffer. All nurses have asked to search for new ways to communicate with patients while wearing the facemask. (See Table 4 for some of the respondents' statements). These results are consistent with results from other research [10].

Theme 4: Aesthetic Ergonomics Concerns. The majority of nurses (09 women and 02 men), explained that the aesthetics of the facemask is of great importance to them. The facemask that looks beautiful in the eye of the nurse does not tire him/her. Moreover, it is nice to wear the facemask that suits you. Nurses indicated that the facemask you wear not only does protect you from the risk of contracting the COVID-19 virus, but it is your public face. Therefore, you have to think about the facemask you are wearing.

Related to this, is the color of the facemask. Nurses have shown that they are obliged to wear the facemasks they are given, regardless of their color, even if you are raised up to dislike it. Almost 47% of the interviewees explained they like to wear facemasks with a color that fits the ward color. However, the other 53% mentioned that they prefer to match the color of the facemask to the one they like. When asked about the solution, nurses suggested that authorities ought to supply facemasks of black color, as they are neutral). It is to note that the gap between ergonomics and aesthetics is gradually fading away. Thus, it is legitimate for nurses to have a facemask designed with the aesthetic qualities they love [11].

4 Conclusion

This study attempted to provide a comprehensive understanding of the nurses' real experience while wearing the facemask the length of months that COVID-19 disease spread (from February 2020 to June 2020), while providing care to patients.

It has been found that the nurses' real experience was embodied in four themes, the first of which was health and safety concerns, the most important of which are redness of the skin, dermatitis, the appearance of icy pimples that the facemask causes when worn for a long period of time. Not one of the nurses has not tested any of these problems. The second theme was the physical ergonomic concerns about the bad design of the facemasks that the nurses wore, as these facemasks were not specifically designed for them and were imported from different countries. The third theme was the communication ergonomics concerns. The nurses showed that wearing facemask caused communication problems. It has become difficult to communicate with the deaf, and with some elderly people who are unable to read the nurses' lips when wearing the facemask. Finally, the fourth theme was aesthetic ergonomics. It has been shown that the nurses' needs are not only represented in the ergonomic properties of the facemask, but rather exceed them to the aesthetic properties that, if available, increase the patience of the nurses for wearing it for long hours.

Acknowledgements. Special thanks go to the hospital staff and nurses who contributed in this research.

References

1. Wu, X., Sun, G., Liu, S., Ding, L., Miao, C., An, K.: Ergonomics considerations of usability test of UAV handheld control unit. In: International Conference on Human-Computer Interaction, pp. 346–356. Springer, Cham, Switzerland (2020)
2. Leung, N.H., Chu, D.K., Shiu, E.Y., Chan, K.H., McDevitt, J.J., Hau, B.J., Yen, H.L., Li, Y., Ip, D.K.M., Malik Peiris, J.S., Seto, W.H., Leung, G.M., Milton, D.K., Cowling, B.J.: Respiratory virus shedding in exhaled breath and efficacy of face masks. Nat. Med. **26**(5), 676–680 (2020)
3. Gefen, A., Alves, P., Ciprandi, G., Coyer, F., Milne, C.T., Ousey, K., Ohura, N., Waters, N., Worsley, P.: Device-related pressure ulcers: SECURE prevention. J. Wound Care **29**(Sup. 2a), S01–S52 (2020)
4. Alves, P., Moura, A., Vaz, A., Ferreira, A., Malcato, E., Sousa, F., Afonso, G., Ramos, P., Dias, V., Homem-Silva, P.: PRPPE GUIDELINEǀ COVID 19. Prevention of skin lesions caused by Personal Protective Equipment (facemasks, respirators, visors and protection glasses). Associação Portuguesa de Tratamento de Feridas (The Portuguese Wound Care Association), Portugal (2020)
5. Gibbs, G.R.: Thematic coding and categorizing. Analyzing Qual. Data **703**, 38–56 (2007)
6. Oliver, D.G., Serovich, J.M., Mason, T.L.: Constraints and opportunities with interview transcription: towards reflection in qualitative research. Soc. Forces **84**, 1273–1289 (2005)
7. Diekelmann, N., Allen, D., Tanner, C.: The NLN Criteria for Appraisal of Baccalaureate Programs: A Critical Hermeneutic Analysis. National League for Nursing, New York (1989)

8. Ong, J.J., Bharatendu, C., Goh, Y., Tang, J.Z., Sooi, K.W., Tan, Y.L., Tan, B.Y.Q., Teoh, H.L., Ong, S.T., Allen, D.M., Sharma, V.K.: Headaches associated with personal protective equipment–a cross-sectional study among frontline healthcare workers during COVID-19. Headache: J. Head Face Pain **60**(5), 864–877 (2020)

9. Salvarzi, E., Choobineh, A., Jahangiri, M., Keshavarzi, S.: Facial anthropometric measurements in Iranian male workers using digimizer version 4.1. 1.0 image analysis software: a pilot study. Int. J. Occup. Saf. Ergonomics **24**(4), 570–576 (2018)

10. Branda, E.: Improving communication with face masks (2020). https://www.signia-lib rary.com/wp-content/uploads/sites/137/2020/06/Signia_white-paper_improving-commun ication-with-face-masks.pdf. Accessed 20 Jan 2021

11. Luo, L., Hu, X.: Study on chinese elderly women's clothing design based on ergonomics. In: International Conference on Human-Computer Interaction, pp. 214–227. Springer, Cham, Switzerland (2020)

Dealing with Medical Errors: A Human Factors/Ergonomics Approach

Mohammed Mokdad$^{1(\boxtimes)}$ ⓘ, Bouhafs Mebarki^2 ⓘ, Imed Eddine Mebarki^3 ⓘ, and Ibrahim Mokdad^4 ⓘ

^{1} College of Arts, University of Bahrain, Zallaq, Bahrain
mmokdad@uob.edu.bh
^{2} Laboratory of Ergonomics, University of Oran 2, Oran, Algeria
mebarki.bouhafs@univ-oran2.dz
^{3} The Public Hospital - Ain Turk, Oran, Algeria
^{4} Mohammed Shaikhedine Establishment, Manama, Bahrain

Abstract. Medical errors are committed by health workers anywhere, and can result in severe patient injuries or death. World Health Organization indicates that medical errors cause great damage to health care systems around the world. Several strategies are used to reduce medical errors, including Human Factors/Ergonomics (HF/E). Accordingly, the present research aims to highlight the contribution of HF/E to the control of medical errors.

This research is based on a literature review carried out on the web search engine Google Scholar. With the selection key "HF/E and medical errors", during the period 2010 to 2020 (17,100) articles were obtained. The articles were shortlisted to include only peer-reviewed articles that directly deal with HF/E and medical errors. After a careful examination of the obtained research, only 42 papers are closely related to the research topic.

Research papers were categorized into four categories: HF/E of medical work, HF/E of medical equipment, HF/E of the physical environment and HF/E of medical drugs naming.

It has been found that the application of HF/E in each of those areas has significantly reduced medical errors.

Keywords: Medical errors · Human Factors/Ergonomics · Medical equipment · Physical environment · Drug naming

1 Introduction

Medical errors are an example of human errors. They are committed by any health worker (doctor, nurse, and others) anywhere, and can result in severe patient injuries or death. World Health Organization (WHO) indicates that medical errors cause a great damage to health care systems around the world. In addition, it indicates that, medical errors cost $ 42 billion annually [1]. In the same context, the American Institute of Medicine stated that every year between (40,000) to (98,000) Americans die from medical errors [2]. Recent studies consider medical errors as the third leading cause of death having

© The Author(s), under exclusive license to Springer Nature Switzerland AG 2021
N. L. Black et al. (Eds.): IEA 2021, LNNS 222, pp. 389–396, 2021.
https://doi.org/10.1007/978-3-030-74611-7_53

surpassed strokes, Alzheimer's, and diabetes [3]. In a study, it was found that (01) in (20) people is exposed to medical errors. The study praised the efforts made to reduce medical errors but indicated that the efforts did not achieve the required success and the desired results. It showed that the more medical errors are controlled, the higher the quality of the medical work [4].

Man-machine system is the backbone of HF/E. The success or failure of man-machine system depends on the success or the failure of its various elements [5]. One of the man-machine system threats is human errors. Between 70% and 90% of man-machine system failures are due to human errors [6]. Human errors are inevitable and thinking about eliminating them altogether could be almost impossible [7].

Literature on medical errors shows that there are strategies, used to reduce medical errors. The major ones are HF/E [8], reporting errors [9], the establishment of safety culture [10], education on medical errors [11], and getting help from health information technology [12].

HF/E by nature, significantly contributes to reducing medical errors [13]. In this context, Mao et al. state; "From an HF/E viewpoint, patient safety activities should reduce and mitigate medical errors, as well as improve human wellbeing, which includes job satisfaction, motivation and technology acceptance" [14].

Accordingly, this research aims to shed light on the HF/E approach, which mitigates medical errors.

2 Methodology

2.1 The Approach Philosophy

The philosophical worldview of this approach is that medical errors are an indication of a problem in the interaction and harmony that must exist between the elements of the man-machine system. Man-machine system is supposed to have consistency between its various elements (human, machine, environment) in order to perform well. The interaction between the elements of the system is very necessary for the normal functioning of the system. Any disruption in the interaction, negatively affects the performance of the system, which leads to many negative results, including medical errors [15].

2.2 The HF/E Studies of the Approach

Researchers searched the freely accessible web search engine Google Scholar, for peer-reviewed articles on HF/E and medical errors. With the selection key "HF/E to reduce medical errors", during the period 2010 to 2020 (17,100) articles were obtained. Researchers carried out the preliminary examination of the retrieved articles, through the title contents of the article, the key words and the abstract. It has been found that a large number of retrieved articles, weren't related to the current research and, accordingly, they were excluded. After careful scrutiny (42) articles that directly deal with HF/E and medical errors, were enrolled.

3 Results and Discussion

This research aims to shed light on the HF/E approach, which controls the occurrence of medical errors. This approach is based on the findings of a number of peer-reviewed studies and research published in scientific journals and conferences. Research articles were categorized into four categories, as follows:

o (12) Articles in HF/E of medical work.
o (10) Articles in HF/E of medical equipment.
o (10) Articles in HF/E of physical environment in medical institutions.
o (10) Articles in HF/E of drugs naming and packaging.

3.1 HF/E of Medical Work

Occupations that involve direct contact with people and require quick decisions such as medical jobs, are among the most stressful jobs. Compared to the general population, health care workers are exposed to high levels of stress, depression, fatigue, anxiety, psychological burnout and suicide [16].

Among the causes of these problems, two are stated: long work hours and sleep deprivation.

Long working hours cause fatigue and exhaustion that cause medical errors [17]. Also, chronic sleep deprivation leads to severe consequences including medical errors [18]. In such circumstances, the result would be medical errors [19].

Here, HF/E helps to increase resiliency among medical staff so that they do their work in a comfortable and error-free work context. What helps build resiliency among medical stuff, various methods are mentioned:

1. Training: It provides the individual with the skills that enable him to properly handle medical tools, so that he uses them effectively and free of risks [20].
2. Mindfulness: It prevents preoccupation with something else while dealing with the patient, which reduces the chances of making mistakes [21].
3. Coping strategies: They help the individual to overcome the difficulties he is facing. Social support from family members and colleagues contribute significantly to reducing medical errors [22].
4. Reflective groups: Reflective groups such as Balint groups, increase the foresight of health professionals. Balint groups, are widely used among health professionals [23].

3.2 HF/E of Medical Equipment

It is worth noting that medical professions are these days among the professions that are highly dependent on technology. Despite the fact that technology, helps the medical practice to develop, but it puts a lot of pressure on the medical staff. Authors found that the continuing use of technology, has given rise to stress (techno-stress) on medical staff [24]. According to Salanova et al. [25], techno-stress is "a negative psychological state associated with the use or the threat to use new technologies, which leads to anxiety, mental fatigue, and sense of ineffectiveness". In such situations, medical staff most probably makes medical errors.

Medical equipment and technology are not friendly to humans unless they are ergonomically designed to fit the capabilities of those who use them [26].

In the last three decades, ergonomists shed light on medical equipment and technology. The laparoscope has attracted the attention of many ergonomists. Current instruments have been found to oblige surgeon to adopt poor working postures while doing the work. Further, they cause pain in the surgeons' upper limbs that causes fatigue and mistakes [27]. Additionally, KC et al. [28] found that most surgeons who use the laparoscope are not aware of the correct directions that they should adhere to in operating rooms. Surgeons with little experience, suffer from varying degrees of physical pain caused by the bad design of the laparoscope. When HF/E principles have been applied in the laparoscope handle re-design, laparoscopes are well designed and comfortable for surgeons [29].

In addition to the laparoscope, Fajobi et al. [30] redesigned the hospital bed in Nigeria showing that the newly designed bed was more comfortable and more secure instigating happiness in both the patient and the nurses, which leads to reducing medical problems.

3.3 HF/E of the Physical Environment

The physical environment includes various variables. Two of them are important to health care systems. They are lighting and noise [31].

As for lighting, good lighting systems (good quantity and good quality), play an important role in improving the medical institutions environment for employees and patients, as they improve vision and professional performance, cause visual comfort, develop social communication between individuals, and inspire happiness in people. Poor lighting works just the opposite [32].

As to noise, the World Health Organization recommends that hospital noise levels do not exceed 30 dB (a) whether during the day or at night. If they are to exceed for some reason and for a short period of time, their peaks do not exceed 40 dB [33]. Unfortunately research shows that noise pervaded these days the hospitals causing health problems and increasing medical errors [34].

The relationship between lighting and medical errors is inverse and strong. The higher the level of lighting, the less medical errors [35]. In 1991, Buchanan, et al. found that poor lighting was associated with increased medical errors [36]. They found that the percentage of medical errors fell to the lowest level when the amount of lighting reached (1570 lx) compared to the levels of lighting (480 lx and 1100 lx). In another study, Brady [37] found that the causes of medical errors are many, including poor lighting. Further, Pennings [38], examined the effect of both daylight and artificial light on the circadian rhythm system, the duration of hospital stay and patient pain levels. She suggested that the design of hospitals that takes into account daylight as the most major variable increases the level of comfort and contentment and reduces number of medical errors among its personnel including patients. Finally, Aarts [39] demonstrated that more light helps both people with perfect vision and with far-sightedness (Hyperopia) to reduce reading errors e.g. when reading text on medication labels. However, its effects on the later ones seem great.

As for noise, HF/E offers three solutions for controlling noise, whether in medical institutions or in others. These solutions are:

– Control at the source, which is the best method to control noise.
– Control at the path through which the noise passes to the individual.
– Control at the individual by requesting him/her to wear earplugs/earmuffs.

As far as medical institutions are concerned, some studies have used the first method to combat noise. They have achieved good results. Boyko et al. [40] reduced the sound volume and stopped talking in the health unit. They have shown that the effect of this intervention improved the patients' sleep level. Likewise, Delaney et al. [41] focused on behavior modification procedures. They included (reducing conversational noise, minimizing nonclinical discussions at the bedside, limiting clinical interactions, titrating alarm volumes, monitoring alarm settings to reduce nuisance alarms, closing patient room doors, modifying workflow, etc.). They found that these procedures helped to reduce noise levels and improve hospital life. On the other hand, there are many studies used the third method. Researchers have shown that the use of earplugs reduces the noise level in the health facility, enabling patients to sleep deeply [40].

3.4   HF/E of Medical Drugs Naming

The similarity of medication names (Look-alike or sound-alike names) and the poor drug packaging are major factors causing medical errors. Center for Drug Evaluation and Research (US Food and Drug Administration) has warned of the problem of similarities in the names of medications. It confirmed that about 10% of medical errors are due to the confusion, caused by their names [42]. Countless number of medical names seems so similar that doctors, nurses, and pharmacists can confuse them, which leads to mistakes in dispensing them to patients. For example, **IODINE**, which is used to treat thyroid problems, and **LODINE**, which is used to relieve pain. **TORADOL**, which is used in the treatment of infections, and **TRAMADOL**, which is used to relieve pain. On the other hand, scientific research has shown that poor packaging and labeling lead to medication errors [43].

To tackle these problems, ergonomists provided a number of strategies, among them the Tall-man lettering and medication indication.

Tall-Man Lettering. Here, letters of two medication names that are not identical are written in capital letters (Tall Man letters) to draw attention to the points of difference between the two medicines. For example, the following medicines are written as follows: (DOBUTamine vs. DOPamine). Researchers have shown that this method is very useful in preventing medical errors [44].

Medication Indication. Here, doctors write the purpose of medication alongside it in the prescription. Many researchers found that this method increases the level of distinction between medications and reduces prescription errors [45].

4 Limitations

1. The sample of accepted articles: The researchers were able to obtain a large number of scientific articles. However, the process of examining all these articles took a great time, but in the end the researchers were able to obtain only a small number of them.
2. Although there are many methods for controlling medical errors, research on how HF/E can contribute to reducing medical errors is not available.
3. Much of the chosen research provides theoretical proposals for how HF/E can contribute to reducing medical errors but does not provide any practical measures that can be used to actually reduce medical errors.

5 Conclusion

The present research aimed to highlight the contribution of HF/E to reduce the occurrence of medical errors. The emphasis has been placed on four areas we believe have a strong correlation with medical errors. These areas are: nature of medical work, HF/E of medical equipment, HF/E of physical conditions, HF/E of drug naming and packaging. It was found in each of these four areas that the application of HF/E is able, directly or indirectly, to eliminate or at least reduce medical errors.

However, these areas are the most stated in the reviewed literature, other HF/E research areas need to be more investigated like the organizational, socio psychological and legal aspects of the medical errors phenomenon that hinder the work of the healthcare giving settings. A holistic HF/E approach can best contribute to minimize or even eradicate many medical errors contributing factors.

References

1. World Health Organization (WHO): Monitoring the building blocks of health systems: a handbook of indicators and their measurement strategies. World Health Organization, Geneva, Switzerland (2017)
2. Donaldson, M.S., Corrigan, J.M., Kohn, L.T. (eds.): To Err is Human: Building a Safer Health System, vol. 6. National Academies Press, USA (2000)
3. Anderson, J.G., Abrahamson, K.: Your health care may kill you: medical errors. Stud. Health Technol. Inform. **234**, 13–17 (2017)
4. Panagioti, M., Khan, K., Keers, R.N., Abuzour, A., Phipps, D., Kontopantelis, E., Ashcroft, D.M.: Prevalence, severity, and nature of preventable patient harm across medical care settings: systematic review and meta-analysis. BMJ **366**(l4185), 1–11 (2019)
5. Tayyari, F., Smith, J.L.: Occupational Ergonomics: Principles and Applications. Chapman & Hall, London (1997)
6. Liu, C.M., Wang, A.H.: A model for predicting the reliability of a man-machine system. Qual. Reliabil. Int. **13**, 159–165 (1997)
7. Wu, A.W., Cavanaugh, T.A., McPhee, S.J., Lo, B., Micco, G.P.: To tell the truth. J. Gen. Intern. Med. **12**(12), 770–775 (1997)
8. Marshall, S.D., Touzell, A.: Human factors and the safety of surgical and anaesthetic care. Anaesthesia **75**, e34–e38 (2020)
9. Levine, K.J., Carmody, M., Silk, K.J.: The influence of organizational culture, climate and commitment on speaking up about medical errors. J. Nurs. Manag. **28**(1), 130–138 (2020)

10. Lee, S.E., Quinn, B.L.: Safety culture and patient safety outcomes in East Asia: a literature review. West. J. Nurs. Res. **42**(3), 220–230 (2020)
11. Kim, Y.S., Kim, H.S., Kim, H.A., Chun, J., Kwak, M.J., Kim, M.S., Hwang, J.I., Kim, H.: Can patient and family education prevent medical errors? a descriptive study. BMC Health Serv. Res. **20**, 1–7 (2020)
12. Sheikh, A.: Realising the potential of health information technology to enhance medication safety. BMJ Qual. Saf. **29**, 7–9 (2020)
13. Song, W., Li, J., Li, H., Ming, X.: Human factors risk assessment: an integrated method for improving safety in clinical use of medical devices. Appl. Soft Comput. **86**, 105918 (2020)
14. Mao, X., Jia, P., Zhang, L., Zhao, P., Chen, Y., Zhang, M.: An evaluation of the effects of human factors and ergonomics on health care and patient safety practices: a systematic review. Plos One **10**(6), 1–19 (2015)
15. Che, H., Zeng, S., Guo, J.: Reliability assessment of man-machine systems subject to mutually dependent machine degradation and human errors. Reliabil. Eng. Syst. Saf. **190**(106504), 1–11 (2019)
16. Yates, S.W.: Physician stress and burnout. Am. J. Med. **133**(2), 160–164 (2020)
17. Caruso, C.C.: Negative impacts of shiftwork and long work hours. Rehabil. Nurs. **39**(1), 16–25 (2014)
18. Czeisler, C.A.: Duration, timing and quality of sleep are each vital for health, performance and safety. Sleep Health J. Nat. Sleep Found. **1**(1), 5–8 (2015)
19. Matyushkina, E.Y., Roy, A.P., Rakhmanina, A.A., Kholmogorova, A.B.: Occupational stress and burnout among healthcare professionals. J. Mod. Foreign Psychol. **9**(1), 39–49 (2020)
20. Ravindran, S., Thomas-Gibson, S., Murray, S., Wood, E.: Improving safety and reducing error in endoscopy: simulation training in human factors. Frontline Gastroenterol. **10**(2), 160–166 (2019)
21. Verweij, H., Waumans, R.C., Smeijers, D., Lucassen, P.L., Donders, A.R.T., van der Horst, H.E., Speckens, A.E.: Mindfulness-based stress reduction for GPs: results of a controlled mixed methods pilot study in Dutch primary care. Br. J. Gen. Pract. **66**(643), e99–e105 (2016)
22. Gardiner, M., Kearns, H., Tiggemann, M.: Effectiveness of cognitive behavioural coaching in improving the well-being and retention of rural general practitioners. Aust. J. Rural Health **21**(3), 183–189 (2013)
23. Antoun, J., BouAkl, I., Halabi, Z., Bou Khalil, P., Romani, M.: Effect of Balint seminars training on emotional intelligence and burnout among internal medicine residents. Health Educ. J. **79**(7), 802–811 (2020)
24. Brivio, E., Gaudioso, F., Vergine, I., Mirizzi, C.R., Reina, C., Stellari, A., Galimberti, C.: Preventing technostress through positive technology. Front. Psychol. **9**, 2569 (2018)
25. Salanova, M., Llorens, S., Cifre, E.: The dark side of technologies: techno stress among users of information and communication technologies. Int. J. Psychol. **48**(3), 422–436 (2013)
26. Carayon, P., Hoonakker, P.: Human factors and usability for health information technology: old and new challenges. Yearb. Med. Inform. **28**(1), 71–77 (2019)
27. Sancibrian, R., Redondo-Figuero, C., Gutierrez-Diez, M.C., Gonzalez-Sarabia, E., Manuel-Palazuelos, J.C.: Ergonomic evaluation and performance of a new handle for laparoscopic tools in surgery. Appl. Ergon. **89**, 103210 (2020)
28. Kc, M.S., Manjunath, K., Krishnappa, R.: Ergonomics in laparoscopy: a questionnaire survey of physical discomfort and symptoms in surgeons following laparoscopic surgery. Int. Surg. J. **4**(12), 3907–3914 (2017)
29. González, A.G., Barrios-Muriel, J., Romero-Sánchez, F., Salgado, D.R., Alonso, F.J.: Ergonomic assessment of a new hand tool design for laparoscopic surgery based on surgeons' muscular activity. Appl. Ergon. **88**, 103161 (2020)

30. Fajobi, M.O., Awoyemi, E.A., Onawumi, A.S.: Ergonomic evaluation of hospital bed design and anthropometric characterization of adult patients in nigeria. Int. J. Sci. Eng. Res. 7(8), 640–651 (2016)
31. Elias, G.A., Calil, S.J.: Evaluation of physical environment parameters in healthcare. In: XIII Mediterranean Conference on Medical and Biological Engineering and Computing 2013, pp. 1178–1181. Springer, Cham (2014)
32. Benedetti, F., Colombo, C., Barbini, B., Campori, E., Kim, E.S.: Morning sunlight reduces length of hospitalization in bipolar depression. J. Affect. Disord. 62, 221–223 (2001)
33. Tijunelis, M.A., Fitzsullivan, E., Henderson, S.O.: Noise in the ED. Am. J. Emerg. Med. 23(3), 332–335 (2005)
34. Al-Tarawneh, O.M., D'emeh, W.M., Yacoub, M.I.: An assessment of nurses' knowledge regarding noise in intensive care units in Jordan. Int. J. Afr. Nurs. Sci. 12, 100183 (2020)
35. Shahrokhi, A., Ebrahimpour, F., Ghodousi, A.: Factors effective on medication errors: a nursing view. J. Res. Pharm. Pract. 2(1), 18–23 (2013)
36. Buchanan, T.L., Barker, K.N., Gibson, J.T., Jiang, B.C., Pearson, R.E.: Lighting and errors in dispensing. Am. J. Hosp. Pharm. 48(10), 2137–2145 (1991)
37. Brady, A.P.: Error and discrepancy in radiology: inevitable or avoidable? Insights Imaging 8(1), 171–182 (2017)
38. Pennings, E.: Hospital Lighting and Patient's Health. BSc Thesis Health and Society. Wageningen University, The Netherlands (2018)
39. Aarts, M.P.J.: Raise the lantern: how light can help to maintain a healthy and safe hospital environment focusing on nurses. Ph.D. Thesis, Department of the Built Environment, Technische Universiteit, Eindhoven, The Netherlands (2020)
40. Boyko, Y., Jennum, P., Nikolic, M., Holst, R., Oerding, H., Toft, P.: Sleep in intensive care unit: the role of environment. J. Crit. Care 37, 99–105 (2017)
41. Delaney, L., Litton, E., Van Haren, F.: The effectiveness of noise interventions in the ICU. Curr. Opin. Anesthesiol. 32(2), 144–149 (2019)
42. US Food and Drug Administration. Draft guidance for industry: safety considerations for container labels and carton labeling design to minimize medication errors. U.S. Department of Health and Human Services Food and Drug Administration, Center for Drug Evaluation and Research, USA (2013)
43. Endestad, T., Wortinger, L.A., Madsen, S., Hortemo, S.: Package design affects accuracy recognition for medications. Hum. Factors 58(8), 1206–1216 (2016)
44. Bryan, R., Aronson, J.K., Williams, A., Jordan, S.: The problem of look-alike, sound-alike name errors: drivers and solutions. Br. J. Clin. Pharmacol. 86, 1–9 (2020)
45. Grissinger, M.: Is an indication-based prescribing system in our future? Pharm. Ther. 44(5), 232–233 (2019)

A Future Patient Transporting Drone Evaluated

Luciana Ribeiro Monteiro[1,2]($\boxtimes$), Michal Adar[2], Riel Bessai[2], Itamar Bukai[2], Lennert van den Boom[2], Alazne Echaniz Jurado[2], Alicia Ville[2], Phillip Essle[2], and Peter Vink[2]

[1] Embraer, Technological Strategy, Amsterdam, The Netherlands
luciana.monteiro@nl.embraer.com

[2] Advanced Embodiment Design Team, Faculty of Industrial Design Engineering, TU Delft, Delft, The Netherlands

Abstract. Soteria is a patient transporting drone, which is part of a living lab setting for Future Mobility, which Embraer is developing. It has been designed in conjunction with the Talaria propulsion system, an autonomous and modular eVTOL flight package. The idea is that during disaster scenarios, Soteria is summoned by first responders to the scene after which a noncritical patient is loaded from the field into the carrier. Soteria then autonomously and independently ferries the patient safely to the closest hospital, where they are unloaded by medical personnel. It is important that handlings are fast and that the patient will fit in the system. Therefore, Soteria was ergonomically tested. The interior of the carrier, the interior layout, and human-machine interface were evaluated with a 1:1 model and compared with guidelines found in the literature. Based on that improvements were made and presented for future design iterations.

Keywords: Patient transportation · Comfort · Drone · Stretcher · Loading

1 Introduction

1.1 Global Context

In recent years, the number of deaths due to natural disasters has decreased substantially due to better disaster preparedness. But even with this decrease, on average there are still around 60,000 deaths each year, as well as many victims left injured, displaced or homeless [1]. Over the past decade, approximately 2 million individuals have been injured and more than 2 billion people affected [2] and with the increasing challenges due to climate change, these numbers might increase.

The current goal of a search and rescue operation following a natural disaster focuses on rescuing the largest number of people in the shortest time. But in instances where the damage of infrastructure, particularly to roads and bridges, is extensive, achieving this goal becomes more difficult as land transportation is obstructed. Under these circumstances, air relief becomes the only effective rescue method [3]. Currently, helicopters are used to locate and carry injured or sick patients to a patient transfer center where these patients are evaluated and transferred to a hospital for further care if necessary.

© The Author(s), under exclusive license to Springer Nature Switzerland AG 2021
N. L. Black et al. (Eds.): IEA 2021, LNNS 222, pp. 397–403, 2021.
https://doi.org/10.1007/978-3-030-74611-7_54

When the use of helicopters for disaster rescues increases, there will also be an increase in the amount of CO2 emissions released. As the effect of climate change worldwide continues to increase ensuring a rise in natural disaster occurrences, the use of helicopters in air rescues will become more common as will the amount of CO2 emission generated during these rescues. On average, helicopters burn much more fuel and emit far more CO2 emissions than a car over the same distance [4]. Additionally, helicopter pilots might not always be available and purchasing a helicopter is expensive. There is a need for the development of a more sustainable patient transportation system that is capable of transferring patients in the same time, if not faster, as helicopters.

As part of a project where living labs are used towards sustainable mobility, this Soteria Storyboard illustrated in Fig. 1 is in development. eVTOLs have the potential to play a crucial role in the future of medical relief. As they take off faster, are able to land in much tighter spaces, and are more electrically efficient than helicopters [5], they have the means to be a huge asset and complement helicopters in the aid and rescue of victims following natural disasters.

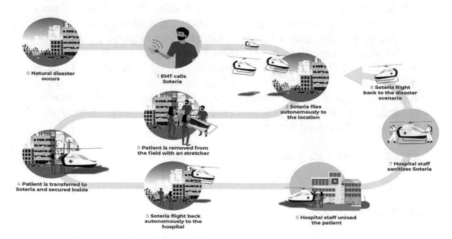

Fig. 1. Soteria storyboard

1.2 Project Goal

The interior layout and sizes of the carrier and human-machine interface were evaluated with a 1:1 model and compared with guidelines found in the literature. Based on that improvements were made and presented for future design iterations. So, the research question for this paper is: what are the interior requests based on ergonomic guidelines and on the way first responders would handle?

Due to payload constraints of the Talaria platform, Soteria will be designed to transport a single patient, falling within the critical care levels 3–5, from a natural disaster site to the nearest medical base or hospital. In this case, patients are relatively stable and do not require urgent care. In addition, first response teams and medical aids are considered to be already at the disaster site when Soteria arrives.

1.3 Target Group

The key users included in the target group are the patients who will be transferred in Soteria from the natural disaster site to the nearest medical base and the EMT or first responder providing the initial medical attention and loading the patient into the vehicle. To better understand the users, existing literature was consulted to determine their emotions, goals, needs, and typical behavior following the natural disaster and into the rescue period.

2 Method

2.1 Exterior

As a starting point a basic design for the exterior form of the vehicle was developed (Fig. 2). The general form of the design featured gullwing doors and a rear trunk, intending to provide easy loading and maximum first responder access to the patient. However, it was not clear how the handlings would take place. Therefore, a 1:1 model was developed, and studies were done on how first responders would load the Soteria.

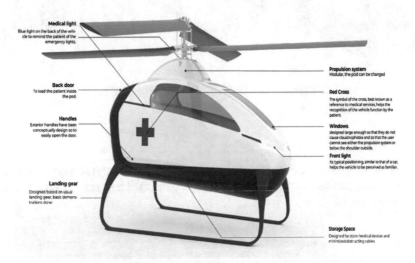

Fig. 2. Soteria exterior final design

2.2 Study on Loading

To study the loading, interviews with first responders were planned and observations were done of how helicopters and ambulances are loaded. Additionally, a overview of equipment needed was made and it was studied where it should be positioned in the Sotaria. Based on that a 1;1 model was made and tests with persons placing a stretcher in the Sotaria were performed. Based on this a patient loading and unloading system is designed, which should enhance user experience (patient and first responders) and reduce the strain imposed on medical aids. Also, a detailed design was made including the stretcher size and space needed for the stretcher, door handles, handles in the cabin, space for the patient and handling first responders. An overall vehicle design including aerodynamics was made as well, which is out of the scope of this paper. Development of the final exterior design of the Soteria patient carrier, included the following steps: 1) Define the loading and unloading process based on observations, ease of procedure and first responder patient access. Some options are shown in Fig. 3; 2) Define the interior size, door length, floor height, stretcher height (it should be minimal to reduce the Soteria size and weight; but patients should fit in it and first responders should be able to work with it comfortably) and handle size and positions; 3) Perform interviews with first responders to get important insights on windows and letting the occupant feel safe.

Fig. 3. Some possibilities to load the Soteria

2.3 Interior

Research on the patient positioning on the stretcher showed that it should be possible to take the Fowler and semi Fowler position in the pod [6]. The stretcher dimensions are shown in Fig. 4.

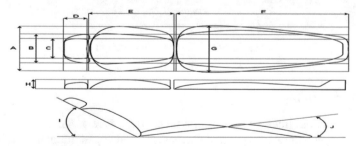

Fig. 4. Stretcher dimensions. A(57–65 cm), B(41–45 cm), C(25 cm), D(20–23 cm), E(82 cm), F(120 cm), G(65 cm), H(30 cm), I(0–60°) and J(0–30°).

3   Results

Observations and recordings at current ambulances showed that a pod floor height relative to ground should be at the height of a P50 man so that the stretcher can be easily placed onto the Soteria carrier.

A 1:1 model was created using PVC installation pipes (see Fig. 5a). Maneuvering in this model showed that loading from the back was easiest, also probably because first responders are used to that in an ambulance. The size of the pod was defined using DINED [7] (see Fig. 5b). The pod door height when opened should be such that it is above the standing height of a P50 man, so those first responders can easily load and unload a stretcher without having to bend too much or strain themselves. Observations and interviews pointed out that the stretcher width should be such that a first responder can easily reach the opposite side of a person lying flat on a stretcher, to perform any medical procedures might be required.

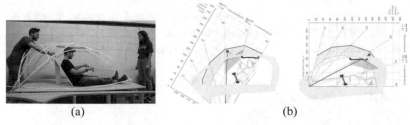

(a)   (b)

Fig. 5. a. 1:1 model was with PVC installation pipes to check maneuverability and b. height in Fowlers position (left) and the reach envelopes of DINED [7] were used to check size and positioning of the handles (middle and right)

The literature also showed that not only a flat position is preferable, but the Fowler and semi-Fowler position should be taken as well patient positioning [6], which means that for a p. 95 1122 mm height is needed. In order to provide maximum comfort, the following stretcher indicated in Fig. 6 was designed.

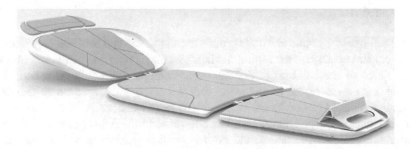

Fig. 6. Final stretcher design

Following expert consultation and the conclusion to move forward with the gull-wing doors, loading the patient into the vehicle was deemed the optimal choice, when compared to loading the patient from the side, see Fig. 7.

Fig. 7. Stretcher loading process

Regarding handles, as considered critical towards helping the patient feel secure during transport [8], research showed that even when patients are secured into their stretchers with seatbelts, they often feel insecure and as if they will fall off [9]. As the aircraft will be moving and slight turbulence may occur, it is imperative to include a form of handles that will offer patient security and allow for them to adjust their position to help enhance comfort. The final handle design, Fig. 8a, and placement, Fig. 8b includes two sets of handles produced from Bcomp material. The selected handle placement and diameter, 30 mm, optimize patient comfort, their feeling of security, and overall grip strength.

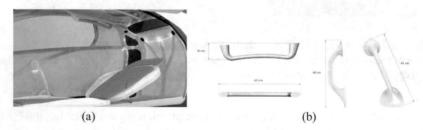

(a)   (b)

Fig. 8. a. Final design and b. Handle design

4   Discussion

Interior shell size was ample and comfortable for all users tested between P5–P95. There is however extra space present behind the headrest that is not used in all circumstances, since the arch of the headrest at different seat configurations follows a curved path while the rear corner of the pod is angular in the side view. Based on further testing investigations should be conducted to potentially decrease the size of the interior, such that the weight of the pod fits within the allowable limit. A heat-map of 10–15 min of a user sitting inside the pod would be beneficial to determine which areas are not completely necessary, and how reducing these areas will make users perceive the comfort of the carrier.

Although the stretcher was comfortable for all users, after testing, it was noticed that the stretcher with hard foam sides should be redesigned to optimize the design for easy loading and unloading, and to avoid any potential elevated points during this activity. It would be beneficial for the stretcher to be flush to the carrier floor or slightly recessed as originally intended.

The top handles were situated to be comfortable in all stretcher positions. After testing however, it was noticed they should be extended towards the front of the pod by 20 cm. The side handles should also be extended towards the front of the pod by 20 cm, and the handle angle should be slightly more vertical for optimal comfort.

References

1. PHYSORG Homepage. https://phys.org/news/2018-10-cascading-natural-disasters.html. Accessed 22 Feb 2021
2. LIVESCIENCE Homepage. https://www.livescience.com/414-scientists-natural-disasters-common.html. Accessed 22 Feb 2021
3. SPRINGER Homepage. https://doi.org/10.1007/s40719-018-0125-3. Accessed 22 Feb 2021
4. Li, X., Zheng, J.: Efficient post-disaster patient transportation and transfer: experiences and lessons learned in emergency medical rescue in aceh after the 2004 asian Tsunami. Mil. Med. **179**(8), 913–919 (2014)
5. VICE Homepage. https://www.vice.com/en_us/article/xwn9bn/what-is-ubercopter-actually-doing-besides-polluting. Accessed 22 Feb 2021
6. EMSWORLD Homepage. https://www.emsworld.com/article/12062118/patientpositioning. Accessed 22 Feb 2021
7. DINED Homepage. https://dined.io.tudelft.nl/en/database/tool. Accessed 21 Feb 2021
8. Kluth, K., Strasser, H.: Ergonomics in the rescue service—Ergonomic evaluation of ambulance cots. Int. J. Ind. Ergon. **36**(3), 247–256 (2006)
9. Suserud, B., Johansson, A., Petzall, K.: Caring for Patients at High Speeds. Keristad: en.rcnpublishing.com (2013)

Changes in Lower Leg Volume Among Health Care Workers During a Working Day

Jonathan Osorio-Vasco[1]([⊠]) [iD] and Yordán Rodríguez[2] [iD]

[1] Centro Regional Aburrá Sur, Corporación Universitaria Minuto de Dios-UNIMINUTO ,
Bello, Colombia
jvascoosori@uniminuto.edu.co
[2] National School of Public Health, Universidad de Antioquia, Medellín, Colombia
yordan.rodriguez@udea.edu.co

Abstract. The objective of this study was to analyze the variation of leg volume in hospital workers, and its relationship with individual factors: sex, age, height, and weight. Cross-sectional study, where leg circumference measurements were taken at the beginning and end of an 8-h workday. Twenty-one workers (12 women, 9 men) working in seven different hospital jobs voluntarily participated. To calculate the volume of the legs, the circumference of the legs was measured in 5 segments every 4 cm (20 cm in total) with the Gulick II tape measure. The average volume in both legs increased (right leg 2.6%, left leg 2.7%), with significant changes in both the right ($Z = -3.1446$, $p = 0.002$) and left ($Z = -3.528$, $p = 0.000$) legs between the beginning and the end of the working day. No relationship was found between leg volume with sex, age, height, and weight. These findings indicate the need to focus more attention on the effects of standing work in health care workers, as increased leg volume has been associated with lower extremity fatigue and discomfort.

Keywords: Leg swelling · Lower extremity · Occupational health · Standing work · Musculoskeletal symptoms · Health care workers

1 Introduction

Standing during the workday is a posture frequently adopted by health care workers [1–3] and has been associated with the development of musculoskeletal symptoms in the lower extremities [4]. One of the reported symptoms is increased leg volume [5–10], which increases due to reduced blood flow in the leg muscles, causing swelling of veins, which may develop into varicose veins or chronic venous insufficiency [6, 10, 11].

Changes in the volume of the legs and the appearance of other musculoskeletal symptoms have been associated with several risk factors: weight [11, 12], age and height [13], flat shoes [14], type of surface [12], standing time [8, 15], among others. On the other hand, Coenen et al. (2017), stated that: "…confounding or mediating variables (including gender, age, other physical or mental work demands, and previous musculoskeletal symptoms) that could explain or modify the association of occupational standing with musculoskeletal symptoms" [7].

© The Author(s), under exclusive license to Springer Nature Switzerland AG 2021
N. L. Black et al. (Eds.): IEA 2021, LNNS 222, pp. 404–409, 2021.
https://doi.org/10.1007/978-3-030-74611-7_55

Several studies report the presence of musculoskeletal symptoms in health care workers [1, 2, 16, 17]. However, there is limited evidence on leg volume changes in health care workers during a working day.

The objective of this study is to analyze the variation of leg volume in hospital workers during a working day and its relationship with individual factors: sex, age, height, and weight.

2 Materials and Methods

2.1 Type of Study and Population

A cross-sectional study in which the circumference of the legs (right and left) was measured in 21 workers (12 women, 9 men) of a hospital in Medellin, Colombia, at the beginning and end of an 8-h working day. Seven different workstations were selected. The number of workers per position was distributed as follows: three in distribution and dietetics, three in pharmacy, five in Intensive Care Units (ICU), three in the laundry, three in maintenance, three in hospitalization, and one cleaner.

Participants were selected based on the number of workers assigned to each job. In jobs with between one and three workers, all workers were selected. In cases where more than three workers were assigned to the job, the selection was random. To participate in the study, workers had to perform their activities in one of the selected positions, be present on the day of data collection, and express their voluntary participation in the study by signing an informed consent form.

Through continuous observation of activities, it was determined that all workers remained standing for at least 80% of the working day.

2.2 Leg Circumference Measuring

Measuring Instrument

To measure the legs' circumference (right and left), the Gulick II tape measure [18] was used. The tape measure is designed to decrease the error in the measurement based on a Newton (1 N) of tension that is in a control device at the time of tensioning the tape through a spring helping the accuracy of the measurements, ensuring that the measurement will have approximately the same tension, unlike standard tape measures [12, 14, 19]. The tape measure proved to be reliable, with a reliability coefficient of 0.97 for the calf and 0.98 for the ankle [20]. Similarly, in a comparison using the Gulick II tape measure and an automated optoelectronic measurement method from Pero-System to measure leg edema, the volume measurements between the two methods had a high correlation with a coefficient of 0.98 for the legs [21].

Measuring Procedure

The work team consisted of two physical therapists, one occupational health and safety professional, and one ergonomist. The two physiotherapists were in charge of field data collection and received prior training. The choice of the day of the week on which the measurements were taken was determined by the availability of access to the hospital. The measurement protocol is described below:

During the first hour of the workday, the workers who participated in this study were taken to a private room, where their weight was measured with a calibrated scale, height with a stadiometer, and leg circumference using the Gulick II tape measure. For left/right leg circumference measurements, participants were asked to sit in a chair, remove their shoes, pull up their left/right leg pant boot, place it on a chair of similar height to the chair they were sitting in, and leave the left/right leg extended for measurements.

Circumference was measured at five points on the leg, each 4 cm apart, starting from the lateral malleolus along the malleolus's longitudinal axis to the calf (20 cm). To facilitate and ensure the consistency of the measurements, the reference points were marked with permanent ink, and a wooden splint was placed on the legs to make the reference marks [12, 14, 22]. This exact procedure was followed during the last hour of the day.

2.3   Calculation of Volume and Percentage of Change

Equation (1) (truncated cone formula) was used for the calculation of leg volume, based on the circumference records [12, 14]:

$$V = \sum (X2 + Y2 + XY)/3\pi \tag{1}$$

Where "V" is the volume of the leg, "X" is the lower circumference of the segment, and "Y" is the upper circumference of the segment 4 cm away from "X".

The equation was used to calculate the volume variation at the beginning (V1) and the end of the working day (V2). Equation (2) was used to calculate the volume variation percentages [14]:

$$\Delta V\% = ((V2 - V1)/V1) \times 100 \tag{2}$$

2.4   Statistical Processing

SPSS software version 23 (SPSS, Inc. 2012) was used for the statistical analysis. A descriptive statistical analysis was performed for the variables: dominant leg, sex, age, height, and weight. The average percentage of leg volume variation was calculated. The Wilcoxon signed-rank test was used to find significant differences in leg volume at baseline and endpoint. Spearman's test was used to analyze the relationship between leg volume and age, height, and weight, while the Whitney U-Mann test was used for sex.

3   Results

The mean age was 35.19 years (SD = 9.91); mean height 165.4 cm (SD = 9.91); mean weight 71.82 kg (SD = 12.64). Regarding the dominant leg, 19 workers reported the right and 2 workers the left.

Table 1. Average variation of volume in the legs, average difference, average percentage of variation (N = 21, P < 0.05).

Leg	Initial volume $\overline{X}$ cm^3	SD	Final volume $\overline{X}$ cm^3	SD	$\Delta \overline{X}$ cm^3	$\Delta V \overline{X}\%$	Wilcoxon test	
							Z	P
Right	1584.2271	245.74	1624.4705	250.87	40.24	2.60	−3.1446	**0.002**
Left	1556.6319	243.58	1597.5876	245.68	40.95	2.70	−3.528	**0.001**

The calculation of the legs' volume presented an increase at the end of the working day with significant differences in the right leg (Z = −3.1446, p = 0.002) and left leg (Z = −3.528, p = 0.000). The left leg had a 0.10% greater increase than the right leg (Table 1).

The correlation between leg volume, sex, age, height and weight were not correlated (Table 2).

Table 2. Relationship between leg volume, sex, age, height and weight. N = 21. P < 0.05.

$\Delta \overline{X}$	Body side	Sex			Age		Height		Weight	
		Men	Woman	P	Rho	P	Rho	P	Rho	P
Volume leg	Right	8.89	12.58	0.177	−0.154	0.505	−0.244	0.287	−0.022	0.924
	Left	10.44	11.42	0.722	−0.169	0.465	0.082	0.723	−0.261	0.254

4 Discussion

This research showed a significant increase in leg volume in health care workers during an 8-h working day. This musculoskeletal symptom can cause vascular damage to the lower extremities and the workers' general well-being [6].

On average, the right leg had the greatest average volume at the beginning and end of the working day (right leg 1624.4705 cm3 and left leg 1597.5876 cm3). However, the left leg (2.7%) had the greatest average percentage change in volume compared to the right leg (2.6%), even though most workers (19) reported the right leg as the dominant leg.

The increase in leg volume found in our investigation coincides with that reported by Zander et al. (2004). In this study, leg circumference was measured in 13 workers during an 8-h workday to evaluate three work surfaces' effect on the change in leg volume. These authors reported that leg volume increased on all surfaces tested, being greater on hard surfaces [12]. Our study differs in that no variables were controlled during the working day, and two additional measurements of leg circumference (5 measurements every 4 cm) were performed in addition to those of Zander et al. (2004).

Increased leg volume is associated with the onset of pain, discomfort, or fatigue [15], hence the importance of analyzing volume change in health care workers.

In our research, no relationship was found between individual factors (age, sex, height, and weight) and volume changes; however, Coenen et al. (2017) highlighted the importance of including these factors in future research since they may explain or modify the occurrence of musculoskeletal symptoms caused by occupational standing work [8]. For example, Zander et al. (2004) found a relationship between weight and increased leg volume [12].

Further studies in real contexts, including a larger number of participants and measurements over several days, could provide evidence on the relationship between individual factors and leg volume changes in health care workers. Besides, other factors to be considered are footwear, type of surface, recovery time, use of pedals, etc., which may influence the increase in leg volume while working while standing.

We believe that research similar to the one presented here can provide evidence on the effects of standing work on the lower limbs of health care workers, allowing a more comprehensive understanding of this phenomenon so that more effective preventive actions can be taken.

5 Conclusions

This research shows a significant increase in leg volume in health care workers between the first and the last hour of an 8-h working day. However, no relationship was found in the increase in volume with individual factors such as sex, age, height, and weight. These findings indicate the need to focus more attention on the effects of standing work in health care workers since increased leg volume has been associated with lower extremity fatigue and discomfort.

References

1. Bernal, D., Campos-Serna, J., Tobias, A., Vargas-Prada, S., Benavides, F.G., Serra, C.: Work-related psychosocial risk factors and musculoskeletal disorders in hospital nurses and nursing aides: a systematic review and meta-analysis. Int. J. Nurs. Stud. **52**, 635–648 (2015)
2. Omokhodion, F.O., Umar, U.S., Ogunnowo, B.E.: Prevalence of low back pain among staff in a rural hospital in Nigeria. Occup. Med. (Chic. Ill). **50**, 107–110 (2000)
3. Ribeiro, T., Serranheira, F., Loureiro, H.: Work related musculoskeletal disorders in primary health care nurses. Appl. Nurs. Res. **33**, 72–77 (2017)
4. Konz, S.: Standing work. International Encyclopedia of Ergonomics and Human Factors, pp. 929–931 (2006)
5. Halim, I., Omar, A.R., Teknikal, U., Jaya, H.T.: A review on health effects associated with prolonged. Int. J. Recent Res. Appl. Stud. **8**, 14–21 (2011)
6. Waters, T.R., Dick, R.B.: Evidence of health risks associated with prolonged standing at work and intervention effectiveness. Rehabil. Nurs. **40**, 148–165 (2015)
7. Coenen, P., Willenberg, L., Parry, S., Shi, J.W., Romero, L., Blackwood, D.M., et al.: Associations of occupational standing with musculoskeletal symptoms: a systematic review with meta-analysis. British Journal of Sports Medicine, pp. 1–10 (2016)
8. Coenen, P., Parry, S., Willenberg, L., Shi, J.W., Romero, L., Blackwood, D.M., et al.: Associations of prolonged standing with musculoskeletal symptoms—a systematic review of laboratory studies. Gait Posture. **58**, 310–318 (2017)

9. Chester, M.R., Rys, M.J., Konz, S.A.: Leg swelling, comfort and fatigue when sitting, standing, and sit/standing. Int. J. Ind. Ergon. **29**, 289–296 (2002)
10. Canadian Centre for Occupational Health and Safety. Working in a Standing Position - Basic Information. https://www.ccohs.ca/oshanswers/ergonomics/standing/standing_basic. html. Accessed 25 Jan 2021
11. Krijnen, R.M., Boer, E.M., de Ader, H.J., Bruynzeel, D.P.: Venous insufficiency in male workers with a standing profession. Part 1: Epidemiology. Dermatology **194**, 111–120 (1997)
12. Zander, J.E., King, P.M., Ezenwa, B.N.: Influence of flooring conditions on lower leg volume following prolonged standing. Int. J. Ind. Ergon. **34**, 279–288 (2004)
13. Orlando, A.R., King, P.M.: Relationship of demographic variables on perception of fatigue and discomfort following prolonged standing under various flooring conditions. J. Occup. Rehabil. **14**, 63–76 (2004)
14. Karimi, Z., Allahyari, T., Azghani, M.R., Khalkhali, H.: Influence of unstable footwear on lower leg muscle activity, volume change and subjective discomfort during prolonged standing. Appl. Ergon. **53**, 95–102 (2016)
15. Antle, D.M., Vézina, N., Messing, K., Côté, J.N.: Development of discomfort and vascular and muscular changes during a prolonged standing task. Occup. Ergon. **11**, 21–33 (2013)
16. Mirmohammadi, S., Yazdani, J., Etemadinejad, S., Asgarinejad, H.: A cross-sectional study on work-related musculoskeletal disorders and associated risk factors among hospital health cares. Procedia Manuf. **3**, 4528–4534 (2015)
17. Meijsen, P., Knibbe, H.J.J.: Prolonged standing in the OR: a dutch research study. AORN J. **86**(3), 399–414 (2007)
18. Country Technology Inc. Gulick II Plus Tape Measure (Model 67019). https://www.fitnes smart.com/collections/gulick-ii-tape-measures-calibrated-for-accuracy-and-repeatability/ products/gulick-ii-plus-tape-measure?variant=291235270471999. Accessed 25 Aug 2020
19. Lin, Y.H., Chen, C.Y., Cho, M.H.: Influence of shoe/floor conditions on lower leg circumference and subjective discomfort during prolonged standing. Appl. Ergon. **43**, 965–970 (2012)
20. Labs, K.-H., Tschoepl, M., Gamba, G., Aschwanden, M., Jaeger, K.A.: The reliability of leg circumference assessment: a comparison of spring tape measurements and optoelectronic volumetry. Vasc. Med. **5**, 69–74 (2000)
21. Mayrovitz, H., Sims, N., Macdonald, J.: Assessment of limb volume by manual and automated methods in patients with limb edema or lymphedema. Adv. Ski. Wound Care **13**, 272–276 (2000)
22. Lin, Y.H., Chen, C.Y., Cho, M.H.: Effectiveness of leg movement in reducing leg swelling and discomfort in lower extremities. Appl. Ergon. **43**, 1033–1037 (2012)

Fitting a Chair to a Surgeon's Body: Mechanism of a Chair for Ophthalmologic Surgeon in an Operating Room

Hideki Oyama[1], Akihisa Watanabe[2], Hidenori Togami[3], Hiroyuki Kondo[2], and Kageyu Noro[4(✉)]

[1] National Institute of Occupational Safety and Health,
1-4-6 Umezono Kiyose, Tokyo 204-0024, Japan
oyama-hideki@s.jniosh.johas.go.jp
[2] Department of Ophthalmology, University of Environmental and Occupational Health,
Tokyo, Japan
[3] Physics, University of Environmental and Occupational Health, Tokyo, Japan
[4] Waseda University/ErgoSeating Co., Ltd., Tokyo, Japan

Abstract. We report the design and testing of a chair to better fit and support an ophthalmologic surgeon during a procedure. The aim of the new chair design is to enhance the surgical performance by reducing physical fatigue. If surgeons are more comfortable, they may make fewer errors, leading to better patient safety. The seat surface is made of fiber-reinforced plastics and molded with a curvature that provides pelvic and side support. The cushioning material is not urethane; instead, it is plastic entwined in a thread structure that can be easily processed. A mechanism that allows the backrest to slide forward and backward allows adjustment for differences in thigh length while enhancing support in the sacral and pelvic regions. The clinical pilot test by surgeons indicated that the prototype chair decreased the pressure on the seat surface and prevented backward tilt of the pelvis compared to a conventional chair. The synergistic effect of the seat surface and backrest allows a stable work posture while minimizing forward displacement.

Keywords: Ophthalmic microsurgery · Posture · Seat surface · Backrest

1 Introduction

In ophthalmic microsurgery, the surgeon sits in a chair while observing the surgical field under a microscope, moving their hands and fingers, operating the foot switch, and moving the microscope vertically with the trunk and upper limbs (Fig. 1). Body movement is restricted by the position of the microscope eyepiece necessarily being located over the site of surgery on the patient. As a result, excessive tension in the surgeon's upper body can lead to fatigue, which may affect surgeon performance and quality of the procedure. Seating problems experienced by ophthalmologic surgeons have been reported and may be associated with the risk of musculoskeletal disorders, including sustained foot elevation, thigh/buttock compression, inadequate arm support,

N. L. Black et al. (Eds.): IEA 2021, LNNS 222, pp. 410–416, 2021.
https://doi.org/10.1007/978-3-030-74611-7_56

excessive neck flexion, inability to recline, inadequate pelvis and back support, prolonged rigid posture, and subjective fatigue of the shoulders and buttocks [1, 2].

In contrast, a newer "heads-up surgery" procedure has been reported to minimize physical and visual fatigue in recent reports [3]. The term "heads-up surgery" is derived from the so-called "head-up display" that was first used in aircraft cockpits to allow pilots to raise their heads to view information without looking down at the instrument panel. In surgery, the surgeon performs the procedure while viewing an image captured by a 3D camera and displayed on a large screen. The microscope eyepieces are not used. Although the heads-up surgery technique prevents neck and back pain during prolonged surgeries, as it allows freedom of body movement, the physical load on the buttocks around the ischial tuberosities remains comparable to the conventional technique [4].

We have been developing a chair to improve seating options for ophthalmic surgeons. The aim of the new design is to enhance surgeon performance by reducing physical fatigue in surgeons. If surgeons are more comfortable, they may make fewer errors, leading to improved patient safety. We have previously reported on the design and testing of a prototype chair backrest [5]. This paper reports on the design of a seat surface and an adjustment mechanism for the seat and backrest to reduce pressure on the thighs/buttocks and to enhance the support of the sacral and pelvic regions.

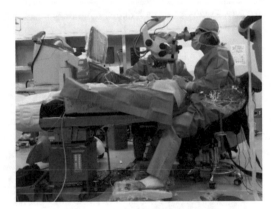

Fig. 1. Ophthalmic microsurgery.

2 Methodology

The study and surgical procedures were performed in the operating room at the University of Environmental and Occupational Health, Kitakyushu, Japan, after the approval of the ethics committee of the university.

2.1 Participatory Ergonomic Approach

A participatory ergonomics approach and prototyping design method were used in this study. Table 1 lists the role of participants in each stage of the project. The prototype chair was developed by a team of ergonomists, surgeons, clinical laboratory technologists, designers, and manufacturers. Ergonomists have consistently participated throughout research and development.

Table 1. Process of research and development of prototype chair.

Phase	Content	Participants				
		E	S	C	D	M
Research	Preliminary study of posture in surgeons	O	O	O		
	Problems extraction	O	O	O		
	Hypothesis planning	O	O	O		
Development	Concept making	O	O	O	O	
	Design and modeling	O			O	
	Specification review	O	O	O	O	
	Production and assembly					O
	Measurement and evaluation	O	O	O		

Abbreviation. E: Ergonomists, S: Surgeons, C: Clinical laboratory technologist, D: Designer, M: Manufacturer.

2.2 Prototyping

We used an iterative approach to prototyping, undertaking multiple rounds of design and testing to incorporate feedback into the design specifications. The seat surface adopts the concept of a high-performance seat pan [6], which divides the muscular regions of the lumbosacral region, buttocks, and thighs based on differences in composition and volume. Figure 2 shows the first study model and a prototype chair that reflects its functions; the seat surface of the study model is divided into pelvic, ischial, and thighs zones. The prototype chair features a curvature to the seat surface that is designed to emulate the shape of the human buttocks and the structure of the study model. The backrest of the prototype is adjusted forward or backward. The backrest consists of two roll supports: the upper part supports the surgeon's lumbar region and the lower part supports the sacral and pelvic regions.

2.3 Clinical Pilot Test

A prototype chair was used by five clinical surgeons during vitreous surgery. Operation times varied from approximately 30 to 120 min. The prototype chair (A) was compared to a conventional chair (B). The pressure on the seat surface was measured using a pressure-sensing device (X-sensor, XSENSOR Co.). The pelvic tilt angle was measured using a gyroscope sensor mounted on the iliac crest of the surgeon's body surface. The relative pelvic angle was calculated in the standing position. A backward pelvic tilt had

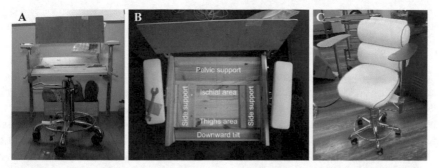

Fig. 2. A: Study model, B: Layout of supports on the seat surface, C: Prototype chair.

a negative value. Data used in the analysis was the mean value of 30 s collected at 30 min after the start of surgery. This was used because the total operation time was different among the surgeons.

3 Results

Figure 3 shows the pressure maps of the seat surface for each subject. The pressure maps of all subjects showed a low pressure around the ischial tuberosities and a wide pressure distribution with the prototype chair (A) compared with the conventional chair (B). The average pressure was 40.5 ± 3.8 mmHg for A and 70.4 ± 12.7 mmHg for B. The maximum pressure was 170.5 ± 38.5 mmHg for A and 242.2 ± 19.7 mmHg for B. The contact area was 1255.9 ± 60.1 cm^2 for A and 906.1 ± 114.5 cm^2 for B. The relative value of the pelvic tilt angle was $-7.1° \pm 4.9°$ for A and $-13.7° \pm 3.7°$ for B.

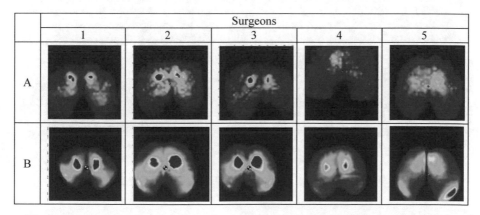

Fig. 3. Pressure map of seat surface in each subject. A: Prototype, B: Conventional chair.

4 Discussions

4.1 Comparison of Chairs

The low pressure and large contact area reported with the prototype chair compared to those with the conventional chair indicate that the prototype succeeds in reducing pressure on the thighs/buttocks. The prototype chair also prevents backward tilt of the pelvis compared to a conventional chair. This indicates that the surgeon is able to maintain a posture that is similar to the pelvic and spinal alignment in the standing position. According to our previous research [5], the backrest of the same prototype is in contact with the surgeon's lower back at a low pressure level (less than 20 mmHg, contact ratio of more than 80%). The synergistic effect of the seat surface and backrest allows a stable work posture while minimizing the reaction force on the backrest and forward displacement on the seat, even when the surgeon's back touches the backrest.

4.2 Ergonomics

This section describes the ergonomics of the chair's design. Figure 4 summarizes the effects on the humans based on the structures of the prototype chair.

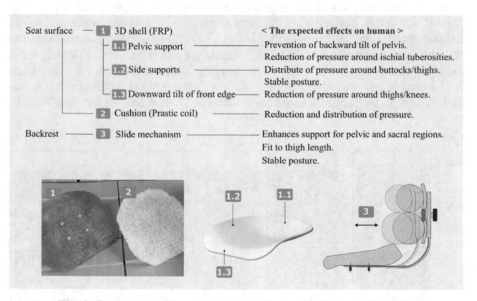

Fig. 4. Ergonomics of the seat surface and backrest in the prototype chair.

Seat Surface. It consists of a "shell" and a "cushion". The shell was molded with a 3D curvature made of fiber-reinforced plastic. The pelvic support, which is wedged shape, with an angle of approximately 20°, is placed at the rear end of the seat to prevent backward tilt of the pelvis, as reported by Wu [7]. This effect is seen in pelvic tilt angle measurements recorded here. It also suggests that the changed position of the ischial tuberosities associated with pelvic rotation contributes to the reduction in seat pressure. The side supports were installed to stabilize the surgeon's posture and distribute pressure. The seat's front edge is also tilted downward to avoid pressure on the thighs/knees, and a pronounced effect is observed in subject 5. The cushioning material is not urethane; instead, it is plastic entwined in a thread structure that can be easily processed. The material contributes to the reduction and dispersion of pressure, which is notable in subjects 4 and 5.

Backrest. A new sliding adjustment mechanism for the backrest enhances support in the sacral and pelvic regions. Adjustment of the backrest can fill the gap that tends to occur between the buttocks and the joint of the seat surface and backrest. When the backrest slides to fill the gap, the two stresses in Fig. 5 will allow the surgeon to maintain a better posture. The slide mechanism also solves the problem of surgeons not using the backrest, so-called "shallow sitting", because it changes the seat depth to accommodate individual differences in thigh length. The importance is that the shaft of the backrest mounted to the backside of the seat can be adjusted. The depth adjustment can be found on the other chairs but is less common on the backrest.

Fig. 5. The two stresses generated by the slide mechanism for the backrest. A is vertical force to push the pelvis upwards on the pelvic support in the seat surface, B is horizontal force to push the sacrum region forward on the backrest, which enhances the effect of A, resulting prevent to backward tilt of the pelvis.

4.3 Research Limitations

A limitation of this study was the small number of surgeons to test the chair. More participants would have increased the validity of the findings; however, we were limited by the number of microsurgeons available at our institution. Another limitation is the relatively short time of data collection. It will be necessary to investigate the effects of longer-term chair use on the fatigue and performance of surgeons. A final limitation is the intervention bias of the participants. Although the participatory ergonomic approach is useful for the development of chairs, the potential for participant bias during evaluation cannot be excluded. Blinded testing with more participants is needed.

5   Conclusions

The prototype chair had lower seat pressure and better posture maintenance than the conventional surgical chair, which may contribute to the improved postural stability of ophthalmologic surgeons in the operating room.

Acknowledgments.   The authors thank HANDAYA Co., LTD for contribution in manufacture of the chair.

References

1. Noro, K., Naruse, T., Lueder, R., Nao-I, N., Kozawa, M.: Application of Zen sitting principles to microscopic surgery seating. Appl. Ergon. **43**(2), 308–419 (2012)
2. Kondo, H., Fujiki, N., Mitsuya, R., Oyama, H., Togami, H., Hachiya, Y., Watanabe, A.: A study on working posture of microsurgeons. Research report, The Daiichi Life Foundation, Tokyo (2016). (in Japanese)
3. Eckardt, C., Paulo, E.B.: Heads-up surgery for vitreoretinal procedures: An experimental and clinical study. Retina **36**(1), 137–147 (2016)
4. Watanabe, A., Oyama, H., Noro, K., Togami, H., Kondo, H.: Analysis and improvement of surgeons' posture during ophthalmic microsurgery (part 1): Heads-up surgery with a 3D monitor. In: Proceedings of 64. Kongress der Gesellschaft für Arbeitswissenschaft (GfA), B. 3.13, pp. 1–6. GfA Press, Dortmund (2018)
5. Oyama, H., Watanabe, A., Togami, H., Kondo, H., Noro, K.: Analysis and improvement of surgeons' posture during ophthalmic microsurgery (part 2): development of a chair with backrest for forward-inclined posture. In: Proceedings of 64. Kongress der Gesellschaft für Arbeitswissenschaft (GfA), B.3.9, pp. 1–6. GfA Press, Dortmund (2018)
6. Noro, K., Lueder, R., Yamada, S., Fujimaki, G., Oyama, H., Hashidate, Y.: Revisiting sitting cross-cultural aspects of seating. In: Proceedings of the Human Factors and Ergonomics Society 50th Annual Meeting, pp. 814–819, SAGE Publishing, San Francisco, CA (2006)
7. Wu, C.S., Miyamoto, H., Noro, K.: Research on pelvic angle variation when using a pelvic support. Ergonomics **41**(3), 317–327 (1998)

Testing Interventions in a Medical Simulator: Challenges and Solutions

Estrella Paterson[1(✉)], Penelope Sanderson[1,2,3], Ismail Mohamed[1], Isaac Salisbury[1], Robert G. Loeb[1,4], and Neil Paterson[3,5]

[1] School of Psychology, The University of Queensland, St Lucia, QLD 4072, Australia
estrella.paterson@uqconnect.edu.au
[2] School of Information Technology and Electrical Engineering, The University of Queensland, St Lucia, QLD 4072, Australia
[3] School of Clinical Medicine, The University of Queensland, St Lucia, QLD 4072, Australia
[4] Department of Anesthesiology, University of Florida College of Medicine, Gainesville, FL 32610, USA
[5] Anaesthesia and Pain Management Services, Queensland Children's Hospital, South Brisbane, QLD 4101, Australia

Abstract. When testing medical interventions in a simulator, establishing an environment that allows findings to generalize to clinical settings; designing scenarios that are representative of clinical situations and that can be delivered consistently; and ensuring correct operation of simulator systems to ensure efficient data collection, can be challenging.

We address these factors using the example of a study that tested auditory displays for the pulse oximeter conducted in a medical simulator with anesthesiologist participants. To establish fidelity of the clinical setting, the simulator was arranged as an operating room (OR) and actors trained to conduct surgery based on real cases. To ensure that scenarios were presented uniformly to each participant, we devised a novel approach: visual displays of vital signs were video-recorded and auditory displays then dubbed into the recordings that were displayed to participants via a monitor. Timing of actors' actions was controlled by the simulator coordinator via verbal cues through earpieces according to a script that corresponded to the recorded displays. To allow for any technical malfunctions and to ensure effective data collection, we established redundant systems for recording scenarios and carried out piloting and training prior to conducting experimental sessions. Taking into account these factors, we were able to show that a novel auditory display was more effective for identifying oxygen saturation values than a standard display. Participants appeared to accept the simulator setting as natural and reacted in ways similar to behavior displayed in the OR. We conducted 20 sessions without any loss of data.

Keywords: Simulator · Medical intervention · Clinical setting · Auditory display · Operating room · Fidelity

N. L. Black et al. (Eds.): IEA 2021, LNNS 222, pp. 417–423, 2021.
https://doi.org/10.1007/978-3-030-74611-7_57

1   Introduction

Researchers can improve the healthcare environment without potentially harming patients by using the simulator to test new technology and protocols [1, 2]. The aim of this paper is to describe the challenges and solutions of simulation testing using the example of a study that investigated two pulse oximetry auditory displays in a simulator arranged as an operating room (OR) [3].

Medical simulation is typically used for training and assessment of clinical performance [4–6]. However, medical simulators can also be used to test research hypotheses [5, 7]. Simulation-based research (SBR) has been used for testing a variety of interventions related to the OR and intensive care unit (ICU), including patient vital sign displays [8–10].

Factors to consider when designing SBR include physical and social fidelity of the work environment [11]; scenario structure; video and audio capture [2]; and piloting. Thus, SBR requires input and collaboration of a variety of experts such as clinicians, engineers, simulator operators and technicians, and human factors specialists.

In this paper, we use as an example a study that assessed anesthesiologists' ability to identify changes in oxygen saturation (SpO_2) range using two auditory displays: a standard pulse oximeter display and a display enhanced with additional sound dimensions to distinguish SpO_2 ranges [3]. We desired participants to behave in the simulator in ways as similar as possible to those manifested in the OR during real cases. Therefore, we aimed to match simulation realism to the OR to support generalizability to the clinical setting. We also designed uniform scenarios to allow for accurate comparison of outcomes, established redundant recording systems to ensure data was captured effectively and conducted extensive piloting to ensure systems worked efficiently.

2   Fidelity

Fidelity is the degree to which the simulation replicates the appearance and behavior of the simulated system [12]. *Physical fidelity* is the extent to which the simulator environment matches the simulated environment, and *social fidelity* is the extent to which the social constructs of the simulation match those of the simulated environment [11]. Together, they can enhance *psychological fidelity* of scenarios: the extent to which behaviors in the OR are captured in the simulated environment [12].

2.1   Physical Fidelity

To maintain physical fidelity, we set up the simulator to closely resemble the ORs of the children's hospital that participants worked in by including a pediatric mannequin as well as equipment sourced from that hospital's operating suite (see Fig. 1). Equipment was set up for airway surgery. Music is often played in the OR [13] so we included a playlist of pop songs that played in the background throughout each session.

2.2 Social Fidelity

Actors dressed in scrubs played the roles of anesthesiologist, surgeon, scrub nurse and anesthetic assistant conducting simulated airway surgery. The role of administrating anesthesiologist was played by a consultant anesthesiologist (NP) who also trained the other actors. During scenarios, actors followed a script based on real airway cases and also engaged in casual conversation. We included two interruptions per scenario: one via telephone and a face-to-face interruption.

3 Scenario Design

To maintain the deterministic nature of the scenarios, participants were not directly involved in patient care [9]. They supervised a more junior colleague administrating an anesthetic (played by NP). Participants sat at a desk near the operating field and performed a patient categorization task throughout the scenario. They verbalized their responses of vital sign changes and were able to converse freely with OR staff. Sessions were video recorded and responses coded.

We constructed two similar scenarios that could be presented in a uniform manner from participant to participant to allow for accurate comparison of their ability to identify changes in vital signs using the two auditory displays. Clinical experts (NP and RGL) based the scenarios on real cases: the removal of laryngeal papillomata and a bronchoscopy to exclude a foreign body inhalation. Patient vital signs (SpO_2, HR, BP and $ETCO_2$) changed frequently during each scenario, providing many stimuli to which the participants reacted (40–43 state changes per scenario). These state changes were

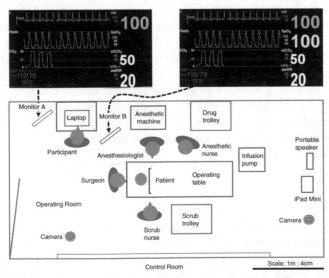

Fig. 1. Layout of simulator (From "Evaluation of an enhanced pulse oximeter auditory display: a simulator study" by Paterson et al. British Journal of Anaesthesia, 125 (5), 826–834 https://doi.org/10.1016/j.bja.2020.05.038)

set at pre-defined intervals so that each participant experienced the changes at exactly the same times within the scenario. This allowed for accurate comparison of detection accuracy rates and latencies of vital sign changes for each of the auditory displays.

It would be difficult for a simulator operator to maintain the timing control of such a large number of state changes within each scenario using an "*on-the-fly*" model as is used for training and performance assessment purposes in the simulator. Therefore, a software engineer (IM) incorporated the state changes into the commercial simulation software (LLEAP Version 6.4.1, Laerdal, Stavanger, Norway). To ensure the timing of events for each scenario was the same for each participant, each scenario was run using the simulator software and the vital signs monitor screen was recorded. The auditory displays were then dubbed into the scenarios with sounds matched to vital sign signals. This was a key step in ensuring control and repeatability of scenarios.

These steps meant the simulator coordinator could simply press the play button to start the relevant video ("set and forget") and then address attention to coordinating the accurate timing of actors' actions. The coordinator provided verbal cues via earpieces according to the scenario scripts. To account for practice and sequence effects we used a counter-balanced, crossover design.

4   Video and Audio Recordings

In simulator research it is essential to obtain clear recordings of participants' reactions to scenario events to allow for accurate analysis of outcomes. Past simulation research reports that technical failures can result in data not being recorded [14]. In our example, participants identified vital sign changes verbally and we used the scenario recordings to code outcome measures. Initially, we tested the existing simulator recording equipment but found that the system was unreliable. Therefore, we established a number of independent recording systems with the aim of providing a high level of redundancy to allow for technical malfunctions. These included a GoPro camera (GoPro, San Mateo, CA) positioned on the participant's head; Open Broadcaster Software (Jim, OBS Studio Contributors, https://obsproject.com) with feeds from two wall-mounted cameras (Logitech, Lausanne, Switzerland); a Nexus 10.10.1 touchscreen tablet (Samsung, Seoul, South Korea) positioned behind the participant that collected video recordings; and Audio-hijack software (Rogue Amoeba, Boston, MA) for audio recording. The hardware set up for the system was run through a Mac Mini (Apple, Cupertino, CA).

5   Piloting

Piloting is important in SBR because simulator and clinician time is expensive. Anesthesiologists have limited availability for research participation because they have clinical duties to perform. In addition, the simulator was located in a busy tertiary hospital and was in high demand for training purposes. Furthermore, we had to schedule numerous people for each session including the participants, actors, simulator controller, software and hardware experts, as well as organize delivery of OR equipment. To ensure that the scenarios ran smoothly and that outcomes were measured accurately, we conducted a number of pilot sessions before we conducted experimental sessions.

6 Outcomes and Discussion

6.1 Fidelity

Participants appeared to accept the simulator setting as natural and behaved in ways similar to those exhibited in the OR. This is evident from the transcriptions of participants' verbal responses that went beyond identifying vital sign changes. For example, participants referred to the patient's treatment:

"Are you happy with your depth of anesthesia?"

"So, he's got propofol, sevoflurane… so it's dexamethasone topical adrenaline?"

"You're happy with the larynx now (surgeon) and looking at the tracheomalacia?"

At one point during the scenario when SpO_2 levels became critical, one participant went as far to ask:

"Do you think (surgeon) should pause the procedure for a moment? Do you think we should call for help? I think we should press the emergency button and get some help for you (surgeon)."

Furthermore, the majority of participants asked the anesthesiologist administering the anesthetic if they would like help. For example,

"Would you like a hand there (anesthesiologist)?"

6.2 Scenario Design

The deterministic nature of the scenarios allowed for robust comparison of the auditory displays. During the 800 total minutes of the experiments, we collected 1890 data points to determine response to changes in oxygen saturation. We showed that participants were more accurate and faster at identifying SpO_2 parameters using the enhanced display compared with the standard display.

6.3 Video and Auditory Recordings

We were able to record and analyze all 20 sessions without losing any data. We used the OBS recordings to code participants' responses for the majority of the 40 scenarios. However, there were 10 sessions where the OBS audio recording was compromised. For these cases we were able to retrieve data from the GoPro and AudioHijack recordings.

6.4 Piloting

Using an iterative approach, we addressed hardware and software issues prior to conducting the experiment. The importance of piloting is illustrated by an incident that occurred after a pilot session. The participant pointed out that the numerical value of the SpO_2 level that was displayed visually to the OR team but not the participant, was reflected in the control room window. Because our hypothesis was based on the premise that participants would be able to identify SpO_2 parameters using the auditory display alone, this confound would have seriously compromised our data. By simply changing the angle of that monitor we were able to avoid this issue.

7 Limitations

There are limitations to simulation research. In the example used, actors' roles were filled by non-clinicians; scenarios were relatively short compared with real cases; and consequences of error were lower than would be the case with real patients. However, participants appeared to accept the simulation and behaved in ways similar to those displayed in the OR.

8 Conclusion

Ideally, a new intervention should be tested in a clinical setting to assess its effect on patient outcomes. However, if the simulator setting accurately represents the OR we can accept that participants behave in a manner similar to how they would in clinical practice. Moreover, if scenarios are rigorously designed, accurate data collected and procedures piloted, we can accept evidence of the efficacy of the intervention. Taken together, we are confident that the finding from this research will transfer to real clinical improvements.

References

1. Leblanc, V.R., Manser, T., Weinger, M.B., Musson, D., Kutzin, J., Howard, S.K.: The study of factors affecting human and systems performance in healthcare using simulation. Simul Healthc. J. Soc. Simul. Healthc. 6(7), S24–S29 (2011)
2. Cheng, A., Auerbach, M., Hunt, E.A., Chang, T.P., Pusic, M., Nadkarni, V., et al.: Designing and conducting simulation-based research. Pediatrics. 133(6), 1091–1101 (2014)
3. Paterson, E., Sanderson, P.M., Salisbury, I.S., Burgmann, F.P., Mohamed, I., Loeb, R.G., et al.: Evaluation of an enhanced pulse oximeter auditory display: a simulator study. Br. J. Anaesth. 125(5), 826–834 (2020)
4. Cook, T.M., Woodall, N., Frerk, C.: Fourth National Audit Project: Major complications of airway management in the UK: results of the fourth national audit project of the royal college of anaesthetists and the difficult airway society. part 1: anaesthesia. Br. J. Anaesth. 106(5), 617–631 (2011)
5. LeBlanc, V.R.: Simulation in anesthesia: state of the science and looking forward. Can. J. Anesth. J. Can. d'anesthésie 59(2), 193–202 (2012)
6. Ryall, T., Judd, B.K., Gordon, C.J.: Simulation-based assessments in health professional education: a systematic review. J. Multidiscipl. Healthc. 9, 60–82 (2016)

7. McNeer, R.R., Dudaryk, R., Nedeff, N.B., Bennett, C.L.: Development and testing of screen-based and psychometric instruments for assessing resident performance in an operating room simulator. Anesthesiol. Res. Pract., 1–13 (2016)
8. Liu, D., Jenkins, S.A., Sanderson, P.M., Watson, M.O., Leane, T., Kruys, A., et al.: Monitoring with head-mounted displays: performance and safety in a full-scale simulator and part-task trainer. Anesth. Analg. 109(4), 1135–1146 (2009)
9. Sanderson, P.M., Watson, M.O., Russell, W.J., Jenkins, S., Liu, D., Green, N., et al.: Advanced auditory displays and head-mounted displays: advantages and disadvantages for monitoring by the distracted anesthesiologist. Anesth. Analg. 106(6), 1787–1797 (2008)
10. McNeer, R.R., Horn, D.B., Bennett, C.L., Edworthy, J.R., Dudaryk, R.: Auditory icon alarms are more accurately and quickly identified than current standard melodic alarms in a simulated clinical setting. Anesthesiology 129(1), 58–66 (2018)
11. Dieckmann, P., Gaba, D.M., Rall, M.: Deepening the theoretical foundations of patient simulation as social practice. Simul. Healthc. 2(3), 183–193 (2007)
12. Maran, N.J., Glavin, R.J.: Low-to high-fidelity simulation–a continuum of medical education? Med. Educ. 37, 22–28 (2003)
13. Weldon, S.M., Korkiakangas, T., Bezemer, J., Kneebone, R.: Music and communication in the operating theatre. J. Adv. Nurs. 71(12), 2763–2774 (2015)
14. Marshall, S.D., Mehra, R.: The effects of a displayed cognitive aid on non-technical skills in a simulated 'can't intubate, can't oxygenate' crisis. Anaesthesia 69(7), 669–677 (2014)

Designing the OR Cockpit - Transfer of Dimensional Layout Conception Used in Vehicle Design to the OR

Stefan Pfeffer[1](), Alexander Mueller[2], and Manuel Weller[1]

[1] Faculty of Industrial Technologies—Furtwangen University, Furtwangen im Schwarzwald, Germany
pfs@hs-furtwangen.de
[2] Hochschule Esslingen – University of Applied Sciences, Esslingen am Neckar, Germany

Abstract. The inadequate anthropometric design of state of the art operation rooms (ORs) is a source of high physical workload for the surgical staff, not least since the advent of minimally invasive surgery. Due to static postural work of the surgeons musculoskeletal complaints are reported by numerous studies. One of the main goals is the transfer and adaptation of digital human modeling (DHM) methods, which have proven themselves in vehicle development, to medical technology in the operating room (OR). The digital human model RAMSIS ® in CATIA V5 CAD environment was used for this purpose, exemplified by a laparoscopic cholecystectomy which is one of the most commonly performed abdominal surgical procedures. First step was to identify factors influencing surgeons' posture. When modeling using DHMs, only the most important influencing factors were considered in this prestudy. In principle, it has been possible to transfer the standardized method of dimensional layout conception used in vehicle design to the OR. The study will be extended in the future by an empirical data collection with motion tracking to show how often and how long the defined extreme body postures are taken. Furthermore, the question arises as to the transferability of the findings to other types of surgery.

Keywords: Dimensional layout conception · Operating Room (OR) · OR-layout · Digital Human Modeling (DHM)

1 The Surgeons' Suffering

Since the early 1990s, laparoscopic surgery has become a common surgical practice in all disciplines. The advantages of laparoscopic procedures and thus the rationale for their advance in operating rooms (henceforth called OR) are on the side of the patients: reduced trauma, faster reconvalescence, better wound healing compared to open surgery [1]. However, for laparoscopic surgeons the working conditions are suboptimal. Due to the specific surgical access to the abdomen, the space limitations at the OR table and the available work equipment, surgeons have to take postures that lead to high physical stress [2, 3]. Figure 1 exemplarily shows an actual surgical situation during a cholecystectomy,

© The Author(s), under exclusive license to Springer Nature Switzerland AG 2021
N. L. Black et al. (Eds.): IEA 2021, LNNS 222, pp. 424–428, 2021.
https://doi.org/10.1007/978-3-030-74611-7_58

in which the surgeon's range of motion in particular overlaps with that of the primary assistant (cp. red circle). The modeling was done on the basis of video analyses, the representation of the surgeons, the assistance as well as the patient was done with the digital human model RAMSIS ®. Based on the type of access and the corresponding patient positioning, the table adjustment as well as the surgical instruments and screen(s) used, the working conditions and thus the anthropometrically describable postures and movement ranges of the surgical team result. Last but not least, the design must take into account different body size groups and somatotypes for all persons involved including the patients. In the present case, the gender as well as the body height were varied; the small woman (5 PF) as well as the tall man (95PM) are shown in each case.

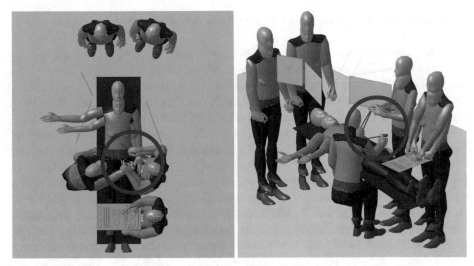

Fig. 1. Modeling of an actual situation for the analysis of anthropometric influencing factors with the digital human model RAMSIS ®

The outlined deficits are based on insufficient consideration of anthropometric and task-related requirements in the design of work equipment and workplace [4, 5]. In a survey of n = 423 surgeons, nearly half of the surgeons working in the OR (44.4%) desired ergonomic improvements in the form of steps and treads [6]. This points to the unbalanced anthropometric conditions, which from an ergonomic point of view only represent a symptom control, which in turn brings problems, such as restricting legroom and causing forced postures. Despite many innovations in the field of medical equipment technology, such as personal assistance systems, exoskeletons or robot-assisted surgery, the ergonomic problem has not yet been solved for the "operating room" system and the OR team as a whole.

The question therefore arises whether a holistic design grid can ensure that anthropometric requirements are taken into account. Based on an underlying dimensional layout conception, medical device manufacturers could design their products for the OR in a user-centered manner and in coordination with other interfaces.

For this purpose, the body and in particular the hand-arm postures of the surgeons must be mapped by means of a digital human model. Consideration should be given to the extent to which the various types of surgery can be combined and possibly standardized from an anthropometric point of view. Furthermore, reference points for the superposition of the different anthropometric user groups have to be found and defined. The standardized superposition of the surgical team results in a dimensional layout that better meets ergonomic requirements.

In the present paper, these issues are addressed with reference to the example of laparoscopic cholecystectomy, which is one of the most commonly performed abdominal surgical procedures.

2 Dimensional Layout Conception for the OR

In vehicle development, the method for the ergonomic design of the cockpit is today standardized and integrated into the design of the so-called dimensional layout [7–9]. The idea of transferring these procedures, which have proven themselves in industrial practice and research to the OR environment is therefore an obvious one. This study therefore focuses on the development of a new method for the systematic dimensioning of a surgical workstation by using adapted vehicle design methods. For this purpose, the digital human model RAMSIS ® in CAD environment CATIA V5 was used.

First, the patients' boundary percentiles were modeled in an H-point overlay on the OR table by varying the ergonometric key dimensions body height, proportion, and corpulence. In addition, the surgeons were modeled in the same way; these were superimposed on the sternum. The basic postures of patients and surgeons were maped based on the standardized standing posture model, which is implemented in the digital human model used. In addition to the basic surgical postures of the patient collective, three extreme operating postures of the surgeon identified through video analysis and interviews were pictured (extreme arm abduction, extreme arm abduction and flexion with back flexion and wrist flexion, extreme wrist ulnar adduction). The patient collective was positioned on the operating table with a small overlap (10 mm), and the surgeon collective was located at a defined distance from the table. For each body posture the individual body angles were modified by taking into account comfort angles ranges. Figure 2 shows the modeling of extreme arm abduction considering comfort angle ranges according to DGUV [10].

On this basis, geometric specifications for geometric design and engineering as well as for evaluation purposes were generated.

As a result, a method for the digital modeling of design-critical postures of the surgical staff in the OR is presented in the paper. With this method, it is possible to design the basic postures for all patient-operator constellations in a manner that the comfort angle ranges are well maintained. The body angles of the extreme postures could be considerably improved by defining the boundary conditions; these are predominantly within an acceptable range. However, for extreme arm abduction and flexion with back flexion and wrist flexion, the body angles cannot be represented acceptably with the formulated boundary conditions.

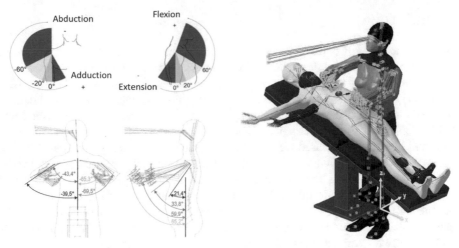

Fig. 2. Top left: comfort angle ranges of the upper arm [10]; Bottom left: Modeling of the upper arm considering the comfort angle ranges; right: H-point superimposed patients and sternum superimposed surgeons with extreme arm abduction.

In addition, the specific case under consideration (laparoscopic procedure, surgical position of OR table: prone) results in reproducible and robust geometric specifications and boundary conditions for geometric design and construction as well as for the evaluation of surgical inventory. In first order this is the OR table.

3 Conclusion

In this study, factors influencing surgeons' posture were determined in case of a laparoscopic cholecystectomy. When modeling using DHMs, only the most important influencing factors were considered. This initial modeling has already shown that from a user-centered perspective, the anthropometric requirements are not met. For example, the situation analyzed so far would indicate that a minimum operating table height of ~540 mm from the floor reference plane would be required for the short female surgeon performing a laparoscopic procedure on a patient with high corpulency.

A quick benchmark analysis of n = 40 operating table models from a total of nine manufacturers showed that only 6 models enable the setting for the short female user.

This first application of digital human modeling has shown that a transfer of the method of dimensional layout conception to the OR is possible and promising. The first study shows the possibilities of an objective description of space requirements. However, it does not yet represent an embedding in an overarching dimensional layout concept. For this, all anthropomeric influencing factors not yet considered must be included in the modeling. One challenge here will be to cluster the different types of surgical interventions with respect to frequency, anthropometric conditions and duration. For this purpose, comprehensive empirical data must be collected so that the human modeling can be based on real body postures and OR conditions such as team constellations.

4 Outlook

The study so far will be extended in the future by an empirical data collection with motion tracking to collect data from real world body postures of different interventions. On this basis extreme body postures can be defined for the digital human modeling. Also the "team perspective" has to be taken into account. For this purpose, empirical data on the postures of the endoscope-guiding assistant and the instrumentation assistant will also be collected and the interdependencies of these three main actors at the operating table will be analyzed. Based on the example of cholecystectomy considered so far, other types of surgery will be analyzed and added to the initially created concept. In case of deviations concerning the anthropometric requirements, a new layout concept will be derived. In this way, design grids will be created that will serve to ensure the most suitable and uniform layout possible. Due to the variety and variance of anthropometric variables, there will not be a one-size-fits-all dimensional concept. But the possibility can be created to work out the best compromise for all involved actors.

References

1. Uhrich, M., Underwood, R., Standeven, J., et al.: Assessment of fatigue, monitor placement, and surgical experience during simulated laparoscopic surgery. Surg. Endosc. **16**(4), 635–639 (2012). https://doi.org/10.1007/s00464-001-8151-5
2. Miller, K., Benden, M., Pickens, A., et al.: Ergonomics principles associated with laparoscopic surgeon injury/illness. Hum. Factors **54**(6), 1087–1092 (2012)
3. Steinhilber, B., Hoffmann, S., Karlovic, K., Pfeffer, S., Maier, T., Hallasheh, O., Kruck, S., Seibt, R., Rieger, M., Heidingsfeld, M., Feuer, R., Sawodny, O., Rothmund, R., Sievert, K.: Development of an arm support system to improve ergonomics in laparoscopic surgery: study design and provisional results. Surg. Endosc. (2015). ISBN https://doi.org/10.1007/s00464-0
4. Ordóñez-Ríos, M., Jara-Díaz, O., Salamea, J.C., Robles-Bykbaev, V.: Ergonomic assessment and analysis of postural load of surgeons performing laparoscopic surgeries in cuenca, ecuador. In: Duffy, V., Lightner, N., (Hrsg.) Advances in Human Factors and Ergonomics in Healthcare and Medical Devices. AHFE 2017. Advances in Intelligent Systems and Computing, vol. 590. Springer, Cham (2018). https://doi.org/10.1007/978-3-319-60483-1_44
5. Pfeffer, S., Hofmann, A., Maier, T., Rothmund, R., Sievert, K., Seibt, R., Rieger, M., Steinhilber, B.: Ergonomics of selected laparoscopic procedures – need for action? In: Biomedical Engineering/ Biomedizinische Technik, Band 58, Heft SI-1 Track J, Usability, Risk Management & Regulatory Affairs. ISSN (Online) 1862–278X (2013). ISSN (Print) 0013-5585, https://doi.org/10.1515/bmt-2013-4228
6. Matern, U., Koneczny, S., Scherrer, M., Gerlings, T.: Arbeitsbedingungen und Sicherheit am Arbeitsplatz OP, Deutsches Ärzteblatt, Jg. **103**(47), 3187–3192 (2006)
7. Bubb, H., Bengler, K., Gruenen, R., Vollrath, M.: Automobilergonomie. Springer, Wiesbaden Germany (2015)
8. Mueller, A.: Systematische und nutzerzentrierte Generierung des Pkw-Maßkonzepts als Grundlage des Interior- und Exteriordesign. IKTD Universität Stuttgart, Stuttgart, Germany (2010)
9. Raabe, R.: Ein rechnergestütztes Werkzeug zur Generierung konsistenter PKW-Maßkonzepte und parametrischer Designvorgaben. IKTD Universität Stuttgart, Stuttgart, Germany (2013)
10. DGUV Homepage, https://www.dguv.de/medien/ifa/de/fac/ergonomic/pdf/bewertung_physischer_belastungen.pdf. Accessed 08 Feb 2021

An Analysis of Usability Levels of Ventilators During Covid-19: A Case Study

Mattia Pistolesi[1]([⊠]) and Stefano Bellucci[2]

[1] Laboratory of Ergonomics and Design (LED), Department of Architecture,
University of Florence, 93 Sandro Pertini Street, 50041 Calenzano, Florence, Italy
mattia.pistolesi@unifi.it
[2] School of Engineering, Department of Information Engineering (DII), University of Pisa,
16 Girolamo Caruso Street, 56122 Pisa, Italy
stefano.bellucci@unipi.it

Abstract. The aim of this study was to investigate the usability levels of some pulmonary ventilators during emergency pandemic caused by COVID-19 for some hospitals of Tuscany Region. The study involved 30 anesthetists with varying age and experience, 5 hospitals of Tuscany Region and 3 different model of pulmonary ventilators. To quantify the usability levels of medical devices the Post-Study System Usability Questionnaire (PSSUQ) was used. The PSSQU was submitted to the operators using the Google Forms platform. This tool allowed us to asses user satisfaction for 4 different dimensions of usability: Overall PSSQU (user satisfaction), system usefulness (SYUSE), information quality (INFOQUAL) and interface quality (INTERQUAL).

Overall, the PSSQU subscale scores show a high overall usability. The results indicate a positive reliability of the pulmonary ventilators studied, although for 2 out of 30 subjects surveyed, the PSSQU subscale score is less than 50%. The PSSQU proved to be a replicable tool for the different ventilator models in use in hospitals, and effective for measuring the usability of pulmonary ventilators, including performance, usability problems and user satisfaction.

The results, although on average high, highlight the need for doctors to have: clearer and more detailed error messages, more usable and less chaotic graphic user interface (GUI), lighter and more intuitive mechanical ventilators during assembly and disassembly of components.

Keywords: Usability · PSSQU · Ergonomics in design · Ventilator · COVID-19

1 Introduction

The current global emergency SARS-CoV-2 (Covid-19) has put enormous pressure on intensive care units (ICU) in all health systems around the world, due to the rapid and exponential growth of new patients requiring intubation and mechanical ventilation.

The contribution of pulmonary ventilators in an ICU is crucial for a high level of care for a critical patient and, now more than ever, in light of the current global COVID-19 emergency.

© The Author(s), under exclusive license to Springer Nature Switzerland AG 2021
N. L. Black et al. (Eds.): IEA 2021, LNNS 222, pp. 429–436, 2021.
https://doi.org/10.1007/978-3-030-74611-7_59

This is the reason why intensive care units are rapidly populated with a wide variety of pulmonary ventilators that differ from each other in terms of type of model, graphic interface, commands, management modes and functions.

For this purpose the usability of the medical device and patient safety are essential requirements, but many errors in healthcare occur because MDs are difficult to use [1] or do not respond to the user's mental models [2].

The major scientific contributions on error in healthcare pointed out that deficiencies in the design of the human-machine interface, both physical and digital, can create the conditions for errors to occur, especially in emergency and unusual conditions [3–5]. Furthermore, incorrect procedures, stress, fatigue and a wide range of medical devices used by the operator during his/her working day can further affect the individual performance.

Scientific evidence [6, 7] shows that one of the most serious consequences of the spread of COVID-19, together with the daily discomfort that health workers are called to face (e.g. management of emergencies, stressful shifts, availability, staff shortages, situation of extreme distress) is that pandemic is putting a strain on all health professionals, whatever their task is. They are the first line defense against an emergency of enormous magnitude, which significantly affects workloads, physical fatigue and psychological health [8].

The motivations above led the researchers to conduct a usability study, using the Post-Study System Usability Questionnaire (PSSQU) method, for 3 models of pulmonary ventilator most commonly used in ICUs of some hospitals in Tuscany.

As suggested by ISO 9241-210:2010, the usability informs about how effective, efficient and satisfactory the use of a device is for the user [9], even under emergency or unusual conditions.

2 Methodology

A focus on the methodology approach is shown in this paper.

The study involved 30 anaesthetists of varying age, experience and gender, contacted through a telephone recruitment campaign and by e-mail (see Table 1).

Table 1. Characterization of subjects

Ventilator	Sex		Age range					Experience range				
	M	F	30–40	41–50	51–60	>61	n/a	<10	11–20	21–30	>31	n/a
Servo I	13	5	3	5	10	1		3	9	5	1	
Hamilton G5	11	2	2	4	4	3		4	5	3	1	
Hamilton C6	14		1	3	6	3	1	4	5	3	1	1

The hospitals at issue are: AUSL Toscana Sud Est, AUSL Toscana Nord Ovest, AUSL Toscana Centro, Azienda Ospedaliera Universitaria Careggi e Azienda Ospedaliera Universitaria Pisana.

For this study, we considered the 3 most commonly used types of pulmonary ventilator in ICUs (Servo I Maquet, Gentinge AB; Hamilton C6, Hamilton Medical AG; Hamilton G5, Hamilton Medical AG), 1 of them recently introduced (Hamilton C6).

It is necessary to specify that many ICUs are equipped with different models of pulmonary ventilators, each one with its own management, assembly and interaction, and that many of the users reported to use several medical devices simultaneously during the working day (see Table 1). This can lead to errors and operational inefficiency by even the most trained and experienced staff. Consequently, considering the total of 30 subjects who took part in the survey, 14 used *Hamilton C6*, 13 used *Hamilton G5* and 18 used *Servo I*.

Usability testing is probably one of the most common methods to assess the usability of a product [10]. Nevertheless, social restrictions, travel limitations and containment measures imposed by COVID-19, made it impossible to observe the users interaction with pulmonary ventilators directly. Not to mention the significant workload that each operator had to and still has to face every day to ensure high care levels. For all these reasons, a case study was conducted using an online questionnaire.

The PSSQU was submitted to the operators using the Google Forms platform, in anonymized form, from June 2020 until September 2020.

In order to receive reliable answers, each participant was asked to fill the PSSQU after using the pulmonary ventilator during his/her work shift.

This tool allowed to assess user satisfaction regarding 4 different dimensions of usability: Overall PSSQU (user satisfaction, the average scores of questions 1–19), SYUSE (system usefulness, the average scores of questions 1–8), INFOQUAL (information quality, the average scores of questions 9–15) and INTERQUAL (interface quality, the average scores of questions 16–18). At the end of the questionnaire each user was asked to describe what they would like to change about the ventilator(s) in their possession.

2.1 Post-study System Usability Questionnaire

To quantify the usability levels of medical devices the Post-Study System Usability Questionnaire (PSSQU) was used [11].

In scientific literature several questionnaires have been conducted for usability measurement of product/service from the user point of view, such as the Software Usability Measurement Inventory (SUMI) [12], the Website Usability Measurement Inventory (WAMMI) [13], the Computer System Usability Questionnaire (CSUQ) [11], Post-Study System Usability Questionnaire (PSSUQ) [11], and the System Usability Scale (SUS) [14].

These questionnaires help researchers and human factors experts to understand the usability of medical devices, revealing users' perceptions of outcomes and interaction [15] with it.

Retrospective usability evaluation requires less expanse and less effort from both users and researchers. Users are not required to complete any tasks but rather they are expected to integrate all their previous experiences with the device and provide their own evaluation.

This retrospective method can be conducted with any validated usability questionnaire, such as the PSSQU [16–18].

The PSSQU tool developed by Human-Computer Interaction expert of IBM, originally called System Usability Metrics (SUMS), is a questionnaire composed of 19 questions [16], where the user is asked to answer each question on a Likert scale from 1 to 7 (1 representing completely agree while 7 completely disagree, and one point not applicable (N/A) outside the scale), where the lower is the answer, the higher is the subject's satisfaction with the analysed system. It is also useful in order to measure the usability of the system, including performance, usability problems and end-user satisfaction.

3 Results

Results are reported below.

Overall, the PPSQU score global values (OVERALL) show a high general usability. The results therefore indicate a positive reliability of the pulmonary ventilators on object, even if the PPSQU score global value is less than 60% for 4 subjects out of 30 interviewed. Respectively the score is 6.32 (11.40%) for the first subject, 4.26 (45.61%) for the second subject, 3.84 (52.63) for the third one and finally for the forth one the score is equal to 3.42 (59.65%), (see Table 2).

Table 2. Users and ventilators: the PSSQU score global values.

User	Ventilator	Overall (%)	Sysuse (%)	Infoqual (%)	Interqual (%)
1	Hamilton C6	1,21 (96,49%)	1,13 (97,92%)	1,29 (95,24%)	1,33 (94,44%)
2	Hamilton C6	1,16 (97,37%)	1,13 (97,92%)	1,29 (95,24%)	1,00 (100%)
	Hamilton G5	2,11 (81,58%)	2,00 (83,33%)	2,29 (78,57%)	2,00 (94,44%)
3	Servo I	1,58 (90,35%)	1,00 (100%)	2,29 (78,57%)	1,67 (88,89%)
4	Servo I	6,32 (11,40%)	6,13(14,58%)	6,29 (11,90%)	6,67 (5,56%)
5	Hamilton G5	1,16 (97,37%)	1,00 (100%)	1,29 (95,24%)	1,33 (94,44%)
	Servo I	2,16 (80,70%)	1,88 (85,42%)	2,43 (76,19%)	2,33 (77,78%)
6	Hamilton G5	2,00 (83,33%)	2,00 (83,33%)	2,00 (83,33%)	2,00 (83,33%)
	Servo I	3,84 (52,63%)	2,63 (72,92%)	4,43 (42,86%)	5,33 (27,78%)
7	Hamilton G5	1,42 (92,98%)	1,63 (89,58%)	1,29 (95,24%)	1,33 (94,44%)
8	Servo I	1,00 (100%)	1,00 (100%)	1,00 (100%)	1,00 (100%)
9	Servo I	1,00 (100%)	1,00 (100%)	1,00 (100%)	1,00 (100%)
10	Servo I	1,68 (88,60%)	1,25 (95,83%)	2,00 (83,33%)	2,33 (77,78%)
	Hamilton G5	2,37 (77,19%)	2,38 (77,08%)	2,43 (76,19%)	2,33 (77,78%)
11	Hamilton G5	2,84 (69,30%)	2,75 (70,83%)	3,00 (66,67%)	3,00 (66,67%)
	Servo I	2,84 (69,30%)	2,75 (70,83%)	3,00 (66,67%)	3,00 (66,67%)

(*continued*)

Table 2. (*continued*)

User	Ventilator	Overall (%)	Sysuse (%)	Infoqual (%)	Interqual (%)
12	Servo I	2,21 (79,82%)	2,25 (79,17%)	2,00 (83,33%)	2,67 (72,22%)
13	Hamilton G5	1,79 (86,84%)	1,75 (87,50%)	2,00 (83,33%)	1,33 (94,44%)
	Servo I	2,21 (79,82%)	2,25 (79,17%)	2,14 (80,95%)	2,33 (77,78%)
14	Hamilton C6	1,63 (89,58%)	1,50 (91,67%)	1,86 (85,71%)	1,67 (88,89%)
	Hamilton G5	1,63 (89,58%)	1,50 (91,67%)	1,86 (85,71%)	1,67 (88,89%)
	Servo I	2,42 (76,32%)	2,50 (75,00%)	2,57 (73,81%)	2,00 (83,33%)
15	Servo I	2,74 (71,05%)	2,86 (69,05%)	2,57 (73,81%)	3,67 (55,56%)
	Hamilton G5	4,26 (45,61%)	4,50 (41,67%)	4,29 (45,29%)	3,67 (55,56%)
16	Hamilton C6	1,84 (85,96%)	2,00 (83,33%)	1,86 (85,71%)	1,67 (88,89%)
	Servo I	1,88 (85,09%)	1,75 (87,50%)	2,00 (83,33%)	2,00 (83,33%)
17	Hamilton C6	1,37 (93,86%)	1,13 (97,92%)	1,43 (92,86%)	1,67 (88,89%)
18	Hamilton G5	1,84 (85,96%)	2,00 (83,33%)	1,86 (85,71%)	1,67 (88,89%)
	Hamilton C6	1,26 (95,61%)	1,25 (95,83%)	1,43 (92,86%)	1,00 (100%)
19	Servo I	2,32 (78,07%)	2,00 (83,33%)	2,71 (71,43%)	2,33 (77,78%)
20	Servo I	2,42 (76,36%)	2,25 (79,17%)	2,43 (76,19%)	2,67 (72,22%)
	Hamilton C6	1,68 (88,60%)	2,13 (81,25%)	1,57 (90,84%)	1,00 (100%)
21	Hamilton C6	1,00 (100%)	1,00 (100%)	1,00 (100%)	1,00 (100%)
	Hamilton G5	1,37 (93,86%)	1,75 (87,50%)	1,14 (97,62%)	1,00 (100%)
	Servo I	2,84 (69,30%)	2,63 (72,92%)	3,00 (66,67%)	3,00 (66,67%)
22	Hamilton C6	2,05 (82,46%)	2,13 (81,25%)	2,00 (83,33%)	2,00 (83,33%)
23	Servo I	3,00 (66,67%)	3,75 (54,17%)	2,43 (76,19%)	2,33 (77,78%)
24	Hamilton C6	2,05 (82,46%)	2,13 (81,25%)	2,00 (83,33%)	2,00 (83,33%)
25	Hamilton G5	1,42 (92,98%)	1,13 (97,92%)	1,86 (85,71%)	1,33 (94,44%)
	Hamilton C6	1,00 (100%)	1,00 (100%)	1,00 (100%)	1,00 (100%)
26	Hamilton C6	1,00 (100%)	1,00 (100%)	1,00 (100%)	1,00 (100%)
27	Hamilton C6	2,00 (83,33%)	2,00 (83,33%)	2,00 (83,33%)	2,00 (83,33%)
28	Hamilton G5	1,00 (100%)	1,00 (100%)	1,00 (100%)	1,00 (100%)
29	Servo I	3,42 (59,65%)	2,88 (68,75%)	4,43 (42,86%)	3,00 (66,67%)
30	Hamilton C6	2,53 (74,56%)	2,63 (72,92%)	2,57 (73,81%)	2,33 (77,78%)

As it can be observed in Table 3, the interface quality (Infoqual) of the three lung ventilators analysed had the worst results, considering the independent subscales. In fact, at the end of the PSSQU, the participants were asked the following question "What would you like to change of the pulmonary ventilator if you could?". 12 out of 30 answered to this question and they all declared that the most critical issues are related to the digital human-machine interface.

Table 3. Ventilators: the PSSQU score global values.

Ventilator	Overall (%)	Sysuse (%)	Infoqual (%)	Interqual (%)
Servo I	2,52 (74,71%)	2,37 (77,14%)	2,60(73,36%)	2,74 (70,99%)
Hamilton G5	1,95 (84,15%)	1,95 (84,15%)	2,05 (82,45%)	1,82 (86,32%)
Hamilton C6	1,57 (90,43%)	1,58 (90,33%)	1,64 (89,33%)	1,48 (92,06%)

Users suggest that a clearer, more efficient, less cluttered interface would allow easier interaction with the device. They also complained about the lack of detailed error messages. Moreover, weight and dimensions of these products, and some of their auxiliary functions led to difficulties in using the equipment.

4   Conclusion

In this study we evaluated how the PSSQU could be a replicable tool for different ventilator models currently in use in some Tuscan hospitals, also effective for measuring the usability of pulmonary ventilators (performance, usability problems, user satisfaction).

Feedbacks from physicians, although positive on average, highlight the need for clearer and more detailed error messages, more usable and less cluttered graphic interfaces, lighter and more intuitive mechanical ventilators during assembly and disassembly of components.

Our study aimed to test the PSSQU as a tool for evaluating the usability of medical devices in the anesthetic and resuscitation fields for possible ergonomic interventions.

In conclusion, usability studies such as the methodology reported in this article are necessary to evaluate the design deficiencies of the device. This will reduce user errors and potential damage, saving time, money and resources in the long term. The reliability of the PSSQU tool, collected from the various studies [16–18] and from the present case study, suggests that the adoption of such a tool in risk management processes can highlight any usability problem and constitute an important part of the production process of future medical devices. Prevention is in fact obtained intervening in the project before the harmful event occurs, using appropriate forecasting methodologies [19–21].

Acknowledgment. The authors would like to thank, for their important contribution, the anaesthetists of AUSL Toscana Sud Est, AUSL Toscana Nord Ovest, AUSL Toscana Centro, Azienda Ospedaliera Universitaria Careggi e Azienda Ospedaliera Universitaria Pisana.

References

1. Ward, J., Clarkson, P.J.: An analysis of medical device-related errors: prevalence and possible solutions. J. Med. Eng. Technol. **28**(1), 2–21 (2004). https://doi.org/10.1080/030919003100 0123747

2. Norman, D.A.: The Design of Everyday Things Revised and Expanded Edition. MIT Press, Cambridge, MA (2014)
3. Drews, F.A.: Human error in health care. In: Carayon, P. (ed.) Handbook of Human Factors and Ergonomics in Healthcare and Patient Safety, 2nd edn., pp. 323–340. CRC Press, Taylor and Francis group, Boca Raton, FL (2012)
4. Weinger, M.B., Wiklund, M., Gardner-Bonneau, D.: Human Factors in Medical Device Design: A Handbook for Designer. CRC Press, Taylor and Francis group, Boca Raton, FL (2011)
5. Weinger, M.B.: Human factors in Anesthesiology. In: Carayon, P. (ed.) Handbook of human factors and ergonomics in health care and patient safety, 2nd edn., pp. 803–823. CRC Press, Taylor and Francis group, Boca Raton, FL (2012)
6. Lancet, T.: COVID-19: Protecting health-care workers. Lancet **395**(10228), 922 (2020). https://doi.org/10.1016/S0140-6736-20-30644-9
7. Vagni, M., Maiorano, T., Giostra, V., Pajardi, D.: Hardiness, stress and secondary trauma in italian healthcare and emergency workers during the COVID-19 pandemic. Sustainability **12**(14), 5592 (2020). https://doi.org/10.3390/su12145592
8. Zaka, A., Shamloo, S.E., Fiorente, P., Tafuri, A.: COVID-19 pandemic as a watershed moment: a call for systematic psychological health care for frontline medical staff. J. Health Psychol. **25**(7), 883–887 (2020). https://doi.org/10.1177/1359105320925148
9. ISO 9241-210:2010: Ergonomics of human-system interaction-part.210: human centered design for interactive systems, International Organization for Standardization (ISO), Geneva (2010)
10. Rubin, J., Chisnell, D.: Handbook of Usability Testing: How to Plan, Design and Conduct Effective Tests. John Wiley & Sons Inc., Hoboken, NJ (2008)
11. Lewis, J.R.: IBM computer usability satisfaction questionnaires: psychometric evaluation and instructions for use. Int. J. Hum.-Comput. Interact. **7**(1), 57–78 (1995). https://doi.org/10.1080/10447319509526110
12. Kirakowski, J., Corbett, M.: SUMI: the software usability measurement inventory. Br. J. Educ. Technol. **24**(3), 210–212 (1993). https://doi.org/10.1111/j.1467-8535.1993.tb00076.x
13. Kirakowski, J., Cierlik, B.: Measuring the usability of web sites. Proc. Hum. Factors Ergon. Soc. Ann. Meet. **42**(4), 424–428 (1998). https://doi.org/10.1177/154193129804200405
14. Brooke, J.: SUS: a quick and dirty usability scale. Usability Eval. Ind. **189**(194), 4–7 (1996). https://doi.org/10.1201/9781498710411-35
15. Hornbæk, K.: Current practice in measuring usability: challenges to usability studies and research. Int. J. Hum.-Comput. Stud. **64**(2), 79–102 (2006). https://doi.org/10.1016/j.ijhcs.2005.06.002
16. Lewis, J.R.: Psychometric evaluation of the PSSQU using data from five years of usability studies. Int. J. Hum.-Comput. Interact. **14**(3&4), 463–488 (2002). https://doi.org/10.1080/10447318.2002.9669130
17. Fruhling, A., Lee, S.: Assessing the reliability, validity and adaptability of PSSQU. In Proceedings of the Eleventh Americas Conference on Information Systems, Omaha, NE, USA, 11th-14th August 2005 pp. 2394–2402 (2005)
18. Gao, M., Kortum, P.: Measuring the usability of home healthcare devices using retrospective measures. In Proceedings of the Human Factors and Ergonomics Society 2017 Annual Meeting, pp. 1281–1285 (2017). https://doi.org/10.1177/1541931213601801
19. Pistolesi, M.: Design Usabilità in ambito sanitario. Il progetto dei dispositivi medici, FrancoAngeli, Milan (2020)

20. Pistolesi, M., Tosi, F.: Design for healthcare. the role of Ergonomics for Design and Human-Centred design approach. In: Sustainable Architecture for Healthcare Facilities, Special issue n. 2/2019, pp. 61–71, Luciano Editore, Naples (2019)
21. Lin, L., Isla, R., Doniz, K., Harkness, H., Vicente, K.J., Doyle, D.J.: Applying human factors to the design of medical equipment: patient-controlled analgesia. J. Clin. Monitor. Comput. **14**, 253–263 (1998)

Evaluation of Physiological Workload of Patient Transport Workers from Their Perceptions and Postural Constraints

Italo Rodeghiero Neto⬩, Eduardo Rocha Garcia⬩, and Fernando Gonçalves Amaral(✉) ⬩

Federal University of Rio Grande do Sul, Porto Alegre, Rio Grande do Sul, Brazil
amaral@producao.ufrgs.br

Abstract. The Physiological Workload (PWL) is a concept that aims to analyze the amount of effort performed by a worker to carry out his activities. In hospitals, certain occupations perform exhausting activities, such as transporting patients and changing positions. Even though several research types are related to the concept, it is impossible to find a standard for this estimate and analysis in the literature. Thus, this research aims to evaluate workers' physiological workload responsible for transporting patients - called stretcher-bearers - based on two different variables: the perception of the worker's effort and the postures used to perform the activities. The analyzed stretcher-bearers work in a public hospital in southern Brazil, in the emergency sector. The applied methodologies contemplated variables related to work and the worker: The Corlett and Bishop Diagram, the Borg scale index, and the Ovako Working Posture Analyzing System (OWAS). Stretcher-bearers' verbalizations were analyzed with the collected data. Thus, it was possible to propose improvements such as the standardization of equipment used, the choice of an optimal path, and workers' need to carry out certain activities together. In the end, it can be concluded that the variables allow an excellent analysis of the physiological workload faced by these hospital workers.

Keywords: Physiological workload · Hospital · Stretcher-bearer · Postural constraints · Worker perception

1 Introduction

Physiological Workload (PWL) is a definition that aims to measure the amount of physical effort expended by a worker to perform a series of activities during their workday [1]. Therefore, PWL concepts need to be studied in hospital activities with excessive dynamic tasks requiring a large amount of energy.

The work dynamics characterize the environment as a complex system, with inaccuracies and uncertainties activities. This complex system can lead to the worker's physical and psychosocial risks (e.g., WMSD, stress, burnout). Therefore, it is necessary to manage the complexity, even if it is inevitable for this system, to reduce the possible problems [2].

N. L. Black et al. (Eds.): IEA 2021, LNNS 222, pp. 437–442, 2021.
https://doi.org/10.1007/978-3-030-74611-7_60

Hospitals have a large number of activities. Several research types are carried out to guarantee improvements to doctors, nurses, and professionals related to cleaning and food [3]. When considering the stretcher-bearer, who are professionals responsible for transporting the patient, it is possible to observe a low number of studies. There are no mechanisms for the evaluation of PWL as assumptions to improve their tasks [4]. These activities can generate significant problems and injuries related to work due to the combination of excess strength, high repetition, and postural constraints [5, 6].

When PWL is analyzed, several considerations can be made in the professional's task, such as changing layout, adapting equipment, investigating the work schedule, and the number of professionals to the activity [7, 8]. It could benefit the worker's health and improve the service provided and reduce management rates as absenteeism and turnover. However, there is no single way to estimate this type of load, but several parameters and methodologies to perform an analysis [3, 9]. Combining different methods for this estimation and analysis generates a different perception about the physiological workload [10]. Still, attention to the perception of the worker's effort and an analysis of the postures performed during the performance of their tasks can bring a reasonable estimate of the PWL. It can generate different importing points for discussion.

This research starts with the question: "is it possible to estimate the physiological workload of stretcher-bearers from their perceptions of effort and postural constraints?". Thus, this research aims to analyze workers' physiological workload transporting patients from a hospital. The analysis takes into account their perception and postural constraints.

2   Methodology

This research is a case study that aims to answer qualitatively whether it is possible to analyze the physiological workload differently. The object of this study is a public hospital located in southern Brazil. As reported by managers, stretcher-bearers perform exhausting activities with an expected high workload. It is a public hospital, which cares for about 6800 urgent patients per month. In this hospital, two stretcher-bearers were analyzed, with the same sex and similar biometric characteristics, such as age, height, and weight. The workers carry out their activities opposite shifts and have no other occupations besides their activities as stretcher-bearers.

The study contemplates three main parts. At first, the workers' biometric characteristics were collected, as well as their social habits. The Corlett and Bishop Diagram were applied to investigate the subjective perception of discomfort and pain caused by work [11]. In a second moment, researchers filmed the performance of stretcher-bearer activities. During this stage, the professionals were questioned to measure the subjective effort from the worker's perception during the execution, using the Borg Scale [12]. After accomplishing the work, Corlett and Bishop Diagram were again applied to compare the beginning and end of their work activity. Finally, in a third moment, the footage was used to apply the Ovako Working Posture Analyzing System (OWAS), a methodology to analyze the postures made during the performance of transport activities [13]. The results were compared to investigate the workers' PWL.

The methods are different and address two different perceptions of the effort made for the job. Borg scale and the Corlett and Bishop Diagram bring a perception of the worker, who is doing the job at that moment. On the other hand, OWAS allows the researcher to evaluate and analyze postural constraints based on observing the activity performed. Thus, different physiological workload perceptions are contemplated, enriching the discussion.

3 Results

The collections were carried out in their respective shifts - morning and afternoon - and lasted an average of two hours with each stretcher-bearer. The sequence of steps was applied and the data obtained are reported below.

The results of the Diagram of Corlett and Bishop were the first found. After collecting the data, it was possible to develop body maps for each of the stretcher-bearers, as shown in Fig. 1. It is possible to identify that the first stretcher-bearer develops discomfort in the shoulders and thighs after performing the activities. This worker has previous pains in the neck and feet, which need investigation. As for the second stretcher-bearer, it was not observed the first discomforts after work.

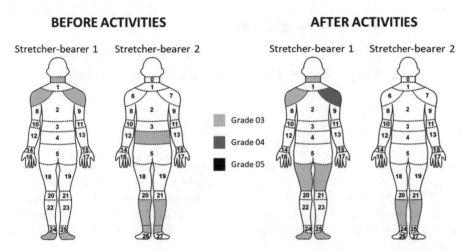

Fig. 1. Body map of the Corlett and Bishop Diagram before and after the activities.

For the Borg scale index, the variation found was large. The workers reported rates ranging from 0 (no effort) to 7 (a lot of effort). As verified by the stretcher-bearers, these efforts occur according to the characteristics of the activity performed, such as the patient's weight, situation and reason for the patient's hospitalization, a path they take, and the material used for transportation. Bedridden patients require more significant effort in transport, as well as those who are overweight. With high elevation ramps and curves, narrow corridors make the activity more exhausting and, consequently, with the demand for more incredible energy to perform it. Finally, transporting patients on stretchers requires more effort than transporting them on wheelchairs, even with another stretcher-bearer.

For the application of the OWAS, four main tasks grouped the activities: commuting without a wheelchair, commuting with the patient, changing decubitus, and commuting with an empty wheelchair. Figure 2 shows the graph prepared for each of the activities performed by the makeup artists. It can be seen, for example, that during transport, the worker's posture is even classified in action category 3 - referring to necessary changes in the workplace. However, in most of its activities, the positions performed reach levels 1 and 2 in the action category.

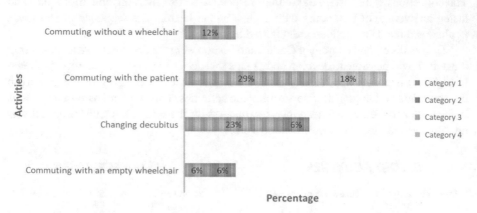

Fig. 2. Example of an OWAS chart, with the score for each activity analyzed.

4   Discussion

When confronting each of the methodologies' results, we can see that it is possible to analyze the stretcher-bearer's physiological workloads from these different factors. After the analysis, it is clear that the patients' transportation tasks can bring problems to health. The Corlett and Bishop Diagram show that the workers' discomfort intensified during the work, mainly related to the effort spent to accomplish the activities - collected from the Borg scale.

The effort to climb ramps, pushing wheelchairs or stretchers, combined with unfavorable postures, is another factor to increase pain in the regions observed. This is an observed point for the appearance of postural constraints, mainly related to the lack of maintenance and adaptation of the professionals' work equipment, corroborated by the OWAS method.

During data collection, the stretcher-bearers were asked about their working conditions. The discussion included the results found to propose adaptations in their activities. For the stretcher-bearers, the lack of standardization of the materials used - wheelchairs and stretchers - make them perform different postures during the activities. These materials, which have other models and dimensions, are different when transporting. Still, reports on environmental conditions corroborate that the excess of ramps and curves must be avoided. A standard path for patients' transport between different hospital wards can be realized, avoiding unnecessary displacement.

5   Conclusion

The analysis shows that it is possible to analyze the PWL from the variables of perception of the worker's effort and postural constraints. When answering the research question, we can state that the variables presented to analyze the physiological workload can investigate whether the materials used are satisfactory and which muscle groups are most required during activities. At the same time, we could explore the energy spent to do the same.

The PWL results could recommend managers and specialists to make decisions about adapting working conditions and investigating absenteeism and turnover rates. The steps developed by this tool serve as a guide to explore possible excess workload faced by workers, especially in the hospital environment.

The study found some limitations during its application. The data collected are from the emergency department of a hospital, where the stretcher-bearer work. The embarrassment of filming was observed, mainly due to the patients' illness conditions, redoubling the risks due to privacy and indiscretion. Another limitation was the low number of stretcher-bearers analyzed. It is not the strong point of the study, but an example of the tool developed and the analysis methodologies.

As suggestions for future works, the addition of other variables, such as heart rate, distance covered, and an analysis of the work, can corroborate for a more robust and complete discussion about the PWL of these professionals.

References

1. Liu, H., Fan, J., Fu, Y., Liu, F.: Intrinsic motivation as a mediator of the relationship between organizational support and quantitative workload and work-related fatigue. Hum. Factors Ergon Manufact. Serv. Ind. **28**(3), 154–162 (2018)
2. Braithwaite, J., Churruca, K., Ellis, L.A., Long, J., Clay-Williams, R., Damen, N., Ludlow, K.: Complexity science in healthcare. Sydney: Australian Institute of Health Innovation, Macquarie University (2017)
3. Khanade, K., Sasangohar, F.: Stress, fatigue, and workload in intensive care nursing: a scoping literature review. In: Proceeding of the Human Factors and Ergonomics Society, vol. 61, no. 1, pp. 686–690 (2017)
4. Rusnock, C.F., Borghetti, B.J.: Workload profiles: a continuous measure of mental workload. Int. J. Ind. Ergon. **63**, 49–64 (2018)
5. Roman-Liu, D.: External load and the reaction of the musculoskeletal system – a conceptual model of the interaction. Int. J. Ind. Ergon. **43**, 356–362 (2013)
6. Ma, L., Chablat, D., Bennis, F., Zhang, W.: A new simple dynamic muscle fatigue model and its validation. Int. J. Ind. Ergon. **39**, 211–220 (2009)
7. Baptiste, A.: An evaluation of nursing tasks. Work **40**, 115–124 (2011)
8. Cooper, G., Gassemieh, E.: Risk assessment of patient handling with ambulance stretcher systems (ramp/(winch), easi-loader, tail-lift) using biomechanical failure criteria. Med. Eng. Phys. **29**, 775–787 (2007)
9. Kwiecien, K., Wujtewicz, M., Medrzycka-Dabrowska, W.: Selected methods of measuring workload among intensive care nursing staff. Int. J. Occup. Med. Environ. Health **25**(3), 209–217 (2012)
10. Neto, I.R., Amaral, F.G.: Identification and estimation of physiological workload in nursing: concepts, methods and gaps in the literature. Int. J. Ind. Ergon. 80, 103016 (2020)

11. Corlett, E.N., Bishop, R.P.: A technique for assessing postural discomfort. Ergonomics **19**(2), 175–182 (1976)
12. Borg, G., Borg, E.: A new generation of scaling methods: level-anchored ratio scaling. Psychologica **28**, 15–45 (2001)
13. Kahru, O., Kansi, P., Kuorinka, I.: Correcting working postures in industry: a practical method for analysis. Appl. Ergon. **4**, 199–201 (1978)

Mid-Air Interaction by Way of a Virtual Slider in a Medical Use Case

Peter Schmid$^{(\boxtimes)}$, Ferdinand Langer, and Thomas Maier

Department of Industrial Design Engineering, University of Stuttgart, Institute for Engineering Design and Industrial Design, Pfaffenwaldring 9, 70569 Stuttgart, Germany
peter.schmid@iktd.uni-stuttgart.de

Abstract. Hygiene standards in hospitals, especially in operating rooms, are a recurring topic in medical research. Contactless technologies could provide a remedy here. However, these technologies currently receive less attention in medicine because a central criterion of human-machine interaction, the feedback to the user, is usually neglected. The systems currently provide only audiovisual feedback, which increasingly strains the highly stressed auditory perception channel. Tactile feedback in the room via ultrasonic waves could provide a remedy here. For this purpose, a virtual slider was implemented in the air with a discrete tactile feedback based on ultrasound in this study. In a test person study, 24 different feedback characteristics were tested. Initial parameters regarding the feedback intensity and the locking point distance of the tactile feedback characteristics were investigated and the results concerning the tactile coding of a slider with regard to a tactile indicator were discussed.

Keywords: Tactile feedback · Ultrasound based feedback · Virtual slider · Human-machine interaction · Human-machine interface · Tactile information coding

1 Introduction

High standards of hygiene in the operating room demand surfaces, which can be disinfected quickly. The current development of human-machine interfaces of medical devices relies mostly on touch displays. They allow direct manipulation on the user interface. Through direct contact during input the user interface contaminates. Hence research focuses on alternative forms of interaction which can be operated via voice or gesture control. These contactless technologies provide a high advantage in terms of hygiene and contamination of user interfaces in the operating room [1].

However, the feedback for the surgeon is not optimally implemented with these contactless technologies. In the design of non-contact human-machine interfaces, feedback plays a particularly important role in operation. Motion feedback in the form of active, tactile feedback is unavoidable in practice [2].

Information from medical products are almost exclusively audio visually transmitted. Hence an overload of the human perception and information processing capacity can

© The Author(s), under exclusive license to Springer Nature Switzerland AG 2021
N. L. Black et al. (Eds.): IEA 2021, LNNS 222, pp. 443–450, 2021.
https://doi.org/10.1007/978-3-030-74611-7_61

be observed. Current studies show that the operating room is subject to high noise levels, which impairs or even makes concentrated work almost impossible [3]. Haptically, however, information is barely transmitted. According to DIN EN ISO 9241-112 the principles for the presentation of information feedback plays an essential role in the design of touchless human-machine interfaces [4]. Hence, this project will evaluate the tactile perception channel of humans with regard to its supporting capacity in terms of tactile feedback design. This idea is addressed by the research of Biermann & Weißmantel [5]. Also Schmid et al. and Winterholler demonstrate the possibility to transfer haptic information by coding of physical rotary control elements [6, 7].

Another investigation of Schmid et al. deals with different tactile coding patterns on a touch user interface which can be used for information coding by intensity modulation of a electro-tactile feedback during a sliding input gesture. Therefore a virtual slider with a discrete feedback is implemented on a touchscreen. During the adjustment process, the user feels individual feedback impulses with his finger, similar to a slider with tick marks [8].

Schmid et al. or Winterholler show in situations with high audio-visual information content, tactile information can be used to support people in the performance of a primary and secondary task.

Within the scope of this study, the information coding of a fine adjustment task in the air is investigated. The investigation addresses thresholds of physical perception of ultrasonic tactile feedback in the air. The focus is on relieving the surgeon's audiovisual perception channel by addressing the tactile perception channel through a virtual slider in the air in order to reduce the noise level in the operating room and to improve the usability of ultrasonic tactile feedback.

2 Methodology

To investigate the tactile feedback in the air, a scenario for the regulation of luminous intensity in the minimal-invasive operating field was set up and a test person study carried out. Thirty-four people (median age 25 years; range 22–66 years; 53% female, 47% male) participated in the study. The participants were 88% right-handed and 12% left-handed. Six participants had experience with minimal-invasive surgery and two had experience in interacting with ultrasonic feedback.

In the test person study, the participants had to perform two parallel tasks and therefore the experimental setup consists of two components. Similar to a surgery as a main task, the test person had to hold a surgical instrument in the form of a wire eyelet as still as possible in the minimal-invasive laparoscopic operating field with their dominant hand. Any contact with the edge of the eyelet was recorded and was judged as an error. The experimental setup was adjusted to the dominant hand of the participant. At the same time, as a secondary task, the test person had to perform various adjustment tasks to artificially regulate the luminosity of the operation field with a virtual slider in the air. The experimental setup for a right-handed participant, consisting of the main task and the secondary task, is shown in Fig. 1.

To identify initial parameters, a slider was implemented using Visual Studio software in form of a tactile indicator. The slider was provided with locking points in the form of

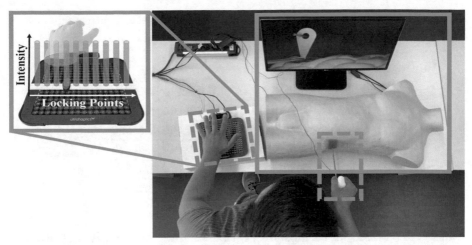

Fig. 1. Experimental setup with a right-handed test person; Ultrahaptics (dotted orange box left) with abstracted illustration of the virtual slider through locking points respectively notches between the tactile feedbacks depicted as pillars, screen with live image from inside the abdomen with laparoscopy phantom (drawn blue box right), surgical instrument (dotted blue box right)

tactile feedback through ultrasound. The tactile feedback characteristics were projected to the proximal middle finger of the palm of the non-dominant hand. If the test person drives along this slider, a feedback impulse at regular intervals, the so-called locking points are felt. The points on the scale were designed as discrete feedback, whereby the intensity and the distance between the points can be changed. A number of locking points with a given feedback intensity were equally distributed on a 30 cm long line in the middle of the ultrasound generating pad (Ultrahaptics STRATOS Explore). The distance of the locking points on the line is defined through the number of notches between the locking points. An abstracted illustration of the virtual slider with ten tactile feedbacks is shown in Fig. 1.

To evaluate the tactile feedback, different locking point distances as well as different feedback intensity levels were tested. In total, there were 4 different locking point distances in combination with 6 intensity levels. The minimum intensity of 30% as well as the number of locking points were defined on preliminary tests. The grading of the number of locking points and intensity levels is based on DIN 323 [9]. The evaluated combination of them is shown in Table 1.

In a short training session, study participants were able to learn how the notches of the ultrasonic feedback feel like and got to know the extreme points of feedback and intensity combination I30LP10, I95LP10, I30LP20 and I95LP20. I30LP10 means an intensity level of 30% (I30) in combination with 10 locking points (LP10).

To objectively evaluate the tactile feedback, the participants had to count a predefined randomized number of notches between the locking points starting from the left beginning of the line of locking points. After counting the requested number of notches the participants stated, that they reached the goal. The position was recorded and thus the difference between the requested number of notches and the counted number of notches

Table 1. Combinations of feedback intensity and number of locking points

Intensity	Locking points			
	10	13	16	20
30%	I30LP10	I30LP13	I30LP16	I30LP20
38%	I38LP10	I38LP13	I38LP16	I38LP20
48%	I48LP10	I48LP13	I48LP16	I48LP20
60%	I60LP10	I60LP13	I60LP16	I60LP20
75%	I75LP10	I75LP13	I75LP16	I75LP20
95%	I95LP10	I95LP13	I95LP16	I95LP20

results in the accuracy of the input by the participant. In addition, a subjective evaluation of the characteristics and precision of the feedback was carried out using a 5-step
Likert scale. In parallel, the error rate in the main task was recorded to draw conclusions
about the participant's distraction during the counting of the notches. This procedure
was repeated in a random order for all combinations of feedback intensity and number
of notches, as stated in Table 1.

3   Results

The results of the study are presented below in Fig. 2. First, the comparative presentation
of the results of the measured values, recorded during operation with tactile feedback
in the air, are presented. The results include the objectively measured parameters such
as the number of errors concerning the main task and the adjustment accuracy of the
second task. The comfort of the feedback as well as the performance measured by the
feedback intensity and the precision of the feedback was recorded by a 5-step Likert-
Scale. Figure 2a shows the number of errors with respect to the main task. The number of
errors increases on average with decreasing locking point distance. The lowest number of
errors is achieved with feedback characteristic I95LP10. The highest number of errors
results from feedback characteristic I60LP20. Looking at the adjustment accuracy in
Fig. 2b, the task is better fulfilled with a larger locking point distance. The adjustment
accuracy also increases with increasing feedback intensity. The smallest deviation is
achieved with the feedback characteristics I95LP16, I60LP20 and I75LP20, followed
by the feedback characteristics I60LP10 and I75LP10. The largest deviation, however,
is achieved with feedback characteristics I30LP20.

The evaluation of the precision of the feedback is shown in Fig. 2c. With an increase
in feedback intensity, the precision is rated better. The feedback characteristics I95LP10
and I95LP13 perform best. The precision rating decreases with decreasing locking point
distance and the feedback characteristics with an intensity of 30% are described as
imprecise regardless of the locking point distance (cf. I30LP10, I30LP13, I30LP16 and
I30LP20).

The evaluation of the feedback's comfort can be seen in Fig. 2d represented through
the feedback intensity. Concerning the median values, the feedback is better rated by

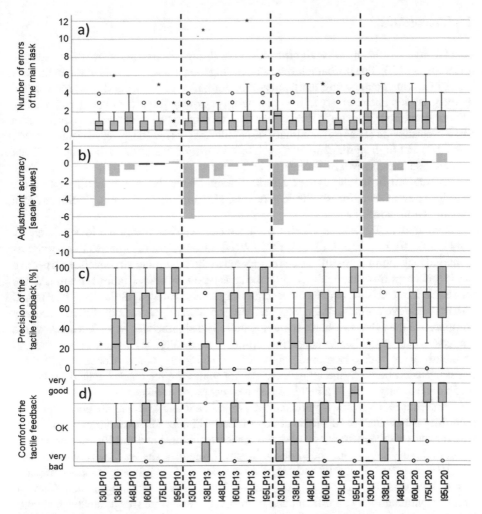

Fig. 2. Results of the test person study concerning the different feedback combination possibilities of the intensity levels and locking points

the test persons with increasing feedback intensity. Feedback I95LP10, I95LP13 and I95LP20 are rated best. The test persons describe these feedback characteristics as very perceptible. Feedback characteristics I60LP10, I75LP10, I60LP13, I75LP13, I60LP16, I75LP16 and I75LP20 are also rated as well perceptible. The feedback characteristics I30LP10, I30LP13, I30LP16 and I30LP20 are rated as not detectable by all test persons. To sum up, the evaluation of the feedback decreases with decreasing locking point distance.

4 Discussion

To identify significant, very significant and high significant differences between the different tactile feedback characteristics regarding the number of errors of the main task, the adjustment accuracy and the feedback performance of the second task, represented by the precision and intensity of the feedback, a Friedman test is conducted, followed by a Dunn Bonferroni's post-hoc test. The evaluation is analyzed with the statistics program SPSS Statistics 22 (IBM). A summary of significant (*: $p < 0.05$) very significant (**: $p < 0.01$) and high significant (***: $p < 0,001$) differences of the individual feedback characteristics are shown in Table 2.

With regard to the number of errors, differences can be determined based on the descriptive representation of the test results, although these are not significant in a statistical evaluation.

If we look at Table 2, especially feedback characteristics with the lowest intensity level (I30LP10, I30LP13, I30LP16, I30LP20) show a hotspot of significant, very significant and high significant differences compared to the other intensity levels, irrespective of the locking point distance. Regarding the adjustment accuracy (Table 2 column A), the feedback characteristics with the lowest intensity levels I30LP10, I30LP13, I30LP16 and I30LP20 achieve a significantly, very and high significantly worse adjustment accuracy compared to the other feedback characteristics. The significance level increases with a decreasing locking point distance. In addition, more differences that are significant can be identified for a scale graduation of 10, 13 and 16 locking points. Consequently, there is a correlation between the adjustment accuracy and the feedback intensity. A higher feedback intensity leads to a better adjustment accuracy in this case.

Furthermore, there are significant, very significant and high significant differences regarding the evaluation of the precision of the feedback. The evaluation of the precision depends on the intensity level of the feedback (Table 2 column P). Concerning the significant, very significant and high significant differences, the feedback characteristics I30LP10, I30LP13, I30LP16 and I30LP20 are assessed significantly worse compared to the other test characteristics. At a scale graduation of 13 locking points, there are further significant, very significant and high significant differences at feedback characteristics with 30% and 38% feedback intensity. The precision at these intensity levels is more unpalatable compared to the feedback characteristics with a higher intensity. Consequently, both the intensity and the locking point distance are crucial for the precise adjustment of a defined scale value in the air.

Significant, very significant and high significant differences could also be identified in the evaluation of the intensity of the feedback (Table 2 column I). Accordingly, a lower intensity of the feedback characteristics I30LP10, I30LP13, I30LP16 and I30LP20 results in a lower evaluation of the expression (Fig. 2). Thus, a scale graduation of 20 locking points in combination with an intensity level of 38% leads to a very and high significant worse assessment. Consequently, not only the feedback intensity but also the locking point distance plays a role in the feedback's comfort.

Table 2. Statistical relevant differences between the test characteristics concerning the adjustment accuracy (A), the precision (P) and the performance of the feedback, represented by the feedback intensity (I)

	I30LP10			I38LP10			I48LP10			I60LP10			I75LP10			I95LP10			I30LP13			I38LP13			I48LP13			I60LP13			I75LP13			I90LP13		
	A	P	I	A	P	I	A	P	I	A	P	I	A	P	I	A	P	I	A	P	I	A	P	I	A	P	I	A	P	I	A	P	I	A	P	I
I30LP10									***	*		*** ***	*		*** ***			*** ***					**							**			*** ***	*		*** ***			*** ***
I38LP10																					**																		
I48LP10		***																		**	***																
I60LP10	*	***	***																	**	*** ***																
I75LP10	*	***	***																*** ***	***																
I90LP10	***	***																		**	*** ***																
I30LP13					**			**	***		**	***	**	*** ***		*** *** ***	*** *** ***			**					*	**	*	*	*** ***	***	**	*** ***	**	*** ***
I38LP13																				**																
I48LP13				**		**													*		**															
I60LP13				***		*													*		***															
I75LP13	*	***	***																**		***															
I95LP13	***	***																	**		***															
I30LP16					**			**	***	*** *** ***	*** *** ***	*** *** ***		**	***	**	** *** ***	*** *** ***
I38LP16	**																		***																	
I48LP16	*		**	**															***	*	**															
I60LP16	*	***	***																**	*** ***																
I75LP16	**	***	***																*** ***	***																
I95LP16	*	***	***																***	***																
I30LP20						***	*** ***	*** ***	*** *** ***	*** *** ***	*** *** ***		***		*** **	*** *** ***	*** *** ***	*** *** ***
I38LP20						**		*** **															*** **	*** ***	
I48LP20		*	**																**		**															
I60LP20	**	*** ***																*** *** ***																	
I75LP20	**	*** ***																*** *** ***																	
I95LP20	***	*** ***																*** *** ***																	

	I30LP16			I38LP16			I48LP16			I60LP16			I75LP16			I95LP16			I30LP20			I38LP20			I48LP20			I60LP20			I75LP20			I95LP20		
	A	P	I	A	P	I	A	P	I	A	P	I	A	P	I	A	P	I	A	P	I	A	P	I	A	P	I	A	P	I	A	P	I	A	P	I
I30LP10		**					*	**	**	*	*** ***	**	***	*	*** ***				***						*	**	**	*** ***	**	*** ***	**	*** ***
I38LP10	***																		***																	
I48LP10	***	***																	*** ***			**														
I60LP10	***	*** ***																	*** *** ***			***	**													
I75LP10	***	*** ***																	*** *** ***																	
I90LP10	***	*** ***																	*** *** ***																	
I30LP13		***		***	*	**	**	*** ***	*** *** ***	*** *** ***					**		**	*** *** ***	*** *** ***	*** *** ***
I38LP13	***		**																***																	
I48LP13	***	**	*																***	**																
I60LP13	***	***	*																*** ***							***									
I75LP13	***	*** ***																	*** ***							***									
I95LP13	***	*** **																	*** ***																	
I30LP16		***		***	*	**	*** *** ***	*** *** ***	*** *** ***				***		**	*** *** ***	*** *** ***	*** *** ***
I38LP16	***																		***																	
I48LP16	***	*	**																***	**	**															
I60LP16	***	*** ***																	*** *** ***			**	**													
I75LP16	***	*** ***																	*** *** ***			*** ***														
I95LP16	***	*** ***																	*** *** ***																	
I30LP20		***		*** **	**	*** *** ***	*** *** ***	*** *** ***					***		**	*** *** ***	*** *** ***	*** *** ***
I38LP20								** **		*** ***									*							*	**	*** ***
I48LP20	***		**																***		**															
I60LP20	***	*** ***																	*** ***	*** ***		*	**												
I75LP20	***	*** ***																	*** *** ***			*** ***	***												
I95LP20	***	*** ***																	*** *** ***																	

5 Conclusion

Ultrasound-based tactile feedback in space is suitable for performing a fine motor gesture-based adjustment task. The empirical studies show that input via a virtual slider in space with ultrasound-based tactile feedback is possible. At an intensity level of 30% and less, the adjustment accuracy becomes significantly more difficult and therefore the task score becomes bad. In terms of the precision and intensity of the feedback, a scale graduation of 20 locking points has an effect on the evaluation of the feedback characteristics. Based on the results of the study, the greatest challenge in designing tactile feedback in the air lies in the feedback characteristics, i.e. the combination of locking point distance and feedback intensity. Further studies are necessary to address this design challenge. Similarly, constraints of different user and age groups need to be considered for the studies. Consequently, with focus on universal design, the generation of initial design guidelines for virtual control elements with tactile feedback in the air could be possible.

References

1. Hurstel, A., Bechmann, D.: Approach for intuitive and touchless interaction in the operating room. Multidiscipl. Sci. J. J2019, **2**, 50–64 (2019)
2. Cabreira, A.T., Hwang, F.: Evaluating the effects of feedback type on older adults' performance in mid-air pointing and target selection. In: Proceedings of the 6th Symposium on Spatial User Interaction. Berlin, Germany (2018)
3. Siegmann, S., Notbohm, G.: Noise in hospitals as a strain for the medical staff. J. Acous. Soc. Am. **133**(5), 3453 (2013)
4. International Organization for Standardization. Ergonomie der Mensch-System-Interaktion. Teil 112-Grundsätze der Informationsdarstellung (EN ISO 9241–112). (2017)
5. Biermann, H., Weißmantel, H.: Regelkatalog SENSI-Geräte – Bedienungsfreundlich und barrierefrei durch das richtige Design. Institut für Elektromechanische Konstruktionen, Darmstadt (1997)
6. Schmid, P., Winterholler, J., Maier, T.: Untersuchung zum Entlastungspotential des visuellen Informationskanals durch das nutzerzentrierte Design eines Drehbedienelements. Stuttgarter Symposium für Produktentwicklung 2019, Stuttgart (2019)
7. Winterholler, J.: Haptische Informationsübertragung von Drehmomentverläufen im Kontext einer Haupt- und Nebenaufgabe. Universität Stuttgart, Stuttgart. Institut für Konstruktionstechnik und Technisches Design, Forschungs- und Lehrgebiet Technisches Design, Dissertation, Stuttgart (2019)
8. Schmid, P., Bader, M., Maier, T.: Tactile Information Coding by Electro-tactile Feedback. In: Proceedings of the 4th International Conference on Computer-Human Interaction Research and Applications – vol. 1: CHIRA, pp. 37–43, (2020)
9. Deutsches Institut für Normung: Normzahlen und Normzahlreihen; Hauptwerte, Genauwerte, Rundwerte (DIN 323–1). (1974)

Vials for Injection and Infusion – A Systems Ergonomics Assessment

Thomas Stüdeli[(⊠)]

F. Hoffmann-La Roche Ltd, Grenzacherstrasse 124, 4070 Basel, Switzerland
thomas.stuedeli@roche.com

Abstract. This research maps out today's use environment and some important use scenarios for vials for injection and infusion in order to inform vial design and to increase the safety and the usability of the next generation of vials and their related accessories.

The vial user interfaces are described, and findings of market research as well as field observations are summarized. Finally, a hierarchical task analysis covering generic user interaction for the main use scenarios is presented.

Based on the current generic hierarchical task analysis, the use-related risks of a specific use scenario can be assessed. The focus on a specific use scenario of a vial-based injection system will take the specific risk profile of the medicine and the clinical practice into account. This risk assessment will complete the here presented context information and the HTA to a holistic systems ergonomics assessment.

Keywords: Ethnography · Market research · Hierarchical task analysis · Usability/ergonomics requirement

1 Introduction

1.1 Vials for Injection and Infusion

A vial is a small glass or plastic bottle used to sell, transport and store medication as liquids, powders or capsules. Vials were, for a long time, the primary containers for medicines for injection and infusion. In the last several decades, a variety of new primary packaging containers have been developed (e.g., cartridges, pre-filled syringes, bags) to support new types of devices for injections, but vials remain the primary packaging containers for infusion.

Medicines are typically injected into the veins, the muscles or the subcutaneous (SC) space (injection routes). Infusions use gravity to administer the medication directly into the blood stream in the vein, the intravenous (IV) injection route. In order to administer a medicine from a vial to a patient, the medicine needs to be transferred from the vial to an injection device or a system for intravenous infusion (IV system) prior to the injection or infusion. These preparations are done with the help of accessories or tools, such as adaptors with spikes and cannulas, or (transfer) needles. From a systems ergonomics

© The Author(s), under exclusive license to Springer Nature Switzerland AG 2021
N. L. Black et al. (Eds.): IEA 2021, LNNS 222, pp. 451–460, 2021.
https://doi.org/10.1007/978-3-030-74611-7_62

point of view [1], the vial as well as all necessary accessories that are used for a successful injection or infusion are part of a system that we call here a "vial-based injection system".

The usability of such systems has not yet been explored in the technical literature, as the developers and manufacturers of the different elements of the vial-based injection systems have typically collaborated mainly on technical aspects, such as specification of dimensions of vials. The developers and manufacturer of the vials are relying on industrial standards, such as ISO 8536 [2–4] to guarantee the technical compatibility of the different accessories and tools.

For the safety and the efficacy of vial-based injection systems, it is important that not only the technical compatibility is considered but also the compatibility in use: that the interaction of the user with the different elements of the system is intuitive and simple. This research aims to apply a user-centered and ergonomic approach to these vial-based injection systems, taking into account the main use scenarios, the main accessories used with the vials, and typical clinical practices (techniques).

1.2   Vial User Interfaces and Accessories

Vials for injection or infusion typically have the user interfaces displayed in Fig. 1.

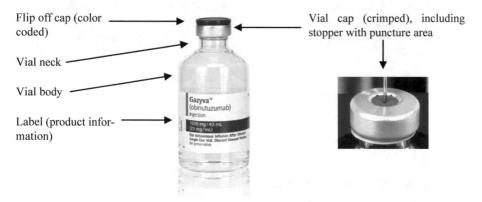

Fig. 1.   Vial user interfaces. Source: https://www.roche.com/products/products-list.htm

The flip off cap protects the puncture area. Once the cap is taken off, the vial typically can't be reclosed. The flip off cap on the vial serves as proof that the vial has not yet been used and serves as a simple Tamper Evident (TE) feature. The vial cap ensures that the rubber stopper is kept in place and the integrity of the vial is maintained. The typically crimped cap leaves an open access to the stopper with the puncture area where the stopper can be pierced with needles, cannulas or spikes to access the content of the vial. In the upper vial neck region the stopper is placed and the vial neck is the place where most accessories are attached to the vial. There are considerable ISO standards, e.g. [2–4] that define some key aspects and dimensions of vials for infusion or injection.

2 Systems Ergonomic Assessment

This work presents a systems ergonomic assessment consisting of the following three sequential activities and objectives:

1. **Market review.** In a first step, the existing primary container solutions (i.e., pre-filled syringes, vials, cartridges) within Roche Pharma (F. Hoffmann-La Roche Ltd Basel, Switzerland) and its associated companies are analyzed by literature review and interviews with internal and external stakeholders. This market review aims to better understand the intended uses and the use environments for vials for injection and infusion.
2. **Field research.** In a second step, the main use scenarios and user needs are explored through observations in the field and interviews with users. This field research aims to re-define the use scenarios and define the scope of vial-based injection systems.
3. **Hierarchical Task Analysis**. In a third step, a high-level Hierarchical Task Analysis (HTA) for the main use scenarios found and described in the previous steps is performed. This HTA aims to be the basis of future work, such as an in depth use-related risk analysis (generic or medicine-specific) for vial-based injection systems.

Ultimately, the initial assessment presented here aims to support and provide usability related design input for the development of new vial-based injection systems.

2.1 Market Review

Container Closing Systems (CCS). In scope of this review were CCSs and devices for already marketed molecules and those under development of Roche Pharma (F. Hoffmann-La Roche Ltd Basel, Switzerland and associated companies). From the 39 molecules in the market, 17 are oral solutions or capsules, one is taken with a nebulizer, and 21 are for injection or infusion. All molecules for injection or infusion have been initially used with a vial during the clinical development. Roche uses standard vial sets from 2 ml to 50 ml according to the ISO standards [2–4]. Most of the marketed molecules to be injected or infused are marketed with more than one CCS or device to accommodate different clinical settings and user needs.

The vial is still the main CCS for intra-venous (IV) injections (infusions) and for clinical trials. For subcutaneous injections, Pre-Filled Syringes (PFS) offer to the user a fixed dose and simplified handling. Roche is using PFSs of different sizes and platforms and with different needle safety systems. More recently, other injection devices like pen injectors, auto-injectors and wearable injectors or "on body devices" (for larger volumes) have been introduced. All off those injection devices aim to further simplify use and typically allow self-medication or injection by a lay-caregiver in home use environments. Self-injection at home is of growing interest as it reduces hospital stays and costs and exerts less burden on the patients. Despite those advantages, self-injection is only possible under certain conditions (e.g., when the risk profile of the molecule allows for unmonitored injection).

From the current molecules in the pipeline, two third are anticipated just for hospital use and one third for home use. For hospital-only molecules the CCS are vials or PFSs.

For home use, the CCS are bottles, blisters, PFSs and PFSs used as CCS for auto-injectors and injection pens.

The market review shows that vials for injection are still an important primary container, although there are newer containers used for needle-based systems like injection pens, auto-injectors, on body devices or PFSs (with safety systems). There are still considerable (older) medications on the market that are distributed in vials. Additionally, for a significant amount of new molecules tested in clinical trials, vials are used for distribution.

Tools, Accessories, and Use Scenarios. The different injection route (injection vs infusion), the devices, and the accessories are the main drivers of the different use scenarios for vial-based injection systems (Table 1).

Table 1. Use scenarios of vial-based injection systems in clinical practice: injection routes, injection devices and accessories.

Main injection route and injection device	Accessory types
Injection *Subcutaneous (under the skin)* or *Intramuscular (in a muscle)* Injection needle	• Adapter • Transfer needle
Infusion *Intravenous (in a vein)* Catheter, Canula, Port etc.	• Adapter • Transfer needle • Closed system transfer Devices (CSTDs)

With vials for injection, the accessories and tools needed for the handling are sometimes co-packed. Such accessories are syringes and transfer needles, or vial adapters (with spikes or cannulas).

Vials for infusion are typically not co-packed with accessories and tools. For the preparation of the infusion the vial content is transferred into an infusion kit or an entire infusion system. For these transfers, the accessories and tools need to be compatible with the vial as well as with the infusion kit or infusion system. On the vial side, these transfer tools are often additionally fixed to the vial neck for a more secure connection.

For hazardous medications, and depending on the clinical practice, Closed System Transfer Devices (CSTDs) are used to increase the safety for the Health Care Providers (HCPs) during handling. These drug transfer devicse prevent environmental contaminants from entering into the system and prevent hazardous medication or vapor concentrations from escaping out of the system. Massoomi [6] analyzed the CSTDs on the US market and distinguished four types of CSTDs. Each type demands a specific user interaction to connect the CSTD with the vial and the infusion kit or infusion system: Luer-lock (turn), Click-to-lock, Color-to-color alignment, and Push-turn-push.

2.2   Field Research

Based on the initial market research, the main use scenario for vial-based injection systems is in the hospital setting. To further explore the vial use in the hospitals, the vial has been followed from the place where the order is processed to the place where the infusions and injections are administered. This research took place at three different locations in Switzerland: the hospital pharmacy and the oncology outpatients' clinics of the university hospital in Basel as well as the cantonal hospital pharmacy of Zurich in Schlieren.

Use Scenarios. The field observations show that the use scenarios for vial-based injection systems (Table 1) are diverse and depend on clinical practices. Although vials for injection and infusion are primarily used in clinical settings, the use scenarios cover a broad range of use environments such as clinics, pharmacies, and home use and they also cover a broad range of users.

Users: Users observed were pharmacy hospital employees and nurses in the outbound clinics. They reported, among others, first time use challenges due to many use steps within each scenario, and multiple use steps that required using several accessories and tools. These professional users highlighted the importance of training and practice.

Vial-Based Injection Systems. The use steps related to the vial itself are comparable for both injection and infusion. Whereas vials for injection are used in a relatively simple system with typically one transfer device and one injection device, the vial-based infusion system is more complex and more difficult to describe and analyze. Here the different accessories and different infusion devices lead to tasks that are comparatively more complex, notably the steps related to the infusion kits and infusion systems.

Use Environments. In the hospital pharmacies, all work steps are defined in detailed work instructions and they are followed closely. One of the main tasks related to the vials is to prepare patient-specific dosing for cytostatic and other hazardous medications. The correct dose is retrieved from the vial and transferred (e.g., in a syringe or an IV bag). The vials are then re-sealed, relabeled, and prepared for re-use. The same or similar tasks are, under certain circumstances, are also done in outpatient clinics. Here, the use of the vial based injection systems can change considerably, depending on clinical practice, the local infrastructure and the availability of materials. Different accessories and tools might be used for the same tasks or purpose and spontaneous workarounds are common practice to overcome complex use steps in the handling of spikes, IV bag spikes, vial adapters, syringes, add on bag access devices, syringe adaptors, spike port adaptors, etc.

2.3   Hierarchical Tasks Analysis for Vial-Based Injection Systems

Table 2 shows the HTAs of the major use scenarios displayed in Table 1 above. The HTA shows all common use steps of these scenarios. Use steps related solely to the IV systems, related to transport and storage, and use steps related to instructions for use are not displayed.

Table 2. Hierarchical tasks analysis for vial-based injection systems (vial and accessories). SC = subcutaneous, IV = intravenous, EXP = expiration, TE = tamper evident.

High level task	Task	Sub-step
1. Transport and store the product	N/A	N/A
2. Vial preparation	2.1 Collect vial	Retrieve carton from refrigerator
		Check the carton for damage and if sealed
	2.2 Unpack vial for use	Check the EXP date on carton *(can be substituted by task 4.1)*
		Open the carton
		Remove contents from carton
	2.3 Perform checks on product/vial	Check the EXP date on vial
3. Injection preparation	3.1 Warm up time	Place the vial on a clean flat surface
		Wait for drug to reach room temperature
		Collect supplies and accessories (e.g., CSTD adaptors for vial and syringe, vial adaptors, transfer and injection needles, alcohol pads, small bandages, sharps container)
	3.2 Clean hands	Clean hands with soap and water
	3.3 Prepare injection site	Select injection site
		Clean injection site with an alcohol pad
		Let the skin dry
4. Vial accessory	4.1 Prepare vial	Remove vial flip off cap
		Interact with TE feature
		Disinfect top of vial with alcohol pad and let it air dry
	4.2 Prepare accessory	Peel off the accessory blister back cover
		Remove transparent blister

(continued)

Table 2. (*continued*)

High level task	Task	Sub-step
		If there is a protective cap on the accessory, remove it
	4.3 Connect accessory with vial	Hold the vial upright on a flat surface
		Center accessory (e.g., spike) over the vial rubber stopper, in some cases an adaptor is needed
		Attach the accessory to the vial
		Check secure connection (visual or audible confirmation)
		Disinfect the lock of the accessory with an alcohol pad
	4.4 Connect syringe with accessory	Peel off syringe blister
		If present, remove the luer-lock and the tip cap from the syringe
		Pull the plunger rod up to the described dose
		If the accessory requires a syringe luer-lock adaptor: a) Remove luer-lock adaptor blister, b) Attach the adaptor to the syringe, c) Check secure connection (visually or audible confirmation), d) Disinfect the lock of the adaptor with an alcohol pad
	4.5 Withdraw medicine from vial	Invert the vial upside down
		Check for particles in the vial
		Withdraw the medicine from the vial
		Check for remaining medication in the vial
		Remove the large bubbles

(*continued*)

Table 2. (*continued*)

High level task	Task	Sub-step
		Turn the vial upright
		Remove the syringe unit from the vial adapter
5. Injection	5.1 Prepare injection SC	Open injection needle blister (or remove needle hub cap)
		Attach the syringe to the injection needle
		Check secure connection (visually or audible confirmation)
		Move the needle safety shield on the side
		Remove the needle cap
		Adjust to the prescribed dose (with the syringe pointing up)
	Note: During the preparation for IV infusion, the content of the vial is transferred into an IV bag. The use-steps depend on the set-up of the IV system.	
	5.2. Perform injection SC	Pinch the skin
		Insert the needle at 45° to 90° into the skin
		Fully depress the plunger (inject the medicine)
		Remove the needle from the skin
		Release the skin
	Note: The use-steps for IV infusion depends on the set-up of the IV system.	
	5.3 Conclude injection	Cover the needle with the needle shield
		Dispose the syringe in a puncture resistant container
		Dispose the remaining material (except vial) in a puncture resistant container

(*continued*)

Table 2. (*continued*)

High level task	Task	Sub-step
		Dispose of the vial if it is empty
		If some product remains in the vial, prepare the vial for re-use
		Place the vial with the vial adapter attached back into the original carton
		If blood and/or leak back at injection site, press cotton ball or gauze after injection

3   Discussion

Today, vials for injection and infusion are primarily used in highly organized and regulated hospital settings. The user interfaces of a vial (Fig. 1) and the main user interactions with this standard CCS itself are simple. The use steps are: unpack the vial, read the label, remove the flip off cap, pierce the stopper with a needle or a spike and remove the vial content, dispose of the vial. However, this research is taking in account also other main elements of vial-based injection systems. The aim is to consider and map all the user interactions needed to safely inject or infuse the prescribed dose, the defined amount of vial content (medicine), into the patient.

On such a systems level the user interactions are obviously more complex, and, as this research shows, more diverse. A generic HTA for SC injections is presented (Table 2) as the different accessories are used similarly. Table 2 maps out all common tasks and steps of SC injections and IV infusions. For the IV infusion with a broader variety of accessories and tools, the use steps related to IV systems are not displayed in Table 2. To map out their concrete user tasks, more specific context around the specific IV system is needed. Earlier ergonomics research on IV pumps and the IV procedures show the challenges of this part of the system [7, 8].

The goal of this systems ergonomics research is to present the use and the use related challenges and risk to achieve better-informed design decisions. It also presents a high-level hierarchical task analysis as a starting framework. In order to inform the design of future vials and improve vial-based injection systems, this task analysis will need to be further refined for the specific products. With additional and more specific information about medication (vial content) and clinical practices, a project specific use-related risk assessment can be fully performed. Applying such a use-related risk assessment, similar to the well established human factors engineering and risk management activities for medical devices [5], allows a risk-based approach to the design input for vial-based injection systems that has been recently promoted for CSTDs by the industry [9]. In order to guarantee safe and usable systems solutions, developers and manufacturers of different elements of vial-based injection systems can use this initial research as a basis for closer collaboration. Understanding the end user and the context of use are key elements in achieving this collaboration and the HFE process [5] as well as a holistic systems approach [1] allows doing so.

4 Conclusion

This research maps out today's use environment and some important use scenarios for vial-based injection systems.

Based on the current generic HTA, use-related risks of specific use scenarios can be assessed. The focus on a specific use scenario of a vial-based injection system will take in account the specific risk profile of the medicine and the clinical practice. This will complete the systems ergonomics assessment.

A complete assessment will complement the design input and increase the safety and the usability of the next generation of vials and their related accessories.

References

1. Carayon, P., Wetterneck, T.B., Rivera-Rodriguez, A.J., Schoofs Hundt, A., Hoonakker, P., Holden, R., Gurses, A.P.: Human factors systems approach to healthcare quality and patient safety, Appl. Ergon. **45**(1), 14–25 (2014)
2. International Standard Organization: 8536–1:2011 Infusion equipment for medical use — Part 1: Infusion glass bottles (2011)
3. International Standard Organization: 8536–2:2010 Infusion equipment for medical use — Part 2: Closures for infusion bottles (2010)
4. International Standard Organization: 8536–3:2009 Infusion equipment for medical use — Part 3: Aluminium caps for infusion bottles (2009)
5. International Electrotechnical Commission: 62366–1:AMD2020 Medical devices - Part 1: Application of usability engineering to medical devices (2020)
6. Massoomi, F.: The Evolution of the CSTD, Oncology Safety **12**(2) (2015). https://www.ppp mag.com/article/1638. Accessed 10 Feb 2021
7. Westbrook, J.I., Rob, M.I., Woods, A., Parry, D.: Errors in the administration of intravenous medications in hospital and the role of correct procedures and nurse experience. BMJ Qual. Safe. **2011**(20), 1027–1034 (2011)
8. Giuliano, K.K.: Intravenous smart pumps - usability issues, intravenous medication administration error, and patient safety, critical care. Nurs. Clin. **30**(2), 215–224 (2018)
9. Besheer, A., Burton, L., Galas, R.J., Gokhale, K., Goldbach, P., Hu, Q., Mathews, L., Muthurania, K., Narasimhan, Ch., Singh, S.N., Stokes, E.S.E., Weiser, S., Zamiri, C., Zhou, S.: An industry perspective on compatibility assessment of closed system drug-transfer devices for biologics. J. Pharm. Sci. **110**(2), 610–614 (2021)

Enhancing Patient Safety in Healthcare Settings: A Systematic Investigation Framework to Reduce Medication Errors

Maryam Tabibzadeh[1]([⊠]) and Mohammad Mokhtari[2]

[1] California State University Northridge, Northridge, CA 91330, USA
maryam.tabibzadeh@csun.edu

[2] Islamic Azad University, Science and Research Branch, Tehran, Iran

Abstract. Preventable medication errors affect more than 7 million patients each year and cost almost $21 billion annually across all healthcare settings. Medication administration errors (MAEs) are identified to be highly occurring and one of the most severe among other categories of medication errors.

Despite some developed studies on analyzing medication errors, there is a need for the development of more robust, systematic methodologies to investigate their contributing causes and provide preventive measures to avoid their recurrence. This study proposes a systematic investigation framework, by adopting the AcciMap methodology originally developed by Rasmussen in 1997, to analyze contributing causes of MAEs and provides context-specific recommendations to reduce the instances of those errors.

The AcciMap methodology is a hierarchical, multi-layered framework with each layer representing a main group of involved players. The layers of the AcciMap framework in this study, from top to bottom, are: Government and Regulatory Bodies; Hospital; Management; Staff (e.g. physicians and nurses administering medications); and Work Processes, Events, and Conditions. It is noteworthy that not only does the AcciMap capture different socio-technical factors that contributed to MAEs across its layers, but also it depicts the interactions of those layers and their involved players.

The analysis of our developed AcciMap framework shows that both internal (to an organization) and external factors contributed to MAEs. Furthermore, organizational factors, among internal factors, have been identified as the root cause of questionable decisions made by staff and management. Factors such as economic pressure, inadequate training infrastructure, and ineffective communication were among influential organizational factors contributed to MAEs.

Keywords: Medication administration errors · Patient safety · Quality of care · Macroergonomics · Socio-technical factors · AcciMap

1 Introduction

Medication errors and adverse drug events (ADEs) due to them have been a major issue in the healthcare industry in the U.S. Preventable medication errors affect more than

N. L. Black et al. (Eds.): IEA 2021, LNNS 222, pp. 461–468, 2021.
https://doi.org/10.1007/978-3-030-74611-7_63

7 million patients each year and cost almost \$21 billion annually across all healthcare settings [1]. Medication errors are usually categorized as prescription, transcription, dispensing, and administration. Based on our comprehensive literature review, medication administration errors are identified to be highly occurring and one of the most severe among other categories of medication errors.

One of the main healthcare settings in which MAEs occur are hospitals. Statistics show that approximately 30% of hospitalized patients have at least one discrepancy on discharge medication reconciliation [1]. This statistic is of paramount importance knowing that there were more than 36 million admissions in the U.S. hospitals in 2020 [2]. It is also noteworthy that medication errors and ADEs are underreported in many cases. Therefore, this issue adversely affects patients, providers, and the economy.

This study proposes a systematic investigation framework, by adopting the AcciMap methodology, to analyze contributing causes of MAEs and provides recommendations to reduce the risks and instances of those errors.

2   Brief Literature Review

Despite some developed studies on analyzing the contributing causes of medication errors, there is a need for the development of more robust, systematic methodologies to identify their contributing causes and provide context-specific recommendations to prevent their recurrence. This study, by developing an AcciMap framework to systematically investigate the contributing causes of medication errors, aims to meet this need.

There have been different studies in the context of medication errors and their adverse effects in the healthcare industry. Some of these studies have utilized methodologies such as Six Sigma Define, Measure, Analyze, Improve and Control (DMAIC); Root Cause Analysis (RCA); Failure Modes and Effects Analysis (FMEA); Fault Tree Analysis (FTA); Reason's model of accident causation; and statistical analysis to analyze some of the contributing causes of medication errors with the purpose of preventing them or reducing the risk of their occurrence.

Buck [3], Kumar and Steinebach [4], and Al-Kuwaiti [5] have applied Six Sigma DMAIC methodology to reduce medication errors. As another category of utilized methods, Teixeira and de Cassiani [6] have used RCA to detect, reduce, and prevent medication (dosage and schedule) errors. In addition, Chiozza and Ponzetti [7] and Montesi and Lechi [8] have applied FMEA to identify the most severe medication errors. FTA has been used as another methodology to analyze the contributing causes of errors in medication delivery [9]. In this domain, Tabibzadeh and Muralidharan [10] have also investigated some of the main contributing and root causes of medication errors using the FTA, which was beyond the depth of the implemented analysis by Cherian [9]. Furthermore, Keers et al. [11, 12] have used the Reason's model of accident causation to investigate causes of MAEs in hospital settings. Finally, some studies such as Tsegaye et al. [13] have used statistical analyses (descriptive and analytical statistics and binary logistic regression in this specific study) to identify factors associated with MAEs.

There are different factors that make our proposed methodology in this study distinct from the existing literature. First of all, some of the existing studies have only analyzed medication errors at a specific hospital or healthcare setting while we have conducted a comprehensive literature research to identify different contributing causes of medication errors. In addition, we have utilized an accident analysis framework; i.e. AcciMap, that prevents unfair blame of frontline operators/staff and enables investigating incidents in a broader socio-technical context. The AcciMap framework has been used for the investigation of accidents in different context. However, due to our knowledge, this is the first attempt to utilize this framework to systematically analyze medication errors in the healthcare industry.

3 Methodology

This study proposes a systematic investigation framework using the AcciMap methodology, originally developed by Rasmussen in 1997 [14]. The AcciMap prevents unfair blame of frontline operators and analyzes incidents in a broader socio-technical context. It was developed in conjunction with a six-layer hierarchical framework (Fig. 1), known as risk management framework. Each layer of the framework represents a main group of involved decision-makers, players, or stakeholders in a studied system. These six layers, from top to bottom, are: Government, Regulators and Associations, Company, Management, Staff, and Work. The analysis of the framework includes assessing the activities of key players in each layer. More importantly, it captures the interactions between those key players within the stated layers [15].

This study adopts the AcciMap framework in the context of healthcare delivery systems, mainly hospitals, to analyze MAEs. In this regard, the main contributing causes of MAEs, which have been identified through an extensive literature research, are captured across each of the layers of the AcciMap framework. The modified layers of this framework in the context of our study, from top to bottom, are as follows: Government and Regulatory Bodies; Hospital; Management; Staff (physicians, nurses, and other staff who administer medications); and Work Processes, Events, and Conditions related to medication administration. We combined the two layers of Government

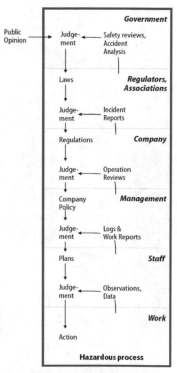

Fig. 1. Risk management framework to analyze socio-technical contributing causes of MAEs (Source of image: [15])

and Regulatory Bodies in this study, as there was no distinction between them while identifying contributing causes of MAEs through literature research.

It is noteworthy that not only does the AcciMap capture different socio-technical factors that contributed to MAEs across its layers, but also it depicts the interactions of those layers and their involved players. Those captured contributing causes across the AcciMap layers and their interactions can be used as a basis for the definition of preconditions of safe operations, as a main focus of proactive risk management systems.

4   The AcciMap Framework for the Analysis of MAEs

This section illustrates the developed AcciMap framework in this study for the analysis of medication administration errors. This framework (Fig. 2) captures and analyzes the contributing causes of MAEs across the five layers of Government and Regulatory Bodies; Company (Hospital); Management; Staff; and Work Processes, Events, and Conditions. It also depicts the interactions and interdependencies between those layers.

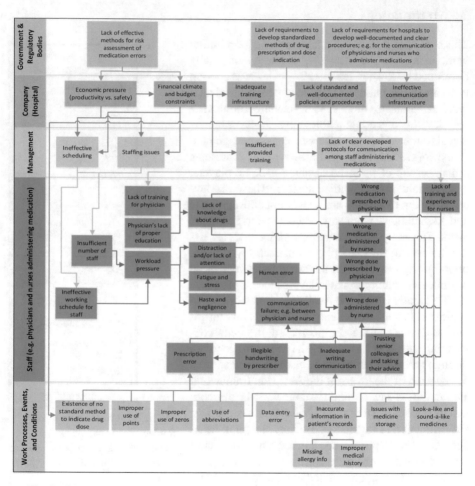

Fig. 2. The developed AcciMap framework to analyze medication administration errors

The captured contributing causes of MAEs across the AcciMap layers have been identified through an extensive literature research and analysis of several studies. Each layer, its captured contributing factors, and arrows showing the impact of those factors on other layers have been differentiate using a distinct color. Due to space limitation, we are not be able to describe each of the layers and its captured factors separately.

We, however, have described some of the captured factors in the Results and Discussion Section.

5   Results and Discussion

The analysis of our developed AcciMap framework shows that both internal (to an organization; i.e. hospital) and external factors contributed to medication administration errors. The captured factors across the first layer of Government and Regulator Bodies constitute the external factors and the other lower layers all capture internal (to an organization) factors.

The three factors of lack of requirements by regulatory bodies for hospitals to develop well-documented and clear procedures; e.g. for the communication of physicians and nurses who administer medications, lack of requirements to develop standardized methods of drug prescription and dose indication, and lack of effective methods for risk assessment of medication errors are among external contributing causes of MAEs.

In the layer of Hospital, economic pressure (imbalance between production and safety), financial climate and budget constraints, ineffective communication infrastructure, as well as lack of standard and well-documented procedures are the main captured organizational factors that contributed to MAEs. These organizational factors have impacted the layer of Management and factors such as ineffective scheduling, insufficient provided training, and lack of clear developed protocols for communication among staff administering medications are examples of captured factors in this layer.

In the layer of Staff, lack of attention to details; fatigue and stress; lack of training and experience; and communication failure between the physician, who prescribes the medication, and the nurse, who administer the medication, are some of the captured contributing causes of MAEs. Finally, inaccurate information in patient's records, existence of no standard method to indicate drug dose, and improper use of points and zeros are some of the captured factors in the layer of Work Processes, Events, and Conditions. Two examples for an improper use of points and zeros are: 1) writing 5 mL instead of 0.5 mL and 2) writing 5.0 mL instead of 5 mL for a drug dose. It is instructed to always use a leading zero before a decimal expression of less than one; e.g., 0.5 mL, since the point might be missed, and conversely, never use a terminal zero; e.g. 5.0 mL, since failure to see the decimal can result in a 10-fold overdose.

Not only does the graphical, multi-layered representation of the AcciMap provide a big-picture to illustrate the context in which an accident occurred, but also it depicts the interactions and the interdependencies between those layers, each representing a main group of involved key players. This is in the form of decisions propagating downwards and information propagating upward across the layers of the framework. These interactions have been illustrated in our developed AcciMap framework in Fig. 2 using arrows. These connections also allow an upward tracking of factors across the layers. For instance, wrong medication administered by the nurse in the layer of Staff can be due to human error in the same layer. One of the contributing causes of human error in this context is distraction and/or lack of attention by the nurse, and that can be because of workload pressure, which is another captured factor in the Staff layer. Insufficient number of staff can contribute to high workload and that itself can be due to ineffective scheduling, which is a captured factor in the Management layer. One of the contributing causes of ineffective scheduling is economic pressure (imbalance between productivity and safety) in the layer of Hospital, and one external factor (from the layer of Government and Regulatory Bodies) contributing to economic pressure is lack of provided effective methods for risk assessment of medication errors.

Furthermore, the analysis of our developed framework indicates that organizational factors, among internal factors, were the root causes of MAEs. They were the root cause of questionable decisions made by staff and management. Economic pressure (compromising safety for productivity), financial and budget constraints, inadequate training infrastructure, and ineffective communication are some influential organizational factors contributed to MAEs. Therefore, developing proper recommendations to address those organizational factors contributing to MAEs is an effective way of reducing the instances of these errors in the healthcare industry.

6 Some Recommendations

Based on the captured contributing causes of medication administration errors across different layers of the AcciMap framework, a series of context-specific recommendations have been developed. This section provides some of those recommendations.

As for the impact of external factors; the layer of Government and Regulatory Bodies, regulatory agencies have to develop system-based risk management programs to holistically assess the safety of operations in healthcare settings, in medications administration in this context. In addition, they have to require hospitals to develop standardized methods of drug prescription and dose indication.

For the layer of Hospital and the impact of organizational factors, improving safety culture and not compromising safety for production; e.g. time and cost saving, is of paramount importance. Hospitals need to establish a balance between production and safety. Strategies such as incorporating equivalent number of performance measures for safety achievements compared to production and cost saving accomplishments, rewarding systems for safe operations, and more appropriate risk analysis practices with concentration on safety are some methods to improve the status of the described organizational factor.

Developing an effective infrastructure for communication and collaboration has to be another focus area for hospitals and healthcare settings. Defining clear lines of communication; e.g. clear interaction protocols for staff who prescribe and administer medications, as well as designing standard and well-understood reporting infrastructures are some strategies toward developing an effective communication infrastructure.

For the Management layer, hiring more staff and scheduling shifts more effectively contribute to minimizing workload pressure for physicians and nurses. This will in turn reduce human errors; e.g. wrong dose and wrong medication, due to fatigue, stress, haste, negligence, and lack of attention. Moreover, developing well-established and sufficient training programs for the staff responsible for prescribing and administering medications reduces risks of MAEs.

The following are some examples of recommendations for the layers of Staff and Work Processes based on the captured contributing factors in these two layers to reduce instances of medication administration errors:

- Physicians have to provide proper instructions regarding the method of administrating the medication to the nurse.
- Nurses should contact the physician in case of any doubts in the method of medication administration and not take their own decisions. They should also not solely take decisions based on senior colleagues' opinions
- Prescription error can be avoided by using computerized prescriptions in hospitals. This will avoid illegible handwriting or ambiguous writing by physicians as well as improper use of zeros and points.
- If using a hand-written prescription, proper use of points and zeros are essential. In addition to what was described before on always using a leading zero before a decimal expression of less than one; e.g., 0.5 mL and conversely, never using a terminal zero; e.g. 5.0 mL, it is recommended to, when possible, avoid the use of decimals. For instance, prescribe 500 mg instead of 0.5 g.
- To "Accurate patients' records such as their allergy information as well as their medical and surgery history should be maintained by hospital administration to avoid wrong medication errors.

7   Conclusion

This study proposed an investigation framework, by adopting the AcciMap framework, to systematically analyze and identify socio-technical contributing causes of medication administration errors, as a main category of medication errors. It also provided recommendations to reduce instances of MAEs by addressing those identified contributing causes.

The AcciMap framework is a powerful tool that through its graphical representation provides a big-picture to illustrate the context in which an incident occurred. Analysis of such a framework emphasizes not only on the assessment of the activities of players in each layer, but more importantly on the analysis of the interactions between key players across those layers. This characteristic prevents unfair blame of frontline operators/staff and enables analyzing the incident in a broader socio-technical context.

The analysis of our developed AcciMap framework showed that both internal (to an organization; i.e. hospital) and external factors contributed to medication administration errors. Furthermore, organizational factors, among internal factors, were identified as the root cause of questionable decisions made by staff and management that contributed to MAEs. Factors such as economic pressure (compromising safety for productivity), inadequate training infrastructure, and ineffective communication were among influential organizational factors contributed to MAEs.

References

1. da Silva, B.A., Krishnamurthy, M.: The alarming reality of medication error: a patient case and review of Pennsylvania and National data. J. Commun. Hosp. Intern. Med. Perspect. **6**(4), 31758 (2016)
2. American Hospital Association (AHA). Fast Facts on US Hospitals. AHA Hospital Statistics. (2020). https://www.aha.org/system/files/media/file/2020/01/2020-aha-hospital-fast-facts-new-Jan-2020.pdf. Accessed 28 Jan 2021

3. Buck, C.: Application of Six Sigma to reduce medical errors. In: ASQ World Conference on Quality and Improvement Proceedings, p. 739. American Society for Quality (January 2001)
4. Kumar, S., Steinebach, M.: Eliminating US hospital medical errors. Int. J. Health Care Qual. Assur. **21**(5), 444–471 (2008)
5. Al-Kuwaiti, A.: Application of Six Sigma methodology to reduce medication errors in the outpatient pharmacy unit: a case study from the King Fahd University Hospital. Saudi Arabia. Int. J. Qual. Res. **10**(2), 267–278 (2016)
6. Teixeira, T.C., de Cassiani, S.H.: Root cause analysis: evaluation of medication errors at a university hospital. Rev. Esc. Enferm. USP **44**, 139–146 (2010)
7. Chiozza, M.L., Ponzetti, C.: FMEA: a model for reducing medical errors. Clin. Chim. Acta **404**, 75–78 (2009)
8. Montesi, G., Lechi, A.: Prevention of medication errors: detection and audit. Br. J. Clin. Pharmacol. **67**, 651–655 (2009)
9. Cherian, S.M.: Fault tree analysis of commonly occurring medication errors and methods to reduce them. Texas A&M University (1994)
10. Tabibzadeh, M., Muralidharan, A.: Reducing medication errors and increasing patient safety: utilizing the fault tree analysis. In: N.J. Lightner (eds), Advances in Human Factors and Ergonomics in Healthcare and Medical Devices. Advances in Intelligent Systems and Computing, vol. 779, pp. 207–218, Springer, Cham (2019)
11. Keers, R.N., William, S.D., Cooke, J., Ashcroft, S.D.: Causes of medication administration errors in hospitals: a systematic review of quantitative and qualitative evidence. Drug Saf. **36**, 1045–1067 (2013)
12. Keers, R.N., William, S.D., Cooke, J., Ashcroft, S.D.: Understanding the causes of intravenous medication administration errors in hospitals: a qualitative critical incident study. BMJ Open **5**, (2015). https://doi.org/10.1136/bmjopen-2014-005948
13. Tsegaye, D., Alem, G., Tessema, Z., Alebachew, W.: Medication administration errors and associated factors among nurses. Int. J. Gen. Med. **13**, 1621–1632 (2020)
14. Rasmussen, J.: Risk management in a dynamic society: a modeling problem. Safe. Sci. **27**(2), 183–213 (1997)
15. Rasmussen, J., Svedung, I.: Proactive Risk Management in a Dynamic Society. First edn, Raddningsverket, Risk and Environmental Department, Swedish Rescue Services Agency, Karlstad, Sweden (2000)

Application of the Ergonomic Checkpoints in Health Care Work: A Case from an Inpatient Service Unit of an Educational Hospital in Colombia

Yaniel Torres[1](✉) ⓘD, Yordán Rodríguez[2] ⓘD, and Néstor R. Buitrago[2] ⓘD

[1] Department of Mechanical Engineering, École de technologie supérieure (ÉTS),
1100 Notre-dame street W, Montreal, QC H3C 1K3, Canada
`yaniel.torres-medina.1@ens.etsmtl.ca`
[2] National School of Public Health, Universidad de Antioquia, Medellín, Antioquia, Colombia
`{yordan.rodriguez,nestor.buitrago}@udea.edu.co`

Abstract. The application of human factors and ergonomics (HFE) in healthcare has been recognized as an essential element to improve patient safety. In this paper, we present the use of the Ergonomic Checkpoints in Health Care Work developed by the International Ergonomics Association (IEA). The checkpoints were used as a guideline to encourage practical and participatory applications of ergonomic principles in a healthcare context. Sixteen nurses from an educational hospital in Colombia participated in the study. A total of 22 points of improvement were identified out of 60 checkpoints proposed in the IEA document. The main points of improvements were associated with material storage and handling (4 points), safe patient handling (3 points), workstations (3 points), infection control (3 points), and work organization (3 points). This study supports the usefulness of applying broad-ranging ergonomic principles in conjunction with a participatory approach to improve healthcare work systems. The intervention presented in this paper represents a novelty in the Colombian healthcare ecosystem. It opens the door to future developments and supports establishing a broader national strategy for patient safety that includes HFE as a fundamental pillar.

Keywords: Patient safety · Nurses · Medication errors · Participatory intervention · Industrially developing countries

1 Introduction

According to the World Health Organisation (WHO), patient safety is a fundamental principle of healthcare and is currently a major global concern [1]. Patient safety focuses on preventing adverse events to avoid harm to patients, which includes the prevention of medical errors, intra hospital infections, and patient falls [2]. Unfortunately, the prevention of adverse events is a challenging issue to tackle within healthcare systems. Data from the European Union consistently show that medical errors and other healthcare-related adverse events occur in 8% to 12% of hospitalizations [3]. Statistics

N. L. Black et al. (Eds.): IEA 2021, LNNS 222, pp. 469–474, 2021.
https://doi.org/10.1007/978-3-030-74611-7_64

show that medical errors account for about two-thirds of all adverse events that cause harm to patients [1].

In the United States, medical error is estimated to be the third leading cause of death after heart disease and cancer, accounting for 251,000 deaths annually [4]. Similarly, the Canadian Patient Safety Institute estimates 28,000 deaths yearly from unintended harm and medication error are also the third leading cause of death in Canada [5]. Furthermore, according to Lane et al. [6] several studies of medical errors have identified medication errors as a major source of adverse events that can cause harm to patients. Ferner and Arason [7] defines a medication error as "a failure in the [drug] treatment process that leads to, or has the potential to lead to, harm to the patient".

Medication errors can occur at any one of the five main drug treatment stages: prescribing, documenting, dispensing or preparation, administering and monitoring. However, the administration stage is frequently associated with the highest error rate, followed by the prescription stage [8–10]. Nurses are one of the health professionals sharing responsibility for drug treatment. Though, the origin of medication errors and other patient safety issues can be found in the design of the work system. For this reason, the WHO endorses Human Factors and Ergonomics (HFE) discipline as an essential component of any Patient Safety strategy aimed at reducing avoidable harm to patients [11].

HFE discipline has been adopted as a patient safety practice by several healthcare systems in industrially advanced countries (IACs) [12, 13]. However, the application of HFE in industrially developing countries (IDCs) has focused, with more emphasis, on the physical elements of work: use of tools, design of workstations, manual material handling, and the evaluation of work environments, especially in tropical climates [14]. Furthermore, healthcare systems in IDCs face different challenges considering the limited availability of infrastructure and the general lack of resources and healthcare professionals in comparison with IACs [15].

For the reasons described below, the application of HFE to healthcare systems within IDCs has been limited, as is the case within the Latin American region [16]. One alternative to this situation is the use of low-cost participatory strategies. This type of approach has been previously explored by developing ergonomic principles guidelines in the form of checklists [17]. More recently, the International Ergonomics Association (IEA) developed the Ergonomic Checkpoints in Health Care Work to encourage the practical applications of ergonomics in a participatory, easy-to-use checkpoints format [18]. The objective of the study is to carry out an ergonomic intervention among a group of nurses aimed to identify areas of improvement within the work system. The focus of the intervention is the reduction of medication errors to improve patient safety.

2   Materials and Methods

A cross-sectional descriptive study was conducted in the inpatient care unit at a major University Hospital in Medellín, Colombia. This service unit has 116 active beds. A group of professional nurses (n = 16) participated in the study. A participatory intervention approach was used to conduct the study which took the form of group interviews. Ergonomic Checkpoints in Health Care Work was used to identify, in a structured manner, areas of improvements in the work system. Group interviews were carried out in the morning during the shift turnover meeting where nurses and supervisors meet. Informed consent was obtained from participants. The fieldwork was led by a postgraduate ergonomics student who acts as a facilitator in close supervision from experienced ergonomics professionals.

2.1 Ergonomic Checkpoints in Health Care Work

The Ergonomic Checkpoints in Health Care Work is a document that presents a compilation of practical improvement actions from an ergonomic perspective. It provides a total of 60 checkpoints grouped in 10 categories (six checkpoints by each category). The ten categories included in the document are materials storage and handling, machine and hand-tool safety, safe patient handling, workstations, physical environment, hazardous substances and agents, infection control, welfare facilities, preparedness, work organization and patient safety. The emphasis throughout the document is placed on presenting simple, low-cost improvements that are practicable in both industrialized and industrializing countries. Checkpoints are easy-to-apply and are readily applicable in varying situations. All checkpoints are presented using images accompanied by an explanatory text. Figure 1 shows two examples of images associated with checkpoint No. 2 and checkpoint No. 4, respectively. Both checkpoints were identified as points of improvement in the study.

Fig. 1. Checkpoint No. 2 (left): Use of small containers and labels makes it easy to store. Checkpoint No. 4 (right): Well-arranged cart for medical treatment materials. Source: IEA 2017 [18].

3 Results

The focus group was able to identify 22 points of improvement among the 60 points proposed in the ergonomics checkpoints. Points of improvement were found in all the 10 technical areas proposed by the IEA document. The main points of improvement were associated with material storage and handling (4 points), safe patient handling (3 points), workstations (3 points), infection control (3 points), and work organization (3 points).

Five priority points were identified, three in the material storage and handling category and one in the work organization and patient safety category. These priority points were: (1) use multi-level shelves or racks and small containers to minimize manual transport of materials, (2), make labels and signs easy to see, easy to read and easy to understand. (3) use carts, hand-trucks and other wheeled devices convenient for moving materials, (4) promote safer healthcare services and a patient safety culture involving personnel, management, and patients.

In Fig. 2, we show two examples of points of improvement that were identified during the study. The first one (on the left) shows that the storage is carried out precariously, potential-ly leading to falling, damage and loss of material and supplies. The second one (on the right) corresponds to the medication cart wich has very few internal divisions. The number of internal divisions helps to better organize the medication delivered to pa-tients in unitary doses.

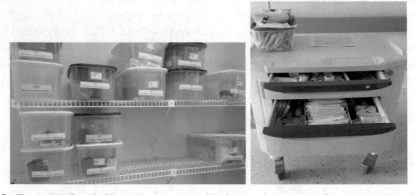

Fig. 2. Example of a shelf used to store medication, and example of a cart used to deliver medication to patients.

4   Discussion

The study constitutes a relatively novel experience in a Colombian hospital in which several stakeholders were mobilized around the subject of patient safety from an ergonomic perspective. Furthermore, the Ergonomic Checkpoints in Health Care Work is a relatively new document [19] and to the best of our knowledge, applications in Colombia have not yet been reported in the literature. However similar, strategies have proven to be effective in IDCs in contexts other than healthcare. i.e., agriculture, general industry, small enterprise [20]. This study supports the usefulness of applying broad-ranging ergonomic principles in conjunction with a participatory approach to improve healthcare work systems. We were able to identify 22 points of improvement that can contribute to patient safety.

The intervention process itself can generate awareness and educate healthcare professionals and different stakeholders about the importance of embracing HFE to improve patient safety. Awareness and education are essential in the Latin American region, where a lack of systematic application of HFE to healthcare systems has been recognized [16]. Similar action-research initiatives could serve as mobilization force within the Latin America region to promote the symbiosis between HFE and patient safety following the long tradition of using this approach [21].

5 Conclusions

In the context of IDCs, using ergonomic principles presented in an easy-to-use format in combination with a participatory approach can serve to identify areas of improvement in the work system and potentially increase the level of awareness among healthcare professionals. This approach to HFE in healthcare and the intervention presented in this paper represents a novelty in the Colombian healthcare ecosystem. It opens the door to future developments. It also supports establishing a broader national strategy for patient safety that includes HFE as a fundamental pillar.

References

1. WHO: Patient Safety: Making health care safer. World Health Organization, Geneva (2017). https://apps.who.int/iris/bitstream/handle/10665/255507/WHO-HIS-SDS-2017.11-eng.pdf;sequence=1. Accessed 10 May 2020
2. WHO: Patient safety: a global health priority. World Health Organization, Geneva (2019). https://www.who.int/patientsafety/policies/global-health-priority/en/. Accessed 23 May 2020
3. WHO: Patient Safety: Data and Statistics. World Health Organization, Geneva (2019). http://www.euro.who.int/en/health-topics/Health-systems/patient-safety/data-and-statistics. Accessed 24 May 2019
4. Makary, M.A., Daniel, M.: Medical error—the third leading cause of death in the US. BMJ **353**, (2016)
5. Risk Analytica.: The Case for Investing in Patient Safety in Canada. Canadian Patient Safety Institute (2017). http://bit.ly/Canadian_Patient_Safety. Accessed 04 Nov 2020
6. Lane, R., Stanton, N.A., Harrison, D.: Applying hierarchical task analysis to medication administration errors. Appl. Ergon. **37**(5), 669–679 (2006)
7. Ferner, R.E., Aronson, J.K.: Medication errors, worse than a crime. Lancet **355**(9208), 947–948 (2000)
8. Gómez-Baraza, C., et al.: Seguridad en la administración intravenosa de medicamentos mediante bombas de infusión inteligentes. Farmacia Hosp. **38**, 276–282 (2014)
9. Karthikeyan, M., Lalitha, D.: A prospective observational study of medication errors in general medicine department in a tertiary care hospital. Drug Metab. Drug Interact. **28**(1), 13–21 (2013)
10. Patel, N., et al.: A study of medication errors in a tertiary care hospital. Perspect. Clin. Res. **7**(4), 168–173 (2016)
11. WHO: Patient Safety Curriculum Guide: Multi-professional Edition. World Health Organization: Geneva (2011)
12. Blouin, A.S., et al.: Caregiver fatigue: implications for patient and staff safety, Part 1. JONA: J. Nurs. Admin. **46**(6) (2016)
13. Carayon, P., Xie, A., Kianfar, S.: Human factors and ergonomics as a patient safety practice. BMJ Qual. Safe. **23**(3), 196 (2014)

14. Huck-Soo, L., Richardson, S.: Ergonomics in industrially developing countries: a literature review. J. Hum. Ergol. **41**(1–2), 1–16 (2012)
15. OECD, Health expenditure and financing. Organisation for Economic Co-operation and Development (OECD) Paris, France (2018)
16. Aceves-González, C., et al.: Frontiers in human factors: integrating human factors and ergonomics to improve safety and quality in Latin American healthcare systems. Int. J. Qual. Health Care 33(Supplement_1), 45–50 (2020)
17. ILO and IEA: Ergonomic Checkpoints: Practical And Easy-To-Implement Solutions for Improving Safety, Health and Working Conditions. International Labour Organization, Geneva (2010)
18. IEA: Ergonomic Checkpoints in Health Care Work. Human Ergology Society and International Ergonomics Association. IEA Press, Geneva (2017). https://www.ioha.net/wp-content/uploads/2019/06/Ergonomic-Checkpoints-in-Health-Care-Work.pdf. Accessed 10 Oct 2020
19. Kogi, K., et al.: The design and use of ergonomic checkpoints for health care work. In: Proceedings of the 20th Congress of the International Ergonomics Association (IEA2018). Springer International Publishing, Cham (2019)
20. Budnick, P., Kogi, K., O'Neill, D.: Examples of practical ergonomics in industrially developing countries. ergonomics in design: Q. Hum. Factors Appl. **20**(4), 5–11 (2012)
21. Helali, F.: Using ergonomics checkpoints to support a participatory ergonomics intervention in an industrially developing country (IDC)-a case study. Int. J. Occup. Safe. Ergon. **15**(3), 325–337 (2009)

Human Factors Methods Applied
to a Healthcare Information Technology Project

Matthew Woodward[1](✉) ⓘ, Nick De Pennington[2], and Lauren Morgan[3] ⓘ

[1] THIS Institute, University of Cambridge, Cambridge, UK
matthew.woodward@thisinstitute.cam.ac.uk
[2] Oxford University Hospitals NHS Trust, Oxford, UK
[3] Morgan Human Systems, Shrewsbury, UK

Abstract. Using a hospital-based improvement project in the UK as a case study, a number of practical human factors/ergonomics (HFE) methods are discussed across four phases of an intervention: analysis, design, implementation and evaluation. The reference project developed and implemented a new web-based referral system which provided shared access to patient details across hospitals. Methods applied were process analysis, software usability studies, prospective hazard analysis (Structured What-If Technique – SWIFT), paper pro formas to collect data in situ, clinical audit and the analysis of electronic health records. The strengths, weaknesses and practical challenges of each are considered.

The referral project resulted in an improvement in the quality of clinical referrals and the availability of patient demographic data. It is recommended that HFE projects collect both process and quality data using mixed methods to gain more robust evidence of an intervention's effects.

Keywords: Health information technology · Usability · SWIFT · Hospital referrals · Human factors

1 Introduction

1.1 Context

Healthcare quality improvement projects often use a narrow range of metrics that provide just one measure of a system [1, 2]. In such cases there is a risk of optimising against one goal to the detriment of others. A systems human factors/ergonomics (HFE) approach, in which implementation is viewed in the context of a sociotechnical system, advocates that a wider range of methods and data sources is encompassed [3–5]. The discipline offers multiple methods for evaluating healthcare interventions, although it has been reported that many of these do not get applied by practitioners on practical projects [6]. Xie and Carayon in their review of healthcare HFE projects defined four phases of redesign: analysis, design, implementation and evaluation. They found that the large majority of studies concerned only the analysis or evaluation phase [7]. This chapter references a recent hospital-based improvement study to illustrate some of the methods and data that can be applied across each phase. The strengths, weaknesses and practical challenges associated with each are discussed.

© The Author(s), under exclusive license to Springer Nature Switzerland AG 2021
N. L. Black et al. (Eds.): IEA 2021, LNNS 222, pp. 475–481, 2021.
https://doi.org/10.1007/978-3-030-74611-7_65

1.2   The Referral System Implementation Project

Context. The project set out to improve the safety of inter-hospital neurosurgery referrals, a transition point in the healthcare system that is vulnerable to failures [8]. In the UK hospitals across a region contact a specialist centre hospital for advice. The requests are typically made by telephone and the advice given may be for local clinical management, direction to other specialist services (such as oncology) or an expedited transfer of the patient to the specialist centre. A roster of different staff fulfilling the role of the on-call registrar, coupled with paper-based recording systems represent risks to patient safety [9].

While the digitisation of such services has potential benefits [10], there are many electronic health record (EHR) systems that neglect basic usability heuristics and user requirements. For example, forcing recall rather than recognition of information, poor navigation leading to long scrolling, and inconsistency across pages [11]. As Weiner et al. note, "Important aspects of ergonomics and human factors engineering frequently appear overlooked during the design and implementation of EHRs" [12].

Project Overview. The project's objective was apply human factors/ergonomics principles and methods to the development, implementation and evaluation of a new electronic referral system. The software was developed over a period of 18 months and delivered into service across a regional network of hospitals in the UK National Health Service (NHS). A detailed account of the project and the results have been published elsewhere [13].

With the lead of a clinician from the neurosurgery department a small team involving software developers and human factors engineers was formed. The study integrated usability considerations into the design from the start with a design process that was informed by the current workflow and a shared understanding of the work system. Use cases were developed to communicate user requirements with the developers, usability studies were conducted and users (referrers, specialists and bed coordinators) were involved throughout.

2   Methods

In common with many HFE studies in healthcare a convergent mixed methods approach was used [5]. Data was collected from across the four system redesign phases as described by Xie and Carayon [7]. A data plan that outlined data types and methods was drafted and discussed with stakeholders (hospital department operations manager, lead clinician, human factors and patient safety specialists) for input.

A distinction was made between four types of data and the associated collection methods: process description, process efficiency, referral quality and usability data. Process data can include a description or quantification of process steps, timings, adherence or potential failure points. Referral quality concerns the information content required for the initiation and progression of care. Usability data refer to the effectiveness, efficiency and user satisfaction with the use of equipment or technology. The methods and approach are summarised in Table 1 and discussed below by project phase.

Table 1. Summary of methods and data collected

System redesign phase	Method	Data content	Data type
Analysis	Swim lane diagrams	Process description	Process description
Design	Usability studies	Errors, difficulties, comments	Software usability
Design	Use cases	Description of task goals and steps	Software usability
Implementation	Retrospective analysis of referrals	System uptake	Process efficiency + usability
Implementation	Structured What-if Technique (SWIFT)	Potential failures and mitigations	Process description
Evaluation	Prospective collection of operational data	Number of referral calls and bleeps	Process efficiency
Evaluation	Retrospective analysis of EPR data	Period to surgery	Process efficiency
Evaluation	Analysis of database content	Completeness of demographic data	Referral quality
Evaluation	Clinical audit	Clinical judgement on content	Referral quality

2.1 Analysis Phase

Firstly, to understand the context of referrals before proposing any change, the current inter-hospital referral process was recorded. Swim lane diagrams were drawn using the notation in which process steps are drawn in rows that represent roles [14]. Meetings with clinicians and field observations of the specialist and bed manager roles were used to collect data. A strength of the swim lane notation was that it made clear the transition of information and responsibility between roles and organisations. It proved to be an effective mechanism for communicating with stakeholders about the different 'states' a referral would move through. A challenge was to effectively capture variation, for example the point at which a consultant review occurs is dependent on when the referral was received and the medical acuity of a patient. This variation can be addressed by including conditional branches or separate diagrams for each case.

2.2 Design Phase

Use cases were written that delineated the user (clinician) goals (e.g. check status of earlier referral) and the steps required to achieve this (e.g. access search function). These were useful to make explicit assumptions and expectations, although in practice the design was also driven by conversations and user interface mock-ups.

During software development two usability studies were run to inform subsequent development. The first used static representations of page layouts and participants conducted walkthroughs of making and receiving a referral whilst thinking aloud (verbalising their thoughts and reactions). Voice recordings were made and difficulties, interpretations and comments about the interaction were noted.

A second study with a fully interactive version of the system was used with participants who worked unaided through a pre-planned series of tasks (for example searching for a specific previous patient referral). Written patient scenarios were used for content and a facilitator (surgeon) acted as the opposite end of the referral to provide appropriate responses. A moderator (human factors engineer) observed for errors, difficulties and comments and interactions were recorded using the Bandicam screen capture software.

Observations were subsequently analysed by counting the type and frequency of difficulties/confusion by task step and summing across participants. These were assigned severity ratings with respect to impact on task completion or risk. Subsequently, these were developed into recommendations and prioritised as either essential, desirable or optional for further development by the project team.

Usability studies have well recognised benefits in the HFE and software engineering disciplines including ensuring user requirements are elicited and identifying problems early in the design cycle [15]. A practical challenge for running such studies in situ is having access to participants for a sufficient period as clinical demands often take precedence. Running a flexible schedule and setting up the test room close to the clinical areas were two ways to mitigate this.

2.3   Implementation Phase

Determining post-implementation uptake of the referral software was a challenge as a reliable data source to record *all* referrals did not exist (a common situation with telephone-based consultations). Instead we used a known, reliable number – patients admitted – and cross-referenced this figure with referrals made via the new system. The proportion of admitted patients that had previously been referred via the new system could then be calculated.

A benefit of using routinely recorded hospital data is the low collection effort as a large number of records can be analysed from a single extraction run. A caution is that hospital episode coding can be unreliable, for example the complexity of comorbidities may be reduced to one or two codes. In practice this meant a clinician was required to review and sense check the disease classifications.

The Structured What-If Technique (SWIFT) provided a top-down approach to establishing potential failure points, resulting risks and mitigations [13]. Guide words from the London patient safety framework [14] were used against steps in the referral process (e.g. register with software). The analysis team comprised a clinician, two software developers and a human factors engineer. An advantage of this method over a bottom-up approach such as the Healthcare Failure Mode and Effects Analysis (HFMEA) is that a detailed description of each task is not required. In practice SWIFT was also used in the design phase as some risks were mitigated through design.

2.4   Evaluation Phase

Process. The process description highlighted that a delay point for referrers was accessing the neurosurgery on-call specialist via the hospital switchboard. This step was thus
selected as a process measure and the number of calls to the specialist on-call bleep
(pager) was collected from automatically generated logs. The limitation with this source
was that no distinction was made between calls originating internally or externally and
there was no indication if the call was ultimately connected. We anticipated that the system would have most benefit for referrals from other hospitals, thus, external calls were
also recorded prospectively by switchboard operators. A paper pro forma was developed
to tally calls and to keep a record if a connection between the caller and specialist had
been established.

An advantage of using this method is that we had greater confidence in establishing
if calls were responded to and as those collecting the data were removed from the referral
task there was no risk of bias. This method relied on the diligence of operators so daily
visits were made to engage with staff, collect the pro formas and provide encouragement.
A practical drawback of this approach was the subsequent time-onerous need to manually
transfer data to spreadsheets.

Routinely collected admissions data was used to calculate the period between
admission and the start of surgery, a proxy for timeliness of care.

Referral Quality. The quality of the referrals was measured with the collection and
analysis of two types of referral data: 1) core information fields, such as patient date of
birth, name of referring clinician and patient location, and 2) clinical details, such as the
reason for referral and the cognitive state of the patient.

For the pre-intervention phase, data was collected by the on-call specialist who was
given a paper form in the format of an easily carried A5-sized book. Fields for patient
name, date of birth and time of referral were marked, otherwise the page was unformatted.
This reflected the blank sheets of paper typically used for recording incoming referrals.
For post-intervention referral information was extracted from the system database and
exported as csv files.

For each core information field referrals (252 pre; 269 post) were tallied for the
presence or absence of core fields and converted to a percentage. A benefit of this
approach was an unambiguous comparison of the pre and post conditions that was
straightforward for a non-clinician to analyse. For the clinical content the specialist's
record of the referral was retrospectively reviewed by two neurosurgery doctors. Using
pre-defined criteria a judgement was made if there was sufficient information recorded
to be able to process the referral. This specialism specific experience was invaluable to
make an informed judgement on quality. A practical disadvantage was obtaining time
from busy clinicians to conduct the audit.

3   Conclusion

In agreement with Carayon et al. [5] we recommend the use of both qualitative and quantitative data when conducted HFE projects in healthcare. In work systems a change rarely

effects just one outcome, by using methods to collect both process and quality/outcome data a more comprehensive understanding of impact can be obtained.

The use of multiple data sources in the referenced referral system project provided greater confidence that the implementation had benefit. For example, in isolation a reduction in the number of calls to the on-call specialist cannot be necessarily interpreted as a benefit – it may mean poorer communication about patients, or that the referral rate has declined. By collecting data in parallel on the number and quality of referrals we observed the quality of information communicated improved and that changes were underpinned by a stable referral rate.

As Shorrock and Williams report, a barrier to the use of HFE methods can be that practitioners view them as not relevant in, or generalisable to, their organisational setting [6]. This chapter has sought to provide some concrete examples of how HFE methods can have relevance to applied hospital improvement projects.

References

1. Subramanyam, R., Mahmoud, M., Buck, D., Varughese, A.: Infusion medication error reduction by two-person verification: a quality improvement initiative. Pediatrics, **138**(6) (2016)
2. Quon, J.S., Dilauro, M., Ryan, J.G.: Disinfection of the radiologist workstation and radiologist hand hygiene: a single institution practice quality improvement project. Can. Assoc. Radiol. J. **68**(3), 270–275 (2017)
3. Wilson, J.R.: Fundamentals of systems ergonomics/human factors. Appl. Ergon. **45**(1), 5–13 (2014)
4. Westbrook, J.I., Braithwaite, J., Georgiou, A., Ampt, A., Creswick, N., Coiera, E., Iedema, R.: Multimethod evaluation of information and communication technologies in health in the context of wicked problems and sociotechnical theory. J. Am. Med. Inform. Assoc. JAMIA. **14**, 746–755 (2007)
5. Carayon, P., Kianfar, S., Li, Y., Xie, A., Alyousef, B., Wooldridge, A.: A systematic review of mixed methods research on human factors and ergonomics in health care. Appl. Ergon. **51**, 291–321 (2015)
6. Shorrock, S.T., Williams, C.A.: Human factors and ergonomics methods in practice: three fundamental constraints. Theor. Issues Ergon. Sci. **17**(5–6), 468–482 (2016)
7. Xie, A., Carayon, P.: A systematic review of human factors and ergonomics (HFE)-based healthcare system redesign for quality of care and patient safety. Ergonomics **58**(1), 33–49 (2015)
8. Amarouche, M., Neville, J.J., Deacon, S., Kalyal, N., Adams, N., Cheserem, B., Curley, D., DeSouza, R.M., Hafiz, F., Jayawardena, T., et al.: Referrers' point of view on the referral process to neurosurgery and opinions on neurosurgeons: a large-scale regional survey in the UK. BMJ Open **7**(11), (2017)
9. Choo, M.C., Thennakon, S., Shapey, J., Tolias, C.M.: A web-based referral system for neurosurgery–solution to our problems? Br. J. Neurosurg. **25**(3), 384–387 (2011)
10. Kim-Hwang, J.E., Chen, A.H., Bell, D.S., Guzman, D., Yee, H.F., Kushel, M.B.: Evaluating electronic referrals for specialty care at a public hospital. J. Gen. Intern. Med. **25**(10), 1123–1128 (2010)
11. Savoy, A., Patel, H., Flanagan, M.E., Weiner, M., Russ, A.L.: Systematic heuristic evaluation of computerized consultation order templates: clinicians' and human factors engineers' perspectives. J. Med. Syst. **41**(8) (2017)

12. Weiner, M., Savoy, A., Barker, B.C.: Gains, losses, and uncertainties from computerizing referrals and consultations. Appl. Ergon. **89**, (2020)
13. Woodward, M., De Pennington, N., Grandidge, C., McCulloch, P., Morgan, L.: Development and evaluation of an electronic hospital referral system: a human factors approach. Ergonomics **63**(6), 710–723 (2020)
14. Jun, G.T., Ward, J., Morris, Z., Clarkson, J.: Health care process modelling: which method when? Int. J. Qual. Health Care **21**(3), 214–224 (2009)
15. Beuscart-Zéphir, M.C,, Aarts, J., Elkin, P.: Human factors engineering for healthcare IT clinical applications. Int. J. Med. Inform. **79**, 223–224 (2010)

The Problems of the Interfaces of the ICU Mechanical Ventilators Evidenced by Covid-19

Maria Clara Muniz Zenderski🆔 and Paulo Miranda de Oliveira(✉)🆔

Federal University of Juiz de Fora, Juiz de Fora, Brazil
mariaclara.zenderski@estudante.ufjf.br,
paulo.miranda@ufjf.edu.br

Abstract. With the COVID-19 pandemic, multiple transformations succeeded, including the demand for ICU mechanical ventilators, the main equipment to meet the most serious manifestations of the disease. The mechanical ventilators companies, however, were unable to respond to the new volume of orders due to logistical, manufacturing, design and financial problems. Emphasizing the scope of ergonomics, works published within the last 15 years that analysed the interfaces of respirators were reviewed, and, as a result, it was possible to verify the various failures of human factors existing in mechanical ventilators. The pandemic scenario, because of the observed consequences, highlighted the importance of a good interface, as well as the simplification of design, which can bring advantages not only for moments of crisis but also for the common hospital routine. It was concluded that, due to their aptitudes, human factors and design are vital disciplines for proposing solutions to the project problems of respirators highlighted during the pandemic.

Keywords: Mechanical ventilators · Interface · COVID-19 · Ergonomics · Design and healthcare

1 Introduction

In 2020 the world was surprised by the emergence of the Coronavirus Disease 19 (COVID-19) pandemic, caused by the Severe Acute Respiratory Syndrome Coronavirus 2 (Sars-CoV-2), until then unknown, and which first cases were recorded at the end of 2019 in the Chinese city of Wuhan [1, 2].

As the months passed, scientists developed studies that aimed to understand the properties of the new virus, while, in parallel, the disease spread across the globe. Because of this, on March 11, 2020, the World Health Organization (WHO) classified this outbreak as a pandemic [2–4].

The analysis of the scenario and the epidemiological curves evidenced the high transmissibility of the new disease, a finding that caused fears about the capacity of hospitals to meet the possible demand of patients. Thus, measures of social distancing were adopted with the intention of preventing the wide contamination of the population in a short period of time and avoiding the overcrowding of Intensive Care Units (ICUs) [5, 6].

Both the disease and the isolation measures adopted to combat it brought changes in multiple areas and on a global scale: the Gross Domestic Product (GDP) of all countries in the second quarter of 2020, with the exception of China and India, has regressed; the consumption in virtual media grew exponentially, with, for example, a 75% increase in delivery services in the United States of America (USA), when compared to 2019; cultural events - like the Olympics or the Cannes Festival - have been postponed [7–10].

The healthcare field, which took on the role of "front of battle", needed to adapt to new demands. In the United States, for example, they predicted that hospitals' capacity might not be sufficient to meet demand expectations. In Italy these predictions came true, with reports from doctors who had to choose which patient would receive treatment as a result of overcrowding and inadequate supply of medical devices. In Deagu, South Korea, there were cases of people dying at home, waiting for a bed in the hospital [11, 12].

Similar situations became even more adverse because of the conflict between the progressive number of patients and the finite number of specialized health professionals, who, in addition to suffering from exhaustion and fatigue, were particularly subject to contracting the pathogen, needing to move away from their work duties. In response to the shortage of professionals, one of the actions embraced consisted of relocating doctors and nurses with other specialties or even students in the health field to work in the care of patients infected with COVID-19 [13–15].

In the medical area, it was necessary to deal with the absence of several products, however, it was the mechanical ventilators that took the protagonism, since they were one of the main medical devices to combat the most serious cases [6, 11]. From the first weeks of pandemics, forecasts indicated that the existing mechanical ventilators would not be sufficient to meet demand. The United Kingdom (UK), for instance, in March, had around 8.000 mechanical ventilators equipment, but estimated that they would need 30.000 machines [16, 17].

In view of this reality, several manufacturers of the device have expanded their production. The market leader, Hamilton, increased its production from 220 mechanical ventilators produced weekly to 400 units in the same period [18]. However, measures like this proved insufficient, since, as Izetzki and Reichardt (2020) showed, the demand for mechanical respirators would be about nine times greater than the global production capacity [17].

In this context, alternative measures have been developed by universities and companies. These included projects of alternative mechanical ventilators that, in some cases, proposed a form to mechanize a Bag-Valve-Mask (BVM), such as the E-vent, developed by the Massachusetts Institute of Technology (MIT). Others have taken different paths, such as *Mechanical Ventilatori Milano* (MVM), which uses pressurized oxygen to activate the equipment. There was also a project that adapted diving masks from the famous chain of Decathlon stores into an emergency mask for hospital respirators. Moreover, there was the use of mechanical ventilators to serve two patients simultaneously [19–22].

The inability of the medical industry to follow the growth of the contagion of the virus was partly resulted from the inherent characteristics of the project and the manufacturing process of the equipment. The device is extremely sensitive and requires time to assemble, being composed of numerous specific parts and complex software [23, 24]. Additionally, to do so, it is necessary "[…] considerable expertise in re-search, design and manufacturing" and "[…] means ensuring reliability, serviceability and adherence to strict regulatory standards." (PANDOLFO, 2020) [21].

Consequently, they have high prices, which varied between $50.000 and $20.000 dollars, when it comes to mechanical ventilators of last generations; transport ventilators ranged from $15.000 to $8.000 dollars while basic ventilators cost between $1.000 and $500 dollars [25].

The equipment factories, in normal periods, usually work close to their capacity. On account of the virus, in March, many of them were already producing more than usual, with manufacturers needing to deal with limitations in the supply of the device's components, which could be considered the main impediment to production [24].

This design complexity and high prices, formerly, already made up the equipment. However, the context of urgency caused by the pandemic was able to highlight the mechanical ventilators, as well as their points of vulnerability, which, if improved, can positively impact the results in daily use, or even in a future health crisis.

2 Analysis of Mechanical Ventilators Interfaces

Since the 1940s and 1950s, with the origin of positive-pressure invasive ventilators for use in ICUs, the device's design has undergone an extensive and significant evolution, which includes the development of techniques to increase patients comfort, addition and improvement of alarms, the use of microprocessors, among many other advances that allowed the best capacity of the most recent mechanical ventilators. On the other hand, the complexity of the interfaces has increased. While in the 1980s the parameters of the ventilator were adjusted by simple and mostly accessible mechanical buttons, the interfaces of the following decades were based on computer screens, with several tabs and between 20 and 40 variables of monitoring information [26, 27].

In order to understand the present condition of the equipment, nine studies were analysed that address the interfaces of the ICU mechanical ventilators belonging to the "Fourth-Generation", according to the classification of Kacmarek (2011). Studies with a publication date prior to 2005 were excluded [26], (Table 1):

Table 1. Articles about the interfaces of ICU mechanical ventilators.

Title	Authors/year/country	Ventilator	Participants	Methodology
Usability heuristics and qualitative indicators for the usability evaluation of touch screen ventilator systems	Katre, Bhutkar and Karmarkar (2014) [28] India	3 touch screen ventilators by different manufacturers. Names of manufacturers and equipment models uninformed	4 usability evaluators that studied ventilator systems with the help of specialist	Heuristic evaluation

(*continued*)

Table 1. (*continued*)

Title	Authors/year/country	Ventilator	Participants	Methodology
The usability of ventilators: a comparative evaluation of use safety and user experience	Morita *et al.* (2016) [29] USA	G5 (Hamilton); PB980 (Covidien); SERVO-U; (Maquet); Evita Infinity V500 (Dräger)	48 critical care respiratory therapists (RTs) with equivalent knowledge of the ventilators tested	Tasks with use errors or close calls (UE/CCs); Post-Study System Usability Questionnaire (PSSUQ); National Aeronautics and Space Administration Task Load Index (NASA-TLX); Debriefing interview
Usability study of the user-interface of intensive care ventilators based on user test and eye-tracking signals	Jiang *et al.* (2018a) [30] China	Evita 4 (Dräger); Servo I (Maquet); Boaray 5000D (Probe)	16 RTs that received a operational training on the tested ventilators before the formal study	Test tasks (completion time and error rate); Eye-Tracking Signals; Questionnaire using Likert scales; Interview
Comprehensive evaluation of user interface for ventilators based on respiratory therapists' performance, workload, and user experience	Jiang *et al.* (2018b) [31] China	Evita 4 (Dräger); Servo I (Maquet); Boaray 5000D (Probe)	16 RTs who had ventilator operation experience, basic knowledge of mechanical ventilation and use of equipment in your work routine. Before the test, the participants received operational training in the studied ventilators	Test tasks (completion time and error rate); Measurement of blink rate and duration; NASA-TLX; USE Questionnaire
The usability of ventilator maintenance user interface: a comparative evaluation of user task performance, workload, and user experience	Jiang *et al.* (2020) [32] China	Evita 4 (Dräger); Servo I (Maquet); Boaray 5000D (Probe)	16 RTs who had experience in ventilator maintenance and before the test received a maintenance training in the ventilators analysed	Test tasks (completion time and error rate); Duration of eye-fixation; NASA-TLX; User experience questionnaire

Jiang *et al.* (2018b) and Katre, Bhutkar and Karmarkar (2014) highlighted the importance of the interface in the results of users actions and in guaranteeing security; Morita *et al.* (2016, p. 7) reached a similar conclusion, detailing that the different results *"could be explained by interaction design, quality of hardware components used in manufacturing, and influence of consumer product technology on users' expectation"*. Jiang *et al.* (2018a), through the analysis of the selected mechanical ventilators, discovered that they had poor ergonomics, high error rates and long task completion times when compared to other studies. Similarly, Katre, Bhutkar and Karmarkar (2014) have noted that the interface design needs improvement. Jiang *et al.* (2020), in a different perspective, evaluated the maintenance interface of mechanical ventilators, but also detected the presence of poor interface design and the high task error rates [28–32].

The studies by Jiang *et al.* (2018b, 2020) recognized difficulty with the on/off button, which position varied between models. Jiang *et al.* (2018a, 2018b) identified a lack of uniformity in the taxonomy of the modes and parameters used between the analysed devices; and Jiang et al. (2020) detected imprecision in the translation of the self-test information. Jiang et al. (2018a) identified variations in the type of adjustment of parameters and modes between the models analysed, which, according to the author, *"[...] resulted in unnecessary operational failures and increased the task completion times"* (JIANG, *et al.*, 2018a, p. 6624); they also informed that the most frequent failure was the recognition of the monitored values, with the recognition of the mode and settings in second place. Alarm identification and management occupied the third position, a function also emphasised by Jiang *et al.* (2018b), which suggests a faster identification of alarmed information. Morita *et al.* (2016) reported in his study problems with the sensitivity of the screens in the equipment they evaluated. Jiang *et al.* (2020) detected adversities in verifying the battery status, difficulty in disassembly and installation of the air filter, and problems in the positioning and font size of the self-test information [29–32].

Of the nine studies analysed, four were highlighted, since they matched better with the objectives of this article.

The Japanese study by Uzawa, Yamata and Suzukawa (2008) performed, with a team of 21 medical residents with basic knowledge of mechanical ventilation, 8 tasks in order to assess the interfaces of mechanical ventilators, using 4 modern ICU respirators - Evita XL (Dräger), Servo-i (Maquet), e500 (Newport) and PB 840 (Medtronic) - with different interface models, whose first contact of the participants occurred just before the tests, through a short manual read in 5 min. Through a subjective evaluation and the analysis of the number of failures and the time spent to complete each task, 23% of total operational failures were registered as a result, which occurred mainly during the configuration of the mechanical ventilator. Difficulties have been reported due to the variation in terminology between the devices, as well as the variation of layouts such as the inspiratory and expiratory ports or the on/off button, which differed from positioning, confusing users and generating errors. It was finally possible to prove the impact of the interface on the result of the doctor's management [33].

The work of Vignaux, Tassaux and Jolliet (2009), analysed 5 pulmonologists and 5 anaesthesiologists with experience in ventilation, but who had no practice with ICU mechanical ventilators in their work routine, performing 8 tasks in a sample of 7 respiratores that have never been used by participating physicians - Elysée (Saime-Resmed), Engström Carestation (GE), Evita XL (Dräger), Servo I (Maquet), G5 (Hamilton), Avea (Viasys), PB840 (Medtronic). The result demonstrated the absence of good ergonomics, since all doctors took longer than expected to perform the proposed tasks. There were, in addition, reports of delayed and impossible user-machine interactions, including difficulties in turning on the device and, among the task which doctors had more difficulties, are the recognition of the mode and parameters, the configuration of the pressure support and finding and activating the NIV mode [34].

Maia's work (2014), developed in Brazil, consisted of an analysis of the mechanical ventilator ix5 (Intermed/Carefusion), based on the heuristic assessment of Jakob Nielsen made after the execution of activities by 8 professionals with experience in mechanical ventilation - 3 doctors, 3 physiotherapists and 2 nurses. As a result, 93 failures were detected, which were classified as aesthetic, minimal, important and critical problems. Among the problems classified as "critical" were, for example: difficulty in accessing some functions and desired information (*weight of the patient by sex; flow sensitivity; ideal weight x height, etc.*); confusions generated by the interfaces (*excess of information on the main screen; "alarms" screen very similar to "adjustments" screen; fast screen change; small numbers; lack of sensitivity on the screen, slow feed-back in some functions, etc.*) [35].

The research by Marjanovic *et al.* (2017), examines the mechanical ventilators by four dimensions - error tolerance; ease of use; efficiency; and engagement. To study ergonomics, 20 experienced ICU doctors were analysed according to time and numbers of failures during 11 monitoring or configuration activities using 6 modern ICU respirators that were not previously known by the participants - V500 (Dräger); PB980 (Covidien); V680 (Philips); S1 (Hamilton); R860 (General Electrics); and Servo-U (Maquet). Psycho-cognitive assessments were performed as well, measuring the usability of the device (System Usability Scale - SUS), the mental workload (NASA– TLX), and physiological parameters (*pupil diameter, heart and respiratory rate and thoracic volume*). As a product of the research, the interface ergonomics was judged as inadequate. The participants had difficulties in crucial functions such as reading the configurations, one of the tasks considered more difficult, regardless of the device, which probable reason derives from the "*[...] absence of a homogenized terminology among manufacturers*". (Marjanovic *et al.* 2017, p.7). It was reported difficulties to turn in some of the models analysed, to activate the NIV and a lack of sensitivity on the screen. In addition, some devices had a high level of failure, high metal workload and low usability score [36].

During medical care, human error is frequent, being one of the main factors responsible for mortality among patients. In the management of a medical equipment, the user's actions can be persuaded by the interfaces, since "*a user's behaviour is directly influenced by operating characteristics of the equipment; user interfaces that are misleading or illogical can induce errors by even the most skilled users*" (Sawyer, 1996, p.3). Although the complete elimination of human error is unreal, it is possible to reduce its indexes in the medical field through the development of interface projects that consider human skills and limitations [36–38].

3 Ergonomics and Design

In the scope of project development and due to the COVID-19 pandemic scenario, two characteristics of respirators stood out: the complexity of the interfaces and the complexity of the project. The first, which was already confusing even for specialized individuals, would be even more complicated for professionals relocated during the health crisis; the second, in turn, contributed to blocking the full attendance of the demand of the device.

This context may have helped in the formation of a new perception of design, focused on a mechanical ventilator that is easier to build and interact with, capable of meeting larger demands in critical times and improving the human-machine relationship. This differs from the direction taken by the ICU ventilator projects in recent decades, which the majority opted for the improvement of technical performance, generated by investments in engineering [26].

To respond to this new design gap, formed by old problems, the simultaneous performance of ergonomics and design is essential.

Ergonomics, also called human factors, is a discipline *"concerned with the understanding of interactions among humans and other elements of a system, and the profession that applies theory, principles, data and methods to design in order to optimize human well-being and overall system performance"* (IEA, 2021). In a broad view, it can be divided into three categories: physical ergonomics, specialized in the study of human physical characteristics; cognitive ergonomics, which focuses on human mental processes; and organizational ergonomics that studies the socio-technical systems [39].

The importance of ergonomics in respirators during the pandemic was highlighted by the Chartered Institute of Ergonomics and Human Factors (CIEHF), which developed documents with comprehensive content to guide the application of human factors in the manufacture and design of the device. CIEHF emphasizes the merit of a good and intuitive interface and the importance of knowing the characteristics and needs of users, with focus on relocated professionals, who commonly have little or no experience with the device. It also addresses the need to think about the device's tasks, the usage environment, the analysis of possible risks, in addition to talking about the instructions for use and training [40].

With its attributes, this faculty, especially cognitive ergonomics, is crucial to lead the development of a mechanical ventilator interface suitable for human skills and limitations, contributing to the reduction of errors during use, increased efficiency and reduced frustration [40].

Design can be a promising partner in the application of ergonomic concepts in a project. Much more than just *"styling"*, design is defined as the development of intelligent solutions for facing problems [41]. It is also a strategic discipline that works using its own methodologies aimed at building an effective final product to meet the needs and desires of the target audience [42]. Baxter (1998), for example, presents a methodology that organizes decisions over the project development, seeking to manage risks and uncertainties. Besides, it guides the unfolding of the creative process, recognizing its flexible and interdisciplinary characteristics, as well the participation of the user's opinion, through market tests. This concept converges with the opinion of Vignaux, Tassaux and Jolliet (2009), who reinforces the value of a close relationship between manufacturers and users since the beginning of the project, in addition to observing them when handling the device, using the data collected for building a successful human-machine interface [34, 43].

In view of its properties, design can also assist in fulfilling the intention of making the design of mechanical ventilators less complex, through concepts such as Design for Manufacturing and Assembly (DFMA), which seeks to facilitate the manufacturing of parts and the assembly of the final product [44]. However, it is essential to underline that the application of DFMA in respirators requires special caution, since the numerous components and the recently improved technological development, promote better performance and, therefore, influence the safety and comfort of the patient [27].

The quest to confront the design problems highlighted in respirators can have positive consequences not only in pandemic contexts. In the common routine, for example, a well-developed interface contributes to a greater effectiveness in the training of professionals [45].

4 Conclusion

Similarly as the contributions related to the improvement of aircraft in World War II, which provided a better clarity on the significance of ergonomics, the pandemic caused by COVID-19 allowed a new look at the design of ICU mechanical ventilators, making evident the problems already existing in the project, such as the complexity of the interface and the complexity of the project, with their respective consequences [46].

According to Marjanovic et al. (2011), ergonomics is as important as the technical performance of mechanical ventilators. When properly applied, it can reduce errors during use, increase efficiency and reduce user frustration. Furthermore, the simplification of the project has a positive impact on the time of manufacture and the final price of the product, a task performed by design and engineering. These qualities can benefit the use and manufacture of the product inside and outside periods of health crisis. To build solutions to these problems, it is essential to use the concepts of ergonomics and design methodology, considering the enormous importance of work at a multidisciplinary level [36, 40, 44].

However, it is worth noting that the norms of design standardization of mechanical ventilators, such as the one advocated by Uzawa, Yamata and Suzukawa (2008), can hinder the development of innovations, which would be essential for the design progress. It is interesting to leave the regulation only for taxonomic topics [33].

References

1. EBSERH - Hospitais Universitários Federais: Plano de contingência com medidas de prevenção e controle a serem adotadas durante a assistência aos casos suspeitos ou confirmados de infecção pelo novo coronavírus (2019-nCoV). Contingency Plan (2020). http://www2.ebserh.gov.br/documents/222842/0/Plano+de+Conting%C3%AAncia+-+COVID-19/af306dee-19d0-4bb1-8403-c236f8b9911e. Retrieved 31 Jan 2020

2. Gorbalenya, A.E., Baker, S.C., Baric, R.S., de Groot, R.J., Drosten, C., Gulyaeva, A.A., Ziebuhr, J.: Coronaviridae study group of the international committee on taxonomy of viruses. The species severe acute respiratory syndrome-related coronavirus: classifying 2019-nCoV and naming it SARS-CoV-2. Nat. Microbiol. **5**, 536–544 (2020)

3. Roser, M.: Our world in data global change data lab, University of Oxford, Oxford Martin Program. Is the world making progress against the pandemic? We built the chart to answer this question. Blog (2020). https://ourworldindata.org/epi-curve-covid-19#licence,%20last% 20accessed%202021/01/27. Retrieved 08 June 2020

4. Ducharme, J.: World Health Organization declares COVID-19 a 'Pandemic.' Here's what that means|Health COVID-19 (2020). TIME USA, LLC., Online News. https://time.com/579 1661/who-coronavirus-pandemic-declaration/. Retrieved 11 Mar 2020

5. Zorzetto, R.: Para conter o avanço explosivo|Redução precoce do contato social favorece o controle mais rápido do espalhamento do novo coronavírus (2020). Revista Pesquisa FAPESP. Revista Online. https://revistapesquisa.fapesp.br/para-conter-o-avanco-explosivo/. Retrieved Apr 2020

6. Iyengar, K., Bahl, S., Vaishya, R., Vaish, A.: Challenges and solutions in meeting up the urgent requirement of ventilators for COVID-19 patients. Diabetes Metab. Syndr. **14**(4), 499–501 (2020). https://www.ncbi.nlm.nih.gov/pmc/articles/PMC7198404/. Retrieved 07 Apr 2020

7. Elias, J.: PIB menos pior: veja o desempenho da economia do Brasil comparada ao mundo (2020). CNN Brasil Business. News Online. https://www.cnnbrasil.com.br/business/2020/09/ 01/pib-menos-pior-porem-mais-mortes-por-covid-19-veja-o-brasil-comparado-ao-mundo. Retrieved 01 Sept 2020

8. Gazeta Esportiva: Olimpíadas de Tóquio têm nova data definida após adiamento (2020). News Online. https://www.gazetaesportiva.com/olimpiadas-2020/olimpiadas-de-toq uio-tem-novas-datas-definidas-apos-adiamento/. Retrieved from 30 Mar 2020

9. Ghosh, I., Visual Capitalist, Markets: How U.S. consumers are spending differently during COVID-19 (2020). News Online. https://www.visualcapitalist.com/how-u-s-consumers-are-spending-differently-during-covid-19/. Retrieved 21 May 2020

10. JORNAL DO COMÉRCIO | O JORNal de economia e negócios do RS. (14/04/2020). Festival de Cannes não terá edição em 2020 por causa do novo coronavírus. News Online. Retrieved from https://www.jornaldocomercio.com/_conteudo/cultura/2020/04/734452-fes tival-de-cannes-nao-tera-edicao-em-2020-por-causa-do-novo-coronavirus.html.

11. Emanuel, E.J., Persad, G., Upshur, R., Thome, B., Parker, M., Glickman, A., Phillips, J.P.: Fair allocation of scarce medical resources in the time of Covid-19. N. Engl. J. Med. **382**, 2049–2055 (2020). https://www.nejm.org/doi/full/10.1056/nejmsb2005114

12. Besser, L., ABC News Australia: Italy's coronavirus disaster: at first, officials urged people to go out for an aperitif. Now, doctors must choose who dies. News Online. https://www.abc. net.au/news/2020-03-18/what-went-wrong-with-how-italy-handled-coronavirus/12062242

13. Bielicki, J.A., Duval, X., Gobat, N., Goossens, H., Koopmans, M., Tacconelli, E., van der Werf, S.: Monitoring approaches for health-care workers during the COVID-19 pandemic. Lancet Infect. Dis. **20**, e261–e267 (2020). https://www.google.com/url?sa=t&rct=j&q=& esrc=s&source=web&cd=&ved=2ahUKEwiG9iY9MvuAhW6KLkGdvZChMQFjAAegQI hAC&url=https%3A%2F%2Fwww.thelancet.com%2Fpdfs%2Fjournals%2Flaninf%2FPIIS 1473-3099(20)30458-8.pdf&usg=AOv-Vaw0sxG7HkTbx2bfxoZkdSrwD

14. Dunn, M., Sheehan, M., Hordern, J., Turnham, H.L., Wilkinson, D.: 'Your country needs you': the ethics of allocating staff to high-risk clinical roles in the management of patients with COVID-19. J. Med. Ethics **46**(7), 436–440 (2020). https://pubmed.ncbi.nlm.nih.gov/324 09625/

15. Mutair, A.A., Amr, A., Ambani, Z., Salman, K.A., Schwebius, D.: Nursing surge capacity strategies for management of critically Ill adults with COVID-19. Nurs. Rep. **10**, 23–32 (2020). https://www.mdpi.com/2039-4403/10/1/4/pdf
16. Jack, S.: BBC News Business: Manufacturers cast doubt on ventilator target, 29 March 2020. News Online. https://www.bbc.com/news/business-52083998
17. Ilzetzki, E., Reichardt, H., VOXeu CEPR: Ramping up ventilator production: lessons from WWII, 17 April 2020. News Online. https://voxeu.org/article/ramping-ventilator-production-lessons-wwii
18. REVISTA EXAME | Ciência: Por que os respiradores viraram o ponto crítico no tratamento da covid-19, 23 March 2020. News Online. https://exame.com/ciencia/por-que-os-respiradores-viraram-o-ponto-critico-no-tratamento-da-covid-19/
19. Slocum, A., Rus, D., Hanumara, N., Kwon, A., Nabzdyk, C., Slocum, A., Diamond, P.: MIT Emergency Ventilator Project, 22 June 2020. Project Online Site. https://emergency-vent.mit.edu/
20. Geggel, L., Live Science | Future US Inc.: Sharing a single ventilator between 4 patients is possible. But it could be disastrous. 26 March 2020. News Online. https://www.livescience.com/coronavirus-emergency-ventillator-capacity-increase.html
21. Pandolfo, B., The Conversation US, Inc.: ICU ventilators: what they are, how they work and why it's hard to make more, 06 April 2020. News Online. https://theconversation.com/icu-ventilators-what-they-are-how-they-work-and-why-its-hard-to-make-more-135423
22. Pooler, M., Miller, J., Kuchler, H., Bushey, C.: The Financial Times Ltd.: The ventilator challenge will test ingenuity to the limit, April 2020. News Online. https://www.ft.com/content/28bc27d1-8561-4838-bd71-0d7884a15dfa.
23. Lee, A.: WIRED Daily: How does a car company make a ventilator? 19 March 2020, News Online. https://www.wired.co.uk/article/car-manufacturers-ventilators
24. Cohn, J.: HuffPost Politics: How to get more ventilators and what to do if we can't, 17 March 2020. News Online. https://www.huffpost.com/entry/coronavirus-ventilators-supply-manufacture_n_5e6dc4f7c5b6747ef11e8134?guccounter=1
25. Yock, P.: Stanford Biodesign: A more affordable ventilator: an interview with Matt Callaghan of OneBreath (n.d.). Site Institucional. https://biodesign.stanford.edu/our-impact/technologies/onebreath.html
26. Kacmarek, R.M.: The mechanical ventilator: past, present, and future. Respir Care. **56**(8), 1170–1180 (2011). http://rc.rcjournal.com/content/56/8/1170/tab-pdf
27. Richard, J.C.M., Kacmarek, R.M.: ICU mechanical ventilators, technological advances vs. user friendliness: the right picture is worth a thousand numbers. Intensive Care. Med. **35**(10), 1662–1663 (2009). https://link.springer.com/content/pdf/10.1007/s00134-009-1581-6.pdf
28. Katre, D., Bhutkar, G., Karmarkar, S.: Usability heuristics and qualitative indicators for the usability evaluation of touch screen ventilator systems. In: HWID: IFIP Working Conference on Human Work Interaction Design, vol. 316, pp. 83–97 (2010). https://link.springer.com/content/pdf/10.1007%2F978-3-642-11762-6_8.pdf.
29. Morita, P.P., Weinstein, P.B., Flewwelling, C.J., Bañez, C.A., Chiu, T.A., Iannuzzi, M., Cafazzo, J.A.: The usability of ventilators: a comparative evaluation of use safety and user experience. Crit. Care **20**(263), 1–9 (2016). https://ccforum.biomedcentral.com/track/pdf/10.1186/s13054-016-1431-1.pdf
30. Jiang, M., Liu, S., Feng, Q., Gao, J., Zhang, Q.: Usability study of the user-interface of intensive care ventilators based on user test and eye-tracking signals. Med. Sci. Monit. **24**, 6617–6629 (2018). https://www.medscimonit.com/download/index/idArt/909933.
31. Jiang, M., Liu, S., Gao, J., Feng, Q., Zhang, Q.: Comprehensive evaluation of user interface for ventilators based on respiratory therapists' performance. Med. Sci. Monit. **24**, 9090–9101 (2018). https://www.medscimonit.com/download/index/idArt/911853

32. Jiang, M., Sun, D., Li, Q., Wang, D.: The usability of ventilator maintenance user interface: a comparative evaluation of user task performance, workload, and user experience. Sci. Prog. **103**(4), 1–18 (2020). https://journals.sagepub.com/doi/pdf/10.1177/0036850420962885
33. Uzawa, Y., Yamada, Y., Suzukawa, M.: Evaluation of the user interface simplicity in the modern generation of mechanical ventilators. Respir. Care **53**(3), 329–337 (2008). https://scholar.google.com/scholar_url?url=http://rc.rcjournal.com/content/respcare/53/3/329.full.pdf&hl=pt-BR&sa=T&oi=ucasa&ct=ufr&ei=0MUZYNryOYOBy9YP0reL0AU&scisig=AAGBfm0jKrb6f-ulozROPQ3ZvhAaxF3kA
34. Vignaux, L., Tassaux, D., Jolliet, P.: Evaluation of the user-friendliness of seven new generation intensive care ventilators. Intensive Care Med. **35**(10), 1687–1691 (2009). https://doi.org/10.1007/s00134-009-1580-7
35. Maia, N.P.S.: A new method based on heuristic evaluation and realistic simulation for the development of mechanical ventilators centered on the user interface (PÓS-GRADUAÇÃO STRICTO SENSU EM CIÊNCIAS MÉDICAS, FAMED - DMC - UFC) (2014). http://www.repositorio.ufc.br/bitstream/riufc/10985/1/2014_dis_npsmaia.pdf
36. Marjanovic, N.S., Simone, A.D., Jegou, G., L'Her, E.: A new global and comprehensive model for ICU ventilator performances evaluation. Ann. Intensive Care **7**(68), 1–13 (2017). https://annalsofintensivecare.springeropen.com/track/pdf/10.1186/s13613-017-0285-2.pdf
37. Richardson, W.C.: The National Academies of Sciences Engineering and Medicine: To Err is Human: Building a Safer Health System, 01 December 1999. Public Briefing. https://www8.nationalacademies.org/onpinews/newsitem.aspx?RecordID=s9728
38. Sawyer, D.: CDRH Work Group: Do it by Design (Guidance). Springfield, Virginia 22161 (January 2007). https://www.google.com/url?sa=t&rct=j&q=&esrc=s&source=web&cd=&cad=rja&uact=8&ved=2ahUKEwjE2uPAnMzuAhXpLLkGWBOMQQFjAAegQIARAC&url=https%3A%2F%2Felsmar.com%2Fpdf_files%2FFDA_fies%2FDOITPDF.PDF&usg=AOvVaw0pqDKafD3lzdhq-SfSsrW8
39. International Ergonomics Association I IEA: Definition, Domains of Specialization, Systemic Approach. IEA Institutional Site (n.d.). https://iea.cc/definition-and-domains-of-ergonomics/
40. Chartered Institute of Ergonomics Human Factors I CIEHF: Human factors in the design and operation of Ventilators for Covid-19 I Guidance from the Chartered Institute of Ergonomics and Human Factors (Guidance). https://www.ergonomics.org.uk/common/Uploaded%20files/HF_in_Design_of_Ventilators_Final_01April.pdf, 01 April 2020
41. Bonsiepe, G.: Design, Cultura e Sociedade, 1st edn. Blucher, São Paulo, SP (2011)
42. Phillips, P.L.: Briefing: A Gestão do Projeto de Design, 1st edn. Blucher, São Paulo, SP (2008)
43. Baxter, M.: Projeto de Produto: Guia Prático Para o Design de Novos Produtos, 3rd edn. Blucher, São Paulo, SP (2011)
44. Boothroyd, G., Dewhurst, P., Knight, W.A.: Product Design for Manufacture and Assembly, 3rd edn. CRC Press, Cleveland, Ohio, EUA (2010)
45. Hodges, E., Griffiths, A., Richardson, J., Blunt, M., Young, P.: Emergency capnography monitoring: comparing ergonomic design of intensive care unit ventilator interfaces and specific training of staff in reducing time to activation. Anaesthesia **67**(8), 850–854 (2012). https://associationofanaesthetists-publications.onlinelibrary.wiley.com/toc/13652044/2012/67/8
46. Hendrick, H.W.: The technology of ergonomics. Theor. Issues Ergon. Sci. **1**(1), 22–23 (2010). https://scholar.google.com/scholar_url?url=https://www.tandfonline.com/doi/pdf/10.1080/146392200308453&hl=pt-BR&sa=T&oi=ucasa&ct=usl&ei=o9oZYMP5CePKsQLKtYWYBw&scisig=AAGBfm1czCn05DK_y8g4d1kS-czbYt6KYA

Part III: HF/E Contribution to Cope with Covid-19 (Edited by Sara Albolino, Tommaso Bellandi, and Andrew Todd)

It Takes Two to Tango: Communication at Work During the COVID-19 Pandemic

Caroline Adam$^{(\boxtimes)}$ and Klaus Bengler

Chair of Ergonomics, Technical University of Munich, Munich, Germany
{caroline.adam,bengler}@tum.de

Abstract. At the beginning of the year 2020, the new coronavirus SARS-CoV-2 triggered a worldwide pandemic. To contain the infections, far-reaching measures were taken that had a major impact on social life. The need to keep physical distance has changed the way employees behave and communicate.

To better understand how the pandemic is changing the daily work of employees, this paper provides initial insights into the communication in terms of *access to information, lack of information, accuracy of the information received*, and *satisfaction with the communication relationship* with superiors, colleagues and subordinates of university staff in the field of mechanical engineering in Germany during the pandemic. Data collection took place on two occasions when the COVID-19 case numbers in Germany were high. In addition to communication, working conditions and the equipment that employees had at their disposal when working from home were analyzed. Finally, changes in the use of digital working resources were investigated and differences between the two periods of data collection were examined.

The results indicate that there is room for improvement regarding working conditions while working from home and that the use of digital means for work changed between the two periods of data collection. Communication in terms of access to information, the accuracy of the information received, and satisfaction with the communication relationship with superiors, as well as the access to information with colleagues, deteriorated between the two data collection periods.

Keywords: COVID-19 · Pandemic · Communication · Work · Ergonomics

1 Background

The COVID-19 pandemic is leading to a rapid and forced transformation at work. Since strict rules and regulations must be implemented in the context of work; face-to-face communication and informal conversations in the corridor, during lunch breaks or after meetings are no longer possible. To maintain the distance between their employees, many companies have introduced remote working in various areas during the lockdowns. The pandemic led to a sharp increase in remote working in numerous companies [1]. Entire departments and teams had to work remotely, some of them for the first time, and did so almost from one day to the next.

© The Author(s), under exclusive license to Springer Nature Switzerland AG 2021
N. L. Black et al. (Eds.): IEA 2021, LNNS 222, pp. 495–503, 2021.
https://doi.org/10.1007/978-3-030-74611-7_67

The spatial distance between employees influences the communication at work. During the pandemic, the number of communication partners declined compared to the situation before COVID-19 and the frequency of communication decreased [2]. In contrast [3] determined an increase in the number of meetings per person and attendees per meeting. However, the length of meetings decreased. Numerous studies postulate the lack of personal and professional communication as a serious problem in the context of the COVID-19 pandemic [2, 4, 5]. Additionally, [6] emphasize the challenge of maintaining the emotional bond with employees despite the physical distances involved. The use of digital communication resources had to be introduced and implemented at extremely short notice and triggered a digitalization push [6]. However, due to the short time available for preparation, ergonomic working conditions, which are clear requirements for offices, could not be achieved in every home.

As we are dealing with an unprecedented situation, there is a great need to understand and explore the changes in the working environment in order to manage the crisis, however long it may last, and to be prepared for a post-pandemic period.

2   Research Objective

There were two survey periods for obtaining information on changes during the pandemic: April/May 2020 and December/January 2020/2021. During both periods, COVID-19 caseloads in Germany were high and working from home was mandatory or strongly recommended. The research questions are:

1. What were the working conditions for the university staff working from home during the pandemic at the different points of time?
2. Which digital working resources were used during the two data collection periods?
3. Are there differences in communication in terms of *access to information, lack of information, accuracy of the information received*, and *satisfaction with the communication relationship* with superiors, colleagues, and subordinates between the two data collection periods?

3   Study Design

To answer the research questions, quantitative data were collected at two different points in time during the pandemic using an online questionnaire in a university context. The sample, the structure of the questionnaire and the data processing are described below.

3.1   Sample

The questionnaire was distributed among mechanical engineering staff at a German university. In the first period of data collection (t_1) n $=$ 179 (n $=$ 106 male, n $=$ 86 female, n $=$ 4 n/a) data sets were included in the analysis, while in the second data collection period (t_2) n $=$ 137 (n $=$ 76 male, n $=$ 57 female, n $=$ 1 other, n $=$ 3 n/a) data sets were analyzed. Of these, $n_{t1} = 140$ and $n_{t2} = 97$ worked as scientific staff, whereas

$n_{t1} = 36$ and $n_{t2} = 31$ of the non-scientific staff participated in the survey ($n_{t1} = 2$ n/a and $n_{t2} = 9$ n/a). The years of birth ranged from 1958 to 1996 (md = 1990; mode = 1990) in the first period of data collection and from 1958 to 2002 (md = 1990; mode = 1994) in the second data collection period. N = 38 participants took part in both surveys. These data sets were excluded from the inferential statistical analysis.

The first period of data collection (April/May 2020) took place during the first lockdown (beginning in March 2020) and all employees, except those in jobs that were of critical importance for the system, had to work from home. The second period of data collection was conducted during the second lockdown (beginning in December 2020), which was also called *lockdown light*. During this period, working from home was strongly recommended but not mandatory.

3.2 Measuring Instrument and Approach

An online questionnaire was designed in English and German. The questionnaire was distributed via e-mail by the management of the faculty of mechanical engineering.

First, the participants were asked questions about their current work situation at home. These questions addressed the equipment employees had at their disposal when working from home, such as a laptop, desktop computer, external monitor, external keyboard, computer mouse, desk lamp, office chair, and other. Furthermore, they were asked about the room in which they mainly worked at home.

To measure aspects of communication, four scales of the standardized communication questionnaire *KomminO* [7, 8] were used, namely access to information (3 items), lack of information (3 items), accuracy of the information received (3 items), and satisfaction with the communication relationship (4 items). Each item was asked three times with reference to the superior, the colleagues and the subordinates. Overall, the participants answered 39 questions on communication on a 5-point Likert scale (2 = *most applicable*; –2 = *not applicable*).

Because employees were encouraged to work from home, communication mainly took place via synchronous and asynchronous digital means. To record the use of digital working resources, it was asked which five means of communication were most frequently used in both survey periods. Since the study focused on digital communication technologies and, in particular, the use of specific programs, the telephone for communication was explicitly excluded.

Finally, demographic data were collected and participants had the opportunity to take part in a raffle for vouchers for online shopping worth €20 to €50.

3.3 Analysis

To answer the first and second research questions, the frequency of mentions was analyzed and a comparison based on descriptive statistics revealed possible differences in the relative distribution between the two data collection periods in terms of the working conditions and the means of communication for work.

Overall values were determined for the four scales (access to information, lack of information, accuracy of the information received, and satisfaction with the communication relationship) for the statistical analysis addressing the third research question.

Negatively polarised items were reversed and the mean values were calculated for each participant and for the three categories of *superior*, *colleagues* and *subordinates*. An independent samples *t*-test (two-tailed) was conducted to analyze whether there was any difference in communication between the two periods of data collection regarding the scales considered. Employees who participated in the survey during both data collection periods were excluded from the independent samples *t*-test.

4   Results

Working conditions for the participants during the pandemic differed slightly between the data collection periods. The relative distribution of the rooms in which the participants mainly worked are displayed in Fig. 1.

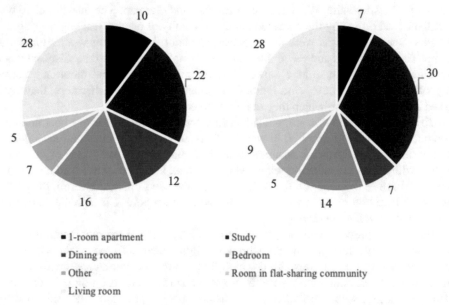

Fig. 1. Relative distribution (%) of rooms in which participants mainly worked during the first (left) and second (right) period of data collection ($n_{t1} = 178$, $n_{t2} = 137$). Numbers are rounded.

In the first survey period, about a quarter of the participants worked in a study, whereas this number increased to about a third in the second survey period. The rest of the participants did not work in rooms dedicated for working; the living room and the bedroom were named most often here.

Figure 2 shows the relative distribution of the working resources the participants had at their disposal in both data collection periods.

Almost all participants worked with a laptop and a computer mouse. About 60% of the participants had an external monitor and approximately half of them had an external keyboard, a desk lamp and an office chair.

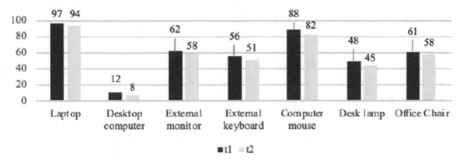

Fig. 2. Relative distribution (%) of working resources in the two data collection periods ($n_{t1} =$ 178, $n_{t2} = 137$). Numbers are rounded.

The ten most frequently mentioned communication programs used are listed below (Fig. 3). When looking at the relative distribution of digital communication for work, e-mail programs such as Outlook were used by almost all the participants and there was practically no difference here between the data collection periods. Zoom was the second most commonly used program, followed by Skype; one difference between the data collection periods became clear in this regard. While the use of Zoom increased, the use of Skype decreased. MS Teams in particular was mentioned far more often in the second data collection period.

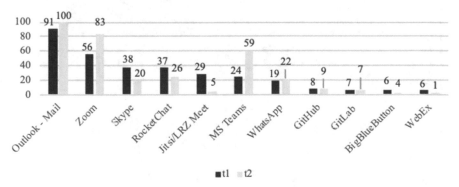

Fig. 3. Relative distribution (%) of programs used for digital communication during the two data collection periods ($n_{t1} = 178$, $n_{t2} = 137$). Numbers are rounded.

Table 1 shows the descriptive and inferential statistics. The mean values and standard deviations, as well as the differences between the mean values of the two periods of data collection are displayed. The biggest differences between the data collection periods can be seen in the measures with superiors and the measures with colleagues. The darkness of the color in the boxes illustrate the size of the differences.

An independent samples t-test was conducted with the aim of showing differences between the two periods of data collection in terms of the access to information, the lack of information, the accuracy of the information received, and the satisfaction with the communication relationship to superiors, colleagues and subordinates. Shapiro-Wilk

Table 1. Descriptive and inferential statistics to identify differences between the two periods of data collection ($n_{t1} = 140$, $n_{t2} = 99$).

		Descriptive statistics			**t-test (Welch's t-test)**			**Effect size**
		Mean t_1 (SD)	Mean t_2 (SD)	Differences mean t_1/t_2	df	t	p	Cohen's d
access to information	superior	1.295 (0.845)	0.936 (0.984)	0.359	190,486	2.945	.004*	0.392
	colleagues	1.631 (0.568)	1.465 (0.69)	0.166	184,558	1.972	.050*	0.263
	subordinates	1.062 (0.903)	0.99 (0.898)	0.072	211,851	0.609	.543	0.080
lack of information	superior	-0.964 (1.116)	-0.677 (1.188)	-0.287	202,847	-1.889	.060	-0.249
	colleagues	-1.305 (0.88)	-1.172 (0.844)	-0.133	216,387	-1.179	.240	-0.154
	subordinates	-0.831 (0.97)	-0.822 (0.854)	-0.009	225,893	-0.079	.937	-0.010
accuracy of the perceived information re-ceived	superior	0.848 (1.049)	0.384 (1.19)	0.464	194,016	3.115	.002*	0.413
	colleagues	1.293 (0.763)	1.098 (0.887)	0.195	190,601	1.774	.078	0.236
	subordinates	0.855 (0.922)	0.724 (0.856)	0.131	220,313	1.127	.261	0.147
satisfaction with the communica-tion relationship	superior	0.877 (0.983)	0.505 (1.127)	0.372	192,443	2.647	.009*	0.352
	colleagues	1.214 (0.828)	1.134 (0.835)	0.080	210,117	0.736	.462	0.097
	subordinates	0.805 (0.919)	0.826 (0.827)	-0.021	223,617	-0.179	.858	-0.023

test showed that the data tested are not normally distributed. Nevertheless, since the data set was relatively large, a *t*-test was conducted, as recommended by [9], for example. Homoscedasticity, assessed by Levene's Test, is given in all variables except *superior: access to information, colleagues: access to information, subordinates: lack of information* and *subordinates: satisfaction with the communication relationship*. Due to the unequal sample sizes and unequal variances, Welch's *t*-test was chosen, as this test is more reliable than Student's *t*-test in the event of unequal variances and sample sizes [10, 11]. The effect size is calculated by Cohen's *d*.

The data showed significant effects between the two periods of data collection on three scales referring to superiors: access to information ($t(190{,}486) = 2.945$, $p = .004$, $d = 0.392$), accuracy of the information received ($t(194{,}016) = 3.115$, $p = .002$, $d = 0.413$), the satisfaction with the communication relationship ($t(192{,}443) = 2.647$, $p = .009$, $d = 0.352$) and on one scale referring to colleagues: access to information ($t(184{,}558) = 1.972$, $p = .050$, $d = 0.263$). The complete list of values can be seen in Table 1.

5 Discussion

The working environment differed greatly between the participants in the two periods of data collection. Most of the participants did not work in rooms devoted to work but in living rooms. In particular, the living rooms and bedrooms became studies during the pandemic. This may have made it less likely for employees to be able to *switch off* after work. If we look at the relative distribution, more people had a study available in the second period of data collection. However, more than 2/3 of the participants still worked in living rooms. Regarding working equipment, the results differed slightly between the two periods of data collection. Most of the participants had a laptop at their disposal. Only very few worked with a desktop computer. However, the spread of external monitors and other ergonomic work equipment was rather rare. About 60% of the participants had an external monitor additional to their computer, meaning that a remarkable number of employees worked without them, which may lead to awkward postures that can increase the risk of neck and back problems. The lighting and seating conditions seemed to be unsuitable for work at most home offices. The availability of working resources decreased slightly between the periods of data collection. This may be the result of the fact that during the first period of data collection, all the employees had to work from home and therefore collected some working equipment from their university offices. After the first lockdown, some working equipment was likely returned to the offices. During the second period of data collection they still had the option of returning to their offices, even though it was strongly encouraged to work from home, and so they may not have taken the equipment home.

The use of digital working practices changed between the two periods of data collection. The variety of media used decreased in the sample considered and there was a clear trend towards the use of Outlook, Zoom and MS Teams – where Zoom is a program systematically introduced by the university. There was a focus on means of communication that have a greater variety of functions (collaboration, video conferencing and chat functions), such as MS Teams, compared to the first period of data collection. In particular, practices that allow video conferencing are widely used.

Between the periods of data collection, communication with superiors became significantly worse on three scales considered, though with minor effects. Participants indicated less access to information in the second period of data collection, as well as a poorer accuracy of the information received. Additionally, the satisfaction with the communication relationship to superiors became significantly worse. This trend was also apparent when the mean values concerning colleagues and subordinates are considered, however, the effects are not significant. The only exception here is the access to information from colleagues, which has also deteriorated significantly. The relatively high standard deviations show that the sample under consideration is a heterogeneous field and for some participants the communication is still considerably better, but for others considerably worse.

Results are not transferable one-to-one to other universities, faculties or beyond Germany. Due to small effect sizes and the non-significant results in some scales considered, it was only possible to derive some cautious trends. Nevertheless, the results should be a warning and lead us to look more closely at how we can achieve good communication through digital working resources.

6 Conclusion

This study shows that working conditions during the pandemic were not ideal for most employees. Communication in terms of access to information, the accuracy of the information received, and satisfaction with the communication relationship with superiors, as well as the access to information with colleagues, deteriorated between the two periods of data collection. The use of various digital working practices changed over the course of the pandemic, and a distinct focus on fewer, more versatile means of communication is emerging. Strategic decisions of the organization show up in the distribution of the means of communication used.

In particular, the data sets of employees who participated in the survey during both data collection periods require further analysis. However, since the results may be of interest for managing the crisis, this contribution provides preliminary insights into the findings.

There is a need to look more closely at the changes in the use of digital technology, communication and at job satisfaction and to explore how these phenomena are interrelated, in order to manage the crisis well and to take as much positive momentum as possible from this crisis into the future.

References

1. DAK.: Digitalisierung und Homeoffice in der Corona-Krise: Sonderanalyse zur Situation in der Arbeitswelt vor und während der Pandemie (2020)
2. FIT: Fraunhofer-Umfrage "Homeoffice": Erste Ergebnisse, 7 Mai 2020. [Press release]
3. DeFilippis, E., Impink, S.M., Singell, M., Polzer, J.T., Sadun, R.: Collaborating during coronavirus: the impact of COVID-19 on the nature of work (No. w27612). National Bureau of Economic Research (2020)

4. Hofmann, J., Piele, A., Piele, C.: Arbeiten in der Corona-Pandemie - Auf dem Weg zum New Normal. Studie des Fraunhofer IAO in Kooperation mit der Deutschen Gesellschaft für Personalführung DGFP e.V. Fraunhofer-Institut für Arbeitswissenschaft und Organisation IAO (2020)
5. Engelhardt, K.: Interne Kommunikation mit digitalen Medien. Essentials (2020). https://doi.org/10.1007/978-3-658-31493-4
6. Krämer, K., Pfizenmayer, A.: Interne Kommunikation in Zeiten von COVID-19: wie die Pandemie die interne Kommunikation verändert hat – eine qualitative Studie (2020)
7. Sperka, M.: Organisationsinterne Kommunikation-Teil II: Zur empirischen Erforschung organisationsinterner Kommunikationsprozesse. Doctoral dissertation, University of Dortmund, Germany (1996)
8. Sperka, M., Rózsa, J.: Fragebogen zur Erfassung der Kommunikation in Organisationen: Kommino. Hogrefe (2007)
9. Luley, T., Diehr, P., Emerson, S., Chen, L.: The importance of the normality assumption in large public health data sets. Annu. Rev. Public Health **23**(1), 151–169 (2002)
10. Ruxton, G.D.: The unequal variance t-test is an underused alternative to student's t-test and the Mann-Whitney U test. Behav. Ecol. **17**(4), 688–690 (2006)
11. Derrick, B., Toher, D., White, P.: Why Welch's test is Type I error robust. Quant. Methods Psychol. **12**(1), 30–38 (2016)

Application of Deep Learning for Ergonomic Data Augmentation and Human State Recognition

Yoshihiro Banchi[1]([⊠]), Takashi Kawai[1], Nagakazu Tomino[2], and Tomohiro Yamagata[2]

[1] Waseda University, Tokyo, Japan
y.banchi@aoni.waseda.jp
[2] FIND Inc., Tokyo, Japan

Abstract. In ergonomic experiments, a small number of participants is often a problem because a sufficient amount of data is not obtained. In recent years, human state recognition is wide-spread, and estimating the human state from biological information acquired from a wearable device, is useful for improving living behavior. While it is necessary to collect a sufficient amount of data in order to perform state estimation with a certain degree of accuracy, collecting the amount of data requires a considerable cost. This study attempted to expand physiological and psychological data using deep learning. Specifically, information on physiological indicators was added to ACGAN. From the verification using the actual experimental results, it was found that the accuracy of recognizing the human state was improved by using the augmented data compared to the case of learning with a small number of original data.

Keywords: Deep learning · Data augmentation · Human state recognition

1 Introduction

In ergonomic experiments, a small number of participants is often a problem. In particular, COVID-19 makes large-scale experiments difficult, making it difficult to obtain data. In recent years, the human state recognition using deep learning has become widespread [1, 2]. For example, estimating the state from the biological information acquired from the wearable device, is useful for improving living behavior. While it is necessary to collect a sufficient amount of data in order to perform state estimation with a certain degree of accuracy, collecting the amount of data requires a considerable cost.

Therefore, this research focused on the issue that how to acquire sufficient ergonomic data. The purpose of this study is to improve the accuracy of state recognition with augmentation by using deep learning, that of the physiological and psychological data acquired under appropriate experimental conditions.

2 Methods

Among Generative Adversarial Nets (GAN) [3], Auxiliary Classifier GAN (ACGAN) [4], which is added with information on multiclass classifications, was used to expand the physiological and psychological data.

The features of this method are the following two points.

1. The noise input to the Generator

Physiological data is generally normally distributed. On the other hand, when under a specific condition (for example, under some sickness state), characteristic physiological data is displayed. Therefore, the noise input to the Generator was created from the distribution according to the physiological data.

2. Pre-learning of Discriminator

Psychological data is used as the objective variable, and the Discriminator is trained in advance. By pre-learning the Discriminator, the initial weight that suits the discrimination of the objective variable is set, and in addition, by learning the authenticity judgment of the Discriminator, data generation that more reflects the characteristics of the characteristic physiological data can be expected.

A proposed GAN model based on 1DCNN was created, and by learning the physiological data during the experiment and the psychological data corresponding to the state, pseudo physiological data of a human being in a specific state was generated. In this study, the data of the 1-min physiological index and the psychological index at that time were augmented (Fig. 1).

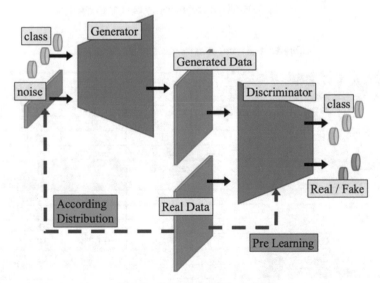

Fig. 1. Proposed GAN model

3 Results

To verify the accuracy, the deep learning model was created that estimates the corresponding psychological index from the 1-min physiological index. Specifically, it was a 1DCNN model consisting of three Convolution layers and two Dense layers. It was compared the cross-validation results that training data and test data using experimental data and results that training data using the data generated by ACGAN or proposed GAN and the test data using the experimental data. As a result, it was confirmed that the accuracy was improved when the training was performed using the augmentation data and the recognition was performed using the acquired experimental data, as compared

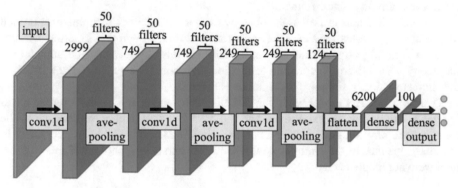

Fig. 2. 1DCNN model to verify the accuracy

Table 1. The confusion matrices on different data

Raw Data		Predicted Class			Recall
		1	*2*	*3*	
Actual Class	*1*	**44**	22	3	63.77%
	2	17	**48**	9	64.86%
	3	7	17	**6**	20.00%
Precision		64.71%	55.17%	33.33%	**56.65%**
ACGAN		Predicted Class			Recall
		1	*2*	*3*	
Actual Class	*1*	**42**	24	3	60.87%
	2	50	**24**	0	32.43%
	3	15	15	**0**	0.00%
Precision		39.25%	38.10%	0.00%	**38.15%**
Proposed GAN		Predicted Class			Recall
		1	*2*	*3*	
Actual Class	*1*	**64**	3	2	92.75%
	2	6	**65**	3	87.84%
	3	2	0	**28**	93.33%
Precision		88.89%	95.59%	84.85%	**90.75%**

with the case where the learning/recognition was performed using only the acquired experimental data (Fig. 2 and Table 1).

4 Discussion

4.1 Strengths, Key Contribution

The possibility of data augmentation by GAN was shown, and it can contribute to the acquisition of ergonomic data. It was confirmed that the accuracy was improved by training the extended data using GAN in the deep learning model. This means that the data has been extended with some features. Therefore, even if the number of participants in the experiment is small, it is possible to perform analysis with sufficient accuracy.

4.2 Limitations

It is important not to create a bias when acquiring experimental data. If the experimental data acquired directly is biased, the augmented data will also be biased, resulting in more biased results. In particular, if the psychological index that is the objective variable is biased, it is considered that it is overfitted because it is not possible to learn a specific state.

5 Conclusions

It was shown that augmented data using the proposed GAN model was reflected human characteristics. It was suggested that a proper design of experiments could enable small-scale experimental design and simulation.

As a future study, it is conceivable that highly accurate results can be obtained in small-scale experiments by conducting an experiment plan that assumes the augmentation of data. Therefore, it is necessary to confirm the accuracy by applying it to other than this experimental data and to improve how to create a model match for other data.

References

1. Song-Mi, L., Sang, M.Y., Heeryon, C.: Human activity recognition from accelerometer data using Convolutional Neural Network. In: 2017 IEEE International Conference on Big Data and Smart Computing (BigComp), Jeju, pp. 131–134 (2017)
2. Liangying, P., Ling, C., Zhenan, Y., Yi, Z.: AROMA: a deep multi-task learning based simple and complex human activity recognition method using wearable sensors. In: Proceedings of the ACM on Interactive, Mobile, Wearable and Ubiquitous Technologies, vol. 2, no. 2, Article 74 (2018)
3. Goodfellow, I.J., Pouget-Abadie, J., Mirza, M., Xu, B., Warde-Farley, D., Ozair, S., Courville, A., Bengio, Y.: Generative adversarial nets. In: Proceedings of the 27th International Conferences on Advances in Neural Information Processing Systems (2014)
4. Odena, A., Olah, C., Shlens, J.: Conditional image synthesis with auxiliary classifier GANs. In: International Conference on Machine Learning on Proceedings, Sydney (2017)

Analysis of Communications from Government Agencies and Stakeholders on Twitter During the COVID-19 in Brazil

Mauro Penha Bastos[1] (ID), Júlio César Bispo Neves[2] (ID), Tiago Cruz de França[3] (ID), Paulo Victor Rodrigues de Carvalho[4] (ID), and José Orlando Gomes[1](✉) (ID)

[1] PPGI, Federal University of Rio de Janeiro, Rio de Janeiro, RJ, Brazil
joseorlando@nce.ufrj.br
[2] TEP, Federal Fluminense University, Niteroi, Brazil
juliobispo@id.uff.br
[3] Federal Rural University of Rio de Janeiro, Seropédica, Brazil
[4] CNEN, Nuclear Engineering Institute, Rio de Janeiro, RJ, Brazil

Abstract. Communication is a fundamental tool in health crisis management, such as the COVID-19 pandemic. This study addressed the communication of the official agencies and the main Brazilian governmental stakeholders on Twitter. The analysis carried out showed inconsistent, incongruous, and conflicting information that includes misinformation and scientific negationism, hindering the implementation of non-pharmacological care strategies measures needed to reduce the virus's spread, contributing to thousands of deaths by COVID-19 reached by the country caused by the pandemic.

Keywords: COVID-19 · Public health · Social media · Network analysis · Human behavior

1 Introduction

There was a lack of policy and strategy for confronting the pandemic by the federal government in Brazil, leading to an absence of coordination within the different government levels (federal, state, and municipality). The unclear criteria for transferring resources to lower state levels, administrative structure problems, and lack of transparency [1] reflect this situation's evidence. Add to this situation the generation of conflicting and inconsistent official information by official agencies and the federal government's negationist behavior.

In the age of Big Social Data, human communication and interaction occur in the digital world (mainly using social media), where technology and society interfere with each other [2]. In this sense, we observe social media's impact on managing the COVID-19 pandemic [3] in Brazil. The messages from governments and agencies were spread on Twitter, with the potential to influence Brazilians' social behavior.

N. L. Black et al. (Eds.): IEA 2021, LNNS 222, pp. 508–514, 2021.
https://doi.org/10.1007/978-3-030-74611-7_69

These communicational actions contributed to creating a context of confusion and misinformation, making it difficult to fight the pandemic, which depends on non-pharmacological strategies that evolve the population's awareness. This scenario, based on the difficulties mentioned above, combined with the state of uncertainty related to the most effective measures to deal with the pandemic, as well as the non-existence of pharmacological solutions, such as effective drugs or vaccines, brought implications of unlike dimensions on different governmental and social stakeholders communication issues. Understanding how government managers communicated policies and actions at all levels of government and their impact on tackling the outbreak provided indications on how this crisis has reached catastrophic dimensions in Brazil.

1.1 The Research Objective and Question

This paper aims to analyze the flow of information at the three levels of government during the first months of the COVID-19 pandemic in Brazil. This study addresses the following research question: How did key government agencies and stakeholders communicate information about COVID-19 on Twitter, and what were the consistency and congruence of the communications?

2 Methodology

2.1 Data Collection

We collect tweets posted by the official accounts of the main government agencies and stakeholders involved at the three levels of government in Brazil as the president of the republic, ministers of state, governors, secretaries, and mayors of the state capitals within the three powers of the republic – Executive, Legislative and Judiciary (see Table 1).

Table 1. Government agencies and stakeholders

Government Level	Power	Authority type	Total
Federal	Executive	Presidency	1
	Executive	Minister of State	22
	Executive	Health Agency	3
	Legislative	President of Legislative House	2
	Judiciary	Minister of Supreme Court	11
State + Federal District	Executive	Governor	27
	Executive	Health Secretary	27
Municipal	Executive	Mayor of State Capitals	27

The analyzed period was from 12/31/2019 to 06/30/2020. From the collected messages, quantitative and qualitative analyzes of the messages were made over time in order to verify the consistency and congruence of the communications.

2.2 Tweets Classification

To create the tweets database, the messages containing words with a sequence of letters related to the terms corona, covid, epidemic, pandemic, sars, or sarscov were collected. Table 2 gives the result of this filter, a bunch of 10,967 messages of 67,027 tweets posted by the selected accounts for the study during the analysis period.

Table 2. Tweets filtered to restrict Covid-19 related messages.

Type of tweet	Tweets collected between 12/31/2019 and 06/30/2020	%
Covid related	10,958	16.3%
Other issues	56,069	83.7%
Total	67,027	100.0%

The analyzed period was from 12/31/2019 to 06/30/2020. After the first filter was applied to the collected messages, the messages were manually classified the Covid-19-related tweets into five kinds of messages. This set was compounded of two categories of messages according to [4, 5] such as "strategies and guidance" and "situational information," and two others as "misinformation," and "scientific negationism [6] and downplaying". See description in Table 3.

Table 3. Categories description.

Categories	Description
Strategies and guidance	The tweets describing strategies or guidance recommended by health agencies to individuals, households, and other stakeholders to minimize the risk of infection or contain the spreading. Example strategies can be "wash hands", "wear masks", and "disinfect the house"
Situational information	The message describing the influence or associated risks of the pandemic, which supports situational awareness of the general public. Examples can be the number of infection cases or deaths or the assessed risks by authoritative agencies
Misinformation	Wrong orientations to prevent the pandemic effects, such as stimulating the use of medicines without scientific evidence of efficacy (e.g., hydroxychloroquine and others)
Negationism and downplaying	Downplaying the pandemic or scientific negationism about Covid-19 outbreak preventive measures

3   Results and Discussion

After classifying the tweets, 1631 messages were discarded as they did not fit the criteria of the categories listed in Table 3. The result of the classification 9,327 remaining messages is shown in Table 4.

Table 4. Tweets filtered to restrict Covid-19 related messages.

Categories	Tweets frequency	%
Strategies and guidance	5,999	64.3%
Situational information	3,155	33.8%
Misinformation	111	1.2%
Negationism and downplaying	62	0.7%
Total		100%

The study shows an underestimation of the pandemic magnitude by the main stakeholders during the period analyzed. The first Covid-19-related tweet message posted by a Brazilian authority was in the fourth week of 2020 when the coronavirus spread was already a reality in the main West-Europe countries (Fig. 1). It also draws attention, the permanent denialism of key-authorities as the Brazilian President always in opposition to the main preventive measures, such as social distancing and encouraging the use of unproven efficacy medicines.

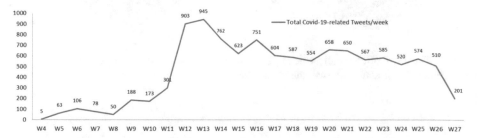

Fig. 1. Frequency of Covid-19-related tweet messages per week.

It was possible to verify an effort from the main agencies and governments of some states and municipalities to inform and sensitize the population about the prevention and care measures to be taken. Although there are many strategic orientation messages and situational information, the qualitative analysis of the messages pointed to inconsistent, incongruous, conflicting information, and scientific negationism. For this reason, this study will focus on messages classified as disinformation and minimization (see Fig. 2 and Fig. 3).

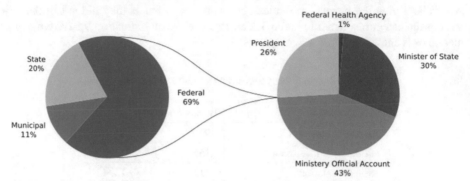

Fig. 2. The distribution of misinformation messages between the three government levels and zoom over the federal level.

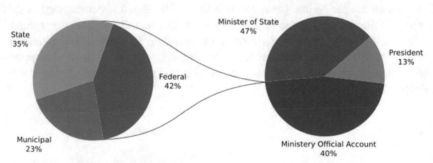

Fig. 3. The distribution of scientific negationism and downplaying messages between the three government levels and zoom over the federal level.

Some non-exhaustive examples of such messages are:

@SaudeMG - "Is it necessary to cancel the carnival because of the coronavirus cases? #carnaval2020 #coronavirus #oms #china https://t.co/vbu9hwi8nq"

The SARS-CoV-2 was already wide-spreading in Europe during that period, impacting those countries' health systems. Even so, the official account of the health department of the state of Minas Gerais informed that it would not be necessary to suspend the carnival. The first justification was the fact that Brazil had no confirmed cases until that moment.

@jairbolsonaro – "hydroxychloroquine increasingly demonstrates its effectiveness in patients with covid-19. https://t.co/ymwnj5hyti" (03/27/2020)

@*jairbolsonaro* – *"Hydroxychloroquine increasingly demonstrates its effectiveness in patients with COVID-19. – I have received reports from all over Brazil in this regard. – Preserve lives and jobs.* - https://youtu.be/vYLlRzhJIoY *"* *(03/29/2020)*

Even though there is no scientific evidence on hydroxychloroquine's effectiveness in the treatment of Covid-19, actors from the Brazilian federal government, as the president of the republic and ministers of state, have posted messages mentioning the alleged effectiveness of the drug in the treatment of Covid-19. In a recent report prepared by the Federal Pharmacy Council, the sale of drugs like hydroxychloroquine more than doubled in Brazil, from 963,000 in 2019 to 2 million units in 2020 [7].

@*casacivil* – *"brazil has the lowest lethality rates of # covid19, in relation to higher economies.* https://t.co/ywu69z0kcc. *"* *(04/23/2020)*

During the period the tweet above was posted, the virus's spread was beginning in Brazil. In that same period, the North of the globe countries, in special Europe, were on the peaks of the first Pandemic wave. The message above clearly inducts a misunderstanding of the Pandemic risk among the population and does not represent the reality.

4   Conclusions

The lack of coordination between the three levels of governmental structure (federal, states, and municipalities) has produced incongruous and inconsistent information during the SARS-CoV-2 crisis. This work enables a discussion on the importance and impact of adequate governments' communications in social networks (focused on Twitter) of non-pharmacological strategies to prevent the spread of the SARS-Cov-2 virus.

Further studies should be done on how the lack of joint strategy and consequent miscommunication has influenced the population behavior and how its behavior contributed to the overall impact of COVID-19 in Brazil. It is necessary to extend the collection and analysis of messages to the pandemic's entire period. It should also expand the analysis to consider the impact and reach of messages with the analyzed accounts' followers and examine the networks' communication dynamics. Further studies could be conducted to analyze the authorities' communications on tools other than Twitter, considering interviews and pronouncements given to supporters through Facebook and YouTube's social networks.

References

1. TCU Tribunal de Contas da União: Acórdão no 1888/2020. Plenário. Relator: Ministro Benjamin Zymler. Sessão de 22/07/2020. https://portal.tcu.gov.br/imprensa/noticias/tcu-avalia-a-governanca-do-ministerio-da-saude-no-combate-a-pandemia.htm
2. Olshannikova, E., Olsson, T., Huhtamäki, J., Kärkkäinen, H.: Conceptualizing big social data. J. Big Data **4**, 3 (2017). https://doi.org/10.1186/s40537-017-0063-x

3. Cuello-Garcia, C., Pérez-Gaxiola, G., van Amelsvoort, L.: Social media can have an impact on how we manage and investigate the COVID-19 pandemic. J. Clin. Epidemiol. **127**, 198–201 (2020). https://doi.org/10.1016/j.jclinepi.2020.06.028
4. Wang, Y., Hao, H., Platt, L.S.: Examining risk and crisis communications of government agencies and stakeholders during early-stages of COVID-19 on Twitter. Comput. Hum. Behav. **114**, 106568 (2021). https://doi.org/10.1016/j.chb.2020.106568
5. Wukich, C.: Government social media messages across disaster phases. J. Contingencies Crisis Manage. **24**, 230–243 (2016). https://doi.org/10.1111/1468-5973.12119
6. Barreto, M.L., Barreto, M.L.: Science, politics, history and the intriguing and persistent mysteries of pandemics. Cien. Saude Colet. **25**, 4094–4095 (2020). https://doi.org/10.1590/1413-812320202510.2.31302020
7. Conselho Federal de Farmácia – Brasil: Notícia: 04/02/2021 - Busca de fórmulas milagrosas contra a Covid-19 continua impulsionando vendas de medicamentos (2021). https://www.cff.org.br/noticia.php?id=6198. Accessed 08 Feb 2021

COVID-19LL: A Systematic Approach to Identify Best Practices and Lessons Learned in German Economic Sectors

Klaus Bengler[1(✉)], Verena Nitsch[2], Martin Schmauder[3], Caroline Adam[1], Sebastian Pütz[2], Christopher Brandl[2], Gritt Ott[3], and Georg Jochum[4]

[1] Chair of Ergonomics, Technical University of Munich, Munich, Germany
{bengler,caroline.adam}@tum.de
[2] Chair and Institute of Industrial Engineering and Ergonomics, RWTH Aachen University, Aachen, Germany
{v.nitsch,s.puetz,c.brandl}@iaw.rwth-aachen.de
[3] Chair of Labour Engineering, Technische Universität Dresden, Dresden, Germany
{martin.schmauder,gritt.ott}@tu-dresden.de
[4] Friedrich Schiedel Chair of Sociology of Science, Technical University of Munich, Munich, Germany
g.jochum@tum.de

Abstract. Due to the coronavirus SARS-CoV-2 outbreak, which led to a worldwide pandemic, many companies were forced to rethink and redefine the working conditions for their employees and the networks with their business partners to secure their productivity and economic survival. Many of these developments have been discussed even before the pandemic as a necessary reaction to economic and societal conditions that are increasingly volatile, uncertain, complex and ambiguous. A situation that has become known by the acronym VUCA. The pandemic has accelerated and changed numerous of those developments.

Through the systematic analysis of lessons learned during the pandemic, the BMBF-funded research project COVID19LL aims to identify successful solutions and measures that have emerged in three different German regions (Bavaria, North Rhine-Westphalia and Saxony). The aim of the project is to identify the problems companies and organizations face and what they have learned from the change process thus far. The project thus aims to ascertain whether innovative and digital forms of work created by the pandemic could lead to positive impulses, which might prove successful in the working world in the medium and long term and the extent to which these can be transferred to other industries. This paper presents the methodological approach and outlines first results of interviews with employers and employee representatives as well as company representatives in order to identify best practices and lessons learned.

Keywords: COVID-19 · Coronavirus · Pandemic · Economic sectors · Work · Best practices

N. L. Black et al. (Eds.): IEA 2021, LNNS 222, pp. 515–522, 2021.
https://doi.org/10.1007/978-3-030-74611-7_70

1 Introduction

The acute infectious lung disease COVID-19 first spread in the city of Wuhan in late 2019. On March 11, 2020, the WHO declared the previous epidemic a global pandemic [1]. In Germany, the first case was recorded in the Bavarian city of Starnberg on January 27, 2020. On March 25, the German Bundestag declared an epidemic situation of national scope. To contain the pandemic, the individual federal states agreed to implement preventive protective measures nationwide [2]. Restrictions on social contact included maintaining a minimum distance, wearing mouth- nose masks on public transport, and enacting a no-contact rule. Additional measures included the closing of numerous businesses, educational institutions, and public facilities. The pandemic and its accompanying measures had significant economic and social consequences.

Beginning in March 2020, companies were confronted by a short-term lockdown and had to fulfill far-reaching hygiene requirements. The changes represented a caesura that triggered a rapid change process in all industries and sectors throughout Germany, as well as internationally. Restrictions and regulations are dynamically evolving. The new day-to-day work thus requires an adaptation in work structures and processes. While home office and virtual meetings were the exception in many organizations prior to the pandemic, with the spread of the virus, they were the only way to continue working under safe conditions. Employees had to learn how to use new technologies and companies equipped their staff to work from home. Stopped or delayed production caused delays in supply chains and at the same time changed demand in the market [3] in both directions – increase and decrease. Many companies adapted their product range, for example by producing disinfectants instead of perfume or masks instead of clothing [4, 5].

As the pandemic eased only locally and temporarily during the year, the work environment remained in a state of limbo between partially pre-pandemic work processes and newly established work methods. The renewed intensification of the pandemic toward the end of 2020, as well as the long period during which the pandemic affects work and life, means that the previously exceptional situation becomes the new norm and new processes and structures gradually become established and consolidated.

2 Research Objective

By systematically analyzing examples of operational measures and lessons learned, the research project aims to identify and make accessible successful approaches to solutions and measures that emerged during the crisis in three different regions (Bavaria, North Rhine-Westphalia and Saxony) and in different value adding sectors. It will be determined what problems the companies and organizations faced and what they learned from the change process. Innovative strategies based on digitalization may not only contribute to overcome the pandemic. Rather, they can promote a general digitalization drive that could have a continued impact beyond the crisis. In this context the following research questions were formulated:

1. Which industries, job profiles and activities are particularly relevant when investigating the effects of the COVID-19 pandemic on work?

2. Which measures and solutions have been introduced by different industries and if necessary modified/optimized to be able to work under the conditions changed by COVID-19?

3. What similarities can be identified between different industries and regions with regard to the measures and best practices introduced?

4. Which best practice examples can be transferred to other industries and might be beneficial after the COVID-19 pandemic?

Since the pandemic has not yet subsided, data collection is still ongoing. In this contribution, the methodological approach to identify best practices and lessons learned is presented. Furthermore, initial findings from the interviews with different stakeholders are outlined.

3 Methodological Approach

Germany being a federal republic, legislations for containing the pandemic as well as governmental support differ substantially between federal states. To take these differences between circumstances for companies in different federal states into account, while also establishing comparability between companies included in the analysis, three federal states were selected to constitute the research scope of this project, namely Bavaria, North Rhine-Westphalia, and Saxony. Beside differences based on location, regulations addressing the pandemic also have different effects on companies within different economic sectors. While companies in most economic sectors were able to continue operating during the pandemic as long as the newly implemented safety and hygiene standards could be met, others such as local retail or gastronomy businesses had to shut down due to federal state regulations during a first lockdown beginning in March 2020 as well as a second lockdown beginning in December 2020. In addition, companies faced with the same regulations are affected differently. For example, employees within the service sector not requiring physical contact with customers can work from home during the lockdown phases. In contrast, typical tasks in manufacturing, construction, agriculture, and forestry require the employees to be on-site. Being confronted with dissimilar challenges, companies in different parts of the economy need to develop different solutions. To capture this multiplicity of approaches to dealing with the COVID-19 pandemic, companies in the primary, secondary, and tertiary sector are being investigated in the three federal states. This way, the full breadth of the economic spectrum can be considered to identify best practices based on fundamentally different prerequisites as well as perspectives and solution strategies.

As the COVID-19 pandemic presents a challenge to the economy unlike any other event over the past decade, the full extent of how the pandemic impacts different companies dealing with, as elaborated, vastly different circumstances can hardly be predicted based on the current state of knowledge. Consequently, an explorative research approach is chosen to address the stated research objective and the open research questions. Rather than focusing on obtaining insights from a maximum number of companies, the goal is to gather an in-depth understanding of the external challenges, internal prerequisites, approaches to finding a solution as well as experiences gained by implementing the solution for each of the investigated companies. To optimize the likelihood of identifying solution strategies that have the potential to form long-term best practices, a set of criteria for selecting companies at the three federal states was developed. On the level of industry membership, the first selection criterion is the extent to which the respective industry is affected by the pandemic. Since companies in industries that are particularly struggling with the challenges of the pandemic have been and continue to be forced to develop short-term solution strategies, these industries offer a high potential for identifying innovative approaches. The regional importance of the industry was defined as a second selection criterion. The regional importance is defined by the number of employees, contributions to economic value and reputation of the industry both in absolute terms and in relation to the German economy as a whole. This criterion supports the supraregional transfer potential of the gained insights. Additional criteria on the industry level are potential for digitalization of work processes and the role in social discourse in regard to the pandemic.

To examine how the investigated companies handled the challenges associated with the pandemic, semi-structured interviews with company representatives were conducted. To structure the interview guideline, a process model was developed, based on the human, technology, and organization (HTO) concept (cf. [7]). This model is intended to help to capture change processes. Figure 1 provides a schematic illustration of the model developed. It is structured into three phases, the status quo ante, the change process itself and the status quo post. Both the status quo ante and the status quo post are described using the three facets of the HTO concept. For each of the facets, an exemplary list of attributes likely to be affected by the pandemic or to influence the company's reaction to the crisis are formulated. The phase describing the transition from the status quo ante to the status quo post is conceptualized as an iterative process. The change process is initiated by the occurrence of external requirements posed by the pandemic and the associated legislations, such as changes in demand, collapsing supply chains, the need for physical distancing, privacy issues and influences from the private environment of employees. These external requirements need to be addressed considering the internal requirements of the respective company including the HTO attributes identified for the status quo ante as well as boundary conditions such as company and collective bargaining agreements, safety standards, or general legislation. Based on both internal and external requirements, a company develops and implements measures and evaluates them in practice. Since the number of new cases and the corresponding federal regulations vary over the course of the pandemic, the external requirements also vary causing the need for adjusting implemented measures resulting in the iterative change process. All these changes in a single company take place in an environment of overall sociological, political, and economic influences.

In the interviews, the status quo ante of the respective company is analyzed first. Second, different measures implemented by the company are examined following the steps of the iterative process model. Third, the interviewee is questioned regarding the status quo post. As the pandemic is still on-going at the time of the data collection, the assessment of the status quo post includes both the current status and expectations for the future. The measures and solution strategies identified in the interviews are evaluated based on their possibility to represent best practices that have the potential to improve

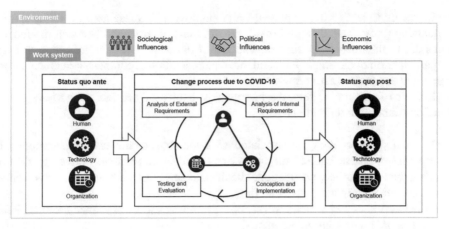

Fig. 1. HTO based model for describing change processes within companies due to the COVID-19 pandemic.

work processes even after the pandemic. The respective evaluation criteria are derived from the two central outcomes considered in the field of ergonomics: employee performance and well-being [6]. Whereas profitability, cooperation/collaboration quality and ecological sustainability are considered for the outcome of performance, job satisfaction, health and safety, opportunities to influence the working process and compatibility of work and personal life reference the well-being of the employees. The evaluation of the measures implemented by a company are conducted both internally, meaning within the interviews by the company representatives, and externally by the researchers. Based on these assessments, best practices examples are identified.

4 Initial Findings

4.1 Interviews with Employers and Employee Representatives

In the three different regions, interviews were conducted with multipliers, especially employers' and employees' representatives.

The interviews (one each with employers' and employees' representatives in North Rhine-Westphalia, Bavaria and Saxony, and one with the Chamber of Industry and Commerce in Saxony) were used to validate the chosen approach to the study concerning the selection of investigated industries, the subject of the study and the evaluation approach. In the interviews, the selected industries were confirmed by most. The hospitality, hotel, and stationary retail industry were named as being particularly affected by the pandemic - which had to close due to the respective general orders.

The remaining industries are viewed differently by the interviewees in terms of how they are affected. Construction, agriculture and forestry are considered to be hardly impeded in their processes. They are also seen as having few options for the increased use of digitization solutions. In the manufacturing sector, the pandemic is mainly perceived as an enforcer/catalyst of transformation processes already initiated, e.g. the transformation in the automotive industry and the increasing digitalization of processes.

In the interviews with employers' and employees' representatives, the proposed evaluation system was also confirmed. No difference is assumed between the federal states due to their sectoral structure. The size of the company, the trade union density, the participation of the employees, and the implementation in company agreements were mentioned as possible differentiation criteria.

In their role as multipliers, the interviewees expressed the following views on the situation concerning their clientele:

- The number of challenges associated with the introduction working remotely is emphasized. These include the necessary technical equipment, preparing and finishing the home office, occupational health and safety in the home office, as well as the separation of work and leisure time.
- In the interviews and various workshops, communication was named a central issue – both work-related and interpersonal.
- The points of view regarding digitization can be summarized in that there are still many unanswered questions associated with it, which currently accumulate in the discussion about mobile work, but also affect traditional workplaces.

4.2   Interviews with Employers and Employees

Until now, 42 interviews with employers and employees have been conducted. All of the interviews confirmed that the work in the companies has changed significantly as a result of the COVID-19 pandemic. The need to reduce physical contact is the main driver of changes in working practices. In the vast number of cases identified so far, this has led to far-reaching hygiene concepts and mandatory use of masks, team formation with spatial and/or temporal separation and significantly increased mobile working as well as a drastically reduced number of business trips. It is already apparent that the scope of the measures is highly dependent on the given spatial infrastructure and the process/product-related distances in production.

- The situation concerning measures and prerequisites for limiting the pandemic in the administrative sector (public administration facilities, administrative departments of hospitals, high schools etc.) is comparable to that in manufacturing companies.
- The internal measures are influenced by the closure of schools and daycare facilities and the general mood of the people, which is also reflected in the companies and in some cases has a negative impact on the ability of measures to be implemented. Especially the long duration of the necessary measures and the partly perceived unequal treatment (especially in the healthcare sector) lead to a decreasing acceptance.
- An essential aspect for managing the necessary changes was the (existing) digital infrastructure of the company and, in particular, the equipment of employees with the necessary tools for mobile work.
- Working from home increasingly forces companies to reconsider and adapt established communication structures and processes. In particular, the loss of informal exchanges between colleagues in the past had to be compensated for. But changes in the interaction between managers and employees must also be managed.

- A partly contrasting picture to manufacturing companies or administrative units can be seen in the healthcare sector interviews. Digitalization of work by relocating activities to the home office is only possible to a limited extent here, as they mostly require a physical presence. Nevertheless, digital technologies are also helping to overcome the crisis here. They assist in coping with the increased need for cooperation between departments due to the pandemic and in ensuring greater flexibility in the use of equipment. The respondents expect that these innovations in the area of in-house organization will continue beyond the pandemic.
- A further central challenge in the health sector is developing and implementing a functioning hygiene concept to reduce the risk of virus transmission. In this regard, conflict area arise between compliance with measures for infection prevention and comprehensive, "good" patient care. The wearing of personal protective equipment represents an increased physical burden for the nursing staff and an impediment to communication with patients, relatives, and colleagues.

From these preliminary findings, it can be deduced that almost all of the companies and organizations surveyed are in a phase of upheaval. More than half a year after the outbreak of the pandemic, most of the respondents have found a way to deal with the new situation to the best of their abilities. In the course of this, experiences were made and lessons learned, which are now to be used in the long term to improve the work processes. This process is mostly on-going. In the interviews conducted so far, it became clear that many of the companies not only react passively to the difficulties associated with the pandemic but are also using the opportunity to test innovative ways of proactively working in a targeted manner to improve existing processes. In some areas, interviewees stated that solutions tested during the pandemic can be directly applied to a post-pandemic period. In other areas, the interviewees saw the challenge in exploring how the experiences gained can be linked to existing working practices in the long term. Here, the shift towards home office concepts can be used as a specific example.

5   Outlook

In a next step, the obtained data will be systematically analyzed and continuously supplemented by further insights. As the pandemic is not yet over, the applicability of lessons learned and best practices identified in the research project will only become apparent at a later stage. However, this project supports the processes of companies to actively start a learning process to plan for a time after the COVID-19 pandemic. The long-term goal is to compare and synthesize the lessons learned in different countries into a cohesive understanding of the circumstances that lead to and enable different solution strategies.

Acknowledgements. This article describes research conducted as part of the research project COVID-19 Lessons Learned (Grant Number 02L18A700), which is funded by the German Federal Ministry of Education and Research (BMBF).

References

1. World Health Organization (WHO).: WHO Director-General's opening remarks at the media briefing on COVID-19 - 11 March 2020. https://www.who.int/director-general/speeches/det ail/who-director-general-s-opening-remarks-at-the-media-briefing-on-covid-19---11-march-2020. Accessed 23 Jan 2021
2. Bundesregierung.: Besprechung der Bundeskanzlerin mit den Regierungschefinnen und Regierungschefs der Länder am 22. März 2020. https://www.bundesregierung.de/bregde/the men/coronavirus/besprechung-der-bundeskanzlerin-mit-den-regierungschefinnen-und-regier ungschefsder-laender-1733248. Accessed 23 Jan 2021
3. Statistisches Bundesamt.: Wirtschaftliche Auswirkungen. Statistiken mit Bezug zu COVID-19. https://www.destatis.de/DE/Themen/Querschnitt/Corona/Wirtschaft/kontextinfor mationen-wirtschaft.html#arbeitsmarkt. Accessed 23 Jan 2021
4. Diebner, R., Silliman, E., Ungerman, K., Vancauwenberghe, M.: Adapting customer experience in the time of coronavirus. McKinsey & Company, pp. 1–7 (2020)
5. George-Parkin, H.: Factories that used to make perfume, T-Shirts, and cars are now making supplies to fight the coronavirus. Accessed 5 Feb 2021. https://www.vox.com/the-goods/2020/ 4/6/21207135/factories-face-masks-ventilators-hand-sanitizer-coronavirus-manufacturing.
6. Dul, J., Bruder, R., Buckle, P., Carayon, P., Falzon, P., Marras, W.S., Wilson, J.R., van der Doelen, B.: A strategy for human factors/ergonomics: developing the discipline and profession. Ergonomics **55**(4), 377–395 (2012)
7. Strohm, O.: Analyse und bewertung von arbeitssystemen. In: Strohm, O., Ulrich, E. (eds.) Unternehmen arbeitspsychologisch bewerten: Ein Mehr-Ebenen-Ansatz unter besonderer Berücksichtigung von Mensch, Technik und Organisation, pp. 135–167. vdf Hochschulverlag, Zürich (1997)

Mental Health Among Workers in Private Medical Clinics in the Era of COVID-19

Lahcene Bouabdellah[1] (ID), Houda Kherbache[1] (ID), Abdenacer Tezkratt[2] (ID),
and Mohammed Mokdad[3](✉) (ID)

[1] University Sétif 2, Setif, Algeria
{doylettres,houdakhe}@univ-setif.dz
[2] University Mohamed El Bachir El Ibrahimi, Bordj Bou Arreridj, Algeria
abdenacer.tezkratt@univ-bba.dz
[3] College of Arts, University of Bahrain, Sakhir, Bahrain
mmokdad@uob.edu.bh

Abstract. In the proposed paper we will present the results of a short study conducted by our research unit (Human Resources Development' URDRH Sétif University 2- Algeria) whose purpose is to determine the various mental health risk factors that may be causing (COVID-19) among doctors and nurses care workers in Algeria; in order to deduce prevention strategies.

The present study took into account in the sample the variables of age, sex, medical specialty, and seniority by following the descriptive method, and the study adopted the mental health scale SCL 90-R [1]. Which was applied to a sample of 200 doctor and nurse from all from some Algerian department; Sétif, Bordj Bou Arreridj, Constantine, Algiers, Tizi Ouzou and Batna.

Finally, the results showed that caregivers, including doctors and nurses, the during coronavirus pandemic, of both sexes and those with more than 10 years of experience in the field that they suffer from psychological imbalances at the level of:

– Physical symptoms such as chronic fatigue and insomnia.
– Compulsive obsession that appear in various fears of transmission even in a safe place.
– Reactive sensitivity and disruption of good communication with others.
– Depressive states of Due to their inability to provide health care for difficult cases of the pandemic.
– Anxiety about continuing to the pandemic situation for a long time.
– Phobias and fears of transmitting the infection to their families.
– Hostility, paranoia and psychosis.

Keywords: Mental health · SARS-CoV-2 · Medical and paramedical personnel · Depression · Obsessive-compulsive disorder · Phobia · Psychosis

1 Introduction

Humanity has experienced many epidemics and deadly diseases, which have spread fear throughout the world. Each period was characterized by the spread of a specific epidemic,

N. L. Black et al. (Eds.): IEA 2021, LNNS 222, pp. 523–531, 2021.
https://doi.org/10.1007/978-3-030-74611-7_71

and each had specific causes, characteristics, and modes of transmission and spread. Perhaps the new COVID-19 virus, is the most of those epidemics that terrorize people, despite its recent spread, it has spread widely and dangerously and has become a global health problem since its emergence in the world. Chinese city of Wuhan in December 2019. This virus is a new strain that has never been before, it mainly targets the human respiratory system and attacks and destroys its cells, which hinders its functions, as it multiplies inside cells leading to its death, and weakens the immune system, so that the body loses its ability to endure and consequently death [2, 3].

As the coronavirus pandemic rapidly sweeps across the world, it is inducing a considerable degree of fear, worry and concern in the population at large and among certain groups in particular, such as older adults, care providers and people with underlying health conditions [4]. In public mental health terms, the main psychological impact to date is elevated rates of stress or anxiety. But as new measures and impacts are introduced especially quarantine and its effects on many people's usual activities, routines or livelihoods levels of loneliness, depression, harmful alcohol and drug use, and self-harm or suicidal behavior are also expected to rise [4].

After months since the outbreak of the Corona pandemic, the number of infections has increased worldwide, surpassing the limit of 29 million cases on September 15, 2020 [5]. The terrible spread of the pandemic originated in societies that developed negative risk factors for cognitive and emotional responses [6]. As a result, there has been a great deficit in the world in controlling this epidemic, on the one hand scientists are still trying to find an effective vaccine, and on the other hand negative feelings have arisen in the community in general and in the medical team. In this regard, Choudhari, [6] confirms that the harmful effects of the Corona virus do not depend only on the level of the body, but also extend to chronic psychological disorders such as depression, anxiety, panic disorder and psychosomatic manifestations.

Healthcare workers, who are at the forefront of the fight against the epidemic, are expected to face an extraordinary workload due to global health measures and regulations [7]. Therefore, ensuring their health is crucial in both preventing the spread of the virus as well as its treatment [8].

Additionally, Lai, et al. [9] assessed the mental health of 1,257 medical personnel working with cases infected with the coronavirus in 34 Chinese hospitals, where the results indicated that the sample exhibited 50.4% symptoms of depression and a rate of 44.6% Among the symptoms of anxiety, 34% of them suffer from insomnia and 71.5% suffer from malaise.

Currently in Algeria, 48,734 cases of coronavirus have been registered on September 15, 2020 [10]. With the intensification of global efforts to fight the virus, Algerian medical staff are also still in continuous work through various public and private health facilities.

In our study, we will try to answer the following questions:

1. What is the mental health level of workers in private medical clinics in the Corona era?
2. Does the mental health of the medical staff differ according to the gender?
3. Does the mental health of the medical staff differ according to their seniority?

2   Methodology

2.1   Research Method

The present study used the descriptive method.

2.2   Sample

The research sample consisted of a total of 200 medical personnel divided between 80 doctors and 120 nurses from different Algerian hospitals; Sétif (18.3%), Bordj Bou Arreridj (13.4%), Constantine (15%), Algiers (22.6%), Tizi Ouzou (13%) and Batna (19.7%). Research took place between April 21 and July 30, 2020.

2.3   Study Tools

The study was conducted using the Mental Health Scale SCL 90-R [1]. This scale aims to identify the general psychological state of individuals. It is made up of 90 items, divided into nine dimensions as follows: physical symptoms, obsessive-compulsive disorder, reactive sensitivity, depression, anxiety, fear, hostility, paranoia and psychosis.

The administration of the questionnaire took place once the reliability and validity criteria were measured and confirmed, (Cronbach alpha reliability: 0.764, Concurrent validity: 0.874).

3   Results and Discussion

Medical and paramedical personnel in normal situations are often confronted with serious and unpredictable situations, which generate intense anxiety and stress that are difficult to control [11] so:

3.1   What Is the Mental Health Level of Workers in Private Medical Clinics in the Corona Era?

Table 1. The levels of mental health for the study sample.

Axes	Mean	Ecart type	Theoretical mean	Mean difference	T
Physical symptoms	29.16	5.455	22	7.160	75.602
O-C-D	28.13	4.539	20	8.130	87.637
Reactive S	24.88	5.044	18	6.880	69.756
Depression	35.91	6.017	26	9.905	84.387
Anxiety	28.50	4.077	20	8.495	98.839
Fear	16.69	3.048	12	4.685	77.407

(continued)

Table 1. (*continued*)

Axes	Mean	Ecart type	Theoretical mean	Mean difference	T
Phobia	20.00	3.452	14	6.000	81.925
Paranoia	16.91	3.029	12	4.910	78.939
Psychosis	28.12	5.206	20	8.115	76.368
Other	22.70	3.802	16	6.695	84.420
Total	**250.71**	**30.85**	**180**	**70.710**	**114.928**

According to the previous Table 1, we see that there are statistically significant differences between the theoretical mean and the arithmetic mean in favor of the theoretical mean. It appears that all the values are statistically significant.

This indicates that the higher the overall score on the mental health scale, the lower the mental health and vice versa. The poor mental health of the study sample is due to the loss of the sense of security and the spread of fear and panic in the social and professional environment. Most Algerian families are extended families, which can also make medical workers fearful of passing the infection on to themselves and their families [12]. These findings align with those of Algeria experienced the first case of Coronavirus on February 17, 2020, from an Italian residing in Algeria [2], and with the passage of several months, a strong wave of the virus appeared around May, June and July.

This has exacerbated the cases and affected various treatment structures, whether governmental or non-governmental, and in view of the deficit recorded in health services in Algeria due to the pandemic, the Algerian government has worked to provide licenses to various private clinics and work on converting some of them into virus detection centers with detection equipment.

In addition, patients turn to general practitioners or specialists with the idea that they have other symptoms such as cold, fever, fatigue and diarrhea while unknowingly infected with the virus. Hence, the fear of spread of infection among doctors has increased.

What has increased the effort of medical staff is that there is still no effective treatment or vaccine against the virus, despite the efforts made. Also, the professional pressures encountered by physicians have increased by reducing the level of motivation to work for them. Unlike the wider society in which the state of quarantine had gathered people into their homes and reduced their movements, and there were those who suffered from stress and tension, whether in their work or in their studies, the confinement provided these people with a bit of calm in their life as it gave them the opportunity to get away from the daily pressures. And rearrange their thoughts. In contrast, confinement imposed social distancing on family, friends, relatives and colleagues [13].

3.2 Does the Mental Health of the Medical Staff Differ According to the Gender?

Table 2. The differences between the mental health averages of doctors and nurses according to the gender variable.

Axes	Sex	N	Mean	Ecart type	T	Sig
Physical symptoms	Male	71	28.83	5.264	−0.632	0.528
	Female	129	29.34	5.568		
O-C-D	Male	71	27.31	4.732	−1.908	0.058
	Female	129	28.58	4.383		
Reactive sensitivity	Male	71	24.17	5.654	−1.483	0.140
	Female	129	25.27	4.652		
Depression	Male	71	34.80	6.596	−1.935	0.054
	Female	129	36.51	5.608		
Anxiety	Male	71	27.52	3.601	−2.540	0.012
	Female	129	29.03	4.235		
Fear	Male	71	16.06	2.868	−2.184	0.030
	Female	129	17.03	3.100		
Phobia	Male	71	19.37	3.457	−1.939	0.054
	Female	129	20.35	3.413		
Paranoia	Male	71	16.58	3.237	−1.153	0.250
	Female	129	17.09	2.906		
Psychosis	Male	71	27.25	5.424	−1.745	0.083
	Female	129	28.59	5.041		
Other symptoms	Male	71	22.04	3.420	−1.812	0.072
	Female	129	23.05	3.963		
Total	**Male**	**71**	**243.24**	**28.721**	**−2.576**	**0.011**
	Female	**129**	**254.82**	**31.314**		

According to the previous Table 2, the value of (T) was reported in: physical symptoms (−0.632), obsessive-compulsive disorder (−1.908), reactive sensitivity (−1.483) depression (−1.935), anxiety (−2.540), hostility (−2.184), phobia (−1.939), paranoia (−1.153), psychosis (−1.745), other statements (−1.812) total mental health score (−2.576) which are all values not statistically significant (P value ≥ 0.01). Except in depression, anxiety, hostility, phobia, and overall mental health scores were in favor of women.

The professional roles of the medical team are performed equally for men and women, but women have shown during the pandemic that they suffer from symptoms of depression, anxiety, hostility and fears, and this may be due to the nature of the psychological structure of women. In addition, the new way of life has appeared in the shadow of the Corona pandemic, which calls for separation this social aspect also includes the professional and the family, which creates a kind of disruption on the relational side with others in the society. Ksour, [13] indicates, "Peoples behaviors have changed because the disease is spreading around them, so they move away from public places and others to control the epidemic". All are of potential carriers of the virus, in previous epidemics, social distancing was present, but to a lesser extent, as the COVID-19 epidemic is characterized by rapid spread and person-to-person transmission. All this created a sort of pathological awakening, which can be translated by the term obsessive-compulsive disorder.

Moreover, most of the countries of the world, after some time after the emergence of the virus, have recognized the coexistence with the pandemic while taking preventive measures. But the community in general has shown its non-compliance, as it has the majority of citizens were found to dispense with wearing masks or respecting distancing altogether, leading doctors and nurses of all genders and seniority to enter a state of desperation resulting from their behavior and fear of an exacerbation of this viral pandemic.

3.3 Does the Mental Health of the Medical Staff Differ According to their Seniority?

Table 3. The differences between the mental health averages of doctors and nurses according to the seniority variable.

Axes	Seniority	N	Mean	Ecart type	T	Sig
Physical symptoms	Under 10	116	28.27	5.674	−2.765	0.006
	Over 11	84	30.39	4.906		
O-C-D	Under 10	116	27.70	4.817	−1.587	0.114
	Over 11	84	28.73	4.079		
Reactive sensitivity	Under 10	116	24.50	5.522	−1.254	0.211
	Over 11	84	25.40	4.274		
Depression	Under 10	116	35.13	6.076	−2.162	0.032
	Over 11	84	36.98	5.802		
Anxiety	Under 10	116	27.99	3.922	−2.070	0.040
	Over 11	84	29.19	4.207		
Fear	Under 10	116	16.28	3.251	−2.253	0.025
	Over 11	84	17.25	2.661		

(*continued*)

Table 3. (*continued*)

Axes	Seniority	N	Mean	Ecart type	T	Sig
Phobia	Under 10	116	19.87	3.290	−0.621	0.535
	Over 11	84	20.18	3.677		
Paranoia	Under 10	116	16.67	3.170	−1.306	0.193
	Over 11	84	17.24	2.810		
Psychosis	Under 10	116	27.44	5.378	−2.176	0.031
	Over 11	84	29.05	4.837		
Other symptoms	Under 10	116	22.15	4.171	−2.427	0.016
	Over 11	84	23.45	3.091		
Total	**Under 10**	**116**	**245.53**	**30.473**	**−2.837**	**0.005**
	Over 11	**84**	**257.86**	**30.103**		

The previous Table 3 shows that, the value of (T) has been reported in physical symptoms (−2.765), obsessive-compulsive disorder (−1.587), reactive sensitivity (−1.254), depression (−2.162), anxiety (−2,070), hostility (−2,253), phobia (−0,621), paranoia (−1,306), psychosis (−2,176), other statements (−2,427) total mental health score (−2,837). Which are all statistically significant values (P value ≥ 0.01) in favor of individuals with more than 10 years of experience except in Reactive sensitivity, phobia and paranoia.

The low level of mental health of the medical staff, according to the statements of most of them, is due to the fact that since the start of the epidemic, the medical staff worked in rotating shifts, which was very exhausting, both physically and psychologically. In addition, most Algerian medical staff live with extended families, making them fearful of passing the infection on to their families.

Likewise, medical staff are met with modern technology, so that they can pass on false information about the emerging virus to each other through unofficial means, which can create an additional state of panic for them [14]. Unofficial organizations, including those working on transmitting false information, which were noticed via social media, where some of them intended to attribute it to official organizations such as the World Organization of Health or Child Health Organization and others, which has increased the level of tension and fear in the community in general and the medical community in particular.

Doctors and nurses are the most vulnerable groups in society to the virus, and their continuous, uninterrupted work is a kind of professional burden, which generates various psychological states of fear, frustration, and tension. Healthcare workers in various parts of the world are recording deaths and infections with the virus along with medical staff. According to Luo, et al. [15] healthcare workers who have been isolated from or worked in Corona virus units or have of family or friends infected with the virus, they suffer from anxiety, depression, frustration, fear and post-traumatic stress more than other people who have not had this experience.

In medical clinics, the tasks are given to the heads of the medical teams, they are usually the oldest in practice, the others are younger and more experienced, they use them as technicians in the treatment, and both are vulnerable to fears of infection and death from daily contact with patients infected with the virus. Heath workers, who are at the forefront of the fight against the epidemic, also face an extraordinary workload due to the health measures and regulations applied around the world,

Choudhari, [6] adds that the damaging effects of Corona virus not only depend on the level of the body, but also cause cases of chronic mental disorders such as depression, anxiety, panic disorder and psychosomatic manifestations. Thus, through our study, it is evident that the aspects of mental disorders do not only depend on the level of the patients, but also include the medical staff. In this regard, Korkmaz, et al. [7] pointed out that the trauma of nurses and doctors of death, and work until late hours of the day with cases exposed to death without sleep on a regular basis. Which is shown by the axis of other sentences that contain questions about the nature of sleep-in individuals all are considered psychosocial factors that generate stress in the work environment.

4   Conclusion

At the end of this research, we can draw several conclusions that caregivers, including doctors and nurses, the during coronavirus pandemic, of both sexes and those with more than 10 years of experience in the field that they suffer from psychological imbalances at the level of:

- Physical symptoms such as chronic fatigue and insomnia and compulsive obsession that appear in various fears of transmission even in a safe place.
- Reactive sensitivity and disruption of good communication with others.
- Depressive states of Due to their inability to provide health care for difficult cases of the pandemic and anxiety about continuing to the pandemic situation for a long time and phobias and fears of transmitting the infection to their families.
- Hostility, paranoia and psychosis.

References

1. Derogatis, L.R.: SCL-90-R, Administration, Scoring and Procedures Manual-I for the Revised Version. Johns Hopkins School of Medicine, Baltimore (1977)
2. Bouamousha, N.: Coronavirus-Covid19- in Algeria, an analytical study. Soc. Empowerment J. **02**(2), 113–151 (2020)
3. Wang, C., Horby, P.W., Hayden, F.G., Gao, G.F.: A novel coronavirus outbreak of global health concern. Lancet **395**(10223), 470–473 (2020)
4. World Health Organization (WHO). Homepage, https://www.euro.who.int/en/health-top ics/noncommunicable-diseases/mental-health/data-and-resources/mental-health-and-COV ID-19. Accessed 01 Sept 2020
5. Worldometer. Homepage. https://www.worldometers.info/coronavirus/. Accessed 15 Sept 2020

6. Choudhari, R.: COVID 19 pandemic: mental health challenges of internal migrant workers of India. Asian J. Psychiatry **54**, 102254 (2020)
7. Korkmaz, S., Kazgan, A., Çekiç, S., Tartar, A.S., Balcı, H.N., Atmaca, M.: The anxiety levels, quality of sleep and life and problem-solving skills in healthcare workers employed in COVID-19 services. J. Clin. Neurosci. **80**, 131–136 (2020)
8. Bashirian, S., Jenabis, E., Khazaei, S., Barati, M., Karimi-Shahanjarini, A., Zareian, S., Rezapur-Shahkolai, F., Moeini, B.: Factors associated with preventive behaviours of COVID-19 among hospital staff in Iran in 2020: an application of the Protection Motivation Theory. J. Hosp. Infect. **105**(3), 430–433 (2020)
9. Lai, J., Ma, S., Wang, Y., Cai, Z., Hu, J., Wei, N., Wu, J.: Factors associated with mental health outcomes among health care workers exposed to coronavirus disease 2019. JAMA Netw. Open. **3**(3), e203976 (2020)
10. Algerian Ministry of Health, Population and Hospital Reform Homepage. https://covid19.sante.gov.dz/carte/. Accessed 15 Sept 2020
11. Halouani, N., Turki, M., Ennaoui, R., Aloulou, J., Amami, O.: La détresse psychologique du personnel médical et paramédical d'anesthésie-réanimation. Pan Afr. Medi. J. **29**, 1–7 (2018)
12. Islam, S.D.U., Bodrud-Doza, M., Khan, R.M., Haque, M.A., Mamun, M.A.: Exploring COVID-19 stress and its factors in Bangladesh: a perception-based study. Heliyon **6**(7), 1–10 (2020)
13. Ksour, A.: The role of the Social Control Authority on the effectiveness of social distancing in the shadow of the COVID-19 pandemic. J. Dev. Hum. Resour. Manag. **08**(1), 103–118 (2020)
14. Ben Ouargla, N., Bilqamari, H.: Ways to circulate the Corona crisis on social media platforms. Afaq Sci. Mag. **05**(4), 209–217 (2020)
15. Luo, M., Guo, L., Yu, M., Wang, H.: The psychological and mental impact of coronavirus disease 2019 (COVID-19) on medical staff and general public–a systematic review and meta-analysis. Psychiatry Res. **291**, 1–9 (2020)

Learning About Healthcare Resilience from the Initial Response to the COVID-19 Pandemic – A Physiotherapy Case Study

Eva-Maria Carman[✉][iD], Laura Evans, and Giulia Miles

Trent Simulation and Clinical Skills Centre, Queen's Medical Centre, Nottingham University Hospitals NHS Trust, Nottingham, UK
eva.burford@nuh.nhs.uk

Abstract. In April 2020, the UK's initial response to the COVID-19 pandemic resulted in drastic and rapid changes to the way work was done within the National Health Service. Despite the difficult times, staff across this healthcare organisation adapted and developed methods of coping to keep the system functioning. This study aimed to capture the changes and adaptive ways of working specifically for one department, namely the physiotherapy service at one large acute NHS hospital trust in the UK. Eight online focus groups were held with a total of 26 physiotherapy staff to explore the changes in their work system as a result of the initial response to the COVID-19 pandemic. The SEIPS 2.0 model was used to provide a system structure for the analysis. The results report the staff's experiences of work during this time, use a systems perspective to depict the changes in the system and new ways of working, and provide some recommendations for preparation for future 'waves' of this pandemic. Furthermore, by positioning the results within the resilience engineering paradigm, a larger theoretical basis is provided for developing recommendations.

Keywords: Systems approach · SEIPS 2.0 · COVID-19 · Adaptations · Resilience engineering

1 Introduction

As a result of the COVID-19 pandemic, the world has witnessed drastic changes in almost all areas of life within a relatively short period of time. Although this pandemic has affected working systems across industries and the everyday life of workers, as it is a health crisis, healthcare systems have had to rapidly adapt and respond to not only maintain general functioning during this time but also to cope with a large number of causalities as a result of this disaster. As part of the initial response to the COVID-19 pandemic, the National Health Service (NHS) in the United Kingdom witnessed drastic changes to the way work was done in a short time span, that before this crisis, many may not have thought feasible. Despite the extensive changes to daily life and the healthcare work system, the NHS saw departments and staff all across the organisation adapt and develop strategies of coping to keep the healthcare system functioning. This initial response to the COVID-19 pandemic can be described as revealing resilience within this healthcare system, as resilience is defined as a system's intrinsic ability to adjust its operation prior to, during or following changes [1].

At the time of the initial response, the pandemic posed an unprecedented event and as a result the duration and extent of this event was unknown. As time has passed and the available knowledge on this virus and pandemic has increased, it has become clear that this event and the effects of it may extend for a much longer period than initially thought. As a result of this, it is essential to extract key learning and insight from the initial response to inform future responses to this type of disaster. As this pandemic is the largest experienced by staff and healthcare organisations in this generation, the initial response provides information previously unavailable regarding the characteristics of phases associated with pandemics, which are necessary for planning response strategies to ensure successful outcomes [2]. Furthermore, the resilience shown during the initial response needs to be understood so that learning can occur to ensure one transitions to organisational resilience that is not as result of individual resilience of staff groups. This would not only assist with protecting staff wellbeing but would also ensure that appropriate responses to changes in the work system caused by the pandemic can occur over an extended period of time.

1.1 Study Aim and Objectives

The purpose of this study was to capture the adaptive ways of working during the initial NHS response to the COVID-19 pandemic (April 2020) within one service, namely the physiotherapy service at one large acute NHS hospital trust in the UK. The research question addressed in this study was: '*What were the changes and adaptations to work during the initial NHS response to the COVID-19 pandemic (April–July 2020)?*'. The objectives included capturing staff's experiences of work during this time, using a systems perspective to depict the changes in the system and new ways of working, and to compile considerations for preparation for a second 'wave' of this pandemic. Furthermore, by framing the changes within the context of resilience engineering, additional suggestions and considerations for enhancing organisational resilience may be compiled.

2   Method

Using Microsoft Teams, eight online focus groups were conducted between the end of June to the beginning of August 2020. Prior to the start of each focus group, consent was obtained from all participants. Each online focus group was approximately 60 min in duration and was recorded. The questions that guided the online focus groups included:

1. What usual (pre-COVID-19) tasks are working more efficiently at the moment due to the unusual situation? Why may this be the case?
2. What strategies have you or your team developed to anticipate and respond quickly to situations (flexibility)?

3. What has the current work climate been like?
4. What aspects have been really challenging?

The audio data from the focus groups were transcribed and analysed using thematic analysis [3] with NVivo 11 Software [4]. The Systems Engineering Initiative for Patient Safety (SEIPS) 2.0 model [5] was used to structure the analysis so that the themes could be placed within the system context from which they emerged. The anonymised results were presented back to staff who participated in the focus group for sense checking. This paper specifically aimed to explore the changes within the work system identified in the focus groups from a resilience engineering perspective and the potential implications in the development of recommendations for future 'waves'.

2.1 Participants

The department that participated in this study provides physiotherapy support for patients within the acute hospital setting and offers care and rehabilitation of patients with and recovering from COVID-19. The department spans across two campuses, has more than 50 staff and works across a range of departments including intensive care, respiratory medicine, infectious diseases, surgical and outpatient services. A total of 26 physiotherapy staff participated in the eight online focus groups. Of the 26 participants, 12 were physiotherapy staff from critical care and surgery, four from medicine and associated specialities and three were from respiratory physiotherapy. The remaining seven participants were redeployed staff from outpatients and inpatient elective services such as orthopaedics, whose work had been paused. The posts held by participants ranged from physiotherapy assistants (unregistered staff) to registered healthcare professionals that include team leaders and rotational roles. The mean age of the participants was 30.59 years (standard deviation ±6.57). The mean number of years involved in patient care was 8.11 years (±7.22) and the mean number of years in the current position was 5.33 years (±7.19).

3 Results

The focus groups revealed not only the changes, challenges and aspects that worked well during the initial response to the COVID-19 pandemic, but also highlighted the connections between these various elements. These results were then used to compile considerations for future pandemic 'waves'.

3.1 Changes to the Healthcare Work System During the Initial Response to the COVID-19 Pandemic

The outbreak of the COVID-19 pandemic resulted in not only changes to the healthcare system, but also numerous elements of social life changed quite drastically and rapidly (e.g. lockdown, social distancing). Some of the changes that occurred were planned or structured changes, whereas some changes were as a result of other changes and

Table 1. Examples of the changes that occurred during the initial response to the COVID-19 pandemic for the different SEIPS 2.0 work system components.

SEIPS 2.0 work system component	Changes
External environment	• Social Aspects: Lockdown, social distancing • NHS (national level): Redefined service scope, changes to guidelines directing work (e.g. PPE requirements) • NHS (Trust level): Redefined service scope, staff redeployment • Availability of PPE supplies
Internal environment	• Available space on the wards and break rooms
Organisation of work	• Enhanced interdepartmental functioning • Departmental changes: Changes to shift length and service cover, interpretation of new guidelines, increased number of staff assigned to the department (due to staff redeployment) • Team changes: New structure and expanded team • Changes to pace of work (e.g. number and time of patient contacts)
Tasks	• New patient type • Reduction in task types • Changes to tasks (e.g. redistribution of administrative work)
Tools and technology	• Required use of PPE and clarity of guidelines on PPE use • Paperless work
Person(s)	• Changes to individual work (e.g. unwillingness to take leave) • Home life changes (e.g. home schooling)

potentially were not anticipated or planned for. A summary of the identified changes per SEIPS 2.0 work system components has been listed in Table 1.

The planned changes at a national and organisational level to prepare the healthcare system so it could respond to the pandemic included redefining the service scope, staff redeployment, changes to national guidelines directing work, the required use of Personal Protective Equipment (PPE) and the national availability of PPE supplies. The redefined service scope that occurred at both a national and organisational level included suspension of certain work structures (e.g. rotations did not occur), changes to working hours and days of specific departments, and reduction in services offered (e.g. certain outpatient services). To deliver the planned changes set out at a national and organisational level (e.g. redefined service scope and new working hours), changes were implemented at a department level that then impacted the work at the person level.

3.2 Challenges and Aspects that Worked Well During the Initial Response to the COVID-19 Pandemic

The changes at the different system levels not only caused changes within other system levels, but these created challenges that staff had to overcome and prompted adaptations to maintain the functioning of their work system. For example, due to the national change of redeploying staff from non-acute areas to assist in the hospital environment to allow for the change in service cover offered by the physiotherapy department, this resulted in changes to team structure and size, redistribution of administrative and management work, as well as having an effect on space on the wards and in break rooms. This last aspect was further influenced by the external social change of social distancing as this had an influence on the number of staff it was safe to have on wards.

Additional challenges staff identified were associated with task and organisation of work aspects, the internal environment, PPE and staff wellbeing. An example of an organisation of work challenge was professional friction which inhibited physiotherapy work due to a lack of clarity regarding the role of therapy services with COVID-19 patients. This is highlighted in the quote below:

> "I think because the physios were very pro rehab early on there was a lot of challenges from nursing staff and doctors - who kind of forgot what we do anyway before COVID. So, we would get in there and rehab people with their tubes in on Ventilators … we got a massive barrier from doctors, nurses, everyone who just said no, you can't do that."

PPE associated challenges included difficulty in determining different staff roles and staff identity, frequently changing guidelines, inconsistent interpretation of PPE guidelines, and required PPE for therapy activities not made readily available on wards. Staff wellbeing challenges included burnout and fatigue, potentially as staff felt reluctant to take time off during this initial response, a conflict between caring for patients and putting oneself at risk and anxiety associated with initial influx and insufficient organisation, communication, and planning regarding redeployment.

Despite the challenges, staff identified numerous aspects that worked well during this time. From a system's perspective, the aspects that worked well were related to improved outcomes, work system components (including tools, organisation of work and tasks) and processes. The tools staff developed to adapt to the changes included compiling a booklet of new fact finding and evidence, ensuring therapy held stocks of PPE and developing local 'PPE on-call bags' as well as using alternative sources for information. The organisation of work elements that functioned well included the longer and more flexible working schedule, alterations to the scheduling of staff and work, the new team structure, that decision making was done more locally, new communication and information transfer methods were used and previously good working relationships with multidisciplinary teams was enhanced. Although the longer and more flexible working schedule was seen as a positive as it allowed for a longer treatment window for patients, greater distribution of the workload throughout the day, and led to more efficient ways of working, this received mixed feedback from staff. Numerous staff felt this worked at the time due to the context but were unsure for how much longer this would be sustainable.

The change in opinion regarding the new schedule and how the context influenced the opinion is highlighted by the following quote:

"I think there was an initial phase of genuine excitement and people loved working shifts and they didn't mind working crazy hours and there was almost like an adrenaline buzz of we are at the forefront of this ... And then ... the excitement died down a little bit, but people were still very willing to work shifts on weekends because everything was shut and things were becoming mundane... then after about 8 or 9 weeks there was a real fatigue."

As highlighted in the quote above a key consideration for challenges and aspects that worked well is the context in which they occurred. To understand how these new ways of working emerged, one needs to understand and explore the connections between the changes within the system. This provides additional insight into some of the requirements and potential costs that may be associated with the aspects that worked well during this time.

3.3   Recommendations for Future Pandemic 'Waves'

The recommendations for future work and future pandemic 'waves' were compiled based on the challenges and aspects that worked well identified during the focus group discussion and confirmed at the sense checking event following the analysis of the data. Seven key recommendations were identified, with two referring to general work system elements and the remaining five associated with specific pandemic response elements. A brief description of the recommendations has been included in Table 2.

Table 2. Considerations for future pandemic 'waves'.

General work system considerations
• Clear, consistent guidance, information and communication: Consistent and definitive information specifically on topics such as infection control, staff exposure, and PPE use
• Promoting staff wellbeing: Ensure staff are actively taking rest and recover through protecting time off and ensuring annual leave is taken regularly. Provide hot and cold debriefing for staff at both a personal and team level
Pandemic specific considerations
• Promoting visibility of the management team: This may be through clear, consistent and regular updates, especially during crisis periods even if there are no new updates
• Earlier changes to service structures (e.g. rostering) if required
• Clear implementation and exit strategies if redeployed staff are to be implemented
• Maintaining the training competencies of staff that were redeployed for the initial response
• Comprehensive PPE plan: This would include sufficient supplies of PPE and communication of the same evidence-based information across all areas within the organization

4 Discussion

Although the COVID-19 pandemic has provided unprecedented challenges for the healthcare system, an unintended positive aspect of work during this time was that it gave staff and the organisation an opportunity to explore new ways of working, that historically may not have been considered as feasible. This may provide insight into enhancing the 'normal' functioning of the system once the pandemic has ended. Furthermore, the initial response to the pandemic highlighted the amount of change that can occur rapidly within a work system to maintain its function and may provide insight into developing organisational resilience that may not have otherwise been visible. By placing these results within the resilience engineering paradigm, previous research and theory may be able to provide guidance on how to move forward to enhance the resilience of the healthcare system. Based on the challenges healthcare systems have had to face worldwide since the start of the COVID-19 pandemic, one could argue that they have had to develop forms of resilience to prevent organisational collapse. Although healthcare staff have shown great resilience in the face of this pandemic, resilience engineering rather focuses on this attribute generated at a team or unit level as a result of organisational processes [6]. Examples of the four cornerstones of organisational resilience [7] are identifiable during the initial response to the pandemic in the different organisation levels within the NHS. An example for each cornerstone and the organisation level it occurred at is described in Table 3.

Table 3. Examples of the four cornerstones of resilience present during the initial response to the COVID-19 pandemic.

The four cornerstones of resilience	Examples from the initial response to the COVID-19 pandemic (organisation level)
Anticipating	Creating a flexible work schedule that would allow the physiotherapy department to be able to respond to a surge in patients (departmental level)
Monitoring	New communication and information transfer methods were used (departmental level)
Responding	Physiotherapy department held their own PPE stocks and developed 'PPE on-call bags' for the staff in response to PPE associated problems (departmental level)
Learning	Physiotherapy department compiled a booklet of new fact finding and evidence as a result of the new and continued situation (departmental level)

By looking at the changes and adaptations that occurred during the initial response to the pandemic from a resilience engineering perspective, insight on the support needed to further embed the quality of resilience within an organisation is provided. For example, the key principles of resilience include top management commitment, flexibility, learning, awareness [8], open communication and a non-punitive approach towards error reporting [9]. By being aware that these principles are required to promote resilience, one can start to identify what structures need to be in place. A theme associated with the challenges, aspects that worked well and recommendations identified in this study was consistent communication. As open communication is a key principle of resilience, it is visible that in some areas communication was functioning better than in other areas. A next step would be to explore if there were pre-existing factors that might have enabled or enhanced communication within certain areas.

5 Conclusion

This case study explored the changes that occurred within one department during the initial response to the COVID-19 pandemic. By considering the changes from a system's perspective, the connections between the different changes were revealed and highlighted how the changes may create challenges for staff and in turn how staff adapted their way of working to overcome these challenges. Although a lot of positive elements were identified by staff during the NHS's response to the initial outbreak of COVID-19, it is important to bear in mind the system inputs that allowed for the changes and the effect of the rapid change on staff's wellbeing and the ability to maintain this. Furthermore, by positioning the results within the resilience engineering paradigm, theories to support promoting some of the aspects that worked well during the initial response are identified.

References

1. Hollnagel, E.: Prologue: the scope of resilience engineering. In: Resilience Engineering in Practice: A Guidebook, pp. xxix–xxxix (2011)
2. Garrett, S.K. Caldwell, B.S.: Human factors aspects of planning and response to pandemic events. In: IIE Annual Conference Proceedings, pp. 705–711 (2009)
3. Braun, V., Clarke, V.: What can 'thematic analysis' offer health and wellbeing researchers? Int. J. Qual. Stud. Health Well-being 9(1), 26152 (2014)
4. QSR International Pty Ltd.: NVivo Qualitative Data Analysis Software (2015)
5. Holden, R.J., et al.: SEIPS 2.0: a human factors framework for studying and improving the work of healthcare professionals and patients. Ergonomics 56(11), 1669–1686 (2013)
6. Anderson, J.E., et al.: Implementing resilience engineering for healthcare quality improvement using the CARE model: a feasibility study protocol. Pilot Feasibility Stud. 2(1), 61 (2016)
7. Hollnagel, E.: The four cornerstones of resilience engineering. In: Resilience Engineering Perspectives: Vol. 2 Preparation and Restoration, Farnham, UK, pp. 117–133. Ashgate Publishing Ltd. (2009)
8. Hollnagel, E.: Resilience Engineering: Concepts and Precepts. Ashgate Publishing Ltd., United Kingdom (2006)
9. Vogus, T.J., Sutcliffe, K.M.: Organizational resilience: towards a theory and research agenda. In: Proceedings of IEEE International Conference on Systems, Man and Cybernetics, pp. 3418–3422 (2007)

A Survey on the Effects of the Covid-19 in the Brazilian Population Lifestyle

Eduardo Ferro dos Santos[1](✉) ⓘ, Paulo Victor Rodrigues de Carvalho[2] ⓘ, and José Orlando Gomes[3] ⓘ

[1] School of Engineering of Lorena, Department of Basic and Environmental Sciences, University of Sao Paulo, Lorena, SP, Brazil
eduardo.ferro@usp.br
[2] Nuclear Engineering Institute, National Nuclear Energy Commission, Rio de Janeiro, RJ, Brazil
paulov195617@gmail.com
[3] Industrial Engineering and Computer Science Program, Federal University of Rio de Janeiro, Rio de Janeiro, RJ, Brazil
joseorlando@nce.ufrj.br

Abstract. How far can a whole social routine be transformed after the restrictions imposed by the Covid-19 pandemic? It is possible that it has impacted human factors and ergonomics, such as sleep, physical activity, mental health and activities of daily living. It is necessary to focus on society currently, and to determine new forms of interaction in search of a better quality of life. The objective of this work is to determine the extent the restrictions imposed by the Covid-19 influenced human behavior in relation to style and quality of life, whether or not imposing new routines, and whether these, such as these, may impact the change of a society. To better understand the impact of the Covid-19 pandemic on society, human factors variables were raised, and a survey study, where several people were able to answer and share their experiences in the midst of the restrictions of the pandemic when answering an online questionnaire. The research seeks by asking questions to the target audience on variables related to the home environment, employment situation, work routine and health in general. In addition, the research explores symptoms of depression and anxiety, as well as sleep, wakefulness, and physical activity levels. There is a need for a new direction in research to monitor the changes across society, seeking a vision of a new society, which emerges in the face of a disruptive period, which impacts the entire planet.

Keywords: Covid-19 · Lifestyle · Quality of life · Human factors

1 Introduction

The effects of the Covid-19 are reflected in several areas of society [1]. It is necessary to focus on society and determine new forms of interaction in search of a better quality of life. The Covid-19 Pandemic consequences may have impacted human factors, such

N. L. Black et al. (Eds.): IEA 2021, LNNS 222, pp. 540–547, 2021.
https://doi.org/10.1007/978-3-030-74611-7_73

as sleep, physical activity, mental health, and daily living activities. These factors have already been seen in research with children [2], mental health [3], and eating habits [4].

The restrictions imposed on society to minimize and mitigate the effects of Covid-19 led to a reduction in social interactions, such as physical distance and changing routines, such as access to work, commerce, and services [5].

These changes may also have influenced certain aspects of our quality of life, such as well-being, sleep, meal times, and even human motivation and employability. These aspects can contain drastic changes, and they can even be irreversible in human factors [6]. People are implementing new routines in a new normal. We still don't know if the changes will be useful, or if people will one day be able to go back to how they were before.

This paper aims to determine how the extent of the restrictions imposed by the Covid-19 pandemic influenced human behavior about lifestyle, and the impact in the way of society, especially in the Brazilian population.

To better understand the impact of the Covid-19 pandemic on Brazilian society, human factors related to the quality of life, lifestyle, and daily routines were raised. A survey type study was carried out [7], where several people were able to answer and share their experiences amid the pandemic restrictions by answering an online questionnaire.

By examining the interactions between changes in human factors resulting from social constraints, such as those imposed by the Covid-19 pandemic, one can predict states of anxiety, depression, or a better lifestyle.

The research seeks questions through variables related to the home environment, employment situation, work routine, and health in general. The study also explores symptoms of depression and anxiety and sleep behavior, wakefulness, and physical activity levels.

2 Methodology

The research was carried out through the collection of quantitative data over the web. The research method used was the internet-based survey [7], non-probabilistic procedures [8], convenience sampling [9], conducted by the snowball method.

This form has the advantages of being able to be developed with low or no cost, applied in a faster and more efficient way, with a readily available sample, fewer rules to follow, and with a better capacity of distinction and analysis of variables due to the use of direct quantitative data, in addition to being applied in a larger geographic area.

The main disadvantage is that the return rate is low, between 5 to 20% of those who receive the access link. The fear can explain it that many people have when clicking on a link they are unaware of, by the fear of containing some malicious file, which could steal data or damage the computer. It is also possible to refuse to answer without anyone knowing.

It is a cross-sectional survey, as it includes a population section encompassing respondents to an online questionnaire developed on Google Forms. The average time to answer the questionnaire was based on a pilot test with a group of people who responded in an average time of twelve minutes.

The questionnaire was sent through an access link in social networks and contacts, who asked the respondents to disclose it. The return was 45 questionnaires.

At the beginning of the questionnaire, they accept the researchers' protocol to obtain if they intend to spontaneously answer the survey in a free and informed consent term. This term follows the ethics protocols of the National Research Ethics Commission in Brazil. Although there is this consent, it is not necessary to identify the respondent.

The elaboration of the questions involved questions from a questionnaire designed to be used in the BRICS ergonomics network, being adapted in each of the countries. Questionnaires are often used interchangeably in various surveys [10].

The questionnaire was adapted for use in Brazil with two sessions. A session is a general presentation with questions containing the age group, gender, city, state, and occupation. The second session relates to lifestyle, physical health, mental health, social relationships, work, routines, food, leisure and sleep. The survey was conducted between November and December 2020.

The research submits variables answered in two scenarios: (1) Before the restrictions imposed by the pandemic, referring to the three months before we entered into social rules and closing of trade in general (i.e., January, February, and March 2020), and (2) During social and commercial restrictions, which refer to the period after the previous scenario (April to September 2020). The differences are apparent in Brazilian society's behavior when buying more online, but they also pointed out several problems.

3   Results

Table 1 shows the age group's relationship, emphasizing the age group from 36 to 45 years old, with 37.8% of the total. The predominance of responses is female, with 62.2% of the total respondents.

Table 1. Respondents' age range.

Age	% of Total	Cumulative %
26–35 yo	22.2%	22.2%
36–45 yo	37.8%	60.0%
46–55 yo	22.2%	82.2%
56–65 yo	15.6%	97.8%
66 yo or more	02.2%	100%

Among Brazilian states, 42.2% live in the state of Rio de Janeiro, 28.9% in the state of São Paulo, and 13.3% in the state of Paraná. The rest are distributed among 7 other states. Regarding occupation, 28.8% of respondents work with education, 22.2% in service provision, 13.3% are students and 8.9% work from home.

Regarding how many people live in the same house, Fig. 1 shows that the vast majority live alone (36.4%) or between 2 to 4 people.

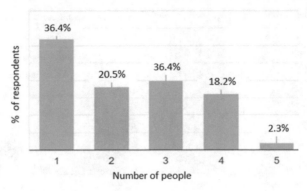

Fig. 1. The number of people in the same house.

Analyzing people's feelings about the danger of Covid-19, the results showed that 37.8% think the virus is dangerous and prefer to stay at home. However, 20% also like to stay at home, but cannot because of work. For 42.2%, the coronavirus is not so dangerous, and with some security measures, one can lead life normally.

Most bother the great majority is the distancing from the family (66.7%) and not being with friends (51.1%). Staying at home and the commerce restrictions with the closing of stores bothered 22.2% in each of these variables since 53.3% of people worked in the home office during the pandemic, 22.2% work by going to the company only essential, predominantly in the home office. Only 13.3% were forced to go to the company every day.

Comparing the working hours per day before and after the pandemic, Fig. 2 shows an apparent increase in the number of hours worked. What previously prevailed between 8 to 10 h of work per day has now been more than 10 h.

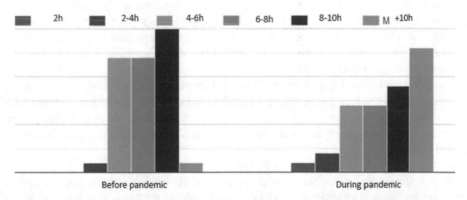

Fig. 2. The number of hours of work per day, before and during the pandemic.

It also changed working hours for 52.4% of people. Figure 3 shows a more significant change in night work, especially at night and in the morning. Regarding the waking time, no differences were noticed.

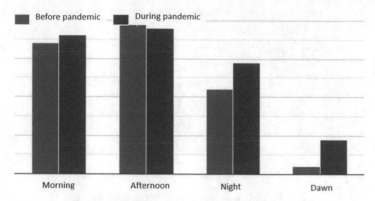

Fig. 3. Work shifts before and after the pandemic.

Leisure activities had a significant impact, with a reduction of 52.2% in outdoor or gym sports, 39% in shopping, and 100% in leisure travel. The increase was seen in watching television and surfing the internet, both with a rise of 25%.

Before the pandemic, the most affected performance issues were waking up, frequent stops at work, and inadequate meals. During the pandemic, the primary references to low productivity were reported to night work, shift shifts, workload, uneven distribution of tasks, and especially the insecurity in being fired, which increased by 700% among respondents.

Another factor that was changed was the number of daily meals, where there were people who answered 5 meals a day, and those who eat all the time. These answers were not found in the questionnaire regarding the period before the pandemic.

These changes reflected some problems, with increased responses regarding decreased mood, restlessness, and agitation, eating disorders, sadness, loneliness, increased consumption of alcohol, tobacco, and drugs, in addition to anxiety, depression, and negative thoughts. These increased values ranged from 300% to 700%.

The condition noted as positive by the respondents was that they became more concerned with themselves (an increase of 500%), the improvement of empathy and patience (both with a 30% increase).

In addition to emotional factors, physical factors were also found. Among them, the biggest was the increase in appetite (2100%), muscle pain (250%), and others with gains more significant than 100%, such as hair loss, change in desire or sexual response, changes in the menstrual cycle, headaches, vision problems, weight gain, and increased blood pressure.

The cognitive system was also affected. Difficulty concentrating was reported with a 100% increase and cases not reported before the pandemic emerged, such as disorientation and mental confusion, in addition to the problem of stopping thinking about unpleasant incidents or situations.

According to those who answered the survey, the leading causes of physical and mental discomfort were social isolation. The usual causes of stress are the fear of losing their job to 66.7% of people, and the concern with family members and the family health, with 44.4% in each variable. On a Likert scale, from 0 to 10, with zero being unable to deal with these problems, 10 being able to deal with these problems and overcome this phase is shown in Fig. 4.

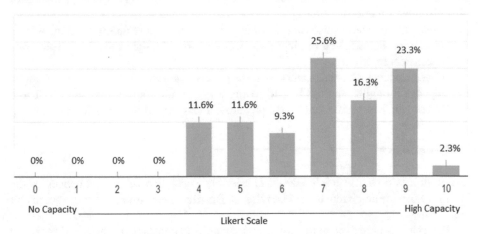

Fig. 4. Individual ability to solve problems

Concerning points noted in the responses were that 7% of people divorced, 45.5% have not rested well, 56.8% work more than before, and 10% seek medical treatment more often. Positive points were noticed in no job loss among the respondents, and 60% reported spending more time with the family, enjoying the benefits of this. In people who work seated, those who exercised home office said a decrease in time in the sitting posture since the domestic environment allows a better postural alteration.

4   Discussion

The differences are apparent in terms of quality of life and behavior of Brazilian society, with positive and negative points.

Among the 27 Brazilian states, the research did not reach 17 states, which brings the need to expand the databases or change how they are collected in the study's progress.

The list of people living alone (36.4%) may explain some of the answers where loneliness, negative thoughts, and the sadness of social isolation were evident since they are far from their families, with restrictions on trade and leisure being imposed across the country.

People's feeling about the danger of Covid-19 was not so significant, as less than half considered Covid-19 dangerous, a situation that goes against the principles of health and safety preservation discussed worldwide.

Working from home in a home office model seems to be the majority's preference, but although they think the virus is not so severe, most people suffer from the fear of losing the job, family, and health.

Working from home also impacts the workload, differently from what people thought. Changes in meal times and rest are added, and leisure hours are consumed, making the relationship that was once dreamed of harms people's health.

People started to eat more, sleep less, be more dispersed in thoughts, show signs of anxiety and depression. Although we have realized the advantage of staying less time in the sitting position in the home office than in the company, it is not suitable for administrative functions.

Staying more at home also caused some people to have more family friction, but this is a point to be investigated in other surveys more specifically, as the 7% divorce rate can be considered normal.

What must be eliminated in any way is the poor distribution of work, excessive hours, and negative thoughts, such as fear of losing a job, health, family, and friends. These factors can lead to a more mental than physical illness, which becomes worrying.

5 Conclusion

Although it is a small sample size, it is possible to see that the consequences of the Covid-19 pandemic changed the behavior of Brazilians and impacted their quality of life.

The changes perceived in this research may point to constant concerns and fears that can have consequences such as anxiety, depression, and panic. The reaction to these problems will depend on each one, as it influences biopsychological factors. However, if the changes were not inserted in the workload that needs to decrease and the hours of rest that need to increase, everything will become a big problem.

It is time to look at how we can organize our work and lifestyle ourselves and realize the values that we are putting ahead of our lives. If it is so problematic to stay at home, with the home office, to be with the family, something is wrong. It's time to rethink what the priorities are and reorganize ourselves.

An analysis of tasks and activities, from the perspective of ergonomics in the organization of work, can reflect benefits and change this excess scenario. The fear of losing a job, health, and family members, on the other hand, should make us recall that we must adopt these actions and keep ourselves safer. Only then will we live better and be productive.

References

1. Atalan, A.: Is the lockdown important to prevent the COVID-19 pandemic? Effects on psychology, environment and economy-perspective. Ann. Med. Surg. **56**, 38–42 (2020). https://doi.org/10.1016/j.amsu.2020.06.010
2. Pietrobelli, A., Pecoraro, L., Ferruzzi, A., Heo, M., Faith, M., Zoller, T., Antoniazzi, F., Piacentini, G., Fearnbach, S.N., Heymsfield, S.B.: Effects of COVID-19 lockdown on lifestyle behaviors in children with obesity living in Verona, Italy: a longitudinal study. Obes. Silver Spring Md. **28**, 1382–1385 (2020). https://doi.org/10.1002/oby.22861
3. Rossi, R., Socci, V., Talevi, D., Mensi, S., Niolu, C., Pacitti, F., Di Marco, A., Rossi, A., Siracusano, A., Di Lorenzo, G.: COVID-19 Pandemic and lockdown measures impact on mental health among the general population in Italy. Front. Psychiatry. **11** (2020). https://doi.org/10.3389/fpsyt.2020.00790.
4. Sidor, A., Rzymski, P.: Dietary choices and habits during COVID-19 lockdown: experience from Poland. Nutrients **12**, 1657 (2020). https://doi.org/10.3390/nu12061657

5. Mucci, F., Mucci, N., Diolaiuti, F.: Lockdown and isolation: psychological aspects of covid-19 pandemic in the general population. Clin. Neuropsychiatry. **17** (2020). https://doi.org/10.36131/CN20200205.

6. Barreto, M.A.M., Vasconcelos, S.S., dos Santos, E.F.: Motivation and work: a survey of the motivational aspects in industries. In: Kantola, J.I., Barath, T., Nazir, S. (eds.) Advances in Human Factors, Business Management and Leadership, pp. 319–328. Springer International Publishing, Cham (2018). https://doi.org/10.1007/978-3-319-60372-8_31.

7. Alvarez, R.M., VanBeselaere, C.: Web-Based Survey. In: Kempf-Leonard, K. (ed.) Encyclopedia of Social Measurement, pp. 955–962. Elsevier, New York (2005). https://doi.org/10.1016/B0-12-369398-5/00390-X.

8. Galloway, A.: Non-probability sampling. In: Kempf-Leonard, K. (ed.) Encyclopedia of Social Measurement, pp. 859–864. Elsevier, New York (2005). https://doi.org/10.1016/B0-12-369398-5/00382-0.

9. Edgar, T.W., Manz, D.O.: Exploratory study. In: Edgar, T.W., Manz, D.O. (eds.) Research Methods for Cyber Security, pp. 95–130. Syngress (2017). https://doi.org/10.1016/B978-0-12-805349-2.00004-2.

10. Toepoel, V., Das, M., Van Soest, A.: Design of web questionnaires: the effects of the number of items per screen. Field Methods. **21**, 200–213 (2009). https://doi.org/10.1177/1525822X08330261

The Effects of the Covid-19 Pandemic on E-Commerce: A Survey on Brazilian Consumer Behavior

Eduardo Ferro dos Santos[1]([⊠]) [iD], Paulo Victor Rodrigues de Carvalho[2] [iD], and José Orlando Gomes[3]([⊠])

[1] School of Engineering of Lorena, Department of Basic and Environmental Sciences, University of Sao Paulo, Lorena, SP, Brazil
eduardo.ferro@usp.br
[2] Nuclear Engineering Institute, National Nuclear Energy Commission, Rio de Janeiro, RJ, Brazil
[3] Industrial Engineering and Computer Sciences Program, Federal University of Rio de Janeiro, Rio de Janeiro, RJ, Brazil
joseorlando@nce.ufrj.br

Abstract. Brazil's e-commerce system has changed around insecurity and low-quality delivery, not being efficient and effective. In response to the Covid-19 pandemic, the Brazilian population was forced to leave insecurity and use e-commerce. But are the significant issues resolved? How do people shop online? What does the Brazilian market like when shopping online? In what ways do Brazilians use e-commerce? Has behavior changed? These are the critical aspects of this study. In an online survey of convenience, a probability sample conducted using a snowball method. The survey pointed out that the acceleration of e-commerce shows the urgency to ensure that the country can better use e-commerce to take advantage of the digitalization opportunities and help the government in its economic recovery.

Keywords: Covid-19 · E-commerce · Consumer behavior · Quality in services

1 Introduction

The Covid-19 has negative impacts on several aspects of society [1]. The research on consumer behavior already describes the extent of consumers and companies [2, 3].

However, in Brazil, e-commerce continues amid insecurity and low quality in deliveries, not being an efficient and effective means. Following the Covid-19 pandemic, the situation forced Brazilian society to put aside its feelings of insecurity and regain its sense of self. Internet shopping, home delivery, among other local services, have become favorable options.

E-commerce encompasses the buying and selling goods and services over the internet by the customer, who is the consumer. Transactions are carried out at retail, serving the company's need, or wholesale, involving bulk purchasing. The e-commerce transaction

N. L. Black et al. (Eds.): IEA 2021, LNNS 222, pp. 548–554, 2021.
https://doi.org/10.1007/978-3-030-74611-7_74

can be carried out in different ways, in cash or installments, called B2B transactions - Business to Business, B2C - Business to Consumer, and C2C - Consumer to Consumer.

The rapid development of information and communication technologies, the steady growth of Internet users, the increasing number of people that use online shopping, and lower prices than face-to-face are facts that drive e-commerce.

With the potential impacts of the Covid-19 pandemic, uncertainties were established, such as the risk of diminished purchasing power due to the adverse effects of the economy. At the same time, due to the fact related to social distance and lockdown, it can drive the growth of the delivery business.

Due to workers with Covid-19 being absent or being blocked from work by public authorities following the current legislation, production is impacted. Some of the rules decrease the production power and supply for certain products and services.

While these technologies continue to develop, the growth of e-commerce is also accelerating. These factors can contribute to the frustration of the consumer who has made the purchase, who needs the product or service, and who may have to wait for the company to overcome the challenges that they face in the business.

Fundamental questions arise in the face of this scenario: What is the impact of the pandemic on the quality of e-commerce services? How did the Brazilian market reinvent itself? What is the Brazilian's satisfaction with online services, and how does he behave? Can new behaviors be maintained in a new normal? What is the impact of the restrictions imposed by the Covid-19 on consumer behavior and the Brazilian e-commerce market? These are questions that guide this research.

The issues related to Brazil are part of this work since other researchers belonging to the collaboration network in ergonomics of the BRICS countries are precisely applying this research in their countries, with results that will be later integrated.

To better understand the impact of Covid-19 on consumer behavior and the Brazilian online market, important variables including quality, safety, and consumer satisfaction were investigated. An internet survey was conducted to determine the system's effectiveness [4], where several people were able to answer and share their experiences amid the pandemic restrictions when answering an online questionnaire.

This research aims to understand country-specific scenarios that will affect the use of e-commerce in Brazil.

2 Methodology

The research was carried out through the collection of quantitative data over the web. The research method used was the internet-based survey [4] non-probabilistic procedures [5] in a convenience sampling and snowball [6].

This form has the advantages of being able to be developed with low or no cost, applied in a faster and more efficient way, with a readily available sample, fewer rules to follow, and with a better capacity of distinction and analysis of variables due to the use of direct quantitative data can be applied in a larger geographic area.

The main disadvantage is that the return rate is low and tends to be standardized under 10%. It can be explained due to the fear that many people have when clicking on a link that they may not know for fear of containing some malicious file that can steal data or damage the computer and the possibility of saying no without anyone knowing.

It is a cross-sectional survey, as it includes a population section encompassing respondents to an online questionnaire developed on Google Forms. The average time to answer the questionnaire was based on a pilot test with a group of people who responded in an average time of five minutes.

The questionnaire was sent to survey respondents through a link in social networks and contacts of the researchers. The response rate was 41 questionnaire surveys.

At the beginning of the questionnaire, respondents answer whether they intend to spontaneously answer the survey by accepting a free and informed consent term, following the National Research Ethics Commission's ethics protocols in Brazil. Although there is this consent, it is not necessary to identify the respondent.

The elaboration of the questions involved questions from a single questionnaire designed to be used in the BRICS ergonomics network, being adapted in each of the countries. Questionnaires are often used interchangeably in various surveys [7]. The questionnaire was then adapted for use in Brazil with 18 main questions, divided into two sessions. The first session consists of general information such as age, gender, city, state, and occupation. The second session was about preferences, satisfaction, difficulties, and security. The survey was conducted from November to December of 2020.

The research submits variables answered in two scenarios: (1) Before the restrictions imposed by the pandemic, referring to the three months before we entered into social restrictions and closing of trade in general (January, February, and March 2020), and (2) During social and commercial restrictions, which refer to the period after the previous scenario (April to September 2020). The differences are apparent in Brazilian society's behavior when buying more online, but they also pointed out several problems.

3   Results

By examining the interactions between consumer behavior changes resulting from social and commercial restrictions such as those imposed by the pandemic, improvements can be envisaged to be implemented in Brazilian e-commerce. These recommendations can be beneficial, efficient, and practical, generating new markets and a better economy.

The study investigates the audience regarding variables that influence service quality, efficiency, safety, and reliability. The study analyses the top products and the strengths and weaknesses of e-commerce in the region.

Table 1 shows the age group's relationship, emphasizing the two age groups, from 36 to 45 years old with more than half of the respondents (51.2%) and 26 to 35 years old, with 26.8% of the total. The predominance of responses is female, with 68.3% of the total respondents.

Among Brazilian states, 41.5% live in the state of São Paulo, 29.3% in the state of Rio de Janeiro, and 12.2% in the state of Paraná. The rest is distributed among 6 other states. About occupation, 26.8% of the respondents work in providing services, 22% at home, 9.8% are students, and 2.4% work in the industry.

In terms of shopping preference, 51.2% prefer to shop online and 29.3% in physical stores. For 19.5%, the way to buy is indifferent. By analyzing the data leading to the

Table 1. Respondents' age group.

Age range	% of total	Cumulative %
26–35 years old	26.8%	26.8%
36–45 years old	51.2%	78.0%
46–55 years old	9.8%	87.8%
56–65 years old	9.8%	97.6%
66 years old or more	2.4%	100.0%

main reasons for purchasing via the internet, we can see that after the pandemic, most causes increased, except for the low price, which was one of the reasons that decreased after the pandemic (Fig. 1).

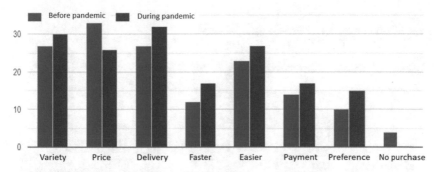

Fig. 1. Top reasons to buy on the internet before and after the pandemic.

Figure 2 shows an increase among those who have already bought online in terms of the frequency of purchases.

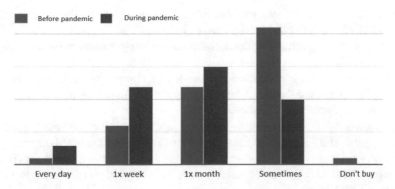

Fig. 2. Frequency of internet shopping before and after the pandemic.

As for the type of products purchased by users on the internet, the buy of electronic products has been down by 3.57% compared to before and after the pandemic. The other products, on the other hand, had an increase, such as 28.5% in shoes, 220% in clothing, 100% in food, 27.2% in medicine, 15% enrollment in digital services, 56.2% in education (courses), and 70% in food and supermarkets.

In terms of satisfaction, the survey showed improvements in product deliveries, with a 25% decrease in late delivery and packaging quality complaints. Besides, there was an improvement of about 20% in the range of products offered by virtual stores and the price. Satisfaction with the service decreased by 20%, exacerbating the pandemic.

Among the main reasons for dissatisfaction, we measure the process of canceling and returning products. Figure 3 shows no relevant situations regarding the problems with which the orders are canceled upon purchases. The number of people who did not experience problems has not changed. The items for compensation and service delays improved in the pandemic. It seems that contact with the company became more difficult, which got worse after the pandemic.

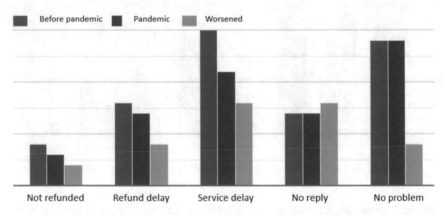

Fig. 3. Problems with purchases before and after the pandemic.

This dissatisfaction also comes from difficulties, in which the respondents claimed an increase of 70% of the products that were not in stock and a price increase of 50% of the items. In terms of payment options, there was an improvement, with more payment options now available.

Even amongst the top companies on the list of companies purchased during the pandemic, Fig. 4 shows the word cloud about the responses. Amazon, Americanas, Magalu were the most cited companies.

It is noteworthy in the responses that in comparison to the previous period to the pandemic period, the 3 most cited companies were the ones that showed the most growth in accesses. Companies like Aliexpress and those related to the hotel chain (Booking, Hotel Urbano, Hotels.com, Accor Hotels) were the ones that presented the most losses (on average 50% below).

The most secure items for purchases were food, medicine, cleaning products, electronics, and subscriptions to television and internet services. However, they feel insecure

Fig. 4. Leading companies accessed in the pandemic.

when buying clothing in general, perishables, and furniture. When delivering the product, they prefer couriers with adequate personal protection and airtight packaging.

At the end of the survey, it was asked what brings more confidence in purchasing products and services over the internet. 78% answered that they trust more leading brands or sites, a reference in the national or international market, and 22% trust the local market.

4 Discussion

The differences are apparent in Brazilian society's behavior when buying more online, but they also pointed out several problems.

During the pandemic, more than half of the survey respondents reported making online purchases more often and relying more on the internet for news, health-related information, and digital entertainment.

Among the 27 Brazilian states, the survey did not reach 18 states, which leads to the need to expand the databases or change how they are collected in research advances. However, the state of São Paulo is the one with the highest consumption in the country.

The predominance of purchases related to the female gender point to a better cultural context. Females are always the best reference for buying. The marketing needs to be well-targeted to this segment.

The number of people who use e-commerce increases every day. In the survey, the reference of more than half of the respondents (51.2%), added to the indifferent ones (19.5%), shows that the future of business is even e-commerce.

The pandemic increased the options available for a purchase payment, the forms, and the Brazilian frequency of purchases. Investing in customer retention systems is necessary to ensure continuity of indices.

The decrease in the purchase of electronics and the increase in clothing (clothes and shoes) may be linked to this change in profile, where women have the most significant purchasing power in their hands.

E-commerce is related to delivery, and fortunately, this item was not wrong. It must be motivated by the expressive increase of moto boys and delivery services, which are no longer dependent only on the Post Office organization, a Brazilian state-owned company.

However, dissatisfaction with the service is a bad sign, which can be related to the teams' lack of preparation for the area's growth.

American companies, Amazon and Magalu, the 4 most cited, point to the return on investment that these companies had already been making, well before the pandemic, in e-commerce. They were already prepared and grew even more in the pandemic, regardless of a possible economic crisis in the population. The hotel industry's decrease is evident, as tourism was one of the main areas affected by the pandemic.

Nowadays, people still trust more in leading brands than in local markets, which grew in the middle of the pandemic but still represent little consumer preference.

5 Conclusion

Although it is a small sample size, it is possible to see that the consequences of the Covid-19 pandemic have changed the Brazilian online shopping behavior.

A peak in Brazilian e-commerce was perceived, mainly due to the purchase of computational resources to establish a home office, home scholar, or even new services. The country's unemployment by the economic crisis resulted from the Covid-19.

Also, some online scammers have increased, and several complaints of customer dissatisfaction have been verified. Some companies were not prepared for an online business, and inexperience contributed to the causes of unfulfilled promises.

Special attention is needed to adapt to companies and consumers so that Brazil can minimize problems and resume the economy with new products and services.

The fact is that the acceleration of online shopping shows the urgency to ensure that Brazil can take advantage of digitalization opportunities as the country goes through its economic recovery. More investment is needed to improve service and regional marketing.

References

1. Atalan, A.: Is the lockdown important to prevent the COVID-19 pandemic? effects on psychology, environment and economy-perspective. Ann. Med. Surg. **56**, 38–42 (2020). https://doi.org/10.1016/j.amsu.2020.06.010
2. Sheth, J.: Impact of Covid-19 on consumer behavior: will the old habits return or die? J. Bus. Res. **117**, 280–283 (2020). https://doi.org/10.1016/j.jbusres.2020.05.059
3. Donthu, N., Gustafsson, A.: Effects of COVID-19 on business and research. J. Bus. Res. **117**, 284 (2020). https://doi.org/10.1016/j.jbusres.2020.06.008
4. Alvarez, R.M., VanBeselaere, C.: Web-based survey. In: Kempf-Leonard, K. (ed.) Encyclopedia of Social Measurement, pp. 955–962. Elsevier, New York (2005). https://doi.org/10.1016/B0-12-369398-5/00390-X
5. Galloway, A.: Non-probability sampling. In: Kempf-Leonard, K. (ed.) Encyclopedia of Social Measurement, pp. 859–864. Elsevier, New York (2005). https://doi.org/10.1016/B0-12-369398-5/00382-0
6. Edgar, T.W., Manz, D.O.: Exploratory study. In: Edgar, T.W., Manz, D.O. (eds.) Research Methods for Cyber Security, pp. 95–130. Syngress (2017). https://doi.org/10.1016/B978-0-12-805349-2.00004-2
7. Toepoel, V., Das, M., Van Soest, A.: Design of web questionnaires: the effects of the number of items per screen. Field Methods **21**, 200–213 (2009). https://doi.org/10.1177/1525822X08330261

Design Solutions to Improve Medical Protective Equipment During COVID-19 Pandemic

Laura Giraldi, Marta Maini[(✉)], and Francesca Morelli

University of Florence, Florence, Italy
{laura.giraldi,marta.maini,francesca.morelli}@unifi.it

Abstract. The current pandemic situation caused by SARS-Cov-2 has high-lighted that collaboration between different sectors can represent a winning way for emergency management. However, even today, the design is often considered an "aesthetic" element and not a strong strategic instrument able to bring innovation to different sectors. This paper, therefore, proposes to highlight how design can be a strategic medium during such situations. The research aims to identify and strategic design solutions to improve first responders' comfort and well-being during the emergency of COVID 19, referring in particular to the medical personnel employed on the frontline during the pandemic. The research investigated the aspects related to the specific scenario of the COVID19 pandemic emergency through different interviews and questionnaires with health workers and a co-working activity with design students. The co-working activity with design students aimed to individuate new technologies and innovative material in relation with health operators' needs and proposed innovative design solutions of PPE. Finally, the research proposed a set of open rules for designing innovative medical PPE to be used during a pandemic, considering the communication aspects in order to improve final user's comfort.

Keywords: Design · Covid-19 · Emergency · Communication design · Education · Interdisciplinarity

1 Introduction

1.1 COVID-19 Pandemic Scenario

COVID-19 is an infectious respiratory disease caused by a coronavirus Sars-cov-2 that has soon become a pandemic. This unexpected infectious disease has hit our society very hard, changing our lifestyle, the interaction between people, and the concept of self-care. In a few weeks, the virus spread worldwide, increasing the number of infected people every day. On the other hand, the Covid-19 pandemic disrupted the health system, forcing it to change entirely in a while. The healthcare professionals are at the frontline working to contain the spread of the epidemic. Doctors, nurses, and paramedic operators were not prepared to face this kind of emergency, and they adapted to the scenario with great difficulty. Environments, clothing, and their working routine were reorganized, and new hard rules and procedures were introduced to ensure medical operators' and patients'

N. L. Black et al. (Eds.): IEA 2021, LNNS 222, pp. 555–563, 2021.
https://doi.org/10.1007/978-3-030-74611-7_75

safety. Consequently, all the healthcare and medical personnel began to use additional personal protective equipment (PPE), trying to avoid infection and ensure their work performance. In March 2020, the Italian Institute of Health published a document indicating the allowed types of personal protective equipment (PPE) and their right use for medical use, first responders, and common citizens according to different uses and scenarios. The document recommended ensuring a set of rules for adequate respiratory protection. Medical staff also has to wear a clear polycarbonate shield to protect themselves from droplets released by infected people through coughing or sneezing, or simply breathing [10]. Facial protections are generally very uncomfortable to use for a long time (the length of a hospital work shift is about six/eight hours) and adhering to the face causes redness and bruising. The infection could also be spread by touching hands, clothes, or objects which have come into contact with sick people because the virions live for many hours also on surfaces. According to these contamination peculiarities, first responders have to wear in addition to the traditional gown another water-repellent garment - often a full jumpsuit - able to protect all the body and protective disposable headgear. The above protective equipment is generally very uncomfortable and requires a very long dressing time, as well as undressing. For this activity, it is often necessary the help of another person to avoid contamination. Moreover, to protect their hands, the healthcare workers have to wear many pairs of gloves on top of each other to avoid contamination during undressing. The number of pairs depends on the use and the scenario. These multiple uses of gloves provoke loss of sensitivity to touch. Consequently, they also have difficulty in the use of medical instruments and the examination of patients. Garments, gloves, healthcare headgears, and masks are generally disposable while the visors are sterilized for multiple uses. Due to the use of a lot of PPE by healthcare professionals during working activities, the communication between them and the patients has been becoming very difficult. Masks and visors reduced quite the visibility between people, making the dialogue impossible and even people recognizability. This situation contributes to the dehumanizing, even more, of the hospital environment and hospitalization path.

1.2   Emergency Design and COVID 19 Pandemic

The emergency scenario is a completely multidisciplinary field. During an emergency, many disciplines are involved with the sole purpose of dealing with and overcoming a crisis with the least possible damage. Many of these disciplines have been so involved in such situations that they have developed branches to study in more depth some particular phenomena. It is important to underline that the actors involved in an emergency are multiple and have very different needs. If, on the one hand, there is the population in difficulty affected by any emergency, on the other, there are all the operators who work non-stop to restore the pre-emergency state. Therefore, it is essential to consider mainly the first responder user, as it is the one subjected to greater prolonged stress as it has an active and indispensable role during the crisis. During an emergency, in addition to the most obvious consequences of the scenario, it is essential to consider all the psychological implications that a given crisis can cause. The type of user-described so far, called "First responders", has specific needs to which you cannot pay attention to make it more bearable and less tiring their work. Despite, as previously explained, the design is a highly cross-disciplinary discipline, it is not yet adequately incorporated into the response phase during an emergency. Even today, the design is often considered an "aesthetic" element and not a strong strategic tool able to bring innovation to different sectors. During the Covid19 epidemic, this problem was often highlighted by numerous international designers, including Neri Oxman, in one of the meetings of the "MoMa Virtual Views" YouTube series organized by Paola Antonelli [12]. Neri Oxman drew attention to the fact that no designer was in one of the scientific committees created to cope with the emergency when instead, other professionals were. At present, there are very few academic courses dealing with this subject. In Italy, regarding university education, the emergency design has not yet codified and structured legitimacy. The only experiences in this regard can be traced back to internal laboratories born on the reference teacher's specific interest. However, design can be a valuable strategic tool to address an emergency better, as it can see foreseeing needs and problems sometimes invisible to other professionals. In this perspective, especially during the current pandemic situation, debates, conferences, and initiatives flourished in which designers from around the world tried to explain how design could help. Worthy of note is the initiative conceived by Paola Antonelli and Alice Rawsthorn, "Design Emergency". The project was born in May 2020, on the Instagram platform, to investigate design response to COVID-19.

2 The Aim of the Research

This paper refers to the study and the analysis of the processes related to the use of the design in First Responders' service, focusing on the application area of design for emergencies caused by the COVID19 pandemic. The main purpose concerns not only a reflection on the ever-new possibilities of using design in this reference field but above all, it is an investigation of its intrinsic ability to adapt, finding different solutions concerning the variables characterizing the other crises and defining its various uses. The areas investigated are related both to operative activities and psychological and emotional approaches. Referring to the first one – operative activities- a focus was directed to the protective uniform and all the other PPE at the disposal of first responders and the medical devices necessary for the routine activity and exceptional one. Referring to the psychological approaches, the research focused on the first responder's necessity to communicate with victims from the welcoming phase to the more strictly operational ones to make them feel comfortable and safe. On the other side the research considers also the needs of the victim to communicate with the healthcare people and be understood. The research aims to investigate in order to find innovative solutions, to improve the following aspects:

1. The ability of medical staff to communicate with other first responders and the victim and the possibility to be easily recognized and the other way around.
2. The comfort and the breathability of the uniforms to ensure a constant body temperature, avoiding dehydration, avoiding sweating, not tightening the various parts of the body, and ensuring freedom of movement.
3. The ease of dressing and undressing in terms of employed time, the necessity not to be helped in dressing up and out by other people, and furthermore, the ease of not being infected during the undressed phase.

4. The possibility to carry and use personal accessories (such as notes, pens).
5. The possibility to comfortable PPE like mask and visors or full mask that do not leave marks on the face or body, allowing to breathe without fogging.
6. Lack of PPE designed specifically for neck, ankles, and wrists.
7. The compatibility of different PPE with the uniform.
8. The difficulty of sterilization of PPE avoiding long times and polluting procedures.
9. The possibility of using the stethoscope to auscultate victims in medical practices and other medical devices.

3 Methodology

The scientific society recognizes the strategic role of design able to establish itself as a collector of different disciplines. This holistic approach is fundamental to designing products and services taking into account different points of view. This multidisciplinary approach of design, in its various forms, is opposite to specialization, and indicates the necessity of going beyond knowledge based on the specificity of a single discipline. This way of designing needs of a constructive exchange of techniques, methodologies and know-how linked together into innovative design solutions. The present research method used a cross-disciplinary approach, involving many different disciplines such as emergency psychology, biology, medicine, and engineering. The contributions of each field represent the key knowledge necessary for the final design proposals. The research refers to the UCD approach as the main method to the design process. Besides, it also concerns the human centered design (HCD), starting with understanding users' needs and behaviors according to the scenario and psychological and emotional traits and features typical for users. This approach also focuses on the importance of involving users in the design processes. The research investigated the aspects of the specific scenario of the COVID19 pandemic emergency through different interviews and questionnaires with health workers to easily understand the strengths and the weaknesses of the existing products and users' habits, behaviors, and points of view. Moreover, the research organized a coworking activity with Design Students of the master's degree in design of the University of Florence. The first purpose of the activity was to individuate new technologies and innovative material concerning health operators' needs. After that, the students involved proposed a series of innovative concepts regarding design solutions of PPE They focused on improving the comfort of health first responder and on the aspect related to different kinds of communication.

3.1 Applied Method

Direct Interviews and Questionnaires with COVID-19 Doctors and Rescuers
The research started investigating the aspects related to the specific scenario of the Covid-19 pandemic emergency, during the first Italian in March and June 2020. Based on the design purpose, a series of different questionnaires were elaborated (using both multiple-choice and free answer) and submitted to different kind of healthcare professionals and volunteers using Google forms in accordance with the privacy legislation

for the processing of sensitive data. Besides, some interviews were conducted in digital mode, using web platforms such as Google Meet. The first objective of the interviews was to identify in detail the real needs of health workers, which, until then, were only hypothesized through the photos and images circulated on the internet and in newspapers around the world. Parallel to identifying the needs, it was necessary, for the purpose of the research, to identify all the problems associated with them, both physical, psychological, and communicative. While the primary need for protection was evident, several problems were caused by the many personal protection systems that had to be worn. Both the above activities involved about 350 health workers from all over Italy, including doctors, nurses, and paramedics, who worked both in COVID units and other departments and general medical practitioners who carried out their activities in a private office or at patients' homes. An accurate evaluation of the PPE they used was requested to questionnaire interviewees (in addition to gender, age group, level of education, and membership category). In particular, the questionnaire aimed to evaluate the PPE in terms of availability, comfort, ease of use, ease of dressing and undressing, risk of contagion, possible difficulty in carrying out work activities, physical discomfort, difficulties in movements, difficulties in communicating with colleagues and patients, difficulties in visiting patients, and also their opinion on the environmental impact assessment of PPE deriving from their sanitation or disposal. Interviews with healthcare staff focused on personal protective equipment and dressing and undressing procedures. In some cases, medical personnel provided photographic documentation of the protective equipment worn. In addition to highlighting the main issues closely related to the comfort, protection, and ease of use of the PPE, the interview activity has highlighted many communication issues. The personal devices, covering most of the body of health care workers, do not allow to recognize each other, and above all, do not allow visual contact with the patient.

The Workshop with Students
According to the research aims, a workshop was organized with the students of the master's degree in Design at the University of Florence. The workshop had the aim of identifying new technologies for the Design of new PPE. The workshop took place in digital mode through the Google Meet platform during the Italian lockdown in March/June 2020. About 50 students were involved and divided into working groups of 2–3 people to optimize the project. The first step of the session was a specific brainstorming for the definition of scenario, in which the first responder works. Working groups focused on different devices: some focused on masks and others on gowns and gloves. Subsequently, each working group carried out an analysis of the state of art on current personal protective equipment for the Covid-19 scenario. This phase highlighted the criticalities of current devices on wearability, material, and waste. As previously mentioned, a problem that has emerged is the disinfection and disposal of PPE. According to the DPR 254/2003, these products are considered "special" and hazardous waste. The students studied a literature review on innovative, smart, and sustainable materials (on the market and in development), guaranteeing the doctor's well-being and facilitating work and communication. The next phase of the workshop was a focus group with some doctors and first responders. The focus group allowed students to understand the operator's real need and the critical issues of the PPE that they wear. In March, the first sketches

and concepts were carried out, and subsequently, they were verified with experts of the reference scenario.

4 Results Analysis

As previously mentioned, the first phase of the research, through interviews and questionnaires to health professionals, has made it possible to highlight recurring and major needs and problems. Through questionnaires, it was also possible to have an accurate assessment of the PPE and identify the different personal protection devices used by operators. Concerning the PPE, following the responses of health professionals, a categorization of the devices was made according to the part of the body of interest (hands, ears, eyes, respiratory system, body, head, feet). The categorization analysis showed how many of the protective devices are worn on the face to protect the respiratory system. It is possible to divide materials into subcategories according to their durability, resistance and also if they are biodegradable. According to this, we could obtain disposable and reusable PPE. This choice is fundamental because disposable PPE usually generates very large quantities of waste, while reusable PPEs have the problem of correct disinfection. All of them represent a threat to the environment in terms of pollution. The questionnaires also highlighted the many related problems. The first, and by far the most frequent, is linked to the physical discomfort and not breathability of the PPE. The device's material, being disposable, does not guarantee adequate breathability. Moreover, the process of dressing and undressing is complicated, in particular, the undressing process exposes staff to a high risk of contamination. The questionnaire and the interviews highlighted that 86.5% of participants believe that the quality of the PPE they use is sufficient or good supplied, 75.9% are equipped with a face shield but do not always use it during all the operations they have to carry out because of discomfort (65.3%). 95.5% use disposable PPE, 97.5% of them consider the environmental impact related to the disposal of these PPE to be significant or very significant for the environment and, finally, 96.5% have positive evaluations regarding the 96.5% have positive evaluations regarding the creation of disposable PPE realized in biodegradable material with antimicrobial and/or antibacterial properties. Starting from the interviews and questionnaires, the students have designed innovative PPE concepts to improve health operators' comfort, usability, and devices' communicative aspects. During the designing process, it is also necessary to consider all the communicative aspects of the PPEs. Health operators have to communicate easily with each other during stressful activities. The communication has to be immediate, accurate, and fast. Sound problems could influence the quality of the communication and directly influence the activity itself. PPEs must not hinder proper communication between health professionals. It is also necessary that each professional and its specialization are properly recognizable in order to facilitate the rescue activities. The communicative aspects are also relevant in order to make patients feel at ease. The hospital environment and the disease could stress and depress the already debilitated patient. Health professionals, wearing the many necessary personal protective equipment, do not appear reassuring to the patient.

5   Conclusions

The results of the analysis of the previous activities are summarized in a set of open rules for designing innovative medical PPE to be used during a biological emergency as follows. The following points indicate the proposed actions necessary to design a new generation of PPE to be used in Covid-19 Department at Hospital starting from users' needs and behaviors. The starting point is to associate a series of requirements to each kind of PPE. The indications try to summarize the wearable PPE into two large categories:

1. PPE to protect the respiratory system of healthcare people to wear on the face;
2. PPE to protect the body.

Each of the above PPE has to contain a series of specific elements necessary to obtain the prefixed goals. These two categories have in common the main function: to totally protect healthcare workers from biological hazards. This peculiarity is reached using specific materials; international standard rules indicate a list of allowed materials for this purpose. It is possible to divide materials into subcategories according to their durability, resistance and eco-compatibility. According to this, we could obtain disposable and reusable PPE. This choice is fundamental because disposable PPE usually generates very large quantities of waste, while reusable PPEs have the problem of correct disinfection. All of them represent a threat to the environment in terms of pollution. The use of specific materials is not sufficient to have a useful and comfortable PPE and the design discipline has the important role to combine user functional and emotional needs together with innovative materials and technologies to design products formally innovative. Referring to the results of the research, it is possible to indicate the following peculiarities of Facial PPE:

1. **Comfortable**. To reach this goal, the PPE has to be ergonomic shapes, adjustable parts, soft surfaces, breathable fabrics, elastic materials, easy to fit, available in different sizes. It could improve comfort, reducing the number of protective facial PPEs, such as integrating the visor with the mask. The PPE should be easy to dress and undress, in order to reduce the risk of contamination of the users.
2. **High Protection**. The use of smart innovative material and coating could improve the PPEs' standard protection. Innovative self-sanitizing biobased fabrics and molecular copper-based coating increase the level of PPEs' protection, reducing the risk of contamination of the users.
3. **Communication aspects and recognizability**. The use of transparent material, the possibility of customization, availability of different colors and applications of logos/pictures could improve the communicative aspects of the PPEs. Moreover, the integration of ITC in PPEs can communication issues related to sound and simplify patients' medical records' monitoring methods.

Referring to PPE for the body they have to be designed according to the following characteristics.

1. **Comfortable.** To reach this goal the PPE has to be ergonomic, designing the model and the pattern according to the ergonomics and the anatomy of the body, able to allow free movements and the natural touch. In addition, the design must take into account the needs of the different areas of the body in terms of breathability, mobility and friction. Moreover, it is necessary to use different sizes of PPE according to the health workers biometric data.
2. **High Protective.** Favoring one-piece suits with easy closure allows dressing and undressing activities alone, without the help of other people and in a few minutes, designing a closure system able to open and close using one hand. Avoiding touching the external part of the garment. Innovative self-sanitizing biobased fabrics and molecular copper-based coating increase the level of PPEs' protection, reducing the risk of contamination for the users.
3. **Communication aspects and recognizability.** The possibility of customization using colors, graphics, allowing to attach pictures/graphics/messages can improve the communicative aspects of PPEs. Different colors and graphic signs can help in identifying the different professionals' workers within the hospital environment, thus facilitating workers/workers and worker/patient communication.
4. **Integration of ICT.** The integration of ICT in PPEs can improve sanitations issues of work daily objects such as pens, notes, smartphones. A removable smart self-sanitizing pocket could reduce the risk of contamination for the users.

Moreover, each type of PPE should consider the Life Cycle Assessment. If not mono material the PPE has to be easy to disassemble. It is preferable to not use glues, to choose Biodegradable or reusable materials, preferring innovative natural biological materials. In conclusion, the analysis highlighted the need for each type of PPE to be compatible with the others, in order to improve user comfort, to reduce the risk of unintended contamination and to simplify the processes of dressing and undressing.

References

1. Antonelli, P.: Safe: Design Takes on Risk. Museum of Modern Art, New York (2005)
2. Antonelli, P.: Design and the Elastic Mind. Museum of Modern Art, New York (2008)
3. Antonelli, P., Tannir, A.: Broken Nature. XXII Triennale di Milano, Electa, Milano (2019)
4. Benyus, J.: Biomimicry: Innovation Inspired by Nature. Harper Perennial, New York (1997)
5. Carlson, R.: Biology is Technology. Harvard University Press, Cambridge (2010)
6. Dargaville, T., Spann, K., Celina, M.: Opinion to address a potential personal protective equipment shortage in the global community during the COVID-19 outbreak. Polym. Degrad. Stab. **176**, 109162 (2020)
7. Khurana, S., Singh, P., Sinha, T.P., Bhoi, S., Mathur, P.: Low-cost production of handrubs and face shields in developing countries fighting the COVID-19 pandemic. Am. J. Infect. Control **48**(6), 726 (2020)
8. Lucibello, S.: Esperimenti di Design: Ricerca e Innovazione con e dei Materiali. LISt Lab, Barcellona-Trento (2018)
9. Myers, W.: Bio Design. The Museum of Modern Art, New York (2012)
10. National Institute of Health. Interim guidelines for the rational use of protection for sars-cov-2 infection in health and social health activities (assistance to subjects affected by covid-19) in the current emergency scenario sars-cov-2, no. 2 (2020)

11. Oxman, N., Antonelli, P.: The Neri Oxman Material Ecology Catalogue. Material Ecology. MoMa. Catalogue. Museum of Modern Art, New York (2020)
12. YouTube. Neri Oxman—Material Ecology | Live Q&A with Paola Antonelli and Neri Oxman | VIRTUAL VIEWS. [File video]. Taken from, 20 May 2020. https://www.youtube.com/watch?v=TUjlAGhukhE

Digital Solutions for Workplace Mental Health Promotion During COVID-19 Pandemic: Taxonomy and Human Factors Issues

Davide Giusino(✉) [iD], Marco De Angelis[iD], and Luca Pietrantoni[iD]

Department of Psychology, Alma Mater Studiorum – University of Bologna, 40126 Bologna, Emilia-Romagna, Italy
davide.giusino2@unibo.it

Abstract. Recent empirical studies have shown the negative psychological impact of the current COVID-19 pandemic. Physical distancing and avoidance of social gatherings are considered among the best public health and safety measures to adopt to counter the outbreak, and governments are establishing subsequent rules worldwide. Consequently, interventions in workplaces need to be implemented remotely, including those regarding mental health. Therefore, the importance of digital solutions for workplace mental health promotion becomes apparent. Meta-analytical and systematic evidence has shown that digital technologies may be useful in improving workers' mental health. Thus, digital-based interventions can be deemed as a feasible solution to deal with the negative psychological impact of the current pandemic. Based on previous literature, we developed a conceptual taxonomy composed of two main functional categories of digital solutions, such as (1) *allowing assessment and intervention*, and (2) *allowing to work remotely*. We also identified three sub-categories of (1), such as digital technologies *for externally provided interventions*, *for stress self-management strategies*, and *for reformatting in-presence interventions*. Human Factors and Ergonomics issues should be considered when dealing with the use of workplace mental health promotion digital technologies, both at the individual and organizational level, as they can be conceived as implementation challenges that may undermine interventions' effectiveness when not managed properly. This paper intends to allow researchers to identify future directions of investigating workplace psychological well-being interventions based on novel technology advancements. Also, the paper provides practitioners with an overview of actionable solutions that can be easily implemented during these organizationally challenging times.

Keywords: Digital technologies · Mental health at work · COVID-19 · Remote work

1 Introduction

Recent empirical studies have extensively shown the negative psychological impact of the current COVID-19 pandemic in terms of increased depression, anxiety, and stress

N. L. Black et al. (Eds.): IEA 2021, LNNS 222, pp. 564–571, 2021.
https://doi.org/10.1007/978-3-030-74611-7_76

within the working population, encompassing not only front-line health care workers as the most at-risk professional group [1], but also other workers providing essential and customer services, for example, those working in grocery stores, transportation, warehouse, construction, retail, and delivery.

Physical distancing and avoidance of social gatherings are considered among the best public health and safety measures to adopt to counter the COVID-19 outbreak [2], and governments are establishing consistent rules worldwide. Therefore, the importance of digital solutions for workplace mental health promotion, which allow work and mental health activities to occur remotely, becomes apparent.

Digital-based solutions for workplace mental health can be defined as structured actions aiming to promote mental health at work by exploiting the potential offered by digital technologies. These may correspond to interventions initially designed to take place in physical presence and subsequently adapted to digital formats provided by online teleconferencing platforms. Besides, they can be interventions available through computer or smartphone apps only. In addition, a specific type of workplace mental health promotion digital-based solutions is represented by products and services which are based on artificial intelligence [3], such as, for instance, chatbots for digital counselling programmes and machine learning-based wearable physiological sensors for detection of work stress. Meta-analyses and systematic reviews [4] have shown that digital technologies may be useful in promoting workers' mental health. Notably, in the COVID-19-related social distancing context, interventions in workplaces may need to be implemented remotely, including those regarding mental health. Therefore, digital-based interventions can be expected to be a feasible solution to deal with the negative psychological impact of the current pandemic.

The present paper is part of the EU-funded H2020 project H-WORK [5], aiming to develop innovative tools for promoting mental health in the workplace. One of the project's objectives has been to explore the role played by digital technologies for promoting workplace mental health in the current pandemic context. As such, this paper aims to outline the multiple roles that digital technologies for promoting mental health at work can play in the current context of social distancing rules due to the COVID-19 pandemic outbreak. Based on the most recent literature on the topic, we developed a conceptual taxonomy based on two main functional categories of digital solutions and three sub-categories. These categories are intended to show which the functions allowed by digital technologies can be to promote workplace mental health despite the COVID-19 pandemic situation.

To the authors' knowledge, this paper constitutes the first attempt to provide such a taxonomy. Also, Human Factors and Ergonomics (HF/E) issues should be considered when dealing with the use of digital technologies, especially for workplace mental health promotion, both at the individual and the organizational level. The abovementioned conceptual taxonomy and HF/E issue are going to be discussed in the remainder of the present paper. As well, research and practical implications will be outlined.

2   A Conceptual Taxonomy for Digital Workplace Mental Health Promotion

The developed taxonomy is based on two main functional categories referring to what digital solutions can offer to workplace mental health promotion in the current context of social distancing rules due to the COVID-19 pandemic outbreak.

The first functional category of the developed taxonomy corresponds to *digital technologies allowing workplace mental health assessment and intervention*. These can be defined as digital technologies whose functions allow to diagnose workplace mental health issues and/or implement actions for improvement of workers' mental health. In turn, three different sub-categories can be distinguished within this domain, such as digital technologies *for externally provided interventions, for stress self-management strategies*, and *for reformatting in-presence interventions*.

Digital technologies for externally provided workplace mental health interventions correspond to the wide range of solutions and online services that the market is currently offering to support users in facing the challenges posed by pandemic, lockdown and quarantine to mental health. As a COVID-19-relevant example, HelloBetter's Corona online course "Calm through the Crisis" (https://hellobetter.de/en/online-courses/corona/) can be mentioned, as well as the European eHealth Hub Platform (https://platform.ehealth-hub.eu). Digital technologies for stress self-management strategies refer to platforms allowing the user to even immediately self-intervene on his or her own mental health issues. As an example, [6] reported that, during the pandemic, medical staff experienced psychological stress or emotional changes, which were mainly caused by family health, disease-related issues and negative news via the internet; however, they managed their emotions and stress by self-control, video calls with family members or colleagues, and communicating with other on WeChat. It can be noticed that digital technologies can be used as a platform allowing to seek and feel psychological and emotional closeness to and from significant persons even when physical proximity to and from them is not allowed, as it is the case within the context of social distancing due to the COVID-19 pandemic. This is made possible by digital information and communication technologies (ICTs) offering video-calling and instant messaging services. In turn, the achieved psychological and emotional closeness can be exploited and leveraged upon in order to interact with significant others with the aim of relieving the stress which has been accumulated throughout the working day. It might also be argued that this type of digital technologies allows the adoption and implementation of individual coping strategies. It is quite straightforward to understand how this might reveal useful especially for frontline health care workers facing COVID-19. Nevertheless, the support that this kind of use of digital technologies can provide to other essential and non-essential workers should not be underestimated in light of how subjective and individually peculiar the human experience of facing COVID-19 can be.

The third and final functional sub-category of (1) corresponds to *digital technologies allowing to reformat in-presence workplace interventions originally*. This category means that psychological interventions originally designed to take place in physical presence can now be adapted to digital formats provided by online teleconferencing platforms. An extensive discussion of the use of new digital information and communication technologies in psychological counseling during the COVID-19 pandemic has been provided by [7], but it is easy to figure out how this could be translated into workplace settings. The authors reported more than one-hundred psychologists to have continued to provide their services during the COVID-19 pandemic due to having adopted information and communication technologies. Although some challenges were identified, psychologists described the experience with the use of ICTs as positive, meeting clients' adherence, and yielding positive results.

The second main functional category of the developed taxonomy corresponds to *digital technologies providing platforms to work remotely*, both individually and in teams. Although this can be considered as not directly linked to workers' mental health, still it can be argued that digital technologies allowing remote work ensure continuity, for instance, in the shift of work activities from office to home, thus preventing unemployment and job insecurity.

3 Human Factors and Ergonomics Issues

Human Factors and Ergonomics issues should be considered when dealing with the use of digital technologies, especially within the domain of workplace mental health promotion. These issues can be analyzed from the individual viewpoint, encompassing the interaction between the technology and the single workers. However, they can also be focused on an organizational level of analysis, including the organizational setting or context as well as the way in which the work activities are designed, managed and organized with regard to the use of digital technologies.

On the one hand, individual-level HF/E issues may refer to acceptance and adoption [8], adherence, digital skills [9] and age-based digital divide, digital fatigue, informational over-exposure, technological readiness, and usability perceptions. In this regard, designing based on end users' needs, requirements and preferences should be considered as a priority challenge to be addressed by workplace mental health digital technologies designers and developers. On the other hand, organizational-level HF/E issues could encompass availability of technological infrastructure (e.g., wi-fi connection), organizational culture, organizational support, organizational openness towards innovation. In this regard, designers and developers should work towards ensuring fit between the proposed technology and the targeted organizational context. Besides, privacy, confidentiality and data protection [10] constitute one additional challenge for organizations, designers and developers, as these features should be embedded into workplace mental health digital technology by design.

From the point of view of the organization implementing remote work digital solutions, the management of remote work should also be paid attention, as both advantages and disadvantages can come with it [11]. Advantages of remote work include better work-life balance, increased flexibility and autonomy, reduction in commuting time, increased productivity, higher morale and job satisfaction, and avoidance of office politics. Disadvantages of remote work include blurring of boundaries between work and home time and overwork, presenteeism, social isolation, lack of support, inadequate equipment, career progression or promotions, resentment from colleagues.

The above listed issues can be conceived as implementation challenges that may undermine the effectiveness of digital technologies for workplace mental health promotion when not managed properly. Effective implementation strategies for digital mental health interventions in the workplace should therefore be deployed [12]. Consistent to traditional approaches in HF/E science and practice, one best manner to deal with this issue would be user-centered design. This would mean developers of workplace mental health digital technologies preventatively taking into account end-users' needs, preferences and requirements with regard to technological features maximizing adoption willingness, actual use and, ultimately, effectiveness of interventions associated with the technology itself. It is a well-known fact that the extent to which intervention users are engaged with and actually use the intervention (i.e., adherence) is likely to influence its effectiveness [13]. Also, people tend to utilize what they perceive to be useful for them. From a methods viewpoint, end users' feedback and insights into their lived work experiences can be gathered through active involvement, participation and empowerment of employees within bottom-up investigation practices, such as surveys, interviews and workshops. Employees are the primary connoisseurs of their job and work environment, which makes them one of the most valuable sources of information concerning mental health risk and protective factors, whose knowledge can subsequently inform and feed the design and development of digital technologies aiming to tackle them. If this is not the case, workers may end up resisting newly introduced digital technologies in the workplace [14] as they might perceive them to be harmful and therefore reject them to autonomously preserve their own well-being at work.

The following Table 1 gives a summary of the functional categories identified within the hereby developed conceptual taxonomy for digital solutions for workplace mental health promotion during the COVID-19 pandemic, as well as of the cross-cutting HF/E issues which can be associated to this type of technologies.

Table 1. Taxonomy of workplace mental health digital technologies (DTs) and HF/E issues.

Functional category	• DTs for assessment and intervention: DTs for externally provided interventions, stress self-management strategies, and to reformat interventions; • DTs for remote work: considering differences and similarities with mandatory and non-mandatory home working and distributed working.
Cross-cutting HF/E issues	• Individual: acceptance, adoption, adherence, digital skills, digital fatigue, informational over-exposure, technological readiness, usability perceptions; • Organizational: availability of technological infrastructure, organizational culture, organizational support, organizational openness towards innovation.
Design and development challenges	• Designing based on end users' needs, requirements and preferences; • Ensuring fit between technology and organizational context; • Embedding confidentiality, data protection and privacy by design.

4   Research and Practical Implications

The present paper intends to allow researchers to identify future directions of investigating the feasibility and effectiveness of workplace psychological well-being interventions based on novel technology advancements. As a first line of future research, it might be interesting to explore which psychosocial working mechanisms promote digital-based workplace mental health interventions' effectiveness that go beyond the ones traditionally investigated in non-digital interventions (e.g., readiness for change, management support, effectiveness beliefs, satisfaction with intervention) and are specific to workplace mental health interventions having a digital nature (e.g., acceptance, adherence and other previously mentioned HF/E variables). Secondly, further empirical support for the proposed conceptual taxonomy might be looked for by investigating differences in the extent to which each functional category applies to various occupational groups, with special reference to those whose work itself is fundamentally based on the use of digital technologies. For instance, whereas health care professionals might be more easily thought of using digital communication technologies to enact stress management and coping strategies during breaks and shifts in real time, it might be interesting to see how this would work for food delivery riders who need to use digital devices between deliveries in order to follow the established work processes and accomplish the given tasks. The ultimate aim would be to develop recommendations about how to best exploit each type of use of digital technologies for workplace mental health promotion depending on the different users.

In addition, occupational health practitioners are hereby provided with an overview of actionable solutions that could be easily implemented each time they would need to manage workplace mental health issues related to COVID-19 during these organizationally challenging times. Particularly, a unique opportunity for evidence-based practice is represented by the possibility to transfer the knowledge that research has collected about telework throughout the last decades [15].

5   Conclusions

It should be underlined that the identified categories within the developed conceptual taxonomy of digital technologies for workplace mental health are not mutually exclusive. Online teleconferencing platforms, for example, can be used both to reformat originally in-presence workplace mental health interventions and to perform remote teamwork. This shows how smart and flexible digital technologies can be, but also how their inherent complexity can be both beneficial and hard to manage (e.g., for the present descriptive research) at the same time. Also, the taxonomy cannot be conceived as definitive, as technological advancements occur seamlessly and rapidly nowadays. Despite the above limitations, given the increasing challenges associated with mental health as a result of the pandemic and its associated changes to working life of people, this paper addresses important questions about how to provide support to workers while at home, while identifying the challenges to this from an HF/E perspective. The use of digital resources to promote mental health in the workplace is vital within the current pandemic context.

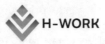

Acknowledgements. This research has received funding from the European Union's Horizon 2020 research and innovation programme under grant agreement No 847386. The material presented and views expressed here are the responsibility of the authors only. The EU Commission takes no responsibility for any use made of the information set out.

References

1. Salari, N., Khazaie, H., Hosseinian-Far, A., Khaledi-Paveh, B., Kazeminia, M., Mohammadi, M., Shohaimi, S., Daneshkhah, A., Eskandari, S.: The prevalence of stress, anxiety and depression within front-line healthcare workers caring for COVID-19 patients: a systematic review and meta-regression. Hum. Res. Health **18**(1), 1–14 (2020). https://doi.org/10.1186/s12960-020-00544-1

2. Luu Duc Huynh, T.: Does culture matter social distancing under the COVID-19 pandemic? Saf. Sci. (2020). https://doi.org/10.1016/j.ssci.2020.104872

3. Puzzo, G., Fraboni, F., Pietrantoni, L.: Artificial intelligence and professional transformation: research questions in work psychology. Rivista Italiana di Ergonomia **21**, 43–60 (2020)

4. Heber, E., Ebert, D.D., Lehr, D., Cuijpers, P., Berking, M., Nobis, S., Riper, H.: The benefit of web- and computer-based interventions for stress: a systematic review and meta-analysis. J. Med. Internet Res. **19**(2), (2017). https://doi.org/10.2196/jmir.5774

5. De Angelis, M., Giusino, D., Nielsen, K., Aboagye, E., Christensen, M., Innstrand, S.T., Mazzetti, G., van den Heuvel, M., Sijbom, R.L., Pelzer, V., Chiesa, R., Pietrantoni, L.: H-WORK project: multilevel interventions to promote mental health in SMEs and public workplaces. Int. J. Environ. Res. Public Health **17**, 8035 (2020). https://doi.org/10.3390/ijerph17218035

6. Luo, L.-S., Jin, Y.-H., Cai, L., Pan, Z.-Y., Zeng, X.-T., Wang, X.-H.: COVID-19: Presumed infection routes and psychological impact on staff in administrative and logistics departments in a designated hospital in Wuhan. China. Front. Psychol. **11**, 1501 (2020). https://doi.org/10.3389/fpsyg.2020.01501

7. Dores, A.R., Geraldo, A., Carvalho, I.P., Barbosa, F.: The use of new digital information and communication technologies in psychological counseling during the COVID-19 pandemic. Int. J. Environ. Res. Public Health **17**(20), 7663 (2020). https://doi.org/10.3390/ijerph17207663

8. Melzner, J., Heinze, J., Fritsch, T.: Mobile health applications in workplace health promotion: an integrated conceptual adoption framework. Procedia Technol. **16**, 1374–1382 (2014). https://doi.org/10.1016/j.protcy.2014.10.155

9. Nguyen, M.N., Hargittai, E., Marler, W.: Digital inequality in communication during a time of physical distancing: the case of COVID-19. Comput. Hum. Behav. (2021). https://doi.org/10.1016/j.chb.2021.106717

10. Lustgarten, S.D., Garrison, Y.L., Sinnard, M.T., Flynn, A.W.P.: Digital privacy in mental healthcare: Current issues and recommendations for technology use. Curr. Opin. Psychol. **36**, 25–31 (2020). https://doi.org/10.1016/j.copsyc.2020.03.012

11. Hayes, S., Priestley, J.L., Ishmakhametov, N., Ray, H.E.: I'm not working from home, I'm living at work: Perceived stress and work-related burnout before and during COVID-19. https://psyarxiv.com/vnkwa/download?format=pdf

12. Graham, A., Lattie, E., Powell, B., Lyon, A., Smith, J., Schueller, S., Stadnick, N., Brown, C., Mohr, D.: Implementation strategies for digital mental health interventions in health care settings. Am. Psychol. **75**(8), 1080–1092 (2020). https://doi.org/10.1037/amp0000686

13. Carolan, S., Harris, P.R., Greenwood, K., Cavanagh, K.: Increasing engagement with an occupational digital stress management program through the use of an online facilitated discussion group: Results of a pilot randomised controlled trial. Internet Interv. **10**, 1–11 (2017). https://doi.org/10.1016/j.invent.2017.08.001

14. Shulzenko, E., Holmgren, J.: Gains from resistance: Rejection of a new digital technology in a healthcare sector workplace. New Technol. Work Employ. **35**(3), 276–296 (2020). ISSN 1468-005X

15. de Macêdo, T.A.M., Cabral, E.L.d.S., Silva Castro, W.R., de Souza Junior, C.C., da Costa Junior, J.F., Pedrosa, F.M., da Silva, A.B., de Medeiros, V.R.F., de Souza, R.P., Cabral, M.A.L., Másculo, F.S.: Ergonomics and telework: a systematic review. Work **66**(4), 777–788 (2020). https://doi.org/10.3233/WOR-203224

Government Strategies in the Confrontation of Covid-19 in the Republic of Cuba

C. Aleida González González[1] ⓘ, Lisandra Leal Rodríguez[1] ⓘ,
Daylí Morales Fonte[1] ⓘ, Adrián González González[1](✉) ⓘ,
and José Orlando Gomes[2] ⓘ

[1] Universidad Tecnológica de La Habana José Antonio Echeverría, La Habana, Cuba
agonza@ind.cujae.edu.cu
[2] Industrial Engineering and Computer Sciences Program, Federal University of Rio de Janeiro,
Rio de Janeiro, RJ, Brazil
joseorlando@nce.ufrj.br

Abstract. The policies that countries develop to face the crisis generated by the COVID-19 pandemic have a strong impact on the impact it causes. In Cuba, the general strategy to confront the pandemic was directed by the government, which, under the guidance of the Ministry of Public Health, drew up an action plan based on stages and phases to comply with the strategy, taking into account the evolution of the disease in the country. The objective of this research is to assess the effectiveness of the government strategy for the treatment of the COVID-19 disease in Cuba, based on the analysis of the integration of the different organizations that participated. The analysis carried out allowed us to find the interrelationships between the different organizations involved with influences in the treatment of the pandemic.

Keywords: COVID-19 · Strategies · Public health · Government

1 Introduction

A new coronavirus, formerly called Severe Acute Respiratory Syndrome Coronavirus (SARS-CoV-2), now officially called by the World Health Organization (WHO) Coronavirus Disease 2019 (COVID-19), caused an outbreak of atypical pneumonia, first in Wuhan, Hubei province, in December 2019 and then spread to more than 180 countries in the world with more than 5 million cases in a short time, because it is highly contagious (Peraza et al. 2020; Galindo et al. 2020).

The virus can kill people of all ages, particularly those with chronic illnesses or the elderly. The new Coronavirus (COVID-19) has been classified by the WHO as a public health emergency of international importance which later on March 11, 2020 it was considered a global pandemic.

This pandemic has affected unprecedented communities and economies around the world. Countries are slow to take a series of measures to stop it, and their current health-care capabilities are insufficient to treat patients, although each country has responded or

N. L. Black et al. (Eds.): IEA 2021, LNNS 222, pp. 572–579, 2021.
https://doi.org/10.1007/978-3-030-74611-7_77

is responding to the same threat with different measures and/or with a different timing. This fact means that the epidemiological curves of the affected countries are behaving differently and that the social and economic cost of the respective responses may be different.

In Cuba, a Preparedness Plan had been applied for this contingency, when the first three cases (all foreign tourists) were identified on March 11, that date represents the starting point of the epidemic for the country. The response of the Cuban Government and the National Health System was immediate, which has led to the epidemiological control of the epidemic in Cuba (Más Bermejo 2020; Díaz-Canel and Núñez 2020).

A peculiarity of the anti-epidemic fight in Cuba has been the active investigation of feverish people and people with respiratory symptoms directly in homes throughout the country, carried out by professionals of Primary Health Care, supported by students from the last years of the careers of Medical Sciences. In this way, tens of thousands of citizens, especially the most vulnerable, are surveyed daily about their state of health. Hospital isolation of suspected cases, modified quarantine for contacts in health centers and immediate personal surveillance for 14 days has also been applied (Galindo and Menéndez 2020).

These constitute some actions carried out by the Cuban Government, which has had great support from the different organizations in the country to confront this disease. We refer to the ministries of Public Health, Construction, Transportation, Information Technology and Communications, Agriculture and Food Industry, which were in charge of ensuring the necessary resources for the fulfillment of the actions defined in the stages and phases. Universities and Research Centers also joined this activity with great prominence, contributing the results and knowledge obtained.

2   Research Objective

This article aims to assess the effectiveness of the government strategy for the treatment of the COVID-19 disease in Cuba, based on the analysis of the integration of the different organizations that participated. Answering the question: how did the Cuban government deal with the COVID-19 pandemic with the support of organizations and institutions?

3   Methodology

A review was carried out of documents issued by the direction of the Ministry of Public Health and other ministries of the country, archive documents of the Department of Teaching of the Pedro Kourí Institute (IPK) and high-impact Cuban journals in the field of medicine. The data were processed with different statistical tools that made it possible to measure the effectiveness of the implemented strategies. The analyzed period comprises the months from March to November 2020.

4   Results

In Cuba, to combat COVID-19, a set of coordinated activities were carried out that involved many of the country's institutions and ministries.

The presence of COVID-19 in Cuba makes it necessary to implement a national protocol of action, which contributes to prevention, control, and better case management, as well as the protection of health workers and the population. For its elaboration, experts took the best existing scientific evidence.

However, the novelty of the disease and the action protocol is under continuous review and subject to modifications according to clinical, epidemiological and therapeutic reports.

The Ministry of Public Health, to carry out the confrontation with this pandemic, drew up an action protocol that is divided into a preventive scenario and one for patient care in their different stages. Figure 1 shows the graphic representation of the above.

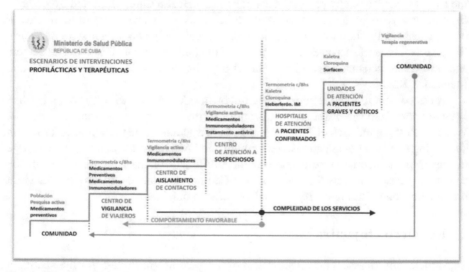

Fig. 1. Diagram of the interventions carried out as part of the care protocol. Source: National Action Protocol for COVID-19 (MINSAP, 2020).

4.1 Preventive Scenario

Composed of actions that begin in the community, at the first level of care (family medical offices) and continue in centers for the isolation of contacts or people from risk areas. Actions on health and auxiliary personnel who necessarily have to work in contact, suspected and confirmed cases, including the asymptomatic, are also included. As shown in Fig. 1, the actions begin in the community in a preventive manner and end in the same, with the actions of surveillance and accompaniment to the recovery of those affected.

Primary Health Care, Traveler Surveillance Centers and Suspect Surveillance Center

An active investigation is carried out, classification of cases, follow-up of contacts, treatment of vulnerable groups and follow-up of the discharge of confirmed cases. Next, the actions that are developed are exposed:

- Differentiated consultation for patients with manifestations of acute respiratory infection is enabled in polyclinics.
- The means of protection are available for the personnel who will work in the differentiated consultation. It is also necessary to protect the rest of the personnel working in health institutions.
- Interrogation and physical examination of the patient is carried out that allows an evaluation of the same and case classification.
- Active investigation of the entire population is carried out to identify cases with acute respiratory infections, as well as contacts and suspects.
- Nursing care is guaranteed in child care centers and schools for the prevention of COVID-19.
- When a case is identified as a contact, admission is made to the contact isolation center for 14 days.
- Biomodulin T and Prevengho-Vir are used in vulnerable groups. This group is made up of people over 60 years of age who reside in nursing homes, people who live in psycho-pedagogical medical centers and children with disabilities or diseases that compromise immunity.
- Temporary isolation is indicated by coordinating the transfer in ambulances to the isolation center defined for contact cases or suspected cases.
- Follow-up of the confirmed case after hospital discharge: home isolation until 14 days after the onset of symptoms, with daily medical supervision. In the case of the obstetric patient, she is kept at home.
- Strict follow-up of patients who are tax graduates of a rehabilitation program that includes regenerative therapy as a result of lung damage.
- Active surveillance and thermometry.

Attention to Patients in Their Different Stages
Set of actions that are developed depending on the type of patient. These treatments start from suspected cases to confirmed ones. Actions on health and auxiliary personnel who necessarily have to work in contact, suspected and confirmed cases, including the asymptomatic, are also included.

Attention to suspected and confirmed patients.

Suspected and confirmed cases are monitored in their respective centers. These cases are admitted to designated hospital units in each territory. The following actions are carried out:

- Daily care report.
- Thermometry at least every 6 h.
- Vital signs at least every 4 h.
- Diet according to patient and underlying diseases.
- Reinforce the necessary protection measures for the transfer and processing of samples.

- Monitor the appearance of warning signs or worsening of the clinical picture.
- Administration of medications to improve the immune activity of these patients.
- Completion of complementary exams.
- Isolation cubicles must meet the minimum requirements for this type of unit.
- The patient will have permanent sanitary gowns and nasobucos as a measure of protection and risk of transmission of the disease.
- Individual means will be used for the protection of healthcare personnel (disposable gowns, gloves, N-95 masks and glasses or masks for facial protection).
- Administration of first-line drugs for the treatment of the disease in confirmed cases.
- Differentiated monitoring of pregnant women and children.

Along with these actions, there is also a set of measures carried out by the organizations and institutions involved in the fight against COVID-19.

The Ministry of Transportation was in charge of carrying out all transportation, whether by land, sea or air:

- Health personnel and priority institutions for production.
- PCR samples carried out daily in the different provinces to the corresponding laboratories.
- Necessary supplies for the isolation centers, be it medicines, food, etc.
- Suspect and confirmed patients with COVID-19.
- Patients with other pathologies that needed medical services in hospitals.

Universities across the country joined this campaign by contributing to:

- Contribution of personnel for work in isolation centers.
- Calls for blood donations.
- Conditioning of isolation centers located within the universities themselves.
- Active participation in the mathematical forecasts made of the behavior of COVID-19.

The Cuban Institute of Radio and Television (ICRT) was dedicated to broadcasting daily informative press conferences on the epidemiological situation of the country by Dr. Francisco Durán García and focused on the publicity of informational and preventive campaigns of everything related to disease.

The Ministry of the Food Industry was in charge of guaranteeing the necessary food to isolation centers throughout the country, hospitals, nursing homes, maternity centers, etc. Food was sold to the population in different municipalities to guarantee a decrease in mobility between municipalities and provinces.

An important element to note within the entire confrontation with the disease in Cuba was the outstanding contribution of Cuban scientists who quickly began the evaluation of drugs for their possible use in the creation of vaccine candidates. Such was the impact that the country currently has 4 vaccine candidates in different phases of testing, which so far have provided positive results. In this way, all the organizations were integrated providing their contribution to the prevention and control of this disease. This individual and at the same time joint contribution created the conditions for the control of the disease in Cuba towards the month of November.

Favorable results are evidenced in the management of the pandemic reflected in the main indicators measured at the international level compared to our geographical area and even at the global level. The synergy between the different organizations responsible for directing the country was consolidated, as well as the integration of universities and scientific institutions in controlling the impacts of this disease.

5 Discussion

The integration between all state and private organizations and institutions achieved compliance with the strategies outlined from the beginning, course and recovery of the pandemic, taking the first steps on the road to the new normal.

Mathematical forecasts were made where the possible behavior of the epidemic in Cuba is evidenced (Escobar and Sánchez 2020). These models were in charge of mathematical professors from the University of Havana.

3 scenarios were defined, starting with a critical scenario, one medium and one favorable. As evidenced in Fig. 2, the behavior of the disease in Cuba was below the favorable scenario, which speaks positively of the strategic management carried out by the country to confront COVID-19.

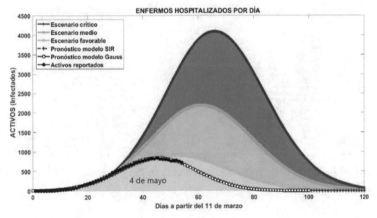

Fig. 2. Predictive mathematical models of the behavior of the pandemic in Cuba. Source: Official Site Cubadebate.

The weekly behavior of cases in the country since its identification on March 11, 2020, initially had a notable increase at the beginning of the pandemic. The peak was reached in week 16 corresponding to the month of April (Fig. 3). Measures to achieve control of COVID-19 were increased, achieving positive results in the coming months.

The continuous improvement of medical protocols allowed an average fatality rate of less than 3% (Fig. 4), an incidence rate per 100,000 inhabitants less than 5.7. These results were supported with communication measures with the people that allowed the population to assume a new mode of action, promoting changes in the culture of Cubans, reflected in an increase in the perception of the risk of COVID-19 in Cuba.

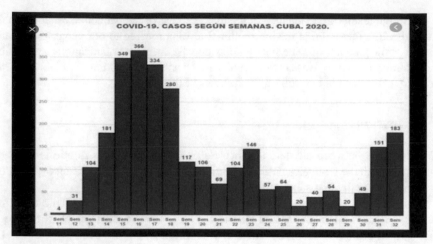

Fig. 3. Behavior of cases per week of the pandemic in Cuba. Source: Official Site Cubadebate.

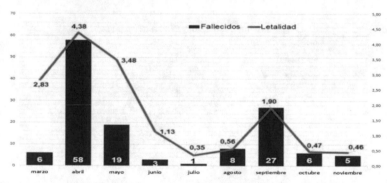

Fig. 4. Behavior of deaths and fatality rate per month of the pandemic in Cuba Source: Official Site Cubadebate.

The positive impact of the government strategies implemented by the country to control the disease in Cuba is evidenced. People and institutions work together to achieve better results every day.

6 Conclusion

- It is adopted as a government strategy, the integration of all state and private bodies and agencies to confront COVID-19.
- Integration of medical specialists with the country's research centers for the creation of vaccine candidates.
- A positive behavior is achieved in the levels of sick and deceased, which are below the average in the American continent and worldwide.

References

Cubadebate. Artículos de salud. Sitio web en Internet. Disponible en: (2020). http://www.cubade bate.cu/categoria/temas/salud-medicina/

Cubadebate. Noticias de Salud. Gobierno cubano actualiza Plan para la prevención y control del COVID-19. La Habana, Cuba. Disponible en: (2020).http://www.cubadebate.cu/noticias/2020/03/05/diaz-canel-el-enfrentamiento-al-nuevocoronavirus-se-gana-con-la-participacion-popular/#.XvUXJv7B_IV

Díaz-Canel, M., Núñez, J.: Gestión gubernamental y ciencia cubana en el enfrentamiento a la COVID-19. Academia Ciencias de Cuba. Disponible en: (2020). http://www.revistaccuba.cu/index.php/revacc/article/view/881/893

Escobar, E.P., Sánchez, D.M.: Modelos estadísticos para las predicciones de la COVID-19 en Cuba. Revista Cubana de Higiene y Epidemiología, 57 (2020)

Galindo, L.F., Barrios, Y.H., Chacón, D.P.: Infectados por SARS CoV-2 y enfermos de COVID-19. Precisiones necesarias. Revista Cubana de Higiene y Epidemiología, 57 (2020)

Galindo, L.F., Menéndez, G.G.: SARS CoV-2 ¿el más letal coronavirus? Revista Cubana de Higiene y Epidemiología, 57 (2020)

Más Bermejo, P.I.: La COVID 19 y la práctica epidemiológica en Cuba. Revista Cubana de Higiene y Epidemiología, 57 (2020)

MINSAP. Protocolo Nacional para el tratamiento a la COVID-19. La Habana, Cuba (2020)

Peraza, M.A.C., Pérez, N.A.J., Marquetti, M.R.C.: Capacitación para la COVID-19: Experiencias del Instituto de Medicina Tropical Pedro Kourí. Revista Cubana de Higiene y Epidemiología, 57 (2020)

Pedestrian Physical-Distancing Strategies During COVID-19

Georgette E. Greenslade, Carolyn G. MacGregor$^{(\boxtimes)}$, and Ai Ching Chang

University of Waterloo, Waterloo, ON N2L 3G1, Canada
carolyn.macgregor@uwaterloo.ca

Abstract. Due to the COVID-19 global pandemic, public health policies urge physical distancing (also known as social distancing) of 2 m (6 feet) when walking outside in public spaces. This survey-based study reports on changes in general pedestrian behaviours due to pandemic conditions such as reduction in frequency of daily walking, and lack of comfort when in proximity of others. Responses to common urban pedestrian scenarios identified emerging adaptive strategies used by adults to maintain physical distancing. The two main strategies are Avoidance (stepping off one's path, crossing the road) and Encounter (stopping to let others pass, continuing the path of travel). Decisions to use one physical distancing strategy over another are related to the perceived traffic safety risks associated with the scenarios. For the low- and moderate-risk traffic scenarios, stepping off the path to avoid others is the preferred strategy. In the high-risk traffic scenarios, stopping on the path to let others pass or continuing to walk are preferred to stepping into traffic, even though physical distancing will not be maintained. Results from the study have implications for educational campaigns to promote effective physical distancing strategies, as well as planning for urban infrastructure to promote walking for health and mobility.

Keywords: Pedestrian behaviours · Physical distancing · Social distancing · Mental models · COVID-19 pandemic

1 Introduction

1.1 Situation of Concern

As a wellness response to the COVID-19 pandemic, the World Health Organization encourages activity, such as walking, to maintain physical and mental health, while at the same time recommending physical distancing, also known as social distancing, of two (2) metres between individuals to reduce risk of virus transmission [1]. Along with physical distancing, the wearing of face masks covering nose and mouth have been sanctioned for indoor use in public spaces, as well as recommended for outdoor use when physical distancing is not possible [2]. Within busy urban environments, the task of consistently maintaining physical distancing can become quite challenging due to the volume of pedestrians on narrow pathways and proximity to oncoming traffic preventing acceptable spacing.

Most adults learn explicit rules for being pedestrians as children (e.g., look both ways before crossing), and unspoken rules like vehicle gap acceptance through experience. The conditions of the pandemic present a unique opportunity to explore how adult pedestrians adapt their mental models and strategies to maintain physical distancing when encountering other pedestrians in outdoor public spaces (e.g., on sidewalks). Understanding emerging pedestrian physical distancing strategies can help with development of public health educational campaigns, as well as design of urban infrastructure to enhance person-focused mobility [3].

1.2 Research Objectives

The survey and results presented are part of a larger mixed-methods research study designed to identify emerging pedestrian mental models and physical distancing rules applied to negotiate common urban walking scenarios [4]. The main objective of the survey was to query residents of an urban community about their self-reported walking habits prior to and during COVID-19 pandemic conditions, and their expected pedestrian actions when presented with common urban walking scenarios.

2 Methodology

2.1 Survey Design

The design of the self-report questions and scenarios were informed by research on general pedestrian behaviours used under pre-pandemic conditions [5–7]. A 60-item online survey using a mix of fixed-choice questions, Likert scales, and open-ended responses was created to capture self-reports on walking behaviours prior to the COVID-19 state of emergency beginning in March 2020 and during pandemic conditions. Pandemic conditions are when local by-laws changed to require the use of masks in indoor public spaces, with recommendations for use of masks in outdoor spaces if physical distancing could not be maintained. To understand emerging pedestrian physical distancing strategies, respondents were presented with ten illustrated scenarios representing common encounters which required making pedestrian physical distancing decisions and selecting actions to continue the walk.

2.2 Recruitment

The research study received approval from the Office of Research Ethics at the University of Waterloo. Recruitment was restricted to adults living in the Waterloo Region, a mid-size urban community of approximately 600,000 people in Ontario, Canada. Restricting participation to a single region allowed for some assurance that the respondents were living with the same municipal by-laws and potential enforcement in outdoor spaces. The online survey was hosted on the Qualtrics Online Surveys system and collected anonymous responses. Invitation to participate was posted to selected social media channels. The survey was available from July 10, 2020 until August 7, 2020., which are summer months when weather is conducive for walking.

Responses from incomplete surveys and individuals indicating they lived outside of the region at the time of the survey were excluded from the analysis. Of the 252 valid responses, 63% identified as female, 34% as male, and 3% identified as other or preferred to not declare. Breakdown by age category were as follows: 18–24 years (24%), 25–34 years (48%), 35–44 years (16%), 45–54 years (6%), 55–64 years (4%), and 65–74 years (2%). According to a 2016 census for the region the median age is 38.5 years, so it is in keeping that most respondents were between 18–44 years.

3   Results

3.1   Analytical Approach

SPSS® was used for data analysis. No significant differences were found for gender and age when chi square analyses were applied to responses on main questions. Thus, response frequencies as percentage are reported collapsed across gender and age categories. When appropriate, Wilcoxon Signed-Rank test with effects size were used to compare self-reports for pre-COVID-19 and during-COVID-19 conditions. Reflexive thematic analysis was used to gain deeper insights from open-ended responses accompanying fixed-choice questions [8, 9].

3.2   General Walking Habits

Respondents were asked about their daily walking frequency, daily walking duration, and general reason(s) for walking both prior to and during COVID-19. Most reported walking in familiar areas (98%) with the primary reason for walking being wellness (81%) both before and during the pandemic. Frequency of daily walks was reported to be significantly lower with the onset of the pandemic [Wilcoxon Signed-Rank Test, $Z = -5.6, p < .001, r = -0.25$]. Based on the open-ended responses, primary reasons for the reduction in daily walking were "increased concern for risk of exposure to COVID-19" and "lack of motivation to go outdoors" even though the weather might be suitable for walking. It is worth noting that while the overall trend was a reduction in daily walking between the pre-pandemic and pandemic conditions, over 20% of respondents reported that "working remotely from home" allowed them more flexibility in taking walks.

3.3   Mask-Wearing Habits

Respondents were asked about their mask wearing habits, prior to COVID-19, as well as their mask wearing habits during COVID-19. As might be expected, the majority (95%) reported never wearing a mask in public prior to March 2020. In contrast, most respondents reported adhering to public health messaging with less than 10% reporting that they never wear a mask in public during the pandemic. It is unclear if self-reports of face mask non-compliance is due to pre-existing health issues or moral grounds.

3.4   Comfort Level Approaching Other Pedestrians

Respondents were asked about their comfort level when approaching other pedestrians both prior to and during the COVID-19 pandemic. A five (5) item Likert-type scale was used, ranging from very uncomfortable to very comfortable. The inclusion of a midpoint in the scale allowed for capturing neutrality in which respondents had no positive or negative feelings when approaching others [10].

Separate questions were asked about comfort level when encountering pedestrians who were known to them (i.e., acquaintances) and those unknown to them (i.e., strangers). Even when walking in familiar areas, respondents reported feeling less comfortable approaching other pedestrians during the pandemic than prior, regardless of whether the other pedestrians were acquaintances [t (249) = 13.6, p < .001], or strangers [t (249) = 14.48, p < .001].

3.5   Encounter and Avoidance Strategies in 10 Walking Scenarios

Contexts for the walking scenarios included whether masks were worn by the respondent or hypothetical pedestrian(s); whether eye contact could be expected (i.e., other person approaching from opposite direction on same path); and whether the adjacent roadway was low, moderate, or high traffic. Choices of actions included two main strategies "Encounter" behaviours (continue on current path; stop moving to let others pass); and "Avoidance" behaviours (step off the current path; cross to the other side of the road). An "other" category was included to allow alternate actions; however, few respondents selected this option.

Scenarios were classified by roadway traffic risk with four low traffic volume scenarios (e.g., quiet neighbourhood), three moderate traffic volume scenarios (e.g., mixed residential-commercial), and three high traffic volume scenarios (busy roadway). When traffic risk was low, avoidance and encounter behaviours were equally distributed (M = 54% and 46%). For moderate traffic risk, avoidance (72%) was chosen more frequently than encounter (28%). For high traffic risk scenarios, encounter behaviours (66%) were selected over avoidance (34%). The presence of masks in the scenarios did not have a notable effect on avoidance or encounter decisions. Table 1 presents a breakdown of pedestrian strategies by traffic risk.

Table 1. Traffic scenario risk levels by pedestrian physical distancing strategies

Traffic scenario	Avoidance behaviours		Encounter behaviours	
Risk level	Cross road	Step off path	Stop while others pass	Continue on path
Low (residential areas)	4.0%	51.4%	11.7%	32.9%
Moderate (mixed use)	28.4%	43.3%	16.5%	11.8%
High (busy roadway)	5.8%	27.9%	40.5%	25.8%

4 Discussion

During COVID-19 pandemic conditions, pedestrians report experiencing reduction in outdoor walking ($p < .001$) and increased unease when approaching others, even when walking in familiar areas ($p < .0001$) and wearing masks. Public health campaigns to wear masks and maintain physical distancing are often in the form of signs or posters with reminders to maintain physical distancing of 2 m. Little if any direction is provided through public health or road safety campaigns as to how to best negotiate physical distancing as a pedestrian when encountering others.

In the absence of educational campaigns providing explicit rules for right-of-way when encountering other pedestrians, the results of this study suggest that the preferred action is to adopt avoidance strategies by leaving the path of travel. The more popular avoidance strategy is to step off the sidewalk or path to give wider berth when approaching or overtaking other pedestrians. If traffic allows, some will opt to cross to the other side of the road to maximize distance between passing pedestrians. When perceived traffic risk is high, preferred action is to encounter the other pedestrian rather than a vehicle. The preference to employ avoidance strategies is supported in part through the thematic analysis of the open-ended survey responses where concerns were raised that even brief exposure to others may increase risk of contracting COVID-19.

Pedestrians relying on "step off the path" as the primary strategy for physical distancing points to a limitation in the current infrastructure within the region of study, particularly in the most heavily walked areas (i.e., downtown, parks/trails and suburban areas). Older neighbourhoods tend to have "traditional" sidewalks that are 1.5 m wide which is insufficient width to allow pedestrians to pass one another while maintaining physical distancing [11]. There is a need for sidewalks that are wide enough, or have sufficient green space adjacent to walking paths, to allow for easier distancing. As a step in this direction, Waterloo Region recently implemented programs to encourage residents to participate in its active transportation campaign [12]. Initiatives include a pilot project with additional separated bicycle lanes and converted shared spaces to allow wider pathways for easier movement and distancing between pedestrians in public. Although not the intended purpose, streets that were a part of the bike pilot program were welcomed by pedestrians, and some participants noted that the presence of bike lanes allowed for easier social distancing compared to streets or sidewalks with no adjacent bicycle lanes. Pedestrians view it safer to maintain physical distancing by stepping off a sidewalk into a designated bicycle lane rather than to walk along the side of the road with traffic. The use of shared expanded pathways has been championed in other locations as a means of responding to mobility needs during the COVID-19 pandemic [2, 13].

5 Conclusions

Patterns of pedestrian strategies are emerging for when to use avoidance and encounter strategies to maintain physical distancing while walking outside, despite absence of educational campaigns providing explicit rules for right-of-way. Design of urban environments and traffic risks play a role in whether the preferred avoidance strategy of "stepping of the path" can be used safely.

References

1. World Health Organization (WHO),# HealthyAtHome – Physical Activity. https://www.who.int/news-room/campaigns/connecting-the-world-to-combat-coronavirus/healthyathome/hea lthyathome---physical-activity. Accessed 8 Feb 2021
2. Kraemer, M.U.G., Yang, C.H., Gutierrez, B., Wu, C.H., Klein, B., Pigott, D.M., Scarpino, S.V.: The effect of human mobility and control measures on the COVID-19 epidemic in China. Science **368**(6490), 493–497 (2020). https://doi.org/10.1126/science.abb4218
3. Barbarossa, L.: Post-pandemic city: challenges and opportunities for a non-motorized urban environment. Overview Ital. Cases Sustain. **12**, 7172 (2020). https://doi.org/10.3390/su1217 7172
4. Greenslade, G.E.: Understanding pedestrian decision-making during the COVID-19 pandemic. Master's Thesis. University of Waterloo, Waterloo ON Canada (2021). UWSpace. http://hdl.handle.net/10012/16770
5. Granié, M.A., Pannetier, M., Guého, L.: Developing a self-reporting method to measure pedestrian behaviors at all ages. Accid. Anal. Prevent. **50**, 830–839 (2013). https://doi.org/10.1016/j.aap.2012.07.009
6. Deb, S., Strawderman, L., Carruth, D.W., DuBien, J., Smith, B., Garrison, T.M.: Development and validation of a questionnaire to assess pedestrian receptivity toward fully autonomous vehicles. Transp. Res. Part Emerg. Technol. **84**, 178–195 (2017). https://doi.org/10.1016/j.trc.2017.08.029
7. McIlroy, R.C., Plant, K.L., Jikyong, U., Nam, V.H., Bunyasi, B., Kokwaro, G.O., Stanton, N.A.: Vulnerable road users in low-, middle-, and high-income countries: validation of a pedestrian behaviour questionnaire. Accid. Analy. Prevent. **131**, 80–94 (2019). https://doi.org/10.1016/j.aap.2019.05.027
8. Braun, V., Clarke, V.: Using thematic analysis in psychology. Qual. Res. Psychol. **3**, 77–101 (2006). https://doi.org/10.1191/1478088706qp063oa
9. Braun, V., Clarke, V.: Successful Qualitative Research a Practical Guide for Beginners. SAGE Publications, New York (2019)
10. Chyung, S.Y., Roberts, K.A., Swanson, I., Hankinson, A.: Evidence-based survey design: the use of the midpoint on the likert scale. Perform. Improve. **56**(10), 15–23 (2017). https://doi.org/10.1002/pfi.21727
11. Waterloo, T.C.: of: Engineering Manual: Chapter 7, Design. Waterloo (2013). https://www.waterloo.ca/en/government/resources/Documents/Development-charges-and-guidelines/Engineering-manual-Part-7.pdf
12. Region of Waterloo: Active Transportation. Waterloo, Ontario, Canada (2020). https://www.regionofwaterloo.ca/en/exploring-the-region/active-transportation.aspx#
13. Zecca, C., Gaglione, F., Laing, R., Gargiulo, C.: Pedestrian routes and accessibility to urban services: An urban rhythmic analysis of people's behaviour during the Covid-19. TeMA **2**, 241–256 (2020). https://doi.org/10.6092/1970-9870/7051

University Student Experiences with Mandated Home Isolation

Hannah R. Griebel and Thomas J. Smith[(⊠)]

University of Minnesota, Minneapolis, MN, USA
{grie0238,smith293}@umn.edu

Abstract. University students were surveyed regarding their experiences with mandated home isolation in response to the COVID-19 pandemic. 42 survey responses were analyzed through the lens of social cybernetics. Key associations between elements of student experiences with social isolation were identified.

Keywords: Social isolation · Social cybernetics · COVID-19 · University student

1 Introduction and Background

Social relationships represent the most significant behavioral design feature on the planet, integral to our evolution and the emergence and expansion of civilization, trade, agriculture, technology and modern cities and nation-states. The 2020–2021 COVID-19 pandemic has cast these claims into stark relief, with mask wearing and social isolation recommended or mandated in numerous countries around the planet. This paper addresses the impact of pandemic-mandated social isolation on the health and wellbeing of students enrolled in universities in a number of U.S. states.

Three lines of inquiry bear upon the present study, namely: 1) empirical research on loneliness; and 2) on pandemic-related social isolation; and 3) conceptual application of social cybernetic theory to understanding social relationships and the effects of social isolation – this theory characterizes such relationships as closed-loop control systems, based on reciprocal social tracking interactions among social participants [1, Chap. 8; 2–4].

1.1 Research on Loneliness and Social Isolation

Loneliness as a manifestation of solitude, its characterization as a distinct emotion, and its adverse social consequences, have been recognized for centuries [5, 6]. More recently, loneliness has been recognized as a distinct public health problem [7–9]. Drawing on recent research, the Economist article [7], and Cacioppo and Cacioppo [8], point out that loneliness is not synonymous with social isolation per se (how often a person meets or speaks to friends and family), but rather is defined by researchers as *perceived* social isolation (a feeling of not having the social contacts one would like). The latter definition

N. L. Black et al. (Eds.): IEA 2021, LNNS 222, pp. 586–594, 2021.
https://doi.org/10.1007/978-3-030-74611-7_79

offers insight into the observed effects of pandemic-imposed social isolation, assuming that those affected typically are accustomed to, indeed perhaps rely upon, face-to-face (FTF) social interaction. These effects represent one focus of a large body of research prompted by the emergence of the pandemic [10].

For example, comparing course withdrawal rates among comparable numbers of university students enrolled in a computer literacy course, taught either online or FTF by the same instructor, Ali and Smith [11] report that the withdrawal rate by online students was almost seven-fold higher. The authors attribute this difference to effects of social isolation on online students.

In a survey of 733 post-secondary students enrolled at a Canadian university, based on a case-control design (e.g., pre-COVID FTF classroom course enrollment; post-COVID online course enrollment), Hamza and colleagues [12] observed that students without preexisting mental health concerns were likely to show declining mental health, which coincided with increased social isolation among these students.

Complementary to, and contemporary with, the report of Hamza and colleagues [12] is the review of Loades and colleagues [13]. These investigators analyzed sixty-three articles published between 1946 and 2020 dealing with the effects of social isolation and loneliness on the mental health of previously healthy children and adolescents. A key conclusion is that the duration of loneliness was more strongly correlated with mental health symptoms than intensity of loneliness. There is an evident parallel between this finding and that of Hamza et al. [12] regarding older university students under COVID-19 related social isolation.

1.2   Social Cybernetics of Social Isolation

Social cybernetic theory offers a comprehensive behavioral interpretation of how people interact socially, and exert control over their social behavioral environment [1, Chap. 8; 2–4; 14]. It represents a behavioral control systems theory that focuses upon the recip-rocal feedback and feedforward control interactions between two or more individuals, a process termed *social tracking*. Social tracking is conceived as a dynamic linking of the social behavior of two or more people which is often goal-oriented as it usually is in the workplace.

Social isolation can perturb and disrupt the integrity of closed-loop social tracking control systems, which can have a deleterious effect on health, as outlined above, as well as on other facets of the human experience. The stay-at-home mandates that went into effect in response to COVID-19 provide conditions for a natural experiment to examine the effects of home isolation on these social systems. The goal of the research described in this report was to collect survey data from university students in order to address the impact of mandated home isolation on university student experiences.

2   Methodology

This IRB-approved, cross-sectional study utilized a 40-question self-report survey, which was distributed via email to nine student chapters of the Human Factors and Ergonomics Society (HFES) across the United States. Student members of these chapters largely are upper level undergraduate as well as graduate students. Students were surveyed to obtain basic demographic information and Likert-scale subjective assessments of quality of social interactions and relationships, quality of physical and mental health, quality of lifestyle and leisure activities, quality of productivity and working from home, evaluations of boredom and loneliness levels, and related topics. Participation was anonymous and voluntary.

Inclusion criteria required that participants were aged 18 or older, had experienced mandated home isolation in response to the COVID-19 pandemic, and were enrolled as a student at a U.S. university at the time of this mandated home isolation. Mandated home isolation was defined to apply to anyone whose State of residence issued a stay-at-home order and leaving the home was restricted; it did not necessarily mean that the participant had been sick and self-isolating, nor did it require that participants lived alone. The term "home" was defined to mean any of the following: my family's residence; a residence that I own; a residence where I pay rent; a residence that someone else rents or owns; a shelter or transitional/temporary housing.

3 Results

3.1 Participant Demographics

A total of 47 surveys were at least partially completed, and 42 were eligible for analysis. The other five surveys were deemed ineligible for analysis because they were not completed. Questions were not forced-response; therefore, the actual number of responses for any given question may be lower than 42 in cases where a respondent answered most questions but skipped one or more.

The 42 analyzed surveys came from 20 undergraduate students, 8 Master's students, and 14 PhD students at the following universities: Michigan Tech (n = 1); Penn State University (n = 1); Purdue University (n = 2); University of Iowa (n = 3); University of Michigan (n = 8); University of Michigan-Dearborn (n = 1); University of Minnesota, Twin Cities (n = 18); University of Wisconsin-Madison (n = 7); and Wichita State University (n = 1). Participant ages ranged from 19–36 years. From these ages, four age groups (see Table 2) were identified: 18–21 (n = 18), 22–25 (n = 8), 26–29 (n = 13), and 30+ (n = 4).

The survey allowed respondents to write in their gender identities via an open-ended question, and responses included 33 females and 9 males. Fourteen participants were unemployed and 28 were employed; employment was defined to include working either on site or from home. When surveyed about living arrangements, six participants indicated they lived alone, 13 lived with family members, 11 lived with non-family roommates, 10 lived with a spouse or significant other only, and 2 listed a combination of the previous arrangements. All participants indicated they had experienced home isolation due to COVID-19 stay-at-home orders.

3.2 Subjective Assessment Survey Responses

Table 1 summarizes participant responses to the survey's subjective assessment questions, presenting the average number of responses for each Likert item. The Likert item most frequently chosen is emphasized in bold text. Questions are grouped based on type of question, either quality attribute, or agree/disagree judgment (N/A responses are not tabulated).

Table 1. Subjective assessments of mandated home isolation (N = 42)

Likert scale-low (1) - high (7)	(1)	(2)	(3)	(4)	(5)	(6)	(7)
Quality of managing mandated home isolation	0.0%	2.4%	9.5%	23.8%	**30.9%**	26.1%	7.1%
Quality of social relationships	0.0%	9.5%	26.1%	**28.6%**	16.7%	9.5%	9.5%
Quality of social interactions	4.8%	**28.6%**	21.4%	11.9%	11.9%	16.7%	4.8%
Quality of mental health	7.1%	19.0%	21.4%	**28.6%**	9.6%	7.1%	4.8%
Quality of physical health	4.8%	4.8%	19.0%	16.7%	**23.8%**	19.0%	9.5%
Quality of eating properly	2.4%	7.1%	9.5%	**23.8%**	19.0%	21.4%	14.3%
Quality of sleep	0.0%	4.8%	19.0%	**21.4%**	16.7%	16.7%	19.0%
Quality of regular physical activity or exercise	2.4%	**26.2%**	19.0%	16.7%	7.1%	11.9%	9.5%
Quality of recreational or leisure activities	4.8%	16.7%	**28.6%**	16.7%	19.0%	2.4%	4.8%
Quality of university academic performance and learning	9.5%	19.0%	**31.0%**	7.1%	11.9%	7.1%	7.1%
Quality of working at home (school or paid work)	14.3%	11.9%	**28.6%**	14.3%	9.5%	9.5%	4.8%
Likert scale-strongly disagree (1) to strongly agree (7)	(1)	(2)	(3)	(4)	(5)	(6)	(7)
Technology enables effective social relationships	0.0%	7.1%	9.5%	9.5%	21.4%	**28.6%**	21.4%
Technology adequate substitution for FTF social interactions	16.7%	21.4%	**28.6%**	19.0%	4.8%	4.8%	2.4%
Decreased feelings of anxiety and stress	21.4%	**26.2%**	19.0%	19.0%	2.4%	4.8%	2.4%
Increased feelings of anxiety and stress	7.1%	7.1%	4.8%	19.0%	**23.8%**	23.8%	9.5%
Decreased feelings loneliness	**33.3%**	30.9%	16.7%	11.9%	2.4%	0.0%	0.0%
Increased feelings loneliness	2.4%	7.1%	2.4%	21.4%	16.7%	19.0%	**26.2%**
Decreased feelings boredom	26.2%	**28.6%**	19.0%	11.9%	0.0%	4.8%	0.0%
Increased feelings boredom	2.4%	4.8%	7.1%	**21.4%**	19.0%	14.2%	**21.4%**
Affected substance use	**52.4%**	11.9%	4.7%	7.1%	11.9%	2.4%	2.4%
Affected sex life	**26.2%**	7.1%	9.5%	11.9%	11.9%	11.9%	14.3%

(continued)

Table 1. (*continued*)

Likert scale-strongly disagree (1) to strongly agree (7)	(1)	(2)	(3)	(4)	(5)	(6)	(7)
Decreased productivity	4.8%	2.4%	11.9%	7.1%	16.7%	23.8%	**26.2%**
Increased productivity	23.8%	**30.9%**	21.4%	11.9%	2.4%	2.4%	0.0%
Affected physical skills	9.5%	19.0%	9.5%	**23.8%**	16.7%	9.5%	4.8%
Affected mental/intellectual skills	7.1%	16.7%	11.9%	19.0%	**23.8%**	11.9%	2.4%
Affected perception of passage of time	0.0%	4.8%	0.0%	7.1%	35.7%	7.1%	**38.1%**

3.3 Comparisons by Age, Gender, Student Type, and Employment Status

Process for Creating Variables. One goal of this research was to evaluate whether there were any differences in subjective experiences with mandated home isolation based on different social, personal, and emotional factors. To this end, survey questions pertaining to similar topics and using the same Likert scale were grouped together. The following question groups were identified: Social Quality (including questions about Overall Quality, Relationships, Interactions, Mobile Relationships, Mobile Interactions); Lifestyle Quality (including questions about Mental Health, Physical Health, Eating, Sleep, Exercise, Leisure); Effect on Feelings (including questions about Anxiety/Stress, Boredom, Loneliness); Other Effects (including questions about Substance Abuse, Sex, Mental Skills, Physical Skills, Perception Passage of Time); and Education Quality (including questions about Quality Academics, Quality Work from Home).

These question groups were made into variables by taking each participants' average response to the questions within each group and creating a single Likert scale response. Each variable was then evaluated using Cronbach's alpha in order to determine if the questions therein were sufficiently related to one another. Adequate internal consistency for comparing groups was found for the following four question groups: Social Quality ($\alpha = 0.77$), Lifestyle Quality ($\alpha = 0.74$), Effect on Feelings ($\alpha = 0.70$), and Education Quality ($\alpha = 0.88$) [16]. The questions clustered into the Other Effects variable had a low internal consistency ($\alpha = 0.57$), and therefore that variable was excluded from the ANOVA analysis (below).

Analysis by ANOVA. ANOVA (Analysis of Variance) examines the possible effect of a categorical independent variable, also called a 'factor', on a dependent variable [17]. For this research, the following between-subjects demographic factors were analyzed, with factor levels listed in parentheses: Age group (18–21; 22–25; 26–30; 30+), gender (male; female), student type (undergraduate; Master's; PhD), and employment status (unemployed; employed). The dependent variables used were Social Quality, Lifestyle Quality, Effect on Feelings, and Education Quality question groups. The goal was to determine whether any differences existed in how participants responded to each variable based on demographic factors.

One-way ANOVAs were conducted for each independent and dependent variable pair. F-values are listed in Table 2, with the first value in parentheses indicating the between-groups degrees of freedom (number of factor levels minus 1), and the second value in parentheses indicating the within-groups degrees of freedom (number of responses minus number of factor levels). The within-groups degrees of freedom vary for each item because the dependent variables were created from grouped survey questions, and there are missing data points from instances where a respondent chose not to answer one or more questions. As outlined in Table 2, there were no significant results found at the level of $p < 0.05$, which means there were no significant differences in how students responded to each question group based on age, gender, student type, or employment status.

Table 2. One-way ANOVA results ($\alpha = 0.05$)

Independent variable	Between-subjects factor levels	Dependent variable	F-value	p-value
Age group	18–21; 22–25; 26–30; 30+	Social quality	$F(3, 37) = 0.242$	$p = .866$
Age group	18–21; 22–25; 26–30; 30+	Lifestyle quality	$F(3, 35) = 0.011$	$p = .998$
Age group	18–21; 22–25; 26–30; 30+	Effect on feelings	$F(3, 34) = 1.998$	$p = .133$
Age group	18–21; 22–25; 26–30; 30+	Education quality	$F(3, 35) = 0.452$	$p = .717$
Gender	Male; Female	Social quality	$F(1, 39) = 0.938$	$p = .339$
Gender	Male; Female	Lifestyle quality	$F(1, 37) = 0.000$	$p = 1.00$
Gender	Male; Female	Effect on feelings	$F(1, 36) = 0.586$	$p = .449$
Gender	Male; Female	Education quality	$F(1, 37) = 0.015$	$p = .902$
Student type	Undergraduate; Master's; PhD	Social quality	$F(2, 38) = 0.035$	$p = .965$
Student type	Undergraduate; Master's; PhD	Lifestyle quality	$F(2, 36) = 0.165$	$p = .848$
Student type	Undergraduate; Master's; PhD	Effect on feelings	$F(2, 35) = 1.659$	$p = .205$
Student type	Undergraduate; Master's; PhD	Education quality	$F(2, 36) = 0.048$	$p = .953$
Employment	Employed; Unemployed	Social quality	$F(1, 39) = 0.021$	$p = .887$

(*continued*)

Table 2. (*continued*)

Independent variable	Between-subjects factor levels	Dependent variable	F-value	p-value
Employment	Employed; Unemployed	Lifestyle quality	$F(1, 37) = 0.186$	p = .669
Employment	Employed; Unemployed	Effect on feelings	$F(1, 36) = 0.010$	p = .921
Employment	Employed; Unemployed	Education quality	$F(1, 37) = 0.085$	p = .772

4 Limitations

The major distinctive feature of this study is that results are based on 42 responses from students enrolled in nine different universities, most in the Midwest, but also including both an Eastern state (Pennsylvania), as well as a Plains state (Kansas) university. The experimental design is a cross-sectional analysis of enrolled online students only, unlike the more robust case-control study by Ali and Smith [11] of students enrolled in both FTF and online classrooms at one university. Student respondents in this study number only about one-third of the 114 reported by Ali and Smith [11], and markedly less than the 773 reported by Hamza and colleagues [12], both at one university. This relatively low number of responses could be considered a limitation of this study.

By contrast, the range of possible effects on student social isolation explored in this study is notably greater than the student withdrawal-from-university effects reported by Ali and Smith [11], and the student mental health effects reported by Hamza and colleagues [12].

Another evident limitation of this study is the disproportionate number of female respondents (over three-fourths) relative to male respondents. Other demographic information, such as race and ethnicity, sexual orientation, income level, and religious affiliation, was not collected; therefore potential differences among those groups were not identified, which could limit the application of these results.

5 Conclusions and Implications

It can fairly be claimed that no other event since WWII has had such dramatic adverse effects on the academic experiences, along with the health and wellness, of university students across the U.S. – indeed worldwide – as the COVID-19 pandemic. Moreover, the rapidity with which these effects have manifested themselves within the space of a year arguably has been unprecedented.

The rating results documented in Table 1 provide insight into the scope of these effects. The top half of Table 1 shows a breakdown of 11 survey questions where participants were asked to rate the quality of several experiences related to mandated home isolation on a scale of Low (1) to High (7). Of these items, 9 of them were rated most frequently as neutral to low quality. Perceived quality of regular physical activity during social isolation, and perceived quality of social interactions, were most frequently rated the lowest relative to the other items. Participants most frequently rated the overall quality of managing home isolation as medium-high, which suggests that although the quality of all but one of the remaining items is rated neutral or low, respondents indicate a degree of resiliency in dealing with self-isolation.

The bottom half of Table 1 shows a breakdown of 15 survey questions where participants were asked to evaluate the degree to which they agree with statements about their experiences with mandated home isolation on a scale of Strongly Disagree (1) to Strongly Agree (7). One provocative finding is that over 80% of respondents agree or strongly agree with the statement that social isolation affects their perception of the passage of time. Of the questions specifically addressing negative emotional and mental effects, the highest response percentages are associated with agreement to strong agreement with all of these effects, including boredom, anxiety and stress, and loneliness. The broader question is what deleterious effects prolonged social isolation might have on emotional and mental health. A troubling answer is provided by a recent Japanese survey [18] of about 1800 teleworkers, 35% of whom said that their mental health had deteriorated as a result of having to work from home.

Most respondents also agree or strongly agree that technology (i.e., cell phones and computers) enables them to maintain effective social relationships, yet a similar number of respondents disagree or strongly disagree that social interactions via these technologies are an adequate substitute for FTF interactions. Considering also that respondents most often rated their social interactions as being low quality, but their social relationships most frequently rated as neutral quality, these results suggest an interesting conclusion: although students may feel that their social relationships are not strongly affected by mandated home isolation, the interactions they have with other people – often remotely via phone or computer – are of a lower quality than in-person interactions. From a social cybernetic perspective, the implication of this finding is that technology-mediated remote social interaction is no substitute for the immediacy and richness of exchange of social tracking feedback during FTF social interaction.

These findings raise the question of when the quality of social relationships might be worsened by continuous low-quality social interactions. Given the already strong agreement that isolation increases loneliness, anxiety, and stress, as well as the continuation of the COVID-19 pandemic into 2021 and beyond, this emerges as an important area for future research.

Inspiration for the content of this survey was a survey employed in an earlier occupancy quality research project [15]. The term *occupancy quality* refers to the degree to which the level of excellence, pertaining to different design features of a given occupancy environment, influence affective feelings such as comfort, satisfaction and usability on the part of the occupants of that environment. The conceptual and empirical basis of this idea is extensive evidence that observed variability in behavior and performance is prominently influenced by design features of the behavioral environment [1].

A final conclusion to be drawn from this research is that there is much more that these students have in common than what divides them. Regardless of differences in age, gender, student type, and employment status, these university students report similar subjective experiences with mandated home isolation, suggested by the lack of significant ANOVA results in Table 2. This reveals a shared experience among students with regard to how they are handling mandated home isolation—blanket interventions to address the effects of mandated home isolation thus might be feasible. It is important to note that given limitations with this study, individual experiences with home isolation could vary broadly.

References

1. Smith, T.J., Wade, M.G., Henning, R., Fisher, T.: Variability in Human Performance. CRC Press, Boca Raton (2015)
2. Smith, K.U.: Industrial social cybernetics. University of Wisconsin Behavioral Cybernetics Laboratory, Madison, WI (1974)
3. Smith, T.J., Henning, R.H., Smith, K.U.: Sources of performance variability. In: Salvendy, G., Karwowski, W. (eds.) Design of Work and Development of Personnel in Advanced Manufacturing (Chap. 11), pp. 273–330. Wiley, New York (1994)
4. Smith, T.J., Henning, R.A., Smith, K.U.: Performance of hybrid automated systems - a social cybernetic analysis. Int. J. Hum. Factors Manuf. **5**(1), 29–51 (1995)
5. Vincent, D.: A History of Solitude. Polity, Cambridge (2020)
6. Alberti, F.B.: A Biography of Loneliness: The History of an Emotion. Oxford University Press, Oxford (2019)
7. The Economist. Alone in the crowd. Loneliness is increasingly being treated as a serious public health problem. The Economist, 1 September, pp. 49–51 (2018)
8. Cacioppo, J.T., Cacioppo, S.: The growing problem of loneliness. Lancet **391**, 426 (2018)
9. DiJulio, B., Hamel, L., Cailey, M., Brodie, M.: Loneliness and Social Isolation in the United States, the United Kingdom, and Japan: An International Survey. Henry J Kaiser Family Foundation, San Francisco (2018)
10. Irmak, R.: The most cited and co-cited COVID-19 articles: knowledge base for rehabilitation team members. Work J. Prev. Assess. Rehabil. **66**(3), 479–489 (2020)
11. Ali, A., Smith, D.: Comparing social isolation effects on students' attrition in online versus face-to-face courses in computer literacy. Issues Informing Sci. Inf. Technol. **12**, 11–20 (2015)
12. Hamza, C.A., Ewing, L., Heath, N.L., Goldstein, A.L.: When social isolation is nothing new: a longitudinal study of psychological distress during Covid-19 among university students with and without preexisting mental health concerns. Can. Psychol./Psychologie Canadienne (2020). https://doi.org/10.1037/cap0000255. Accessed Jan 2021
13. Loades, M.E., Chatburn, E., Higson-Sweeney, N., Reynolds, S., Shafran, R., Brigden, A., Linney, C., McManus, M.N., Borwick, C., Crawley, E.: Rapid systematic review: the impact of social isolation and loneliness on the mental health of children and adolescents in the context of COVID-19. J. Am. Acad. Child Adolesc. Psychiatry **59**(11), 1218–1239 (2020)
14. Smith, T.J., Henning, R.A.: The nature of the firm – a social cybernetic analysis. Work J. Prev. Assess. Rehabil. **64**, 641–650 (2019)
15. Smith, T.J., Orfield, S.J.: Occupancy quality predictors of office worker perceptions of job productivity. In: Proceedings of the Human Factors and Ergonomics Society Annual Meeting, vol. 51, pp. 539–543 (2007)
16. Bland, M.J., Altman, D.G.: Statistics notes: Cronbach's alpha. BMJ **314**, 572 (1997)
17. Maxwell, S.E., Delaney, H.D., Kelley, K.: Designing Experiments and Analyzing Data: A Model Comparison Perspective, 3rd edn. Taylor & Francis Group, Oxfordshire (2017)
18. The Daily Yomiuri – The Japan Times. As work boundaries blur, teleworkers report drop in mental health. Minneapolis, MN, Star Tribune, 3 May, SH4 (2020)

Confirmation of the Significance of Facial Images in Online Learning Using Eye Gaze Tracking Measurement

Satori Hachisuka[1]([✉]), Kayoko Kurita[2], and Shin'ichi Warisawa[1]

[1] Graduate School of Frontier Sciences, The University of Tokyo, Tokyo, Japan
hachisuka@edu.k.u-tokyo.ac.jp
[2] Graduate School of Education, The University of Tokyo, Tokyo, Japan

Abstract. In this study, we examined the significance of facial images of a lecturer in online learning both quantitatively and qualitatively. We conducted an experiment to confirm how the lecturer's facial image affects the learner's impression and eye gaze duration during online learning. The experiment consisted of an eye gaze tracking measurement and a semi-structured interview for six participants. Based on multimedia learning theory, we hypothesized that placing a lecturer's facial image on the screen during online learning would improve the impression of the lecture for the learner. However, from the experimental results, the average time ratio for gazing at the lecturer's facial image was 2% or less. In addition, 83% of the participants answered in the semi-structured interview that it would be better not to display the lecturer's facial image, which was contrary to the hypothesis. The novel point of this paper is that it shows the results of those who have newly experienced online learning and/or online lecture in daily life for approximately one year. This result is one of the important factors in considering the design of online learning, which has rapidly become widespread in recent years.

Keywords: Lecturer's facial image · Facial expression · Eye gaze tracking · Online learning

1 Introduction

Recently, online learning is rapidly expanding as a countermeasure against infectious diseases. However, in online learning, the pros and cons of displaying facial images of oneself and others have not been established. According to the multimedia learning theory, the lecturer's facial information is considered to improve the learning effect [1]. Generally, it is also reported that the display of facial images brings a secure feeling. On the other hand, it is also reported that the display of facial images leads tense and annoyance due to the appearance of each other's facial expressions. In some studies, superimposing a lecturer's facial image on lecture material, for example, a digital slide, did not affect the learner's ability to recall the lecture contents [2], and learners prefer the overlay mode to the picture-in-picture mode [3]. In addition, if it is selectable, some learners chose a learning video without the lecturer's facial image more than the learning

© The Author(s), under exclusive license to Springer Nature Switzerland AG 2021
N. L. Black et al. (Eds.): IEA 2021, LNNS 222, pp. 595–599, 2021.
https://doi.org/10.1007/978-3-030-74611-7_80

video with a facial image for avoiding distraction [4]. However, now, the learning form is changing rapidly with the spread of infectious diseases, and the way of thinking and the common sense of learners is greatly changing. Therefore, in this paper, we clarified the latest basic answers to the questions which "When studying using the learning materials displayed on the screen, is a lecturer's facial image needed or not?" and "If it is needed, what kind of effect does it have?"

The objective of this study is to clarify the fundamental knowledge of a facial image of the lecturer, whether it should be displayed and how it should be displayed. We consider the lecturer's facial image has an important function in online learning. Essentially, there are various subjects and contents in learning, and it is expected that the learner's condition will differ for each subject. Therefore, in this paper, we used the content of common sense, which is unrelated to school subjects.

2   Experimental Method

We conducted the experiment using a general online communication tool (Zoom) and displayed the presentation materials for learning on the full screen (2880 × 1920 pixels). Lecturer's facial image was overlaid displayed at the top right of the screen as picture-in-picture mode. The theme of the learning content was the traffic safety course quiz provided online by the Cabinet Office of Japan [5]. The learning form was an on-demand format, and there is no interactive communication between lecturer and learner. In the learning content, an illustration of the front view from the driver's seat was displayed for 10 s, and a participant was instructed to find three traffic risks. There was text information as a question or explanation on the same screen as the illustration. The instructions, questions, and explanations displayed on the screen were read aloud by the lecturer at the same time and were also provided to the learner as audio information. Figure 1 shows a simplified schematic figure of the learning video presented to the participants.

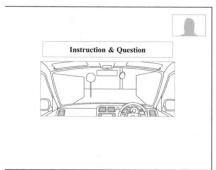
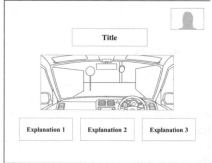

(a) Instruction and question screen   (b) Correct answer and explanation screen

Fig. 1. (a) was shown during thinking time and (b) was shown for self-confirmation of answers.

2.1 Experimental Condition

Participant. Participants were six healthy males and females in their 20s to 40s. They had experiences of attending lectures and meetings online on a daily basis for approximately one year.

Measured Data. Participant's eye gaze point coordinates on a display, and free answers to the semi-structured interview were measured.

Participant's eye gaze point was tracked and measured by calibration-free eye mark recorder (EMR ACTUS, nac Image Technology Inc.).

Impression for the lecture videos was orally asked by the experimenter after all videos were shown. The semi-structured interview began with fixed questions such as: (1) Recognized differences in three videos, (2) Preference ranking of display format among three videos, (3) Preference of existence or not of lecturer's facial image on a screen, and (4) Preference of size of lecturer's facial image on a screen.

Parameters. The size of the lecturer's facial image and the content of the illustration quiz were different in the three videos. The size parameters of the lecturer's facial image such as: (1) not displayed (0×0 pixels), (2) small (450×250 pixels), and (3) large (640×360 pixels). The content of the illustration quiz was different in every three videos, but each illustration had three points of traffic risks to find. Lecturer's voice guidance existed in all three videos.

Procedure. After obtaining informed consent, the participants voluntarily participated in the experiment. Participants were instructed to sit in front of the display with a distance of approximately 1 m and to watch three different learning videos for approximately 80 s for each. Participants did not have to answer the quiz verbally, and the correct answer for each video quiz was shown on the screen immediately after 10 s of thinking time with descriptive text and audio. Participants took off the mask only during eye gaze measurements and put on the mask for the subsequent semi-structured interviews. The interview was conducted with sitting; the angle between the participant and experimenter was 90°. The entire procedure of the experiment is shown in Fig. 2.

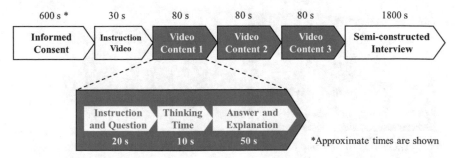

Fig. 2. The experiment was conducted according to this procedure.

2.2 Data Analysis

Eye Gaze Point as Objective Data. For the eye gaze data, we analyzed (A) the area of contents (text, illustration, and facial image), which the eye gaze point existed at the beginning of each video, and (B) the area of contents (text, illustration, and facial image) which the eye gaze point existed in long periods. As the result of the gaze time, the percentage value of the gaze time obtained by dividing the gaze time of each area of content by the total gaze time for one video was adopted.

Answer to Semi-structured Interview as Subjective Data. In the semi-structured interview, by continuing to ask additional questions based on the answers to the fixed questions, the participants' impressions of the video contents and the reasons for it were extracted. The overall tendency was quantified as a percentage of the number of people from the contents and words commonly obtained from the answers of all participants. What the participants felt during their usual online learning was also verbally extracted.

3   Results and Considerations

According to the results, eye gaze transition followed the lecturer's voice guidance, and those were distributed on text and illustration contents most of the time. The example results of the heatmap and the names of the content areas are shown in Fig. 3. The average time ratio for gazing at the lecturer's facial image was 2% or less (Fig. 4). Comparing two videos that included the lecturer's facial image, there was no tendency of the relation between the gaze time and the size of the facial image.

On the other hand, according to the subjective evaluation, 83% of participants preferred a video without the lecturer's facial image. The summarized reason for the answers was that participants felt distracted by the facial image. Some of them felt the tension, like being monitoring from the facial image. In addition, 83% of participants answered that the facial image of the lecturer is unnecessary even in the usual online lectures because it distracts concentration. However, they answered that they feel anxious without other person's facial images during the interactive online meetings.

(a) Overlayed heatmap result

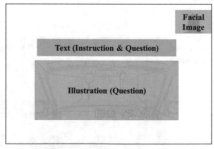
(b) Names of content areas on the screen

Fig. 3. (a) indicates the gaze points results, and names in (b) were used in gaze time analysis.

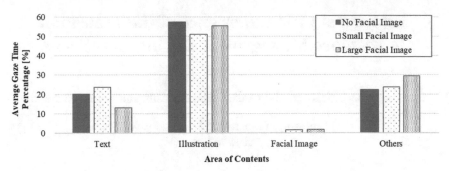

Fig. 4. Most of the participants gazed at the illustration related to the main task.

4   Conclusion

In this paper, it is suggested that the lecturer's facial image has a possibility to be a distraction noise in on-demand type online learning without interaction between a lecturer and learners. According to the eye gaze tracking measurement, the lecturer's facial image was rarely gazed at, with an average gaze time ratio of less than 2%. Some participants answered that they were aware of the presence of the facial image but did not intentionally look at it in order to focus on the task. The novel and valid point of this study are that the experiments were conducted for participants who have experienced online learning and online lectures on a daily basis with the actual tools.

The limitation of this study is the number of participants and the variety of age groups, learning styles, and contents. Our goal is to develop a novel learning system that brings a secure feeling to learners and keeps the concentration of them. In the next step, we will conduct the experiments to clarify the effective parameters such as exist timing, period, size of the lecturer's facial image. We believe that there is a possibility for a facial image to help learners' understandings, feelings, and motivation.

References

1. Mayer, R.E.: Multimedia Learning. Cambridge University Press, Cambridge (2001)
2. Kizilcec, R.F., Papadopoulos, K., Sritanyaratana, L.: Showing face in video instruction: effects on information retention, visual attention, and affect. In: Proceedings of the SIGCHI Conference on Human Factors in Computing Systems 2014 (CHI 2014), Toronto, pp. 2095–2102. ACM (2014)
3. Bhat, S., Chinprutthiwong, P., Perry, M.: Seeing the instructor in two video styles: preferences and patterns. In: Proceedings of the 8th International Conference on Educational Data Mining, pp. 305–312. IEDMS, Madrid (2015)
4. Kizilcec, R.F., Bailenson, J.N., Gomez, C.J.: The instructor's face in video instruction: evidence from two large-scale field studies. J. Educ. Psychol. **107**(3), 724–739 (2015)
5. Cabinet Office, Government of Japan, Traffic safety course PDF file (in Japanese). https://www8.cao.go.jp/koutu/kyouiku/pdf/elderly_drivers.pdf. Accessed 9 Feb 2021

Managers' First Experience of the Transition to Distance Management During COVID-19

Christine Ipsen(✉), Kasper Edwards, Giulia Nardelli, and Nelda Vendramin

Technical University of Denmark, 2800 Kgs. Lyngby, Denmark
chip@dtu.dk

Abstract. Managers at all levels have been forced to change their managerial activities during COVID-19 lockdowns. This paper describes early findings of a case study of 13 Danish first- and second-line managers' experiences with distance management during COVID-19. The qualitative study collected data from May to December 2020 during six rounds. The analysis shows that the managers take the responsibility on them to make working from home function for their employees and seek new ways of organizing and manage work from home. They appreciate the flexibility and that meetings have become more efficient but also equal and inclusive. The new role provide them with new skills and tasks. However, distance management also comes with a cost i.e. longer workdays and awkward working hours, the tasks are demanding and require planning. The managers miss the social interaction that the office provides and work hard to create a sense of proximity and trust across distance. The study shows that the lockdowns have impacted managers' experiences of their management job in a positive and negative way. If workplaces are to continue with WFH or hybrid-remote-work workplaces they are to ensure that managers' wellbeing is safeguarded by new efficient ways of working rather than working harder and longer.

Keywords: Managers · Experiences · Distance management · Working from home · Hybrid remote work · COVID-19

1 Introduction

The COVID-19 pandemic has created substantial changes within organizations and its members. Managers at all levels have been forced to change their managerial activities during COVID-19 and there has been a strong focus on how to safeguard employees' wellbeing and performance across distance. However, less attention has been paid to the managers and their experience of the lockdown during the pandemic. Research has primarily focused on employees and their experiences and wellbeing rather that managers [1–4]. A study of the experiences of working from home (WFH) shows that Danish managers found the lockdown period more challenging than their employees [5]. The question remains; how do managers experience the new ways of working as distance managers, with the majority of their workforce working from home? Hence, the aim of this study was to explore how managers conducted their new role and how they experienced managing from a distance during the lockdown.

© The Author(s), under exclusive license to Springer Nature Switzerland AG 2021
N. L. Black et al. (Eds.): IEA 2021, LNNS 222, pp. 600–606, 2021.
https://doi.org/10.1007/978-3-030-74611-7_81

2 Literature

2.1 Managers' Wellbeing

Managers' job performance is key to organizational performance [6] and their wellbeing has a potential effect on their employees' wellbeing [7] and employees' loyalty and job security [8]. Despite the awareness of managers' role in safeguarding the performance and wellbeing and that stressors and environmental pressure also affect managers [6], only recently the topic has gained research attention. Managers' wellbeing has shown to be associated with job demands like workload, managerial role and personal responsibility and organizational change [8, 9]. Recent studies have examined the link between managers' happiness and performance and presented the "Happy-Performing Managers" [6, 10] as an extension of the happy productive worker. The latter study examines how role stressors (ambiguity, conflict and overload) impact on manager's wellbeing and job satisfaction and how that in turn ultimately influenced their contextual performance.

Regarding organizational change, a study by Worrall and Cooper (2006) shows that while the proportion of managers experiencing symptoms increased during and post organizational changes, their absence and willingness to take time off decreased [11, 12]. Where work-life balance may affect employee wellbeing, a study on managers' wellbeing shows that it can have similar negative effects on them [13]. While existing research mainly has focused on managers in general, few researchers have addressed managers' wellbeing from a distance management perspective. However, a new study of WFH during the national lockdowns suggests that Danish managers found managing from a distance more demanding than the employees [14].

2.2 Experiences of WFH

One of the effects of the COVID-19 outbreak was the massive increase in people WFH as governments demanded that as much work as possible should be done from home. Previous studies have outlined the advantages and disadvantages of WFH [15–17]. Examples of perceived advantages of distance work are increased productivity, less stress, a better work–life balance [18], reduced commuting time [19, 20], increased control of work patterns and being in less contact with others [21, 22]. Conversely, examples of potential disadvantages associated with distance work are isolation, misunderstandings, decreased interpersonal contact and role ambiguity [23–26]. Other studies have found that the work–life balance may also be challenged since boundaries become blurry, people work more hours, there can be a lack of support and visible leadership, and there may be less social interaction when isolated and detached from the workplace [27–29].

3 Methods

This longitudinal single case-study of an international pharmaceutical company was initiated in May 2020. The company employs more than 45.000 people and have production facilities around the world. This study focuses on knowledge intensive work where both managers and employees are highly specialized, work in project teams. Due to COVID-19 lockdowns managers and employees worked at different sites, primarily from home. The thirteen first and second line managers have their base in Denmark. To gain insights into the managers' experience we conducted online interviews, over 6 rounds from May 2020 to December 2020 (See Table 1).

Table 1. Overview of number of interviews conducted with 1st and 2nd line managers.

Round	Interview time	1st line	2nd line
1st	May	7	6
2nd	June	6	6
3rd	Aug	6	5
4th	Oct	7	6
5th	Nov	5	5
6th	Dec	5	6

In the interviews, we obtained the managers' view about the current situation focusing on their experience and perception of their work as distance managers as we asked about the pros and cons of the work and their perception of the organizational support. All interviews were recorded and then transcribed by otter.ai and checked for accuracy by the authors. The aim of the analysis was to condense the extensive data from the 67 interviews into a brief format. The data was analyzed in Atlas.ti software using a thematic analysis to cluster the data into positive and negative experiences [30].

4   Results

4.1   Positive Experiences

The managers expressed that WFH provided diverse benefits, e.g., more flexibility and ability to plan workdays according to own needs, and that working from home was possible and functions well. Furthermore, the managers noticed that the meetings had become more efficient and structured, and that meeting online provided opportunities for increased global engagement i.e., coworkers working abroad could participate in meetings in a more equal and inclusive way from a distance than prior the pandemic.

Even though the managers were managing from a distance, they experienced that they have become closer to their employees and learned more about them personally due to the increase in informal events, virtual coffee gatherings, and frequent one to one meetings. Throughout the lockdown, managers approached problems in innovative ways through experimentation with different tools and approaches to solve emerging issues. The experimentation and trying out new things had given the managers both new skills and expanded their skillset.

4.2 Negative Experiences

Distance management during the lockdown also presented several challenges. The managers perceived distance management as more demanding and requiring more planning because managers lost the daily unplanned touch points with employees and compensated by scheduling one-to-one meetings. WFH implied longer working hours (more time spent on work) and the perception of spending days from one online meeting to another. Furthermore, the managers expressed the need for establishing better structures for their workdays as lack of these structures led to spending whole days in front of their computers. Consequently, when the manager was working from home, daily movement was minimized compared to navigating around more when they were in the office.

Managers found it difficult to identify employees who were struggling due to lack of contact. It was a challenge to bridge hybrid-remote work i.e. a combination of employees WFH and on-site, and ensuring that people in both places had equal opportunities. Finally, the managers acknowledged that they missed their teams' and would wish to have regular informal interaction with their employees on-site as these interactions facilitate knowledge sharing which was impeded in distance work. Due to the distance, the managers expressed difficulties initiating new projects and as a result, they feared missing out on good initiatives. Because of these challenges, managers expressed that the preferable way of working would include management from on-site and WFH maximum three days a week, where each mode would be dedicated to different tasks e.g., on-site work linked with project initiation processes and WFH linked to focus time. All managers expressed that distance management required trust, but also systematic follow up to get information about how people were doing and progressing with their tasks. They all expressed having experienced full top management support in the first months and had experienced the freedom to decide themselves how to act as distance manager.

5 Discussion

Building on the positive experiences of WFH, more workplaces are likely to offer people the opportunity to continue WFH post COVID-19 to meet the increased demand for flexibility [4, 31, 32]. Internationally, public and private companies have already taken the first steps in this direction [33, 34], and the expectation is that it is possible to maintain high performance, support well-being and potentially reduce office space.

5.1 New Level of Trust

In line with previous studies [35–37], all managers found trust to be key to good distance management, but also that being familiar with each and having a close relation in advance made trust easier. The managers were surprised by the adaptability, flexibility and the team spirit among their employees to make it work, but also the level of collaboration. That indicates that managers may not be aware of the hidden resources of the workforce or the benefits of distance work.

5.2 Flexibility Requires Structures

The study also shows that flexibility comes with a cost, as distance management is time consuming due to increased meeting activity. The increased use of formal meetings might be due to a perceived loss of control or the need for social interaction. Following the recommendations by Hosie et al. (2009) changes in the workplace are needed to ensure managers, who are stressed, can retain and improve their positive affective wellbeing by working smarter and faster, rather than harder and longer [10].

5.3 Preference for Hybrid Remote Work

WFH during the lockdown demonstrated that managers and employees can be both productive and efficient, however, the overall preference across all the managers is to return to the office and manage their employees primarily on-site with the room for occasional WFH. The hybrid remote work may be organized around tasks where tasks requiring deep focus are accomplished from home, while the project initiation processes and informal interactions are conducted on-site. As a consequence, the hybridway of working may affect the design of future workplaces especially meeting rooms and focus areas.

6 Conclusion

The purpose of this study was to gain insights into the experiences of WFH among distance managers during months of national restrictions and lock-downs. Replies from six rounds of interviews with thirteen first and second line managers formed the dataset for this study. This paper describes early findings of a single case study of Danish first- and second-line managers' experiences with distance management during COVID-19. We explored how lockdowns have impacted managers' experiences of their management job. COVID-19 has profoundly affected how managers and employees relate to each other and "go to work". The study shows that the managers take the responsibility on them to make WFH work and seek new ways of organizing and managing the hybrid remote work. However, distance management require dedicated structures and organizational support.

Acknowledgement. We want to thank Professor John Paulin Hansen at DTU Management, Denmark who has made substantial conceptual research design contributions, gathered important data and commented on this chapter.

References

1. Vargas, O.L.: COVID-19 unleashed the potential for telework – How are workers coping? | Eurofound, Bruxelles (2020)
2. Eurofound. Living, working and COVID-19. COVID-19 Series (2020). https://www.eurofo und.europa.eu/publications/report/2020/living-working-and-covid-19. Accessed 09 Feb 2021

3. Center for Workplace Mental Health: Your Mental Health & Well-Being. https://workplace mentalhealth.org/. Accessed 09 Feb 2021
4. The European Commission's Science and Knowledge Center: Telework in the EU before and after the COVID-19: where we were, where we head to. https://ec.europa.eu/jrc/sites/jrcsh/files/jrc120945_policy_brief_-_covid_and_telework_final.pdf. Accessed 09 Feb 2021
5. Ipsen, C., Kirchner, K., Hansen, J.P.: Experiences of Working from Home in Times of COVID-19 International survey conducted the first months of the national lockdowns. DTU, Denmark (2020)
6. Hosie, P., Sharma, P., Kingshott, R.P.J.: "Happy-performing managers" thesis: testing the mediating role of job-related affective outcomes on the impact of role stressors on contextual performance. Int. J. Manpow. **40**(2), 356–72 (2019)
7. Skakon, J., Nielsen, K., Borg, V., Guzman, J.: Are leaders' well-being, behaviours and style associated with the affective well-being of their employees? A systematic review of three decades of research. Work Stress **24**(2), 107–139 (2010)
8. Lindorff, M., Worrall, L., Cooper, C.: Managers' well-being and perceptions of organizational change in the UK and Australia. Asia Pac. J. Hum. Resour. **49**(2), 233–254 (2011)
9. Hujala, A., Rissanen, S., Vihma, S., Unigrafia: Designing wellbeing in elderly care homes. School of Arts, Design and Architecture, Aalto University (2013)
10. Hosie, P.J., Sevastos, P.: Does the "happy-productive worker" thesis apply to managers? Int. J. Work Health Manag. **2**(2), 131–60 (2009)
11. Worrall, L., Cooper, C.L.: The quality of working life: managers' health and well-being. Chartered Management Institute, London (2006)
12. Worrall, L., Cooper, C.: The quality of working life: managers' wellbeing, motivation and productivity. Eur. Bus. Rev. **July–August**, 49–52 (2013)
13. Haar, J.M., Roche, M., ten Brummelhuis, L.: A daily diary study of work-life balance in managers: utilizing a daily process model. Int. J. Hum. Resour. Manag. **29**(18), 2659–81 (2018)
14. Kirchner, K., Ipsen, C., Hansen, J.P.: COVID-19 leadership challenges in knowledge work. Knowl. Manag. Res. Pract. (2021). https://doi.org/10.1080/14778238.2021.1877579
15. Kurland, N.B., Bailey, D.E., Kurkland, N.B., Bailey, D.E.: Telework: the advantages and challenges of working here, there anywhere, and anytime. Organ. Dyn. **28**(2), 53–68 (1999)
16. Bailey, D.E., Kurland, N.B.: A review of telework research: findings, new directions, and lessons for the study of modern work. J. Organ. Behav. **23**(4), 383–400 (2002)
17. Charalampous, M., Grant, C.A., Tramontano, C., Michailidis, E.: Systematically reviewing remote e-workers' well-being at work: a multidimensional approach. Eur. J. Work Organ. Psychol. **28**(1), 51–73 (2019)
18. Staples Inc.: There's No Place Like a Home Office: Staples Survey Shows Telecommuters are Happier and Healthier, With 25% Less Stress When Working from Home. https://www.businesswire.com/news/home/20110719005318/en/There%E2%80%99s-No-Place-Like-a-Home-Office-Staples-Survey-Shows-Telecommuters-are-Happier-and-Healthier-With-25-Less-Stress-When-Working-from-Home. Accessed 09 Feb 2021
19. Fonner, K.L., Roloff, M.E.: Why teleworkers are more satisfied with their jobs than are office-based workers: when less contact is beneficial. J. Appl. Commun. Res. **38**(4), 336–61 (2010)
20. Anderson, A.J., Kaplan, S.A., Vega, R.P.: The impact of telework on emotional experience: when, and for whom, does telework improve daily affective well-being? Eur. J. Work Organ. Psychol. **24**(6), 882–97 (2015)
21. Biron, M., van Veldhoven, M.: When control becomes a liability rather than an asset: comparing home and office days among part-time teleworkers. J. Organ. Behav. **37**(8), 1317–37 (2016)

22. Kurland, N.B., Bailey, D.E.: When workers are here, there, and everywhere: a discussion of the advantages and challenges of telework. Organ. Dyn. **28**, 53–68 (1999)
23. Cooper, C.D., Kurland, N.B.: Telecommuting, professional isolation, and employee development in public and private organizations. J. Organ Behav. **23**(SPEC. ISS.), 511–32 (2002)
24. Hertel, G., Geister, S., Konradt, U.: Managing virtual teams: a review of current empirical research. Hum. Resour. Manag. Rev. **15**(1), 69–95 (2005)
25. Stich, J.-F.: A review of workplace stress in the virtual office. Intell. Build. Int. **12**(3), 208–20 (2020)
26. Kurland, N.B., Bailey, D.E.: Telework: the advantages and challenges of working here, there anywhere, and anytime. Organ. Dyn. **28**(2), 53–68 (1999)
27. Gurstein, P.: Wired to the World, Chained to the Home: Telework in Daily Life, vol. 1. UBC Press, Vancouver (2001)
28. Jackson, P.J.: Virtual working: Social and organisational dynamics. Routledge (2001)
29. Mitchell, D.: 50 Top Tools for Employee Engagement: A Complete Toolkit for Improving Motivation and Productivity, vol. 1. Kogan Page Publishers (2017)
30. Crabtree, B., Miller, W.: Doing Qualitative Research, vol. 2. Sage, London (1999)
31. Lister, K.: Work-at-Home After Covid-19—Our Forecast. Global Workplace Analytics (2020)
32. Gartner: Gartner HR Survey Reveals 41% of Employees Likely to Work Remotely at Least Some of the Time Post Coronavirus Pandemic (2020)
33. Washington Post: Twitter employees can now work from home forever. Washington Post (2020). https://www.washingtonpost.com/technology/2020/10/01/twitter-work-from-home/?arc404=true. Accessed 09 Feb 2021
34. The Economist: The future of work - Is the office finished. The Economist (2020)
35. Ipsen, C., Poulsen, S., Nielsen, L.: Management across distances – how to ensure performance and employee well- being. In: Proceedings of the 19th Triennial Congress of the International Ergonomics Association 2015 (2015)
36. Fisher, K., Fisher, M.D.: The Distance Manager. A Hands-On Guide to Managing Off-Site Employees and Virtual Teams, vol. 1. McGraw-Hill, New York (2001)
37. Peñarroja, V., Orengo, V., Zornoza, A., Hernández, A.: The effects of virtuality level on task-related collaborative behaviors: the mediating role of team trust. Comput. Hum. Behav. **29**(3), 967–74 (2013)

An Ergonomic, Safety and Wellness Perspective of a Screener Role During the COVID-19 Pandemic

Anita Jogia(✉), Amanda Stuyt, Angela Santos, Shawna Tomlinson, Sherri Cheadle,
Ashleigh Van Ryn, Katie Willing, Vanessa Case, Cathy Zantingh, Nancy Lawrence,
Ali Ismail, Greg Leblanc, Jill Smith, Cathy Stark, Mac Barry, Emily Hahn-Trnka,
and Andy Rombouts

London Health Sciences Centre, London, ON, Canada
Anita.Jogia@lhsc.on.ca

Abstract. A Screener role was created at the London Health Sciences Centre during the COVID-19 Pandemic to 'screen-out' staff, patients and visitors entering the hospital who may potentially have COVID-19, and to re-direct them appropriately. This paper shares the experiences of the hospital's Ergonomist and safety team in relation to this role from the start of the role to current state.

Keywords: COVID-19 · Ergonomics · Safety · Screening · Wellness

1 Introduction

The COVID-19 Pandemic was officially announced on March 13, 2020. Following guidelines from the Ministry of Health (MOH), the London Health Sciences Centre established a Pandemic Incident Management Team (PIMT). Directives from this team included the need to manage access into and out of the hospital, thereby identifying the need for a Screener role. The Ergonomist and some safety team members were re-deployed to the Screener role at the onset of the pandemic from March to April, 2020. The role continued to evolve based on updates from the PIMT.

As a scientific discipline, ergonomics and human factors looks at interactions between humans and other elements of a system [1]. Re-deployment to the Screener role during the pandemic provided the hospital's Ergonomist with a unique opportunity to not only observe but experience the system changes first hand. The hospital ergonomic program was temporarily placed on hold with the challenge of maintaining existing health and safety procedures while prioritizing tasks in response to COVID-19.

While not directly screening, other members of Occupational Health and Safety Services (OHSS) were impacted with the introduction of the Screener role including applying controls to mitigate risks associated with infection control hazards, noise concerns, workplace violence, safe food and beverage locations and slip/trip/falls. Safety staff were also involved with training Screeners on personal protective equipment (PPE)

N. L. Black et al. (Eds.): IEA 2021, LNNS 222, pp. 607–614, 2021.
https://doi.org/10.1007/978-3-030-74611-7_82

and members of the Occupational Health team followed up with staff who 'failed' screening requirements. The Where Wellness Works team provided initial and ongoing support to Screeners throughout the changes.

The Ergonomist and some safety team members were re-deployed as Screeners for approximately one and half months from mid-March to April 2020, at which time the hospital was reducing its regular services to prepare bed capacity in response to the pandemic. In July 2020, the hospital gradually began resuming services based on updates from the PIMT.

Two types of screening stations were set up at the Victoria Hospital (VH) and University hospital (UH). One station for screening patients/visitors and another for staff screening. The initial workstation set up consisted of a table and chair with Screeners donning PPE (gloves, level 2 isolation gown, face mask with shield and routine hand hygiene). As the pandemic continued, the workstations included Plexiglas barriers, microphones and laptops. Health, safety, ergonomic and wellness supports continued from the onset of the role to current date.

Occupational Health and Safety Services (OHSS) in a large acute care teaching hospital are well placed to provide health, safety and ergonomic services during a pandemic and re-deployment to new roles provides a unique opportunity to experience the effect of those changes on hospital staff. Staff safety, well-being and psychological safety can strengthen the system and environment during a pandemic [1].

2 Method

A field study approach was used and both qualitative and quantitative data was collected. Qualitative feedback was received from the Ergonomist and safety team members regarding their experiences during the Screener role.

As a means to quantify the data, Screeners were surveyed on September 17, 2020 on physical ergonomics for the period of March 16 to August 21, 2020. Other safety issues were being addressed by leaders during this time and therefore an additional survey was not considered to be value added. A comparison of health and safety statistics for the same time period in 2019 was also completed by reviewing statistical data gathered through the hospital's Adverse Event Management system (AEMs) to compare any changes in incident reporting during the pandemic.

3 Findings

The Ergonomist and safety team members information was captured based on informal discussions with them. Quantitative feedback from the survey results and AEMS statistical data was reviewed and are represented in the graphs below.

3.1 Ergonomist Experience

The Ergonomist's work schedule was immediately changed from a five day weekly 8-h work day to 12-h day shifts with a continental shift rotation of two days on, two days off, three days on, repeat. The impact of the schedule change was not immediately apparent, however following the second rotation of three days on, fatigue was notable by the end of the third 12-h day shift. Although the Ergonomist was not scheduled to work afternoon or night shifts, there was a notable change with sleep and eating habits specifically during the third day of the 12-h shift. Falling asleep at a timely hour to arise for the next seven am shift in the three-day stretch was a challenge. Eating lighter snacks more frequently on work days, and performing regular physical and breathing exercises seemed to help break up the day and maintain regular digestion and sleep schedule.

The original screening workstation was set up with a table and chair for seated work. Given the urgent response required for screening, ergonomics of the table or chair were not considered. Four legged and single post tables were used with a basic four-legged wooden chair. Immediately recognizing ergonomic challenges of the equipment, the Ergonomist frequently and intermittently stood up and walked around and when possible screened people while standing. Fortunately, there was opportunity to stand up and move around as needed based on self-awareness of the workstation challenges. The Ergonomist readily shared this information with other Screeners.

The task demands were not physically challenging. A series of questions were asked to determine if patients or staff had possible exposure to COVID-19 and then directing them as needed. A written script was provided with the questions and directions on how to direct patients and staff based on their responses. Cognitive and psychosocial demands such as communication, decision making and emotional intelligence became apparent based on unpredictable responses from some patients and the general anxiety around the pandemic such as patients whose surgery was re-scheduled or those awaiting updates on tests with potential life altering consequences.

3.2 Safety Analyst Experience

Becoming a screener required the ability to quickly adapt and exercise flexibility and resilience in the face of rapid and ongoing changes. Changes included rotating through different patient or staff screening work stations without having a designated work area. Without having a designated work area, there was a limited ability to ergonomically adjust the station with some stations having different furniture and resources available than others. As time went on, this became increasingly difficult and it was evident the role was evolving to a more complex role.

It was important to have wipeable chairs in this setting, however this led to the use of hard, unpadded wooden chairs which were not 12-h shift friendly. As safety team members and other Screeners became more familiar in their setting, they altered their position to a greater extent and took stretch breaks resulting in the reduction of bodily discomfort from static postures.

If not accustomed to a rotating continental shift schedule, one of the most challenging aspects of the screening role was switching to overnight shifts. This role was created quickly and the body had to adjust rapidly to shift work.

Overall it was easier than expected and the greater the duration in the role, the easier shift rotation became. A more uncomfortable chair at the beginning surprisingly helped one to stay more alert. This coupled with wearing full PPE prior to the installation of the Plexiglas barrier created some discomfort.

In this role there was a risk of potential COVID-19 exposure from those who were entering the facility so mitigation of risk and promotion of staff and patient/visitor safety was a priority. Proper training was provided related to PPE use with supplies being readily available to the worker despite challenges with supply chain across the province or conservation measures in place. To address some of the potential reactive or responsive behaviours in light of the many changes, security was present at patient/visitor screening entrances should an escalating situation arise. While Plexiglas barriers were not immediately available, they were quickly sourced and installed during the initial phases of the pandemic response as an engineered means to control any potential exposure and mitigate the overall risk to the worker which provided another layer of comfort.

At the conclusion of a shift, the voice became hoarse as a result of multiple screeners and patient/visitors being screened simultaneously thus requiring voice projection. There were several screening stations placed six-feet apart in a long hallway which often echoed. It was important to project loudly enough for the individual to hear and comprehend the questions with the Screener also relying on visual cues to ascertain that patients or staff were understanding and responding. It was cognitively exhausting repeating the same questions, however there were opportunities during shift rotations when the volume of staff or patients was significantly diminished providing a rest period for the Screener.

This role blended many redeployed staff from many vastly different areas across the acute care teaching hospital allowing Screeners to share experiences and perspective with others and make valuable and lasting connections with many dedicated health care workers which otherwise would not have occurred without re-deployment to this role.

3.3 Ergonomic Survey Results

A total of 150 Screeners were surveyed on Sept. 17, 2020. The response rate was 75%. Survey questions included a combination of choice, rating, and open response. See Table 1 for questions.

Table 1. Screener survey questions

Survey Question	Response Type
1. Which Screener role did you work in	Patient/Visitor/Both
2. When did you do the Screener role	March-May or June to Current (September),
3. Which of the following ergonomic factors is the most challenging in the Screener role. Select One Only:	Posture, Repetitive Work, Lifting/lowering/pushing/pulling/carrying
4. How Would You Rate Your Physical Comfort at The Screener Workstation	Very uncomfortable/uncomfortable/ somewhat comfortable/comfortable very comfortable
5. How Helpful Did You Find The Laptop in the Role	Open response
6. Do you feel you have the ability to sit and stand and move around as needed	Yes/No, If no, explain
7. Given that task variety is important, what type of things did you do in the Screener role to add variety	Open response
8. What Ergonomic Factors would you change in the Screener role and why	Open response

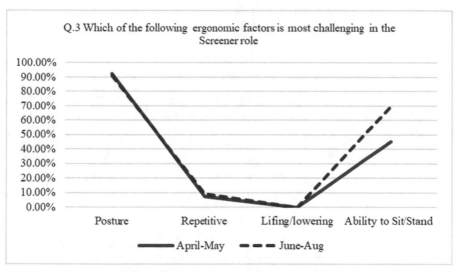

Fig. 1. Screener response differences to ergonomic factor question from April-May to June-August, 2020

Based on survey results, 90.5% of Screeners who worked from April to August felt that posture was the primary ergonomic concern (Fig. 1) and 55% didn't feel they could sit and stand as needed from April to May compared to 70% from June to August who felt they could sit and stand as needed. Overtime, comfort parameters improved slightly between April-May and June-August with majority of responses related to the ergonomic factors that Screeners would change relating to the ability to adjust the chair and workstation.

3.4 Health and Safety Statistical Data

Initially, there was no specific department assigned for Screeners to report in the AEMS reporting system so staff would often use their own home department. Currently, Screeners report under Support Services. A general comparison of workplace incidents in Support Services showed an increase of 45 workplace incidents for the period of March 16 to August 21, 2020 compared to the same time period in 2019. It was determined that a separate new screener category under Support Services was required to further delineate and better direct AEMS for improved statistical analysis. Following this, additional data up to Oct. 15, 2020 showed Screeners reported a total 25 incidents including musculoskeletal disorders (MSDs). As a result of this new role and increased AEMS, a Job Demands Description (JDD) was created. Further review of the AEMS data would be required for further root cause analysis (Fig. 2).

4 Discussion

There were challenges in tracking changes to the Screener role as it evolved quickly as per updates from the PIMT. The opportunity for some safety team members and the

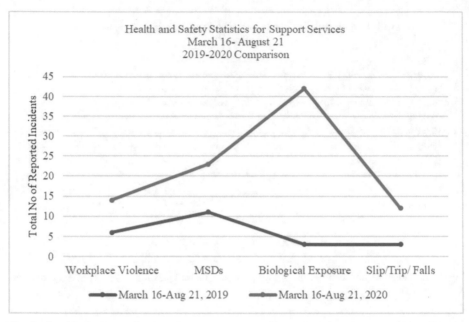

Fig. 2. Specific health and safety data in support services comparison between 2019–2020 for the period of March 16 to August 21

Ergonomist to have first-hand experience as a Screener provided the chance to experience the challenges that other Screeners encountered such as: changes in work tasks, shifts and work environment. During the initial changes, ongoing communication with the Screener leadership team was invaluable in permitting concerns to be addressed in the moment, and providing immediate on-site training on donning and doffing PPE was also beneficial. Screener workstations initially had to be setup quickly, using existing hospital furniture and workstation ergonomics were not of primary concern at the time. Wooden chairs were later replaced with padded chairs and Screeners could use empty totes/boxes to place their laptops on to intermittently stand and screen.

Following return to regular duties, the Ergonomist collaborated with the Where Wellness Works team to develop a brochure for future Screeners. It provided guidance on: how to change position/posture throughout the shift, packing smaller portable snacks that could be consumed during slower times or between workflow/during breaks. One of the Screener leads initiated a new "Screening Health and Wellness Section" to the 'Microsoft Teams' environment to help support their staff in direct relation to the Wellness Brochure and rounds. As an immediate support, the Where Wellness Works Team started implementing Micro-Breaks (ten-minute stretching and breathing sessions led by LHSC Staff Fitness Trainers) for all Screeners at VH and UH in July. Each week the trainers lead forty-five breaks at VH and twenty-four breaks at UH. This may have attributed to why Screeners from June to August reported the ability to move between a seated to standing position more frequently than Screeners in April-May. For immediate support, Screeners were also encouraged to sign up for the hospital's virtual fitness program on

Instagram, created and implemented in April, 2020 providing on-going physical, mental and emotional support services during COVID-19.

A violence risk assessment was performed in compliance with the Occupational Health and Safety Act [2]. This assessment addressed issues related to harassment, working with objects of value and potential triggers for reactive behaviours. As such, a script for common questions, review of communication tools and supports, storage of personal valuables and means of readily obtaining assistance along with reporting were advised and implemented.

Increased line-ups may be a potential trigger for reactive behaviours, so a screener application (app) was developed and implemented for staff eliminating the requirement of the Screener to verbally question staff upon entrance improving the speed and efficiency of the process. Currently, an app is not available at the patient/visitor entrances, as a means to address line-ups, additional patient/visitor locations were created or altered to accommodate the increased volumes and reduce wait-times. Signage was strategically placed to improve communication with wayfinding along with other supports such as portering services and security.

Specified locations were assessed and allocated for the safe storage and consumption of food and drink as per O. Reg 67/93 [3]. Areas were assessed to be non-clinical spaces, free of any chemical or biological contaminant, soiled patient equipment or narcotics. Safe locations were assessed to be reasonably geographically located to screening stations to balance worker well-being and comfort to attain nutrition/hydration while maintaining safety in a clean area.

The Screening Team continues to evolve to support hospital requirements. The role allows for temporary accommodation of injured staff as a means of early and safe return to work and potential reduction of WSIB lost time costs. The size of the team (165 people) and standards of practice are regularly updated to support the needs of the organization and the hazards encountered within the department. As the hospital transitions towards regular capacity, wellness indicators show an increase in the "self-perception of stress" and indicated decrease in the "self-perception of leadership support", These indicators will once again be evaluated to ensure appropriate support is provided to effectively manage transition and change. Computer-based tools have also been developed to support flow, crowding and efficiencies and compliance with usage of these tools will be monitored. The Ergonomist, Safety Team and Wellness team continue to support the Screening Team in addressing ongoing concerns.

5   Conclusion

Future work should review the type of roles required during a pandemic and recognize the physical and psychological impact of involuntary relocation to these roles. Safety and ergonomic professionals collaborating with multiple stakeholders inclusive of employer and worker partnerships can enhance an acute care hospitals response to a pandemic. The Screener role had many changes as it evolved including: persons performing the role, leadership, workstation ergonomics, and safety factors. A topic of discussion would be how to take the information learned from this experience to develop a standard approach in addressing ergonomic, safety and wellness when people are needed to assist during a pandemic.

References

1. Staines, A., Amalberti, R., Berwick, D.M., Braithwaite, J., Lachman, P., Vincent, C.A.: COVID-19: patient safety and quality improvement skills to deploy during the surge. Int. J. Qual. Health Care **2020**, 1–3 (2020)
2. Ontario Occupational Health and Safety Act. Sect.32.0.3 (1). Thompson Reuters Canada Ltd. (2019)
3. Ontario Regulations 67/93. Healthcare and Residential Facilities. Sect.32.0.3. Thompson Reuters Canada Ltd. (2019)

Contactless and Low-Burden Measurement of Physiological Signals and Comparison of Obtained Indices

Yoshiyuki Kamakura[1](✉), Hiroki Takeuchi[2], and Mieko Ohsuga[3]

[1] Faculty of Information Science and Technology, Osaka Institute of Technology, Hirakata, Osaka 573-0196, Japan
yoshiyuki.kamakura@oit.ac.jp

[2] Graduate School of Robotics and Design, Osaka Institute of Technology, Hirakata, Osaka, Japan
d1d21r02@st.oit.ac.jp

[3] Faculty of Robotics and Design, Osaka Institute of Technology, Osaka, Japan
mieko.ohsuga@oit.ac.jp

Abstract. It is important for human adaptive systems, especially those living with or having survived the COVID-19 crisis, to obtain the usual human state continuously and non-intrusively. Our research is focused on non-intrusive measurement of physiological signals and a comparison of the methods of measurement and indices thus obtained.

Keywords: Psychophysiology in ergonomics · Contactless measurement method · Camera-based photoplethysmography (cbPPG)

1 Introduction

Recently, human adaptive ICT systems, such as IoT, remote working and automated driving technology, have gained widespread use and their importance is increasing in life with/after the COVID-19 crisis. For these human adaptive systems, it is necessary to continuously obtain the human usual state in daily life; therefore, physiological indices must be acquired by low-burden or contactless non-intrusive methods of measurement. However, most devices do not provide instantaneous information, but yield measurements such as average pulse rate, respiratory rate, and blink rate only that are not suitable for detailed analysis. In this study, we examined the suitability of non-intrusive methods of measurement of ECG, waveforms of pulse, respiration, and blink, and compared the indices thus obtained. We carried out contactless measurement of (a) waveforms of pulse and blink with an RGB camera and (b) waveform of respiration with an RGB-D camera. A low-burden measurement of ECG and waveform of respiration was also made by using smart shirts.

2 Objectives and Questions

It is known that pulse signals can be detected from changes in the skin color captured from a distance with an RGB camera [1] by a method called camera-based photoplethysmography (cbPPG). This is a contactless method of measurement using natural light.

N. L. Black et al. (Eds.): IEA 2021, LNNS 222, pp. 615–619, 2021.
https://doi.org/10.1007/978-3-030-74611-7_83

The results obtained thereby are strongly affected by changes in the light environment and movements of the person [2]. This is because the image sensor is not in contact with the skin and reflected natural light is not bright enough as compared to that obtained by directly irradiating the skin with a red or green LED. The signal-to-noise ratio is compromised for the convenience of acquiring images from a distance. Furthermore, there is a difference in the waveforms of the electrocardiogram (ECG) and PPG/cbPPG. We simultaneously obtained blink signals using an RGB camera and respiration signals with an RGB-D camera in this study, and faced the same issues as in the case of cbPPG, namely the effect of light environment and the person's body movement, and a low signal-to-noise ratio. Therefore, it is necessary to examine whether contactless measurement of physiological indices is sufficient for the purpose of measurement.

3   Methods

3.1   Proposed Contactless Measurement of Physiological Indices Method

First, our proposed methods detected the face and the facial landmarks in each video frame with a face detection Kazemi algorithm [3], which is registered in the dlib C++ library [4], and a template matching algorithm, and physiological signals were obtained in each case. In the case of pulse detection, the ROI pixels were determined based on facial landmarks. The pulse waveform was detected by applying frequency filters to the average of the green components in the ROI pixels. The blink waveform was detected from the change in the distance between the upper and lower eyelid points on the facial landmarks. For the detection of respiration waveform, we used an RGB-D camera such as Intel RealSense [5] that can measure depth with near infrared (NIR) radiation. The respiration waveform was also detected by the back and forth body movement by measuring the change in distance between the camera and the part of the body from the breast to shoulders.

3.2   Face and Facial Landmarks Detection Adapted to Facial Mask

Wearing a face mask has become a part of daily life under the COVID-19. It has many problems to detect facial landmarks in a face image wearing the face mask. Therefore, we re-train the face detector and the facial landmarks detector in the dlib C++ library with following 3 steps.

1. detect 68 facial landmarks from face images without face mask
2. paint with black/white the region surrounded by landmarks of the lower face and the nose in the results of Step1
3. extract 28 points which are a part of the head near the temple, the eyebrows and the eyelids from 68 landmarks

In Step 2, it makes possible to create the face image worn white/black-colored face mask from results in Step 1 (see Fig. 1). Eventually, it's obtained the re-trained files, both "face object detector" and "28 facial landmarks detector", which make possible to detect them from faces wearing black/white/none face mask (see Fig. 2).

Fig. 1. Original image with 68 facial landmarks (left) and created white/black-colored face mask images (center and right)

Fig. 2. Results of the face and the 28 facial landmarks detection with re-trained detector files (l to r: without the mask, wearing the white-colored mask, wearing the black-colored mask)

3.3 ROI for Pulse Detection

In the method of 3.1, ROI (Region of Interest) for pulse detection defined the area around cheek. In the situation who wearing a face mask, cheek area is mostly hidden with face mask. Therefore, we changed ROI to between the eyebrows (see Fig. 3).

Fig. 3. Location of ROI for pulse detection (yellow: cheek area, green: between the eyebrows)

The forehead is one of the good areas for pulse detection with skin color, but the forehead is sometimes hidden with bangs like as in Fig. 3.

In Fig. 4, it suggested that change ROI to between the eyebrows could detect pulse wave same as the proposed ROI.

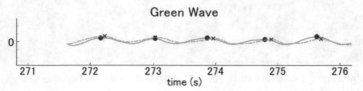

Fig. 4. Sample of pulse waves (green: ROI sets between the eyebrows, yellow: ROI sets around cheek)

4   Results

In Fig. 5, it's obtained the pulse waveform, the blink waveform, and the respiration waveform with the proposal method.

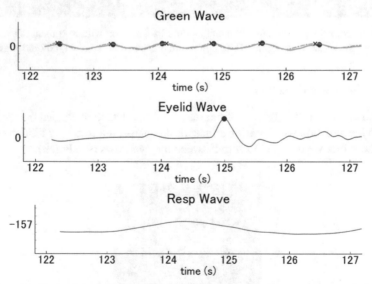

Fig. 5. Sample of physiological signals with proposal contactless measurements (top: pulse waveform, middle: blink waveform, bottom: respiration waveform)

The results revealed that the most important condition in a contactless method of measurement is to maintain the sampling interval correctly, with particular attention to missing video frames. The respiration waveform obtained with the RGB-D camera and that with smart shirts (Hexoskin Smart Shirts [6]) was similar i.e., the pulse rate obtained with the RGB camera generally matched the heart rate obtained with smart shirts.

A reduction of the variations in the peak interval in the waveforms obtained by the contactless method can improve the accuracy of the measured indices. The following methods can be adopted to further improve the accuracy: replacing the green components in cbPPG detection with Hue or PCA components and choosing an appropriate size and area of the ROI.

5   Discussion

We demonstrated the possibility of measuring pulse waveform and respiration waveform by using contactless and low-burden methods. In future, we wish to make a quantitative comparison of the accuracy of the proposed methods and their improved versions. Further, we intend to increase the number of participants in the experiment and verify the results in daily situations for a longer duration.

Acknowledgments. A part of this work was conducted by New Media Development Association supported by Japan Keirin Autorace foundation (JKA) and its promotion funds from KEIRIN RACE.

References

1. Trumpp, A., Lohr, J., Wedekind, D., Schmidt, M., Burghardt, M., Heller, A.R., Malberg, H., Zaunseder, S.: Camera-based photoplethysmography in an intraoperative setting. BioMed. Eng. OnLine **17**(1), 33, 1–19 (2018)
2. Kumar, M., Veeraraghavan, A., Sabharval, A.: DistancePPG: robust non-contact vitalsigns monitoring using a camera. Biomed. Opt. Express **6**(5), 1565–1588 (2015)
3. Kazemi, V., Sullivan, J.: One millisecond face alignment with an ensemble of regression trees. In: 2014 IEEE Conference on Computer Vision and Pattern Recognition, Columbus, OII, pp. 1867–1874 (2014)
4. dlib C++ Library. https://dlib.net. Accessed 05 Feb 2021
5. Intel RealSense Computer Vision. https://www.intelrealsense.com/. Accessed 05 Feb 2021
6. Hexoskin Smart Shits. https://www.hexoskin.com/. Accessed 05 Feb 2021

The Burnout Among Female Hospital Workers During the COVID-19 Pandemic in Algeria

Houda Kherbache[1]([⊠]) [iD], Lahcene Bouabdellah[1] [iD], Asma Hammoudi[1] [iD],
and Mohammed Mokdad[2] [iD]

[1] University Sétif 2, Sétif, Algeria
{houdakhe,doylettres}@univ-setif.dz
[2] College of Arts, University of Bahrain, Sakhir, Bahrain
mmokdad@uob.edu.bh

Abstract. Psychological burnout is a relatively new term used to describe the physical and emotional responses to work pressures and exhaustion of workers in the humanitarian professions such as hospital workers. A lot has been written about the burnout among the Algerian hospital workers. However within the limits of our research, we did not find any research which deal with the burnout in the female workers during the pandemic COVID-19.

This study measured the level of burnout among female hospital workers during the COVID-19 pandemic in Algeria.

The sample consisted of 104 hospital female employees of which 100 completed the questionnaire, participants are randomly chosen from different department of the university hospital of Setif in Algeria. Our sample included nurses, administrators, physicians, radiographers, speech therapist, psychologists, cleaning women, pharmacists.

The study used Maslach Burnout Inventory (MBI). It was found that the burnout was high among female hospital workers of all categories. Based on these findings, some recommendations were given to the responsible authorities of the health in Algeria to intensify their efforts to improve the situation.

Keywords: Burnout · Female hospital workers · COVID-19 pandemic

1 Introduction

Algerian hospital workers suffer from many occupational pressures according to different sources, resulting in high levels of burnout, which has been proven by many Algerian studies [1–3]. A lot of foreign studies have proven the suffering of hospital workers from varying levels of psychological burnout. Among these studies, what focused on the category of physicians (doctors) [4], and some of them focused on the category of nurses [5–7]. Other studies, concerned both doctors and nurses simultaneously [8]. As for the other categories of hospital workers, we may have obtained a few studies, one of which concerned psychologists, the other concerned radiologists, and the third, brought together psychologists and doctors [9].

N. L. Black et al. (Eds.): IEA 2021, LNNS 222, pp. 620–624, 2021.
https://doi.org/10.1007/978-3-030-74611-7_84

Coinciding with the emergence of the COVID-19 pandemic in Algeria since mid-February, the severity of the suffering of the Algerian hospital workers increased due to the difficult conditions imposed on them, both in terms of the lack of material resources or in terms of the lack of necessary means to take care of the affected cases. Adding to that the fear of the contamination, the doubling night shifts number, the imposition of requisition to specialized services in confronting the pandemic, the resulting quarantine that may last for months with the disability to visit their homes and families because of the fear of transmitting the infection. All these factors exacerbate the burnout felt by female hospital workers.

The study of Wu, et al. [10] conducted in Wuhan, indicated that the burnout level is higher among doctors working in the specialized services of COVID-19. But if we want to focus on the category of women among them we will find that the nature of the Algerian environment endure additional hardships. As Algerian women, whether employed or non-employed, have not been able to get rid of the traditional role that the customs and traditions impose on them. As women must take care of all the housework, raising the children, and caring for their husbands. The study of Jediat, [2] confirmed that women suffer from higher levels of burnout than men. Regarding the central role that employed women in hospitals play in confronting this pandemic, attention must be paid to their mental and physical health.

On the national level, studies that dealt with nurses have taken the lion's share compared to other categories of workers [3, 11–15]. We also obtained only two local studies that concerned physicians (doctors), the first included resident physicians and the second general physicians [16, 17].

The aim of this study is to determine the level of the burnout among female hospital workers in Setif, during the COVID-19 pandemic and spans female hospital workers from various departments. The study answers the following question:

– What is the level of burnout among female hospital workers in Setif during the COVID-19 pandemic?

2 Methodology

2.1 Method

We carried out a quantitative descriptive study; a self-administered questionnaire was distributed to our sample.

2.2 Sample

We administered the inventory to 104 female hospital employees of which 100 completed the questionnaire. Participants were randomly chosen from different departments of the University Hospital of Setif in Algeria (Otolaryngology Department, Ophthalmology Department, Maxillofacial Surgery, Pediatric Department, and Hospital Administration). Our sample included nurses, administrators, physicians, radiographers, speech therapist, psychologists, cleaning women, pharmacists ranging between 24 and 49 years of age (SD 3.86).

2.3 Data Collection Tool

The collection of information was used through Maslach Burnout Inventory (MBI). It is a validated tool to assess the prevalence of burnout. It consists of 22 questions divided in three sequential subscales (Emotional exhaustion, Depersonalization, personal accomplishment). This tool is widely used, and it is considered the standard measure for burnout [18]. An Algerian version was offered in the study of [18]. The participants answer according to the degree of agreement with different situations related to their job environment during the pandemic COVID-19. The study was conducted from 10–09-2020 to 27–11-2020.

3   Results

3.1   What is the Level of Burnout Among Female Hospital Workers in Setif During the COVID-19 Pandemic?

Mean and standard deviation (SD) for the three stages were obtained. The mean (SD) score for emotional exhaustion, depersonalization and personal accomplishment were 29.50 (11.11), 12.85 (6.68), 30.11 (10.42) respectively (Table 1) Those results showed: higher mean of emotional exhaustion (29.50), higher mean of depersonalization (12.85) and low mean for personal accomplishment (30.11) comparing with MBI norms.

Table 1. Mean and standard deviation for subscale scores of the sample.

MBI subscales	Mean	SD
Emotional exhaustion	29.50	11.11
Depersonalization	12.85	6.68
Personal accomplishment	30.11	10.42

The percentage of the subjects of this study who were at high risk of burnout for emotional exhaustion depersonalization and personal accomplishment were 32%, 48% and 24% respectively, while the percentage of the subjects of this study who were at low risk of burnout for emotional exhaustion depersonalization and personal accomplishment were 10%, 19% and 51% respectively (Table 2).

Table 2. Percentage of MBI subscales scores (N = 100).

MBI subscales	Low	Moderate	High
Emotional exhaustion	10 (10%)	43 (43%)	32 (32%)
Depersonalization	19 (19%)	23 (23%)	48 (48%)
Personal accomplishment	51 (51%)	13 (13%)	24 (24%)

4 Discussion

The results of our study show that 43% of our sample suffer from high level of emotional exhaustion, 48% suffer from high level of depersonalization, and 51% suffer from low personal accomplishment. According to the interpretation of the MBI results, we can say that the majority of our sample suffer from a high level of burnout during the pandemic COVID-19.

The results of this study are consistent with the findings of the study [10] which found that the doctors suffer from a high level of burnout during the pandemic COVID-19. Similar results are obtained by [19, 20]. This result can be explained by a set of factors: The weakness of the health system, the bad conditions that are provided for work on one hand. Hospital workers suffer in Algeria in normal conditions before the outbreak of the pandemic [1, 3] not to mention the difficult circumstances caused by this pandemic, which developed countries were unable to manage. On the other hand, it can be explained by the nature of the tasks entrusted to Algerian women and their multiplicity due to the characteristics of the environment in which they live and which still adheres to the traditional role of women, whether they are employed or housewives. We refer to the imposed conditions by the Algerian environment for women, which burden them with family and marital tasks that add to the work requirements.

5 Conclusions

The psychological burnout of female workers in the hospital would affect their performance and quality at work, and it would affect their mental and physical health greatly. Its harms spread even to their life outside of work, so the responsible authorities should ensure that their working conditions are improved as much as possible especially during extreme cases (outbreaks of a specific epidemic, natural disasters, wars...etc.) to reduce the expected damage resulted from their burnout.

Acknowledgement. The authors wish to acknowledge all participants who took part in this study.

References

1. Makhlouf, S.: Supplication and its relationship to the level of psychological burnout of the surgeon. A thesis for a doctorate in Clinical Psychology, University of Mentouri Constantine, Algeria (2011)
2. Jediat, A.: Psychological exhaustion and its relationship to marital compatibility among public health doctors and nurses. A note to obtain a master's degree in psychology of work and organization, University of Algiers 2, Algeria (2012)
3. Taibi, N.: The relationship of burnout with some psychosomatic disorders among nurses. A thesis for a doctorate in clinical psychology, University of Algiers 2, Algeria (2013)
4. Rivera, R.R., Alfaro, L.D.C.F., Gutiérrez, T., Guillén, I.R.: Burnout syndrome in medical staff and their relationship to quality of care. Int. J. Innov. Sci. Res. Technol. 5(6), 539–541 (2020)
5. Sasaki, M., Kitaoka-Higashiguchi, K., Morikawa, Y., Nakagawa, H.: Relationship between stress coping and burnout in Japanese hospital nurses. J. Nurs. Manag. 17(3), 359–365 (2009)

6. Van Bogaert, P., Meulemans, H., Clarke, S., Vermeyen, K., Van de Heyning, P.: Hospital nurse practice environment, burnout, job outcomes and quality of care: test of a structural equation model. J. Adv. Nurs. **65**(10), 2175–2185 (2009)
7. Sahraian, A., Fazelzadeh, A., Mehdizadeh, A.R., Toobaee, S.H.: Burnout in hospital nurses: a comparison of internal, surgery, psychiatry and burns wards. Int. Nurs. Rev. **55**(1), 62–67 (2008)
8. Escribà-Agüir, V., Martín-Baena, D., Pérez-Hoyos, S.: Psychosocial work environment and burnout among emergency medical and nursing staff. Int. Arch. Occup. Environ. Health **80**(2), 127–133 (2006)
9. Okuda, Y., Iwasaki, S., Deguchi, Y., Nitta, T., Mitake, T., Sakaguchi, A., Niki, A., Inoue, K.: Burnout and occupational stressors among non-medical occupational health staff. Occup. Med. **70**(1), 45–51 (2020)
10. Wu, Y., Wang, J., Luo, C., Hu, S., Lin, X., Anderson, A.E., Bruera, E., Yang, X., Wei, S., Qian, Y.: A comparison of burnout frequency among oncology physicians and nurses working on the front lines and usual wards during the COVID-19 epidemic in Wuhan, China. J. Pain Symptom Manag. **60**(1), e60–e65 (2020)
11. Abdi, I.: Psychological burnout among nurses and night work. A memorandum for obtaining a master's degree in work psychology, organization and management of human resources. Arabi Ben Mahidi University, Umm El Bouaghi, Algeria (2014)
12. Mihoubi, F.: The organizational climate prevailing within the health institution and its relationship to psychological burnout among nurses. A note to obtain a master's degree in psychology of work and organization. University of Algiers, Algeria (2007)
13. Bin Dorf, S.: Burnout level and job satisfaction among nurses. Al-Riwaq J. Soc. Hum. Stud. **6**(1), 127–140 (2020)
14. Wakely, B.: Burnout and its relationship to self-efficacy among nurses - a field study at Setif Hospital. Al-Murshid Mag. **7**(1), 222–203 (2018)
15. Slimani, S., Waddah, F.: Psychological burnout among a sample of nurses on night shift in the medical and surgical urgent service in the valley. In: International Forum: Suffering at Work among Nursing Staff. University of Batna, Algeria (2020)
16. Samani, M.: Coping strategies for those suffering from psychological burnout among parents residing in the University Hospital of Oran. Graduation notes for a master's degree in mental health and school adaptation. University of Oran, Algeria. (2012)
17. Jabbar, N.: Psychological Burnout among General Practitioners (field study at Mostaganem Hospital). A thesis for a master's degree in Clinical Psychology and Mental Health. Mostaganem University, Algeria (2015)
18. Nbar, R., Geagea, A.: Legalizing the psychological burnout scale (maslach) on the algerian environment - a field study on a sample of nurses. Al-Turath Mag. **8**(1), 517–540 (2018)
19. Chernoff, P., Adedokun, C., O'Sullivan, I., McManus, J., Payne, A.: Burnout in the emergency department hospital staff at Cork University Hospital. Irish J. Med. Sci. (1971-) **188**(2), 667–674 (2019)
20. Głębocka, A.: The relationship between burnout syndrome among the medical staff and work conditions in the Polish healthcare system. In: Influenza and Respiratory Care, pp. 61–70. Springer, Cham (2017)

Usability Review of Mask Extenders and Ear Savers

Jason Kumagai[1]([✉]), Lorena Kembel[2], and Tanya Ewashko[3]

[1] Human Factors Specialist, Provincial Patient Safety Department, Quality and Healthcare Improvement, Alberta Health Services, Alberta, Canada
jason.kumagai@albertahealthservices.ca
[2] Research and Evaluation Consultant, Health Systems Evaluation and Evidence, Alberta Health Services, Alberta, Canada
[3] Innovation, Evidence and Impact, Provincial Clinical Excellence, Alberta Health Services, Alberta, Canada

Abstract. Continuous masking at Alberta Health Services (AHS) was required when a Healthcare Worker (HCW) was involved in direct patient contact or where a two-metre distance between patients and/or co-workers could not be maintained. In response, many AHS personnel employed mask extenders, or ear savers, to relieve the pressure and abrasion on their ears. A two-part review was conducted to investigate if mask extenders can be removed and reused safely and effectively. Part 1 involved an on-line survey that identified the variety of mask extenders used by AHS staff and some of the issues experienced with extended use. Part 2 involved an end-user review of five different styles of mask extenders. Results identified the features most liked about mask extenders, as well as the challenges presented by some mask extender designs. The comparison of mask extenders identified pros and cons of various mask extender designs. These results can help to inform HCWs as the need for continuous masking persists in healthcare.

Keywords: Covid 19 · Mask · PPE · Usability · Ear saver · Mask extender · Healthcare

1 Introduction

1.1 Background

In response to the COVID-19 pandemic, Alberta Health Services (AHS) mandated continuous masking in AHS facilities in April 2020. Continuous masking was required when a Healthcare Worker (HCW) was involved in direct patient contact or where a two-metre distance between patients and/or co-workers could not be maintained. The extended use of masks can place contact pressure and abrasion at the back of the ear, contributing to discomfort, pain and bruising. In response, many AHS personnel employed mask extenders, or ear savers, to relieve the pressure on their ears. Several different designs of mask extenders were reportedly employed by AHS personnel, with many variations in material, design and size.

N. L. Black et al. (Eds.): IEA 2021, LNNS 222, pp. 625–630, 2021.
https://doi.org/10.1007/978-3-030-74611-7_85

1.2   Purpose

To gather information on the mask extenders, the AHS Personal Protective Equipment (PPE) Task Force requested that AHS Human Factors, along with the newly formed AHS PPE Innovation Review Team (PIRT), review the use of the mask extenders. PIRT is a group of AHS representatives who provide knowledge and experience for review of PPE (and related) innovations introduced to AHS for the COVID-19 pandemic response. A two-part review was conducted to investigate if mask extenders can be used safely and effectively.

2   On-line Review (Part 1)

2.1   Method

An on-line survey was issued to all AHS employees to investigate the types of mask extenders in use and to obtain feedback on the usability and preferences. The survey was open from April 29 to May 8, 2020.

2.2   Survey Results

The survey received 3521 staff responses. Key findings of the survey indicated that mask extenders are widely used across the province and roles, including nursing, allied health, support services and management. Most respondents (84%) received their mask extenders free of charge, either homemade or donated by the community. Few commercially available options were mentioned by the respondents. Mask extenders styles are made from a range of materials and methods: 60% were made of plastic, many manufactured with 3D printers; 18% were hand-made knitted or crocheted styles with buttons; 15% were made of cloth, such as a head band with buttons or a scrub cap with buttons; and 7% used unique versions including silicon material, paperclips, hair barrettes, or chip bag clips.

Some respondents (7%) reported concerns with the ease of taking off their mask when using an extender. Some respondents (7%) also expressed concerns with self-contamination when putting on or removing the mask and extender. More than 90% of respondents reused their extenders and cleaned or disinfected them. Some respondents wearing cloth or knitted/crocheted styles were not sure of the best method for disinfection.

Results of the survey were used to inform the review team on the styles of mask extenders to include in the end-user review. The styles most frequently used by the respondents included: multi-hook 3D printed plastic (several variations); laser cut foam; and headband or scrub cap with buttons.

3   End-User Review (Part 2)

3.1   Method

The end-user review involved distribution of five different mask extender styles to participants for a within-subject evaluation of fit, comfort, cleaning and functionality.

The order of use was at the users' discretion. The study was conducted between June 18 to July 10, 2020 with participants from Foothills Medical Center in Calgary, Alberta, Canada. Descriptions and measurements of the five different mask extenders are described in Table 1 below.

Table 1. Descriptions of the five mask extender styles.

Type	Description	Image
1. Multi-hook 3D printed plastic	A popular design for 3D printing based on the template files available from the National Institute of Health (UK). Made from PETG material. Size: 157 mm long x 27 mm wide x 1 mm thick (2mm thick hooks). Length adjustments to 145, 121, 98, and 74 mm.	
2. Multi-hook injected plastic	Made from EVA PE injection molded material. Size: 180 mm long x 23 mm wide x 1 mm thick. Length adjustments to 165 mm, 144 mm, 123 mm, 102 mm.	
3. Scrub cap with buttons	Made from cloth material. Buttons ranged in size from 15 mm to 28 mm diameter. Buttons were located 150-180 mm from front/centre seam and 60-80 mm above bottom hem. Button location was not adjustable.	
4. Snowboard shaped injected plastic	Made from medical grade EVA polyethylene that is non-porous and non-hydroscopic. The hooks include a nub to help secure the mask strap. Size: 100 mm long x 30 mm wide x 2 mm thick (5 mm thick hooks). Length adjustments to 81 mm and 49mm	
5. Tongue depressor shaped laser cut foam	Closed cell foam cut with a laser cutter. Size: 198mm long x 25 mm wide x 4 mm thick. Includes 3 adjustment levels at 165 mm, 122 mm and 81 mm.	

Participants were asked to use each style for an entire shift (12 h) and complete an on-line questionnaire at the end of each shift. Participants completed exit questions once they had used all the styles to help compare the mask extenders. Some participants were asked to perform a donning and doffing task under observation (including video) to help make a visual assessment of the possibility for self-contamination.

3.2 Results

Demographics: There were 26 participants from a large acute care hospital, including the Emergency Department, Cardiovascular Intensive Care Unit, and Labour and Delivery. Several roles were represented in the study, including Registered Nurses, Respiratory Therapists, Unit Clerks, Health Care Aides, Service Workers, Housekeeping and Orthopedic Technician. Head circumferences were measured at a horizontal level above the eyebrows, included the hair, and ranged between 39 cm to 61 cm. The average head circumference was 55.53 cm (SD 4.07). There were a range of hairstyles, including long, short, medium, clipped and head covering. A large majority of participants had long hair (69.23%), followed by short hair (19.23%).

Utility: All the mask extenders, except for the multi-hook 3D printed plastic, were rated to have reduced or prevented irritation to the back of the ears for all participants that were having problems with the ear loops. Some participants also indicated that the masks were too loose without the mask extender and that they "don't feel comfortable using masks without an extender." Participants used disposable medical masks.

Usability: All the mask extenders were rated on usability criteria. Results are provided in Table 2 and described below.

Table 2. Average rating on usability criteria on a 5-point scale performance (5 = excellent, 4 = good, 3 = neutral, 2 = fair, 1 = poor).

Usability criteria	Multi-hook 3D printed mean (SD)	Multi-hook injected plastic mean (SD)	Scrub cap with buttons mean (SD)	Snowboard shaped injected plastic mean (SD)	Laser cut foam mean (SD)
Ease of putting mask on	4.0 (1.2)	3.6 (1.1)	4.6 (0.5)	4.1 (1.1)	3.3 (1.4)
Ease of taking the mask off	3.1 (1.3)	3.5 (0.9)	4.5 (0.5)	3.8 (1.3)	3.6 (1.2)
Ease of avoiding self-contamination	3.5 (1.1)	3.4 (1.1)	4.4 (0.7)	3.9 (1.2)	3.6 (1.3)
Fit	4.1 (0.9)	3.9 (0.9)	3.8 (1.6)	3.7 (1.1)	4.0 (1.3)
Comfort	3.9 (0.9)	3.9 (0.9)	4.1 (1.2)	3.8 (1.3)	4.2 (1.0)
Ease of cleaning the mask extender	4.5 (0.5)	4.2 (0.9)	3.6 (1.4)	4.3 (0.7)	2.6 (1.5)
Overall experience	3.7 (1.2)	3.6 (1.0)	4.0 (1.1)	3.5 (1.1)	3.2 (1.3)

Ease of Putting On/Taking Off the Mask: The scrub cap with buttons was rated highest for ease of putting on and taking off the mask. The benefit of the scrub cap is that it stays secured to the head when the mask is donned and doffed. The laser cut foam was rated the lowest for ease of putting the mask on because participants found it difficult to find, manipulate and push out the foam tabs to securely hook on the mask straps. The multi-hook 3D printed devices were rated the lowest for ease of taking the mask off because the hooks were more prone to get tangled in the hair or with the mask straps.

Ease of Avoiding Self-contamination: The scrub cap with buttons was rated highest for ease of avoiding self-contamination. The scrub cap does not need to be removed when donning or doffing the mask, reducing the handling and opportunities for self-contamination. The multi-hook options were rated the lowest because they were more prone to get tangled in the hair or mask which resulted in mishandling of the device where it might touch the hair, face, mask, or fall to the floor.

Fit: The multi-hook 3D printed device was rated highest for fit because it provided a long adjustment of 157 mm. The multi-hook injected plastic and laser cut foam were also rated high because of their long adjustments of 165 mm. The long adjustments were important to accommodate larger head circumferences (including hair). The snowboard shaped device was rated lowest for fit because its longest adjustment was 81 mm. The shorter adjustment can cause the mask to be pulled tight. The scrub cap only came in one size. Although the lip could be folded up, or the ties could be pulled tighter, the scrub cap was too large for participants with smaller head circumference and too small for participants with long, voluminous hair.

Comfort: The laser cut foam was rated highest for comfort, closely followed by the scrub cap with buttons. The foam and scrub cap were made of soft materials so that it did not scratch or cause pressure points. The snowboard shaped device was rated lowest for comfort because its shorter adjustment caused the mask to be pulled tight for those with larger head circumferences. The multi-hook 3D printed device was also rated low for comfort because the plastic hooks can scratch the neck or cause pressure points on the skin.

Ease of Disinfecting/Cleaning the Mask Extender: The multi-hook 3D printed extender was rated highest for ease of disinfecting/cleaning. This was a bit surprising given the small grooves that result from the 3D printing process, which could require more diligence to disinfect. The laser cut foam rated the lowest for ease of disinfecting/cleaning. Participants expressed concern that the foam could absorb contaminants which caused uncertainty in the success of the efforts to disinfect.

Overall Experience Using the Mask Extender: The scrub cap with buttons was rated highest overall. This reflects the high ratings for ease of taking the mask on and off, avoiding contamination and comfort. Ratings may have been even better if additional size options were available to improve the fit. The laser cut foam was rated the lowest overall. The laser cut foam was more difficult to put on, but the low rating was primarily related to the uncertainty of effectively disinfecting/cleaning the mask extender.

Infection Prevention and Control Assessment: Representatives from Infection Prevention and Control (IP&C) were provided with samples of each of the ear savers, as well as donning and doffing videos of some participants. Based on their review of the videos, they reported that the mask extenders carried an increased risk of self-contamination and/or clean supplies contamination if proper hand hygiene and extender cleaning were not followed. From an IP&C perspective, the mask extender must be cleanable after each use to meet the criteria for the PPE that can be reused. The biggest concern with mask extenders is the risk of self-contamination during doffing.

4   Conclusion

The two-part review investigated if mask extenders can be removed and reused safely and effectively. Results of the on-line survey identified that a variety of mask extenders are being used by AHS staff. The end-user review compared five different styles of mask extenders to help identify the features most liked in mask extenders, as well as the challenges presented by some mask extender designs.

The results were used to communicate to staff the various options available and the usability criteria. Based on the results, a 5-min video [1] was generated to advise staff on when and how to use mask extenders. As well, a tip sheet [2] was developed to provide guidance. The most important criteria to consider in selecting an ear extender are described below.

Comfort: A rigid plastic may irritate or scratch the head or back of neck. Softer, lightweight plastics are preferred.

Ease of Donning and Doffing the Mask: Mask extenders that cover and contain the hair (e.g. scrub caps with buttons, headbands with buttons, or head coverings used with a mask extender) make it easier to put the mask on or off and help to avoids self-contamination. Mask extender designs with hooks are more prone to get caught on the mask or in hair, which can also contribute to self-contamination and discomfort.

Ease of Disinfecting/Cleaning: Mask extenders made of cloth, yarn, or foam may be more prone to contamination and will need to be disposed of or replaced and cleaned regularly. Plastic that have ridges or hard to clean areas should also be avoided.

Fit: Many mask extenders have multiple hooks for adjustment. However, select a longer mask extender for a larger head and/or lots of hair. Also, consider that use of a head covering will add to the length required. If the mask extender is too short, it may pull the mask tightly on the face causing discomfort. Shorter mask extenders may be suitable for a smaller head and/or the mask is very loose with the ear loops. A good fit will also help to prevent the mask extender from falling down the back of the head to the neck which may cause the mask to be pulled down.

The review demonstrated the value of involving the end user in evaluations of new and innovative products. These results can be shared broadly to help other healthcare organizations, as well as other industries, consider if mask extenders may help to relieve discomfort, and potential injury, in their workforce. The test protocol may inform future research, as there are new styles of mask extenders to evaluate.

References

1. Alberta Health Services PPE Question of the Week: Mask Extenders: when & how to use, and use safely. https://youtu.be/k0vpMFSyU8c, Accessed 15 Feb 2021
2. Alberta Health Services webpage: Personal Protective Equipment (PPE) Covid-19. "Tips: Using Mask Extenders". https://www.albertahealthservices.ca/assets/info/ppih/if-ppih-covid-19-tips-on-the-use-of-mask-extenders.pdf, Accessed 15 Feb 2021

The Maker Movement Response to COVID-19: What Was Considered in the Development and Sharing of Emergency Protective Equipment?

Renato L. R. Souza[1](✉) ⓘ, Esdras Paravizo[2] ⓘ, Larissa Oliveira dos Santos[2] ⓘ, Gustavo Souza de Almeida[1] ⓘ, and Daniel Braatz[2] ⓘ

[1] Department of Industrial Engineering, Federal University of Triângulo Mineiro, Uberaba, MG, Brazil

[2] Department of Industrial Engineering, Federal University of São Carlos, São Carlos, SP, Brazil

Abstract. The design and production of protective equipment by makers was among the many actions undertaken by society in the fight against the COVID-19 pandemic. These decentralized initiatives sought to solve a low supply of medical inputs and individual protection devices by sharing these devices through online repositories. However, it is known that personal protective equipment may cause discomfort and pain in situations of prolonged use, even when they are designed and approved through traditional processes. In this context, this paper aims to analyze COVID-19-related protective equipment (PE) models and files shared in online repositories to understand to what extent aspects related to ergonomics, safety and manufacturing were considered in their design and sharing. This study takes an exploratory qualitative and comparative approach. The models' analysis focused on their description and related information, looking specifically for mentions to ergonomics, safety and manufacturing (model printing and quality) aspects. One hundred models were analyzed, and of these, 60% presented information related to ergonomics and safety, while 80% presented information related to manufacturing. Specifically, the concern in describing the ergonomics and safety aspects was below those related to manufacturing, especially when considering the level of detail of this information. The findings show that developing and sharing solutions, in online, collaborative, and free to use platforms has a great potential to solve the lack of protective equipment, in face of extreme situations. However, this initiative should be better understood and directed to reduce possible comfort and effectiveness problems that may arise from poor information and design of the devices.

Keywords: Covid-19 · Maker community · Ergonomic · Safety

1 Introduction

The COVID-19 pandemic is an international public health crisis with impacts in diverse aspects of human life. At the onset of the pandemic several countries' health systems

N. L. Black et al. (Eds.): IEA 2021, LNNS 222, pp. 631–638, 2021.
https://doi.org/10.1007/978-3-030-74611-7_86

were overwhelmed by the sheer number of cases demanding attention and the lack of information on this new disease. This increased demand affected the availability of personal protective equipment for the healthcare workers who are on the frontlines of health service. In Brazil this same trend was seen, and several healthcare workers reported working without or with improvised protective equipment.

The use of the appropriate PPE by health professionals minimizes the chances of becoming infected, ensuring that they are not exposed to occupational diseases and accidents that can compromise their health, work capacity and life of professionals during, and after the active phase of work (Guimarães et al. 2011; Cohen e Rodgers 2020; Silva Filho et al. 2020). Furthermore, Cohen e Rodgers (2020) indicate that sick healthcare professionals contribute to viral transmission, increase the demand for care, and at the same time reduce the capacity of the healthcare system. Thus, the pandemic outbreak generated by COVID-19 highlights the importance of the use of PPE to minimize viral transmissions (Delgado et al. 2020; Silva Filho et al. 2020).

The use of surgical masks and respiratory protection are essential for controlling the spread of SARS-Cov-2 (Silva Filho et al. 2020). Nonetheless, unwanted effects of using PPE are being reported. Ong et al. 2020draws attention to the emergence and aggravation of headaches in health professionals due to prolonged use of conventional protective equipment (e.g., N95 masks and safety glasses) in the context of the pandemic caused by the new coronavirus. This situation highlights that even the safety equipment that already validated and commercialized are sources of discomfort that get worse in situations of long period of use.

In this context a number of initiatives from the maker community (here broadly considered designers, hobbyists, engineers and general public who design, create and share 3D models and other designs for 3D printings and other rapid prototyping techniques), universities and other organizations tried to supply healthcare professionals with the equipment they were lacking. These equipment, designed and shared in a decentralized fashion in online repositories and platforms allowed for the exchange of solutions across countries and regions, and for their production to be done locally.

Santos et al. (2020) highlight how 3D model sharing repositories, commonly used by the maker community, were used to share models that could be used to protect against COVID-19. The authors show an increase in the sharing of these types of models and raise in their discussion, the need for standardization of information available in the repositories.

The contribution of the maker community in the fight against COVID-19 was also highlighted by Corsini et al. 2020a at a macro level, considering global projects, and at a detailed level in the contributions evidenced in the United Kingdom. The authors also discuss, the dichotomy between the models developed by the maker community and the need for standardization of these models. In another study, Corsini et al. 2020b based on solutions developed by makers groups in two countries, Italy and India, discuss the importance of frugal innovations developed by maker groups in response to COVID-19.

Despite the relevance of such actions in a time of crisis, the problem investigated in this paper is centered around the design features and use of these equipment, namely if ergonomics and safety aspects wcre taken into account in the development and sharing of the equipment files and models.

The aim of this paper is to analyze COVID-19-related protective equipment (PE) models and files that were shared in online repositories to understand to what extent aspects related to ergonomics, safety and manufacturing were considered in their design and sharing.

2   Methods

The process of maker repositories and models' selection is detailed in Santos et al. (2020), but a brief overview is given here. Five main 3D models online repositories commonly used for sharing 3D printing models and specifications were selected based on their relevance (Thingiverse, Cults3D, PrusaPrinters, Pinshape and NIH 3D Print Exchange). On each of these repositories the 20 most relevant 3D models (based on number of likes, downloads and similar metrics) that were characterized as PE against COVID-19 were compiled, registering their description and instructions of fabrication and use.

The analysis of this pool of 100 3D models of intended PE against COVID-19 (ranging from face-shields, respirators, masks and ear protectors) considered three main aspects: Ergonomics, Safety and Manufacturing. The goal of this analysis was to identify the information available on the 3D models' description and information on the ergonomics, safety and manufacturing aspects.

For the category of analysis related to Ergonomics aspects, three main elements were considered: use, fit and comfort. Use information comprised the orientations that could help the user on how to effectively use the PE. Fit information considered the explanations on adjustments that could be made so that the model could be used adapted to each person's needs. Finally, comfort information comprised the mentions that aimed to improve comfort during the use of the PE.

Similarly, for the Safety category, the three main elements considered were: tests, effectiveness, and associated risks. Tests information considered if there was available information related to trials that had already been carried out with the PE model. Effectiveness information aimed to explicitly identify the details provided on the efficacy of the model for user protection. Finally, the associated risks information comprised mentions to the risks present in the use of the PE.

Finally, for the Manufacturing category, the three main elements considered were: 3D printing; assembly and quality. 3D printing information comprised specifications related to equipment settings in order to print the model. Assembly information comprised details on how to assembly the model. Lastly, quality information comprised details on the model characteristics in terms of different materials used, different printing configurations, among other parameters.

To each of the 100 models selected, the researchers read their description and additional details and evaluated the information for each of the 3 aspects in a 4-point scale (high, medium, low and none), determining the degree in which each of the aspects were present in the models' description. Data collection was conducted in April/2020, and the focus of the analysis was models' description rather than an evaluation of their features itself.

More specifically, the qualitative criteria for the evaluation of models' description followed the structure presented in the Table 1.

Table 1. Qualitative criteria for the evaluation of models' information on the target aspects

Level/Aspect	Ergonomics	Safety	Manufacturing
High	Includes use, fit and comfort information (3/3)	Includes tests, effectiveness and associated risks information (3/3)	Includes 3D printing, assembly and quality information (3/3)
Medium	Includes use and fit or comfort information (2/3)	Includes tests and effectiveness or associated risks information (2/3)	Includes 3D printing, assembly or quality information (2/3)
Low	Information on use, fit or comfort is minimal (1/3)	Information on tests, effectiveness or associated risks is minimal (1/3)	Information on 3D printing, assembly or quality information is minimal (1/3)
None	No information on either use, fit or comfort available	No information on either tests, effectiveness or associated risks available	No information on 3D printing, assembly or quality available

3 Results

Overall, the 100 models analyzed could be grouped in seven categories (masks, face-shields, respirators, comfort-focused items (e.g., ear saver for masks), valves, adapters and daily life accessories), with most models (76%) being either masks or face-shields. Figure 1 shows a few examples of the 3D models found on the repositories.

Results from the 100 models' descriptions analysis indicate that aspects related to ergonomics and safety appeared in 60% of the models' descriptions, while manufacturing aspects were present in 80% of the models' descriptions.

Among the 60% of ergonomics mentions identified, most mentions were at the low degree (53%, n = 32), followed by the medium degree (28%, n = 17) and high degree (18%, n = 11) of discussion of the ergonomics aspects in the models' description. With regards to the 60% of safety mentions identified, the distribution among the degrees of the topics' discussion was relatively even, with the medium degree (35%, n = 21) being the highest one, followed by high degree (33%, n = 20) and low degree (32%, n = 19). On the 80% of fabrication mentions identified, most were on the medium degree (63%, n = 38), then on the low degree (45%, n = 27) and finally on the high degree (25%, n = 15). Figure 2 summarizes the number of mentions identified to each aspects and levels.

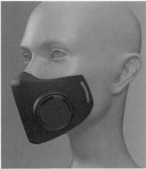

Fig. 1. Example of models analyzed on the repositories; face-shield (left) (Model uploaded by Print-T3D, available on: https://cults3d.com/en/3d-model/tool/covid-19-prusa, last accessed on 09/02/2021), mask (center) (Model uploaded by Copper3D, available on: https://cults3d. com/en/3d-model/tool/n95-masks-against-coronavirus-covid19-hackthepandemic, last accessed on 09/02/2021) (Model uploaded by Copper3D, available on: https://cults3d.com/en/3d-model/ tool/n95-masks-against-coronavirus-covid19-hackthepandemic, last accessed on 09/02/2021) (Model uploaded by Copper3D, available on: https://cults3d.com/en/3d-model/tool/n95-masks-against-coronavirus-covid19-hackthepandemic, last accessed on 09/02/2021) and "safegrabber", daily life accessory (right) (Model uploaded by Coolioiglesias, available on: https://www.thingi verse.com/thing:4192643, last accessed on 0902/2021.).

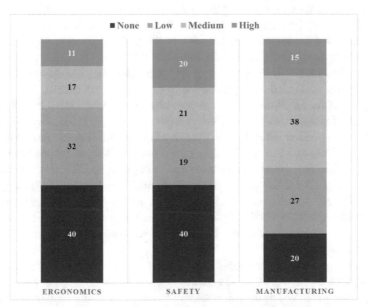

Fig. 2. Summary of the analysis of ergonomics, safety and manufacturing aspects mentions on models' descriptions.

4 Discussion

The results reflect the overwhelming preoccupation of designers with aspects related to the 3D printing of the components, instead of the equipment's ergonomics and safety aspects.

The descriptions and guidelines that refer to the manufacturing aspects of the components and models were the most detailed, focusing on enabling the repository user to produce the models. This finding is aligned with the core purpose of such repositories, which is to enable the greatest number of people to manufacture of the 3D models following the descriptions provided. The information that is made available, such as equipment configuration guidelines, filament type and assembly guidelines, are crucial so that the available model can be reproduced by users without having to contact the user who shared the model. Some descriptions even had links to videos in which the assembly was detailed.

On the other hand, the concern to provide a complete description regarding safety and ergonomics aspects was presented with a low and/or medium degree of detail. Here it is worth mentioning that the developed and shared items are part of a group effort to solve a temporary demand for protection items and that in the context of the pandemic caused by the new coronavirus this information gap is expected, since some models were tested (in best case scenarios) by a small group of people and possibly in situations that did not account to the professional use, long term use of the model.

It is also necessary to consider that most of the models were designed so that a production scale was sought (trying to match the increased demand for this type of PE) using additive manufacturing technologies (e.g., 3D printers using fused filament fabrication technology), an unconventional use of this type of technology. Adjustments to minimize the amount of material spent and also in the dimensions of the models are common to achieve a reasonable production in this type of equipment.

Thus, it becomes a challenge for the user who searches the models in the bases of sharing, either for own use or for production and distribution of the items in civil society organizations, to understand and identify among the available models those that meet the requirements of use and safety. This may be a problem if the model produced and used causes discomfort and, even more, is not effective in protecting the user. Such situations are further aggravated if the model is being produced on a larger scale by groups for donations to health professionals. The comments made by other users and the number of downloads from the model in the repository may be important information for choosing the model, but may not be enough, especially if we consider the models that are for protection purposes.

The challenge pointed out by this study is how to ensure that safety items shared in the context, such as the COVID-19 pandemic, meet the requirements of ergonomics and safety. This study allowed us to understand that there is a limitation in the initial concept that permeates these sites (except for NIH 3D Print) since they were designed precisely for this simplified sharing, decentralized production and experimentation of solutions. Thus, they are not repositories that aim to certify the use of shared models according to technically established criteria.

However, it is noteworthy that at the beginning of the pandemic and in the face of a shortage of protective equipment for health professionals, different state control and regulatory bodies changed guidelines regarding the manufacture, import and acquisition of medical devices in order to simplify and facilitate the access to professionals on the front line.

In this sense, it may be appropriate to learn from these experiences so that, in extreme situations, in addition to making it more flexible, there may be efforts by these bodies to indicate good practices, general guidelines, or even to open a close dialogue with the maker community mobilized to assist the community.

5 Conclusion

This study showed that there was a lack of information on aspects of ergonomics and safety in PE models related to Covid-19 shared in online repositories. In the future, it may be useful for designers, repositories and platforms to explicitly request/ make this information available, especially for such sensitive and crucial equipment in times of crisis.

However, the PE shared in these repositories has in some ways helped health professional in a time of crisis. The ability to share and exchange solutions around the world has a great potential benefit, although it needs to be better understood and directed to reduce the problems presented in this study.

Finally, it is highlighted that the lack of consideration given to ergonomics (for example, use, adjustments and comfort) and safety aspects (tests, efficiency and risks) of the equipment can affect the final performance of the user and the real safety conditions that are being obtained in the workplace.

The present research did not focus on understanding how this impact actually occurred, especially due to the limited access to workers and the ongoing pandemic still impacting the daily lives of these professionals. Future studies can devise ways to test these PE both in laboratory and real-life settings to provide an in-depth, experimental, understanding of their characteristics.

Finally, the diversity of models of protective equipment, the differences between the repositories that provide such models and the constant changes that occur in the insertion, modification and use of these platforms, are intrinsic features of this object of study, but could be addressed in future studies.

References

Guimarães, E.A. de A., Araújo, G.D., Bezerra, R., da Silveira, R.C., de Oliveira, V.C.: Percepção de técnicos de enfermagem sobre o uso de equipamentos de proteção individual em um serviço de urgência. Cienc. y Enfermería. **17**, 113–123 (2011). https://doi.org/10.4067/S0717-955320 11000300010

Cohen, J., Rodgers, Y. van der M.: Contributing factors to personal protective equipment shortages during the COVID-19 pandemic. Prev. Med. (Baltim). **141**, 1–7 (2020). https://doi.org/10.1016/j.ypmed.2020.106263

Silva Filho, P.S. da P., et al.: The importance of using individual protection equipment (IPE) in times of covid-19. Res. Soc. Dev. **9**, 1–14 (2020). https://doi.org/10.33448/rsd-v9i7.4610

Ong, J.J.Y., et al.: Headaches associated with personal protective equipment – a cross-sectional study among frontline healthcare workers during COVID-19. Headache. **60**, 864–877 (2020). https://doi.org/10.1111/head.13811

Santos, L.O. Dos, Paravizo, E., De Souza, R.L.R., Braatz, D.: Análise de repositórios utilizados pela comunidade maker mundial para auxílio no combate à COVID-19. In: XL Encontro Nacional de Engenharia de Produção. p. 1 a 16. ABEPRO, Foz do Iguaçu (2020). https://doi.org/10.14488/ENEGEP2020_TN_STO_346_1779_40865

Corsini, L., Dammicco, V., Bowker-lonnecker, L., Blythe, R.: The Maker movement and its impact in the fight against COVID-19. (2020a). https://doi.org/10.17863/CAM.60248

Corsini, L., Dammicco, V., Moultrie, J.: Frugal innovation in a crisis: the digital fabrication maker response to COVID-19. R&D Manag. **19**, 16 (2020b). https://doi.org/10.1111/radm.12446

Delgado, D., Wyss Quintana, F., Perez, G., Sosa Liprandi, A., Ponte-Negretti, C., Mendoza, I., Baranchuk, A.: Personal safety during the COVID-19 pandemic: realities and perspectives of healthcare workers in Latin America. Int. J. Environ. Res. Public Health. **17**, 2798 (2020). https://doi.org/10.3390/ijerph17082798

Ergonomics in the Time of the Coronavirus

Micheline Marier[(⊠)]

Occupational Health Advisor – Ergonomist, UQAM (SDO), C.P.8888 Succ. Centre-Ville,
Montréal H3C 3P8, Canada
michelinemarier@contrechamps.ca

Abstract. The eruption of the SARS-CoV-2 virus in March 2020 created an unprecedented situation in workplaces as a whole, and universities were no exception. It has been necessary to learn about the new virus and to adapt preventive measures to a multifaceted environment in order to protect not only students, but also professors, support staff and managerial personnel. The aim of this paper is to describe the interventions of an ergonomics advisor in occupational health, with a view to presenting the contribution made by activity analysis, co-construction as part of a project approach, and the application of the precautionary principle in responding to the pandemic.

Keywords: COVID-19 · Activity analysis · Precautionary principle · Co-construction · Communication · University

I am an ergonomics practitioner and I have worked as an occupational health advisor at the Université du Québec à Montréal for 16 years. At the university, I have worked in office ergonomics and on architectural projects, while dealing with problems related to noise, lighting, materials handling and working at heights. As a result of the pandemic, I was thrust into preventing a biohazard that was poorly understood, namely, that posed by the SARS-CoV-2 coronavirus.

Our university, with its more than 5 300 employees – professors, lecturers, support staff, and managerial personnel – plus nearly 40 000 students during the fall and winter terms is a bit like a large village.

I belong to the university's global health team, along with three other professionals and a technician. We quickly shared all COVID-19 interventions, namely, providing assistance to employees working remotely, preventing psychological risks, and warding off the risk that the virus would be transmitted on our campuses. Since I was already in charge of physical risk prevention on our global health team and because of my experience at the university, I was assigned the responsibility of adapting the authorities' recommendations to the specific characteristics of the working environment.

1 Introduction

The first COVID-19 case was diagnosed in Québec on February 27, 2020 and the province went into lockdown on March 13.

The first wave of the pandemic began in the middle of the winter term and continued throughout the summer term. The only people present at the university were managerial personnel and employees required to be on site in order to maintain the university's facilities. Teaching and support activities were conducted mostly online. During this period, my work consisted in familiarizing myself with crucial information for designing preventive measures and in summarizing this data for my department or the operational services concerned.

In mid-April, Québec authorized a gradual lifting of restrictions. The university then had to prepare for the gradual resumption of activities that could not be carried out remotely, starting first and foremost with research in science and arts. In May, the university began to prepare for the fall term, which was to take place mainly remotely. I then provided support and assistance to the people in charge of the various services and departments in preparation for the resumption of activities that would take place on site.

However, on September 2, Québec officially entered the second wave of the pandemic and on September 28, the city of Montréal was designated a red zone. For us, this meant that as many teaching and operational activities as possible would be carried out remotely. Since most of my recommendations had already been submitted, my job was to ensure that they would be applied during activities where staff and students would continue to be present at the university.

To illustrate all the work that was done, I have decided to describe the steps I took at the registrar's office of the university.

2   The Registrar's Office, an Essential University Service

The registrar's office is one of the university's essential services. It comprises four main sectors: recruitment, admissions, management of university records from registration to graduation, and administrative services, which consist of client services, operational support and computer systems.

The office has nearly 80 employees, spread out over three floors. In March, all of them began to work remotely. Their computers were moved to their homes and, since then, all operations that can be performed remotely have been done in that way. However, although the registrar's admissions, registration and recruitment officers, as well as its computer analysts, have continued to work remotely, this is not the case of clerks, some of whose tasks cannot be performed at a distance. At the end of May, operational support clerks took turns returning to work at the university in order to issue diplomas. In early July, clerks in the admissions and university records management sectors took turns providing telephone service and, in late August, they resumed reception services. This was a major challenge for the registrar's office.

The director in charge of organizing the employees' return to work contacted me on May 21 about organizing a training session on safety rules for clerks who had to return to campus. We knew each other well as I had already led several initiatives in her department in connection with workstation analysis, while designing the admissions sector, as well as with noise and materials handling problems and a records digitization project.

The plan was for all registrar employees to return to work on site on August 17 in order to prepare for the students' return to school in September. When we met on the premises on June 17 to prepare for the students' return, the director had drawn up, for each sector of the registrar's office, a series of very precise questions concerning the maximum number of people who could be present in the office, two-metre distancing, plexiglass, protective equipment, employee traffic, shared equipment and spaces, and the protection of employees who were at risk of complications from the virus or who were potential vectors of transmission.

These questions echoed the recommendations of the public health authorities, who considered that respiratory droplets excreted by an infected person were the main mode of transmission of the virus, through direct or indirect contact. At the time, aerosol transmission was considered unlikely.

In late March, the Institut national de santé publique du Québec (INSPQ) identified four risk levels in workplaces, ranging from low (no or minimal contact with other people) to very high (medical or paramedical procedures that generate aerosols among people who are probably or definitely infected).

We do not have a faculty of medicine or a health clinic at the university. I estimated that our work situations entailed low to moderate risk levels. In such cases, the INSPQ recommended first and foremost remote working and avoiding contact with others, followed by hand hygiene, respiratory etiquette, keeping premises clean and maintaining a distance of one metre between individuals. This distance was soon increased to two metres. In situations where the two-metre rule could not be respected, physical barriers had to be set up between people or, as a last resort, personal protective equipment had to be provided.

On March 13, I assigned a moderate risk level to the university's various service and payment counters. At the end of April, I assigned the same level of risk to people meeting at workstations, especially to greet different segments of the public, as well as to on-site work on equipment or workstations, deliveries in the presence of users or colleagues and, lastly, the maintenance of surfaces. I drew up a table detailing potential risks, physical organization recommendations and the hygiene measures that had to be introduced for each typical situation.

At the registrar's office, the main situations involved clerks greeting students at the reception desk, employees being asked to provide information at their workstations, and computer technicians.

2.1 Client Services: At the Reception Desk, by Telephone or by Email

Client services at the registrar's office are delivered in three ways: by telephone, at the reception desk or by email. Usually, the clerks take turns delivering these services by telephone or at the reception desk, three hours a day.

Students are greeted on the main floor, where there is a reception desk with six windows. Since none of the windows had a glass separation between the users and the clerks, plexiglass panels had to be installed so that documents or an Interact terminal could be handed back and forth and a computer screen could be turned towards the students to show them information. Since the space between each window was not wide enough for clerks to be two metres apart, it was decided that only four windows would remain open after making them compliant with the safety rules.

Cash payments were eliminated, and each window was provided with an Interact terminal and stamps, as well as a bottle of hydroalcoholic solution for sanitizing hands and another bottle containing a solution for cleaning surfaces. The goal was to limit contacts between clerks when they went to the central island where the cash register and the photocopier were located.

If necessary, the clerks at the reception desk consulted the technician or the specialized clerks working at the back of the office. Consultations with the specialized clerks were generally short and took place standing up. A mark was placed on the floor to indicate the distance that had to be maintained. Consultations with the technician were usually longer and often concerned documents. In such situations, plexiglass panels had to be installed. Two of the clerks' workstations were located in a very busy passageway, so they also had to be made compliant with the safety rules, especially since one of the clerks was at risk of developing complications from the virus. Two adjacent workstations that could not be placed at the required distance were also rendered compliant (Fig. 1).

The clipboard shows the position of the plexiglass panel that allowed computer screens to be shared.	The sides of the stations were open to facilitate communication and ensure that everyone had access to light.

Fig. 1. Reception desk and Admissions sector

As for telephone service, it could not be provided remotely for technical reasons when people were working from home, and when it was offered once again on site, it was available in offices located five stories up from the reception desk.

Each of the clerks in the admissions and university records management sectors had their own workstation, laid out on a U-shaped plan. The stations were separated by tall dividers when they were face to face; however, their sides were open except in one small area. This layout was designed to facilitate communication and ensure that everyone had access to light. The distance of two metres between two adjacent workstations was respected when the clerks were seated in the middle of their stations, but not when they worked on the sides. This posed a problem during the pandemic, especially since it was impossible to install a plexiglass panel between each station given the large number of panels that had to be installed throughout the university. Therefore, the clerks were instructed to use the adjoining surfaces along the sides of their workstations solely for storing files that were waiting to be processed. Portable screens were to be provided in cases where this rule could not be obeyed.

Due to the width of the passageways, it was impossible for employees to circulate without passing within less than two metres of a colleague seated at his or her workstation; however, the risk of contracting the virus was considered low as long as the clerks did not stop to talk to one another. It was recommended that shelves and filing cabinets located near certain workstations be moved so as to limit small gatherings. It was also agreed that the workstation of the team leader, with whom the clerks often met, and that of the administrative secretary, which was next to the door of the director's office, would be made compliant with the safety rules.

2.2 Occupant Density, Ventilation and Masks

I was concerned about the question of occupant density as of early May, when the INSPQ and other scientific sources began to talk about the risk of large viral loads being generated in indoor air in the absence of respiratory etiquette. The INSPQ added that there was growing suspicion that the virus could potentially be spread indoors, making it important to ensure that indoor areas were well ventilated and that filters were properly maintained. I then began to ask questions to the service in charge of ventilation, heating and air-conditioning in our buildings, and it provided me with a chart indicating ventilation levels according to the type of space involved. Ventilation of the registrar's office was described as sustained, so I focused the main preventive measures on ensuring adequate distancing between workstations and, where that was impossible, on making the stations safe with plexiglass panels. I did not consider that mask wearing was necessary because I felt that all of the measures proposed were sufficient in the context of a moderate level of risk.

However, during the summer, clerks who were worried about the risk of COVID-19 transmission raised the question of employee traffic. We had suggested using Teams software to communicate with colleagues seated in other parts of the office, but people of course preferred to talk to each other face to face. As of July 18, Québec made it mandatory for employees to wear a face covering whenever they left their work station, but this did not reassure the clerks seated near passageways. Their concern was still obvi-ous in the fall, especially due to the delays that had been incurred in the implementation of preventive measures: shelving had still not been moved and the plexiglass panels were not all installed.

In May, I also became concerned about the quality of face coverings. The Institut de recherche en santé et sécurité du travail had published its work on the highly variable, particle filtering capacity of the fabric used to make these coverings. The professional in charge of testing this equipment had given me the names of manufacturers whose washable masks filtered out 50 to 65% of particles, depending on the model. When the director of the register's office asked me in early August for advice on the purchase of masks, I recommended that it approach these manufacturers.

However, during the summer, the Commission des normes, de l'équité et de la santé et sécurité du travail required that procedural masks be used by people working less than two metres apart. Therefore, in early September, I recommended the purchase of procedural masks, for even though plexiglass panels had been installed at the reception desk on the ground floor, and the workstation of the clerk at risk of complications from

COVID-19 had been made compliant with the safety rules, the rest of the work still had to be done.

Due to the lower-than-expected number of people coming to the reception desk, only two of its windows were open from August 31 to September 5. After that, only one remained open until October 14. Montréal had just been designated a red zone and the government insisted that priority be given to remote working. Therefore, the administration of the registrar's office decided to close the reception desk and keep on site only telephone service and work on paper files that had still not been digitized. The clerks who were present in the office were spaced further apart, and all of the plexiglass panels were finally installed despite the logistical problems encountered in implementing the recommendations.

2.3   Implementing the Recommendations – Logistical Challenges

Carpenters at the university made the plexiglass panels. During the summer, it soon became obvious that they would not be able to make and install the 100 or so panels that we had requested in time for the students' return to school, especially if the carpenters had to take measurements on site. They were under-staffed and their holidays had to be taken into account. Moreover, making and installing the panels was on top of their other duties. The carpenters had designed three models that could be made very quickly, and we agreed that my recommendations would indicate which of the three models had to be provided in each situation. Made-to-measure models were reserved for special situations.

The janitor service coordinated the delivery of the panels with that of the masks and visors. This was a colossal job for the director and the assistant director, with whom I was collaborating. We had to develop joint order monitoring tools from scratch so that changes in recommendations could be taken into account as they occurred.

One of the problems stemmed from the fact that the activity forecasts for the registrar's office, like those for the university's other departments and services, fluctuated with the impacts of the pandemic and the authorities' directives.

While I was writing this paper, after all the operations had been completed in preparation for the winter term, the university issued a new directive that prompted us to review prevention strategies at the registrar's office. Given that the second wave was still under way and the risk that more contagious variants of the virus might spread in the community, the Ministère de l'Enseignement supérieur recommended that masks be worn at all times. From then on, this requirement applied to everyone at the university, except employees who had their own office or were protected by dividers. As we saw earlier, the dividers at the registrar's office did not protect the entire area occupied by the workstations. However, it was impossible to provide phone service while wearing a mask. I had to place an urgent order for more plexiglass panels. I will have to determine if similar situations have occurred elsewhere in the university.

2.4   Situating Preventive Action in a Context of Constant Change

The directives of the public health authorities, the government and the university administration changed in step with our understanding of the virus, and our directives had to follow suit.

From the beginning of the pandemic, the university set up various committees to manage the COVID-19 crisis, without neglecting its missions or operations. In May, it created five steering committees to plan the lifting of safety restrictions in teaching, research, work, access, traffic and, lastly, student life and common areas. A sixth committee was also created to manage any COVID-19 cases that might occur at the university.

Of course, it was impossible for our small global health team to sit on all of these committees. An advisor with the organizational development service to which we are attached and our director took part in the Work and Access committees, but not in the Teaching, Research or Student Life committees. I sent opinions to the first two committees on the measures to be taken and was informed about some of their decisions; however, it was more difficult to work this way with the three other committees. Nonetheless, I was asked to answer questions from faculty administrators about teaching and research facilities, as well as the preventive measures that had to be applied to students who were on site.

When a steering committee was set up in mid-April to prioritize the opening up of certain research sectors, I was invited to participate in the committee. I was able to make relevant recommendations for research activities that would soon begin in remote regions – recommendations I probably wouldn't have thought of had I not sat on the committee. In addition, the fact that I was able to attend a meeting on the reopening of the psychology, sexology, remedial education and career choice clinics – all of which are needed to allow students in the departments concerned to graduate – led me to meet with the professors in charge in order to jointly determine what measures had to be taken, which is something I would not have done otherwise.

However, it was hard for me to define my role in the process as a whole, to obtain the information required to intervene in a proactive manner and to find out who to contact for short-term authorization of preventive measures with a potential impact on teaching activities.

3   Advantages and Challenges in Complex Organizations

The university is a complex organization. It comprises research and teaching faculties as well as vice-rectors' offices in charge of managing the operational (administrative and technical) services needed to support the university's missions. In this context, what advantages did I have as an ergonomist to take action during the pandemic and what challenges did I encounter?

3.1   An Approach Involving Activity Analysis and the Precautionary Principle

The fact that I had experience in activity analysis, as carried out in ergonomics, was definitely an advantage when it came to adapting the recommendations made by the public health authorities. Obviously, I had not done this type of analysis in emergency situations, but the fact that I was used to doing it as part of office planning or occupational health projects, coupled with the practical experience I had gained from doing thousands of workstation analyses and hundreds of group interventions, enabled me to anticipate the specific characteristics of many work situations and thus to ask questions so that I could adapt my recommendations to the realities in the different services.

We value the precautionary principle in occupational health and safety. Of course, we base our actions on conclusive scientific data, but when studies agree that a risk is probable, we must act to prevent it even though definitive proof is still lacking.

Therefore, as early as May, information I had found on scientific websites aroused my concern about the possibility of aerosol transmission and I decided to put some questions to the service in charge of our ventilation systems. Since this service considered that the ventilation was low in offices measuring 10 m^2, I soon recommended that staff members not meet in enclosed office even when they were equipped with plexiglass barriers.

3.2 Students' Health and Safety – Outside My Sphere of Activity?

The global health team is responsible for the health and safety of the university's employees – professors, lecturers, support employees, administrators, and student employees. Student Life services is responsible for the health and safety of university users.

However, in the case of internships and practicums in science, arts and communications, where students, teachers and technicians mingle with one another, we cannot reflect on the safety of one group separately from that of the others. Therefore, I included student activities in my recommendations for the faculties concerned, which is something I had done on a few occasions in the past, during interventions concerned with working at heights or handling toxic resins.

3.3 Project Approach and Horizontal and Vertical Communication

Our use of a project approach like the one implemented in ergonomic design, in a spirit of co-construction, facilitated collaboration with managers in determining the preventive measures to be introduced, whether these measures were related to organization, facilities and equipment to be provided, or hygiene practices to be promoted. Projects are rarely linear. Changes often occur along the way any recommendations made must be adapted to those changes and implemented in a flexible manner.

As soon as preparations were made to lift restrictions in spring 2020, managers were invited to contact the global health team that I belong to in order to take advantage of the advice and assistance the team offered for preparing the return to campus. These contacts were originally made at the request of those in charge of priority services, who had approached us directly to discuss what they were thinking of doing or what had to be done. These were services or faculties that I had worked with in previous years. Communications were direct and the rules were adapted fairly rapidly as knowledge and the general situation evolved. Unfortunately, however, we had no control over the situation in services we were not familiar with because we had never worked with them.

It was more difficult for us to adapt our actions to changes in the directives issued by senior management, for we often learned about these changes through other concerned parties or only shortly before they were implemented. As for any compromises that may have needed to be made, we weren't really in a position to participate.

4 Conclusion

While I was writing this paper, a new lockdown was declared in Québec for the Christmas holidays and it will probably last until after February 8. Since the necessary measures are already in place, we basically have to respond to situations that have not yet been assessed or to new directives.

Activity analysis, the use of a project approach and the application of the precautionary principle have helped us to adapt our recommendations to the specific characteristics of each situation. One of the positive outcomes of our work for the future is perhaps the fact that the action of ergonomic advisors in risk prevention has not been focused solely on biomechanical risks.

Taking the risks faced by students into account is perhaps what prompted the university to create a student health and safety advisory position that will be in the office of the vice-rector (academic life). As ergonomists, we consider student activities to be work that cannot be view separately from that of the teachers and technicians who supervise them. To design effective prevention programs in faculties, it will be essential to think together about the safety of all the people who work on the same premises.

To facilitate communication, we will have to rethink how to better align formal organizations with informal ones. This reflection process could take place within the framework of defining a "pandemic" type action plan that could be adapted to the specific risks involved. Obviously, such a plan would incorporate issues of ventilation and eco-responsibility, occupant density, and distancing to make it easier to transition from a normal health situation to a pandemic one, without having to rethink everything. Thought should also be given to methods of communication between decision-making and operational levels, be it in the context of long-term planning or short-term changes.

Detection of Deviations from a Calm State of Mind Using Respiratory Waveforms and HRV - Aiming to Grasp the Driver's Condition Remotely

Chizuru Nakagawa$^{(\boxtimes)}$, Takahiro Watanabe, Naohiro Akiu, and Ayako Suzuki

Railway Technical Research Institute, 2-8-38, Hikari 185–8540, Japan
nakagawa.chizuru.55@rtri.or.jp

Abstract. It is important for drivers who are responsible for the lives of passengers to remain in a calm state of mind and body suitable for driving. The objective of this study is to grasp the driver's state by using physiological data that can be continuously and relatively easily measured. To provide support in a timely manner, changes in the driver's state must be detected with high time resolution and reliability. The spread of Covid-19 across the world has emphasized the importance of technology to remotely monitor physiological conditions in real time and provide support. This study attempted to improve the accuracy of estimation by using the appropriate indices for individuals. Specifically, we tried to estimate the tension state of drivers using both respiration-wave and ECG data. The results demonstrated that different individuals have different valid indicators and it is possible to improve the accuracy of estimation by using the appropriate indices for each individual.

Keywords: Physiological measurement · Respiration · ECG · Estimation of drivers condition · Railway

1 Introduction

A train driver is essentially a one-man crew. It is important that the driver, who is responsible for the lives of passengers, remain in a calm state of mind and body suitable for driving.

To ensure the driver remains in good condition, it is effective to continuously monitor the condition from the outside and provide appropriate support [1]. The spread of Covid-19 across the world has emphasized the importance of technology to remotely monitor physiological conditions in real time and provide support.

The objective of this study is to grasp the driver's state by using physiological data that can be continuously and relatively easily measured. To provide support in a timely manner, changes in the driver's state must be detected with high time resolution and reliability. Since the physiological indices vary from one individual to another, it is difficult to quantify them.

This study attempts to improve the accuracy of estimation by using the appropriate indices for each individual. The "tense" states were selected as the detection targets.

N. L. Black et al. (Eds.): IEA 2021, LNNS 222, pp. 648–651, 2021.
https://doi.org/10.1007/978-3-030-74611-7_88

Valid indicators were extracted from situations where "tension" is likely to occur, as a way to obtain the correct answer without relying on subjective evaluation.

2 Methods

We used a simplified railway driving simulator and conducted physiological measurements during the operation. The experiments were subjected to an ethical review.

There were ten voluntary participants who received sufficient explanation. As the participants were not train drivers, they drove through the practice tasks seven times to familiarize themselves with train driving.

These practice tasks were followed by four "Accident Tasks" and various "Time Pressure Tasks (TP-Tasks)". Both tasks involved driving between four stations with a 90-s rest period before and after. The duration of each task was about ten minutes.

Although various data (e.g., electroencephalogram, respiration, and sweating data) were measured, this paper reports the analysis results using only the heart rate and respiration data, which are relatively easy to obtain.

3 Data Analysis

The analysis was performed using the data of nine participants who had no problems measuring their data.

On the basis of the R-waves detected from the ECG, the heart rate (HR) and heart rate regularity (HRR) were obtained. The respiratory rate (RR) and the respiratory rate regularity (RRR) were calculated from the time points of inhalation on the respiratory waveform. HR and RR were judged to be "increasing" when the value was more than the median plus half of standard deviation (SD), and "decreasing" when the value was less than the median minus half of SD. HRR and RRR were judged to be "regular" when all differences between four consecutive values were less than or equal to half of SD, and "irregular" when all differences were greater than or equal to half of SD [2].

We extracted valid indices from situations in which the "tense" state is likely to occur, as a method of obtaining correct answers without relying on subjective evaluation. The operation of stopping a train at a station tends to make the drivers tense because the train must be stopped at a precisely fixed position. The section of the operation to stop at the station in the TP-Task was designated as section-A1, and the section in the first and second tests of the practice task was designated as section-A2.

For comparison, the Rest section of the practice task was chosen as a scene where it was difficult to become tense (Section R). However, since participants were more likely to be tense the first and second time they performed the practice task, we chose the third to seventh times as the target.

4 Results

The occurrence rates of the judgment results in Section-R, Section-A1, and Section-A2 are shown in Fig. 1.

HR increase, RR increase, HRR, and RRR were classified as "Tension Judgment", while HR decrease, RR decrease, HR irregularity, and RR irregularity were classified as "Non-Tension Judgment". For each participant, the characteristic index in the TP-Task was defined as "individual tension index (Indx-A1)".

Indx-A1 was defined as the index in which the percentage of occurrences in Section-A1 was 85% or more of the total number of occurrences in Section-R and Section-A1 combined. Indx-A2 was selected in the same way. In the figure, the bar of Indx-A1 and Indx-A2 is marked with▼.

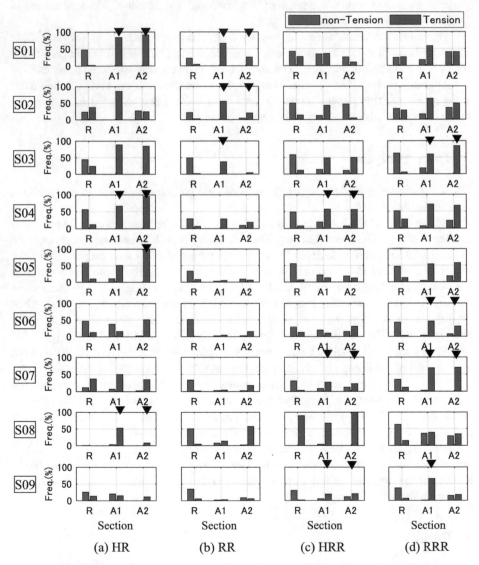

Fig. 1. Frequency of occurrence of each indicator judgment in each section.

The results showed that the indicators selected for either Indx-A1 or Indx-A2 were 4 of 9 for HR increase, 3 of 9 for RR increase, 3 of 9 for HRR, and 4 of 9 for RRR. Among the indicators selected for both sections, 3 of 4 were selected for HR increase, 2 of 3 for RR increase, 3 of 3 for HRR, and 3 of 4 for RRR.

Several indices were extracted as Indx-A1 or Indx-A2 for all participants.

5   Discussion

In all nine participants, 14 indices were selected for either Indx-A1 or Indx-A2, of which 11 (79%) were selected for both. This suggests that these tension indices are reproducible within individuals.

6   Conclusion

In this study, we attempted to estimate the tension state of drivers by using respiration-wave and ECG data. The results demonstrate that this estimation is possible if we use the appropriate indices for individual participants.

References

1. Nakagawa, C., Akiu, N., Watanabe, T., Kojma, T., Yoshie, S., Suzuki, A.: Basic study on assessment of the driver's condition based on physiological indices. Q. Rep. RTRI **60**(4), 281–285 (2019)
2. Task Force of The European Society of Cardiology and The North American Society of Pacing and Electrocardiology: Heart rate variability –Standards of measurement, Physiological Interpretation, and Clinical Use. Eur. Heart J. **17**, 354–381 (1996)

Low Burden Measurement of Autonomic Indices for Self-measurement or Longtime Measurement in the Field

Mieko Ohsuga[1]([⊠]), Yoshiyuki Kamakura[2], Hiroki Takeuchi[2], and Haruya Koba[1]

[1] Faculty of Robotics & Design, Osaka Institute of Technology, Osaka, Japan
mieko.ohsuga@oit.ac.jp
[2] Osaka Institute of Technology, Information Science and Technology, Osaka, Japan

Abstract. A low-burden method that allows the heartbeat and respiration to be measured is important for estimating a person's mental state. We examined the possibility of using smart clothing and a prototype device consisting of a low-cost kit, and assess the validity of the acquired data.

Keywords: Psychophysiology in Ergonomics · Autonomic indices · Wearable devices

1 Introduction

The need to continuously measure the human mental state without burdening the person has arisen because of the increase in the number of remote workers as a result of COVID-19. Although online work has advantages, it has many disadvantages compared with face-to-face work. Complaints abound that additional effort is required to attract attention and that mental fatigue sets in and accumulates. We are developing a low-burden method for measuring the heart rate and respiration, which is useful for estimating a person's mental state. Low-burden measurement methods can be broadly divided into three types: incorporating the sensor in a chair [1] or in the floor, using a wearable sensor, and capturing an image of the participant's face and/or body. Our aim is to develop a method that allows participants in the experiment to collect their own physiological signals and to allow them ample time to practice in an environment in which no experimenters are present, without using large-scale and expensive experimental equipment.

In terms of wearable devices, we introduced a commercially available smart garment (Hexoskin (HxS)) and a prototype device using a low-cost biosensor kit (BITalino). We examined their validity by comparing their output with the measurements of analog amplifiers for laboratory biometrics. We also discuss the acceptability of long-term measurements in the field.

2 Method

2.1 Participants

The experiment was conducted with the permission of the ethics committees of the Osaka Institute of Technology (Approved Number: 2020–7). One healthy female aged

N. L. Black et al. (Eds.): IEA 2021, LNNS 222, pp. 652–657, 2021.
https://doi.org/10.1007/978-3-030-74611-7_89

63 years participated in the experiment. The number of participants in the experiment could not be increased due to restrictions to prevent COVID-19 infection.

2.2 Measurement

An HxS device [2] was used to record the electrocardiogram (ECG), chest and abdominal respiration, and 3-axis acceleration. The BITalino [3] recorded the electrocardiogram using disposable electrodes attached to the abdomen, abdominal respiration, 3-axis acceleration, and illuminance. The BITalino circuit was placed in a case, which was attached to the belt with the breathing sensor (Fig. 1). An 8-channel analog bio-amplifier (BA 1008, Nihon Suntech) and respiratory pickup sensor (TR-751T, Nihon Kohden) of which the validity has been verified was used as the gold standard. Data obtained by both the bio-amplifier and BITalino were sampled at 1000 Hz and data from the HxS were resampled at 1000 Hz.

Fig. 1. The BITalino circuit and a wearing scenery (The model person is not the experiment participant. An illuminance sensor for time adjustment is in hand. See 2.4 for details.)

2.3 Protocol

Measurements were acquired for two different postures (sitting and standing) and under various respiratory conditions. Each trial lasted approximately 90 s. Following this, measurements were recorded for 30 min or more while the participant was working freely in the sitting position. The respiratory conditions were breathing mode (chest breathing and compound breathing) × 2 respiratory rates (inspiration: exhalation; 2: 3 s and 4: 6 s).

2.4 Data Analysis

Electrocardiogram (ECG), respiration (chest and abdomen), and acceleration for synchronization were acquired with a HxS. The sampling rates were 265 Hz, 128 Hz, and 64 Hz, respectively. These data were up-sampled to 1000 Hz by 3D spline interpolation.

The corresponding changes in acceleration were used for time adjustment between the HxS and BITalino system. The time adjustment between the analog bio-amplifier and BITalino system was executed using a LED circuit. The voltage output the circuit was input to the amplifier and the Illuminance sensor of BITalino detected the onset of LED.

The peaks of the R wave were detected after applying the R wave enhancement filter to ECG, where the threshold values were adaptively determined from past peak values. The RR intervals were converted to the instantaneous heart rate values, and the values within the set range were converted to 50 Hz equi-time interval data by three-dimensional spline interpolation. The upper and lower limits of the accepted heart rate were obtained by multiplying the median value of the surrounding data by the set ratio. The range of heart rates to be accepted was determined by setting the ratio of the surrounding data to the median. This procedure is for dealing with R wave detection errors and omissions.

The averaged heart rate (HRmean) was obtained for every 30 s frames shifted by 1 s by applying a low-pass filter with a high cutoff frequency of 0.05 Hz to the equi-time interval instantaneous heart rate. The heart rate variability (HRV) indices were calculated by applying the short-time Fast Fourier Transform (STFFT) to the same data to obtain the amplitude spectrum; Low frequency component of heart rate variability (HRVLF) in the range of 0.04–0.15 Hz and high frequency component of heart rate variability (HRVHF) in the range of 0.15–0.6 Hz were obtained. The reason for expanding the range of HF to higher frequencies than usual is that breathing becomes faster during work. For the STFFT, a humming window was applied to the data for about 30 s shifted by 1 s, and both sides were filled with zeros so that the number of data points was 2 to the 12th power (=4096) to make one frame.

The respiratory waveform was also indexed by performing spectral analysis in the same manner as for heart rate variability. The mean respiratory amplitude (RspAmp), peak respiratory frequency (PF), center of gravity frequency within half width of amplitude value at PF (GF), and the absolute value of the difference between PF and GF (|PF-GF|) as an index of respiratory instability were calculated.

3 Result

3.1 Feasibility

If we choose the size of HsX that suits the body, it will not give a feeling of oppression, there are no restrictions on physical activity, and we can wear it continuously for several hours or more. The BITalino system also imposes a small burden, but at this stage the electrodes are directly attached to the skin, so we would like to consider substituting with pulse waves in the future. In the experiment, a conventional respiratory pickup and chest electrocardiogram electrodes were attached, so that the total burden was not low.

3.2 Assessment

The ECG measurement was assessed with the performance of R wave detection and the time series data of the instantaneous heart rate value after conversion to equi-interval data. ECG obtained by the analog bio-amplifier made no detection deficiencies other than

Table 1. Experimental conditions

No.	extracted duration[s]	posture	condition	resp style	resp period
1	60	Sitting	rest	free	free
2	60	Sitting	resp control	Chest breathing	2:3
3	60	Sitting	resp control	Chest breathing	4:6
4	60	Sitting	resp control	Abdominal breathing	2:3
5	60	Sitting	resp control	Abdominal breathing	4:6
6	60	Standing	resp control	Chest breathing	2:3
7	60	Standing	resp control	Chest breathing	4:6
8	60	Standing	resp control	Abdominal breathing	2:3
9	60	Standing	resp control	Abdominal breathing	4:6
10	600	Sitting	PC work	free	free

errors observed when participants jumped at the start and end of the recording. As to the ECG by BITalino, no R wave detection error (false positive: FP) was observed except when changing postures; sitting to standing and vice versa, while a several omissions (false negative, FN) were found during the deep breath conditions. HxS also generally delivered good measurement performance; however, more numbers of FP and PN were found especially when standing. It is considered that the contact condition of the electrodes in HeX deteriorates due to the change in posture.

Figure 2 compares the time variation of the HRmean, HRVLF, HRVHF among the three devices for 11 conditions. See Table 1 for details of the conditions. It is considered that the differences in HRmean are suppressed to small values because the measurement accuracy of RR intervals is improved by up-sampling and the interpolation performed by removing the outliers by the adaptive range setting. The effect of R wave detection failure is greater in HRV, especially in HRVHF than in HRmean.

The respiratory waveforms are different because the time constants are different depending on the device and the wearing site cannot be the same. In this experiment, there was a measurement deficiency period in the measurement of the commercially available pickup and analog amplifier, which should be the gold standard. Figure 3 compares the time variation of RspAmp, GF, PF, |PF-GF|. Since it is difficult to make an absolute comparison of respiratory amplitudes, relative values are used for comparison. The differences in measures between devices are larger than HRV indices, which indicates the difficulty of respiratory measurement. The respiratory frequency indices are greatly affected by waveform distortion. The quantification method of applying a humming window to a 30-s frame is suitable for capturing rapid changes, however when a large transient breath is mixed, both PF and GF are affected by its waveform and size. This is also considered to make the differences between devices large.

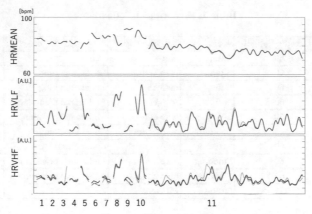

Fig. 2. Comparison in HRmean, HRVLF, HRVHF among devices (magenta:bio-amplifier, green:HxS,blue:BITalino)

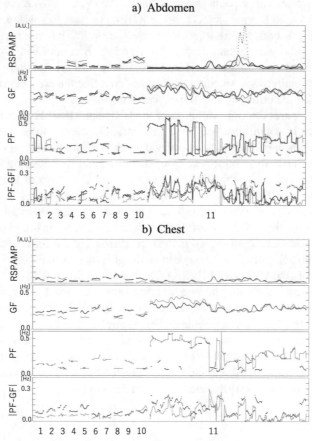

Fig. 3. Comparison in RspAmp, GF, PF, |PF-GF| among devices (magenta:bio-amplifier, green:HxS,blue:BITalino) a) Abdomen, b) Chest

4 Discussion

HxS can be worn for an entire day provided the garment fits the person snugly, and provided the resilience of respiratory measurement is high against posture changes and exercise. Although the electrocardiogram is vulnerable to body movement, the measurement situation is expected to improve when sweating occurs during exercise. It was shown again that it is necessary to pay close attention to measurement deficiencies when using the heart rate variability indices. A method to automatically detect measurement deficiencies is needed. It is also desirable to output the reliability of the evaluation value as well. It means that the processing of measurement deficiencies and outliers should not be performed in a black box.

The current prototype using BITalino can measure only one respiratory channel, hence the device is useful to estimate the respiratory rate. However, the estimation of the ventilation volume is highly likely to be incorrect as a result of changes in the breathing pattern.

5 Conclusion

Our results suggested the suitability of using a smart garment and a prototype device to record heart rate and respiration measurements in the field. In future, we aim to increase the number of participants and to proceed with quantitative validation studies involving long-term measurements. We also plan to compare the results with those obtained using wristband and ring-type mobile devices.

References

1. Ohsuga, M.: Development of chairs for nonintrusive measurement of heart rate and respiration and its application. In: Congress of the International Ergonomics Association, pp. 392–404 (2018)
2. Montes, J., Young, J.C., Tandy, R., Navalta, J.W.: Reliability and validation of the hexoskin wearable bio-collection device during walking conditions. Int. J. Exerc. Sci. **11**(7), 806 (2018)
3. Batista, D., da Silva, H.P., Fred, A., Moreira, C., Reis, M., Ferreira, H.A.: Benchmarking of the BITalino biomedical toolkit against an established gold standard. Healthc. Technol. Lett. **6**(2), 32–36 (2019)

Attitudes to Teaching and Learning Online in Higher Education During the COVID-19 Pandemic

Olga Voronina[1] ⓘ, Aleksandra Sopina[2](✉) ⓘ, Aleksandr Volosiuk[3] ⓘ,
and Julia Ostanina-Olszewska[4] ⓘ

[1] Saint Petersburg State University, Saint Petersburg, Russia
[2] Saint Petersburg Electrotechnical University, Saint Petersburg, Russia
[3] Saint Petersburg Electrotecnical University, ITMO University, Saint Petersburg, Russia
[4] Pedagogical University of Cracow, Kraków, Poland

Abstract. Currently, almost a year into the COVID-19 pandemic, the transfer to an online mode of learning does not seem to be a temporary measure anymore, but rather a viable way of studying. This study explores how people often involuntarily involved in this type of work evaluate the process and considers potential consequences. The pandemic of 2020 has brought rapid and dramatic changes in the lives of educators and students across the world. In Russia, both students and academics in higher education institutions had to adapt within a week to an online mode of working. Education process implies joint work where the course and success of the process heavily depends on the ability and readiness of all actors to contribute and respond timely. Despite reported stress both from academics and students, many universities have opted to continue online studying as a measure to prevent the spread of the disease. This study aims at analyzing the way academics and students working online conceptualize the process of online learning. Students and professors of four state universities of Saint Petersburg participated in a survey that asked to both directly evaluate the process of online learning and to give metaphorical associations. The study has revealed persistent negative psychological patterns both among students and among academics that may cause resistance to the development of a new learning space and undermine the success of the education process. The results can be used as the basis for designing adaptation trainings needed for a smoother transfer to online learning.

Keywords: Online learning · Pandemic · Conceptual metaphor · Working environment · Higher education

1 Introduction

The COVID-19 pandemic has caused an unprecedented disruption to education systems, affecting nearly 1.6 billion students in over 190 countries [1]. Lockdowns imposed all over the world and closures of educational institutions have limited physical access to

N. L. Black et al. (Eds.): IEA 2021, LNNS 222, pp. 658–663, 2021.
https://doi.org/10.1007/978-3-030-74611-7_90

educational facilities for many. In the light of this change, new online learning technologies offered educators the last lifeline and, thus, transformed the studying environment and methods of providing education irrevocably.

Despite all the benefits of online technologies, studies show that the lack of face-to-face social contact caused by the physical distancing measures due to the COVID-19 pandemic might have far-reaching consequences in the youth and it is still not clear if the access to digital forms of social interaction can mitigate the detrimental effect of social deprivation [2]. In general, according to a review study by Brooks S. K. et al., many factors associated with quarantines have a negative psychological impact on people including post-traumatic stress symptoms, confusion, and anger [3] and this impact may concern adolescents even more than adults [4, 5].

Among 38 publications in Psychology and Education about the impact of COVID-19 on education in Russia (https://elibrary.ru/), the authors of this study found only 8 concerned with higher education and aimed at revealing major psychological problems associated with online learning during the pandemic. The main psychological problems that are described by psychologists and education specialists [6–12] may be summarized as follows: suddenness of the transfer to distance learning and the lack of mental readiness for the change, lack of peer interaction, poor feedback provision, poor time management, excessive homework that does not improve academic performance, fatigue, and unevenness of the workload among students and teachers (the motivated part of students and teachers give away much physical and mental reserves). The studies also stress some advantages of online learning, such as: limited contacts with the virus carriers, the ability to study anywhere in the world and meaningfully different distribution of time.

In the spring of 2020 universities in St. Petersburg were ordered to transfer all educational processes online within weeks. This prompt decision in many cases left academics and students alone with the problem of adapting to the new sudden reality. First organized trainings, seminars, consultations and master classes on mastering programs that facilitate distant learning (Moodle, Zoom, MS Teams, Cisco Webex Meetings) appeared only in the summer of 2020. It would be expected then that in such circumstances both students and academics were particularly subjected to stress in the beginning of the pandemic and that students, who are in the most socially active stage of their lives, were hit even more than the academics.

This study, thus, aims to compare the attitudes of students and academics towards online learning during the first (the spring of 2020) and the second wave (the fall of 2020) of the COVID-19 pandemic and to determine the main factors that influenced their attitudes.

2   Method

The authors conducted two online surveys in May-June, 2020 (the end of the first semester under the COVID-19 quarantine), and in November-December, 2020 (the end of the second semester under the COVID-19 quarantine). The surveys were designed to both elicit direct comments and metaphorical associations related to online learning.

Metaphor relates to conceptualization and is often used to understand abstract or complex ideas [13, 14]. Therefore, the metaphor elicitation method was used to reveal not ready-formulated judgements, but rather beliefs and evaluations that might not have been subjected to much critical thinking. The survey asked the participants to give a metaphorical description of online learning and then to give a rationale for the choice of a specific metaphor. After that, the participants were asked to give comments about online learning in a free form. The direct and metaphorical comments were then cross-compared and analyzed.

The study involved 24 academics (8 participants in the first wave, and 16 in the second wave) and 53 students (22 and 31 participants, respectively) from four state Saint Petersburg universities (ETU, SPbU, SPbPU, SPbSUT).

The collected answers were divided into three groups: positive reactions, neutral reactions and negative reactions. Then, the metaphorical associations were annotated according to a predefined set of content analysis units to determine the factors that defined the attitudes. The units were determined in accordance with the previous findings about the most common psychological problems associated with online learning during the pandemic (see Introduction) and included concerns about the following: price/quality, basic needs (health saving), safety and stability needs, social belonging needs (affiliating, being part of a group), self-regulation needs (time management), self-actualization needs.

3   Results

Table 1. Content analysis results (shown in percentage)

Units of analysis	Students		Academics	
	Spring	Fall	Spring	Fall
Positive reactions	17.4	19.3	0	0
Neutral reactions	8.7	6.4	0	0
Negative reactions	73.2	74.2	100.0	100.0
Overall	100.0	100.0	100.0	100.0
Basic needs (health saving)	7.7	5.7	25.0	0
Safety and stability needs	7.7	17.1	8.3	23.4
Social belonging needs	3.8	22.9	33.3	72.1
Price/quality dissatisfaction	46.1	28.6	25.0	4.5
Self-regulation (time management) needs	23.1	17.1	8.3	0
Self-actualization needs	11.5	8.6	0	0
Overall	100.0	100.0	100.0	100.0

The results (see Table 1) showed a general negative attitude towards online learning both among students and academics ("bad coffee on a cold day", "loneliness in a crowd", "a hemorrhoid"). Notably, academics in this study gave no positive reactions in relation to online learning. The students appeared to be more satisfied with the new mode of studying than academics ("a game", "a hobby", "a fridge full of food"). Contrary to the expectations, the results revealed no major shift in the attitude during the second wave of the pandemic in both groups, which demonstrated that the trainings and seminars offered by the universities in the summer of 2020 could not fully meet the needs of the academics and students. The factors that defined the attitude towards online learning during the second wave, however, changed.

The main factors that determined the attitude of the students in the first wave are price/quality dissatisfaction ("a parody", "delivery of a very expensive pizza", "Schrodinger's studying"). In their comments, some students openly stated that the quality of the provided online education is not worth the money paid. In addition, many metaphors revealed concerns about self-regulation and motivation of the students ("slavery because of your own lack of action", "a fight with yourself"). It appears that the students feel more strain working on their own and that online learning does not provide enough supervision and encouragement to keep students active.

In the second wave, students became less concerned with the price/quality issue and self-regulation problems, some even gave positive comments (not metaphorical ones, though) about new time management opportunities, such as saving time on commute, flexibility in choosing time for classes. At the same time, in their metaphorical answers, students emphasized two more negative factors, which are: unmet safety and stability needs ("the great unknown", "turning everything upside down", "to swim in the ocean without a lifeline", "struggle", "pour a bucket of cold water on your head", "trying to get out of the forest") and social belonging needs, affiliating and being part of a group ("a solo dance", "a bird in a cage", "distance relationships"). This may indicate the accumulative effects of social deprivation and uncertainty with continuously changing regulations. In their comments in both waves students also identified problems associated with fatigue ("… in the beginning there was a terrible load, endless homework, from which the eyes and head literally hurt"), but this was not reflected in their metaphorical associations.

The analysis of the metaphorical answers given by academics demonstrated that two notable in the first wave factors, namely price/quality ("a labour of Sisyphus", "thumping on the closed door - useless") and unmet basic needs (health saving) ("schizophrenia - too many tasks", "a hemorrhoid"), almost completely disappeared in the second wave. To the contrary, academics showed more concern with their social belonging needs ("you sit in your mini-vacuum", "dialogue with yourself", "performance in front of Malevich's black square"). This factor became more prevalent in determining their attitude towards online learning than any other factor. Direct comments on their dissatisfaction with the feedback from their students demonstrated the same results ("you don't have the slightest idea of what is happening on the other side of the screen", "it is not clear what the students are doing when you give them a lecture").

Interestingly, the results showed that the transfer to online learning motivated self-actualization thoughts only among students ("exploration of an unknown planet", "the way of Samurai"). It appears that academics do not see this new mode of learning as a ground for self-development.

4 Conclusions

The study revealed some dynamics in the attitudes of academics and students towards online learning during the COVID-19 pandemic. Initial concerns about the price/quality ratio of online learning, among students in particular, significantly decreased during the second wave. Open criticism of the work of academics in the spring wave of the pandemic may have been associated with the rigidity of academics who were unable to respond promptly and creatively to the changes or did not have enough technical skills for that. It seems that the seminars and master-classes on new online platforms offered before the second wave helped to partially resolve this issue.

At the same time academics seem to be completely dissatisfied with the new form of teaching and especially concerned about their unmet social belonging needs. The results report a similar kind of dissatisfaction among the students. Policy makers, education specialists, and engineers should work on the development of new methods of online interaction that could mitigate the lack of face-to-face interaction and feedback.

Students are also concerned with their self-regulation abilities and lack of motivation, which proves that they need additional support and encouragement. Educational institutions should provide more tools for students to develop their time management skills and self-motivation.

Consideration of these factors, on an equal basis with the development of relevant software and infrastructure, is paramount for further incorporation of online learning in educational processes, as satisfaction of students and educators defines their joint contribution and results.

References

1. Policy Brief: Education during COVID-19 and beyond. https://www.un.org/development/desa/dspd/wp-content/uploads/sites/22/2020/08/sg_policy_brief_covid-19_and_education_august_2020.pdf. Accessed 31 Jan 2021
2. Orben, A., et al.: The effects of social deprivation on adolescent development and mental health. Lancet. Child Adolesc. Health **4**(8), 634–640 (2020)
3. Brooks, S.K., et al.: The psychological impact of quarantine and how to reduce it. Rapid Rev. Evid. **395**, 912–920 (2020)
4. Sorokin, M.: Psihologicheskie reakcii naseleniya kak faktor adaptacii k pandemii COVID – 19. Obozrenie psihiatrii i medicinskoj psihologii **2**, 87–94 (2020)
5. Arbuzova, E.: Ocenka psihologicheskogo sostoyaniya i resursov sovladayushchego povedeniya obuchayushchihsya obrazovatel'noj organizacii MVD Rossii v usloviyah samoizolyacii. Vestnik Sankt – Peterburgskogo universiteta MVD Rossii **3**(87), 218–226 (2020)
6. Kartezhnikov, D., Kartezhnikova, A.: Psihologicheskie trudnosti u studentov pri distancionnogo obuchenii vo vremya pandemii. https://www.elibrary.ru/item.asp?id=44311012. Accessed 20 Jan 2021
7. Malyh, S.: Adaptaciya prepodavatelej universiteta k distancionnomu obucheniyu vo vremya pandemii. V sbornike: V poiskah social'noj istiny. Materialy II Mezhdunarodnoj nauchno-prakticheskoj konferencii. Red: Polyushkevich O., Druzhinina G., pp. 349–352 (2020)
8. Harlamova, T.: Specifika psihicheskogo sostoyaniya i koping-strategij studentov pri distancionnom obuchenii v usloviyah pandemii COVID-19. Vestnik Permskogo gosudarstvennogo gumanitarno -pedagogicheskogo universiteta. Psihologicheskie i pedagogicheskie nauki **1**, 26–39 (2020)

9. Vahanceva, O., Almazova, O., Novikova, Y.U.: Riski onlajn obucheniya: Prokrastinaciya u studentov v period samoizolyacii v svyazi s pandemiej COVID-19. Gercenovskie chteniya: Psihologicheskie issledovaniya v obrazovanii **3**, 750–756 (2020)

10. Yakobyuk, L.: Izuchenie vliyaniya distancionnoj formy obucheniya vo vremya pandemii na rezul'taty obucheniya.Mir nauki, kul'tury, obrazovaniya **5**(84), 179–181 (2020)

11. Adil'gazinov, G.: Distancionnoe obuchenie v usloviyah pandemii koronavirusa - glazami prepodavatelej. Annali d'Italia **10**(3), 52–58 (2020)

12. Tsabolova, O.: Global'nye riski i problemy distancionnogo obucheniya do i posle pandemii COVID-19. Obshchestvo, doverie, riski, pp. 275–280 (2020)

13. Lakoff, G., Johnson, M.: Metaphors we live by. University of Chicago Press, Chicago (1981)

14. Wan, W., Low, G.: Elicited Metaphor Analysis in Educational DIscourse. John Benjamins Publishing Co, Amsterdam (2015)

Covid 19 - Limiting and Managing Risk in a Physiotherapy School

William Suarez[✉]

Hôpitaux Saint-Maurice, 94069 Saint-Maurice, France
William.suarez@ght94n.fr

Abstract. The Covid 19 pandemic has changed our working and our living conditions, the environment has become hostile. We propose to briefly present an ergonomic intervention aiming at resuming classes in a physiotherapy school in the Parisian suburbs in this crisis context. The intervention was a confrontation of Covid's recommendations (evolving regularly) with the functioning of the lessons. The main problems questioned were: the school being closed during the intervention there was no activity, how to intervene without observing the activity? How to take into account that the privet's practices of the students' school have an influence on the health situation inside? Therefore, we imagined with the trainers a phase of perceptive simulation activity (PS) on the "residual" activity in order to have a representation of the organization of the lessons. In a second time, a transparent relationship with the students was established with the main idea "what you do outside has an influence inside (the school)". Intervening in pandemic was new conditions. It was therefore necessary to adapt the methods of intervention to the situation and ergonomics allows this adaptability to situations. In the idea of empowering interventions, the system and the individuals (teachers and students) have adapted, evolved over the course of the recommendations and the appearance of Covid 19 cases. Both groups have probably developed their theoretical, practical and organizational knowledge of infectiology, which is an asset for caregivers or future caregivers. Finally, the ergonomist has also developed and adapted his practice to the singular situation.

Keywords: Covid 19 · Ergonomics · Hostile environment · Perceptive simulation activity · Enabling environments

1 Problem

Training as a masseur-physiotherapist is a combination of theoretical scientific contributions (anatomy, biomechanics, physiology…), practical teaching (manipulations, massages…) and professional elements through internships in professional environments (hospital or private practice).

The challenge of resuming teaching during the pandemic crisis was to preserve the quality of a maximum of these components of this training while minimizing the *Covid 19* risk, in this population of students, teachers, professionals and patients.

N. L. Black et al. (Eds.): IEA 2021, LNNS 222, pp. 664–670, 2021.
https://doi.org/10.1007/978-3-030-74611-7_91

The approach we have taken is innovative on several points: a health crisis of this magnitude has never been experienced and managed by our generations, the *Covid 19* risk goes beyond the framework of the school and/or the internship. Individuals, generally considered as resources for collective performance, become dangerous for each other and the environment becomes hostile.

The activity analysis approach, which is the basis of ergonomic intervention, has not been carried out in the traditional way in the sense that teaching activity was suspended. It was therefore necessary to adapt the approach to this new context: a new way of intervening for the development of a future activity in a non-activity context was developed.

In this new context, in addition to organizing flows and adapting teaching methods, a relationship of trust had to be created with the students. This process enabled us to get feedback on their festive gatherings outside the institution for example, to find out about the conditions of these gatherings and to give recommendations on their organization. The implementation of vigilance on their part and on our part on the appearance of signs (linked to the *Covid 19* disease) following these gatherings was facilitated.

This last point is new because it goes beyond the responsibility of the structure but "what happens outside can have consequences inside (the school) and vice versa".

2   Context

The Physiotherapy school is located inside a hospital on the suburbs of Paris. It depends administratively on the hospital but also on the university. In this context, Covid 19 risk management is shared but for reasons of proximity it is mainly managed by the school director, his team and the hospital ergonomist.

2.1   Covid 19, a Hostile Environment [1]

A hostile environment is one in which human activity is complex, restrictive and extremely hazardous to health. This is the case, for example, for manned flights [2] or activities in the Antarctic [3, 4].

Working in the world of care has exposed caregivers to a number of specific risks such as accidents involving exposure to blood or the risk of infection. These are known and often limited. For example, a contagious patient will be identified and isolated in his room during his care.

The emergence of a *SARS-Cov 2* pandemic has created a change in the work environment and more broadly in society. At the hospital, the risk of infection was essentially on the "patient side". It is now ubiquitous: co-workers are also becoming a threat. There is therefore a shift from a known and controlled (although dynamic) environment to a dangerous, hostile environment.

One of the major differences with environments such as manned flight or exercise in Antarctica is that the operators working there have chosen to work there with knowledge of the risks already present. Moreover, in any activity, the work collective is a resource for developing performance and safety [5]. The *SARS-Cov 2* pandemic has led to a change in the working environment: everyone becomes at risk for each other. Evolving in this new environment is a constraining factor and requires adaptation in line with changes in national and local health conditions.

2.2   Finding an Alternative to "traditional" Activity Analysis in a Hostile Environment Without Activity

The demand was finally a perspective of future organization with the appearance of new constraints linked to *Covid 19*. In "normal" times, a phase of understanding the activity would have been set up and then a phase of organizational simulation of the future activity would have followed [6].

This method could not be put in place because the students were not present and therefore the teaching activity did not exist and could not be analyzed. It was therefore necessary to deal with this singularity. A "perceptive simulation" (SP) was initially carried out with the teachers in order to understand the organization of the teaching of (specific) practical work, in amphitheaters and in (more traditional) direct work.

One point, not the least, was that even masked we could not spend hours discussing and debating because the *Covid 19* risk would become too important for all of us.

3   Actions

At the end of the holidays (time without students), the school director asked the ergonomist to work on the organization of the new school year in September.

The first step was to understand the nominal teaching situations. While taking into account this "perceptual simulation" would be incomplete because part of the actors (students) could not be consulted. The teachers "played" their lessons in order to gain an understanding of how they were conducted. The ergonomist's questions, aimed at clarifying a certain number of practices, enabled him to gain knowledge (although partial) of the operation of the different types of teaching.

The second step was to imagine together a *Covid* compatible organization that respects the recommendations as much as possible but preserves the quality of the teaching: the teachers again played their future courses essentially practical work.

At the end of these "perceptive simulations" carried out in the places concerned, a global point was made with the team, some members of which were not present during the *SPs*. The objectives were to present to the whole team the axes of evolution of their activity and to open them to debate.

The proposals were not standard but adapted to each activity and the specificity of each premise. The ergonomist managed these different steps in collaboration with the teachers.

The wearing of masks was imposed. For the practical work where physical efforts could be made, the wearing of masks was discussed and finally adopted, the efforts being of moderate intensity.

3.1   Teachings

During the teachings in the amphitheater, there was a debate: what protection for the microphone in order to protect the various speakers during the passage of the microphone, what number of people can be accommodated, at what moment the presence is limited, for example.

Practical work was the most discussed part. It was necessary to combine maintaining the quality of the practical work with the *Covid* risk. The group logic was adopted: groups of students will be able to work together, without rotating with other groups and designing the specific material for each group.

3.2 Administrative Part

The flows were studied for the administrative premises, in particular the enrolments phases, but also in the various movements within the establishment.

The use of cloakrooms and toilets and the documentation center were also discussed along the same lines.

3.3 The Process of Collaboration with Student

It was decided to give the student a briefing on the organization of the school with regard to the *Covid 19* risk at each promotion. He took over the national health measures as well as the specific organization set up within the school. A large part of these interventions was reserved for questions about *Covid 19* (preventive measures, population at risk, tests…). A specific and new point was strongly discussed: the relationship of trust to be established between the teaching team and the students on the activities outside school. The aim is not to forbid everything (which the school cannot do…) but to have a feedback on extra-activities, and potentially give an opinion on specific activities (such as sports "Olympics" organized for new students).

Exchanges with the student office in charge of organizing events such as the integration of new students have been set up.

4   Outcomes

The first physical contact with the students was the registration. They took place as planned, but in the open air with appointments being made. For the handing over of documents, the personal protective equipment used were masks and visors for the agents receiving the students. Hand hygiene using hydro-alcoholic solution was adopted by everyone.

The lectures started normally at the beginning and then quickly with part of the classes present, the other part by videoconference and an established rotation.

Practical work was one of the most worked points: the quality of the teaching is based on the students' ability to handle various templates. The group logic was adopted: for example, for a group of 12 students, 2 groups of 6 were formed, they rotate among these groups with rehabilitation material specific to each group. Usually the teachers stayed in their classrooms and the students changed, but now it is the other way around in order to limit the number of people moving around. Soon, the classrooms were moved to the amphitheaters in order to benefit from a much larger volume and to limit the risks linked to transmission by air.

A relationship with the students was established following meetings with the students' office and "*Covid*" topos' at each promotion by the ergonomist. The objectives being to present some notions of infectiology and the state of knowledge of *Covid 19*. The new organization was of course discussed as well as the fact that the "outside" activities of all have an influence on the activities of the school.

A "transparent" relationship of students is in place: they report to each other when they are *Covid* + or suspects, isolate themselves and transmit the list of potential contacts cases of the school.

These exchanges with the students are new, as the health situation requires it, and have made it possible to maintain the quality of teaching at a level that is not very poor and to avoid any contamination acquired within the school during the first semester. The ergonomist collaborates with a *Covid* reference teacher to answer questions about the *Covid* from certain students, in particular about screening and isolation procedures.

5   Discussion

The questioning of organizations (flow management, organization of signs) and means of prevention are in the end fairly standard whatever the environment.

The national health situation and the local situation where the activity had to be understood when it was not being carried out require an adaptation of the activity analysis methods, and a form of "perceptive simulation" has been adopted. It was piloted by the ergonomist who presented the method to the teachers. Openness to debate was, of course, one of the main threads of the approach.

Another specific feature of this intervention was the relationship of trust established with the trio of students, the teaching team and the ergonomist. This results in almost daily exchanges between the students and the teacher-referral-ergonomist duo. The students who identify themselves as *Covid* + and or contact cases isolate themselves spontaneously or ask for advice on how to proceed. They also provide a list of potential contact cases among their fellow students if necessary. At the beginning, as national recommendations evolved, exchanges were on a multi-daily basis. Then the ergonomist was informed, but students and teachers have acquired the *Covid* management logic so that the ergonomist was only consulted in cases deemed to be complex. This perhaps reveals the developmental and sustainable aspect of the intervention.

The increase in students' skills concerning the *Covid* risk is probably broader: they have acquired knowledge about risk management but also about the risk of infection, which is interesting for future caregivers. This opens up a possible field of study on the contribution of the *Covid* crisis and its consequences for the training of care workers. These skills were later mobilized during the risk management lessons given by the ergonomist in December, with the case of *Covid 19* experienced by the students serving as a basis for the teaching. It is clear that, compared with subsequent courses of the same type, the current students had a more solid foundation in risk management, particularly infectious risks, than former groups of students. This is a subjective reflection linked to certain exchanges during the courses.

Another study would be interesting to carry out: it would focus on the physiological and psychological constraints linked to the wearing of masks. The current studies are essentially laboratory studies but few are in active situations. It could even be the subject of a collaboration within the framework of a work at the end of a physiotherapy study.

6 Conclusion

Crisis intervention is complex. It is all the more so for the health crisis that we are going through, because this pandemic is global and is not limited to an environment of work, the educational sphere or private life: the environment is hostile. The *Covid 19* and trans-environment crisis and intervention must also try to be.

One of the bases of the success of the management of this crisis among this population of student masseur-physiotherapists is based on a collaboration in which the main actors are the teaching team, the students and the ergonomist with the idea that "what happens outside the school can have an impact on the inside".

The intervention briefly developed in this communication has allowed on the one hand to manage the *Covid* risk in this training institute while conceiving a quality teaching.

The constraints imposed by the crisis made it possible to develop new ways of intervention, an example of which we briefly develop with the "perceptive simulations", a form of activity analysis without directly observable activity.

This unprecedented health situation implies a re-conception of a certain number of work tasks, some of which were quickly set up on the arrival of the financial crisis (teleworking, videoconferencing meetings, tele-consultations, etc.). This constructive, developmental and adaptive aspect of working environments is not new. It is studied and developed in particular through constructive ergonomics [7] and encouraged by the implementation of so-called enabling environments [8].

The forced introduction of new ways of working has been an opportunity to test them, even if their effectiveness has been only partial. The de-confinement offers an opportunity to reflect on their maintenance in routine and/or their development.

In spite of the obligation to adapt quickly, the system has held and even developed, probably because of its resilience. The teams have adapted to the changing environment by coping. Some of them have come out of it, probably better.

References

1. Suarez, W.: SARS-Cov 19 : une mutation de l'environnement de travail hospitalier, naissance d'un environnement hostile. Techniques Hospitalières (2020)
2. Rivolier, J.: L'homme dans l'espace : Une approche psycho-écologique des vols habités. Paris : PUF (1997)
3. Palinkas, L.A., Johnson, J.C., et al.: Effect of culture on social dynamics and individual performance in Antarctica. In: Peri, A., (ed.) Proceedings of the Second Italian Workshop on Human Adaptation in Antarctica and Extreme Environments. Rome (2001)
4. Villemain, A.: Etude exploratoire de la construction de la sécurité en environnement hostile : L'exemple du raid polaire (2014)
5. Caroly, S., Barcellini, F.: Le développement de l'activité collective. Ergonomie constructive 33–45 (2013)

6. Van Belleghem, L.: La simulation de l'activité en conception ergonomique : acquis et perspectives. Activités 15–1 (2018)
7. Falzon, P.: Ergonomie constructive. PUF, Paris (2013)
8. Falzon P.: Ergonomics, knowledge development and the design of enabling environments, Humanizing Work and Work Environments, Guwahati, India (2005)

The Application of Systems Ergonomics to the Design of a Mobile COVID-19 Laboratory

Abigail R. Wooldridge$^{(\boxtimes)}$ (iD)

University of Illinois At Urbana-Champaign, Urbana, IL 21801, USA
arwool@illinois.edu

Abstract. The development of affordable, efficient, effective and accessible surveillance testing has been a focus since the emergence of SARS-CoV-2 coronavirus (i.e., COVID-19) in December 2019. Systems ergonomics can play an important role in pandemic response efforts beyond formal health care settings, including the translation of those tests to support community health. In this paper, the important role systems ergonomics on a project to design and prototype a mobile COVID-19 laboratory are described. In future, we should develop methods and strategies that are rapid and support use by individuals with limited training in systems ergonomics.

Keywords: Systems ergonomics · Macroergonomics · COVID-19 · Community health · Translational research

1 Introduction

COVID-19 was first reported in China in December 2019, becoming a pandemic by March 2020 (Zhou et al. 2020). Many governments limited activities beyond the essential to contain the disease. Continued cessation of activity presents economic and social challenges, and secondary surges of infection are occurring as activities resume. Previous outbreaks demonstrated the importance of surveillance testing to resume activity (Kelly-Cirino et al. 2019). Researchers developed novel tests that could support community surveillance if translated properly, e.g., the saliva to RT-qPCR test developed at the University of Illinois at Urbana-Champaign (Ranoa et al. 2020). Systems ergonomics was a critical component to translate this test beyond campus.

A translational research project, called mobileSHIELD, led by the author, was supported by the University of Illinois System to design, prototype and pilot a mobile laboratory that could make the RT-qPCR COVID-19 test available where additional testing capacity is needed – for example, in communities with limited testing access to reduce health inequities, on other college campuses, or to support reopening of businesses. See https://grainger.illinois.edu/news/features/illinois-mobile-shield for more details about the project. Given the author's background, various systems ergonomics principles were used at various stages throughout the project.

© The Author(s), under exclusive license to Springer Nature Switzerland AG 2021
N. L. Black et al. (Eds.): IEA 2021, LNNS 222, pp. 671–673, 2021.
https://doi.org/10.1007/978-3-030-74611-7_92

2 Objective

The objective of this proposal is to describe and reflect on the application of systems ergonomics to the design and implementation of the saliva to RT-qPCR COVID-19 test, i.e., throughout mobileSHIELD.

3 Systems Ergonomics in MobileSHIELD

The goal of the project was to design and pilot a system to conduct COVID-19 testing that is not fixed in a specific geographic location. This system includes the registration of patients, collection of specimens, laboratory analysis and reporting of results. mobileSHIELD was interdisciplinary, spanned organizational boundaries (i.e., multiple colleges, institutes and industrial partners) and was led by a systems ergonomist. As such, much of the project was structured following systems ergonomics principles, as follow.

1. Clearly defined and agreed upon system scope (Edwards and Jensen 2014): at the outset, the systems ergonomist defined a proposed scope from target site identification through setup, testing and site breakdown.
2. Identification and participation of stakeholders (Dul et al. 2012; Edwards and Jensen 2014): by conducting rapid interviews with subject-matter experts, the ergonomist was able to identify system actors and experts to include on the design team and system decision makers and influencers to engage as needed.
3. Gathering process knowledge with focus on interactions and context (Edwards and Jensen 2014; Wilson 2014): with the team, the initial scope was refined and narrowed. The team conducted observations and interviews to gather process and system knowledge for modeling, analysis and design. In addition to adapting the SEIPS-based process modeling method (Wooldridge et al. 2017), the ergonomist developed diagrams to support multiple perspectives and identify important interactions between work system elements (Wooldridge & Hale-Lopez, Accepted).
4. Building explicit feedback loops in the system for continuous design improvement (Edwards and Jensen 2014; Wilson and Carayon 2014): the ergonomist and information technology designers worked together to develop usable dashboards and metrics that would support daily operations in the laboratory and provide insight into overall performance.
5. Consideration of outcomes including and beyond well-being and performance (Edwards and Jensen 2014; Zink 2014): by definition, this project focuses on important societal and economic outcomes (e.g., containment of COVID-19 and reopening of businesses and other activities); however, environmental outcomes were not examined. While special attention was paid to minimize waste, many supplies and materials are plastic, biohazardous waste, precluding recycling. This is an important opportunity for future work.

4 Discussion and Conclusion

Ergonomics and human factors, in particular systems ergonomics, can and should play a central role in responses to global emergencies like pandemics. This proposal describes one such application to enable affordable, efficient, effective and equitably accessible surveillance testing to support community health during the COVID-19 pandemic. The mobileSHIELD project highlights the use of systems ergonomics approaches and methods while identifying specific opportunities to enhance future impact. Notably, methodologies that are rapid and can be applied by individuals with limited-to-no training in systems ergonomics are needed; for example, checklists and a toolkit could be very useful. As a discipline, we could contribute strategies to sustainably handle medical and biohazard waste from health care systems. We also need continued efforts to broaden awareness of the ergonomics/human factors discipline to ensure we are included in responses to societal crises.

References

Dul, J., Bruder, R., Buckle, P., Carayon, P., Falzon, P., Marras, W.S., Wilson, J.R., van der Doelen, B.: A strategy for human factors/ergonomics: developing the discipline and profession. Ergonomics 55(4), 377–395 (2012). https://doi.org/10.1080/00140139.2012.661087

Edwards, K., Jensen, P.L.: Design of systems for productivity and well-being. Appl. Ergon. 45(1), 26–32 (2014)

Kelly-Cirino, C.D., Nkengasong, J., Kettler, H., Tongio, I., Gay-Andrieu, F., Escadafal, C., Piot, P., Peeling, R.W., Gadde, R., Boehme, C.: Importance of diagnostics in epidemic and pandemic preparedness. BMJ Global Health 4(Suppl 2), e001179–e001179 (2019). https://doi.org/10.1136/bmjgh-2018-001179

Ranoa, D., Holland, R., Alnaji, F.G., Green, K., Wang, L., Brooke, C., Burke, M., Fan, T., Hergenrother, P.J.: Saliva-Based Molecular Testing for SARS-CoV-2 that Bypasses RNA Extraction. BioRxiv (2020)

Wilson, J.R.: Fundamentals of systems ergonomics/human factors. Appl. Ergon. 45(1), 5–13 (2014)

Wilson, J.R., Carayon, P.: (2014, 1//). Systems ergonomics: looking into the future–editorial for special issue on systems ergonomics/human factors. Appl. Ergon. 45(1), 3–4. https://doi.org/10.1016/j.apergo.2013.08.007

Wooldridge, A.R., Carayon, P., Hundt, A.S., Hoonakker, P.L.T.: SEIPS-based process modeling in primary care. Appl. Ergon. 60, 240–254 (2017). https://doi.org/10.1016/j.apergo.2016.11.010

Wooldridge, A.R., Hale-Lopez, K.: (Accepted). Human Factors/Ergonomics-Based Process Analysis and Improvement of a COVID-19 Laboratory Testing Process Healthcare Systems Process Improvement Conference 2021 (2021)

Zhou, P., Yang, X.-L., Wang, X.-G., Hu, B., Zhang, L., Zhang, W., Si, H.-R., Zhu, Y., Li, B., Huang, C.-L., Chen, H.-D., Chen, J., Luo, Y., Guo, H., Jiang, R.-D., Liu, M.-Q., Chen, Y., Shen, X.-R., Wang, X., Zheng, X.-S., Zhao, K., Chen, Q.-J., Deng, F., Liu, L.-L., Yan, B., Zhan, F.-X., Wang, Y.-Y., Xiao, G.-F., Shi, Z.-L.: (2020, 2020/03/01). A pneumonia outbreak associated with a new coronavirus of probable bat origin. Nature 579(7798), 270–273. https://doi.org/10.1038/s41586-020-2012-7

Zink, K.J.: (2014, 2014/01/01/). Designing sustainable work systems: the need for a systems approach. Appl. Ergon. 45(1), 126–132. https://doi.org/10.1016/j.apergo.2013.03.023

Part IV: Musculoskeletal Disorders
(Edited by Ann Marie Dale)

Work-Related Exposures and Musculoskeletal Disorder Symptoms Among Informal E-Waste Recyclers at Agbogbloshie, Ghana

Augustine A. Acquah[1] (iD), Clive D'Souza[2](✉) (iD), Bernard Martin[2] (iD),
John Arko-Mensah[1], Isabella A. Quakyi[1], Niladri Basu[3] (iD), Thomas G. Robins[4] (iD),
and Julius N. Fobil[1] (iD)

[1] Department of Biological, Environmental and Occupational Health Sciences,
School of Public Health, University of Ghana, P.O. Box LG13, Accra, Ghana
[2] Center for Ergonomics, Department of Industrial & Operations Engineering,
University of Michigan, Ann Arbor, MI 48109-2117, USA
crdsouza@umich.edu
[3] Faculty of Agricultural and Environmental Sciences, McGill University, Montréal,
QC 9X 3V9, Canada
[4] Department of Environmental Health Sciences, University of Michigan, Ann Arbor,
MI 48109-2029, USA

Abstract. Recycling of electrical and electronic waste (e-waste) in developing countries is mostly conducted in the informal sector consisting of low skilled workers. Informal e-waste recycling predominantly involves the physically demanding work of manually collecting, dismantling and burning of e-waste items to extract reusable components and valuable metals including gold or copper. This cross-sectional study investigated the effects of manual e-waste recycling work on the musculoskeletal health of 176 workers at Agbogbloshie in Accra, Ghana – the largest informal e-waste dumpsites in Africa. Findings indicate significant associations between prolonged walking and weighted MSD symptom scores for the lower extremities, and between manual material handlings tasks and weighted MSD symptom scores for the upper extremities and lower back. The study calls attention to the need for ergonomics research in the informal work sector to promote safer practices and address a range of worker health concerns.

Keywords: Electronic waste · Informal work · Musculoskeletal disorders · Exposure

1 Introduction

High demand and overconsumption of electronic and electrical appliances (e.g., computers, cellphones, and refrigerators) has created a global challenge of managing discarded and waste products [1, 2]. Each year vast amounts of discarded electronic and electrical waste (e-waste) from Europe and North America make their way into developing countries under the guise of donations and end up at dumpsites [3, 4].

© The Author(s), under exclusive license to Springer Nature Switzerland AG 2021
N. L. Black et al. (Eds.): IEA 2021, LNNS 222, pp. 677–681, 2021.
https://doi.org/10.1007/978-3-030-74611-7_93

The processing and recycling of e-waste in developing countries is almost exclusively manual, informal, unregulated and conducted by low-skilled workers, with little or no attention to occupational health and safety practices such as the use of personal protective equipment or properly designed workstations [5].

This study focused on Agbogbloshie in Accra, Ghana. Agbogbloshie is the largest dumping ground for e-waste in sub-Saharan Africa and among the busiest informal e-waste recycling sites in the world [3, 6]. Multiple recent studies conducted at Agbogbloshie document the environmental effects of informal, unregulated e-waste recycling [7, 8]. Studies also suggest a high level of manual material handling (MMH; e.g., lifting, carrying) in a harsh outdoor environment [9–12]. These conditions are known risk factors for work-related musculoskeletal disorders (MSDs), however, little is known about their effects on the musculoskeletal health of informal e-waste workers (EWWs).

The objective of this study was to investigate the relationship between self-reported ergonomic exposures and work-related MSD symptoms in a diverse cohort of EWWs at the Agbogbloshie e-waste dumpsite and non-EWWs at a comparison site.

2 Methodology

2.1 Study Sample

The study was conducted from August to October 2018 using a cross-sectional design. The study recruited 176 EWWs (including 73 e-waste collectors, 82 dismantlers and 21 burners) at the Agbogbloshie site, and 41 reference workers from a comparison site – Madina Zongo (MZ), that were not engaged in e-waste processing. The ethical review committee of the University of Ghana, College of Health Sciences approved the study. All participants provided written informed consent.

2.2 Data Collection Procedure

First, participants were administered a questionnaire to obtain information on age, gender, primary job category, years of working in the current job, typical hours worked per day, and days worked per week.

Next, the Cornell Musculoskeletal Discomfort Questionnaire (CMDQ) was administered to obtain information about MSD symptoms [13, 14]. The CMDQ assesses musculoskeletal symptoms collectively described as discomfort, aches and pains experienced in the last 7 days for 11 different body parts on three rating scales, *frequency*, *severity*, and *work interference*. An aggregate MSD symptom score, referred to as *pain score* was computed by multiplying the weighted *frequency* (0, 1.5, 3.5, 5.0, 10.0), *severity* (1.0, 2.0, 3.0) and *work interference* (1.0, 2.0, 3.0) ratings. Weighted scores were obtained for four body regions, lower extremities (sum of both knees, lower legs, thighs, and hips/buttocks), upper extremities (sum of both shoulders, upper arms, forearms, and wrists), the upper back and neck, and the lower back.

Lastly, a modified Occupational Physical Activity Questionnaire (Reis et al., 2005) was used to assess self-reported exposure to physical work factors characterized as the frequency of prolonged (> 4 h) sitting, standing, and walking, and frequency of performing lifting, carrying, and pushing-pulling in a typical work-week on a 5-point ordinal scale [15]. For the present analyses, exposures were re-categorized as either 'high' (once daily or more) vs. 'low' (ranging from never to '3–4 times a week'). OPAQ also asks for the maximum weight handled during MMH on a 5-point scale in 5 kg increments. For analysis, we re-categorized the maximum weight handled as either 'high' (> 10 kg) vs. 'low' (≤ 10 kg).

When responding to the CMDQ and OPAQ, participants were instructed to use the previous full workweek as the reference period (i.e., a 7-day period starting Monday morning). Questionnaires were administered in English, and when needed, explanations were given in Dagbani, the local dialect spoken by e-waste workers.

2.3 Statistical Analyses

Descriptive statistics for demographics, weighted pain scores, and physical exposures (binary) were computed for the EWW and MZ groups. Mixed effects analyses were used to examine the relationship between pain scores for each body region as the outcome variable, and demographics and binary exposure variables as predictors. We present only the reduced models. Statistical analyses were conducted in IBM SPSS v24.

3 Results

3.1 Summary Statistics

Participants were all men with an average ± SD age of 25.9 ± 7.3 years, work experience of 6.7 ± 5.8 years, and worked 6 ± 1 days/week and 9.9 ± 2.7 h/day. Pain scores were significantly higher in the EWW vs. MZ group for the lower extremities (mean ± SD: 20.7 ± 32.6 vs. 7.3 ± 18.5; $p = 0.051$), upper extremities (21.0 ± 39.1 vs. 8.5 ± 21.7; $p = 0.012$), but not for lower back (12.1 ± 16.3 vs. 7.2 ± 13.0; $p = 0.077$) nor the upper back & neck (6.2 ± 12.1 vs. 3.3 ± 8.3; $p = 0.148$). Self-reported exposure to prolonged walking (53 vs. 16%), daily lifting (79 vs. 39%), carrying (77 vs. 29%), pushing-pulling (42 vs. 12%), and heavy load handling (90 vs. 42%) were higher in the EWW vs. MZ group; but similar in terms of prolonged standing (22 vs. 24%) and sitting (32 vs. 33%).

3.2 Associations Between Work Exposures and MSD Symptoms

Mixed effect analysis for lower extremity pain scores indicated significant effects of age ($B = -0.9 ± 0.4$ unit decrease per 1-year age increase; $p = 0.017$), of days worked per week ($B = 5.8 ± 2.6$ increase for every additional day worked per week; $p = 0.026$), for prolonged walking ($B = 15.0 ± 5.4$; $p = 0.006$) and prolonged standing ($B = -24.9 ± 6.4$; $p < 0.001$). Negative associations with age might suggest a healthy worker effect (i.e., affected workers leaving the work force over time), and for prolonged standing possibly due to less strenuous activity among workers standing compared to walking, respectively. Significant predictors of upper extremity pain scores were days worked per week ($B = 4.9 ± 2.2$; $p = 0.025$) and maximum weight handled ($B = 11.9 ± 5.3$; $p = 0.025$). Frequent lifting ($B = 4.7 ± 2.3$; $p = 0.048$) was the only significant predictor of pain scores for the lower back. Pain scores for the upper back & neck were generally low and did not yield any significant predictors.

4 Discussion

EWWs at Agbogbloshie experience MSD symptoms substantially worse compared to a reference group of non-EWWs. Exposure to long bouts of walking, as well as frequent and heavy manual material handling by EWWs are directly associated with MSD symptoms in the lower and upper extremities and lower back, respectively. The equipment used for transporting (e.g., hand-drawn carts, wheelbarrows), dismantling (e.g., hammers, chisels, pliers) and burning (i.e., long metal rods for handling burning items) e-waste items is rudimentary and worn out [9]. Only 25% of e-waste workers wear any PPE, e.g., safety shoes and/or gloves [12].

Limitations of this study include its reliance on self-reported data (e.g., recall bias), the cross-sectional study design, and potential selection bias due to a healthy worker effect. Longitudinal studies using direct observations and instrumentation are warranted; however, these methods require extensive resources and ergonomics expertise.

5 Conclusion

This initial study provides evidence about the detrimental physical effects of informal e-waste recycling. By fostering international collaborations, the broader ergonomics community can help address some of the disproportionate occupational health and safety burden experienced by EWWs in developing countries. Example contributions include assisting with ergonomic exposure and MSD assessment research; facilitating dialog aimed at the development, implementation and evaluation of locally adapted injury prevention strategies, providing occupational health and safety training, and promoting awareness about and use of personal protective equipment. Potential ergonomics interventions would need to balance the objectives of reducing occupational and environmental exposures with maintaining job availability/security for the many workers who rely on informal e-waste recycling for their livelihood.

Acknowledgements. The authors are grateful to the e-waste workers at Agbogbloshie for their participation in this study. The authors also thank the field team and colleagues at the University of Ghana School of Public Health for their assistance in data collection.

This research was supported by the 1/2 West Africa-Michigan CHARTER in GEOHealth with funding from the US National Institutes of Health / Fogarty International Center (NIH/FIC) (paired grant nos. 1U2RTW010110–01 and 5U01TW010101) and Canada's International Development Research Center (IDRC; grant no. 108121–001). Co-authors C.D. and B.M. were partially supported by the training grant T42-OH008455 from the National Institute for Occupational Safety and Health (NIOSH), US Centers for Disease Control and Prevention (CDC). The views expressed in this publication do not necessarily reflect the official policies of nor endorsement by NIH, NIOSH, CDC, and/or the Canadian and US Governments.

References

1. Bakhiyi, B., Gravel, S., Ceballos, D., Flynn, M.A., Zayed, J.: Has the question of e-waste opened a Pandora's box? An overview of unpredictable issues and challenges. Environ. Int. **110**(August 2017), 173–192 (2018). https://doi.org/10.1016/j.envint.2017.10.021

2. Perkins, D.N., Brune Drisse, M.-N., Nxele, T., Sly, P.D.: E-waste: a global hazard. Ann. Global Health **80**(4), 286–295 (2014). https://doi.org/10.1016/J.AOGH.2014.10.001
3. Maphosa, V., Maphosa, M.: E-waste management in sub-saharan africa: a systematic literature review. Cogent Bus. Manage. **7**(1) (2020). https://doi.org/10.1080/23311975.2020.1814503
4. Forti, V., Baldé, C.P., Kuehr, R., Bel, G.: The Global E-waste Monitor 2020: Quantities, flows, and the circular economy potential (2020). https://ewastemonitor.info/wp-content/upl oads/2020/07/GEM_2020_def_july1_low.pdf. Accessed 25 Oct 2020
5. Oteng-Ababio, M.: When necessity begets ingenuity: e-waste scavenging as a livelihood strategy in Accra, Ghana. Afr. Stud. Q. **13** (Spring 2012), 1–21 (2012)
6. Amoyaw-Osei, Y., Agyekum, O.O., Pwamang, J.A., Mueller, E., Fasko, R., Schluep, M.: Ghana e-Waste Country Assessment: SBC e-Waste Africa Project, Secretariat of the Basel Convention, Châtelaine, Switzerland (2011). https://www.basel.int/Portals/4/BaselConvent ion/docs/eWaste/E-wasteAssessmentGhana.pdf. Accessed 21 Nov 2020
7. Srigboh, R.K., Basu, N., Stephens, J., Asampong, E., Perkins, M., Neitzel, R.L., Fobil, J.: Multiple elemental exposures amongst workers at the Agbogbloshie electronic waste (e-waste) site in Ghana. Chemosphere **164**, 68–74 (2016). https://doi.org/10.1016/j.chemosphere.2016. 08.089
8. Akormedi, M., Asampong, E., Fobil, J.N.: Working conditions and environmental exposures among electronic waste workers in Ghana. Int. J. Occup. Environ. Health **19**(4), 278–286 (2013). https://doi.org/10.1179/2049396713Y.0000000034
9. Acquah, A.A., D'Souza, C., Martin, B., Arko-Mensah, J., Nti, A.A., Kwarteng, L., Takyi, S., Quakyi, I.A., Robins, T.G., Fobil, J.N.: Processes and challenges associated with informal electronic waste recycling at Agbogbloshie, a suburb of Accra, Ghana. In: Proceedings of the 2019 Human Factors and Ergonomics Society Annual Meeting, Seattle, WA, vol. 63(1), pp. 938–942 (2019). https://doi.org/10.1177/1071181319631219
10. Acquah, A.A., D'Souza, C., Martin, B., Arko-Mensah, J., Botwe, P.K., Tettey, P., Nti, A.A., Kwarteng, L., Takyi, S., Quakyi, I.A., Robins, T.G., Fobil, J.N.: A preliminary assessment of physical work exposures among electronic waste workers at Agbogbloshie, Accra Ghana. Int. J. Ind. Ergon. **82**(March 2021), 103096 (2021). https://doi.org/10.1016/j.ergon.2021.103096
11. Acquah, A.A., Arko-Mensah, J., D'Souza, C., Martin, B., Quakyi, I.A., Robins, T.G., Fobil, J.N.: Prevalence of work-related musculoskeletal disorders among e-waste workers at Agbogbloshie in Accra, Ghana. In: Proceedings of the 2019 International Society of Environmental Epidemiology Conference, Utrecht, Netherlands, October 2019, vol. 3, pp. 2–3 (2019). https:// doi.org/10.1097/01.EE9.0000605616.87684.ec
12. Fischer, D., Seidu, F., Yang, J., Felten, M.K., Garus, C., Kraus, T., Fobil, J.N., Kaifie, A.: Health Consequences for E-Waste workers and bystanders - a comparative cross-sectional study. Int. J. Environ. Res. Public Health **17**(5), 1534 (2020). https://doi.org/10.3390/ijerph 17051534
13. Hedge, A., Morimoto, S., McCrobie, D.: Effects of keyboard tray geometry on upper body posture and comfort. Ergonomics **42**(10), 1333–1349 (1999). https://doi.org/10.1080/001401 399184983
14. CU Ergo: Cornell Musculoskeletal Discomfort Questionnaires (CMDQ), Cornell University Ergonomics Web (CU Ergo), Cornell, NY. https://ergo.human.cornell.edu/ahmsquest.html (n.d.). Accessed 20 Nov 2020
15. Reis, J.P., DuBose, K.D., Ainsworth, B.E., Macera, C.A., Yore, M.M.: Reliability and validity of the occupational physical activity questionnaire. Med. Sci. Sports and Exerc. **37**(12), 2075–2083 (2005). https://doi.org/10.1249/01.mss.0000179103.20821.00

CAD and MODAPTS Models for Assessing Localized Fatigue

Thomas J. Armstrong$^{(\boxtimes)}$ (iD)

University of Michigan, Ann Arbor, USA
tja@umich.edu

Abstract. This work demonstrates the use of CAD-based workstation models that describe the spatial aspects and predetermined time systems, specifically MODAPTS, that show the temporal aspects of a given job provide an underlying model assessing localized fatigue with respect the ACGIH TLV®. This work shows that CAD and predetermined time systems can provide an underlying model for predicting and interpreting WMSD risk. It also provides a framework for interpreting observation-based results, for identifying specific risk factors, and for designing engineering interventions.

Keywords: Job analysis · Job design · Localized fatigue · Musculoskeletal disorders · MODAPTS

1 Introduction

Localized fatigue is a significant problem for workers engaged in repetitive hand work. It also is regarded as a harbinger of chronic musculoskeletal disorders. Tools are needed that can be used to predict and manage localized fatigue based on workstation design, material parameters and standard methods.

Tools such as include RULA, Strain Index, OCRA, ACGIH TLV®s, are widely used to assess risk of work-related musculoskeletal disorders, WMSDs (Kong et al. 2018). These tools are most frequently based on subjective estimates of posture and may be supplemented with selected measurements such as the weight of work objects. As such the results may vary based on who is observed, when that person is observed, and on the observer.

To address the problem of inter subject and observer variability, predetermined time systems, PTS, such as MTM, MOST, and MODAPTS, that predict the normal time for each movement are now widely used in place of traditional time study methods and performance ratings (Freivalds and Niebel 2013).

For application of a PTS, it is first necessary to describe the sequence of steps or the method required to complete the task and certain qualities of each step, such as reach and move distances. Reach and move distances can be determined from physical measurements of a workstation or from a virtual CAD model. This work aims to demonstrate the use of CAD and PTSs to estimate work methods and load patterns necessary for application of the ACGIH TLV for localized fatigue. This work is particularly focused on the use of MODAPTS because of its simplicity and widespread use.

N. L. Black et al. (Eds.): IEA 2021, LNNS 222, pp. 682–687, 2021.
https://doi.org/10.1007/978-3-030-74611-7_94

2   Methods

The ACGIH localized fatigue TLV® is based on duty cycle, DC, and the time-weighted relative force, $\%MVC_{twa}$. The TLV is applicable to the hand/forearm, the elbow and the shoulder. For the purpose of this demonstration, only the hand/forearm are considered. A case packing job in which a worker packs 150 cases per hour (24 s per case), which was previously used to demonstrate time-based analysis of force and posture patterns, was used for this demonstraton (Armstrong et al. 2003). The steps for determining DC and $\%MVC_{twa}$ were as follows:

1) Sketchup (Sketchup 2020) was used to construct a 3D model of the workstation (Fig. 1). Any number of commercial or open-source CAD packages can be used for this purpose.
2) The work method was determined by observing an experienced worker performing the job. The work method also can be constructed from observations of a similar job or inferred from knowledge of the materials and where they are located and the sequence in which they must be processed. While there are many ways to perform any job, it is desirable to select one that minimizes time and effort (Freivalds and Niebel 2013). The important thing is to establish a standard method that will serve as benchmark for determining the effects of possible material, equipment, process or worker variations on work performance and fatigue.
3) MODAPTS was used to determine the time required to perform each step. MODAPTS times are expressed as integer values of Mods (1 Mod = 0.129 s). Move distances are mapped into body parts, which are used to determine move times. Get and put times were determined based on the actions based on how objects are grasped, interference and precision.
4) Forces as %MVC were estimated for each step as described by Ebersole et al. (2005). In the absence of job observations, they can be calculated using biomechanical analyses or in some cases inferred from published studies.
5) The time-weight average force, $\%MVC_{twa}$, was computed based on MODAPTS elements with an estimated force greater than 7%MVC.
6) The duty cycle was computed as the sum of element times in which the force was > 7%MVC for each hand divided a) by the sum of the elements used to determine total work cycle time and b) by the process or Takt time.
7) The resulting DC and $\%MVC_{twa}$ were then compared with the ACGIH TLV® for hand/forearm fatigue. For comparison purposes, the DC also were computed using observed times (Armstrong et al. 2003).

3   Results

A 3-D Sketchup Model is shown in Fig. 1. Packing cases can be divided into 3 tasks: 1) get and erect case, 2) pack 12 boxes of product into the case, and 3) close and aside case into tapping machine. The basic movement patterns required to complete each task are shown by the arrows in the figure. The left hand is used to reach for the flat case. The right hand is used to help position it and both hands are used to erect the cases.

The boxes of product arrived two at a time. From observations it was determined that the worker transferred them two at a time from the chute to the case. It was possible for the worker to transfer them one at a time or to use just one hand to transfer them. After filling the case, the worker folded the flaps down and pushed the filled case into the tapping machine with the left hand while holding the flaps down with the right hand.

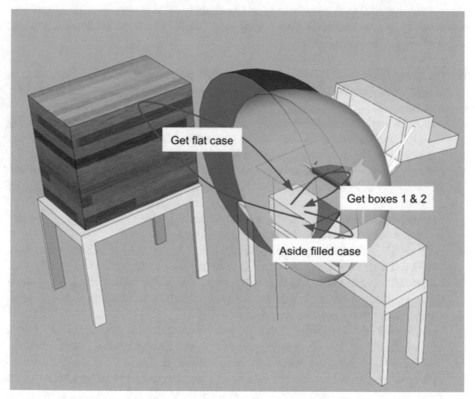

Fig. 1. 3D CAD model of case pack station showing work locations and basic movement patterns. Created using SketchUp (2020).

The MODAPTS steps along with estimated %MVC for the right and left hands are shown in Table 1. The estimated time to complete one cycle based on the MODAPTS analysis were 20.8 s (161 Mods) and 19.2 (149 Mods) respectively for the right and left hands. The Duty cycles were computed as 42% and 44% and the time-weighted %MVC$_{twa}$ were computed as 27% and 28% respectively for the right and left hands.

The DC %MVC$_{twa}$ were compared with the ACGIH TLV as show in Fig. 2. It can be seen that the combination of DC and time-weighted %MVC$_{twa}$ exceed TLV® for both the right and hands. Either the DC must be reduced through additional recovery time or the %MVC$_{twa}$ must be decreased. This DC was based on the MODAPTS time to pack each case. The production rate for this job is actually 1,800 boxes of product per hour or 24 s/case. This provides an additional 3.2 s and 4.8 s recovery time for the right and left hands which results in DCs of 37% and 35% respectively. It can be seen that this combination of DC and %MVC is closer to the TLV®, but the TLV® is still exceeded. The %MVC$_{twa}$ either needs to be reduced to 21%MVC and 23%MVC, or additional recover time must be allocated to decrease the DC to 27% and 24% respectively.

Table 1. Standard method, MODAPTS codes, and duty cycle and %MVC$_{twa}$ calculations.

Step	Hand	MODAPTS Code	Freq	Mods Total	%MVC	Mods %MVC>7%	Duty Cyle MODAPTS	Duty Cyle Takt Time*	Time x %N
1 Get flat case	RH	M4G1M4P0	1	9	20	5			100
	LH	M5G1M5P0	1	11	15	6			90
2 Get corners & move to center to erect case	RH	M3G0M4P0	1	7	20	4			80
"	LH	M3G0M4P0	1	7	20	4			80
3 Get & fold flap 1	RH	M3G1M3P0	1	7	10	4	ı		40
	LH	hold/rest	1	7	0	0			0
4 Get & fold flap 3	RH	hold/rest rest	1	7	0	0			0
	LH	M3G1M3P0	1	7	15	4			60
5 Get & fold flap 2	RH	M4G1M3P0	1	8	15	4			60
	LH	hold/rest	1	3	0	0			0
6 Get & fold flap 4	RH	hold rest	1	8	0	0			0
	LH	M4G1M3P0	1	8	15	4			60
7 Get & Rotate case 180° into position	RH	M4G1M4P0M4P0	1	13	15	8			120
Rotate case 45°	LH	M4P0M4G1	1	9	15	4			60
8 Move & rest hands on flaps 1 & 3	RH	M4G1	1	4	0	0			0
	LH	hold/rest	1	3	0	0			0
9 Get boxes 1 & 2 from chute & place in case	RH	M4G1M4P0M4P2	3	45	40	33			1320
Hold/rest Flap 3	LH	M4G0	3	33	0	0			0
10 Hold/rest Flap 1	RH	M4G0 rest	3	33	0	0			0
Get boxes 3 & 4 from chute & place in case	LH	M4G1M4P0M4P2	3	45	40	33			1320
Repeat steps 9 & 10 2x each for boxes 5-12									
11 Get & close flap 1	RH	M3G0M3P0	2	12	10	6			60
Get & close flap 3	LH	M3G0M3P1	2	12	10	6			60
reapet step 11 to close flaps 2 & 4									0
12 Get end of box	RH	M4P0	1	4	0	0			0
Hold & push box into tapping machine	LH	M4P0	1	4	20	4			80
13 Push carton into tapping machine	RH	M4P0	1	4	20	4			80
Step 1	LH	M6G1							
Total	RH			161	27%	68	42%	37%	1860
	LH			149	28%	65	44%	35%	1810

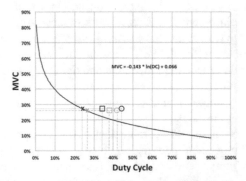

Fig. 2. %MVC$_{twa}$ and DC versus ACGIH TLV® for localized fatigue. (DC based on the total MODAPTS time, ·, the Takt time, O, and the TLV®, X) (Right hand ....; left hand ----)

4 Discussion

The predicted DC were compared with those obtained using time-based analysis at 3 samples/sec for a typical cycle (Armstrong et al. 2003). The DC was computed as 43% and 38% based on the total MODAPTS time versus 37% and 35% based on process or Takt time. The MODAPTS time does not account for the time waiting for boxes of product to arrive. The recovery time only occurs when the estimated hand force is less than 7%MVC or while one hand is waiting for the other. The total work time is estimated as 161 Mods (20.8 s) for the right hand and 149 Mods (19.2 s) for the left hand. The Takt time is 24 s, which provides and additional 3.2 s and 4.8 s recovery time. This translates to a rest allowances of 13% and 20% for the right and left hand. This might seem very generous, except that the TLV® (Fig. 2) is still exceeded. In addition, any irregular tasks such as restocking flattened cartons, adjusting the tapping machine or housekeeping would cut into this allowance.

MODAPTS and other PTSs are based on an assumed "standard" method for performing that job. They are not subject to statistical variations as observed methods. This is an important reason for using a PTS to define the standard method. Deviations from the standard method can result in extra work and reduce available recovery time. The causes of these variations should be investigated, e.g., equipment, process, or worker variations. For example, if the boxes stick together, if damage product is received that must be repaired or set aside, or if the tapping machine requires adjustment, additional motions may be required which may increase the duty cycle. If the worker does not follow the standard method, it may change the movement pattern, DC and %MVC$_{twa}$ – and affect product quality and worker safety. For example, it would be possible for the worker to do all of the packing with one hand. This would greatly increase the DC.

One of the appeals of MODAPTS is its simplicity, but this simplicity comes at the possible cost of overlooking small but important details. MODAPTS utilizes only six categories for Move and only three categories each for Reach and Move. MTM includes many separate categories each for Reach, Grasp, Move and Put. MTM requires much greater training to use and greater time to apply than MODAPTS.

Regardless, which PTS is used, it is necessary to determine the location of the work objects, the reach/move distances, the size and accessibility of the work objects and the precision required placement precision of work objects. Any changes in the spatial relationship between the worker and the work objects will affect the move distances and times. The distance between the delivery location and the boxes of products and the case might be reduced to reduce the move time and the DC. The CAD model might be used to redesign the chute to reduce the reach distance and the time required to pack the cases. The flattened cases might be put on a lift and located closer to the packing point to reduce the time to get the cases.

We are seeing increased use of wearable devices and computer vision for the study of work postures and movement patterns. 3D models and standard work methods are of great value for the interpretation of data collected using these methods. Aside from their value for conducting a basic analysis, they provide insights into how equipment can be rearranged to reduce reaching. Work equipment that is not bolted down sometimes gets rearranged. Workstation models can be used to identify changes that might increase reaching and the time to get and place parts.

This work focused primarily on the spatial and temporal aspects of the job/task analysis. Forces estimates were taken from a previous study. There is quite a bit of force data available in the literature for various jobs that can be used for at least first order force estimates in some cases. In many case forces can be computed using biomechanical analyses. This work focused only factors related to hand/forearm fatigue, but it could be expanded to the elbow and shoulder. The 3D workstation model provides a bases for determining reach distances and computing elbow and shoulder moments. It should be possible to integrate the available tools and data for estimating forces into a decision support system (Gusich et al. 2018).

5   Conclusions

CAD and predetermined time systems provide an underlying model for predicting and interpreting WMSD risk. They also provide a framework for interpreting results, for identifying specific risk factors and for designing engineering interventions.

Acknowledgements. The author wishes to acknowledge Ms. Megan Liu from the University of Michigan and Drs. Roberto Bonfiglioli from the University of Bologna and Francesca Gratiosi for their assistance with this work. This work was made possible by a Safety Education Training grant from the State of Michigan.

References

American Conference of Governmental Industrial Hygienists (ACGIH®): Upper Limb Localized Fatigue TLV®. 2019 Threshold Limit Values and Biological Exposure Indices, pp. 209–211 (2020)

Armstrong, T.J., Keyserling, W.M., Grieshaber, D.C., Ebersole, M., Lo, E.: Time based job analysis for control of work-related musculoskeletal disorders. In: 15th Triennial Congress of the International Ergonomics Association, Seoul, Korea (2003)

Ebersole, M.L., Armstrong, T.J.: Analysis of an observational rating scale for repetition, posture, and force in selected manufacturing settings. Hum. Factors **48**(3), 487–498 (2006)

Freivalds, A., Niebel, B.: Niebel's Methods, Standards, & Work Design. McGraw-Hill higher education (2013)

Gusich, B.R., Armstrong, T.J., Seo, N.J., Grieshaber, D.C.: Development of a computerized model for evaluation of manual insertion of flexible hoses in automobile assembly. In: Proceedings of the Human Factors and Ergonomics Society Annual Meeting, vol. 52, No. 19, pp. 1498–1502. SAGE Publications, Los Angeles, CA, September 2008

Kong, Y.K., Lee, S.Y., Lee, K.S., Kim, D.M.: Comparisons of ergonomic evaluation tools (ALLA, RULA, REBA and OWAS) for farm work. Int. J. Occup. Saf. Ergon. **24**(2), 218–223 (2018)

MODAPTS: International MODAPTS Association, 5119 Kara Dr., Jonesboro, AR 72401, US (2020). https://modapts.org/

Sketchup: 3D Design Software, Trimble (2020)

Ergonomic Assessment of Indian Dentists Using the Assessment of Repetitive Tasks (Art) Technique

Vibha Bhatia[1]([⊠]), Jagjit Singh Randhawa[1], Ashish Jain[2], and Vishakha Grover[2]

[1] Department of Production and Industrial Engineering, Punjab Engineering College, Chandigarh, India
vibhabhatia.phdidp17@pec.edu.in, jagjitsingh@pec.ac.in
[2] Harvansh Singh Judge Institute of Dental Sciences and Hospitals, Punjab University, Chandigarh, India
ashish@pu.ac.in, vishakha_grover@rediffmail.com

Abstract. Prevalence of Musculoskeletal Disorders is high amongst dental practitioners all over the world. Indian population comprises of nearly three lakh dentists, making it crucial to ergonomically assess the dental occupation using different methods of an ergonomic assessment. The dental profession comprises of highly frequent hand-arm motions and necessitates the implementation of the appropriate ergonomic assessment tools. Assessment of Repetitive Tasks (ART) has been created primarily to evaluate the risk involved in the repetitive movement of upper extremity body parts such as arms and hands. Umpteen numbers of studies have been done using other ergonomic tools (RULA, REBA, SI, and OCRA) in dentistry. Limited investigations have been conducted using the ART technique for assessing the dental profession ergonomically. In the study, ART was used as the key tool to assess the risk levels involved in the Indian population of dentists. The study deduced that the new improved ergonomic methods like ART may prove effective in determination of risk factors responsible for prevalent MSDs in dentistry.

Keywords: Dentists · Assessment of repetitive tasks · Ergonomics · Musculoskeletal disorders

1 Introduction

Globally, workers are exposed to Work-related musculoskeletal disorders (WMSDs) which lead to least productivity, reduction in working days and expensive work injuries. Most of the industrial countries are facing this issue of occupation related health problems and WMSDs constitute the major percentage of these problems and needs ergonomists to address it [1]. The body parts involved in movement like muscles, ligaments, tendons, nerves, joints and blood vessels constitutes the musculoskeletal system of the human body and the injuries related to them are Musculoskeletal disorders. The major responsible ergonomic factors of occurrence of these disorders are awkward static postures,

© The Author(s), under exclusive license to Springer Nature Switzerland AG 2021
N. L. Black et al. (Eds.): IEA 2021, LNNS 222, pp. 688–696, 2021.
https://doi.org/10.1007/978-3-030-74611-7_95

force exertions, repetitive body movements, biomechanical pressures and vibrations [2].
In earlier studies, discomfort in different body parts related to the human musculoskeletal system was reported. Absenteeism due to the occurrence of WMSDs has been on rise. Prevention of WMSDs has now become the priority issue and necessity nationally and internationally.

In dentistry, high prevalence of musculoskeletal disorders in body parts like neck, back, hands and shoulders is reported. The literature based upon different studies suggests that the 63% to 93% of the dentist around the world are suffering from one or more symptom related to musculoskeletal disorder [3]. The repetitive nature of actions, badly designed tool usage, high exertion requirement and longer duration tasks in dental profession while following an unbalanced posture are responsible for high probability of occurrence of the muscular injuries in dental practitioners [4]. The work related muscular injuries not only reduces the work efficiency but also affects the quality of work. Therefore, ergonomics plays a vital role proper functioning of a dental work environment [1].

Due to the higher occurrence of MSDs in dentists of India and abroad, the implementation of suitable ergonomic assessment techniques involving repetitive upper extremity motions becomes crucial. Despite the appropriateness of the ART technique for repetitious dental tasks, limited exploratory studies have been conducted using ART.

The present study aimed to assess the risk of musculoskeletal disorders (MSDs), and to determine the responsible risk parameters of musculoskeletal problems among the Indian population of dentists in Chandigarh city by using the ART method.

2 Methods

Ergonomic Assessment was done on the randomly selected cross-sectional data from the Indian cohort of dentists (n = 68) of Chandigarh city. Subjects were pre-screened for having any Work-Related Musculoskeletal Disorder (WMSD) in their upper extremity body parts. The study was conducted after taking ethical permission from the Ethical Department of the Panjab University, Chandigarh. The subjective data like age, height, weight were collected. Questionnaire data containing personalized and professional information (like gender, years of experience, type of dental practice, number of work hours per week, etc.) of dentists were also collected. Dentists doing the dental practice of more than 20 h a week were selected for the current study. Assessment of Repetitive Tasks (ART) technique was used to assess the MSDs risk factors in practicing the dental profession. The image stream data was collected by using the videography method using a high-technology still camera (SONY, Model: HDR-XR550) having a frame rate of 30 fps.

The video stream data was collected while the dentists were working on a typical Pelton and Crane dental chair. The videography camera was placed at 3.6 m from the dental chair center and the height of 1.2 m, radially at roughly 9' o clock position to the dental chair. The continuous image stream data was collected while the dental practitioner finished the dental scaling task and further image stream data was analyzed with the help of the ergonomics expert. Statistical software SPSS was used to analyze the data collected. Logistic regression modeling technique was used to detect risk parameters leading to musculoskeletal disorders.

3 Results

Demographic data of all the dentists participating in the study was recorded which are mentioned in the Table 1 and Table 2.

Table 1. Demographic parameters of dentists (n = 68)

Variable	Mean	Range
Age (years)	29.3	24.8–33.8
Weight (kg)	64.64	56.24–73.04
Height (cm)	166.3	159–173.6

Table 2. Other demographic and occupational parameters of the participants (n = 68)

	Characteristics	Percentage (%)	Musculoskeletal disorders		p-value
			No (n =) frequency (percentage)	Yes (n =) frequency (percentage)	
Gender	Male	55.88	10 (76.92)	28 (50.90)	< 0.0001
	Female	44.11	3 (23.07)	27 (49.09)	
Marital status	Married	45.58	2 (15.38)	29 (52.72)	0.46
	Single	54.41	11 (84.61)	26 (47.27)	
Level of expertise	General	25	8 (61.53)	9 (16.36)	< 0.0001
	Specialized	75	5 (38.46)	46 (83.63)	
Out-of-clinic activity	Yes	16.17	2 (15.38)	9 (16.36)	0.72
	No	83.82	11 (84.61)	46 (83.63)	
Exercise	Yes	39.70	12 (92.30)	15 (27.27)	< 0.001
	No	60.29	1 (7.69)	40 (72.72)	
Duration of working	< 8	8.82	6 (46.15)	0 (0)	< 0.001
	≥ 8	91.176	7 (53.84)	55 (100)	
Type of activity	Sedentary	94.41	10(76.92)	54(98.18)	0.643
	Standing and sedentary	5.88	3(23.07)	1(1.18)	
Number of children	No child	70.58	4(30.76)	44(64.7)	0.71
	More than one child	29.41	9(69.23)	11(16.17)	

The mean age, height, and weight of the participants were 29.3 ± 4.5 years, 166.3 ± 7.3 cm, and 64.64 ± 8.4 kg, respectively. More number of male dentists participated

in the study (55.88% of the participant s population). Percentage of unmarried participants was more than the married participants but the occurrence of symptoms related to
musculoskeletal disorders were more common in married participants (52.72%). As the
study was conducted in the Periodontology department of the Dental Institute, 75% of
the participants were Periodontists and were specialised in the area of dental hygiene,
rest 25% of the participants belonged to the general dental background. According to the
data recorded, most of the dentists (94.41%) preferred to work in sedentary work posture. While taking individual data, it was mentioned that exercise should be any physical
activity conducted at least for half an hour per day. More than half of the participants
(60.29%) were not involved in any kind of physical exercise and out of which most of
them (72.72%) experienced related symptoms of musculoskeletal disorders. The highest
frequency of participants bears no child (70.58%). Rest period is the rest time taken by
dentist after the treatment of each patient which is usually of 5 min. The subjective data
taken from the Nordic Musculoskeletal Questionnaires was summarised in the Table 3.

Table 3. Prevalence of MSDs among the subjects

Body part	N (%)	95% confidence interval
Neck	27(39.70)	36.31–43.09
Shoulder	29(42.64)	38.13–47.15
Elbow	32(47.05)	42.6–51.5
Wrist	47(69.11)	65.74–72.48
Upper back	29(42.64)	37.5–47.78
Lower back	26(38.23)	35.11–41.35
Hips and thighs	20(29.41)	25.79–33.03
Knee	18(26.47)	22.06–30.88
Ankle	15(22.05)	17.1–27

Out of all the dentists who were having one or more symptoms of Musculoskeletal Disorders, maximum number of participants were having MSDs related to wrist
(69.11%), followed by pain or discomfort in body parts like elbow (47.05%), shoulder
(42.64%), Upper back (42.64%), neck (39.70%), Lower Back (38.23%), Hips/Thighs
(29.41%), Knee (26.47%) and ankle joint (22.05%) respectively.

An illustrative of dentist working in the dental environment is shown in the Fig. 1.
Tables 4 and 5 which describes the exposure level estimation and random participant's
study worksheet prepared using ART gives the illustrative representation of the ART
method.

The level of risks (using ART method as the basic assessment tool) associated with
the occurrence of musculoskeletal disorders in both right and left side of the dentists
body was tabulated in the Table 6.

It was concluded that left and right final scores varied significantly with $p \leq 0.001$
using Wilcoxon test where right side of the dentists were exposed to significantly higher

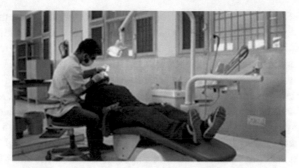

Fig. 1. Dental practitioner and the work environment

Table 4. Exposure level determination using exposure score in ART method

Exposure score	Exposure level	Recommendation
0–11	Low	Take personal conditions into account
12–21	Medium	More examination is necessary
22 or higher	High	More immediate examination is necessary

risk level. The average total score of prevalent risk in right and left side of the dentist's body using ART method were 33.48 ± 4.12 and 9.92 ± 4.12 respectively. The results of ART assessment tool resulted in the notion that most of the dental postures need ergonomic interventions and required prioritised corrective methods. The insights were drawn on the use of the ART ergonomic assessment tool for the data analysis. The ART tool revealed that the higher MSDs risk was observed on the right-hand side of the body of the dental practitioner. The ART also suggested that the risk of MSDs was higher among certain groups. Considering the gender factor, the female dentists were more prone to MSDs than male dentists. On dentistry based professional classification, the periodontists were more susceptible than other dental professional groups. Dental professionals who worked more than 40 h a week (8 h a day*5 workdays = 40 h)and who were having work experience of more than 20 years were most exposed to the dental occupational risk of developing MSDs. Professionals who regularly do some kind of physical activity or exercise were comparatively at lower risk of exposure level.

The number of risk factors affecting the occurrence of MSDs was shortlisted to be assessed by using the total scores from the ART evaluation. These factors included gender, dental specialisation, number of working hours per week, work experience in years and physical activity. The body regions which showed high percentage occurrence of MSDs symptoms (wrist, elbow, upper back, shoulder) were considered for regression analysis to determine the contributing factors of MSDs. The results are summarised in Table 7.

Table 5. Worksheet illustration of assessment of risk factors in dental workplace using ART method

Name of unit: 01-left hand	Observation date:	Observation time:		
Department: periodontology				
Assessment factors		Left side score	Right side score	
A1 arm movement		3	3	
A2 repetition (movement of hands and arms)		0	3	
B force		1	8	
C1 head and shoulders		2	2	
C2 back(Waist)		2	3	
C3 arms		4	4	
C4 wrists		2	2	
C5 hands and fingers		0	2	
D1 restless working		0	2	
D2 speed of working		0	1	
D3 other factors		1	2	
Total job factors		15	32	
D4 duration coefficient		X1	X1	
Exposure score		15	32	
D5 psychosocial factors	High level of attention and concentration			
Determination of exposure score	Exposure level based on exposure score Suggested exposure level			
0–11	Low	Take personal conditions into account		
12–21	Medium	Further examination is required		
22 ≥	High	Further immediate examination is required		

4   Discussion

The ART tool was developed and validated by UK's Health and Safety Executive body to protect employers from risks involved in repetitive tasks [5]. The study could potentially determine the risk exposure levels of Musculoskeletal Disorders using ART ergonomic assessment tool among the dental community of the Chandigarh area. In the present study, the more risk exposure to the right side of the dentist's body was observed which may be

Table 6. ART exposure scores of left and right side of the dentist's body

Level of risk	Right frequency of occurrence	Right side percentage	Left frequency of occurrence	Left side percentage	Recommendation
Low	3	4.41	30	44.11	Take personal condition into consideration
Medium	12	17.64	35	51.47	Further investigation is needed
High	53	77.94	3	4.41	Further immediate investigation is needed

Table 7. Regression models indicating risk factors with association with symptoms of MSDs in various body parts of the dentists (n = 68)

Body part	Risk factor	Odds ratio	p value
Wrist	Gender-female	31.01	< 0.0001
	Expertise-Periodontists	10.63	< 0.0001
	Work hours-more than 40 h per week	24.87	< 0.0001
	Exercise-performed no exercise	8.53	< 0.0001
Elbow	Gender-female	23.52	< 0.0001
	Expertise-Periodontists	5.56	< 0.0001
	Work hours-more than 40 h per week	16.87	< 0.0001
	Exercise-performed no exercise	7.39	< 0.0001
Upper Back	Gender-female	10.54	< 0.0001
	Expertise-Periodontists	4.5	< 0.0001
	Work hours-more than 40 h per week	17.71	< 0.0001
	Exercise-performed no exercise	13.83	< 0.0001
Shoulder	Gender-female	12.51	< 0.0001
	Expertise-Periodontists	6.1	< 0.0001
	Work hours-more than 40 h per week	12.44	< 0.0001
	Exercise-performed no exercise	6.4	< 0.0001

due to the reason that most of the participants involved in the study were right-handed and used right-sided upper extremity body parts more often. This fact was also supported by the previous studies conducted by Abbaszadeh et al., Sohrabi et al., Hosseini et al. and Jafari Rodbandi et al. [6–9]. The study revealed the more risk level to the female dentists and subjects who were not having a proper exercise regime. Many studies had stated that the prevalence of Musculoskeletal Disorders in females was more than that in males where the odds ratio of all the body parts was greater than one [10, 11]. For wrist, shoulder, elbow and upper back, the female gender and long working hours came out to be significant factors when the regression model was implemented. Years of working experience in dentistry holds a direct relation to the occurrence of Carpal Tunnel Syndrome (CTS) [12] and supports the results of the present study. The Periodontists were more exposed to risk levels which may be due to the reason that the average pinch strength during dental scaling is 11–20% of the maximum [13].

5   Conclusion

In the present study, the ergonomic evaluation of Indian dentists and the assessment of MSDs among them revealed the prominent existence of musculoskeletal injuries. The regression analysis of risk factors suggested gender and long working hours maybe responsible for MSDs in dentists. The current study suggests that the innovative and novel ergonomic evaluation methods like ART may prove an assistive tool to assess MSDs in dentists.

References

1. Hadler, N.M., Tait, R.C., Chibnall, J.T.: Back Pain in the Workplace.Occupational Musculoskeletal Disorders. 3th ed. Philadelphia: Lippincott Williams & Wilkins, pp. 94–96 (2005)
2. Valachi, B., Valachi, K.: Mechanisms leading to musculoskeletal disorders in dentistry. J. Am. Dent. Assoc. **134**, 1344–1350 (2003)
3. Loeppke, R., Taitel, M., Richling, D., Parry, T., Kessler, R.C., Hymel, P.: Health and productivity as a business strategy. J. Occup. Environ. Med. **49**, 712–721 (2007)
4. Dehghan, M.F., Amiri, Z., Rabiei, M.: Prevalence of musculoskeletal pain among a group of iranian dentists, (Tehran-1999). J. Dental School Summer. **21**, 185–192 (2003)
5. HSE Homepage. https://www.hse.gov.uk/msd/uld/art/whatis.htm. Accessed 8 Feb 2021
6. Abbaszadeh, M., Zokaei, M., Zakerian, S., Hassani, H.: Using assessment repetitive task (ART) tool in an assembly industry. Iran Occup. Health J. **10**, 1–15 (2013)
7. Sohrabi, M., Faridizad, A.M., Farasati, F.: Comparing results of musculoskeletal disorders assessment in computer users by CMDQ, RULA, and ROSA methods. J. Ilam Univ. Med. Sci. **23**, 53–62 (2015)
8. Hosseini, A., Choobineh, A., Razeghi, M., Pakshir, H.R., Ghaem, H., Vojud, M.: Ergonomic assessment of exposure to musculoskeletal disorders risk factors among dentists of Shiraz, Iran. J. Dent. (Shiraz) **20**(1), 53–60 (2019)
9. Jafari, R., Karimi, A., Mardi, H., Nadri, F., Nadri, H.: The Prevalence of musculoskelet al disorders and posture assessment by ART method in Mosaic art in Kerman city. J. Neyshabur. Univ. Med. Sci. **2**, 38–42 (2014)
10. Alghadir, A., Zafar, H., Iqhbal, Z.: Work-related musculoskeletal disorders among dental professionals in Saudi Arabia. J. Phys. Ther. Sci. **27**(5), 1107–1112 (2015)
11. Saraji, J.N., Hosseini, M., Shahtaheri, S., Golbabaei, F., Ghasemkhani, M.: Evaluation of ergonomic postures of dental professions by rapid entire body assessment (REBA), in Birjand, Iran. J. Dent. Med. **18**, 61–67 (2005)

12. Ashwini, R., Shenoy, R.G., Pai, R., Mithun, B.H.: Symptoms of Carpal Tunnel Syndrome in a dental work force of a developing country Department of Public Health Dentistry, Manipal College of Dental Sciences, Manipal University, Mangalore, Karnataka, India.
13. Bramson, J.B., Smith, S., Romagnoli, G.: Evaluating dental office ergonomics. Risk factors and hazards. J. Am. Dental Assoc. **129**(2), 174–183 (1998)

Exposure to Regular Sit-stand Changes During Office Work Changes Limb Posture

Nancy L. Black[1]([✉]) [iD], Jenna Smith[1], Mathieu Tremblay[2] [iD],
and Fandresena Ranaivosoa[1]

[1] Université de Moncton, Moncton, NB E1A3E9, Canada
nancy.black@umoncton.ca
[2] Université du Québec à Rimouski, Rimouski, QC, Canada

Abstract. Sixteen full-time office-based workers were exposed to extended periods working with regularly sit-stand changing table surface. The angular adduction and flexion deviations of upper arms (mousing and keying), thighs and shins were measured with 2-D inclinometers and average value calculated over one hour. Comparing average segmental deviation from standing neutral showed significant variations across the study population. Mousing arm was affected by exposure, reducing average deviation significantly from Pre to Post exposure to regular sit-stand changes. Only right shin adduction varied significantly across Pre, Post and 0% standing conditions, whereas more lower limb segment deviations changed significantly across the different standing durations. Left (but not right) thigh adduction and flexion deviations varied significantly across sit-stand conditions varying from 0% to 50% standing. Flexion of both right and left shins varied significantly, but only right shin adduction varied significantly across these same sit-stand conditions. Considering Pre-Post, Pre-Post-0% standing and five alternating sit-stand periods, shin flexion and left thigh abduction conditions significantly varied but differently. The greatest number of significant segmental angular variations occurred when considering 0% to 50% standing, although those have been ignored by previous studies which report only upper body and trunk posture angles.

Keywords: Sit stand changes · Posture · Upper arm · Lower limb

1 Introduction

Rather than sitting or standing continuously, experts recommend standing for between 25% and 50% of the time and alternating between sitting and standing postures [1]. Past studies have shown improvement in physical and perceived factors when using sit-stand desks [2], and reduced slouching when sit-stand changes are programmed regularly [3], but studies have generally ignored sit-stand alternating effects on upper and lower limb posture. One recent publication studied mean and minute-to-minute changes in upper body posture including neck, trunk and upper arms, without controlling for varying sit-stand ratios [4]. The current study considers upper arm and lower limb (thigh,

N. L. Black et al. (Eds.): IEA 2021, LNNS 222, pp. 697–702, 2021.
https://doi.org/10.1007/978-3-030-74611-7_96

shin) average angular deviations in frontal and sagittal planes over eight conditions: three continuously sitting (before "Pre", after "Post", and during 0% standing), and five controlled sit-stand alternation conditions. We hypothesize that average deviations of these segments will differ across these conditions. Significant differences in limb deviations across these conditions would indicate a need to consider these segments when describing postural variability and musculoskeletal discomfort.

1.1 Study Objective

The objective of this study was to determine the presence of significant differences in average angular deviation of left and right upper arms, thighs, and shins across continuous sitting at baseline (Pre), and following exposure (Post), as well as during a series of five periodic, controlled sit-stand ratios within 30-min cycles.

2 Methodology

The methodology of data collection was approved by Research Ethics Board of the Université de Moncton. All sixteen participants were full-time office-based university employees without physical limitations affecting their ability to work sitting or standing. Two conditions (Baseline or Pre, and Post) were measured using the participant's regular fixed-height table. After the Pre condition, we replaced their regular desk work surface with one of six identical electric height-adjustable tables (by ErgoTables.com) with a programmable controller that changed table height between individual relaxed sitting or standing elbow height. The table movement cycled over 30-minutes, remaining at standing height for 0%, 10%, 20%, 30%, 40% or 50%, of that period, with the remainder at sitting height. Following exposure to those six controlled conditions, the height-adjusting table was removed, and the 'Post' condition was measured using the participant's regular fixed height table. Each condition was used for at least two working days before researchers recorded the participant for one hour while using the table and continuing their regular work. The ordering of controlled table conditions varied randomly across the participant population to avoid biasing data due to an ordering effect. Postural deviations measured both flexion and abduction of the right (mousing) and left (keyboarding) upper arms, thighs and shins with wireless 2-D inclinometers sampling at 16 Hz and recording to the wireless T-Log to be analyzed with the CAPTIV Premier system (TEA Ergo).

Deviation angles were measured for each of the segments relative to the standing relaxed neutral posture. Deviations were compiled to a single mean value for each of the six conditions with the controlled sit-stand table as well as prior to installing the table ('Pre' condition) and after table removal ('Post' condition).

To determine the effect of Table condition on limb deviation, a Linear Mixed Effects (LME) model was programmed in RStudio (version 1.2.1335) using the LMER4 package (version 1.1.21 [5]). This model included participant as a random factor, as well as potential contributing factors classified in two levels: age (at least 40 years of age), years of similar experience (over 10 years), and any pre-existing reported musculoskeletal discomfort in three grouped body regions: (1) head-neck-trunk, (2) shoulders- upper limbs, and (3) hips and legs. This article describes ANOVA comparison of LME model run with and without Table as a factor. Comparing the results of these two models using a simple ANOVA determined if Table condition contributed significantly to the model. Significance was set at $p = 0.05$, and values of $p < 0.01$ were considered highly significant.

3 Results

Seven men and nine women participated, although 'Post' data was missing for one woman. Participants were 43.8 ± 10.1 years of age and possessed 16.1 ± 10.2 years' experience. Three were left-handed, but all used the computer mouse with their right hand, so the right arm will be referred to as the "mousing arm" and the left arm as the "keying arm".

Data includes 15 (with Post) or 16 participants (otherwise). Some data points were missing due to non-standard standing duration or inclinometer malfunction. Average angular deviations across the available data points are found in Table 1. These angles consider values recorded over the entire hour-long recorded period whether in standing or sitting posture. Since the 2-D inclinometers used to measure deviation were only sensitive to deviations up to $45°$ from the reference angle, and when sitting, angles were close to $90°$ physically, recorded thigh angles in both planes were consistently less than $90°$. Since comparison is made across different conditions using the same sensors, such errors are not crucial for the current analysis.

Four LME models determined if significant variation in average angular deviation existed: (1) Pre-Post (continuously sitting using participants' regular work surface revealing a change in behavior following forced sit-stand alternation); (2) Pre-Post and 0% standing (all continuously sitting conditions); (3) all six controlled conditions (0% to 50% standing); and (4) alternating sit-stand controlled conditions (10% to 50% standing). Significant results are presented in Table 2.

Pre-Post deviation differed significantly only for the mousing arm (both planes) and right shin adduction. Flexion of the mousing arm variation was highly significant, and adduction was nearly significant ($p = 0.07$); average angular deviation was similar, but standard deviation was greatest in both planes for Pre. In contrast, right shin adduction was more deviated Pre with somewhat higher standard deviation Post. The Pre-Post-0% stand LME model found deviations varied significantly for both planes of the mousing upper arm (flexion highly significant), right shin adduction (highly significant) and left shin flexion. Left shin flexion had lowest average deviation values in the 0% stand condition, and greatest in Post. Right shin adduction varied more across the participant population. Thus, the condition impacting the variation most varied by limb segment.

When comparing mean deviation across the six or five conditions using controlled alternating sit-stand table conditions (LME models 3 and 4), neither upper arm average angular deviations varied significantly in adduction or flexion. In contrast, left thigh (both planes), right shin (both planes) and left shin (flexion only) varied highly significantly. Considering only 10%–50% standing conditions, the significance reduced somewhat but remained high. Ordering from most to least impactful condition for left thigh adduction was 40% - 30% - 50% - 20% - 10% and 0%. In contrast, right shin adduction in descending

Table 1. Average angular deviations over one-hour recordings (mean ± standard deviation) in degrees across N participants by sit-stand Table condition and body segment.

% Stand	N	Mousing arm (R)		Thigh (R)		Shin (R)	
		Adduction	Flexion	Adduction	Flexion	Adduction	Flexion
0	13	21.1 ± 8.2	11.8 ± 10.2	40.4 ± 46.9	11.6 ± 13.5	4.3 ± 17.5	−14.5 ± 8.9
10	12	19.2 ± 16.1	8.2 ± 8.3	34.6 ± 39.4	−3.8 ± 22.5	−8.7 ± 12.6	−11.1 ± 7.5
20	13	23.1 ± 14.6	7.6 ± 7.5	35.9 ± 29.3	0.5 ± 18.5	−5.3 ± 14.4	−11.5 ± 7.3
30	12	22.8 ± 7.0	5.9 ± 12.1	31.7 ± 30.5	1.3 ± 13.8	−6 ± 11	−12.6 ± 7.6
40	14	22.4 ± 10.6	5 ± 10.8	28.9 ± 27.5	−1 ± 10.3	−0.8 ± 15.8	−9.6 ± 6.5
50	12	16.7 ± 11.3	6.9 ± 9	23.4 ± 20.2	−4.8 ± 9.2	−1.6 ± 9.8	−7.6 ± 7.5
Pre	12	20.1 ± 11.6	7.5 ± 16.9	25.2 ± 59.3	−2.6 ± 15.9	8.6 ± 10.5	−18.9 ± 11
Post	10	21.3 ± 8.9	7.1 ± 9.9	54.6 ± 29.4	6.7 ± 8.3	2.7 ± 13.2	−13 ± 6.2

% Stand	N	Keying arm (L)		Thigh (L)		Shin (L)	
		Adduction	Flexion	Adduction	Flexion	Adduction	Flexion
0	13	−4.6 ± 28.7	−7.9 ± 13.6	−59 ± 20.1	0.1 ± 17.1	2.2 ± 13	9.7 ± 14.4
10	12	−17 ± 10	−4 ± 14.6	−38.7 ± 36.7	−6.9 ± 15.4	11.1 ± 17.3	10 ± 12.5
20	13	−11.6 ± 23.7	−1 ± 11	−45.3 ± 11.2	−0.4 ± 14.5	4.1 ± 12.9	10.5 ± 10.6
30	12	−7 ± 21.6	−8.4 ± 9.9	−37.9 ± 8.7	1 ± 14.3	6.8 ± 12.7	16.5 ± 8.1
40	14	−5.6 ± 23.5	−5.7 ± 10.2	−39 ± 8.4	4 ± 5.9	5.1 ± 10.2	9.8 ± 8.6
50	12	−5.5 ± 18.6	−6.8 ± 6.8	−23.8 ± 13.1	6.8 ± 11.4	5.7 ± 7.4	7.9 ± 11.5
Pre	12	2.4 ± 37.2	−12.2 ± 13.1	−43 ± 19.7	−7.7 ± 19.9	2.1 ± 16.1	15.5 ± 12.2
Post	10	−15.9 ± 14.7	−2 ± 14	−60.4 ± 17.8	−0.9 ± 16.1	−2.3 ± 16.6	17.3 ⊥ 10.3

Table 2. Mean angular deviations differing significantly with table condition by LME model.

Model	Mousing arm R		Keying arm L		Thigh (R)		Thigh (L)		Shin (R)		Shin (L)	
	Add.	Flex.	Add.	Flex.	Add.	Flex.	Add.	Flex.	Add.	Flex.	Add.	Flex.
Pre – Post	0.07	<0.01							0.02			
Pre – post −0% stand	0.04	<0.01							<0.01			0.03
0%−50% stand							<0.01	<0.01	<0.01	0.01		<0.01
10%−50% stand							<0.01	0.01	<0.01	0.01		<0.01

order of impact was 30% - 0% - 40%- 20% - 10% - 50%. In right shin flexion, descending order of impact was 0% - 10% - 30% - 20% - 50% - 40%. Finally, left shin flexion descending order of impact was 30% - 40% - 10% - 0%- 20% - 50%. No clear pattern of favorable alternating sitting percentage appeared.

4 Discussion

This study presents significant average adduction and flexion variations in the upper arms and lower limbs when engaging in computer-intensive work in an office environment, particularly focusing on the effect of regular sit-stand periodic changes during work and the impact of those changes after returning to the regular fixed seated-height desk.

Except for mousing arm adduction, all average deviation angles during all conditions studied remained under 20°, signifying low postural risk relative to ergonomic upper limb assessment categorization like RULA in flexion [6], and Keyserling in adduction [7]. Similarly, average deviations of the lower limbs typically remained under 10°, although they varied significantly across sit-stand conditions.

Significant changes in average angular deviation varied across upper arms and lower limbs. Upper arm deviations only changed significantly on the mousing side, and this only when comparing Pre-, Post and 0% standing (all continuous sitting conditions). Having been exposed to regular sit-stand changes, mousing arm flexion was reduced and less variable across the population, suggesting a benefit to past exposure to regular sit-stand changes. Similarly, average shin flexion reduced Post relative to Pre, with 0% standing being intermediate in value.

When comparing six different percent standing conditions, the most impactful table condition varied by both body segment and deviation plane.

5 Conclusions

This study shows that average limb segment deviation varies significantly when exposed to regular sit-stand changes during normally sedentary office work, particularly for the lower limbs. Interestingly, keying (left) arm deviations did not vary significantly, but mousing (right) arm flexion deviation was significantly reduced after exposure, which would positively affect shoulder and neck discomfort. In contrast, abduction of the mousing arm varied significantly, with more variability prior to sit-stand exposure, but no average decrease in deviation. Significant leg postural deviations which only occurred across sit-stand varying conditions are more difficult to interpret since they combine differing standing and seated durations.

This study grouped deviation into a single average value affected by both seated and standing periods within a given condition. Further analysis of variability separating seated from standing periods may reveal significant variations across the sit-stand conditions that are currently hidden. Furthermore, using other descriptive statistics across the population and table conditions, like standard deviation of the angles may provide further insight. The fact that some statistically significant variations were found in the upper arms and lower limbs, suggests that considering such analysis indeed adds information to the more standard head and trunk postural variations to provide a more complete understanding of office worker postural behavior.

Acknowledgements. The data collection was supported by the Office Ergonomics Research Committee (2016) and analysis was supported financially by the Natural Sciences and Engineering Research Council's Discovery Development Grant awarded to the first author 2018.

References

1. Buckley, J.P., Hedge, A., Yates, T., Copeland, R.J., Loosemore, M., Hamer, M., et al.: The sedentary office: an expert statement on the growing case for change towards better health and productivity. Br. J. Sports Med. **49**, 1357–1362 (2015)
2. Chambers, A.J., Robertson, M.M., Baker, N.A.: The effect of sit-stand desks on office worker behavioral and health outcomes: a scoping review. Appl. Ergon. **78**, 37–53 (2019)
3. Black, N., Fortin, A.-P., Handrigan, G.A.: Postural and perception variations when using manually adjustable and programmable sit-stand workstations in an emergency call center. IIE Trans. Occup. Ergon. Hum. Factors **3**, 127–138 (2015)
4. Barbieri, D.F., Srinivasan, D., Mathiassen, S.E., Oliveira, A.B.: Variation in upper extremity, neck and trunk postures when performing computer work at a sit-stand station. Appl. Ergon. **75**, 120–128 (2019)
5. Bates, D., Maechler, M., Bolker, B., Walker, S.: Fitting linear mixed-effects models using lme4. J. Stat. Softw. **67**, 1–48 (2015)
6. McAtamney, L., Corlett, E.N.: RULA: a survey method for the investigation of work-related upper limb disorders. Appl. Ergon. **24**, 91–99 (1993)
7. Keyserling, W.M.: Postural analysis of the trunk and shoulders in simulated real time. Ergonomics **29**, 569–583 (1986)

Occupational Disease Compensation and Update on the Musculoskeletal Health of Office Employees in Hong Kong

Justine M. Y. Chim[1,2(✉)] and Tienli Chen[3]

[1] Student of Doctoral Program in Design, College of Design, National Taipei University of Technology, Taipei, Taiwan
jchim@my-ergonomics.com

[2] Principal Consultant, Chim's Ergonomics and Safety Limited, Hong Kong, 17/F, No. 80 Gloucester Road, Wan Chai, Hong Kong

[3] Professor of Department of Industrial Design, College of Design, National Taipei University of Technology, Taiwan, 1, Sec. 3, Zhongxiao E. Rd., Taipei 10608, Taiwan

Abstract. The aims of this paper include introduction of the Employees' Compensation Ordinance in relation to occupational disease in cases of musculoskeletal disorders. The paper also gives updates on the musculoskeletal health of office-based computer users from 2018 to 2019 and 2020 during COVID-19 pandemic.

In Schedule 2 of the Employees' Compensation Ordinance, compensable occupational disease concerning musculoskeletal issues caused by prolonged use of computers only include injuries to the hand or forearm (including elbow). If office employees suffer from lower back or shoulder pain, any application for compensation may not be practicable and feasible.

Statistics indicate that 96% of office employees in Hong Kong spent at least six hours a day on computer work in the years 2018 and 2019. A total of 78% of office employees reported musculoskeletal discomfort and among all cases, Shoulder, Neck and Lower Back were the three highest reported body regions to have discomfort in past research from 2011 till 2020.

In terms of the musculoskeletal health of computer-based users during COVID-19 in 2020, 80% of respondents self-reported musculoskeletal discomfort during the pandemic season of COVID-19. A high percentage of respondents who suffered from musculoskeletal health issues did not seek medical treatment. In addition, about one-third of the respondents had a basic workstation setup with the use of a laptop, tablet or phone only for work/study from home. 54% of the survey respondents perceived no suitable work/study space at home, but only 10% of the survey respondents were dissatisfied with their workstation setup at home.

Keywords: Employees' compensation · Musculoskeletal disorders · Computer workstation · COVID-19 pandemic

N. L. Black et al. (Eds.): IEA 2021, LNNS 222, pp. 703–709, 2021.
https://doi.org/10.1007/978-3-030-74611-7_97

1 Introduction

The World Health Organization (WHO) describes musculoskeletal health as affecting physical mobility and functional ability, which is also linked with mental well-being and chronic health situations. As per the International Classification of Disease, musculoskeletal conditions affect the joints, bones, muscles, spine as well as multiple body systems. The development of musculoskeletal issues can arise suddenly and last for a short period of time; however, it could possibly become a lifelong condition with suffering from ongoing and persistent pain and even disability (WHO, 2021).

Many studies have reported the prevalence rate of musculoskeletal disorders among office employees: musculoskeletal disorders are caused by prolonged working hours, repetitive movements and improper working posture (Akrouf et al. 2010).

In Hong Kong, previous studies have reported that the percentage of office employees who spend at least six hours a day doing computing work increased from 73% in 2011 to 2012 to 96% from 2015 to 2017. From 2015 to 2017, among 74% of subjects who reported musculoskeletal discomfort, 69% of them reported shoulder discomfort which was the highest reported body region with musculoskeletal discomfort. Moreover, the three highest reported body regions with musculoskeletal symptoms were neck, shoulders and lower back from three studies for the period from 2011 to 2017. The time and medical cost of seeking medical treatment is another concern of employers. During 2015 to 2017, 39% of sample office employees required medical treatment for musculoskeletal problems. In summary, the reported rate of musculoskeletal discomfort among office employees has seen an alarming prevalence rate (Chim 2013, 2015, 2018).

2 Aims

The paper aims to introduce the Employees' Compensation Ordinance in Hong Kong in particular occupational disease in relation to the task nature and activities of office employees with prolonged use of computers. The paper also reports an update on the musculoskeletal health condition of office employees in Hong Kong for the period from 2018 to 2019 as well as 2020 during the COVID-19 pandemic.

3 Methodology

The legislation on Employees' Compensation Ordinance in Hong Kong was reviewed with consideration of the associated areas between the job nature of office employees with the use of computers and the potential outcome of work-related musculoskeletal injuries relevant to occupational disease compensation.

Regarding occupational health statistics, a quantitative method using face-to-face structured questions was used in this study. The data were collected by an ergonomics consultancy company in Hong Kong during the ergonomics workstation assessment for the period of 2018 to 2019. A total of 83 face-to-face structured interviews were conducted and questions on the average working hours of computer user at work, self-reported body region with musculoskeletal discomfort, and whether medical treatment had been received were asked. Regarding occupational health statistics, workstation setup and workspace condition during COVID-19 concerning work/study from home, a survey was used for collecting the data during a postgraduate online lecture at a University in Hong Kong. Two sets of data (N = 50 and N = 54) were collected in August 2020 during COVID-19.

4 Result and Discussion

4.1 Employees' Compensation Ordinance (Chap. 282) in Hong Kong

The Employees' Compensation Ordinance (Chap. 282) in Hong Kong applies to all employees no matter whether they are employed on a full-time or part-time basis under a contract of service. There are two types of liability for compensation under the Employees' Compensation Ordinance for an employee suffering incapacity arising from injury due to an accident or occupational disease. Concerning musculoskeletal disorders of office employees in relation to computer work, the compensation for temporary incapacity could be relevant to occupational disease cases under the Employees' Compensation Ordinance (Labour Department 2019).

In the legislation, an employer has the right to arrange for new employees to undertake a medical examination before job commencement so the employer has an opportunity to understand any pre-existing musculoskeletal medical condition and also, the employer can modify the computer workstation, design suitable tasks and work arrangements for minimizing the development or aggravation of musculoskeletal health (Labour Department 2019). However, a pre-employment medical examination of musculoskeletal condition is not usually arranged in Hong Kong. In addition, it could be more important to ensure the selection of suitable furniture, office workstation setup, training and education on office ergonomics.

Schedule 2 of the Employees' Compensation Ordinance specifies compensable occupational diseases by law. Among all items in the list of compensable occupational diseases, only item A8 on the condition of "Traumatic inflammation of the tendons of the hand or forearm (including elbow), or of the associated tendon sheaths" could be relevant to the task nature of office employees with prolonged hours of computer work in which the tasks are frequent or repeated movements of the hand or wrist as per the description in Schedule 2. The compensation covers the medical expenses, loss of earnings during temporary incapacity as well as the permanent loss of earning capacity as per the legislation and is borne by the insurer (Labour Department 2019).

In reality, both the employer and employee bear significant uninsured costs associated with work-related musculoskeletal injuries. These include the cost of medical services, loss of skill and experience of the employee, training cost to replace the injured employee, loss of company goodwill, increased labour conflict, and the cost of investigation and reporting. If an office employee suffers from musculoskeletal disorders such as neck, shoulder or back pain which are other than that included in item A8 of Schedule 2 of the Employees' Compensation Ordinance, the medical expenses may be covered by the employer if the company's voluntary medical insurance benefits have been provided. If there is a high percentage of office employees who require medical treatment for their musculoskeletal health, the ultimate insurance premium will then be increased.

4.2 Update on the Musculoskeletal Health Condition of Office Employees during 2018 to 2020

Time Spent on Computing Work
The result shown in Table 1 indicates that from 2018 to 2019, 96% of 83 employees spent at least six hours a day on computing work. The percentage of prolonged hours spent on a computer during 2018 to 2019 was the same as for the period of 2015 to 2017.

For the year 2020 during the COVID-19 pandemic, the survey found that among the respondents, 58% of them had spent at least four days a week working/studying at home with a computer/laptop.

Table 1. Time Spent on computing work (2011 to 2020)

Items	2011–2012	2013–2014	2015–2017	2018–2019	2020
Sample size (number of office employees)	618	245	1618	83	54*
Time spent at least six hours a day in computing work (%)	73%	87%	96%	96%	58%**

(Chim 2013, 2015, 2018).
* The sample refers to work from home/study during COVID-19 pandemic
** The result refers to time spent at least four days a week working/studying with a computer/laptop at home during COVID-19 pandemic.

Self-reported Musculoskeletal Symptoms
Table 2 shows the self-reported musculoskeletal health statistics for the period from 2011 to 2020. During the period of 2018 to 2019, 78% of sample employees reported musculoskeletal symptoms. Among all reported discomfort cases, Shoulder (78%), Neck (65%) and Lower Back (26%) were three highest reported body regions.

For the year 2020 during the COVID-19 pandemic, the results showed that 80% of respondents self-reported suffering from musculoskeletal discomfort. Among the reported cases, 50% had discomfort in one body region and 50% had discomfort in more than one body region. The survey results concluded that the neck, lower back and shoulder are three commonly reported body regions with one body region discomfort. The continuous high percentage of self-reported musculoskeletal symptoms was noted.

Seeking of Medical Treatment
Table 3 shows the statistical result of the self-reported health condition of office employees who sought medical treatment during 2011 to 2020. During 2018 to 2019, the percentage of self-reported musculoskeletal symptoms was similar to previous years. However, only 8% of sample employees reported musculoskeletal symptoms and required medical treatment which was comparatively low compared to previous years of 39% to 52%. It is noted that the sample size was relatively smaller for 2018 to 2019 comparative to previous studies. This was caused by the Hong Kong protests with less office ergonomics assessment completed due to the protests affecting business operation and day to day personal life in 2019/2020.

Table 2. Self-reported musculoskeletal symptoms (2011 to 2020)

Items	2011–2012	2013–2014	2015–2017	2018–2019	2020
Sample Size (number of office employees)	618	245	1618	83	50
Reported Musculoskeletal Symptoms (%)	81%	91%	74%	78%	80%
Commonly reported body region with discomfort	Neck, Shoulder, Lower Back	Shoulder *(31%)* Lower Back *(26%)* Neck *(14%)*	Shoulder *(69%)* Neck *(49%)* Lower Back *(39%)*	Shoulder *(78%)* Neck *(65%)* Lower Back *(26%)*	Discomfort for More than One Body Regions *(50%)* Discomfort for One Body Region Neck *(17.5%)* Lower Back *(15%)* Shoulder *(10%)* Others *(7.5%)*

(Chim 2013, 2015, 2018).

Table 3. Seeking of medical treatment (2011 to 2020)

Items	2011–2012	2013–2014	2015–2017	2018–2019	2020
Sample size (number of office employees)	618	245	1618	83	50
Seeking of medical treatment	52%	42%	39%	8%	22.5%

(Chim 2013, 2015, 2018).

For the year 2020 during the COVID-19 pandemic, among 80% of the respondents who reported musculoskeletal discomfort, 76.5% of them did not visit a doctor or therapist in the past 6 months. The result could be related to the COVID-19 pandemic as people were highly advised to keep a physical distance and stay at home so people who may have suffered from musculoskeletal condition had less intention to visit a doctor or therapist for consultation.

5 Workstation Setup and Workspace Condition for Work/Study from Home During the COVID-19 pandemic in 2020

The results in Table 4 show that 34% of the respondents use laptops, tablets or phones for work/study from home. It is not a satisfactory computer workstation setup for prolonged computer user. In addition, 28% of the respondents had a fully equipped workstation setup for using a laptop/desktop connected to a separate monitor screen, keyboard and computer mouse. This is a more ideal setup with a separate monitor screen and input devices so the computer user can properly maintain a good working posture. It will rely on the company promoting computer ergonomics practice for working from home so the computer user can acquire the knowledge and skill for a proper workstation setup and adopt a healthy posture.

In Tables 5 and 6, among all respondents, only 54% believed that their work/study space at home was unsuitable although 80% self-reported musculoskeletal discomfort and 71% did not have a full workstation setup. In addition, the survey also showed that 74% of the respondents were moderately satisfied with their workstation setup at home and only 5% were unsatisfied with their workstation setup at home.

The high rate of self-reported musculoskeletal discomfort and unsatisfactory computer workstation and equipment setup suggests that the respondents were not well aware of the musculoskeletal health hazard in light of the perceived suitability of their work/study space at home and perceived satisfaction with their workstation setup.

Table 4. Computer workstation and equipment use for work/study from home

Items		Frequency	Percent
Basic setup	Laptop/tablet/phone only	17	34%
Laptop setup	Laptop + mouse or + separate keyboard & mouse	18	36%
Full setup	Desktop computer or Laptop + external monitor + separate keyboard & mouse	14	28%
	None of above	1	2%

Computer users are advised to set up their home office depending on their work activities, the home environment and individual needs. In addition, healthy computer practice involves regular stretching and moving to avoid the development of musculoskeletal pain.

Table 5. Perceived suitability of work/study space at home

Items	Frequency	Percent
Yes, I think so	23	46%
No	27	54%

Table 6. Perceived satisfaction of workstation setup at home

Items	Frequency	Percent
Satisfied	8	16%
Moderately satisfied	37	74%
Unsatisfied	5	10%

6 Conclusion

This paper concludes that musculoskeletal health has been an area of considerable concern in regard to office employees' well-being. Office employees in Hong Kong spend long hours with computers. Especially in the new norm of working from home, the potential for musculoskeletal health issues will be more significant as computer workstations may not be properly equipped and set up in the home environment. The selection of appropriate furniture and workstation setup are required for the prevention of musculoskeletal discomfort.

Acknowledgements. This work was supported by Chim's Ergonomics and Safety Limited.

References

Akrouf, Q.A.S., Crawford, J.O., Al Shatti, A.S., Kamel, M.I.: Musculoskeletal disorders among bank office workers in Kuwait. EMHJ-East. Mediterr. Health J. **16**(1), 94–100 (2010)

Chim, J.M.Y.: Musculoskeletal disorders among office employees in Hong Kong and best practice office ergonomics solutions. In Proceedings of the 8th International Conference on Prevention of Work-Related Musculoskeletal Disorders, Busan, Korea, pp. 330–331 (2013)

Chim, J.M.Y.: Update on the musculoskeletal health of office employees in Hong Kong. In: Congress of the International Ergonomics Association, pp. 432–437. Springer, Cham (August 2018)

Labour Department: A Concise Guide to the Employees' Compensation Ordinance, Labour Department of HKSAR. https://www.labour.gov.hk/eng/public/ecd/pco360.pdf. Accessed 18 Jan 2020

Chim, J.M.Y.: Healthy computing and ergonomics: review of musculoskeletal health problems and workplace setting. In: Proceedings 19th Triennial Congress of the IEA, Melbourne (August 2015)

World Health Organization, Musculoskeletal condition dated 8 February 2021. https://www.who.int/news-room/fact-sheets/detail/musculoskeletal-conditions. Accessed 22 April 2021

Development of Criteria and Practical Methods to Study the Risks by Biomechanical Overload as an Aid Focused to Study Production Process Present in Companies Operating in Civil Construction Sector

Daniela Colombini[1]([✉]), Ariel Orlei Michaloski[2], Antonio Augusto de Paula Xavier[2], and Juliano Prado Stradioto[2]

[1] Scientific Association EPMIES, Milan, Italy
epmies.corsi@gmail.com
[2] Federal University of Technology - Paraná, Ponta Grossa, Brazil
{ariel,augustox}@utfpr.edu.br, juliano.stradioto@gmail.com

Abstract. The civil construction sector has difficulties in applying effective risk assessment methods for studying the biomechanical overhead, due to the complex work organization of tasks in situ and lack of ergonomics professionals. The biggest challenge in this sector is the fact that workers perform variable tasks, not just on a daily basis, but during all work activity (which can be weekly, monthly or even annually). Given that the organization of work in this sector includes a large number of manual tasks, each with a different level of exposure patterns to biomechanical risks, the working structure makes task analysis and risk evaluation very complex. This article presents a general model adapted to prevention of musculoskeletal diseases in the construction sector, in order to improve the health and safety of workers. Considering the presence of rotations between several repetitive tasks that are completed in periods longer than the day (macrocycles with annual turnover) the OCRA method (the only one that allows this type of risk analysis) was used. The study of biomechanical overload from manual handling of loads and posture is completed by using the adapted NIOSH method and the TACOs method respectively. The evaluation examples presented confirm that the methods proposed here for the study of biomechanical overload, both first and second level, allow to obtain risk evaluation also in this complex sector.

Keywords: Construction · Risk assessment · Biomechanical overload · Awkward postures · Multitask analysis · Manual lifting

1 Introduction

Work Related Musculoskeletal Disorders (WMSD) are the most common work-related illnesses among construction workers (Colombini 2012; Michaloski et al. 2020, Stradioto et al. 2020) [1–3].

The sector includes an immense diversity of skill sets and categories of workers. In addition, the size, structure and market of construction companies can also be extremely variable. The sector employs on average between 5 to 10% of the workforce in most countries, indicating that construction is a significant component of the global economy and is one of the largest employers in the world. Globally, musculoskeletal disorders are the major cause of work-related illnesses, accounting for more than 33% of all occupational diseases, with the prevalence becoming 65% for construction workers [4].

There are also indirect socio-economical implications due to job loss, absenteeism, health costs and even worker hospitalization [5, 6]. There is no doubt that the prevention of WMSDs may significantly contribute to reduce economic and social impact: the OCRA method offers the possibility to study the risk that can cause them.

The OCRA method in fact [7] takes into account action frequency, awkward postures (of arm, elbow, wrist and hand), force value, additional factors (mechanical, environmental and organizational), recovery periods and duration of the repetitive and non-repetitive tasks. The ISO 11228–3 Standard [8] recommends the use of OCRA to assess and classify risks in situations of upper limbs repetitive stress. Therefore, OCRA method was selected as the repetitive task design tool for this study.

Beyond repetitive movements, other causes of WMSDs are manual handling, heavy physical work, inadequate postures.

2 Scope of Proposed Project and Normative References

This project has the goal of defining the basic criteria and practical methods to assess the occupational risks in the civil construction sector, with more specific attention to the prevention of musculoskeletal disorders basically, following ISO 11228 series, of ISO 11226 and of ISO TR 12295 [5, 6, 8–10] guideline. Specifically, the project is aimed at providing the potential users with additional information on how to use existing standards in a world widespread working sector, where, also if with different characteristics, biomechanical overload is a relevant aspect and where preventive actions are needed.

One of the main goals is therefore to provide all users, and particularly those who are not experts in ergonomics, with criteria and procedures:

- To identify the situations in which they can apply the standards of the ISO 11228 series and/or ISO 11226 and ISO TR 12295 in different construction contexts (*key-enter level*).
- To provide a *quick assessment* method (according to the criteria given in the relative standard) to easily recognize activities that are "*certainly acceptable*" or "*certainly critical*".

If an activity is "not acceptable because critical" it is necessary to proceed as soon as possible with the subsequent improvement actions. Where the quick assessment method shows that the activity risk falls between the two exposure conditions, then it is necessary to refer to the detailed methods for risk assessment set out in the relevant standard.

3 Materials

To explain the complexity of the subject, reference is made in the following to the experience carried out in Brazil in conjunction with a team of construction engineers from the UTFPR Technological University – Brazil and EPMIES (Ergonomics of Posture and Movements. International Ergonomics School)-Italy. The ergonomic analysis in the construction industry was studied with qualitative and quantitative approach, through field research and case studies. In the first phase the data were collected through a survey with interviews and questionnaires applied in loco in seven construction sites (buildings with an average of fifteen floors) in Ponta Grossa, Paraná, Brazil.

In the second more analytical phase, filming and photographs were taken over a ten-month period (2018 and 2019), due to the complexity and availability of the activity at each participating construction site. More than 300 tasks were recorded and analyzed. The study project was analyzed by the Committee of Ethics in Research of the Federal University of Technology, Paraná - Brazil and received the authorization to be conducted in June 07, 2018, under the no. CAAE 83437517.0.0000.5547, in accordance with the Declaration of Helsinki.

4 Methods: General Outline of the Working Process in Annual Multi-task Analysis in Construction: Qualitative Tasks Distribution Over the Year and Research of the Homogeneous Groups of Workers

Task rotation is when a worker alternates between two or more tasks during a certain period of time. In special situations, such as in construction, where the worker has to perform a large number of tasks and the tasks are distributed "asymmetrically" throughout the shift, risk assessments can become extremely complex. This is why it is necessary to carry out a thorough preliminary study of how the work is organized.

In this contest it is necessary, for starting the risk process analysis, to define a set of procedures and criteria for estimating risk in more complex situations, where workers perform multiple tasks variously distributed in qualitative and quantitative terms over the year (annual cycle). It is an anything but simple matter to identify tasks, which may be very numerous and performed by different workers or groups of workers. At the outset, therefore, it is necessary (as shown in Table 1) to:

- Identify a specific building site;
- Break down the growing activities work into *macro-phases* and *phases*: all of the relevant tasks must be identified;
- List all the tasks required annually, regardless of who performs them: then allocation of tasks to workers (either on an individual basis or as a homogeneous group for risk exposure).

The next step is to assign tasks to an *individual worker* or *group of workers exposed to the same risk*, to identify *homogeneous groups*. The different tasks, present in building site, will be assigned to different groups of workers. When *tasks of the same nature and duration* are assigned to the same group of workers, we may speak of a *homogeneous group in terms of risk exposure*. Due to space constraint Table 1 shows only some of the 300 tasks carried out: in the example those actually performed by a single homogeneous group (No.1), during the entire year, broken down into each month.

5 Pre-mapping of Danger and Discomfort: Contents, Criteria and Preliminary Results

The main aim is to rapidly but accurately identify the presence of possible sources of risk, using instruments that can easily be used by accident prevention officers, occupational physicians, business owners, workers, trade union representatives and security services. This objective also reflects the criteria set forth in ISO/TR 12295 with respect to the risk of biomechanical overload [8].

Table 1. Example of semi-quantitative description of tasks per month among homogeneous group of workers n°1.

	No. hours worked by the homogeneous group per month											
	0	0	0	0	0	195	200	200	195		0	0
All the repetitive tasks	Jan	Feb	Mar	Apr	May	Jun	Jul	Aug	Sep	Oct	Nov	Dec
Crane operating from the ground						5%	5%	5%	5%			
-Manual pallet transport (strong force)						5%	5%	5%	5%			
-Manual pallet transport (strong force)						5%	5%	5%	5%			
-Material transport with wheelbarrow						5%	5%	5%	5%			
Transport manual weight> 40kg						10%	10%	10%	10%			
-External wall cover with projector						5%	5%	5%	5%			
-External spoon coating						5%	5%	5%	5%			

(continued)

Table 1. (*continued*)

	No. hours worked by the homogeneous group per month											
	0	0	0	0	0	195	200	200	195		0	0
-Spray with sarrafo - regua						10%	10%	10%	10%			
-Spread with spoon						10%	10%	10%	10%			
External spoon coating - instable						10%	10%	10%	10%			
-Short sarrafo spread - instable						10%	10%	10%	10%			
-Finishing with unhandless hand instable						10%	10%	10%	10%			
-Performance finishing - instable						10%	10%	10%	10%			
						100	100	100	100			

Against this backdrop, the "problem" of WMSDs must be considered together with other occupational "hazards" (be they physical, chemical, or other), for the more general purposes of prevention. Aim here is to suggest a methodology and some simple tools for bringing together various parties to undertake a preliminary *mapping of discomfort/danger* (i.e., to identify *risk sources in the work cycle*) in the workplace.

The procedure presented here demands a cooperative approach towards assessing and managing risk, as it also entails interviews with workers.

As it is inherently difficult to identify macro-phases, phases and tasks in building construction, they have been collected in kind of *universal building construction library* that will enable even beginners to conduct a preliminary organizational analysis in building construction setting.

The specific worksheet, **EPMIES-costruERGOCHECKpreconstructionENG** (now in validation) includes the library with the universal building construction organisation.

The model (implemented in the spreadsheet) provides a general preliminary overview of all the main risk factors that may be present, regardless of the size of the manufacturing facility, and is underpinned by the basic tenets of ergonomics, entailing a global interpretation of the worker's discomfort deriving from the task or the workplace. Figure 1 shows an example of "pre-mapping" results obtained from of the homogeneous group NO.1

(part time, 4 months), generated automatically by the software, depicting histograms for all possible risks. These histograms give merely descriptive scores, to be used to "rank" events from the best to the worst. The scores do not reflect an analysis or assessment of risk: they are simply descriptive scales designed to help not only to identify problems but also to set priorities for the analyses and evaluations that will have to be undertaken to adopt immediate measures to reduce risk, especially for conditions defined as "critical".

While describing only the priorities of intervention with respect to exposure at risk, the method is still very sensitive to exposition times, thanks to its careful initial organizational and exposition analysis. In the example of Fig. 2, in fact, the final result of the evaluation for a homogeneous group (n°. 2) is shown, the same for the tasks carried out as the homogeneous group n°.1, but different for the exposure times (in this case a full time, 11 months): the histograms indicate scores much higher than the previous ones.

6   Analytical Study of Working Process in Annual Multi-task Analysis: the Typical Working Day and the Quantitative Tasks Distribution

To switch from pre-mapping of discomfort and dangers (first level of the evaluation), the actual assessment phase of the risk, whatever the risk to be analyzed, it is necessary to deepen the organizational studies with data no longer just only qualitative but also quantitative. Three phases are necessary: Phase a – Description of a typical working day; Phase b – Estimation of the total number of hours worked every month of the year; Phase c – Assignment of tasks to a homogeneous group (or individual worker) and calculation of their proportional duration in each individual month.

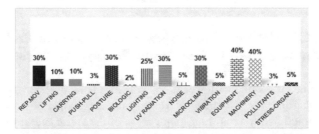

Fig. 1. Final summary results generated automatically by the software, depicting histograms for all possible risks presented by homogeneous group n°.1 part time, 4 months (example in Table1).

Before going on to complete the organizational analysis of the risk-exposed worker or homogeneous group of workers, the exposure constants to which reference is made for calculating exposure time to various tasks, for reconstructing the *artificial working day representative of the year,* are to be used [7]. It has been found to be necessary to adopt the exposure constants representing the typical exposure level used in the industry.

Once obtained the duration of tasks in each month (as in Table 1), the figure enabling the final risk can be evaluated: the *total number of hours worked per year on each task* by each member of the homogeneous group.

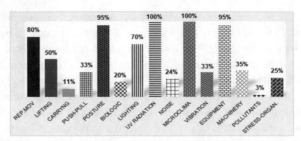

Fig. 2. Final summary results generated automatically by the software, depicting histograms for all possible risks presented by homogeneous group NO.2 full time 11 months.

7 Annual Multitask Risk Assessment of Biomechanical Overload for Upper Limbs: Contents, Criteria and Preliminary Results

To arrive at a final risk index with use of the OCRA method for multi-analysis tasks, it is necessary to proceed by the following successive steps [7]:

– *Phase a* – Analysis of each individual task using the OCRA checklist to calculate the intrinsic score [7] and prepare the "basic tasks risk evaluation" for a building site.
– *Phase b* - Application of mathematical models: preliminary preparation of *artificial working day representative of the whole year* and of every month of the same.

Figure 3 compares, month-by-month, the checklist OCRA risk index obtained in two homogeneous groups, doing the same tasks for 420 min. a shift but the homogeneous group n°.1 working 4 month a year and homogeneous group n°.2 working eleven months.

8 The TACOS Method: Contents and Criteria and Preliminary Results for Back and Lower Limbs Posture Analysis

The TACOs studies the spine an lower limbs posture (Time assessment computerized system) [4]. Regarding the examples of Homogeneous groups, n° 1 and 2, the final results are presented divided into four major areas of the spine and lower limbs and in their entirety (Fig. 4).

9 Annual Multitask Risk Assessment of Manual Material Handling: Manual Lifting and Pushing-Pulling

In order to study the annual exposure risk for manual lifting of loads and pushing-pulling, it is necessary to start again from the quantitative organisational studies. Start ng from Table 1, dedicated to identifying the tasks involving upper limbs repetitive tasks, we now have to activated only tasks where the manual lifting and pushing-pulling are present [8], also if without risk: these last are to be included, assigning them a risk value equal or less than 1 (acceptable risk, green band).

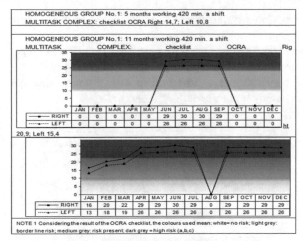

Fig. 3. Risk index scores (for homogeneous group n°.1 and n°.2, plotted by month over the whole year using Multitask Complex formula.

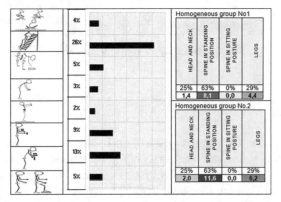

Fig. 4. Application of TACOs for an additional study of back and lower limb postures in two different exposure settings (homogeneous group n°1 and 2).

Always following the same criteria used for other hazards that may cause biomechanical overload, we will calculate, for each task, the intrinsic risk, with the calculation techniques defined in ISO standards [6, 8]. We will present only the results obtain regarding manual lifting. The tasks performed may be characterized by manual lifting of loads of type *mono task,* or *composite task* or *variable task.* When calculating the intrinsic indexes for MMH in construction, the frequency/duration multiplier for *long duration* is to be used [1, 6].

The intrinsic values are calculated separately for adult male, adult female, younger/older male, younger/older female [1, 6]. Now having the intrinsic risk indices and the proportional duration of each task, both within each month of the year and throughout the year, becomes possible calculate risk indices through the reconstruction of new *artificial working days*, specific for manual lifting of loads, representative of each month and of the year.

This procedure is the same as used for calculating exposure to repetitive movements with OCRA method and awkward postures with TACOS method.

Examples of application are proposed in Fig. 5 concerning manual lifting risk assessment in the homogeneous groups n°.1 and n°.2.

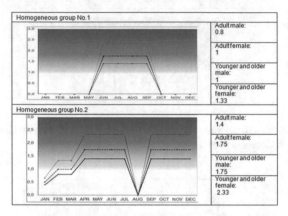

Fig. 5. Examples of homogeneous groups.

10   Conclusion

The complex procedures for addressing the biomechanical overload in construction have be developed, including the study of the risk of repetitive upper limb movements, manual lifting and awkward postures (including lower limb and spine studies).

Criteria and measurement methods already present in the ISO standards dedicated to biomechanics have been proposed and adapted to the characteristics of build construction work that involves annual cycle organization, with exposure to more work tasks, which diversify qualitatively and quantitatively over the course of the year.

Given the clear complexity of the risk assessment, to start with a first qualitative and simple analysis (using the *key questions* and *quick assessment*) is illustrated. It is extended not only to biomechanical risk factors but to all risks, so as to obtain a sort of *global risk pre-mapping*, which points out the presence of discomforts and dangers and with priorities for more precise risk assessments. A simple tool to deal with this first phase of analysis is available. Methodologies for actual risk assessment level applicable to the construction complex case have been developed by applying OCRA, NIOSH and TACOs methodologies.

References

1. Colombini, D., Occhipinti, E., Alvarez, C., Waters, T.: Manual Lifting: A Guide to Study of Simple and Complex Lifting Tasks. CRC Press by Taylor & Francis, New York (2012)

2. Michaloski, A.O., Stradioto, J.P., de Paula Xavier, A.A.: Ergonomics study in the productive process in civil construction in the external plastering activity. In: Goossens R., Murata A. (eds.) Advances in Social and Occupational Ergonomics. AHFE 2019. Advances in Intelligent Systems and Computing, vol. 970, pp. 245–255. Springer, Washington (2020). https://doi.org/10.1007/978-3-030-20145-6_24
3. Stradioto, J.P., Michaloski, A.O., de Paula Xavier, A.A., Colombini, D.: Comparison of RULA and checklist OCRA ergonomic risk methods for civil construction. Ind. Eng. Manag. Syst. **19**(4), 790–802 (2020). https://doi.org/10.7232/iems.2020.19.4.790
4. Colombini, D., Occhipinti, E.: Working Posture Assessment: The TACOs Method, Time-Based Assessment Computerized Strategy. CRC Taylor & Francis, New York (2018)
5. ISO 11226, Ergonomics—Evaluation of static working posture.
6. ISO 11228–1, Ergonomics—Manual handling—Part 1: Lifting and carrying
7. Colombini, D., Occhipinti, E.: Risk Analysis and Management of Repetitive Actions: A guide for Applying the OCRA System (Occupational Repetitive Actions). CRC Press by Taylor & Francis, New York (2016)
8. ISO/TR 12295, Ergonomics—Application document for International Standards on manual handling (ISO 11228–1, ISO 11228–2 and ISO 11228–3) and evaluation of static working postures (ISO 11226).ISO 12100, Safety of machinery—General principles for design
9. ISO 11228–2, Ergonomics—Manual handling—Part 2: Pushing and pulling
10. ISO 11228–3, Ergonomics—Manual handling—Part 3: Handling of low loads at high frequency

Musculoskeletal Disorders in Unstructured, Unregulated Work: Assessment Methods and Injuries

Clive D'Souza[1]([⊠]) [iD], Bernard Martin[1] [iD], Julius N. Fobil[2] [iD], Andrew Todd[3] [iD], and José Orlando Gomes[4] [iD]

[1] Center for Ergonomics, Department of Industrial & Operations Engineering, University of Michigan, Ann Arbor, MI 48109-2117, USA
crdsouza@umich.edu
[2] Department of Biological, Environmental & Occupational Health Sciences, School of Public Health, University of Ghana, P.O. Box LG13, Accra, Ghana
[3] Department of Human Kinetics and Ergonomics, Rhodes University, Grahamstown, South Africa
[4] Department of Industrial Engineering, Federal University of Rio de Janeiro, Rio de Janeiro, Brazil

Abstract. Unstructured and unregulated work is expanding fast among low- and middle-income countries (LMICs). Furthermore, accumulation of urban waste resulting from overconsumption is a global concern. Hence, waste management and recycling have received increased attention. One specific waste category pertaining to electrical and electronic waste (e-waste) is growing at a higher rate than other waste streams. Recycling of e-waste is largely informal and disproportionately relies on LMICs, exposing workers to various occupational and environmental health risks. In order to promote safer work practices and limit a broad range of occupational health and safety concerns associated with informal manual work, the broader psychosocial and sociocultural environment also deserves attention. This symposium will discuss contemporary issues in informal, unregulated, unstructured work in LMICs, primarily in Africa and South America. The goal of the symposium is to call attention to both, the unique occupational context of informal work, and the need for new ergonomics methods to address occupational exposure assessment and musculoskeletal injury prevention adapted to informal work in limited resource settings.

Keywords: Electronic waste · Informal work · LMIC · Musculoskeletal disorders · Exposure assessment

1 Introduction

The ILO estimates that nearly two billion people, or about 61% of the world's employed population, make their living in the informal economy [1]. Particularly notable is that LMICs and emerging countries employ 93% of the world's informal worker population.

N. L. Black et al. (Eds.): IEA 2021, LNNS 222, pp. 720–727, 2021.
https://doi.org/10.1007/978-3-030-74611-7_99

The informal sector makes up 85.8% of employment in Africa compared to 25.1% in Europe [1].

Informal work is characterized by work conducted in unstructured and unregulated conditions, and is typically based on casual employment, kinship or personal and social relations rather than contractual arrangements with formal guarantees. This implies a lack of social protection, worker rights and decent working conditions. Specific to human factors and ergonomics (HF/E), this also means that informal work has little to no implementation of occupational health and safety (OHS) guidelines. Consequently, informal workers are exposed to significant risk for adverse health effects, including acute injuries, musculoskeletal disorders (MSDs) from cumulative trauma, and work disability through poor working conditions and environments.

1.1 Informal Waste Processing

Accumulation of urban waste resulting from overconsumption is a global concern. Informal workers mostly perform the collection, processing and recycling of urban waste in LMICs. This is a source of livelihood for low skill, low-wage workers [2].

Waste from used electrical and electronic equipment, commonly known as e-waste, is growing at a higher rate than the regular municipal waste streams. High demand and overconsumption of electronic and electrical appliances (e.g., computers, cellphones) has created a global crisis in e-waste management [3]. Globally, generation of e-waste in 2019 was 53.6 million tons (MT) and projected to reach 74.7MT by 2030 [3]. Recycling of e-waste disproportionately relies on LMICs [3, 4]. Vast amounts of e-waste from Europe and North America make their way into LMICs each year disguised as donations that end up at dumpsites [3, 4]. E-waste processing in LMICs is almost exclusively informal and conducted by low-skilled workers, with little attention to OHS practices, e.g., PPE use, proper work tools and/or workstations [2, 5, 6].

1.2 Goals of This Symposium

The goal of this symposium is to call attention to both, the unique occupational context of informal work, and the need for new ergonomics methods to address occupational exposure assessment and MSD prevention adapted to informal work in limited resource settings. The symposium will discuss contemporary issues in informal, unregulated, unstructured work in LMICs, primarily in Africa and South America.

The specific objectives of the symposium are to:

- Discuss specific examples and lessons from first-hand experience of conducting research with informal e-waste processing in Ghana, and waste collection in South Africa as case examples.
- Present the contextual factors that pose unique challenges to conducting ergonomic research in unstructured, informal work settings,
- Identify research needs and knowledge gaps related to MSD risk assessment and injury prevention specific to informal worker populations in LMICs.

2 Methodology

2.1 Overview of the Interdisciplinary Panel

This symposium brings together an interdisciplinary panel of researchers. The symposium organizers, Profs. Clive D'Souza and Bernard Martin are experienced in the field of occupational ergonomics, assessment of physical work exposures, and MSD prevention. Prof. Julius Fobil is an expert in environmental epidemiology, the exposure assessment, surveillance and control of environmental pollution, waste management research in LMICs, and co-leads the West Africa-Michigan CHARTER II for GEO Health. Mr. Andrew Todd is a senior lecturer and experienced in embedding HF/E research within real-world contexts to ensure validity of findings. His particular focus is on the informal economy in South Africa, with an emphasis on understanding waste pickers and the challenges faced in their work. Prof. José Orlando Gomes conducts research on ergonomic work analyses in the wild/real-world in several domains including complex systems, with a particular focus on methodology oriented to reducing the gap between work-as-imagined versus work-as-done.

2.2 Informal, Unstructured Work Settings

A growing number of studies call attention to the musculoskeletal health effects of informal, unstructured work encountered in manual processing/recycling of municipal solid waste, medical waste, and e-waste. The informal waste processing sector is plagued by high rates of MSD symptoms, particularly in the low back, shoulders, neck, and knees [7]. A survey of 340 solid waste collectors (e.g., sweepers, garbage collectors, garbage van and tricycle drivers) in Accra, Ghana found high pain prevalence in the back (73.5%), wrist (48.2%) and neck (44.7%), with 80 to 90% of the respondents developing pain symptoms subsequent to joining their current job [8]. Studies from India, Egypt, Colombia, Philippines, and Iran indicate similar MSD trends among urban waste workers [7–9]. These studies also identify potential risk factors including heavy material handling (e.g., lifting, carrying, pushing-pulling), bending and repetitive tasks, and prolonged sitting and standing, environmental factors (e.g., heat, harsh outdoor conditions), personal factors (e.g., low literacy, smoking, drug use) and psychosocial factors (e.g., work stress, poor job security) [7].

Case Example: Informal E-Waste Processing in Ghana: Agbogbloshie is the largest dumping grounds for e-waste in sub-Saharan Africa and among the busiest informal e-waste recycling sites in the world [3, 4]. Multiple recent studies conducted at Agbogbloshie report high rates of work-related MSD symptoms, e.g., chronic body pain, discomfort, from informal e-waste recycling [5, 6, 10]. Studies on e-waste workers in other LMICs suggest similar trends [11, 12]. Studies also report high rates (96%) of acute injuries, e.g., cuts, lacerations, and scars among e-waste workers [10].

Most e-waste workers in Ghana are young, typically between 14 to 40 years old. They regularly work between 10 to 12 h per day or 300 to 360 h per month, [4, 5]. Work continues every day of the week, with workers taking either Fridays or Sundays off based on religious affiliation [6, 13]. These conditions suggest limited rest/recovery, increased cumulative fatigue and MSD risk. Not surprisingly, workers at this dumpsite have a short work tenure (i.e., high turnover) of 3 to 7 years [4].

E-waste workers at Agbogbloshie also self-medicate on painkillers, traditional medications, and other substances (e.g., smoking cannabis) to treat body pain [5, 10, 14]. Overuse or abuse of such treatments may potentially mask symptoms of underlying work-related MSDs reported in some studies.

The majority of studies on exposure assessment in the informal waste sector are based either on observational or self-reported data. Observational methods used in ergonomics are mostly suited to repetitive jobs with structured sampling. Adaptive sampling methods suited to informal work settings are few [13]. Body-worn video cameras are another option, but labor intensive to code video and/or image stills, may not capture all of the relevant work methods (e.g., hand tools) and body postures, and potential privacy concerns. Understanding cause-effect relationships between exposures and MSD causation from informal work needs prospective studies, however, these methods require extensive resources and trained personnel – which is scarce.

Informal waste recycling worksites present challenges to research, such as difficulties in collecting work-related, time-varying, job-specific exposure data and guide the design of locally-adapted strategies for injury prevention. Overcoming these research challenges will require new ergonomics perspectives, exposure assessment tools and methods suited to informal work settings.

2.3   The Big Picture: Effects on Environmental Health

Lessons learnt from the GEO-Health Project include the many studies conducted assessing health effects of exposure to particulate matter, rare metals and toxic chemicals associated with informal e-waste processing in Ghana and other countries in Africa [6, 10, 14]. Some key findings include:

- High levels of particulate matter affecting lung function and respiratory ailments
- Traces of aluminum, copper, iron, lead, and zinc in soil and/or air samples
- Toxic chemicals in the soil and vegetables resulting in non-communicable diseases
- Cancer, asthma, neurodevelopmental conditions, obesity, and chronic diseases due to noxious exposure in early childhood
- Restricted thyroid function, cellular expression and function, adverse neonatal outcomes, changes in temperament and behavior.

Environmental health challenges within the informal sector economy are pervasive, largely understudied and may require simple innovative methods for resolution compared to the formal sector while amendable to the application of interdisciplinary collaborations and broader systems approaches. The HF/E community could benefit from learning about these research experiences in allied OHS professions in terms of research methodology as well as identifying opportunities for taking a systems approach to OHS in the informal work sector.

2.4 Cultural Sensitivity, Trust and Community Embedded Research

Informal worker populations and stakeholder audiences can be very diverse in terms of linguistic, cultural, and economical background. Researchers administering questionnaires may need to be fluent in multiple languages to provide explanations in the local dialect to minimize translation errors and information loss. For example, in a study with e-waste workers, questionnaires were administered in English, with explanations given in Dagbani – the local dialect spoken by e-waste workers [13]. Similarly, in the South African study on waste pickers, questionnaires needed translation from English to isiXhosa. The lead researcher being a native English-speaker and unable to speak isiXhosa necessitated use of translators. Significant barriers were uncovered in translating ergonomics terminology into isiXhosa. Achieving consistency and reliability may need careful adaptation and piloting.

Certain worker groups in Africa still maintain a strong ethnic/tribal identity with a hierarchical structure, tribal Chiefs and noblemen. Research conducted with such worker populations requires approval and buy-in from tribal leaders. For example, research conducted at the Agbogbloshie e-waste dumpsite was preceded by a durbar (i.e., public gathering) with tribal leadership, representatives of the scrap dealers association, and available e-waste workers. The research team explained the study objectives and procedures in order to obtain buy-in from local/tribal leaders [13].

In post-apartheid countries like South Africa, low wage informal worker populations still bear a distrust of white-majority academic institutions. The distrust may stem from the long history of oppression and inequality [15]. Rhodes University (where the current research was undertaken) was initially established as an "Oxford in the bush" based on imperialistic western values [15]. Within this context there is need for carefully consideration of ergonomics methods for assessing exposures and MSD risk that rely on direct observations, video and/or photographs of workers and what this means on the part of communities in relation to academic institutions. Research with informal traders and waste pickers in South Africa reported reluctance to study participation due to data privacy concerns, i.e., unsure of where the data would end up and if it could be used against them at a later time [16]. These issues present challenges to obtaining reliable and valid data on exposure to potential MSD risk factors, hinders the embedding of researchers within the system, and impedes efforts to understand work-as-done vs. work-as-described or work-as-imagined. This made it difficult to gain a systemic understanding of the interactions leading to MSDs in waste pickers.

Stakeholder engagement is critical to conducting participatory research. Wilson (2014) warned against the charlatans of manual handling research of the past who took a narrow non-systems approach [17]. He contended "….a musculoskeletal disorders (MSD) investigation or improvement which does not account for psychological/emotional/social influences, on MSD causation or success of solutions, is not properly E/HF" [17]. Accordingly, good ergonomics research requires a systems approach focused on understanding interactions holistically within context whilst acknowledging emergence. To achieve this, Wilson (2014) argued an embedded approach as necessary, suggesting that any research not conducted "in the wild" should not have a primary role in HF/E [17]. Engagement with stakeholders should focus not just on external research goals but also align with internal objectives of the stakeholders. Workplace interventions focused on worker safety but perceived as reducing earnings/employment may get disused or abandoned. For example, adoption of a newly introduced powered wire-stripper/shredder at Agbogbloshie to isolate metal from insulated cables/wire required e-waste burners to fundamentally alter their work behaviors and overcome concerns of lower yield and decreased income – aspects that relied on mutual trust. From a South African research perspective, a key lesson learnt was to shift the focus from doing research *on* people to doing research *with* people. This strongly aligns with principles of both sociotechnical systems theory and participatory ergonomics that emphasize valuing all stakeholders within the system [18, 19].

2.5 Ergonomics and the Global Divide

Outreach and communication strategies with informal worker populations need to consider the context and purpose of the interaction. Informal workers may be hesitant to seek information about safer working conditions due to language barriers and low agency. Hence, outreach is critical. The design of communication products needs to follow principles of plain language and effective design, writing, and translation. Engagement of stakeholders such as community leaders and/or local health workers can also benefit in translating and communicating OHS research into prevention practices. The HF/E community needs to develop innovative approaches for action-oriented research and for disseminating case studies on the successes/failures of engaging informal worker communities to prevent workplace injuries and illnesses.

The lack of trained HF/E researchers and practitioners also hampers research on MSD causation and prevention. This spans formal and informal work settings, and government and regulatory agencies. Lack of HF/E training opportunities, for students in university curricula and for working professionals in government and industry, often results in a limited use or even misuse/misapplication of HF/E methods, analysis tools and workplace interventions borrowed from developed countries. Cross-country collaborations and research partnerships can help to build capacity for training-the-trainers in LMICs and address some of these gaps in HF/E education, training and practice.

3 Conclusion

Informal waste workers face substantial risk from hazardous exposures and work conditions. The high rates of MSDs and work disability among informal workers is likely a confluence of multiple factors, including high physical work demands, young worker population, long work hours, low literacy, polluted work environment, limited PPE and work tools, and psychosocial stressors [5–7, 13].

New ergonomics methods are required to address risk assessment and injury prevention adapted to informal work in limited resource settings. The HF/E community needs to foster international collaborations to help address some of the disproportionate OHS burden experienced by workers in the informal sector, particularly in LMICs. Interventions aimed at MSD prevention needs to consider the six key HF/E components proposed by Wilson (2014), namely, a systems focus, concern for context, interactions, holism, recognizing emergent properties, and embedded HF/E practice [17].

Acknowledgements. Symposium organizers C.D. and B.M. were partially supported by the training grant T42-OH008455 from the National Institute for Occupational Safety and Health (NIOSH), US Centers for Disease Control and Prevention (CDC).

J.N.F. was supported by the 1/2 West Africa-Michigan CHARTER in GEOHealth with funding from the US National Institutes of Health/Fogarty International Center (NIH/FIC) (paired grant nos. 1U2RTW010110–01 and 5U01TW010101) and Canada's International Development Research Center (IDRC; grant no. 108121–001).

The views expressed do not necessarily reflect the official policies of nor endorsement by NIH, NIOSH, CDC, and/or the Canadian and US Governments.

References

1. ILO: Women and men in the informal economy: A statistical picture. Third edition. International Labor Organization (ILO) (2018). https://www.ilo.org/global/publications/books/WCMS_626831/lang--en/index.htm, Accessed 12 Feb 2021
2. Oteng-Ababio, M.: When necessity begets ingenuity: e-waste scavenging as a livelihood strategy in Accra, Ghana. African Studies Quarterly **13**, 1–21 (2012)
3. Forti, V., Baldé, C.P., Kuehr, R., Bel, G.: The Global E-waste Monitor 2020: Quantities, flows, and the circular economy potential (2020). https://ewastemonitor.info/wp-content/uploads/2020/07/GEM_2020_def_july1_low.pdf, Accessed 25 Oct 2020
4. Amoyaw-Osei, Y., Agyekum, O.O., Pwamang, J.A., Mueller, E., Fasko, R., Schluep, M.: Ghana e-Waste Country Assessment: SBC e-Waste Africa Project, Secretariat of the Basel Convention, Châtelaine, Switzerland (2011). https://www.basel.int/Portals/4/BaselConvention/docs/eWaste/E-wasteAssessmentGhana.pdf, Accessed 21 Nov 2020
5. Acquah, A.A., D'Souza, C., Martin, B., Arko-Mensah, J., Nti, A.A., Kwarteng, L., Takyi, S., Quakyi, I.A., Robins, T.G., Fobil, J.N.: Processes and challenges associated with informal electronic waste recycling at Agbogbloshie, a suburb of Accra, Ghana. In: Proceedings of the 2019 Human Factors and Ergonomics Society Annual Meeting, Seattle, WA, vol. 63, no. 1, pp. 938–942 (2019). https://doi.org/10.1177/1071181319631219
6. Akormedi, M., Asampong, E., Fobil, J.N.: Working conditions and environmental exposures among electronic waste workers in Ghana. Int. J. Occup. Environ. Health **19**(4), 278–286 (2013). https://doi.org/10.1179/2049396713Y.0000000034
7. Emmatty, F.J., Panicker, V.V.: Ergonomic interventions among waste collection workers: a systematic review. Int. J. Ind. Ergonomics **72**, 158–172 (2019). https://doi.org/10.1016/j.ergon.2019.05.004
8. Norman, I.D.: Neck, wrist and back pain among solid waste collectors: case study of a Ghanaian waste management company. Open Public Health J. **6**(1), 59–66 (2013). https://doi.org/10.2174/1874944501306010059
9. Reddy, E., Yasobant, S.: Musculoskeletal disorders among municipal solid waste workers in India: a cross-sectional risk assessment. J. Family Med. Prim. Care **4**(4), 519 (2015). https://doi.org/10.4103/2249-4863.174270
10. Fischer, D., Seidu, F., Yang, J., Felten, M.K., Garus, C., Kraus, T., Fobil, J.N., Kaifie, A.: Health consequences for e-waste workers and bystanders - a comparative cross-sectional study. Int. J. Environ. Res. Public Health **17**(5), 1534 (2020). https://doi.org/10.3390/ijerph17051534
11. Ohajinwa, C., van Bodegom, P., Vijver, M., Olumide, A., Osibanjo, O., Peijnenburg, W.: Prevalence and injury patterns among electronic waste workers in the informal sector in Nigeria. Injury Prev. **24**(3), 185–192 (2018). https://doi.org/10.1136/injuryprev-2016-042265

12. Yohannessen, K., Pinto-Galleguillos, D., Parra-Giordano, D., Agost, A., Valdés, M., Smith, L.M., Galen, K., Arain, A., Rojas, F., Neitzel, R.L., Ruiz-Rudolph, P.: Health assessment of electronic waste workers in chile: participant characterization. Int. J. Environ. Res. Public Health **16**(3), 386 (2019). https://doi.org/10.3390/ijerph16030386
13. Acquah, A.A., D'Souza, C., Martin, B., Arko-Mensah, J., Botwe, P.K., Tettey, P., Nti, A.A., Kwarteng, L., Takyi, S., Quakyi, I.A., Robins, T.G., Fobil, J.N.: A preliminary assessment of physical work exposures among electronic waste workers at agbogbloshie, Accra Ghana. Int. J. Ind. Ergonomics **82**, 103096 (2021). https://doi.org/10.1016/j.ergon.2021.103096
14. Asampong, E., Dwuma-Badu, K., Stephens, J., Srigboh, R., Neitzel, R., Basu, N., Fobil, J.N.: Health seeking behaviours among electronic waste workers in Ghana. BMC Public Health **15**(1), 1065 (2015). https://doi.org/10.1186/s12889-015-2376-z
15. Maylam, P.: 'Oxford in the bush': the founding (and diminishing) ethos of Rhodes University. Afr. Hist. Rev. **48**(1), 21–35 (2016). https://doi.org/10.1080/17532523.2016.1231443
16. Redman, C.: Stakeholder identification in the makana municipal solid waste management system and stakeholder perceptions of waste pickers and their inclusion into the system: an ergonomics approach. Unpublished Masters thesis, Rhodes University, Grahamstown, SA (2020)
17. Wilson, J.R.: Fundamentals of systems ergonomics/human factors. Appl. Ergonomics **45**(1), 5–13 (2014). https://doi.org/10.1016/j.apergo.2013.03.021
18. Read, G.J., Salmon, P.M., Goode, N., Lenné, M.G.: A sociotechnical design toolkit for bridging the gap between systems-based analyses and system design. Hum. Fact. Ergonomics Manuf. Serv. Ind. **28**(6), 327–341 (2018). https://doi.org/10.1002/hfm.20769
19. Thatcher, A., Todd, A.: HFE in underdeveloped countries: how do we facilitate equitable, egalitarian, and respectful progress? In: Roscoe, R.D., Chiou, E.K., Wooldridge, A.R. (eds.) Advancing Diversity, Inclusion, and Social Justice through Human Systems Engineering, pp. 31–50. CRC Press, Boca Raton (2020). ISBN: 9780429425905

Work-Related Musculoskeletal Symptoms and Associated Factors in Laparoscopic Surgeons of Peruvian Hospitals

Carlos Manuel Escobar Galindo(✉), Alexandra Lang, Brendan Ryan, and Sue Cobb

Faculty of Engineering, Human Factors Research Group, University of Nottingham, Nottingham, UK
manuel.escobar@nottingham.ac.uk

Abstract. The study aimed to determine the prevalence of Work-related Musculoskeletal Symptoms (WRMS) and associated work system factors impacting laparoscopic surgery in Peruvian Hospitals. **Methods:** An online survey with 17 questions was sent to 320 laparoscopic surgeons in different hospitals in Perú. The survey was distributed by email and paper format and consisted of six sections: informed consent, demographic data, physical symptoms, working conditions, impact on surgeons and others. Descriptive data were presented in tables and figures while associations were established using chi-square and fisher´s exact tests with a significance of 0.05. **Results:** 140 surgeons responded to the survey. Most surgeons worked more than 5 years (57%) and belong to the age group 30–60 years (87%). The prevalence rate of WRMS in survey respondents was 89%, with targeted WRMS identified in the following body regions: shoulders (59%), neck (51%), hand/wrist (41%) and upper back (43%). Duration and complexity of surgeries (nature of tasks) and inadequate table height (technology) were considered as highly contributing factors to WRMS by more than 50% of surgeons surveyed. 40% of surgeons considered the lack of suitable equipment and inadequate training as a highly contributed factor to WRMS. **Conclusion:** The study determined a high rate of WRMS, especially in the upper body region. These WRMS were associated with several work factors mainly related to inadequate operating table height, duration and complexity of surgeries, lack of suitable equipment and training.

Keywords: Laparoscopic surgery · Minimally invasive surgery · Ergonomics · Surgery · Physical discomfort

1 Introduction

Laparoscopic surgery (LAPS) is a surgical technique that consists of operating on patients without making large incisions in the skin and through the use of a camera that displays images on a monitor. Because of the short hospital stay and short recovery period, LAPS is preferred by patients but the work can be more challenging for surgeons and assistants [1]. Unlike open surgery, LAPS demands special psychomotor skills and working

© The Author(s), under exclusive license to Springer Nature Switzerland AG 2021
N. L. Black et al. (Eds.): IEA 2021, LNNS 222, pp. 728–737, 2021.
https://doi.org/10.1007/978-3-030-74611-7_100

with sensory restriction by using long surgical instruments of about 35 cm length. Before surgery, the patient's abdomen is insufflated with CO_2 until it is large enough to introduce the trocars, which consist of small tubes that allow maintaining the insufflation and the introduction of laparoscopic surgical tools to operate. To display images on the monitor, an assistant conducts the laparoscope (camera) that is introduced into the abdomen of patients and guides the laparoscope according to instructions from the surgeon. Hence, LAPS demands a high level of interaction with different elements of the surgical work system. A work system consists of a set of elements that interact dynamically with a specific objective. Elements in the system include tasks, technology, internal /external environment, organization and person(s) [2]. Poor interactions between system components can negatively impact the behaviour and wellbeing of people (individuals and teams) and overall performance and safety of the system [2] As a result, demands of the system may overtake the physical and mental capacities of persons, so they may experience as primary response work-related musculoskeletal symptoms (WRMS) including pain, fatigue, heat and tremors [3]. Symptoms may lead to severe limitations and restrictions in the performance of tasks reducing the response capacity of individuals [4]. Thus, ongoing and high exposure to sub-optimal work system factors without control and balance may lead to Work-related musculoskeletal disorders [WRMSD]. This condition is the most prevalent work-related health issue affecting workers from different occupations, with high impact on work performance [5].

Studies in developed countries (DC) indicate that the prevalence rates of WRMS in surgeons is high, reaching a range of 74%–95%, with a predominance in the neck, shoulders and back region [6–8]. Despite the high rates of symptoms, rates of clinically diagnosed WRMSD are comparatively low, with 17 and 19% of reports among laparoscopic surgeons [9]. The main trigger conditions are work-related factors present in operating rooms (OR) especially in DC [7, 8, 10, 11]. There are few studies from industrial developing countries (IDC) such as Perú where the healthcare system has limitations, adverse event rates in surgery are high and access to technology can be restricted. Peruvians are among the shortest populations not only in Latin America but also in the world due to the high native american genetic load [14, 15]. These physical characteristics of Peruvian surgeons and other personnel working in the OR, can mean that they experience difficultly and discomfort when interacting with medical equipment that is mainly manufactured in DC and designed to fit the requirements and characteristics of taller people [16]. Internal and external conditions of the fragmented Peruvian healthcare system has several limitations that affect the medical management, medical technology availability, surgical training patient safety culture and occupational health policies [12, 17]. There is a gap in the academic literature regarding LAPS related WRMSD within IDCs and specifically Peru. As such, there is a need to investigate the main issues related to LAPS within the Peruvian surgical system and the factors associated with WRMS of surgeons to prioritize further actions. The study aimed to determine the prevalence of WRMS and associated work system factors impacting surgeons performing LAPS in Peruvian Hospitals.

2 Method

A descriptive cross-sectional study was carried out from 2018 to 2019, applying a virtual survey to Peruvian surgeons with accredited experience in LAPS recognized by the Peruvian medical college. Students, residents, and physicians still in training were excluded. The survey was designed to be completed online through the JISC survey server (Bristol online survey)™ and on a paper format. For the electronic version of the survey, a hyperlink was provided to participants to complete it by phones or pc. The survey consisted of six sections: 1) participant´s information sheet and consent form; 2) demographic data, 3) WRMS divided into body regions, 4] work factors in LAPS, 5) impact on surgeons and 6) general questions about interaction and training. Questions were formulated based on previous studies related to LAPS and ergonomics considering work system elements in LAPS [7, 8, 18, 19]. Section three included questions based on the standard Nordic Questionnaire [20]. The total number of questions was 17 (only two were open questions) with an average time to complete of ten minutes (measured through a pilot study).

The survey was distributed to 320 surgeons with the support of Peruvian Society of Endoscopic Surgery through the associated members. In addition, the survey was shared to surgeons of six Peruvian hospitals with the previous permission of authorities. To promote a higher response rate the survey was resent to participants after one week as a reminder to participate. The paper format was distributed during two annual congresses of LAPS at north and south of Peru recruiting surgeons from different regions between 2018 and 2019. Results were imported from the online webpage of JISC to Microsoft Excel and then processed in SPSS v.24™. Descriptive analysis of categorical variables was presented in frequency and proportions and the numerical variables were summarized in averages and standard deviation (eg. Stature). The chi-square test of independence and Fisher´s exact test were used to examine associations. A significance value of $p < 0.05$; $p < 0.01$ and $p < 0.001$ was accepted. Responses to open questions were analysed thematically based on possible risk factors related to the system analysis and surgery complexity [2]. The study was approved by the Faculty of Engineering Ethics Committee of the University of Nottingham.

3 Results

A total of 140 surgeons across different specialities responded to the survey. Participants were mainly men (76%) with a range of age between 30–60 years old (87%) with more than 5 years of experience (57%) and with a medical speciality in general surgery (92%). The majority of surgeons worked in different hospitals in the city of Lima (45%) and the rest from different regions of Peru (55%). The mean stature was 169 cm (5.6) for men and 161 cm (6.3) for women. The prevalence of WRMS was 89% of which more than half of surgeons (56%) claimed symptoms in more than three body regions. Reported symptoms were higher in shoulders (59%) and neck (51%), followed by the hand/wrist (41%) and upper back segment (43%), while lower back (36%), elbows and lower limbs had the lowest proportion of reports. There was no statistical difference between male and female surgeons ($p > 0.05$) (see Table 1). The prevalence rate of 12-month symptoms was high especially in the shoulder (37%) and neck (36%) while participants who reported 7-day symptoms in those body parts were lower, reaching 21% and 15% respectively.

Figure 1 illustrates the frequency of 18 work factors based on the opinion of surgeons and the level of contribution to WRMS. Over half of surgeons reported the duration of surgery (59%), inadequate operating table height (57%) and the complexity of the surgery (54%) as highly contributing factors.

Table 1. Work-related musculoskeletal symptoms reported by surgeons.

	Total, prevalence		Female = 33		Male = 107		
	n	%	n	%	n	%	p
Body regions							
Neck	72	51%	16	48%	56	52%	0.69
Shoulder	82	59%	22	67%	60	56%	0.28
Elbow	18	13%	5	15%	13	12%	0.65
Hand/wrist	57	41%	11	33%	46	43%	0.32
Upper back	57	41%	13	39%	44	41%	0.86
Lower back	50	36%	12	36%	58	54%	0.92
Hip/thighs	9	6%	4	12%	5	5%	0.12
Knee/Legs	36	26%	9	27%	27	25%	0.81
Ankle/feet	36	26%	11	33%	25	23%	0.25
Body regions with complaints							
None	16	11%	5	15%	10	9%	0.72
More than one	124	89%					

*Note. P: Chi- square test of independence and Fishers´s exact; * p < 0.05*

Many surgeons also reported, lack of suitable equipment (41%), lack of training in LAPS (34%), the position of surgeons in surgery (31%), the position of monitor display (29%) and patient´s shape (26%) were as highly contributing factors, with more than 25% of respondents indicating they were related to WRMS. Conversely, time pressure (62%) and use of double gloves (68%) were perceived by the majority as a non-contributing factor. The lack of microbreaks (45%) and use of disposable tools (36%) were perceived mainly as low-contributing factors. Surgeons reported that cholecystectomy with complications (26.3%), complex appendectomy (16.3%), inguinal hernia repair (16.3%) and bariatric surgery (Whipple bypass) (8.8%) were the more complex procedures that required more than 1 h and a high physical and mental demand. More than three-quarters of surgeons (79%) indicated that they did not receive formal training in LAPS and ergonomics but would be interested in being trained, while 17% reported that they had received training and barely 4% said that they would not be interested.

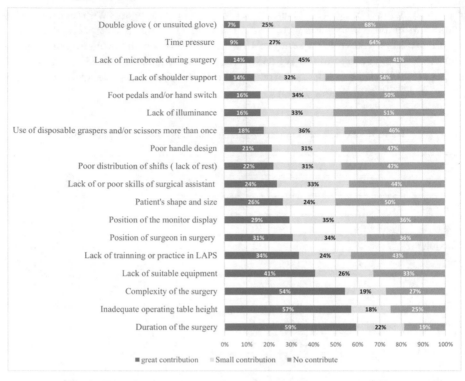

Fig. 1. Work factors and level of contribution to the presence of WRM

With regards to organizational factors, 41% of participants stated that they had difficulties interacting with surgical staff such as nurses, assistants and residents. The lack of collaboration with the team (34%) and the presence of inexperienced residents (44%) were the most recurrent factors affecting surgical performance. Within the survey 25% of surgeons reported changing the way they work in the following ways: 46% of surgeons avoided being booked in to carry out additional surgeries, 37% reduced the number of complex LAPS procedures and 29% reduced their workload by reducing the number of surgeries that they carried out. Also, 17% of surgeons reduced the number of surgeries of high Body mass index (BMI) patients and emergency LAPS. The study revealed association between WRMS and time as a laparoscopic surgeon ($x^2_{(1)} = 10.3$; $p < 0.05$), especially in the upper back segment ($x^2_{(1)} = 20.5 p < 0.001$). Several work factors were associated with the total prevalence of WRMS such as: duration ($x^2_{(1)} = 21.1; p < 0.001$) and complexity of surgeries ($x^2_{(1)} = 9.84; p < 0.001$), lack of suitable equipment ($x^2_{(1)} = 22.1; p < 0.001$), inadequate table height ($x^2_{(1)} = 8.0; p < 0.01$), the position of monitor display ($x^2_{(1)} = 10.4; p < 0.01$), reuse of disposable tools ($x^2_{(1)} = 7.4; p < 0.01$), position to operate ($x^2_{(1)} = 8.5; p < 0.01$) and lack of microbreaks during surgery ($x^2_{(1)} = 10.3; p < 0.01$). Neck, shoulders, and upper back were the main body regions with a high number of associations with work factors ($p < 0.05$) (see Table 2).

Table 2. Work factors and associations with WRMS by body regions

Work system factors	Body regions (p-value)							
	Total	Neck	Shoulders	Elbow/Forearm	Wrist/hands	Upper Back	Lower back	Ankle/feet
Demographics factors								
Age group						*		
Time as laparoscopic surgeon	*	*	*			***		*
Work factors								
Duration of the surgery	***	*	**		*	*		**
Inadequate operating table height	**		*		***			
Complexity of the surgery	**	**	**			**		
Lack of suitable equipment	***	**	**	*	***	***		**
Lack of practice or training	*	**	**		*	**		*
Position of surgeon in surgery	**	*	**			*		
Position of the monitor display	**	***	***		**			**
Patient's shape and size	*	**	*			*	**	*
Lack of surgical assistant								
Poor distribution of shifts	*	*	**			*		
Poor handle design		*	**					
Reuse of disposable tools more than once	**	**	***		**	*		*
Lack of illuminance	*	**	**	*	*	**		

(*continued*)

Table 2. (*continued*)

Work system factors	Total	Neck	Shoulders	Elbow/Forearm	Wrist/hands	Upper Back	Lower back	Ankle/feet
			Body regions (p-value)					
Foot pedals and/or hand switch		**	**			**	**	***
Lack of shoulder support		**	***					*
Lack of microbreak during surgery	**	*	**			**	*	
Time pressure			**			*	*	
Use of Double glove or unsuited glove								

Note. Chi- squared and Fisher's exact test of independence, P < 0.05*; P < 0.01**; P < 0.001***

4 Discussion

A total of 140 surgeons responded to the survey reaching a response rate of 43.7%, higher than other similar studies in LAPS using surveys in DC [7]. The survey was responded to predominantly by men, due to the low presence of female surgeons in Peru who represent about 9.4% of surgeons [21], lower in contrast to DC such as the UK where female surgeons represent 12.9% [22]. The total rate of WRMS was 89% of which more than half of surgeons reported symptoms in more than three body regions. This suggested a high rate of WRMS, exceeding other at-risk occupational groups, such as skilled agricultural forestry, assemblers or plant operators [5] as well also rates of surgeons from DC who perform LAPS [6]. However, these results may be even higher because surgeons usually underestimate pain for the "surgical culture" that discourages complaints and demands performance[11]. Hallbeck et al [23]indicated that surgeons "put everything out of their mind" even pain to complete the surgery in favour of the patient. Shoulders and neck symptoms were reported as the most prevalent body segments and highly associated with multiple factors, being similar to other studies in LAPS except for the lower back that reached a lower percentage [6, 7, 9]. This difference may be attributed to responses that may over or under-estimate symptoms but also by factors related to surgeons' characteristics such as the short stature proper of the Peruvian population. Over half of surgeons indicated that three main highly contributing factors were complexity and duration of the surgery and the inadequate height of the operating table to perform LAPS. These results align with the model of discomfort explained by De Looze et al. [4] who argued that physical discomfort is the result of the imbalance not only from factors related to the product, such as laparoscopic instruments, but also of the context in which human interact. At the context or system level, this includes factors related to "tasks" such as level of difficulty to perform surgery, as well as the physical environment where surgeons operate, and includes equipment and technology such as the poor working height as a consequence of inadequate operating tables [2].

Duration and complexity of surgery are factors related to the nature of tasks [2]. High duration is related to the level of complexity of surgeries and possible unanticipated events during the procedure which may prolong the surgeon´s exposure. For example, emergency surgery that requires advanced techniques, increase the intraoperative time and thus the total duration of surgery. To address this issue, the development of training skills is imperative to improve surgical technique, reduce discomfort and time in surgery [24]. Based on the results of the survey, only a few surgeons considered that they were properly trained in LAPS and ergonomics, so a formal program should be set up in hospitals and universities to respond to this urgent necessity. The long duration of surgeries may increase the WRMS due to the high exposure to physical factors such as awkward postures, overexertion and repetition [3]. This was evidenced, for example, when surgeons reported ankle/feet symptoms due to surgeons keep standing for a long time without support and for the use of foot pedals to activate electrocautery. Matern [10] observed that the bending movements of ankles to activate pedals and the instability on one foot increased the physical overload, especially in overweighted surgeons triggering symptoms of numbness and pain. Issues with operating table height was reported as the main contributor factor related to technology. This result contrasts with other studies that found that this was not the priority [7, 25]. It may be explained by two aspects: 1) the limitation of adjustability of current operating tables designed to be used in open surgery but not in LAPS and 2) the short stature of Peruvians which reduces the chances of a suitable fit with the table. Current clinical guidelines suggest working heights based on anthropometry measures of people from DC [10, 25] and thus it will be difficult to fit table heights to the current Peruvian population [14, 15]. Furthermore, the patient´s size, such as obese patients (related to the nature of LAPS task) raise the working height, and this may increase physical discomfort of the surgeon, especially in the upper limbs. Similar issues could be explained in regard to screen position and handle design of tools. Currently, there is poor knowledge of Peruvian surgical contexts and as such, as an importing country of medical technology [26], there are difficulties associated with the transfer of technology and processes from DC, which put at risk not only surgeons but also patient safety.

More than 50% of surgeons reported that lack of microbreaks with stretching was a small contributing factor to WRMS, however, it is highly associated with symptoms of all body regions. Studies carried out in DC evidenced the importance of setting up microbreaks during LAPS to reduce pain, fatigue, stress and improving physical performance [11]. The establishment of microbreaks demands organizations to establish a culture of safety and ergonomics, otherwise, they may be perceived as non-essential elements. In Peru, many companies adopt microbreaks as part of their occupational health and safety program [27] but hospitals do not have well-established safety programs, which may difficult its implementation [17]. The demand for LAPS is increasing in hospitals due to the benefits for the patient but this may be highly demanding and challenging for surgeons [1]. It is necessary to rethink and redesign to optimise the system of work and to eliminate negative factors such as WRMSD. Furthermore, solutions must be focused not only on surgeons but also on surgical staff such as camera assistants and nurses who participate directly in surgery. Limitations of the study included the focus only on surgeons but not on other members of surgical staff and the method that not allowed to explore directly ORs.

The study contributed to the analysis of LAPS system in Peru and identified factors that are relevant for high impact on the physical load of surgeons helping us to design further strategies. The introduction of ergonomics in LAPS training is necessary to increase ergonomics awareness in the surgical team and improve the LAPS technique to reduce time and exposition. It is also important to develop ergonomics guidelines in LAPS based on limitations of Peruvian hospitals and its application. The inclusion of microbreaks with muscle stretching during surgeries may be a short-term solution especially when the surgery takes more than one hour. In addition, the development of local technology that may offset limitations of technology, for instance, the design of an adjustable low-cost platform to adapt surgeons and assistants at suitable working heights without changing current operating tables.

The data presented in the study was the first diagnosis of the current situation of ORs in Peru and how it may affect to surgeons. The study determined a high rate of WRMS, especially in upper limbs, associated with work factors such as inadequate operating table height, duration and complexity of surgeries, lack of suitable equipment and LAPS training. Further studies should be focused on all humans within the system such as surgeons and assistants, and also all other system factors of Peruvian context to ultimately improve conditions and reduce physical risk factors and WRMSD.

References

1. Berguer, R., Smith, W.D., Chung, Y.H.: Performing laparoscopic surgery is significantly more stressful for the surgeon than open surgery. Surg. Endosc. **15**(10), 1204–7 (2001)
2. Carayon, P., Schoofs Hundt, A., Karsh, B.-T., Gurses, A.P., Alvarado, C.J., Smith, M., et al.: Work system design for patient safety: the SEIPS model. Qual. Saf. Health Care. **15**(1), i50–i58 (2006)
3. Armstrong, T.J., Buclkle, P., Fine, L.J., Hagberg, M., Jonsson, B., Kilborn, A., et al.: A conceptual model for work-related neck and upper-limb musculoskeletal disorders. Scand. J. Work Environ. Health **19**, 73–84 (1993)
4. De Looze, M.P., Kuijt-Evers, L.F.M., Van Dieën, J.: Sitting comfort and discomfort and the relationships with objective measures. Ergonomics **46**(10), 985–997 (2003)
5. EU-OSHA. Work-related musculoskeletal disorders: prevalence, costs and demographics in the EU. Publication Office of the European Union (2019)
6. Alleblas, C.C.J., de Man, A.M., van den Haak, L., Vierhout, M.E., Jansen, F.W., Nieboer, T.E.: Prevalence of musculoskeletal disorders among surgeons performing minimally invasive surgery: a systematic review. Ann. Surg. **266**(6) (2017)
7. Park, A., Lee, G., Seagull, F.J., Meenaghan, N., Dexter, D.: Patients benefit while surgeons suffer: an impending epidemic. J. Am. Coll. Surg. **210**(3), 306–313 (2010)
8. Sutton, E., Irvin, M., Zeigler, C., Lee, G., Park, A.: The ergonomics of women in surgery. Surg. Endosc. **28**(4), 1051–1055 (2014)
9. Epstein, S., Sparer, E.H., Tran, B.N., et al.: Prevalence of work-related musculoskeletal disorders among surgeons and interventionalists: a systematic review and meta-analysis. JAMA Surg. **153**(2), e174947 (2018).
10. Matern, U.: Ergonomic deficiencies in the operating room: Examples from minimally invasive surgery. Work **33**(2), 165–168 (2009)

11. Park, A., Zahiri, H., Susan Hallbeck, M., Augenstein, V., Sutton, E., Denny, Y., Lowndes, B., Bingener, J.: Intraoperative "micro breaks" with targeted stretching enhance surgeon physical function and mental focus: a multicenter cohort study. Ann. Surg. **265**(2), 340–346 (2017)
12. La Contraloria General de la Republica. Gestion y Control. Report No: 42 (2016)
13. World Health Organization. IBEAS: a pioneer study on patient safety in Latin America: towards safer hospital care. World Health Organization (2011)
14. NCD Risk Factor Collaboration (NCD-RisC). A century of trends in adult human height. Franco E, editor. ELife 5, e13410 (2016)
15. Escobar Galindo, C.M.: Perfil antropométrico de trabajadores del Perú utilizando el método de escala proporcional. Ergonomía, Investigación y Desarrollo **2**(2), 96–111 (2020)
16. Pheasant, S., Haslegrave, C.M.: Human diversity. In: Bodyspace: Anthropometry, ergonomics and the design of work, p. 65. CRC Press (2006)
17. Mejia, C.R., Scarsi, O., Chavez, W., Verastegui-Díaz, A., Quiñones-Laveriano, D.M., Allpas-Gomez, H.L., et al.: Conocimientos de Seguridad y Salud en el Trabajo en dos hospitales de Lima-Perú. Rev Asoc Esp Espec Med Trab. **25**, 211–219 (2016)
18. Hignett, S., Gyi, D., Calkins, L., Jones, L., Moss, E.: Human factors evaluation of surgeons' working positions for gynecologic minimal access surgery. J. Minim. Invasive Gynecol. **24**(7), 1177–1183 (2017)
19. Shepherd, J.M., Harilingam, M.R., Hamade, A.: Ergonomics in laparoscopic surgery—a survey of symptoms and contributing factors. Surg. Laparosc. Endosc. Percutaneous Tech. **26**(1), 72–77 (2016)
20. Kuorinka, I., Jonsson, B., Kilbom, A., Vinterberg, H., Biering-Sørensen, F., Andersson, G., et al.: Standardised Nordic questionnaires for the analysis of musculoskeletal symptoms. Appl. Ergonomics **18**(3), 233–237 (1987)
21. Colegio Médico del Perú. https://www.cmp.org.pe/conoce-a-tu-medico/, Accessed 2021
22. Royal College of Surgery. Women In surgery. https://www.rcseng.ac.uk/careers-in-surgery/women-in-surgery/statistics/, Accessed 2019
23. Hallbeck, M.S., Lowndes, B.R., Bingener, J., Abdelrahman, A.M., Yu, D., Bartley, A., et al.: The impact of intraoperative microbreaks with exercises on surgeons: a multi-center cohort study. Appl. Ergonomics **60**, 334–341 (2017)
24. Fried, G.M.: FLS assessment of competency using simulated laparoscopic tasks. J. Gastrointest. Surg. **12**(2), 210–212 (2008)
25. Wauben, L.S.G.L., van Veelen, M.A., Gossot, D., Goossens, R.H.M.: Application of ergonomic guidelines during minimally invasive surgery: a questionnaire survey of 284 surgeons. Surg. Endosc. **20**(8), 1268–1274 (2006)
26. Camara de Comercio de Lima. COMSALUD:. Diario Medico. https://www.diariomedico.pe/?p=12987, Accesed 2020
27. Cáceres-Muñoz, V., Magallanes-Meneses, A., Torres-Coronel, D., Copara-Moreno, P., Escobar-Galindo, M., Mayta-Tristán, P.: Efecto de un programa de pausa activa mas folletos informativos en la disminución de molestias musculoesqueléticas en trabajadores administrativos. Rev Ped Med Exp **34**, 611–618 (2017)

Work-Home System Analysis
and Musculoskeletal Discomfort of Workers
in Covid-19 Pandemic Context

Carlos Manuel Escobar Galindo[1]([✉]), Richard Raitt Rodriguez Rojas[2],
José Enrique Villalobos Tupia[2], and Paula Martha Veliz Terry[2]

[1] Facultad de Medicina, Universidad Peruana Cayetano Heredia, Lima, Peru
manuel.escobar@nottingham.ac.uk
[2] Escuela de Tecnología Médica, Universidad Nacional Mayor de San Marcos, Lima, Peru

Abstract. The study aimed to analyse work-home system factors and their connection with workers' comfort, musculoskeletal discomfort (MSD) and perceived quality of work. **Methods**: A virtual survey was given to 196 administrative workers of a bank in Lima Peru. The survey consisted of four sections: consent form, sociodemographic data, risk factors of the work system and questions about comfort and MSD. Descriptive data was presented in percentages and associations were established with the chi-square statistic test. The significance level was 0.05. **Results:** The rate of musculoskeletal discomfort reached 96%, the most frequent body regions being the neck (91%), upper back (89%) and lower back region (89%). Regarding the work-home system, 49% of the study subjects worked in the bedroom and/or the living room, 32% had a desk, 18% used an adjustable chair, 37% worked at a dining table and 34% indicated that domestic activities overlapped with their work activities. The workers' greatest perceived benefit was spending time with their families (59%). MSD was associated mainly with organisational factors ($p < 0.01$). Comfort was associated with the backrest and type of seat, along with factors related to the environment and work tasks ($p < 0.05$). **Conclusion:** Work-home systems are not prepared for performing office work. They raise MSD rates and reduce the quality of work, as perceived by workers. Spending time with family acted as a protective and negative factor.

Keywords: Home office · Ergonomics · Work system · Musculoskeletal disorders

1 Introduction

The current COVID-19 pandemic forced many companies in Peru to restructure their work systems in order to avoid possible infection among their workers. As an immediate response, the companies set up a remote system enabling employees to continue working without being exposed to possible contagion. New offices were moved to the workers' homes, where the workers do not have a clear overview of the work system environment, exposing them to different risk factors that may negatively impact their

© The Author(s), under exclusive license to Springer Nature Switzerland AG 2021
N. L. Black et al. (Eds.): IEA 2021, LNNS 222, pp. 738–745, 2021.
https://doi.org/10.1007/978-3-030-74611-7_101

well-being and overall performance [1, 2]. Current guides establish ergonomic recommendations for how to adapt work systems in offices and industries; however, they do not consider work-systems at home [3–8]. As a result, remote work may substantially increase musculoskeletal discomfort (MSD) in employees. The current reported rates of employee MSD may differ in different offices [9–15]. Remote work also reduces the ability of workers to perceive comfort in their workplace, which is necessary in order to achieve acceptable well-being and productivity levels [13, 14]. Furthermore, Peru has several limitations in terms of occupational health and safety culture [11], access to the internet [18] and ergonomics awareness, which may make the successful implementation of work-home programmes difficult.

Hence, there is a clear knowledge gap concerning the current context that users are experiencing when working at home. Based on the ergonomics systemic perspective [2], this study aims to analyse factors of the work-home system and their connection with comfort, MSD and perceived quality of work.

2 Methods

The study design was cross-sectional and was carried out through the application of a virtual survey. The survey was applied to office workers of a banking company in Peru who worked under the modality of remote work from April to June 2020. A total of 352 administrative workers with more than one year of experience in the bank were selected to participate in the study. Participants with clinically diagnosed musculoskeletal disorders were excluded from the study. The survey used in this study was designed in the Microsoft Forms software™ with single and multiple response options. It consisted of 40 questions divided into four sections: 1) consent form, 2) sociodemographic data, 3) risk factors of the work system and 4) questions about comfort and MSD. Questions were formulated based on different ergonomics guides and system analysis studies [3–7, 15].

The banking company's database was used to identify the workers in a home office setup as part of the preventive measures in the COVID-19 pandemic context. Authorisation to make contact with their work teams was requested from the leaders. The employees were then invited to voluntarily participate in a virtual survey delivered via email. To distribute the survey to the workers, the Microsoft form system generated a hyperlink that was shared to their emails to be responded to by phone or PC at any time of the day. Every week, a reminder email with the survey was sent to the workers who did not answer. Descriptive data was presented in percentages and associations were established with the chi-square statistic test, with a significance level of 0.05.

3 Results

The survey was sent to 352 workers. Of these, 196 responded, accounting for a rate of 55.7%. The sample consisted predominantly of women (56.6%) (43.4% percent were men) and the mean sample age was 31.8 years. Of all survey participants, 77%, worked two to eight hours a day.

Only 18% of the participants took three active pauses during their working hours and 72% of workers did not establish a defined work schedule. The main work environments were the bedroom (49%) and the living room (49%). Among the utilised work surfaces were the dining table (37%) and a common desk (32%). A laptop was used among 55% of the workers, 46% of which did not use any adaptation element. Only 18.4% had an adjustable office chair. Over half of the workers (52%) considered their functions to have varied too much while 34% reported that existed an overlapped of domestic tasks with work.

More than half of the study sample indicated an overlap of work and domestic activities. Perceived drawbacks were coordination difficulty (43%), internet instability (35%) and distractions (27%). Conversely, perceived benefits were spending time with family (59%), having flexible hours (56%) and working from home (50%). Working at home was considered comfortable by 56% of the survey participants.

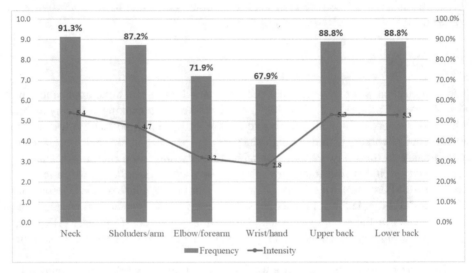

Fig. 1. Musculoskeletal discomfort reported by workers at home

In terms of impact, 96% of the participants reported MSD, the highest rate being in the neck (91%), upper back (89%), lower back (89%) and shoulders (87%). The highest MSD intensity means corresponded with the neck (5.40/10), upper back (5.3/10) and the lower back (5.2/10) (see Fig. 1). In the study, 56% of the workers perceived comfort when working at home, while 20% perceived that their work had increased too much. In the study, MSD was associated mainly with the work schedule and active pauses ($p < 0.01$). Comfort was associated with the type of backrest and seat as well as factors related to the work environment and tasks ($p < 0.05$). Associations were observed between the number of working hours per day and the reported MSD levels in the neck ($p < 0.05$), shoulders ($p < 0.05$), elbow/forearm ($p < 0.05$), upper back ($p < 0.05$) and lower back ($p < 0.01$). Likewise, discomfort of elbows/forearm and wrist/hand were associated with the overlap of domestic and work activities ($p < 0.05$).

The greater the number of daily work hours, the greater the perception of MSD in all body regions. On the other hand, the perception of work-seat comfort was associated with the type of seat ($p < 0.001$) and backrest ($p < 0.001$). The comfort of the work

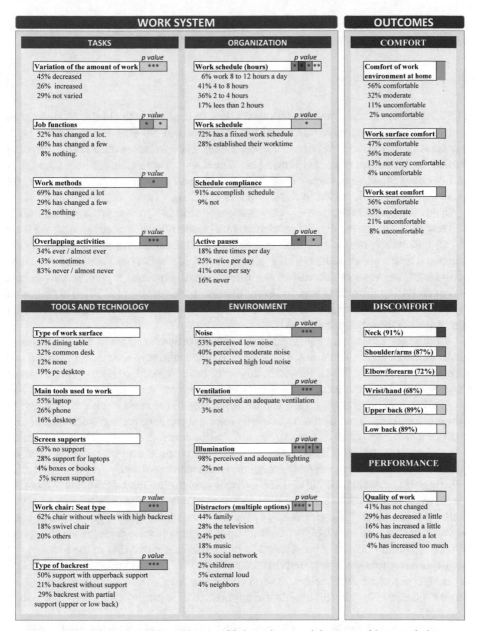

Note. * p<0.05; ** p<0.01; *** p<0.001; multiple option: participants could responded more than one alternative

Fig. 2. Work-home system factors and associations.

surface was related to the type of work surface, the desk being perceived as the most comfortable. The general comfort of the workstation was associated with the impact of the environment on the worker (p < 0.001), variation of the functions (p < 0.05) and methods of work (p < 0.05), the overlap of domestic tasks (p < 0.001) and the presence of distractors, such as family and pets, (p < 0.001) (Fig. 2).

4 Discussion

The final MSD rates reached an impressive 96% in contrast with studies carried out in conventional administrative offices, which reached about 54–80% (up to 80% in bank workers) [9–11]. These values even exceed other occupations with a higher physical burden, such as farmers and fishermen [12]. The discomfort rates in the neck, shoulders and back segments were higher than 85%, with a level of intensity above the average, exceeding other statistics in similar populations [12, 16, 17].

Body region discomfort was highly associated with factors related to work duration and rest time. Due to the current pandemic, most workers were forced to virtualise their job and, therefore, recondition their homes for work and maintain unstable and poorly organised hours. As a result, working hours reached 12 continuous hours in almost half of the study population, increasing exposure to static postures, repetitive movements and overexertion. This may lead to severe discomfort responses [13, 14]. This duration is also associated with reduced number of active pauses, which was associated with discomfort in the elbows and wrists.

Companies are usually equipped with standard office furniture, such as adjustable chairs and desk tables, that follows specific recommendations based on occupational and safety standards [3, 5, 7, 18]. However, this study has revealed that home is not the most suitable environment to work in. Only 31% of the workers had a suitable desk, 63% had no monitor support and only 18% had an adjustable office chair, which is essential to office work [4, 6]. Most of the participants used a fixed-height chair, such as a dining chair or a common bench, for work. Several studies concluded that not using a suitable office chair may prompt the adoption of awkward postures and increase pressure on buttocks and back, which added to a high exposure increase the physical discomfort [6, 19]. Besides, prolonged sitting at a sub-optimal workstation may significantly increase MSD, especially in the back, shoulders and neck, due to the constant tension of upper body muscle groups [20]. Helander [4] indicates that a lack of height and seat back adjustability, as well as a lack of lumbar support, may increase pressure on the spine. Thus, workers at home may be exposed to the development of MSD in the back.

In addition, this study revealed that the perception of chair comfort is mainly linked to the type of chair and backrest and not to the seat or material as is suggested by other studies [6, 19]. This highlights the importance of selecting a suitable chair with a backrest.

The majority of the study participants used a dining table, which height may vary depending on the model (76–88 cm), for work [21, 22], exceeding the regular height of an office desk, which reaches 72 cm on average [5, 23]. The raised height may be compensated by adjusting the seat height or raising the user's shoulders to achieve an optimal position of comfort [24]. However, the study revealed that only 18% of workers had an adjustable-height chair, which may result in the users without suitable furniture compensating for the raised height of a fixed chair with their body. Furthermore, over half of the participants used a laptop without suitable elements, such as an external keyboard, laptop support (dock stations), footrests or regulation systems of surfaces, for work. Combined with working at dining tables (37%), this could increase the overload in upper body regions, especially in the neck and back [8, 22].

Participants perceived that work at home did not produce major limitations; however, distraction by family members was a relevant factor that was perceived as both positive and negative. This may be explained with the possible conflict between internal and external work factors within the same environment, which may generate greater conflicts but at the same time behave as a protective factor [25]. For example, hearing noise from family members, carrying out household chores and assisting relatives are negative factors. However, they can be compensated with additional time with the family, greater schedule flexibility and control over domestic activities, etc. As a result, the overall comfort perception at home is relatively high, successfully improving the work experience, which may compensate the perceived high discomfort [17].

The use of the internet was considered negative, especially when it was not supported by employers. The home network is different than usual work networks in terms of speed and connectivity, especially in Peru, where limited access to a high-quality internet connection is evident [26]. Internet connectivity issues may increase the physical and mental load of responding efficiently to work demands, especially when workers do not directly control their home connection [27]. Although 41% of the participants did not perceive any change in the quality of their work, 39% perceived a reduction and 20% and increase. This could be due to the modification of tasks, poor clarity of the workers' roles and changes in the overall system [2, 28], all of which raise feelings of uncertainty regarding the external factors causing the COVID-19 pandemic.

Despite the limitations in the work system, over half of the workers perceived working at home as comfortable. This may be explained by De Looze [14] in the comfort theory, who states that comfort is related not only to physical or environmental factors of the system but also to the needs, expectations and emotions of workers, which may reduce the feeling of physical discomfort and improve user experience. Hence, comfort should not only be considered the absence of discomfort but also the pleasant state or relaxed feeling of people in reaction to their environment [29]. Based on this approach, factors such as tasks, organisation and the physical environment may be key aspects to improving comfort. However, it is not implied that we should not focus on physical factors, but that we should work with a consideration for the whole system in order to achieve employee wellbeing.

The study has contributed to analysing the new work-home system, which has allowed us to understand the situation of workers in the current pandemic. As a result of the analysis, we suggest three key aspects to improving the work-home system:

1) Developing ergonomics guidelines to help workers orient themselves in the best suitable recommendations to organising their work at home. For instance, by using boxes or books as support for the screen or as a footrest to support the lower limbs, using cushions to improve back support and compensate the height of the chair in relation to the table, among others.

2) Setting up a remote ergonomics program with an aim to identify specific issues that the company may facilitate to workers. For instance, providing adjustable office chairs or internet connection to improve the experience of working at home.

3) Increasing ergonomics awareness among workers, for instance, by setting up a participate ergonomics program, so that they are able to identify their issues and apply ergonomics principles of the work system in their homes.

The study provides evidence that work at home demands adapting to a different work system, in terms of organisation, environment, furniture, tools and tasks, which also has an impact on the workers' well-being, comfort and performance. Besides, the use of regular ergonomics recommendations in offices may not be applicable in the majority of work-home systems. The results of this study should be taken with caution, as the home environment may change drastically among workers depending on socio-economical aspects and context of work.

References

1. Dul, J., Bruder, R., Buckle, P., Carayon, P., Falzon, P., Marras, W.S., et al.: A strategy for human factors/ergonomics: developing the discipline and profession. Ergonomics **55**(4), 377–95 (2012)
2. Carayon, P., Smith, M.J.: Work organization and ergonomics. Appl. Ergon. **31**(6), 649–62 (2000)
3. Cosar, R.C.: NTP 242: Ergonomía: análisis ergonómico de los espacios de trabajo en oficinas. Recuperado El. 13 (2012)
4. Helander, M.: A guide to human factors and ergonomics. CRC Press, Routledge (2005)
5. ISO. ISO 24496:2017(en) Office furniture — Office chairs — Methods for the determination of dimensions [Internet]. (2017). https://www.iso.org/obp/ui/fr/#iso:std:iso:24496:ed-1:v1:en
6. Pheasant, S., Haslegrave, C.M.: Ergonomics in the office. In: Bodyspace: Anthropometry, Ergonomics and the Design of Work, pp. 160–81. CRC Press, Routledge (2006)
7. Vega, M.F., Cuixart, C.N.: NTP 602: El diseño ergonómico del puesto de trabajo con pantallas de visualización: el equipo de trabajo (2001)
8. Sarsak, H.I.: Working from home: Self-assessment computer workstation set-up. World Fed Occup Ther Bull, pp. 1–8 (2020)
9. Akrouf, Q., Crawford, J., Al Shatti, A., Kamel, M.: Musculoskeletal disorders among bank office workers in Kuwait. EMHJ-East Mediterr. Health J. **16**(1), 94–100 (2010)
10. Eltayeb, S., Staal, J.B., Kennes, J., Lamberts, P.H., de Bie, R.A.: Prevalence of complaints of arm, neck and shoulder among computer office workers and psychometric evaluation of a risk factor questionnaire. BMC Musculoskelet Disord. **8**(1), 1–11 (2007)
11. MARSH REHDER. Realidad en la Gestión de Seguridad y Salud en el trabajo [Internet] (2019). https://www.Descargas/mc-realidad-de-seguridad-y-salud-en-el-trabajo.pdf
12. EU-OSHA. Work-related musculoskeletal disroders: prevalence, costs and demographics in the EU. Publ Off Eur Union (2019
13. Cáceres-Muñoz, V.S., Magallanes-Meneses, A., Torres-Coronel, D., Copara-Moreno, P., Escobar-Galindo, M., Mayta-Tristán, P.: Efecto de un programa de pausa activa mas folletos informativos en la disminución de molestias musculoesqueléticas en trabajadores administrativos. Rev. Peru Med. Exp. Salud Publica. **34**, 611–8 (2017)
14. Vinothini, P., Halim, I., Radin Umar, R.Z., Too, Y.W., Halim, I.: A future framework for musculoskeletal disorders symptoms among computer office workers. Int. J. Physiother. [Internet], 5(6) 2018 [cited 25 Apr 2020]. https://www.ijphy.org/index.php/journal/article/view/379
15. Aarås, A., Horgen, G., Bjørset, H.-H., Ro, O., Thoresen, M.: Musculoskeletal, visual and psychosocial stress in VDU operators before and after multidisciplinary ergonomic interventions. Appl. Ergon. **29**(5), 335–54 (1998)

16. Armstrong, T.J., Buckle, P., Fine, L.J., Hagberg, M., Jonsson, B., Kilbom, A., et al.: A conceptual model for work-related neck and upper-limb musculoskeletal disorders. Scand. J. Work Environ. Health **19**(2), 73–84 (1993)
17. De Looze, M.P., Kuijt-Evers, L.F.M., Van Dieën, J.: Sitting comfort and discomfort and the relationships with objective measures. Ergonomics **46**(10), 985–97 (2003)
18. Trimmel, M., Meixner-Pendleton, M., Haring, S.: Stress response caused by system response time when searching for information on the internet. Hum. Factors **45**(4), 615–22 (2003)
19. Kuorinka, I., Jonsson, B., Kilbom, A., Vinterberg, H., Biering-Sørensen, F., Andersson, G., et al.: Standardised Nordic questionnaires for the analysis of musculoskeletal symptoms. Appl. Ergon. **18**(3), 233–7 (1987)
20. Besharati, A., Daneshmandi, H., Zareh, K., Fakherpour, A., Zoaktafi, M.: Work-related musculoskeletal problems and associated factors among office workers. Int. J. Occup. Saf. Ergon. **26**(3), 632–8 (2020)
21. Shikdar, A.A., Al-Kindi, M.A.: Office ergonomics: deficiencies in computer workstation design. Int. J. Occup. Saf. Ergon. **13**(2), 215–23 (2007)
22. Parotas: A Guide To Calculating Your Standard Table & Chair Heights [Internet] [cited 25 Jan 2021] (2019). https://www.parotas.com/en/standard-table-chair-heights-guide/#:~:text= above%20the%20floor.-,Standard%20Dining%20Table%20Height,average%20around% 2029%20inches%20tall
23. Pheasant, S., Haslegrave, C.M.: Ergonomics in the home. In: Bodyspace: Anthropometry, Ergonomics and the Design of Work, p. 184. CRC Press, Routledge (2006)
24. Pheasant, S., Haslegrave, C.M.: Working design. In: Bodyspace: Anthropometry, Ergonomics and the Design of Work, p. 65. CRC Press, Routledge (2006)
25. Grandjean, E., Kroemer, K.: Fitting task to be Human, 4th edn. CRC Press, Routledge (1995)
26. Golden, T.D.: Telework and the Navigation of Work-Home Boundaries. Organ Dyn. 100822 (2021)
27. Flores-Cueto, J.J., Hernández, R., Argandoña, R.: Tecnologías de información: Acceso a internet y brecha digital en Perú. Revista venezonala de Gerencia. **25**(90) (2020)
28. Van Niekerk, S.-M., Louw, Q.A., Hillier, S.: The effectiveness of a chair intervention in the workplace to reduce musculoskeletal symptoms. a systematic review. BMC Musculoskelet Disord. **13**, 145 (2012)
29. Vink, P., Hallbeck, S.: Editorial: comfort and discomfort studies demonstrate the need for a new model. Spec. Sect. Prod. Comf. **43**(2), 271–6 (2012)

Occupational and Environmental Health Effects of Informal Electronic Waste Recycling – A Focus on Agbogbloshie, Ghana

Julius Fobil[1]([✉]) [iD], Priscillah Abotsi[2], Augustine A. Acquah[1] [iD],
John Arko-Mensah[1] [iD], Clive D'Souza[3] [iD], and Bernard Martin[3] [iD]

[1] Department of Biological Environmental and Occupational Health Sciences, School of Public Health, University of Ghana, P.O. Box LG13, Legon, Accra, Ghana
jfobil@ug.edu.gh
[2] Legon Center for International Affairs and Diplomcy (LECIAD), University of Ghana, P.O. Box LG25, Legon, Accra, Ghana
[3] Center for Ergonomics, Department of Industrial and Operations Engineering, University of Michigan, Ann Arbor, MI 48109-2117, USA

Abstract. The unregulated and unorganized structure of informal electronic waste recycling worksites exposes workers to numerous occupational hazards. This context also presents research challenges in collecting exposure data to establish linkages with adverse health effects and development of risk-mitigating strategies. This paper presents some findings from a 5-year multinational and multi-institutional collaboration of academic and government partners, which documented extensive occupational and environmental health conditions at the Agbogbloshie electronic waste site in central Accra, Ghana.

Keywords: Agbogbloshie · Electronic waste · Ergonomics · Occupational health

1 Introduction

1.1 Background

Electronic waste (e-waste) is believed to be one of the most rapidly increasing components of the global waste stream [1]. The increase in e-waste has been fuelled by the increase in obsolescence and the desire to keep up with global advancement in technology. Large volumes of e-waste are legally and illegally dumped in developing countries such as Ghana where they are recycled as a form of livelihood [1–3]. Recycling of valuable metals including gold or copper contained in e-waste (e.g., discarded cell phones, computers, televisions, refrigerators, and automobiles) has become an important source of income, largely in the informal sector of emerging/developing or less-industrialized nations. These countries often lack the technical know-how and technological infrastructure to recycle e-waste in an ecologically safe and sustainable manner and this poses serious public health and environmental concerns. Informal e-waste recycling and scrap metal recovery consists primarily of scavenging and collecting e-waste items, sorting out

N. L. Black et al. (Eds.): IEA 2021, LNNS 222, pp. 746–752, 2021.
https://doi.org/10.1007/978-3-030-74611-7_102

items that can be reused or repaired and manual dismantling of items that are irrepara-ble and/or non-functional [4, 5]. The recycling process is carried out by low-wage, low skilled workers who are largely unaware about the associated exposure risks or about safe work practices to prevent or mitigate related adverse effects [1, 2, 6].

Agbogbloshie in Accra Ghana is one of the major e-waste recycling hubs in the world [7]. The recycling processes used at this site are predominantly manual and simple. Basic tools such as hammer and screw drivers are used for breaking apart (dismantling) electrical items to retrieve valuable metals such as copper, aluminium, silver and gold [2, 3]. Open air burning, especially of insulated wires, is used to recover copper, iron and aluminium from items that cannot be dismantled [4]. Non-valuable fractions of e-waste are discarded at the dumpsite and subsequently burnt to reduce the volume of waste accumulated [8].

1.2 Problem Statement

The informal recycling process consists of the use of rudimentary methods which are hazardous and poses huge safety risks to workers and the environment [6, 9–11]. A defining characteristic of workers in informal sectors is that they are not subject to national labor laws and standards. As a result, these workers are likely exposed to hazardous work conditions, including high levels of toxic chemicals with little or no social, economic or occupational protections. For the estimated two billion informal sector workers around the globe, there is a clear need for identifying and implementing the appropriate context-specific interventions in challenging work environments where unprotected workers face substantial risk from hazardous exposures and work conditions.

1.3 Objective

The objectives of this paper are to: (1) highlight some of the adverse health consequence of fast-growing e-waste in the global waste stream by showcasing such conditions at Agbogbloshie – the largest e-waste dumpsite in Africa, and (2) call attention to the need for continued research, including by the ergonomics community, to characterize and reduce work exposures and promote worker health and safety measures associated with informal e-waste recycling in emerging/developing economies.

2 Methodology

This study uses a hybrid design drawing up materials from both extant literature and new empirical studies conducted at the Agbogbloshie e-waste dumpsite in Accra, Ghana. These empirical studies include our own research and experiences during the 5-year collaborative research. The broad aim of this multinational collaboration was to increase multi-disciplinary understanding of the occupational and environmental risks associated with informal e-waste recycling, and to use the project's findings to inform evidence-based work interventions and policy.

In this collaboration various studies [3, 9–14] used multidisciplinary combination of methods to investigate the environmental and health effects of e-waste recycling in

Agbogbloshie. We collected and analyzed in the laboratory both biological and environmental samples in a longitudinal design at 4 time-points. Direct field observations were conducted to supplement quantitative data collected in the field. The areas of investigation included: evaluation of ergonomic risk factors and work-related musculoskeletal disorders among e-waste workers [3, 14, 15]; investigating the adverse cumulative exposures [11], including particulate matter discharge that determined air quality [9, 13] and its effects on workers respiratory health. The results from these and other relevant studies on e-waste worker health are synthesized and summarized in this paper.

3 Results

Summary of findings of our research studies at Agbogbloshie speaks to significant health consequences of informal e-waste recycling activities on both environment and human health. Primitive recycling methods such as manual dismantling of electrical appliances and open air burning of predominantly copper wires at low temperatures are used in the recycling process. These rudimentary methods; including heavy and stressful lifting, are a source of high exposure to toxic chemicals and physical risk factors leading to undesirable health implications such as musculoskeletal pain and various adverse cardiovascular and respiratory health outcomes. The use of personal protective equipment by workers at Agbogbloshie is extremely rare despite all the health hazards associated with the manual recycling of e-waste.

3.1 Physical/Ergonomic Exposures and Work-Related Musculoskeletal Disorders

A preliminary investigation of the processes involved in manual e-waste recycling at Agbogbloshie and the associated ergonomic risk factors revealed that, self-reported sitting, standing, walking and manual material handling such as carrying, lifting and pushing/pulling of collecting carts were performed at varied frequency and intensity among e-waste workers [3, 15]. Lifting and carrying activities were performed on five or more days in the workweek by dismantlers (60%) as well as collectors and burners (nearly 90%). Prolonged walking, sitting and standing was frequently reported by collectors (87%), dismantlers (82%) and burners (60%), respectively [15].

Dismantlers of e-waste assume non-neutral seated postures with excessive forward flexion and twisting of the trunk as well as high force exertion from manual use of hammers in the dismantling of non-functional electrical appliances. Collectors of e-waste were often exposed to high force exertion and contact stress as a result of pulling/pushing loaded collection carts over long distances [16].

An alarmingly high prevalence (90%) of work-related MSDs exists among e-waste workers [14] in Agbogbloshie, Ghana. Work-related musculoskeletal disorder symptoms were mostly reported in the lower back (65%), knee (39%), shoulder (37%), upper arm (30%), lower leg (27%) and neck (26%) (14). Prolonged work duration was significantly associated with MSDs, which were also significantly associated with the primary e-waste job category [14].

In addition, evidence of acute injuries such as cuts, lacerations, abrasions and scars were observed in 96.2% of e-waste workers [10]. Scars were prevalent on the skins of 93.6% of workers while 23.1% of workers had burns [10].

3.2   Environmental Health Effects

Manual dismantling of appliances and open air burning to isolate valuable metals create very harmful ambient conditions [11]. Styrofoam food containers and car tires are often added as fuel to sustain the burning process. These conditions expose child- and adult-workers as well as their family members and the general population to excessive doses of hazardous substances [17]. For example, burning of copper wires results in emission of dioxins and furans [18] while breaking (dismantling) of Cathode Ray Tubes (CRT) monitors with rudimentary tools to recover copper and steel, result in the release and inhalation of organic compounds such as flame retardants, formaldehyde and combustion products such as polychlorinated biphenyls (PCBs), polybromated diphenyl ethers (PBDE), furans and dioxins as well as hazardous cadmium dust and other pollutants [18]. Other harmful substances resulting from informal e-waste recycling include oxides of: a) Lead, b) Chromium and c) Mercury, often as toxic fumes, as well as other heavy metal accumulation in water, soil and food [19–22].

Besides the hazardous components being processed, e-waste also produces several toxic by-products likely to affect the health of the adjacent general population [17], particularly children who need more specific protection [5, 23, 24]. For instance, while still growing, children's intake of water, air and food as a proportion of body weight is significantly larger compared with adults; thus, considerably increasing the risk of hazardous chemical absorption. Additionally, functional systems such as the: (i) immune system, (ii) digestive system, (iii) reproductive system and (iv) central nervous system are still developing and exposure to toxic substances, by hampering further development, might cause irreversible damage.

E-waste workers at Agbogbloshie are also exposed to high levels of particulate matter [9, 11] which predisposes them to a decline in lung function and the risk of developing small airway diseases like asthma or chronic obstructive pulmonary disease [9].

4   Discussion

Agbogbloshie has been the dumping ground for discarded electronic products, mainly from Europe and North America. Besides harbouring one of Accra's largest food markets, some 40,000 people are said to live and work in the wider area and all together, some 250,000 people including a floating day-time population are likely to be directly exposed to the fumes released during e-wastes recycling activities. Some 1.5 million people are believed to be indirectly exposed via the food chain. The unregulated and unorganized structure of informal e-waste recycling worksites leads to a hazardous work environments.

The high physical demands of manual recycling activities subject workers to high risk of acute injuries and work-related musculoskeletal disorders, predominantly low back pain. Our studies reported high prevalence of low back pain among the e-waste workers as a result of frequent manual material handling tasks such as carrying, lifting, pushing and pulling of loaded collecting carts, which exposes workers to non-neutral work postures and high force exertion over prolonged work durations. The use of hammer and chisel to break apart electronic waste may have accounted for the prevalence of upper limb musculoskeletal pain. Prolonged walking over uneven ground in search of e-waste from neighboring communities could be contributing to the high prevalence of lower extremity disorders among e-waste collectors.

Informal e-waste recycling worksites present challenges to research, such as difficulties in collecting work-related, time-varying, job-specific exposure data that would establish linkages with adverse health effects and guide the design of locally-adapted risk-mitigating strategies. New ergonomics perspectives, exposure assessment tools and methods suited to informal work settings are needed to overcome some of these research challenges.

5   Conclusion

E-waste represents a major global health challenge in the 21st Century. Growing evidence of hazardous work conditions and diverse sources of environmental pollution driven by practices used to recover valuable metals and dispose waste in the informal e-waste recycling sector have raised considerable global concerns. Upstream and downstream solutions are therefore urgently needed to redesign the structures for handling fast growing global e-waste production. Confronting this challenge will require interdisciplinary cooperation of multiple international stakeholders.

Acknowledgements. This research was supported by the 1/2 West Africa-Michigan CHARTER in GEOHealth with funding from the US National Institutes of Health/Fogarty Interna-tional Center (NIH/FIC) (paired grant nos. 1U2RTW010110-01 and 5U01TW010101) and Canada's International Development Research Center (IDRC; grant no. 108121-001). Co-authors C.D. and B.M. were partially supported by the training grant T42-OH008455 from the National Institute for Occupational Safety and Health (NIOSH), US Centers for Disease Control and Prevention (CDC). The views expressed in this publication do not necessarily reflect the official policies of nor endorsement by NIH, IDRC, NIOSH, CDC, and/or the Canadian and US Governments.

References

1. Lundgren, K.: The global impact of e-waste: Addressing the challenge (2012). https://ilo.org/sector/Resources/publications/WCMS_196105/lang--en/index.htm
2. Amankwaa, E.F.: Livelihoods in risk: exploring health and environmental implications of e-waste recycling as a livelihood strategy in Ghana. J. Mod. Afr. Stud. 51(4), 551–575 (2013). https://doi.org/10.1017/S0022278X1300058X
3. Acquah, A.A., D'Souza, C., Martin, B., Arko-Mensah, J., Nti, A.A., Kwarteng, L., Fobil, J.N.: Processes and challenges associated with informal electronic waste recycling at Agbogbloshie, a suburb of Accra, Ghana. Proc. Hum. Factors Ergon. Soc. Annu. Meet. 63(1), 938–942 (2019). https://doi.org/10.1177/1071181319631219
4. Akormedi, M., Asampong, E., Fobil, J.N.: Working conditions and environmental exposures among electronic waste workers in Ghana. Int. J. Occup. Environ. Health 19(4), 278–286 (2013). https://doi.org/10.1179/2049396713Y.0000000034
5. Binion, E., Gutberlet, J.: The effects of handling solid waste on the wellbeing of informal and organized recyclers: a review of the literature. Int. J. Occup. Environ. Health 18(1), 43–52 (2012). https://doi.org/10.1179/1077352512Z.0000000001

6. Yu, E.A., Akormedi, M., Asampong, E., Meyer, C.G., Fobil, J.N.: Informal processing of electronic waste at Agbogbloshie, Ghana: workers' knowledge about associated health hazards and alternative livelihoods. Glob. Health Promot. **24**(4), 90–98 (2017). https://doi.org/10.1177/1757975916631523
7. Davis, J.M., Akese, G., Garb, Y.: Beyond the pollution haven hypothesis: where and why do e-waste hubs emerge and what does this mean for policies and interventions? Geoforum **98**, 36–45 (2019). https://doi.org/10.1016/j.geoforum.2018.09.020
8. Amoyaw-Osei, Y., Agyekum, O.O., Pwamang, J.A., Mueller, E., Fasko, R., Schluep, M.: SBC e-Waste Africa Project Ghana e-Waste Country Assessment Yaw Amoyaw-Osei-Green Advocacy Ghana Obed Opoku Agyekum-Green Advocacy Ghana (2011). https://www.basel.int/Portals/4/BaselConvention/docs/eWaste/E-wasteAssessmentGhana.pdf
9. Amoabeng Nti, A.A., Arko-Mensah, J., Botwe, P.K., Dwomoh, D., Kwarteng, L., Takyi, S.A., Fobil, J.N.: Effect of particulate matter exposure on respiratory health of e-waste workers at Agbogbloshie, Accra, Ghana. Int. J. Environ. Res. Pub. Health **17**(9), 3042 (2020). https://doi.org/10.3390/ijerph17093042
10. Adusei, A., Arko-Mensah, J., Dzodzomenyo, M., Stephens, J., Amoabeng, A., Waldschmidt, S., Fobil, J.: Spatiality in health: the distribution of health conditions associated with electronic waste processing activities at Agbogbloshie Accra. Ann. Glob. Health **86**(1), 31 (2020). https://doi.org/10.5334/aogh.2630
11. Kwarteng, L., Baiden, E.A., Fobil, J., Arko-Mensah, J., Robins, T., Batterman, S.: Air quality impacts at an e-waste site in Ghana using flexible, moderate-cost and quality-assured measurements. GeoHealth **4**(8) (2020). https://doi.org/10.1029/2020GH000247
12. Laskaris, Z., Milando, C., Batterman, S., Mukherjee, B., Basu, N., O'neill, M.S., Fobil, J.N.: Derivation of time-activity data using wearable cameras and measures of personal inhalation exposure among workers at an informal electronic-waste recovery site in Ghana. Ann. Work Exposure. Health (2019). https://doi.org/10.1093/annweh/wxz056
13. Takyi, S.A., Basu, N., Arko-Mensah, J., Botwe, P., Amoabeng Nti, A.A., Kwarteng, L., Fobil, J.N.: Micronutrient-rich dietary intake is associated with a reduction in the effects of particulate matter on blood pressure among electronic waste recyclers at Agbogbloshie, Ghana. BMC Pub. Health **20**(1), 1067 (2020). https://doi.org/10.1186/s12889-020-09173-8
14. Acquah, A.A., Arko-Mensah, J., D'Souza, C., Martin, B., Quakyi, I.A., Robins, T.G., Fobil, J.N.: Prevalence of work-related musculoskeletal disorders among electronic waste workers at Agbogbloshie in Accra, Ghana. In: Proceedings of the Annual Conference of the International Society for Environmental Epidemiology, p. 92. Utrecht, Netherlands, August 2019, vol. 3, pp. 2–3 (2019). https://doi.org/10.1097/01.EE9.0000605616.87684.ec
15. Acquah, A.A., D'Souza, C., Martin, B., Arko-Mensah, J., Botwe, P.K., Tettey, P., Dwomoh, D., Nti, A.A., Kwarteng, L., Tyaki, S., Quaki, I., Robins, T., Fobil, J.N.: A preliminary assessment of physical work exposures among electronic waste workers at Agbogbloshie, Accra Ghana. International Journal of Industrial Ergonomics, in press (2021). https://doi.org/10.1016/j.ergon.2021.103096
16. Acquah, A.A., D'Souza, C., Martin, B., Arko-Mensah, J., Nti, A.A., Kwarteng, L., Fobil, J.N.: Development of an observation-based tool for ergonomic exposure assessment in informal electronic waste recycling and other unregulated non-repetitive work. Proc. Hum. Factors Ergon. Soc. Annu. Meet. **64**(1), 905–909 (2020). https://doi.org/10.1177/1071181320641216
17. Fischer, D., Seidu, F., Yang, J., Felten, M.K., Garus, C., Kraus, T., Kaifie, A.: Health consequences for e-waste workers and bystanders—a comparative cross-sectional study. Int. J. Environ. Res. Pub. Health **17**(5), 1534 (2020). https://doi.org/https://doi.org/10.3390/ijerph17051534

18. Prakash, S., Manhart, A., Amoyaw-Osei, Y., Agyekum, O.: Socio-economic assessment and feasibility study on sustainable e-waste management in Ghana. Öko-Institut e.V. - Institute of Applied Ecology, vol. 49 (2010). https://ressourcenfieber.org/publications/reports/2010-105-en.pdf

19. Srigboh, R.K., Basu, N., Stephens, J., Asampong, E., Perkins, M., Neitzel, R.L., Fobil, J.: Multiple elemental exposures amongst workers at the Agbogbloshie electronic waste (e-waste) site in Ghana. Chemosphere **164**, 68–74 (2016). https://doi.org/10.1016/j.chemosphere.2016.08.089

20. Caravanos, J., Clark, E., Fuller, R., Lambertson, C.: Assessing worker and environmental chemical exposure risks at an e-waste recycling and disposal site in Accra, Ghana. J. Health Pollut. **1**(1), 16–25 (2011). https://doi.org/10.5696/jhp.v1i1.22

21. Asante, K.A., Agusa, T., Biney, C.A., Agyekum, W.A., Bello, M., Otsuka, M., Tanabe, S.: Multi-trace element levels and arsenic speciation in urine of e-waste recycling workers from Agbogbloshie, Accra in Ghana. Sci. Total Environ. **424**, 63–73 (2012). https://doi.org/10.1016/j.scitotenv.2012.02.072

22. Feldt, T., Fobil, J.N., Wittsiepe, J., Wilhelm, M., Till, H., Zoufaly, A., Göen, T.: High levels of PAH-metabolites in urine of e-waste recycling workers from Agbogbloshie, Ghana. Sci. Total Environ. 466–467, 369–376 (2014). https://doi.org/10.1016/j.scitotenv.2013.06.097

23. Robinson, B.H.: E-waste: an assessment of global production and environmental impacts. Sci. Total Environ. **408**(2), 183–191 (2009). https://doi.org/10.1016/j.scitotenv.2009.09.044

24. Porta, D., Milani, S., Lazzarino, A.I., Perucci, C.A., Forastiere, F.: Systematic review of epidemiological studies on health effects associated with management of solid waste. Environ. Health A Glob. Access Sci. Source. BioMed Central (2009). https://doi.org/10.1186/1476-069X-8-60

Musculoskeletal Complaints and Their Associations with Health and Work-Related Factors: A Cross-Sectional Study in a Beverage Company

Marisa de Cássia Registro Fonseca[1]([⊠]), Vinicius Restani Castro[1], Ester R. C. Lopes[1], Lisandra V. Martins[2], and Leonardo D. S. Mauad[1]

[1] University of São Paulo, Ribeirão Preto, Brazil
[2] Federal University of Espírito Santo, Vitória, Brazil

Abstract. Introduction: Work-related Musculoskeletal Disorders include the musculoskeletal clinical conditions related to work. This study aimed to describe the prevalence of musculoskeletal pain and discomfort and to analyze the association of individual, physical/biomechanical, psychosocial, cognitive and organizational risk factors in a beverage company.

Methods: Observational and cross-sectional study carried out in all sectors of a beverage company. The following questionnaires were applied: sociodemographic information, the Nordic questionnaire, Corlett's Body Map, Short Form Health Survey (SF-36), the Work Ability Index, the Need for Recovery Scale, and the Quick Exposure Check - Br. The analysis was performed by the associations using Fisher's Exact Test and logistic regression using the Odds Ratio (OR) ($p < 0.05$, 95% Confidence Interval).

Results: A total of 100 volunteers participated in the study. The sample has predominance of male (69%), mean age of 33.76 years. 57% of the participants reported musculoskeletal pain/discomfort, mainly in the region of the lumbar spine, of moderate intensity. Individual factors such as age over 40 years (OR 7.40; 1.87–29.25), time in function (OR 4.12; 1.43–11.84), absenteeism (OR 7.35; 2.68–20.14), non-adherence to workplace exercises (OR 2.95; 1,28–6.80). SF-36 questionnaire Functional Capacity (OR 6.13; 2.34–16.06), Physical Aspects (OR 10.25; 2.23–46.97), Social Aspects (OR 4.96; 1.89–12.99), Mental Health (OR 3.01; 1.27–7.11), Pain (OR 77.68; 9.93–607.20) and General Health Status (OR 5.17; 1.88–14.16), Work Ability Index questionnaire (OR10.45; 3.58–30.47) and Need for Recovery Scale OR3.40; 1.38–8.36) were associated with musculoskeletal pain/discomfort.

Conclusions: Emphasis in workplace exercises, pauses, physical activities and mental/psychosocial support are mandatory in addition to ergonomics preventive approach.

Keywords: Pain · Risk factors · Musculoskeletal disorders · Assessment · Association

© The Author(s), under exclusive license to Springer Nature Switzerland AG 2021
N. L. Black et al. (Eds.): IEA 2021, LNNS 222, pp. 753–762, 2021.
https://doi.org/10.1007/978-3-030-74611-7_103

1 Introduction

Work-related musculoskeletal disorders can be related to factors such as repetitive movements, awkward and sustained postures, which can affect the neck, upper limbs and lumbar spine [1, 2]. The effects on musculoskeletal symptoms can be associated to several risk factors as individual/personal as age, gender, previous diseases, hormonal changes, Body Mass Index (BMI), family history, smoking, alcohol consumption, physical activity level, motor skills and training; organizational, cognitive or psychosocial factors as the possibility of breaks during activities, rotation or alternation of activities, relationship with colleagues and superiors, cognitive demand for tasks) and/or physical or biomechanical factors (extreme or uncomfortable postures, excessive use of force, handling loads, repetitive movements, excessive temperatures and the presence of vibration [3–6].

Cognitive or psychosocial risk factors are critical components of the multifactorial nature of work-related musculoskeletal disorders and need to be evaluated to plan prevention and monitoring programs for successive musculoskeletal disorders in the workplace, as a strategy in health promotion [1, 3]. Psychosocial exposures include high work demands, low job control, high job stress and low support from supervisors and co-workers [5]. Risk ergonomic assessment is also important to provide favorable working conditions, in order to improve productivity, through a safe and healthy work environment [2, 6]. The programs of quality of life at work search to incorporate environments by offering a range of activities, such as workplace exercises as a preventive action for workers' health, acting in the prevention and reduction musculoskeletal complaints, carried out voluntarily, in groups, in the work environment, during office hours [7–9].

So, this study aimed to describe the prevalence of musculoskeletal pain and discomfort and to analyze the association of individual, physical/biomechanical, psychosocial, cognitive and organizational risk factors in a beverage company which offers workplace exercises as part of its quality of life program.

2 Methodology

This was an observational and cross-sectional study in a convenience sample of a beverage company. All company employees were invited to participate in the survey during the period from January 2018 to January 2020. Initially, the company had 1,429 employees, distributed in sectors such as production line (production, potting), inventory, distribution, building maintenance (mechanics and electricians), sales, call center (telemarketing agents), administrative (human resources, legal and work safety) and medical outpatient (physiotherapist, physicians, occupational nursing technicians, speech therapist and physical educators), in addition to security, cleaning, and maintenance work at heights. During the collection data period, there was a gradual reduction in the number of employees, when the company started to count with just over 1,000 active employees. The volunteers answered the questionnaires at their workplace during their working day, in just one opportunity, in a private room at the company's outpatient clinic.

All participants answered a sociodemographic questionnaire with items related to age, sex, lifestyle and occupational aspects. The questionnaires Medical Outcome

Study 36-item Short Form (SF-36) [10] Nordic Questionnaire [11] Corlett's Body Map [12]; Work Ability Index (WAI) [13]; Need for Recovery Scale (NRS) [14] and Quick Exposure Check (QEC) [15, 16] were collected.

This study was approved by the Local Ethical Committee (CAAE: 89764418.7.0000.5440). Written consent was obtained from all participating and the company.

A descriptive analysis of the data was performed to characterize the sample. To verify the association between qualitative variables, the data were submitted to Fisher's Exact Test [17]. The quantification of this association was measured using logistic regression models where the gross Odds ratio was calculated with their respective 95% confidence intervals. All statistical analyzes were performed using the SAS statistical software.3.

3   Results

One hundred employees accepted to participate in the study. In the sample there was a predominance of men (69%), with a mean age of 33.76 years (±8.51 years), normal body mass index (BMI) in 60% of the sample, with the majority being right-handed (95%). 51% performed functions in the company in which they did not perform lifting, transportation and handling of loads, while 49% performed functions that performed lifting, transportation and handling of loads, with time in the function varying between 8 months and 23 years, 70% have been working in the same function for up to 5 years, 63% had no history of absenteeism, 59% did not practice physical activity, 55% of the participants did workplace exercises. 57% of the sample reported musculoskeletal pain/discomfort.

There was a prevalence of pain/discomfort in the low back region (43%), most reported as a complaint in the last 12 months, with greater impediments to perform activities, greater need to search for health professionals' aids and greater number of pain complaints/discomfort in the last seven days by the Nordic questionnaire. Corlett's Body Map also showed greater reports of pain/discomfort in the low back region, most of moderate intensity (12%). No intensity of intolerable pain was verified by any participant.

The scores obtained in the SF-36 questionnaire presented the best mean values for the Functional Capacity components with 88.00 and the Social Aspects with 81.26 and, as the worst ones for the Vitality components with 67.20 and Mental Health with 69.56. The mean value for the WAI questionnaire was 36.92, referring to a low work capacity. For the NRS questionnaire was 12.29, classified as moderate after-work fatigue. The QEC presented mean value of 126.82, which points to a moderate occupational risk, regarding exposure to biomechanical, organizational and psychosocial factors (Table 1).

Individuals factors as age over 40 years, time in function greater than 5 years, absenteeism due to musculoskeletal disease, non-adherence to workplace exercises, incapacity for work and the need for recovery were associated with the presence of musculoskeletal pain/discomfort [18, 19]. In our study we did not find significant differences in pain between workers who performed functions with or without weightlifting, which may indicate that both situations can be harmful to the appearance of low back pain.

As individual characteristics, we first found that age and time in function were associated with pain complaints. With increasing age and working time, the individual

Table 1. Frequency, Fisher's exact test and logistic regression in relation to the self-reported pain

| | Pain | | | | |
| | No (43%) | Yes (57%) | | | |
	n (%)	n (%)	Total	p-value*	Raw odds ratio (CI 95%)
Age (years)					
Below 30	25 (58.14)	18 (41.86)	43 (100.00)	0.00.6	1.00 (Reference)
Between 30 to 40	15 (39.47)	23 (60.53)	38 (100.00)		2.13 (0.87; 5.18)
Between 40 a 60	3 (15.79)	16 (84.21)	19 (100.00)		7.40 (1.87; 29.25)
Gender					
Male	31 (44.93)	38 (55.07)	69 (100.00)	0.663	1.00 (Reference)
Female	12 (38.71)	19 (61.29)	31 (100.00)		1.29 (0.54; 3.06)
Dominance					
Right-handed	41 (43.16)	54 (56.84)	95 (100.00)	1.000	1.00 (Reference)
Left-handed	2 (40.00)	3 (60.00)	5 (100.00)		1.13 (0.18; 7.13)
Load lifting					
Yes	18 (36.73)	31 (63.26)	49 (100.00)	0,233	1.65 (0.74; 3.68)
No	25 (49.02)	26 (50.98)	51 (100.00)		1.00 (Reference)
Time in function (years)					
Below 2	21 (60.00)	14 (40.00)	35 (100.00)	0,021	1.00 (Reference)
Between 2 to 5	14 (40.00)	21 (60.00)	35 (100.00)		2.25 (0.86; 5.85)
More than de 5 years	8 (26.67)	22 (73.33)	30 (100.00)		4.12 (1.43; 11.84)
Absenteeism due to musculoskeletal diseases					
Yes	6 (16.22)	31 (83.78)	37 (100.00)	<0,001	7.35 (2.68; 20.14)
No	37 (58.73)	26 (41.27)	63 (100.00)		1.00 (Reference)

(*continued*)

Table 1. (*continued*)

| | Pain | | | | |
| | No (43%) | Yes (57%) | | | |
	n (%)	n (%)	Total	p-value*	Raw odds ratio (CI 95%)
BMI					
Normal	30 (50.00)	30 (50.00)	60 (100.00)	0.153	1.00 (Reference)
Overweight	9 (37.50)	15 (62.50)	24 (100.00)		1.66 (0.63; 4.39)
Obesity	4 (25.00)	12 (75.00)	16 (100.00)		3.00 (0.86; 10.36)
Physical activity					
Yes	19 (46.34)	22 (53.66)	41 (100.00)	0,681	1.00 (Reference)
No	24 (40.67)	35 (59.32)	59 (100.00)		1.25 (0.56; 2.81)
Workplace exercises					
Yes	30 (54.54)	25 (45.46)	55 (100.00)	0.014	1.00 (Reference)
No	13 (28.89)	32 (71.11)	45 (100.00)		2.95 (1.28; 6.80)
SF-36 – Functional capacity					
<93,5	7 (18.42)	31 (81.58)	38 (100.00)	<0,001	6,13 (2.34; 16.06)
≥93,5	36 (58.06)	26 (41.93)	62 (100.00)		1.00 (Reference)
SF-36 - Physical aspects					
<80	2 (9.52)	19 (90.48)	21 (100.00)	<0.001	10,25 (2.23; 46.97)
≥80	41 (51.90)	38 (48.10)	79 (100.00)		1.00 (Reference)
SF-36 – Pain					
<82.8	1 (2.63)	37 (97.37)	38 (100.00)	<0,001	77.68 (9.93; 607.20)
≥82.8	42 (67.74)	20 (32.26)	62 (100.00)		1.00 (Reference)
SF-36 - General Health Status					
<75.75	6 (18.75)	26 (81.25)	32 (100.00)	0,001	5.17 (1.88; 14.16)
≥ 75.75	37 (54.41)	31 (45.59)	68 (100.00)		1.00 (Reference)

(*continued*)

Table 1. (*continued*)

	Pain				
	No (43%)	Yes (57%)			
	n (%)	n (%)	Total	p-value*	Raw odds ratio (CI 95%)
SF-36 – Vitality					
<73.8	17 (36.17)	30 (63.83)	47 (100.00)	0.227	1.69 (0.76; 3.79)
≥73.8	26 (49.06)	27 (50.94)	53 (100.00)		1.00 (Reference)
SF-36 - Social aspects					
<86.25	7 (20.00)	28 (80.00)	35 (100.00)	<0.001	4.96 (1.89; 12.99)
≥86.25	36 (55,38)	29 (44,62)	65 (100,00)		1.00 (Reference)
SF-36 - Emotional Aspects					
<80	5 (23.81)	16 (76.19)	21 (100.00)	0.051	2.96 (0.99; 8.88)
≥80	38 (48.10)	41 (51.90)	79 (100.00)		1.00 (Reference)
SF-36 - Mental health					
<74.8	11 (27.50)	29 (72.50)	40 (100.00)	0.013	3.01 (1.27; 7.11)
≥74.8	32 (53.33)	28 (46.67)	60 (100.00)		1.00 (Reference)
WAI					
Reduced	5 (13.16)	33 (86.84)	38 (100.00)	<0.001	104.5 (3.58; 30.47)
Good	38 (61.29)	24 (38.71)	62 (100.00)		1.00 (Reference)
NRS					
Low	34 (53.12)	30 (46.88)	64 (100.00)	0.009	
Moderate	9 (27.27)	24 (72.73)	33 (100.00)		
High	0 (0.00)	3 (100.00)	3 (100.00)		
NRS					
Low	34 (53.12)	30 (46.88)	64 (100.00)	0.006	1.00 (Reference)
Moderate/High	9 (25.00)	27 (75.00)	36 (100.00)		3.40 (1.38; 8.36)

(continued)

Table 1. (*continued*)

	Pain				
	No (43%)	Yes (57%)			
	n (%)	n (%)	Total	p-value*	Raw odds ratio (CI 95%)
QEC					
Low	5 (62.50)	3 (37.50)	8 (100.00)	0,436	1.00 (Reference)
Moderate	23 (43.40)	30 (56.60)	53 (100.00)		2.17 (0.47; 10.04)
High	15 (38.46)	24 (61.54)	39 (100.00)		2.66 (0.55; 12.81)

*p-value related to Fisher's Exact Test.
Legend- WAI: Work ability index; NRS: Need for Recovery Scale; QEC: Quick Exposure Check.

was more and more likely to have musculoskeletal pain/discomfort. From the age of 30, workers were 2.13 times more likely to experience pain/discomfort, and from the age of 40 this chance increased to 7.40 times. In Finland in 2018, the average retirement age was 61.3 years and the most common reason for early retirement was problems of the musculoskeletal system (33%) and the second most common reason was mental problems (31%) [20].

We also found as an individual factor the absenteeism because of musculoskeletal disease; 7.35 times more likely to have pain than workers who did not were out of work. Workers who reported pain and work-related psychosocial factors were at a higher risk of severance and/or retirement due to disability [21], up to 15 to 20 times [22].

Another individual factor that was associated with pain was the non-participation in the voluntary workplace exercises. We found that workers who did not participate in the voluntary and supervised workplace exercises offered by the company had 2.95 times more complaints of musculoskeletal pain compared to workers who participated. Workplace exercises can bring benefits provided for both the employee and the company. With regard to employees, there are physiological benefits; improving posture and reducing muscle tension; improving muscle strength and endurance, motor coordination, concentration, as well as well-being and quality of life. Regarding to the company, there are reduced health care costs and absenteeism rates; healthy habits improvement and reduction of accidents at work. Although, evidence is lacking about its effectiveness, promising results have been reported [23–25].

Regarding the association of pain with the SF-36 domains, we found that the domains related to functional capacity, physical aspects, pain, general health, social aspects and mental health showed an association between complaints of musculoskeletal pain reported by workers in a beverage production company. Because it is a generic questionnaire that seeks broader information on the individual's biopsychosocial issues [8]. The study of Müller et al., (2016) corroborate with our findings regarding the use of SF-36, which also indicated an association between the presence of pain and the general health, social aspects and mental health domains. Thus, in addition to the preventive approach to musculoskeletal pain and discomfort, issues related to mental health and social support are also useful in improving the general quality of life of workers [8].

In both WAI and NRS questionnaires, we found an association between pain and risk factors at work represented by such instruments. In relation to these two questionnaires, our study pointed out that workers who reported pain had reduced rates of work capacity, as well as a moderate to high need for recovery. So, the lower the WAI score, the greater the complaints of pain and the lesser the ability to work. Similar results have also been reported on a sample of tertiary hospital employees [13].

In addition to the ability to work, personal characteristics, psychosocial factors and quality of life are associated with the presence of pain in the present study. In the study by Sewell et al. [26], pain also showed a significant association with the physical domain and the social domain. Sörensen et al. [27] showed that there was a relationship between work ability and quality of life in middle-aged men working in physically demanding jobs. It can be suggested that the promotion of work ability can influence the overall quality of life.

Multimorbidity has been shown to reduce quality of life and increase mortality. People with multimorbidity are more dependent on health services and have worse work results. In addition, these conditions have been shown to reduce quality of life, increase incapacity for work, increase treatment burden and health costs. For people living with multimorbidity, musculoskeletal disorders can impair the ability to cope and maintain health and independence, leading to a precipitous physical and social decline [28].

The QEC questionnaire presented moderate occupational risk for the volunteers. Statistically, it was not associated with the dependent variable "pain", however, it is worth noting that such data found points to an important issue of ergonomics at work. When filling out this questionnaire, ergonomics is taken into account, from the perspective of the examiner and the perception of the worker. Adopting good ergonomic practices is one way to prevent occupational diseases. In addition, good ergonomic practices are essential for the company's success, as they directly affect the worker's quality of life [29].

As limitations, this study did not focus on ergonomics analysis by subgroups, that could bring additional findings.

This study had its relevance in the general scope of occupational health, however, was focused on verifying the prevalence of the complaints, as well as the association of musculoskeletal pain/discomfort with individual, physical/biomechanical, psychosocial, cognitive risk factors and organizational in workers of a beverage company. Furthermore, this study did not perform any intervention, indicating that further studies that investigate the effectiveness of the workplace exercises may be relevant for this population.

4   Conclusion

The most affected area by pain between these workers was the lower back. The musculoskeletal pain/discomfort found in the workers of this beverage company was associated with individual, physical and psychosocial risk factors, reducing quality of life, capacity for work and increasing the need for recovery between working hours.

References

1. Akrouf, Q.A., Crawford, J.O., Al-Shatti, A.S., Kamel, M.I.: Musculoskeletal disorders among bank office workers in Kuwait. East. Mediterr. Health J. **16**, 94–100 (2010)
2. Chiasson, M.E., Imbeau, D., Major, J., Aubry, K., Delisle, A.: Influence of musculoskeletal pain on worker's ergonomic risk-factor assessments. Appl. Ergon. **49**, 1–7 (2015)
3. Antonopoulou, M.D., Alegakis, A.K., Hadjipavlou, A.G., Lionis, C.D.: Studying the association between musculoskeletal disorders, quality of life and mental health. A primary care pilot study in rural Crete, Greece. BMC Musculoskelet. Disord. **10**(1), 143 (2009)
4. Widanarko, B., Legg, S., Devereux, J., Stevenson, M.: The combined effect of physical, psychosocial/organizational and/or environmental risk factors on the presence of work-related musculoskeletal symptoms and its consequences. Appl. Ergon. **45**, 1610–1621 (2014)
5. Mather, L., et al.: Health, work and demographic factors associated with a lower risk of work disability and unemployment in employees with lower back, neck and shoulder pain. BMC Musculoskelet. Disord. **20**(1), 1–10 (2019)
6. Hembecker, P.K., et al.: Investigation of musculoskeletal symptoms in a manufacturing company in Brazil: a cross-sectional study. Braz. J. Phys. Ther. **21**(3), 175–183 (2017)
7. Bonge, P.M., Ijmker, S., Van de Heuvel, S., Blatter, B.M.: Epidemiology of work related neck and upper limb problems: psychosocial and personal risk factors (Part 1) and effective interventions from a biobehavioural perspective (Part II). J. Occup. Rehabil. **16**, 279–302 (2006)
8. Müller, J.D.S., Falcão, I.R., Couto, M.C.B.M., Viana, W.D.S., Alves, I.B., Viola, D.N., Woods, C.G., Rêgo, R.F.: Health-related quality of life among artisanal fisherwomen/shellfish gatherers: lower than the general population. Int. J. Environ. Res. Public Health **13**, 466 (2016)
9. Sundstrup, E., Jakobsen, M., Brandt, M., Jay, K., Persson, R., Aagaard, P., Andersen, L.: Workplace strength training prevents deterioration of work ability among workers with chronic pain and work disability: a randomized controlled trial. Scand. J. Work Environ. Health **40**, 244–251 (2014)
10. Oakman, J., et al.: Workplace interventions to improve work ability: a systematic review and meta-analysis of their effectiveness. Scand. J. Work Environ. Health **44**(2), 134–146 (2018)
11. Prieske, O., et al.: Effects of physical exercise training in the workplace on physical fitness: a systematic review and meta-analysis. Sports Med. **49**, 1903–1921 (2019)
12. Hemingway, H., Stafford, M., Stansfeld, S., Shipley, M., Marmot, M.: Is the SF-36 a valid measure of change in population health? BMJ **315**(7118), 1273–9 (1997)
13. Kuorinka, I., Jonsson, B., Kilbom, A., Vinterberg, H., Biering-Sorensen, F., Andersson, G., Jorgensen, K.: Standardised Nordic questionnaires for the analysis of musculoskeletal symptoms. Appl. Ergon. **18**(3), 233–7 (1987)
14. Corlett, E.N., Bishop, R.P.: A technique for assessing postural discomfort. Ergonomics **19**, 175–182 (1976)
15. Souza, D.B.O., Martins, L.V., Marcolino, A.M., Barbosa, R.I., Tamanini, G., Fonseca, M.C.R.: Work capability and musculoskeletal symptoms in workers at a public hospital. Fisioter. Pesqui. **22**, 182–190 (2015)
16. Jansen, N.W.H., Kant, I., Van Den Brandt, P.A.: Need for recovery in the working population: Description and associations with fatigue and psychological distress. Int. J. Behav. Med. **9**, 322–40 (2002)
17. Comper, M.L.C., Macedo, F., Padula, R.S.: Musculoskeletal symptoms, postural disorders and occupational risk factors: correlational analysis. Work **41**, 2445–2448 (2012)
18. David, G., Woods, V., Li, G., Buckle, P.: The development of the quick exposure check (QEC) for assessing exposure to risk factors for work-related musculoskeletal disorders. Appl. Ergon. **39**, 57–69 (2008)

19. Fisher, R.A.: The logic of inductive inference. J. R. Stat. Soc. **98**(1), 39–82 (1935)
20. Kwon, B.K., Roffey, D.M., Bishop, P.B., Dagenais, S., Wai, E.K.: Systematic review: occupational physical activity and low back pain. Occup. Med. **61**, 541–548 (2011)
21. Odebiyi, D.O., Olawale, O.A., Adeniji, Y.M.: Impact of computer related posture on the occurrence of musculoskeletal discomfort among secondary school students in Lagos, Nigeria. Nig. Q. J. Hosp. Med. **23**, 237–42 (2013)
22. Eläketurvakeskus. https://www.etk.fi/en/the-pension-system/international-comparison/retirement-ages/. Accessed June 2019
23. Shelerud, R.A.: Epidemiology of occupational low back pain. Clin. Occup. Environ. Med. **5**(3), 501–28 (2006)
24. Dorner, T.E., Alexanderson, K., Svedberg, P., Tinghög, P., Ropponen, A., Mittendorfer-Rutz, E.: Synergistic effect between back pain and common mental disorders and the risk of future disability pension: a nationwide study from Sweden. Psychol. Med. **46**(2), 425–36 (2016)
25. Eerd, D.V., Munhall, C., Irvin, E., Rempel, D., Brewer, S., van der Beek, A.J., Dennerlein, J.T., Tullar, J., Skivington, K., Pinion, C., Amick, B.: Effectiveness of workplace interventions in the prevention of upper extremity musculoskeletal disorders and symptoms: an update of the evidence. Occup. Environ. Med. **73**, 62–70 (2016)
26. Ris, I., Sogaard, K., Gram, B., Agerbo, K., Boyle, E., Juul-Kristensen, B.: Does a combination of physical training, specific exercises and pain education improve health-related quality of life in patients with chronic neck pain? A randomized control trial with a 4–month follow up. Manual Ther. **26**, 132–140 (2016)
27. Shariat, A., Cardoso, J.R., Cleland, J.A., Danaee, M., Ansari, N.N., Kargarfard, M., Mohd Tamrin, S.B.: Prevalence rate of neck, shoulder and lower back pain in association with age, body mass index and gender among Malaysian office workers. Work **60**, 191–199 (2018)
28. Sewell, M., Churilov, L., Mooney, S., Ma, T., Maher, P., Grover, S.R.: Chronic pelvic pain–pain catastrophizing, pelvic pain and quality of life. Scand. J. Pain **18**, 441–448 (2018)
29. Sörensen, E.L., Pekkonen, M.M., Männikkö, H.K., Louhevaara, A.V., Smolander, J., Alén, J.M.: Associations between work ability, health-related quality of life, physical activity and fitness among middle-aged men. Appl. Ergon. **39**, 786–791 (2008)
30. Duffield, S.J., Ellis, B.M., Goodson, N., Walker-Bone, K., Conaghan, P.G., Margham, T., Loftis, T.: The contribution of musculoskeletal disorders in multimorbidity: implications for practice and policy. Best Pract. Res. Clin. Rheumatol. **31**, 129–144 (2017)
31. Haukka, E., Pehkonen, I., Leino-Arjas, P., Viikari-Juntura, E., Takala, E.P., Malmivaara, A., Hopsu, L., Mutanen, P., Ketola, R., Virtanen, T., Leino-Holtari, M., Nykänen, J., Stenholm, S., Ojajärvi, M., Riihimäki, H.: Effect of a participatory ergonomics intervention on psychosocial factors at work in a randomized controlled trial. Occup. Environ. Med. **67**(3), 170–7 (2010)

A Low-Cost Sensor-Based Smartphone App for Wrist Velocity Measurements

Mikael Forsman[2,1]([✉]) [ID], Liyun Yang[1,2] [ID], Filipe Chinarro[1], and Jonas Willén[1] [ID]

[1] Division of Ergonomics, CBH, KTH Royal Institute of Technology, Stockholm, Sweden
[2] IMM, Karolinska Institutet, Stockholm, Sweden
miforsm@kth.se

Abstract. A quantitative wrist angular velocity to wrist-related disorders relation have been reported in hand intensive work. This velocity has been complicated to measure. A new sensors and smartphone method was developed and tested. The result indicate the prototype as a promising tool, which in the future may support researchers and practitioners in exposure quantification and risk assessment of hand intensive repetitive work tasks.

Keywords: Hand intensive work · Goniometers · IMUs · Musculoskeletal disorders · Risk assessments

1 Introduction

Work-related musculoskeletal disorders in e.g. the hand/wrist are common in all countries and in different hand intensive work industries, such as assembling, construction and food industries.

In practice risk assessments are often performed by observations. There are many developed observational risk assessment methods for repetitive work tasks. They are easy to use, and they can cover a large spectrum of risk factors, but they have often show rather low reliability, especially so for hand and wrist postures and movements [1, 2].

A quantitative wrist angular velocity to wrist-related disorders relation have been demonstrated by Nordander et al. [3]. The group have also studied quantitative exposure-response relationships for occupational physical exposures of the neck and upper extremity and disorders of the neck, shoulders and hands [4], and recommended to measure wrist and arm velocity. They also recommended a median level action limit of 20 °/s for wrist velocity. The common way today to measure wrist velocity is to use electro-goniometers. They are, however, expensive and because their mechanical construction they often break. The analyses are today complex; these kind of measurement projects are very rarely carried out by practitioners; only by researchers.

This study is a part of a larger project, with plans to carry out wrist velocity measurements in several occupational groups, by the regional Centres for Occupational and Environmental Medicine, in Sweden. Unfortunately, because of the Covid-19 pandemic, the field data collection is delayed.

N. L. Black et al. (Eds.): IEA 2021, LNNS 222, pp. 763–767, 2021.
https://doi.org/10.1007/978-3-030-74611-7_104

1.1 Objective

The aim of this study was to develop and test an inexpensive and practical method for workplace wrist velocity measurements.

2 Methods

2.1 The Prototype

A prototype of a wrist velocity measuring method was developed. Two Movesense inertial measurement units (so-called IMUs; Movesense.com, owned by Suunto, Vantaa, Finland) were attached, the first with double-sided tape on the back of the hand, and the second on the lower arm, as a watch, with an armband. See Fig. 1.

Fig. 1. The prototype for smartphone measurements of wrist velocity

An app was developed. In the prototype app, the gyroscope data of each sensor is sampled at a frequency of 50 Hz, and transmitted via low energy Bluetooth to an iPod Touch or iPhone device (Apple Inc.). In order to obtain the wrist velocity, the absolute angular velocity of the lower arm sensor is subtracted from the velocity of the hand sensor. The angular velocity is displayed and saved in the app. Directly after a measurement, statistical results, i.e. the mean value, and 50th and 90th percentiles, may be seen in the app.

2.2 Tests

Three novel validity tests were first carried out: 1) Two sensors of the kind used in the prototype, were, together with three other IMUs pairs (from other companies) attached to a bicycle wheel, which was rotated back and forth at different speeds, for about two minutes [5], see Fig. 2. The difference of the two sensors, should be zero; anything above zero should be seen as an error. To test if there is a dependence on differences in

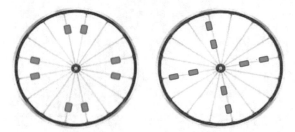

Fig. 2. Schematic illustration of the four pairs of sensors attached to the wheel. To the left, at equal distances from the center, and to the right at different distances from the center.

acceleration within the pair, the test was repeated with the sensor in each pair at different distances from the center.

The Movesense sensors were then attached a) firstly to a non-flexible ruler, which were attached to the right lower arm and hand of a 44-year old man. In this experiment, since the wrist is 'stiff', the true wrist velocity is zero. The subject moved his arm and hand, as he was performing a manual task, during more than two minutes. In similar way the sensors were in a later trial attached to a stiff book, and during a two-hour recording (with an iPod Touch). Every 10th minute, a 28-year old woman, moved the book around somewhat quicker than usually during manual work tasks.

Then tests were performed in a motion tracking lab, to compare with velocity computed from optical markers. Six subjects performed three simulated work tasks, hair drying, folding paper plane and sorting mail. These experiments are described more in detail in another chapter [6].

Finally, in a battery test, the app was used for 11 h, continuously sampling data.

3   Results

3.1   Tests Simulating a Stiff Wrist

From the bicycle wheel test two pairs showed error levels, i.e. 99% of the values, was below 2 °/s, Movesense was one of those pairs, while the other two pairs showed somewhat higher error levels, about 3 °/s. The trial with different distances from the wheel center, did not increase those errors. Hence there was no significant dependence on the distance from the center.

In the test with the stiff ruler the mean absolute velocity error during the two-minute task was 2.7 °/s. Early trials had shown an error dependent on a random component of the delay in sending data from the sensors to the iPod Touch. These errors were reduced in the app by averaging the time difference between sensor 1 and sensor 2. That function made the increased synchronization of the velocity signals. It also seemed to handle any drift between the two sensors' clocks. Figure 3 shows velocity signals of the two sensors on the stiff book, before and after the synchronization function. In a 30 s window more than two hours after start, the mean absolute error was 2.1 °/s, see diagram to the right in Fig. 3.

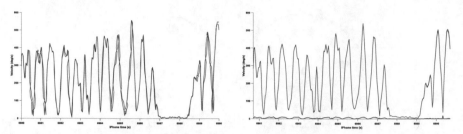

Fig. 3. Velocity signals of the two sensors (blue and red) on the stiff book, to the left without, and to the right, with the synchronization function. The right figure also shows the absolute difference signal, i.e. the black. In the ideal case, that signal should be zero, since the two sensors are rotated simultaneously.

In the motion tracking lab, for the three simulated work tasks, the mean the mean absolute difference, between the velocity measured with the app, and the velocity from the optical motion tracking system ranged between 4 and 12 °/s. The subjects reported that the equipment was possible to use in simulated work tasks, without interfering the tasks.

In the battery test, the app did still sample data, when it was stopped after 11 h.

4 Discussion

The present study was conducted in order to test the feasibility of a new prototype, designed to measure wrist velocity in MSD risk assessments.

Among the three accuracy tests, the ones with a known zero inter sensor velocity showed low errors, while the simulated work test showed larger differences to the gold standard signal. One could claim that the motion capture lab test should be the most important one, but wrist velocity is hard to measure also with optical markers. Since both types of sensors are attached to the skin, and at different places, none is perfectly measuring the joint velocity, and a difference should be expected. Also in the "ruler" and stiff book experiments, the sensors were rotated in different planes; so that low error estimate may well be close to what may be expected under real working life conditions.

However, in the measurements of the total velocity, which in this study was computed as the total velocity of the lower arm sensor subtracted from ditto of the hand sensor, there will be an underestimation when, which may occur during e.g. hair blowing, the hand and the lower arm are rotating in opposite directions.

It has been shown that important risk factors in manual work are highly repetitive tasks and high force demands. Repetitive tasks are difficult to assess by observations. Also, observational methods may be used for a limited time, while a workday rarely is similar during the whole time. So there is also a difficulty of sampling strategy. Technical methods, on the other hand, are highly reliable and may be used for a full workday. And as velocity may be seen as a combination of amplitude and repetitiveness in movements, it does not need a cut-off limits to decide how much do you need to move the hand to be counted as one movement. The force demands is still harder to measure. Electromyography or grip force sensors may be used, but they are still more complicated and often expensive to use. However, in both of two large studies [3, 4] clear associations have been seen between wrist velocity and neck/shoulder and elbow/hand complaints.

During its use, the smartphone app shows the estimated wrist velocity in real time, and directly after a measurement, the app shows velocity statistics. Such an app may be useful for practitioners to in, an easy way, obtain research quality measurements of the wrist velocity. This measure is a good quantization of repetitive work, which is difficult to quantify by observation, and it is practically impossible to observe for a full day.

5 Conclusion

The result indicated that the prototype is promising as an objective tool, which in the future may support researchers and practitioners in exposure quantification and risk assessment of hand intensive repetitive work tasks.

Acknowledgements. The participation of the subjects in the experiment is greatly acknowledged, as well as the support from MSc Karnica Manivasagam and MSc Mikael Reimeringer, who both worked hard and professionally in the experimental data collection. We are also grateful to PT Karin Berglund, who performed the battery test. This study was financially supported by Forte dnr 2017-01209.

References

1. Takala, E.P., Pehkonen, I., Forsman, M., Hansson, G.Å., Mathiassen, S.E., Neuman, P., Sjøgaard, G., Veiersted, K.B., Westgaard, R., Winkel, J.: Systematic evaluation of observational methods assessing biomechanical exposures at work. Scand. J. Work Environ. Health **36**(1), 3–24 (2010)
2. Rhén, I.M., Forsman, M.: Inter- and intra-rater reliability of the OCRA checklist method in video-recorded manual work tasks. Appl. Ergon. **84**, 103025 (2020). https://doi.org/10.1016/j.apergo.2019.103025
3. Nordander, C., Ohlsson, K., Akesson, I., Arvidsson, I., Balogh, I., Hansson, G.Å., Strömberg, U., Rittner, R., Skerfving, S.: Exposure-response relationships in work-related musculoskeletal disorders in elbows and hands - a synthesis of group-level data on exposure and response obtained using uniform methods of data collection. Appl. Ergon. **44**(2), 241–53 (2013)
4. Balogh, I., Arvidsson, I., Björk, J., Hansson, G.Å., Ohlsson, K., Skerfving, S., Nordander, C.: Work-related neck and upper limb disorders - quantitative exposure-response relationships adjusted for personal characteristics and psychosocial conditions. BMC Musculoskelet Disord. **20**(1), 139 (2019). https://doi.org/10.1186/s12891-019-2491-6
5. Chinaro, F.: A study of the performance of IMU sensors - Can IMU sensors be used to prevent work injuries on the wrist? KTH Royal Institute of Technology, Sweden. Batchelor Thesis (2020)
6. Yang, L., Manivasagam, K., Forsman, M.: Comparison of measurement accuracy of inertial measurement units and goniometer for wrist velocity assessment. In: Proceedings of IEA 2021 (2021)

Investigating Musculoskeletal Injury Risk: A Field Study on the Influence of Typical Assembly Activities on the Physiological Response of Industrial Workers

Tobias Hellig[⊠] [iD], Alexander Mertens[iD], Verena Nitsch[iD],
and Christopher Brandl[iD]

Chair and Institute of Industrial Engineering and Ergonomics, RWTH Aachen University,
Aachen, Germany
t.hellig@iaw.rwth-aachen.de

Abstract. Musculoskeletal disorders (MSD) are the most common cause of sick leave and the second most common cause of early retirement for health reasons. High incidence of MSDs is found in the shoulder and neck region. A major risk factor for developing MSDs in the shoulder and neck region is work above shoulder level. However, it is often assumed that at least short-term work above shoulder level is tolerable for well-trained and experienced working persons. Up to now, there are only few data describing the amount of effort exerted by different postures during industrial working tasks among industrial workers. In contrast, the findings of this study show that such working tasks may comprise a higher level of musculoskeletal injury risk. Repeated-measures ANOVA and subsequent conducted post-hoc analyses revealed a significant influence of work height on muscle activity of trapezius pars descendens, anterior deltoideus, erector spinae and rectus femoris. Furthermore, results show that working above shoulder level has significant influence on workload in other body regions. Based on the results, it can be assumed that industrial working persons are also exposed to a higher risk for the development of MSDs through activities with inappropriate work heights, i. e. above shoulder level.

Keywords: Musculoskeletal disorders · Surface electromyography · Assembly work · Field study

1 Introduction

Musculoskeletal disorders (MSDs) and work-related injuries contribute towards sickness-related absenteeism, reduced work capacity and early retirement, and as such they present significant challenges to individuals, companies, societies, and insurance systems (Jakobsen et al. 2018). Some MSDs are on the rise, in particular for the neck and shoulder area, Vos et al. (2017) indicate an increase in years lived with disability (YLD) of 21.9% for the year 2016 compared to 2006.

N. L. Black et al. (Eds.): IEA 2021, LNNS 222, pp. 768–775, 2021.
https://doi.org/10.1007/978-3-030-74611-7_105

A high incidence of diseases in the shoulder region gives rise to the need investigating factors contributing to the development of MSDs in the shoulder region. A rate of shoulder pain between 7% and 43% have been observed among American workers (Silverstein et al. 2006), Finnish workers (Miranda et al. 2001), French workers (Bodin et al. 2012) and recently recruited working persons (Harkness et al. 2003).

In many industrial manufacturing systems, a high workload is caused by a missing individual adaptation of workplaces, e.g. to body size, due to the large number of workers with different heights and to limiting factors caused by the production environment and the work piece to be produced (Bodin et al. 2020). This results in a high exertion of the musculoskeletal system and in particular for the shoulder and neck area. However, it is often assumed that exposures of the musculoskeletal system are at a lower level for experienced and well-trained working persons than for inexperienced working persons (Gagnon et al. 2016; Marras et al. 2006; Riley et al. 2015).

Up to now, there are only few data describing the amount of effort exerted by different postures during industrial working tasks among industrial working persons in the neck and shoulder muscles (Ng et al. 2014). Furthermore, it is exceedingly difficult to quantify the risk of musculoskeletal injury among industrial working persons due to work above shoulder level since relevant data describing the amount of effort exerted by neck and shoulder muscles are missing. Finally, due to interaction effects of body part postures, the musculoskeletal injury risk in other parts of the body arising by work above shoulder level could be significant, too.

An experiment was conducted in order to assess muscle activity among a sample of male blue-collar workers during assembly work in a truck trailer manufacturing company. In particular, the objective was to determine the influence of the height of the assembly objects on the muscle activity in different parts of the body of the working persons. It was hypothesized that muscle activity varies due to the different height of the assembly objects, especially in the neck and shoulder area.

2 Methodology

2.1 Participants

For the experiment, an opportunity sample of 47 male working persons between the ages of 18 and 62 years and mean (SD) age of 39.67 years (12.69 years) participated in a three-level univariate study design. The sample was limited to male participants, as only a very small number of female potential participants were available for this field study, thus making it difficult to achieve gender balance within this sample. Participants provided informed consent prior to their participation.

2.2 Experimental Design

Participants were required to perform a typical assembly task of screwing four screws into a device at three different levels of height. A univariate (work height) within-subject design was devised to measure muscle activity, whereby work height was set at three different heights. The order of the factor levels was systematically varied to reduce order effects.

As dependent variables, unilateral muscle activity of four muscles of the right body part and perceived exertion were collected. Muscle activity was sampled from the following muscles by using surface electromyography (EMG): trapezius pars descendens, anterior deltoideus, erector spinae and rectus femoris. The selected muscles are depicted in Fig. 1.

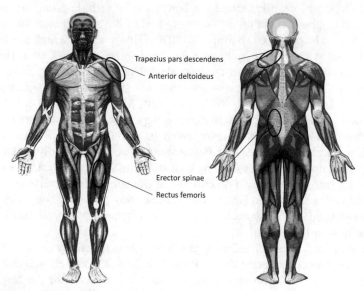

Fig. 1. The four selected muscles for electromyography analysis of the muscle activity. (Illustration by Termininja/CC BY-SA 3.0).

Selection of the trapezius pars descendens and anterior deltoideus was based on their function as arm lifter and shoulder stabiliser (Kadefors et al. 1999; Roman-Liu and Tokarshi 2005). Erector spinae and rectus femoris were chosen as representatives of the back and the legs and therefore responsible for an upright working posture (Perotto and Delagi 2011).

2.3 Procedure

Prior to the experimental task, sensors and electrodes were placed according to the European Recommendations for Surface Electromyography (SENIAM) (Hermens et al. 1999). Maximal voluntary contraction (MVC) values were observed during isometric contraction of each investigated muscle as reference contraction value. MVC tests were performed for each investigated muscle separately. In the following step, participants were instructed on the experimental task.

During the experimental task, participants screwed four screws out of a device with a cordless drill and then screwing them back in. This task was carried out on three different heights of 0.45 m, 1.25 m and 2.05 m. Such a task is carried out, for example, during the assembly of the eyelets for the tarpaulin on a truck.

2.4 Data Recording and Analysis

In this experimental procedure, an EMG device (Desktop DTS Receiver, Noraxon, AZ, USA) was used to measure bilateral muscle activity of four muscles. Ag/AgCl self-adhesive 8-shaped dual electrodes (dimensions of adhesive: 4×2.2 cm; diameter of the two circular adhesives: 1 cm; inter-electrode distance: 1.75 cm) were used. Signals were amplified with a gain of 1,000 V/V, input impedance of 100 MΩ and a common mode rejection ratio of 100 dB. Signals were sampled with a sampling frequency of 1,500 Hz and digitally band-pass filtered (10–500 Hz) with a first-order high-pass filter. Signals were recorded using the analysis software MyoResearch 3.8 (Noraxon, Scottsdale, AZ, USA). Root mean square (RMS) amplitude was calculated with an overlapping moving window of 100 ms (Hermens 1999). In order to compare EMG data for different conditions of working postures, RMS values were normalised to percent muscle activation by using the peak of the corresponding MVC reference contraction obtained prior to the experiment.

All statistical analyses were conducted using IBM SPSS Statistics 25. A repeated-measures ANOVA was used to identify the effects of work height on muscle activity. Where the assumption of sphericity was violated, p-values were ascertained based on degrees of freedom with Greenhouse–Geisser correction (for $\varepsilon < 0.75$) (Greenhouse and Geisser 1959). Significance was accepted at the α-level of $p < 0.05$. A post-hoc analysis of the mean values was conducted with Bonferroni adjustment of the α-level of $p < .05$.

3 Results

The results show that muscle activity of all four muscles was affected significantly by the work height. Results of ANOVAs are presented in Table 1. As post-hoc tests revealed (see Table 2), a work height of 1.25 m causes significantly lower muscle activity in the muscles of the neck and shoulder than a low work height or a work height above shoulder level. Conversely, a low working height causes significantly higher muscle activity in the muscles of the lower back and thigh.

Table 1. Results of univariate ANOVAs for effect of work height.

Dependent variable	F	$df1$	$df2$	p	η_p^2
Trapezius pars descendens (UT)	11.607	1.435	66.026	<.001	.201
Anteroior deltoideus (AD)	39.633	1.208	55.563	<.001	.463
Erector spinae (ES)	8.066	1.335	61.415	.003	.149
Rectus femoris (RF)	17.338	.1095	50.392	<.001	.274

In addition, the study shows that assembling activity under shoulder level leads to muscle activity of more than 20% MVC in the lower back (see Fig. 2). Assembling activity above shoulder level leads to muscle activity of more than 20% in the shoulder muscles.

Table 2: Results of post-hoc tests

Factor	p (UT)	p (AD)	p (ES)	p (RF)
low vs. middle	<.001	<.001	.060	<.001
low vs. high	1.000	<.001	.006	.006
high vs. middle	<.001	<.001	.083	<.001

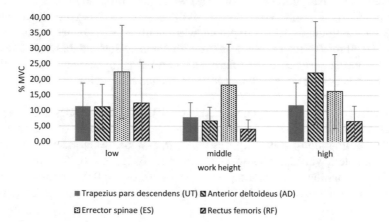

Fig. 2. Averaged muscle activity and standard deviation of muscle activity of four muscles according to working height.

4   Discussion

Previous investigations have shown significantly increased muscle activity in the neck and shoulder regions among working persons suffering from MSDs (Ng et al. 2014; Veiersted et al. 1993). However, the amount of data on musculoskeletal exertion of well-trained and experienced workers in real working systems is low. It is often assumed that there is a lower musculoskeletal injury risk for experienced and well-trained workers (Gagnon et al. 2016; Marras et al. 2006; Riley et al. 2015). However, in contrast to this thesis, our study shows significant neuromuscular responses early during work activity, which reached muscle activity amplitudes of more than 20% of MVC. In contrast to the hypothesis of lower musculoskeletal injury risk for experienced and well-trained workers, the findings of our study show that such working tasks may comprise a higher level of injury risk even for a well-trained and experienced working person. The results point out to the need to adapt workplaces to the individual characteristics and needs of workers. Despite the restrictive conditions in practice described in the introduction, adaptations in the design of workplaces and/or work activities should be made in order to reduce the musculoskeletal injury risk for all workers, regardless of their training level.

As the results of this study revealed, work height has a significant influence on muscle activity in different parts of the body and consequently on musculoskeletal injury risk of several body regions, such as the lower back or lower limbs. However, the higher muscle activity in the lower limb and lower back muscles during work at low heights emphasises the need to base an assessment of the load on a comprehensive view of the musculoskeletal system. According to the results of this study, workers should be given the opportunity to change their working postures frequently during their work activities in order to allow a distribution of the loads on the different parts of the body. Changing of working postures can help to avoid overloading specific parts of the body.

Furthermore, studies by Björkstén and Jonsson (1977), Kroemer (1989) and McNeil et al. (2015) showed that increased musculoskeletal injury risk is associated with muscle activity amplitudes of more than 15%–20% of maximum voluntary contraction. Exceeding this limit of maximum contraction would cause an internal muscle pressure which exceeds the blood pressure, leading to a shortage of oxygen in the muscle. Therefore, according to the muscle activity values of this study, even short-term work above shoulder level must be considered as a musculoskeletal injury risk.

However, some limitations to this study have to be considered in the interpretation of the results. The fixed working height of the experimental task must be characterised as a limiting factor of the study. Due to the practical test environment, it was not possible to adjust the height to the individual body height of the participants. Nevertheless, it can be assumed that adjusting the working height in accordance with a worker's individual body height can contribute to a further reduction of muscle activity.

Finally, during this investigation effect of repetition, work duration or rest allocation on physiological response were not considered. However, according to studies of Kakarot et al. (2012), Mathiassen (1993), Mathiassen and Winkel (1996) and Veiersted et al. (2013) this effect has been suggested by others and should be kept in mind when designing work tasks.

5 Conclusion

In summary, the muscle activity of four muscles among well-trained and experienced working persons were investigated using surface electromyography. The findings of our study provide new insights into surface muscle activity during real assembly work among well-trained and experienced workers. Based on the results, it can be assumed that such persons are also exposed to a higher risk for the development of MSDs through activities on inappropriate work heights, i. e. above shoulder level.

References

Björkstén, M., Jonsson, B.: Endurance limit of force in long-term intermittent static contractions. Scand. J. Work Environ. Health 3(1), 23–27 (1977)

Bodin, J., Garlantézec, R., Costet, N., Descatha, A., Viel, J.-F., Roquelaure, Y.: Shoulder pain among male industrial workers: validation of a conceptual model in two independent French working populations. Appl. Ergonomics 85, 103075 (2020)

Bodin, J., Ha, C., Sérazin, C., Descatha, A., Leclerc, A., Goldberg, M., Roquelaure, Y.: Effects of individual and work-related factors on incidence of shoulder pain in a large working population. J. Occup. Health 54(4), 278–288 (2012)

Gagnon, D., Plamondon, A., Larivière, C.: A biomechanical comparison between expert and novice manual materials handlers using a multi-joint EMG-assisted optimization musculoskeletal model of the lumbar spine. J. Biomech. **49**(13), 2938–2945 (2016)

Greenhouse, S.W., Geisser, S.: On methods in the analysis of profile data. Psychometrika **24**(2), 95–112 (1959)

Harkness, E.F., Macfarlane, G.J., Nahit, E.S., Silman, A.J., McBeth, J.: Mechanical and psychosocial factors predict new onset shoulder pain: a prospective cohort study of newly employed workers. Occup. Environ. Med. **60**(11), 850–857 (2003)

Hermens, H.J., Freriks, B., Merletti, R., Stegeman, D., Blok, J., Rau, G., et al.: European recommendations for surface ElectroMyoGraphy: results of the SENIAM project. In: SENIAM, vol. 8. Roessingh Research and Development, Enschede (1999)

Jakobsen, M.D., Sundstrup, E., Brandt, M., Persson, R., Andersen, L.L.: Estimation of physical workload of the low-back based on exposure variation analysis during a full working day among male blue-collar workers: cross-sectional workplace study. Appl. Ergonomics **70**, 127–133 (2018)

Kadefors, R., Forsman, M., Zoéga, B., Herberts, P.: Recruitment of low threshold motor-units in the trapezius muscle in different static arm positions. Ergonomics **42**(2), 359–375 (1999)

Kakarot, N., Mueller, F., Bassarak, C.: Activity-rest schedules in physically demanding work and the variation of responses with age. Ergonomics **55**(3), 282–294 (2012)

Kroemer, K.H.E.: Cumulative trauma disorders: their recognition and ergonomics measures to avoid them. Appl. Ergonomics **20**(4), 274–280 (1989)

Marras, W.S., Parakkat, J., Chany, A.M., Yang, G., Burr, D., Lavender, S.A.: Spine loading as a function of lift frequency, exposure duration, and work experience. Clin. Biomech. (Bristol, Avon) **21**(4), 345–352 (2006)

Mathiassen, S.E.: The influence of exercise/rest schedule on the physiological and psychophysical response to isometric shoulder-neck exercise. Eur. J. Appl. Physiol. Occup. Physiol. **67**(6), 528–539 (1993)

Mathiassen, S.E., Winkel, J.: Physiological comparison of three interventions in light assembly work: reduced work pace, increased break allowance and shortened working days. Int. Arch. Occup. Environ. Health **68**(2), 94–108 (1996)

McNeil, C.J., Allen, M.D., Olympico, E., Shoemaker, J.K., Rice, C.L.: Blood flow and muscle oxygenation during low, moderate, and maximal sustained isometric contractions. Am. J. Physiol. Regul. Integr. Comp. Physiol. **309**(5), R475–R481 (2015)

Miranda, H., Viikari-Juntura, E., Martikainen, R., Takala, E.P., Riihimäki, H.: A prospective study of work related factors and physical exercise as predictors of shoulder pain. Occup. Environ. Med. **58**(8), 528–534 (2001)

Ng, D., McNee, C., Kieser, J., Farella, M.: Neck and shoulder muscle activity during standardized work-related postural tasks. Appl. Ergonomics **45**(3), 556–563 (2014)

Perotto, A., Delagi, E.F.: Anatomical Guide for the Electromyographer: The Limbs and Trunk, 5th edn. Charles C. Thomas, Springfield (2011)

Riley, A.E., Craig, T.D., Sharma, N.K., Billinger, S.A., Wilson, S.E.: Novice lifters exhibit a more kyphotic lifting posture than experienced lifters in straight-leg lifting. J. Biomech. **48**(10), 1693–1699 (2015)

Roman-Liu, D., Tokarski, T.: Upper limb load as a function of repetitive task parameters: part 2–an experimental study. Int. J. Occup. Saf. Ergonomics JOSE **11**(1), 103–112 (2005)

Silverstein, B.A., Viikari-Juntura, E., Fan, Z.J., Bonauto, D.K., Bao, S., Smith, C.: Natural course of nontraumatic rotator cuff tendinitis and shoulder symptoms in a working population. Scand. J. Work Environ. Health **32**(2), 99–108 (2006)

Veiersted, K.B., Westgaard, R.H., Andersen, P.: Electromyographic evaluation of muscular work pattern as a predictor of trapezius myalgia. Scand. J. Work Environ. Health **19**(4), 284–290 (1993)

Veiersted, K.B., Forsman, M., Hansson, G.-Å., Mathiassen, S.E.: Assessment of time patterns of activity and rest in full-shift recordings of trapezius muscle activity - effects of the data processing procedure. J. Electromyogr. Kinesiol. Off. J. Int. Soc. Electrophysiological Kinesiol. **23**(3), 540–547 (2013)

Vos, T., Abajobir, A.A., Abate, K.H., Abbafati, C., Abbas, K.M., Abd-Allah, F., et al.: Global, regional, and national incidence, prevalence, and years lived with disability for 328 diseases and injuries for 195 countries, 1990–2016: a systematic analysis for the global burden of disease study 2016. Lancet **390**(10100), 1211–1259 (2017)

Previous Shoulder and Low Back Injury, Kinesiophobia, and Fear-Avoidance in Young Adult Asymptomatic Participant Groups

Heather Johnston[1,2](✉) and Janessa Drake[1]

[1] York University, Toronto, ON, Canada
haj18@yorku.ca
[2] Institute for Work and Health, Toronto, ON, Canada

Abstract. Ergonomics, biomechanics, and clinical human movement studies often describe the use of an asymptomatic young adult cohort as a control group or uninjured population for the study of shoulder and low back musculoskeletal disorders (MSD). While it is acknowledged that psychosocial factors play a role in work-related shoulder and low back musculoskeletal disorder, participant characterization and descriptives emphasize current physical characteristics (anthropometrics, demographics, injury status), without accounting for potentially latent characteristics like previous injury. It is well established that previous injury experience impacts an individual's emotional and behavioural responses [1], however, previous experiences with work-related injury are often overlooked when recruiting asymptomatic controls. This study reports previous shoulder and low back injury, fear of movement, and fear-avoidance beliefs in 134 asymptomatic university-aged young adults and demonstrates that previous injury experiences impact current beliefs, and opens discussion to including additional participant characteristics in addition to traditional descriptive measures.

Keywords: Musculoskeletal disorders · Fear-avoidance beliefs · Health psychology · Participant characteristics

1 Introduction

Shoulder and low back musculoskeletal disorders (MSD) remain common concerns in MSD research. Recruitment and study design are important considerations for successful investigation of risk factors and as such is necessary to address concerns of participant variability. Incorporating anthropometric and other descriptive characteristics, such as sex, age, and injury status, is one component of characterizing participant populations to address some of the variability in study outcomes [1]. However, there are still challenges in recruitment and appropriate characterization of sample populations and asymptomatic controls. Often samples of convenience are used as asymptomatic comparisons, for example, many research institutions are based within undergraduate university settings. Assumptions that an individual who is currently asymptomatic as a comparison for shoulder and low back MSD research, dismisses potential confounders such as previous injury experience, emotions, and fear of re-injury. The fear-avoidance model, as a theoretical framework, demonstrates how acute pain experience can manifest into chronic pain or future risk of injury [2], highlighting the role of a person's previous experience with injury and potential for anticipatory response of fear and subsequent avoidance behaviour [2]. While university aged comparison groups may mitigate participant variability due to age and physical symptomology, typically collected descriptive characteristics may not account for previous injuries and subsequent fear-avoidance beliefs which may benefit from sub-categorization or covariates of participants when it comes to understand complex disorders like shoulder and low back MSD.

2 Objectives

The primary objectives of this study were to 1) determine the prevalence of previous shoulder and low back pain injuries in a sample of asymptomatic young adults; and 2) measure kinesiophobia and fear-avoidance beliefs pertaining to work.

3 Methods

3.1 Participants

A cross-sectional study was completed following approval through an institutional ethics board. Participants were recruited from a sample of convenience through a university student population and provided written informed consent. Participants were eligible for the study if they were aged 18–35 years, had no prior injury to their shoulder, hip, and/or low back that required any medical care or loss time at work within the last 12 months, were current students. Participants were excluded if they had current or unresolved low-back, hip, or shoulder injuries or pain, or if any previous injury had required change to the anatomical arrangement of their joint (i.e., orthopaedic implants; tissue reconstruction, spinal fusion).

3.2 Anthropometrics

Participant anthropometric characteristics were measured prior to collection of the questionnaires. Characteristic measures included age (years), height (cm), weight (kg), waist circumference (cm), body fat percentage (BIA%).

3.3 Fear-Avoidance Model and Questionnaire

The fear-avoidance model of pain was developed to expand beyond typical biomedical and mechanical understandings of chronic low back pain [1]. Two questionnaires reflecting this model were included in this study. The first questionnaire included the measure of fear of movement and fear of reinjury using the Tampa scale of Kinesiophobia (TSK) [3]. The TSK is a 17-item self-report checklist using a 4-point Likert scale with a total score range of 17 through 68, where each question has an answer of "strongly disagree" to "strongly agree". High values on the TSK indicate higher degrees of fear of movement where a high scoring individual would have a cutoff score of 37 [3]. The avoidance of activity for work was captured using the Fear-Avoidance Beliefs Questionnaire, using the subscale of work (FABQ-W) [4]. The scale is a 6-point likert scale ranging from "completely disagree" to "completely agree". Following in-laboratory collection of anthropometrics, participants were emailed a brief survey that asked questions pertaining to previous injuries and the TSK-17, and the FABQ. Both scales have been demonstrated to be reliable in young adults and acute pain LBP populations [5]. The following three questions were asked regarding previous injury: 1) Have you ever experienced [insert shoulder or low back] pain due to an injury? 2) Was this caused by a work activity? 3) Did you seek medical care? The average total time of completion of the questionnaires was 5.5 min.

3.4 Analyses

A sample size calculation resulted in a sample of 114 participants, with an assumed prevalence of 0.05, and precision of 0.04. Anthropometrics were calculated as percentiles for the male and female data respectively. Questionnaire data was collected using Qualtrics software and analyses were performed using (version 24.0; IBM Corp., Armonk, NY, USA) with an alpha of 0.05. A participant was considered as having current kinesiophobia and FABQw if their scores were greater than the established cutoffs [3, 4], as such kinesiophobia and FABQw scores were also dichotomized into high and low. A descriptive analysis was performed, with categorical data analyses, presented as counts (#) and percentage (%), and the differences between sex were analyzed using a chi-square test. Pearson's correlation was used to determine the association between the two scores.

4   Results

4.1   Participant Characteristics

170 participants were recruited for this study, 153 were eligible based on the inclusion and exclusion criteria. The response rate of the questionnaires was 87.6%, with a total of 134 participants completing the questionnaires. The average age of participants, not significantly different between males and females, was 21 ± 6 years. The percentiles of a height, weight, waist circumference, and body fat percentage (BIA) are reported in Table 1.

Table 1. Brief anthropometrics presented by percentiles of male and female data.

		Min	Max	5th	25th	75th	95th	99th
Female	Height (cm)	149	183.5	154	158.5	167.9	175.6	182
(n = 87)	Weight (kg)	38	132	45.5	53.5	67	83	112
	Waist Circ. (cm)	67	114	70	77.8	88	100	113
	BIA (%)	6.9	39.6	12	17.2	24.8	34.3	35.8

(continued)

Table 1. (*continued*)

		Min	Max	5th	25th	75th	95th	99th
Male	Height (cm)	163	191	165.3	171	183	190	191
	Weight (kg)	50.5	112	54	67.9	83.5	100	112
(n = 47)	Waist Circ. (cm)	68.5	117	73	81	93	105	117
	BIA (%)	4.1	31.4	6.4	10.3	17	24.3	31.4

4.2 Previous Pain Due to Injury, Kinesiophobia, and Fear-Avoidance Beliefs

Out of the 134 participants, 40.3% of participants reported having either previous low back pain or shoulder pain that required time off occupation and medical care due to an injury (Table 2). The majority of previously injured participants reported previous low back pain (n = 35), followed by both having both shoulder and low back pain (n = 10), and those with only previous shoulder pain (n = 9). There were no differences in the proportions of the injury type between females and males. Of those who had experienced previous low back pain, 22.8% (n = 8 of 35) reported this previous injury was due to work, and one third (n = 3 out of 9) of those shoulder group reported their injury was caused by a work activity. Of the 32 female participants who had experienced either previous pain of the shoulder or low back from injury, 78% currently had kinesiophobia (average TSKscore = 42 ± 3). Of the 22 males who had experienced previous pain of the shoulder or low back from injury, 68% currently had kinesiophobia (average TSKscore = 42 ± 3). TSK scores were significantly higher for those who had a previous shoulder

Table 2. Previous injuries, kinesiophobia and fear-avoidance for male and female participants, categorical data presented as high and low scores on the TSK and FABQ-w.

		Female (n = 87)		Male (n = 47)		Difference	
		n	%	n	%	x^2	p-val
Previous back or shoulder injury	Yes	32	36.8	22	46.8		
	No	55	63.2	25	53.2	1.28	0.259
		Female *previous injury* (n = 32)		Male *previous injury* (n = 22)			
TSK	High	25	78.1	15	68.1		
	Low	7	21.9	7	31.8	0.671	0.412
FABQw	High	9	28.1	2	9.1		
	Low	23	71.8	20	90.9	2.91	0.088

or low back injury compared to participants with no previous injury ($t_{(132)} = 2.08$, p = 0.028, cohen's d = 9.12). All 11 participants who reported their injury was due to work scored high on the FABQw (Table 2). Scores for FABQw were significantly higher for those that had a previous shoulder or low back injury attributed to work compared to those without any previous injury ($t_{(132)} = 2.22$, p = 0.041, cohen's d = 6.12). Overall, the proportion of participants who scored high on the TSK was greater than the proportion of participants who scored high on the FABQw $\chi 2$ (n = 54) = 3.2, p < 0.001). There were no associations between these two scores.

5 Discussion

This study aimed to recruit and collect descriptive data on a sample of asymptomatic young adults aged 18–35 with no current injuries to represent a typical asymptomatic sample of convenience of a university aged population. Despite all participants being self-reported as presently asymptomatic, a modest percentage (40.3%) of this population had experienced a previous shoulder or low back injury. Of those who reported previous injury, 20.3% of these individuals reported it was due to work. Recognizing, that this young adult university population (average age of 21 years), was not working full time it was surprising to note the percentage of individuals that had experienced previous shoulder or low back injuries attributed to work. Demonstrating a continued concern over MSDs of these two regions, collecting this information prior to research protocols may be advantageous for further understanding risk factors in younger adults for early intervention and education and presents important characteristics for participant characterization or classification.

The use of the TSK suggests that the fear of reinjury may be an important consideration for classifying asymptomatic participants, as 74.0% of those with a previous shoulder or low back injury presently scored high on fear of reinjury and movement, even though they had not experienced injury or pain within the last 12 months. Despite not having previous injury etiology and full medical history, the fear-avoidance model highlights the potential long-lasting latent effects of previous injury that may impact participant categorization [5]. In previous studies of workers, the Tampa scale has provided a uni-dimensional construct of fear of movement across pain levels, ages and genders [6]. Therefore, a quick screening for previous injury with the addition of a scale such as the TSK could add value to participant recruitment or be a potential confounder or covariable in research design. Fear-avoidance behaviours relating to work were reported for all 11 participants who reported a previous injury due to work. As the FABQw has been validated for work-related low back pain in a variety of studies [7], it is unsurprising that this content of the FABQ was only applicable to those who had experienced a previous work injury. As such, it was successful in distinguishing potential long-lasting psychosocial concerns for work-related injury [7]. Considering that these participants joined the study as asymptomatic, free from injury in the past 12 months, the FABQw may be a useful starting for research protocols to further identify factors that require greater attention for young-adults who have experienced a work-related injury. However, it is clear that it is only applicable to those participants who have experienced a previous work-related injury and may not be a useful classification for all participants in comparative studies. Future studies that quantify musculoskeletal patterns in manual materials handling or work-related simulations will be required to determine if asymptomatic controls who have had a previous injury and still currently have kinesiophobia generate different musculoskeletal patterns than asymptomatic controls without previous injury [3].

The descriptive analyses presented here are not surprising from a clinical standpoint, as rehabilitation, pain, and return to work research highlights the impact of acute injury and pain beliefs [1, 7]. However, these findings do warrant attention to participant recruitment when investigating shoulder and low back MSD with the following limitations considered. There are a variety of methods in screening and classifying groups of participants and the surveys presented here may not be applicable to all populations. Their measurement properties are debated in the literature and warrant attention to validity and reliability in specific samples. Additionally, as a cross-sectional descriptive study, potential associations or relationships with respect to shoulder and low back MSD risk is not demonstrated and it is recognized that previous injury, kinesiophobia, and fear-avoidance on their own may not be sufficient for classification of a group as there is no knowledge of beliefs or behaviour prior to the injury.

6 Conclusions

The shoulder and low back remain common areas of interest in human factors and ergonomics MSD research. Previous shoulder and low back injuries, kinesiophobia, and fear-avoidance beliefs relating to work, collected in young adult university asymptomatic controls emphasized that individuals may have previous experiences like injury and pain that may impact their classification as asymptomatic participants or control groups. The findings motivate researchers to investigate ways of better classifying research control groups and participant populations to account for potential variability, especially in ergonomics and occupational biomechanics protocols where research questions focus on potential musculoskeletal pattern differences for the prevention of shoulder and low back MSD.

References

1. Vlaeyen, J., Linton, S.: Fear-avoidance and its consequences in chronic musculoskeletal pain: a state of the art. Pain **85**(3), 317–332 (2000)
2. Westgaard, R.H.: Work-related musculoskeletal complaints: some ergonomics challenges upon the start of a new century. Appl. Ergon. **31**(6), 569–580 (2000)
3. Miller, R., Kori, S., Todd, D.: The Tampa Scale: a measure of kinesiophobia. Clin. J. Pain **7**(1), 51 (1991)
4. Waddell, G., et al.: A Fear-Avoidance Beliefs Questionnaire (FABQ) and the role of fear-avoidance beliefs in chronic low back pain and disability. Pain **52**(2), 157–168 (1993)
5. Swinkels-Meewisse, E., et al.: Psychometric properties of the Tampa Scale for kinesiophobia and the fear-avoidance beliefs questionnaire in acute low back pain. Manual Ther. **8**(1), 29–36 (2003)

6. Jørgensen, M., et al.: Properties of the Tampa Scale for kinesiophobia across workers with different pain experiences and cultural backgrounds: a rasch analysis. J. Appl. Meas. **16**(2), 218–227 (2015)
7. Iles, R., Davidson, M., Taylor, N.: Psychosocial predictors of failure to return to work in non-chronic non-specific low back pain: a systematic review. Occup. Environ. Med. **65**(8), 507–517 (2008)

The Relationship Between Fidgeting, Posture Changes, Physical Activity, and Musculoskeletal Discomfort in Office Workers

Athena Nguyen[1]([⊠]), Federico Arippa[1,2], Matthew Kiok[1,3], Massimiliano Pau[2], and Carisa Harris-Adamson[1,3]

[1] School of Public Health, University of California, Berkeley, CA 94720, USA
anguyen01@berkeley.edu

[2] Department of Mechanical, Chemical and Materials Engineering, University of Cagliari, Cagliari, Italy

[3] Department of Medicine, University of California, San Francisco, CA 94143, USA

Abstract. Background: Increasing standing and walking time has been proposed to mitigate the risk of musculoskeletal discomfort (MSD) associated with prolonged sitting. However, the duration, frequency, and timing of standing and walking required to reduce risk of MSD is less understood. **Objective**: The primary aim of this cross-sectional study was to 1) understand the relationship between daily movement patterns and MSD among office workers; and 2) determine whether daily movement patterns and MSD differed between those with different sitting strategies during prolonged work. **Methods**: 26 participants completed baseline questionnaires and wore an inertial measuring unit to quantify posture and movement over a 48-h period, stratified by work and leisure time. Participants were then classified as "breakers" and "prolongers" based on breaks taken during a 2-h sitting bout. The relationships between posture, movement and MSD were assessed using Spearman correlation coefficients, two-sample t tests, and Mann Whitney U tests, then stratified by and compared between breakers and prolongers. **Results**: Step count($r^2 = -0.26$), standing time($r^2 = -0.39$), and walking time($r^2 = -0.31$) were negatively associated with MSD, whereas sitting duration was positively($r^2 = 0.20$) associated with MSD; posture, activity, and MSD correlations were similar between work and leisure time. Prolongers(10.55(1.28)) spent more hours sitting compared to breakers(9.01(3.02)) and tended to have more overall MSD(p < 0.05). **Conclusion**: Increased time spent standing and walking while decreasing sitting time during both work and leisure time may help reduce risk of MSD. Those who did not change posture during the work bout tended to spend more time sitting and less time standing and walking during both work and leisure time. Future interventions should consider encouraging increased standing and walking during both work and leisure time to reduce MSD among office workers.

Keywords: Musculoskeletal discomfort · Posture · Sedentary workers

N. L. Black et al. (Eds.): IEA 2021, LNNS 222, pp. 783–793, 2021.
https://doi.org/10.1007/978-3-030-74611-7_107

1   Background

Sedentary behavior has increased due to the growing number of work and leisure activities performed while seated [1–4]. Research has shown that sedentary time can account for almost 81.8% of work hours for office employees, which includes long durations (>30 minutes) of sedentary time and few durations (0-10 minutes) of activity [5]. Additionally, slumped or forward postures commonly observed while sitting have been associated with low back discomfort [6]. Evidence has shown that 20% to 60% of office workers have some form of MSD [7]. As a result, MSD is a pertinent problem for sedentary office workers.

Some research indicates that postural transitions throughout the day can reduce MSD, especially frequent breaks from prolonged sitting [8–11]. For example, one study used reminder software that prompted participants to stand, move around, or adjust their sit-stand station every 30 minutes; the results showed reductions in shoulder, hand/wrist, and upper/lower back discomfort [9]. Accelerometer-measurement studies have also identified the beneficial outcomes associated with breaks in sedentary time. In one study, researchers noted interruptions in sedentary time if the accelerometer counts rose to or greater than 100 counts per minute and defined breaks to include transitions from sitting to standing and from standing to walking [11]. Researchers found that more frequent breaks in sedentary time were negatively associated with body mass index, waist circumference, 2-h plasma glucose, and triglycerides; however, the relationship between taking frequent breaks and MSD was not assessed [11].

Other strategies to reduce sedentary behavior include increasing standing and walking time at work. In a systematic review of fourteen studies, researchers identified seven studies that recorded either local, whole body, or both local and whole-body discomfort scores in sedentary workers; six of the seven studies showed that sit-stand work led to decreased trends in discomfort [12]. A meta-analysis of randomized controlled trials also found that walking mitigated chronic LBP and discomfort [13]. A 1-year prospective study among 287 workers used regression models to examine the relationship between daily walking steps and incidence of neck and low back pain [14]. Although there were no significant associations between daily steps and low back pain, researchers identified that an increase of 1,000 daily steps reduced the risk of neck pain by 14% [14].

In addition to the frequency of posture changes [8–11] and time spent standing or walking [12–14], moving while sitting, such as fidgeting or shifting in one's chair [10, 15–18] has also been recommended to mitigate LBP related to prolonged sitting. Of interest is the relationship between these various movement behavior strategies including fidgeting, posture transitions and time spent in different postures and MSD. Furthermore, the differences among the associations between these movement behaviors and MSD during work and leisure time are poorly understood. For instance, some studies have found that interventions at work do not lead to positive behavior change outside of work. One study on sit-stand desks in an office setting found that the participants had reduced workday (344 ± 107 to 186 ± 101 min/day) and total (645 ± 140 to 528 ± 91 min/day) sitting time, but showed no differences in sitting time, standing time or steps per day during leisure time [19]. Another study found that while a sit-stand workstation intervention led to reduced sitting time and increased light activity levels during working hours, participants compensated by increasing sedentary time and decreasing activity levels during leisure time [20]. More specifically, a study of 40 office workers discovered that while the proportion of time spent sitting while working during week 1 and week 6 of the intervention significantly decreased (75% ± 13% vs 52% ± 16% to 56% ± 13%) from baseline, the proportion of time spent sitting during leisure time significantly increased (60% ± 11% vs 66% ± 12% to 68% ± 12%) [20]. As a result, it is possible that MSD risk mitigation is optimized by using a comprehensive approach addressing frequency and duration of movement throughout the day.

The Total Worker Health Initiative (TWH), introduced by the National Institute for Occupational Safety and Health, emphasizes the combination of health protection with health promotion [21]. We hope to advance TWH by identifying how movement behaviors can impact MSD inside and outside of work. If there is interaction between work and leisure movement behavior and MSD, interventions that address both may be more effective than either alone. Thus, the aims of this cross-sectional analysis include 1) understanding the association between daily movement patterns and MSD among office workers, identifying differences between work and leisure time activity; and 2) comparing daily movement patterns among those who sit for longer periods versus those who do not.

2 Methodology

2.1 Participants

Twenty-six office workers recruited from a sample of convenience at the University of California, Berkeley were included in this study. Recruiting methods included posting flyers throughout campus and sending emails through department listservs. The inclusion criteria specified that participants must have a sit-stand desk, work at the desk for at least thirty hours per week and be capable of standing for at least twenty minutes. Exclusion criteria included any MSD or illness that would prevent the worker from standing.

2.2 Procedure

All data were collected at the UC Berkeley campus in a newly constructed building with the same sit-stand desks and office chairs throughout. Upon arrival, participants signed a consent form and anthropometric measurements were collected. Subjects completed a baseline survey through a Qualtrics link sent via SMS text message. The survey gathered data on demographic characteristics, activity levels, and MSD using the 0 to 10 Numeric Pain Rating Scale (NPS). The MSD scores were grouped into four regions: 1) head, neck, shoulders; 2) upper and lower back; 3) hips, knees, feet, and ankles; and 4) elbows, hands, and wrists and analyzed both separately and as a composite (sum of all regions) score.

A pressure sensitive mat (Tekscan Inc., Boston, USA) was placed on the seat-pan of the chair and participants were asked to make final adjustments to their workstation and chair to ensure that the seat back and armrests could be utilized. Contact pressure was continuously recorded while participants were working at their computer during their regular work-shift. During the test, participants were asked to continuously perform their normal work and to take short breaks only if needed; the test duration lasted up to 3 h to ensure that at least 2 h of sitting data were collected.

2.3 Measures

Physical activity (walking time, step count), posture (time spent in standing and sitting) and posture shifts (frequency of changes in posture) were recorded for 48 h for each subject using the activPAL monitor (Glasgow, Scotland) and categorized into leisure and work time based on self-reported work hours start and stop time. Fidgeting (movement while seated) was measured using the overall distance traveled by the center of pressure during the two-hour work session. Based on the two-hour sitting bout, participants were identified as "breakers" (BRK) if they changed posture from sitting to standing lasting more than one minute during the test and categorized as "prolongers" (PRO) if no breaks were taken.

2.4 Analysis

Spearman correlation coefficients were used to explore the relationship between movement and MSD. Self-reported work hours from the baseline survey were used to stratify the analysis by work and leisure time. Two-sample t-tests and Mann Whitney U tests were used to assess differences in measures of movement and MSD between prolongers and breakers for parametric and non-parametrically distributed data, respectively. Two-sample t-tests and Mann Whitney U tests were also used to compare differences between measures of posture and activity during leisure and work times.

3 Results

Demographic analysis showed that most of the participants were female and of normal weight (Table 1). The average age of subjects was 33.23 ± 9.37 years old. There were 17 subjects who reported a pain score of 2 or more in at least one of the four regions (head/neck/shoulders; upper/lower back; hips/knees/feet/ankles; elbows/hands/wrists). Participants slept an average of 8.38 ± 0.90 h.

Breakers took an average of 2.16 ± 0.92 breaks during their 2-h sitting bout. When assessed for in chair movement, prolongers fidgeted less (PRO $= 461.48 \pm 241.64$ mm/min) over the 2-h sitting period compared to breakers (BRK $= 755.30 \pm 477.08$ mm/min) ($p < 0.01$).

Table 1. Demographics of subjects

Characteristics	Total (%)	Prolonger (%)	Breaker (%)
N	26	10	16
Gender			
Male	9 (35%)	5 (50%)	4 (25%)
Female	16 (61%)	5 (50%)	11 (69%)
Other	1 (4%)	0 (0%)	1 (6%)

(continued)

Table 1. (*continued*)

Characteristics	Total (%)	Prolonger (%)	Breaker (%)
Age (years)			
<30	12 (46%)	3 (30%)	9 (56%)
≥30 & <40	8 (31%)	5 (50%)	3 (19%)
≥40 & <50	4 (15%)	2 (20%)	2 (13%)
≥50	2 (8%)	0 (0%)	2 (13%)
Children			
No	20 (77%)	7 (70%)	13 (81%)
Yes	6 (23%)	3 (30%)	3 (19%)
Body mass index			
<25kg/m^2: Normal	15 (58%)	4 (40%)	11 (69%)
≥25 kg/m^2 & <30 kg/m^2: Overweight	8 (31%)	5 (50%)	3 (19%)
≥30 kg/m^2: Obese	3 (11%)	1 (10%)	2 (13%)
Number who reported MSD ≥ 2			
Head/Neck/Shoulders	12 (46%)	6 (60%)	6 (38%)
Upper/Lower back	14 (54%)	8 (80%)	6 (38%)
Hips/Knees/Feet/Ankles	8 (31%)	4 (40%)	4 (25%)
Elbows/Hands/Wrists	12 (46%)	5 (50%)	7 (44%)

Overall, participants took approximately 497 steps more at work compared to leisure time (Table 2). Additionally, subjects spent 34.8 and 115.2 more minutes standing and sitting at work compared to leisure time. These differences could be partially influenced by participants spending more time at work (8.5 h) compared to leisure time (7.0 h). Prolongers sat for a longer duration and spent less time walking and standing than breakers (Table 3), though differences were not statistically significant. These trends were consistent during both work and leisure time. For example, prolongers spent 61.2 more minutes sitting at work and 24.6 more minutes sitting during leisure time compared to breakers (Table 3). In contrast with prolongers, breakers spent approximately 36.6 more minutes standing at work and 10.8 more minutes standing during leisure time. Furthermore, breakers took 305 and 1,064 more steps than prolongers during work and leisure time (Table 3).

The study population had a median composite pain score of 6.50 (Table 4). Stratified analysis showed prolongers reported higher MSD scores across all four regions compared to prolongers. More specifically, prolongers had a nearly 3-fold increase in composite pain ($p = 0.05$) and 6-fold increase in upper/lower back pain ($p = 0.01$) compared to breakers.

Among all participants, there were weak negative correlations among steps, time spent standing, time spent walking and MSD, while there were weak positive correlations between posture transitions and sitting time and MSD (Table 5). Among both prolongers

Table 2. Summary median (IQR) of posture and activity during the entire day, working hours and leisure time (non-working hours) among all participants (n = 26).

	Daily	Work	Leisure
Hours per day	–	8.5 (1.0)	7.0 (1.5)
Steps	9,632 (4,281)	4,568 (2,955)	4,071 (2,380)
Transitions	47.50 (16.25)	24.50 (7.62)	25.00 (13.75)
Hours standing	5.63 (2.24)	3.31 (1.89)	2.73 (0.88)
Hours walking	1.74 (0.74)	0.81 (0.46)	0.84 (0.44)
Hours sitting	10.02 (2.36)	5.90 (1.85)	3.98 (0.93)

Table 3. Summary median (IQR) of posture and activity during the entire day, working hours and leisure time (non-working hours) among prolongers (no breaks during 2-h bout) and breakers (at least 1 break during 2-h bout).

	Prolonger (n = 10)			Breaker (n = 16)		
	Daily	Work	Leisure	Daily	Work	Leisure
Hours per day	–	8.5 (1.0)	7.0 (1.5)	–	8.5 (1.0)	7.0 (1.5)
Steps	7,271 (2,872)	4,500 (2,606)	3,805 (2,207)	9,985 (3,135)	4,805 (4,173)	4,869 (2,461)
Transitions	50.00 (14.88)	24.75 (9.12)	26.75 (14.75)	46.00 (16.88)	24.50 (8.75)	24.75 (12.50)
Hours standing	5.56 (0.76)	2.91 (1.28)	2.66 (1.17)	6.23 (3.18)	3.52 (2.62)	2.84 (0.78)
Hours walking	1.33 (0.37)	0.75 (0.37)	0.80 (0.30)	1.82 (0.41)	0.85 (0.70)	0.89 (0.43)
Hours sitting	10.55 (1.28)	6.36 (0.76)	4.13 (0.59)	9.01 (3.02)	5.34 (2.23)	3.71 (1.12)

There were no significant differences in measures between prolongers and breakers.

Table 4. Summary median (IQR) of MSD levels from baseline survey

MSD	All (n = 26)	Prolonger (n = 10)	Breaker (n = 16)	p
Head/Neck/Shoulders	1.00 (3.00)	2.50 (2.00)	0.50 (2.00)	0.11
Upper/Lower back	2.00 (3.00)	3.00 (2.75)	0.50 (2.00)	0.01
Hips/Knees/Feet/Ankle(s)	1.00 (2.00)	1.00 (3.25)	0.00 (1.25)	0.17
Elbow(s)/Hands/Wrists	1.00 (2.00)	1.50 (1.75)	0.50 (2.00)	0.42
Composite	6.50 (9.00)	9.00 (7.00)	3.50 (7.63)	0.05

and breakers, there were weak negative correlations between steps per day, daily hours spent walking and MSD and weak to moderately positive correlations between postural transitions and MSD (Table 6). Among prolongers, there was a weak negative association between sitting and MSD, but there was a weak positive association between sitting and MSD among breakers (Table 6). Similar patterns were reflected in correlations for work and leisure activities for prolongers and breakers.

Table 5. Correlation between daily activity levels vs composite musculoskeletal discomfort

	Overall (N = 26)		
	Daily	Work	Leisure
Steps	−0.26	−0.10	−0.18
Posture transitions	0.38	0.46*	0.20
Hours standing	−0.39*	−0.27	−0.30
Hours walking	−0.31	−0.09	−0.21
Hours sitting	0.20	0.29	0.13
Hours sleeping	0.21	−	−

Spearman correlation. The symbols * and ** indicate significant differences for comparisons at baseline ($p < .05$ and $p < .01$ respectively).

Table 6. Correlation between daily activity levels vs composite musculoskeletal discomfort

	Prolonger (n = 10)	Breaker (n = 16)
Steps	−0.04	−0.29*
Posture transitions	0.62**	0.30*
Hours standing	0.01	−0.49**
Hours walking	−0.38	−0.26*
Hours sitting	−0.26*	0.39**
Hours sleeping	0.15	0.30

Spearman correlation. The symbols * and ** indicate significant differences for comparisons at baseline ($p < .05$ and $p < .01$ respectively).

4   Discussion

In this cross-sectional study, we explored differences in sitting, standing, and walking during work and leisure time and assessed whether their associations with MSD differed. Among our study population, participants took slightly more steps and spent more time standing and sitting at work compared to leisure time, whereas walking time was approximately the same; this could be due to participants spending approximately 1.5 more hours work versus leisure time. Although associations were weak, time spent sitting was positively correlated with MSD while time spent walking and standing were negatively correlated with MSD. Stronger associations were observed for work-based sitting time and daily walking time. Increased standing time both at work and during leisure hours had similar negative associations with MSD in this sedentary group of office workers. Thus, it appears that there is no one posture or time of day that sedentary office workers can intervene to reduce MSD; instead, a comprehensive approach of decreased sitting, increased standing and increased walking throughout the day may be warranted. More research is needed to understand whether interventions should target different movement behavior strategies during certain points throughout the day.

The minor differences between leisure and work time posture and activity were consistent for prolongers and breakers. However, there were interesting differences in the summary values and associations between these movement behavior measurements and MSD. Breakers tended to have a higher overall step count, particularly during leisure time while having increased standing time and only slight increases in walking time. This may indicate that breakers tend to move or fidget more while standing just as they do while sitting. Further research using pressure insoles to measure movement while standing is needed to understand standing movement patterns in this group and whether movement while standing helps to abate MSD. Additionally, breakers sat about 93 min less per day than the prolongers. Although both groups sat long enough to increase health risks [22–27], reducing total sitting time to less than 10 h per day to reduce risk is an important metric. About one hour (two-thirds) of this differential between breakers and prolongers occurred while at work indicating that increasing intermittent standing at work could be an important strategy to reducing overall sitting time. When comparing daily behavior movement pattern totals between prolongers and breakers, there was a stronger negative correlation between standing time, step count and MSD among breakers versus prolongers; this supports the possibility that increased fidgeting while standing may be an important strategy that breakers have to reduce sitting time and reduce risk of MSD.

When comparing sitting time between prolongers and breakers, prolongers spent a median time of 6.36 h at work in a seated position compared to breakers who spent a median time of 5.34 h. A separate study found that people who sit for an average of 6.29 h of an 8-h shift report discomfort, fatigue, and musculoskeletal discomfort in the shoulders, lower back, and knees [28]. These findings are reflected in our study population: prolongers reported higher MSD in all four categories (head/neck/shoulders; upper/lower back; hips/knees/feet/ankle[s]; elbow[s]/hands/wrists) and composite pain compared to breakers. More specifically, prolongers had significantly higher lower/upper back (p = 0.01) and composite pain scores (p = 0.05) compared to breakers.

Of interest is the slightly higher number of transitions observed in prolongers compared to the breakers despite the increase in sitting time and decrease in standing and walking time throughout the day. This could indicate that although prolongers change position as much (or slightly more) as breakers, they do not spend as much time in these alternative postures. It could be that the transitions are occurring due to MSD, particularly in the low back and that once relieved, the individuals are returning to a seated position. This is supported by the moderate positive correlations between posture transition and MSD, particularly during work time which was stronger in prolongers than in breakers. A prior study found that people with back pain move more frequently than those without low back pain [29]. If prolongers are changing posture due to MSD but not staying in alternative postures, they may not get the full benefit of the posture change. This is important since many interventions focus on reminding people to change their posture but may not track whether the change in posture is of adequate duration to be beneficial. More research is needed to understand the relationship between transitions, time spent in non-sitting postures and MSD.

In this study, the breaks during the 2-h sitting bout that separated breakers from prolongers showed interesting differences between these office workers in overall movement behaviors throughout the day. First, breakers moved more while sitting, as evidenced by the increased distance traveled by their center of pressure. Breakers also spent more time walking and standing, and less time sitting throughout the entire day and reported less discomfort than prolongers. Determining how to facilitate a reduction in overall sitting time and increase movement while sitting may be an important strategy for office workers. This analysis shows that an integrated approach that incorporates strategies during both work and leisure time is important to reducing MSD.

Given the numerous movement behavior metrics, having an aggregate measure or an integrated index has the potential to be incredibly useful. For instance, an index that integrates the duration and frequency of non-sitting postures and in-chair movements may provide a holistic approach to reducing the negative impacts of prolonged sitting.

Some limitations of this analysis include its cross-sectional design and the sample of convenience which may be a healthier cohort than typical sedentary workers. Additionally, this study was interrupted by the COVID-19 pandemic and thus was underpowered. Despite this, these results indicate that posture variation must be accompanied by time spent in non-sitting postures, and that strategies need to incorporate both work and leisure time. Interventions that encourage spending more work and leisure time in non-static sitting postures (i.e., standing and walking) may be most effective in preventing MSD in sedentary workers.

5 Conclusions

In this cross-sectional analysis, there were negative correlations between measures of non-sitting time, including standing and walking, and musculoskeletal discomfort, and a positive correlation between hours sitting and discomfort. Based on a 2-h sitting bout, workers classified as "breakers" spent more time moving and less time sitting throughout the entire day and reported less discomfort than "prolongers."

Acknowledgements. We would like to thank the Office Ergonomics Research Committee for their support of this study.

References

1. Bontrup, C., et al.: Low back pain and its relationship with sitting behaviour among sedentary office workers. Appl. Ergon. **81**, 102894 (2019)
2. Jans, M.P., Proper, K.I., Hildebrandt, V.H.: Sedentary behavior in Dutch workers: differences between occupations and business sectors. Am. J. Prev. Med. **33**, 450–454 (2007)
3. Koohsari, M.J., et al.: Neighborhood environmental attributes and adults' sedentary behaviors: review and research agenda. Prev. Med. **77**, 141–149 (2015)
4. Saidj, M., et al.: Descriptive study of sedentary behaviours in 35,444 French working adults: cross-sectional findings from the ACTI-cités study. BMC Public Health **15**, 379 (2015)
5. Parry, S., Straker, L.: The contribution of office work to sedentary behaviour associated risk. BMC Public Health **13**, 296 (2013)
6. Callaghan, J.P., Dunk, N.M.: Examination of the flexion relaxation phenomenon in erector spinae muscles during short duration slumped sitting. Clin. Biomech. **17**, 353–360 (2002)
7. Hoe, V.C., Urquhart, D.M., Kelsall, H.L., Zamri, E.N., Sim, M.R.: Ergonomic interventions for preventing work-related musculoskeletal disorders of the upper limb and neck among office workers. Cochrane Database Syst. Rev. (2018)
8. Callaghan, J.P., De Carvalho, D., Gallagher, K., Karakolis, T., Nelson-Wong, E.: Is standing the solution to sedentary office work? Ergon. Des. **23**, 20–24 (2015)
9. Davis, K.G., Kotowski, S.E., Sharma, B., Herrmann, D., Krishnan, A.P.: Combating the effects of sedentary work: postural variability reduces musculoskeletal discomfort. Proc. Hum. Factors Ergon. Soc. Annu. Meet. **53**, 884–886 (2009)
10. Davis, K.G., Kotowski, S.E.: postural variability: an effective way to reduce musculoskeletal discomfort in office work. Hum. Factors **56**, 1249–1261 (2014)
11. Owen, N., Healy, G.N., Matthews, C.E., Dunstan, D.W.: Too much sitting: the population-health science of sedentary Behavior. Exerc. Sport Sci. Rev. **38**, 105–113 (2010)
12. Karakolis, T., Callaghan, J.P.: The impact of sit–stand office workstations on worker discomfort and productivity: a review. Appl. Ergon. **45**, 799–806 (2014)
13. Sitthipornvorakul, E., Klinsophon, T., Sihawong, R., Janwantanakul, P.: The effects of walking intervention in patients with chronic low back pain: a meta-analysis of randomized controlled trials. Musculoskelet. Sci. Pract. **34**, 38–46 (2018)
14. Sitthipornvorakul, E., Janwantanakul, P., Lohsoonthorn, V.: The effect of daily walking steps on preventing neck and low back pain in sedentary workers: a 1-year prospective cohort study. Eur. Spine J. **24**, 417–424 (2015)
15. Vergara, M., Page, Á.: Relationship between comfort and back posture and mobility in sitting-posture. Appl. Ergon. **33**, 1–8 (2002)
16. Aarås, A., Horgen, G., Ro, O.: Work with the visual display unit: health consequences. Int. J. Human-Computer Interact. **12**, 107–134 (2000)
17. Pynt, J., Higgs, J., Mackey, M.: Seeking the optimal posture of the seated lumbar spine. Physiother. Theory Pract. **17**, 5–21 (2001)
18. Srinivasan, D., Mathiassen, S.E.: Motor variability in occupational health and performance. Clin. Biomech. **27**, 979–993 (2012)
19. MacEwen, B.T., Saunders, T.J., MacDonald, D.J., Burr, J.F.: Sit-stand desks to reduce workplace sitting time in office workers with abdominal obesity: a randomized controlled trial. J. Phys. Act. Health **14**, 710–715 (2017)
20. Mansoubi, M., Pearson, N., Biddle, S.J.H., Clemes, S.A.: Using sit-to-stand workstations in offices: is there a compensation effect? Med. Sci. Sports Exerc. **48**, 720–725 (2016)
21. Schill, A.L., Chosewood, L.C.: The NIOSH Total worker health[TM] program: an overview. J. Occup. Environ. Med. **55**, S8 (2013)

22. Chau, J.Y., et al.: Daily sitting time and all-cause mortality: a meta-analysis. PLOS ONE **8**, e80000 (2013)
23. Bailey, D.P., Hewson, D.J., Champion, R.B., Sayegh, S.M.: Sitting time and risk of cardiovascular disease and diabetes: a systematic review and meta-analysis. Am. J. Prev. Med. **57**, 408–416 (2019)
24. Katzmarzyk, P., Church, T., Craig, C., Bouchard, C.: Sitting time and mortality from all causes, cardiovascular disease, and cancer. Med. Sci. Sports Exerc. **41**, 998–1005 (2009)
25. Carter, S., Hartman, Y., Holder, S., Thijssen, D.H., Hopkins, N.D.: Sedentary behavior and cardiovascular disease risk: mediating mechanisms. Exerc. Sport Sci. Rev. **45**, 80–86 (2017)
26. van der Ploeg, H.P.: sitting time and all-cause mortality risk in 222 497 Australian adults. Arch. Intern. Med. **172**, 494 (2012)
27. Patterson, R., et al.: Sedentary behaviour and risk of all-cause, cardiovascular and cancer mortality, and incident type 2 diabetes: a systematic review and dose response meta-analysis. Eur. J. Epidemiol. **33**, 811–829 (2018)
28. Daneshmandi, H., Choobineh, A., Ghaem, H., Karimi, M.: Adverse effects of prolonged sitting behavior on the general health of office workers. J. Lifestyle Med. **7**, 69–75 (2017)
29. Scholtes, S.A., Gombatto, S.P., Van Dillen, L.R.: Differences in lumbopelvic motion between people with and people without low back pain during two lower limb movement tests. Clin. Biomech. **24**, 7–12 (2009)

Validation of the OCRA Checklist Score as Predictive of the Occurrence of UL-WMSDs in Workers Exposed to Manual Repetitive Tasks

Enrico Occhipinti[✉] and Daniela Colombini

EPM International Ergonomics School, Milan, Italy
epmenrico@tiscali.it

Abstract. ISO 11228–3 and ISO TR 12295 recommend the OCRA Checklist as a useful method for screening exposure to manual repetitive tasks. The aim of this study is to define forecasting models for the expected prevalence of UL-WMSDs in groups of exposed workers based on the OCRA Checklist scores. A database of 11,734 workers divided into 30 groups featuring different exposure levels and different prevalences of UL-WMSDs was analyzed. The association between the independent variable "Checklist score" (CK) and the dependent variable "% of workers with UL-WMSDs" (PA) was researched: a convincing association (R^2 = 0.86) resulted from the linear regression equation PA = 0.742($\pm$0.055) x CK, which may be used (within defined limits) as a model for forecasting the occurrence of UL-WMSDs based on the OCRA Checklist score. By using pre-established OCRA Checklist key-values, macro-groups with different exposure levels were created and the Prevalence Odds Ratio (POR) of each group was computed versus the "non-significant exposure" group. The POR for "borderline", "low", "medium" and "high" exposure groups was respectively 2.18, 2.77, 4.36 and 3.78. These results confirm the overall effectiveness of the current classification of the OCRA Checklist scores, while also suggesting that an OCRA Checklist score of 16 should be the cutoff for identifying low and medium exposure.

Keywords: Repetitive task · Risk assessment · OCRA method · UL-WMSDs

1 Introduction and Aim

The OCRA method for assessing risk associated with repetitive movements of the upper limbs consists of two tools, the OCRA Index and the OCRA Checklist [2, 3, 6, 8], which feature different analytical details and purposes, although both are inspired by the same conceptual model. The OCRA Index is more detailed and was chosen as the reference risk assessment method by international standards relating to high-frequency repetitive manual work [1, 4]; the OCRA Checklist is the simpler one used for the initial screening of workstations, as suggested by ISO TR 12295 [5].

The OCRA Checklist consists of five sections focusing on the four main risk factors (frequency, force, awkward posture/stereotyped movement, lack of recovery periods) and a number of additional risk factors (vibrations, low temperatures, precision work,

N. L. Black et al. (Eds.): IEA 2021, LNNS 222, pp. 794–801, 2021.
https://doi.org/10.1007/978-3-030-74611-7_108

repeated impacts, etc.). It also factors into the final risk estimate the net duration of repetitive jobs. The OCRA Checklist analysis entails using pre-assigned scores (the higher the score, the higher the risk factor) to define the level of exposure associated with each of the aforementioned factors. The sum and product of partial values generate a final score that estimates the overall exposure level (Fig. 1).

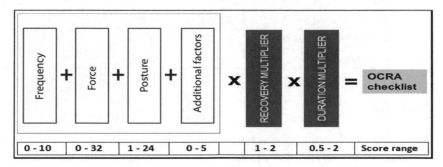

Fig. 1. OCRA Checklist: final score calculation

In the early 2000s, studies involving over 5,000 variously exposed workers found a significant association between exposure levels assessed by the OCRA Index and the overall prevalence of UL-WMSDs (PA) in exposed working populations [7, 9]. A linear regression equation forecasts (within defined limits) the expected PA based on the OCRA Index:

$$PA = 2.39\,(\pm 0.14) \times OCRA\,Index \tag{1}$$

These studies [7, 9], which also considered the overall prevalence of UL-WMSDs (PA) in working populations with non-significant exposure levels, defined OCRA Index "key-values" for classifying exposure as: acceptable (green), borderline (yellow), low-risk (red-low), medium risk (red-medium) and high-risk (red-high or purple). Since a very strong association exists between the OCRA Index and OCRA Checklist values [7], it was possible to obtain "key-values" for classifying OCRA Checklist results and for making "indirect gross estimations" (by linking with OCRA Index values) of the expected prevalence (PA) of workers affected by UL-WMSDs. Table 1 compares the OCRA Index and OCRA Checklist classification systems.

Since the mid-2000s, more data has been added to the existing database. The data regards the OCRA Checklist as an exposure assessment tool and includes matched results for prevalence among workers with one or more clinically diagnosed UL-WMSDs.

The aim of this study is therefore to use the extended database to define a model for forecasting the expected prevalence of UL-WMSDs in groups of exposed workers based directly on the results of the OCRA Checklist.

A secondary aim is to verify the general adequacy of the current classification of OCRA Checklist scores (see Table 1), or determine whether adjustments are necessary.

Table 1. OCRA Index and OCRA Checklist score classification based on key-values.

Zone	Ocra index values	Ocra checklist values	Risk classification
Green	Up to 2.2	Up to 7.5	Acceptable
Yellow	2.3–3.5	7.6–11	Borderline
Red-low	3.6–4.5	11.1–14	Low
Red-medium	4.6–9.0	14.1–22.5	Medium
Red-high	Over 9.0	Over 22.5	High

2 Methods

The study examined over 11,000 workers (including the original reference group used in 2004 and 2007 studies) divided into 30 groups featuring different exposure levels. A representative OCRA Checklist score was calculated for each group and the prevalence of workers affected by one or more clinically diagnosed UL-WMSDs was reported. Figure 2 shows the most significant data in the database used in the study.

The association and regression models between the independent variable "OCRA Checklist score" and the dependent variable "% of workers with UL-WMSDs" (PA) were explored (with SPSS© software). Data was processed by weighting the compared groups based on their numerical size and without considering the constant in the models (i.e. OCRA Checklist = 0; PA $\approx$ 0).

By using pre-established OCRA Checklist key-values (see Table 1), macro-groups with different exposure levels were aggregated and the Prevalence Odds Ratio (POR) of each "aggregated" group was computed versus the "non-significant exposure" group.

This last procedure was repeated with respect to the preliminary results and considering alternative OCRA Checklist key-values for grouping.

3 Results

The relationship between the OCRA Checklist score and PA (Percentage of workers affected by UL-WMSDs) variables is reported graphically in Fig. 3.

The strength of the association between the two variables was rather high (Pearson correlation coefficient = 0.722; $p < 0.00001$).

A simple linear regression function between the OCRA Checklist Score and PA is expressed by the following general equation:

$$PA = 0.742(\pm 0.055) \times OCRA\ CK \tag{2}$$

This function shows a fairly strong association between the two variables (adjusted $R^2 = 0.86$) and is statistically highly significant ($p < 0.00001$).

Since the regression function (2) can be used as a forecasting model to estimate the number of workers potentially affected by one or more UL-WMSDs based on the OCRA

JOB/TASK	TOTAL	Nr. MALES	Nr. FEMALES	CHECKLIST SCORE	% PERSONS AFFECTED (PA)
Electric motors assembly 1	431	126	305	15.2	11.37
Electric motors assembly 2	288	173	115	12.0	8.68
Freezer Assembly	374	264	110	11.5	8.56
Refrigerator Assembly A	350	270	80	14.7	15.43
Refrigerator Assembly B	42	32	10	13.0	14.29
Refrigerator Assembly C	31	31	0	14.4	19.35
Refrigerator Assembly D	118	63	55	15.0	15.25
Refrigerator Ass+Cablage	42	22	20	19.4	30.95
Oven Assembly	650	150	500	10.2	13.23
Shock-absorber assembly	242	158	83	19.5	23.97
Meat processing (chickens)	943	0	943	20.0	22.38
Assembly motor 1	467	355	112	10.0	3.85
Assembly motor 2	53	37	16	12.0	7.55
Assembly motor 3	105	42	63	17.0	13.33
Upholsterers A	783	783	0	25.0	18.60
Hide cutters A	514	488	26	21.7	8.20
Stitchers A	840	4	836	23.2	11.30
Preparers A	205	196	9	20.6	13.20
Upholsterers B	85	85	0	24.9	20.00
Hide cutters B	54	50	4	20.4	10.00
Stitchers B	143	0	143	24.3	8.40
Preparers B	56	56	0	20.0	7.10
Upholsterers C	76	76	0	23.0	28.90
Hide cutters C	25	24	1	15.2	16.00
Stitchers C	75	1	74	20.9	9.30
Preparers C	33	33	0	17.7	15.20
Blue collars not exposed	1383	1306	77	7.4	6.10
VDU 20-30 hours	577	329	248	6.2	4.33
VDU >30 hours	1440	792	648	7.4	3.13
Reference group	749	310	439	1.5	4.41

Fig. 2. Main features of groups included in the study: breakdown by gender, OCRA Checklist score and prevalence of workers affected by one or more UL-WMSDs (PA).

Checklist value, the 95% confidence interval of the function was computed:

$$\text{Lower 95\% limit: } PA = 0.629 * CK \tag{3}$$

$$\text{Upper 95\% limit: } PA = 0.856 * CK \tag{4}$$

In order to check PA trends as a function of the OCRA Checklist classification (green; yellow; red-low; red-medium; red-high) the groups of subjects were aggregated based on the "traditional" OCRA Checklist key-scores shown in Table 1.

The results are reported in Table 2 and show a positive incremental trend as exposure shifts from very low to very high, but with no progression from yellow to red-low.

Considering these results, the Prevalence Odds Ratio (POR) and 95% confidence limits were initially computed, further aggregating the red-low and red-medium exposed groups.

Table 3 reports the Prevalence Odds Ratio (POR) and 95% confidence limit relating to this further grouping. PORs were computed in relation to the "green" exposed group (POR = 1).

The results in Table 3 can be considered satisfactory as they show an increasing POR trend when exposure levels shift from borderline to very high.

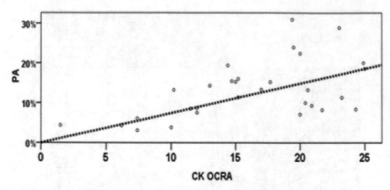

Fig. 3. Association between OCRA Checklist score (CK OCRA) and Percentage of workers Affected by UL-WMSDs (PA)

Table 2. Percentage of workers affected by UL-WMSDs when groups are aggregated based on the "traditional" OCRA Checklist classification (see Table 1)

Checklist scores	Checklist exposure level	Nr. Total	Nr. affected	PA % affected
≤7.5	Green	4,149	187	4.52
7.6–11	Yellow	1,117	104	9.31
11.1–14	Red-low	757	67	8.85
14.1–22.5	Red-medium	3,224	518	16.05
>22.5	Red-high or purple	1,927	292	15.13

However, PORs do not distinguish between low and medium exposure. This differentiation was originally set at an OCRA Checklist score of 14 but was found to be inconsistent; a different cut-off point was consequently sought.

Table 3. Prevalence Odds Ratios (PORs): central values and 95% confidence limits in four groups of workers with different exposure levels (according to OCRA Checklist scores)

CK scores	Exposure level	Total	Nr. affected	PA % affected	POR central value	POR lower 95% CL	POR upper 95% CL
≤7.5	Green	4,149	187	4.52	1.00	=	=
7.6–11	Yellow	1,117	104	9.31	2.18	1.69	2.80
11.1–22.5	Red-low + medium	3,981	585	14.68	3.65	3.08	4.33
>22.5	Red-high	1,927	292	15.13	3.78	3.12	4.59

For this particular purpose, the criteria and procedures used to search for OCRA Index key-values were adopted [7, 9]. These range from estimating the standardized rate (by gender and age) of PAs in a working population with no or very low exposure to biomechanical overload of the upper limbs and initially applying its upper 95% confidence limit and then its multiples (2x, 3x and 4x), to the regression equations associating OCRA Checklist values and PA in the sample.

In previous studies [7, 9], the standardized PA rate for non-exposed populations was equal to 3.7% and the upper 95% confidence limit was equal to 4.8%. In this study, these values were used as driving values and inserted into Eqs. (3) and (2) to find suitable OCRA Checklist key-values for distinguishing different exposure levels.

The application of the procedure, as here briefly reported, confirmed all the "traditional" OCRA Checklist key-values shown in Table 1, with the exception of the key-value of 14 as a cut-off between low and medium exposure levels. This key-value should thus be replaced by a score of 16, the level resulting from using Eqs. (2) and (3), combined with 3 times the standardized rate of PA estimated in the non-exposed reference working population.

Taking the new key-value of 16, the groups in Fig. 2 were re-aggregated according to the updated classification of the OCRA Checklist results, and the Prevalence Odds Ratios (PORs) and 95% confidence limits were computed, this time distinguishing different groups broken down into low and medium exposure.

Table 4 reports the Prevalence Odds Ratios (PORs) and 95% confidence limits for these 5 groups. Again, PORs are computed versus the "green" exposed group (POR = 1).

Table 4. Prevalence Odds Ratios (PORs): central values and 95% confidence limits in five groups of workers with different exposure levels (according to an updated classification of OCRA Checklist scores)

CK scores	Checklist exposure level	Nr. TOTAL	Nr. Affected	PA % Affected	POR central value	POR lower 95% CL	POR upper 95% CL
≤7.5	Green	4,149	187	4.52	1.00	=	=
7.6–11	Yellow	1,117	104	9.31	2.18	1.69	2.80
11.1–16	Red-low	1,712	198	11.57	2.77	2.25	3.41
16.1–22.5	Red-medium	2,269	387	17.04	4.36	3.63	5.24
>22.5	Red-high	1,927	292	15.13	3.78	3.12	4.59

4 Discussion and Conclusions

The results generated by the OCRA Checklist, which is a tool recommended by international standards [4, 5] for quantifying exposure to biomechanical overload of the upper limbs, show a strong association with the prevalence of UL-WMSDs in groups of exposed workers.

Although the analysis presented here is based exclusively on prevalence studies with intrinsic limits for confirming potential relationships between exposure and corresponding collective health outcomes, the final OCRA Checklist score was found capable of effectively predicting the expected occurrence of UL-WMSDs in exposed working populations.

Forecasts of the expected prevalence of UL-WMSDs should be based on Eq. (2) and its 95% confidence limits (Eqs. (2) and (3)).

The OCRA Checklist predictive model can now be used directly without interpolations with the original OCRA Index classification system.

It should be noted, however, that based on a more detailed analysis of some of the results reported in the present study, when the OCRA Checklist final scores are between 20 and 30 or more, the outcome of the predictive model may be less accurate, but will certainly still be relevant compared with the one for reference populations (no or low exposure).

The OCRA Checklist classification system is substantially confirmed also in relation to the OCRA Index classification. The only significant exception is that the red-light zone now applies to OCRA Checklist scores ranging from 11 to 16. Consequently, the red-medium area ranges from 16 to 22.5. Table 5 shows the updated OCRA Checklist classification system.

It should, however, be emphasized that the classification and key-values reported in Table 5 should be used to better frame the risk assessment and more effectively guide preventative actions, rather than be taken as mere numbers for breaking down results into rigidly defined "risk" levels.

Table 5. Updated OCRA Checklist score classification by key-values.

Zone	Ocra checklist values	Risk classification
Green	Below 7.5	Acceptable
Yellow	7.6–11	Borderline
Red-low	11.1–16	Low
Red-medium	16.1–22.5	Medium
Red-high	Above 22.5	High

References

1. CEN (European Committee for Standardization): EN 1005–5. Safety of machinery: Human physical performance. Part 5—Risk assessment for repetitive handling at high frequency. CEN Management System, Bruxelles, Belgium (2007)

2. Colombini, D., Occhipinti, E., Grieco, A.: Risk Assessment and Management of Repetitive Movements and Exertions of Upper Limbs. Book Elsevier Science, Amsterdam (2002)
3. Colombini, D., Occhipinti, E.: Risk Analysis and Management of Repetitive Actions - A Guide for Applying the OCRA System (Occupational Repetitive Action). CRC Press - Taylor & Francis, Boca Raton and New York (2017)
4. ISO (International Organization for Standardization): ISO 11228–3. Ergonomics - Manual handling - Handling of low loads at high frequency. ISO, Geneva, Switzerland (2007)
5. ISO (International Organization for Standardization): ISO TR 12295. Ergonomics—Application document for International Standards on manual handling (ISO 11228–1, ISO 11228-2 and ISO 11228-3) and evaluation of static working postures (ISO 11226). ISO, Geneva, Switzerland (2014)
6. Occhipinti, E.: OCRA: A concise index for the assessment of exposure to repetitive movements of the upper limbs. Ergonomics $41(9)$, 1290–1311 (1998)
7. Occhipinti, E.: Colombini, D: Metodo OCRA: Aggiornamento dei valori di riferimento e dei modelli di previsione dell'occorrenza di UL-WMSDs nelle popolazioni lavorative esposte a movimenti e sforzi ripetuti degli arti superiori. La Medicina del Lavoro $95(4)$, 305–319 (2004)
8. Occhipinti E., Colombini D.: The occupational repetitive action (OCRA) methods: OCRA index and OCRA checklist. In: Stanton, N. et al. (eds.) Handbook of Human Factors and Ergonomics Methods, Chap. 15, pp. 1–14. CRC Press, Boca Raton (2004)
9. Occhipinti, E., Colombini, D.: Updating reference values and predictive models of the OCRA method in the risk assessment of work-related musculoskeletal disorders of the upper limbs. Ergonomics $50(11)$, 1727–1739 (2007)

An Experimental Study to Analyze the Effects of Self Stretching and Postural Re Education Program for Classical Carnatic Violin Artistes in Reducing Playing Related Musculoskeletal Disorder (PRMD) of Cervical Flexor Muscle Group

Srinath and Venkatesh Balasubramanian[✉]

RBG Labs, Department of Engineering Design, Indian Institute of Technology Madras, Chennai 600036, India
chanakya@iitm.ac.in

Abstract. Playing Related Musculoskeletal Disorder (PRMD) among musicians especially violinists are one of the prevailing concerns in Performing Arts Medicine and least explored from human factors perspective. In this study, effects of self-stretching & postural reeducation program towards reduction of PRMD in Neck flexor muscle group among Classical Carnatic violinists is studied. Experimental study design with a convenient sampling method was used for the study. 40 Eligible violinists from Harish Raghavendra School of Music, West Mambalam, Chennai were selected, of which, 10 violinists chose not to participate. Hence, after taking study participation consent, 30 young Violinists between 15–25 years across gender with a criteria of minimum five years professional music training under the same tutelage were selected and divided in to two groups (Group A-Sample & Group B- Experimental) with 15 participants in each. Both the groups were studied for a duration of 7 h (with two 15 min break every two hours) during their continuous musical concert performance. Group A Violinists performing music conventionally without any intervention & Group B Violinists performing the concert with a trained self-stretch (done before concert beginning & during the two 15 min breaks) to cervical flexor muscle group (10 Reps) and informed awareness on postural correction before the start of concert. To determine the comparative outcome on flexor muscle tightness, Range of Motion (ROM) of neck flexors are measured through a standardized Manual Goniometry method. As studies have established the correlation of performance anxiety with poor posture, MPAI (Music Performance Anxiety Inventory) tool was used. Quick DASH (Disabilities of Arm, Shoulder and Hand) was used to determine the effect of intervention towards preventing PRMD among neck flexor muscle group. Statistical value difference signifies that, there is a marginal reduction in PRMD of cervical flexors among violinists in the experimental group validating the Alternate Hypothesis.

Keywords: Playing related musculoskeletal disorder · Classical carnatic violinists · Self-stretching · Postural reeducation

N. L. Black et al. (Eds.): IEA 2021, LNNS 222, pp. 802–811, 2021.
https://doi.org/10.1007/978-3-030-74611-7_109

1 Introduction

Indian classical carnatic musicians can be segmented as vocalist, percussionist and stringed instrument players. On an Average, A traditional carnatic music concert is performed over a duration of two hours. In the involvement to give the best performance, String instrument player (Violinists) adopt a poor posture during the concert & pre dispose themselves to muscular fatigue/Pain in short term & degenerative conditions in long term. And not just that, even for a seasoned performing artist, it takes hours of vigorous training & rehearsals prior to a scheduled concert, Hence, Training sessions must also be considered as a pre-disposing factor that attributes to the mental & physical stress of the musicians [1]. Thus, the term," Playing Related Musculoskeletal Disorder (PRMD)" was coined to address the collective occupational hazard faced by the musicians/Performing artists at large [2]. There are numerous study articles in the literature that defines the terminology "PRMD" [3] & its prophylactic management through preventive interventions. However, the study sample chosen were western musicians, with interventions & management catering to their specific needs desired. There is a dearth of literature knowledge to define the concept of PRMD and its associated influence on performing artists from an Indian population perspective, Especially, Specific studies to conceptualize the terminology among southern classical musicians is the need of the hour. Owing to a broad range of traditional & classical instruments played individually/collectively on a musical troupe for a given performance, Scope of studying ergonomic behavior among performing artistes has huge potential & needs many more explorative literature studies in the days to come.

Evolution of Indian Music is phenomenal in the past century, with Carnatic music becoming more popular among the international audience and trending fusion music has opened doors for many promising artistes to perform on world stage. For any performing musician from southern India, what is looked upon as hobby playing has now become a promising career to many brooding youngsters, who opt & dedicate their focus in shaping themselves as a Music professional. Adding fortune to it, many reality shows have drawn attention & attraction for budding musicians in creating newer opportunities. Tamil month "Margazhi" is becoming famous internationally, as it is the time when dedicated classical Carnatic music concerts take place at Tamilnadu and Chennai in specific. The whole Month is power packed with the musical performances from Leading musical Stalwarts on a tight schedule. The very same opportunity has also changed equations among musicians, with more mental stress & physical strain levied upon them. However, there is no proper study or documentation about their exact experience on physical health associated to musical performance.

Although performing arts medicine is a growing field, the health problems of musicians remain under-recognized and under-researched [3]. India, with its biggest strength of having highest youth population, Sound health & Productivity among the young population is a much-needed trait for a sustained growth of our country.

The current topic is hence chosen to identify the effect of self-stretching & posture correction in reducing the effects of PRMD on cervical flexor muscle group among classical Carnatic Violinists. Biomechanical analysis of stringed instrument players has been carried out in western population and many contemporary methods in establishing the relationship between musicians and playing related musculoskeletal disorder has been Published [4]. However, since this particular study is contemporary for classical Carnatic violinists & Indian performing arts medicine study literature at large, it is intended to be carried out by taking a collective study references from multiple topic related Evidence based study articles carried out on western population than a single mother article.

2 Materials and Methods

2.1 Subjects Summary

40 Eligible violinists from Harish Raghavendra School of Music, West Mambalam, Chennai were selected, of which, 10 violinists chose not to participate. Convenient sampling method was chosen for the study and the Sample size chosen was 30 violinists. Participants with tutelage from the same teacher and similar experience skills are included as study participants and subjects with known history of hyperthermia, low back ache and muscle stiffness are excluded from the study.

2.2 Experimental Design

Procedure for Performing Self Stretch. Violinists belonging to experimental group were told orally about brief anatomy of neck and significance of self-stretching. They were also taught and demonstrated to do self-stretch of neck flexor. Violinist were also shown a you tube video on Self stretch published by Manual Therapy association, Indianapolis. Finally, At the end of their playing session, experimental group were also taught

Fig. 1. Self-stretch of neck flexor taught and demonstrated to a participant

& trained to do cool down exercises that involved mobility exercises & mild stretching of neck muscles (Fig. 1).

Procedure for Performing Posture Re-education. All the subjects under experimental group were made to perform and Visually observed for the method of playing & posture they adopted while Playing. In available cases, Video of their performance in earlier concerts were analyzed. In Broad, Posture corrective inputs were given to ensure following aspects

1. Keep the spine erect while playing, cueing technique for reminder like, after finishing every note, remember to straighten your spine, were taught & trained
2. Minimal cervical flexion by elevating the thigh with a pillow or folded cloth & keeping the chin holder of violin as high as possible
3. While bowing, play without shoulder abduction (arm separation) is also trained and ensured (Figs. 2 and 3).

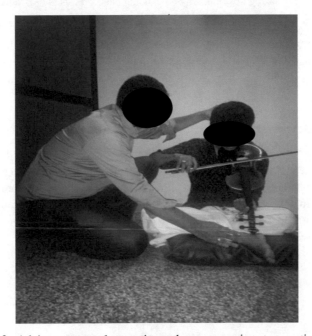

Fig. 2. Advise on postural correction and awareness given to a participant

Avoiding proper cross-legged sitting and Resting the Violin on the ankle joint without pressure.

Following to the correctives advise & self-stretching by the experimental group and conventional playing method by the control group, both the groups did continuous playing of Violin for 7 h with two breaks for twenty minutes each. Practise session was performed in group for their upcoming concert, Hence, time duration of practise, instrument, rehearsal environment is exactly the same for both groups without any bias. At the

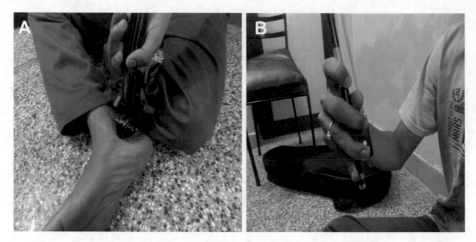

Fig. 3. A - violin resting position, B - bow holding position was taught to the participant

end of the 7 h practise session, both the groups were asked to fill out the questionnaire and in the mean while post-test goniometric values were measured and documented for both groups respectively.

2.3 Statistical Analysis

The outcome values obtained were tabulated in Microsoft Excel 10 spread sheet, and were exported to SPSS Statistics 17.0 version for Windows 7 for statistical analysis. The effects of the intervention on the Range of Motion of Cervical flexors from pre to posttest values in both groups were analyzed using Paired 'T' Test for within group analysis and Independent Sample 'T' test for between Group analyses. The P value was chosen as per the description given by SPSS Statistics for Windows 7 Ultimate Version (Tables 1 and 2).

Table 1. Statistical reference values

P value	Description
< 0.001	Extremely significant
0.001 to 0.01	Very significant
0.01 to 0.5	Significant
> 0.05	Not significant

When violinists performed their rehearsals conventionally without any intervention, there is a very minimal and skewed difference of pre-test mean value of 49.9 with a standard deviation value of 2.4 in comparison to the post test mean value of 49.3 with

Table 2. Comparison of pre and post-test value of Group- A

| | | Pre - Test | | | Post - Test | | |
S. No	Variable	Mean	SD	SEM	Mean	SD	SEM
1.	Range of motion	49.9	2.4	.628	49.33	2.6	.695

Table 3. Comparison of pre and post-test value of Group- B

| | | Pre - Test | | | Post - Test | | |
S. No	Variable	Mean	SD	SEM	Mean	SD	SEM
1.	Range of motion	50.2	2.36	.611	51.8	2.6	.696

a standard deviation of 2.6. This difference can be attributed to the mild playing related musculoskeletal strain on cervical flexors experienced by the subjects (Table 3).

When violinists performed their rehearsals with Posture re-education & trained self-stretches to cervical flexors, there is a comparatively striking difference of pre-test mean value of 50.2 with a standard deviation value of 2.36 to that of Post-test mean value of 51.8 with a standard deviation of 2.6. This difference can be attributed to the effect of self-stretches & postural re-education on cervical flexors of the subjects (Table 4).

Table 4. Paired difference – Group A

| | | | | | 95% confidence interval of the difference | | | | |
S. No	Variable	Mean	SD	SEM	Lower	Upper	Df	t Value	Sig (2tailed)
1.	Pre & Post test range of motion (in degrees)	.600	.910	.235	0.96	1.104	14	2.553	.023

When subjects on Group-A were made to play conventionally without any intervention, mean value is .600 with a SD value of .910. At 95% confidence interval of the difference, 14 and "t" value 2. 553. The above readings shows the transition of difference in the reading values prior and post-performance (Table 5).

Paired samples test to determine Range of Motion, when done on subjects belonging to Group-B, with Trained self-stretches & Postural Re-education, mean value is −1.667 with a SD value of 2. 992. At 95% confidence interval of the difference, 14 and "t" value −2. 157. The above readings shows the transition of difference in the reading values prior and post-performance (Table 6).

Table 5. Paired difference – Group B

| S. No | Variable | Mean | SD | SEM | 95% confidence interval of the difference | | Df | t Value | Sig (2tailed) |
					Lower	Upper			
1.	Pre & Post test range of motion	1.667	2.992	.773	−3.324	−0.10	14	−2.157	.049

Table 6. Music performance anxiety index (MPAI)

| S. No | Variable | Group A | | | Group B | | |
		Mean	SD	SEM	Mean	SD	SEM
1.	MPAI	30.93	1.8	.483	28.2	1.4	.368

Music Performance anxiety index is a questionnaire filled by the candidates one week later to the date of assessment, to understand their psychological impact on PRMD. Group-A without intervention showed a mean of 30.93 with a standard deviation of 1.8, whereas, Group-B that underwent self-stretching and posture re-education, showed a decreased mean of 28.2 with a standard deviation of 368 (Table 7).

Table 7. Quick dash (Disability of Arm, Shoulder, Hand) scale

| S. No | Variable | Group A | | Group B | |
		Mean rank	Sum of ranks	Mean rank	Sum of ranks
1.	Quick DASH	18.93	284	12.07	181

After performing Quick DASH and statistically comparing the ranks through Mann-Whitney Test method, Experimental group (Group-B) has obtained a reduced score of mean 12.07 with 181 as sum of ranks, whereas Group-A has obtained a mean rank of 18.93 with 284 as sum of ranks. This indicates reduced PRMD in Group-B in comparison to Group-A.

3 Results

This study was done for 30 subjects who consist of 15 subjects in each group with the duration of one day. Mean value of Mann Whitney Test of the Control and Experimental group shows statistically significant difference in reduction of PRMD among cervical neck flexors of classical carnatic violinists. The result on analysis between the groups shows a significance by Mann Whitney Test value ($p < 0.05$) proving that Alternate Hypothesis is valid (Figs 4, 5 and 6).

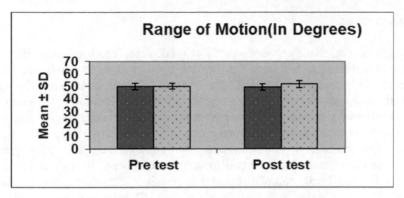

Fig. 4. Range of motion – pre-test and post- test values

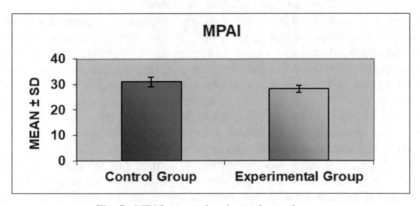

Fig. 5. MPAI – control and experimental group

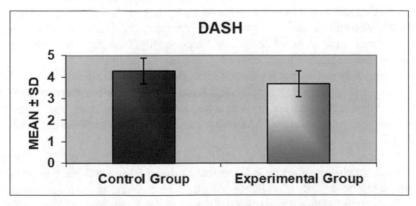

Fig. 6. DASH – control and experimental group

4 Discussion

Performing arts medicine especially "Playing related musculoskeletal disorder" is one of the most under researched subject in the contemporary era of Physiotherapy [2]. This statement stands absolutely valid to Indian Literature context, as the word "Performing Arts Medicine" remains unknown to many of the practising Healthcare professionals in India. Good news is, as such, "Ergonomics" as a stream of speciality is gaining popularity among both healthcare practitioners and common man.

Height of ignorance is, even musicians who undergoes the said "Playing related Musculoskeletal disorder" doesn't realize the terminology [4], it's effects and ways to overcome it. They hardly complain about their physical discomfort due to playing and assumes that, this discomfort is short lived and they will soon overcome it without any medical intervention. But the fact remains that, they have learnt to live with their bodily discomfort without taking preventive care to prevent deterioration.

Journey of this study, will make one to realize, how effective is preventive healthcare than a reactive intervention measure. Though there are mention about self-stretching & postural re-education as a prevention strategy in several literature articles [5]. When these are applied to young budding violinists, not just the statistical significance, but also perceptually heart-warming response is seen among musicians. Even if it's applied for a day's practise, if this study can show a marginal difference, just imagine the positive influence of these preventive strategies adopted by musicians throughout their career.

There is a specific reason for choosing Cervical neck flexor group, Unlike Western method of playing orchestral Violin, Classical Carnatic Violinists tend to play the instrument by flexing their neck to hold the instrument on their chin throughout the concert. To worsen this, there is also a non-paradox Slough sitting posture with a completely cross-legged sitting coupled with arm movements to handle bowing. In all true possibilities, the above said posture is least recommended for a musician who is going pursue their career as Violinist in future and play for significantly longer hours.

Indeed, Cervical flexor muscles is one of the aspects in Violinists to study about [6] and it's the pronounced region of discomfort perceived and experienced by musicians & hence brought in to scope of this study. Subsequently, other regions with respect to playing can also be studied to understand its influence on musicians.

Thus, this study not just proves the statistical significance of self-stretches & postural re-education in reducing PRMD of cervical flexors among classical Carnatic violinists, but also has shown the potential for literature studies based on these topic lines. It has always been believed that, reduced Mortality rate is not fruitful until there is a reduction in morbidity.

Given the increasing cases of occupational illness & reduced productivity, work based health hazards are the biggest threat to our human kind and irony is, Musicians who intend to entertain their audience with their best efforts in performance land up hurting themselves [7]. In nut shell, this defines the in depth meaning of "Playing Related Musculoskeletal Disorder".

5 Conclusion

The result of the study concludes, there is a marginal difference in reduction of PRMD of Cervical neck flexors seen in Group B violinists who are intervened with Self - stretches & Postural Re-education compared to Group A who were under the conventional method of playing violin. Further studies with a larger sample size and duration can substantiate the findings and bring about new horizons in the field of performing arts medicine benefitting the musicians at large.

References

1. Se Suza Moraes, G.F., Antuines, A.P.: Musculoskeletal disorders in professional violinists and violists- systematic review. Acta Ortop Bras. **20**(1), 43–47 (2012)
2. Foxman, I., Burgel, B.J.: Musician health and safety preventing playing-related musculoskeletal disorders. AAOHN J. **54**(7), 309–316 (2005)
3. Steinmetz, A., Moller, H.: Playing related musculoskeletal disorders in music students - associated musculoskeletal signs. Eur. J. Phys. Rehabl. Med. **48**(4), 625–633 (2012)
4. Barbara, P., Christine, H.: The Athlete Musician: A Guide to Playing Without Pain. Scarecrow Press, Lanham (1997)
5. Paarup, H.M., Baelum, J., Manniche, C.: Occurrence and co-existence of localized musculoskeletal symptoms and findings in work attending orchestra musicians - an explanatory cross-sectional study. BMC Res. Notes Stud. **5**(1), 1–15 (2012)
6. Zaza, C., Charles, C., Muszynski, A.: The meaning of playing related musculoskeletal disorders to classical musicians. Soc. Sci. Med. **47**(12), 2013–2023 (1998)
7. Ostwald, P.E., Baron, B.C., Byl, N.M., Wilson, F.R.: Performing arts medicine. West. J. Med. **160**(1), 48 (1994)

Prevalence of Musculoskeletal Symptoms in Dental Students

Yordán Rodríguez$^{(\boxtimes)}$ [ID], Hugo Grisales-Romero [ID], Leidy C. Botero,
and Marisol Arroyave

National School of Public Health, Universidad de Antioquia, Medellín, Antioquia, Colombia
yordan.rodriguez@udea.edu.co

Abstract. The study of musculoskeletal symptoms in dental professionals has
been a topic of interest for several years. However, few studies have focused on
student populations, even though they are exposed to similar professional dentists'
conditions during their clinical practices. The aim of this study was to determine
the prevalence of musculoskeletal symptoms in a population of dental students
at a public university in Colombia. Cross-sectional study, where 106 dental students who were studying between the fifth and tenth semester of a public university in Colombia were randomly selected. Students answered a questionnaire
composed of 22 questions and structured in three sections: (1) sociodemographic
characteristics, (2) clinical practice data, and (3) musculoskeletal symptoms. Students spend an average of 10.5 h per week (SD = 4.1 h) in clinical practice.
27.4% reported that musculoskeletal pain had interfered with their daily activities. Also, students reported other symptoms such as tiredness (60.4%), muscle
fatigue (41.5%), numbness in wrist hands (21.7%), and (17.9%) weakness in the
grip of instruments and muscle spasms. The prevalence of musculoskeletal pain
in the student population was 82.1%, being significantly greater prevalence in
women (89.7%) than in men (68.4%) (p = 0.0133) and CI (95%: 2.8%–4.0%). A
greater proportion of pain prevalence was also found in women than in men by
body region. The body regions most affected, both by frequency and severity of
pain, were the lower and upper back, neck, hands-wrists, and shoulders. Findings
show university authorities the need for a systemic ergonomic analysis of clinical
practices to improve students' well-being and health.

Keywords: Musculoskeletal symptoms · Musculoskeletal pain · Dentistry · Risk
factors · Dental students

1 Introduction

The study of musculoskeletal symptoms in dental professionals has been a topic of
interest for several years [1–4]. However, few studies have focused on student populations
[3, 5], even though they are exposed to similar professional dentists' conditions during
their clinical practices.

In Colombia, dental students have to perform clinical practices as part of their academic program. Although the student population is usually very young, and clinical

© The Author(s), under exclusive license to Springer Nature Switzerland AG 2021
N. L. Black et al. (Eds.): IEA 2021, LNNS 222, pp. 812–817, 2021.
https://doi.org/10.1007/978-3-030-74611-7_110

practices are not conducted on a continuous schedule, students sometimes complain of musculoskeletal discomfort that could lead to disease. Therefore, the study of the prevalence of these musculoskeletal symptoms is necessary to quantify the problem's magnitude and identify the related risk factors to take preventive actions.

The aim of this study was to determine the prevalence of musculoskeletal symptoms in a population of dental students at a public university in Colombia.

2 Materials and Methods

2.1 Study Population

A cross-sectional descriptive study was conducted in a population of dental students studying between the fifth and tenth semester of a public university in Colombia. From a total of 302 dental students, 106 were randomly selected.

2.2 Study Design

The dental students answered a questionnaire composed of 22 questions grouped in three sections: (1) sociodemographic characteristics, (2) clinical practice data, and (3) musculoskeletal symptoms. The body map proposed by (ISO/TS 20646: 2014), divided into 21 body regions, was adapted to record musculoskeletal symptoms [6]. The severity of musculoskeletal pain was evaluated with a visual analog scale of 100 mm in length. The value zero (0) indicated no pain in the scale, and the value one hundred (100) indicated maximum pain. To classify the presence or absence of musculoskeletal pain in dental students, we considered the following: (pain) if the student had reported pain (value > 0) in at least one body region, and (no pain) if the student did not report pain in any body region. The Borg CR-10 scale was used to determine the perceived exertion by students during their clinical practice. Before answering the questionnaire, each student signed an Informed Consent. The questionnaire was administered by two dental professionals who recently graduated from the same university.

2.3 Statistical Analysis

A descriptive analysis of the variables was conducted, reporting the mean and standard deviation for quantitative variables and percentages for qualitative variables. The prevalence of musculoskeletal pain was calculated by dividing the total number of students who reported at least one body region with musculoskeletal pain by the sample size (n = 106). To establish the association between pain by body region and sex, Pearson's Chi-square test of independence was used. In cases where the expected frequencies were less than 5, Fisher's Exact Test was used. We also calculated prevalence ratios (PRs) using a 95% confidence interval (95% CI) as a measure of association, adjusted by sex. The statistical software SPSS version 27.0 was used.

3 Results

64.2% of the students are women. Average age was 24.3 years (SD = 3.1 years); average weight and height were 63.6 kg (SD = 11.1 kg) and 165.3 cm (SD = 9.0 cm), respectively. 92.5% are right-handed, 4.7% are left-handed, and 2.8% are ambidextrous. According to the Borg-10 scale, the intensity of the effort was on average 1.9 (SD = 0.8), which is equivalent to weak (light) perceived exertion.

Students reported that they spend an average of 10.5 h per week (SD = 4.1 h) in clinical practice and attend an average of 2.5 child patients (SD = 1.3) and 3.0 adult patients (SD = 1.7) per week.

82.1% of the students reported suffering musculoskeletal pain in at least one part of the body during the clinical practices (p = 0,0133, IC 95%: 74,3%–89,8%). In analyzing the prevalence by sex, we found a higher prevalence of musculoskeletal pain in women (89.7%) than in men (68.4%). For the difference in proportions (p = 0.0133) and CI (95%: 2.8%–4.0%). Figure 1 shows the prevalence of pain by sex.

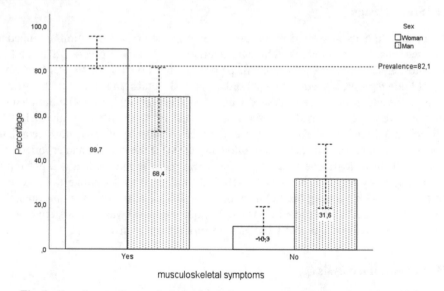

Fig. 1. Prevalence of musculoskeletal pain by sex among dental students (n = 106).

27.4% reported that musculoskeletal pain had interfered with their daily activities, and only 3.8% consulted a physician for these complaints. In addition to musculoskeletal pain, students reported other symptoms such as: tiredness (60.4%), muscle fatigue (41.5%), numbness in wrist hands (21.7%), and 17.9% weakness in the grip of instruments and muscle spasms. To alleviate musculoskeletal pain and discomfort, students' two most frequent actions were stretching (58.5%) and pauses (31.1%).

The body regions with the highest frequency of pain were (n = 106): lower back (61), upper back (58), neck (58), the left-hand wrist (44) and right hand (34), right shoulder (32) and left shoulder (29). Also, these same body regions presented the greatest severity of pain (n = 106): lower back 29.1 (SD = 30.6), upper back 24.3 (SD = 27.3), neck

20.5 (SD = 24.7), left hand wrist 14.6 (SD = 24.0), right hand wrist 9.7 (SD = 20.0), left shoulder 9.6 (SD = 20.9) and right shoulder 8.6 (SD = 18.9). The number of body regions with pain among students who reported musculoskeletal pain (n = 87) ranged from 1 to 21 (mean 7.1) and (median 4).

3.1   Prevalence of Pain for Body Region Discriminated by Sex

Table 1 shows the prevalence of pain by gender for each of the 21 body regions analyzed.

Table 1. Prevalence of musculoskeletal pain by body region among dental students (n = 106).

Body region	Pain	Women n (%)	Men n (%)	PRs (95% CI)	p
Neck	Yes	46 (67,6)	12 (31,6)	2,1 (1,3–3,5)	**0,0000**
	No	22	26		
Upper back	Yes	40 (58,8)	18 (47,3)	1,2 (0,8–1,8)	0,3106
	No	28	20		
Left shoulder	Yes	24 (35,2)	8 (21,1)	1,7 (0,3–3,4)	0,0936
	No	44	30		
Left upper arm	Yes	17 (25,0)	5 (13,2)	1,9 (0,8–4,7)	0,1152
	No	51	33		
Left elbow	Yes	13 (19,1)	5 (13,2)	1,5 (0,6–3,8)	0,3087
	No	55	33		
Lower back	Yes	43 (63,2)	18 (47,4)	1,3 (0,9–2,0)	0,0840
	No	25	20		
Left lower arm	Yes	17 (20,0)	4 (9,5)	2,1 (0,8–5,9)	0,073
	No	68	38		
Left-hand wrist	Yes	28 (41,2)	6 (15,8)	2,6 (1,2–5,7)	**0,0070**
	No	40	32		
Left hip-thigh	Yes	13 (19,1)	6 (15,8)	1,2 (0,5–2,9)	0,6680
	No	55	32		
Left knee	Yes	20 (29,4)	5 (13,2)	2,2 (0,9–5,5)	0,0590
	No	48	33		
Left leg	Yes	15 (22,1)	4 (10,5)	2,1 (0,7–5,9)	0,1380
	No	53	34		
Left ankle-foot	Yes	14 (20,.6)	6 (15,8)	1,3 (0,5–3,1)	0,5450
	No	54	32		

(continued)

Table 1. (*continued*)

Body region	Pain	Women n (%)	Men n (%)	PRs (95% CI)	p
Right shoulder	Yes	23 (33,8)	6 (15,8)	2,1 (1,0–4,8)	**0,0460**
	No	45	32		
Right upper arm	Yes	19 (27,9)	5 (13,2)	2,1 (0,9–5,2)	0,0810
	No	49	33		
Right elbow	Yes	13 (19,1)	3 (7,9)	2,4 (0,7–8,0)	0,1220
	No	55	35		
Right lower arm	Yes	16 (23,5)	4 (10,5)	2,2 (0,8–6,2)	0,1010
	No	52	34		
Right hand-wrist	Yes	35 (51,5)	9 (23,7)	2,2 (1,2–4,0)	**0,0050**
	No	33	29		
Right hip-thigh	Yes	15 (22,1)	5 (13,2)	1,7 (0,7–4,3)	0,2610
	No	53	33		
Right knee	Yes	19 (27,9)	4 (10,5)	2,7 (1,0–7,2)	**0,0370**
	No	49	34		
Right leg	Yes	17 (25,0)	4 (10,5)	2,4 (0,9–6,5)	0,0730
	No	51	34		
Right ankle-foot	Yes	15 (22,1)	5 (13,2)	1,7 (0,7–4,3)	0,2613
	No	53	33		

% = prevalence, X^2 test $p < 0.05$, PR = prevalence ratio; 95%, CI = 95% confidence interval.

4 Discussion

This study's results are consistent with musculoskeletal symptoms reports in professional dentists [1–4], showing that dental students can also be affected by their clinical practices.

The prevalence of musculoskeletal pain obtained in our study (82.1%) corresponds to literature reports. For example, a review by Hayes et al. reported that the prevalence of general musculoskeletal pain ranges between 64% and 93% [1]. Another study conducted in a student population found a prevalence of pain between 41% and 71% [5]. While in a review among dental professionals in Western countries, the prevalence ranged from 10.8% to 97.9% [4].

In our study, the prevalence of musculoskeletal pain was greater in women than in men in general and by all body region; being significant ($p < 0.05$) only for the neck, left hand-wrist, right shoulder, right hand-wrist, and right knee (see Table 1). Similar findings have been reported both in a professional [7] and in a student population [5], also in the Colombian population [8].

The body regions with the greatest prevalence of pain found in our study (n = 106) were: lower back (57.5%), upper back (54.7%), neck (54.7%), the left-hand wrist (41.5%), and right hand (32.0%), right shoulder (30.1%) and left shoulder (27.3%). These results are consistent with reports of the most affected body regions in dental students and dental professionals [1, 3–5]. For instance, Hayes et al. reported the back (36.3–60.1%), the neck (19.8–85%), and the wrist (60–69.5%) as the body regions with the highest prevalence of pain [1]. Moreover, Lietz et al. reported the neck (58.5%), the lower back (56.4%), the shoulder (43.1%), and the upper back (41.1%) [4].

As mentioned, our results agree with the reports of other studies of musculoskeletal symptoms in dental professionals and students. They also suggest the need for ergonomic analysis of the conditions under which our dental student population perform their clinical practices [3]. We hope to carry out this analysis in the second part of the project.

5 Conclusions

The prevalence of musculoskeletal pain in the student population was 82.1%, a significantly greater prevalence in women (89.7%) than in men (68.4%). Also, a greater prevalence of pain by body region was found in women than in men. The body regions most affected, both by frequency and severity of pain, were the lower and upper back, neck, hands-wrists, and shoulders. Findings show university authorities the need for a systemic ergonomic analysis of clinical practices to improve students' well-being and health.

References

1. Hayes, M., Cockrell, D., Smith, D.R.: A systematic review of musculoskeletal disorders among dental professionals. Int. J. Dent. Hyg. **7**, 159–165 (2009)
2. Alexopoulos, E.C., Stathi, I.-C., Charizani, F.: Prevalence of musculoskeletal disorders in dentists. BMC Musculoskelet. Disord. **5**, 16 (2004)
3. Gupta, A., Ankola, A.V., Hebbal, M.: Dental ergonomics to combat musculoskeletal disorders: a review. Int. J. Occup. Saf. Ergon. **19**, 561–571 (2013)
4. Lietz, J., Kozak, A., Nienhaus, A.: Prevalence and occupational risk factors of musculoskeletal diseases and pain among dental professionals in Western countries: a systematic literature review and meta-analysis. PLoS One **13**, e0208628 (2018)
5. Rising, D.W., Bennett, B.C., Hursh, K., Plesh, O.: Reports of body pain in a dental student population. J. Am. Dent. Assoc. **136**, 81–86 (2005)
6. ISO 20646: Ergonomics guidelines for the optimization of musculoskeletal workload (2014). Accessed 8 Feb 2021
7. Pejčić, N., Petrović, V., Marković, D., Miličić, B., Dimitrijević, I.I., Perunović, N., Čakić, S.: Assessment of risk factors and preventive measures and their relations to work-related musculoskeletal pain among dentists. Work **57**, 573–593 (2017)
8. Ramírez-Sepúlveda, K.A., Gómez-Arias, M.Y., Agudelo-Suárez, A.A., Ramírez-Ossa, D.M.: Musculoskeletal disorders and related factors in the Colombian orthodontists' practice. Int. J. Occup. Saf. Ergon., 1–10 (2020)

Inter-rater Reliability of the Individual Risk Assessment (ERIN) Method

Yordán Rodríguez[1]([⊠]) [iD] and Paola Monsalve[2] [iD]

[1] National School of Public Health, Universidad de Antioquia, Medellín, Antioquia, Colombia
yordan.rodriguez@udea.edu.co
[2] Consultoría en Gestión del Riesgo Suramericana, Medellín, Antioquia, Colombia
pmonsalve@sura.com.co

Abstract. ERIN is an observational method developed for non-expert personnel to assess the exposure to risk factors related to musculoskeletal disorders. Since its initial publication, its use has gradually spread in Latin American countries and other regions. However, few reliability studies of the method have been reported. The purpose of this work was to determine the inter-rater reliability of the ERIN method. Thirty-nine raters (physiotherapists) evaluated eight tasks from video recordings. Each task was evaluated simultaneously while the video was projected in a room. The inter-rater reliability of the categorical variables was evaluated using the statistical index kappa Fleiss (K), while for the continuous variable (total risk), the intraclass correlation coefficient ICC (2.1) was used. Sixteen categorical variables were analyzed. In eight, the agreement was moderate, the K values varied between 0.45 and 0.59, and in the other eight variables, the agreement was substantial; the K values varied between 0.61 and 0.80. When unifying the four ERIN risk levels into "No risk" (low and medium risk levels) and "Risk" (high and very high-risk levels), the agreement was almost perfect (K = 0.86). A good agreement was obtained for the total risk variable; the average value was ICC (2,1) = 0.62. The results of this study indicate that the ERIN method has acceptable levels of inter-rater reliability.

Keywords: ERIN method · Inter-rater reliability · Observational methods · Posture · Risk assessment · Assessment tool

1 Introduction

The prevention of musculoskeletal disorders (MSDs) has been an area of interest for ergonomics researchers and practitioners for several years [1]. These diseases are related to non-ergonomic working conditions where workers are exposed to various risk factors [2]. Consequently, several methods/tools have been developed to assess exposure to risk factors related to MSDs [3–5].

Among the available methods, observational methods have been the most widely used by ergonomics practitioners [3–5]. However, the proper use of these methods requires personnel with knowledge and experience in ergonomics [3] and adequate training in the use of each method to avoid errors in the assessment [6]. The availability of personnel

© The Author(s), under exclusive license to Springer Nature Switzerland AG 2021
N. L. Black et al. (Eds.): IEA 2021, LNNS 222, pp. 818–824, 2021.
https://doi.org/10.1007/978-3-030-74611-7_111

with these characteristics is scarce, at least in Latin American countries. This situation has slowed down the performance of job/task evaluations as part of MSD prevention actions.

In response to the situation described above, the observational Individual Risk Assessment (ERIN) method was developed [7, 8]. During its development, the needs, limitations, and capabilities of non-expert personnel to assess exposure to MSD risk factors in real contexts were taken into account. The use of ERIN has gradually grown in Latin American countries and other regions of the world since its initial publication. However, few reliability studies of the ERIN have been reported [9, 10].

The purpose of this research was to determine the inter-observer reliability of the ERIN method.

2 Materials and Methods

Thirty-nine physiotherapists were trained in the use of the ERIN method. Each physiotherapist assessed eight different video tasks.

2.1 ERIN Method

ERIN can be used to evaluate static and dynamic tasks [7, 8]. For its use, the task must be observed during several work cycles, and the critical posture of the trunk, arm, wrist, and neck body segments must be evaluated, as well as the frequency of movement for each body segment. The work rhythm (a combination of work speed and effective duration of the task); the intensity of effort (a combination of perceived effort using the modified Borg scale and the frequency of effort); and self-assessment (perception of the stress referred by the worker on the task being performed) are also evaluated [7, 8]. Table 1 shows the risk levels and actions according to the total risk value. The additive model used in ERIN to calculate the total risk facilitates identifying those aspects of the task that should be intervened to reduce the risk level.

Table 1. Risk and action levels recommended in the ERIN method.

Zone	Total risk	Risk level	Action
Green	6–14	Low	No changes are required
Yellow	15–24	Medium	Further investigation is needed and changes may by required
Orange	25–34	High	Investigation and changes are required soon
Red	≥ 35	Very high	Investigation and changes are required immediately

Source: [10]

2.2   Video Tasks

Eight video tasks from different economic sectors were selected (Fig. 1). The videos had to meet the following criteria: high definition with minimum resolution 1280 × 720 p, duration not less than 2 min, recording at least 18 work cycles, stable image, and full view of the workstation. A brief description of the task was included at the beginning of each video.

Fig. 1. Tasks evaluated from video recordings.

2.3 Raters

Thirty-nine physiotherapists (31 women, 8 men) participated in this study. Their age ranged from 27 to 48 years (mean 34.9 years). The physiotherapists had completed postgraduate studies lasting approximately one year: thirty-six in Occupational Safety and Health and three in Ergonomics. All physiotherapists had previous experience in ergonomic workplace assessment of more than three years.

2.4 Training

The 39 physiotherapists received a three-hour training in the use of the ERIN method. This training was led by an ergonomist and focused on explaining the ERIN variables and using the ERIN worksheet's assessment. Finally, to practice what they had learned, the physiotherapists evaluated a video task chosen exclusively for the training.

2.5 Task Assessment Procedures

The evaluation of the eight selected video tasks was performed immediately after the training. All raters performed the assessments simultaneously in a room where the videos were projected. For the evaluation, they used the ERIN worksheet, which they had to hand to an assistant once they finished evaluating each video task. The next evaluation did not begin until all the raters had finished their evaluation. Raters were not allowed to exchange opinions and conversations with each other during the evaluations.

2.6 Statistical Analysis

The Fleiss Kappa (K) was used to evaluate the level of agreement in categorical variables. The interpretation of the values of agreement was as follows: poor (< 0), slight (0.01–0.20), fair (0.21–0.40), moderate (0.41–0.60), substantial (0.61–0.80), and almost perfect (0.81–0.99) [11]. For continuous variables (e.g., ERIN total risk), the Intraclass Correlation Coefficient (ICC) was used. ICC can be used in different forms. In this study, a two-way single-measure random effect model was used (ICC, 2.1) and reported the average [12]. The interpretation of the values of agreement was as follows: poor (ICC $<$ 0.4), moderate to good (ICC $=$ 0.4–0.7), and excellent (ICC $>$ 0.7) [13]. The statistical software SPSS version 25.0 was used.

3 Results

The K values obtained for the ERIN categorical variables analyzed were between 0.50 and 0.86, with a moderate or substantial agreement for all variables except for the Risk/No risk variable (K $=$ 0.86) with almost perfect agreement (Table 2). For the total risk variable (sum of risk scores per variable), the average agreement reached (ICC $=$ 0.62; 95% CI 0.41 - 0.88) was good. An analysis of the agreement obtained according to ERIN risk levels for each video task was also performed (Table 3). As shown in Table 3, no task was classified as low risk, and only in task # 4, the agreement reached was almost perfect.

Table 2. Inter-rater agreement among physiotherapists (n = 39) from eight video tasks.

ERIN variables		Fleiss Kappa (K)*	Interpretation
Trunk	Posture	0.61	Substantial
	Frequency of movement	0.45	Moderate
	Adjust	0.65	Substantial
Shoulder/arm	Posture	0.61	Substantial
	Frequency of movement	0.54	Moderate
	Adjust	0.77	Substantial
Wrist	Posture	0.74	Substantial
	Frequency of movement	0.58	Moderate
	Adjust	0.80	Substantial
Neck	Posture	0.80	Substantial
	Frequency of movement	0.50	Moderate
	Adjust	0.69	Substantial
Intensity of effort	Intensity	0.50	Moderate
	Frequency of efforts	0.59	Moderate
Speed of work		0.59	Moderate
Risk levels (Low, Medium, High and Very High)		0.56	Moderate
No-Risk (Low-Medium)/Risk (High–Very High)		0.86	Almost perfect

*(K) values interpretation: poor (< 0), slight (0.01–0.20), fair (0.21–0.40), moderate (0.41–0.60), substantial (0.61–0.80), and almost perfect (0.81–0.99).

Table 3. Inter-rater agreement among physiotherapists (n = 39) according to the ERIN risk level for each task assessed.

# Video tasks	Risk Levels				Kappa (K)*
	Low	Medium	High	Very high	
1	0	4	13	4	0.43
2	0	19	20	19	0.49
3	0	1	26	1	0.53
4	0	0	3	0	0.85
5	0	0	16	0	0.50
6	0	6	28	6	0.54
7	0	2	30	2	0.62
8	0	0	24	0	0.51
Overall					0.56

*(K) values interpretation: poor (< 0), slight (0.01–0.20), fair (0.21–0.40), moderate (0.41–0.60), substantial (0.61–0.80), and almost perfect (0.81–0.99).

4 Discussion

The aim of this study was to determine inter-rater reliability in a group of physiotherapists using the ERIN method evaluating eight video tasks.

Of the 17 categorical variables analyzed for reliability, it was obtained that: in eight variables, the agreement was substantial K = (0.61–0.80), and in eight variables, it was moderate K = (0.61–0.80). When considering the unification of the low and medium risk levels in the "No risk" category and the high and very high-risk levels in the "Risk" category (Table 1), the agreement was almost perfect (K = 0.86). Therefore, based on the results obtained, we can state that the agreement was generally moderate to substantial.

In general, the results of inter-rater reliability obtained in this study are better than those previously reported [10, 14], although the statistical indices used were different, making comparison difficult. Firstly, this could be since all participants in this study (physiotherapists) had previous experience in ergonomic workplace assessment of more than three years. Whereas in the previous reports [10, 14], the participants (students) had no experience. Secondly, the assessment of angular ranges and joint movements is regularly performed by physiotherapists as part of their professional practice, which may have facilitated the assessment.

In terms of training time (3 h) and how the assessment was carried out (video tasks), there are no differences between this study and those previously reported [10, 14].

It should also be highlighted that changes made in the limit of the angle of flexion/extension of the wrist from 20° to 45° improved the reliability results for this variable compared with previous studies [10, 14].

For variables related to the frequency of movement per body segment, the agreement was moderate. As in previous studies [10, 14], this indicates the need to emphasize this aspect during training sessions and the difficulty for raters to accurately evaluate the frequency of body movements in real-time (the video could not be stopped). The inter-rater reliability of these variables could be improved by conducting video evaluations, in which the observers could stop or put in slow motion filming. These circumstances would facilitate the assessment process with ERIN and lead to better reliability results than those obtained in this study.

5 Conclusions

The results of this study indicate that the ERIN method has acceptable levels of inter-rater reliability. Professionals interested in MSDs prevention can find in ERIN a valuable tool to consistently evaluate jobs/tasks and quickly identify which preventive actions can be applied.

References

1. Dempsey, P.G.: Effectiveness of ergonomics interventions to prevent musculoskeletal disorders: Beware of what you ask. International Journal of Industrial Ergonomics **37**, 169–173 (2007)
2. Bernard, B.P., Putz-Anderson, V.: Musculoskeletal disorders and workplace factors. A critical review of epidemiologic evidence for work-related musculoskeletal disorders of the neck, upper extremity, and low back (1997). https://doi.org/10.26616/NIOSHPUB97141
3. Takala, E.-P., Pehkonen, I., Forsman, M., Hansson, G.-A., Mathiassen, S.E., Neumann, W.P., Sjogaard, G., Veiersted, K.B., Westgaard, R.H., Winkel, J.: Systematic evaluation of observational methods assessing biomechanical exposures at work. Scand J Work Environ Health **36**, 3–24 (2010)
4. Li, G., Buckle, P.: Current techniques for assessing physical exposure to work-related musculoskeletal risks, with emphasis on posture-based methods. Ergonomics **42**, 674–695 (1999)
5. David, G.C.: Ergonomic methods for assessing exposure to risk factors for work-related musculoskeletal disorders. Occup Med (Lond) **55**, 190–199 (2005)
6. Diego-Mas, J.-A., Alcaide-Marzal, J., Poveda-Bautista, R.: Errors Using Observational Methods for Ergonomics Assessment in Real Practice. Hum Factors **59**, 1173–1187 (2017)
7. Rodríguez, Y., Viña, S., Montero, R.: ERIN: A practical tool for assessing work-related musculoskeletal disorders. Occupational Ergonomics **11**, 59–73 (2013)
8. Rodriguez, Y., Vina, S., Montero, R.: A Method for Non-experts in Assessing Exposure to Risk Factors for Work-related Musculoskeletal Disorders-ERIN. Ind Health **51**, 622–626 (2013)
9. Rodríguez, Y.: ERIN: a practical tool for assessing exposure to risks factors for work-related musculoskeletal disorders. In: Bagnara, S., Tartaglia, R., Albolino, S., Alexander, T., Fujita, Y. (eds.) Proceedings of the 20th Congress of the International Ergonomics Association (IEA 2018), pp. 369–379. Springer International Publishing, Cham (2019)
10. Rodríguez, Y.: Individual risk assessment (ERIN): method for the assessment of workplace risks for work-related musculoskeletal disorders. In: Handbook of Research on Ergonomics and Product Design, pp. 1–27. IGI Global (2018)
11. Landis, J.R., Koch, G.G.: The measurement of observer agreement for categorical data. Biometrics **33**, 159–174 (1977)
12. Shrout, P.E., Fleiss, J.L.: Intraclass correlations: Uses in assessing rater reliability. Psychol Bull **86**, 420–428 (1979)
13. Stevens, E.M., Vos, G.A., Stephens, J.-P., Moore, J.S.: Inter-rater reliability of the strain index. J Occup Environ Hyg **1**, 745–751 (2004)
14. Rodríguez, Y., Heredia, J.: Confiabilidad ínter-observador del método de Evaluación de Riesgo Individual. Revista Hacia la Promoción de la Salud 18 (2013)

A Comparison of Forklift Operator Whole-Body Vibration Exposures When Operating Forklifts with and Without a Mast Damping System

Hyoung Frank Ryou[1(✉)], Peter W. Johnson[2], Jeong Ho Kim[3], and Edmund Seto[2]

[1] LG Electronics, Clarksville, TN, USA
[2] Department of Environmental and Occupational Health Science, University of Washington, Seattle, WA, USA
[3] College of Public Health and Human Sciences, Oregon State University, Corvallis, OR, USA

Abstract. Forklift operators are frequently exposed to a high level of whole-body vibration (WBV), a leading risk factor for low back pain. The purpose of this study was to determine whether a mast damping system of forklift was effective in reducing forklift operators' WBV exposures compared to forklifts without mast damping systems. The results showed that the forklifts with the mast damping system significantly reduced the 8-h normalized weighted average vibration [A(8)] at the floor and seat level. While the mast damping system significantly reduced vibration dose value [VDV(8)] at the forklift floor, it had a limited effect on the seat-measured VDV(8) exposures. The study findings indicate that a mast damping system may have potential to reduce forklift operators' WBV exposures. However, given the differences in the seat-measured A(8) and VDV(8) exposures between forklifts, more rigorous evaluations of the forklift and seat suspensions may be merited.

Keywords: Occupational health · Musculoskeletal disorders · Low back pain

1 Introduction

Forklift operators are frequently exposed to whole-body vibration (WBV), which can contribute to the onset and development of low back pain (Bovenzi et al. 2006; Schwarze et al. 1998; Wegscheider 2014). The high levels of WBV exposures in forklift operators are partly due to the limited capabilities of the forklift suspension. Most forklift suspension systems are designed to have limited travel/displacement for better load stability.

To address forklift operators' exposure to WBV, previous studies have evaluated forklift seats and tires as engineering controls (Blood et al. 2010; Joubert 2002). Since vibrations and impacts can be transmitted through the mast during loading and unloading, an effective mast damping system may further reduce forklift operators' WBV exposures. However, the effects that mast damping have on WBV exposures have not been evaluated in a field setting. Therefore, the objective of this study was to determine whether there were differences in WBV exposures between forklift operators using forklifts equipped with and without a mast damping system.

© The Author(s), under exclusive license to Springer Nature Switzerland AG 2021
N. L. Black et al. (Eds.): IEA 2021, LNNS 222, pp. 825–828, 2021.
https://doi.org/10.1007/978-3-030-74611-7_112

2 Methods

2.1 Subjects

Ten professional forklift operators who were employees of a manufacturing facility were recruited to operate the two types of forklifts during their regular work shift. The subjects were divided into two groups of five operators each based on the forklift they regularly operated. With multiple forklifts available, a total of eight unique operator-forklift combinations were collected from each type of forklift. To determine homogeneity between the two groups, relevant demographic, anthropometric (height, weight and BMI) and work history data were collected and statistically compared using the Wilcoxon signed-rank tests. No significant differences were found in the demographics and work history between the two groups.

2.2 Forklifts

Two different forklifts were used in this study and had the same load-carrying capacity (5,000 kgs) and the same tires (size, tire pressure, manufacturer and model). However, one had a mast damping system (Model H50, Linde Material Handling, Aschaffenburg, Germany) while the other one did not (Model H100, Hyster-Yale, Cleveland, OH).

2.3 Data Collection

To assess forklift operators' WBV exposures during their regular work, a seat-pad tri-axial accelerometer was mounted on the driver seat top, and an additional single-axis accelerometer was magnetically mounted on the floor of the forklift (i.e., the base of the seat) per ISO 2631-1. A GPS device was placed on the forklift dashboard to collect forklift speed and location concurrently.

2.4 Data Analysis

The raw unweighted acceleration data were analyzed according to ISO 2631-1. Weighted average acceleration (A_w) and Vibration Dose Value (VDV) were calculated and normalized to reflect 8-h daily exposures: A(8) and VDV(8). Due to the small sample size and the potential for the data to not be normally distributed, non-parametric tests (Wilcoxon rank-sum) were used for comparing WBV exposures between two forklift groups.

3 Results

The forklift with a mast damping system had significantly lower floor-measured A(8) and VDV(8) vibration levels compared to the forklift without the mast damping system (Fig. 1). The seat-measured A(8) WBV exposures were also significantly lower in the forklift with the mast damping system. However, there were no differences in the seat-measured VDV(8) exposures between two forklifts. As shown in Fig. 1, the seat-measured A(8) values in both forklifts were below the EU daily vibration action limit (0.5 m/s^2), but the VDV(8) values were above action limits (9.1 m/s$^{1.75}$).

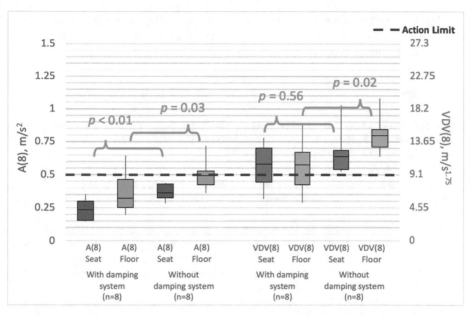

Fig. 1. Comparisons of Daily equivalent weighted average vibration [A(8)] and vibration dose value [VDV(8)] between the forklifts with and without a mast damping system. The red dashed line indicates the European Union's daily vibration action limits [A(8) = 0.5 m/s²; VDV(8) = 9.1 m/s$^{1.75}$]. The boxes indicate interquartile ranges; the horizontal line in the boxes are median values; whiskers indicate maximum and minimum values.

4   Discussion and Conclusions

The aim of this study was to determine whether a mast damping system reduced forklift operators' exposure to WBV in a real field setting. The results showed that the forklift with the mast damping system had significantly lower A(8) and VDV(8) vibration levels at the forklift floor. However, these differences were not observed at the seat level. While the seat-measured A(8) was lower with the mast damping system, no differences in the seat-measured VDV(8) were found between the two forklifts. This indicates potential interactions between the forklift and seat suspensions. Therefore, it may be important to evaluate such interaction and optimize the performance and interactions between the forklift and seat suspensions.

In addition, the WBV data showed that VDV(8) values were above the EU daily exposure limit (9.1 m/s$^{1.75}$), suggesting that forklift operators are exposed to a high level of impulsive exposures during their regular work. Previous studies have shown that these impulse shock exposures can be a better indicator of low back pain (Bovenzi et al. 2009) and have more detrimental effects on spine degenerative conditions than the more continuous oscillating A(8) exposures (Mayton et al. 2008). This indicates that there is a critical need to identify effective vibration mitigation strategies to reduce forklift operators' exposure to WBV.

Despite the aforementioned important study implications, the results should be interpreted with caution due to a few limitations. For example, the small sample size may have reduced statistical power and generalizability of the study findings.

References

Blood, R.P., Ploger, J.D., Johnson, P.W.: Whole body vibration exposures in forklift operators: Comparison of a mechanical and air suspension seat. Ergonomics **53**(11), 1385–1394 (2010). https://doi.org/10.1080/00140139.2010.519053

Bovenzi, M., Rui, F., Negro, C., D'Agostin, F., Angotzi, G., Bianchi, S., Bramanti, L., Festa, G.L., Gatti, S., Pinto, I., Rondina, L., Stacchini, N.: An epidemiological study of low back pain in professional drivers. J. Sound Vib. **298**(3), 514–539 (2006). https://doi.org/10.1016/j.jsv.2006.06.001

Bovenzi, M.: Metrics of whole-body vibration and exposure–response relationship for low back pain in professional drivers: a prospective cohort study. Int. Arch. Occup. Environ. Health **82**, 893–917 (2009)

Joubert, M.: Whole-body vibration exposures in a developing country: a pilot study in South Africa amongst forklift drivers at the port of Durban (2002)

Mayton, A.G., Kittusamy, N.K., Ambrose, D.H., et al.: Jarring/jolting exposure and musculoskeletal symptoms among farm equipment operators. Int. J. Ind. Ergon. **38**, 758–766 (2008)

Schwarze, S., Notbohm, G., Dupuis, H., Härtung, E.: Dose-response relationships between whole-body vibration and lumbar disk disease - a field study on 388 drivers of different vehicles. J. Sound Vib. **215**(4), 613–628 (1998). https://doi.org/10.1006/jsvi.1998.1602

Viruet, H.B., Genaidy, A., Shell, R., Salem, S., Karwowski, W.: Effect of forklift operation on lower back pain: An evidence-based approach. Hum Factors Ergon. Manuf. **18**(2), 125–151 (2008). https://doi.org/10.1002/hfm.20105

Waters, T., Genaidy, A., Viruet, H.B., Makola, M.: The impact of operating heavy equipment vehicles on lower back disorders. Ergonomics **51**(5), 602–636 (2008). https://doi.org/10.1080/00140130701779197

Wegscheider, P.: Development and Assessment of a Virtual Reality Forklift Simulator as a Research Tool to Study Whole-Body Vibration. Electronic Thesis and Dissertation Repository. http://ir.lib.uwo.ca/etd/2405

Ergonomic Assessment of Exposure to Musculoskeletal Disorders Risk Factors Among Canadian Truck Drivers

Firdaous Sekkay[1(✉)], Daniel Imbeau[1], Yuvin Chinniah[1], Philippe-Antoine Dubé[1], Nathalie de Marcellis-Warin[1], Nancy Beauregard[2], and Martin Trépanier[1]

[1] Department of Mathematics and Industrial Engineering,
Polytechnique Montreal, Montreal, Canada
firdaous.sekkay@polymtl.ca
[2] School of Industrial Relations, University of Montreal, Montreal, Canada

Abstract. The transport trucking industry is an important industrial sector that contributes greatly to the Canadian economy. Nevertheless, it is an industry that faces important challenges in terms of occupational health and safety (OHS). This paper summarizes a set of studies that documented the prevalence of self-reported musculoskeletal (MS) pain, self-reported MSD risk factors, and work-related physical demands among truck drivers working for the same company specializing in industrial gas production and delivery in Canada. Multiple data sources (i.e., video-based observations, direct measurements, and self-reports) were used in this study. Among all drivers, the overall prevalence of MS pain in at least one body area investigated for the past 12-month period was 43.1%. Prevalence of MS pain was higher among Bulk drivers than in P&D drivers. MS pain in Bulk drivers was mainly associated with psychosocial risk factors and lifestyle whereas MS pain in P&D drivers was mainly associated with physical risk factors. Bulk drivers' work was characterized by long working days ranging from 9.9 to 15.1 h (mean = 11.4 h), with half (49%) of the total working time spent behind the wheel. The average work metabolism of P&D drivers and Bulk drivers during the delivery tasks correspond to the upper bound of the "Moderate" work rate range. The results of this study bring a more differentiated picture of the prevalence of MS pain, exposures to MSD risk factors and work demands in these two groups of drivers.

Keywords: Musculoskeletal pain · Risk factors · Professional truck drivers · Risk assessment

1 Introduction

Truck drivers are a high-risk group for musculoskeletal disorders (MSD) to the low back (Bovenzi et al. 2006; Goon et al. 2010), shoulders, neck and knee joints (Robb and Mansfield 2007). The driving part of their work exposes them to static postures and whole-body vibration (Bovenzi et al. 2006), whereas the non-driving tasks (Robb and

© The Author(s), under exclusive license to Springer Nature Switzerland AG 2021
N. L. Black et al. (Eds.): IEA 2021, LNNS 222, pp. 829–836, 2021.
https://doi.org/10.1007/978-3-030-74611-7_113

Mansfield 2007; Reiman et al. 2014) often expose them to strenuous physical work such as manual materials handling (MMH). Exposures to MSD risk factors can be expected to vary between short-haul and long-haul truck drivers since for the former, the workday is often characterized by short task cycles composed of driving, MMH, and working in numerous and varied customer environments, while for long haul truck drivers the daily work is often characterized by much longer hours of driving to and from one or just a few clients. In other words, with longer distances the amount of time spent driving increases, while the proportion of time spent loading and unloading decreases (van der Beek et al. 2005). Exposure to MSD risk factors has been assessed for short-haul truck drivers (Okunribido et al. 2006; Chih-Long Lin and Chen 2010), and long-haul truck drivers as well (Kim et al. 2016; Awang Lukman et al. 2017). Studies suggest that truck drivers should not be considered as a homogeneous group in term of exposures to MSD risk factors, however, it is still unclear to what extent the work demands, and consequently the exposures, are different between both groups.

This paper summarizes a set of studies that documented the prevalence of self-reported musculoskeletal (MS) pain, self-reported MSD risk factors, and work-related physical demands through field observations among two groups of Canadian truck drivers (short- and long-haul) all employed by a same multinational company specializing in industrial gas production and delivery.

2   Methodology

The research began with a questionnaire survey, which was then followed by field observations and direct measurements to assess the physical work demands and MSD risk factors, in the work of both groups of truck drivers.

2.1   Questionnaire Survey

The questionnaire was adapted from the EQCOTESST (Vézina et al. 2011) and was administered anonymously between May and October 2016 at company locations in 6 Canadian provinces (Quebec, Ontario, Alberta, New Brunswick, British Columbia, Nova Scotia). The questionnaire documented the prevalence of musculoskeletal pain (MS) in drivers and investigated associations with self-reported exposures to MSD-related physical (e.g., postures, application of forces, manual handling…) and psychosocial (e.g., level of decisional latitude in the work, social support of superiors and colleagues) risk factors. The reader is referred to Sekkay et al. (2018) for more details on the questionnaire survey.

All 249 delivery truck drivers from the company had been targeted across Canada for the survey. The inclusion criterion was to be employed as a full-time truck driver by the company for the twelve months prior to the study. The truck drivers were either Pick up & Delivery (P&D) drivers responsible for picking-up and delivering gas cylinders of different sizes, or Bulk delivery drivers responsible for delivering gas from large tanker trucks. P&D work involves MMH of empty or full gas cylinders, short driving distances, and many deliveries per day (Fig. 1a). On the other hand, Bulk delivery involves driving over long distances primarily, connecting/disconnecting hoses between the tanker and the client's reservoirs, and supervising the gas loading/unloading process (Fig. 1b). A total of 123 drivers from the 6 provinces across Canada, agreed to participate in the study by signing the informed consent form, and produced usable data (63 Bulk and 60 P&D) resulting in a response rate of 49%.

(a) (b)

Fig. 1. Truck used to transport gas cylinders (a) and gas in bulk (b)

The participants were between 27 and 71 years old and had been working for this company between 1 and 35 years (Table 1). Average age and Body Mass Index (BMI) were significantly higher for the Bulk driver group.

Table 1. Main characteristics of participants to the questionnaire survey

	Bulk N = 63	P&D N = 60
Age (years)*	52 ± 8.1 (35–71)	46 ± 9 (27–66)
Stature (m)	1.75 ± 0.11 (1.55–2.03)	1.76 ± 0.11 (1.54–2.10)
Weight (kg)	98.0 ± 16.6 (65.8–145)	92.0 ± 19.0 (63.5–163.3)
BMI (kg/m²)*	32.0 ± 6.1 (24.3–52.9)	29.8 ± 6.1 (17.8–45.3)

*The overall t-student test is statistically significant at the threshold p < 0.05

The prevalence of MS pain reported by the truck drivers for each body part was determined. Answers to MS pain questions were dichotomized into a No MS pain group (those who reported "never" having pain or "from time to time") and a MS pain group (those who reported having pain "often" or "all the time") for each body area, as in Vézina et al. (2011).

Univariate logistic regression analyses were first conducted to examine associations between each independent variable (work-related and individual factors) and MS pain.

Crude odds ratios (ORs) and 95% confidence intervals (CIs) were computed. Independent variables that were significant at $p < 0.05$ (Hosmer and Lemeshow 2000) were used next to conduct a multivariate logistic regression with dummy coding (Tabachnick and Fidell 2001).

2.2   Observational Field Study

Field observations involved 31 volunteer drivers: 12 Bulk drivers (for a total of 13 driver-days of data collection) and 19 P&D drivers. They were conducted over two time periods: between May and October 2016 (summer), and between February and March 2017 (winter) in two Canadian provinces (Quebec and Ontario).

The two driver groups were comparable in terms of age and BMI but mean aerobic fitness (or maximum work capacity - MWC) of Bulk drivers was significantly lower (34.1 mlO2/kg/min vs 38.3 mlO2/kg/min) (Table 2). Heart rate (HR) was recorded during a submaximal step-test and during the whole work shift (Polar RS800CX), together with video sequences, direct observations of the work activities, and measurement of force exertions on equipment during normal work. A research assistant accompanied each participant and made video recordings of his work, while noting the work tasks and the main events throughout the day. The reader is referred to Sekkay et al. (2020, 2021) for more details.

Table 2. Main characteristics of participants to field observations

	Bulk N = 12	P&D N = 19
Age (years)	48.9 ± 7.4 (37.0–62.0)	48.8 ± 4.8 (40.0–56.0)
Stature	1.82 ± 0.09 (1.69–1.90)	1.75 ± 0.05 (1.67–1.85)
Weight (kg)	98.3 ± 16.6 (72.6–124.3)	86.5 ± 17.1 (68.0–131.5)
BMI (kg/m^2)	29.7 ± 4.0 (24.8–37.2)	28.6 ± 5.6 (22.2–42.9)
MWC* (mlO$_2$/kg/min)	34.1 ± 6.4 (25.4–43.8)	38.3 ± 8.9 (28.0–56.3)

*The overall t-student test is statistically significant at the threshold $p < 0.05$.

Task Analysis: The video recordings were analyzed with the Video Event Analysis (VEA) software (Chappe Software). The results and statistics output by VEA were exported to Microsoft Excel for further analysis, where tasks were grouped into five categories: "Driving"; "Delivering to clients"; "Preparing loads at home terminals"; "Other tasks"; "Non-work-related tasks". For each category, total duration and percent of shift total work time (TWT) were calculated.

Physiological Data: For each driver, the task analysis and measured HR data were associated to enable calculation of average HR_{work} over the whole workday as well as for the different task categories. Relative heart rate (RHR) was also calculated as: $RHR = 100 \times (HR_{work} - HR_{rest}) \div (HR_{max} - HR_{rest})$ (Wu and Wang 2002; Chengalur et al. 2004). HR_{rest} corresponded to the 1st percentile of measured HR over the workday (Mairiaux and Malchaire 1990), and HRmax was estimated at 220 minus age in years (Åstrand and Rodahl 1977; Dubé et al. 2015). Maximum acceptable work time (MAWT) defined as the maximum amount of time which the worker could work without developing excessive fatigue was calculated from RHR using the model proposed by Wu and Wang (2002): MAWT (h) $= 26.12 \times e^{(-4.81 \times RHR)}$.

3   Results and Discussion

3.1   Prevalence and Risk Factors for MS Pain Over Past 12 Months

Table 3 summarizes the prevalence of MS pain according to the body area in each driver group. The overall prevalence of MS pain in at least one body area investigated for the past 12-month period was 43.1%. Among all drivers reporting MS pain in the past 12 months, low back was the area with the highest prevalence (21.1%), followed by shoulders (20.3%), and neck (14.6%). Prevalence was highest for the low back (33.3%) and the shoulders (28.6%) among Bulk drivers, whereas it was highest for the shoulders (11.7%) and in the forearms, wrist or hand (11.7%) among P&D drivers. Prevalence of MS pain in any body area (57.1% vs 28.3%) and in the neck (19.0% vs 10.0%) were twice as high among Bulk drivers than in P&D drivers.

Table 3. Prevalence of reported MS pain among truck drivers (Bulk and P&D) over the past 12-month period

	All drivers N = 123	Bulk N = 63	P&D N = 60
Neck	14.6%	19.0%*	10.0%*
Shoulders	20.3%	28.6%	11.7%
Upper back	6.5%	9.5%	3.3%
Arms	8.1%	9.5%	6.7%
Elbows	5.7%	4.8%	6.7%
Lower back	21.1%	33.3%	8.3%
Forearm, wrist or hand	12.2%	12.7%	11.7%
Hips or thighs	8.9%	12.7%	5.0%
Knees	7.3%	7.9%	6.7%
Legs, calves	3.3%	1.6%	5.0%
Ankles or feet	5.7%	4.8%	6.7%
Any MS pain	43.1%*	57.1%*	28.3%*

*The overall t-student test is statistically significant at the threshold $p < 0.05$.

Among Bulk drivers, "High effort-reward imbalance" was strongly associated with MS pain in any body area (OR = 6.47 p = 0.01), with shoulder pain (OR = 4.95 p = 0.016), and with low back pain (OR = 4.51 p = 0.02). In the P&D driver group, "Working with hands above shoulders" (OR = 6.58 p = 0.009) and "Whole-body vibration" (OR = 5.48 p = 0.018) were significant factors for MS pain in any body area. Hand-arm vibration was strongly associated with MS pain in the shoulders (OR = 7.27 p = 0.041) among P&D drivers.

Exposures to work-related risk factors were different between the driver groups of this study, which likely explains the different associations observed with MS pain outcomes (Hanowski et al. 2000, Olson et al. 2009). This study shows the importance of analysing these driver groups separately whenever possible, as pooling all subjects would have led to mistakenly suppose associations to apply to all drivers when in fact they were group specific, or would have been missed as Table 3 shows nicely for prevalence of reported MS pain (Messing et al. 2009).

3.2 Composition of a Workday

Table 4 provides an overview of the composition of the workday in terms of duration and proportion of the total work time (TWT) of main task categories. Observation results indicate that Bulk drivers worked longer hours than P&D drivers (mean daily working

Table 4. Duration mean, standard deviation (SD), range and % of total working time (TWT), of tasks, with number of deliveries per working day.

	Bulk N = 13	P&D N = 19
Total working time (min)	682 ± 91.5 (593–907)	479 ± 53 (347–585)
Number of deliveries per day	2 ± < 1 (1–4)	9 ± 3 (2–14)
Driving		
Duration (min)	333 ± 90 (153–482)	208 ± 56 (102–340)
%TWT	49% ± 10% (24–62%)	43% ± 10% (27–63%)
Delivering		
Duration (min)	132 ± 44 (88–222)	134 ± 43 (50–200)
%TWT	20% ± 8% (11–35%)	28% ± 9% (11–40%)
Other tasks		
Duration (min)	83 ± 34.1 (41–147)	72 ± 37 (27–153)
%TWT	12% ± 4% (7–21%)	15% ± 7% (5–30%)
Preparing loads		
Duration (min)	49 ± 40 (0–114)	39 ± 35 (0–101)
%TWT	7% ± 6% (0–19%)	8% ± 7% (0–23%)
Non-work-related task		
Duration (min)	72 ± 70 (4–197)	29 ± 23 (1–65)
%TWT	10% ± 8% (<1–26%)	6% ± 5% (<1–15%)

time of 682 min vs 479 min), which is coherent with the fact the Bulk drivers work overtime more frequently. The drivers drove during about half of their working time as other researchers have observed (Beek and Frings-Dresen 1995; Hedberg and Niemi 1986). On average, delivering gas represented 20% of the work time for Bulk drivers and 28% for P&D drivers.

3.3 Physical Work Demands

P&D drivers had a significantly higher mean work metabolism (WM) over the entire working day (7.3 vs 5.9 mlO_2/kg/min), and during the delivering task (10.4 vs 8.3 mlO_2/kg/min). According to Chengalur et al. (2014), the average WM of P&D drivers and Bulk drivers during the delivery tasks corresponded to the upper bound of the Moderate work rate range (>7.0–10.7 mlO_2/kg/min) for whole-body physical work.

The mean RHR of Bulk drivers over a full workday was 18.7%. According to Wu and Wang (2002) this translates to a 10.6 h maximum acceptable work time (MAWT), that is to be compared to an actual 11.4 h observed; Bulk drivers are thus exposed to an increased risk of excessive fatigue. For P&D drivers, this risk is absent since the MAWT at the observed mean 19% RHR, is longer than the observed mean 8 h workday.

3.4 Conclusion

In this study, we used multiple data sources (i.e., self-reports, field observation and direct measurements) to document prevalence of self-reported pain over the past 12 months and conduct an ergonomic assessment of work-related MSD risk factors and work demands among two different groups of Canadian truck drivers working for the same company. The results of this study bring a more differentiated picture of the prevalence of MS pain, exposures to MSD risk factors and work demands in these two groups of drivers.

Acknowledgments. This work was supported jointly by a research sponsorship from our industrial partner; Mitacs Accelerate program (IT06366); funds provided by the Mathematics and Industrial Engineering Department of Polytechnique Montreal and the Natural Sciences and Engineering Research Council of Canada (NSERC) (RGPIN-2017–05629).

References

Åstrand, P.O., Rodahl, K.: Textbook of Work Physiology, 2nd edn. McGraw-Hill, New York (1977)

Lukman, K.A., Jeffree, M.S., Rampal, K.G.: Lower back pain and its association with whole-body vibration and manual materials handling among commercial drivers in Sabah. Int. J. Occup. Saf Ergon. **25**(1), 8–16 (2019)

Bovenzi, M., Rui, F., Negro, C., D'Agostin, F., Angotzi, G., Bianchi, S., Bramanti, L., Festa, G., Gatti, S., Pinto, I., Rondina, L., Stacchin, N.: An epidemiological study of low back pain in professional drivers. J. Sound Vib. **298**(3), 514–539 (2006)

Chengalur, S.N., Rodgers, S.H., Bernard, T.E.: Kodak's Ergonomics Design for People at Work, 2nd edn. Wiley, Hoboken (2004)

Chih-Long Lin, Y.T.H., Chen, M.J.W.J.P.: The investigation of low back problems among home delivery drivers. Adv. Hum. Factors Ergon. Saf. Manuf. Serv. Ind. **384** (2010)

Dubé, P.A., Imbeau, D., Dubeau, D., Auger, I., Leone, M.: Prediction of work metabolism from heart rate measurements in forest work: some practical methodological issues. Ergonomics. **58**(12), 2040–2056 (2015)

Goon, M., Ghoshal, S., Chandrasekaran, B., Sharma B.C.: Prevalence of low back pain in long-distance truck drivers of mountainous terrain. In: Salvendry, G., Karwowski, W. (eds.) Advances in Occupational, Social, and Organizational Ergonomics, Chap. 55 pp. 516–522. CRC Press (2010)

Hedberg, G.E., Niemi, K.: Physical and muscular strain in Swedish tanker truck drivers. Ergonomics **29**(6), 817–826 (1986)

Hosmer, D.W., Lemeshow, S.: Applied Logistic Regression. Wiley, New York (2000)

Kim, J.H., Zigman, M., Aulck, L.S., Ibbotson, J.A., Dennerlein, J.T., Johnson, P.W.: Whole body vibration exposures and health status among professional truck drivers: a cross-sectional analysis. Ann. Occup. Hyg. **60**(8), 936–948 (2016)

Mairiaux, P., Malchaire, J.: Le travail en ambiance chaude: Principes, méthodes, mise en oeuvre. Masson, Paris (1990)

Meyer, J.P., Flenghi, D.: Détermination de la dépense énergétique de travail et des capacités cardiorespiratoires maximales à l'aide d'un exercice sous maximal sur step test. Documents pour le Médecin du Travail **64**(4), 245–251 (1995)

Reiman, A., Pekkala, J., Väyrynen, S., Putkonen, A., Forsman, M.: Participatory video-assisted evaluation of truck drivers' work outside cab: deliveries in two types of transport. Int. J. Occup. Saf. Ergon. **20**(3), 477–489 (2014)

Robb, M.J., Mansfield, N.J.: Self-reported musculoskeletal problems amongst professional truck drivers. Ergonomics **50**(6), 814–827 (2007)

Sekkay, F., Imbeau, D., Chinniah, Y., Dubé, P.A., de Marcellis-Warin, N., Beauregard, N., Tré-panier, M.: Risk factors associated with self-reported musculoskeletal pain among short and long distance industrial gas delivery truck drivers. Appl. Ergon. **72**, 69–87 (2018)

Sekkay, F., Imbeau, D., Dubé, P.A., Chinniah, Y., de Marcellis-Warin, N., Beauregard, N., Tré-panier, M.: Assessment of physical work demands of long-distance industrial gas delivery truck drivers. Appl. Ergon. **90**, 103224 (2021)

Sekkay, F., Imbeau, D., Dubé, P.A., Chinniah, Y., de Marcellis-Warin, N., Beauregard, N., Tré-panier, M.: Assessment of physical work demand of short distance industrial gas delivery truck drivers. Appl. Ergon. **89**, 103222 (2020)

Tabachnick, B.G., Fidell, L.S.: Using Multivariate Statistics. Pearson, Boston (2001)

Van der Beek, A.J., Mathiassen, S.E., Windhorst, J., Burdorf, A.: An evaluation of methods assessing the physical demands of manual lifting in scaffolding. Appl. Ergon. **36**(2), 213–222 (2005)

Vézina, M., Cloutier, E., Stock, S., Lippel, K., Fortin, É., Delisle, A., St-Vincent, M., Funes, A., Duguay, P., Vézina, S., Prud'homme, P.: Enquête québécoise sur des conditions de travail, d'emploi, et de santé et de sécurité du travail (EQCOTESST). Institut de recherche Robert-Sauvé en santé et sécurité du travail - Institut national de santé publique du Québec et Institut de la statistique du Québec, Québec (2011)

Wu, H.C., Wang, M.J.J.: Relationship between maximum acceptable work time and physical workload. Ergonomics **45**(4), 280–289 (2002)

Ergonomic Risk Assessment in Kerbside Waste Collection Through Dynamic REBA Protocol

Alessio Silvetti[1](✉), Lorenzo Fiori[1], Antonella Tatarelli[1], Alberto Ranavolo[1], Eleonora Spagnoli[2], and Francesco Draicchio[1]

[1] DIMEILA, INAIL Research Area, Monte Porzio Catone, Rome, Italy
{al.silvetti,lo.fiori,a.tatarelli,a.ranavolo,
f.draicchio}@inail.it
[2] Università Cattolica del Sacro Cuore, Colleferro, Rome, Italy

Abstract. Literature shows that biomechanical risk in kerbside waste collection is high and widespread. The different work environments and working conditions make hard to use standardized protocols. Moreover, the lifting index limitations and restrictions (handling overhead, temperature and humidity) do not allow the use of the NIOSH protocol in this kind of activity. Manual handling of bins was investigated in four different operating modes: through 1) a lorry side window; 2) at the back of the lorry; 3) in a certified container; 4) in a non-certified container. Dynamic REBA was applied for risk assessment. The most dangerous one is mode 2 where the mean REBA scores were 9.8 for the right upper limb and 8.5 for the left upper limb. The posture above shoulder height adopted by the upper limbs contributed to reach these values. The emptying technique that presented the lowest risk level was mode 3. With this technique, the mean REBA scores were 8.8 for the right upper limb and 6.7 for the left upper limb. However, the reduced capacity of the certified container resulted in a significant time increase in the collection round. It would be useful to design larger containers to be mechanically poured so optimizing collection times and reduce biomechanical risk. Synergic effects with other risk factors (vibrations, weather conditions, etc.) are not assessed in this paper.

Keywords: Ergonomic · MSDs · Muscle fatigue · Biomechanical load

1 Introduction

Italian INAIL data [1] shows that work-related musculoskeletal disorders (MSDs) are constantly increasing. They account for two-thirds of all claims of occupational disease reported to the Institute in 2019 (66,51%).

Scientific literature from different countries highlights that kerbside waste collection presents high level of biomechanical load related to several body joints: Brazil [2], Denmark [3], Taiwan [4], Netherlands [5, 6], United States [7], Iran [8], Great Britain [9, 10], Turkey [11], Italy [12].

Markslag et al. [6] examined the metabolic cost in kerbside waste collection workers. Their results show a high level of energy expenditure when throwing 7 kg bags.

N. L. Black et al. (Eds.): IEA 2021, LNNS 222, pp. 837–844, 2021.
https://doi.org/10.1007/978-3-030-74611-7_114

Pinder [9] investigated biomechanical overload in waste sorting workers through metabolic cost and compressive forces. He found high levels of biomechanical load. For the reduction of the biomechanical load, Pinder suggests to perform waste collection using wheelie bins instead of sacks or boxes.

In 2002, An [7] conducted an epidemiological study in Florida in which he identified three main categories of health risks for workers employed in waste collection: respiratory injuries, dermal injuries and strains in the back. He found that Monday was the most common day for injuries. This is probably dues to increased waste accumulation during the weekend resulting in a higher workload.

In 2012 do Nascimento [13] conducted a study in Brazil to evaluate postures and to identify risk factors for an early detection of symptoms associated with MSDs in waste collection workers. This study showed that, according to 88.6% of the 44 workers interviewed, the work was monotonous and repetitive. Another finding of the study was the lack of workers training on the risks.

In Italy [12] it was found that considering the working hours, breaks and time spent driving, the time of performing manual material handling activities was about 260 min in a day. The authors did a risk assessment of kerbside using the NIOSH protocol [14] that, although its limitations, (particularly environmental limitations), would not allow its use. The lifting indexes at the origin fell largely in the green-yellow risk zone (23 out of 28–82%) and only 5 in the red one. The lifting indexes at the destination were all in the red-violet risk zone. The study was conducted in urban areas characterized by high population density. The authors suggested a waste collection schedule in which the workforce alternatively operates in the different municipal zones.

In an epidemiological study from Iran [8], it was found that workers were exposed to high levels of risk of biomechanical overload while carrying bags and bins. The research also revealed that 92.5% of workers reported MSDs in at least one body area in the last 12 months. Lower back and knee injuries were more prevalent and more severe. Another relevant issue, in 39% of workers, was the work-related stress due to time pressure to complete the collection round. Time pressure was also identified as a risk factor in a previous study conducted in Brazil [15].

The biomechanical risk of kerbside waste collection workers was explored also by Oxley [10]. Oxley found an excessive depth of bins used for collecting. Oxley also proposed a lifting weight threshold of 11.38 kg, with a frequency of twice per minute during the eight working hours. This threshold would be protective for 90% of the male and 20% of the female working population. Oxley, moreover, applied REBA protocol in the task of emptying bins inside the lorry [16]. He showed high levels of risk, due to the posture of the arms that mostly of the time over the shoulder.

Finally, a survey from South Korea [17] showed as municipal solid workers suffer of MSDs. Workers involved in the waste collection are among those with the highest number of claims to the Korean Workers' Compensation Institute.

Aim of this study is a biomechanical risk assessment of kerbside waste collection workers in the task of bins emptying in the lorry. The task could be performed in four different technique. The most overloading technique was identified and suggestions for risk reduction were provided. The analysis that is carried out differs from those of the cited studies for the use of dynamic REBA [18], for the morphology of the land in which the collection is performed, the vehicles used and the timetable.

2   Material and Methods

The task studied was the emptying of the bin in the lorry. The bin weight was 10 kg; it was lower than the 11.38 kg recommended by Oaxley [10]. The task was investigated in the four (Fig. 1, 2, 3 and 4) technique usually adopted from the workers:

1) emptying in the lorry by a side window (WIN), height 135 cm;
2) emptying in the lorry from the back (POST), height 200 cm;
3) Emptying in a certified container to be mechanically unloaded in the lorry (HOM), height 90 cm;
4) emptying in a non-certified container to be mechanically unloaded in the lorry (NHOM), height 110 cm.

The lorry used in the simulation was the standard one (Iveco Daily).

Figure 5 shows the worker starting the lifting. All techniques had the same movement.

Video recordings of the workers were made during the task simulations. From video recordings, frames were sampled and studied by KINOVEA software (https://www.kinovea.org/). The software allows to measure the joints angles requested in REBA protocol [16]. Dynamic REBA [18] was then computed as the mean value of the 6 frames sampled for each handling technique.

Fig. 1. WIN technique

Fig. 2. POST technique

Fig. 3. HOM technique

Fig. 4. NHOM technique

Fig. 5. Lifting start

3   Results

For the four different operating modes Tables 1, 2, 3 and 4 show REBA show Right upper limb and left upper limb results of each frame and relative mean REBA score.

3.1   Handling Directly into the Lorry by a Side Window (WIN)

Table 1 shows REBA scores of each of the 6 analyzed frames. The frame with the highest REBA score was frame 2. The highest score was 11 on the right side and 9 on the left side, both corresponding to a very high risk level. Handled load, trunk and neck torsion/bending and right shoulder flexion/abduction contributed to reach these scores.

The mean REBA scores were 9.3 for the right upper limb and 8.2 for the left upper limb, both corresponding to a high-risk level.

Table 1. REBA score for each of the six examined frame and mean REBA score with the WIN technique.

	Right	Left
Frame 1	9	7
Frame 2	11	9
Frame 3	9	6
Frame 4	9	9
Frame 5	9	9
Frame 6	9	9
Mean	**9.3**	**8.2**

3.2   Handling Directly into the Lorry from the Backside (POST)

Table 2 shows REBA protocol scores for each of the 6 analyzed frames. The highest REBA score was 11 (corresponding to a very high-level risk) and was obtained for the right side in frame 2. The frames with the highest overall score (right and left) were respectively 5 and 6. Both upper limbs in these two frames showed a REBA score of 10 corresponding to a high risk level. The handled load and the elevation of both shoulders over the head level contributed to those scores. The mean REBA scores were 9.8 for the right upper limb and 8.5 for the left upper limb both corresponding to a high risk level.

Table 2. REBA score for each of the six examined frame and mean REBA score with the POST technique.

	Right	Left
Frame 1	9	7
Frame 2	11	8
Frame 3	10	8
Frame 4	9	8
Frame 5	10	10
Frame 6	10	10
Mean	**9.8**	**8.5**

3.3 Handling into a Certified Container to Be Mechanically Unloaded in the Lorry (HOM)

Table 3 shows REBA protocol scores for each of the 6 analyzed frames. The frame 2 had the highest REBA scores. The scores were 11 for the right upper limb, and 9 for the left upper limb, both corresponding to a high risk level. Handled load, trunk and neck torsion/lateral bending and right shoulder flexion/abduction contributed to reaching these scores. The mean REBA scores were 8.8 for the right upper limb corresponding to a high risk level and 6.7 for the left upper limb corresponding to an average risk level.

Table 3. REBA score for each of the six examined frame and mean REBA score with the HOM technique.

	Right	Left
Frame 1	6	4
Frame 2	11	9
Frame 3	9	5
Frame 4	9	7
Frame 5	9	7
Frame 6	9	8
Mean	**8.8**	**6.7**

3.4 Handling into a Non-certified Container to Be Routinely Unloaded in the Lorry (NHOM)

Table 4 shows REBA protocol scores for each of the 6 analyzed frames. The frame with the highest REBA score of right upper limb was frame 3 (score 11, very high risk level). The frame with the highest REBA score for left upper limb was frame 6 (score 9, high risk level). Trunk and neck torsion/lateral bending and right shoulder flexion/abduction contributed to reaching these risk levels. The mean REBA scores were 9 for the right upper limb and 7.8 for the left upper limb both corresponding to a high risk level.

Table 4. REBA score for each of the six examined frame and mean REBA score with the NHOM technique.

	Right	Left
Frame 1	8	8
Frame 2	9	7
Frame 3	11	8
Frame 4	9	7
Frame 5	9	8
Frame 6	8	9
Mean	**9.0**	**7.8**

4 Discussion

Scientific literature showed that in kerbside waste collection the risk of biomechanical load is high and widespread.

The various work environments and operating modes make difficult to use standardized tools such as NIOSH protocol for these reasons we used the dynamic REBA protocol [18]. Our results agree with those of Oxley who used standard REBA tool [16].

The most hazardous mode, among those investigated, was the one in which the worker handled the bin directly into the lorry from the backside (POST). This handling technique showed mean REBA scores of 9.8 for the right upper limb and 8.5 for the left one, both corresponding to a high risk level. The elevation of both upper limbs overhead played a significant role in determining these values. The handling in the side window (WIN) showed mean REBA scores of 9.3 for right upper limb and 8.2 for left upper limb which correspond to high risk levels. In this handling technique, the risk was related to flexion and abduction of the right shoulder as well as trunk asymmetry which was in torsion and laterally bended. The HOM handling technique had the lowest risk level. Anyway, HOM mean REBA scores fell into high risk level for right upper limb (mean REBA score 8.8) and into medium risk for left upper limb (mean REBA score 6.7).

To reduce the biomechanical risk in kerbside waste collection, it would be desirable to redesign the lorry in such a way that workers do not have to rise the arms up to the limit of postural ranges and can reduce trunk flexion-extension.

Our data shows that the POST handling technique is the one at highest risk. The least demanding technique is the HOM one, but anyway, this technique has criticalities related to trunk flexion. Moreover, HOM handling technique presents problems from an operational perspective. The limited storage capacity of the container would determine a remarkable time increase to complete the collection round. This has also been highlighted in two previous papers [8, 15].

It would be desirable to replace the certified container with a larger one, of a more durable material, which can be periodically mechanically emptied into the lorry so optimizing the collection time.

A multifactorial movement analysis, integrating inertial motion unit sensors and surface electromyography could be useful in future research for a more accurate risk assessment.

Acknowledgement. We would like to thank Rubes Triva foundation for promoting this study.

References

1. INAIL – Relazione Annuale 2019 del Presidente – Appendice statistica (2020). https://www.inail.it/cs/internet/docs/alg-appendice-statistica-relazione-annuale-anno-2019.pdf. Accessed 08 Jan 2020
2. Velloso, M.P., et al.: The labor process and workrelated accidents among garbage collectors in Rio de Janeiro. Brazil. Cad Saude Publica **13**, 693–700 (1997)
3. Ivens, U.I., Lassen, J.H., Kaltoft, B.S., et al.: Injuries among domestic waste collectors. Am. J. Ind. Med. **33**, 182–189 (1998)
4. Yang, C.H., Chang, W.T., Chuang, H.Y., et al.: Adverse health effects among household waste collectors in Taiwan. Environ. Res. **85**, 195–199 (2001)
5. Kuijer, P.P., Hoozemans, M.J., Kingma, I., et al.: Effect of a redesigned two-wheeled container for refuse collecting on mechanical loading of low back and shoulders. Ergonomics **46**, 543–560 (2003)
6. Markslag, A.M.T., Stassen, A., de Looze, M.P., Kemper, H.C.G., Frings-Dresen, M., Toussaint, H.M.: Biomechanische energetische belasting van huisvuilbeladers. Academisch Medisch Centrum, Amsterdam, pp. 1–40 (1993)
7. An, H., Englehardt, J., Fleming, L., et al.: Occupational health and safety amongst municipal solid waste workers in Florida. Waste Manag. Res. **17**, 369–377 (1999)
8. Ziaei, M., Choobineh, A., Abdoli-Eramaki, M., Ghaem, H.: Individual, physical, and organizational risk factors for musculoskeletal disorders among municipality solid waste collectors in Shiraz. Iran. Ind. Health **56**(4), 308–319 (2018)
9. Pinder, A.: Manual handling in refuse collection HSL/2002/21, pp. 1–5 (2002)
10. Oxley, L., Pinder, A., Cope, M.: Manual handling in kerbside collection and sorting of recyclables. HSL/2006/25 (2006)
11. Bulduk, E.: Work-related stress levels and musculoskeletal disorders among municipal solid waste collectors in Ankara. Work **63**(3), 427–433 (2019)
12. Battini, D., Persona, A., Sgarbossa, F.: Innovative real-time system to integrate ergonomic evaluations into warehouse design and management. Comput. Ind. Eng. **77**, 1–10 (2014)
13. do Nascimento, L.S., Pessoa, J.C.: Analysis of urban cleanness agents' workstation on the appearance of work related musculoskeletal disorders. Work **41**(Suppl 1), 2482–2486 (2012)

14. Waters T, Putz-Anderson V, Garg, A. (eds.): Applications Manual for the Revised Lifting Equation, (DHHS/NIOSH) Pub. No. 94-110. CDC, NIOSH, Cincinnati, Ohio (1994)
15. Camada, I.: Heavy physical work under time pressure: the garbage collection service- a case study. Work **41**(Suppl 1), 462–469 (2012)
16. Hignett, S., McAtamney, L.: Rapid entire body assessment (REBA). Appl. Ergon. **31**, 201–205 (2000)
17. Choi, H.W.: Characteristics of occupational musculoskeletal disorders of five sectors in service industry between 2004 and 2013. Ann. Occup. Environ. Med. **29**, 41 (2017)
18. Jones, A., Hignett, S.: Safe access/egress systems for emergency ambulances. Emerg. Med. J. **24**, 200–205 (2007)

Ergonomic Evaluation of Home Workspaces During the Coronavirus Pandemic

Samuelle St-Onge and Nancy L. Black$^{(\boxtimes)}$ (iD)

Mechanical Engineering, Université de Moncton, Moncton, NB E1A3E9, Canada
nancy.black@umoncton.ca

Abstract. This study describes a methodology used to measure the working conditions experienced by people who normally work in an office, but who have worked from their home because of the Covid-19 pandemic. An online survey and two photographs showing the participant in their principal work location were used. Photo instructions supplied requested a sagittal view and a second perpendicular view of the participant in their usual working posture to allow full analysis applying the Rapid Office Strain Assessment using Kinovea software. Despite the ease of an on-line questionnaire, subsequent reception of photos has been problematic, and recruitment efforts via emails have had limited success. While the current participant population is limited (15), the methodology has been proved operational. This methodology can include participants from various employers to provide a general understanding of how working at home conditions compare with those previously experienced in-office. Photos are not always sent with the questionnaire which precludes ROSA use, but allows other complementary analyses.

Keywords: Work from home · Covid-19 · Posture

1 Introduction

1.1 Problem Statement

With the current coronavirus pandemic, working from home is more common than ever, particularly for people working principally with computers. As of June 2020, people able to engage in "Telework" saw only one-third the reduction in employment relative to those unable to telework in the first months of the Covid-19 pandemic [1]. While adapting to this new lifestyle, it is essential to find ways to create an ergonomic workspace at home in order to reduce the risk of injuries and musculoskeletal disorders particularly associated with poor posture at work [2]. The first step is understanding home-based working conditions.

1.2 Objective

This communication describes a method assessing physical workspaces and postures of employees who are currently working from home due to the coronavirus, identifying

© The Author(s), under exclusive license to Springer Nature Switzerland AG 2021
N. L. Black et al. (Eds.): IEA 2021, LNNS 222, pp. 845–851, 2021.
https://doi.org/10.1007/978-3-030-74611-7_115

and quantifying physical risks of musculoskeletal injuries and diseases associated with the participants' home workspaces based on published tools. The study is similar to research performed among faculty and staff members of the University of Cincinnati to evaluate their current workspaces at home [3] but considers a more diverse population. Initial results are presented.

2 Methodology

Data collection is divided into two main components: a survey evaluation and a photo analysis. Together these collect data to apply the Rapid Office Strain Assessment (ROSA) [4] to evaluate the participants' workspaces at home.

The survey questions related to home-based working modalities (Table 1), inspired by the research of the Occupational Health Clinics for Ontario Worker [5]. The survey used images and text to identify the most common postures used, referring to ROSA categories (Table 2), and overall posture (Fig. 1) inspired by the Canadian Centre of Occupational Safety and Health [6]. In the final section of the survey, participants recorded their age, gender, and height.

Table 1. Variables measured by survey including responses and references.

Question (source)	Measure	Responses possible
How long working from home? [5]	Ordinal scale	# months { <1, 1, 2, 3, ≥ 4}
How different is home office from work office? [5]	Likert-type scale	{1 (no different), 2, 3, ..., 9, 10 (completely different)}
Location of home workspace [5]	Choose one	{Bedroom, Kitchen, Living room, Spare room, Other}
Daily hours spent on computer work [4]	Ordinal classification	1: < 0.5 consecutive hours OR < 1 h total 2: 0.5 to < 1 consecutive hour OR 1-4 h total 3: > 1 consecutive hour OR > 4 h total
Number of daily hours spent seated [4]	Ordinal classification	1: < 30 consecutive minutes OR < 1 h total 2: 0.5 to < 1 consecutive hour OR 1-4 h total 3: > 1 consecutive hour OR > 4 h total
Impact of working from home on perceived productivity [5]	Yes/No + Checklist	If 'Yes' Selection of one or more probable elements resulting in 'more productive' and 'less productive'
Type of chair used [5]	Choose one	{Adjustable, Non-adjustable, Kitchen chair/stool, Foldable, Bed, Couch, Other}
Adjustable chair components [4]	Choose all applicable	{height, depth, armrests, lumbar support, back tilt, seat tilt}
Phone located within arm's reach? [4]	Choose one	Yes/No

(continued)

Table 1. (*continued*)

Question (source)	Measure	Responses possible
Device used most often for phone calls [4]	Choose one	{Headset, Phone held in one hand, Phone held between neck and shoulder, Phone on speaker mode, Other}
Number of daily hours spent on phone calls [4]	Ordinal classification	1: < 30 consecutive minutes OR < 1 h total 2: 0.5 to < 1 consecutive hour OR 1-4 h total 3: > 1 consecutive hour OR > 4 h total
Intensity of typical pain/fatigue by body region after a day of working at home [5]	Likert-type scale	{1 (none), 2, 3, …, 9, 10 (maximum)} for each of overall, neck, upper back, lower back, shoulders, hands, eyes

The subsequent photo analysis used two photos per participant: one in the sagittal plane and the other perpendicular to the first. These photos captured the participant's posture as well as their most commonly-used home workstation. Instructions described how to take the photo in the sagittal plane to capture the angles of the knees, hips, ankles, trunk, elbow, arm (on the side of the camera) and neck, as well as the visual angle between participants' eyes and their computer screen. Postural measurements used Kinovea software (Version 0.8.15) to quantify values required for ROSA scoring (Fig. 2). The second photo, taken from overhead, from behind or in front above the computer screen, captured elements not visible in the first image and allowed qualitative assessment of participants' office equipment (type of screen used, keyboard, location of equipment on the work surface, etc.).

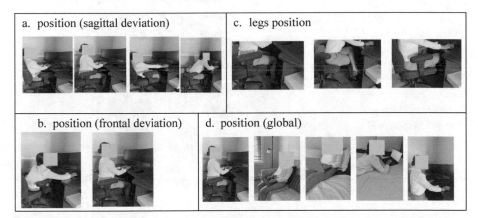

Fig. 1. Postural categories by plane (a, b) and body region (c, d) in Survey with photographic supports supplied (percentage time in each posture selected in 10% increments) inspired by the CCOHS [6]

To add value to participation, at the end of the survey, electronic links were provided to reliable resources suggesting methods to inexpensively improve the physical workspace at home.

Table 2. Survey images to classify posture measurements for ROSA [4].

Question	Measurement	Responses possible		
Position of arms on arm-rests in most frequent working posture	Classification			OR chair does not have armrests
Arm position while using an external computer mouse in most frequent working posture	Choose one			
Position of hand while using an external computer mouse in most frequent working posture	Choose one			
Mouse and keyboard located on same work surface	Yes/No			
Position of hands while using keyboard in most frequent working posture (top view)	Choose one			
Position of hands while using keyboard in most frequent working posture (side view)	Choose one			
Position of shoulders while using keyboard in most frequent working posture	Choose one			
Position of shoulders on work surface in most frequent working posture	Choose one			
Position of principal computer screen or monitor in most frequent working posture	Choose one			

This structure describes posture in light of workstation elements (chair style) and location, perceived productivity, relevant demographics, localized discomfort, and ROSA scoring.

Participants were recruited through electronic communications via workplaces and word of mouth through the research team's network (in the local area and beyond).

Fig. 2. Sagittal view analysis using Kinovea software with reference angles for elbow visible.

3   Results

This research received ethical approval and data collection began in October 2020. As of December 2020, fifteen participants completed the survey and twelve of these provided photos. Participants' age varied between 30 and 59 years and half of the participants were female.

Survey responses showed all participants have been working from home for 3 months or more and were not working from home on a regular basis prior to the coronavirus pandemic. All respondents spent at least one consecutive hour or more than four hours in total on the computer per workday. Most respondents (93.33%) used an adjustable office chair; one used a non-adjustable office chair. 60% of participants responded that working from home impacted their productivity; of these, 22.22% noted both positive and negative impacts and one only positive impacts. Most participants' (86.67%) required phone calls. Similarly, 80% used an external mouse. 46.67% worked from a spare room, 20% in their bedroom, 13.33% in the basement and the remaining responded 'other'. 26.67% of respondents noted feeling more pain when working from home compared to working at the office.

Photos complemented the survey for 12 participants, providing additional information for the ROSA score calculation. Sagittal views were particularly useful as illustrated in Fig. 2. Photos showed that 66.67% have hips flexed over 90 degrees due to the knees being positioned too high. For 50% the seat is too long, providing less than 7.5 cm free behind the knee. The photos illustrated adequate lumbar support in 66.66% of participants, while 16.67% were angled too far back. The remaining participants were leaning forward, not using any back support. Most (83.33%) participants had their primary monitor at eye level, while the rest had neck extension caused by a monitor placed too high. Nearly half (41.67%) had their monitor at a distance within arm's reach and 33.33% had their monitor placed too far away, the rest not being visible. When looking at their principal monitor, 25% of participants had a neck rotation greater than 30 degrees. Two of the 12 (16.67%) had glare on their screen, caused by location of lamps or windows. One-quarter (25%) of participants were using documents without a document holder.

4 Discussion

This methodology includes exact and easily measured data. ROSA results are complemented by demographics and perception data providing a rich database structure. A previous publication found that five photographs were sufficient to describe ROSA parameters [8] but in this case we reduced that number to two to encourage participation, knowing that some information would be captured through the survey. We estimate 40 participants are required to move analysis beyond qualitative statistics. The preliminary results presented here show promise. The current methodology requires that participants provide their informed consent on an electronic form which then gives them access to the questionnaire and can be associated with the photos submitted. Drop out occurs between receiving the questionnaire and photos. A more integrated data collection would likely improve participation and data completeness (integrity).

This pilot group had worse posture than university employees studied by Davis et al. [3], which found 43% of 41 participants sat at the wrong height but better back support usage (69% of which 73% had improper lumbar support).

5 Conclusions

The methodology can easily be used at a distance relative to workers at minimal cost to quantify priorities for home offices as they are set up. With greater participation, future analyses will link discomfort with measured conditions.

Providing a cross-sectional sample of actual working conditions of a representative population when working at home will help focus employer and employee efforts to adapt to their unexpected home-office work environment.

Acknowledgement. Funding for this project was provided through a Mitacs Research Training Award (2020).

References

1. Dey, M., Frazis, H., Loewenstein, M.A., Sun, H.: Ability to work from home: evidence from two surveys and implications for the labor market in the COVID-19 pandemic. Mon Labor Rev US Bur Labor Stat [Internet]. USA; Jun [cited 7 Feb 2021] (2020). https://www.bls.gov/opub/mlr/2020/article/ability-to-work-from-home.htm
2. Marcus, M., Gerr, F., Monteilh, C., Ortiz, D.J., Gentry, E., Cohen, S., et al.: A prospective study of computer users: II. Postural risk factors for musculoskeletal symptoms and disorders. Am. J. Ind. Med. **41**, 236–49 (2002)
3. Davis, K.G., Kotowski, S.E., Daniel, D., Gerding, T., Naylor, J., Syck, M.: The Home Office: Ergonomic Lessons From the "New Normal." Ergon Des. SAGE Publications Inc; 1064804620937907 (2020)

4. Sonne, M., Villalta, D.L., Andrews, D.M.: Development and evaluation of an office ergonomic risk checklist: ROSA – rapid office strain assessment. Appl. Ergon. **43**, 98–108 (2012)
5. OHCOW. Ergonomic Tips for Temporary Home Workstations…3 Months Later [Internet]. [cited 8 Feb 2021]. https://www.ohcow.on.ca/news/ergonomic-tips-for-temporary-home-wor kstations3-months-later.html
6. Government of Canada CC for OH and S. Work-related Musculoskeletal Disorders (WMSDs) - Risk Factors : OSH Answers [Internet]. [cited 10 Feb 2021] (2021). https://www.ccohs.ca/
7. Occupational Safety and Health Administration – US Department of Labor, Computer Work-stations eTool, Workstation Components – Chairs – Armrest, [cited 20 Apr 2021]. https://www. osha.gov/SLTC/etools/computerworkstations/components_chair.html
8. Liebregts, J., Sonne, M., Potvin, J.R.: Photograph-based ergonomic evaluations using the rapid office strain assessment (ROSA). Appl. Ergon. **52**, 317–24 (2016)

Poultry Slaughterhouse Workers: Finger Temperatures and Cold Sensation in the Hands

Adriana Seara Tirloni[1](✉) ⓘ, Diogo Cunha dos Reis[2] ⓘ,
and Antônio Renato Pereira Moro[1,2] ⓘ

[1] Technological Center, Federal University of Santa Catarina,
Florianópolis, SC, Brazil
adri@tilroni.com.br
[2] Biomechanics Laboratory, CDS, Federal University of Santa Catarina,
Florianópolis, SC, Brazil

Abstract. Many employees work in Brazilian slaughterhouses and are exposed to several ergonomic risks; one of them is cold temperatures. This cross-sectional study aimed to analyze the finger temperatures of poultry slaughterhouse workers, and its associations with sociodemographic, work and cold sensory variables. The research included 142 workers from two poultry slaughterhouses that operated in a cold environment (10–12 °C). The data were obtained through interviews and thermographic images (palm and dorsum of the hands). For this, a Flir® T450SC infrared camera and the Flir® Tools software were utilized. Binary logistic regression models were employed to assess the association between finger temperatures ($\leq$15 °C) and the independent variables. Half of the workers wore three overlapping gloves, despite this, most workers presented at least one finger with a mean temperature $\leq$ 15 °C (76%), $\leq$ 24 °C (98%) and felt cold in their hands (75%). There was an association between the finger temperatures $\leq$ 15 °C and feeling cold in the hands, where most workers with fingers $\leq$ 15 °C experienced a cold sensation in the hands (84%). The binary logistic revealed that the chance of a slaughterhouse worker feeling cold in the hands as well as presenting finger temperatures $\leq$ 15 °C was three times greater than a worker who did not feel cold in their hands (OR = 3.54). Therefore, the health and safety team must monitor the workers' finger temperatures inserted in cold environments. In addition, efficient gloves for thermal protection should be developed and offered to these workers.

Keywords: Ergonomics · Slaughterhouse · Thermography · Skin temperature · Worker

1 Introduction

Many employees work in Brazilian poultry slaughterhouses, since Brazil was the world leader in exports in this sector in 2019, as cuts were the most commercialized products (67%) [1]. These workers are exposed to several ergonomic risks; one of them is cold temperatures [2].

© The Author(s), under exclusive license to Springer Nature Switzerland AG 2021
N. L. Black et al. (Eds.): IEA 2021, LNNS 222, pp. 852–859, 2021.
https://doi.org/10.1007/978-3-030-74611-7_116

Humans residing or working in cold environments exhibit a stronger cold-induced vasodilation (CIVD) reaction in the peripheral microvasculature than those living in warm regions of the world, leading to a general assumption that thermal responses to local cold exposure can be systematically improved by natural acclimatization or specific acclimation [3]. However, these authors carried out a systematic review about the trainability of CIVD, concluding that repeated local cold exposure does not alter circulatory dynamics in the peripheries, and that humans remain at risk of cold injuries even after extended stays in cold environments. Tirloni et al. [4] verified that most workers felt bodily discomfort (71.5%), besides, the cold perception was associated with bodily discomfort perception of poultry slaughterhouse workers.

According to the Technical Regulation of the Technological and Hygienic-Sanitary Inspection of Poultry Meat, the cutting rooms of Brazilian poultry slaughterhouses that perform cuts and/or chicken deboning must have their own exclusive air-conditioned room with an ambient temperature that does not exceed 12 °C [5].

Regulatory norm 36 (NR-36), regarding slaughterhouses, recommends that the Personal Protective Equipment (PPE) and clothing must be compatible with the temperature of the working environment, in order to promote thermal comfort [6]. Therefore, studies showed that poultry slaughterhouse workers felt cold in their hands (78% and 49%, respectively) and most workers had finger temperatures below 24 °C [7, 8], despite using PPE (gloves).

International Organization for Standardization (ISO 11079) titled "Ergonomics of the thermal environment" institutes that finger temperatures ≤ 24 °C cause low physiological strain and ≤ 15 °C is considered high physiological strain [9].

Although there is a study that evaluated the hand temperatures of poultry slaughterhouse workers before the implantation of NR-36 [7], this did not address how many workers were exposed to high thermal stress (≤ 15 °C), acceptable only in sporadic situations [10]. Only one research post NR-36 analyzed this variable and verified that most poultry slaughterhouse workers had at least one finger with a temperature ≤ 15 °C (66.4%) [8]. Additionally, it established that there were no associations between finger temperatures (≤ 15 °C) and personal and organizational variables, cold perception, and bodily discomfort in workers in adjusted models.

For that reason, further studies are required to map the effects of environmental conditions and the hand protection of workers in poultry slaughterhouses after the publication of NR-36. Therefore, the aim of this study was to analyze the finger temperatures of the poultry slaughterhouse workers, and its associations with sociodemographic, work and cold sensory variables.

2   Method

The Committee of Ethics in Research with Human Beings in Brazil, protocol n° 2098/2011, approved this research. The cross-sectional study included 142 workers from two Brazilian poultry slaughterhouses that operated in a cold environment (10–12 °C), with 108 women (34.0 ± 9.6 years) and 34 men (33.9 ± 9.6 years).

Data collections were performed approximately two years after the publication of NR-36. The data were obtained through employee interviews and the health and safety team of the slaughterhouses. In one slaughterhouse, there were 3,970 employees in which 350,000 chicken were slaughtered per day and in another, 1,252 employees slaughtered 91,000 chicken per day.

To participate in this study, the worker would have to perform the same activity at the workstation for at least 15 min prior to data collection. In addition, he/she would answer questions about sociodemographic (age), work (number of overlapping gloves and knife use) and cold sensory variables ("Do you feel cold in the hands?"). Other variables about cold were verified in the thermographic images (body side – dominant or non-dominant hand and surface of finger that had the lowest temperature – dorsal or palmar).

A Flir® T450SC infrared camera and the Flir® Tools software were utilized to record the two thermographic images (palm and dorsum of the hands) (Fig. 1). The ISO 11079 classification "Ergonomics of the thermal environment" was used to determine the finger temperature limit that causes cold stress [9], $\leq 15\ °C$ or $\leq 24\ °C$.

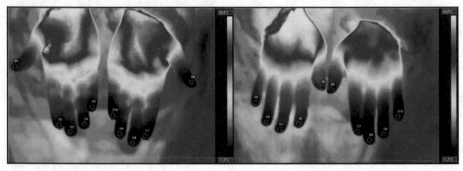

Fig. 1. Identification of the coldest areas of each finger in the thermographic images of the palmar and dorsal surfaces of the hands.

Two groups were analyzed; one used a knife and the other did not. In the group that used a knife, the non-dominant hand manipulated the products and the dominant hand held the knife. The difference between the non-dominant and dominant hand temperatures was calculated and the criteria adopted for acceptable limits of thermal asymmetry between both hands was $< 1\ °C$, as proposed by Hong et al. [11].

Binary logistic regression models were employed to assess the association between finger temperatures ($\leq 15\ °C$) and the independent variables: sociodemographic (age, gender), work conditions (use of tool, number of overlapping gloves) and the cold sensory variables (feeling cold in the hands, the fingers' coldest side - non-dominant or dominant and the surface - palmar or dorsal). When the number of gloves was analyzed, the largest number of overlapping gloves that the worker wore, regardless of the hand, was considered. The binary logistic regression between feeling cold in the hands and knife use were carried out. The odds ratio and confidence intervals for finger temperatures were estimated for crude and adjusted analyses. To compare the temperature values between the fingers of both hands, the paired Student test was applied and $p \leq 0.05$ was adopted.

3   Results

Half of the workers wore three overlapping gloves, despite this, most workers presented at least one finger with a mean temperature $\leq 15\,°C$ (76%), $\leq 24\,°C$ (98%) and felt cold in their hands (75%). There was an association between the finger temperatures $\leq 15\,°C$ and feeling cold in the hands (p $= 0.008$), in which most of the workers who showed fingers with these temperatures ($\leq 15\,°C$) experienced a cold sensation in the hands (84%) (Table 1). Results showed that the chance of a poultry slaughterhouse worker feeling cold in the hands as well as presenting finger temperatures $\leq 15\,°C$ was three times greater than a worker who did not feel cold in their hands (OR $= 3.54$, 95% CI 1.38;9.06) (Table 1).

Table 1. Frequency and percent of the variables in relation to hand temperature and crude and adjusted associations between finger temperature and personal and organizational variables, as well as thermal sensation of cold and bodily discomfort.

	Finger temperature ($\leq 15\,°C$)			Crude		Adjusted[#]	
	No n (%)	Yes n (%)	Total n (%)	OR (95%CI)	p-value	OR (95%CI)	p-value
Age (mean ± SD)	34.9 ± 11.8	33.7 ± 8.8	34.0 ± 9.6	0.99 (0.95; 1.03)	0.516		-
Gender					0.028[*]		0.643
Female	21 (19)	87 (81)	108 (76)	2.57 (1.11; 5.94)		1.27 (0.47; 3.46)	
Male	13 (38)	21 (62)	34 (24)	1		1	
Number of overlapping gloves					0.034[*]		0.136
1	12 (35)	22 (65)	34 (24)	1		1	
2	19 (27)	52 (73)	71 (50)	1.49 (0.62; 3.59)		1.16 (0.45; 3.02)	
≥ 3[†]	3 (8)	34 (92)	37 (26)	6.18 (1.56; 24.43)		4.04 (0.96; 16.99)	
Knife use					0.668		-
No	20 (25)	59 (75)	79 (56)	1.19 (0.54; 2.59)			
Yes	14 (22)	49 (78)	63 (44)	1			
Felt cold in the hands					< 0.001[*]		0.008[*]
No	17 (47)	19 (53)	36 (25)	1		1	
Yes	17 (16)	89 (84)	106 (75)	4.68 (2.03; 10.8)		3.54 (1.38; 9.06)	
Hand that had the lowest finger temperature					0.528		-
Dominant	14 (27)	38 (73)	52 (37)	0.78 (0.35; 1.71)			
Non-dominant	20 (22)	70 (78)	90 (63)	1			

(*continued*)

Table 1. (*continued*)

	Finger temperature ($\leq 15\ °C$)			Crude		Adjusted[#]	
	No n (%)	Yes n (%)	Total n (%)	OR (95%CI)	p-value	OR (95%CI)	p-value
Finger surface that had the lowest temperature					0.561		-
Palmar	16 (22)	57 (53)	73 (51)	1.26 (0.58; 2.72)			
Dorsal	18 (26)	51 (74)	69 (49)	1			
Total	34 (24)	108 (76)	142 (100)				

[#] Adjusted for age, length of time working at the company, work shifts, tool use and perception of cold hands. * Factors were removed from the logistic model (p > 0.20); ** $p \leq 0.05$; [†] Only one worker wore four overlapping gloves and one used five.

The percentage of workers with hands $\leq 15\ °C$ was similar among those who used a knife (78%) along with those who did not (75%) (p = 0.668) (Table 1). However, for a worker who used a knife, the chance of feeling cold in the hands was greater than a worker who did not use a knife (OR = 0.32, 95% CI 0.14;0.75).

It was observed that there was only a temperature difference between the thumbs of both surfaces for workers who did not use a knife (p < 0.05), and the thumb of the dominant hand was the coldest (Table 2). Conversely, there was a significant difference between the average finger temperatures of the non-dominant and dominant sides, in all fingers and surfaces (p < 0.001) for the group that used a knife (coldest non-dominant hand fingers) (p < 0.001) (Table 2).

Table 2. Comparison between workers' finger temperatures and knife use.

	Without tool									
	Minimum		Maximum		Mean			ΔT		
Palmar surface	D	ND	D	ND	D	ND	p	Mean	SD	% $\Delta T >$ 1 °C[†]
Thumb	8.3	9.6	27.3	27.9	16.7	17.0	0.028*	1.4	1.2	49
Index	8.0	8.2	27.0	28.5	15.5	15.6	0.648	1.4	1.5	46
Middle	7.8	7.5	27.2	26.9	15.2	15.2	0.839	1.1	1.1	35
Ring	8.2	7.4	27.9	29.5	15.6	15.8	0.282	1.1	1.2	37
Little	7.7	8.6	30.3	30.3	16.4	16.3	0.566	1.3	1.6	42
Dorsal surface										
Thumb	9.2	10.3	27.6	27.8	16.3	16.7	0.021*	1.2	1.4	33
Index	8.7	8.1	26.2	27.7	15.6	15.7	0.561	1.3	1.5	41
Middle	7.6	7.0	26.3	27.7	15.3	15.3	0.994	1.1	1.2	35
Ring	8.3	6.9	28.2	27.4	15.7	15.6	0.588	1.0	1.0	41
Little	8.2	8.1	29.2	28.5	16.4	16.1	0.308	1.3	1.5	35

(*continued*)

Table 2. (*continued*)

| | Without tool | | | | | | | ΔT | | |
| | Minimum | | Maximum | | Mean | | | | | |
Palmar surface	D	ND	D	ND	D	ND	p	Mean	SD	% ΔT > 1 °C[†]
	With tool							ΔT		
	Minimum		Maximum		Mean					
Palmar surface	D	ND	D	ND	D	ND	p	Mean	SD	% ΔT > 1 °C[†]
Thumb	12.1	10.2	28.8	25.8	17.5	15.4	$< 0.001^*$	2.3	2.0	64
Index	11.0	9.6	29.0	24.4	16.8	14.6	$< 0.001^*$	2.7	2.7	59
Middle	11.7	9.2	30.7	24.9	17.0	14.3	$< 0.001^*$	3.2	3.2	67
Ring	11.3	10.0	30.8	27.0	17.3	14.6	$< 0.001^*$	3.3	3.0	75
Little	11.2	10.6	30.9	26.2	18.1	15.3	$< 0.001^*$	3.4	2.8	79
Dorsal surface										
Thumb	12.0	11.1	28.7	24.7	17.3	15.6	$< 0.001^*$	2.1	1.9	54
Index	11.1	9.4	27.1	23.7	16.6	14.5	$< 0.001^*$	2.5	2.7	60
Middle	11.6	8.7	28.4	25.7	16.5	14.2	$< 0.001^*$	2.8	2.7	70
Ring	11.3	9.5	29.8	26.6	16.9	14.3	$< 0.001^*$	2.9	2.7	78
Little	12.3	10.5	30.0	25.3	17.7	15.2	$< 0.001^*$	3.2	2.5	75

D – Dominant; ND – Non-dominant; [*] $P \leq 0.05$; ΔT – Difference between temperature averages of the fingers (D and ND); [†] % of workers with ΔT > 1 °C.

In both groups, there were temperature differences ≥ 1 °C between the non-dominant and dominant hands, in all fingers and both surfaces (Table 2).

4 Discussion

Two studies corroborated with this research, as they verified that 78% and 72.7% of poultry slaughterhouse workers felt cold in their hands [7, 8]. However, it noted that pig slaughterhouse workers also feel cold in their hands (66%) and workers who used a knife felt the coldest [12]. Not specifying the body region, results of a study performed prior to NR-36 with 925 workers of three poultry slaughterhouses showed that 59.2% of these workers felt cold [4]. These authors revealed that the risk of a slaughterhouse worker feeling bodily discomfort was 105% higher for those who feel cold compared with those who do not.

Cold temperatures are an ergonomic risk present in poultry slaughterhouses [2], evidenced in the plants analyzed in the current study. Considering that most of the fingers had temperatures ≤ 15 °C (76%), both groups (knife use or not) showed a difference between the temperature of each finger with its respective contralateral ≥ 1 °C on both hand surfaces, and the chance of a worker feeling cold and presenting finger temperatures ≤ 15 °C was greater than those who did not feel cold. Unlike the study by Tirloni et al.

[8], in which a finger temperature $\leq 15\ °C$ was not associated with feeling cold in the hands (p = 0.377).

In addition to this paper, another analysis also evidenced that most workers (66.4%) had at least one finger with a temperature $\leq 15\ °C$ [8], which is a high physiological strain condition [9]. Nevertheless, examining one worker for two hours performing one cutting task, Güths et al. [13] established that the non-dominant hand finger temperature reached more than 16 °C during most of the analyzed time.

The fingers' ideal temperature on both hands (> 24 °C) without presenting low physiological strain [9] was found in a few workers in this study (2%), as well as in the studies by Ramos et al. [7] (7%) and Tirloni et al. (0.7%) [8].

There was no association between knife use and a temperature $\leq 15\ °C$. However, for a worker who used a tool, the chance of feeling cold was greater than for those who did not, identical to the outcome presented by Tirloni et al. (OR = 3.19 95% CI 1.46; 6.94) [8]. Although workers wore several overlapping gloves on the non-dominant hand, Ramos et al. [7] and Tirloni et al. [8] proved that the hand that handled the product (non-dominant) and used a chain-mail glove was significantly colder than the hand that held the knife, except the thumb and little finger, respectively. This was contrary to the present study, in which there was a difference between all fingers.

Studies show a mean delta temperature between the dominant and non-dominant hands of poultry slaughterhouse workers > 1 °C, regardless of knife use [7, 8, 12]. However, most workers who used a knife presented the $\Delta T \geq 1\ °C$ [7, 12].

Just like the current study, some investigations demonstrated that using several overlapping gloves was not enough to promote thermal insulation of the hands in slaughterhouses [8, 12, 14]. For this reason, urgent and effective measures must be taken to modify this reality experienced by slaughterhouse workers, providing investigations about the use of different types of gloves (PPE) and their effects on hand thermal protection.

5 Conclusion

Gloves did not protect the workers' fingers, because most employees presented finger temperatures $\leq 15\ °C$ and felt cold in their hands. Workers who used knives presented significant differences between the average temperatures of the non-dominant and dominant sides in all fingers, with temperature deltas > 1 °C. Therefore, the slaughterhouse health and safety team must monitor the workers' finger temperatures inserted in cold environments. In addition, efficient gloves for thermal protection should be developed, tested and provided for these workers.

References

1. Brazilian Association of Animal Protein: Annual Report 2020. https://www.abpa-br.org/rel atorios. Accessed 08 Dec 2020
2. Occupational Safety and Health Administration (OSHA): Prevention of musculoskeletal injuries in poultry processing (2013). https://www.osha.gov/Publications/OSHA3213.pdf. Accessed 10 Jan 2021
3. Cheung, S.S., Daanen, H.A.M.: Dynamic adaptation of the peripheral circulation to cold exposure. Microcirculation **19**, 65–77 (2012)

4. Tirloni, A.S., Reis, D.C., Borgatto, A.F., Moro, A.R.P.: Association between perception of bodily discomfort and individual and work organisational factors in Brazilian slaughterhouse workers: a cross-sectional study. BMJ Open. **9**, e022824 (2019)
5. Brasil: Ministério da Agricultura e do Abastecimento. Portaria n° 210 de 10 de novembro de 1998. Dispõe sobre o regulamento técnico da inspeção tecnológica e higiênico-sanitária de carnes de aves. MAPA, Brasília. https://www.agencia.cnptia.embrapa.br/Repositorio/Portaria-210_000h19kjcan02wx7ha0e2uuw60rmjy11.pdf. Accessed 16 Dec 2020
6. Brasil: Norma Regulamentadora 36. Segurança e Saúde no Trabalho em Empresas de Abate e Processamento de Carnes e Derivados, Ministério do Trabalho e Emprego, Portaria MTE n. 555, de 18 de abril de 2013, Diário Oficial da União (2013)
7. Ramos, E., Reis, D.C., Tirloni, A.S., Moro, A.R.P.: Thermographic analysis of the hands of poultry slaughterhouse workers exposed to artificially cold environment. Procedia Manuf. **3**, 4252–4259 (2015)
8. Tirloni, A.S., Reis, D.C.D., Dias, N.F., Moro, A.R.P.: The use of personal protective equipment: finger temperatures and thermal sensation of workers' exposure to cold environment. Int. J. Environ. Res. Pub. Health **15**, 2583 (2018)
9. International Organization for Standardization: Ergonomics of the thermal environment - Determination and interpretation of cold stress when using required clothing insulation (IREQ) and local cooling effects. (ISO 11079). ISO, Geneva, Switzerland (2007)
10. Holmér, I.: Evaluation of cold workplace: an overview of standards for assessment of cold stress. Ind. Health **47**, 228–234 (2009)
11. Hong, Y.-P., Ryu, K.-S., Cho, B.-M., Oh, S.-M., Park, S.-H.: Evaluation of thermography in the diagnosis of carpal tunnel syndrome: comparative study between patient and control groups. J. Korean Neurosurg. Soc. **39**, 423–426 (2006)
12. Tirloni, A.S., Reis, D.C.D., Ramos, E., Moro, A.R.P.: Thermographic evaluation of the hands of pig slaughterhouse workers exposed to cold temperatures. Int. J. Environ. Res. Pub. Health **14**, E838 (2017)
13. Güths, S., Santos, V.A., Takeda, F., Reis, D.C., Moro, A.R.P.: Body Temperature monitoring system for slaughterhouse workers. In: Ahram, T., Karwowski, W. (eds.) Advances in Human Factors, Software, and Systems Engineering. AHFE 2017. Advances in Intelligent Systems and Computing, vol 598. Springer, Cham. (2018)
14. Takeda, F., Moro, A.R.P., Güths, S.: Sistema de monitoramento de temperatura corporal para atividades com exposição ao frio artificial controlado. Revista Produção online **19**, 229–248 (2019)

Musculoskeletal Ergonomic Implications in Smartphone Users: A Systematic Review

Danilo Fernandes Vitorino[1]([⊠]) [iD], Walter Franklin Marques Correia[1] [iD],
and Márcio Alves Marçal[2] [iD]

[1] Federal University of Pernambuco, Av. Prof. Moraes Rêgo, sn, Cidade Universitária, Recife,
PE 50670420, Brazil
{danilo.fernandesvitorino,walter.franklin}@ufpe.br
[2] Federal University of the Valleys of Jequitinhonha and Mucuri, Rodovia MGT 367 - Km 583,
nº 5000, Diamantina, Brazil
marcio@nersat.com.br

Abstract. This article aims to investigate ergonomic implications with musculoskeletal consequences caused in smartphone users, as well as the identification of methods, techniques and tools that are being used in current studies for the physical evaluation of users of these interfaces. Thus, a systematic review of the literature was performed through the Scopus database, using the Snowballing approach (C. Wohlin, "Guidelines for snowballing in systematic literature studies and a replication in software engineering," in Proceedings of the 18th international conference on evaluation and assessment in software engineering, 2014, pp. 1–10, https://doi.org/10.1145/2601248.2601268.) to form the most robust set of documents on the subject addressed. During the document collection processes, 341 articles were found, followed by readings of titles, abstracts and verification of previously established inclusion and exclusion criteria, leaving 27 articles, which were completely analyzed in search of relevant information to fulfill the research objective.

Keywords: Smartphone · Ergonomics · Musculoskeletal · Systematic review

1 Introduction

Studies indicate that smartphones are used by billions of users worldwide [2–5]. However, despite their rapid acceptance, ergonomic issues are still being studied, and the consequences for the health of their followers are not fully known. Thus, this systematic review intends to collect the studies related to the use of smartphones that contemplate ergonomic issues of physical order, to understand the strategies adopted by researchers and identify issues that still need to be researched.

1.1 Systematic Literature Review

In order to collect information in an objective and impartial manner, taking into account the large amount of data found on the topics involving this study, a literature review

N. L. Black et al. (Eds.): IEA 2021, LNNS 222, pp. 860–867, 2021.
https://doi.org/10.1007/978-3-030-74611-7_117

was carried out in order to find more specific, relevant and reliable research on the topic addressed. Thus, a document search was performed through the Scopus database, using Wohlin's Snowballing approach [1] which uses documents found in the search, its references and subsequent works that mentioned it, to form the most robust set of documents on the subject addressed (see Fig. 1).

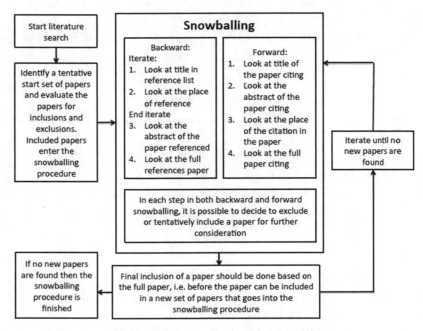

Fig. 1. Wohlin snowballing procedure [1].

1.2 Search Strategy

Therefore, we have outlined as a strategy the search by means of terms that are more related to the focus of this search, where the keywords: "smartphone" AND "ergonomics" AND "musculoskeletal" located in the title, abstract, or keywords of the document were selected as descriptors. The objective criteria of the search were: publication period = from 2015, document type = all, language = English, and that the number of articles found could not be less than 10 publications, otherwise the keywords should be changed.

The Snowballing procedure used for systematic review followed 3 steps, which are: Start Set (1), are the documents found in the search with the keywords; Backward (2), are the references cited in the Start Set documents; and Forward (3), are later works that cited the Start Set.

1.2.1 Inclusion and Exclusion Criteria

The inclusion and exclusion criteria can be checked in the tables (see Table 1 and 2).

Table 1. Inclusion criteria (IC).

Criteria	Description
IC1	+ Publications can be selected that present methods, techniques or tools applied for ergonomic evaluation of the touchscreen interface of smartphones;
IC2	+ Publications may be selected that present a literature review related to the musculoskeletal consequences of the use of smartphones;
IC3	+ Publications that present studies on musculoskeletal problems resulting from the use of smartphones can be selected

Table 2. Exclusion criteria (EC).

Criteria	Description
EC1	- Publications that do not meet any inclusion criteria will not be selected;
EC2	- Publications of duplicate articles will not be selected;
EC3	- Publications that do not have full content available for reading and data analysis will not be selected;
EC4	- Publications from before 2015 will not be selected

1.2.2 Selected Documents

Finally, after the 3 stages of document selection, 51 articles were added up for complete reading, content analysis and extraction of relevant data. For a selection of the most relevant articles, taking as a criterion those with the greatest impact on the scientific environment, the Field-Weighted Citation Impact (FWCI) was used, which is a metric that evaluates the impact of citations according to the field of the subject, the value greater than 1.00, means that the document is more cited than expected [6], being selected only those articles that scored in this regard. Thus, 24 were excluded with an impact score of "0.0", leaving 27 documents (see Fig. 2).

1.3 Data Extraction

After the complete reading, analysis and data extraction of the articles, Table 3 was developed and organized in descending order according to the FWCI score.

From this selection and reading, information was extracted from the articles to identify the most affected body regions in this type of interaction and that were explored in the studies, being the neck region the most cited area (n = 13) and then parts of the upper limbs, which were: shoulder, arm, forearm, hands, fingers and thumb (n = 12). Some studies presented a general approach to musculoskeletal problems (n = 5) checking all areas affected by interaction with smartphones, including a study (n = 1) indicating inappropriate lower limb postures.

Regarding the neck region, there is great concern about its high flexion during long periods, being one of the main evidences of musculoskeletal disorders in smartphone

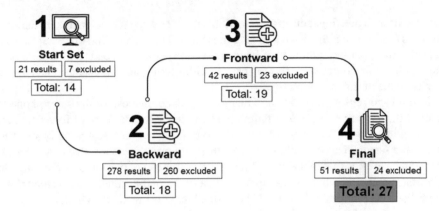

Fig. 2. Scheme of the snowballing systematic review process.

Table 3. Final papers analyzed.

Author, Year	FWCI	Author, Year	FWCI
1. Xie et al., 2016 [7]	7,0	15. Toh et al., 2017 [4]	2,33
2. Lee et al., 2015a [8]	5,34	16. Xie et al., 2017 [5]	2,3
3. Kim e Koo, 2016 [9]	4,31	17. Stalin et al., 2016 [10]	2,11
4. Gustafsson et al., 2017 [11]	4,12	18. Gustafsson et al., 2018 [12]	1,11
5. Yang et al., 2017 [13]	3,65	19. Lee et al., 2018 [14]	1,11
6. Kim, 2015 [15]	3,62	20. Akurke et al., 2018 [16]	1,09
7. İnal et al., 2015 [17]	3,39	21. Tegtmeier, 2018 [3]	1,01
8. Kietrys et al., 2015 [18]	3,1	22. Liang et al., 2016 [19]	0,87
9. Xiong et al., 2016 [20]	2,8	23. Lee e Shin, 2015 [21]	0,77
10. Namwongsa et al., 2018a [22]	2,71	24. Eitivipart et al., 2018 [2]	0,48
11. Kim e Kim, 2015 [23]	2,67	25. Asakawa et al., 2017 [24]	0,47
12. Xie et al., 2018 [25]	2,60	26. So et al., 2017 [26]	0,36
13. Ning et al., 2015 [27]	2,39	27. Namwongsa et al., 2018b [28]	0,33
14. Lee et al., 2015b [29]	2,36	**Total Documents = 27**	

users. The so-called "Text Neck" caused by high neck flexion, associated with the weight of the head and consequently the weight on the spine, mainly the cervical region, causing pain and discomfort [8, 9, 12, 15, 22, 27]. Moreover, its association to the use with two hands (bilateral) causes greater neck flexion, while with one hand (unilateral) results in asymmetric cervical posture [5].

Regarding the upper limbs, practically all their divisions are related in the studies: shoulders, arms, forearms, fists, hands and fingers, the thumb being the most cited component in the articles [2, 3, 12, 20]. This is due to a greater activity and repetition of movements with this finger during interaction with the device screen, mainly in unilateral activities (with one hand), causing greater muscle load [5]. According to Gustafsson et al. [12], in a study on the influence of hand size on messages and text, thumb kinematics tends to be more affected in shorter hands, while long hands present greater muscle activity in the thumb and forearm.

In the hand region, there is an indication that excessive use of the smartphone can increase the median nerve, cause thumb pain and decrease the force of forceps, among other hand functions [17]. According to Kietrys et al. [18], in research on types of text entries and screen sizes on mobile devices, there are some measures that can reduce the biomechanical exposure of the upper limbs such as: the use of two hands at the same time (bilateral), smaller and lighter smartphones. In a study on the dimensions of smartphones in one-handed activities, Lee et al. [14] identified that the greater the width of the screen, the worse the performance of users, and that tasks become more and more difficult to perform with the decrease of the lower frame, resulting in a greater occupation of the screen in this area that is difficult to reach.

Regarding the methods, techniques and tools used in the ergonomic analyses, the following were identified and accounted for: Posture Analysis (n = 10), Surface Electromyography (n = 7), Movement Analysis (4), Ultrasonography (n = 1), Algometry (n = 2), Questionnaire (n = 9) and Form (n = 4). The Systematic Literature Reviews (n = 4) used a bibliographic research approach, but presented a rich contribution on the biomechanical risks of smartphone use [3], which can contribute to musculoskeletal alterations [2] as well as the need for more studies to evidence this association [4, 5].

1.4   Results Discussion

After the study was completed, the most affected body regions were identified and studied in the interaction with smartphones, which are: neck and upper limbs (in different regions), and that these were studied to verify variables such as posture, strength, repeatability and duration. Thus, these variables were evaluated through the use of methods, techniques and tools such as: structured questionnaire, posture analysis, surface electromyography (sEMG), form, movement analysis, algometry and ultrasonography, which were combined to check more than one variable in each study.

However, some of the techniques used require specialized knowledge and expensive equipment, such as sEMG and Ultrasonography, making it difficult to include them in the process of interface development. Research is needed to identify more viable ways of evaluating biomechanical issues in digital interfaces, making this type of evaluation feasible for the reality of digital application development offices or even the insertion of professionals specialized in ergonomics to participate in the development and evaluation of these interfaces before they are launched on the market.

1.5   Future Works Indications

After identifying the future work indications of each publication, we found some similarities in the authors' proposals and summarized in the following points: 1) To use a consistent and representative sample of users, and to use comparison groups; 2) To conduct longitudinal studies with high scientific quality; 3) To develop ergonomic guidelines for the use of smartphone interfaces; 4) To evaluate realistic situations of use to obtain accurate data, considering the different postures and habits of users; 5) To verify the use of smartphones in work and productivity situations; 6) To consider the different gestures made in the smartphones; 7) To measure the level of discomfort of interaction; 8) To discover new risk potentials, going beyond those already discovered; 9) To carry out a study on the tasks performed in media or social networks, considering the large amount of daily hours dedicated to their use.

1.6 Conclusion

In the end, it was possible to realize the importance of conducting more studies on the subject that involves the ergonomics of the gestural interface of smartphones devices, such as the indications of future works presented in the revised articles, as well as taking advantage of the methods, techniques and tools that can be used in further research. However, in view of the market reality of digital interface development offices, these forms of evaluation need to be made possible for their use in the evaluation of interfaces, as well as the need to hire ergonomists to contribute to the development team.

We realized that although there are several studies and evidences that prove the skeletal muscle problems in smartphone users, it is necessary to go further, verifying what can be added to improve this interaction, such as the development of ergonomic guidelines for this type of interface, considering that it is an artifact present in the daily life of a large part of the world population, tending to increase more and more.

References

1. Wohlin, C.: Guidelines for snowballing in systematic literature studies and a replication in software engineering. In: Proceedings of the 18th International Conference on Evaluation and Assessment in Software Engineering, pp. 1–10 (2014). https://doi.org/10.1145/2601248.2601268

2. Eitivipart, A.C., Viriyarojanakul, S., Redhead, L.: Musculoskeletal disorder and pain associated with smartphone use: a systematic review of biomechanical evidence. Hong Kong Physiother. J. **38**(2), 77–90 (2018). https://doi.org/10.1142/S1013702518300010

3. Tegtmeier, P.: A scoping review on smart mobile devices and physical strain. Work **59**(2), 273–283 (2018). https://doi.org/10.3233/WOR-172678

4. Toh, S.H., Coenen, P., Howie, E.K., Mukherjee, S., Mackey, D.A., Straker, L.M.: Mobile touch screen device use and associations with musculoskeletal symptoms and visual health in a nationally representative sample of Singaporean adolescents. Ergonomics **62**(6), 778–793 (2019). https://doi.org/10.1080/00140139.2018.1562107

5. Xie, Y., Szeto, G., Dai, J.: Prevalence and risk factors associated with musculoskeletal complaints among users of mobile handheld devices: a systematic review. Appl. Ergon. **59**, 132–142 (2017). https://doi.org/10.1016/j.apergo.2016.08.020

6. ELSEVIER, "What is Scopus Preview? - Scopus: Access and use Support Center (2020). https://service.elsevier.com/app/answers/detail/a_id/15534/supporthub/scopus/#tips. Accessed 15 Apr 2020

7. Xie, Y., Szeto, G.P.Y., Dai, J., Madeleine, P.: A comparison of muscle activity in using touchscreen smartphone among young people with and without chronic neck-shoulder pain. Ergonomics **59**(1), 61–72 (2016). https://doi.org/10.1080/00140139.2015.1056237

8. Lee, S., Kang, H., Shin, G.: Head flexion angle while using a smartphone. Ergonomics **58**(2), 220–226 (2015). https://doi.org/10.1080/00140139.2014.967311
9. Kim, S.-Y., Koo, S.-J.: Effect of duration of smartphone use on muscle fatigue and pain caused by forward head posture in adults. J. Phys. Ther. Sci. **28**(6), 1669–1672 (2016). https://doi.org/10.1589/jpts.28.1669
10. Stalin, P., Abraham, S.B., Kanimozhy, K., Prasad, R.V., Singh, Z., Purty, A.J.: Mobile phone usage and its health effects among adults in a semi-urban area of Southern India. J. Clin. Diagn. Res. JCDR **10**(1), LC14–16 (2016). https://doi.org/10.7860/JCDR/2016/16576.7074.
11. Gustafsson, E., Thomée, S., Grimby-Ekman, A., Hagberg, M.: Texting on mobile phones and musculoskeletal disorders in young adults: a five-year cohort study. Appl. Ergon. **58**, 208–214 (2017). https://doi.org/10.1016/j.apergo.2016.06.012
12. Gustafsson, E., Coenen, P., Campbell, A., Straker, L.: Texting with touchscreen and keypad phones - a comparison of thumb kinematics, upper limb muscle activity, exertion, discomfort, and performance. Appl. Ergon. **70**, 232–239 (2018). https://doi.org/10.1016/j.apergo.2018.03.003
13. Yang, S.-Y., Chen, M.-D., Huang, Y.-C., Lin, C.-Y., Chang, J.-H.: Association between smartphone use and musculoskeletal discomfort in adolescent students. J. Community Health **42**(3), 423–430 (2017). https://doi.org/10.1007/s10900-016-0271-x
14. Lee, S.C., Cha, M.C., Hwangbo, H., Mo, S., Ji, Y.G.: Smartphone form factors: effects of width and bottom bezel on touch performance, workload, and physical demand. Appl. Ergon. **67**, 142–150 (2018). https://doi.org/10.1016/j.apergo.2017.10.002
15. Kim, M.-S.: Influence of neck pain on cervical movement in the sagittal plane during smartphone use. J. Phys. Ther. Sci. **27**(1), 15–17 (2015). https://doi.org/10.1589/jpts.27.15
16. Akurke, S., Li, Y., Craig, B.: Effect of smartphone use on upper extremity and neck. Adv. Intell. Syst. Comput. **588**, 241–249 (2018). https://doi.org/10.1007/978-3-319-60582-1_24
17. İnal, E.E., Demirci, K., Çetİntürk, A., Akgönül, M., Savaş, S.: Effects of smartphone overuse on hand function, pinch strength, and the median nerve. Muscle Nerve **52**(2), 183–188 (2015). https://doi.org/10.1002/mus.24695
18. Kietrys, D.M., Gerg, M.J., Dropkin, J., Gold, J.E.: Mobile input device type, texting style and screen size influence upper extremity and trapezius muscle activity, and cervical posture while texting. Appl. Ergon. **50**, 98–104 (2015). https://doi.org/10.1016/j.apergo.2015.03.003
19. Liang, H.-W., Hwang, Y.-H.: Mobile phone use behaviors and postures on public transportation systems. PloS One, **11**(2) (2016). https://doi.org/10.1371/journal.pone.0148419
20. Xiong, J., Muraki, S.: Effects of age, thumb length and screen size on thumb movement coverage on smartphone touchscreens. Int. J. Ind. Ergon. **53**, 140–148 (2016). https://doi.org/10.1016/j.ergon.2015.11.004
21. Lee, S., Shin, G.: Relationship between smartphone use and the severity of head flexion of college students, (2015-Jan), 1788–1790 (2015) https://doi.org/10.1177/1541931215591386
22. Namwongsa, S., Puntumetakul, R., Neubert, M.S., Boucaut, R.: Factors associated with neck disorders among university student smartphone users. Work **61**(3), 367–378 (2018). https://doi.org/10.3233/WOR-182819
23. Kim, H.-J., Kim, J.-S.: The relationship between smartphone use and subjective musculoskeletal symptoms and university students. J. Phys. Ther. Sci. **27**(3), 575–579 (2015). https://doi.org/10.1589/jpts.27.575
24. Asakawa, D.S., Crocker, G.H., Schmaltz, A., Jindrich, D.L.: Fingertip forces and completion time for index finger and thumb touchscreen gestures. J. Electromyogr. Kinesiol. **34**, 6–13 (2017). https://doi.org/10.1016/j.jelekin.2017.02.007
25. Xie, Y.F., Szeto, G., Madeleine, P., Tsang, S.: Spinal kinematics during smartphone texting - a comparison between young adults with and without chronic neck-shoulder pain. Appl. Ergon. **68**, 160–168 (2018). https://doi.org/10.1016/j.apergo.2017.10.018

26. So, B.C.L., Cheng, A.S.K., Szeto, G.P.Y.: Cumulative IT use is associated with psychosocial stress factors and musculoskeletal symptoms. Int. J. Environ. Res. Public. Health, **14**(12) (2017). https://doi.org/10.3390/ijerph14121541
27. Ning, X., Huang, Y., Hu, B., Nimbarte, A.D.: Neck kinematics and muscle activity during mobile device operations. Int. J. Ind. Ergon. **48**, 10–15 (2015). https://doi.org/10.1016/j.ergon. 2015.03.003
28. Namwongsa, S., Puntumetakul, R., Neubert, M.S., Chaiklieng, S., Boucaut, R.: Ergonomic risk assessment of smartphone users using the Rapid Upper Limb Assessment (RULA) tool. PLoS One, **13**(8) (2018). https://doi.org/10.1371/journal.pone.0203394
29. Lee, M., et al.: The effects of smartphone use on upper extremity muscle activity and pain threshold. J. Phys. Ther. Sci. **27**(6), 1743–1745 (2015). https://doi.org/10.1589/jpts.27.1743

Comparison of Accuracy of Inertial Measurement Units, Goniometer and Optical Tracking System for Wrist Velocity Assessment

Liyun Yang[1,2](✉) , Karnica Manivasagam[2], and Mikael Forsman[1,2]

[1] Institute of Environmental Medicine, Karolinska Institutet, Stockholm, Sweden
Liyun.yang@ki.se
[2] Division of Ergonomics, School of Engineering Sciences in Chemistry, Biotechnology and Health, KTH Royal Institute of Technology, Stockholm, Sweden

Abstract. Wrist angular velocity assessment is important for assessing the risks in hand-intensive work. This study compared the measurement accuracy of an inertial measurement unit (IMU)-smartphone system, an electronic goniometer and an optical tracking system (OTS) for measuring wrist flexion velocity. Six participants performed three sets of standard hand/wrist movements and three simulated work tasks. The results showed the IMUs had adequate accuracy comparing to the OTS during standard movements of low to medium pace. The accuracy of the IMUs compared to the OTS was lower during fast pace movements and simulated work tasks. Still, the IMUs had in general small differences compared to the goniometer in flexion/extension and simulated work tasks. Therefore, the IMU system may be used by researchers and practitioners for assessing wrist flexion velocity in hand-intensive work. Future studies need to explore algorithms to improve the IMU-smartphone system and reduce errors.

Keywords: Wrist movements · Hand-Intensive work · Inertial measurement unit · Goniometer · Smartphone application

1 Introduction

Wrist angular velocity is one critical risk factor for work-related musculoskeletal disorders in the elbow/hand [1–3]. A quantitative exposure-response relationship was established with an action limit at 20°/s for wrist flexion velocity [2]. The postures and movements of the wrist and hand are especially difficult to assess by observational methods [4]. One commonly used technical method for assessing wrist velocity is the electronic goniometer, which has been applied by various researchers in both laboratory and field studies [5–7]. However, the electronic goniometer is relatively expensive, fragile and resource-demanding for data analysis. The inertial measurement units (IMUs) with embedded gyroscope and Bluetooth connection provide the opportunity to assess wrist velocity easily for practitioners using a smartphone application. In order to apply such IMU-smartphone systems for assessing the wrist velocity in the field, the accuracy

N. L. Black et al. (Eds.): IEA 2021, LNNS 222, pp. 868–873, 2021.
https://doi.org/10.1007/978-3-030-74611-7_118

of the method need to be examined. It is also of interest to know how the IMU-smartphone system performs comparing to the electronic goniometer, as the proposed action limit was established based on measurement data using goniometers in the field.

The aim of this study was to compare the measurement methods of an IMU-smartphone system, an electronic goniometer and an optical tracking system (OTS) for assessing wrist flexion velocity during both standard wrist movements and simulated work tasks.

2 Methods

Six participants (three men and three women, all right-handed) gave their informed-consent and joined the experiment. The electronic goniometer (Biometrics Ltd., Newport, UK) was placed on the dominant wrist, and the two IMU sensors (Movesense, Suunto, Helsinki) were placed on top of the goniometer endblocks; one on the middle of the hand, and one the forearm (Fig. 1a). A third IMU was placed on the upper arm, which was not used in this study. Optical markers were placed at the carpal end of third metacarpal (hand), the thumb and little finger side of the wrist, and the lateral epicondyle (elbow). The participants were instructed to perform standard wrist movements for flexion/extension (Fig. 1b), radial/ulnar deviation and pronation/supination (Fig. 1c) at three paces, following a metronome of 30, 60, and 90 beat-per-minute (BPM). The participants also performed three simulated work tasks including hair drying (Fig. 1d), folding paper plane (Fig. 1e), and mail sorting, each task lasting one minute.

The wrist flexion velocities from the three systems were calculated and compared using MATLAB (2018a, MathWorks, Inc., USA). The sampling frequencies of the goniometer, IMUs and optical system were 20, 52 and 100 Hz, respectively. For the goniometer, the output in flexion/extension angles was low-pass filtered at 5 Hz [8], and then the derivatives of the flexion angle was calculated into wrist flexion velocity. For the IMUs, the gyroscope outputs in the x-axis of the hand and forearm IMUs were first synchronised, low-pass filtered (6th order Butterworth with a cut-off frequency at 8 Hz), down-sampled to 20 Hz and then subtracted as the wrist flexion velocity. For the optical system, a mid-point of the two wrist markers was calculated, two vectors connecting hand–wrist and elbow–wrist were created and the angles between them were calculated as the wrist flexion angle. Further, the derivatives of the flexion angle were calculated as the wrist flexion velocity, and then low-pass filtered (6th order Butterworth with a cut-off frequency at 8 Hz) and down-sampled to 20 Hz. All signals were synchronised and the 50th percentile of the wrist flexion velocity was calculated for each standard movement and simulated work task. The mean absolute errors (MAE) were computed for each pair of the three systems.

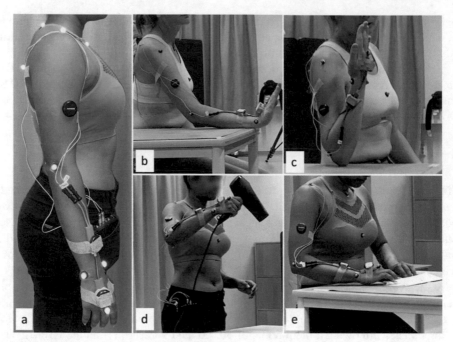

Fig. 1. a) Placement of the electronic goniometer, the inertial measurement units (IMUs) and the optical markers, with detailed placement descriptions in the text; b) standard movement of wrist flexion/extension; c) standard movement of wrist supination/pronation; d) simulated work task of hair drying; and e) simulated work task of folding paper plane.

3   Results

Comparisons between the three systems: the IMU-smartphone system, the electronic goniometer and the optical tracking system (OTS) for assessing wrist flexion velocities during standard wrist movements and simulated work tasks are shown in Table 1. During the standard wrist flexion/extension movements, the mean absolute errors (MAE) of the median flexion velocity between the IMUs and the OTS ranged from 0.9 to 22.6°/s, with the largest error during the flexion/extension at 90 BPM. The goniometer and the OTS had larger differences in the flexion/extension of lower pace (30 and 60 BPM) but smaller differences in the highest pace at 90 BPM. Errors were observed during the deviation and pronation/supination wrist movements from all systems, where the wrist flexion velocity should be close to zero.

For the three simulated work tasks, the MAEs between the two comparisons of IMU–OTS and goniometer–OTS were on a similar level: the mail sorting task had the highest difference, with a MAE of 11.6°/s and 10.3°/s respectively. The task of folding paper plane showed smallest differences at 4.5°/s for the comparison between IMU–OTS and 4.7°/s for the comparison between goniometer–OTS. When comparing the IMUs and the goniometer, the MAEs during simulated work tasks were generally smaller, ranging from 1.4 to 6.2°/s.

Table 1. The mean absolute errors (MAE) of the median flexion velocity measurement between the IMUs, the goniometer and the optical tracking system (OTS) during the three standard wrist movements at the paces of 30, 60 and 90 BPM, and three simulated work tasks. Values from OTS are given as a reference for the median flexion velocity. Data from six participants are presented.

(°/s)	Mean absolute errors between measurements			(Values from OTS)
	IMU–OTS	Gonio–OTS	IMU–Gonio	
Flexion/Extension				
30 BPM	3.4	5.0	2.7	(39.2)
60 BPM	7.4	10.6	5.2	(76.6)
90 BPM	22.6	16.5	15.0	(125.6)
Deviation				
30 BPM	0.9	0.4	0.5	(3.4)
60 BPM	1.1	0.7	0.5	(4.0)
90 BPM	2.5	2.3	1.4	(7.2)
Pronation/Supination				
30 BPM	2.9	3.9	5.9	(7.5)
60 BPM	6.5	8.0	13.9	(15.2)
90 BPM	9.6	7.1	16.7	(20.7)
Simulated work tasks				
Hair dressing	10.9	8.9	6.2	(32.2)
Folding paper plane	4.5	4.7	1.4	(19.3)
Mail sorting	11.6	10.3	4.8	(41.4)

4 Discussion

This study aimed at comparing the methods for assessing wrist flexion velocity using an IMU-smartphone system, an electronic goniometer and an optical tracking system (OTS) during standard wrist movements and simulated work tasks. The results showed that in standard wrist movements, the errors between the IMU and OTS system during the slow-to-medium paced movements were small, which were similar to those between the goniometer and OTS, but larger differences were observed as the pace increased. During simulated work tasks, for both comparisons of IMU–OTS and gonio–OTS, larger differences were observed for the hair drying and mail sorting tasks whilst smaller differences were observed for the task of folding paper plane. Still, the IMUs had in general small differences compared to the goniometer, which has been used in the field studies.

It is worth noting that during the deviation and pronation/supination wrist movements, the wrist flexion velocities were supposed to be close to zero as ground truth values. However, the values obtained from the OTS, which were used as a reference, were deviated from zero. This pointed to the limitations of the model used in the OTS, which could further lead to errors when comparing the methods during simulated work tasks with wrist movements in multiple planes. Therefore the model in the OTS needs to be improved in future studies if it will be used as a gold standard measurement for validating the accuracy of other systems. In addition, since the calculation of flexion velocity from the IMU-smartphone system assumed the alignment of the x-axes of the hand and forearm IMUs, a potential misalignment would lead to increased errors for the measurement. Future studies will look at algorithms to calibrate the potential misalignment before practitioners can use this method for wrist velocity assessment of work tasks in the field.

Another limitation of the study was that the IMUs were placed on the goniometer endblocks on the participants' hand and forearm in order to compare the three systems. This may lead to extra errors for the IMU system when calculating the relative velocity between the two sensors, as the forearm IMU was placed further away from the wrist joint than in a normal case without the goniometer.

5 Conclusions

The measurement accuracy of wrist velocity is important for performing risk assessment of hand-intensive work. The study showed that the IMU-smartphone system had adequate accuracy comparing to the optical tracking system (OTS) during standard hand/wrist movements of low to medium pace. The accuracy of the IMUs compared to the OTS was slightly lower during simulated work tasks. Still, the IMU-smartphone system had in general small differences compared to the goniometer during simulated work tasks. The results indicate that the IMU-smartphone system have a potential to be used by both researchers and practitioners for assessing wrist flexion velocity in hand-intensive work. Future studies need to explore algorithms to improve the alignment of the two IMUs on hand and forearm and reduce errors.

References

1. Seidel, D.H., Ditchen, D.M., Hoehne-Hückstädt, U.M., Rieger, M.A., Steinhilber, B.: Quantitative measures of physical risk factors associated with work-related musculoskeletal disorders of the elbow: a systematic review. Int. J. Environ. Res. Public Health 16, 1–23 (2019)
2. Balogh, I., et al.: Work-related neck and upper limb disorders - Quantitative exposure-response relationships adjusted for personal characteristics and psychosocial conditions. BMC Musculoskelet. Disord. 20, 1–19 (2019)
3. Nordander, C., et al.: Exposure-response relationships in work-related musculoskeletal disorders in elbows and hands - a synthesis of group-level data on exposure and response obtained using uniform methods of data collection. Appl. Ergon. 44, 241–53 (2013)
4. Takala, E.-P.P., et al.: Systematic evaluation of observational methods assessing biomechanical exposures at work. Scand. J. Work. Environ. Health 36, 3–24 (2010)
5. Arvidsson, I., Åkesson, I., Hansson, G.Å.: Wrist movements among females in a repetitive, non-forceful work. Appl. Ergon. 34, 309–316 (2003)
6. Balogh, I., Ohlsson, K., Nordander, C., Skerfving, S., Hansson, G.Å.: Precision of measurements of physical workload during standardized manual handling part III: goniometry of the wrists. J. Electromyogr. Kinesiol. 19, 1005–1012 (2009)

7. Bartnicka, J., Zietkiewicz, A.A., Kowalski, G.J.: An ergonomics study on wrist posture when using laparoscopic tools in four techniques in minimally invasive surgery. Int. J. Occup. Saf. Ergon. **24**, 438–449 (2018)
8. Hansson, G.Å., Balogh, I., Ohlsson, K., Rylander, L., Skerfving, S.: Goniometer measurement and computer analysis of wrist angles and movements applied to occupational repetitive work. J. Electromyogr. Kinesiol. **6**, 23–35 (1996)

Author Index

N. L. Black et al. (Eds.): IEA 2021, LNNS 222, pp. 875–879, 2021.
https://doi.org/10.1007/978-3-030-74611-7

Printed in the United States
by Baker & Taylor Publisher Services